CIVIL PROCEDURE

ASPEN CASEBOOK SERIES

CIVIL PROCEDURE

Tenth Edition

STEPHEN C. YEAZELL

David G. Price & Dallas P. Price Distinguished Professor of Law Emeritus
University of California, Los Angeles

JOANNA C. SCHWARTZ

Vice Dean for Faculty Development and Professor of Law
University of California, Los Angeles

Wolters Kluwer

Published by Wolters Kluwer in New York.

Wolters Kluwer Legal & Regulatory U.S. serves customers worldwide with CCH, Aspen Publishers, and Kluwer Law International products. (www.WKLegaledu.com)

To contact Customer Service, e-mail customer.service@wolterskluwer.com, call 1-800-234-1660, fax 1-800-901-9075, or mail correspondence to:

> Wolters Kluwer
> Attn: Order Department
> PO Box 990
> Frederick, MD 21705

Printed in the United States of America.

1 2 3 4 5 6 7 8 9 0

ISBN 978-1-4548-9788-0

Library of Congress Cataloging-in-Publication Data

Names: Yeazell, Stephen C., author. | Schwartz, Joanna C., author.
Title: Civil procedure / Stephen C. Yeazell, David G. Price & Dallas P. Price Distinguished
  Professor of Law Emeritus, University of California, Los Angeles; Joanna
  C. Schwartz, Vice Dean for Faculty Development and Professor of Law, University of
  California, Los Angeles.
Description: Tenth edition. | New York: Wolters Kluwer, [2019] | Series:
  Aspen casebook series | Includes bibliographical references and index.
Identifiers: LCCN 2018043033 | ISBN 9781454897880
Subjects: LCSH: Civil procedure—United States. | LCGFT: Casebooks (Law)
Classification: LCC KF8839.Y43 2019 | DDC 347.73/5—dc23
LC record available at https://lccn.loc.gov/2018043033

Certified Chain of Custody
Promoting Sustainable Forestry
www.sfiprogram.org
SFI-01681

SFI label applies to the text stock

About Wolters Kluwer Legal & Regulatory U.S.

Wolters Kluwer Legal & Regulatory U.S. delivers expert content and solutions in the areas of law, corporate compliance, health compliance, reimbursement, and legal education. Its practical solutions help customers successfully navigate the demands of a changing environment to drive their daily activities, enhance decision quality and inspire confident outcomes.

Serving customers worldwide, its legal and regulatory portfolio includes products under the Aspen Publishers, CCH Incorporated, Kluwer Law International, ftwilliam.com and MediRegs names. They are regarded as exceptional and trusted resources for general legal and practice-specific knowledge, compliance and risk management, dynamic workflow solutions, and expert commentary.

For Ruth, Owen, and Emmet—SCY
and
For Teddy, Kate, and Julian—JCS

Summary of Contents

Contents

PART I: THE CONSTITUTIONAL FRAMEWORK FOR U.S. LITIGATION

Chapter 2: Personal Jurisdiction 67

PART II: THE PROCESS OF LITIGATION

Chapter 5: Incentives to Litigate   293

Chapter 7: Discovery   455

Chapter 10: Appeal   661

Chapter 11: Respect for Judgments   703

PART III: PROBING THE BOUNDARIES: ADDITIONAL CLAIMS AND PARTIES

Preface

Process lies at the core of our legal system: It expresses many of our culture's basic ideas about the meaning of fairness; it determines the victor in close cases; and it further determines which cases will be close ones. Procedure is also the area of law least understood and most maligned by lay observers. We root for underdogs and insist that rules not be stacked against them. But we are equally quick to condemn a case for having been decided on a "legal technicality," a phrase commonly signifying that a procedural rule has come into operation.

A similar ambivalence pervades debate about the behavior of courts and lawyers. As a society we demonstrate a strong belief in the efficacy of lawsuits to solve social, business, and personal problems, and we extol the rule of law as a distinguishing virtue of our culture. But at the same time we worry about what many believe is an excessive willingness to seek legal solutions. The ensuing debate ranges from the role of courts in restructuring social institutions to the question of whether lawyers exacerbate disputes and waste social resources by reflexively behaving in competitive, adversarial ways.

All these issues are procedural. Lawyers thus need to understand process as a tool of their trade, as a constitutive element of the legal system, and as a focus of debate about social values. Yet civil procedure is, by most accounts, a difficult and frustrating first-year course. Students come to law school with little experience in thinking explicitly about procedure and with an impression that cases simply arrive at the point of decision. Moreover, students sense that procedure may be the area in which lawyers' skill counts most; the notion that meritorious cases can be lost because of bad lawyering outrages their sense of justice even as it creates anxiety.

This book seeks to show procedure as an essential mechanism for presenting substantive questions and as a system that itself often raises fundamental issues regarding social values. We hope that students will begin to appreciate that lawyers move the system and that, to a large extent, clients' fates depend on the wisdom, skill, and judgment of their lawyers. Moreover, although all would agree that cases should not be decided on the basis of "mere" technicalities, fierce debate quickly arises when one tries to distinguish rules that merely direct traffic from those that guard the boundaries of fairness.

In addition to considering such theoretical issues, the book has some practical goals. It seeks to give students a working knowledge of the procedural system and its sometimes arcane terminology. The course also introduces the techniques of statutory analysis. It should give students a better understanding of the procedural context of the decisions they read in other courses. To these ends we have tried to select cases that are factually interesting and do not involve substantive matters beyond the experience of first-year students. The problems following the cases are intended to be answerable by first-year students and to present real-life issues. Finally, the book incorporates a number of dissenting opinions to dispel the notion that most procedural disputes present clear-cut issues.

The organization of the book adapts it to the most common sequences in contemporary procedure courses. After a brief overview of the procedural system in Chapter 1, some courses will initially consider the materials in Part I, which covers jurisdiction and choice of law. Other courses will begin with discussion of remedies, pleading, discovery, resolution without trial, identifying the trier, trial, appeal, and former adjudication, which are addressed in Part II. Part III, on joinder and complex litigation, recapitulates much of the material in Parts I and II and can be used either as a culmination of the course or as an insertion that follows pleading.

Cases have been severely edited to eliminate citations (without indicating their omission), and they read somewhat differently from real case reports; we hope they err in the direction of smoothness. Citations are retained only when they seem significant. Footnotes have been eliminated without indication. Those that survive retain their original numbers, while the editor's footnotes employ symbols. We have used several special citation forms: F. James, G. Hazard, and J. Leubsdorf, Civil Procedure (5th ed. 2001), is cited as James, Hazard, and Leubsdorf; C. Wright, Federal Courts (5th ed. 1994), is cited as Wright, Federal Courts; J. Moore, Federal Practice and Procedure (1969), is cited as Moore; C. Wright, A. Miller, and E. Cooper, Federal Practice and Procedure (1969), is cited as Wright and Miller.

Those whose assistance was acknowledged in the prefaces of earlier editions created the foundations on which this book rests. We additionally wish to thank two UCLA colleagues, Joel Feuer and Clyde Spillenger—and a former colleague, Maureen Carroll—who have gone above and beyond to help improve the tenth edition.

Finally, both of us want to thank many teachers and students who have used previous editions for detailed, thoughtful, and constructive suggestions. As with past editions, this one has been greatly improved by the library staff at UCLA's Hugh & Hazel Darling Law Library, whose ingenuity is exceeded only by their helpfulness.

We hope you like the result.

Joanna C. Schwartz
Stephen C. Yeazell

November 2018

Acknowledgments

CIVIL PROCEDURE

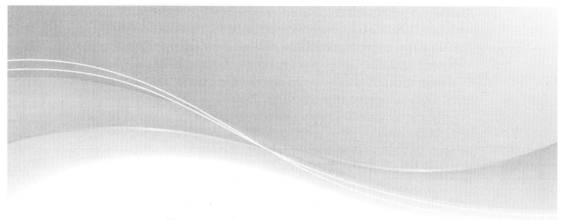

CHAPTER 1

An Overview of Procedure

A. THE IDEA AND THE PRACTICE OF PROCEDURE

1. Locating Procedure

Civil procedure is a course about truth and justice—about how we define those words, how we seek the goals they express, and how we sometimes lose sight of them. It is also, inevitably, a course about greed, venality, and oppression, and the running battle waged against these fundamental human characteristics.

Mixed with these lofty themes are the minutiae of lawyers' work. Civil procedure is about lawyers—about their relation to their clients, to their profession, and to the courts. Most of the first year of law school concerns what lawyers call substantive law, the rules governing behavior in ordinary life: property, criminal law, torts, and contract. Everyone needs to know at least a little about these topics simply to function in the everyday world. But procedure is insiders' law, of special importance to those administering the legal system.

Those insiders turn to procedure to describe the rules of the elaborate game called litigation. At one level, procedure is the etiquette of ritualized battle, defining the initiation, development, and conclusion of a lawsuit. What does one have to say to get a court to pay attention? Suppose my adversary wants to invoke a court's help—can I instead take the dispute to a different forum? From whom may a person with a grievance seek relief? What kind of relief? If I believe my adversary has information that would help me to prove my case, may I demand it of her? All these questions—involving what lawyers would call pleading, forum selection, joinder, remedies, and discovery—are dealt with in civil procedure. The answers to such questions are important to any lawyer who needs to help a client in a lawsuit. Although one might think that the underlying merits of the case are all that matters at the end of the day, procedural rulings—about where a case can be filed, whether a case can proceed to discovery, and whether a party is entitled to the discovery he seeks—can determine who wins and who loses.

But if procedure were only a set of rules about the etiquette of lawsuits, it would be hard to justify its place in the first-year curriculum. Another facet of procedure justifies that place: Procedure mirrors our most basic notions of fairness and the meaning of justice. If coming to a quick decision were all that mattered, we could flip coins to decide lawsuits. We don't flip coins because solving an important dispute without reference to its merits strikes us as unjust. This bedrock principle of fairness and justice finds expression both in the details of procedural design and in several parts of the U.S. Constitution, most notably the Due Process Clauses of the Fifth and Fourteenth Amendments.

Commentators, litigants, and courts do not, however, agree about what procedural mechanisms best reflect these overarching values. Some argue that our system is overly obsessed with permitting the adversarial airing of grievances. Proposed solutions range from streamlining adjudication to nonadjudicative dispute resolution. The system's defenders argue both that the critics overstate the pathologies of modern civil litigation and that adjudication has proved to be a major force for social justice, economic growth, and political stability over the past two centuries. Such conflicting views lurk in the background at every turn of our path.

This chapter seeks to give you some feel for procedural issues as they arise in the life cycle of a civil lawsuit. It will raise more questions than it answers, but it will offer you a sense of the course of civil litigation and a taste of the kinds of problems lawyers describe as procedural. Seeing the whole picture all at once will make more meaningful our closer investigation of these issues in the weeks to come.

We start with a simple and plausible fact situation: Peters, a student at the University of Michigan, spent his winter vacation in Champaign, Illinois, where his parents have recently moved from Milwaukee, Wisconsin. While visiting his parents, Peters was seriously injured in an automobile accident with Dodge, a lifelong resident of Champaign and owner of a popular ice cream parlor in the town. The remainder of this chapter deals with issues that might flow from this everyday occurrence.

2. Clients, Lawyers, Procedure, and Strategy

Consider first whether and how this accident might enter the formal legal system. Most such episodes will never get near lawyers or courts. If Peters had adequate medical insurance and no lost wages, he might have little reason to sue Dodge. Or Dodge (or his insurer) might well offer Peters a satisfactory settlement before a suit is filed. Or Peters might want to sue but be unable to find a lawyer who would take his case.

These three alternatives describe the fate of most disputes that arise in our society, with the consequence that they will never enter the official judicial system. For the rest of this book—and for the rest of law school—you will be dealing with the exceptional instances, the disputes that do find their way into court.

What would need to happen? First, Peters would probably need to find a lawyer. (In the United States individuals can prosecute their cases themselves—*in pro. per.* or *pro se,* in the jargon of the law*—but most consider lawyers worthwhile for litigation, in part because lawyers know their way around the procedural system.) We'll deal later, in Chapter 5, with how people in Peters's situation might find a lawyer; this matters a good deal, and because it does, it deserves more attention than it can get in this introduction.

But—even in this introduction—it bears emphasizing that the lawyer-client relationship involves *two* decisions at the outset. First, Peters, the prospective client, must locate a lawyer. For clients like Peters, that can be a bewildering process. Most individuals deal with lawyers quite infrequently, and therefore lack knowledge about what qualities to look for. Rules of professional ethics allow lawyers to advertise, but only in a limited way, and we have yet to develop a robust and reliable way of rating lawyers. So it's likely that someone in Peters's position would have to rely on word-of-mouth recommendations: Did a friend or relative have a lawyer she would recommend?

Suppose Peters does get such a recommendation and approaches Ursula Sands, a lawyer who practices in Champaign, where the accident occurred and where Peters's family lives. Further suppose that Sands's practice includes the kind of case Peters contemplates (as opposed, say, to a practice limited to wills or business transactions). When he visits Sands's office, the second decision must be made: Does Sands want to represent Peters? Experienced lawyers will tell you that the most important decision they make in a lawsuit is whether to take on a particular client. That initial decision derives its importance from the fact that professional rules prevent lawyers from simply abandoning clients if they become unhappy with the progress of the case. So Sands wants to be sure about at least two things before she takes on Peters as a client. First, she wants to know whether she can rely on his truthfulness and candor. It's a dreadful thing for a lawyer to discover, halfway through a case, that her client has fabricated part of the story or has omitted critical facts. We will learn a bit more in Chapter 6 about an attorney's obligation to double check her client's claims. Second, for reasons you'll better understand after reading Chapter 5, Sands will likely want to know whether the stakes of the case will warrant the investment it requires. In the United States today, almost all cases like Peters's will be handled on the plaintiff's side by a contingent fee agreement, in which the client pays nothing if the case fails but pays a percentage of any recovery to his lawyer. So Sands will care about the likely recovery in relation to the amount she will need to invest—in terms of her time and other expenses. If Peters's only injury is a broken ankle, but the case will require multiple experts, it's likely not worth his—or Sands's—while to pursue it. So, to reiterate, Peters must decide if he wants to retain Sands as his lawyer, and Sands must similarly decide whether she wants to represent Peters in this matter.

If Peters decides to hire Sands (and Sands agrees to take Peters on as a client), Peters and Sands have to divide responsibilities. Common sense and codes of

---

* *In pro. per.* is an abbreviation for the Latin *in propria persona,* meaning "in his or her own person" (rather than by an agent or attorney). *Pro se* means "for him- or herself."

professional ethics agree that clients make major decisions about the goals of litigation. A lawyer can get disbarred if she files suit, settles a case, or refuses a settlement without consulting her client. By contrast, questions of tactics belong to the lawyer: what court to sue in, whether to request a jury trial, how to develop the facts of the case, what evidence to present in what order, and more. A lawyer should keep her client informed about these matters and would certainly explain her thinking if a client asked, but generally would not seek a client's permission or advice concerning them. Because tactics, including procedural tactics, lie in the hands of the lawyer, the lawyer needs, besides good judgment, a good grounding in the available procedural tools. How well Sands uses these tools may, in a close case, spell the difference between victory and defeat for Peters. As you encounter cases in this course you will have two questions to answer: What principle of law determined who prevailed in this situation?; and which lawyer picked this particular fight and why—what strategic or tactical advantage was she hoping to achieve?

Having divided responsibilities between lawyer and client, the system has to decide how to handle problems that arise from this division of responsibilities. For representation to work, the legal system has to treat the lawyer's choices as if they were Peters's choices. In legal and economic terms Sands is Peters's "agent," acting for him in the lawsuit. When Peters's lawyer does a fine job, everyone (except Dodge) is happy. But what if she doesn't? Suppose Sands files a suit seeking recovery for personal injuries but not for damage to Peters's car. The legal system will treat that choice as if Peters himself had made it. But what if Sands's behavior results not from Peters's choice but from Sands's carelessness—forgetting to ask Peters whether his car was damaged? In that situation, the procedural system faces a dilemma. If the system lets Sands fix her mistake by later adding the claim for property damage, it will thereby harm Dodge, who may have been relying on the original claim to be a complete statement of Peters's grievance (and thus failed to preserve evidence showing that Peters's car was not in fact damaged). But if the procedural system insists that Peters stand by the original version of the claim—without the claim for property damage—it will thereby harm Peters, by blocking him from recovering for damage to his car.

This problem has no good solution, but the system tries to solve it in three ways. The first is to make the party who made the mistake suffer: Peters can sue Sands for malpractice if her negligence has caused him to forgo part of his recovery. The second is to tell the party suffering the harm—Dodge—that the harm really isn't so bad, and that he should suffer the expense and inconvenience of allowing Peters to fix the mistake. Finally, the system can try to wriggle out of the problem by allowing Peters to amend his claim but granting Dodge extra time to prepare a defense. Each solution has a corresponding drawback. If the system insists that Peters is bound by his lawyer's slip—and that his only remedy is a malpractice action—it will force him to start a second lawsuit (against his lawyer), with all the attendant uncertainty, expense, and delay. (Moreover, his lawyer may not have the assets or insurance to cover his losses.) If the system allows Peters's lawyer to cure her slip by amending the complaint, it will undermine the efficiency that flows from treating lawyers' actions as those of their clients and will inflict the costs of Peters's lawyer's sloppiness on Dodge. And if it crafts a solution that hurts neither Peters nor Dodge but extends the litigation, it may inflict costs on other litigants by making them wait longer to have their cases resolved.

Because procedural choices have consequences for parties and other litigants, you will repeatedly encounter courts trying to resolve this trilemma. As you do, consider whether the choices they make are reasonable.

WHAT'S NEW HERE?

If you've absorbed the preceding few pages, you have—even before encountering your first case or Rule or statute—learned something fundamental about the practice of law: that lawyers and clients stand in a relationship. Many layers of law and professional ethics define the lawyer-client relationship and most of them lie beyond the scope of this course. But each is assigned a role, and must have confidence that the other will do their part. The client, in choosing his lawyer, must keep in mind that the lawyer will be responsible for making tactical decisions about the litigation—including where to file the case, what evidence to seek, and how to present the claims—that could spell victory or defeat in the case. The lawyer, in accepting a case, must keep in mind that the client will have authority to accept or reject settlement offers, regardless of the attorney's view of whether the case should go to trial. So—for *both* lawyer and client—it's a very good idea to do some investigating and some thinking before entering the relationship.

B. WHERE CAN THE SUIT BE BROUGHT?

Once Peters has selected Ursula Sands as his lawyer, Sands will have to begin making procedural choices, each of which may have consequences for the outcome of the suit. One of the first such choices may not have occurred to you: where to file the case. The 50 states and the federal government all operate systems of courts, and Sands must find out whether she has a choice of courts. If she has a choice, she will have to decide which would be most advantageous.

Why should Sands care in which state Peters's case is heard? Convenience provides one possible answer: Recall that Peters is likely to return to Ann Arbor for classes, but Sands, his lawyer, operates out of Champaign. For Peters it would likely be more convenient to have the case heard in Ann Arbor, Michigan. For Sands, this may involve some headaches: If she is not licensed to practice in Michigan, she must refer the case to a lawyer who is. On the other hand, recall that Dodge is a long-established business owner in Champaign and Peters and his family are relative newcomers. A Champaign jury might be less sympathetic to Peters than to Dodge—in which case it may be worth Sands's time to find that Ann Arbor lawyer. Moreover, convenience for Peters is likely to mean inconvenience for Dodge (or his insurer), a possibility that may not make Sands unhappy. Will an Ann Arbor jury—with perhaps a University of Michigan student or two on it—be more sympathetic to Peters? Do courts in one state or the other have large case backlogs that would delay Peters's claim? Or maybe Sands is trying to avoid a particular judge, whom she believes to be unsympathetic or ill-tempered.

With a sense in mind of where she might prefer to bring suit, Sands now needs to know what the possibilities are. The rules governing where a suit can be brought come under the headings of personal jurisdiction, subject matter jurisdiction, and venue.

1. Personal Jurisdiction

A court in the United States cannot exercise power over a defendant—here Dodge— if doing so would "deprive any person of life, liberty, or property, without due process of law." Out of this phrase in the U.S. Constitution* the United States Supreme Court has woven an elaborate doctrinal fabric that limits the power of courts over defendants. As you will see in Chapter 2, this doctrine defines the *personal jurisdiction* of courts. To condense a great deal of law into a few words, a court cannot exercise power over Dodge unless the state in which that court sits has some connection with him or with the accident that gave rise to Peters's claim. Because Dodge lives in Illinois and the accident occurred there, courts in Illinois would have the power to hear the case, but not a court in Texas or California—unless Dodge lived there when the suit was later filed or had some other significant connection with those states.

What about Michigan, where Peters goes to school? Probably not, unless Dodge consented. The doctrine of personal jurisdiction focuses on the defendant, who is being taken to court against his will. That does not mean that defendants can only be sued in their home states—but it does mean that a state cannot enter a judgment against a defendant like Dodge who has no connection with the state. So our case is almost certain to be brought in a court in Illinois.

2. Subject Matter Jurisdiction

Assuming for now that Peters will have to bring suit in Illinois, does he have any other choices among courts available to him? Specifically, does he have his choice between a state court and a federal court? As already noted, Sands will want to choose the court that offers her client the greatest advantages—and fewest disadvantages.

All states have at least one court of general jurisdiction that could hear Peters's state law tort claim. In Illinois that court is the circuit court, but in other states it may be called a district court, superior court, court of common pleas, or, in New York, the Supreme Court. Thus one alternative open to Peters is the Circuit Court of Illinois.

Sands may also be able to file Peters's case in federal court. If she can, some additional elements enter the calculation. All federal judges are appointed for life

---

* There are, in fact *two* Due Process Clauses, one found in the Fifth Amendment, which applies only to the federal government, the other in the Fourteenth Amendment, which applies to the states.

(Article III of the U.S. Constitution permits their removal only by impeachment). Most state judges are subject to some electoral approval. That difference can be important in a case in which judicial insulation from political pressure may play a role (hardly likely in the Peters-Dodge case). Second, most federal districts are larger than their state equivalents (usually counties), so jurors will be drawn from a broader pool—not just Ann Arbor or Champaign but several surrounding counties. Consider how this fact might have affected the strategy of the plaintiffs' lawyer in the next case, *Hawkins v. Masters Farms*.

Though at this point in your study the idea may seem strange, federal courts have limited jurisdiction. Article III, §2 of the federal Constitution set the outer bounds of that jurisdiction. Within those bounds it is up to Congress to decide the precise subject matter jurisdiction of the federal courts. Congress has enacted a number of statutes authorizing federal district courts (the trial courts of the federal system) to hear certain kinds of cases. The most important statutes at this point in our exploration are 28 U.S.C. §§1331 and 1332(a).* Read those two statutes and decide which might apply to *Peters v. Dodge*. Then read the following case. Does it tell Peters's lawyer whether she can file his claim in federal court?

Hawkins v. Masters Farms, Inc.

2003 WL 21555767 (D. Kan. 2003)

VAN BEBBER, S.J.

Plaintiffs, Mary Ann Hawkins, as Personal Representative to the Estate of James Patrick Creal, and Rachel Baldwin, as heir of Mr. Creal, bring this action . . . against Defendants, Masters Farms, Inc., Harhge Farms, Inc., and Jack E. Masters. Plaintiffs' claims arise from a December 8, 2000 traffic accident in which a tractor driven by Defendant Masters collided with Mr. Creal's automobile, resulting in the death of Mr. Creal. Plaintiffs filed this action in federal court alleging the existence of diversity jurisdiction under 28 U.S.C. §1332. Defendants dispute that there is complete diversity among the parties, and the matter is before the court on Defendants' motion to dismiss for lack of subject matter jurisdiction. For the reasons set forth below, Defendants' motion is granted.

I. Rule 12(b)(1) Motion to Dismiss Standard

Fed. R. Civ. P. 12(b)(1) motions for lack of subject matter jurisdiction generally take one of two forms: (1) a facial attack on the sufficiency of the complaint's allegations as to subject matter jurisdiction; or (2) a challenge to the actual facts upon which subject matter jurisdiction is based. . . . Here, Defendants mount a factual attack on

---

* This citation form means that the text of this statute is found in section 1332 of title 28 of the United States Code, a compilation of the statutes that make up part of federal law. The "titles" are divisions of the code according to topic; title 28 is also known as the Judicial Code, and governs matters of procedure in federal courts.

Plaintiffs' allegations of diversity subject matter jurisdiction. In addition to Plaintiffs' complaint itself, deposition testimony and other documents have been submitted for the court's review. As the party seeking to invoke federal jurisdiction, Plaintiffs bear the burden of proving that jurisdiction is proper. Because federal courts are courts of limited jurisdiction, the presumption is against federal jurisdiction.

II. Factual Background

On December 8, 2000, Mr. Creal was killed in an automobile accident on Mineral Point Road, just south of Troy, Kansas, when his 1988 Chevrolet van collided with a New Holland tractor driven by Defendant Masters [a citizen of Kansas]. At the time of his death, Mr. Creal was living in Troy with his wife, Elizabeth Creal, and her children. He was approximately forty-four years old when he died.

James and Elizabeth Creal first met in St. Joseph, Missouri in November 1999. Mr. Creal had lived in St. Joseph for most of his life, while Mrs. Creal resided in Troy for the majority of her life. When the couple first met, Mr. Creal was living at his mother's home in St. Joseph, where he had been residing since obtaining a divorce from his previous wife.

Beginning in January 2000, Mr. Creal began spending the night at the apartment Mrs. Creal shared with her children on South Park Street in Troy. Initially, Mr. Creal would return to his mother's house every evening after work, shower, gather some clothes, and proceed to the apartment to retire for the evening. Mrs. Creal paid the rent for the apartment on South Park Street, while Mr. Creal contributed by buying the groceries for himself, Mrs. Creal, and her two children. Mr. and Mrs. Creal split the cost of utilities for the apartment.

When Mrs. Creal and her children moved into an apartment on 1st Street in Troy in March 2000, Mr. Creal brought his clothes, some furniture, pictures, photo albums, and other memorabilia to the new apartment. Mr. and Mrs. Creal also purchased a bedroom set for the apartment. When they moved into the apartment, Mr. Creal stopped going to his mother's house in St. Joseph to shower and change after work, and instead came directly back to Troy to spend the night. Also at that time, Mr. and Mrs. Creal opened a joint checking account into which Mr. Creal began depositing his paychecks to help pay the household bills. Mr. and Mrs. Creal were married in July 2000.

In November 2000, Mr. and Mrs. Creal moved into a house on Streeter Creek Road in Troy. Mr. Creal died approximately two weeks later. His death certificate lists Kansas as his residence.

From the time Mr. and Mrs. Creal first met until Mr. Creal's death in December 2000, Mr. Creal retained certain connections with the State of Missouri. In November 1999, he applied for a Missouri title and license for his Chevrolet van using his mother's St. Joseph address. In December 1999, he applied for automobile insurance on the van using the same address. In March 2000, he listed the address when he took out a loan and applied for a new Missouri title on the van to name a new lien holder. In April 2000, he renewed his Missouri driver's license for three more years under the address. In May 2000, he filled out a form for life insurance listing the address. Mr. Creal also received mail and his paycheck stubs at his mother's house, where he stopped by every week to visit. After his death, an estate was opened for Mr. Creal in Buchanan County, Missouri alleging that he resided at his mother's address at the time of his death.

Finally, although Mr. and Mrs. Creal left open the possibility of leaving Troy to move to a location closer to Kansas City, Missouri, such as Platte City or Faucett, Missouri, they never looked for houses elsewhere and never made any specific plans to leave. Mrs. Creal testified in deposition that she was, for the most part, satisfied living in Troy.

III. Discussion

. . . The parties do not dispute that all Defendants are citizens of the State of Kansas and that Plaintiff Baldwin is a citizen of the State of Missouri. Although Plaintiff Hawkins, as an individual, is also a citizen of the State of Missouri, her role in this case as Personal Representative of the Estate of Mr. Creal mandates that the court focus on the citizenship of Mr. Creal at the time of his death, not the citizenship of Plaintiff Hawkins herself. 28 U.S.C. §1332(c)(2) ("[T]he legal representative of the estate of a decedent shall be deemed to be a citizen only of the same State as the decedent . . ."). Whether Mr. Creal was a citizen of the State of Kansas or the State of Missouri at the time of his death is the central dispute currently before the court.

For purposes of determining whether diversity jurisdiction exists, a person is a "citizen" of the state in which he or she is "domiciled." "For adults, domicile is established by physical presence in a place in connection with a certain state of mind concerning one's intent to remain there." Miss. Band of Choctaw Indians v. Holyfield, 490 U.S. 30, 48 (1989).

Here, the court concludes that at the time of his death, Mr. Creal had not only established a physical presence in the State of Kansas, but also displayed an intent to remain there. Although Mr. Creal lived the majority of his life in St. Joseph, Missouri, he had been living in Troy, Kansas with his wife of five months for nearly one year at the time he died. Among other things, he had moved his clothes, some furniture, pictures, photo albums, and other memorabilia into the home he shared with Mrs. Creal and her children; he contributed to household costs; and he purchased a new bedroom set with his wife. Although Mr. Creal retained some connections with the State of Missouri, the court does not find these connections sufficient to overcome the evidence that his actions from January 2000 until the time of his death demonstrated an intent to remain with his wife in the State of Kansas. In fact, the only evidence presented by Plaintiffs that directly calls Mr. Creal's intent into question is the deposition testimony of Mrs. Creal that the couple left open the possibility of leaving Troy to move to a location like Platte City or Faucett, Missouri, but that they never looked for houses there or made any specific plans to leave. At most, Mrs. Creal's testimony evidences a "floating intention" of Mr. Creal to return to his former domicile, which is insufficient to overcome the evidence that he was domiciled in the State of Kansas at the time of his death.

In conclusion, the court has considered all of the evidence and arguments presented by the parties and holds that Mr. Creal was a citizen of the State of Kansas at the time of his death. Because Plaintiffs have failed to carry their burden of showing that complete diversity exists among the parties, the court grants Defendants' motion to dismiss for lack of subject matter jurisdiction.

IT IS, THEREFORE, BY THE COURT ORDERED that Defendants' motion to dismiss is granted.

The case is closed.

WHAT'S NEW HERE?

- *Hawkins* is a quintessential case about procedure. What does that mean? For starters, the case talks not at all about whether the driver of the tractor was careless—a question that will surely matter if the case goes to trial. Instead, it focuses on an apparently strange question: of what state Mr. Creal was a "citizen"? That matters because a federal statute, 28 U.S.C. §1332, confers subject matter jurisdiction on federal district courts in controversies between "citizens of different states." For over two centuries courts have interpreted that phrase in ways this short opinion elaborates.
- But—and this is what makes this a quintessential procedural case—after we know the answer to this question, we will still not have resolved the question of negligence (what lawyers would call the "substantive" issue in the case). Instead we will know *where* (in what court system) the rest of the case will proceed.

Notes and Problems

1. Focus on what the parties did that led to this decision.

   a. The plaintiffs filed a "complaint" (stay tuned) stating a claim for damages for wrongful death.

   b. The defendant then filed a "motion" (a request that the court do something).

      i. In this case it was a motion authorized by Rule 12(b)(1) of the Federal Rules of Civil Procedure. Read that Rule.

      ii. The motion asked the court to dismiss the case because the federal court lacked jurisdiction. The opinion doesn't tell us exactly what the motion papers said, but we can infer a good deal from the opinion. What do you suppose the defendants' lawyer said in the effort to get the case dismissed?

      iii. Once the defendants made this motion, the plaintiffs' lawyer resisted it, by filing more papers arguing against dismissal. Again, what can you infer the plaintiffs said to try to persuade the court not to dismiss the case?

2. Why do the plaintiffs lose?

   a. Troy, Kansas, where the Creals lived during their short marriage, is about 16 miles from St. Joseph, Missouri, which lies on the eastern bank of the Missouri River. Mr. Creal still conducted most of his business affairs in Missouri—his mother's address was on his car registration and insurance, life insurance, and paycheck. Why wasn't this enough to make him a "citizen" of Missouri?

   b. What's the smallest factual change that would, you think, lead to a different outcome? If the Creals had signed a lease in St. Joseph, but had not yet moved there? If Mr. Creal had not moved his "memorabilia" into their Kansas apartment? If the Creals had not married?

3. What does it mean that plaintiffs have lost this motion?

   a. Can plaintiffs file the claim again in federal court?

   b. Can plaintiffs file the claim again in a state court?

   c. The answer to 3a is almost certainly no, for reasons that we will discuss in Chapter 11. Although, as a technical matter, the plaintiffs could file the case again in federal court, it would quickly be dismissed because the issue of federal court jurisdiction has already been conclusively answered.

   d. The answer to 3b is "probably." The court held there was no subject matter jurisdiction in federal court, but a Kansas state court of general jurisdiction would be able to hear the case. One might think that during the federal litigation the statute of limitations would expire, but Kansas, like many states, has a "savings" statute, which provides:

   > If any action be commenced within due time, and the plaintiff fail in such action otherwise than upon the merits, and the time limited for the same shall have expired, the plaintiff, or, if the plaintiff die, and the cause of action survive, his or her representatives may commence a new action within six (6) months after such failure.
   >
   > K.S.A. §60-518.

   The action in federal court apparently "was commenced within due time," that is, within the statute of limitations, and it failed for a reason "otherwise than upon the merits," namely a jurisdictional dismissal.

4. How did the court come to know all the facts about the Creals that the court relied upon in making its ruling?

   a. For the most part, issues that arise before trial are decided based on motions written by a lawyer. Often motions include presentations of evidence, usually affidavits (sworn statements) from witnesses. The affidavits may incorporate documentary evidence: bills, correspondence, photographs, and the like. If you were representing the plaintiffs, whom would you have contacted to obtain an affidavit?

   b. In this case, because there was a dispute over the facts relating to the question of jurisdiction, the court says that it considered deposition testimony as well. At a deposition, a witness is questioned under oath before a court reporter by a lawyer for each party, usually at one attorney's office. The witness can also be requested to bring to the deposition documents in her possession, which then can be reviewed and possibly marked as exhibits. Lawyers can then use portions of the transcript and exhibits from the deposition to support motions they submit to the court. If you were representing the defendant, whom would you have liked to depose to obtain evidence to support your argument that the court lacked jurisdiction? What documents would you have asked the witnesses to bring to the deposition? What questions would you have asked?

c. As you read cases in this book and in your other law school courses, consider in each instance how the court came to know the facts that the court relies upon in its opinion. Much of lawyering consists of marshalling the facts and trying to persuade the court that your client's version of the facts is more credible than your opponent's version.

Procedure as Strategy

If it was clear that plaintiffs (the executor and heir of the estate) could have filed— and probably still can file—their claim in state court, why did the defendants' lawyer (most likely hired by their insurance carrier) spend time and money trying to get it dismissed from federal court? Conversely, if there was any doubt about the existence of federal diversity jurisdiction, why did plaintiffs (or, likely, their lawyer, who is probably working on a contingent fee basis) waste time and effort on a losing gamble when they could have been proceeding with state court litigation?

Your authors don't know for sure the answers to these questions. But reading the depositions taken in this case offers some clues that permit speculation. The plaintiffs requested a jury trial, as is common in automobile tort cases. Troy, Kansas is the seat of Doniphan County, located in northeast Kansas; a state court jury would have been drawn from the citizens of Doniphan County. If, however, the case were brought in federal court, the jury would be drawn from a much larger population pool, one that would include a number of city-dwellers.

Masters, a defendant, was a long-time resident of Troy, active in civic affairs, and known to many of its residents, including Elizabeth Creal. We know that Mr. Creal was a relative newcomer. The depositions reveal some more information about Mr. Creal: His marriage to Elizabeth Creal was his fourth marriage, and he appears not to have had close relationships with his adult children from his previous marriages. Nor was he connected with the religious or civic organizations in Troy. The fatal accident occurred when Creal was returning—alone—from a solitary day spent deer hunting.

Which jury pool would plaintiffs' lawyer want? Which jury pool would defendants' lawyer want? If this speculation is correct, notice something else: the decision's absolute silence about this factor. Judge Van Bebber, who grew up in Troy and may well have had a pretty good inkling about why this case was on the federal docket, applies the law to the facts and renders a decision. You will repeatedly encounter cases where your guess about trial strategy is not reflected in the court's application of the law.

5. On the basis of cases like *Hawkins*, Sands decides to bring Peters's case in a federal court. Dodge is indisputably a resident of Champaign, Illinois and thus a citizen of that state within the meaning of the statute. Where might Sands argue that Peters is domiciled to establish federal subject matter jurisdiction? Given what you know about students' lives, what sort of evidence would Sands want to gather to support her contention that diversity jurisdiction is appropriate here?

3. Service of Process

Once Sands has decided where to bring the suit, she must begin the action and notify the defendant that it has begun. The first thing to do is to draft a *complaint*. A copy of the complaint must be filed with the court. Rule 3.

Then the plaintiff's lawyer must formally notify the defendant of the suit. (It's quite likely that informal conversations with the defendant's insurance carrier will have suggested that a lawsuit is coming, but formal notice is necessary.) Rule 4 sets forth two basic means of notice, one inexpensive and informal, the other more expensive and formal. The inexpensive method, called waiver of service, involves mailing the defendant the complaint; if the defendant agrees to waive service the suit can proceed. The more expensive method, used if the defendant refuses to cooperate, requires the lawyer to draft a summons (an order to appear), and take it to the clerk of the court, who will sign and seal it. See Rule 4(a) and (b). The summons and complaint must then be "served" — that is, delivered to the defendant in one of the ways authorized by Rule 4 — by private process servers or, in exceptional cases, a federal marshal. The expense comes because process servers require a fee for their work. See Rule 4(c). These topics are covered in more depth in Chapter 2.

C. STATING THE CASE

1. The Lawyer's Responsibility

The preceding paragraphs referred in passing to the lawyer's drafting of a complaint. Do not be misled by that casual reference: A complaint asks the legal system to use governmental power to grant plaintiff relief; it sets out the plaintiff's claims against the defendant; leads to the exchange of discovery; and, if the facts warrant it, the entry of judgment against the defendant. Those filing a complaint bear the responsibility not to invoke the formal legal system for claims that lack factual or legal basis, and not to bring claims for improper purposes. Lawyers bear special burdens in this respect. Read Rule 11(b) and consider it in connection with the next case.

Bridges v. Diesel Service, Inc.

1994 U.S. Dist. LEXIS 9429 (E.D. Pa. 1994)

HUYETT, J.

I. Background

James Bridges ("Plaintiff") commenced this action against Diesel Service, Inc. ("Defendant") under the Americans with Disabilities Act ("ADA"), 42 U.S.C. §12101 et seq. [Bridges alleged that Diesel Service dismissed him from his job as a result of a disability and thus violated the ADA.] By Order dated June 29, 1994, the Court dismissed Plaintiff's Complaint without prejudice for failure to exhaust administrative remedies. In particular, Plaintiff did not file a charge with the Equal Employment Opportunity Commission ("EEOC") until after commencement of this action. Defendant now moves for sanctions pursuant to Fed. R. Civ. P. 11. . . .

II. Discussion

. . . [A]s explained in this Court's June 29 Order, the filing of a charge with the EEOC is . . . a condition precedent to maintenance of a discrimination suit under the ADA. The parties do not dispute that administrative remedies must be exhausted before commencement of an action under the ADA. . . .

Rule 11 "imposes an obligation on counsel and client analogous to the railroad crossing sign, 'Stop, Look and Listen.' It may be rephrased, 'Stop, Think, Investigate and Research' before filing papers either to initiate the suit or to conduct the litigation." Gaiardo v. Ethyl Corp., 835 F.2d 479, 482 (3d Cir. 1987). Rule 11 is violated only if, at the time of signing, the signing of the document filed was objectively unreasonable under the circumstances. "The Rule does not permit the use of the 'pure heart and an empty head' defense." Gaiardo. Rather, counsel's signature certifies the pleading is supported by a reasonable factual investigation and "a normally competent level of legal research." Lieb v. Topstone Industries, Inc., 788 F.2d 151, 157 (3d Cir. 1986).

The Court is not convinced that Plaintiff's counsel displayed a competent level of legal research. A brief review of case law would have revealed the EEOC filing requirement. Further, an award of sanctions for failure to exhaust administrative remedies is not unprecedented.

Notwithstanding, the Court will not grant sanctions. Rule 11 is not intended as a general fee-shifting device. The prime goal of Rule 11 sanctions is deterrence of improper conduct. In this case, monetary sanctions are not necessary to deter future misconduct. Plaintiff's counsel immediately acknowledged its error and attempted to rectify the situation by filing a charge with the EEOC and moving to place this action in civil suspense. In fact, the Complaint has been dismissed without prejudice. The Court expects that Plaintiff's counsel has learned its lesson and will demonstrate greater diligence in future.

Further, Rule 11 sanctions should be reserved for those exceptional circumstances where the claim asserted is patently unmeritorious or frivolous. The mistake in the present case was procedural rather than substantive. It is also possible that Plaintiff's counsel was confused by the different interpretations of the Supreme Court's holding in [a case interpreting the EEOC filing requirement]. Finally, the Court is aware of the need to avoid "chilling" Title VII litigation.

III. Conclusion

For the above stated reasons, Defendant's motion pursuant to Fed. R. Civ. P. 11 is DENIED. However, this Opinion should not be read as condoning the conduct of Plaintiff's counsel. As stated above, the standard of pre-filing research was below that required of competent counsel. Plaintiff's case has been dismissed without prejudice. If the action is refiled, the Court fully expects to see a high standard of legal product from Plaintiff's counsel—in particular attorney London, who signed the Complaint.

WHAT'S NEW HERE?

- Most Rules tell lawyers how to run the procedural system: where to file the complaint, how to notify the defendant, and so on.
- Rule 11 does something different: It tells lawyers and parties to be careful, diligent, and honest. And it sets forth some consequences if they are not.

Notes and Problems

1. The court concludes that the plaintiff's counsel did not "display[] a competent level of legal research." What did they do wrong? What provision of Rule 11(b) was violated?

2. The court concludes that the plaintiff's counsel violated Rule 11 by signing and filing a complaint that was "objectively unreasonable under the circumstances." But the court nevertheless declines to impose a sanction. What aspect of Rule 11(c) gives the court this discretion?

Procedure as Strategy

The judge, the defendant, and the plaintiff agreed that the complaint was defective and that it would be easy to cure the defect by filing the right piece of paper with the Commission. If the defect is so minor and so easy to cure, why did the defendant bother to file a motion for sanctions? One possibility is that the defendant hoped to collect fees for the relatively small amount of time necessary to bring the motion to dismiss. Possible, but not likely: Most judges would view such a sanctions motion as a waste of time—and think ill of the defendant's lawyer for imposing on the court.

Consider another possibility. Many employment discrimination lawyers would say that the EEOC filing requirement as a precondition of suit was quite elementary, and that a lawyer unfamiliar with it was likely not familiar with this area of the law. Supposing such an assessment to be correct, consider what signals the defendant's lawyer would be sending to the judge with this Rule 11 motion. Locate the signs in the opinion that the judge has heard those implicit signals.

Despite the plaintiff's attorneys' error, the court declines to impose sanctions. Why might that be? Note that, when Bridges's attorneys learned of the failure to exhaust, they agreed to dismiss the complaint without prejudice on the condition that defendant did not file a motion for sanctions.

The current Rule 11(c)(2)—not in effect at the time of the *Bridges* decision—requires that a party first serve his opponent with a motion for sanctions, then give her 21 days to fix the error. Only if the error remains uncorrected is the party allowed to provide the court with a copy of the motion. Were this rule followed in *Bridges*, the court would never have known of the plaintiff's attorneys' failure to exhaust—assuming that the plaintiff's lawyers withdrew the complaint within the 21 days.

Note: Reading the Rules—Process and Politics

In *Masters Farms* and in *Bridges* you have encountered references to various Federal Rules of Civil Procedure. What are these Rules? Where do they come from? How are they related to other sources of law that shape civil procedure: the Constitution, statutes, and cases?

Briefly put, the Rules are like statutes and the Constitution in that they state general principles rather than dealing with their application in specific instances, which is the task of courts. But the Rules differ from statutes in two important ways.

- Unlike statutes, they are not directly enacted by a legislature. Instead, Congress in 1935 empowered judges to write the Rules. A statute, 28 U.S.C. §2072 (called the Rules Enabling Act), empowers the U.S. Supreme Court to promulgate "rules of practice and procedure . . . for cases in the United States district courts."
- Also, unlike federal statutes, which can deal with any topic concerning which the Constitution allows Congress to legislate, the Rules may *only* deal with "practice and procedure." Emphasizing this point, 28 U.S.C. §2072(b) provides, "Such rules shall not abridge, enlarge, or modify any substantive right." To give a crude example, a Rule could not establish principles governing damages for breach of contract; that would be "substantive." A Rule could, however, tell the parties how they have to go about claiming whatever damages they have suffered; Rules 8(a)(3)

and 26(a)(1)(A)(iii) do just that. As you will learn in your studies this year, defining the boundary between substance (which the Rules may not regulate) and procedure (which they may) can be difficult, but Congress has made it clear that it wants the Rules to confine themselves to the latter. You will also notice that, in theory, a Rule could violate the Rules Enabling Act if it crossed the line and regulated a "substantive right"— if, for example, a Rule tried to establish the principles of contractual damages. The Supreme Court has never found such a violation, though on several occasions parties have argued that some Rule crossed this line.

The original set of Federal Rules became effective in 1938. The Supreme Court Justices did not write the original Rules themselves nor do they now serve as the primary body considering amendments to the Rules. Instead, as provided in 28 U.S.C. §§2073-2077, a series of committees, appointed by the Chief Justice of the United States Supreme Court, do this work. A Committee on Civil Rules, consisting of judges, lawyers, and a professor or two, considers proposed amendments to the Rules. This group circulates proposed changes, holds public hearings, revises the changes in light of the hearings, and submits the results to the Standing Committee on Rules of Practice, Procedure, and Evidence, again with members from the bench and bar. The Standing Committee further considers and refines the proposed amendments, passing them in turn to the Judicial Conference of the United States. The Conference, consisting entirely of federal judges and presided over by the chief justice, is the senior administrative body of the federal courts. Its tasks include everything from judicial discipline to assigning visiting judges, approving requests for new courthouse buildings, and passing on proposed amendments to the Rules.

If the Conference approves a change, it passes the proposed Rule to the Supreme Court. With all these layers in place, it may not be surprising to learn, first, that amending a Rule takes a long time, and, second, that the Court has rarely rejected outright a Rules amendment, although on occasion individual justices have dissented from the promulgation of a proposed Rule.

Even after all these steps the proposed Rule still is not law. Under 28 U.S.C. §2074 the Court, if it too approves the proposed change, must "transmit [it] to Congress not later than May 1 of the year in which such a rule . . . is to become effective." Congress has until December 1 to act: If it disagrees with a proposed change it can pass a statute blocking or altering the proposed Rule. Congress has only on a very few occasions blocked or amended a Rule.

Since their promulgation in 1938 the Rules have undergone a number of revisions, some minor (adding a new holiday to the list of days that do not "count" for time limits) and some major (creating the modern class action, a change that some thought came close enough to being "substantive" that it violated the Rules Enabling Act).

After a number of decades during which the Rules and the process that produced them were seen as essentially technical, recent years have seen both individual Rules and the process surrounding them become the source of controversy. Briefly put, that controversy has taken two forms. Some have criticized specific Rules as favoring one group over another. For example, some say that the recent changes in discovery rules came at the behest of repeat defendants (generally large public and private institutions) and will handicap those who more often find themselves as plaintiffs—those challenging the actions of such defendants. (We'll explore this branch of the controversy more thoroughly in Chapter 7, on discovery.) The other form of criticism focuses on the courts, which, some charge, have interpreted Rules in ways unintended by the drafters and which, again, favor institutional defendants over plaintiffs. As examples, critics cite the U.S. Supreme Court's recent reinterpretation (as the critics would have it) of Rule 8, governing pleading; and the same Court's interpretation of Rule 23, governing class actions. As you will see in later chapters, these decisions raised barriers for plaintiffs that, critics say, betray the original principles behind the Rules and distort access to justice. In the pages that follow, we shall try to highlight such examples of controversy—we aim not to resolve these disputes, but to lay out their bases and sometimes point to data that would enable one to decide who has the stronger argument.

Finally, one should note that the Rules have had an influence far beyond the courts for which they were written. Federal courts hear only 2 percent of the civil cases in the United States. But the model represented by the Rules—merger of law and equity, relaxed pleading, flexible joinder of claims and parties, and broad discovery—has deeply influenced the procedure of state courts. Though it was not the case in 1938, *every* state now uses a procedural model that embraces most of these principles. At one time, 30-plus states went so far as to adopt the "federal" Rules as their own procedural code. This trend has declined; as of 2003, one scholar found "no true replicas" of the Federal Rules adopted by any state, but concluded that "the federal model of civil procedure remains substantially influential at the state level." John B. Oakley, *A Fresh Look at the Federal Rules in State Courts*, 3 Nev. L.J. 354 (2003). So when you are studying the Rules, you are studying the most influential procedural reform of the last 200 years. Note also that the states' adoption of a Rules-model procedure makes state courts a forum for the political controversies just noted. To use just one example, when the U.S. Supreme Court interpreted Rule 8 (the pleading rule) in a way said to handicap plaintiffs, that interpretation bound all federal courts, but left state courts free to interpret their analogous rule in a different way. So when, in the coming pages, you read a federal court's interpretation of a federal Rule, you might ponder whether you think a state should follow the same path or diverge from it.

2. The Complaint

Bridges illustrates one facet of a lawyer's responsibility in drafting a complaint. But even if Peters's lawyer is entirely comfortable that the claim is well grounded in fact and in law, she must still confront the task of setting forth that claim in a formal document. What should be in a complaint? Should it contain a simple statement that Peters is suing Dodge for injuries suffered in an accident, or a detailed recitation of what each party did on the day of the accident, and a blow-by-blow account of plaintiff's injuries and recovery? As we will explore in Chapter 6, we are now in the midst of a revived debate over that question. The next case captures what was, until recently, the answer in federal courts and continues to be the rule in most state courts.

Bell v. Novick Transfer Co.

17 F.R.D. 279 (D. Md. 1955)

THOMPSEN, J.

In this tort action, originally filed in the Court of Common Pleas of Baltimore City, and removed to this court pursuant to 28 U.S.C. §§1441 and 1446, defendants have moved to "dismiss the Declaration" because (1) it "fails to state a claim against the defendants and each of them upon which relief can be granted"; (2) it "alleges only that an accident occurred due to the negligence of the defendants as a result of which the plaintiffs were injured"; and (3) it "fails to allege the specific acts of negligence by the defendants of which the plaintiffs complain."

The [complaint, known in Maryland as a] declaration[,] alleges that [1] "on or about August 14, 1954, while the Infant Plaintiff, Ronald Bell, was riding in an automobile headed in a northerly direction on Race Road at its intersection with Pulaski Highway, both said road and highway being public highways of Baltimore County, State of Maryland, the automobile in which the infant plaintiff was riding was run into and struck by an automobile tractor-trailer outfit owned by the Defendants, Novick Transfer Company, Inc., and Katie Marie Parsons, and operated at the time by their agent, servant or employee, the Defendant, Morris Jarrett Coburn, III, in a careless, reckless and negligent manner, in a westerly direction on Pulaski Highway at the intersection aforesaid, [2] so that" the infant plaintiff was injured. The declaration also alleges the injuries and damage, and that they were "the direct result of the negligence on the part of the defendants" without any negligence on the part of the plaintiffs contributing thereto.

Although this declaration may not be sufficient under Maryland practice, it meets the requirements of Rule 8, Fed. Rules Civ. Proc., which requires only "a short and plain statement of the claim showing that the pleader is entitled to relief."

Nor is defendant entitled in this case to "a more definite statement" by motion under Rule 12(e). Although some courts have held that such a motion is the correct procedure to follow if a party needs further information to prepare his defense, the better rule of law is that such information should be obtained by interrogatories under Rule 33, or other discovery procedure, unless it is really necessary to enable the party to frame his responsive pleading.

Defendant may obtain by interrogatories or other discovery procedure the facts upon which plaintiff based its allegations that the truck was being operated in a careless, reckless and negligent manner, and that such negligence was the direct cause of the injury to the infant plaintiff.

The motion is hereby overruled.

Notes and Problems

---

1. To understand what this fight is about, reread the second paragraph of the opinion, which quotes the significant parts of the complaint, which are preceded by numbers in square brackets (e.g., [1]). Imagine yourself in the position of the defendant. What other information would the defendant want the complaint to contain?

    a. Why might the plaintiff not include all the detail desired by the defendant?

    b. Why doesn't the court require the plaintiff to include additional detail in the complaint?

    c. If the plaintiff did not know this information, would filing the complaint violate Rule 11? (The case arose before the current version of Rule 11.) Presumably not, so long as there was a factual basis for the claims made in the complaint.

2. The court, in passing, notes that the complaint was not sufficiently detailed to pass muster under the then-prevailing Maryland state court pleading rules. That statement references a debate that has recently taken on new salience.

    a. One school of thought says that a detailed complaint will enable courts to screen out weak claims early in the process. That desirable result will, however, come at the cost of eliminating a certain number of claims that *would be strong* if they gained access to the discovery mechanism that is one hallmark of modern procedure.

    b. The other school of thought says that "notice pleading"—a regime like that endorsed in *Bell*, that gives the defendant only a general idea of the nature of the claim—will lead to more claims being resolved justly, on their factual merits. That desirable result will, however, come at the cost of allowing some weak claims to survive to a later stage of litigation—thus increasing the defendant's litigation expense.

3. The case accurately describes the approach long understood to be prescribed by the Federal Rules—allowing sketchy pleadings and leaving until a later stage the elimination of unsubstantiated claims. As you will see in Chapter 6, over the last several years the U.S. Supreme Court has revisited this debate, interpreting Rule 8 with more stringency than does the opinion in *Bell v. Novick Transfer*. Stay tuned.

Procedure as Strategy

We have thus far focused on procedural maneuvers in which the adversaries have sought to use procedural rules to gain tactical or procedural advantage. Consider the possibility that Novick Transfer's lawyer may have outsmarted himself. Unlike *Hawkins v. Masters Farms*, Bell's lawyer originally filed suit in a state court. The opinion tells us in passing that the very general complaint it quotes would at the time not have passed muster in Maryland state courts. But defendant, presumably seeking some tactical advantage, "removed" the case to federal court alleging that the parties were of diverse citizenship. (As you will see in Chapter 3, under some circumstances it is possible for a defendant to reject plaintiff's original choice of a court.) Explain how this opinion suggests that the decision to remove was a tactical error.

On the basis of *Novick Transfer Co.*, Peters's attorney has drafted the following complaint:

United States District Court for the Central District of Illinois

---

Paul Peters,
    Plaintiff

                                            COMPLAINT FOR NEGLIGENCE
                                                    File No. _____

v.

Dan Dodge,
    Defendant

Plaintiff, Paul Peters, for his complaint, alleges as follows:

1. Plaintiff, Paul Peters, is a citizen of the state of Michigan, and defendant, Dan Dodge, is a citizen of the state of Illinois. The matter in controversy exceeds $75,000, exclusive of interest and costs.

2. On January 1, 2019, Paul Peters was operating his car on Main Street in Champaign, Illinois.

3. At 4:00 P.M. on that date, a car owned and operated by defendant Dan Dodge negligently collided with plaintiff's car, causing damage to plaintiff's car and injury to plaintiff's person.

4. Plaintiff suffered a sprained neck, broken arm, and numerous bruises and lacerations, and incurred medical expenses in the amount of $25,000.

WHEREFORE, plaintiff demands judgment for $100,000, together with the costs of this action.

Ursula Sands
Attorney for Plaintiff
123 Church Street
Champaign, Illinois 61820
sands@sandslaw.com
217/353-5775

---

3. The Response—Motions and Answer

Once defendant receives proper notice of the complaint, attention shifts to his response—the defense of the action. In the United States in the twenty-first century, most defendants in cases like *Peters v. Dodge* will be represented by a lawyer hired by their automobile insurer.

Liability policies typically contain two promises—that the insurer will pay damages (up to the amount of the policy limits) *and* that the insurer will provide a legal defense. Dodge will have notified his insurer immediately after the accident (liability policies require prompt notification of accidents so the insurer's staff can gather information with which to defend against possible claims). When Dodge is served with the complaint, he may be upset that he's being sued, but he'll again contact his insurer, who will inform him that the insurer will provide a lawyer. The insurer will then contact a local lawyer, with whom the insurer likely has a standing arrangement, giving the lawyer any information already in the file. The lawyer will contact Dodge directly and proceed from there with Dodge as her client. The relationship between Dodge and his attorney will mirror that between Peters and his attorney, with one important exception. Almost all liability policies give the insurer—not the insured—authority to settle the case. So an insurer could decide that Peters's claim was strong and pay him the damages he demanded (or whatever smaller sum was agreed on), even if Dodge vehemently denied any liability. Conversely, even if Dodge wanted his insurer to enter into a quick settlement so he could focus all his attention on his ice cream shop, the insurer could decide to contest liability and litigate.*

Assume that Dodge and his insurer do not want to settle, at least at this stage. How does Dodge's lawyer proceed? Her first procedural task is to respond to the complaint. Although it would be possible to have a system in which a defendant was not required to do anything until trial, both the Federal Rules and state codes of procedure require some response by the defendant. Generally, that response takes one of two forms: a *motion* attacking the complaint in some way or a pleading responding to the allegations in the complaint (usually called an *answer*).

a. Pre-Answer Motions

Motions is lawyer-talk for requests that a court do something; lawyers speak of "moving" or of "making a motion" to have the court take some step—dismiss the case, require an adversary to disclose certain information, enter judgment on a verdict, and so on. At the early stages of litigation, there are several motions that a defendant may make to end the case or to alter its shape, set out in Rule 12(b).

There may be reasons, having nothing to do with the merits of the claim, why a case should be dismissed. These reasons typically relate to the court in which the action is brought or the method by which the defendant was brought into that court. For example, the defendant may contend that the case should be dismissed because it does not belong in federal court (subject matter jurisdiction); such a motion prompted the decision in *Hawkins v. Masters Farms*, the first case in this chapter. See Rule 12(b)(1).

---

* As you may learn in another course, there may be penalties if an insurer *unreasonably* refuses to settle a case, but we ignore these refinements for now.

The defendant may also say that, even if everything in the complaint is true, under the substantive law plaintiff has no right to relief. An obvious if unrealistic example is a complaint that alleges that the defendant made a face at the plaintiff or that the defendant drove a car of an offensive color. At common law, the defendant would *demur* to such claims; now we say that the defendant moves to dismiss on the ground that the complaint fails to state a claim upon which relief can be granted. See Rule 12(b)(6). The opinion you read in *Bell v. Novick Transfer* was written in response to the defendant's Rule 12(b)(6) motion.

Notice an important characteristic of these pre-answer motions: *They take no position on the truth or falsity of plaintiff's factual allegations* (for example, that Dodge was driving negligently). That, as you will see in a moment, is the job of the answer.

Notes and Problems

---

1. If Dodge wants to make a pre-answer motion to dismiss for lack of subject matter jurisdiction, he will prepare and file a series of papers with the court and serve them on Peters:

   a. A notice of the motion—which simply tells the other side that the defendant plans to make a motion, what that motion is (here, a motion to dismiss for want of subject matter jurisdiction), and the time and place at which the motion will be heard by the judge;

   b. A memorandum of points and authorities (a short brief discussing his case and the reasons the court should grant his motion);

   c. Any evidence pertinent to the motion—perhaps an affidavit (a sworn declaration) and copies of documents concerning Dodge's and Peters's residence and local affiliations.

2. What next? It has become common for motions to be decided without any oral hearing—"on the papers." In that event the judge will simply issue a ruling. If there is a hearing, the judge will typically have read the motion papers beforehand. The judge will either hear oral argument from the lawyers or ask them questions about any aspects of the case not clear from the papers. She may decide the motion on the spot or she may reserve her ruling, making it after additional thought or research. Sometimes a judge will issue a tentative ruling based on the papers, which is given to the lawyers when they arrive for the hearing. The judge then allows the losing party to argue against the tentative ruling.

   If the defendant does not make a pre-answer motion or if the court denies a pre-answer motion, the defendant must then answer. See Rules 7(a), 12(a).

b. *The Answer*

In contrast to a pre-answer motion, an *answer*, as the name suggests, does respond to the allegations of the complaint, paragraph by paragraph. There are only two essential variations on the answer:

1. In the most common response to a complaint, the defendant denies the truth of one or more of the allegations of the complaint, or, if after reasonable investigation the defendant does not know whether an allegation is true, he may deny the allegation. See Rule 8(b). (At common law, this move was called a *traverse**; today it's a *denial*.) The defendant will also likely admit some of the facts in the complaint, for example, the day the accident occurred, or the citizenship of the parties.

2. The defendant may want to assert defenses that will wholly or partially defeat plaintiff's claim. For example, the defendant may contend that the applicable statute of limitations has run or that the plaintiff has released her claim. At common law, such matters were called *confession and avoidance*; today we call them *affirmative defenses*. See Rule 8(c).

3. The defendant may also wish to assert a claim against the plaintiff that would entitle him to relief. These are called *counterclaims*. See Rule 13.

Turning to Peters's case, let us suppose that Dodge's attorney decides there is no question relating to personal jurisdiction and that there are no problems with notice or service of process. On the other hand, Dodge may very well believe that the federal court does not have subject matter jurisdiction over the claim because the parties are not diverse (as in *Hawkins*). Dodge probably will want to deny certain allegations of the complaint, such as the allegation that he was negligent. He also may want to allege various affirmative defenses to Peters's claims. For example, in such a case it is quite common for a defendant to claim that the plaintiff's contributory negligence was, at least in part, the cause of the accident. Such contributory negligence will act as a complete or partial defense to recovery. And, if Dodge was injured or his vehicle damaged in the accident, he will want to assert a counterclaim, alleging Peters's negligence caused injuries to Dodge, which could enable Dodge to get compensation for his injuries and property damage. Indeed, as you will discover in Chapter 12, if Dodge has a counterclaim arising from the accident, he *must* assert it in his answer, or lose it.

After considering the possible responses and possible counterclaims, Dodge's attorney drafts the following answer to Peters's complaint.

---

* From an obsolete sense of the word: "something that crosses, thwarts, or obstructs."

United States District Court for the Central District of Illinois

Paul Peters,
  Plaintiff

              ANSWER AND COUNTERCLAIM
                File No. _____

v.

Dan Dodge,
  Defendant

Defendant, Dan Dodge, answers the complaint of plaintiff herein as follows:

 1. Admits that defendant is a citizen of the state of Illinois, and, except as admitted, denies the allegations of paragraph 1 of the complaint.

 2. Admits that, at approximately 4:00 P.M. on January 1, 2019, plaintiff was operating a car on Main Street in Champaign, Illinois, and, except as admitted, states that defendant is without information sufficient to form a belief as to the truth of the allegations in paragraph 2 of the complaint and, on that basis, denies the allegations of paragraph 2 of the complaint.

 3. Admits that, at approximately 4:00 P.M. on January 1, 2019, there was a collision between a car owned and operated by defendant and a car owned and operated by plaintiff and that plaintiff's vehicle was damaged and plaintiff suffered some injury as a result of said collision and, except as admitted, defendant denies the allegations of paragraph 3 of the complaint.

 4. Defendant states that he is without information sufficient to form a belief as to the truth of the allegations in paragraph 4 of the complaint and, on that basis, denies the allegations of paragraph 4 of the complaint.

First Defense

 5. The court lacks jurisdiction over the subject matter of this action because plaintiff and defendant are not citizens of different states.

Second Defense

 6. Defendant alleges that plaintiff drove his car carelessly and recklessly, and that such careless and reckless operation was a cause of the accident.

Counterclaim

 7. On January 1, 2019, at approximately 4:00 P.M. at Main Street in Champaign, Illinois, Paul Peters drove a car in a careless, reckless, and negligent manner and thereby caused said car to collide with a car owned and operated by Dan Dodge.

 8. As a result of said collision, Dodge's car was damaged, and Dodge also suffered a whiplash injury, as well as numerous cuts and bruises, and incurred expenses for medical treatment of $1,800.

WHEREFORE, defendant demands judgment dismissing Peters's action and judgment against Peters on the counterclaim in the amount of $12,000, together with the costs thereof.

Yvonne O. Upton
Attorney for Defendant
125 Church Street
Champaign, Illinois 61820
upton@uptonlaw.com
217/353-7531

Notes and Problems

1. Contrast this answer with the hypothetical pre-answer motion discussed in the previous section.

   a. Note first the difference in scope. Unlike the motion, the answer responds to all the paragraphs of the complaint, rather than selecting one or two aspects.

   b. Unlike the motion, the answer seeks no immediate relief from the court; instead it sets the stage for various future battles. For example, filing an answer raising the defense of Peters's negligence does not ask the court to dismiss the case on this ground. Instead, it notifies Peters and the court that Dodge may raise this defense at summary judgment or trial.

2. What would happen if the answer failed to respond to some of the allegations of the complaint? See Rule 8(b)(6).

3. What is the point of stating that the defendant lacked information or belief sufficient to admit or deny some of the allegations of the complaint? See Rule 8(b)(5).

4. Are the allegations in paragraph 7 of the answer ambiguous? What exactly does Dodge mean when he writes: "Peters drove a car in a careless, reckless, and negligent manner"? Having filed such a counterclaim, could Dodge seek to introduce evidence that Peters's brakes failed because he had not properly maintained them? Perhaps, if a court read the paragraph broadly. If not, Dodge could only introduce this evidence if he was able to amend his answer to add an additional counterclaim—a topic we are turning to now.

WHAT'S NEW HERE?

- With the sample complaint and answer, we've moved from the conceptual to the practical: What words does a lawyer put down on what kind of paper to achieve what effect? Spend a few minutes looking first at the relevant Rules (8 and 12, in this case) and comparing their general directives to the specific embodiment in the complaint and answer and in the cases interpreting their scope.

4. Amendment of Pleadings

In discussing complaints and answers, we have been speaking of what the Rules call "pleadings"; Rule 7(a) contains a complete list. The Federal Rules reject the view that the case is set in stone once the pleadings are completed. Instead, the Rules reflect a liberal policy toward changes (called *amendments*) to the pleadings. The discovery rules, which enable parties to gather information about the case, would mean little if new information could not be reflected in amended pleadings. For example, the *Peters v. Dodge* complaint assumes that Dodge was both the owner and driver of the vehicle. Discovery might reveal that Dodge's daughter holds title to the vehicle (suppose Dodge bought the car as a graduation present for the daughter, but was borrowing it for the day while his own car was in the shop). Under the substantive law, owners of a vehicle are liable for accidents negligently caused by a permissive driver. Having learned of this circumstance, Peters's lawyer could seek to amend the complaint to add Dodge's daughter as a defendant.

Rule 15(a) sets forth the basic amendment rules and states that "[t]he court should freely give leave [to amend] when justice so requires." What this seemingly simple phrase means is open to interpretation, as we will see in Chapter 6. Rule 15(c) deals with amendments that add a new claim or party after the statute of limitations has run.

D. PARTIES TO THE LAWSUIT

Our Peters-Dodge lawsuit is an action by a single plaintiff against a single defendant, but litigation often is not so simple; the events giving rise to a lawsuit may affect more than two persons, sometimes many more. The procedural issues raised by the involvement of multiple parties are addressed by a number of Rules. First, who *may* be joined as a plaintiff or a defendant in the lawsuit? See Rule 20. Second, who *must* be joined as a plaintiff or a defendant in the lawsuit? See Rule 19. Third, are there persons who are not in the lawsuit who can join as parties if they so choose? See Rule 24. Fourth, may some of the parties in the lawsuit represent others who are not in the lawsuit, so that the final decision will determine the rights of all? See Rule 23. There are other party issues as well, and we turn to them in Chapter 12.

In this quick survey, we will focus on one joinder rule: Rule 20, which governs permissive joinder. Note that the plaintiff has a choice of whom to join as a coplaintiff as well as whom to join as codefendants. Imagine that Peters was riding in the car with Penny, his sister, who was also injured in the collision. Could Peters and Penny sue Dodge in one lawsuit? Read Rule 20, then consider how it applies to the following case, and what might be at stake for the parties.

Fisher v. Ciba Specialty Chemicals Corp.

245 F.R.D. 539 (S.D. Ala. 2007)

STEELE, J.

I. Background

This action involves claims brought by five individual plaintiffs who own property in or around Washington County, Alabama alleging diminution in value to their real estate caused by environmental contamination from a nearby chemical manufacturing facility . . . owned at various times by defendants. Plaintiffs contend that their properties are contaminated by DDT emanating from Ciba's McIntosh plant. . . .

On April 27, 2007, defendants filed a Motion to Sever pursuant to Rules 20 and 21, Fed. R. Civ. P., seeking to splinter the trial of these proceedings (which is slated for the August 2007 trial term) into five separate trials, one for each plaintiff. Defendants ground their Motion on assertions that a common trial would be inefficient and prejudicial. Plaintiffs oppose the Motion, arguing that severing the plaintiffs' essentially identical claims would effect great inefficiency, undue delay and undue expense, while also burdening the Court with presiding over a largely similar trial five times in a row.

II. Analysis

A. Legal Standard

. . . The determination of whether to grant a motion to sever is left to the discretion of the trial court. . . . Among the factors considered in exercising that discretion include whether the claims arise from the same transaction or occurrence, whether they present some common question of law or fact, whether severance would facilitate settlement or judicial economy, and the relative prejudice to each side if the motion is granted or denied. . . .

In assessing whether severance is appropriate under Rules 20 and 21, one factor is whether the claims arise from the same transaction. The Eleventh Circuit has opined that the term "transaction is a word of flexible meaning" that "may comprehend a series of many occurrences, depending not so much upon the immediateness of their connection as upon their logical relationship." *Alexander*, 207 F.3d at 1323 (citations omitted). Likewise, for purposes of the commonality element, the *Alexander* panel stressed that "Rule 20 does not require that *all* questions of law and fact raised by the dispute be common, but only that *some* question of law or fact be common to all parties." *Id.* at 1324.

B. Application of Standard

Defendants articulate four different grounds for their contention that severance of each plaintiff's claims from each other plaintiff's claims for trial purposes is appropriate. In particular, defendants argue that (i) plaintiffs' claims do not arise from the same transaction or occurrence; (ii) plaintiffs will rely on individualized evidence to prove their claims; (iii) defendants will invoke individual-specific defenses; and (iv) a common trial will be prejudicial to defendants.

The first three of defendants' contentions logically should be considered together, because they all are fundamentally challenges to the efficiency of trying all five plaintiffs' claims in a single trial. . . .

Plainly, to conduct a single joint trial would be a strategy marked by both efficiencies, inasmuch as the issues of common proof need only be presented and decided once, and inefficiencies, inasmuch as there will be a certain degree of unique evidence and argument as to each plaintiff's claims that is not germane to the other plaintiffs' claims. . . . After careful consideration of the respective arguments of counsel, the Court is persuaded that, while neither approach is optimal, the interests of efficiency would be best served by keeping the plaintiffs' claims together for trial in their present consolidated posture. The Court anticipates that there will be substantial overlapping background evidence for all plaintiffs' claims concerning the environmental history and activities of the Ciba plant, and the interactions of Ciba with the media, government regulators, and alleged co-conspirators. Moreover, plaintiffs have argued, and defendants have not disputed, that it is probable that the same roster of nine expert witnesses (three for plaintiffs and six for defendants), all of whom live out of state, will be called to testify with respect to each plaintiff's claims. To require these nine experts (not to mention counsel, many of whom live in Texas and Louisiana) to travel to Mobile, Alabama five times in quick succession (or to sit and wait in a hotel for days on end) to testify in five different trials would be financially foolhardy and needlessly wasteful of the parties' economic resources, potentially even rendering these trials cost-prohibitive.* Moreover, if these nine experts would be testifying to substantially similar, partially overlapping opinions in each of these five trials, the attendant drag on the efficient administration of justice would be considerable, as this Court would be subjected to something akin to a judicial *Groundhog Day.* Under the specific circumstances of this case, it appears far preferable from a judicial economy standpoint to hear all of the evidence once, including both common and plaintiff-specific facts, in a single trial proceeding than to hear the common evidence five times, with plaintiff-specific testimony being confined to

---

* To illustrate the point, the aggregated hourly rate of these nine expert witnesses approaches $3,000, which equals or exceeds the county-assessed property values of four of the five plaintiffs' property at issue herein.

each plaintiff's individual trial. Accordingly, the Court finds that considerations of efficiency and delay do not militate in favor of severance.

Defendants also maintain that a joint trial would be "extremely prejudicial" to them. This objection is apparently threefold, to-wit: (a) a multiplicity of plaintiff-specific facts will confuse the jury; (b) to the extent that one plaintiff's claims are stronger than the others', evidence as to that plaintiff may unfairly taint the jury as to the other plaintiffs' claims; and (c) consolidation for trial will allow plaintiffs to "bolster [ ] their individually weak cases by a suggestion that contamination is widespread." None of these considerations are persuasive. . . . Federal juries are routinely asked to parse facts that are relevant to particular claims or particular parties, and are able to do so without difficulty so long as counsel presents the evidence in a cogent, orderly fashion that makes clear which evidence attaches to which particular claims or defenses. Furthermore, defendants' "taint" argument disregards the ready availability of limiting instructions (should counsel draft and propose same) . . . as well as pattern charges stressing that the claims and defenses of each party must be considered separately and independently from those of each other party. There is no reason to believe that a jury would be unwilling or unable to follow such instructions in this case; therefore, defendants' protestations of prejudice are misplaced.

Finally, as for defendants' stated concern that the joinder of plaintiffs' claims in one trial might give rise to a suggestion that contamination from the Ciba plaint is widespread, the Court fully anticipates that plaintiffs' evidence—whether presented in one trial or five trials—will be that the alleged contamination is, in fact, widespread. Thus, this "suggestion" will be before the jury in plaintiffs' evidentiary submission at trial, irrespective of whether severance is granted.

In short, the Court finds that defendants have failed to make a showing of prejudice sufficient to justify the heavy burden that would be visited on the litigants and this Court alike by virtue of the proposed fragmentation of the plaintiffs' claims into five overlapping trials.

. . . [T]he Motion to Sever is **denied**. The claims of all five plaintiffs will be tried concurrently, before a single jury, in the August 2007 trial term.

Notes and Problems

---

1. Be sure that you understand what the plaintiffs and defendants want. How, if the defendants had their way, would plaintiffs' claims be tried? What, in contrast, would plaintiffs prefer? Why do you imagine they have these preferences?

2. Put yourself in the role of the attorneys arguing this motion.

   a. What was the defendants' best argument regarding the inefficiencies and prejudice of having all five plaintiffs try their claims together?

   b. What were the plaintiffs' best arguments?

Procedure as Strategy

Whether five plaintiffs can bring their claims against defendants in one case or must file five separate lawsuits may seem mundane, akin to the question of whether to drive separate cars to a restaurant or carpool. Either way, one may assume, each of the plaintiffs are equally likely to have their day in court. Yet this may not be so. Note that it would cost $3,000 to have the plaintiffs' experts testify at one trial; five trials would raise the experts' expenses to $15,000. Note also that four of the five plaintiffs' properties at issue in the case are valued at less than $3,000. So a decision to sever the cases might well mean that it would be prohibitively expensive for four of the five plaintiffs to proceed to trial. Now consider the defendants' perspective on joinder. Presumably, these cost considerations are among the very reasons defendants oppose joinder. Additionally, defending against five plaintiffs with similar claims of environmental contamination would be far more challenging than addressing the cases one by one; particularly if, as the opinion suggests, defendants believe some of the plaintiffs' claims are stronger than others.

Rule 20 gives you just a taste of the possibilities and problems created by joinder of parties. For now it is enough to understand that broad joinder of parties is one of the distinctive marks of modern civil procedure. You will get a much more comprehensive view of joinder in Chapter 12.

E. FACTUAL DEVELOPMENT—DISCOVERY

If relaxed pleading and broad joinder comprise two foundational characteristics of modern procedure, the third would be extensive discovery. Questions of jurisdiction, pleading, and parties typically arise at what may be called the "pleading stage" of a lawsuit, so called because most of the questions emerge in the process of drafting or challenging complaints or answers. During discovery, parties seek out facts to support or deny their usually contradictory allegations about what happened.

Do not equate "discovery," the legal machinery for unearthing information that comes after the pleading stage, with fact investigation. Before drafting a complaint or answer, the parties must do some investigation regarding the facts underlying the suit. Lawyers can gather those facts in any of the ways in which ordinary citizens, unaided by official sanction, find out about things—through observation, personal knowledge, conversations with anyone who will talk to them, Internet searches, and public records requests. (Ethical rules do, though, prevent lawyers from speaking with people represented by counsel without their lawyer present.) Before the Federal Rules there was limited provision for discovery, and so factual development largely came about through these types of informal efforts by the parties. Much of it still does. This type of factual investigation is not set out in the Rules, and is consequently often overlooked in Civil Procedure courses. Let us take a moment to consider its benefits and limitations.

For example, in the Peters-Dodge case, assume that one of the issues in the suit is the seriousness of Peters's injuries. Peters has been active on his college's basketball team and claims that he cannot play for at least the remainder of the season. Upton (Dodge's counsel) can speak to coaches and the athletic department about Peters's performance pre-accident and post-accident, if they are willing to speak with her. She can search for online evidence of Peters's participation in basketball games—including whatever he might post about himself on social media. And she might be able to hire a photographer to stand on the edge of the court where Peters's team practices. But she would run afoul of the law were she to tap his telephone or install hidden cameras in his dorm room.

In many cases, however, private inquiry by the parties simply won't uncover key information. For example, neither Peters nor Dodge is likely to voluntarily provide information to opposing counsel, and Dodge's likelihood of obtaining information from witnesses aligned with Peters—his parents, friends, or coach—is low. Even more neutral witnesses may be reluctant to become involved in litigation or to produce information without legal compulsion. Accordingly, the Rules provide mechanisms for a party to obtain information about the case both from other parties in the case and from third parties not in the case. These rules are grouped under the heading of *discovery*.

The discovery rules are a major innovation of modern procedure (though they have antecedents in earlier practices). They are also a source of much dispute, both among the parties seeking and resisting discovery and among commentators debating whether the effort and expense involved in discovery yields real returns to the parties, the judicial system, or society at large.

Rules 26-37 and 45 give parties broad powers of investigation, backed by court-imposed sanctions. Rule 26(a)(1) requires a party, without being asked, to disclose certain basic information supporting that party's claims or defenses—names of witnesses, the existence of documents, bases for damage calculations, and the like.

Beyond these *disclosures*, the parties may seek additional information through several means: asking written questions (*interrogatories*) of parties to the suit (Rule 33); requiring the production of records from parties to the suit (Rule 34) and from others (Rule 45(a)(1)(A)(iii)); asking parties and witnesses oral questions under oath (*depositions*) (Rules 30 and 45); and compelling physical or mental examinations (Rule 35).

Notice that a party to a civil lawsuit may be compelled to provide the other side with information that weakens his claim or defense; not surprisingly, parties are often reluctant to produce such information and often try to use procedural tools to avoid doing so.

Three restrictions limit the otherwise broad powers of civil discovery. First, parties may discover only evidence that is *relevant* to a claim or defense in the case and *proportional* to the needs of the case. Rule 26(b). Second, even if relevant, the requested information may be protected if *privileged*. Rule 26(b). For example, the privilege against self-incrimination, and attorney-client and doctor-patient privileges, may bar discovery even of relevant information. Third, even relevant, unprivileged information may be undiscoverable if a party can convince a court that one of the limitations in Rules 26(b)(2)(C) or 26(c) applies; if, for example, the discovery sought is "unreasonably cumulative or duplicative," or its potential for "annoyance, embarrassment, oppression, or undue burden or expense" outweighs its evidentiary value.

Several of these limitations are at issue in the next case. One bit of background may be helpful before reading the next case. In addition to federal district judges, Congress has provided for the appointment of a group of magistrate judges to assist district court judges in their work. District court judges typically assign magistrates to resolve discovery disputes, oversee settlement, and do other tasks described as "non-dispositive" (meaning rulings that will not, in themselves, end a case). Magistrate Judge Carman was referred the defendant's motion to compel discovery in *Gordon v. T.G.R. Logistics, Inc.*, and issued the order that follows.

Gordon v. T.G.R. Logistics, Inc.

2017 WL 1947537 (D. Wyo. 2017)

CARMAN, M.J.

This comes before the Court on the Defendant T.G.R. Logistics, Inc.'s motion to compel discovery production.

Background

Plaintiff was driving her motor vehicle on June 28, 2015 on U.S. Highway 309 in Lincoln County, Wyoming. As she was executing a left-hand turn she was struck by a tractor-trailer unit owned and operated by Defendant T.G.R. Logistics, Inc. and driven by Defendant Varga which was attempting to execute a pass in the left lane. As a result of this collision Plaintiff alleges numerous physical injuries, pain (back, neck and jaw), traumatic brain injury, posttraumatic stress disorder, anxiety and depression.

[Defendant served the following Request for Production on Plaintiff:

REQUEST NO. 11: Utilizing the instructions attached hereto, download and produce an electronic copy of your Facebook account history to the enclosed flash drive.]

Defendant asserts that Plaintiff's Facebook account history is relevant and necessary to its defense of the damages claimed by Plaintiff.

The Plaintiff responds that the request for the Facebook account history exceeds the permissible discovery limits of Federal Rule of Civil Procedure 26. Plaintiff further asserts that the request is unduly burdensome, lacks relevance and is overly invasive of Plaintiff's privacy. Plaintiff emphasizes that she has downloaded and produced the information from her Facebook accounts that references the accident or her injuries. Further the Plaintiff has provided the Facebook information for the following keywords as set forth by Defendant in its request for production number 12. Those keywords are: accident; attorney; TGR; Igor Varga; Kemmerer; Lincoln County, Wyoming; brain injury; concussion; posttraumatic stress disorder; and PTSD.

Discussion

[The court quotes Rule 26(b)(1).]

There are three basic steps for the court to consider when determining the appropriate scope of discovery under Rule 26(b)(1). Those steps are: (1) is the information

not privileged info

privileged; (2) is it relevant to a claim or defense; and (3) is it proportional to the needs of the case. There being no claim of privilege asserted herein, this matter will resolve with a review of the final two criteria.

The courts have a long history of attempting to define the proper scope of discovery. The federal discovery rules were initially adopted in 1938 and have been described as a striking and imaginative departure from tradition. In the 1980s it became apparent that excessive discovery was becoming a problem. . . . With the amendments of the Rules beginning in 1983, the issue of proportionality was introduced into the scope of discovery evaluations.

This effort to properly limit the scope of discovery comes at a time when the amount of available data for discovery is growing exponentially. More data has been created in the last two years than in the entire previous history of the human race and the amount of data is predicted to grow 10-fold by 2020. A great deal of that data will involve social media.

Social media presents some unique challenges to courts in their efforts to determine the proper scope of discovery of relevant information and maintaining proportionality. While it is conceivable that almost any post to social media will provide some relevant information concerning a person's physical and/or emotional health, it also has the potential to disclose more information than has historically occurred in civil litigation. While we can debate the wisdom of individuals posting information which has historically been considered private, we must recognize people are providing a great deal of personal information publicly to a very loosely defined group of "friends," or even the entire public internet. People have always shared thoughts and feelings, but typically not in such a permanent and easily retrievable format. No court would have allowed unlimited depositions of every friend, social acquaintance, co-employee or relative of a plaintiff to inquire as to all disclosures, conversations or observations. Now far more reliable disclosures can be obtained with a simple download of a social media history. A few clicks on the computer and you shortly have what can consist of hundreds of pages of recorded postings and conversations of a party. There can be little doubt that within those postings there will be information which is relevant to some issue in the litigation. It is equally clear that much of the information will be irrelevant.

Just because the information can be retrieved quickly and inexpensively does not resolve the issue. Discovery can be burdensome even as it is inexpensive. Courts have long denied discovery of information which was easy to obtain, but which was not discoverable. "The court may, for good cause, issue an order to protect a party or person from annoyance, embarrassment, oppression, or undue burden or expense." Fed. R. Civ. P. 26(c)(1). Upon a finding of good cause a court may prohibit the production of relevant information. The recent inclusion of proportionality within Fed. R. Civ. P. 26(b)(1) further emphasizes this point.

Time & expense not an issue

The Defendant correctly observes that there would be very little time or expense involved in the initial production of Plaintiff's Facebook history. That's true on the front end. The problem is that such vast information has the potential to generate additional discovery or impact trial testimony. It's not difficult to imagine a plaintiff being required to explain every statement contained within a lengthy Facebook history in which he or she expressed some degree of angst or emotional distress or discussing life events which could be conceived to cause emotional upset, but which is extremely personal and embarrassing. . . . That being said, Defendant has a legitimate interest in discovery which is important to the claims and damages it is being asked to pay. Information in social media which reveals that the plaintiff is lying or exaggerating his or her injuries should not be protected from disclosure. . . .

Defendant, in apparent recognition that its initial request was overly broad, has offered to limit its request for social media temporally for three years prior to the motor vehicle accident to present. Defendant asserts that it will be unable to defend Plaintiff's damage claims without access to information regarding Plaintiff's emotional state prior to the accident. In this Court's opinion that is casting the net too wide. . . . From what has been presented this case is . . . [a] "garden variety" emotion[al] distress claim. . . . Granting access to Plaintiff's entire Facebook history would provide minimal relevant information while exposing substantial irrelevant information. As such the discovery would exceed the proper limits of proportionality.

The Defendant's claim that it would be unable to challenge Plaintiff's damage claims is exaggerated. Defendants have been effectively defending such garden variety emotional distress claims for many years and such claims typically make up a small part of the damages in physical injury cases. The Plaintiff also alleges a traumatic brain injury. Such damages have long been a subject of the evaluation and diagnosis by experts using proven testing protocols. . . . Therefore the Court will deny Defendant's request for social media discovery prior to the date of the accident of June 28, 2015. Nevertheless, the Court is not convinced that all relevant social media subsequent to that date has been produced. The Plaintiff will be required to produce all relevant history which addresses Plaintiff's significant emotional turmoil, any mental disability or ability, or relate significant events which could reasonably be expected to result in emotional distress.[1] Plaintiff will also be required to produce all Facebook postings which reference the accident, its aftermath, and any of her physical injuries related thereto, insofar as such has not already been produced by Plaintiff. In its reply brief Defendant discusses the impact of Plaintiff's injuries on activities she enjoyed before the accident. The Court has not been provided any guidance as to what activities of the Plaintiff may have been impacted by this accident. The Court will order the production of Facebook history and photos which relate or show the Plaintiff's level of activity after the accident.

The Defendant's Motion to Compel Discovery is GRANTED in the following respects:

1. The Plaintiff is ordered to produce all post-June 28, 2015 Facebook history and photos which relate to Plaintiff's significant emotional turmoil, any mental disability or ability, or relate significant events which could reasonably be expected to result in emotional distress.

2. The Plaintiff is ordered to produce all post-June 28, 2015 Facebook history and photos which address or relate to the accident and its aftermath or any of her resulting physical or emotional injuries.

3. The Plaintiff is ordered to produce all post-June 28, 2015 Facebook history and photos which relate or show the Plaintiff's level of activity.

The Defendant's Motion to Compel Discovery is DENIED in all other respects.

---

1. The Plaintiff is to err on the side of disclosure and if the Plaintiff is uncertain, the relevant documents shall be provided to the Court for in camera review. The use of the term "significant" is to avoid disclosure of transient and trivial emotional distress.

WHAT'S NEW HERE?

- Unlike some previous cases in this chapter, the case would proceed no matter who prevailed on this motion.
- Instead, the parties are jockeying for strategic advantage, something that will help them in later stages of the suit. Many procedural disputes have this characteristic, and a student's job often lies in thinking about *how* the parties believe that winning (or losing) this small battle will affect the outcome of the war.

Notes and Problems

1. First, make sure you understand what is at issue in this discovery dispute. The plaintiff has already produced information from her Facebook account that references the accident, her injuries, and the defendants. Why you think that T.G.R. Logistics wants Gordon's entire Facebook account history? What does the defendant hope to find?

2. The court concludes that there would be little time or expense in producing plaintiff's entire Facebook history, but still concludes that the request "would exceed the proper limits of proportionality." What is the basis for the court's conclusion?

3. Note the ways in which the scope of the discovery at issue shifts during the course of the litigation. The defendant initially sought plaintiff's entire Facebook account history. Then, during the discovery dispute, the defendant offered to limit its request to three years prior to the motor vehicle accident. Finally, the court's order to compel requires production of all Facebook history and photos on or after the date of the accident that relate to the accident and her resulting injuries, or describe any other emotional turmoil, mental disability, emotionally distressing events, or physical activities. Courts have great discretion to adjust the scope of discovery requests as a means of achieving a just outcome.

4. Note also that the court's efforts to reach a just outcome may lead to more time and expense for the plaintiff. Were the plaintiff to produce her entire Facebook history, the production would be quick and cheap. Now, the plaintiff must go through each of her posts and photos and determine whether they are responsive.

5. Note also that the court's strategy may be paving the way for future disputes.

   a. How will the defendant know whether plaintiff is producing all responsive posts and photos? Would footnote 1 reassure you, were you representing T.G.R. Logistics?

   b. Reread the order. Will the plaintiff (and her lawyer) think that it invites or allows her to respond only with Facebook postings that support her contentions that she is suffering great pain and emotional turmoil? Might she or her lawyer, for example, think the terms of the ruling allowed her to ignore postings that show her having a fine time with her friends, or engaging in leisure activity incompatible with her contentions of pain?

F. PRETRIAL DISPOSITION—SUMMARY JUDGMENT

Imagine that the *Peters v. Dodge* case survives the pleading stage and the parties engage in discovery. After submitting document requests and taking depositions of witnesses and each other, the parties gather all of the information that they can about the underlying facts of the case. There is, then, another opportunity for a court to decide whether the case should proceed to trial: *summary judgment.*

Rule 56(a) requires that a court should grant summary judgment when there is "no genuine dispute as to any material fact."

What does that mean? Suppose in *Peters v. Dodge* that Dodge moves for summary judgment and asserts that the collision occurred at the intersection of Main and Walnut Streets, and that the light was green for Walnut traffic (Dodge's street) and red for Main traffic, where Peters was driving. To support the motion, Dodge submits his own affidavit stating that the Walnut light was green and submits the affidavit of a truck driver who was immediately behind Peters on Main saying that the light on Main was red. On this showing, with no evidence to the contrary offered by Peters, most courts would grant summary judgment for Dodge. There is no dispute that Dodge's light was green and Peters's light was red. No reasonable jury could conclude, given these facts, that Dodge was in the wrong.

What if, instead, Peters submitted his own affidavit in opposition stating that he had the green light? At that point we have a factual issue for trial: Who was accurately perceiving and telling the truth about the traffic lights? In such a situation, a court would deny Dodge's motion for summary judgment. The court would reason that summary judgment is not for weighing evidence but for determining whether there is any evidence to weigh; the conflicting affidavits would establish that there was an issue for trial.

Sometimes, however, it is not as easy to tell whether there is a genuine factual dispute. Consider the following case.

Houchens v. American Home Assurance Co.

927 F.2d 163 (4th Cir. 1991)

ERVIN, J.

Alice Houchens brought suit against American Home Assurance Company ("American") for breach of contract involving two insurance policies in the United States District Court for the Eastern District of Virginia. American made a motion for summary judgment, and a hearing was held on the motion. The district court granted American's motion for summary judgment, and Houchens appealed. Finding no error in the granting of summary judgment in favor of American, we affirm.

I

Coulter Houchens disappeared in August 1980 and has not been heard from since. His wife, Alice Houchens, is trying to collect upon either of two life insurance policies issued by American, which covered Mr. Houchens. One policy was an occupational accidental injury and death insurance policy. The other policy was a non-occupational accident insurance policy. . . . Both policies required that the insured's death be caused by accident in order to be covered.

Evidence shows that Mr. Houchens was . . . [employed by the] International Civil Aviation Organization in Montreal, Canada (ICAO) . . . [and] stationed in Dharan, Saudi Arabia.

Sometime around August 14, 1980, Mr. Houchens received a week of vacation leave. He traveled to Bangkok, Thailand on or before August 14 via Thai Airlines. Immigration records show that he arrived in Bangkok on August 15, 1980. His entry permit was valid through August 29, 1980.

No one has heard from Mr. Houchens since that time. The State Department, the FBI, ICAO, Mrs. Houchens, and the Red Cross have searched for him to no avail. In 1988, Mrs. Houchens brought an action to declare Mr. Houchens legally dead under Virginia law. On April 29, 1988, an order was issued by the Circuit Court of Loudoun County, Virginia, declaring that Mr. Houchens is presumed to have died between August 15 and August 29, 1980.

Houchens sued American for breach of contract because American refused to pay under either of two accidental death policies covering Mr. Houchens, which were issued by American. Both policies provided coverage in the event of death by accident. American maintained that there was no evidence of Mr. Houchens' death, nor was there evidence of *accidental death*. American moved for summary judgment, and the district court granted the motion. This appeal followed. . . .

II

Section 64.1-105 of the Virginia Code provides that a person who has been missing for 7 years is presumed to be dead. Va. Code Ann. §64.1-105 (1987). Therefore, Mr. Houchens is presumed to be dead, and Mrs. Houchens is entitled to that presumption. However, in order for Mrs. Houchens to recover under the American policies, she must prove that Mr. Houchens died as a result of an accident. The term "accident" is not defined in the policies. In such cases, the courts of Virginia have said that an accident is an "event that takes place without one's foresight or expectation; an undesigned, sudden, and unexpected event." Harris v. Bankers Life & Cas. Co., 222 Va. 45, 46 (1981) (quoting Ocean Accident & Guaranty Corp. v. Glover, 165 Va. 283, 285 (1935)).

"Under the general rule . . . a beneficiary who makes a death claim under an accident policy or the double indemnity clause of a life policy, has the burden of proving that the insured's death was caused by violent, external and accidental means within the terms of the policy." Life & Cas. Ins. Co. of Tennessee v. Daniel, 209 Va. 332, 335 (1968). Therefore, the burden is on Mrs. Houchens to prove that her husband died by accidental means.

The district court granted summary judgment to American in this case under the rationale of Celotex Corp. v. Catrett, 477 U.S. 317 (1986). The Supreme Court set out the standard for granting summary judgment as follows:

> In our view, the plain language of Rule 56[(a)] mandates the entry of summary judgment, after adequate time for discovery and upon motion, against a party who fails to make a showing sufficient to establish the existence of an element essential to that party's case, and on which that party will bear the burden of proof at trial.

Celotex, 477 U.S. at 322. We elaborated on that standard in *Helm v. Western Maryland Ry. Co.*:

> The appellate court, therefore, must reverse the grant of summary judgment if it appears from the record that there is an unresolved issue of material fact; the inferences to be drawn from the underlying facts contained in the materials before the trial court must be viewed in the light most favorable to the party opposing the motion.

838 F.2d 729, 734 (4th Cir. 1988). On this appeal, then, we must view the evidence in the light most favorable to Houchens to ascertain whether she made a sufficient showing that Mr. Houchens died accidentally.

Mrs. Houchens asserts that the presumption that Mr. Houchens is dead somehow translates into the presumption that he died accidentally; therefore, she made a sufficient showing. She relies upon three cases from the western part of the country as support for the fact that she met her burden. [The court described these cases—*Martin, Englehart,* and *Valley National.*]

These three cases are readily distinguishable from the case at bar. Here, there is only evidence of a disappearance. Mr. Houchens went to Bangkok and was never heard from again. There are no bizarre circumstances surrounding his disappearance. He was not last seen in a position of peril as in *Martin.* He simply vanished. The circumstances surrounding his disappearance do not give us a clue that he actually died, as did the circumstances in *Martin, Englehart,* and *Valley National.* Viewed in the light most favorable to Mrs. Houchens, we can only conclude that Mr. Houchens disappeared, and then presume that he died under Virginia law. We cannot conclude that he died accidentally. . . .

This is a case where the inferences show equal support for opposing conclusions. Mr. Houchens might have died accidentally. However, it is equally likely that he was murdered, that he died of natural causes, that he took his own life, or that he just went away somewhere and lives yet. "It is our function . . . to ascertain whether the evidence, considered in the light most favorable toward plaintiff affords room for men of reasonable minds to conclude that there is a greater probability that the ultimate fact did happen than that it did not happen." [quoting one of the distinguishable cases]. The ultimate fact at issue here is whether the death occurred by accident. We cannot conclude that there is a greater probability that the death was caused by accident than by other means.

The Virginia Supreme Court gave guidance in this area in General Accident & Casualty Corp. v. Murray, 120 Va. 115, [126] (1916). There the court wrote:

> The right to recover upon the policy sued on must be established by a preponderance of the evidence deduced in the case, and not be based merely upon conjecture, guess or random judgment, that is, upon mere supposition without a single known fact.
>
> The [burden is upon plaintiff] to bring herself within the provisions of the contract of insurance by proving an accidental injury to the assured, and there is no presumption to aid her in this proof, since the well-established rule of law, according to all the authorities, is, that when death occurs it is presumed to be the result of natural dissolution rather than of accidental injury. . . .

III

To summarize, Houchens relies on the presumption given her by §64-1.105 of the Virginia Code to establish that Mr. Houchens is dead. She then relies upon the facts surrounding his disappearance as a basis for a jury finding that his death was accidental. However, the meager circumstances would not allow a jury to reasonably conclude that it is more likely that Mr. Houchens died from an accident than in some other manner. Because of the sparse evidence concerning his disappearance, we cannot say that the district court erred in granting summary judgment in favor of American under the *Celotex* standard. Therefore, the order of the district court is affirmed. . . .

WHAT'S NEW HERE?

- Up to this point we have dealt either with "allegations"—assertions made in a complaint or answer but not yet supported by evidence—or with uncontested assertions from which various inferences might be drawn (no one denied that Creal had a Missouri driver's license; the question was what to make of that).

- With summary judgment we're in the realm of factual disputes: *A* says "*X*," *B* says "not *X*."
- *Houchens* adds a layer of complexity. We don't know for sure that Mr. Houchens is dead, let alone that he died accidentally. But the law of Virginia (which controls in this diversity case; see below) says that a person unaccountably missing for seven years may be "presumed" dead. It thus relieves Mrs. Houchens of the need to show that her husband has died. But it does not satisfy her burden of showing that he died accidentally.

Notes and Problems

---

1. Would it be irrational to conclude that Mr. Houchens died accidentally? If such a conclusion would not be irrational, why did the court not permit the case to go to trial? What does its ruling tell us about the function of a trial and the burdens placed on the parties at summary judgment?

2. To understand summary judgment, one needs to understand what additional evidence would have enabled Mrs. Houchens to avoid summary judgment. Consider several possibilities; in each the question is whether there is a genuine issue of material fact, making summary judgment improper.

   a. Suppose Mrs. Houchens produced a witness, a former college friend of Mr. Houchens who had not seen him for more than ten years. The friend is prepared to testify that, while vacationing in Thailand during the time in question, he saw Mr. Houchens (or someone who looked like him) hit by a bus in a busy intersection. He caught only a brief glimpse; moreover, his vision is not good. The Thai police have no record of a bus accident on the day in question. Can Mrs. Houchens avoid summary judgment with this showing?

   b. What if, in response to Mrs. Houchens's production of the witness above, the insurance company comes forward with two affidavits, from two Thai government officials, stating that Mr. Houchens was shot and killed by Thai police when they intercepted a drug smuggling effort. (Assume that such a death would not be accidental, as the Virginia courts define that term.) In support of these affidavits, the Thai officials state that they are prepared to produce Mr. Houchens's passport. The judge is then faced with conflicting affidavits—one from the near-sighted former roommate, the other from Thai government officials. Summary judgment for the insurer?

   c. Finally, what if, as in *Houchens* itself, neither side had been able to find information about the circumstances of Mr. Houchens's death. But assume that Virginia law specified that seven years' unexplained absence would give rise to a presumption of death, and, in the absence of contrary evidence, such presumed death would be further presumed to be accidental. Summary judgment for the insurer? For Mrs. Houchens?

d. In the first two scenarios, Mrs. Houchens should be able to defeat the summary judgment motion. Even if Mrs. Houchens's witness does not seem particularly credible, credibility is not for the judge to assess. Juries should assess material factual disputes. In the third scenario, Mrs. Houchens would probably win summary judgment herself, not because the facts are different but because the law has stepped in.

3. One aspect of *Houchens* having nothing to do with summary judgment may have puzzled you: The case is heard in federal court, but the court mostly discusses Virginia law (and that of other states); why not federal law? The answer, as you will see in Chapter 4, is that in *Erie Railroad v. Tompkins*, a leading constitutional opinion, the Supreme Court held that in a case that is in federal court only because of diversity jurisdiction, state *substantive* law applies. According to this line of cases, Virginia substantive law, including such matters as presumptions of death, governs. The law of other states comes into the picture because the federal court apparently believes that Virginia courts would look to them as persuasive, though not binding, authority.

There are other methods of pretrial disposition that should be briefly mentioned here. In some cases, defendant will fail to answer the complaint entirely, or will otherwise fail to defend, and a *default judgment* will be granted. See Rule 55. Similarly, if plaintiff does not obey an order of the court during the proceedings, a *dismissal* may be granted. The most common reasons for dismissal are persistent failure to comply with discovery orders, failure to prosecute the case, and failure to appear for calendar calls, motions, or pretrial conferences. See Rule 41(b). In addition, plaintiff may seek a so-called *voluntary dismissal* of the case if the case settles or, for some reason, he thinks that he would be better off starting over. See Rule 41(a). We discuss these matters in more detail later; for now, you simply should be aware of their existence.

G. TRIAL

All pretrial activities, from pleading through summary judgment, anticipate the ultimate trial, yet few cases actually reach that point. Fewer than 5 percent of all cases commenced in the federal courts go to trial. Nevertheless, the trial process exercises a dominant influence on pretrial behavior because during the pretrial period the parties have to gather all the information that would be necessary at trial if it did occur. Moreover, for the majority of cases that settle, they do so on terms dictated by the parties' estimates of what the outcome at trial would be, estimates shaped by the information gathered in the pretrial phase.

If trial does occur, it consists of an elaborate pattern of symmetrical opportunities for the parties to present their cases. Plaintiff will have an opportunity to make an opening statement, following which defendant will get the same opportunity.

Plaintiff can then present his case offering witnesses and documents; defendant can cross-examine each of plaintiffs' witnesses to test their recollection and credibility. Defendant can then present his evidence, with plaintiff having the same opportunity for cross-examination. It all ends with both parties making closing statements. This pattern reflects two principles: that parties (not, as in many other systems, the judge) are responsible for proof; and that the party going first bears the burden of producing evidence and of persuading the trier of fact that his version of the case is more likely than not to be true.

In U.S. courts, that trier of fact will sometimes be a jury. The Seventh Amendment of the U.S. Constitution and comparable provisions in state constitutions demonstrate a strong commitment to the idea of civil jury trial, an almost uniquely American institution.

But that ideal has limits. Just as a judge may head off trial entirely by granting summary judgment, at trial a judge may refuse to submit a case to a jury or, after a jury has rendered its verdict, may grant judgment notwithstanding the verdict. See Rule 50(a). Under what circumstances should a judge grant such a motion for "judgment as a matter of law"? There is general agreement that if a party who has the burden of proof on an issue offers no evidence at all on that issue, judgment must be directed against him. There is similar agreement in cases in which the party with the burden of proof offers evidence that is simply too weak for any reasonable juror to believe. But what about a case involving evidence that, although weak, conceivably could be credited?

Courts insist that it is the jury's job to evaluate the credibility of witnesses and that, in passing on such motions, they will not consider whether witnesses are telling the truth. Courts are equally firm, however, in their belief that the function of judgment as a matter of law is to avoid (or overrule) jury deliberations in cases in which a jury could reasonably come to only one verdict. The next case involves a collision of these two principles. It uses two different terms for different stages at which the power of taking a case from the jury is exercised: "directed verdict,"* to describe the exercise of judicial power before the case is given to the jury; and "judgment notwithstanding the verdict" to describe post-verdict reversal of the jury's decision.

Norton v. Snapper Power Equipment
806 F.2d 1545 (11th Cir. 1987)

CLARK, J.

Plaintiff James L. Norton was injured while using a riding lawn mower manufactured by defendant Snapper Power Equipment. The issue on appeal is whether the district court erred in granting a judgment notwithstanding the verdict to Snapper on Norton's strict liability claim. We reverse.

---

* The term comes from earlier practice, in which the judge instructed the jury to deliberate but told them what decision to reach, thus "directing" their verdict. An occasional jury refused to follow judicial instructions, which led to awkward standoffs; current practice simply allows the judge to enter the judgment without the jury's action.

I. Facts

Norton was, and still is, in the commercial lawn mowing business. He bought a Snapper riding mower in July 1981. On January 24, 1983, Norton was using this mower to clear leaves from a yard . . . adjacent to a creek. At the end of his third circular route through the yard, he drove up an incline, traveling in the direction away from the creek. Norton testified that as he reached the top of the incline, approximately six feet from the creek, the mower began to slide backwards toward the creek. Norton says he applied the brakes, but he continued to slide backwards. The lawn mower, with Norton still aboard, crashed into the creek. Norton testified that he kept both hands on the handle bars until the impact of the mower hitting the water knocked him off the seat. . . . [A]t some point during this crash, Norton's hand was caught in the lawn mower's blades, thereby amputating four of his fingers. It is not known . . . precisely how the injury occurred. . . .

At the close of the plaintiff's case, and again at the close of all evidence, Snapper moved for a directed verdict. The court dismissed Norton's negligence and warranty claims, but left the strict liability "defect" claim for the jury. The jury returned a verdict for Norton, holding Snapper liable for 80% of the injuries.

Immediately after dismissing the jury, the district court indicated it would enter a judgment notwithstanding the verdict.

[Plaintiff appealed from this ruling.]

II. Substantive Objections to Judgment Notwithstanding the Verdict

The test for granting a judgment notwithstanding the verdict is the same as the test for granting a directed verdict. The court considers the evidence in the light most favorable to the non-moving party and should grant the judgment notwithstanding the verdict only where the evidence so strongly and so favorably points in the favor of the moving party that reasonable people could not arrive at a contrary verdict. . . .

The issues in this case were: (1) whether the failure to install "dead man" devices rendered the 1981 Snapper mower defective; and (2) if the lawn mower was defective, whether the lack of a "dead man" control caused Norton's injury. . . .

Norton claims the Snapper mower was unreasonably dangerous because it did not have a "dead man" device. Although there are several types of such devices, the basic principle is the same in each type. In order to keep the lawn mower blades spinning, the operator has to remain in a certain position or has to continuously apply pressure to a pedal or handle. When the operator disengages the blades, they are quickly brought to a stop. The 1981 Snapper mowers were designed so that the blades would spin for three to five seconds after the power was turned off. Norton offered evidence that more sophisticated "dead man" devices are able to stop the blades in less than one second after the operator applies the brakes or releases the handle.

[After reviewing the law on product defects, the appellate court concluded that the jury could reasonably have found the mower defective. The court then considers whether a jury could reasonably have found that the defect caused Norton's injury.]

. . . Since Norton did not know exactly when or how his hand got caught in the blades, and since a reconstruction of the accident was impossible, Snapper contends that the jury could not determine whether a blade stopping device would have eliminated or lessened Norton's injury.

Snapper correctly points out that "plaintiffs are not entitled to a verdict based on speculation and conjecture." Fenner v. General Motors Corp., 657 F.2d 647, 651 (5th Cir. 1981), cert. denied, 455 U.S. 942 (1982). . . . The jury is, however, permitted to "reconstruct the series of events by drawing an inference upon an inference." Id. at 650.

In *Fenner*, plaintiff contended his automobile veered off the highway because of a defective steering mechanism. The steering problem would only manifest itself if a stone got caught in the steering mechanism. Because plaintiff's vehicle was not examined by any experts and since plaintiff's experts were only able to say that theoretically the accident could have been caused by a stone in the steering mechanism, the district court entered a judgment notwithstanding the verdict for defendant. . . .

The causation evidence in this case, although circumstantial, was far more impressive than the evidence presented in *Fenner*. Norton testified that the lawn mower slid six feet from the top of the hill into the creek. . . . Expert testimony revealed that when Norton applied the brakes, an effective dead man device could have stopped the blades in as little as .7 seconds. The blades on the 1981 Snapper would continue to spin for three to five seconds. . . . Each of Snapper's experts testified that, given the amount of time the mower would have taken to slide six feet and given Norton's testimony that both of his hands were on the handle bars until the mower hit the creek, a two or three second difference in blade stopping time would have avoided the injury. . . . Snapper was given every opportunity to point out the weaknesses in Norton's proof, but apparently was unpersuasive. . . .

Reversed and Remanded.

WHAT'S NEW HERE?

- For the first time we see a jury hearing evidence and rendering a verdict.
- But then we see a judge overriding the jury's verdict and instead granting judgment to the side that lost the verdict—followed by an appellate reversal instructing the district court to reinstate the verdict.

Notes and Problems

1. In a motion for judgment as a matter of law the court is deciding whether a reasonable jury could reach a verdict in favor of the party opposing the motion.

    a. The jury's verdict depended on its finding that the absence of a "dead man" device on the mower caused Norton's injury. The trial court ruled that there was insufficient evidence for the jury to reach this conclusion; the court of appeals ruled that the jury could reasonably have reached such a verdict.

    b. Although we have juries decide questions of fact, we also empower trial judges to reverse juries' verdicts if they are unreasonable, and we have appellate courts that can reverse the decision of a trial judge about the reasonableness of the jury's decision.

2. Is *Norton* distinguishable from *Houchens*? That question can be addressed on two levels—of procedural theory and of factual inference.

    a. Start with procedural theory.

        i. *Houchens* was decided on a motion for summary judgment, under Rule 56; *Norton* was decided after trial on a motion for judgment notwithstanding the verdict (now called a renewed motion for judgment as a matter of law) under Rule 50. So the two motions come at different stages: The summary judgment motion usually comes at the end of discovery and always *before* trial commences. By contrast, a motion for judgment as a matter of law comes *during* or *after* trial when the evidence for one or both sides has already been presented. But both ask the same question: Is one party entitled to victory because there just isn't any evidence to support the other side?

        ii. If the two motions cover similar ground, why is there ever any need for judgment as a matter of law? Shouldn't summary judgment have been granted if there really was no evidence to support one side? Logically, the answer would be that, in a perfect world, there should never be a successful motion for judgment as a matter of law—because all the cases in which one would be granted have been eliminated at the summary judgment stage. The real world is not so tidy. It often happens that what looks at the pretrial stage like an evidentiary conflict evaporates at trial: A witness fails to appear or tells a different story at trial than in the lawyer's office. In that situation the motion for judgment as a matter of law serves as a back-up to summary judgment.

    b. Now turn to the facts of the two cases. In *Houchens* the court affirmed a grant of summary judgment while conceding it was possible that Houchens had died accidentally. Does the jury verdict in *Norton* rest on more than a finding that the absence of a dead-man mechanism *might* have caused the accident?

3. What will happen to this case now? The court of appeals has "reversed" and "remanded" the trial court's decision, which means that the entry of judgment notwithstanding the verdict is reversed, and the case is remanded to the trial court. The district court should then enter judgment on the jury's verdict.

Procedure as Strategy

Thus far, we have focused on the ways in which procedural rules create tactical opportunities for parties. Now, consider procedure as strategy for the judge. The trial judge in *Norton* denied a defense motion for a directed verdict: Doing so was tantamount to saying that a reasonable jury could find for the plaintiff. Then, when the jury did find for the plaintiff, the judge—looking at exactly the same evidence that was before him when he denied the directed verdict motion and applying the same legal standard—made the opposite ruling: that no reasonable jury could find for the plaintiff and judgment notwithstanding the verdict was appropriate. At the level of logic, the judge has to be wrong at least once—either when he denied the directed verdict motion or when he granted judgment notwithstanding the verdict.

Maybe there's a deeper procedural logic at work here, a logic that emerges if one contemplates the interplay of trial and appellate courts and the costs of a second trial. When judges make rulings, they want them to be correct—at least in the sense that they will be affirmed on appeal. But a wise judge knows that not all her rulings will be affirmed, so sometimes judges take that into account. While we don't know the thought processes of the trial judge in *Norton*, suppose he thought as follows: "I think I'm right in believing that there's no proof of causation, but it's a close case and an appellate court might reverse me. If I grant the directed verdict and send the jury home, and it then turns out that I'm wrong on causation, we'll have to have a second trial—and product liability cases, with dueling expert testimony, take a good bit of time. Suppose, then, I deny the motion for a directed verdict, and let the jury decide the case. If they agree with me that there's no causation, fine. But if they don't—if they find for the plaintiff—I can still grant judgment notwithstanding the verdict. And, if the case is appealed and the appellate court disagrees with my ruling, we won't have to try the case again. I'll simply enter judgment on the original jury verdict." Make sense?

H. FORMER ADJUDICATION

Most of us are vaguely familiar with the criminal law notion of double jeopardy, which prevents a person from being tried twice for the same crime. Not surprisingly, there is a similar notion in civil procedure. If Peters sues Dodge for injury to his car and loses, he should not be allowed to refile the same case, seeking damages for those same injuries, again. Lawyers speak of such questions under the general heading of former adjudication. There are actually two branches of former adjudication: claim preclusion (or, in its Latin equivalent, *res judicata* (literally, (some) thing adjudicated)) and issue preclusion (*collateral estoppel*). Claim preclusion prevents a case from being brought again (as in the *Peters v. Dodge* example). Issue preclusion prevents an issue from being revisited: If Peters sues Dodge for damage to his car and loses because the court finds the car did not actually belong to Peters, Peters would likely be bound by that finding in a future case.

For claim preclusion to apply, the claim must be the same in both the first and second action. As might be expected, deciding what is and is not the same claim is sometimes difficult. In Chapter 11, we will consider different understandings of what constitutes the "same claim," and see how courts have considered close cases. For now, we stick with a straightforward example.

Ison v. Thomas

2007 WL 1194374 (Ky. App. 2007)

ABRAMSON, J.

George Ison appeals from a January 30, 2006 summary judgment of the Pendleton Circuit Court dismissing his claim against Anthony Thomas for personal injury damages. Ison contends that the trial court misapplied the rule against splitting one's cause of action, an aspect of the doctrine of *res judicata*. We disagree and so affirm.

Ison alleges that in July 2003 Thomas injured him in an automobile accident on Kentucky Highway 9 near Foster in Pendleton County. Soon after the accident, in August 2003, Ison sued Thomas and Thomas's insurer for losses arising from the damage to Ison's vehicle. . . . A jury awarded him about $5,000.00 for his property losses. . . . Ison brought the present personal injury action against Thomas in April 2005. The trial court, noting the long standing rule in Kentucky that "one may not split up his cause of action and have it tried piecemeal," Hays v. Sturgill, 302 Ky. 31, 34 (1946), ruled that Ison's personal injury claim was part of the same cause of action as his property damage claim and so had merged with the prior judgment. We agree.

> As the Kentucky Court of Appeals, then the state's highest Court, stated in *Hays*: when a matter is in litigation, parties are required to bring forward their whole case; and the plea of *res judicata* applies not only to the points upon which the court was required by the parties to form an opinion and pronounce judgment, but to every point which properly belonged to the subject of litigation, and which the parties, exercising reasonable diligence, might have brought forward at the time.

Applying this rule in Kirchner v. Riherd, 702 S.W.2d 33 (Ky. 1985), a case, like this one, involving an automobile accident and successive suits for property and personal injury damages, our Supreme Court ruled that "the law will not permit a party who has sued for a part of an entire demand to sue for the residue in another action." In [that case] the Court reaffirmed its adoption of Restatement (Second), Judgments, §24 (1982), which provides in part that:

> [w]hen a valid and final judgment rendered in an action extinguishes the plaintiff's claim . . . the claim extinguished includes all rights of the plaintiff to remedies against the defendant with respect to all or any part of the transaction, or series of connected transactions, out of which the action arose.

Our Supreme Court so held in *Kirchner*, and the trial court did not err by so holding here.

Ison's contention that the rule against splitting one's cause of action does not apply if the plaintiff prevails in the prior action is without merit. . . . If the plaintiff prevails on his initial claim, other claims arising from the same transaction are said to merge with his judgment, and if the plaintiff loses initially, that judgment is said to bar any such subsequent claim. Restatement (Second), Judgments, §§18, 19 (1982). In either case, the subsequent action is precluded.

Finally, Ison contends that Thomas waived the affirmative *res judicata* defense by failing to plead it in his answer to Ison's complaint. He notes, correctly, that CR 8.03 [analogous to Federal Rule 8(c)(1)] requires affirmative defenses such as *res judicata* to be "set forth affirmatively" in the answer, that is, that the pleading should give fair notice of the particular defense and a short statement of its grounds. . . . We agree with Ison that Thomas's Answer . . . did not satisfy a notice standard for any particular affirmative defense. Nevertheless, CR 8.03 is not to be applied mechanically, and waiver need not be found where the affirmative defense is raised by timely motion that does not prejudice the plaintiff.

In this case, Thomas raised the *res judicata* defense in a motion for summary judgment in September 2005, only about five months into the case and before either party had expended much on discovery. . . .

In sum, our law requires that all claims against a single defendant arising from a single negligent incident be brought in a single action. Ison improperly split his claim for property damages from his claim for personal injury damages, where both claims arose against a single defendant as a result of a single automobile accident. The damages claims should have been brought together, and because they were not, the trial court correctly ruled that the subsequent action is barred. Accordingly, we affirm the January 30, 2006 order of the Pendleton Circuit Court.

ALL CONCUR.

WHAT'S NEW HERE?

- Up to now we've been looking at how courts decide disputes—which courts have power to hear which disputes (jurisdiction), how disputes are framed (pleading), how evidence is gathered (discovery), and how opposing factual contentions are resolved (summary judgment, trial).
- We're now looking back at a lawsuit that's over, and deciding what it resolved, and what it left open.

Notes and Problems

1. Notice that the court twice describes the legal principles underlying its decision, but does so in different ways.

    a. First it quotes *Hays v. Sturgill*, an earlier Kentucky case, which describes the principle in broad terms: "parties are required to bring forward their whole case; and the plea of *res judicata* applies not only to the points upon which the court was required by the parties to form an opinion and pronounce judgment, but *to every point which properly belonged to the subject of litigation*, and which the parties, exercising reasonable diligence, might have brought forward at the time" (emphasis supplied).

b. Then it quotes from the Restatement (Second) Judgments: "a valid and final judgment rendered in an action extinguishes the plaintiff's claim. . . . [T]he claim extinguished includes all rights of the plaintiff to remedies against the defendant with respect to all or any part of the transaction, or series of connected transactions, out of which the action arose."

c. Most observers would say that the Restatement quote more accurately reflects the trend of the law in this area because it defines precluded claims as involving those that arise from the same transaction as the original claim as opposed to the "subject of litigation." In *Ison v. Thomas*, what was that "transaction"?

2. The Restatements, which you will encounter in a number of other courses, are not official pronouncements of law, like legislation or cases.

a. Instead they represent efforts by a private, purportedly non-partisan organization, the American Law Institute, to distill existing law (or, if the law is conflicting or uncertain, to announce what the Institute believes is the preferable principle).

b. Note that in the other cases in this chapter, the result flowed from interpreting and applying a Rule or a statute. Not here; why? Because, unlike the other areas encountered in this chapter—and in most of the rest of this course— the principles of former adjudication have been developed by courts on a case-by-case basis rather than being set forth in statutes or Rules. Nothing in principle prevents there being such a statute, but the effort of drafting one has not recommended itself to Congress or to state legislatures. When you study the principles of former adjudication in greater detail in Chapter 11 you may better understand why legislatures have left this area to the courts.

c. Although Congress and legislatures may be wise to avoid legislating former adjudication, this decision makes this topic relatively unusual in your Civil Procedure course. It stands out as an island in a sea of legislation and Rule-making. A thousand years ago—even two hundred years ago—the geography of procedure looked different. For many centuries judges made most procedural law in the course of adjudication, with the occasional statute standing out as an island in a sea of common law. Two great movements of procedural reform starting in the second half of the nineteenth century gave legislatures (and later Rule-makers) the dominant position they enjoy today, leaving only a few common law islands (such as former adjudication) remaining.

I. APPEALS

Our judicial system permits a losing party to appeal an adverse judgment of the trial court to a higher court. One might imagine that an appellate court can correct any errors that the trial court has made. Yet procedural rules limit in two significant respects appellate courts' power of review.

The first limitation concerns the standard of the appellate courts' review. Put in very simplified form, existing doctrine tells the appellate courts that they should affirm findings of fact unless "clearly erroneous." By contrast, rulings of law should only be affirmed if the appellate court would have reached the same conclusion. But, regardless of the standard of review, the court of appeals should not reverse unless the lower court's error affected the outcome of the lawsuit. Finally, in many areas, the law itself gives the trial judge discretion to balance competing concerns in making a ruling—for example, whether the potential information to be gained from a particular discovery request is outweighed by the financial burden of complying with that discovery request. In those areas, the issue on appeal is not whether the appellate court judges would themselves have balanced the competing interests the same way, but whether the trial court can be said to have abused its discretion.

The second limitation concerns the timing of appellate review. Imagine that a trial judge has made an important discovery ruling, one that both parties believe will affect the outcome of the case. Further, suppose that the ruling is at least questionable and that the party on the losing end of the ruling appeals. Read 28 U.S.C. §1291, which defines the jurisdiction of the federal courts of appeals: "The courts of appeals . . . shall have jurisdiction of appeals from all *final* decisions of the district courts. . . ." (emphasis added). That bland statement has a negative implication: that the courts of appeals do *not* have jurisdiction over an effort to appeal from an order that is not a "final decision." Lawyers call a non-final order "interlocutory." The next case shows "the final judgment rule," as it is often called, applied to a discovery order under Rule 35 for a mental examination of the plaintiff.

Reise v. Board of Regents of the University of Wisconsin
957 F.2d 293 (7th Cir. 1992)

EASTERBROOK, J.

E.H. Reise, who was graduated in the top 5% of his class from the Law School of the University of Wisconsin at Madison, applied for a position on its faculty. The Law School did not hire him. He believes that his race and sex account for the decision, that in recent years the Law School has been unwilling to consider anyone, no matter how skilled, who is not black, female, or otherwise eligible for preferential treatment. According to Reise, only one of the last thirteen appointments to the faculty has been a white male, and that appointment was made in 1985. The Law School says that the persons it hired are better lawyers and scholars than Reise. The district court has set a trial for this coming April to get at the truth.

[Reise has filed an appeal] . . . asking us to reverse the judge's order that he submit to a mental examination under Fed. R. Civ. P. 35. Reise demands $4 million in compensatory damages on account of the mental anguish, emotional distress, and illness that he says he has endured as a result of the Law School's decision not to hire him. Not surprisingly, the Law School wants to obtain a medical opinion on Reise's mental state, so that it may present evidence on that subject at trial. Reise insists that because he is over his distress and is not seeking damages on account of his *current* mental condition, an examination would reveal nothing of value. Again not surprisingly, the Law School is not content with Reise's say-so and wants to check. The district judge, siding with the Law School, ordered Reise to undergo an examination.

Although Reise contends that the examination is unnecessary and that the judge should at all events have ensured that the physician would be independent of the University, we shall have nothing to say about [those contentions]. Details of discovery are a long way from final decision [and the discovery order is therefore "interlocutory" and the Court of Appeal thus lacks jurisdiction to consider Reise's argument, 28 U.S.C. §1291]. . . .

It is too late in the day to waste words explaining why interlocutory orders, and discovery orders in particular, are not appealable despite their irreversible costs. Because almost all interlocutory appeals from discovery orders would end in affirmance (the district court possesses discretion, and review is deferential), the costs of delay via appeal, and the costs to the judicial system of entertaining these appeals, exceed in the aggregate the costs of the few erroneous discovery orders that might be corrected were appeals available. . . .

Discovery orders, including orders to submit to an examination, are readily reviewable after final decision. A party aggrieved by the order assures eventual review by refusing to comply. The district judge then imposes sanctions under Fed. R. Civ. P. 37(b)(2). The probable sanction in a case such as this is an order striking Reise's claim for damages on account of mental and physical distress. If Reise should prevail on the merits but not obtain damages because of the order striking his claim, he may obtain full review on appeal: if the district judge abused his discretion in requiring Reise to submit to an examination, we will remand for further proceedings. True, this procedure creates a potential for two trials, but then so does any other discovery order, or an order disqualifying or failing to disqualify counsel, or any order granting or denying partial summary judgment. . . . And requiring the complaining party to take some risk—to back up his belief with action—winnows weak claims. Only persons who have *substantial* objections to the examination and believe their legal positions strong will follow a path that could end in defeat. Among those who take the risk by balking at the order, some will lose on the merits, and their discovery disputes will become moot. Most of the remaining cases will end in affirmance, given deferential review. The number of retrials entailed by the procedure is small, the number of appeals avoided large.

As an order to submit to a physical or mental examination is not appealable. . . . Appeal No. 91-3844 is dismissed for want of jurisdiction.

Notes and Problems

1. Be sure you understand what has happened in this case. Did the court rule on plaintiff's contention that the ordered mental examination was improper? What *did* it do? Why?

2. The court not only dismissed plaintiff's appeal; it also offered several justifications for the final judgment rule. Be sure that you understand what they are. Another justification for the rule is that many trial court decisions that seem wrong at the time turn out not to matter because the party on the losing end of that decision goes on to prevail.

3. The argument against the final judgment rule relies on a different kind of pragmatic reasoning. Most cases will not end in a judgment of any sort—the parties will settle. Judicial rulings that precede settlements are not appealable, but those rulings may have dictated the terms of the settlement by greatly advantaging one party. In those settled cases—the majority of all cases—it seems unjust to allow what may be practically dispositive judicial rulings to escape appellate review. Some states, New York most notable among them, have adopted this reasoning by providing for liberal interlocutory appeal of significant trial court rulings. Others (the federal courts included) create some statutory exceptions to the final judgment rule and weasel a bit with judge-made doctrines that slightly soften its impact. It is nevertheless still fair to say that the rule poses an insuperable barrier to immediate appeal of many trial court rulings.

4. Apply the final judgment rule to some of the cases we have already considered in this chapter. From which of the following decisions would an immediate appeal lie assuming the order in question were entered by a federal district judge:
    a. a trial court order granting dismissal for want of subject matter jurisdiction (as in *Hawkins v. Masters Farms*);
    b. a trial court order refusing to dismiss for want of subject matter jurisdiction;
    c. a trial court order denying a 12(b)(6) motion (as in *Bell v. Novick Transfer*);
    d. a trial court order granting a 12(b)(6) motion;
    e. an order denying a defendant's motion to sever several plaintiffs' joint complaints (as in *Fisher v. Ciba Specialty Chemicals Corp.*);
    f. an order denying permission to amend a pleading and add an additional party;
    g. an order granting or denying requested discovery?

WHAT'S NEW HERE?

- Most of us would intuit that an appellate court corrects any errors the trial court made.
- You now understand that intuition is doubly wrong. First, appellate courts will never review most trial court rulings. Second, of those they can review, they will reverse only for some kinds of error.

● That means that you, as a lawyer at the start of your career, need to understand that in most instances the trial court is the *only* place you can present your case—there won't be another chance.

Procedure as Strategy

Consider how the final judgment rule affects the dynamics of litigation. Plaintiff files a lawsuit and defendant, before answering, makes a modest settlement offer. Plaintiff's lawyer advises plaintiff to reject the offer, which he does. Defendant answers and the parties head into discovery. Plaintiff seeks discovery of some information vital to the lawsuit, but the defendant objects and the judge refuses to grant the requested discovery. Plaintiff cannot appeal unless the case goes to final judgment, but it will cost plaintiff considerable time and money to get to that stage. Will the defendant's original settlement offer look better? Will defendant still be willing to make that modest offer, having won the battle over discovery?

Implications

In *Reise*, the defendant university sought to have its own physician conduct a mental examination. Suppose instead—or in addition to—this exam, the university had sought Reise's medical records, hoping to be able to show that his emotional distress predated, and therefore was not caused by, the university's failure to employ him. Relevant? Surely yes. Privileged? Yes but no: Before Reise filed this lawsuit, his disclosures to his health care professionals were privileged. But, when Reise sued claiming damages for mental distress, he *waived* that privilege and rendered the records discoverable for the purposes of this lawsuit.

Note on Appellate Structure and Jurisdiction

In this and other law school courses you will read a good many appellate opinions from state and federal courts. What determines which court will hear such an appeal?

The most basic proposition is that the appellate courts of whatever system the case starts in will hear subsequent appeals. Thus in the federal system, parties who lose a "final decision" in the district court can appeal to the court of appeals. The courts of appeals hear cases from district courts in regions covering several states, each region being called a "circuit." There are 11 circuits covering the 50 states, a twelfth for the District of Columbia, and a thirteenth, the Court of Appeals for the Federal Circuit, which hears appeals in certain specialized cases—patent actions, for example. Thus the Court of Appeals for the Second Circuit hears cases from the district courts in Connecticut, Vermont, and New York; the Court of Appeals for the Seventh Circuit hears cases from the district courts in Indiana, Illinois, and Wisconsin. Atop the courts of appeals is the Supreme Court of the United States.

The same principle applies in the state courts. *Ison v. Thomas* was decided by the Kentucky Court of Appeals because the case was initially heard by a Kentucky trial court. Most states have an appellate structure resembling the federal system— a trial court of general jurisdiction, an intermediate appellate court to which all cases may be appealed, and a state supreme court* that has discretion over which cases it will hear. In some states, however, there is no intermediate appellate court, so appeals go directly to the state supreme court.

How and when does the U.S. Supreme Court get into the act? Cases reach the Supreme Court in two ways—from federal courts and from state courts. In both instances Supreme Court review is discretionary: The Justices pick and choose which cases they will hear. Thus, parties who lose in the highest state court or federal court of appeals must apply to the Supreme Court to have their case heard, which they do by asking the Court to grant a *writ of certiorari*. See 28 U.S.C. §§1253-1258.

There is an additional barrier to U.S. Supreme Court review of state court cases. The Supreme Court may hear a state court case *only* if it presents an issue of federal law. It cannot hear cases from the state supreme court that involve solely questions of state law. In other words, cases like *Ison* that exclusively concern state law— there, state law rules governing former adjudication—cannot be heard by the U.S. Supreme Court. This rule does not stop people from trying to get their case heard by the Supreme Court. How might they do so? If they can "make a federal case" out of it—perhaps by arguing that Kentucky's laws governing former adjudication violate the U.S. Constitution's Due Process Clause. (That's a losing argument on *Ison's* facts, but it would be the only imaginable way of dragging federal law into the case.)

Finally, because the Court enjoys broad discretion in selecting which cases it will hear, a decision not to review a case does not signify approval of the decision rendered by the court below. So, if the U.S. Supreme Court denies petition for certiorari, that doesn't mean it affirmed the lower court's ruling; it just decided not to review the case.

Note: Civil Procedure in Your Substantive Courses

During the year you will encounter repeated discussion of procedural issues in various substantive courses. Discussing a case in Contracts, your instructor may

---

*New York has particularly challenging terminology: The state calls its trial court of general jurisdiction the "Supreme Court," its intermediate appellate court the "Appellate Division," and its highest court the "Court of Appeals."

ask about the procedure by which the case reached the appellate court; a Torts class may focus on the question of what additional evidence would have enabled a plaintiff to avoid a directed verdict for the defendant. A Property class may explore the defects in a plaintiff's complaint for trespass that led the court to grant a motion to dismiss. These scenarios do not represent efforts by your other instructors to seize pedagogical territory by conquest. Instead they reflect the role that substantive law plays in procedural decisions and that procedure plays in substantive law.

Lawsuits grow from disputes. Parties may dispute what happened and what consequences the law attaches to those happenings. At several stages of litigation, procedure establishes hurdles that a party must jump. Demurrers or Rule 12(b)(6) motions are one such hurdle; motions for summary judgment, a directed verdict, or a judgment notwithstanding the verdict are others. All these procedural devices require the judge to reflect on the substantive law that applies to the case and to describe the way in which that law applies to the facts as they then appear: that makes such cases good teaching tools for the substantive law involved.

Focusing on the procedural stance of the case clarifies two points. First, seeing that the case arises on an appeal from a motion to dismiss, an objection to jury instructions, or the like explains *why* the judge is engaging in a recitation of the substantive law. Second, understanding the procedural stance of the case enables you to see how much of what the court says depends purely on a legal assessment of the case and how much depends on a factual assessment. For example, on a Rule 12(b)(6) motion, the court considers whether the plaintiff's allegations in the complaint, if proved, would entitle him to the court's help; it does not consider whether it is likely that the plaintiff could prove the truth of those statements. On a motion for summary judgment or a directed verdict, by contrast, the court must consider both the law that applies to the case and the evidence that the parties have gathered and presented.

Procedure will thus play two roles in your substantive courses. First, various procedural hurdles will provide the occasion for judicial expositions of the law of torts, property, contract, and crimes. Second, by understanding the procedural stage at which the issue under discussion arose, you will also understand the extent to which the court is considering the facts of the particular case. Comprehending this dual role will enable you to see both the way in which procedure shapes substantive law and the reason procedural discussions will often play a central role in learning that substantive law.

Assessment Questions—And a Word About Using These Questions

At the end of every chapter will appear a set of questions we've written to help you test your mastery of the material in that chapter. Following the questions are analyses of each of them, together with brief explanations of why various responses are correct or incorrect. We hope both will be useful to you. But, we'd also like to make a suggestion about how to use these questions to best effect. You'll get almost nothing out of the questions if you use them as one of your authors used such questions in his high-school algebra text—looking quickly from the problem to the solution and then mentally telling himself, "Yes, I knew that." Much better is to work through each question, write down your responses, and only after completing all the questions consult the analyses. Even better—counterintuitive as it may seem—is to work through the problems and then wait a day to consult the responses. Though it sounds odd, that method has a great deal of cognitive science research behind it: Apparently our minds retain things better when we space rather than bunch our learning. So give it a try—what can you lose?

Q1. Peters, involved in a collision with Dodge under the circumstances described earlier in this chapter, consults a lawyer about bringing a lawsuit. After hearing Peters's version of the facts, the lawyer is likely to (choose as many as are accurate):

    A. Ask Peters whether he would want to bring the case in state or federal court.

    B. Tell Peters he wants to do some investigation and research before reaching a conclusion about whether to offer to represent him.

    C. Draft a complaint alleging the circumstances of the accident based solely on Peters's recollection.

    D. *If* Peters's lawyer concludes the case will fare best in federal court, offer Peters some suggestions about steps he might take after returning to Ann Arbor.

Q2. Peters's lawyer files his case in federal district court in the appropriate district of Illinois (where Dodge resides). The complaint reads like the one on page 21. Dodge might appropriately respond by (choose as many as apply):

    A. Filing a 12(b)(1) motion challenging the court's subject matter jurisdiction.

    B. Answering the complaint denying that he was negligent.

    C. Filing a 12(b)(6) motion seeking to have the claim dismissed on the grounds that the complaint misstates the date of the accident, which happened three days before the date indicated in the complaint.

    D. Answering the complaint denying that he was negligent and asserting as affirmative defenses that the statute of limitations had run and that the court lacked subject matter jurisdiction.

Q3. Suppose that Dodge's lawyer answers by denying the allegations of negligence and counterclaiming for his own injuries, and the case proceeds. During discovery, the two sides seek various pieces of information; which of the following statements is accurate?

    A. If Dodge seeks Peters's medical records, hoping to be able to show that some of the symptoms of which he complains predated the accidents, Peters can successfully resist on grounds of doctor-patient privilege.

    B. If Peters seeks to depose two witnesses who were at the intersection where the accident occurred, they can successfully resist on grounds that they are not parties to the lawsuit and therefore should not be inconvenienced.

    C. If Dodge seeks the maintenance records for the past decade on Peters's automobile, Peters may be able to resist on the grounds that it will be difficult and expensive for him to reconstruct these records and that the older records will be at best of marginal relevance.

    D. The party losing the types of discovery rulings described above will be unable to get an immediate appellate ruling reviewing the trial court's decision.

Q4. Discovery comes to a close in *Peters v. Dodge.* Peters deposed four apparently impartial witnesses, all of whom support his version of the facts; Dodge has only his own word against these witnesses. But Dodge has uncovered something he thinks useful: two previous lawsuits by Peters—in both, he claimed injuries from similar auto accidents and the courts found for the defendants. Which of the following statements is accurate?

    A. On this state of the evidence, the case of *Peters v. Dodge* would be submitted to a jury.

    B. If Dodge moves for summary judgment on the basis of this evidence, the court would grant it.

    C. If this information was presented at trial and Dodge at trial moves for judgment as a matter of law on the basis of this evidence, the court would grant it.

    D. If Dodge brings to the court's attention the previous lawsuits, the court will conclude that *res judicata* precludes Peters from moving forward with this case.

Analysis of Assessment Questions

Q1. B and D are the correct responses. B is correct because Rule 11—as well as analogous rules of professional responsibility—require the lawyer to investigate his client's version of the facts before filing a complaint (and so it makes sense to do this investigation before deciding whether to assume the responsibilities of representation). D is correct because Peters will have to rely on diversity jurisdiction to make it into federal court and, as *Hawkins* (and a thousand other cases) teach, determining diversity involves both physical residence and objective indications of an intent to remain indefinitely. Taking steps like registering to vote and registering his motor vehicle in Michigan may help Peters make such a showing. A is wrong because such tactical decisions are for the lawyer rather than the client; even a law student like Peters is unlikely to be able to make a sensible choice about such a matter. C is wrong because the lawyer will want to verify Peters's story before drafting any complaint.

Q2. A, B, and D are correct responses. A: A pre-answer motion may be made on any of the grounds listed in Rule 12(b). B: An answer is always an appropriate response to a complaint, and the most common response in an answer is a denial of one or more key allegations of the complaint. D: One may make a pre-answer motion, but one may equally decide instead to answer and to assert as defenses matters that might have been the subject of a pre-answer motion (such as lack of subject matter jurisdiction). C is wrong: A 12(b)(6) motion assumes—for the purposes of argument—that all the allegations of the complaint are true. To dispute those allegations—including the allegation of the date of the accident—one would file an answer denying whichever allegations one wants to dispute and then marshal evidence supporting one's claim during discovery, to be used at summary judgment.

Q3. C and D are correct responses. C is correct because, as in *Gordon*, a party can resist discovery on grounds of proportionality, including expense in relation to likely relevance. D is correct because none of the discovery rulings described will be a final judgment. A is wrong because by bringing suit to recover for his injuries Peters has waived the privilege. B is wrong because our legal system requires nonparties to offer any relevant, unprivileged evidence they possess.

Q4. A is the only correct response. B is incorrect because, even though the evidence appears to favor Peters, the witnesses could be mistaken and the jury's central function is to sort out the truth from the clash of testimony. C is incorrect for the same reason. D is wrong because preclusion would apply only if Peters had previously brought *this* claim against Dodge (as was the case in *Ison v. Thomas*).

PART I

THE CONSTITUTIONAL FRAMEWORK FOR U.S. LITIGATION

A. APPROACHING CIVIL PROCEDURE

One can study the procedural system from the top down or from the bottom up. The top-down approach starts with the constitutional environment in which the individual lawsuit exists. That approach takes the student into both the history and the current interpretation of the Constitution of the United States. Studying the Constitution reveals several limits on the ways in which state and federal court systems conduct their business—limits that have major consequences for individual litigants. The bottom-up approach begins with the life cycle of an individual lawsuit: how the parties initially state their grievances, develop information about them, and bring them to resolution. This approach emphasizes features and problems of the contemporary procedural system, which is in many respects a bold experiment. Studying the process of litigation reveals how these features shape and constrain the litigants' responsibilities and choices.

As you have probably already guessed, anyone wanting to become a lawyer has to understand both approaches, to comprehend the constitutional environment as well as the modes for processing disputes. This book accordingly contains materials about both approaches, and most courses will examine both. But one can with equal validity start at the top and work down or begin at the bottom and work up. The three parts of this book are labeled to emphasize these different starting points. Some courses may begin with Part I: The Constitutional Framework for U.S. Litigation, comprising Chapters 2-4. This starting point represents the "top-down" approach. Other classes may move first to Part II: The Process of Litigation, comprising Chapters 5-11 and representing the "bottom-up" approach. The last part of this book, Part III: Probing the Boundaries: Additional Claims and Parties, combines significant elements of both the other parts and may be studied either at the end of the course, as a reprise, or in conjunction with either of the other two parts. The next three chapters represent an approach to litigation starting at the top—with the constitutional framework.

B. CONSTITUTIONAL LIMITS IN LITIGATION

The U.S. Constitution dictates many fundamental aspects of a lawsuit—not only in landmark cases but in ordinary civil litigation. For example, someone looking at the U.S. system from the outside might conclude that it would be more efficient to have a single, unitary court system for all disputes rather than 51 separate systems (one for each state and one for the federal government). Efficient it might be, but it would also be unconstitutional, for reasons you will come to understand. The next three chapters develop several of the most important ways the Constitution shapes litigation in the United States. Two of those ways involve "jurisdiction," a protean and important word in U.S. litigation; a third involves "choice of law."

1. The Idea of Jurisdiction

No legal system in the world claims the power to decide all disputes arising anywhere. Which cases, then, will a legal system resolve? Consider this question concretely. Imagine that you live in Illinois and come to California to attend law school. A particularly contentious sort, you become involved in two disputes during your first year there: You think your landlord is failing to maintain your apartment, and you think one of your instructors unfairly rejects you for a position as a part-time research assistant. In the first case, you might start by complaining to the landlord; in the second, to the instructor or the dean. You would *not* seek relief from the landlord of the building next door or from the dean of another law school. You would not do so because the landlord of the other building and the dean of the other school have no power over the conditions in your apartment or school. Putting the matter very loosely, one could say the condition of your apartment and the employment decision fall outside of their *jurisdictions*: Say what they might about the poor state of garbage collection or the unfairness of failing to hire you, they are powerless to remedy either.

You will repeatedly encounter the concept of jurisdiction while studying law and will soon discover that the term is used in several different ways. More or less literally, "jurisdiction" means the power to declare the law. By extension, it has acquired several other meanings. Lawyers may speak of "the law of a jurisdiction" or "legislative jurisdiction," using the term in both instances to signify a state or territory whose government has the power to make law within its bounds. In civil procedure it has a narrower meaning. Lawyers sometimes refer to jurisdiction in this narrower sense as "judicial jurisdiction": the power of a court to render a judgment that other courts and government agencies will recognize and enforce.

You might encounter jurisdiction in this narrower legal sense if your two imaginary disputes escalated and you sued either the landlord or the instructor. If during the dispute with your landlord you returned to Illinois for the summer and there filed an action against your California landlord, you might well be met with the defense that courts in Illinois have no jurisdiction over the landlord. If you filed suit in federal court in California against the instructor, a different kind of jurisdiction question might arise. While conceding that the instructor could be sued in California, the defendants might challenge the jurisdiction of *federal* courts over the lawsuit: Whether the challenge was successful would depend on whether you could either frame your challenge to the hiring decision as a claim "arising under federal law" or convince the court that you were still a "citizen" of Illinois and that you and the defendant(s) were thus of diverse citizenship.

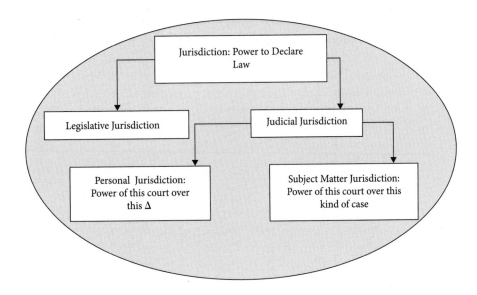

2. Jurisdiction and the Constitution

The next two chapters explore the ways in which courts in the United States conceive of and resolve questions like those raised in the preceding hypothetical case. Exploring the topic will be easier if you have some sense of both the terminology and the context in which jurisdictional issues arise. The basic terminology requires the student to distinguish between "personal" jurisdiction, the focus of Chapter 2, and "subject matter" jurisdiction, the focus of Chapter 3. Lawyers would describe the challenge to the Illinois suit against your California landlord as involving a question of *personal jurisdiction*—the power of an Illinois court to render a judgment binding someone who may have never set foot in Illinois. They would describe the challenge to the federal courts' power to decide the question whether you were wrongly refused a part-time job as raising the issue of federal courts' *subject matter jurisdiction*—the power of federal (as opposed to state) courts to decide certain kinds of cases. At the outset you need only bear in mind that personal and subject matter jurisdiction are *both* necessary ingredients of any court's power to render a binding decision in a case; that is, a court must have both subject matter and personal jurisdiction to render a valid judgment.

The deep concern with jurisdiction ranks high among the distinguishing characteristics of the Anglo-American legal system. The concept has special significance in the United States, where government power is divided among states and between the states as a whole and the federal government: No single government entity has plenary power. This system of limited and overlapping authority means that government agencies—including courts—must repeatedly decide which agency has the power to exercise authority in a given situation. Because the federal Constitution defines the lines of authority among the competing centers of power, courts look to the Constitution for their basic framework in deciding issues of judicial jurisdiction. This aspect of civil procedure will be for many students their first law school encounter with the Constitution, the text of which appears in the supplement that accompanies this casebook.

Three parts of the Constitution bear on jurisdiction. Article III authorizes the establishment of the system of federal courts and in §2 sets the limits of federal judicial authority. Federal courts cannot exceed those jurisdictional boundaries, and Congress has the power in many instances to restrict the scope of federal judicial authority more narrowly than does the Constitution. The constraints imposed by Article III and the legislation implementing it are the focus of Chapter 3, on subject matter jurisdiction.

Article IV, §1 requires that "Full Faith and Credit . . . be given in each State to judicial proceedings of every other State." The Supreme Court has interpreted this clause to require that one state recognize and enforce judgments of another state. For example, suppose a court in State *A* enters a judgment for $100,000 against *D*, but plaintiff cannot find any assets of *D* within State *A* to satisfy the judgment. *D*'s only assets turn out to be a large bank account at a bank located in State *B*. Under the Full Faith and Credit Clause (and state legislation implementing it), plaintiff commences a summary proceeding in a court in State *B*, records State *A*'s judgment, and can then obtain a writ of execution from the State *B* court enforcing State *A*'s judgment against any assets of *D* located in State *B*. As you are about to see, however, the Full Faith and Credit Clause has an important unstated condition—such judgments are entitled to full faith and credit only if the court rendering them had jurisdiction to do so.

Finally, §1 of the Fourteenth Amendment provides that no "State [shall] deprive any person of life, liberty or property without due process of law." This clause, known as the Due Process Clause, has proved to be one of the cornerstones of modern constitutional and procedural theory. It derives its relation to jurisdiction from *Pennoyer v. Neff*, a case that might be termed the great-grandparent of personal jurisdiction, the topic of Chapter 2. As you will see, *Pennoyer* made the question of what we now call personal jurisdiction part of the Constitution.

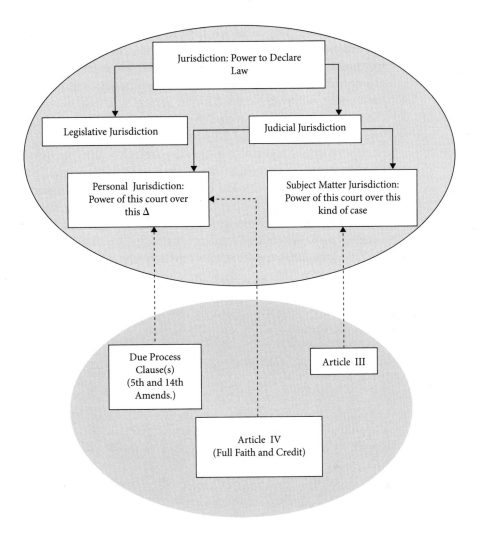

3. The Constitution and Choice of Law

Beyond personal and subject matter jurisdiction, the Constitution shapes U.S. litigation in a third way: It sometimes dictates which set of laws a court must apply to a dispute. There are two key ways in which the Constitution dictates choice of law. First, Article VI provides that the Constitution and federal laws "shall be the supreme Law of the Land; and the Judges in every State shall be bound thereby, any Thing in the Constitution or Laws of any State to the Contrary notwithstanding." This provision is commonly referred to as the Supremacy Clause. Although the Supremacy Clause typically arises in a Constitutional Law class rather than in Civil Procedure, for present purposes it is enough to understand that the clause means that if Congress has validly enacted a statute dealing with a particular subject, both federal and state courts are required to enforce the federal statute, regardless of whether there is a contrary state statute or state common law rule.

The second way in which the Constitution dictates choice of law is that, in the absence of a controlling federal statute, the federal court system is required to respect both the statutory and common law rules of the several states. For an example of how such an issue might arise, imagine that your hypothetical dispute with your California landlord found its way to a federal court. Which law would the court apply to the dispute? Would it be bound by the California law of landlord and tenant? Or would it be free to apply what it thought was a more sensible or just system of regulation to the dispute before it? That question is the focus of Chapter 4, and is answered in significant part by the Supreme Court's decision in *Erie Railroad v. Tompkins. Erie* is a case of constitutional dimensions—or so it insists—but, unlike personal or subject matter jurisdiction, one cannot readily locate the constitutional provisions from which it flows; that enigma itself is part of the problem. Together with personal and subject matter jurisdiction, the Supremacy Clause and the *Erie* doctrine shape the environment in which U.S. litigation operates.

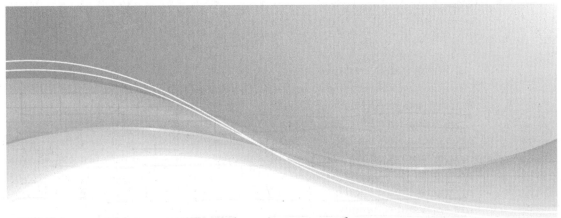

CHAPTER 2

Personal Jurisdiction

A. THE ORIGINS

Personal jurisdiction doctrine concerns, in the simplest terms, a state's ability to assert power over a defendant in a civil lawsuit. It became part of U.S. constitutional law because of *Pennoyer v. Neff*, a case whose facts spawned a truly splendid doctrinal elaboration. To understand those facts you need to have some background. One of the more difficult parts of a lawsuit often comes at its end, when a victorious plaintiff tries to collect the judgment from the defendant, who declines to pay. When this happens, the plaintiff may obtain a writ of execution from the court, which will authorize the sheriff to seize any property belonging to the defendant, sell it (typically through an auction), and give the resulting money to the plaintiff (up to the amount of the judgment). When that sale occurs, the sheriff gives to whomever buys the defendant's property a "sheriff's deed" as evidence of title. The second piece of background you need for *Pennoyer* concerns the idea of "constructive" notice. In law "constructive" generally means "fictional" or "pretend." Defendants generally receive service of process, but what happens if no one can find the defendant? Under those conditions some states provide for a notice in a newspaper—in those fine-print columns no one reads. Under such conditions notice is "constructive" because it is highly unlikely that the defendant will actually see it. Finally, you need to know that "attachment" is the legal term for an officially sanctioned seizure of property; Real estate, cars, and other property may be "attached." Sometimes "attachment" means literal seizure; other times it means posting notices on property or on records of title so that prospective buyers know it cannot be sold by the owner with title.

Pennoyer v. Neff

95 U.S. 714 (1877)

FIELD, J., delivered the opinion of the Court.

[The case concerned two lawsuits. The first suit grew from an unpaid legal fee. Marcus Neff hired Mitchell, a lawyer living and practicing in Oregon, to do some legal work. When Neff failed to pay Mitchell's fee (evidently less than $300), Mitchell sued him in state court. At the time of this first suit Neff was, in the court's words, "a non-resident of the State [who] was not personally served with process, and did not appear [i.e., did not come to court or otherwise resist the lawsuit]. . . . [J]udgment was entered upon his default in not answering the complaint, upon a constructive service of summons by publication." *After* this default judgment, Neff acquired 300 acres of land (allegedly worth $15,000) in Oregon from the federal government. To satisfy his judgment Mitchell had the sheriff seize and sell Neff's land. Pennoyer bought it and received a sheriff's deed as evidence of title. The sheriff then turned the sale proceeds over to Mitchell. Sometime after these events Neff reappeared, and when he discovered what had become of his land, he brought the second lawsuit with which *Pennoyer* is concerned. Neff sued Pennoyer in federal court "to recover the possession of [the] tract of land." As evidence of their respective titles, Neff pointed to the original government deed, and Pennoyer pointed to the sheriff's deed. In this second suit the court thus had to decide whether the first lawsuit and the sheriff's sale had extinguished Neff's title. The opinion begins with an analysis of the form of notice in the first suit.]

The Code of Oregon provides for such [constructive] service when an action is brought against a non-resident and absent defendant, who has property within the State. It also provides, where the action is for the recovery of money or damages, for the attachment of the property of the non-resident. And it also declares that no natural person is subject to the jurisdiction of a court of the State, "unless he appear in the court, or be found within the State, or be a resident thereof, or have property therein; and, in the last case, only to the extent of such property at the time the jurisdiction attached." Construing this latter provision to mean that, in an action for money or damages where a defendant does not appear in the court, and is not found within the State, and is not a resident thereof, but has property therein, the jurisdiction of the court extends only over such property, the declaration expresses a principle of general, if not universal, law. The authority of every tribunal is necessarily restricted by the territorial limits of the State in which it is established. Any attempt to exercise authority beyond those limits would be deemed in every other forum, as has been said by this court, an illegitimate assumption of power, and be resisted as mere abuse. D'Arcy v. Ketchum et al., 11 How. 165. In the case against the plaintiff, the property here in controversy sold under the judgment rendered was not attached, nor in any way brought under the jurisdiction of the court. Its first connection with the case was caused by a levy of the execution. It was not, therefore, disposed of pursuant to any adjudication, but only in enforcement of a personal judgment, having no relation to the property, rendered against a non-resident without service of process upon him in the action, or his appearance therein. The court below did not consider that an attachment of the property was essential to its jurisdiction or to the validity of the sale, but held that the judgment was invalid from defects in the affidavit upon which the order of publication was obtained, and in the affidavit by which the publication was proved.

There is some difference of opinion among the members of this court as to the rulings upon these alleged defects [about whether the statute required an affidavit from the "printer," as the statute specified, or whether one from the editor would suffice]. If, therefore, we were confined to the rulings of the court below upon the defects in the affidavits mentioned, we should be unable to uphold its decision. But it was also contended in that court, and is insisted upon here, that the judgment in the State court against the plaintiff was void for want of personal service of process on him, or of his appearance in the action in which it was rendered, and that the premises in controversy could not be subjected to the payment of the demand of a resident creditor except by a proceeding in rem; that is, by a direct proceeding against the property for that purpose. If these positions are sound, the ruling of the Circuit Court as to the invalidity of that judgment must be sustained, notwithstanding our dissent from the reasons upon which it was made. And that they are sound would seem to follow from two well-established principles of public law respecting the jurisdiction of an independent State over persons and property. The several States of the Union are not, it is true, in every respect independent, many of the rights and powers which originally belonged to them being now vested in the government created by the Constitution. But, except as restrained and limited by that instrument, they possess and exercise the authority of independent States, and the principles of public law to which we have referred are applicable to them. One of these principles is, that every State possesses exclusive jurisdiction and sovereignty over persons and property within its territory. As a consequence, every State has the power to determine for itself the civil status and capacities of its inhabitants; to prescribe the subjects upon which they may contract, the forms and solemnities with which their contracts shall be executed, the rights and obligations arising from them, and the mode in which their validity shall be determined and their obligations enforced; and also to regulate the manner and conditions upon which property situated within such territory, both personal and real, may be acquired, enjoyed, and transferred. The other principle of public law referred to follows from the one mentioned; that is, that no State can exercise direct jurisdiction and authority over persons or property without its territory. Story, Confl. Laws, c. 2; Wheat. Int. Law, pt. 2, c. 2. The several States are of equal dignity and authority, and the independence of one implies the exclusion of power from all others. And so it is laid down by jurists, as an elementary principle, that the laws of one State have no operation outside of its territory, except so far as is allowed by comity; and that no tribunal established by it can extend its process beyond that territory so as to subject either persons or property to its decisions. "Any exertion of authority of this sort beyond this limit," says Story, "is a mere nullity, and incapable of binding such persons or property in any other tribunals." Story, Confl. Laws, sect. 539.

But as contracts made in one State may be enforceable only in another State, and property may be held by non-residents, the exercise of the jurisdiction which every State is admitted to possess over persons and property within its own territory will often affect persons and property without it. To any influence exerted in this way by a State affecting persons resident or property situated elsewhere, no objection can be justly taken; whilst any direct exertion of authority upon them, in an attempt to give ex-territorial operation to its laws, or to enforce an ex-territorial jurisdiction by its tribunals, would be deemed an encroachment upon the independence of the State in which the persons are domiciled or the property is situated, and be resisted as usurpation.

Thus the State, through its tribunals, may compel persons domiciled within its limits to execute, in pursuance of their contracts respecting property elsewhere situated, instruments in such form and with such solemnities as to transfer the title, so far as such formalities can be complied with; and the exercise of this jurisdiction in no manner interferes with the supreme control over the property by the State within which it is situated.

So the State, through its tribunals, may subject property situated within its limits owned by non-residents to the payment of the demand of its own citizens against them; and the exercise of this jurisdiction in no respect infringes upon the sovereignty of the State where the owners are domiciled. Every State owes protection to its own citizens; and, when non-residents deal with them, it is a legitimate and just exercise of authority to hold and appropriate any property owned by such non-residents to satisfy the claims of its citizens. It is in virtue of the State's jurisdiction over the property of the non-resident situated within its limits that its tribunals can inquire into that non-resident's obligations to its own citizens, and the inquiry can then be carried only to the extent necessary to control the disposition of the property. If the non-residents have no property in the State, there is nothing upon which the tribunals can adjudicate. . . .

If, without personal service, judgments *in personam*, obtained ex parte against non-residents and absent parties, upon mere publication of process, which, in the great majority of cases, would never be seen by the parties interested, could be upheld and enforced, they would be the constant instruments of fraud and oppression. Judgments for all sorts of claims upon contracts and for torts, real or pretended, would be thus obtained, under which property would be seized, when the evidence of the transactions upon which they were founded, if they ever had any existence, had perished.

Substituted service by publication, or in any other authorized form, may be sufficient to inform parties of the object of proceedings taken where property is once brought under the control of the court by seizure or some equivalent act. The law assumes that property is always in the possession of its owner, in person or by agent; and it proceeds upon the theory that its seizure will inform him, not only that it is taken into the custody of the court, but that he must look to any proceedings authorized by law upon such seizure for its condemnation and sale. Such service may also be sufficient in cases where the object of the action is to reach and dispose of property in the State, or of some interest therein, by enforcing a contract or a lien respecting the same, or to partition it among different owners, or, when the public is a party, to condemn and appropriate it for a public purpose. In other words, such service may answer in all actions which are substantially proceedings in rem. But where the entire object of the action is to determine the personal rights and obligations of the defendants, that is, where the suit is merely in personam, constructive service in this form upon a nonresident is ineffectual for any purpose. Process from the tribunals of one

State cannot run into another State, and summon parties there domiciled to leave its territory and respond to proceedings against them. Publication of process or notice within the State where the tribunal sits cannot create any greater obligation upon the non-resident to appear: Process sent to him out of the State, and process published within it, are equally unavailing in proceedings to establish his personal liability. . . .

[The Court then responded to Pennoyer's argument that it should make no difference whether Oregon had attached Neff's property at the outset of Mitchell's lawsuit against Neff, or whether Oregon seized Neff's property after Mitchell had obtained the judgment against Neff for the unpaid attorneys' fees.] [The Oregon court's] jurisdiction in that respect cannot be made to depend upon facts to be ascertained after it has tried the cause and rendered the judgment. If the judgment be previously void, it will not become valid by the subsequent discovery of property of the defendant, or by his subsequent acquisition of it. The judgment, if void when rendered, will always remain void: it cannot occupy the doubtful position of being valid if property be found, and void if there be none. . . . [T]he validity of every judgment depends upon the jurisdiction of the court before it is rendered, not upon what may occur subsequently. . . .

In *Webster v. Reid*, reported in 11th of Howard, the plaintiff claimed title to land sold under judgments recovered in suits brought in a territorial court of Iowa, upon publication of notice under a law of the territory, without service of process; and the court said: "These suits were not a proceeding in rem against the land, but were in personam against the owners of it. . . . No person is required to answer in a suit on whom process has not been served, or whose property has not been attached. In this case, there was no personal notice, nor an attachment or other proceeding against the land, until after the judgments. The judgments, therefore, are nullities, and did not authorize the executions on which the land was sold."

The force and effect of judgments rendered against non-residents without personal service of process upon them, or their voluntary appearance, have been the subject of frequent consideration in the courts of the United States and of the several States, as attempts have been made to enforce such judgments in States other than those in which they were rendered, under the provision of the Constitution requiring that "full faith and credit shall be given in each State to the public acts, records, and judicial proceedings of every other State"; and the act of Congress [current version at 28 U.S.C. §1738] providing for the mode of authenticating such acts, records, and proceedings, and declaring that, when thus authenticated, "they shall have such faith and credit given to them in every court within the United States as they have by law or usage in the courts of the State from which they are or shall be taken." In the earlier cases, it was supposed that the act gave to all judgments the same effect in other States which they had by law in the State where rendered. But this view was afterwards qualified so as to make the act applicable only when the court rendering the judgment had jurisdiction of the parties and of the subject-matter, and not to preclude an inquiry into the jurisdiction of the court in which the judgment was rendered, or the right of the State itself to exercise authority over the person or the subject-matter. M'Elmoyle v. Cohen, 13 Pet. 312. . . .

Since the adoption of the Fourteenth Amendment to the Federal Constitution, the validity of such judgments may be directly questioned, and their enforcement in the State resisted, on the ground that proceedings in a court of justice to determine the personal rights and obligations of parties over whom that court has no jurisdiction do not constitute due process of law. Whatever difficulty may be experienced in giving to those terms a definition which will embrace every permissible exertion of power affecting private rights, and exclude such as is forbidden, there can be no doubt of their meaning when applied to judicial proceedings. They then mean a course of legal proceedings according to those rules and principles which have been established in our systems of jurisprudence for the protection and enforcement of private rights. To give such proceedings any validity, there must be a tribunal competent by its constitution—that is, by the law of its creation—to pass upon the subject-matter of the suit; and, if that involves merely a determination of the personal liability of the defendant, he must be brought within its jurisdiction by service of process within the State, or his voluntary appearance.

Except in cases affecting the personal status of the plaintiff, and cases in which that mode of service may be considered to have been assented to in advance, as hereinafter mentioned, the substituted service of process by publication, allowed by the law of Oregon and by similar laws in other States, where actions are brought against non-residents, is effectual only where, in connection with process against the person for commencing the action, property in the State is brought under the control of the court, and subjected to its disposition by process adapted to that purpose, or where the judgment is sought as a means of reaching such property or affecting some interest therein; in other words, where the action is in the nature of a proceeding in rem. As stated by Cooley in his Treatise on Constitutional Limitations, 405, for any other purpose than to subject the property of a non-resident to valid claims against him in the State, "due process of law would require appearance or personal service before the defendant could be personally bound by any judgment rendered." . . .

It follows from the views expressed that the personal judgment recovered in the State court of Oregon against the plaintiff herein, then a non-resident of the State, was without any validity, and did not authorize a sale of the property in controversy.

To prevent any misapplication of the views expressed in this opinion, it is proper to observe that we do not mean to assert, by anything we have said, that a State may not authorize proceedings to determine the status of one of its citizens towards a non-resident, which would be binding within the State, though made without service of process or personal notice to the non-resident. The jurisdiction which every State possesses to determine the civil status and capacities of all its inhabitants involves authority to prescribe the conditions on which proceedings affecting them may be commenced and carried on within its territory. The State, for example, has absolute right to prescribe the conditions upon which the marriage relation between its own citizens shall be created, and the causes for which it may be dissolved. . . .

Neither do we mean to assert that a State may not require a non-resident entering into a partnership or association within its limits, or making contracts enforceable there, to appoint an agent or representative in the State to receive service of process and notice in legal proceedings instituted with respect to such partnership, association, or contracts, or to designate a place where such service may be made and notice given, and provide, upon their failure, to make such appointment or to designate such place that service may be made upon a public officer designated for that purpose, or in some other prescribed way, and that judgments rendered upon such service may not be binding upon the nonresidents both within and without the State. . . . Nor do we doubt that a State, on creating corporations or other institutions for pecuniary or charitable purposes, may provide a mode in which their conduct may be investigated, their obligations enforced, or their charters revoked, which shall require other than personal service upon their officers or members. Parties becoming members of such corporations or institutions would hold their interest subject to the conditions prescribed by law.

In the present case, there is no feature of this kind, and, consequently, no consideration of what would be the effect of such legislation in enforcing the contract of a non-resident can arise. The question here respects only the validity of a money judgment rendered in one State, in an action upon a simple contract against the resident of another, without service of process upon him, or his appearance therein.

Judgment affirmed.

[Mr. Justice HUNT dissented.]

WHAT'S NEW HERE?

Pennoyer established fundamental jurisdictional doctrine, the main outlines of which prevailed for a century and which is still good law in many respects. *Pennoyer* proclaims that its holding rests on the Constitution, and the opinion mentions both the Due Process and the Full Faith and Credit Clauses. That assertion has two entailments.

- First, because the Due Process Clause restricts the power of state governments, the boundaries of personal jurisdiction proclaimed by the Supreme Court bind state courts. (They also bind federal courts for an additional reason: Rule 4(k)(1)(A) provides that the personal jurisdiction of a federal court shall be the same as the court of a state in which the federal court is sitting, unless a federal statute provides otherwise.)

- *Pennoyer's* mention of the Full Faith and Credit Clause (U.S. Const. Art. IV, §1) points to a second constitutional issue. The opinion links full faith and credit to personal jurisdiction: The courts of State *Y* need not enforce a judgment against a defendant entered by the courts of State *X* if *X* lacked personal jurisdiction over the defendant.

- *Pennoyer* also makes, in passing, a point about the nature of appellate review in the U.S. legal system. Consider the sentence: "If these positions are sound, the ruling of the Circuit Court as to the invalidity of that judgment must be sustained, notwithstanding our dissent from the reasons upon which it was made." Appellate courts in the United States review *outcomes*, not reasoning; because in the Supreme Court's view the lower court had reached the correct outcome, it affirmed, even though it came to that outcome by an entirely different—and at the time novel—line of reasoning.

Notes and Problems

1. Before considering anything else, look back at the facts.

   a. Do we know whether Neff ever learned about the existence of Mitchell's original lawsuit?

   b. If not, isn't the absence of notice a strong objection to the way in which the first lawsuit was conducted?

   c. Did the Court discuss this objection?

2. The case operates on two levels—simple facts and lofty doctrine. According to the opinion, what facts would have to be different for the Oregon courts to have had jurisdiction to enter a valid judgment in Mitchell's original suit against Neff?

3. The Supreme Court confronted not just a case but a significant political and economic problem. The Court had to steer between two rocks: stopping interstate commerce and permitting interstate "piracy by judgment."

   a. As an example of the first problem, suppose a transaction much like that in *Pennoyer*: A New York purchaser buys a piece of property in Oregon. If title proves defective, could Purchaser sue Seller in New York? If Purchaser's check bounces, could Oregon Seller sue Purchaser in Oregon? Unless distant parties can reliably resolve disputes, they will not deal with each other. How does *Pennoyer* answer these questions?

   b. As an example of the second problem, imagine a world with the Full Faith and Credit Clause but without *Pennoyer*. Unscrupulous litigants in a distant state could file meritless complaints, recover default judgments, and then bring those judgments to the defendants' home state for execution. The opinion hints at this concern:

   > If, without personal service, judgments *in personam*, obtained ex parte against non-residents and absent parties, upon mere publication of process, which, in the great majority of cases, would never be seen by the parties interested, could be upheld and enforced, they would be the constant instruments of fraud and oppression. Judgments for all sorts of claims upon contracts and for torts, real or pretended, would be thus obtained, under which property would be seized, when the evidence of the transactions upon which they were founded, if they ever had any existence, had perished.

   c. As you read the cases that follow *Pennoyer*, consider how they steer between these two dangers—blocking commerce and avoiding abusive litigation.

4. After announcing that it would be affirming the judgment on grounds different from those articulated by the lower court, the opinion has an odd structure.

   a. Starting with the sentence (partway through the third paragraph of the edited opinion), "And that they are sound would seem to follow from two well-established principles . . . ," the opinion enunciates a series of broad categorical propositions: "every State possesses exclusive jurisdiction and sovereignty"; "no State can exercise direct jurisdiction and authority over persons or property without its territory"; "Any exertion of authority of this sort beyond this limit, is a mere nullity, and incapable of binding such persons or property in any other tribunals."

b. The remainder of the opinion (starting with the paragraph that begins, "But as contracts made in one State . . . ,") the opinion qualifies and takes back some of its more extreme statements about states' jurisdictional authority.

c. It thus becomes important both to recognize the conceptual structure implied by the extreme statements and then to understand how the opinion qualifies them.

5. Let us start with the conceptual structure, which the opinion describes in the lofty Latinate phrases that divide the world into two jurisdictional categories: *in personam* and *in rem*. The case assumes that jurisdiction is about power and that one can divide power into two apparently distinct categories—power over persons and power over property. Making that distinction implies that one could sensibly think about Oregon's having power over Neff's property (had it gone about acquiring it in the proper way) as a question separate from its having power over Neff himself. Power over Neff himself came to be known as jurisdiction *in personam* (over the person); power over his property came to be known as jurisdiction *in rem* (over the thing). Modern legal scholars doubt that the distinction holds up. The best critique appears in Geoffrey C. Hazard, Jr., *A General Theory of State-Court Jurisdiction*, 1965 S. Ct. Rev. 241. As you will see, in recent years the Supreme Court has reconsidered this distinction.

a. *In personam* jurisdiction looks, at first, refreshingly simple, as described by *Pennoyer*. To obtain jurisdiction over a nonresident defendant the plaintiff must arrange to have defendant personally served with process within the borders of the state in question. So, in the hypothetical in Note 3, Purchaser could sue Seller in New York only if he could serve him with process in New York; otherwise Seller would be beyond the range of the New York court's power. In *Pennoyer*'s view, serving Neff by other means (e.g., by mail) or by personal service in a different state does not work. Working with the facts of *Pennoyer*, explain why the Oregon court did not obtain *in personam* jurisdiction over Neff.

b. *In rem* jurisdiction, the more obscure category, flows from a problem created by the rules for *in personam* jurisdiction: People sometimes own property distant from their usual personal residence. In the hypothetical case in Note 3, suppose that, after Purchaser of the Oregon land returned to New York, the check bounced, and Seller argued that he still owns the property. Can Purchaser, by remaining out of state—perhaps indefinitely—prevent Oregon from giving clean title back to Seller (and thus enabling him to sell to a solvent purchaser)? If *in personam* jurisdiction were the only possibility, nothing could be done until Purchaser returned to Oregon and could be served with process. Unwilling to see that result, the court created a procedure by which a court located in the same state as the property could enter a judgment disposing of that property—by seizing it at the outset of the lawsuit. *Pennoyer* calls that procedure *in rem* jurisdiction. Working with the facts of *Pennoyer*, explain why the Oregon court did not obtain *in rem* jurisdiction over Neff.

6. So far, so good in the world of concepts. The waters begin to cloud in the paragraph that begins "To prevent any misapplication . . . ," in which the opinion qualifies and retracts some of its broad statements. It does so in two ways:

   a. It says that a state has jurisdiction over "the status of one of its citizens towards a non-resident." What does that mean? The same paragraph tells us: it's marriage and divorce. Without this paragraph Marcus Neff could abandon his wife in Oregon, move to another state, and leave her unable to obtain a divorce. The phrase just quoted suggests the hypothetical Mrs. Neff could obtain an Oregon divorce, because Oregon would have jurisdiction over her "status" as a married person, even if she could not locate or serve her husband in Oregon. In fact, courts wrestled with this situation for a century, wishing to allow abandoned spouses to obtain divorces, but not to allow abandoning spouses to move to another state and obtain a divorce without satisfying their obligations of support.

   b. The next paragraph of the opinion says that states can require someone doing business there "to appoint an agent or representative in the State to receive service of process and notice in legal proceedings instituted with respect to such" business. By thus "consenting" to service of process one would, in the world of *Pennoyer*, consent to jurisdiction. In the wake of *Pennoyer* many states passed statutes requiring those doing business in the state to appoint an agent—often a state official—empowered to receive process on their behalf.

PERSPECTIVES

[John] Mitchell was a well-known Portland lawyer specializing in land litigation and railroad right-of-way cases[, who in] 1872 was elected a United States Senator. Allegations of vote fraud were made against [him], and indictments were sought but later dismissed. Interestingly, Judge Deady—who rendered the lower court decision in *Pennoyer*—actively supported the attempts to seek indictments for vote fraud. It is somewhat surprising that Mitchell was ever elected to public office given his somewhat sordid past. At the age of 22, [he] was forced to marry a fifteen-year-old girl "he had seduced and made pregnant." He soon abandoned his first wife and took up with a "schoolmarm." Mitchell next entered a bigamous marriage, and eventually fell "in love with his

John Mitchell

wife's sister and carr[ied] on an open affair for many years." [Citing and quoting from E.E. MacColl, The Shaping of a City 201-03 (1976).]

Pennoyer was also active in public life. Educated at Harvard, he was both governor of Oregon and mayor of Portland. Something of a political maverick, Pennoyer proclaimed Oregon's Thanksgiving Day holiday one week later than the rest of the Nation.

Linda Silberman, Shaffer v. Heitner: *The End of an Era*, 53 N.Y.U. L. Rev. 33, 44 n.53 (1978).

Is it ironic—or entirely appropriate—that a case that created a century of developing procedural doctrine had its genesis in a lawsuit brought by a lawyer trying to collect his fee? Many twenty-first-century lawyers dispense the advice never to sue for a fee, on the grounds that such a lawsuit will often draw a counterclaim for malpractice. Now you have a second basis for this maxim of practice: You might also create a whole new chapter in civil procedure casebooks!

Unfortunately, no picture exists of Marcus Neff, who started all this, but on the evidence of the pictures here, can one say that possession of a beard was a key feature of the early law of personal jurisdiction?

Sylvester Pennoyer

Justice Stephen Field

B. THE MODERN CONSTITUTIONAL FORMULATION OF POWER

Pennoyer has its feet planted in a pre-industrial world with communications that by modern standards seem slow and uncertain. The decade following *Pennoyer* saw enormous railroad construction. The last quarter of the nineteenth century also witnessed both a great expansion of industrial production and the proliferation of often interlocking corporations organizing that production. Within 50 years of the decision, other developments—the automobile, telegraph, and telephone—had nationalized economic life and even leisure activities in a way unforeseen by *Pennoyer*'s authors. As a consequence, many of the most difficult problems facing the courts after *Pennoyer* dealt with entities and situations to which *Pennoyer* only passingly alluded. Chief among those was the business corporation, a legal entity that could, through its employees, be "present" in many places at once.

Over the century following *Pennoyer*, the courts tried to work out how to apply principles of personal jurisdiction to corporations, and how to think about principles limiting state power when transportation, communication, and commerce had reshaped the nation.

Each of the elements found in *Pennoyer*—power, consent, and notice—continues to play a role in modern jurisdictional thought. But each has taken on a different shape, one that sometimes makes the original assumptions difficult to recognize. This chapter traces the evolution of these three themes in the modern law of personal jurisdiction.

1. Redefining Constitutional Power

Operating under the framework established by *Pennoyer*, state and federal courts encountered several situations for which its schema seemed ill adapted. As noted above, one of the most frequent involved *in personam* jurisdiction over a defendant corporation. Ironically, the way out of the tangled path was suggested in a case involving not a corporation but a person. In *Milliken v. Meyer*, 311 U.S. 457 (1940), two partners in an oil well sued each other. Meyer, the defendant, had been a resident of Wyoming but at the time of the suit was served personally in Colorado; Meyer did not appear in Wyoming, where the court rendered a judgment against him. Meyer attacked the Wyoming judgment collaterally (does this sound a lot like *Pennoyer* so far?). The U.S. Supreme Court held that the Wyoming judgment was valid, and in a paragraph that laid the groundwork for much future law said:

> Domicile in the state is alone sufficient to bring an absent defendant within the reach of the state's jurisdiction for purposes of a personal judgment by means of appropriate substituted service. Substituted service [i.e., service other than personal service in the forum state] in such cases has been quite uniformly upheld where the absent defendant was served at his usual place of abode in the state as well as where he was personally served without the state. That such substituted service may be wholly adequate to meet the requirements of due process was recognized by this Court in *McDonald v. Mabee* despite earlier intimations to the contrary. See Pennoyer v. Neff, 95 U.S. 714. Its adequacy so far as due process is concerned is dependent on whether or not the form of substituted service provided for such cases and employed is reasonably calculated to give him actual notice of the proceedings and an opportunity to be heard. If it is, the traditional notions of fair play and substantial justice (*McDonald v. Mabee, supra*) implicit in due process are satisfied. Here there can be no question on that score. Meyer did not merely receive actual notice of the Wyoming proceedings. While outside the state, he was personally served in accordance with a statutory scheme which Wyoming had provided for such occasions. And in our view the machinery employed met all the requirements of due process. Certainly then Meyer's domicile in Wyoming was a sufficient basis for that extraterritorial service. As in [the] case of the authority of the United States over its absent citizens, the authority of a state over one of its citizens is not terminated by the mere fact of his absence from the state. The state which accords him privileges and affords protection to him and his property by virtue of his domicile may also exact reciprocal duties. "Enjoyment of the privileges of residence within the state, and the attendant right to invoke the protection of its laws, are inseparable" from the various incidences of state citizenship. The responsibilities of that citizenship arise

out of the relationship to the state which domicile creates. That relationship is not dissolved by mere absence from the state. The attendant duties, like the rights and privileges incident to domicile, are not dependent on continuous presence in the state. One such incidence of domicile is amenability to suit within the state even during sojourns without the state, where the state has provided and employed a reasonable method for apprising such an absent party of the proceedings against him.

Id. at 462-63. The next case took these suggestions and ran with them, rearranging the landscape of personal jurisdiction; most contemporary debate concerns its application and interpretation.

International Shoe Co. v. Washington
326 U.S. 310 (1945)

STONE, C.J., delivered the opinion of the Court.

The questions for decision are (1) whether, within the limitations of the due process clause of the Fourteenth Amendment, the appellant, a Delaware corporation, has by its activities in the State of Washington rendered itself amenable to proceedings in the courts of that state to recover unpaid contributions to the state unemployment compensation fund enacted by state statutes, Washington Unemployment Compensation Act, and (2) whether the state can exact those contributions consistently with the due process clause of the Fourteenth Amendment.

The statutes in question set up a comprehensive scheme of unemployment compensation, the costs of which are defrayed by contributions required to be made by employers to a state unemployment compensation fund. The contributions are a specified percentage of the wages payable annually by each employer for his employees' services in the state. The assessment and collection of the contributions and the fund are administered by appellees. Section 14(c) of the Act authorizes appellee Commissioner to issue an order and notice of assessment of delinquent contributions upon prescribed personal service of the notice upon the employer if found within the state, or, if not so found, by mailing the notice to the employer by registered mail at his last known address. . . .

In this case notice of assessment for the years in question was personally served upon a sales solicitor employed by appellant in the State of Washington, and a copy of the notice was mailed by registered mail to appellant at its address in St. Louis, Missouri. Appellant appeared specially before the office of unemployment and moved to set aside the order and notice of assessment on the ground that the service upon appellant's salesman was not proper service upon appellant; that appellant was not a corporation of the State of Washington and was not doing business within the state; that it had no agent within the state upon whom service could be made; and that appellant is not an employer and does not furnish employment within the meaning of the statute. . . .

The facts as found by the appeal tribunal and accepted by the state Superior Court and Supreme Court, are not in dispute. Appellant is a Delaware corporation, having its principal place of business in St. Louis, Missouri, and is engaged in the manufacture and sale of shoes and other footwear. It maintains places of business in several states, other than Washington, at which its manufacturing is carried on and from which its merchandise is distributed interstate through several sales units or branches located outside the State of Washington.

Appellant has no office in Washington and makes no contracts either for sale or purchase of merchandise there. It maintains no stock of merchandise in that state and makes there no deliveries of goods in intrastate commerce. During the years from 1937 to 1940, now in question, appellant employed eleven to thirteen salesmen under direct supervision and control of sales managers located in St. Louis. These salesmen resided in Washington; their principal activities were confined to that state; and they were compensated by commissions based upon the amount of their sales. The commissions for each year totaled more than $31,000. Appellant supplies its salesmen with a line of samples, each consisting of one shoe of a pair, which they display to prospective purchasers. On occasion they rent permanent sample rooms, for exhibiting samples, in business buildings, or rent rooms in hotels or business buildings temporarily for that purpose. The cost of such rentals is reimbursed by appellant.

The authority of the salesmen is limited to exhibiting their samples and soliciting orders from prospective buyers, at prices and on terms fixed by appellant. The salesmen transmit the orders to appellant's office in St. Louis for acceptance or rejection, and when accepted the merchandise for filling the orders is shipped f.o.b. from points outside Washington to the purchasers within the state. All the merchandise shipped into Washington is invoiced at the place of shipment from which collections are made. No salesman has authority to enter into contracts or to make collections. . . .

Appellant . . . insists that its activities within the state were not sufficient to . . . [confer] jurisdiction. . . . And appellant further argues that since it was not present within the state, it is a denial of due process to subject it to taxation or other money exaction. It thus denies the power of the state to lay the tax or to subject appellant to a suit for its collection.

Historically the jurisdiction of courts to render judgment in personam is grounded on their de facto power over the defendant's person. Hence his presence within the territorial jurisdiction of a court was prerequisite to its rendition of a judgment personally binding him. *Pennoyer v. Neff*. But now that the capias ad respondendum has given way to personal service of summons or other form of notice, due process requires only that in order to subject a defendant to a judgment in personam, if he be not present within the territory of the forum, he have certain minimum contacts with it such that the maintenance of the suit does not offend "traditional notions of fair play and substantial justice." Since the corporate personality is a fiction, although a fiction intended to be acted upon as though it were a fact, it is clear that unlike an individual its "presence" without, as well as within, the state of its origin can be manifested only by activities carried on in its behalf by those who are authorized to act for it. To say that the corporation is so far "present" there as to satisfy due process requirements, for purposes of taxation or the maintenance of suits against it in the courts of the state, is to beg the question to be decided. For the terms "present" or "presence" are used merely to symbolize those activities of the corporation's agent within the state which courts will deem to be sufficient to satisfy the demands of due process. Those demands may be met by such contacts of the corporation with the state of the forum as to make it reasonable, in the context of our federal system of government, to require the corporation to defend the particular suit which is brought there. An "estimate of the inconveniences" which would result to the corporation from a trial away from its "home" or principal place of business is relevant in this connection.

"Presence" in the state in this sense has never been doubted when the activities of the corporation there have not only been continuous and systematic, but also give rise to the liabilities sued on, even though no consent to be sued or authorization to an agent to accept service of process has been given. Conversely it has been generally recognized that the casual presence of the corporate agent or even his conduct of single or isolated items of activities in a state in the corporation's behalf are not enough to subject it to suit on causes of action unconnected with the activities there. To require the corporation in such circumstances to defend the suit away from its home or other jurisdiction where it carries on more substantial activities has been thought to lay too great and unreasonable a burden on the corporation to comport with due process.

While it has been held, in cases on which appellant relies, that continuous activity of some sorts within a state is not enough to support the demand that the corporation be amenable to suits unrelated to that activity, there have been instances in which the continuous corporate operations within a state were thought so substantial and of such a nature as to justify suit against it on causes of action arising from dealings entirely distinct from those activities.

Finally, although the commission of some single or occasional acts of the corporate agent in a state sufficient to impose an obligation or liability on the corporation has not been thought to confer upon the state authority to enforce it, other such acts, because of their nature and quality and the circumstances of their commission, may be deemed sufficient to render the corporation liable to suit. True, some of the decisions holding the corporation amenable to suit have been supported by resort to the legal fiction that it has given its consent to service and suit, consent being implied from its presence in the state through the acts of its authorized agents. But more realistically it may be said that those authorized acts were of such a nature as to justify the fiction.

It is evident that the criteria by which we mark the boundary line between those activities which justify the subjection of a corporation to suit, and those which do not, cannot be simply mechanical or quantitative. The test is not merely, as has sometimes been suggested, whether the activity, which the corporation has seen fit to procure through its agents in another state, is a little more or a little less. Whether due process is satisfied must depend rather upon the quality and nature of the activity in relation to the fair and orderly administration of the laws which it was the purpose of the due process clause to insure. That clause does not contemplate that a state may make binding a judgment in personam against an individual or corporate defendant with which the state has no contacts, ties, or relations.

But to the extent that a corporation exercises the privilege of conducting activities within a state, it enjoys the benefits and protection of the laws of that state. The exercise of that privilege may give rise to obligations, and, so far as those obligations arise out of or are connected with the activities within the state, a procedure which requires the corporation to respond to a suit brought to enforce them can, in most instances, hardly be said to be undue.

Applying these standards, the activities carried on in behalf of appellant in the State of Washington were neither irregular nor casual. They were systematic and continuous throughout the years in question. They resulted in a large volume of interstate business, in the course of which appellant received the benefits and protection of the laws of the state, including the right to resort to the courts for the enforcement of its rights. The obligation which is here sued upon arose out of those very activities. It is evident that these operations establish sufficient contacts or ties with the state of the forum to make it reasonable and just, according to our traditional conception of fair play and substantial justice, to permit the state to enforce the obligations which appellant has incurred there. Hence we cannot say that the maintenance of the present suit in the State of Washington involves an unreasonable or undue procedure.

We are likewise unable to conclude that the service of the process within the state upon an agent whose activities establish appellant's "presence" there was not sufficient notice of the suit, or that the suit was so unrelated to those activities as to make the agent an inappropriate vehicle for communicating the notice. It is enough that appellant has established such contacts with the state that the particular form of substituted service adopted there gives reasonable assurance that the notice will be actual. Nor can we say that the mailing of the notice of suit to appellant by registered mail at its home office was not reasonably calculated to apprise appellant of the suit. . . .

Appellant having rendered itself amenable to suit upon obligations arising out of the activities of its salesmen in Washington, the state may maintain the present suit in personam to collect the tax laid upon the exercise of the privilege of employing appellant's salesmen within the state. For Washington has made one of those activities, which taken together establish appellant's "presence" there for purposes of suit, the taxable event by which the state brings appellant within the reach of its taxing power. The state thus has constitutional power to lay the tax and to subject appellant to a suit to recover it. The activities which establish its "presence" subject it alike to taxation by the state and to suit to recover the tax.

Affirmed.

BLACK, J., delivered the following opinion. . . .

I believe that the Federal Constitution leaves to each State, without any "ifs" or "buts," a power to tax and to open the doors of its courts for its citizens to sue corporations whose agents do business in those States. Believing that the Constitution gave the States that power, I think it a judicial deprivation to condition its exercise upon this Court's notion of "fair play," however appealing that term may be. Nor can I stretch the meaning of due process so far as to authorize this Court to deprive a State of the right to afford judicial protection to its citizens on the ground that it would be more "convenient" for the corporation to be sued somewhere else.

There is a strong emotional appeal in the words "fair play" "justice," and "reasonableness." But they were not chosen by those who wrote the original Constitution or the Fourteenth Amendment as a measuring rod for this Court to use in invalidating State or Federal laws passed by elected legislative representatives. No one, not even those who most feared a democratic government, ever formally proposed that courts should be given power to invalidate legislation under any such elastic standards. . . .

True, the State's power is here upheld. But the rule announced means that tomorrow's judgment may strike down a State or Federal enactment on the ground that it does not conform to the Court's idea of natural justice. . . .

WHAT'S NEW HERE?

- *International Shoe* "modernizes" the law in several ways. (Even the entrance of the then-headquarters of the company, shown below, was self-consciously "modern" when redesigned in 1930.)
- The case dealt with what was then a new phenomenon—unemployment insurance, a creation of the New Deal.
- Doctrinally, it moves the question of personal jurisdiction from a yes/no inquiry (in which there either is or isn't personal jurisdiction) to an "it depends" analysis. A sound-bite or Twitter® version of the difference says that *International Shoe* changed the jurisdiction inquiry from "Is s/he (or it) *there* [in the forum state]" to "Is it *fair*?"
- After *International Shoe*, jurisdiction depends on the extent of the defendant's contacts in the state in relation to the claim asserted. That move, which you will see in many later cases, has the advantage of allowing courts to consider a broad range of factors. It has the disadvantage of making it harder to predict the outcome of close cases.

Notes and Problems

1. The case holds that International Shoe is subject to personal jurisdiction in the State of Washington in a suit brought to collect unemployment taxes. After rereading the two paragraphs of the opinion starting with "'Presence' in the state in this sense . . . ," consider their implications.

   a. Suppose that right after the Supreme Court decision a Missouri citizen injured by one of International Shoe's trucks backing out of its Missouri factory sued in Washington state court. Jurisdiction? If you have the (correct) intuition that the answer is no—why not?

   b. In the key paragraph of the opinion the Court writes that, to be subject to a state's jurisdiction, a defendant must "have certain minimum contacts with it such that the maintenance of suit does not offend 'traditional notions of fair play and substantial justice.'" A perfectly good principle, but not exactly a clear recipe. One commentator has suggested that the basic test of *International Shoe* is a good one but that because of its generality it must be subjected to a process of "arbitrary particularization" in order to come up with workable rules. Geoffrey C. Hazard, Jr., *A General Theory of State-Court Jurisdiction*, 1965 Sup. Ct. Rev. 241, 283. One can read the chain of cases following *International Shoe*, several examples of which you will encounter in this chapter, as examples of Hazard's arbitrary particularization.

2. To understand the key development in *International Shoe* try this idea out on a set of simple hypothetical cases. Assume that International Shoe is incorporated in Delaware and has its headquarters and principal manufacturing operations in Missouri. Further assume that International Shoe has no salespeople in Wyoming, sells no shoes there, buys no cowhide there, and does no business there of any sort—except to use Wyoming roads for transporting its wares to other states.

   a. A truck loaded with shoes, owned by International Shoe Co. and driven by one of its employees, travels through Wyoming on its way to the State of Washington. While in Wyoming, the truck collides with a pickup driven by a rancher, who is injured in the accident. The rancher files suit against International Shoe in Wyoming, alleging negligence by the International Shoe driver. Jurisdiction in Wyoming?

   b. In Wyoming there also lives a former employee of International Shoe who used to work for the company at its Missouri headquarters. Alleging that she was wrongfully discharged from her job in Missouri, she files suit against International Shoe in Wyoming. Jurisdiction? What is the rationale on which one could explain a different outcome in 2a and 2b?

   c. Now imagine the plaintiffs in 2a and 2b file suit in Missouri. In determining whether the state has personal jurisdiction over International Shoe, would it make any difference whether the plaintiff was the rancher in 2a or the former employee in 2b?

3. One explanation of why "no jurisdiction" is the answer to Notes 1a and 2b is that *International Shoe* creates a sliding scale, in which a high level of activities will support jurisdiction even over claims unrelated to those activities. By contrast, a low level of activity ("contact," in the jargon) will support jurisdiction, but only over claims related to that contact. The opinion hints at this idea, which has been elaborated in subsequent cases and commentary:

> While it has been held, in cases on which appellant relies, that continuous activity of some sorts within a state is not enough to support the demand that the corporation be amenable to suits *unrelated to that activity*, there have been instances in which the continuous corporate operations within a state were thought so substantial and of such a nature as to justify suit against it on causes of action arising from dealings *entirely distinct from those activities*. (Emphasis added.)

From the idea of a sliding scale for personal jurisdiction courts and scholars have implied an entire vision of jurisdiction.

a. *General jurisdiction.* In some cases the defendant will have such substantial contacts with the forum state to make it fair to assert jurisdiction even over claims unrelated to those contacts. For example, suppose an individual is a resident of California. She could be sued in California even over contracts or torts concluded or committed in other states or nations. Likewise, take a corporation like Microsoft, which has its chief place of business in Washington State. Under the theory of general jurisdiction, Microsoft could be sued in Washington even over contracts or torts concluded or committed in Idaho or Germany. As *Daimler AG v. Bauman* (infra page 133) put it, "A court may assert general jurisdiction over foreign (sister-state or foreign-country) corporations to hear any and all claims against them when their affiliations with the State are so 'continuous and systematic' as to render them essentially at home in the forum State." Later in this chapter we return to the question of general jurisdiction; for now, keep in mind the basic proposition that every individual and business entity in the United States has at least one state where they can be sued on any claim. To use the language of *Daimler*, an individual will be "at home" (and thus amenable to suit on all claims) in the state of her domicile. Corporations will similarly be "at home" both in the state of their incorporation and in the state that is their principal place of business (if that differs from their state of incorporation). In later cases, we will consider where *else* they can be sued.

b. *Specific jurisdiction.* Where the defendant's activities fall short of general jurisdiction, the minimum contacts analysis of *International Shoe* becomes important. In those cases courts worry both about the extent of those contacts and about the relation between defendants' contacts with the state and the claim on which plaintiff is suing. Suppose, for example, Driver has never been in Missouri but, in the course of a vacation, enters the state, and injures a pedestrian. Specific jurisdiction would allow the injured pedestrian to sue Driver in Missouri on a claim arising from that accident—but not on other, unrelated claims. As the *Daimler* Court put it, "*International Shoe* recognized, as well, that 'the commission of some single or occasional acts of the corporate agent in a state' may sometimes be enough to subject the corporation to jurisdiction in that State's tribunals with respect to suits relating to that in-state activity." Commentators describe such cases as instances of specific jurisdiction, in which jurisdiction exists for the specific claim in question but not necessarily for other claims. In the decades following *International Shoe,* courts tried to work out its application to varying factual patterns. In particular, they wrestled with the question of whether the holding of *International Shoe* provided any limits: Was every defendant (at least every business defendant) subject to jurisdiction anywhere it did any business? Two cases decided by the Supreme Court about a decade after *International Shoe* gave contrasting answers to that question. Both are still frequently cited and present paradigmatic instances of the issues that arise in applying *International Shoe*.

McGee v. International Life Insurance Co.
355 U.S. 220 (1957)

Opinion of the Court by BLACK, J., announced by DOUGLAS, J.

The material facts are relatively simple. In 1944, Lowell Franklin, a resident of California, purchased a life insurance policy from [an insurer subsequently bought by respondent, which] then mailed a reinsurance certificate to Franklin in California offering to insure him. . . . He accepted this offer and from that time until his death in 1950 paid premiums by mail from his California home to respondent's Texas office. [When the beneficiary notified International Life of Franklin's death,] it refused to pay, claiming that he had committed suicide[, a cause of death excluded by the policy]. It appears that neither [the original insurer] nor respondent has ever had any office or agent in California. . . .

Looking back over this long history of [jurisdiction cases] a trend is clearly discernible toward expanding the permissible scope of state jurisdiction over foreign corporations and other nonresidents. In part this is attributable to the fundamental transformation of our national economy. . . . With this increasing nationalization of commerce has come a great increase in the amount of business conducted by mail across state lines. At the same time modern transportation and communication have made it much less burdensome for a party sued to defend himself in a State where he engages in economic activity. Turning to this case we think it apparent that the Due Process Clause did not preclude the California court from entering a judgment binding on respondent. It is sufficient for purposes of due process that the suit was based on a contract which had substantial connection with that State. The contract was delivered in California, the premiums were mailed from there and the insured was a resident of that State when he died. It cannot be denied that California has a manifest interest in providing effective means of redress for its residents when their insurers refuse to pay claims. These residents would be at a severe disadvantage if they were forced to follow the insurance company to a distant State in order to hold it legally accountable. . . . There is no contention that respondent did not have adequate notice of the suit or sufficient time to prepare its defenses and appear.

Hanson v. Denckla

57 U.S. 235 (1958)

WARREN, C.J., delivered the opinion of the Court.

[The case arose from a family fight over a trust established by Mrs. Donner, funded primarily with publicly traded stocks. When she created the trust, she lived in Pennsylvania, but the trust was created in Delaware, with a Delaware bank as trustee. After creating the trust she moved to Florida, and later died there. Her will was probated in Florida. The case concerns whether the Florida court could obtain jurisdiction over the trust. That issue turned on whether Florida could acquire jurisdiction over the Delaware trustee. If Florida had jurisdiction, two daughters received everything, and a third daughter got nothing. If Florida did not have jurisdiction, the three daughters shared equally. The Supreme Court concluded that Florida lacked jurisdiction.]

. . . [P]rogress in communications and transportation has made the defense of a suit in a foreign tribunal less burdensome. In response to these changes, the requirements for personal jurisdiction over nonresidents have evolved from the rigid rule of *Pennoyer v. Neff* to the flexible standard of *International Shoe Co. v. Washington*. But it is a mistake to assume that this trend heralds the eventual demise of all restrictions on the personal jurisdiction of state courts. Those restrictions are more than a guarantee of immunity from inconvenient or distant litigation. They are a consequence of territorial limitations on the power of the respective States. However minimal the burden of defending in a foreign tribunal, a defendant may not be called upon to do so unless he has had the "minimal contacts" with that State that are a prerequisite to its exercise of power over him. See *International Shoe Co. v. Washington*.

We fail to find such contacts in the circumstances of this case. The defendant trust company has no office in Florida, and transacts no business there. . . . [T]he record discloses no solicitation of business in that State either in person or by mail. . . .

The first relationship Florida had to the agreement was years later when [Mrs. Donner] became domiciled there, and the trustee remitted the trust income to her in the State. From Florida Mrs. Donner carried on several bits of trust administration. . . . But the record discloses no instance in which the trustee performed any acts in Florida. . . .

The unilateral activity of those [like Mrs. Donner] who claim some relationship with a nonresident defendant [the Delaware trustee] cannot satisfy the requirement of contact with the forum State. The application of that rule will vary with the quality and nature of the defendant's activity, but it is essential in each case that there be some act by which the defendant purposefully avails itself of the privilege of conducting activities within the forum State, thus invoking the benefits and protections of its laws. *International Shoe Co. v. Washington*. . . .

[Justices BLACK, BURTON, BRENNAN, and DOUGLAS dissented, the latter separately.]

Notes and Problems

1. *McGee* and *Hanson*, decided a year apart, come to different conclusions about jurisdiction on remarkably similar facts: business conducted by mail with an out-of-state financial institution, which was then sued in plaintiff's state. Notice as well the emphasis both cases place on modern transport and communication. Can you identify a factual difference that justifies the difference in outcomes in the two cases?

2. The decades after *McGee* and *Hanson* saw two developments: a continued attempt to apply *International Shoe*'s open-ended doctrine to varying factual situations; and a decision to curtail the availability of one of *Pennoyer*'s results—*in rem* jurisdiction. We deal first with the latter development.

2. Absorbing *In Rem* Jurisdiction

International Shoe provided a new framework for thinking about *in personam* jurisdiction over corporations. But the case left open other jurisdictional questions.

International Shoe involved a corporate defendant (as did many of the most difficult jurisdictional questions), and it therefore did not discuss the applicability of its approach to jurisdiction over individuals. The second issue left untouched by *International Shoe* was *in rem* and *quasi in rem* jurisdiction. Under the line of cases descended from *Pennoyer*, the presence of property in the forum state could be the basis for jurisdiction over claims of any sort.

Here it makes sense to pause and offer a note on terminology. Some courts—like the *Pennoyer* Court—use *in rem* to describe all cases in which property is used as the basis for jurisdiction. Other courts distinguish between *in rem* and *quasi in rem* jurisdiction. They use the former term to describe cases in which ownership of the property itself is at stake: Does *X* own Blackacre? Such courts use *quasi in rem* to describe cases in which the property is used only as a jurisdictional hook to allow the litigation of a claim not related to that property. In this stricter terminology *Pennoyer* itself was a *quasi in rem* case; Mitchell was not claiming that he rather than Neff owned the property in question; he was instead trying to use the property as the basis for Oregon's jurisdiction over his claim for an unpaid legal fee.

While it lasted, *quasi in rem* jurisdiction created some strange doctrinal possibilities. The most unexpected elaboration of this branch of *Pennoyer* came in a series of cases holding that plaintiffs could obtain jurisdiction by seizing not only tangible property—land and chattels—but also debts owed to the defendant. Harris v. Balk, 198 U.S. 215 (1905), is probably the most bizarre of this line of cases. Harris owed Balk money, and Balk owed Epstein money; Balk lived in North Carolina, Epstein in Maryland. Harris journeyed from North Carolina to Maryland. While Harris was in Maryland, Epstein had him served with process, and a Maryland court entered a judgment saying that Harris should pay the money he owed Balk to

Epstein instead. Balk challenged the Maryland court's power to enter this judgment (arguing that only personal service on him in Maryland would have justified such a judgment), but the Supreme Court upheld it. The consequence of *Harris* was that a state could acquire jurisdiction over persons whenever their debtors were present in that state by "attaching" the debts. The result was to make creditors liable (to the extent of amounts owed them) in any state in which their debtors set foot.

Under *Harris*'s extension of *Pennoyer*, for example, if Alfred Manhattanite had lent money to his friend Jane Gotham and she took a trip to Florida, that state had the power to enter a judgment directing Jane to pay someone besides Alfred the money she owed him—if Jane's debt to Alfred were "attached" during her visit.

Lurking behind these somewhat extreme results was an undiscussed circumstance: *In rem* jurisdiction provided an escape from the results yielded by *Pennoyer*'s somewhat restrictive doctrines. To the extent, then, that *International Shoe* provided a more sensible way of thinking about *in personam* jurisdiction, one might not need *quasi in rem* jurisdiction—at least not in its more extravagant applications.

These two themes—the applicability of *International Shoe* to individuals and the role of *in rem* jurisdiction—came together in *Shaffer v. Heitner*, the most important jurisdictional case after *International Shoe*.

PERSPECTIVES ON THE BUSINESS CORPORATION

Many U.S. businesses take the form of corporations. A corporation is an entity, typically chartered under the laws of a state. For a business, the corporate form has some advantages: It can outlast the lives of individual owners; it can make it easier to raise capital (by selling shares); it can insulate its owners from personal liability (the corporation, rather than individual shareholders, is liable for corporate obligations). It also has some disadvantages: Many states as well as the federal government impose taxes on corporations as well as their shareholders; and the corporation must comply with whatever regulations the chartering state imposes.

In the United States, many substantial corporations have chosen Delaware as their state of incorporation. It has relatively low corporate taxes and its laws allow the corporation great flexibility in conducting its affairs.

Moreover, Delaware maintains a separate Court of Chancery, whose judges become, in effect, corporate law specialists, allowing greater predictability in suits involving corporate matters.

One such matter involves the fiduciary obligations of corporate directors. The members of the board of directors of a corporation owe it fiduciary obligations: The law requires directors to prudently conduct the affairs of the corporation—monitoring its financial and other affairs; hiring and firing its officers, who conduct day-to-day operations; and directing or overseeing major decisions of the corporation.

Like trustees, directors can be sued by their beneficiaries. But because the corporation is the beneficiary and is controlled by the directors, the prospect of such a suit to enforce the directors' fiduciary duties is nil—unless a representative of the corporation who is independent of the directors may sue. American law has developed such a procedure, called the shareholder's derivative suit. In a derivative action, a shareholder steps forward and sues the directors or officers in the name of the corporation, alleging some breach of fiduciary duty. If the suit is successful, the proceeds go to the corporation. Such suits have spawned numerous complex issues of procedural and corporate law as well as a good deal of controversy.

Shaffer v. Heitner

433 U.S. 186 (1977)

MARSHALL, J., delivered the opinion of the Court.

The controversy in this case concerns the constitutionality of a Delaware statute that allows a court of that State to take jurisdiction of a lawsuit by sequestering any property of the defendant that happens to be located in Delaware. Appellants contend that the sequestration statute as applied in this case violates the Due Process Clause of the Fourteenth Amendment both because it permits the state courts to exercise jurisdiction despite the absence of sufficient contacts among the defendants, the litigation, and the State of Delaware and because it authorizes the deprivation of defendants' property without providing adequate procedural safeguards. We find it necessary to consider only the first of these contentions.

I

Appellee Heitner, a nonresident of Delaware, is the owner of one share of stock in the Greyhound Corporation, a business incorporated under the laws of Delaware with its principal place of business in Phoenix, Ariz. On May 22, 1974, he filed a shareholder's derivative suit in the Court of Chancery for New Castle County, Del., in which he named as defendants . . . 28 present or former officers or directors of one or both of the corporations. In essence, Heitner alleged that the individual defendants had violated their duties to Greyhound by causing it and its subsidiary to engage in actions that resulted in the corporation's being held liable for substantial damages in a private antitrust suit and a large fine in a criminal contempt action. The activities which led to these penalties took place in Oregon.

Simultaneously with his complaint, Heitner filed a motion for an order of sequestration of the Delaware property of the individual defendants pursuant to 10 Del. C. §366. This motion was accompanied by a supporting affidavit of counsel which stated that the individual defendants were nonresidents of Delaware. The affidavit identified the property to be sequestered as

> common stock, 3% Second Cumulative Preferred Stock and stock unit credits of the Defendant Greyhound Corporation, a Delaware corporation, as well as all options and all warrants to purchase said stock issued to said individual Defendants and all contractral [sic] obligations, all rights, debts or credits due or accrued to or for the benefit of any of the said Defendants under any type of written agreement, contract, or other legal instrument of any kind whatever between any of the individual Defendants and said corporation.

The requested sequestration order was signed the day the motion was filed. Pursuant to that order, the sequestrator "seized" approximately 82,000 shares of Greyhound common stock belonging to 19 of the defendants, and options belonging to another two defendants. These seizures were accomplished by placing "stop transfer" orders or their equivalents on the books of the Greyhound Corporation. So far as the record shows, none of the certificates representing the seized property was physically present in Delaware. The stock was considered to be in Delaware, and so subject to seizure, by virtue of 8 Del. C. §169, which makes Delaware the situs of ownership of all stock in Delaware corporations.

All 28 defendants were notified of the initiation of the suit by certified mail directed to their last known addresses and by publication in a New Castle County newspaper. The 21 defendants whose property was seized (hereafter referred to as appellants) responded by entering a special appearance for the purpose of moving to quash service of process and to vacate the sequestration order. They contended that the ex parte sequestration procedure did not accord them due process of law and that the property seized was not capable of attachment in Delaware. In addition, appellants asserted that under the rule of *International Shoe Co. v. Washington*, they did not have sufficient contacts with Delaware to sustain the jurisdiction of that State's courts.

[The Delaware courts rejected all of defendants' arguments. They distinguished seizure for jurisdictional purposes from other forms of ex parte seizure. And they contended that the assertion of jurisdiction need not meet *International Shoe* standards because Delaware was asserting *in rem*, rather than *in personam*, jurisdiction.]

II

The Delaware courts rejected appellants' jurisdictional challenge by noting that this suit was brought as a quasi in rem proceeding. Since quasi in rem jurisdiction is traditionally based on attachment or seizure of property present in the jurisdiction, not on contacts between the defendant and the State, the courts considered appellants' claimed lack of contacts with Delaware to be unimportant. This categorical analysis assumes the continued soundness of the conceptual structure founded on the century-old case of *Pennoyer v. Neff*.

[The Court discussed the development of jurisdictional ideas from the time of *Pennoyer v. Neff*. In reviewing *International Shoe* itself the opinion explained in footnote 19 that "the *International Shoe* court believed that the standard it was setting forth governed actions against natural persons as well as corporations, and we see no reason to disagree. The differences between individuals and corporations may, of course, lead to the conclusion that a given set of circumstances establishes State jurisdiction over one type of defendant but not over the other." The note cited *McGee v. International Life* as a "see also" citation for this proposition.] [T]he relationship among the defendant, the forum, and the litigation, rather than the mutually exclusive sovereignty of the States on which the rules of *Pennoyer* rest, became the central concern of the inquiry into personal jurisdiction.[20] The immediate effect of this departure from *Pennoyer*'s conceptual apparatus was to increase the ability of the state courts to obtain personal jurisdiction over nonresident defendants.

No equally dramatic change has occurred in the law governing jurisdiction in rem. There have, however, been intimations that the collapse of the in personam wing of *Pennoyer* has not left that decision unweakened as a foundation for in rem jurisdiction. [The Court cited lower court opinions, commentators, and oblique hints in Supreme Court cases.]

It is clear, therefore, that the law of state-court jurisdiction no longer stands securely on the foundation established in *Pennoyer*. We think that the time is ripe to consider whether the standard of fairness and substantial justice set forth in *International Shoe* should be held to govern actions in rem as well as in personam.

III

The case for applying to jurisdiction in rem the same test of "fair play and substantial justice" as governs assertions of jurisdiction in personam is simple and straightforward. It is premised on recognition that "[t]he phrase, 'judicial jurisdiction over a thing,' is a customary elliptical way of referring to jurisdiction over the interests of persons in a thing." Restatement (Second) of Conflict of Laws §56, introductory note. This recognition leads to the conclusion that in order to justify an exercise of jurisdiction in rem, the basis for jurisdiction must be sufficient to justify exercising "jurisdiction over the interests of persons in a thing."[23] The standard for determining whether an exercise of jurisdiction over the interests of persons is consistent with the Due Process Clause is the minimum contacts standard elucidated in *International Shoe*.

This argument, of course, does not ignore the fact that the presence of property in a State may bear on the existence of jurisdiction by providing contacts among the forum State, the defendant, and the litigation. For example, when claims to the property itself

---

20. Nothing in *Hanson v. Denckla* [supra page 87] is to the contrary. The *Hanson* Court's statement that restrictions on state jurisdiction "are a consequence of territorial limitations on the power of the respective states," simply makes the point that the States are defined by their geographical territory. After making this point, the Court in *Hanson* determined that the defendant over which personal jurisdiction was claimed had not committed any acts sufficiently connected to the State to justify jurisdiction under the *International Shoe* standard.

23. It is true that the potential liability of a defendant in an in rem action is limited by the value of the property but that limitation does not affect the argument. The fairness of subjecting a defendant to state-court jurisdiction does not depend on the size of the claim being litigated.

are the source of the underlying controversy between the plaintiff and the defendant, it would be unusual for the State where the property is located not to have jurisdiction. In such cases, the defendant's claim to property located in the State would normally indicate that he expected to benefit from the State's protection of his interest. The State's strong interests in assuring the marketability of property within its borders and in providing a procedure for peaceful resolution of disputes about the possession of that property would also support jurisdiction, as would the likelihood that important records and witnesses will be found in the State.[28] The presence of property may also favor jurisdiction in cases, such as suits for injury suffered on the land of an absentee owner, where the defendant's ownership of the property is conceded but the cause of action is otherwise related to rights and duties growing out of that ownership.

It appears, therefore, that jurisdiction over many types of actions which now are or might be brought in rem would not be affected by a holding that any assertion of state-court jurisdiction must satisfy the *International Shoe* standard. For the type of quasi in rem action typified by *Harris v. Balk* and the present case, however, accepting the proposed analysis would result in significant change. These are cases where the property which now serves as the basis for state-court jurisdiction is completely unrelated to the plaintiff's cause of action. Thus, although the presence of the defendant's property in a State might suggest the existence of other ties among the defendant, the State, and the litigation, the presence of the property alone would not support the State's jurisdiction. . . .

Presence alone & State jurisdiction

Since acceptance of the *International Shoe* test would most affect this class of cases, we examine the arguments against adopting that standard as they relate to this category of litigation. Before doing so, however, we note that this type of case also presents the clearest illustration of the argument in favor of assessing assertions of jurisdiction by a single standard. For in cases such as *Harris* and this one, the only role played by the property is to provide the basis for bringing the defendant into court. Indeed, the express purpose of the Delaware sequestration procedure is to compel the defendant to enter a personal appearance. In such cases, if a direct assertion of personal jurisdiction over the defendant would violate the Constitution, it would seem that an indirect assertion of the jurisdiction should be equally impermissible.

The primary rationale for treating the presence of property as a sufficient basis for jurisdiction to adjudicate claims over which the State would not have jurisdiction if *International Shoe* applied is that a wrongdoer "should not be able to avoid payment of his obligations by the expedient of removing his assets to a place where he is not subject to an in personam suit." Restatement §66, Comment a. This justification, however, does not explain why jurisdiction should be recognized without regard to whether the property is present in the State because of an effort to avoid the owner's obligations. Nor does it support jurisdiction to adjudicate the underlying claim. . . .

It might also be suggested that allowing in rem jurisdiction avoids the uncertainty inherent in the *International Shoe* standard and assures a plaintiff of a forum.[37] . . . [W]hen the existence of jurisdiction in a particular forum under *International Shoe*

---

28. We do not suggest that these illustrations include all the factors that may affect the decision, nor that the factors we have mentioned are necessarily decisive.

37. This case does not raise, and we therefore do not consider, the question whether the presence of a defendant's property in a State is a sufficient basis for jurisdiction when no other forum is available to the plaintiff.

is unclear, the cost of simplifying the litigation by avoiding the jurisdictional question may be the sacrifice of "fair play and substantial justice." That cost is too high.

We are left, then, to consider the significance of the long history of jurisdiction based solely on the presence of property in a State. . . . "[T]raditional notions of fair play and substantial justice" can be as readily offended by the perpetuation of ancient forms that are no longer justified as by the adoption of new procedures that are inconsistent with the basic values of our constitutional heritage. The fiction that an assertion of jurisdiction over property is anything but an assertion of jurisdiction over the owner of the property supports an ancient form without substantial modern justification. Its continued acceptance would serve only to allow state court jurisdiction that is fundamentally unfair to the defendant.

We therefore conclude that all assertions of state court jurisdiction must be evaluated according to the standards set forth in *International Shoe* and its progeny.[39]

IV

The Delaware courts based their assertion of jurisdiction in this case solely on the statutory presence of appellants' property in Delaware. Yet that property is not the subject matter of this litigation, nor is the underlying cause of action related to the property. Appellants' holdings in Greyhound do not, therefore, provide contacts with Delaware sufficient to support the jurisdiction of that State's courts over appellants. If it exists, that jurisdiction must have some other foundation.

Appellee Heitner did not allege and does not now claim that appellants have ever set foot in Delaware. Nor does he identify any act related to his cause of action as having taken place in Delaware. Nevertheless, he contends that appellants' positions as directors and officers of a corporation chartered in Delaware provide sufficient "contacts, ties, or relations," *International Shoe Co. v. Washington*, with that State to give its courts jurisdiction over appellants in this stockholder's derivative action. This argument is based primarily on what Heitner asserts to be the strong interest of Delaware in supervising the management of a Delaware corporation. That interest is said to derive from the role of Delaware law in establishing the corporation and defining the obligations owed to it by its officers and directors. In order to protect this interest, appellee concludes, Delaware's courts must have jurisdiction over corporate fiduciaries such as appellants.

This argument is undercut by the failure of the Delaware Legislature to assert the state interest appellee finds so compelling. Delaware law bases jurisdiction not on appellants' status as corporate fiduciaries, but rather on the presence of their property in the State. Although the sequestration procedure used here may be most frequently used in derivative suits against officers and directors, the authorizing statute evinces no specific concern with such actions. Sequestration can be used in any suit against a nonresident, and reaches corporate fiduciaries only if they happen to own interests in a Delaware corporation, or other property in the State. But as Heitner's failure to secure jurisdiction over seven of the defendants named in his complaint demonstrates, there is no necessary relationship between holding a position as a corporate fiduciary and owning stock or

---

39. It would not be fruitful for us to re-examine the facts of cases decided on the rationales of *Pennoyer* and *Harris* to determine whether jurisdiction might have been sustained under the standard we adopt today. To the extent that prior decisions are inconsistent with this standard, they are overruled.

other interests in the corporation. If Delaware perceived its interest in securing jurisdiction over corporate fiduciaries to be as great as Heitner suggests, we would expect it to have enacted a statute more clearly designed to protect that interest. . . .

Appellee suggests that by accepting positions as officers or directors of a Delaware corporation, appellants performed the acts required by *Hanson v. Denckla*. He notes that Delaware law provides substantial benefits to corporate officers and directors, and that these benefits were at least in part the incentive for appellants to assume their positions. It is, he says, "only fair and just" to require appellants, in return for these benefits, to respond in the State of Delaware when they are accused of misusing their powers.

But like Heitner's first argument, this line of reasoning establishes only that it is appropriate for Delaware law to govern the obligations of appellants to Greyhound and its stockholders. It does not demonstrate that appellants have "purposefully avail[ed themselves] of the privilege of conducting activities within the forum State," *Hanson v. Denckla*, in a way that would justify bringing them before a Delaware tribunal. Appellants have simply had nothing to do with the State of Delaware. Moreover, appellants had no reason to expect to be haled before a Delaware court. Delaware, unlike some States, has not enacted a statute that treats acceptance of a directorship as consent to jurisdiction in the State. And "[i]t strains reason . . . to suggest that anyone buying securities in a corporation formed in Delaware 'impliedly consents' to subject himself to Delaware's . . . jurisdiction on any cause of action." Appellants, who were not required to acquire interests in Greyhound in order to hold their positions, did not by acquiring those interests surrender their right to be brought to judgment only in States with which they had "minimum contacts." The Due Process Clause "does not contemplate that a state may make binding a judgment . . . against an individual or corporate defendant with which the state has no contacts, ties, or relations." *International Shoe Co. v. Washington*. Delaware's assertion of jurisdiction over appellants in this case is inconsistent with that constitutional limitation on state power. The judgment of the Delaware Supreme Court must, therefore, be reversed.

It is so ordered.

REHNQUIST, J., took no part in the consideration or decision of this case.

POWELL, J., concurring.

I agree that the principles of *International Shoe Co. v. Washington* should be extended to govern assertions of in rem as well as in personam jurisdiction in state court. I also agree that neither the statutory presence of appellants' stock in Delaware nor their positions as directors and officers of a Delaware corporation can provide sufficient contacts to support the Delaware courts' assertion of jurisdiction in this case.

I would explicitly reserve judgment, however, on whether the ownership of some forms of property whose situs is indisputably and permanently located within a State may, without more, provide the contacts necessary to subject a defendant to jurisdiction within the State to the extent of the value of the property. In the case of real property, in particular, preservation of the common law concept of quasi in rem jurisdiction arguably would avoid the uncertainty of the general *International Shoe* standard without significant cost to "traditional notions of fair play and substantial justice." Subject to that reservation, I join the opinion of the Court.

STEVENS, J., concurring in the judgment.

The Due Process Clause affords protection against "judgments without notice." *International Shoe Co. v. Washington* (opinion of Black, J.). . . .

One who purchases shares of stock on the open market can hardly be expected to know that he has thereby become subject to suit in a forum remote from his residence and unrelated to the transaction. As a practical matter, the Delaware sequestration statute created an unacceptable risk of judgment without notice. . . . I therefore agree with the Court that on the record before us no adequate basis for jurisdiction exists and that the Delaware statute is unconstitutional on its face.

How the Court's opinion may be applied in other contexts is not entirely clear to me. . . . My uncertainty as to the reach of the opinion, and my fear that it purports to decide a great deal more than is necessary to dispose of this case, persuade me merely to concur in the judgment.

BRENNAN, J., concurring and dissenting.

I join Parts I-III of the Court's opinion. I fully agree that the minimum contacts analysis developed in *International Shoe Co. v. Washington* represents a far more sensible construct for the exercise of state court jurisdiction than the patchwork of legal and factual fictions that has been generated from the decision in *Pennoyer v. Neff*. It is precisely because the inquiry into minimum contacts is now of such overriding importance, however, that I must respectfully dissent from Part IV of the Court's opinion. . . .

I, therefore, would approach the minimum contacts analysis differently than does the Court. Crucial to me is the fact that appellants voluntarily associated themselves with the State of Delaware, "invoking the benefits and protections of its laws," *Hanson v. Denckla*; *International Shoe Co. v. Washington*, by entering into a long term and fragile relationship with one of its domestic corporations. They thereby elected to assume powers and to undertake responsibilities wholly derived from that State's rules and regulations, and to become eligible for those benefits that Delaware law makes available to its corporations' officials. E.g., 8 Del. C. §§143 (interest-free loans); 145 (indemnification). While it is possible that countervailing issues of judicial efficiency and the like might clearly favor a different forum, they do not appear on the meager record before us; and, of course, we are concerned solely with "minimum" contacts, not the "best" contacts. I thus do not believe that it is unfair to insist that appellants make themselves available to suit in a competent forum that Delaware might create for vindication of its important public policies directly pertaining to appellants' fiduciary associations with the State.

WHAT'S NEW HERE?

- Attaching property—here the "sequestered" shares belonging to the 21 directors—does not, by itself, establish jurisdiction. This part of *Shaffer* overrules *Harris v. Balk* and limits or abolishes *quasi in rem* jurisdiction.

- Jurisdictional cases involving property post-*Shaffer* undergo the same analysis as other jurisdictional cases: What are the contacts in relation to the claim? Is the assertion of jurisdiction reasonable under the circumstances?
- After *Shaffer, International Shoe* applies to individuals as well as corporations. So the previously multiple lines of jurisdictional analysis (individuals vs. corporations; *in personam* vs. *in rem*) seem to merge in a single analysis. But stay tuned for *Burnham v. Superior Court*, infra page 148.

Notes and Problems

---

1. Do not let the corporate context or the caption of this suit mislead you into assuming that jurisdiction over the corporation was at issue. As you have already seen, Greyhound Corporation would undoubtedly be subject to jurisdiction in Delaware—because that was the state of its incorporation. The defendants challenging jurisdiction were 21 of the 28 individual members of Greyhound's board of directors; none were residents of Delaware, but they did hold stock in Greyhound.

2. Explain why *Shaffer* did not decide:
   a. that property is irrelevant to the existence of jurisdiction;
   b. that stock is not property;
   c. that directors of a corporation cannot be sued in the state of incorporation;
   d. that Greyhound's board of directors had not "consented" to be sued in Delaware;
   e. that attachment of property is an unconstitutional way for a state to assert its jurisdiction.

3. We can understand what *Shaffer* does by imagining two variations on *Pennoyer*. How would these variations be decided under *Pennoyer*? Does *Shaffer* alter that result?
   a. Neff, who has never been to Oregon, inherits property there. Mitchell, from whom Neff has previously borrowed money (the transaction occurring in California), sues Neff in Oregon for the unpaid debt, asserting jurisdiction by attaching the property.
   b. Neff, who has never been to Oregon, hires Mitchell to help him buy some property in Oregon. Mitchell does so, but Neff fails to pay Mitchell's fees. Mitchell sues Neff in Oregon.

4. The majority suggested that Delaware could have required the corporate officers to submit to Delaware jurisdiction as a condition of becoming corpo-

rate officers. After the decision in *Shaffer*, the Delaware legislature enacted a statute purporting to give its courts jurisdiction over officers and directors of Delaware corporations in cases related to their corporate activities. See 10 Del. Code §3114. The Delaware Supreme Court upheld the statute against constitutional attack in Armstrong v. Pomerance, 423 A.2d 174 (Del. 1980). Suppose Delaware courts read that statute to assert such jurisdiction—limited to suits challenging actions taken as corporate leaders—regardless of the extent of directors' and officers' other contacts with the state. Defend that result using the categories of *International Shoe*.

5. Notice Justice Brennan's contention that one ought to take into account not only the defendant's circumstances but also the interests of the forum state. As you will see in subsequent cases, the justices have not entirely agreed about whether and how to take this factor into account. Notice that it will usually favor the assertion of jurisdiction and the plaintiff, who is likely to be at least a temporary resident of the forum state.

6. Though *Shaffer* holds that the mere seizure of property does not establish jurisdiction, parties continue to seize property for other purposes: to prevent a party from moving assets out of the country pending litigation; or to satisfy judgments. We will see in Chapter 5 that such cases of prejudgment seizure of property, even when there are minimum contacts, may require prior notice and the opportunity for a hearing to the owner of the property.

Implications

In rem jurisdiction, an old idea, and the Internet, a newer one, have come together in an interesting way. Like other trademarks, Internet domain names are valuable pieces of intellectual property, and legislation protects them from various sorts of abuse and poaching. Because of the ease of registering a domain name and the ubiquity of the Internet, plaintiffs seeking to protect domain names sometimes have difficulty in locating the defendant. Even if the defendant's whereabouts are known, the defendant may not be subject to personal jurisdiction in the United States. Congress responded with the Anti-Cybersquatting Consumer Protection Act (15 U.S.C. §1125(d)(2) (2011)), whose procedural portions exploit the architecture of the Internet and the concept of *in rem* jurisdiction. Individual computers connected to the Internet have numerical addresses. But long strings of numbers are more difficult to remember than, for example, google.com, so the Internet uses a domain name system, which is a table of names associated with computer addresses. Whenever an Internet user requests a domain name site by typing its name in a browser, its numerical address has to be matched with a number by searching a list acquired from directory computers that maintain lists matching site names with numerical addresses. The domain name registrar keeps the most current tables matching names and numbers. The registrar thus functions both as a keeper of title records and as a continually updated directory that facilitates the matching process that allows the Internet to function.

In addition to establishing liability for various forms of "cybersquatting," the statute exploits this system. It allows a plaintiff to bring an *in rem* action in the location of the registrar of domain names:

> The owner of a mark may file an in rem civil action against a domain name in the judicial district in which the domain name registrar, domain name registry, or other domain name authority that registered or assigned the domain name is located if: . . .
> (A) (ii) the court finds that the owner—
> (I) is not able to obtain in personam jurisdiction over a person who would have been a defendant in a civil action under paragraph (1); or
> (II) through due diligence was not able to find a person who would have been a defendant in a civil action under paragraph (1) by—
> (aa) sending a notice of the alleged violation and intent to proceed under this paragraph to the registrant of the domain name at the postal and e-mail address provided by the registrant to the registrar; and
> (bb) publishing notice of the action as the court may direct promptly after filing the action.
> (B) The actions under subparagraph (A)(ii) shall constitute service of process.

Upon receiving such a notice, the domain name registrar is to "deposit" the disputed domain name with the court during the suit's pendency.

3. Specific Jurisdiction: The Modern Cases

Pennoyer established the concept of personal jurisdiction; 75 years later, *International Shoe* modernized the framework; and 30 years after that, *Shaffer v. Heitner* eliminated *quasi in rem* jurisdiction and consolidated the regime of *International Shoe*. In more recent cases, the Supreme Court has struggled with how to apply the concepts of *International Shoe* and shown some restlessness with its doctrinal categories. The Court's restlessness raises a question that you should consider as you work through the intricacies of modern jurisdictional doctrine: Does the current doctrinal framework make sense?

The following cases represent a sampling of the Supreme Court's decisions in the years since *International Shoe*. As you read them, work on two levels of analysis. Initially, consider the analytical framework the Court is applying: To what extent is it working within, and to what extent modifying or departing from, the framework of *International Shoe*? Second, try to understand how the particular facts of each case led to its holding; what is the smallest alteration in facts that would lead the Court to a different result?

Don't be misled by the concentration of U.S. Supreme Court cases in this section: Federal district courts and courts of appeals are deciding these questions every day. State courts decide questions of personal jurisdiction as well, as you will see with *Abdouch*, at page 121.

World-Wide Volkswagen Corp. v. Woodson

444 U.S. 286 (1980)

WHITE, J., delivered the opinion of the Court.

The issue before us is whether, consistently with the Due Process Clause of the Fourteenth Amendment, an Oklahoma court may exercise in personam jurisdiction over a nonresident automobile retailer and its wholesale distributor in a products-liability action, when the defendants' only connection with Oklahoma is the fact that an automobile sold in New York to New York residents became involved in an accident in Oklahoma.

I

Respondents Harry and Kay Robinson purchased a new Audi automobile from petitioner Seaway Volkswagen, Inc. (Seaway) in Massena, N.Y., in 1976. The following year the Robinson family, who resided in New York, left that State for a new home in Arizona. As they passed through the State of Oklahoma, another car struck their Audi in the rear, causing a fire which severely burned Kay Robinson and her two children.[1] The Robinsons subsequently brought a products-liability action in the District Court for Creek County, Okla. claiming that their injuries resulted from defective design and placement of the Audi's gas tank and fuel system. They joined as defendants the automobile's manufacturer, Audi NSU Auto Union Aktiengesellschaft (Audi); its importer, Volkswagen of America, Inc. (Volkswagen); its regional distributor, petitioner World-Wide Volkswagen Corporation (World-Wide); and its retail dealer, petitioner Seaway. Seaway and World-Wide entered special appearances,[3] claiming that Oklahoma's exercise of jurisdiction over them would offend the limitations on the State's jurisdiction imposed by the Due Process Clause of the Fourteenth Amendment.

The facts presented to the District Court showed that World-Wide is incorporated and has its business office in New York. It distributes vehicles, parts and accessories, under contract with Volkswagen, to retail dealers in New York, New Jersey, and Connecticut. Seaway, one of these retail dealers, is incorporated and has its place of business in New York. Insofar as the record reveals, Seaway and World-Wide are fully independent corporations whose relations with each other and with Volkswagen and Audi are contractual only. Respondents adduced no evidence that either World-Wide or Seaway does any business in Oklahoma, ships or sells any products to or in that State, has an agent to receive process there, or purchases advertisements in any media calculated to reach Oklahoma. In fact, as respondents' counsel conceded at oral argument, there was no showing that any automobile sold by World-Wide or

---

1. The driver of the other automobile does not figure in the present litigation.

3. Volkswagen also entered a special appearance in the District Court, but unlike World-Wide and Seaway did not seek review in the Supreme Court of Oklahoma and is not a petitioner here. Both Volkswagen and Audi remain as defendants in the litigation pending before the District Court in Oklahoma.

Seaway has ever entered Oklahoma with the single exception of the vehicle involved in the present case. . . .

. . . Petitioners then sought a writ of prohibition in the Supreme Court of Oklahoma to restrain the District Judge, respondent Charles S. Woodson, from exercising in personam jurisdiction over them.

The Supreme Court of Oklahoma denied the writ. . . . The Court's rationale was contained in the following paragraph:

> In the case before us, the product being sold and distributed by the petitioners is by its very design and purpose so mobile that petitioners can foresee its possible use in Oklahoma. This is especially true of the distributor, who has the exclusive right to distribute such automobile in New York, New Jersey and Connecticut. The evidence presented below demonstrated that goods sold and distributed by the petitioners were used in the State of Oklahoma, and under the facts we believe it reasonable to infer, given the retail value of the automobile, that the petitioners derive substantial income from automobiles which from time to time are used in the State of Oklahoma. This being the case, we hold that under the facts presented, the trial court was justified in concluding that the petitioners derive substantial revenue from goods used or consumed in this State.

We granted certiorari to consider an important constitutional question with respect to state-court jurisdiction and to resolve a conflict between the Supreme Court of Oklahoma and the highest courts of at least four other States. We reverse.

II

. . . As has long been settled, and as we reaffirm today, a state court may exercise personal jurisdiction over a nonresident defendant only so long as there exist "minimum contacts" between the defendant and the forum State. *International Shoe Co. v. Washington*. The concept of minimum contacts, in turn, can be seen to perform two related, but distinguishable functions. It protects the defendant against the burdens of litigating in a distant or inconvenient forum. And it acts to ensure that the States, through their courts, do not reach out beyond the limits imposed on them by their status as coequal sovereigns in a federal system.

The protection against inconvenient litigation is typically described in terms of "reasonableness" or "fairness." We have said that the defendant's contacts with the forum State must be such that maintenance of the suit "does not offend 'traditional notions of fair play and substantial justice.' " *International Shoe Co. v. Washington*, quoting *Milliken v. Meyer*. The relationship between the defendant and the forum must be such that it is "reasonable . . . to require the corporation to defend the particular suit which is brought there." Implicit in this emphasis on reasonableness is the understanding that the burden on the defendant, while always a primary concern, will in an appropriate case be considered in light of other relevant factors, including the forum State's interest in adjudicating the dispute; the plaintiff's interest in obtaining convenient and effective relief, at least when that interest is not adequately protected by the plaintiff's power to choose the forum, cf. *Shaffer v. Heitner*; the interstate judicial system's interest in obtaining the most efficient resolution of controversies; and the shared interest of the several States in furthering fundamental substantive social policies.

The limits imposed on state jurisdiction by the Due Process Clause, in its role as a guarantor against inconvenient litigation, have been substantially relaxed over the years. As we noted in *McGee v. International Life Ins. Co.*, this trend is largely attributable to a fundamental transformation in the American economy. . . .

The historical developments noted in *McGee*, of course, have only accelerated in the generation since that case was decided. Nevertheless, we have never accepted the proposition that state lines are irrelevant for jurisdictional purposes, nor could we and remain faithful to the principles of interstate federalism embodied in the Constitution. The economic interdependence of the States was foreseen and desired by the Framers. In the Commerce Clause, they provided that the Nation was to be a common market, a "free trade unit" in which the States are debarred from acting as separable economic entities. But the Framers also intended that the States retain many essential attributes of sovereignty, including, in particular, the sovereign power to try causes in their courts.

The sovereignty of each State, in turn, implied a limitation on the sovereignty of all of its sister States—a limitation express or implicit in both the original scheme of the Constitution and the Fourteenth Amendment. . . .

Thus, the Due Process Clause "does not contemplate that a state may make binding a judgment in personam against an individual or corporate defendant with which the state has no contacts, ties, or relations." *International Shoe Co. v. Washington.* Even if the defendant would suffer minimal or no inconvenience from being forced to litigate before the tribunals of another State; even if the forum State has a strong interest in applying its law to the controversy; even if the forum State is the most convenient location for litigation, the Due Process Clause, acting as an instrument of interstate federalism, may sometimes act to divest the State of its power to render a valid judgment. *Hanson v. Denckla.*

III

Applying these principles to the case at hand, we find in the record before us a total absence of those affiliating circumstances that are a necessary predicate to any exercise of state-court jurisdiction. Petitioners carry on no activity whatsoever in Oklahoma. They close no sales and perform no services there. They avail themselves of none of the privileges and benefits of Oklahoma law. They solicit no business there either through salespersons or through advertising reasonably calculated to reach the State. Nor does the record show that they regularly sell cars at wholesale or retail to Oklahoma customers or residents or that they indirectly, through others, serve or seek to serve the Oklahoma market. In short, respondents seek to base jurisdiction on one, isolated occurrence and whatever inferences can be drawn therefrom: the fortuitous circumstance that a single Audi automobile, sold in New York to New York residents, happened to suffer an accident while passing through Oklahoma.

It is argued, however, that because an automobile is mobile by its very design and purpose it was "foreseeable" that the Robinsons' Audi would cause injury in Oklahoma. Yet "foreseeability" alone has never been a sufficient benchmark for personal jurisdiction under the Due Process Clause. In *Hanson v. Denckla*, supra, it was no doubt foreseeable that the settlor of a Delaware trust would subsequently move to Florida and seek to exercise a power of appointment there; yet we held that Florida courts could not constitutionally exercise jurisdiction over a Delaware trustee that had no other contacts with the forum State. . . .

If foreseeability were the criterion, a local California tire retailer could be forced to defend in Pennsylvania when a blowout occurs there; a Wisconsin seller of a defective automobile jack could be haled before a distant court for damage caused in New Jersey; or a Florida soft drink concessionaire could be summoned to Alaska to account for injuries happening there. Every seller of chattels would in effect appoint the chattel his agent for service of process. His amenability to suit would travel with the chattel. We recently abandoned the outworn rule of *Harris v. Balk*, that the interest of a creditor in a debt could be extinguished or otherwise affected by any State having transitory jurisdiction over the debtor. *Shaffer v. Heitner*. Having interred the mechanical rule that a creditor's amenability to a quasi in rem action travels with his debtor, we are unwilling to endorse an analogous principle in the present case.

This is not to say, of course, that foreseeability is wholly irrelevant. But the foreseeability that is critical to due process analysis is not the mere likelihood that a product will find its way into the forum State. Rather, it is that the defendant's conduct and connection with the forum State are such that he should reasonably anticipate being haled into court there. The Due Process Clause, by ensuring the "orderly administration of the laws," gives a degree of predictability to the legal system that allows potential defendants to structure their primary conduct with some minimum assurance as to where that conduct will and will not render them liable to suit.

When a corporation "purposefully avails itself of the privilege of conducting activities within the forum State," it has clear notice that it is subject to suit there, and can act to alleviate the risk of burdensome litigation by procuring insurance, passing the expected costs on to customers, or, if the risks are too great, severing its connection with the State. Hence if the sale of a product of a manufacturer or distributor such as Audi or Volkswagen is not simply an isolated occurrence, but arises from the efforts of the manufacturer or distributor to serve, directly or indirectly, the market for its product in other States, it is not unreasonable to subject it to suit in one of those States if its allegedly defective merchandise has there been the source of injury to its owner or to others. The forum State does not exceed its powers under the Due Process Clause if it asserts personal jurisdiction over a corporation that delivers its products into the stream of commerce with the expectation that they will be purchased by consumers in the forum State. Cf. *Gray v. American Radiator*.

But there is no such or similar basis for Oklahoma jurisdiction over World-Wide or Seaway in this case. Seaway's sales are made in Massena, N.Y. World-Wide's market, although substantially larger, is limited to dealers in New York, New Jersey, and Connecticut. There is no evidence of record that any automobiles distributed by World-Wide are sold to retail customers outside this tri-State area. It is foreseeable that the purchasers of automobiles sold by World-Wide and Seaway may take them to Oklahoma. But the mere "unilateral activity of those who claim some relationship with a nonresident defendant cannot satisfy the requirement of contact with the forum State." *Hanson v. Denckla.*

In a variant on the previous argument it is contended that jurisdiction can be supported by the fact that petitioners earn substantial revenue from goods used in Oklahoma. The Oklahoma Supreme Court so found, drawing the inference that because one automobile sold by petitioners had been used in Oklahoma, others might have been used there also. While this inference seems less than compelling on the facts of the instant case, we need not question the Court's factual findings in order to reject its reasoning.

This argument seems to make the point that the purchase of automobiles in New York, from which the petitioners earn substantial revenue, would not occur but for the fact that the automobiles are capable of use in distant States like Oklahoma. Respondents observe that the very purpose of an automobile is to travel, and that travel of automobiles sold by petitioners is facilitated by an extensive chain of Volkswagen service centers throughout the Country, including some in Oklahoma.[12] However, financial benefits accruing to the defendant from a collateral relation to the forum State will not support jurisdiction if they do not stem from a constitutionally cognizable contact with that State. In our view, whatever marginal revenues petitioners may receive by virtue of the fact that their products are capable of use in Oklahoma is far too attenuated a contact to justify that State's exercise of in personam jurisdiction over them.

Because we find that petitioners have no "contacts, ties, or relations" with the State of Oklahoma, the judgment of the Supreme Court of Oklahoma is reversed.

BRENNAN, J., dissenting.

. . . Because I believe that the Court reads *International Shoe* and its progeny too narrowly, and because I believe that the standards enunciated by those cases may already be obsolete as constitutional boundaries, I dissent. . . .

The Court's opinions focus tightly on the existence of contacts between the forum and the defendant. In so doing, they accord too little weight to the strength of the forum State's interest in the case and fail to explore whether there would be any actual inconvenience to the defendant. . . .

[T]he interest of the forum State and its connection to the litigation is strong. The automobile accident underlying the litigation occurred in Oklahoma. The plaintiffs were hospitalized in Oklahoma when they brought suit. Essential witnesses and evidence were in Oklahoma. See *Shaffer v. Heitner.* The State has a legitimate interest in enforcing its laws designed to keep its highway system safe, and the trial can proceed at least as efficiently in Oklahoma as anywhere else.

The petitioners are not unconnected with the forum. Although both sell automobiles within limited sales territories, each sold the automobile which in fact was driven to Oklahoma where it was involved in an accident. It may be true, as the Court suggests, that each sincerely intended to limit its commercial impact to the limited territory, and that each intended to accept the benefits and protection of the laws only of those States within the territory. But obviously these were unrealistic hopes that

---

12. As we have noted, petitioners earn no direct revenues from these service centers.

cannot be treated as an automatic constitutional shield.[9] An automobile simply is not a stationary item or one designed to be used in one place. An automobile is intended to be moved around. Someone in the business of selling large numbers of automobiles can hardly plead ignorance of their mobility or pretend that the automobiles stay put after they are sold. It is not merely that a dealer in automobiles foresees that they will move. The dealer actually intends that the purchasers will use the automobiles to travel to distant States where the dealer does not directly "do business." The sale of an automobile does *purposefully* inject the vehicle into the stream of interstate commerce so that it can travel to distant States. . . .

The Court accepts that a State may exercise jurisdiction over a distributor which "serves" that State "indirectly" by "deliver[ing] its products into the stream of commerce with the expectation that they will [be] purchased by consumers in other States." It is difficult to see why the Constitution should distinguish between a case involving goods which reach a distant State through a chain of distribution and a case involving goods which reach the same State because a consumer, using them as the dealer knew the customer would, took them there. In each case the seller purposefully injects the goods into the stream of commerce and those goods predictably are used in the forum State. . . .

It may be that affirmance of the judgments in these cases would approach the outer limits of *International Shoe*'s jurisdictional principle. But that principle, with its almost exclusive focus on the rights of defendants, may be outdated. . . .

The Court's opinion suggests that the defendant ought to be subject to a State's jurisdiction only if he has contacts with the State "such that he should reasonably anticipate being haled into court there."[18] There is nothing unreasonable or unfair, however, about recognizing commercial reality. . . .

[Two dissenting opinions, one by Justice MARSHALL, joined by Justice BLACKMUN, and another by Justice BLACKMUN writing separately, are omitted.]

WHAT'S NEW HERE?

● At one level, not much is new here: The Court applies *International Shoe* and finds the affiliations supporting jurisdiction are lacking for World-Wide and Seaway.

---

9. Moreover, imposing liability in this case would not so undermine certainty as to destroy an automobile dealer's ability to do business. According jurisdiction does not expand liability except in the marginal case where a plaintiff cannot afford to bring an action except in the plaintiff's own State. In addition, these petitioners are represented by insurance companies. They not only could, but did, purchase insurance to protect them should they stand trial and lose the case. The costs of the insurance no doubt are passed on to customers.

18. The Court suggests that this is the critical foreseeability rather than the likelihood that the product will go to the forum State. But the reasoning begs the question. A defendant cannot know if his actions will subject him to jurisdiction in another State until we have declared what the law of jurisdiction is. . . .

- At another level, the case tightens the test for jurisdiction. Seaway and World-Wide could "foresee" that their cars might end up in Oklahoma, or for that matter in any part of the world with paved roads connected to those in upstate New York, where Seaway was located; after all, cars are *supposed* to be mobile—that's why advertisements show them zooming along open highways. Not enough, says the majority. Looking back to *Hanson v. Denkla*, the Court says the local dealer and the regional distributor did not purposefully avail themselves—did not seek out, by advertising or in other ways—the Oklahoma market, so jurisdiction does not lie. By contrast, the opinion suggests, though does not hold (because the issue was not presented), that the manufacturer and the national distributor did avail themselves—by buying advertising and establishing dealerships—of the Oklahoma market.

- Also notice a pattern present here and in most of the other cases in this chapter: A state court—here the Oklahoma Supreme Court—first applies what it understands to be existing constitutional doctrine. That is where most personal jurisdiction cases end: with a state court applying existing doctrine. Out of the hundreds of such state court decisions—all interpreting and applying the Due Process Clause of the U.S. Constitution, only a minute proportion will ever be reviewed by the U.S. Supreme Court, although in theory all could be. Here the U.S. Supreme Court does grant review and decides that the Oklahoma court did not correctly apply the doctrine. Its analysis will now become part of the accumulating doctrine that both state and federal courts will apply when considering questions of personal jurisdiction.

Notes and Problems

1. Consider the case as doctrine, as strategy, and as a guide to future litigation. Begin by clarifying what the case did and didn't decide:

   a. Which defendants were before the Supreme Court?

   b. Audi, the manufacturer, did not challenge personal jurisdiction; Volkswagen of America, the national distributor, originally objected to the Oklahoma court's jurisdiction, but did not appeal the trial court's rejection of that defense. Because their claims were not before the Court, the opinion does not hold that these parties are subject to personal jurisdiction, but suggests that they would be:

      > Hence if the sale of a product of a manufacturer or distributor such as Audi or Volkswagen is not simply an isolated occurrence, but arises from the efforts of the manufacturer or distributor to serve, directly or indirectly, the market for its product in other States, it is not unreasonable to subject it to suit in one of those States if its allegedly defective merchandise there has been the source of injury to others. . . .

c. Apply *World-Wide Volkswagen* to the following hypothetical: Assume that, as purchased, the Robinsons' car lacked a radio. Before leaving on the trip to Arizona, they went to a Massena, N.Y., retailer who specialized in sound equipment for cars and purchased a sound system for the Audi. The system was manufactured in Japan and sold all over the United States. The national distributor was located in California. Further assume that the cause of the car fire was traced to defective wiring in the sound system. If the Robinsons sue in Oklahoma, naming the Massena retailer, the Japanese manufacturer, and the California distributor, who will be subject to personal jurisdiction?

2. If Audi and its national distributor are subject to jurisdiction in Oklahoma, but the regional distributor and dealer are not, *World-Wide Volkswagen* can result in inconsistent lawsuits. Suppose Audi had discovered a gas tank problem and sent a service bulletin to Seaway and World-Wide requiring them to correct the problem—but they had failed to do so. Their failure to correct the defect would not be a defense in the Robinsons' actions against Audi, but it might be the basis for requiring Seaway and World-Wide to indemnify Audi. Under these circumstances, Audi, after paying a judgment to the Robinsons, would have to sue Seaway and World-Wide separately, probably in New York. But because World-Wide and Seaway would not have been parties to the Oklahoma litigation, they would not be bound by the finding of a product defect. The result might be inconsistent judgments—Oklahoma holding Audi responsible for a design defect, but New York courts finding that there was no defect and that Audi was therefore not entitled to indemnity.

Procedure as Strategy

Personal jurisdiction motions are strategic tools in a defendant's arsenal, and therefore something plaintiffs must anticipate. In theory, a successful motion to dismiss for want of personal jurisdiction only delays the suit: At least as to a U.S. defendant, there will be some jurisdiction (permanent domicile, state of incorporation) where suit can be brought. So why do defendants bother?

In a marginal case, the suit might go away entirely. The statute of limitations in the new forum state may have run. Or, unlike the Robinsons' case, which involved very serious permanent injuries, there could be a much lower damage bill. Plaintiff's lawyer has to locate a competent practitioner in another state and arrange for her to take over the case, a process involving some expense. If witnesses have to travel, the added expense might make bringing the suit irrational.

Even if the case persists, the defendant has done two things. He's delayed the date at which he may have to pay damages (in many tort suits interest does not run until judgment is entered). And he's moved the case to a different forum, which, for reasons having nothing to do with jurisdiction, may be friendlier.

But plaintiffs too can behave strategically. Modern jurisdictional doctrine often permits plaintiff a choice of several fora in which to sue. In *World-Wide*, the plaintiffs could have sued Audi in New York, in Oklahoma, and perhaps in Arizona, where the Robinsons were moving on their ill-fated trip. The plaintiffs' lawyer doubtless considered which of these fora would be most sympathetic to their case.

In fact, *World-Wide Volkswagen* displays both sides maneuvering for strategic advantage by deploying jurisdictional doctrine. Reading the case, you may have wondered why the driver of the car that collided with the plaintiffs did not seem to be in the case, and why the plaintiffs bothered to name the local dealer and regional distributor as defendants in a product design defect case. Professor Charles Adams, who has looked into the story behind the case in World-Wide Volkswagen v. Woodson—*The Rest of the Story*, 72 Neb. L. Rev. 1122 (1993), provides an account that may answer the first of these questions:

> Lloyd Hull knew he had a serious drinking problem. Ever since his retirement from the Navy two years before, it seemed as though he needed to get a little high, or better, every day. After getting off work on September 21, 1977, in Berryville, Arkansas, Lloyd was on his way to visit his older sister in Okarche, Oklahoma. Next to the bottle of Jim Beam on the front seat was a loaded .22 Magnum pistol for shooting jack rabbits on his sister's farm. . . .
>
> As he drove along, Lloyd took shots from the bottle of bourbon. . . . Later he assumed he must have been driving too fast on account of the liquor. Lloyd did not notice the small car ahead of him until he was nearly on top of it. . . .
>
> Lloyd Hull was an obvious defendant, but he had no liability insurance. . . .

Id. at 1122-23, 1127. Hull's lack of resources likely explains why the Robinsons did not name him as a defendant.

And why did the Robinsons name the New York dealer and regional distributor? The answer may lie in where the parties would want the case to be tried. Start with the plaintiff, who has the initial choice. Why did the Robinsons' lawyer choose Oklahoma? According to Professor Adams, Creek County, Oklahoma, where the crash had occurred, was "a blue collar community that . . . [had] become known to personal injury lawyers throughout the state as being particularly sympathetic to personal injury plaintiffs." Id. at 1128.

But a successful strategy to try the case in Creek County would not only have to bring it there but keep it there. As you will see in the next chapter, noncitizen defendants may "remove" to federal court an action if the requisites of diversity have been met. Any good plaintiff's lawyer would know that if he sued a German manufacturer and its national distributor (located in Michigan), the defendants could remove the case to a federal district court by invoking diversity jurisdiction. Since the federal district court nearest to Creek County is in Tulsa, and since that court would draw its jurors from a number of counties in the Eastern District of Oklahoma, the defendants could, by making such a move, dilute what plaintiff hoped would be a favorable jury pool.

Could the plaintiff prevent such removal? For diversity jurisdiction to exist, none of the defendants can be of the same state as the plaintiffs (a principle explored more fully in the next chapter). The Robinsons' lawyer argued that the Robinsons, although they were on their way to Arizona, remained New York citizens until they had permanently settled in their new home. Hence the importance of naming World-Wide and Seaway, both New York corporations, as defendants: So long as they remained in the lawsuit, the case could not be removed to federal court and would therefore be tried before a Creek County jury.

The defendants' counter was the motion to dismiss the two New York defendants for want of personal jurisdiction. Do you now understand why there was such a fierce battle about personal jurisdiction over two apparently irrelevant defendants?

Given this background, what would you expect to be the remaining defendants' next procedural move after the case has been sent back to Oklahoma courts with the holding that there is no jurisdiction over Seaway and World-Wide?

3. Five years after *World-Wide*, the Court decided Burger King v. Rudzewicz, 471 U.S. 462 (1985). Burger King sells franchises for its fast food outlets to investors. To establish quality control and national brand uniformity Burger King requires its franchisees to adhere to a number of standards, including attendance at "Burger King University" in Miami, Florida, where franchise owners are trained in creating a uniform product. John Rudzewicz (a partner in a national accounting firm) and Brian MacShara, an acquaintance—both Michigan residents—applied to take over an existing Burger King franchise in a Detroit suburb. The Florida headquarters approved the application and MacShara, who was to supervise day-to-day operations, thereafter trained in Florida. When the franchise began to lose money and the partners fell behind in their payments, Burger King terminated the franchise and brought suit in Florida, invoking federal diversity jurisdiction. Rudzewicz and MacShara challenged the personal jurisdiction of the Florida district court, arguing that the franchise was in Michigan, and that their limited contact with Florida did not support jurisdiction over this claim. The Supreme Court disagreed, holding that by entering into a long-term agreement with a corporation known to be based in Florida, in a contract that called for the application of Florida law, and training in Florida, the partners had purposefully availed themselves of Florida law—enough to warrant the exercise of Florida jurisdiction over them in a suit seeking to enforce terms of the franchise agreement. In the process the majority opinion, written by Justice Brennan, enunciated principles that Brennan had espoused in other opinions (including his dissents in *Shaffer* and *World-Wide Volkswagen*) but had never previously won the day.

> Once it has been decided that a defendant purposefully established minimum contacts within the forum State, these contacts may be considered in light of other factors to determine whether the assertion of personal jurisdiction would comport with "fair play and substantial justice." *International Shoe Co. v. Washington.* Thus courts in "appropriate [cases]" may evaluate "the burden on the defendant," "the forum State's interest in adjudicating the dispute," "the plaintiff's interest in obtaining convenient and effective relief," "the interstate judicial system's interest in obtaining the most efficient resolution of controversies," and the "shared interest of the several States in furthering fundamental substantive social policies." *World-Wide Volkswagen Corp. v. Woodson.* These considerations sometimes serve

to establish the reasonableness of jurisdiction upon a lesser showing of minimum contacts than would otherwise be required. On the other hand, where a defendant who purposefully has directed his activities at forum residents seeks to defeat jurisdiction, he must present a compelling case that the presence of some other considerations would render jurisdiction unreasonable.

471 U.S. at 476-77. This view of personal jurisdiction is a break from earlier cases: The Supreme Court's majority opinions up until this point focused almost exclusively on whether there were sufficient "minimum contacts" between the defendant and the forum state without paying more than lip service to considerations of "fair play and substantial justice." Justice Brennan's analysis has neither found an echo in later cases nor been explicitly repudiated.

Procedure as Strategy

Notice that Rudzewicz could have avoided this fight by preemptively filing suit—perhaps seeking a declaratory judgment—in Michigan. Explain why, on the basis of what you already know, it is clear that Michigan courts would have had jurisdiction over Burger King.

Conversely, Burger King could have avoided this fight by having a forum selection clause—specifying that all disputes arising from the agreement had to be litigated in Florida—in its franchise agreement. As you will see later in this chapter, in 2019 it is clear that such a clause would be enforceable. But in 1985 that result lay in doubt—probably explaining why Burger King's lawyers did not put one in the contract.

4. Unlike *World-Wide Volkswagen*, *Burger King* was initiated in a federal court. The *Burger King* opinion silently assumes that the analysis is identical—that the jurisdictional reach of a federal court matches that of a state court sitting in the same state. That assumption is correct, but it may be worth taking the steps to see why.

   a. Read Rule 4(k)(1)(A), which generally gives a federal court the same jurisdictional reach as a court of the state in which it sits. So a federal district court sitting in Florida has the same jurisdictional reach as a Florida state court.

   b. Exceptions to this provision occur when a specific federal statute or Rule authorizes more extensive personal jurisdiction. Rule 4(k)(1)(B)-(C). In several notable instances, Congress has purported to give the federal courts expansive powers of personal jurisdiction. For example, the Federal Interpleader Act, 28 U.S.C. §2361, gives federal courts the power to serve process anywhere in the nation, a power that has been interpreted to include personal jurisdiction. Various laws regulating federal securities do the same.

c. Both of these aspects of Rule 4(k)(1) are described in more detail at page 174.

5. In *World-Wide Volkswagen*, the plaintiffs sued both the national distributor (Volkswagen of America) and the German manufacturer. Under the substantive law of most states the distributor as well as the manufacturer would be liable for injuries caused by a defective product. If we assume the distributor is well capitalized or insured, plaintiff could collect a judgment from either. But not all distributors are solvent. In the next case, a tort plaintiff faced a national distributor who, after selling the allegedly defective product, went bankrupt. The question was whether the plaintiff could obtain jurisdiction over the manufacturer. In *World-Wide Volkswagen*, the manufacturer thought the answer was sufficiently self-evident that it did not challenge jurisdiction. In the next case, the manufacturer did challenge personal jurisdiction—and prevailed.

J. McIntyre Machinery, Ltd. v. Nicastro
564 U.S. 873 (2011)

KENNEDY, J., announced the judgment of the Court and delivered an opinion, in which THE CHIEF JUSTICE, SCALIA, J., and THOMAS, J., join.

Whether a person or entity is subject to the jurisdiction of a state court despite not having been present in the State either at the time of suit or at the time of the alleged injury, and despite not having consented to the exercise of jurisdiction, is a question that arises with great frequency in the routine course of litigation. The rules and standards for determining when a State does or does not have jurisdiction over an absent party have been unclear because of decades-old questions left open in Asahi Metal Industry Co. v. Superior Court of Cal., Solano Cty., 480 U.S. 102 (1987).

Here, the Supreme Court of New Jersey, relying in part on *Asahi*, held that New Jersey's courts can exercise jurisdiction over a foreign manufacturer of a product so long as the manufacturer "knows or reasonably should know that its products are distributed through a nationwide distribution system that might lead to those products being sold in any of the fifty states." Applying that test, the court concluded that a British manufacturer of scrap metal machines was subject to jurisdiction in New Jersey, even though at no time had it advertised in, sent goods to, or in any relevant sense targeted the State.

That decision cannot be sustained. . . . As a general rule, the exercise of judicial power is not lawful unless the defendant "purposefully avails itself of the privilege of conducting activities within the forum State, thus invoking the benefits and protections of its laws." Hanson v. Denckla, 357 U.S. 235, 253 (1958). There may be exceptions, say, for instance, in cases involving an intentional tort. But the general rule is applicable in this products-liability case, and the so-called "stream-of-commerce" doctrine cannot displace it.

I

This case arises from a products-liability suit filed in New Jersey state court. Robert Nicastro seriously injured his hand while using a metal-shearing machine manufactured by J. McIntyre Machinery, Ltd. (J. McIntyre). The accident occurred in New Jersey, but the machine was manufactured in England, where J. McIntyre is incorporated and operates. The question here is whether the New Jersey courts have jurisdiction over J. McIntyre, notwithstanding the fact that the company at no time either marketed goods in the State or shipped them there.

At oral argument in this Court, Nicastro's counsel stressed three primary facts in defense of New Jersey's assertion of jurisdiction over J. McIntyre.

First, an independent company agreed to sell J. McIntyre's machines in the United States. J. McIntyre itself did not sell its machines to buyers in this country beyond the U.S. distributor, and there is no allegation that the distributor was under J. McIntyre's control.

Second, J. McIntyre officials attended annual conventions for the scrap recycling industry to advertise J. McIntyre's machines alongside the distributor. The conventions took place in various States, but never in New Jersey.

Third, no more than four machines, including the machine that caused the injuries that are the basis for this suit, ended up in New Jersey.

In addition to these facts emphasized by respondent, the New Jersey Supreme Court noted that . . . the U.S. distributor "structured [its] advertising and sales efforts in accordance with" J. McIntyre's "direction and guidance whenever possible," and that "at least some of the machines were sold on consignment to" the distributor. . . .

In light of these facts, the New Jersey Supreme Court concluded that New Jersey courts could exercise jurisdiction over petitioner. . . .

This Court's *Asahi* decision [described below] may be responsible in part for [the New Jersey] court's error regarding the stream of commerce, and this case presents an opportunity to provide greater clarity.

II

A court may subject a defendant to judgment only when the defendant has sufficient contacts with the sovereign "such that the maintenance of the suit does not offend 'traditional notions of fair play and substantial justice.'" International Shoe Co. v. Washington, 326 U.S. 310, 316 (1945) (quoting Milliken v. Meyer, 311 U.S. 457, 463 (1940)). Freeform notions of fundamental fairness divorced from traditional practice cannot transform a judgment rendered in the absence of authority into law. As a general rule, the sovereign's exercise of power requires some act by which the defendant "purposefully avails itself of the privilege of conducting activities within the forum State, thus invoking the benefits and protections of its laws," *Hanson*, though in some cases, as with an intentional tort, the defendant might well fall within the State's authority by reason of his attempt to obstruct its laws. In products-liability cases like this one, it is the defendant's purposeful availment that makes jurisdiction consistent with "traditional notions of fair play and substantial justice."

A person may submit to a State's authority in a number of ways. There is, of course, explicit consent. Presence within a State at the time suit commences through service of process is another example. See *Burnham* [casebook page 148]. Citizenship or domicile—or, by analogy, incorporation or principal place of business for corporations—also indicates general submission to a State's powers. *Goodyear Dunlop Tires Operations, S.A. v. Brown* [casebook page 129]. Each of these examples reveals circumstances, or a course of conduct, from which it is proper to infer an intention to benefit from and thus an intention to submit to the laws of the forum State. Cf. *Burger King Corp. v. Rudzewicz* [casebook page 109]. These examples support exercise of the general jurisdiction of the State's courts and allow the State to resolve both matters that originate within the State and those based on activities and events elsewhere. By contrast, those who live or operate primarily outside a State have a due process right not to be subjected to judgment in its courts as a general matter.

There is also a more limited form of submission to a State's authority for disputes that "arise out of or are connected with the activities within the state." *International Shoe Co.* Where a defendant "purposefully avails itself of the privilege of conducting activities within the forum State, thus invoking the benefits and protections of its laws," *Hanson*, it submits to the judicial power of an otherwise foreign sovereign to the extent that power is exercised in connection with the defendant's activities touching on the State. In other words, submission through contact with and activity directed at a sovereign may justify specific jurisdiction "in a suit arising out of or related to the defendant's contacts with the forum."

The imprecision arising from *Asahi*, for the most part, results from its statement of the relation between jurisdiction and the "stream of commerce." The stream of commerce, like other metaphors, has its deficiencies as well as its utility. It refers to the movement of goods from manufacturers through distributors to consumers, yet beyond that descriptive purpose its meaning is far from exact. This Court has stated that a defendant's placing goods into the stream of commerce "with the expectation that they will be purchased by consumers within the forum State" may indicate purposeful availment. *World-Wide Volkswagen Corp. v. Woodson* (finding that expectation lacking). But that statement does not amend the general rule of personal jurisdiction. It merely observes that a defendant may in an appropriate case be subject to jurisdiction without entering the forum—itself an unexceptional proposition—as where manufacturers or distributors "seek to serve" a given State's market. The principal inquiry in cases of this sort is whether the defendant's activities manifest an intention to submit to the power of a sovereign. In other words, the defendant must "purposefully avai[l] itself of the privilege of conducting activities within the forum State, thus invoking the benefits and protections of its laws." *Hanson*; Insurance Corp. [of Ireland v. Compagnie des Bauxites de Guinee, 456 U.S. at 704-05 (1982)] ("[A]ctions of the defendant may amount to a legal submission to the jurisdiction of the court"). Sometimes a defendant does so by sending its goods rather than its agents. The defendant's transmission of goods permits the exercise of jurisdiction only where the defendant can be said to have targeted the forum; as a general rule, it is not enough that the defendant might have predicted that its goods will reach the forum State.

In *Asahi*, an opinion by Justice Brennan for four Justices outlined a different approach. It discarded the central concept of sovereign authority in favor of considerations of fairness and foreseeability. As that concurrence contended, "jurisdiction premised on the placement of a product into the stream of commerce [without more] is consistent with the Due Process Clause," for "[a]s long as a participant in this process is aware that the final product is being marketed in the forum State, the possibility of a lawsuit there cannot come as a surprise." It was the premise of the concurring opinion that the defendant's ability to anticipate suit renders the assertion of jurisdiction fair. In this way, the opinion made foreseeability the touchstone of jurisdiction.

The standard set forth in Justice Brennan's concurrence was rejected in an opinion written by Justice O'Connor; but the relevant part of that opinion, too, commanded the assent of only four Justices, not a majority of the Court. That opinion stated: "The 'substantial connection' between the defendant and the forum State necessary for a finding of minimum contacts must come about by an action of the defendant purposefully directed toward the forum State. The placement of a product into the stream of commerce, without more, is not an act of the defendant purposefully directed toward the forum State." Id., at 112 (emphasis deleted; citations omitted).

Since *Asahi* was decided, the courts have sought to reconcile the competing opinions. But Justice Brennan's concurrence, advocating a rule based on general notions of fairness and foreseeability, is inconsistent with the premises of lawful judicial power. This Court's precedents make clear that it is the defendant's actions, not his expectations, that empower a State's courts to subject him to judgment. . . .

Two principles are implicit in the foregoing. First, personal jurisdiction requires a forum-by-forum, or sovereign-by-sovereign, analysis. The question is whether a defendant has followed a course of conduct directed at the society or economy existing within the jurisdiction of a given sovereign, so that the sovereign has the power to subject the defendant to judgment concerning that conduct. Personal jurisdiction, of course, restricts "judicial power not as a matter of sovereignty, but as a matter of individual liberty," for due process protects the individual's right to be subject only to lawful power. But whether a judicial judgment is lawful depends on whether the sovereign has authority to render it.

The second principle is a corollary of the first. Because the United States is a distinct sovereign, a defendant may in principle be subject to the jurisdiction of the courts of the United States but not of any particular State. This is consistent with the premises and unique genius of our Constitution. Ours is "a legal system unprecedented in form and design, establishing two orders of government, each with its own direct relationship, its own privity, its own set of mutual rights and obligations to the people who sustain it and are governed by it." For jurisdiction, a litigant may have the requisite relationship with the United States Government but not with the government of any individual State. That would be an exceptional case, however. If the defendant is a domestic domiciliary, the courts of its home State are available and can exercise general jurisdiction. And if another State were to assert jurisdiction in an inappropriate case, it would upset the federal balance, which posits that each State has a sovereignty that is not subject to unlawful intrusion by other States. Furthermore, foreign corporations will often target or concentrate on particular States, subjecting them to specific jurisdiction in those forums.

It must be remembered, however, that although this case and *Asahi* both involve foreign manufacturers, the undesirable consequences of Justice Brennan's approach are no less significant for domestic producers. The owner of a small Florida farm might sell crops to a large nearby distributor, for example, who might then distribute them to grocers across the country. If foreseeability were the controlling criterion, the farmer could be sued in Alaska or any number of other States' courts without ever leaving town. And the issue of foreseeability may itself be contested so that significant expenses are incurred just on the preliminary issue of jurisdiction. Jurisdictional rules should avoid these costs whenever possible.

The conclusion that the authority to subject a defendant to judgment depends on purposeful availment, consistent with Justice O'Connor's opinion in *Asahi*, does not by itself resolve many difficult questions of jurisdiction that will arise in particular cases. The defendant's conduct and the economic realities of the market the defendant seeks to serve will differ across cases, and judicial exposition will, in common-law fashion, clarify the contours of that principle.

III

In this case, petitioner directed marketing and sales efforts at the United States. It may be that, assuming it were otherwise empowered to legislate on the subject, the Congress could authorize the exercise of jurisdiction in appropriate courts. That circumstance is not presented in this case, however, and it is neither necessary nor appropriate to address here any constitutional concerns that might be attendant to that exercise of power. Nor is it necessary to determine what substantive law might apply were Congress to authorize jurisdiction in a federal court in New Jersey. A sovereign's legislative authority to regulate conduct may present considerations different from those presented by its authority to subject a defendant to judgment in its courts. Here the question concerns the authority of a New Jersey state court to exercise jurisdiction, so it is petitioner's purposeful contacts with New Jersey, not with the United States, that alone are relevant.

Respondent has not established that J. McIntyre engaged in conduct purposefully directed at New Jersey. . . . Indeed, after discovery the trial court found that the "defendant does not have a single contact with New Jersey short of the machine in question ending up in this state." These facts may reveal an intent to serve the U.S. market, but they do not show that J. McIntyre purposefully availed itself of the New Jersey market. . . .

* * *

Due process protects petitioner's right to be subject only to lawful authority. At no time did petitioner engage in any activities in New Jersey that reveal an intent to invoke or benefit from the protection of its laws. New Jersey is without power to adjudge the rights and liabilities of J. McIntyre, and its exercise of jurisdiction would violate due process. The contrary judgment of the New Jersey Supreme Court is *Reversed*.

BREYER, J., with whom ALITO, J., joins, concurring in the judgment.

The Supreme Court of New Jersey adopted a broad understanding of the scope of personal jurisdiction based on its view that "[t]he increasingly fast-paced globalization of the world economy has removed national borders as barriers to trade." I do not doubt that there have been many recent changes in commerce and communication, many of which are not anticipated by our precedents. But this case does not present any of those issues. So I think it unwise to announce a rule of broad applicability without full consideration of the modern-day consequences.

In my view, the outcome of this case is determined by our precedents. Based on the facts found by the New Jersey courts, respondent Robert Nicastro failed to meet his burden to demonstrate that it was constitutionally proper to exercise jurisdiction over petitioner J. McIntyre Machinery, Ltd. (British Manufacturer), a British firm that manufactures scrap-metal machines in Great Britain and sells them through an independent distributor in the United States (American Distributor). On that basis, I agree with the plurality that the contrary judgment of the Supreme Court of New Jersey should be reversed. . . .

I

None of our precedents finds that a single isolated sale, even if accompanied by the kind of sales effort indicated here, is sufficient. Rather, this Court's previous holdings suggest the contrary. . . .

There may well have been other facts that Mr. Nicastro could have demonstrated in support of jurisdiction. And the dissent considers some of those facts. But the plaintiff bears the burden of establishing jurisdiction, and here I would take the facts precisely as the New Jersey Supreme Court stated them.

Accordingly, on the record present here, resolving this case requires no more than adhering to our precedents.

II

I would not go further. Because the incident at issue in this case does not implicate modern concerns, and because the factual record leaves many open questions, this is an unsuitable vehicle for making broad pronouncements that refashion basic jurisdictional rules.

A

The plurality seems to state strict rules that limit jurisdiction where a defendant does not "inten[d] to submit to the power of a sovereign" and cannot "be said to have targeted the forum." But what do those standards mean when a company targets the world by selling products from its Web site? And does it matter if, instead of shipping the products directly, a company consigns the products through an intermediary (say, Amazon.com) who then receives and fulfills the orders? And what if the company markets its products through popup advertisements that it knows will be viewed in a forum? Those issues have serious commercial consequences but are totally absent in this case. . . .

GINSBURG, J., with whom SOTOMAYOR, J., and KAGAN, J., join, dissenting.

A foreign industrialist seeks to develop a market in the United States for machines it manufactures. It hopes to derive substantial revenue from sales it makes to United States purchasers. Where in the United States buyers reside does not matter to this manufacturer. Its goal is simply to sell as much as it can, wherever it can. It excludes no region or State from the market it wishes to reach. But, all things considered, it prefers to avoid products liability litigation in the United States. To that end, it engages a U.S. distributor to ship its machines stateside. Has it succeeded in escaping personal jurisdiction in a State where one of its products is sold and causes injury or even death to a local user?

Under this Court's pathmarking precedent in *International Shoe Co. v. Washington* and subsequent decisions, one would expect the answer to be unequivocally, "No." But instead, six Justices of this Court, in divergent opinions, tell us that the manufacturer has avoided the jurisdiction of our state courts, except perhaps in States where its products are sold in sizeable quantities. Inconceivable as it may have seemed yesterday, the splintered majority today "turn[s] the clock back to the days before modern long-arm statutes when a manufacturer, to avoid being haled into court where a user is injured, need only Pilate-like wash its hands of a product by having independent distributors market it." Weintraub, A Map Out of the Personal Jurisdiction Labyrinth, 28 U.C. Davis L. Rev. 531, 555 (1995).

I

On October 11, 2001, a three-ton metal shearing machine severed four fingers on Robert Nicastro's right hand. Alleging that the machine was a dangerous product defectively made, Nicastro sought compensation from the machine's manufacturer, J. McIntyre Machinery Ltd. (McIntyre UK). Established in 1872 as a United Kingdom corporation, and headquartered in Nottingham, England, McIntyre UK "designs, develops and manufactures a complete range of equipment for metal recycling." The company's product line, as advertised on McIntyre UK's Web site, includes "metal shears, balers, cable and can recycling equipment, furnaces, casting equipment and . . . the world's best aluminum dross processing and cooling system." McIntyre UK holds both United States and European patents on its technology.

The machine that injured Nicastro, a "McIntyre Model 640 Shear," sold in the United States for $24,900 in 1995, and features a "massive cutting capacity." According to McIntyre UK's product brochure, the machine is "use[d] throughout the [w]orld." McIntyre UK represented in the brochure that, by "incorporat[ing] off-the-shelf hydraulic parts from suppliers with international sales outlets," the 640 Shear's design guarantees serviceability "wherever [its customers] may be based." The instruction manual advises "owner[s] and operators of a 640 Shear [to] make themselves aware of [applicable health and safety regulations]," including "the American National Standards Institute Regulations (USA) for the use of Scrap Metal Processing Equipment."

Nicastro operated the 640 Shear in the course of his employment at Curcio Scrap Metal (CSM) in Saddle Brook, New Jersey. "New Jersey has long been a hotbed of scrap-metal businesses. . . ." In 2008, New Jersey recycling facilities processed 2,013,730 tons of scrap iron, steel, aluminum, and other metals—more than any other State—outpacing Kentucky, its nearest competitor, by nearly 30 percent.

CSM's owner, Frank Curcio, "first heard of [McIntyre UK's] machine while attending an Institute of Scrap Metal Industries [(ISRI)] convention in Las Vegas in 1994 or 1995, where [McIntyre UK] was an exhibitor." ISRI "presents the world's largest scrap recycling industry trade show each year." The event attracts "owners

[and] managers of scrap processing companies" and others "interested in seeing—and purchasing—new equipment." According to ISRI, more than 3,000 potential buyers of scrap processing and recycling equipment attend its annual conventions, "primarily because th[e] exposition provides them with the most comprehensive industry-related shopping experience concentrated in a single, convenient location."

McIntyre UK representatives attended every ISRI convention from 1990 through 2005. These annual expositions were held in diverse venues across the United States; in addition to Las Vegas, conventions were held 1990-2005 in New Orleans, Orlando, San Antonio, and San Francisco. McIntyre UK's president, Michael Pownall, regularly attended ISRI conventions. He attended ISRI's Las Vegas convention the year CSM's owner first learned of, and saw, the 640 Shear. McIntyre UK exhibited its products at ISRI trade shows, the company acknowledged, hoping to reach "anyone interested in the machine from anywhere in the United States."

Although McIntyre UK's U.S. sales figures are not in the record, it appears that for several years in the 1990's, earnings from sales of McIntyre UK products in the United States "ha[d] been good" in comparison to "the rest of the world." In response to interrogatories, McIntyre UK stated that its commissioning engineer had installed the company's equipment in several States—Illinois, Iowa, Kentucky, Virginia, and Washington.

From at least 1995 until 2001, McIntyre UK retained an Ohio-based company, McIntyre Machinery America, Ltd. (McIntyre America), "as its exclusive distributor for the entire United States." Though similarly named, the two companies were separate and independent entities with "no commonality of ownership or management." In invoices and other written communications, McIntyre America described itself as McIntyre UK's national distributor, "America's Link" to "Quality Metal Processing Equipment" from England.

In a November 23, 1999 letter to McIntyre America, McIntyre UK's president spoke plainly about the manufacturer's objective in authorizing the exclusive distributorship: "All we wish to do is sell our products in the [United] States—and get paid!" Notably, McIntyre America was concerned about U.S. litigation involving McIntyre UK products, in which the distributor had been named as a defendant. McIntyre UK counseled McIntyre America to respond personally to the litigation, but reassured its distributor that "the product was built and designed by McIntyre Machinery in the UK and the buck stops here—if there's something wrong with the machine."

Over the years, McIntyre America distributed several McIntyre UK products to U.S. customers, including, in addition to the 640 Shear, McIntyre UK's "Niagara" and "Tardis" systems, wire strippers, and can machines. In promoting McIntyre UK's products at conventions and demonstration sites and in trade journal advertisements, McIntyre America looked to McIntyre UK for direction and guidance. To achieve McIntyre UK's objective, i.e., "to sell [its] machines to customers throughout the United States," "the two companies [were acting] closely in concert with each other." McIntyre UK never instructed its distributor to avoid certain States or regions of the country; rather, as just noted, the manufacturer engaged McIntyre America to attract customers "from anywhere in the United States."

In sum, McIntyre UK's regular attendance and exhibitions at ISRI conventions was surely a purposeful step to reach customers for its products "anywhere in the United States." At least as purposeful was McIntyre UK's engagement of McIntyre

America as the conduit for sales of McIntyre UK's machines to buyers "throughout the United States." Given McIntyre UK's endeavors to reach and profit from the United States market as a whole, Nicastro's suit, I would hold, has been brought in a forum entirely appropriate for the adjudication of his claim. He alleges that McIntyre UK's shear machine was defectively designed or manufactured and, as a result, caused injury to him at his workplace. The machine arrived in Nicastro's New Jersey workplace not randomly or fortuitously, but as a result of the U.S. connections and distribution system that McIntyre UK deliberately arranged.[3] On what sensible view of the allocation of adjudicatory authority could the place of Nicastro's injury within the United States be deemed off limits for his products liability claim against a foreign manufacturer who targeted the United States (including all the States that constitute the Nation) as the territory it sought to develop?

II

. . . [I]n *International Shoe* itself, and decisions thereafter, the Court has made plain that legal fictions, notably "presence" and "implied consent," should be discarded, for they conceal the actual bases on which jurisdiction rests. "[T]he relationship among the defendant, the forum, and the litigation" determines whether due process permits the exercise of personal jurisdiction over a defendant, and "fictions of implied consent" or "corporate presence" do not advance the proper inquiry . . . .

This case is illustrative of marketing arrangements for sales in the United States common in today's commercial world. A foreign-country manufacturer engages a U.S. company to promote and distribute the manufacturer's products, not in any particular State, but anywhere and everywhere in the United States the distributor can attract purchasers. The product proves defective and injures a user in the State where the user lives or works . . . .

The modern approach to jurisdiction over corporations and other legal entities, ushered in by *International Shoe*, gave prime place to reason and fairness. Is it not fair and reasonable, given the mode of trading of which this case is an example, to require the international seller to defend at the place its products cause injury? Do not litigational convenience and choice-of-law considerations point in that direction? On what measure of reason and fairness can it be considered undue to require McIntyre UK to defend in New Jersey as an incident of its efforts to develop a market for its industrial machines anywhere and everywhere in the United States? Is not the burden on McIntyre UK to defend in New Jersey fair, *i.e.*, a reasonable cost of transacting business internationally, in comparison to the burden on Nicastro to go to

---

3. McIntyre UK resisted Nicastro's efforts to determine whether other McIntyre machines had been sold to New Jersey customers. McIntyre did allow that McIntyre America "may have resold products it purchased from [McIntyre UK] to a buyer in New Jersey," but said it kept no record of the ultimate destination of machines it shipped to its distributor. A private investigator engaged by Nicastro found at least one McIntyre UK machine, of unspecified type, in use in New Jersey. But McIntyre UK objected that the investigator's report was "unsworn and based upon hearsay." Moreover, McIntyre UK maintained, no evidence showed that the machine the investigator found in New Jersey had been "sold into [that State]."

Nottingham, England to gain recompense for an injury he sustained using McIntyre's product at his workplace in Saddle Brook, New Jersey?

McIntyre UK dealt with the United States as a single market. Like most foreign manufacturers, it was concerned not with the prospect of suit in State X as opposed to State Y, but rather with its subjection to suit anywhere in the United States . . . . If McIntyre UK is answerable in the United States at all, is it not "perfectly appropriate to permit the exercise of that jurisdiction . . . at the place of injury"? . . .

* * *

For the reasons stated, I would hold McIntyre UK answerable in New Jersey for the harm Nicastro suffered at his workplace in that State using McIntyre UK's shearing machine. While I dissent from the Court's judgment, I take heart that the plurality opinion does not speak for the Court, for that opinion would take a giant step away from the "notions of fair play and substantial justice" underlying *International Shoe*, 326 U.S., at 316, 66 S. Ct. 154 (internal quotation marks omitted).

Notes and Problems

---

1. The plurality opinion starts by saying that it hopes to clear up confusion created by the plurality opinion in a preceding case, *Asahi Metal*. It might have done so had the plurality been a majority. But, as Justice Ginsburg's dissent points out, Justice Kennedy's opinion got only four votes—another plurality. So the case stands for the proposition that six Justices thought that jurisdiction did not lie under the circumstances described—and that four of those six would reject the "foreseeability" principle set forth by four Justices in *Asahi*.

   a. Do the six Justices that agreed on the outcome of the case (no personal jurisdiction) agree about anything else?

   b. Do the concurring Justices—Breyer and Alito—agree with the dissent about anything? They write: "There may well have been other facts that Mr. Nicastro could have demonstrated in support of jurisdiction. And the dissent considers some of those facts." Might this suggest that Breyer and Alito would have voted in favor of personal jurisdiction had the plaintiff introduced the facts that Ginsburg describes in her dissent? If so, a majority of Justices would have found personal jurisdiction.

2. What are the plurality and the concurrence disagreeing about, if they agree on the result? (The answer matters to anyone litigating future such cases or trying to arrange her business affairs.)

   a. The plurality wants to organize all personal jurisdiction (except for intentional torts) on the basis of consent, real or implied. Is that a convincing reading of the cases since *International Shoe*?

   b. Justices Breyer and Alito resist the plurality's generalizations. Why?

3. Why did the plaintiff care whether it obtained jurisdiction over the English manufacturer?

4. The record indicated that the now-bankrupt distributor had been incorporated in Ohio, where the English manufacturer communicated with the distributor on various matters. Did the plaintiff make a mistake by suing in New Jersey rather than in Ohio, where the manufacturer's contacts had been more extensive?

5. It is both a strength and a weakness of contemporary jurisdictional doctrine that the broad categories of *International Shoe* require contextualization in differing circumstances. Two lines of case law—one dealing with intentional torts, the other with the Internet—come together in the next case.

   a. Suppose I stand on the border of State *A* and throw a rock aimed at someone in State *B*. Am I subject to jurisdiction in State *B*? Yes, says a series of cases, applying the tort version of "purposeful availment": Where defendant engages in behavior designed to inflict harm in another jurisdiction, he is subject to jurisdiction there. E.g., Calder v. Jones, 465 U.S. 783 (1984).

   b. What if I create a website in State *A* that causes harm in State *B*? Early cases confronting this question quickly concluded that the wide availability of the Internet did not mean that the creator of a website was subject to jurisdiction wherever the site could be viewed. But cases also have held that if the site was "active"—if the defendant who created the site entered into contracts and exchanged files and other information over the site, he was "purposefully availing" himself of that state and thus subject to jurisdiction there. Zippo Manufacturing Co. v. Zippo Dot Com, Inc., 952 F. Supp. 1119 (W.D. Pa. 1997).

Abdouch v. Lopez
285 Neb. 718, 829 N.W.2d 662 (2013)

McCormack, J.

I. Nature of Case

Helen Abdouch filed suit against an out-of-state defendant, Ken Lopez, individually and as owner and operator of his company, Ken Lopez Bookseller (KLB), under Neb. Rev. Stat. §20-202 (Reissue 2012) for violating her privacy rights by using an inscription in Abdouch's stolen copy of a book entitled "Revolutionary Road" to advertise on the KLB rare books Web site. . . . Lopez and KLB filed, and the district court sustained, a motion to dismiss for lack of personal jurisdiction. Abdouch now appeals.

II. Background

Abdouch is a resident of Omaha, Nebraska. In 1960, Abdouch was the executive secretary of the Nebraska presidential campaign of John F. Kennedy. In 1963,

Abdouch received a copy of the book, which was inscribed to her by the late author Richard Yates. The inscription stated: "For Helen Abdouch—with admiration and best wishes. Dick Yates. 8/19/63." At some time not specified by the record, Abdouch's inscribed copy of the book was stolen. Lopez and his company, KLB, bought the book in 2009 from a seller in Georgia and sold it that same year to a customer not in Nebraska. In 2011, Abdouch, who does not own a computer, learned from a friend that Lopez had used the inscription in the book for advertising purposes on his Web site, http://www.lopezbooks.com. The commercial advertisement had been used with the word "SOLD" on the Web site for more than 3 years after the book was sold. The advertisement associated with a picture of the inscription stated in relevant part:

> This copy is *inscribed by Yates*: "For Helen Abdouch—with admiration and best wishes. Dick Yates. 8/19/63." Yates had worked as a speech writer for Robert Kennedy when Kennedy served as Attorney General; Abdouch was the executive secretary of the Nebraska (John F.) Kennedy organization when Robert Kennedy was campaign manager. The book is cocked; the boards are stained; the text is clean. A very good copy in a near fine, spine-tanned dust jacket. A scarce book, and it is extremely uncommon to find this advance issue of it signed. Given the date of the inscription—that is, during JFK's Presidency—and the connection between writer and recipient, it's reasonable to suppose this was an author's copy, presented to Abdouch by Yates. [# 028096] SOLD

Lopez is the owner and sole proprietor of KLB, which is a rare book business based in Hadley, Massachusetts. KLB buys and sells rare books and manuscripts. KLB sells these books and manuscripts through published catalogs and through the Web site. Generally, the Web site contains KLB's inventory of rare books and manuscripts. Individuals that visit the Web site can browse and search the inventory. If individuals or entities choose to, they can purchase through the Web site.

In addition to selling books through catalogs and online, KLB attends and has exhibits at various antiquarian bookfairs. Over the past 25 years, Lopez and/or KLB have attended and exhibited at an estimated 300 to 400 bookfairs in various locations within the United States, as well as overseas. Lopez and KLB have never exhibited at or attended a book fair in Nebraska.

KLB has an active mailing list for its catalogs of approximately 1,000 individuals and entities. Among that list, only two are located in Nebraska. According to Lopez' affidavit, KLB did not solicit the two Nebraska members; rather, the two individuals solicited contact with KLB and requested to be placed on the mailing list. Neither of these two individuals has any connection to the claims at issue in this lawsuit.

Neither Lopez nor KLB is registered to do business in Nebraska in any capacity. Lopez and KLB do not own or lease real estate in Nebraska, do not maintain an office in Nebraska, and have never conducted or attended meetings in Nebraska. Neither Lopez nor KLB has paid any Nebraska sales tax.

Lopez and KLB do not advertise in any publication that is published in or that otherwise originates from Nebraska. Lopez and KLB do not advertise in any publication that specifically targets potential customers in Nebraska. Beyond the two customers on the mailing list, Lopez and KLB do not target or reach out to customers or potential customers in Nebraska in any way.

The amount of contact with Nebraska and Nebraska residents is also demonstrated by KLB's sales. KLB's total sales for 2009 through 2011 were approximately $3.9 million. In 2009, KLB sold three books to a single Nebraska customer, earning a total of $76. In 2010, KLB sold three books to two Nebraska customers for $239.87. In 2011, two books were sold to a Nebraska customer for $299. All of these sales were initiated by the customers through the Web site.

Abdouch alleges that Lopez knew she was a resident of Nebraska when he violated her privacy. Lopez avers in his affidavit that he did not know that Abdouch was a resident of Nebraska until in or around June 2011, at which time he was contacted by someone and told that Abdouch lived in Nebraska. In Abdouch's affidavit, she counters that she has been informed that she can be easily found and identified as a Nebraska resident on the Internet and that there are only two people named "Helen Abdouch" in the entire United States.

After discovering Lopez and KLB's use of the inscribed book as an advertisement, Abdouch brought suit pursuant to §20-202 against Lopez and KLB for violating her vigilantly protected right of privacy. In a relevant part of the complaint, she alleged:

5. That . . . Lopez did an internet search for "Helen Abdouch" and found a brief reference to her as "executive secretary of the Nebraska (John F.) Kennedy campaign" in an October 10, 1960, *Time Magazine* article entitled: "DEMOCRATS: Little Brother is Watching" based on an interview with Robert F. Kennedy, campaign manager of his brother's John F. Kennedy's presidential campaign.

6. That based on this article, . . . Lopez wrote an ad for the sale of Abdouch's book on his online catalogue linking [Abdouch] to Yates through the Kennedy connection . . . and placed on [the KLB Web site] at www.lopezbooks.com and which was "broadcast" or sent out over the world wide web.

7. That by his own admission, . . . Lopez did not search the internet to determine whether . . . Abdouch was still alive and assumed she was dead so he made no further effort to get her permission.

Lopez and KLB filed a motion to dismiss for lack of personal jurisdiction, alleging that they do not have sufficient contacts with Nebraska for purposes of personal jurisdiction and have not purposefully availed themselves of the benefits and protections of the forum state. The district court granted the motion and dismissed the case. . . .

V. Analysis

Abdouch argues that the district court erred in finding that the State lacked personal jurisdiction over Lopez and KLB. Abdouch argues that Lopez and KLB's active Web site deliberately targeted Abdouch with tortious conduct. She alleges these contacts are sufficient to create the necessary minimum contacts for specific jurisdiction. [The court concludes that Nebraska's long-arm statute "extends Nebraska's jurisdiction over nonresidents having any contact with or maintaining any relation to this state as far as the U.S. Constitution permits." Note that state long-arm statutes are discussed infra page 177.] . . .

A. "Sliding Scale" Test

The Internet and its interaction with personal jurisdiction over a nonresident is an issue of first impression for this court. . . . [T]he Eighth Circuit, as well as the majority of circuits, has adopted the analytical framework set forth in *Zippo Mfg. Co. v. Zippo Dot Com., Inc.*, for internet jurisdiction cases. In that case, Zippo Manufacturing Company [which made cigarette lighters] filed a complaint in Pennsylvania against nonresident Zippo Dot Com, Inc.[, a news service], alleging causes of action under the federal Trademark Act of 1946. Zippo Dot Com's contact with Pennsylvania consisted of over 3,000 Pennsylvania residents subscribing to its Web site. The district court in *Zippo Mfg. Co.* famously created a "sliding scale" test that considers a Web site's interactivity and the nature of the commercial activities conducted over the Internet to determine whether the courts have personal jurisdiction over nonresident defendants. The court in *Zippo Mfg. Co.* explained the "sliding scale" as follows:

> At one end of the spectrum are situations where a defendant clearly does business over the Internet. If the defendant enters into contracts with residents of a foreign jurisdiction that involve the knowing and repeated transmission of computer files over the Internet, personal jurisdiction is proper. . . . At the opposite end are situations where a defendant has simply posted information on an Internet Web site which is accessible to users in foreign jurisdictions. A passive Web site that does little more than make information available to those who are interested in it is not grounds for the exercise [of] personal jurisdiction. . . . The middle ground is occupied by interactive Web sites where a user can exchange information with the host computer. In these cases, the exercise of jurisdiction is determined by examining the level of interactivity and commercial nature of the exchange of information that occurs on the Web site.

The district court held that Pennsylvania had personal jurisdiction over Zippo Dot Com and the causes of action. In doing so, the district court made two important findings. First, the district court found that the Zippo Dot Com Web site was a highly interactive commercial Web site. Second, and more important, the district court found that the trademark infringement causes of action were related to the business contacts with customers in Pennsylvania.

In the case at hand, it is evident that the Web site is interactive under the *Zippo Mfg. Co.* sliding scale test. In his affidavit, Lopez admits that customers can browse and purchase books from the online inventory. Lopez admits that he has two customers in Nebraska who are on the mailing list for KLB's catalogs. He admits that from 2009 through 2011, a total of $614.87 in sales from the Web site was made to Nebraska residents out of an estimated $3.9 million in total sales.

But, beyond the minimal Web site sales to Nebraska residents and mailing catalogs to two Nebraska residents, Lopez' and KLB's contacts with Nebraska are nonexistent. Lopez and KLB do not own, lease, or rent land in Nebraska. They have never advertised directly in Nebraska, participated in bookfairs in Nebraska, or attended meetings in Nebraska, and neither has paid sales tax in Nebraska.

Furthermore, the Seventh Circuit has recently stated that when "the plaintiff's claims are for intentional torts, the inquiry focuses on whether the conduct underlying the claims was purposely directed at the forum state." The reason for requiring purposeful direction is to "'ensure that an out-of-state defendant is not bound to appear to account for merely "random, fortuitous, or attenuated contacts" with the forum state.'" Here, Abdouch's cause of action is an intentional tort based on Nebraska's privacy statute. There is no evidence, as discussed in greater detail later in the opinion, that Lopez and KLB purposefully directed the advertisement at Nebraska. Further, there is no evidence that Lopez and KLB intended to invade Abdouch's privacy in the State of Nebraska. Rather, the limited Internet sales appear to be random, fortuitous, and attenuated contacts with Nebraska.

Therefore, although Lopez and KLB's Web site is highly interactive, all of the contacts created by the Web site with the State of Nebraska are unrelated to Abdouch's cause of action.

B. *Calder* Effects Test

Abdouch argues that the effects test formulated by the U.S. Supreme Court in *Calder v. Jones* creates personal jurisdiction over Lopez and KLB, because Lopez and KLB aimed their tortious conduct at Abdouch and the State of Nebraska. In *Calder,* two Florida residents participated in the publication of an article about a California resident who brought a libel action in California against the Florida residents. Both defendants asserted that as Florida residents, they were not subject to the jurisdiction of the California court in which the libel action was filed. The Supreme Court rejected the defendants' argument and noted that the defendants were not charged with mere untargeted negligence. Rather, their intentional, and allegedly tortious, actions were expressly aimed at California. Petitioner[s] wrote and . . . edited an article that they knew would have a potentially devastating impact upon respondent. And they knew that the brunt of that injury would be felt by respondent in the State in which she lives and works and in which the National Enquirer [where the article was published] has its largest circulation. Under the circumstances, petitioners must "reasonably anticipate being haled into court there" to answer for the truth of the statements made in their article.

In coming to its holding, the U.S. Supreme Court created a test, now known as the *Calder* effects test, which has been explained by the Eighth Circuit [in *Johnson v. Arden*]:

> "[A] defendant's tortious acts can serve as a source of personal jurisdiction only where the plaintiff makes a prima facie showing that the defendant's acts (1) were intentional, (2) were uniquely or expressly aimed at the forum state, and (3) caused harm, the brunt of which was suffered—and which the defendant knew was likely to be suffered—[in the forum state]."

The Third Circuit has noted that the effects test "can only be satisfied if the plaintiff can point to contacts which demonstrate that the defendant *expressly aimed* its tortious conduct at the forum, and thereby made the forum the focal point of the tortious activity." Stated another way by the Third Circuit, "the effects test asks whether the plaintiff felt the brunt of the harm in the forum state, but it also asks whether defendants *knew* that the plaintiff would suffer the harm there and whether they *aimed* their tortious conduct at that state." Similarly, the Eighth Circuit has stated that the *Calder* effects test "allows the assertion of personal jurisdiction over non-resident defendants whose acts 'are performed for the very purpose of having their consequences felt in the forum state.'"

. . . Lopez and KLB's placement of the advertisement online was directed at the entire world, without expressly aiming the posting at the State of Nebraska. Abdouch pleaded in her complaint that the advertisement was "'broadcast' or sent out over the world wide web," but Abdouch failed to plead facts that demonstrate that Nebraska residents were targeted with the advertisement. Although the advertisement does mention that "Abdouch was the executive secretary of the Nebraska (John F.) Kennedy organization," the advertisement does not expressly direct its offer of sale to Nebraska. As in *Johnson*, the mention of Nebraska here is incidental and was not included for the purposes of having the consequences felt in Nebraska. . . . Lopez did not know that Abdouch was a resident of Nebraska. He assumed that she had passed away and thus had no way of knowing that the brunt of harm would be suffered in Nebraska. Abdouch's complaint fails to demonstrate that Lopez and KLB had an intent to target and focus on Nebraska residents . . . .

VI. Conclusion

We conclude that Abdouch's complaint fails to plead facts to demonstrate that Lopez and KLB have sufficient minimum contacts with the State of Nebraska. Although the Web site used to post the advertisement is interactive, the contacts created by the Web site are unrelated to Abdouch's cause of action. Furthermore, under the *Calder* effects test, the pleadings fail to establish that Lopez and KLB expressly aimed their tortious conduct at the State of Nebraska. For these reasons, Lopez and KLB could not have anticipated being haled into a Nebraska court for their online advertisement.

WHAT'S NEW HERE?

- Doctrinally, *Abdouch* displays a court applying *International Shoe* to a new domain—the Internet. One of the virtues of *International Shoe*'s open-ended formulation is that it enables courts to apply it to new contexts. One of its vices is that each new context will require courts to think through the analogies to other cases and situations.

- *Abdouch* displays a state court, rather than the U.S. Supreme Court, working with familiar jurisdictional doctrine. Most civil litigation occurs in state courts. Because the Due Process Clause addresses itself to states, most challenges to personal jurisdiction will be decided in state courts, with the U.S. Supreme Court granting review only occasionally. But for the most part the system assumes that state courts will faithfully apply constitutional doctrine. Because *Abdouch* is a state court decision, even though it applies and interprets a clause of the U.S. Constitution, it will have precedential value within Nebraska, but only illustrative and persuasive power elsewhere.

Notes and Problems

---

1. The opinion refers to two lines of authority.

   a. One line, flowing from the *Zippo* case, is specific to the Internet and employs the sliding scale test described in the opinion. The court finds that the Internet site is interactive, yet concludes that there is no personal jurisdiction over the defendant in Nebraska. Why?

   b. The second line draws on cases, including *Calder*, in which a defendant takes some action in State *A* that has effects in State *B*. (The classic example is standing by the state line and throwing a rock at someone in the adjacent state.) According to this line of cases, the knowledge of where the effect will occur and the intent to cause that effect will support jurisdiction. So far as you can judge, what facts would have had to be different to support a finding of jurisdiction in Nebraska?

2. The *Zippo* interactivity test has been criticized for asking not quite the right question.

   a. One criticism of the *Zippo* test is that the Internet operates differently now than it did in 1997, when *Zippo* was decided. "Virtually all websites . . . are now interactive in nature" and most "also interact with the user 'behind the scenes' through the use of 'cookies.' Thus, even a website that appears 'passive in nature' may actually be interacting with the user's data and custom-tailoring the content based on the user's identity, demographics, browsing history, and personal preferences." Kindig It Design, Inc. v. Creative Controls, Inc., 157 F. Supp. 3d 1167 (D. Utah 2016).

   b. Some have argued that the focus should not be on the extent of interactivity, but rather the features of the site that demonstrate purposeful availment of the benefits and protections of the state. According to this criticism, a site that was intensely interactive—allowing visitors to post comments and pictures, and play games, for example—might nevertheless fail to support jurisdiction if the creator of the site did not target users in the state. Conversely, a very modestly interactive site on which shoppers could order and pay for products—that in the process ascertained the address and contact information for users—would support jurisdiction for claims arising out of those orders. Persuasive?

3. The *Calder* knowledge/intent issue came before the U.S. Supreme Court in yet another guise in Walden v. Fiore, 134 S. Ct. 1115 (2014). Gina Fiore and her companion were professional gamblers. Returning from a gambling trip to Puerto Rico, they were carrying hand luggage containing $97,000 in cash, their gambling "bank" and winnings. While in the process of changing planes in Atlanta to board a flight to Nevada, they were questioned by federal Drug Enforcement Agents who seized the funds as suspected proceeds of drug trafficking. Fiore's Nevada attorney contacted the DEA and submitted various forms of evidence supporting the claim that the funds were derived from gambling, not narcotics. While these conversations were going on, Walden, the agent who had first seized the cash, drafted an allegedly false affidavit supporting an effort to have the money forfeited as the proceeds of drug sales. Fiore filed suit in federal court for the District of Nevada, alleging violations of constitutionally protected rights and seeking damages. Defendant challenged the assertion of personal jurisdiction over him, pointing out that the seizure had occurred in Georgia and defendant had no contacts with Nevada. Plaintiff countered that at the time the false affidavit was drafted, defendant knew that his action would affect her in Nevada (because he knew that was one of her residences) and that such knowledge sufficed. No, held a unanimous Court: "A forum State's exercise of jurisdiction over an out-of-state intentional tortfeasor must be based on intentional contact by the defendant that creates the necessary contacts with the forum." The opinion sought to distinguish *Calder v. Jones*, described above in *Abdouch*. In *Calder*, the *Fiore* Court pointed out, it wasn't just the plaintiff's California residence that mattered, but the phone calls to California sources for the story and the substantial sales of the tabloid in California. In *Fiore*, by contrast, the only link to Nevada was the defendant's knowledge that Nevada was one of the states in which plaintiff resided—not enough.

4. General Jurisdiction

The cases in the previous section all concern the relationship to the forum state necessary to support specific jurisdiction. For example, *Burger King* holds that Florida had jurisdiction to hear a lawsuit against Mr. Rudzewicz arising out of his dealings with Burger King. The case does not stand for the proposition that Florida could hear a lawsuit brought by Mr. Rudzewicz's Michigan neighbor claiming that his tree roots had clogged the neighbor's drains, or a suit by an Iowa motorist claiming that Rudzewicz had collided with her on a Colorado road.

Under what circumstances will defendant be subject to jurisdiction for all claims—even those without any connection to the forum state? In passing, *International Shoe* suggests that, at least for U.S. defendants, there will always be a state in which suit may be brought on all claims. For corporations, the state of incorporation will be such a forum; so will the state that is the principal place of business (if different from the state of incorporation). General Motors (GM), incorporated in Delaware and with its principal place of business in Michigan, may be sued in either of those states even for claims unrelated to its activities there. Thus an Oregon automobile owner claiming injuries due to a defectively designed GM vehicle could sue in either Michigan or Delaware. That would be true even if the vehicle had been manufactured at a GM plant in Texas, Mexico, or Germany.

A similar situation holds true for individuals. As already noted, *Milliken v. Meyer* (supra page 78) stands for the proposition that individuals can be sued in the state of their domicile for all claims. Thus a resident of Michigan could be sued there for claims arising out of an auto accident that occurred while he was vacationing in Colorado.

The states of domicile (for individuals) and incorporation and principal place of business (for corporations) comprise the easy instances of general jurisdiction, instances where defendants are being sued in what is self-evidently their "base of operations." In the next two cases, the Supreme Court considers whether and under what circumstances the principle of general jurisdiction extends beyond these limited bounds: not very far, it appears.

Goodyear Dunlop Tires Operations, S.A. v. Brown
564 U.S. 915 (2011)

GINSBURG, J., delivered the opinion of the Court.

This case concerns the jurisdiction of state courts over corporations organized and operating abroad. We address, in particular, this question: Are foreign subsidiaries of a United States parent corporation amenable to suit in state court on claims unrelated to any activity of the subsidiaries in the forum State?

A bus accident outside Paris that took the lives of two 13-year-old boys from North Carolina gave rise to the litigation we here consider. Attributing the accident to a defective tire manufactured in Turkey at the plant of a foreign subsidiary of The Goodyear Tire and Rubber Company (Goodyear USA), the boys' parents commenced an action for damages in a North Carolina state court; they named as defendants Goodyear USA, an Ohio corporation, and three of its subsidiaries, organized and operating, respectively, in Turkey, France, and Luxembourg. Goodyear USA, which had plants in North Carolina and regularly engaged in commercial activity there, did not contest the North Carolina court's jurisdiction over it; Goodyear USA's foreign subsidiaries, however, maintained that North Carolina lacked adjudicatory authority over them.

A state court's assertion of jurisdiction exposes defendants to the State's coercive power, and is therefore subject to review for compatibility with the Fourteenth Amendment's Due Process Clause. *International Shoe Co. v. Washington*. Opinions in the wake of the pathmarking *International Shoe* decision have differentiated between general or all-purpose jurisdiction, and specific or case-linked jurisdiction.

A court may assert general jurisdiction over foreign (sister-state or foreign-country) corporations to hear any and all claims against them when their affiliations with the State are so "continuous and systematic" as to render them essentially at home in the forum State. Specific jurisdiction, on the other hand, depends on an "affiliatio[n] between the forum and the underlying controversy," principally, activity or an occurrence that takes place in the forum State and is therefore subject to the State's regulation. von Mehren & Trautman, Jurisdiction to Adjudicate: A Suggested Analysis, 79 Harv. L. Rev. 1121, 1136 (1966) (hereinafter von Mehren & Trautman); see Brilmayer et al., A General Look at General Jurisdiction, 66 Texas L. Rev. 721, 782 (1988) (hereinafter Brilmayer). In contrast to general, all-purpose jurisdiction, specific jurisdiction is confined to adjudication of "issues deriving from, or connected with, the very controversy that establishes jurisdiction." von Mehren & Trautman 1136.

Because the episode-in-suit, the bus accident, occurred in France, and the tire alleged to have caused the accident was manufactured and sold abroad, North Carolina courts lacked specific jurisdiction to adjudicate the controversy. The North Carolina Court of Appeals so acknowledged. Were the foreign subsidiaries nonetheless amenable to general jurisdiction in North Carolina courts? Confusing or blending general and specific jurisdictional inquiries, the North Carolina courts answered yes. Some of the tires made abroad by Goodyear's foreign subsidiaries, the North Carolina Court of Appeals stressed, had reached North Carolina through "the stream of commerce"; that connection, the Court of Appeals believed, gave North Carolina courts the handle needed for the exercise of general jurisdiction over the foreign corporations.

A connection so limited between the forum and the foreign corporation, we hold, is an inadequate basis for the exercise of general jurisdiction. . . .

Endeavoring to give specific content to the "fair play and substantial justice" concept, the Court in *International Shoe* classified cases involving out-of-state corporate defendants. First, as in *International Shoe* itself, jurisdiction unquestionably could be asserted where the corporation's in-state activity is "continuous and systematic" and *that activity gave rise to the episode-in-suit.* Further, the Court observed, the commission of certain "single or occasional acts" in a State may be sufficient to render a corporation answerable in that State with respect to those acts, though not with respect to matters unrelated to the forum connections. The heading courts today use to encompass these two *International Shoe* categories is "specific jurisdiction." See von Mehren & Trautman 1144-1163. Adjudicatory authority is "specific" when the suit "aris[es] out of or relate[s] to the defendant's contacts with the forum." . . .

In only two decisions postdating *International Shoe* has this Court considered whether an out-of-state corporate defendant's in-state contacts were sufficiently "continuous and systematic" to justify the exercise of general jurisdiction over claims unrelated to those contacts: Perkins v. Benguet Consol. Mining Co., 342 U.S. 437 (1952) (general jurisdiction appropriately exercised over Philippine corporation sued in Ohio, where the company's affairs were overseen during World War II); and *Helicopteros* (helicopter owned by Colombian corporation crashed in Peru; survivors of U.S. citizens who died in the crash, the Court held, could not maintain wrongful-death actions against the Colombian corporation in Texas, for the corporation's helicopter purchases and purchase-linked activity in Texas were insufficient to subject it to Texas court's general jurisdiction).

B

To justify the exercise of general jurisdiction over petitioners, the North Carolina courts relied on the petitioners' placement of their tires in the "stream of commerce." The stream-of-commerce metaphor has been invoked frequently in lower court decisions permitting "jurisdiction in products liability cases in which the product has traveled through an extensive chain of distribution before reaching the ultimate consumer." 18 W. Fletcher, Cyclopedia of the Law of Corporations §8640.40, p. 133 (rev. ed. 2007). Typically, in such cases, a nonresident defendant, acting *outside* the forum, places in the stream of commerce a product that ultimately causes harm *inside* the forum. . . .

The North Carolina court's stream-of-commerce analysis elided the essential difference between case-specific and all-purpose (general) jurisdiction. Flow of a manufacturer's products into the forum, we have explained, may bolster an affiliation germane to *specific* jurisdiction. See, e.g., *World-Wide Volkswagen* (where "the sale of a product . . . is not simply an isolated occurrence, but arises from the efforts of the manufacturer or distributor to serve . . . the market for its product in [several] States, it is not unreasonable to subject it to suit in one of those States if its allegedly defective merchandise *has there been the source of injury to its owner or to others*" (emphasis added)). But ties serving to bolster the exercise of specific jurisdiction do not warrant a determination that, based on those ties, the forum has *general* jurisdiction over a defendant. . . .

A corporation's "continuous activity of some sorts within a state," *International Shoe* instructed, "is not enough to support the demand that the corporation be amenable to suits unrelated to that activity." Our 1952 decision in *Perkins v. Benguet Consol. Mining Co.* remains "[t]he textbook case of general jurisdiction appropriately exercised over a foreign corporation that has not consented to suit in the forum."

Sued in Ohio, the defendant in *Perkins* was a Philippine mining corporation that had ceased activities in the Philippines during World War II. To the extent that the company was conducting any business during and immediately after the Japanese occupation of the Philippines, it was doing so in Ohio: the corporation's president maintained his office there, kept the company files in that office, and supervised from the Ohio office "the necessarily limited wartime activities of the company." Although the claim-in-suit did not arise in Ohio, this Court ruled that it would not violate due process for Ohio to adjudicate the controversy. . . .

Measured against *Helicopteros* and *Perkins*, North Carolina is not a forum in which it would be permissible to subject petitioners to general jurisdiction. Unlike the defendant in *Perkins*, whose sole wartime business activity was conducted in Ohio, petitioners are in no sense at home in North Carolina. Their attenuated connections to the State, fall far short of the "the continuous and systematic general business contacts" necessary to empower North Carolina to entertain suit against them on claims unrelated to anything that connects them to the State. *Helicopteros*, 466 U.S., at 416, 104 S. Ct. 1868, 80 L. Ed. 2d 404.[5] . . .

For the reasons stated, the judgment of the North Carolina Court of Appeals is *Reversed*.

---

5. As earlier noted, the North Carolina Court of Appeals invoked the State's "well-recognized interest in providing a forum in which its citizens are able to seek redress for injuries that they have sustained." But "[g]eneral jurisdiction to adjudicate has in [United States] practice never been based on the plaintiff's relationship to the forum. There is nothing in [our] law comparable to . . . article 14 of the Civil Code of France (1804) under which the French nationality of the plaintiff is a sufficient ground for jurisdiction." When a defendant's act outside the forum causes injury in the forum, by contrast, a plaintiff's residence in the forum may strengthen the case for the exercise of specific jurisdiction.

Notes and Problems

1. Take the case in pieces.
   a. As a review, focus first on why plaintiffs failed to make the case for specific jurisdiction. Recall that of the four defendants, the only ones challenging jurisdiction were three Goodyear subsidiary corporations—one each in France, Luxembourg, and Turkey. Although some of the products of each of these corporations reached North Carolina, explain why that did not suffice to give the North Carolina court specific jurisdiction.
   b. Now turn to the plaintiffs' main contention—which the Court rejected in its unanimous opinion.
      i. First, explain what it was: What was plaintiffs' argument about "general jurisdiction"?
      ii. Having articulated plaintiffs' argument, explain why it failed. One way of doing that would be to compare the facts of this case with the only case in which the Supreme Court has upheld general jurisdiction—*Perkins v. Benguet Mining.*

2. What difference does this decision make to the plaintiffs' case? The parent company, Goodyear USA, did not challenge personal jurisdiction so they are before the court. But, under the law of most states only the entity that designed, manufactured, marketed, and distributed the product would be liable, not the parent, unless the plaintiffs could show that the subsidiary was not truly operated as a separate corporation.
   a. So unless the plaintiffs could obtain jurisdiction over the foreign subsidiary in the United States they could not pursue their claim in the United States. (They could, of course, sue abroad, but that would mean forgoing a jury trial, and most other nations' discovery rules are substantially more limited than in the United States.)
   b. Suing outside the United States also has many collateral difficulties. A few examples: Most other countries bar the contingent fee, so hiring a lawyer could be difficult; many countries limit wrongful death damages to a much greater extent than in the United States; collecting a judgment can be more difficult than it is in the United States; and in many nations the loser pays the winner's attorneys' fees—making the bringing of a less-than-certain claim a risky proposition.

3. You will regularly see case-law references to general jurisdiction. But, as Prof. Mary Twitchell argues in the article cited in the opinion, most of those references come in cases in which a court says something resembling that said in *Goodyear*: There's no specific jurisdiction in this case and, though plaintiff argues valiantly, there's no general jurisdiction either. One can see this pattern at work in the next case, in which the plaintiffs ignored the subsidiaries and took direct aim at the parent. A word of introduction about the federal statute that formed the basis for the substantive claim may help. The Alien

Tort Statute, 28 U.S.C. §1350, grants jurisdiction to the federal courts for "civil action[s] by an alien for a tort only, committed in violation of the law of nations or a treaty of the United States." Enacted in 1789, apparently out of the embarrassed discovery that the young federal courts lacked jurisdiction to hear a civil claim arising out of an assault on a diplomat by a foreign national, the statute lacks both a clarifying legislative history or much case law. In recent decades, it served as a vehicle for those seeking to redress abuses of human rights occurring outside the United States. The Supreme Court limited the reach of the Alien Tort Statute in Kiobel v. Royal Dutch Petroleum Co., 133 S. Ct. 1659 (2013) (invoking presumption that U.S. statutes were not intended to have extra-territorial reach). The next case creates an additional barrier to liability under the Alien Tort Statute based in its analysis of the scope of general jurisdiction.

Daimler AG v. Bauman
571 U.S. 117 (2014)

GINSBURG, J., delivered the opinion of the Court.

This case concerns the authority of a court in the United States to entertain a claim brought by foreign plaintiffs against a foreign defendant based on events occurring entirely outside the United States. . . . In *Goodyear Dunlop Tires Operations, S.A. v. Brown*, we addressed the distinction between general or all-purpose jurisdiction, and specific or conduct-linked jurisdiction. As to the former, we held that a court may assert jurisdiction over a foreign corporation "to hear any and all claims against [it]" only when the corporation's affiliations with the State in which suit is brought are so constant and pervasive "as to render [it] essentially at home in the forum State." Instructed by *Goodyear*, we conclude Daimler is not "at home" in California, and cannot be sued there for injuries plaintiffs attribute to MB Argentina's conduct in Argentina.

I

In 2004, plaintiffs (respondents here) filed suit in the United States District Court for the Northern District of California, alleging that MB Argentina collaborated with Argentinian state security forces to kidnap, detain, torture, and kill plaintiffs and their relatives during the military dictatorship in place there from 1976 through 1983, a period known as Argentina's "Dirty War." Based on those allegations, plaintiffs asserted claims under the Alien Tort Statute, 28 U.S.C. §1350, and the Torture Victim Protection Act of 1991, note following 28 U.S.C. §1350, as well as claims for wrongful death and intentional infliction of emotional distress under the laws of California and Argentina. The incidents recounted in the complaint center on MB Argentina's plant in Gonzalez Catan, Argentina; no part of MB Argentina's alleged collaboration with Argentinian authorities took place in California or anywhere else in the United States.

Plaintiffs' operative complaint names only one corporate defendant: Daimler, the petitioner here. Plaintiffs seek to hold Daimler vicariously liable for MB Argentina's alleged malfeasance. Daimler is a German *Aktiengesellschaft* (public stock company) that manufactures Mercedes-Benz vehicles in Germany and has its headquarters in Stuttgart. At times relevant to this case, MB Argentina was a subsidiary wholly owned by Daimler's predecessor in interest.

Daimler moved to dismiss the action for want of personal jurisdiction. Opposing the motion, plaintiffs submitted declarations and exhibits purporting to demonstrate the presence of Daimler itself in California. Alternatively, plaintiffs maintained that jurisdiction over Daimler could be founded on the California contacts of MBUSA, a distinct corporate entity that, according to plaintiffs, should be treated as Daimler's agent for jurisdictional purposes.

MBUSA, an indirect subsidiary of Daimler, is a Delaware limited liability corporation.[1] MBUSA serves as Daimler's exclusive importer and distributor in the United States, purchasing Mercedes-Benz automobiles from Daimler in Germany, then importing those vehicles, and ultimately distributing them to independent dealerships located throughout the Nation. Although MBUSA's principal place of business is in New Jersey, MBUSA has multiple California-based facilities, including a regional office in Costa Mesa, a Vehicle Preparation Center in Carson, and a Classic Center in Irvine. According to the record developed below, MBUSA is the largest supplier of luxury vehicles to the California market. In particular, over 10% of all sales of new vehicles in the United States take place in California, and MBUSA's California sales account for 2.4% of Daimler's worldwide sales.

The relationship between Daimler and MBUSA is delineated in a General Distributor Agreement, which sets forth requirements for MBUSA's distribution of Mercedes-Benz vehicles in the United States. That agreement established MBUSA as an "independent contracto[r]" that "buy[s] and sell[s] [vehicles] . . . as an independent business for [its] own account." The agreement "does not make [MBUSA] . . . a general or special agent, partner, joint venturer or employee of DAIMLERCHRYSLER or any DaimlerChrysler Group Company"; MBUSA "ha[s] no authority to make binding obligations for or act on behalf of DAIMLERCHRYSLER or any DaimlerChrysler Group Company."

After allowing jurisdictional discovery on plaintiffs' agency allegations, the District Court granted Daimler's motion to dismiss. Daimler's own affiliations with California, the court first determined, were insufficient to support the exercise of all-purpose jurisdiction over the corporation. . . . Next, the court declined to attribute MBUSA's California contacts to Daimler on an agency theory, concluding that plaintiffs failed to demonstrate that MBUSA acted as Daimler's agent. . . .

The Ninth Circuit [reversed, ruling that] the agency test was satisfied and considerations of "reasonableness" did not bar the exercise of jurisdiction. . . .

We granted certiorari to decide whether, consistent with the Due Process Clause of the Fourteenth Amendment, Daimler is amenable to suit in California courts for claims involving only foreign plaintiffs and conduct occurring entirely abroad. . . .

---

1. At times relevant to this suit, MBUSA was wholly owned by DaimlerChrysler North America Holding Corporation, a Daimler subsidiary.

III

[The opinion recounted the emergence of the distinction between general and specific jurisdiction in the case law.]

Since *International Shoe*, "specific jurisdiction has become the centerpiece of modern jurisdiction theory, while general jurisdiction [has played] a reduced role." . . . Our subsequent decisions [since *International Shoe*] have continued to bear out the prediction that "specific jurisdiction will come into sharper relief and form a considerably more significant part of the scene."[7] . . .

Most recently, in *Goodyear*, we answered the question: "Are foreign subsidiaries of a United States parent corporation amenable to suit in state court on claims unrelated to any activity of the subsidiaries in the forum State?" . . .

As is evident from *Perkins*, *Helicopteros*, and *Goodyear*, general and specific jurisdiction have followed markedly different trajectories post-*International Shoe*. Specific jurisdiction has been cut loose from *Pennoyer*'s sway, but we have declined to stretch general jurisdiction beyond limits traditionally recognized. As this Court has increasingly trained on the "relationship among the defendant, the forum, and the litigation," *Shaffer*, *i.e.*, specific jurisdiction, general jurisdiction has come to occupy a less dominant place in the contemporary scheme.

IV

With this background, we turn directly to the question whether Daimler's affiliations with California are sufficient to subject it to the general (all-purpose) personal jurisdiction of that State's courts. In the proceedings below, the parties agreed on, or failed to contest, certain points we now take as given. Plaintiffs have never attempted to fit this case into the *specific* jurisdiction category. Nor did plaintiffs challenge on appeal the District Court's holding that Daimler's own contacts with California were, by themselves, too sporadic to justify the exercise of general jurisdiction. While

---

7. See, e.g., Asahi Metal Industry Co. v. Superior Court of Cal., Solano Cty., 480 U.S. 102, 112 (1987) (opinion of O'Connor, J.) (specific jurisdiction may lie over a foreign defendant that places a product into the "stream of commerce" while also "designing the product for the market in the forum State, advertising in the forum State, establishing channels for providing regular advice to customers in the forum State, or marketing the product through a distributor who has agreed to serve as the sales agent in the forum State"); World-Wide Volkswagen Corp. v. Woodson, 444 U.S. 286, 297 (1980) ("[I]f the sale of a product of a manufacturer or distributor such as Audi or Volkswagen is not simply an isolated occurrence, but arises from the efforts of the manufacturer or distributor to serve, directly or indirectly, the market for its product in other States, it is not unreasonable to subject it to suit in one of those States if its allegedly defective merchandise has there been the source of injury to its owner or to others."); Calder v. Jones, 465 U.S. 783, 789-790 (1984) (California court had specific jurisdiction to hear suit brought by California plaintiff where Florida-based publisher of a newspaper having its largest circulation in California published an article allegedly defaming the complaining Californian; under those circumstances, defendants "must 'reasonably anticipate being haled into [a California] court'"); Keeton v. Hustler Magazine, Inc., 465 U.S. 770, 780-781 (1984) (New York resident may maintain suit for libel in New Hampshire state court against California-based magazine that sold 10,000 to 15,000 copies in New Hampshire each month; as long as the defendant "continuously and deliberately exploited the New Hampshire market," it could reasonably be expected to answer a libel suit there).

plaintiffs ultimately persuaded the Ninth Circuit to impute MBUSA's California contacts to Daimler on an agency theory, at no point have they maintained that MBUSA is an alter ego of Daimler . . . .

Daimler, on the other hand, failed to object below to plaintiffs' assertion that the California courts could exercise all-purpose jurisdiction over MBUSA.[12] . . . We will assume then, for purposes of this decision only, that MBUSA qualifies as at home in California.

A

[The Court describes and criticizes the Ninth Circuit's conclusion that MBUSA acted as Daimler's agent for jurisdictional purposes.]

B

Even if we were to assume that MBUSA is at home in California, and further to assume MBUSA's contacts are imputable to Daimler, there would still be no basis to subject Daimler to general jurisdiction in California, for Daimler's slim contacts with the State hardly render it at home there.

Goodyear made clear that only a limited set of affiliations with a forum will render a defendant amenable to all-purpose jurisdiction there. "For an individual, the paradigm forum for the exercise of general jurisdiction is the individual's domicile; for a corporation, it is an equivalent place, one in which the corporation is fairly regarded as at home." . . . (citing Brilmayer et al., A General Look at General Jurisdiction, 66 Texas L. Rev. 721, 728 (1988)). With respect to a corporation, the place of incorporation and principal place of business are "paradig[m] . . . bases for general jurisdiction." . . . See also Twitchell, 101 Harv. L. Rev., at 633. Those affiliations have the virtue of being unique—that is, each ordinarily indicates only one place—as well as easily ascertainable. . . .

Goodyear did not hold that a corporation may be subject to general jurisdiction *only* in a forum where it is incorporated or has its principal place of business; it simply typed those places paradigm all-purpose forums. Plaintiffs would have us look beyond the exemplar bases *Goodyear* identified, and approve the exercise of general jurisdiction in every State in which a corporation "engages in a substantial, continuous, and systematic course of business." That formulation, we hold, is unacceptably grasping. . . .

Accordingly, the inquiry under *Goodyear* is not whether a foreign corporation's in-forum contacts can be said to be in some sense "continuous and systematic," it is whether that corporation's "affiliations with the State are so 'continuous and systematic' as to render [it] essentially at home in the forum State."[19] . . .

---

12. MBUSA is not a defendant in this case.

19. We do not foreclose the possibility that in an exceptional case, see, *e.g., Perkins*, described *supra*, a corporation's operations in a forum other than its formal place of incorporation or principal place of business may be so substantial and of such a nature as to render the corporation at home in that State. But this case presents no occasion to explore that question, because Daimler's activities in California plainly do not approach that level. It is one thing to hold a corporation answerable for operations in the forum State, quite another to expose it to suit on claims having no connection whatever to the forum State.

Here, neither Daimler nor MBUSA is incorporated in California, nor does either entity have its principal place of business there. If Daimler's California activities sufficed to allow adjudication of this Argentina-rooted case in California, the same global reach would presumably be available in every other State in which MBUSA's sales are sizable. Such exorbitant exercises of all-purpose jurisdiction would scarcely permit out-of-state defendants "to structure their primary conduct with some minimum assurance as to where that conduct will and will not render them liable to suit." . . .

It was therefore error for the Ninth Circuit to conclude that Daimler, even with MBUSA's contacts attributed to it, was at home in California, and hence subject to suit there on claims by foreign plaintiffs having nothing to do with anything that occurred or had its principal impact in California.

C

Finally, the transnational context of this dispute bears attention. . . .

The Ninth Circuit . . . paid little heed to the risks to international comity its expansive view of general jurisdiction posed. Other nations do not share the uninhibited approach to personal jurisdiction advanced by the Court of Appeals in this case. In the European Union, for example, a corporation may generally be sued in the nation in which it is "domiciled," a term defined to refer only to the location of the corporation's "statutory seat," "central administration," or "principal place of business." European Parliament and Council Reg. 1215/2012, Arts. 4(1), and 63(1), 2012 O. J. (L. 351) 7, 18. . . . The Solicitor General informs us, in this regard, that "foreign governments' objections to some domestic courts' expansive views of general jurisdiction have in the past impeded negotiations of international agreements on the reciprocal recognition and enforcement of judgments." . . . Considerations of international rapport thus reinforce our determination that subjecting Daimler to the general jurisdiction of courts in California would not accord with the "fair play and substantial justice" due process demands. . . .

For the reasons stated, the judgment of the United States Court of Appeals for the Ninth Circuit is

Reversed.

SOTOMAYOR, J., concurring in the judgment.

I agree with the Court's conclusion that the Due Process Clause prohibits the exercise of personal jurisdiction over Daimler in light of the unique circumstances of this case. I concur only in the judgment, however, because I cannot agree with the path the Court takes to arrive at that result.

The Court acknowledges that Mercedes-Benz USA, LLC (MBUSA), Daimler's wholly owned subsidiary, has considerable contacts with California. It has multiple facilities in the State, including a regional headquarters. Each year, it distributes in California tens of thousands of cars, the sale of which generated billions of dollars in the year this suit was brought. And it provides service and sales support to customers throughout the State. Daimler has conceded that California courts may exercise general jurisdiction over MBUSA on the basis of these contacts, and the Court assumes that MBUSA's contacts may be attributed to Daimler for the purpose of deciding whether Daimler is also subject to general jurisdiction.

Are these contacts sufficient to permit the exercise of general jurisdiction over Daimler? The Court holds that they are not, for a reason wholly foreign to our due process jurisprudence. The problem, the Court says, is not that Daimler's contacts with California are too few, but that its contacts with other forums are too many. In other words, the Court does not dispute that the presence of multiple offices, the direct distribution of thousands of products accounting for billions of dollars in sales, and continuous interaction with customers throughout a State would be enough to support the exercise of general jurisdiction over some businesses. Daimler is just not one of those businesses, the Court concludes, because its California contacts must be viewed in the context of its extensive "nationwide and worldwide" operations. In recent years, Americans have grown accustomed to the concept of multinational corporations that are supposedly "too big to fail"; today the Court deems Daimler "too big for general jurisdiction."

The Court's conclusion is wrong as a matter of both process and substance. As to process, the Court decides this case on a ground that was neither argued nor passed on below, and that Daimler raised for the first time in a footnote to its brief. As to substance, the Court's focus on Daimler's operations outside of California ignores the lodestar of our personal jurisdiction jurisprudence: A State may subject a defendant to the burden of suit if the defendant has sufficiently taken advantage of the State's laws and protections through its contacts in the State; whether the defendant has contacts elsewhere is immaterial.

Regrettably, these errors are unforced. The Court can and should decide this case on the far simpler ground that, no matter how extensive Daimler's contacts with California, that State's exercise of jurisdiction would be unreasonable given that the case involves foreign plaintiffs suing a foreign defendant based on foreign conduct, and given that a more appropriate forum is available. Because I would reverse the judgment below on this ground, I concur in the judgment only. . . .

WHAT'S NEW HERE?

- In both *Goodyear* and *Daimler*, the plaintiffs were suing on claims unrelated to the defendants' activities in the forum state. They were arguing that defendants' activities in the forum state were so substantial that they would support jurisdiction over unrelated claims—so-called general jurisdiction.
- In the years leading up to these cases, some suggested that, where the defendants' activities in the forum were extensive, they would support jurisdiction over claims unrelated to those activities. In both cases the Court rather firmly rejected that proposition.

Notes and Problems

1. To see what the case does and does not stand for, imagine that the plaintiff was a California resident injured in a Mercedes-Benz auto in Los Angeles and that the plaintiff alleged that a defect in the design or manufacture of the car caused his injuries. Assuming that MBUSA's actions are attributable to Daimler AG (the German parent company), as it was assumed in *Daimler*, the plaintiff would be able to establish personal jurisdiction over both MBUSA and Daimler AG in California. Why? Why is this factual scenario distinguishable from *Daimler AG v. Bauman*?

2. After *Goodyear* and *Daimler* when, if ever, will a corporate defendant be "at home" in a state other than that of its principal place of business or state of incorporation? Consider a hypothetical suit against Boeing Aircraft, incorporated in Delaware. For many decades, Boeing's headquarters was in the State of Washington, and almost all of its manufacturing operations occurred in Washington, where it was considered to be a core employer. It has now relocated its headquarters to Chicago, Illinois, but the bulk of its manufacturing operations continue to occur in Washington. Suppose there was an air crash involving a Boeing plane not manufactured in Washington, with suit brought in that state. Might Boeing be sufficiently "at home" there to satisfy the court's general jurisdiction test?

3. *Daimler* restates the proposition that a corporation will be subject to general jurisdiction in the state where it "has its principal place of business." As you will see, that concept recurs in several contexts—(1) in personal jurisdiction; (2) in venue (treated later in this chapter); and (3) in the context of federal diversity jurisdiction (discussed in Chapter 3). As you will see, in the latter context the U.S. Supreme Court has interpreted the relevant diversity statute to define a corporation's principal place of business as being the state where its "officers direct, control, and coordinate the corporation's activities." Hertz Corp. v. Friend, 599 U.S. 77 (2010) (infra page 225). It would be lovely, would it not, for us to be able to report that the same test also controls in the case of personal jurisdiction and venue? But we cannot: There is no definitive ruling that the same phrase means the same thing in all three settings. Just as "citizen" may mean one thing for naturalization purposes, another for getting a driver's license, and a third for in-state university tuition, it is possible that courts will give the same phrase somewhat different meanings in these contexts as well.

4. In *Daimler* the defendant's California activities had no connection to the claim. What if activities in the forum state had given rise to some—but not all—of the claims? This is the question the Supreme Court faced in the next case. Do you think it answered the question correctly?

Bristol-Myers Squibb Co. v. Superior Court

137 S. Ct. 1773 (2017)

ALITO, J., delivered the opinion of the Court.

More than 600 plaintiffs, most of whom are not California residents, filed this civil action in a California state court against Bristol-Myers Squibb Company (BMS), asserting a variety of state-law claims based on injuries allegedly caused by a BMS drug called Plavix. The California Supreme Court held that the California courts have specific jurisdiction to entertain the nonresidents' claims. We now reverse.

I

A

BMS, a large pharmaceutical company, is incorporated in Delaware and headquartered in New York, and it maintains substantial operations in both New York and New Jersey. Over 50 percent of BMS's work force in the United States is employed in those two States.

BMS also engages in business activities in other jurisdictions, including California. Five of the company's research and laboratory facilities, which employ a total of around 160 employees, are located there. BMS also employs about 250 sales representatives in California and maintains a small state-government advocacy office in Sacramento.

One of the pharmaceuticals that BMS manufactures and sells is Plavix, a prescription drug that thins the blood and inhibits blood clotting. BMS did not develop Plavix in California, did not create a marketing strategy for Plavix in California, and did not manufacture, label, package, or work on the regulatory approval of the product in California. BMS instead engaged in all of these activities in either New York or New Jersey. But BMS does sell Plavix in California. Between 2006 and 2012, it sold almost 187 million Plavix pills in the State and took in more than $900 million from those sales. This amounts to a little over one percent of the company's nationwide sales revenue.

B

A group of plaintiffs—consisting of 86 California residents and 592 residents from 33 other States—filed eight separate complaints in California Superior Court, alleging that Plavix had damaged their health. All the complaints asserted 13 claims under California law, including products liability, negligent misrepresentation, and misleading advertising claims. The nonresident plaintiffs did not allege that they obtained Plavix through California physicians or from any other California source; nor did they claim that they were injured by Plavix or were treated for their injuries in California.

Asserting lack of personal jurisdiction, BMS moved to quash service of summons on the nonresidents' claims, but the California Superior Court denied this motion, finding that the California courts had general jurisdiction over BMS "[b]ecause [it] engages in extensive activities in California." BMS unsuccessfully petitioned the State Court of Appeal for a writ of mandate, but after our decision on general jurisdiction in *Daimler AG v. Bauman* [casebook page 133], the California Supreme Court instructed the Court of Appeal "to vacate its order denying mandate and to issue an order to show cause why relief sought in the petition should not be granted."

The Court of Appeal then changed its decision on the question of general jurisdiction. Under *Daimler*, it held, general jurisdiction was clearly lacking, but it went on to find that the California courts had specific jurisdiction over the nonresidents' claims against BMS.

The California Supreme Court affirmed. The court unanimously agreed with the Court of Appeal on the issue of general jurisdiction, but the court was divided on the question of specific jurisdiction. The majority applied a "sliding scale approach to specific jurisdiction." Under this approach, "the more wide ranging the defendant's forum contacts, the more readily is shown a connection between the forum contacts and the claim." Applying this test, the majority concluded that "BMS's extensive contacts with California" permitted the exercise of specific jurisdiction "based on a less direct connection between BMS's forum activities and plaintiffs' claims than might otherwise be required." This attenuated requirement was met, the majority found, because the claims of the nonresidents were similar in several ways to the claims of the California residents (as to which specific jurisdiction was uncontested). The court noted that "[b]oth the resident and nonresident plaintiffs' claims are based on the same allegedly defective product and the assertedly misleading marketing and promotion of that product." And while acknowledging that "there is no claim that Plavix itself was designed and developed in [BMS's California research facilities]," the court thought it significant that other research was done in the State.

Three justices dissented.

II

It has long been established that the Fourteenth Amendment limits the personal jurisdiction of state courts. . . . The primary focus of our personal jurisdiction inquiry is the defendant's relationship to the forum State.

Since our seminal decision in *International Shoe*, our decisions have recognized two types of personal jurisdiction: "general" (sometimes called "all-purpose") jurisdiction and "specific" (sometimes called "case-linked") jurisdiction. *Goodyear* [casebook page 129]. "For an individual, the paradigm forum for the exercise of general jurisdiction is the individual's domicile; for a corporation, it is an equivalent place, one in which the corporation is fairly regarded as at home." *Id.* A court with general jurisdiction may hear *any* claim against that defendant, even if all the incidents underlying the claim occurred in a different State. But "only a limited set of affiliations with a forum will render a defendant amenable to" general jurisdiction in that State. *Daimler*.

Specific jurisdiction is very different. In order for a state court to exercise specific jurisdiction, "the *suit*" must "aris[e] out of or relat[e] to the defendant's contacts with the *forum*." *Id.* In other words, there must be "an affiliation between the forum and the underlying controversy, principally, [an] activity or an occurrence that takes place in the forum State and is therefore subject to the State's regulation." *Goodyear.* For this reason, "specific jurisdiction is confined to adjudication of issues deriving from, or connected with, the very controversy that establishes jurisdiction." *Ibid.* . . .

In determining whether personal jurisdiction is present, a court must consider a variety of interests. These include "the interests of the forum State and of the plaintiff in proceeding with the cause in the plaintiff's forum of choice." But the "primary concern" is "the burden on the defendant." Assessing this burden obviously requires a court to consider the practical problems resulting from litigating in the forum, but it also encompasses the more abstract matter of submitting to the coercive power of a State that may have little legitimate interest in the claims in question. As we have put it, restrictions on personal jurisdiction "are more than a guarantee of immunity from inconvenient or distant litigation. They are a consequence of territorial limitations on the power of the respective States." *Hanson,* [casebook page 87]. "[T]he States retain many essential attributes of sovereignty, including, in particular, the sovereign power to try causes in their courts. The sovereignty of each State . . . implie[s] a limitation on the sovereignty of all its sister States." *World-Wide Volkswagen,* [casebook page 100]. And at times, this federalism interest may be decisive. As we explained in *World-Wide Volkswagen,* "[e]ven if the defendant would suffer minimal or no inconvenience from being forced to litigate before the tribunals of another State; even if the forum State has a strong interest in applying its law to the controversy; even if the forum State is the most convenient location for litigation, the Due Process Clause, acting as an instrument of interstate federalism, may sometimes act to divest the State of its power to render a valid judgment."

III

Our settled principles regarding specific jurisdiction control this case. In order for a court to exercise specific jurisdiction over a claim, there must be an "affiliation between the forum and the underlying controversy, principally, [an] activity or an occurrence that takes place in the forum State." *Goodyear.* When there is no such connection, specific jurisdiction is lacking regardless of the extent of a defendant's unconnected activities in the State.

For this reason, the California Supreme Court's "sliding scale approach" is difficult to square with our precedents. Under the California approach, the strength of the requisite connection between the forum and the specific claims at issue is relaxed if the defendant has extensive forum contacts that are unrelated to those claims. Our cases provide no support for this approach, which resembles a loose and spurious form of general jurisdiction. For specific jurisdiction, a defendant's general connections with the forum are not enough. As we have said, "[a] corporation's 'continuous activity of some sorts within a state . . . is not enough to support the demand that the corporation be amenable to suits unrelated to that activity.'"

The present case illustrates the danger of the California approach. The State Supreme Court found that specific jurisdiction was present without identifying any adequate link between the State and the nonresidents' claims. As noted, the nonresidents were not prescribed Plavix in California, did not ingest Plavix in California, and were not injured by Plavix in California. The mere fact that *other* plaintiffs were prescribed, obtained, and ingested Plavix in California—and allegedly sustained the same injuries as did the non-residents—does not allow the State to assert specific jurisdiction over the nonresidents' claims . . . . Nor is it sufficient—or even relevant—that BMS conducted research in California on matters unrelated to Plavix. What is needed—and what is missing here—is a connection between the forum and the specific claims at issue . . . .

In a last ditch contention, respondents contend that BMS's "decision to contract with a California company [McKesson] to distribute [Plavix] nationally" provides a sufficient basis for personal jurisdiction. But as we have explained, "[t]he requirements of *International Shoe* . . . must be met as to each defendant over whom a state court exercises jurisdiction." In this case, it is not alleged that BMS engaged in relevant acts together with McKesson in California. Nor is it alleged that BMS is derivatively liable for McKesson's conduct in California. And the nonresidents have adduced no evidence to show how or by whom the Plavix they took was distributed to the pharmacies that dispensed it to them. The bare fact that BMS contracted with a California distributor is not enough to establish personal jurisdiction in the State.

IV

Our straightforward application in this case of settled principles of personal jurisdiction will not result in the parade of horribles that respondents conjure up. Our decision does not prevent the California and out-of-state plaintiffs from joining together in a consolidated action in the States that have general jurisdiction over BMS. BMS concedes that such suits could be brought in either New York or Delaware. Alternatively, the plaintiffs who are residents of a particular State—for example, the 92 plaintiffs from Texas and the 71 from Ohio—could probably sue together in their home States. In addition, since our decision concerns the due process limits on the exercise of specific jurisdiction by a State, we leave open the question whether the Fifth Amendment imposes the same restrictions on the exercise of personal jurisdiction by a federal court. . . .

* * *

The judgment of the California Supreme Court is reversed, and the case is remanded for further proceedings not inconsistent with this opinion.

It is so ordered.

SOTOMAYOR, J., dissenting.

Three years ago, the Court imposed substantial curbs on the exercise of general jurisdiction in its decision in *Daimler AG v. Bauman*. Today, the Court takes its first step toward a similar contraction of specific jurisdiction by holding that a corporation that engages in a nationwide course of conduct cannot be held accountable in a state court by a group of injured people unless all of those people were injured in the forum State.

I fear the consequences of the Court's decision today will be substantial. The majority's rule will make it difficult to aggregate the claims of plaintiffs across the country whose claims may be worth little alone. It will make it impossible to bring a nationwide mass action in state court against defendants who are "at home" in different States. And it will result in piecemeal litigation and the bifurcation of claims. None of this is necessary. A core concern in this Court's personal jurisdiction cases is fairness. And there is nothing unfair about subjecting a massive corporation to suit in a State for a nationwide course of conduct that injures both forum residents and nonresidents alike . . . .

II

[T]he California courts appropriately exercised specific jurisdiction over respondents' claims.

First, there is no dispute that Bristol-Myers "purposefully avail[ed] itself" of California and its substantial pharmaceutical market. Bristol-Myers employs over 400 people in California and maintains half a dozen facilities in the State engaged in research, development, and policymaking. It contracts with a California-based distributor, McKesson, whose sales account for a significant portion of its revenue. And it markets and sells its drugs, including Plavix, in California, resulting in total Plavix sales in that State of nearly $1 billion during the period relevant to this suit.

Second, respondents' claims "relate to" Bristol-Myers' in-state conduct. A claim "relates to" a defendant's forum conduct if it has a "connect[ion] with" that conduct. So respondents could not, for instance, hale Bristol-Myers into court in California for negligently maintaining the sidewalk outside its New York headquarters—a claim that has no connection to acts Bristol-Myers took in California. But respondents' claims against Bristol-Myers look nothing like such a claim. Respondents' claims against Bristol-Myers concern conduct materially identical to acts the company took in California: its marketing and distribution of Plavix, which it undertook on a nationwide basis in all 50 States. That respondents were allegedly injured by this nationwide course of conduct in Indiana, Oklahoma, and Texas, and not California, does not mean that their claims do not "relate to" the advertising and distribution efforts that Bristol-Myers undertook in that State. All of the plaintiffs—residents and nonresidents alike—allege that they were injured by the same essential acts. Our cases require no connection more direct than that.

Finally, and importantly, there is no serious doubt that the exercise of jurisdiction over the nonresidents' claims is reasonable. Because Bristol-Myers already faces claims that are identical to the nonresidents' claims in this suit, it will not be harmed by having to defend against respondents' claims: Indeed, the alternative approach—litigating those claims in separate suits in as many as 34 different States—would prove far more burdensome. By contrast, the plaintiffs' "interest in obtaining convenient and effective relief" is obviously furthered by participation in a consolidated proceeding in one State under shared counsel, which allows them to minimize costs, share discovery, and maximize recoveries on claims that may be too small to bring on their own. California, too, has an interest in providing a forum for mass actions like this one: Permitting the non-residents to bring suit in California alongside the residents facilitates the efficient adjudication of the residents' claims and allows it to regulate more effectively the conduct of both nonresident corporations like Bristol-Myers and resident ones like McKesson . . . .

Nothing in the Due Process Clause prohibits a California court from hearing respondents' claims—at least not in a case where they are joined to identical claims brought by California residents. . . .

I fear the consequences of the majority's decision today will be substantial. Even absent a rigid requirement that a defendant's in-state conduct must actually cause a plaintiff's claim,[3] the upshot of today's opinion is that plaintiffs cannot join their claims together and sue a defendant in a State in which only some of them have been injured. That rule is likely to have consequences far beyond this case.

First, and most prominently, the Court's opinion in this case will make it profoundly difficult for plaintiffs who are injured in different States by a defendant's nationwide course of conduct to sue that defendant in a single, consolidated action. The holding of today's opinion is that such an action cannot be brought in a State in which only some plaintiffs were injured. Not to worry, says the majority: The plaintiffs here could have sued Bristol-Myers in New York or Delaware; could "probably" have subdivided their separate claims into 34 lawsuits in the States in which they were injured; and might have been able to bring a single suit in federal court (an "open . . . question"). Even setting aside the majority's caveats, what is the purpose of such limitations? What interests are served by preventing the consolidation of claims and limiting the forums in which they can be consolidated? The effect of the Court's opinion today is to eliminate nationwide mass actions in any State other than those in which a defendant is "'essentially at home.'"[4] See *Daimler*. Such a rule hands one more tool to corporate defendants determined to prevent the aggregation of individual claims, and forces injured plaintiffs to bear the burden of bringing suit in what will often be far flung jurisdictions. . . .

Second, the Court's opinion today may make it impossible to bring certain mass actions at all. After this case, it is difficult to imagine where it might be possible to bring a nationwide mass action against two or more defendants headquartered and incorporated in different States. There will be no State where both defendants are "at home," and so no State in which the suit can proceed. What about a nationwide mass action brought against a defendant not headquartered or incorporated in the United States? Such a defendant is not "at home" in any State. . . .

The majority chides respondents for conjuring a "parade of horribles," but says nothing about how suits like those described here will survive its opinion in this case. The answer is simple: They will not.

* * *

---

3. Bristol-Myers urges such a rule upon us, but its adoption would have consequences far beyond those that follow from today's factbound opinion. Among other things, it might call into question whether even a plaintiff injured in a State by an item identical to those sold by a defendant in that State could avail himself of that State's courts to redress his injuries—a result specifically contemplated by World-Wide Volkswagen Corp. v. Woodson, 444 U.S. 286, 297, 100 S. Ct. 559, 62 L. Ed. 2d 490 (1980). See Brief for Civil Procedure Professors as Amici Curiae 14-18; see also J. McIntyre Machinery, Ltd. v. Nicastro, 564 U. S. 873, 906-907, 131 S. Ct. 2780, 180 L. Ed. 2d 765 (2011) (Ginsburg, J., dissenting). That question, and others like it, appears to await another case.

4. The Court today does not confront the question whether its opinion here would also apply to a class action in which a plaintiff injured in the forum State seeks to represent a nationwide class of plaintiffs, not all of whom were injured there. Cf. Devlin v. Scardelletti, 536 U.S. 1, 9-10, 122 S. Ct. 2005, 153 L. Ed. 2d 27 (2002) ("Nonnamed class members . . . may be parties for some purposes and not for others"); see also Wood, Adjudicatory Jurisdiction and Class Actions, 62 Ind. L.J. 597, 616-617 (1987).

It "does not offend 'traditional notions of fair play and substantial justice'" to permit plaintiffs to aggregate claims arising out of a single nationwide course of conduct in a single suit in a single State where some, but not all, were injured. But that is exactly what the Court holds today is barred by the Due Process Clause.

This is not a rule the Constitution has required before. I respectfully dissent.

Notes and Problems

1. Start by using the case to review.
   a. What prior case(s) made it likely that the Court would be unanimous in rejecting a claim of general jurisdiction? The Court makes clear that it views the claim of general jurisdiction to be foreclosed by *Daimler*. But was there any possible argument that could have been made to differentiate this case from *Daimler*?
   b. Though Justice Sotomayor in dissent worries that the decision will make it difficult for plaintiffs spread all over the country—but allegedly injured by the same defect in a drug or other product—to consolidate all claims in a single suit, you know that there are at least a couple of states in which such a suit could be brought against Bristol-Myers. What are those states and what is your authority for so thinking?
   c. The California Supreme Court said it was applying a sliding scale test for the existence of specific jurisdiction—requiring less connection between the in-state activities and the claim as the level of those in-state activities increased (and, conversely, requiring a closer connection as the claim-creating in-state activities declined). The Supreme Court rejected this approach. But what decisions might the California Supreme Court have cited to support its view that there should be a sliding scale test?

2. Now to the case itself.
   a. Of the jurisdiction cases you have already studied, which seems closest to the *Bristol-Myers* facts?
   b. Judging from the majority opinion, what's the smallest change in facts that would have led to a different outcome?

3. Though the opinion does not say so, does it implicitly undermine the outcome of or the assumptions underlying any of the cases you have previously read?
   a. The notes after *Nicastro* suggest that the plaintiff could have sued McIntyre in Ohio, where the national distributor was located. But the Court here rejects the notion that Bristol-Myers could be sued in California simply because it has a California distributor.
   b. Sotomayor, in footnote 3 of her dissent, observes that the majority's decision calls into question assumptions made in prior cases, including *World-Wide Volkswagen*, that "a plaintiff injured in a State by an item identical to those sold by a defendant in that State could avail himself of that State's courts to redress his injuries."

4. Justice Sotomayor worries that *Bristol-Myers* will make it difficult for plaintiffs injured by a widely distributed product to come together to sue in a single location. How serious is this problem? Consider several scenarios—keeping in mind that your responses to some of the scenarios may require some knowledge of the financing of litigation and the organization of the plaintiffs' bar—topics touched on in Chapter 5.

   a. From the plaintiffs' standpoint, the easiest cases to bring will be those in which a defective product seriously injures or kills a number of people. Because damages in each case will be substantial, it will usually be possible for such plaintiffs to find competent counsel to represent each plaintiff (or small groups of plaintiffs) individually—in which case it will not matter whether the cases can be consolidated. That leaves, however, the *Nicastro* situation: a product manufactured outside the United States and not widely distributed—but which inflicts a serious injury.

   b. And, even if there are substantial individual damages, where can those persons sue? One might assume that they could do so in whatever state they purchased the drug in question. But consider a possibly significant sentence toward the end of the majority opinion: "Alternatively, the plaintiffs who are residents of a particular State—for example, the 92 plaintiffs from Texas and the 71 from Ohio—could *probably* sue together in their home States." (Italics added.) "Probably" may merely represent Justice Alito exercising the caution of a good judge in a common law system: Don't make unnecessary pronouncements about cases not before the court. Or might he mean something else, suggesting that for jurisdiction to lie a defendant must have "purposefully directed" (*Nicastro*) activity toward the state in question? One feels certain that defendants will probe this question in future cases.

   c. Now consider: What if damages in individual cases were insufficient to warrant individual representation—as may have been the situation in *Bristol-Myers*?

      i. From the plaintiffs' standpoint, the ideal would be either a class action (unlikely for reasons you'll better understand when you encounter that device in Chapter 12) or, putting that aside, "bundling" a number of individual cases together as the lawyers in *Bristol-Myers* sought to do. How difficult will that be to do? The answer may well depend on how well organized the segment of the plaintiffs' bar that handles such cases is. For example, the "pharmaceutical bar" on the plaintiffs' side in the United States is relatively small (comprising scores or perhaps a hundred or so lawyers who regularly handle such cases and who can deploy the considerable resources, intellectual and financial, needed to prosecute them), and the members of this bar have various informal arrangements with each other that facilitate cooperation. One imagines that they would be able to organize aggregate representation of the *Bristol-Myers* plaintiffs without much difficulty if the stakes warranted it. And there are many such specialized "bars," with expertise ranging from cruise ship accidents to tire safety and on and on.

    ii. On the other hand, if the injury involved a more obscure corner of litigation, such a segment of the bar might not be readily available, in which case Justice Sotomayor's concerns might be more salient.

5. Finally, note the curious phrase at the end of the majority opinion: "we leave open the question whether the Fifth Amendment imposes the same restrictions on the exercise of personal jurisdiction by a federal court." This statement seems to suggest that federal courts might have a broader jurisdictional reach under the Fifth Amendment than state courts do under the Fourteenth. This is not a topic that the Supreme Court has frequently addressed, but perhaps, given this statement, it will do so soon. Or, is the Court pointing toward Congress? Consider the bearing of Rules 4(k)(1)(C) and 4(k)(2).

    a. The former provides that personal jurisdiction lies "when authorized by a federal statute." Could Congress constitutionally provide that the manufacturer of any product is subject to jurisdiction on a claim of product defect wherever it sold that product within the United States? No such legislation exists.

    b. The latter, presumably with a *Nicastro* scenario in mind, imagines a federal statute subjecting a foreign defendant who has sufficient contacts with the United States as a whole (but not with any given state) would be subject to jurisdiction on a claim arising under federal law.

6. Now that we have considered general jurisdiction over corporations, let us consider general jurisdiction over individuals. We know that individuals are subject to general jurisdiction in the state where they are domiciled. Where else are they subject to general jurisdiction? The next case offers an answer.

Burnham v. Superior Court
495 U.S. 604 (1990)

SCALIA, J., announced the judgment of the Court and delivered an opinion in which THE CHIEF JUSTICE and KENNEDY, J., joined, and in which WHITE, J., joined as to Parts I, II-A, II-B, and II-C.

The question presented is whether the Due Process Clause of the Fourteenth Amendment denies California courts jurisdiction over a nonresident, who was personally served with process while temporarily in that State, in a suit unrelated to his activities in the State.

I

Petitioner Dennis Burnham married Francie Burnham in 1976, in West Virginia. In 1977 the couple moved to New Jersey, where their two children were born. In July 1987 the Burnhams decided to separate. They agreed that Mrs. Burnham, who intended to move to California, would take custody of the children. Shortly before Mrs. Burnham departed for California that same month, she and petitioner agreed that she would file for divorce on grounds of "irreconcilable differences." In October

1987, petitioner filed for divorce in New Jersey state court on grounds of "desertion." Petitioner did not, however, obtain an issuance of summons against his wife, and did not attempt to serve her with process. Mrs. Burnham, after unsuccessfully demanding that petitioner adhere to their prior agreement to submit to an "irreconcilable differences" divorce, brought suit for divorce in California state court in early January 1988.

In late January, petitioner visited southern California on business, after which he went north to visit his children in the San Francisco Bay area, where his wife resided. He took the older child to San Francisco for the weekend. Upon returning the child to Mrs. Burnham's home on January 24, 1988, petitioner was served with a California court summons and a copy of Mrs. Burnham's divorce petition. He then returned to New Jersey.

[The California courts refused to dismiss for want of personal jurisdiction.] We granted certiorari.

II

A

. . . To determine whether the assertion of personal jurisdiction is consistent with due process, we have long relied on the principles traditionally followed by American courts in making out the territorial limits of each State's authority. That criterion was first announced in *Pennoyer v. Neff*, in which we stated that due process "mean[s] a course of legal proceedings according to those rules and principles which have been established in our systems of jurisprudence for the protection and enforcement of private rights," including the "well-established principles of public law respecting the jurisdiction of an independent State over persons and property." In what has become the classic expression of the criterion, we said in International Shoe Co. v. Washington, 326 U.S. 310 (1945), that a State Court's assertion of personal jurisdiction satisfies the Due Process Clause if it does not violate "'traditional notions of fair play and substantial justice'" [quoting *Milliken v. Meyer*]. Since *International Shoe*, we have only been called upon to decide whether these "traditional notions" permit States to exercise jurisdiction over absent defendants in a manner that deviates from the rules of jurisdiction applied in the 19th century. We have held such deviations permissible, but only with respect to suits arising out of the absent defendant's contacts with the State. The question we must decide today is whether due process requires a similar connection between the litigation and the defendant's contacts with the State in cases where the defendant is physically present in the State at the time process is served upon him.

B

Among the most firmly established principles of personal jurisdiction in American tradition is that the courts of a State have jurisdiction over nonresidents who are physically present in the State. The view developed early that each State had the power to hale before its courts any individual who could be found within its borders, and that once having acquired jurisdiction over such a person by properly serving him with process, the State could retain jurisdiction to enter judgment against him, no matter how fleeting his visit. See, e.g., Potter v. Allin, 2 Root 63, 67 (Conn. 1793);

Barrell v. Benjamin, 15 Mass. 354 (1819). That view had antecedents in English common-law practice, which sometimes allowed "transitory" actions, arising out of events outside the country, to be maintained against seemingly nonresident defendants who were present in England. . . .

Recent scholarship has suggested that English tradition was not as clear [as Supreme Court Justice and treatise writer Joseph Story thought it was]. . . . Accurate or not, however, judging by the evidence of contemporaneous . . . decisions, one must conclude that Story's understanding was shared by American courts at the crucial time for present purposes: 1868, when the Fourteenth Amendment was adopted.

C

Despite this formidable body of precedent, petitioner contends, in reliance on our decisions applying the *International Shoe* standard, that in the absence of "continuous and systematic" contacts with the forum, a nonresident defendant can be subjected to judgment only as to matters that arise out of or relate to his contacts with the forum. This argument rests on a thorough misunderstanding of our cases. . . .

[Cases following *International Shoe* upheld jurisdiction over defendants who were *not* present in the forum state.]

Nothing in *International Shoe* or the cases that have followed it, however, offers support for the very different proposition petitioner seeks to establish today: that a defendant's presence in the forum is not only unnecessary to validate novel, nontraditional assertions of jurisdiction, but is itself no longer sufficient to establish jurisdiction. . . .

The short of the matter is that jurisdiction based on physical presence alone constitutes due process because it is one of the continuing traditions of our legal system that define the due process standard of "traditional notions of fair play and substantial justice." That standard was developed by analogy to "physical presence," and it would be perverse to say it could now be turned against that touchstone of jurisdiction.

D

Petitioner's strongest argument, though we ultimately reject it, relies upon our decision in *Shaffer v. Heitner.*

It goes too far to say, as petitioner contends, that *Shaffer* compels the conclusion that a State lacks jurisdiction over an individual unless the litigation arises out of his activities in the State. *Shaffer*, like *International Shoe*, involved jurisdiction over an absent defendant, and it stands for nothing more than the proposition that when the "minimum contact" that is a substitute for physical presence consists of property ownership it must, like other minimum contacts, be related to the litigation. Petitioner wrenches out of its context our statement in *Shaffer* that "all assertions of state-court jurisdiction must be evaluated according to the standards set forth in *International Shoe* and its progeny." When read together with the two sentences that preceded it, the meaning of this statement becomes clear:

> The fiction that an assertion of jurisdiction over property is anything but an assertion of jurisdiction over the owner of the property supports an ancient form without substantial modern justification. Its continued acceptance would serve only to allow state-court jurisdiction that is fundamentally unfair to the defendant.

"We *therefore conclude* that all assertions of state-court jurisdiction must be evaluated according to the standards set forth in *International Shoe* and its progeny." Ibid. (emphasis added).

Shaffer was saying, in other words, not that all bases for the assertion of in personam jurisdiction (including, presumably, in-state service) must be treated alike and subjected to the "minimum contacts" analysis of *International Shoe*; but rather that quasi in rem jurisdiction, that fictional "ancient form," and in personam jurisdiction, are really one and the same and must be treated alike—leading to the conclusion that quasi in rem jurisdiction, i.e., that form of in personam jurisdiction based upon a "property ownership" contact and by definition unaccompanied by personal, in-state service, must satisfy the litigation-relatedness requirement of *International Shoe*. . . . *International Shoe* confined its "minimum contacts" requirement to situations in which the defendant "be not present within the territory of the forum," and nothing in *Shaffer* expands that requirement beyond that.

It is fair to say, however, that while our holding today does not contradict *Shaffer*, our basic approach to the due process question is different. . . . While in no way receding from or casting doubt upon the holding of *Shaffer* or any other case, we reaffirm today our time-honored approach. For new procedures, hitherto unknown, the Due Process Clause requires analysis to determine whether "traditional notions of fair play and substantial justice" have been offended. *International Shoe*. But a doctrine of personal jurisdiction that dates back to the adoption of the Fourteenth Amendment and is still generally observed unquestionably meets that standard. . . .

III

A few words in response to Justice Brennan's opinion concurring in the judgment. . . .

The subjectivity, and hence inadequacy, of [Justice Brennan's] approach becomes apparent when the concurrence tries to explain why the assertion of jurisdiction in the present case meets its standard. . . . Justice Brennan lists the "benefits" Mr. Burnham derived from the State of California—the fact that, during the few days he was there, "[h]is health and safety [were] guaranteed by the State's police, fire, and emergency medical services; he [was] free to travel on the State's roads and waterways; he likely enjoy[ed] the fruits of the State's economy." Three days' worth of these benefits strike us as powerfully inadequate to establish, as an abstract matter, that it is "fair" for California to decree the ownership of all Mr. Burnham's worldly goods acquired during the 10 years of his marriage, and the custody over his children. We daresay a contractual exchange swapping those benefits for that power would not survive the "unconscionability" provision of the Uniform Commercial Code. . . .

Suppose . . . that a defendant in Mr. Burnham's situation enjoys not three days' worth of California's "benefits," but 15 minutes' worth. Or suppose we remove one of those "benefits"—"enjoy[ment of] the fruits of the State's economy"—by positing that Mr. Burnham had not come to California on business, but only to visit his children. . . .

. . . What if Mr. Burnham were visiting a sick child? Or a dying child? Cf. Kulko v. Superior Court of California, City and County of San Francisco, 436 U.S. 84, 93 (1978) (finding the exercise of long-arm jurisdiction over an absent parent unreasonable because it would "discourage parents from entering into reasonable visitation agreements"). . . .

The difference between us and Justice Brennan has nothing to do with whether "further progress [is] to be made" in the "evolution of our legal system." It has to do with whether changes are to be adopted as progressive by the American people or decreed as progressive by the Justices of this Court. . . .

[Justice WHITE's concurrence is omitted.]

BRENNAN, J., with whom MARSHALL, J., BLACKMUN, J., and O'CONNOR, J., join, concurring in the judgment.

I agree with Justice Scalia that the Due Process Clause of the Fourteenth Amendment generally permits a state court to exercise jurisdiction over a defendant if he is served with process while voluntarily present in the forum State.[1] I do not perceive the need, however, to decide that a jurisdictional rule that "'has been immemorially the actual law of the land,'" quoting Hurtado v. California, 110 U.S. 516, 528 (1884), automatically comports with due process simply by virtue of its "pedigree." Although I agree that history is an important factor in establishing whether a jurisdictional rule satisfies due process requirements, I cannot agree that it is the only factor such that all traditional rules of jurisdiction are, ipso facto, forever constitutional. Unlike Justice Scalia, I would undertake an "independent inquiry into the . . . fairness of the prevailing in-state service rule." I therefore concur in the judgment.

I

I believe that the approach adopted by Justice Scalia's opinion today—reliance solely on historical pedigree—is foreclosed by our decisions in *International Shoe Co. v. Washington* and *Shaffer v. Heitner*. . . . The critical insight of *Shaffer* is that all rules of jurisdiction, even ancient ones, must satisfy contemporary notions of due process. . . .

II

. . . Tradition, though alone not dispositive, is of course relevant to the question. . . .

. . . [T]he historical background [is] relevant because, however murky the jurisprudential origins of transient jurisdiction, the fact that American courts have announced the rule for perhaps a century (first in dicta, more recently in holdings) provides a defendant voluntarily present in a particular State *today* "clear notice that [he] is subject to suit" in the forum. Regardless of whether Justice Story's account of the rule's genesis is mythical, our common understanding now, fortified by a century of judicial practice, is that jurisdiction is often a function of geography. The transient rule is consistent with reasonable expectations and is entitled to a strong presumption that it comports with due process. . . . "If I visit another State, . . . I knowingly assume some risk that the State will exercise its power over my property or my person while there. My contact with the State, though minimal, gives rise to predictable

---

1. I use the term "transient jurisdiction" to refer to jurisdiction premised solely on the fact that a person is served with process while physically present in the forum State.

risks." *Shaffer* (Stevens, J., concurring in judgment). . . .[11] By visiting the forum State, a transient defendant actually "avail[s]" himself of significant benefits provided by the State. His health and safety are guaranteed by the State's police, fire, and emergency medical services; he is free to travel on the State's roads and waterways; he likely enjoys the fruits of the State's economy as well. Moreover, the Privileges and Immunities Clause of Article IV prevents a state government from discriminating against a transient defendant by denying him the protections of its law or the right of access to its courts. . . . Without transient jurisdiction, an asymmetry would arise: a transient would have the full benefit of the power of the forum State's courts as a plaintiff while retaining immunity from their authority as a defendant.

The potential burdens on a transient defendant are slight. . . . That the defendant has already journeyed at least once before to the forum—as evidenced by the fact that he was served with process there—is an indication that suit in the forum likely would not be prohibitively inconvenient. . . .

In this case, it is undisputed that petitioner was served with process while voluntarily and knowingly in the State of California. I therefore concur in the judgment.

STEVENS, J., concurring in the judgment.

As I explained in my separate writing, I did not join the Court's opinion in *Shaffer v. Heitner* because I was concerned by its unnecessarily broad reach. The same concern prevents me from joining either Justice Scalia's or Justice Brennan's opinion in this case. For me, it is sufficient to note that the historical evidence and consensus identified by Justice Scalia, the considerations of fairness identified by Justice Brennan, and the common sense displayed by Justice White, all combine to demonstrate that this is, indeed, a very easy case.*

WHAT'S NEW HERE?

- Does *Burnham* take us back full circle to the rule of *Pennoyer* where service of process within the state established jurisdiction over the person served?
- How big a hole does *Burnham* make in *Shaffer's* pronouncement that all assertions of jurisdiction are to be measured under the criteria of *International Shoe*? A big hole for those who signed Justice Scalia's opinion, suggesting that this "traditional" method of asserting jurisdiction had always existed alongside the other means described in *International Shoe*. No hole at all for those who signed Justice Brennan's concurrence, because his analysis concluded that under the criteria of *International Shoe* California had contacts with Mr. Burnham sufficient to support jurisdiction.

---

11. As the Restatement suggests, there may be cases in which a defendant's involuntary or unknowing presence in a State does not support the exercise of personal jurisdiction over him. The facts of the instant case do not require us to determine the outer limits of the transient jurisdiction rule.

* Perhaps the adage about hard cases making bad law should be revised to cover easy cases.

Notes and Problems

1. The Court in *Burnham* is unanimous as to the result but sharply divided as to how to reach that result with no opinion getting a majority vote.

   a. Justice Stevens characterizes *Burnham* as an easy case; is it? Perhaps the answer to this question turns on how broadly one reads *Burnham*: as a marital property case or a case applicable to all settings. If one limits *Burnham* to its domestic relations context, it begins to look easy. After all, there are only two possible states that could take jurisdiction (New Jersey, where the husband lives, and California, where the wife lives); isn't one as reasonable as the other? Moreover, Mr. Burnham, having allegedly reneged on his pre-separation agreement to divide marital property equally with Mrs. Burnham, was not a particularly sympathetic litigant.

   b. But nothing in the opinion suggests such a limitation. Read broadly, it revives "tag" jurisdiction, in which mere presence and service with process conclusively establishes jurisdiction.

   c. In *Burnham*, all justices found personal jurisdiction despite their differences. But could the reasoning used by Justice Scalia and Justice Brennan lead to different conclusions in some instances? Can you imagine a scenario in which Justice Scalia would find personal jurisdiction but Justice Brennan would not?

2. *Burnham* suggests that the courts applying its principles will need to confront an issue that arose regularly under the regime of *Pennoyer*: Does service of process obtained by force or fraud confer jurisdiction? Consider the following examples.

   a. If the defendant were kidnapped, brought across state borders, served with process, and then released, would that establish jurisdiction? A number of cases assert in dicta that under such conditions service of process would not establish jurisdiction, although the situation seems to have arisen so infrequently in civil suits that it is difficult to locate a holding on point.

   b. What would have happened if Mrs. Burnham had contacted Mr. Burnham and falsely told him one of the children was seriously ill, and, when he arrived to visit the "sick" child, had served him with process? On analogous facts the court in Wyman v. Newhouse, 93 F.2d 313 (2d Cir.), cert. denied, 303 U.S. 664 (1937), held that the court lacked personal jurisdiction. See also Voice Systems Marketing Co. v. Appropriate Technology Corp., 153 F.R.D. 117 (E.D. Mich. 1994) (called to state to resolve customer problems, defendant was asked to extend stay for a day for a "meeting," at which he was served with process; service quashed).

3. Could Mr. Burnham (or his lawyer) have avoided this outcome?

   a. Recall that Mr. Burnham had filed a divorce action in New Jersey, but he had not served Mrs. Burnham. If he had done so—and divorce and marital property litigation was underway in another state—California courts would not have proceeded with the action. Could New Jersey have acquired jurisdiction over the absent Mrs. Burnham based on the substantial duration of the marriage and location of at least some of the marital property in that state?

  b. The Uniform Interstate Family Support Act, now mandatory in all states by virtue of federal law, seeks to establish guidelines for jurisdiction over child and marital property litigation. The Act, of course, cannot establish jurisdiction on an unconstitutional basis, but one could argue that a court facing a due process claim under this Act should be cognizant of the kinds of mess, represented by *Burnham,* into which matters fall if unregulated by statutory guidelines.

4. Note that the divorce proceeding would be captioned *Burnham v. Burnham*—the Supreme Court's decision, however, is captioned *Burnham v. Superior Court.* Why? Because as a matter of California procedure, a writ of mandamus challenging the decision of a trial court is brought "against" the trial court. (A similar device was at work in *World-Wide Volkswagen:* The Woodson in that case was the trial court judge, and defendants brought a writ of prohibition to prevent Woodson from exercising personal jurisdiction over them.)

Note on the Mechanics of Jurisdiction: Challenge and Waiver

Now, armed with a better grasp of the doctrine of personal jurisdiction, it is important to understand how lawyers bring jurisdictional challenges to bear on actual cases. The workings of such procedures expose some otherwise hidden assumptions about the meaning of jurisdiction, and display legal tactics at work on the ground.

Assume Abe, a resident of Illinois, sues Barbara, a resident of California, in Illinois, and notifies Barbara of the suit. Barbara thinks that she is not subject to personal jurisdiction. What does her lawyer do?

The simplest but riskiest course is for Barbara's lawyer to do nothing. If she is very sure indeed that the court lacks jurisdiction (and she has no assets in Illinois), she may simply decline to appear, suffer a default judgment, and attack the judgment when Abe seeks to enforce it in a subsequent proceeding. Before Abe can enforce the Illinois judgment in California, he must file it with a California court. Barbara will receive notice of that filing, and with it an opportunity to contest the Illinois court's jurisdiction over her before the California court issues a writ of execution against Barbara's assets in California. Even before *Pennoyer,* that route—known as collateral attack—lay open. *D'Arcy v. Ketchum,* 52 U.S. 165 (1850). It carries, however, a serious risk, for if the second court rejects the jurisdictional challenge, Barbara can raise no other defenses on the merits. Jurisdiction, but only jurisdiction, is open to collateral attack.

What happens if Barbara wishes to pursue a less risky course of action? How does she raise jurisdictional objections in the first proceeding?

a. Under the Federal Rules (and state statutes patterned on them), Barbara may raise her jurisdictional defense either in the answer or, if she makes a pre-answer motion, at that time. Read Rule 12(b), (h), and (g). These provisions of Rule 12 make sequencing critical. Making any pre-answer motion that omits a defense of personal jurisdiction is treated as a waiver of objection to jurisdiction. By the same token, making an appearance or litigating other issues but failing to challenge personal jurisdiction in one of these two ways results in waiver of the jurisdictional defense. If Barbara raises the objection at the proper time, she does not waive it by joining it with other defenses or objections, but she must raise it the first time she raises any issue, either by way of motion, appearance, or answer. Moreover, she must litigate the defense promptly. This happens as a matter of course if she makes a pre-answer motion. If she makes no such motion but challenges jurisdiction in her answer, she must promptly move for dismissal on this ground. Although the Rules do not say so explicitly, courts will not look kindly on a defendant who waits until the end of discovery to see how the wind is blowing on the merits of the case before moving to dismiss for want of personal jurisdiction.

b. In a few state systems (and in many older cases), Barbara would raise the jurisdictional claim by making a "special appearance." See, e.g., Tex. R. Civ. P. 120a (Bender 2011). This is what Dennis Burnham did. The procedure is so called for reasons you can now understand: Otherwise, a defendant who "appeared" might be held to have consented to the state's exercise of power. What was needed was a form of "appearance" that would not be treated as presence or consent. A "special" appearance permitted the defendant to object to jurisdiction without the action of objecting being itself the basis for jurisdiction.

c. Finally, what happens if the defendant has availed herself of the system's opportunity to challenge jurisdiction but loses? May she immediately appeal that decision? Some states do permit such an immediate appeal; indeed sometimes they require an immediate appeal of the jurisdictional ruling—treating the choice to litigate on the merits as waiving the jurisdictional defense. Other states and the federal system treat a jurisdictional defense like other pretrial rulings and require that an appeal await final judgment. If you were a defendant with a jurisdictional defense, which pattern would you prefer? If you were a plaintiff, which would you prefer?

Notes and Problems

1. Jurisdictional challenges raise technical, strategic, and theoretical issues. Start with the technical. Reread Rule 12(b), (h), and (g) and apply it to the following

scenarios. Each assumes that the plaintiff has filed a complaint and the defendant then makes one of the following responses. The question is whether the defendant has waived her jurisdictional objection. (These questions of timing and strategy are revisited in Chapter 6, pages 421-24, where we examine Rule 12 in earnest.)

    a. Defendant makes a pre-answer 12(b)(6) motion; upon its denial she files a second pre-answer motion based on Rule 12(b)(2), seeking a dismissal for want of personal jurisdiction.

    b. Defendant makes a pre-answer 12(b)(6) motion; upon its denial she files an answer containing both a defense on the merits and a 12(b)(2) defense, asserting no personal jurisdiction.

    c. Defendant makes no pre-answer motion but answers the complaint, including in her answer a defense based on personal jurisdiction.

    d. Defendant makes a pre-answer 12(b)(1) motion, which is denied; she then makes a 12(b)(2) motion.

2. Other actions by the defendant, apart from motions under Rule 12(b) and answers to the complaint, may result in waiver of the personal jurisdiction defense. As a result, a defendant who wishes to object to personal jurisdiction must carefully consider any litigation activity preceding such an objection. For example, litigating the propriety of a preliminary injunction or filing a permissive counterclaim before an answer or 12(b) motion have sometimes been held to constitute waiver. See Wright, Federal Courts 463.

3. Now that you have avoided future malpractice claims with this technical knowledge, consider what the technical pattern means. Why is such a premium placed upon arguing the jurisdictional issue at the same time as or before other issues? What does that say about the nature of this defense that defendants can so easily—even by inattention—waive objections to personal jurisdiction?

Procedure as Strategy

As you have seen, Rule 12(b) allows a defense of lack of personal jurisdiction to be raised either by pre-answer motion or as part of the answer (if, but only if, there has been no pre-answer motion). Why would a defendant choose a pre-answer motion rather than simply bundling everything into her answer to the complaint?

    One straightforward answer is that with a 12(b) motion, the defendant stands to get the case against him dismissed. But there are some other, less obvious reasons a defendant might prefer moving instead of answering in some cases. To get an idea of one possible reason, read Rules 8(b) and 11, which put the lawyer's professional standing—and also her pocketbook—behind the allegations of an answer: Rule 8(b) requires that an answer respond to each allegation in a complaint—either admitting or denying it; Rule 11 requires that each such admission or denial be adequately grounded in law and fact—with court-ordered sanctions possible for violations. Accordingly, an attorney answering a complaint on behalf of a defendant must take the time (and, sometimes, money) to ensure that her answers to each paragraph in the complaint comport with Rule 11. For a short, straightforward complaint, answering will likely take less time than moving to dismiss for lack of personal jurisdiction (particularly if briefing the jurisdictional issue requires investigation and discovery, as it did in *Hawkins,* in Chapter 1). But in a case with complex facts and a straightforward jurisdictional defense, it might be more efficient to move to dismiss than to answer.

Rule 13 supplies another reason: It requires that an answer contain any counterclaim arising out of the same transaction as the claim. In some cases it might require substantial factual and legal research to decide if a viable counterclaim exists.

Not only money and professional requirements but also time is at stake. Rule 12(b) gives the defendant just 21 days to answer (unless time is extended or the defendant waives service of process). That may be a short time if the lawyer has to do substantial factual investigation to decide on the strategy of the answer. Rule 12(a)(4) extends the time to answer until 14 days after the court has ruled on a pre-answer motion; accordingly a Rule 12 motion buys the defendant additional weeks or months before any answer is required (if it is required at all—the defendant, of course, need not answer a complaint once it has been dismissed!). But be wary about treating a Rule 12 motion as a "free" time extension: The lawyer's required signature on such a motion constitutes a certificate that "it is not being presented for any improper purpose, such as to . . . cause unnecessary delay." Rule 11(b)(1).

C. CONSENT AS A SUBSTITUTE FOR POWER

Recall *Pennoyer's* indication that either power or consent could establish jurisdiction. That proposition remains true today: A defendant may, either at the outset of the lawsuit itself or before it, consent to jurisdiction in a forum. As we have just noted, the Rules reflect this principle: A party with a potential defense based on personal jurisdiction waives that defense by failing to assert it at an early stage of litigation—either in a pre-answer motion or in the answer.

But the broader significance of consent as a basis for jurisdiction long remained buried. Before *International Shoe* the cases that spoke of "consent" often referred to consent implied from presence, or from what modern jurisdictional analysis would refer to as contacts. Such contacts can provide a perfectly adequate basis for jurisdiction, but they are not consent in any strong sense of the word. Since *International Shoe* recharacterized those implied consent cases as contacts, it has become easier to focus on what one might call "real" consent, a specific agreement to submit to jurisdiction. Cases since *International Shoe* have greatly expanded parties' ability to use consent as a jurisdictional tool; as you would expect, this tool finds its most frequent use in cases in which the parties have some prior contractual dealings.

The starting point is National Equipment Rental v. Szukhent, 375 U.S. 311 (1964). The Szukhents, Michigan farmers, leased farm equipment from a New York concern. On the back of the lease form was a clause saying that the Szukhents "designate[] Florence Weinberg [at a New York City address] as agent for the purpose of accepting service of process." When the Szukhents defaulted on the lease, plaintiff sued in New York, serving process on Ms. Weinberg (who notified defendants of the suit), and basing jurisdiction on such service. The Supreme Court upheld this procedure, treating the quoted clause as consent to personal jurisdiction and holding that under the circumstances the clause did not violate due process.

Why would National Equipment want such a clause? The most likely reason is that it would reduce costs and increase convenience—National Equipment could use its regular lawyer, who would be a member of the New York bar, and would not have to incur the costs of finding lawyers in whatever states it rented its farm equipment. If required to testify, the company's officers could do so without disrupting its business. Moreover, National Equipment might have liked that lower costs and greater convenience for it meant increased costs and inconvenience for the Szukhents and others similarly situated. And, in the event a dispute went to trial, it would be before a New York rather than a Michigan jury, which might view the New Yorkers less favorably in a dispute with "one of their own."

In *National Equipment Rental*, the parties manipulated jurisdictional rules contractually, the Szukhents consenting to a New York jurisdiction that would not likely have existed without that clause. Notice, however, that the clause in *National Equipment Rental* permitted service in New York but did not require suit to be brought there; so far as the contract was concerned, the Szukhents could have sued National Equipment Rental in Michigan, and National Equipment could have sued the Szukhents there as well. The next case takes matters further. (A word about substantive background may ease understanding: Federal courts have subject matter jurisdiction over admiralty matters, which include the interpretation of contracts calling for carriage of passengers by sea.)

Carnival Cruise Lines, Inc. v. Shute

499 U.S. 585 (1991)

BLACKMUN, J., delivered the opinion of the Court.

In this admiralty case we primarily consider whether the United States Court of Appeals for the Ninth Circuit correctly refused to enforce a forum-selection clause contained in tickets issued by petitioner Carnival Cruise Lines, Inc., to respondents Eulala and Russel Shute.

I

The Shutes, through an Arlington, Wash., travel agent, purchased passage for a 7-day cruise on petitioner's ship, the *Tropicale*. Respondents paid the fare to the agent who forwarded the payment to petitioner's headquarters in Miami, Fla. Petitioner then prepared the tickets and sent them to respondents in the State of Washington. The face of each ticket, at its left-hand lower corner, contained this admonition: "SUBJECT TO CONDITIONS OF CONTRACT ON LAST PAGES IMPORTANT!

PLEASE READ CONTRACT—ON LAST PAGES 1, 2, 3." The following appeared on "contract page 1" of each ticket:

Terms and Conditions of Passage Contract Ticket . . .

3. (a) The acceptance of this ticket by the person or persons named hereon as passengers shall be deemed to be an acceptance and agreement by each of them of all of the terms and conditions of this Passage Contract Ticket. . . .

8. It is agreed by and between the passenger and the Carrier that all disputes and matters whatsoever arising under, in connection with or incident to this Contract shall be litigated, if at all, in and before a Court located in the State of Florida, U.S.A., to the exclusion of the Courts of any other state or country.

The last quoted paragraph is the forum-selection clause at issue.

II

Respondents boarded the *Tropicale* in Los Angeles, Cal. The ship sailed to Puerto Vallarta, Mexico, and then returned to Los Angeles. While the ship was in international waters off the Mexican coast, respondent Eulala Shute was injured when she slipped on a deck mat during a guided tour of the ship's galley. Respondents filed suit against petitioner in the United States District Court for the Western District of Washington, claiming that Mrs. Shute's injuries had been caused by the negligence of Carnival Cruise Lines and its employees.

Petitioner moved for summary judgment, contending that the forum clause in respondents' tickets required the Shutes to bring their suit against petitioner in a court in the State of Florida. . . .

III

We begin by noting the boundaries of our inquiry. First, this is a case in admiralty, and federal law governs the enforceability of the forum-selection clause we scrutinize. Second, we do not address the question whether respondents had sufficient notice of the forum clause before entering the contract for passage. Respondents essentially have conceded that they had notice of the forum-selection provision. Brief for Respondents 26 ("The respondents do not contest the incorporation of the provisions nor [sic] that the forum selection clause was reasonably communicated to the respondents, as much as three pages of fine print can be communicated."). . . .

[In an earlier case, *The Bremen,* the Court had approved a forum selection clause negotiated between two large commercial entities, with dicta suggesting general approval of such clauses.] Within this context, respondents urge that the forum clause should not be enforced because, contrary to this Court's teachings in *The Bremen,* the clause was not the product of negotiation, and enforcement effectively would deprive respondents of their day in court. . . .

IV

A

. . . . [R]espondents' passage contract was purely routine and doubtless nearly identical to every commercial passage contract issued by petitioner and most other cruise lines. In this context, it would be entirely unreasonable for us to assume that respondents—or any other cruise passenger—would negotiate with petitioner the terms of a forum-selection clause in an ordinary commercial cruise ticket. Common sense dictates that a ticket of this kind will be a form contract the terms of which are not subject to negotiation, and that an individual purchasing the ticket will not have bargaining parity with the cruise line. . . .

Including a reasonable forum clause in a form contract of this kind well may be permissible for several reasons: First, a cruise line has a special interest in limiting the fora in which it potentially could be subject to suit. Because a cruise ship typically carries passengers from many locales, it is not unlikely that a mishap on a cruise could subject the cruise line to litigation in several different fora. Additionally, a clause establishing ex ante the forum for dispute resolution has the salutary effect of dispelling any confusion about where suits arising from the contract must be brought and defended, sparing litigants the time and expense of pretrial motions to determine the correct forum and conserving judicial resources that otherwise would be devoted to deciding those motions. Finally, it stands to reason that passengers who purchase tickets containing a forum clause like that at issue in this case benefit in the form of reduced fares reflecting the savings that the cruise line enjoys by limiting the fora in which it may be sued. . . .

It bears emphasis that forum-selection clauses contained in form passage contracts are subject to judicial scrutiny for fundamental fairness. In this case, there is no indication that petitioner set Florida as the forum in which disputes were to be resolved as a means of discouraging cruise passengers from pursuing legitimate claims. Any suggestion of such a bad-faith motive is belied by two facts: Petitioner has its principal place of business in Florida, and many of its cruises depart from and return to Florida ports. Similarly, there is no evidence that petitioner obtained respondents' accession to the forum clause by fraud or overreaching. Finally, respondents have conceded that they were given notice of the forum provision and, therefore, presumably retained the option of rejecting the contract with impunity. In the case before us, therefore, we conclude that the Court of Appeals erred in refusing to enforce the forum-selection clause. . . .

STEVENS, J., with whom MARSHALL, J., joins, dissenting. . . .

Forum-selection clauses in passenger tickets involve the intersection of two strands of traditional contract law that qualify the general rule that courts will enforce the terms of a contract as written. Pursuant to the first strand, courts traditionally have reviewed with heightened scrutiny the terms of contracts of adhesion, form contracts offered on a take-or-leave basis by a party with stronger bargaining power to a party with weaker power. Some commentators have questioned whether contracts of adhesion can justifiably be enforced at all under traditional contract theory because the adhering party generally enters into them without manifesting knowing and voluntary consent to all their terms. . . .

The second doctrinal principle implicated by forum-selection clauses is the traditional rule that "contractual provisions, which seek to limit the place or court in which an action may . . . be brought, are invalid as contrary to public policy." Although adherence to this general rule has declined in recent years, particularly following our decision in The Bremen v. Zapata Off-Shore Co., 407 U.S. 1 (1972), the prevailing rule is still that forum-selection clauses are not enforceable if they were not freely bargained for, create additional expense for one party, or deny one party a remedy. . . .

[For both reasons noted above, the dissenters would have declined to enforce the forum selection clause in the ticket.]

WHAT'S NEW HERE?

- At one level, not much is new here: The Supreme Court, interpreting federal maritime law, decided that a forum selection clause on the back of a ticket was enforceable in a suit brought by a passenger. That holding, while an authoritative interpretation of federal maritime law, did not control in other contracts governed by state law or other aspects of federal law.
- But, to the extent that the Supreme Court's reasoning was persuasive, other courts might follow it. And they have: Federal courts have enforced forum selection clauses in numerous contexts, and many state courts have followed suit.

Notes and Problems

1. To see the effect of the forum selection clause in this case, begin by imagining that the ticket had contained no such clause. Under such circumstances the questions that arise recapitulate the material in the preceding sections of this chapter:

   a. Review the jurisdictional contacts and identify the plausible forum states.
   b. What jurisdictional issues would arise in each of those locations?

2. Now consider the forum selection clause. One of the hallmarks of U.S. law is the extent to which the rules of procedure are "default" rules, rules that govern if the parties have not agreed to something else. Forum selection clauses provide an example of the parties' ability to make agreements that displace ordinary procedural rules. The clause is a contractual provision. As Justice Stevens's dissent suggests, courts approaching such clauses will always have at least two questions to consider:

   a. First, as a matter of contract law, is the clause enforceable? (The same question arises in respect to agreements to arbitrate, as you will learn in Chapter 8.)
   b. Second, apart from the law of contract, is there some overriding reason that such clauses should not be enforced?

      c. Does the majority suggest any circumstances under which it would have been unwilling to enforce a forum selection clause?

      d. Because it would have been easy to distinguish *The Bremen* (as concerning a contract negotiated by commercially sophisticated parties of equal standing), *Carnival Cruise Lines* stands as strong evidence of the Court's willingness to enforce forum selection clauses. Notice, however, that the Court reserved the right not to enforce these types of clauses under some circumstances, and that reservation has remained in the background in subsequent cases (compare *Atlantic Marine Construction* at the end of this chapter)—even when the Court ultimately enforces the clause.

3. Forum selection clauses lie in the middle of a spectrum of contractual provisions that affect procedure; all are common parts of many contracts. Lawyers drafting contracts must consider whether any or all of these types of clauses would be helpful to their clients.

      a. *Choice of law* clauses do not purport to say where suit shall be brought but do provide that the substantive law of a particular jurisdiction will govern disputes arising under the contract. The contract in *Burger King* (supra page 109) contained such a clause, which specified that Florida law would govern the agreement. (The Burger King franchise agreement did not contain a forum selection clause; compare the date of that case to *Carnival Cruise Lines* and imagine why Burger King's lawyers may have hesitated to insert a forum selection clause in that contract.)

      b. *Consent-to-jurisdiction* clauses say that the parties (or one of the parties) consent to suit in a particular place, thus waiving challenges to personal jurisdiction. Such clauses permit, but do not require, that the suit be brought in the consented-to place. The Supreme Court upheld such a clause in *National Equipment Rental v. Szukhent*, described supra page 158.

      c. *Forum selection clauses*, exemplified in *Carnival Cruise Lines*, take things one step further, limiting the forum to a single location.

      d. *Arbitration clauses* (discussed in Chapter 8 infra) take disputes out of the hands of the judicial system and place them in an arbitration system largely beyond judicial review.

D. NOTICE

1. The Constitutional Requirements

Pennoyer established an analytic scheme with three branches—power, consent, and notice. This exploration of personal jurisdiction has so far focused on the first two of these branches. Reflecting on the case law examined so far, one could conclude that in order to exercise jurisdiction over a defendant a forum state must have *either* power (flowing from the kind of relationships discussed in the contacts cases) *or* the defendant's consent. Consent may come either in the form of a prelitigation agreement (as in *Carnival Cruise Lines v. Shute*) or by waiver (when defendant appears but fails to challenge jurisdiction).

The facts of *Pennoyer*, however, suggested another basic objection to the exercise of a state's power. In *Mitchell v. Neff*, the lawsuit preceding *Pennoyer v. Neff*, the only notice given to the defendant was a small-print advertisement appearing in the pages of a legal newspaper. In the lower court Neff argued that the statute authorizing notice in this form had not been complied with, and the lower court had reversed on this ground. The U.S. Supreme Court split on the question of statutory interpretation and went on to rest its decision on the absence of power. Because the Court equated power with personal service of process, the question of notice remained buried for some decades: Personal service of process on the defendant within the state simultaneously asserted power and gave notice.

The issues of power and notice began to diverge as states expanded the concept of consent. For example, in Wuchter v. Pizzutti, 276 U.S. 13 (1928), a precursor of *Mullane v. Central Hanover Bank & Trust*, infra, the Supreme Court considered a New Jersey nonresident motorist statute. It treated the use of the state's roads by nonresidents as consent to both jurisdiction in auto accident cases and to the appointment of the Secretary of State as the agent of the defendant for service of process. But the statute did not explicitly direct the Secretary to give notice to the nonresident driver. Even though the defendant had in fact received notice, the Court struck down the statute.

Cases like *Wuchter* made it clear that individuals being sued *in personam* must receive some form of notice. But again recall the distinction, recognized by *Pennoyer*, between *in personam* and *in rem* jurisdiction. As the *Pennoyer* Court saw things, because it was perfectly permissible for a state to assume that people kept an eye on their property, a state could presume that the seizure of property (a necessary prerequisite to *in rem* jurisdiction, you will recall) would also accomplish notice. Behind this rather cavalier assumption may have been an understandable concern. If states were to exercise control over land titles, they had to have some method of rendering binding judgments; a rule that permitted landowners to avoid jurisdiction simply by wandering off without leaving an address would be intolerable. The willingness to presume notice from seizure was a rough but effective way of ensuring that this situation did not arise. But it also posed a potentially troubling question—could a state also dispense with notice if the whereabouts of the property owner *were* known? The next case, a constitutional landmark, addresses that question.

PERSPECTIVES

Justice Robert H. Jackson was the last Justice appointed to the U.S. Supreme Court without graduating from law school. After a year of law school, he had studied law "in chambers," by apprenticing himself to an experienced lawyer.

Raised in a small upstate New York town, he returned there to practice for 20 years while participating in civic and political activities that brought him to wider notice and gained him increasingly responsible appointments in the national

government: General Counsel of the Internal Revenue Service, Solicitor General of the United States, Attorney General, and Associate Justice of the U.S. Supreme Court.

Extraordinarily, he took leave from the Court to serve for a year as chief U.S. prosecutor at the Nuremburg trials of accused Nazi war criminals: The picture above shows him making his opening statement in those trials. So impressive was his advocacy that even one of the defendants admiringly described Jackson's opening statement as a "grand, devastating" address.

Returning to the U.S. Supreme Court, Jackson, believing that President Roosevelt had promised to appoint him Chief Justice, expressed public disappointment when President Truman nominated Fred Vinson for the position.

A stylist in the grand manner, Jackson wrote many memorable sentences, including one from *Mullane*: "[W]hen notice is a person's due, process which is a mere gesture is not due process."

Mullane v. Central Hanover Bank & Trust Co.
339 U.S. 306 (1950)

JACKSON, J., delivered the opinion of the Court.

This controversy questions the constitutional sufficiency of notice to beneficiaries on judicial settlement of accounts by the trustee of a common trust fund established under the New York Banking Law. . . .

[Common trust funds allow banks to pool a number of small trusts that would otherwise be too small to warrant the bank's supervision.] The income, capital gains, losses and expenses of the collective trust are shared by the constituent trusts in proportion to their contribution. By this plan, diversification of risk and economy of management can be extended to those whose capital standing alone would not obtain such advantage.

[Banks and other fiduciaries make periodic "accountings," which allow beneficiaries to challenge the fiduciary's actions for a stated prior period—but insulate the fiduciaries from later challenges.] The decree, in each such judicial settlement of accounts, is made binding and conclusive as to any matter set forth in the account upon everyone having any interest in the common fund or in any participating estate, trust or fund. . . .

In January, 1946, Central Hanover Bank and Trust Company established a common trust fund and in March, 1947, it petitioned the Surrogate's Court [which in New York has jurisdiction over trusts] for settlement of its first account as common trustee. . . . The record does not show the number or residence of the beneficiaries, but they were many and it is clear that some of them were not residents of the State of New York.

The . . . only notice required [to beneficiaries of the trust, as a matter of New York law], and the only one given, was by newspaper publication setting forth merely the name and address of the trust company, the name and the date of establishment of the common trust fund, and a list of all participating estates, trusts or funds. [The Court notes that same statute required the bank, when the trust was established, to send each beneficiary a letter setting forth the procedure for notifying beneficiaries of the accountings.]

Upon the filing of the petition for the settlement of accounts, appellant [Mullane] was, by order of the court . . . appointed special guardian and attorney for all persons known or unknown not otherwise appearing who had or might thereafter have any interest in the income of the common trust fund; and appellee Vaughan was appointed to represent those similarly interested in the principal. There were no other appearances on behalf of any one interested in either interest or principal.

Appellant [Mullane] appeared specially, objecting that notice and the statutory provisions for notice to beneficiaries were inadequate to afford due process under the Fourteenth Amendment, and therefore that the court was without jurisdiction to render a final and binding decree. Appellant's objections were . . . overruled, [and] the Surrogate* [entered a] final decree accepting the accounts. . . .

The effect of this decree, as held below, is to settle "all questions respecting the management of the common fund." We understand that every right which beneficiaries would otherwise have against the trust company, either as trustee of the common fund or as trustee of any individual trust, for improper management of the common trust fund during the period covered by the accounting is sealed and wholly terminated by the decree.

[The Court first rejects the argument that New York does not have power to adjudicate claims against beneficiaries who reside outside New York and were not personally served.] [W]hatever the technical definition of its chosen procedure, the interest of each state in providing means to close trusts that exist by the grace of its laws and are administered under the supervision of its courts is so insistent and rooted in custom as to establish beyond doubt the right of courts to determine the interests of

---

* [In New York, the court with subject matter jurisdiction over trusts and estates is the Surrogate's Court; its judges are known as Surrogates.—Eds.]

all claimants, resident or non-resident, provided its procedure accords full opportunity to appear and be heard.

Quite different from the question of a state's power to discharge trustees is that of the opportunity it must give beneficiaries to contest. Many controversies have raged about the cryptic and abstract words of the Due Process Clause but there can be no doubt that at a minimum they require that deprivation of life, liberty or property by adjudication be preceded by notice and opportunity for hearing appropriate to the nature of the case.

In two ways, this proceeding does or may deprive beneficiaries of property. It may cut off their rights to have the trustee answer for negligent or illegal impairments of their interests. Also, their interests are presumably subject to diminution in the proceeding by allowance of fees and expenses to one who, in their names but without their knowledge, may conduct a fruitless or uncompensatory contest. Certainly the proceeding is one in which they may be deprived of property rights and hence notice and hearing must measure up to the standards of due process.

Personal service of written notice within the jurisdiction is the classic form of notice always adequate in any type of proceeding. But the vital interest of the State in bringing any issues as to its fiduciaries to a final settlement can be served only if interests or claims of individuals who are outside of the State can somehow be determined. A construction of the Due Process Clause which would place impossible or impractical obstacles in the way could not be justified.

Against this interest of the State we must balance the individual interest sought to be protected by the Fourteenth Amendment. This is defined by our holding that "[t]he fundamental requisite of due process of law is the opportunity to be heard." This right to be heard has little reality or worth unless one is informed that the matter is pending and can choose for himself whether to appear or default, acquiesce or contest.

The Court has not committed itself to any formula achieving a balance between these interests in a particular proceeding or determining when constructive notice may be utilized or what test it must meet. Personal service has not in all circumstances been regarded as indispensable to the process due to residents, and it has more often been held unnecessary as to nonresidents. We disturb none of the established rules on these subjects. No decision constitutes a controlling, or even a very illuminating, precedent for the case before us, but a few general principles stand out in the books.

An elementary and fundamental requirement of due process in any proceeding which is to be accorded finality is notice reasonably calculated, under all the circumstances, to apprise interested parties of the pendency of the action and afford them an opportunity to present their objections. The notice must be of such nature as reasonably to convey the required information, and it must afford a reasonable time for those interested to make their appearance. But if with due regard for the practicalities and peculiarities of the case these conditions are reasonably met, the constitutional requirements are satisfied. . . .

But when notice is a person's due, process which is a mere gesture is not due process. The means employed must be such as one desirous of actually informing the absentee might reasonably adopt to accomplish it. The reasonableness and hence the constitutional validity of any chosen method may be defended on the ground that it is in itself reasonably certain to inform those affected, or, where conditions do not reasonably permit such notice, that the form chosen is not substantially less likely to bring home notice than other of the feasible and customary substitutes.

It would be idle to pretend that publication alone, as prescribed here, is a reliable means of acquainting interested parties of the fact that their rights are before the courts. It is not an accident that the greater number of cases reaching this Court on the question of adequacy of notice have been concerned with actions founded on process constructively served through local newspapers. Chance alone brings to the attention of even a local resident an advertisement in small type inserted in the back pages of a newspaper, and if he makes his home outside the area of the newspaper's normal circulation the odds that the information will never reach him are large indeed. The chance of actual notice is further reduced when, as here, the notice required does not even name those whose attention it is supposed to attract, and does not inform acquaintances who might call it to attention. In weighing its sufficiency on the basis of equivalence with actual notice, we are unable to regard this as more than a feint.

Nor is publication here reinforced by steps likely to attract the parties' attention to the proceeding. It is true that publication traditionally has been acceptable as notification supplemental to other action [such as attachment or seizure] which in itself may reasonably be expected to convey a warning. [But, the Court finds, there is no comparable other action providing notice here.]

This Court has not hesitated to approve of resort to publication as a customary substitute in another class of cases where it is not reasonably possible or practicable to give more adequate warning. Thus it has been recognized that, in the case of persons missing or unknown, employment of an indirect and even a probably futile means of notification is all that the situation permits and creates no constitutional bar to a final decree foreclosing their rights.

Those beneficiaries represented by appellant whose interests or whereabouts could not with due diligence be ascertained come clearly within this category. As to them the statutory notice is sufficient. However great the odds that publication will never reach the eyes of such unknown parties, it is not in the typical case much more likely to fail than any of the choices open to legislators endeavoring to prescribe the best notice practicable.

Nor do we consider it unreasonable for the State to dispense with more certain notice to those beneficiaries whose interests are either conjectural or future or, although they could be discovered upon investigation, do not in due course of business come to knowledge of the common trustee. . . . [W]e have no doubt that . . . impracticable and extended searches are not required in the name of due process. . . . These are practical matters in which we should be reluctant to disturb the judgment of the state authorities.

Accordingly we overrule appellant's constitutional objections to published notice insofar as they are urged on behalf of any beneficiaries whose interests or addresses are unknown to the trustee.

As to known present beneficiaries of known place of residence, however, notice by publication stands on a different footing. Exceptions in the name of necessity do not sweep away the rule that within the limits of practicability notice must be such as is reasonably calculated to reach interested parties. Where the names and post-office addresses of those affected by a proceeding are at hand, the reasons disappear for resort to means less likely than the mails to apprise them of its pendency.

The trustee has on its books the names and addresses of the income beneficiaries represented by appellant, and we find no tenable ground for dispensing with a serious effort to inform them personally of the accounting, at least by ordinary mail to the record addresses. Certainly sending them a copy of the statute months and perhaps years in advance does not answer this purpose. The trustee periodically remits their income to them, and we think that they might reasonably expect that with or apart from their remittances word might come to them personally that steps were being taken affecting their interests.

We need not weigh contentions that a requirement of personal service of citation on even the large number of known resident or nonresident beneficiaries would, by reasons of delay if not of expense, seriously interfere with the proper administration of the fund. . . . However, no such service is required under the circumstances. This type of trust presupposes a large number of small interests. The individual interest does not stand alone but is identical with that of a class. The rights of each in the integrity of the fund and the fidelity of the trustee are shared by many other beneficiaries. Therefore notice reasonably certain to reach most of those interested in objecting is likely to safeguard the interests of all, since any objection sustained would inure to the benefit of all. We think that under such circumstances reasonable risks that notice might not actually reach every beneficiary are justifiable. . . . The statutory notice to known beneficiaries is inadequate, not because in fact it fails to reach everyone, but because under the circumstances it is not reasonably calculated to reach those who could easily be informed by other means at hand. However it may have been in former times, the mails today are recognized as an efficient and inexpensive means of communication. Moreover, the fact that the trust company has been able to give mailed notice to known beneficiaries at the time the common trust fund was established is persuasive that postal notification at the time of accounting would not seriously burden the plan. . . .

Certainly it is instructive, in determining the reasonableness of the impersonal broadcast notification here used, to ask whether it would satisfy a prudent man of business, counting his pennies but finding it in his interest to convey information to many persons whose names and addresses are in his files. We are not satisfied that it would. . . .

We hold that the notice of judicial settlement of accounts required by the New York Banking Law §100-c(12) is incompatible with the requirements of the Fourteenth Amendment as a basis for adjudication depriving known persons whose whereabouts are also known of substantial property rights. Accordingly the judgment is reversed and the cause remanded for further proceedings not inconsistent with this opinion.

WHAT'S NEW HERE?

- The Court said that *all* cases required a form of notice that was sensible under the circumstances and reasonably likely to actually inform interested parties of the lawsuit.
- The Court suggested that due process did not always require personal service of process.
- The Court remade the doctrine for constitutionally required notice into the same "it depends on all the circumstances" principle that *International Shoe* used for jurisdictional power.

Notes and Problems

1. Imagine the thought processes of the drafters of the New York Banking Law: Explain why they thought that published notice would be constitutionally adequate. What was wrong with their thinking, according to the Court?

2. What does the decision mean in practical terms? After the decision, what steps would have to occur to assure that the proceeding would bind the beneficiaries? For the approach taken by the State of New York, see N.Y. CLS Bank §100-c(6) (Matthew Bender 2011) (requiring mail notice to all beneficiaries whose addresses appear in bank's records or were known to claim any part of the common trust funds).

3. Note that in *Mullane* those who have to receive adequate notice were not, as in most cases, defendants, but rather prospective *plaintiffs*: those who might wish to challenge the bank's stewardship of their trust funds. But the case has had its most significant applications in cases involving notice to defendants.

4. Written in broad terms, *Mullane* interprets the meaning of due process in civil litigation with a reach extending far beyond its specialized facts. But it is less explicit about its implications than about its holding:

   a. In *Mullane*, mass mailings were deemed satisfactory. The Court acknowledged that some letters would not get through to their intended recipients but reasoned that because all intended recipients had the same interests, contacting a certain number of people in the group would serve approximately the same function as contacting them all. How would this principle apply to ordinary litigation, in which only a few parties are involved: Is mail adequate then? The answer matters because mail notice reduces the cost of serving process while also increasing the risk that the mail will not reach its addressee.

b. Does *Mullane* require individual notice whenever one can identify and locate a person whom litigation may affect—even if the cost of such notice will be high? The issue matters greatly in class actions—where both sides in the debate cite *Mullane*, one stressing its requirement of individual notice, the other stressing its emphasis on practicality. Rule 23(c)(2) straddles the question, requiring individualized notice for some classes with others receiving only "appropriate" notice. See Chapter 12 for further discussion of class action requirements.

c. The drafters of the New York statute that was struck down had counted on the language in *Pennoyer* stating that notice by publication would suffice for *in rem* and *quasi in rem* cases. *Mullane* changed the doctrinal landscape by saying that the label attached to the action didn't change the obligation to give notice.

5. Although the *Mullane* Court dropped hints, some legislators, courts, and lawyers thought it did not answer the question whether notice was required in other forms of actions. Those courts and lawyers turned out to be wrong:

   a. Subsequent cases have made it clear that only very unusual circumstances justify failure to give personal notice to any defendant whose identity and whereabouts are known and who is not seeking to evade service. E.g., Walker v. Hutchinson, 352 U.S. 112 (1956) (property seized for condemnation); Tulsa Professional Collection Services, Inc. v. Pope, 485 U.S. 478 (1985) (settlement of decedent's estate; published notice to creditors in general insufficient when estate knew of claim of particular creditor); Connecticut v. Doehr, 501 U.S. 1 (1991) (prejudgment attachment of real property).

   b. One case in this line, Jones v. Flowers, 547 U.S. 220 (2006), goes further—extending to a situation where the owner's location was not known. In a tax sale, the state authorities sent two certified mail notices to the last known address of the owner who, however, had moved after a marital separation. After the sale had occurred the owner sued to set it aside, citing his failure to get notice. The Supreme Court agreed, indicating that the state should have taken additional steps, without precisely specifying what they were—except that it rejected the idea that the authorities had the obligation to consult other sources, such as the telephone directory or income tax rolls, which would have revealed the new address. Given the low cost of digital searches under current conditions, one can imagine circumstances in which a court would hold that due process requires such a search in order to notify one whose property is about to be taken.

   c. At least one court has taken the availability of digital technology a step further. A New York wife was seeking a divorce. She could not locate her husband to serve process in a conventional way, but he maintained a Facebook account. The judge granted the wife permission to serve process via a Facebook message—so long as the defendant's Facebook account acknowledged receipt of the notice. http://time.com/3772614/facebook-divorce-summons-blood-dzraku/.

6. Be alert to a potential confusion that arises when courts or statutes speak of "service of process" and "personal jurisdiction."

   a. By "service of process," courts sometimes refer to the way in which the defendant is given notice of the action—the question with which *Mullane* deals. At other times they use the same phrase to refer instead to the extent of a court's adjudicatory power—minimum contacts and the like. This blending occurs because, so long as transient jurisdiction is valid, service of process within a state's borders may confer jurisdiction as well as giving notice (as in *Burnham v. Superior Court,* supra page 148). Courts and statutes thus speak of "service of process" when they mean jurisdiction or a combination of jurisdiction and service. (The Federal Interpleader Act, 28 U.S.C. §2361, for example, speaks of nationwide "process," but has been uniformly interpreted to mean nationwide personal jurisdiction.)

   b. Conversely, courts that conclude that a defendant did not receive constitutionally adequate notice (as in *Mullane*) will sometimes express that conclusion by saying that the court lacked "jurisdiction"; that is, it lacked one of the constitutional requisites for exercising adjudicatory power—proper notice.

7. *Mullane* completes the conceptual renovation of *Pennoyer. Pennoyer* posited three central categories for thinking about judicial authority: power, consent, and notice. Subsequent cases have reinterpreted each. As a summation of the chapter so far, identify the ways in which each of *Pennoyer*'s categories have been reinterpreted over the past 50 years.

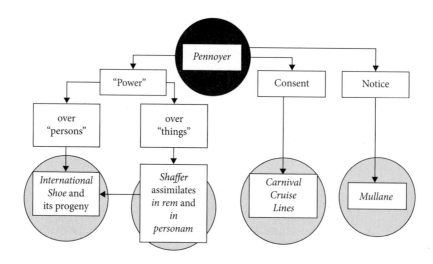

2. Beyond the Constitutional Requirements: The Mechanics of Notice and Service

Assuming that some constitutionally adequate notice is required, one must then decide what exact form notice must take. That form is widely regulated by statute. Rule 4 provides that regulation in federal courts. The current Rule 4 consolidates a gradual informalizing of the practice of service of process that has taken place over the last few decades, an evolution enabled in part by *Mullane*'s suggestion that forms of notice other than personal service would satisfy due process. In pursuit of informality, Rule 4 makes service by an officer of the court (a U.S. marshal) exceptional rather than ordinary. In its place, the Rule provides for service by any person who is not a party and is at least 18 years old. More fundamentally, Rule 4 proposes to replace even this personal but "unofficial" service with a still less formal procedure called "waiver of service" (see Rule 4(d)). Waiver of service uses first-class mail to send a copy of the complaint to the defendant, together with a request that the defendant return a form (found after Rule 4) by mail, waiving formal service of a summons. If the defendant returns that form, the case proceeds as if process had been served. If the defendant does not return the form within the time specified in the Rule, the plaintiff must then proceed to have a summons served more formally, using the procedures set forth in Rule 4(e)-(j). The defendant who waives service does not thereby waive objections to venue or jurisdiction, or any defenses to the merits of the lawsuit. By waiving service the defendant does, however, waive any objections to the sufficiency of the summons or the method by which it was served (Rule 12(b)(4) and (5)).

WHAT'S NEW HERE?

- Rule 4 avoided a long-simmering debate about whether ordinary mail is good enough for personal service of process. It uses ordinary mail, all right, but not to *serve* process; instead it requests a "waiver" that makes formal service unnecessary—even though the request for waiver accomplishes exactly the same notice function as service.

Why should the defendant want to make things easy for the plaintiff by waiving formal service of process? Rule 4 provides two answers to that question—a stick for failing to waive and a carrot for doing so. Rule 4(d)(1) imposes on defendants the "duty to avoid unnecessary expenses of serving the summons." The "stick" enforcing that duty is Rule 4(d)(2) requiring a "defendant located within the United States" to pay the costs of subsequent service if he has without good cause refused to waive service of process. The carrot appears in Rule 12(a)(1)(A)(ii), which extends the time to answer the complaint—from 21 to 60 days for domestic defendants and from 21 to 90 days for foreign defendants. The accompanying notes reflect a hope that this combination of procedural sticks and carrots will make waiver the predominant form of service in federal litigation. If the defendant fails to waive service, Rule 4 goes on to specify various means by which a plaintiff may serve defendants. Plaintiff must also use these means to serve defendants from whom a waiver of service cannot be demanded. Such defendants include the U.S. government, minors and incompetents, and others whose service is thought to require special formality so as to reduce the possibility of inadvertent default. Anecdotal accounts suggest that neither the carrot nor the stick has been large enough to make waiver the dominant form of notice.

Where formal service is required, its form depends on the nature of the defendant—individuals and corporations, domestic and foreign defendants, and federal and state government entities all have sections. The Rule specifies the means of serving foreign defendants, a source of special problems and growing concern as the volume of international business increases. Rule 4(f) and (h) set forth a list of ways in which such foreign defendants may be served, incorporating the provisions of the Hague Service Convention of 1969, an important international treaty.

1. Read Rule 4 and answer the following questions:
   a. Plaintiff wishes to sue an individual located in the United States and wants to commence the suit at minimum cost. What steps should she take?
   b. Defendant, located in the United States, receives a complaint together with copies of the designated forms appended to Rule 4, requesting waiver of service of summons. The request is dated September 1. If Defendant wishes to waive service, by when must she respond? See Rule 4(d)(1)(F).
   c. Plaintiff requests a waiver of service of summons from Defendant located in the United States, receives no waiver, and incurs the costs of personal service. After service has been completed, Plaintiff moves pursuant to Rule 4(d)(2) to recover the increased costs from Defendant. Defendant resists the motion, arguing that the underlying lawsuit is without merit and that it denies him due process of law to require him to help his adversary bring a meritless action. How will a court likely rule?

2. Service of process gives a defendant notice and thus overcomes what would otherwise be a constitutional obstacle to a valid judgment. Service may also avoid a defense based on the statute of limitations; in many states the statute is satisfied not by filing the suit but only by serving defendant with process. For claims based on federal law, Rule 3 provides that the statute of limitations stops running when the complaint is filed with the court; but defendant must still be notified. The Supreme Court has twice made clear that in diversity actions to which such state statutes apply, actual service (or waiver) is required to satisfy the statute of limitations—in spite of whatever Rule 3 says.

3. Rule 4 makes one proposition explicit that has been implicit since *Pennoyer v. Neff* and another that the Rules have long skirted: the relation between personal jurisdiction and service of process, and the relation between the reach of personal jurisdiction of the state and federal courts.
   a. On the first issue, Rule 4(k)(1) states that service (or waiver) establishes jurisdiction over defendants subject to personal jurisdiction. That formula is as important for what it does not say as for what it does. It does *not* say that service establishes jurisdiction. That had been the assumption of *Pennoyer*, at least for defendants served in the forum state. Instead, the Rule states that *if* the requisites of personal jurisdiction exist, proper service establishes jurisdiction. Thus a defendant who waives process, or who has been properly served, remains free to challenge the existence of personal jurisdiction.

b. On the second issue—the personal jurisdiction of federal courts—Rule 4 establishes a four-tier scheme. First, it says that federal courts, at a minimum, have personal jurisdiction over any defendant over whom the state court of the forum state would have such jurisdiction (Rule 4(k)(1)(A)). To that extent—and this provision covers the vast majority of all cases—the personal jurisdiction of state and federal courts "match." Thus a federal court sitting in California or Georgia has the same jurisdictional reach as a state court in that state—no less, but also no more.

c. The three remaining provisions deal with situations in which the Rule defines a longer jurisdictional reach for the federal courts than the state courts would have. One occurs when a party is joined to litigation under Rule 14 or 19; in these instances, the Rules provide for a "100-mile bulge" in the personal jurisdiction of a federal district court, even if a state court would not have had such jurisdiction (Rule 4(k)(1)(B)). This provision is particularly useful where federal district courts lie close to state lines: the Southern and Eastern Districts of New York (Manhattan and Brooklyn) and the district courts in New Jersey, Washington, D.C., Philadelphia, and Delaware are examples.

Another special situation arises when federal legislation specifically provides for broad, national power of a federal court. One example is a federal statute providing for nationwide service of process (for example, see 28 U.S.C. §1335); another is the enforcement of a civil contempt order arising from litigation involving a federal question Rule 4.1(b).

Finally, the Rule purports to define a new form of personal jurisdiction, limited to federal claims against defendants not subject to personal jurisdiction in any state. Such defendants will inevitably be foreign persons or entities that have insufficient contacts with any single state to create personal jurisdiction. In that situation, Rule 4(k)(2) provides:

> For a claim that arises under federal law, serving a summons or filing a waiver of service establishes personal jurisdiction over a defendant if:
>
> > (A) the defendant is not subject to jurisdiction in any state's courts of general jurisdiction; and
> > (B) exercising jurisdiction is consistent with the United States Constitution and laws.

This provision rests on the proposition that the Due Process Clause permits aggregation of the defendant's contacts with the United States as a whole for jurisdictional purposes—a question raised in several cases but not definitively resolved. As a quick review of this chapter so far, explain why Rule 4(k)(2) would not have helped the plaintiff in *J. McIntyre Machinery, Ltd. v. Nicastro*, supra page 111.

4. Assuming one knows the proper mode of service, questions still arise over whether the attempted service conformed to the statutory requirements. For example, has the process server left process "with someone of suitable age and discretion" as required by Rule 4(e)(2)(B)? Or what if the process server submits an affidavit that the defendant was served, but defendant denies it? Such questions will often require a hearing and judicial resolution. They may arise, for example, in a motion made under Rule 60(b) to set aside a default judgment (as in *Peralta*, at page 525). They may also arise in those states in which the statute of limitations does not stop running until process is served. And, service may be quashed on defendant's motion at the preliminary stages of the case for improprieties of form even though the service has performed its chief function—that of notifying the defendant of the commencement of the case.

a. Failure to deliver service may benefit the process server if his failures are not caught, because he can collect the fees and not do the work. Such intentional failure to serve process, accompanied by a false affidavit of service, is called "sewer service" by reference to the place where process eventually finds itself. Such abuses may also benefit the plaintiff, who may be able to collect a default judgment based on the sewer service because the defendant was intimidated by the judgment collection process, was ignorant of his rights, or could not afford a lawyer.

b. On the other side of the coin, defendants may sometimes take unfair advantage of service-of-process rules. Wily prospective defendants have sometimes dodged process for long periods, thereby requiring process servers to display ingenuity and sometimes even physical bravery. What should be done with such defendants, who refuse to waive service and then evade the process server? Rule 4(d), which imposes the duty to minimize costs of service on defendants and shifts those costs to a defendant who makes expensive personal service necessary, is one response; Rule 4(m), extending the time for service "if the plaintiff shows good cause," is another. But such a defendant must be served as a prerequisite even for collecting those costs of service, not to speak of the relief sought on the merits of the lawsuit.

Implications

As international litigation grows with international trade and travel, more lawyers find themselves faced with the need to serve process on foreign defendants. In many nations in the civil law tradition, only governmental officials can serve process: for a private person to do so (as Rule 4 permits) would be the rough equivalent of impersonating a police officer.

To save parties from such potential problems the Hague Service Convention, an important international treaty covering service of process, aims at clarifying the means of serving judicial process abroad. The Hague Convention would, for example, guide a Japanese firm seeking to serve a U.S. defendant in a suit brought in Japanese courts; it would also guide a U.S. plaintiff seeking to sue a Spanish defendant in Spain. The Convention provides that each signatory nation must designate a "Central Authority"* responsible for serving process on its nationals. So long as a plaintiff submits its request to this Central Authority in

---

* In the United States, the Central Authority is a division of the U.S. Department of Justice, which takes responsibility for serving process on U.S. defendants.

proper form, the Central Authority assumes responsibility for serving process in whatever way plaintiff directs. Unfortunately, the Convention's flexibility sometimes creates compli-cations, and other complications arise from the interaction of the Convention and Rule 4—problems with technical aspects beyond the scope of this course.

E. SELF-IMPOSED RESTRAINTS ON JURISDICTIONAL POWER: LONG-ARM STATUTES, VENUE, AND DISCRETIONARY REFUSAL OF JURISDICTION

Our discussion of jurisdiction has thus far proceeded as if the only relevant questions are constitutional power and notice. Each case has silently assumed that the state or federal court in question was authorized to assert jurisdiction if doing so was constitutionally permissible. The issue has been whether the Constitution permitted such an assertion of jurisdiction. We now go behind that assumption in three settings: long-arm statutes, venue laws, and the doctrine of forum non conveniens. Each represents a situation in which the legislature or courts have framed rules that restrict where a lawsuit may take place—even when the Constitution would pose no obstacles.

1. Long-Arm Statutes as a Restraint on Jurisdiction

A court may exercise jurisdiction over a defendant only when the state or federal government authorizes it to do so (and the authorization must be constitutional as applied to the case in question). In the world of *Pennoyer* such authorization was usually a simple matter: Had the state provided for service of process on a defendant in this situation? As the doctrines of personal jurisdiction expanded (especially in the years after *International Shoe*), many states began to authorize service (sometimes by mail) on defendants beyond their borders. Because *Pennoyer* had conceived of such extensions of state court jurisdiction as near-physical exertions of state power, statutes authorizing courts to reach beyond their own borders came to be known as "long-arm" statutes: States were extending their jurisdictional "arms." The name has stuck.

Some states have enacted long-arm statutes that reach for as much jurisdiction as the Constitution allows. California provides a well-known example:

California Code of Civil Procedure §410.10

A Court of this state may exercise jurisdiction on any basis not inconsistent with the Constitution of this state or of the United States.

Under such a statute there is no separate problem of analyzing the coverage of the long-arm statute: If jurisdiction is constitutional, it is also authorized by the statute. Other states have long-arm statutes limiting jurisdiction to specified situations. The next case displays a court applying such a statute.

Gibbons v. Brown
716 So. 2d 868 (Fla. Dist. Ct. App. 1998)

PER CURIAM.

[In 1994, Martine Gibbons and Mr. and Mrs. Brown were driving together in Montreal, Canada. Ms. Gibbons was giving directions to Mr. Brown, who was driving. The car turned the wrong way onto a one-way street, resulting in a head-on collision that injured both passengers. In 1995, Ms. Gibbons, a Texas resident, sued Mr. Brown in Florida alleging his negligent driving caused the accident; Mrs. Brown was not a party. Two years later, Mrs. Brown, seeking to recover for her own injuries, brought this Florida action against Ms. Gibbons alleging that her faulty directions caused the crash.]

In her complaint . . . Mrs. Brown alleged 1) that she is a resident of Florida; 2) that Ms. Gibbons has subjected herself to the personal jurisdiction of the Florida court by bringing [the prior] lawsuit. . . . In her motion to quash service of process and, alternatively, motion to dismiss, Ms. Gibbons . . . challenged the allegations in the . . . complaint as . . . inadequate to satisfy the strict requirements of the Florida long-arm statute. . . .

Obtaining in personam jurisdiction over a non-resident defendant requires a two-pronged showing. First, the plaintiff must allege sufficient jurisdictional facts to bring the defendant within the coverage of the long-arm statute, section 48.193, Florida Statutes. If that prong is satisfied, then the second inquiry is whether sufficient "minimum contacts" are shown to comply with the requirements of due process. *International Shoe Co. v. Washington.* Generally speaking, Florida's long-arm statutes are of a class that requires more activities or contacts to allow service of process than are currently required by the decisions of the United States Supreme Court.

As to the first part of the inquiry, Mrs. Brown contends that the allegations in her complaint satisfy section 48.193(2), Florida Statutes (1995), which states:

A defendant who is engaged in substantial and not isolated activity within this state, whether such activity is wholly intrastate, interstate, or otherwise, is subject to the jurisdiction of the courts of this state, whether or not the claim arises from that activity.

The parties agree that as a general rule in Florida, a plaintiff, by bringing an action, subjects herself to the jurisdiction of the court and to subsequent lawful orders entered regarding the same subject matter of that action. Mrs. Brown broadly construes this general rule to mean that by initiating the 1995 action, Ms. Gibbons subjected herself to Florida jurisdiction with respect to any "lawful orders" that were entered subsequently regarding "the subject matter of the action." On the other hand, Ms. Gibbons notes that her prior suit was brought in 1995, whereas Mrs. Brown did not file her complaint until October 20, 1997. Although Ms. Gibbons acknowledges that her prior action arose from the same vehicular accident as Mrs. Brown's instant suit, Ms. Gibbons notes that Mrs. Brown was not a party in the earlier action. Furthermore, several years separate the filing of the two proceedings. For purposes of the resolution of the question on appeal, we assume that the 1995 proceedings were over by the time Mrs. Brown brought her 1997 suit.

In Milberg Factors, Inc. v. Greenbaum, 585 So. 2d 1089 (Fla. 3d DCA 1991), . . . [o]bserving that an entity cannot control where its account debtors choose to relocate, the court stated that "the filing of lawsuits unrelated to this action against account debtors in Florida does not subject Milberg to the jurisdiction of our courts." Even if we assume (without deciding) that bringing an action in a Florida court can constitute a "substantial and not isolated activity" in some instances, we nevertheless note that Mrs. Brown has not shown that Ms. Gibbons "is engaged" in any activity in this state whatsoever other than defending the present suit. A current defendant's prior decision to bring a suit in Florida should not act indefinitely as a sword of Damocles hanging perilously over the head of that defendant if she later challenges jurisdiction in a separate suit (albeit a suit arising from the same subject matter). . . . Given the length of time between the two actions and the fact that the prior suit named as the defendant a non-party in the instant proceedings, we conclude that Mrs. Brown has not alleged a satisfactory ground for personal jurisdiction pursuant to statutory subsection (2). The appellee does not suggest, nor do we find, that the appellant's filing the 1995 action in the Florida court would, by itself, satisfy any of the alternative grounds for jurisdiction set forth in section 48.193(1)(a)-(1)(h). . . .

Absent sufficient jurisdictional allegations to show that Ms. Gibbons' acts satisfy the prerequisites in the Florida long-arm statute . . . the trial court is directed to DISMISS Mrs. Brown's complaint.

WHAT'S NEW HERE?

- Up until now, this chapter has dealt with situations in which a state has sought to assert jurisdiction over a defendant, and the question has been whether doing so violated the United States Constitution.
- *Gibbons* and cases like it represent a state legislature choosing not to go as far as the Constitution might permit. The *Gibbons* court decides it need not decide whether Florida *could have* exercised jurisdiction because, as it reads the statute, Florida chose not to.
- For litigants in such states, many personal jurisdiction inquiries have two steps:
- Does the long-arm statute in this state allow its courts to assert jurisdiction in such circumstances? If not, as in *Gibbons*, the case ends there.
- If so, is asserting jurisdiction on the facts of this case constitutional (a question the *Gibbons* court did not need to face)?

Notes and Problems

1. Be sure you understand why the opinion above does not say that it would be unconstitutional for Florida to assert personal jurisdiction over Ms. Gibbons.

   a. Why does Ms. Gibbons's activity not satisfy the Florida statute?

   b. Suppose Florida had a long-arm statute like that of California (quoted supra) extending state court jurisdiction to the boundaries permitted by the Due Process Clause. On the facts of this case, would it have been constitutional for Florida to exercise jurisdiction over Ms. Gibbons?

   c. In answering the preceding question, compare the facts of *Gibbons* to those of Adam v. Saenger, 303 U.S. 59 (1938). Saenger, a Texas citizen, brought suit in California against Adam, a California resident. Adam counterclaimed against Saenger, whereupon Saenger abandoned his lawsuit. Adam then recovered a default judgment on the counterclaim against Saenger. When Adam sued in Texas to enforce his judgment, Saenger defended on the ground that the California court lacked personal jurisdiction. So far as the record showed, Saenger's one and only contact with California was the filing of the lawsuit in question. That was enough, held the U.S. Supreme Court: "The plaintiff having, by his voluntary act in demanding justice from the defendant, submitted himself to the jurisdiction of the court, there is nothing arbitrary or unreasonable in treating him as being there for all purposes for which justice to the defendant demands his presence." Id. at 67-68. Is *Gibbons* distinguishable?

2. *Gibbons* points out that "Florida's long-arm statutes are of a class that requires more activities or contacts to allow service of process than are currently required by the decisions of the United States Supreme Court."

   a. New York is another populous state that has decided not to extend its jurisdictional reach to the full extent permitted by the Constitution:

   > [NY] CPLR 302(a)(3), the provision of New York's long-arm statute at issue here, permits a court to exercise personal jurisdiction over a nondomiciliary who:
   >
   > > 3. commits a tortious act without the state causing injury to person or property *within the state* . . . if he
   > >
   > > (i) *regularly* does or solicits business, or engages in any other persistent course of conduct, or derives substantial revenue from goods used or consumed or services rendered, *in the state*, or
   > >
   > > (ii) expects or should reasonably expect *the act to have consequences in the state* and derives substantial revenue from *interstate* or international *commerce*."
   >
   > (CPLR 302[a][3] [emphasis supplied]).
   >
   > Under this provision, the appellant must show both that an injury occurred "within the state," and that the elements of either clause (i) or (ii) have been

satisfied. It is appropriate to point out that establishment of long-arm jurisdiction in connection with a New York injury under either clause does not
implicate constitutional due process concerns. "[T]he subdivision [302(a)(3)]
was not designed to go to the full limits of permissible jurisdiction. The limitations contained in subparagraphs (i) and (ii) were deliberately inserted to
keep the provision 'well within constitutional bounds'" (1 Weinstein Korn
Miller, N.Y. Civ. Prac. P. 302.14, quoting 12th Ann. Report of N.Y. Jud. Conf.,
at 341).

Ingraham v. Carroll, 90 N.Y.2d 592, 596 (1997).

   b. Apply the New York statute to the following facts. Mrs. Ingraham "was
   a patient of Community Health Plan (CHP), a New York HMO with [a]
   clinic located in Hoosick Falls, New York," near the Vermont border. On
   several occasions her HMO physicians referred her to Dr. Carroll, who
   practices in Bennington, Vermont. Dr. Carroll is not under contract with
   CHP for consultation services. However, he frequently sees CHP patients
   on an ad hoc/fee-for-service basis, on referral. Dr. Carroll allegedly mis-
   diagnosed Mrs. Ingraham, whose survivors sued in New York. Assuming
   that defendant's contacts satisfied the Due Process Clause, did they fall
   within the New York statute? Held, no. Ingraham v. Carroll, 90 N.Y.2d 592
   (1997).

3. Note that although long-arm statutes are often products of state law, they
still bind federal courts. In other words, if Mrs. Brown brought suit against
Ms. Gibbons in Florida federal court, the district judge would also have to
assess whether her contacts with the state satisfy the Florida long-arm statute.
Rule 4(k)(1)(A).

4. In several notable instances, Congress has enacted federal long-arm statutes,
which purport to give the federal courts expansive powers of personal jurisdiction. Provisions of the federal securities laws provide one example. Another is
the Federal Interpleader Act, 28 U.S.C. §2361, which gives federal courts the
power to serve process anywhere in the nation, a power that has been interpreted to include personal jurisdiction.

2. Venue as a Further Localizing Principle

Like personal jurisdiction, *venue* determines where litigation will take place. Unlike
personal jurisdiction, venue flows solely from statutory—not constitutional—
sources. Also unlike personal jurisdiction, which is generally directed to which
state a suit can be brought in, venue determines within which federal judicial district suit can be brought. (States are divided into federal judicial "districts," with the
count ranging from one in less populated states to four (in California, New York,
and Texas).)

The general federal venue statute is 28 U.S.C. §1391. Its goal is to place suits in
judicial districts connected either to the parties or to the events giving rise to the

action. See, for example, 28 U.S.C. §1391(b), which puts venue "where any defendant resides" if all defendants reside in the same state or where "a substantial part of the events or omissions giving rise to the claim occurred." Because of this, the inquiries necessary under the venue statutes duplicate those involved in personal jurisdiction questions, but focus on contacts with a judicial district within a state, not with the state as a whole.

Why, then, have both a law of personal jurisdiction and one of venue? At a technical level the answer to that question is easy: Unlike personal jurisdiction, venue locates litigation not just in a state but in a particular federal judicial district within that state. For example, suppose a defendant is clearly subject to personal jurisdiction in Florida, which has three federal judicial districts. See 28 U.S.C. §133(a). Principles of personal jurisdiction tell plaintiff that she can sue in Florida, but the venue statutes and cases interpreting them will tell her in which of the three districts venue will lie, and thus whether she needs to file the complaint at a courthouse in Tallahassee, Tampa, or Miami.

The federal venue statute took its present form in 2011, following a century-long evolution during which it was occasionally impossible to find a judicial district in which venue lay even when there was both personal and subject matter jurisdiction over the case and parties.

The statute's structure is straightforward. Subsection (a) makes it clear that §1391 provides the venue provisions for all civil actions in federal courts—unless a specific statute provides otherwise. (For an example of a special venue provision, see 28 U.S.C. §1397, which provides that in an interpleader action—covered in Chapter 12—venue lies in any district where any claimant resides.)

Subsection (b) then provides three potential alternative venues. The first two are primary and the third (in (b)(3)) comes into play only if the first two do not yield an appropriate venue.

Subsections (c) and (d) clarify an issue that had proved vexing under previous versions of the statute: Given that "residency" often establishes venue, how does one define that term?

For this analysis, entities are treated differently than natural persons. The statute has separate definitions for persons and for entities (corporations, limited liability companies, and the like). Though the statute does not say so, for venue purposes the principal place of business of an entity will likely be defined the same way under the venue statute as it is for diversity jurisdiction—as the "nerve center" of the entity. *Hertz Corp. v. Friend*, infra page 225. If a state has more than one district? See §1391(d).

The statute also addresses the issue of residency for citizens of other countries. The statute makes clear that non-citizens who have been admitted by the United States as permanent residents are to be treated as citizens for venue purposes under subsection (c)(1). Courts are split about whether *all* non-citizens, regardless of whether they are lawful permanent residents, reside in the judicial district in which they are domiciled for venue purposes under subsection (c)(1). For a case concluding they do, see *Alvardo v. United States*, 2017 WL 2303758 (D.N.J. May 25, 2017).

Notes and Problems

Review 28 U.S.C. §1391 and answer the following questions by deciding the districts in which venue lies. (You may assume that federal subject matter and personal jurisdiction exist.)

1. Plaintiff sues defendant, a resident of the Southern District of New York, on a claim of breach of contract. The contract called for the manufacture and delivery of a machine. The machine was designed in New Mexico and assembled in the Northern District of Illinois from parts made in Ohio, California, and Pennsylvania.
   a. Where will venue certainly lie?
   b. What additional information would one need to decide whether there were other available venues?

2. Plaintiff sues *A*, a resident of the Southern District of New York, and *B*, who resides in New Jersey but conducts his business from an office in the Southern District of New York, on a claim of breach of contract. The contract, which was executed in Mexico, called for the assembly and delivery of a machine in Mexico, from parts made in Japan.

3. Plaintiff sues *B*, a lawful permanent resident who lives in Los Angeles (part of the Central District of California) and *C*, a resident of San Francisco (part of the Northern District of California).

4. Plaintiff sues defendant, a citizen of Belize, who has lived in California for 30 years but has not been admitted as a lawful permanent resident.

5. Plaintiff sues BigSoftware Corp., headquartered in the Western District of Washington, which does substantial business in every state, for a breach of contract arising out of the failure of software that occurred in New Mexico.

6. Plaintiff, a California resident, sues CarCorp, a Japanese corporation that sells cars all over the United States, on a product defect claim allegedly leading to personal injuries that occurred in an accident in Montana.
   a. For convenience's sake, plaintiff would like to sue in California. If, as courts have held, foreign corporations are treated for venue purposes the same as non-residents, will venue lie in California?
   b. Assuming venue will lie in California, can the suit be brought there? What more do you need to know?
   c. Notice that in practice the very generous venue provisions for non-residents will often be narrowed substantially by the principles of personal jurisdiction.

7. Finally, as background for the next case, look at 28 U.S.C. §1406, which addresses situations in which a case has been brought in a district where venue does not lie.

Thompson v. Greyhound Lines, Inc.

2012 WL 6213792 (S.D. Ala. 2012)

STEELE, J.

This matter is before the Court on the motion of defendant Greyhound Lines, Inc. ("Greyhound") to dismiss.... The appearing parties have filed briefs in support of their respective positions ... and the motion is ripe for resolution.

Background

According to the complaint ... on March 14, 2011, the plaintiff purchased from Greyhound in Pensacola a one-way ticket to Tunica, Mississippi, to arrive at 5:05 P.M. on March 15. A Greyhound bus delivered the plaintiff from Pensacola to Mobile just after midnight on March 15. Seven hours later, Greyhound personnel directed the plaintiff to board a Colonial Trailways bus. The driver, defendant Terry Reeves, announced that the bus was traveling only to Jackson, Mississippi and would thereafter return to Mobile. Reeves also announced that his bus was scheduled to arrive in Jackson at 12:05 P.M. and that a bus would depart Jackson at 12:30 P.M., arriving in Tunica at 5:05 P.M. The plaintiff, upon hearing this, decided it was time for a nap.

So far, so good. But when the plaintiff awakened, he realized it was almost 2:30 P.M. and that the bus was now headed back to Mobile. He and Reeves exchanged words, but the bus continued to Mobile, where the plaintiff remained for over nine hours before his brother sent him a pre-paid ticket back to Pensacola. Because of these events, the plaintiff "missed his court-date and was found guilty in absentia." The plaintiff sues Greyhound, Colonial Trailways and Reeves on several state law causes of action. Subject matter jurisdiction is based on diversity of citizenship.

Discussion

Greyhound argues that the action should be dismissed for improper venue or, in the alternative, for failure to state a claim. It is well established that a court should address challenges to subject matter jurisdiction under Rule 12(b)(1) and challenges to personal jurisdiction under Rule 12(b)(2) before considering a Rule 12(b)(6) motion based on failure to state a claim.... For similar reasons, the Court concludes that it should resolve Greyhound's challenge to venue under Rule 12(b)(3) before addressing its Rule 12(b)(6) motion. See Arrowsmith v. United Press International, 320 F.2d 219, 221 (2d Cir. 1963) (venue should be resolved before addressing failure to state a claim).

Although unnoted by the parties, "[t]he plaintiff has the burden of showing that venue in the forum is proper." ... However, "[w]hen a complaint is dismissed on the basis of improper venue without an evidentiary hearing, 'the plaintiff must present only a prima facie showing of venue.'" ... "Further, '[t]he facts as alleged in the complaint are taken as true to the extent they are uncontroverted by defendants' affidavits.'" ... Greyhound did not request an evidentiary hearing, so the plaintiff need present only a prima facie showing of venue. Neither side presented affidavits or other evidence, so the Court's review is limited to the complaint. As discussed below, that document does not suffice to meet the plaintiff's burden of making a prima facie showing of proper venue.

The propriety of venue in this case is to be measured by 28 U.S.C. §1391(b). This statute provides two means of establishing proper venue, with a third means available if proper venue cannot be established under either of the first two.

Venue is proper in "a judicial district in which any defendant resides, if all defendants are residents of the State in which the district is located." 28 U.S.C. §1391(b)(1). For purposes of this provision, an individual resides "in the United States district in which that person is domiciled." §1391(c)(1). According to the complaint, Reeves "is a citizen of Florida with his domicile residence in the State of Florida." . . . Because Reeves does not reside in Alabama, venue is not proper under Section 1391(b)(1).

Venue is also proper in "a judicial district in which a substantial part of the events or omissions giving rise to the claim occurred." 28 U.S.C. §1391(b)(2). Under this provision, "[o]nly the events that directly give rise to a claim are relevant." . . . The only event that occurred in this District was that the plaintiff changed buses here, and that event did not "directly give rise to a claim." The plaintiff does not allege that the transfer constituted a breach of contract, only that Greyhound had not told him, when he purchased the ticket to Tunica the previous day, that he would be transferring to a Colonial Trailways bus. Greyhound's alleged negligence and breach of contract, according to the complaint, derive from its failure to safely and successfully transport the plaintiff to Tunica, and nothing that occurred in Alabama caused or contributed to such failure. According to the complaint, Greyhound contracted to get him to Tunica at 5:05 P.M. on March 15, and taking the Colonial Trailways bus to Jackson would have (but for his sleeping through the transfer) gotten him to Tunica at precisely that time. The mere fact that the plaintiff passed through this District and changed buses here is not a "part of the events or omissions giving rise to the claim," much less a "substantial" part. Accordingly, venue is not proper under Section 1391(b)(2).

However, a substantial part of the events or omissions giving rise to the plaintiff's claims certainly occurred in the Southern District of Mississippi. Greyhound explicitly concedes the propriety of venue in that District. . . . Because proper venue can be established under Section 1391(b)(2) (only not in this District), the plaintiff cannot rely on Section 1391(b)(3) to establish venue.

"The district court of a district in which is filed a case laying venue in the wrong division or district shall dismiss, or if it be in the interest of justice, transfer such case to any district or division in which it could have been brought." 28 U.S.C. §1406(a). To the extent the phrase "in which it could have been brought" requires that personal jurisdiction over the defendants exist in the transferee district, specific personal jurisdiction exists in the Southern District of Mississippi, as the plaintiff's claims arise from and relate to the defendants' contacts with that District—Reeves' driving of the plaintiff there (and not waking him up in Jackson), Colonial Trailways' operation of the bus there, and Greyhound's sale of a ticket to transport the plaintiff through there. The parties make no argument to the contrary.

Greyhound requests the Court to dismiss rather than transfer, but it offers no explanation why this route should be preferred. As this Court has noted, "[g]enerally, the interests of justice [favor] transferring a case to the appropriate judicial district rather than dismissing it." Boutwell v. Advance Construction Services, Inc., 2007 WL 2988238 at 3 (S.D. Ala. 2007) (internal quotes omitted). For the reasons set forth in that decision, and in light of Greyhound's inability to articulate any reason why the action should be dismissed, the Court exercises its discretion in favor of transfer.

Conclusion

For the reasons set forth above, Greyhound's motion to dismiss for improper venue is denied. This action is transferred to the Southern District of Mississippi. Greyhound's motion to dismiss for failure to state a claim remains pending and ripe and will be considered by the transferee Court.

DONE and ORDERED.

Notes and Problems

---

1. Use *Thompson* to review your grasp of venue.

    a. The court gives two grounds for its ruling that venue did not lie in Alabama; what are they?

    b. The court does not explicitly say so, but it's fair to infer that Alabama had personal jurisdiction over Greyhound on this claim; why could plaintiff not resort to (b)(3) to rescue his chosen Alabama venue?

2. The court notes that it could have dismissed the case, leaving Thompson free to refile in Mississippi, assuming the statute of limitations had not run in the meantime. Why do you suppose the judge decided instead on the transfer alternative permitted by §1406?

3. What motion do you expect Greyhound to make as soon as the federal court in Mississippi accepts the transfer?

4. The opinion suggests, though it does not hold, that venue would have been proper in Alabama if the plaintiff had not joined Terry Reeves, the bus driver, who resided in Florida. Suppose the plaintiff had foreseen the venue problem: Was there any reason to join Reeves? (Even if he had been found liable, he was not likely to have significant assets to pay a damage judgment and, if he had been found liable for something that happened in the course of employment, his employer would be liable under the doctrine of respondeat superior.) So why bother to join Reeves?

    a. If you have already encountered the discovery materials in Chapter 7, you will know that some discovery devices are available as to a party that are not available as to a nonparty.

    b. Beyond that, there may be tactical reasons for joining Reeves: So long as he remains possibly liable as an individual defendant, he may have more incentive to testify as to various aspects of company policy ("Don't bother waking up passengers") that might help the plaintiff pursue his case against the bus companies.

Implications

When an action is brought in state court, federal venue statutes are irrelevant; they only apply to actions originally brought in the federal courts. (Cases removed to the federal courts from state courts are similarly not subject to federal venue requirements; venue lies in the district encompassing the state court from which the case is removed.) States, however, have their own venue statutes that indicate in which county an action must be brought. Professors James, Hazard, and Leubsdorf have summarized the state venue rules as follows:

> In other actions, state venue rules—in contrast to federal venue rules—follow variegated patterns that employ one or more of the following tests: (a) where the cause of action, or part of it, arose or accrued; (b) where some fact is present or happened; (c) where the defendant resides; (d) where the defendant is doing business; (e) where the defendant has an office or place of business, an agent, or representative, or where an agent or officer of defendant resides; (f) where the plaintiff resides; (g) where the plaintiff is doing business; (h) where the defendant may be found; (i) where the defendant may be summoned or served; (j) in the county designated in the plaintiff's complaint; (k) in any county; (l) where the seat of government is located. The tests that give plaintiff the widest choice are often applicable only when defendant is a nonresident of the state. The defendant's residence is the most common provision for venue.

James, Hazard & Leubsdorf 146, citing George Neff Stevens, *Venue Statutes: Diagnosis and Proposed Cure*, 49 Mich. L. Rev. 307, 315 (1951).

Another principle that is sometimes given the label "venue" is the local-action rule for certain causes of action, chiefly those involving real property. The rule states that only the courts of the state where land is located will hear cases that raise any question concerning title to the land. In the early case of Livingston v. Jefferson, 15 F. Cas. 660 (C.C.D. Va. 1811) (No. 8,411), Livingston sought to sue Thomas Jefferson for trespass to land located in Louisiana. As Jefferson was a resident of Virginia and not subject to jurisdiction elsewhere, and as the court ruled that under English common law the action was local and had to be brought where the land was located, the plaintiff was effectively left without a remedy. The rule has since been changed by statute in many states and was rejected by court decision in Reasor-Hill Corp. v. Harrison, 220 Ark. 521, 249 S.W.2d 994 (1952). Another traditional local action is an action by a state to collect taxes, although increasingly that restriction has been abandoned. E.g., Oklahoma ex rel. Oklahoma Tax Committee v. Neely, 225 Ark. 230, 282 S.W.2d 150 (1955).

3. Declining Jurisdiction: Transfer and Forum Non Conveniens

Both state and federal courts may decline to exercise jurisdiction even though they possess it. You have already encountered one example of this power: long-arm statutes that do not extend as far as the Constitution would permit. As personal jurisdiction has expanded under modern cases, courts have more frequently exercised the power of declining to hear cases. Both statutes and common law decisions express this power to decline jurisdiction. This section examines two of the rationales for declining to exercise jurisdiction. One—the common law doctrine of forum non conveniens*—affects both state and federal courts. The other—transfer among federal judicial districts under 28 U.S.C. §1404—applies only to the federal courts, allowing them to move cases around the country "for the convenience of parties and witnesses, in the interests of justice."

Both §1404(a) transfer and forum non conveniens dismissals flow from the same perception: that there will be circumstances in which a court has the power to hear a case but, for reasons of justice or efficiency, should not do so. For example, the judge may conclude that although jurisdiction is clear, the preponderance of witnesses, perhaps some of them severely disabled, will have to travel long distances to testify. Under these or similar circumstances, a federal court may decide to either transfer the case to another federal court under §1404(a) or dismiss it under the forum non conveniens doctrine for trial in another country. A state court might take a similar action, transferring (under a state statute analogous to §1404(a)) to another court in the same state or dismissing under the forum non conveniens doctrine for refiling in another state or country. We start with the more basic doctrine, forum non conveniens.

Piper Aircraft v. Reyno
454 U.S. 235 (1981)

MARSHALL, J., delivered the opinion of the Court....

I

A

In July 1976, a small commercial aircraft crashed in the Scottish highlands during the course of a charter flight from Blackpool to Perth. The pilot and five passengers were killed instantly. The decedents were all Scottish subjects and residents, as are their heirs and next of kin. There were no eyewitnesses to the accident. At the time of the crash the plane was subject to Scottish air traffic control.

The aircraft, a twin-engine Piper Aztec, was manufactured in Pennsylvania by petitioner Piper Aircraft Co. (Piper). The propellers were manufactured in Ohio by petitioner Hartzell Propeller, Inc. (Hartzell). . . . [The aircraft was owned and maintained by Air Navigation and] was operated by McDonald Aviation, Ltd. (McDonald), a Scottish air taxi service. Both Air Navigation and McDonald were organized in the United Kingdom. The wreckage of the plane is now in a hangar in Farnsborough, England.

[A] British Department of Trade [report] . . . found no evidence of defective equipment and indicated that pilot error may have contributed to the accident. The

---

* Inconvenient forum.

pilot, who had obtained his commercial pilot's license only three months earlier, was flying over high ground at an altitude considerably lower than the minimum height required by his company's operations manual.

In July 1977, a California probate court appointed respondent Gaynell Reyno administratrix of the estates of the five passengers. Reyno is not related to and does not know any of the decedents or their survivors; she was a legal secretary to the attorney who filed this lawsuit. Several days after her appointment, Reyno commenced separate wrongful-death actions against Piper and Hartzell in the Superior Court of California, claiming negligence and strict liability.... Reyno candidly admits that the action against Piper and Hartzell was filed in the United States because its laws regarding liability, capacity to sue, and damages are more favorable to her position than are those of Scotland. Scottish law does not recognize strict liability in tort. Moreover, it permits wrongful-death actions only when brought by a decedent's relatives. The relatives may sue only for "loss of support and society."

[The defendants first removed to federal district court in California invoking diversity jurisdiction. Piper then sought transfer under §1404(a) to the Middle District of Pennsylvania, where Piper does business, on grounds of convenience. Hartzell moved to dismiss for want of personal jurisdiction, or in the alternative to transfer the case to the Middle District of Pennsylvania under 28 U.S.C. §1404(a), where Hartzell's business with Piper supported jurisdiction; the district court transferred. With the case now moved to federal district court in Pennsylvania, both defendants then sought to dismiss the case on grounds of forum non conveniens.]

B

... The District Court granted these motions in October 1979. It relied on the balancing test set forth by this Court in Gulf Oil Corp. v. Gilbert, 330 U.S. 501 (1947), and its companion case, Koster v. Lumbermens Mut. Cas. Co., 330 U.S. 518 (1947). In those decisions, the Court stated that a plaintiff's choice of forum should rarely be disturbed. However, when an alternative forum has jurisdiction to hear the case, and when trial in the chosen forum would "establish . . . oppressiveness and vexation to a defendant . . . out of all proportion to plaintiff's convenience," or when the "chosen forum [is] inappropriate because of considerations affecting the court's own administrative and legal problems," the court may, in the exercise of its sound discretion, dismiss the case. To guide trial court discretion, the Court provided a list of "private interest factors" affecting the convenience of the litigants, and a list of "public interest factors" affecting the convenience of the forum.[6]

---

6. The factors pertaining to the private interests of the litigants included the "relative ease of access to sources of proof; availability of compulsory process for attendance of unwilling, and the cost of obtaining attendance of willing, witnesses; possibility of view of premises, if view would be appropriate to the action; and all other practical problems that make trial of a case easy, expeditious and inexpensive." Gilbert, 330 U.S., at 508. The public factors bearing on the question included the administrative difficulties flowing from court congestion; the "local interest in having localized controversies decided at home"; the interest in having the trial of a diversity case in a forum that is at home with the law that must govern the action; the avoidance of unnecessary problems in conflict of laws, or in the application of foreign law; and the unfairness of burdening citizens in an unrelated forum with jury duty.

[The Third Circuit reversed, on the ground that dismissal for forum non conveniens is never appropriate where the law of the alternative forum is less favorable to the plaintiff.]

II

The Court of Appeals erred in holding that plaintiffs may defeat a motion to dismiss on the ground of forum non conveniens merely by showing that the substantive law that would be applied in the alternative forum is less favorable to the plaintiffs than that of the present forum. The possibility of a change in substantive law should ordinarily not be given conclusive or even substantial weight in the forum non conveniens inquiry.

We expressly rejected the position adopted by the Court of Appeals in our decision in Canada Malting Co. v. Paterson Steamships, Ltd., 285 U.S. 413 (1932). . . .

The Court of Appeals' decision is inconsistent with this Court's earlier forum non conveniens decisions in another respect. Those decisions have repeatedly emphasized the need to retain flexibility. . . .

[I]f conclusive or substantial weight were given to the possibility of a change in law, the forum non conveniens doctrine would become virtually useless. Jurisdiction and venue requirements are often easily satisfied. As a result, many plaintiffs are able to choose from among several forums. Ordinarily, these plaintiffs will select that forum whose choice-of-law rules are most advantageous. Thus, if the possibility of an unfavorable change in substantive law is given substantial weight in the forum non conveniens inquiry, dismissal would rarely be proper. . . .

Upholding the decision of the Court of Appeals would result in other practical problems. At least where the foreign plaintiff named an American manufacturer as defendant, a court could not dismiss the case on grounds of forum non conveniens where dismissal might lead to an unfavorable change in law. The American courts, which are already extremely attractive to foreign plaintiffs, would become even more attractive. The flow of litigation into the United States would increase and further congest already crowded courts.[19] . . .

We do not hold that the possibility of an unfavorable change in law should never be a relevant consideration in a forum non conveniens inquiry. Of course, if the remedy provided by the alternative forum is so clearly inadequate or unsatisfactory that it is no remedy at all, the unfavorable change in law may be given substantial weight; the district court may conclude that dismissal would not be in the interests of

---

19. In holding that the possibility of a change in law unfavorable to the plaintiff should not be given substantial weight, we also necessarily hold that the possibility of a change in law favorable to defendant should not be considered. Respondent suggests that Piper and Hartzell filed the motion to dismiss, not simply because trial in the United States would be inconvenient, but also because they believe the laws of Scotland are more favorable. She argues that this should be taken into account in the analysis of the private interests. We recognize, of course, that Piper and Hartzell may be engaged in reverse forum-shopping. However, this possibility ordinarily should not enter into a trial court's analysis of the private interests. If the defendant is able to overcome the presumption in favor of plaintiff by showing that trial in the chosen forum would be unnecessarily burdensome, dismissal is appropriate—regardless of the fact that defendant may also be motivated by a desire to obtain a more favorable forum.

justice. In these cases, however, the remedies that would be provided by the Scottish courts do not fall within this category. Although the relatives of the decedents may not be able to rely on a strict liability theory, and although their potential damages award may be smaller, there is no danger that they will be deprived of any remedy or treated unfairly. . . .

III

The Court of Appeals also erred in rejecting the District Court's *Gilbert* analysis. . . .

A

The District Court acknowledged that there is ordinarily a strong presumption in favor of the plaintiff's choice of forum, which may be overcome only when the private and public interest factors clearly point towards trial in the alternative forum. It held, however, that the presumption applies with less force when the plaintiff or real parties in interest are foreign.

The District Court's distinction between resident or citizen plaintiffs and foreign plaintiffs is fully justified. In *Koster*, the Court indicated that a plaintiff's choice of forum is entitled to greater deference when the plaintiff has chosen the home forum. When the home forum has been chosen, it is reasonable to assume that this choice is convenient. When the plaintiff is foreign, however, this assumption is much less reasonable. Because the central purpose of any forum non conveniens inquiry is to ensure that the trial is convenient, a foreign plaintiff's choice deserves less deference.

B

The forum non conveniens determination is committed to the sound discretion of the trial court. It may be reversed only when there has been a clear abuse of discretion. . . .

(1)

In analyzing the private interest factors, the District Court stated that the connections with Scotland are "overwhelming." This characterization may be somewhat exaggerated. Particularly with respect to the question of relative ease of access to sources of proof, the private interests point in both directions. As respondent emphasizes, records concerning the design, manufacture, and testing of the propeller and plane are located in the United States. She would have greater access to sources of proof relevant to her strict liability and negligence theories if trial were held here.[25] However, the District Court did not act unreasonably in concluding that fewer evidentiary problems would be posed if the trial were held in Scotland. A large proportion of the relevant evidence is located in Great Britain. . . .

---

25. In the future, where similar problems are presented, district courts might dismiss subject to the condition that defendant corporations agree to provide the records relevant to the plaintiff's claims.

The District Court correctly concluded that the problems posed by the inability to implead potential third-party defendants clearly supported holding the trial in Scotland. Joinder of the pilot's estate, Air Navigation, and McDonald is crucial to the presentation of petitioners' defense. If Piper and Hartzell can show that the accident was caused not by a design defect, but rather by the negligence of the pilot, the plane's owners, or the charter company, they will be relieved of all liability. . . .

(2)

The District Court's review of the factors relating to the public interest was also reasonable. On the basis of its choice-of-law analysis, it concluded that if the case were tried in the Middle District of Pennsylvania, Pennsylvania law would apply to Piper and Scottish law to Hartzell. It stated that a trial involving two sets of laws would be confusing to the jury. It also noted its own lack of familiarity with Scottish law. Consideration of these problems was clearly appropriate under *Gilbert*. . . .

Scotland has a very strong interest in this litigation. The accident occurred in its airspace. All of the decedents were Scottish. Apart from Piper and Hartzell, all potential plaintiffs and defendants are either Scottish or English. As we stated in *Gilbert*, there is "a local interest in having localized controversies decided at home." Respondent argues that American citizens have an interest in ensuring that American manufacturers are deterred from producing defective products, and that additional deterrence might be obtained if Piper and Hartzell were tried in the United States, where they could be sued on the basis of both negligence and strict liability. However, the incremental deterrence that would be gained if this trial were held in American court is likely to be insignificant. The American interest in this accident is simply not sufficient to justify the enormous commitment of judicial time and resources that would inevitably be required if the case were to be tried here.

IV

The Court of Appeals erred in holding that the possibility of an unfavorable change in law bars dismissal on the ground of forum non conveniens. It also erred in rejecting the District Court's *Gilbert* analysis. The District Court properly decided that the presumption in favor of the respondent's forum choice applied with less than maximum force because the real parties in interest are foreign. It did not act unreasonably in deciding that the private interests pointed towards trial in Scotland. Nor did it act unreasonably in deciding that the public interests favored trial in Scotland. Thus, the judgment of the Court of Appeals is

Reversed.

[Justices POWELL and O'CONNOR took no part in the decision of these cases. The concurring opinion of Justice WHITE and the dissent of Justices STEVENS and BRENNAN are omitted.]

WHAT'S NEW HERE?

- Up until now, this chapter has considered cases in which the plaintiff has asserted and the defendant denied that the court possessed authority to hear *this* case against *this* defendant in *this* place. In *Piper* and cases like it, the defendant is saying something different: Yes, the court has the *power* to hear this case, but there are good reasons it, as a matter of discretion, should decline to exercise that power.
- Conceptually the two doctrines sound quite different. In practice, some think that forum non conveniens replays many of the same themes—convenience, basic justice, fairness—that one hears in modern personal jurisdiction cases.

Notes and Problems

1. Be sure you understand the issue at stake. By the time the case came to rest in Pennsylvania, defendants were not challenging the court's jurisdiction; what were they arguing?

2. Which changes in facts should lead to a different outcome—that is, the denial of the motion to dismiss for forum non conveniens?

   a. If the decedents had been U.S. citizens?
   b. If the plane had crashed into the sea, making it unavailable for examination?
   c. If Scotland permitted no recovery for wrongful death?

3. What will happen now that the case has been dismissed? One (likely) possibility is that the plaintiffs, deprived of the advantageous U.S. product liability and damages law, will drop the lawsuit. Another possibility is that they will refile in Scotland. But what if, in the meantime, the statute of limitations has run? It seems unfair to permit a defendant to move for dismissal on the grounds that forum *A* is less convenient than forum *B*, only to raise a defense that makes forum *B* entirely unavailable.

   a. To prevent this unfairness, courts regularly require that a defendant moving to dismiss on grounds of an inconvenient forum agree in advance to waive the statute of limitations defense in the alternative forum.
   b. The same requirement sometimes applies to personal jurisdiction and venue: Occasionally defendants will argue that a forum lacking either jurisdiction or venue is more convenient. When courts accept such arguments, they often condition dismissal on an agreement to waive jurisdictional or venue defenses in the new forum.

4. *Piper* exemplifies two adversaries determined to wring every ounce of advantage from the procedural system. Consider the steps in the case as examples of high-stakes, high-powered tactical maneuvering for advantage.

   a. Who was the plaintiff? Why do you suppose she filed suit in California, where none of the relevant events occurred?

   b. How did defendants respond to plaintiff's initial strategy? Enumerate the steps defendants used as they maneuvered toward the eventual outcome.

5. Contrast two applications of *Piper*'s doctrine. Are the cases distinguishable?

   a. Guidi v. Inter-Continental Hotels Corp., 224 F.3d 142 (2d Cir. 2000). Plaintiffs were U.S. citizens, survivors and heirs of the victims of shootings in an Egyptian hotel operated by defendant, where a gunman, apparently motivated by political and religious animus, had shot six people. Plaintiffs brought a federal diversity action in New York against the New York-based corporate hotel operator. The district court dismissed on forum non conveniens grounds, finding that an Egyptian court would be more familiar with Egyptian law, which governed the action, that Egypt's commitment to tourism assured that the suit would be handled properly, and that there was already related litigation pending in Egypt—suits brought by the families of French and Italian victims. The Second Circuit reversed, holding that the district court had abused its discretion in dismissing. The inconvenience and "emotional burden" on plaintiffs outweighed the "slight[ly]" greater convenience of litigation in Egypt, said the court. Can you distinguish *Piper*?

   b. Gonzalez v. Chrysler Corp., 301 F.3d 377 (5th Cir. 2002). Plaintiff, a Mexican national, sued in Texas for the wrongful death of his child as a result of an air bag accident. The court explained:

   > Mexican law caps the maximum award for the loss of a child's life at approximately $2,500 (730 days' worth of wages at the Mexican minimum wage rate). Thus, according to Gonzalez, Mexico provides an inadequate alternative forum for this dispute. . . .
   >
   > Gonzalez argues that because of the damage cap, the cost of litigating this case in Mexico will exceed the potential recovery. As a consequence, the lawsuit will never be brought in Mexico. Stated differently, the lawsuit is not economically viable in Mexico. . . .
   >
   > The practical and economic realities lying at the base of this dispute are clear. At oral argument, the parties agreed that this case would never be filed in Mexico. In short, a dismissal on the ground of forum non conveniens will determine the outcome of this litigation in Chrysler's favor.[9] We nevertheless are unwilling to hold as a legal principle that Mexico offers an inadequate forum

---

9. This fact is not unique to this lawsuit. A survey found that between 1945 and 1985, of 85 transnational cases dismissed on the ground of forum non conveniens, only 4 percent ever reached trial in a foreign court. See David Robertson, Forum Non Conveniens in America and England: "A Rather Fantastic Fiction," 103 L.Q. Rev. 398, 418-19 (1987).

simply because it does not make economic sense for Gonzalez to file this lawsuit in Mexico. . . .

[I]f we allow the economic viability of a lawsuit to decide the adequacy of an alternative forum, we are further forced to engage in a rudderless exercise of line drawing with respect to a cap on damages: At what point does a cap on damages transform a forum from adequate to inadequate? Is it, as here, $2,500? Is it $50,000? Or is it $100,000? Any recovery cap may, in a given case, make the lawsuit economically unviable. We therefore hold that the adequacy inquiry under *Piper Aircraft* does not include an evaluation of whether it makes economic sense for Gonzalez to file this lawsuit in Mexico.

Is *Piper* distinguishable? Is *Guidi,* described in Note 5a?

6. *Piper* portrays both §1404 and the common law doctrine of forum non conveniens in action. Add now two additional ingredients, both of which you have already met: an additional statute, 28 U.S.C. §1406 (encountered in *Thompson v. Greyhound Lines,* supra page 184), which allows a federal court to transfer to a proper district a case filed in a district lacking jurisdiction or venue; and a forum selection clause, which after *Carnival Cruise Lines v. Shute* (supra page 159) is an increasingly common feature of contracts. Consider the resulting interaction.

Atlantic Marine Construction Co. v. United States District Court
571 U.S. 49 (2013)

ALITO, J., delivered the opinion of the Court.
The question in this case concerns the procedure that is available for a defendant in a civil case who seeks to enforce a forum-selection clause. . . .

I

Petitioner Atlantic Marine Construction Co., a Virginia corporation with its principal place of business in Virginia, entered into a contract with the United States Army Corps of Engineers to construct a child-development center at Fort Hood in the Western District of Texas. Atlantic Marine then entered into a subcontract with respondent J-Crew Management, Inc., a Texas corporation, for work on the project. This subcontract included a forum-selection clause, which stated that all disputes between the parties "'shall be litigated in the Circuit Court for the City of Norfolk, Virginia, or the United States District Court for the Eastern District of Virginia, Norfolk Division.'" . . .

When a dispute about payment under the subcontract arose, however, J-Crew sued Atlantic Marine in the Western District of Texas, invoking that court's diversity jurisdiction. Atlantic Marine moved to dismiss the suit, arguing that the forum-selection clause rendered venue in the Western District of Texas "wrong" under §1406(a) and "improper" under Federal Rule of Civil Procedure 12(b)(3). In the alternative, Atlantic Marine moved to transfer the case to the Eastern District of Virginia under §1404(a). J-Crew opposed these motions. . . .

The District Court denied both motions [and the Fifth Circuit affirmed]. . . .

Relying on Stewart Organization, Inc. v. Ricoh Corp., 487 U.S. 22 . . . (1988) [noted at page 282], the Court of Appeals agreed with the District Court that §1404(a) is the exclusive mechanism for enforcing a forum-selection clause that points to another federal forum when venue is otherwise proper in the district where the case was brought. . . .[1] The court stated, however, that if a forum-selection clause points to a nonfederal forum, dismissal under Rule 12(b)(3) would be the correct mechanism to enforce the clause because §1404(a) by its terms does not permit transfer to any tribunal other than another federal court. . . . The Court of Appeals then concluded that the District Court had not clearly abused its discretion in refusing to transfer the case after conducting the balance-of-interests analysis required by §1404(a). . . . That was so even though there was no dispute that the forum-selection clause was valid. . . . We granted certiorari. . . .

II

Atlantic Marine contends that a party may enforce a forum-selection clause by seeking dismissal of the suit under §1406(a) and Rule 12(b)(3). We disagree. Section 1406(a) and Rule 12(b)(3) allow dismissal only when venue is "wrong" or "improper." Whether venue is "wrong" or "improper" depends exclusively on whether the court in which the case was brought satisfies the requirements of federal venue laws, and those provisions say nothing about a forum-selection clause.

A

Section 1406(a) provides that "[t]he district court of a district in which is filed a case laying venue in the wrong division or district shall dismiss, or if it be in the interest of justice, transfer such case to any district or division in which it could have been brought." Rule 12(b)(3) states that a party may move to dismiss a case for "improper venue." These provisions therefore authorize dismissal only when venue is "wrong" or "improper" in the forum in which it was brought.

This question—whether venue is "wrong" or "improper"—is generally governed by 28 U.S.C. §1391.[2] That provision states that "[e]xcept as otherwise provided by *law* . . . this section *shall* govern the venue of *all civil actions* brought in district courts of the United States." §1391(a)(1) (emphasis added). . . . Whether the parties entered into a contract containing a forum-selection clause has no bearing on whether a case falls into one of the categories of cases listed in §1391(b). As a result, a case filed in a district that falls within §1391 may not be dismissed under §1406(a) or Rule 12(b)(3).

---

1. Venue was otherwise proper in the Western District of Texas because the subcontract at issue in the suit was entered into and was to be performed in that district. . . .

2. Section 1391 governs "venue generally," that is, in cases where a more specific venue provision does not apply. Cf., e.g., §1400 (identifying proper venue for copyright and patent suits).

Petitioner's contrary view improperly conflates the special statutory term "venue" and the word "forum." It is certainly true that, in some contexts, the word "venue" is used synonymously with the term "forum," but §1391 makes clear that venue in "all civil actions" must be determined in accordance with the criteria outlined in that section. That language cannot reasonably be read to allow judicial consideration of other, extrastatutory limitations on the forum in which a case may be brought.

The structure of the federal venue provisions confirms that they alone define whether venue exists in a given forum. In particular, the venue statutes reflect Congress' intent that venue should always lie in *some* federal court whenever federal courts have personal jurisdiction over the defendant. . . . As we have previously noted, "Congress does not in general intend to create venue gaps, which take away with one hand what Congress has given by way of jurisdictional grant with the other." . . .

B

Although a forum-selection clause does not render venue in a court "wrong" or "improper" within the meaning of §1406(a) or Rule 12(b)(3), the clause may be enforced through a motion to transfer under §1404(a). That provision states that "[f]or the convenience of parties and witnesses, in the interest of justice, a district court may transfer any civil action to any other district or division where it might have been brought or to any district or division to which all parties have consented." Unlike §1406(a), §1404(a) does not condition transfer on the initial forum's being "wrong." And it permits transfer to any district where venue is also proper (i.e., "where [the case] might have been brought") or to any other district to which the parties have agreed by contract or stipulation.

Section 1404(a) therefore provides a mechanism for enforcement of forum-selection clauses that point to a particular federal district. And for the reasons we address in Part III, a proper application of §1404(a) requires that a forum-selection clause be "given controlling weight in all but the most exceptional cases." *Stewart* . . . (Kennedy, J., concurring).

Atlantic Marine argues that §1404(a) is not a suitable mechanism to enforce forum-selection clauses because that provision cannot provide for transfer when a forum-selection clause specifies a state or foreign tribunal, . . . and we agree with Atlantic Marine that the Court of Appeals failed to provide a sound answer to this problem. The Court of Appeals opined that a forum-selection clause pointing to a nonfederal forum should be enforced through Rule 12(b)(3), which permits a party to move for dismissal of a case based on "improper venue." As Atlantic Marine persuasively argues, however, that conclusion cannot be reconciled with our construction of the term "improper venue" in §1406 to refer only to a forum that does not satisfy federal venue laws. If venue is proper under federal venue rules, it does not matter for the purpose of Rule 12(b)(3) whether the forum-selection clause points to a federal or a nonfederal forum.

Instead, the appropriate way to enforce a forum-selection clause pointing to a state or foreign forum is through the doctrine of *forum non conveniens*. Section 1404(a) is merely a codification of the doctrine of *forum non conveniens* for the subset of cases in which the transferee forum is within the federal court system; in such cases, Congress has replaced the traditional remedy of outright dismissal with transfer. . . . For the remaining set of cases calling for a nonfederal forum, §1404(a) has no application, but the residual doctrine of *forum non conveniens* "has continuing application in federal courts." Sinochem [Intl. Co. v. Malaysia Intl. Shipping, 549 U.S. at 430 (2007)] (noting that federal courts invoke *forum non conveniens* "in cases where the alternative forum is abroad, and perhaps in rare instances where a state or territorial court serves litigational convenience best"). . . . And because both §1404(a) and the *forum non conveniens* doctrine from which it derives entail the same balancing-of-interests standard, courts should evaluate a forum-selection clause pointing to a nonfederal forum in the same way that they evaluate a forum-selection clause pointing to a federal forum. . . .

III

Although the Court of Appeals correctly identified §1404(a) as the appropriate provision to enforce the forum-selection clause in this case, the Court of Appeals erred in failing to make the adjustments required in a §1404(a) analysis when the transfer motion is premised on a forum-selection clause. When the parties have agreed to a valid forum-selection clause, a district court should ordinarily transfer the case to the forum specified in that clause.[5] Only under extraordinary circumstances unrelated to the convenience of the parties should a §1404(a) motion be denied. And no such exceptional factors appear to be present in this case. . . .

When parties have contracted in advance to litigate disputes in a particular forum, courts should not unnecessarily disrupt the parties' settled expectations. A forum-selection clause, after all, may have figured centrally in the parties' negotiations and may have affected how they set monetary and other contractual terms; it may, in fact, have been a critical factor in their agreement to do business together in the first place. In all but the most unusual cases, therefore, "the interest of justice" is served by holding parties to their bargain. . . .

We reverse the judgment of the Court of Appeals for the Fifth Circuit. Although no public-interest factors that might support the denial of Atlantic Marine's motion to transfer are apparent on the record before us, we remand the case for the courts below to decide that question.

It is so ordered.

Notes and Problems

---

1. Where did J-Crew, the plaintiff, file suit?

   a. Ignoring the forum selection clause, did venue lie in that district?
   b. Why?

2. To what forums did the forum selection clause point?

---

5. Our analysis presupposes a contractually valid forum-selection clause.

3. By what procedural devices did the defendant seek to invoke the forum selection clause?
    a. Putting yourself in defendant's position, why might you want to invoke all three of these devices?
    b. In particular, why might the defendant want to invoke §1406 and Rule 12(b)(3) in addition to §1404, which earlier cases had made clear was one route by which forum selection clauses might be enforced? About what language in §1404 might defendant be concerned?
4. By the time the dust has settled, it looks very much as if the defendant will be able successfully to invoke the forum selection clause.
    a. If that's accurate, and if on remand the district court enforces the forum selection clause via §1404, to which court will the case be transferred?
    b. Suppose there is a variation on the forum selection clause in which the only court specified was the Circuit Court for the City of Norfolk, Virginia (a state court).
        i. Explain why the federal district court could not use §1404 to send the case there.
        ii. In that situation, what would be the right order for the federal district court to enter?

* * *

This chapter has explored the elaborate law developed to answer a single question: In which court(s) can this lawsuit against this defendant be brought? The complexity of the doctrine answering that question testifies both to its practical importance and to a constitutional structure that recognizes a degree of independent autonomy and sovereignty in the several states. Simply put: It matters whether Alabama or California courts will hear a case because constitutional structure gives the governments of Alabama and California, including their respective courts, the last word on many important questions. Under our federal structure, however, there is an overarching—but limited—federal sovereignty with its own court system. So, in each case, the question is not simply whether the case belongs in State *A* or State *B*, but whether the case can be heard in a federal court instead of a state court. The next chapter explores the answer to that question.

Assessment Questions

Q1. Jane, fired by GrowCo, moves from Utah, where GrowCo is incorporated and has its only place of business, to California. In California she files suit in federal court for employment discrimination. Choose as many responses as are accurate.

   A. GrowCo cannot challenge personal jurisdiction because the case is in federal court.
   B. GrowCo can challenge personal jurisdiction.

C. If GrowCo could challenge personal jurisdiction, on these facts that challenge would probably prevail.

D. GrowCo need not challenge personal jurisdiction because the court will dismiss Jane's case on its own motion.

Q2. Jane, fired by GrowCo, moves from Utah, where GrowCo is incorporated and has its only place of business, to California. In California she files suit in federal court for employment discrimination. The employment agreement between Jane and GrowCo contains a clause specifying that any suit arising from the employment will be filed in federal district court in Utah. Which of the following statements accurately reflect the law? GrowCo . . .

A. Would prevail on a 12(b)(3) motion to dismiss for improper venue.

B. Would prevail on a motion under 28 U.S.C. §1406 to have the case moved to Utah.

C. Might prevail on a motion under 28 U.S.C. §1404 to have the case transferred to Utah.

D. Would prevail on a 12(b)(6) motion to have the claim dismissed because Jane has not honored the forum selection clause.

Q3. Same case as in Q2. GrowCo receives Jane's complaint and immediately answers, denying that it discriminated against her and asserting a counterclaim alleging that Jane stole trade secrets when she left GrowCo's employ. Discovery ensues. In a motion for summary judgment GrowCo challenges the court's personal jurisdiction.

A. GrowCo should prevail because it has no contacts with California.

B. GrowCo should lose because summary judgment is about the facts of the case, not the law of jurisdiction.

C. GrowCo should lose because it has waived its challenge.

D. None of the above.

Q4. Same case, except that upon receiving the complaint, GrowCo files a Rule 12(b)(2) challenge to personal jurisdiction. The district court rules against GrowCo. Which of the following is accurate?

A. If it litigates on the merits, GrowCo will lose the right to appeal the jurisdictional ruling.

B. GrowCo can litigate on the merits and, if it loses, still appeal the jurisdictional ruling.

Q5. *Mullane* . . .

A. "Overruled" the dicta in *Pennoyer* suggesting that seizure of property plus publication gave constitutionally adequate notice in all cases.

B. Created a sliding scale "it depends" test of constitutional adequacy of notice.

C. Suggested that people who had received no notice whatsoever could under some circumstances be constitutionally bound by a judgment.

D. Demonstrates that one doesn't need to graduate from law school to write a pretty fancy constitutional opinion.

Q6. Defendant receives a summons and complaint issued by a federal district court. With the summons and complaint is a request for waiver of service of process. Which of the following is accurate?

A. If defendant signs the waiver he cannot thereafter make a Rule 12(b)(2) motion.

B. If defendant signs the waiver, he has 60 days in which to answer the complaint.

C. If defendant does not sign the waiver, he will have a default judgment entered against him.

D. If defendant fails to sign the waiver, he may be responsible for the costs of serving him with process.

Q7. Sam starts a software business in Michigan. His principal product is an application that helps pet owners keep track of medical records of their animals. He sells the product through a website he maintains, allowing customers who have paid by credit card to download the software. Nora, who lives in North Carolina, buys the product and later brings suit against Sam in that state, alleging that the application's failure resulted in serious and expensive medical problems for her dogs. Sam challenges the jurisdiction of the North Carolina courts. Which of the following is accurate?

A. Nora will prevail so long as Sam's website is at all interactive.

B. Sam will prevail so long as nothing about his product makes it especially attractive to North Carolina customers.

C. Sam will prevail because he has never travelled to North Carolina.

D. Nora is more likely to prevail if as part of the purchase she was required to list her North Carolina address.

Q8. Auto Maker's vehicles have been recalled because faulty ignition switches cause the cars to lose critical safety systems, including power steering and air bag deployment. Purchaser, who lives in Seattle, Washington, brings suit against Auto Maker in federal district court for the Western District of Washington, seeking to recover for injuries sustained in such an episode. Which of the following is accurate?

A. Auto Maker can successfully challenge personal jurisdiction if it is incorporated and has its principal place of business in Michigan.

B. Purchaser need not worry about a challenge to personal jurisdiction so long as there is complete diversity between Purchaser and Maker and more than $75,000 in controversy.

C. To prevail against a challenge to personal jurisdiction, Purchaser will want to demonstrate that Auto Maker sought to market its vehicles in Washington.

D. *Daimler* and *Nicastro* will allow Maker to prevail so long as it distributed its cars through a subsidiary corporation.

Q9. Same failure of ignition switches, but the plaintiffs now include both the Washington purchasers and those throughout the country injured by the failure of the switches. Which of the following statements about personal jurisdiction is accurate?

  A. Jurisdiction lies in Washington so long as Auto Maker purposefully availed itself of that state by doing business there.
  B. Jurisdiction will lie in Washington if Auto Maker sold more cars there than in any other state.
  C. Jurisdiction will lie as to the Washington plaintiffs but likely not as to those from other states.

Analysis of Assessment Questions

Q1. B and C are the correct responses. B is correct because Rule 12(b)(2) authorizes such a challenge. C is correct because, in the absence of any contacts with California, jurisdiction would not lie against an out-of-state defendant. A is wrong because of Rule 12(b)(2). D is wrong because, unlike federal subject matter jurisdiction, which can be raised on the court's own motion, personal jurisdiction is waived unless raised by the defendant.

Q2. A, B, and C are correct responses. A is correct because, unlike *Atlantic Marine Construction*, no district in California has venue according to 28 U.S.C. §1391 and venue is therefore improper. B is correct because, again in contrast to *Atlantic Marine Construction,* venue is improper in any district in California, and *Thompson v. Greyhound Lines* teaches us that, when venue does not lie, one of the options is to move under §1406 for transfer to a district where venue is proper. C is correct because *Atlantic Marine Construction* leaves this issue open: If venue is *improper,* does a motion to transfer under a forum selection clause lie—or is that motion appropriate only when, disregarding the forum selection clause, venue would be proper? D is wrong because a 12(b)(6) motion goes to the validity of the complaint, not the appropriate location of the court.

Q3. C is the only correct response. C is correct because, by failing to raise the question of personal jurisdiction either in a pre-answer motion or in its answer, GrowCo has waived the defense. Rule 12(h)(1). A is wrong because, even if its contentions about contacts are correct, GrowCo has waived. B is doubly wrong: both because personal jurisdiction *is* often about facts and because defendant has waived the defense.

Q4. B is the only accurate response. The federal courts, and most state systems, allow one to challenge jurisdiction, litigate on the merits, and then to argue on appeal that both the refusal to grant a jurisdictional dismissal as well as other errors on the merits warrant reversal.

Q5. All responses are correct. A is correct because some of *Mullane's* power came from its ruling against a litigant relying on "seizure" plus published notice. B is correct because the opinion is full of this kind of language. C is correct because that was *Mullane's* answer to the problem of unnotified beneficiaries: They would be bound because adequately represented by someone with the same interests. D is correct because Justice Jackson had only one year of law school.

Q6. B and D are the correct responses. A is wrong because Rule 4(d)(1) makes it explicit that waiver of service is not a waiver of jurisdictional objections. C is wrong because failure or refusal to waive creates liability for costs of service, but has no further consequence. B is correct because the extension of time to answer is one of the carrots contained in Rule 4(d)(3). D is correct because 4(d)(2) provides for the imposition of costs "unless good cause [for failure to waive] be shown."

Q7. D is the correct response. A is wrong because even the cases that list interactivity as an element in jurisdictional analysis make use of a sliding scale in which the amount of interactivity is relevant. B is wrong because the relevant question will be whether Sam purposefully availed himself of the North Carolina market; while making a product especially suitable for North Carolina would be one way of demonstrating that availment, there are many others—such as shipping his product to a North Carolina buyer—that indicate purposeful availment. C is wrong because, given the substance of the lawsuit, it will be Sam's product, not Sam's personal travels that will be relevant. D is correct because the ability to know that one is doing business with a North Carolina customer is highly relevant to the question of purposeful availment.

Q8. C is the correct response. A is wrong because Purchaser can demonstrate specific jurisdiction if the facts warrant it. B is wrong because federal courts need both subject matter jurisdiction (here based on diversity) *and* personal jurisdiction. C is correct because under the stream-of-commerce cases as well as *Hanson v. Denkla* the relevant question will be the extent to which Maker sought to avail itself of business opportunities in Washington. D is wrong because both *Nicastro* and *Daimler* say that the relevant question is the extent to which Maker tried to sell its cars in Washington, not the precise corporate structure involved; see, e.g., footnote 7 in *Daimler.*

Q9. C is probably the correct response. *Bristol-Myers Squibb v. Superior Court* held that California lacked jurisdiction over the out-of-state plaintiffs under similar circumstances. A is wrong because, for states in which general jurisdiction does not lie, the cases require a connection between defendant's actions and this claim against this plaintiff—not just a general effort to do business in the state. B is wrong: *Daimler AG v. Bauman* held that even a high volume of business was not enough to support jurisdiction over claims unrelated to that business.

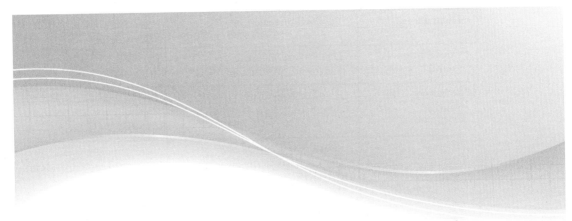

CHAPTER 3

Subject Matter Jurisdiction of the Federal Courts

A. THE IDEA AND THE STRUCTURE OF SUBJECT MATTER JURISDICTION

Personal jurisdiction doctrine limits both state and federal courts in relation to particular defendants. If the defendant lacks connection with the forum state, due process forbids courts sitting in that state from rendering a judgment that will bind that defendant.

Courts and lawyers in the United States must also cope with a second jurisdictional boundary—this one between the powers of state and federal courts. The Constitution created a federal government but made the federal government supreme only in certain areas. In other areas the states are sovereign, and in still others federal and state governments share power.

The centuries since the ratification of the Constitution have seen numerous political struggles and a bloody civil war fought over the location of the line between state and federal powers. That continuing struggle is reflected in the realm of civil procedure. State and federal governments both have court systems. But because of limits on federal power, federal courts can hear only certain kinds of cases. Consequently, litigants, their lawyers, and federal judges need to know whether a particular kind of case must be filed in federal court. Other kinds of cases can only be filed in state court. And in many others, both state *and* federal courts are available. Lawyers describe this sorting of cases between court systems as "subject matter jurisdiction."

Doctrine	Personal Jurisdiction	Federal Subject Matter Jurisdiction
Constitutional Source	Due Process Clause of the Fourteenth Amendment	Article III
Statutory Source	State and federal long-arm statutes (e.g., Rule 4(k)(1)(A))	Federal jurisdictional statutes (e.g., 28 U.S.C. §§1331, 1332, etc.)
Effect	Limits power of state *and* federal courts in any given state over cases involving defendants without sufficient connections to that state	Limits power of federal courts to certain kinds of cases

WHAT'S NEW HERE?

- In Chapter 2, we assumed that the court in question could hear the *kind of case* at issue—Neff's trespass action against Pennoyer, the Robinsons' tort claim against World-Wide and Audi, Ms. Abdouch's right-of-privacy claim against Mr. Lopez, and so on. The only question was whether the court had the power to enter a judgment against a particular *defendant*—given the defendant's connection with the state.
- In this chapter we will flip those assumptions, taking for granted that the court has personal jurisdiction over the defendant. Instead we'll ask whether the Constitution and the relevant statutes authorize a *federal court* to hear this case or whether only a state court can hear it.
- To have the requisite authority, a federal district court must have *both* personal jurisdiction over the defendant *and* subject matter jurisdiction over the kind of case. The two forms of jurisdiction are *not* substitutes for each other, a point reflected in the circumstance that Rule 12 devotes separate subsections (12(b)(1) and 12(b)(2)) to these distinct challenges.
- This chapter will not explore questions of subject matter jurisdiction as they arise in state courts. Some states have special courts for, say, traffic offenses or will probates. One could not bring a tort suit or contract action in such courts because these cases would lie outside their jurisdiction.

A sketch of constitutional history reveals several political compromises that shape the structure of federal judicial jurisdiction. Read Article III, the portion of the Constitution devoted to the judiciary. You won't be surprised to see that §1 of this Article establishes a Supreme Court. But you may be surprised to learn that the Constitution views other federal courts as optional. Section 1 authorizes, but does not require, Congress to establish lower federal courts—what we know today as the courts of appeals and the district courts. Putting the question of lower federal courts into Congress's hands represented a compromise between those who feared an overly powerful federal government and those who viewed the establishment of federal courts as one of the most important goals of the new government. The compromise left the issue subject to changeable legislative wishes. In fact, the first Congress created lower federal courts, and their existence has never been in serious doubt since, though the exact scope of their powers has often been questioned.

Section 2 of Article III contains a second compromise, one whose terms have been fiercely contested for more than 200 years. Article III, §2 limits federal courts' jurisdiction to the list set forth in §2. By implication a case not listed in Article III, §2 may not be heard in a federal court. Such a case could be heard only in a state court. Within the boundaries of Article III, however, Congress remains free to bestow all or some of the constitutionally permissible jurisdiction on the lower federal courts.

This history has implications even in ordinary lawsuits. Because the federal courts are courts of *limited jurisdiction,* two questions lurk at the threshold of every case brought in a federal court: Does the case fall within one of the enumerated categories of Article III, §2; and has Congress further authorized the lower federal courts to assume that jurisdiction?

Rule 8(a)(1) reflects these concerns by requiring every federal complaint to begin with a "short and plain statement of the grounds for the court's jurisdiction." In judging those jurisdictional statements, the courts look to three bodies of law—the Constitution, the statutes conferring jurisdiction, and the case law interpreting both.

Skimming the jurisdictional statutes, one might not suspect another important feature: Federal courts share much of their jurisdiction with state courts.

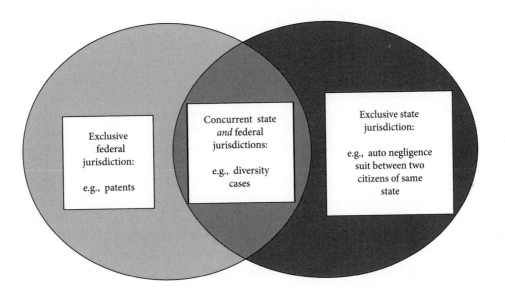

Look, for example, at the so-called general federal question statute, 28 U.S.C. §1331. It grants federal courts jurisdiction over cases that arise under federal law. That federal courts have such jurisdiction does not seem surprising, but it may be surprising to learn that they do not have exclusive jurisdiction over such cases. So far as Congress and the Constitution are concerned, cases arising under federal law can be brought in state as well as federal courts. Lawyers describe such shared jurisdiction as *concurrent*. Like general federal question cases, diversity jurisdiction (28 U.S.C. §1332) is also concurrent. In some instances Congress has made federal jurisdiction exclusive. (28 U.S.C. §§1333 (admiralty), 1334 (bankruptcy), and 1346(b) (tort suits based on negligence of a federal employee).) For an example of a statute carefully discriminating between grants of concurrent and exclusive federal jurisdiction, read 28 U.S.C. §1338. In still other instances Congress has specifically forbidden federal courts from hearing cases that might otherwise fall within their jurisdiction; for example, 28 U.S.C. §1341 forbids federal courts from enjoining state tax collection in most circumstances.

Why would a lawyer or a litigant care whether a state or federal court heard her case? Assuming some court is available, why should it matter which one? The answer has both practical and political dimensions. As a tactical matter, the reasons for seeking a federal rather than a state court range from the practical (some federal courts presently have shorter waiting times until trial than their state counterparts) to the strategic (is the defendant likely to get a more sympathetic hearing from the local state judge than from the federal judge in a city at the other end of the state; will a six-person federal jury, drawn from a broader geographic area and required to reach a unanimous verdict, be likely to award higher—or lower—damages than the state jury, which may have 12 members and may be allowed to reach a non-unanimous majority verdict; is the federal bench generally more liberal or conservative than the state court bench in the particular jurisdiction?) to the crafty (is the opposing lawyer uncomfortable with the generally more formal conduct and faster pace of federal litigation?).

On a different plane, note that Article III, §1 gives federal judges lifetime tenure, a protection that shields them from political pressure. So a litigant with a legally strong but unpopular claim or defense might prefer federal court. The limited jurisdiction of the federal courts also shields them, however, from certain kinds of cases: Family law disputes, for example, are not part of the federal docket. These dual insulations—from political pressure and from a broad caseload—may work in opposite directions. Arguing that federal courts possess a range of virtues ranging from greater competence to "class-based predilections favorable to constitutional enforcement," a civil rights litigator once argued that in virtually every conceivable situation the federal courts would be more hospitable to his clients' claims. Bert Neuborne, *The Myth of Parity*, 90 Harv. L. Rev. 1105 (1977). More recently, another similar litigator argued that for his gay and lesbian clients, the state courts' closer ties both to the local community and their broad mix of cases made them the superior forum. William Rubenstein, *The Myth of Superiority*, 16 Const. Comment. 599 (2000). So even experienced lawyers believe it matters whether a state or a federal court hears the case—even in instances when the two courts would be applying the same substantive law. This proposition sets the stage for an exploration of federal subject matter jurisdiction.

B. FEDERAL QUESTION JURISDICTION

PERSPECTIVES

The Shifting Pattern of Federal Subject Matter Jurisdiction

Today, most would intuitively assume that federal trial courts have jurisdiction to hear all cases involving federal law. In fact, that assumption has not been true for much of the nation's history and is true today only in a limited form. Why? To answer that question, we must look again at constitutional history.

In 1789, Congress exercised its authority under Article III to create what the Constitution calls "inferior" federal courts. But Congress has only bestowed upon those courts some of the jurisdiction allowed under Article III. Among the most important early grants of jurisdiction were diversity and admiralty. Combined, these two jurisdictional grants gave federal courts jurisdiction over most significant interstate and international trade.

Most striking from a modern perspective was the absence of any general federal question jurisdiction. There were individual statutes allowing suits invoking patent and federal pension laws, but federal courts had no general power to entertain claims based on federal law. That may not have mattered much in an age when there weren't enough federal statutes to create a lot of such claims.

After the Civil War had reshaped understandings of federalism and, in particular, the federal courts' role in the enforcement of civil rights, Congress in 1875 enacted a general federal question statute.

Today, three kinds of cases dominate the federal district court civil docket—federal question cases are almost half, diversity cases a bit more than a third, and cases that land in federal court because the United States is a party, 15 percent.

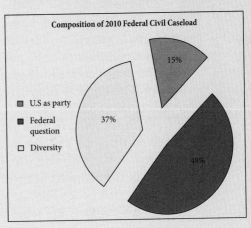

Composition of 2010 Federal Civil Caseload

- U.S as party
- Federal question
- Diversity

15%

37%

48%

The broadest grant of federal question jurisdiction appears in 28 U.S.C. §1331. The key provision of that statute gives district courts jurisdiction over cases "arising under" the Constitution, statutes, or treaties of the federal government.

The difficulty comes in deciding what it means for a case to "arise under" federal law. Before you despair, bear in mind that the basics are quite straightforward, although not intuitive. As a preface to our exploration, consider the following two cases.

1. Worker contends that Employer has violated the federal Fair Labor Standards Act, which, among other things, establishes a minimum wage for certain employees. Employer does not contest the applicability of the statute or the amount of the minimum wage but instead asserts that Worker has overstated the number of hours he has worked and is for that reason not entitled to the pay he seeks. Consider what issues will be contested.

2. Plaintiff claims that Newspaper has libeled her. Newspaper's defense rests on a body of law that the courts have extrapolated from the First Amendment. Specifically, it relies on a set of U.S. Supreme Court cases holding that media defendants in libel cases may prevail—even if they have published false and injurious information—so long as they have not been negligent in, for example, checking their sources. Newspaper concedes the inaccuracy of its article but nevertheless believes that it has such a First Amendment defense. Consider what the contested issues in the second case will be.

As an intuitive matter, which of these cases arises under federal law and, therefore, should be in federal court? Now consider how the following case affects the answer to this question.

Louisville & Nashville Railroad v. Mottley
211 U.S. 149 (1908)

[Erasmus and Annie Mottley were injured in a railway accident. To settle their claims, the railroad in 1871 gave them a lifetime pass good for free transportation on the line. Several decades later, Congress, believing that railroads were using free transportation to bribe public officials, made free passes unlawful. The railroad thereupon refused to honor the Mottleys' passes, citing the new federal legislation. The Mottleys sued in federal court seeking specific performance of their settlement. "The bill[, that is, the complaint,] further alleges: First, that the act of Congress referred to does not prohibit the giving of passes under the circumstances of this case; and, second, that if the law is to be construed as prohibiting such passes, it is in conflict with the Fifth Amendment of the constitution, because it deprives the plaintiffs of their property without due process of law. The defendant demurred to the bill." The federal trial court overruled the demurrer and granted the Mottleys the relief they had requested. Defendant railroad appealed to the Supreme Court.]

MOODY, J., . . . delivered the opinion of the Court.

Two questions of law were raised by the demurrer to the bill, were brought here by appeal, and have been argued before us. They are, first, whether that part of the act of Congress of June 29, 1906 (34 Stat. 584), which forbids the giving of free passes or the collection of any different compensation for transportation of passengers than that specified in the tariff filed, makes it unlawful to perform a contract for transportation of persons, who in good faith, before the passage of the act, had accepted such contract in satisfaction of a valid cause of action against the railroad; and, second, whether the statute, if it should be construed to render such a contract unlawful, is in violation of the Fifth Amendment of the Constitution of the United States. We do not deem it necessary, however, to consider either of these questions, because, in our opinion, the court below was without jurisdiction of the cause. Neither party has questioned that jurisdiction, but it is the duty of this court to see to it that the jurisdiction of the Circuit Court, which is defined and limited by statute, is not exceeded. This duty we have frequently performed of our own motion.

There was no diversity of citizenship and it is not and cannot be suggested that there was any ground of jurisdiction, except that the case was a "suit . . . arising under the Constitution and laws of the United States." [The Court cited the then-current version of the "arising under" jurisdiction statute.] It is the settled interpretation of these words, as used in this statute, conferring jurisdiction, that a suit arises under the Constitution and laws of the United States only when the plaintiff's statement of his own cause of action shows that it is based upon those laws or that Constitution. It is not enough that the plaintiff alleges some anticipated defense to his cause of action and asserts that the defense is invalidated by some provision of the Constitution of the United States. Although such allegations show that very likely, in the course of the litigation, a question under the Constitution would arise, they do not show that the suit, that is, the plaintiff's original cause of action, arises under the Constitution. In Tennessee v. Union & Planters' Bank, 152 U.S. 454, the plaintiff, the State of Tennessee, brought suit in the Circuit Court of the United States to recover from the defendant certain taxes alleged to be due under the laws of the State. The plaintiff alleged that the defendant claimed an immunity from the taxation by virtue of its charter, and that therefore the tax was void, because in violation of the provision of the Constitution of the United States, which forbids any State from passing a law impairing the obligation of contracts. The cause was held to be beyond the jurisdiction of the Circuit Court, the court saying, by Mr. Justice Gray, "a suggestion of one party, that the other will or may set up a claim under the Constitution or laws of the United States, does not make the suit one arising under that Constitution or those laws." Again, in Boston & Montana Consolidated Copper & Silver Mining Company v. Montana Ore Purchasing Company, 188 U.S. 632, the . . . cause was held to be beyond the jurisdiction of the Circuit Court, the court saying, by Mr. Justice Peckham:

> It would be wholly unnecessary and improper in order to prove complainant's cause of action to go into any matters of defence which the defendants might possibly set up and then attempt to reply to such defence, and thus, if possible, to show that a Federal question might or probably would arise in the course of the trial of the case. To allege such defence and then make an answer to it before the defendant has the opportunity to

Does the Constitution trump this fed law [handwritten marginal note]

itself plead or prove its own defence is inconsistent with any known rule of pleading so far as we are aware, and is improper.

The rule is a reasonable and just one that the complainant in the first instance shall be confined to a statement of its cause of action, leaving to the defendant to set up in his answer what his defence is and, if anything more than a denial of complainant's cause of action, imposing upon the defendant the burden of proving such defence.

Conforming itself to that rule the complainant would not, in the assertion or proof of its cause of action, bring up a single Federal question. The presentation of its cause of action would not show that it was one arising under the Constitution or laws of the United States.

The only way in which it might be claimed that a Federal question was presented would be in the complainant's statement of what the defence of defendants would be and complainant's answer to such defence. Under these circumstances the case is brought within the rule laid down in Tennessee v. Union & Planters' Bank, 152 U.S. 454 [holding that such cases do not arise under federal law].

. . . The application of this rule to the case at bar is decisive against the jurisdiction of the circuit court.

It is ordered that the judgment be reversed and the case remitted to the circuit court with instructions to dismiss for want of jurisdiction.

WHAT'S NEW HERE?

- Everyone agreed that the only significant questions in the case were how to interpret a federal statute and whether that statute, if interpreted to cover the Mottleys, was constitutional. But the Supreme Court held that the lower court lacked jurisdiction to hear that case and, because the lower court lacked jurisdiction, the Supreme Court could not hear the appeal.
- Why did the trial court lack jurisdiction? Because at its heart the Mottleys' complaint was for breach of contract (the settlement agreement). Yes, the complaint referred to various defenses the railroad might (and did) raise, but those anticipated defenses were not part of a "well-pleaded complaint" for breach of contract.

Notes and Problems

1. Explain why the federal trial court lacked jurisdiction.

2. Look back at the two hypothetical cases in the text preceding *Mottley—Worker v. Employer* and *Plaintiff v. Newspaper*. Under the principle applied in *Mottley*, which case will "arise under" federal law?

3. Who raised the question of federal jurisdiction in *Mottley*?
   a. If both parties were prepared to argue the merits of the case, how could a court justify dismissal on a ground unrelated to those merits? See Federal Rule 12(h)(3) for another example of the importance federal courts attach to their subject matter jurisdiction.
   b. After suffering dismissal in the Supreme Court, the Mottleys refiled their suit in state court. It again made its way to the U.S. Supreme Court. The Mottleys lost again, this time on the merits. 219 U.S. 467 (1911). Is this any way to run either a railroad or a judicial system? Before answering, consider the "Implications" box below and the note following it.

Implications

PLEADING RULES AND JURISDICTIONAL TESTS

Mottley exemplifies the "well-pleaded complaint" rule, one rather rigid but widely used approach to a difficult problem. Can one justify this approach? An enormous number of claims have some federal ingredient in their background. For example, as Charles Wright pointed out, land title in most western states can be traced back to U.S. land grants. Wright, Federal Courts 104. Large numbers of checks and online payments clear through Federal Reserve banks. Does every question of land title or every suit on a bad check arise under federal law and thus belong in federal court? If one answers that question "no," then one has to find a principled way of sorting claims in which federal questions have some central importance from those in which they are merely background assumptions.

Mottley chooses to sort roughly, based on the pleadings: The federal claim must appear as part of a well-pleaded complaint. That approach has at least one important advantage: It permits the sorting to occur at the start of the lawsuit before the parties and court have invested much time. To see the force of this point, consider the opposite extreme: One could, theoretically, postpone a decision on jurisdiction until after trial, to see whether an important question of federal law had emerged, and dismiss if it had not, allowing the case to start all over in state court. Not too surprisingly, not even the fiercest critic of *Mottley* has suggested taking things this far. Yet the *Mottley* approach eliminates cases from federal court, like *Mottley* itself, in which the central issue was a federal defense rather than a part of the plaintiff's claim.

---

4. It is clear that the restrictive reading *Mottley* (and numerous other cases) gives to "arising under" is not constitutionally required. Why? After all, both Article III and §1331 speak of cases "arising under" federal law; could that phrase mean different things in the Constitution and in the statute? Yes: The Supreme Court in several cases has said that the meaning of "arising under" in Article III is broader than the same phrase in §1331. Consider what that means.

a. Because the constitutional meaning of "arising under" is broader than its statutory meaning, the Supreme Court (operating under the broader constitutional definition) had jurisdiction to hear and decide *Mottley* the second time around, even though it previously decided that the district court (operating under the narrower statutory definition) did not have jurisdiction. Be sure you understand why before moving on.

b. As a further corollary, Congress could change the result in *Mottley* by amending §1331. It might, for example, provide that the district courts have original jurisdiction over cases "in which an essential element either of a claim or defense rests on federal law." Should Congress do so?

5. When a defendant challenges federal question jurisdiction in district court, one of three questions commonly arises:

a. Is there a federal issue at all? If the plaintiff's claim is based on some federal statute or regulation, the problem consists in interpreting legislation. If the plaintiff claims the right to relief under federal common law, the question is whether such federal common law exists.

b. Assuming there is a federal issue, does it "give rise to" plaintiff's claim? That is the question in *Mottley*.

c. If there is a federal issue that is not the basis for plaintiff's claim, is it sufficiently important to "federalize" the case?

6. Although *Mottley*'s bright-line test suggests that the answer to 5c is a simple "no," it turns out that things are a bit more complicated.

a. Alongside the broad and straight mainstream view reflected in *Mottley* flows a narrow and meandering rivulet. In this second line of cases the federal courts have assumed "arising under" jurisdiction on the basis of something less—or different—than a claim depending on federal law. Smith v. Kansas City Title & Trust Co., 255 U.S. 180 (1921), is the poster child for this more expansive view. In *Smith*, the plaintiff alleged that the defendant bank as trustee had violated a state law allowing it to invest only in legal securities. Thus stated, the suit would seem to arise entirely under state law regulating trustees. But the allegedly "illegal" securities were bonds issued by a federal agency under a federal law that plaintiff claimed was unconstitutional. Held: "arising under" jurisdiction. Is *Mottley*, not cited in *Smith*, distinguishable?

b. The Supreme Court has repeatedly tried to define this line of cases, without bringing great clarity to the topic. The Supreme Court's most recent effort came in Grable & Sons Metal Prod. Inc. v. Darue Eng'g & Mfg., 545 U.S. 308 (2005). Land was sold to satisfy an Internal Revenue Service lien for unpaid taxes. To assure that it had clean title, the purchaser of the land brought a quiet title action in state court, at which point the original owner of the land challenged title, alleging that the notice of the tax lien sale was inadequate. Defendant sought to remove to federal court, arguing that the underlying issue was the adequacy of the IRS system of notice in its tax sales. Federal question jurisdiction was proper, said the Court. In a unanimous opinion, *Grable* set out a three-part test for such federalized claims: "[T]he question is, does a state-law claim [1] necessarily raise a federal issue, [2] actually disputed and substantial, [3] which a federal forum may entertain without disturbing any congressionally approved balance of federal and state judicial responsibilities." Id. at 314. Lower courts interpreting this test have overwhelmingly remanded such cases to state courts, usually concluding, without much analysis, that the case fails the third of the *Grable* criteria.

c. What's going on in this "broader" *Smith* line of cases, cases like *Grable*? One way of explaining them is to say that the courts thought the federal law interests were important. Important in what way? A monumentally important case with a federal ingredient will eventually make its way to the Supreme Court, which, you'll recall, has a broader "arising under" jurisdiction than do the district courts. For these cases it makes little difference whether the case is initially heard in a state or federal court.

d. But the Supreme Court currently hears fewer than a hundred cases a year. So as a practical matter most federal issues litigated in state courts will never reach any federal court. The battle in the statutory "arising under" cases is fought over which federal issue cases should be heard in federal trial and intermediate appellate courts. One thoughtful analysis puts the question like this:

> Federal issues might be raised in a large number of cases, but the claimants of federal rights often are wrong in their view that federal law protects them. They would therefore lose on the federal issue, and they could win only on state law grounds. If "arising under" were interpreted expansively, many cases in federal court on the basis of "arising under" jurisdiction would be disposed of on state law grounds. . . . What is needed is a test that will screen out cases in which federal interests are unlikely to be strongly implicated. Can the following considerations be combined to produce a "test"? (i) What is the national interest in disposing of the case as a whole—with federal fact-finding—in the federal courts, as compared to the interest of disposing of it in the state courts? (ii) How likely is it that the national interest will in fact be implicated? (iii) How likely is it that the Supreme Court will use its limited resources to decide the federal issue where the record is made in the state court?

> Howard Fink & Mark Tushnet, Federal Jurisdiction:
> Policy and Practice 396 (2d ed. 1987).

Recall that these questions—if these are the right questions—must be decided at a very early stage, with nothing more than the pleadings before the court, and you will understand why courts and scholars have struggled over the question for a century.

7. As you will see in Chapter 5, the federal Declaratory Judgment Act, 28 U.S.C. §§2201-2202, empowers federal district courts to hear certain cases in which a potential defendant seeks not a coercive remedy but a declaration of rights. Thus, for example, an insurance company might seek a declaration of nonliability under an insurance contract, or a manufacturer might seek a declaration that a device did not infringe an existing patent.

a. How does one apply the well-pleaded complaint rule to such cases? The question is made more difficult by a well-established understanding that the Declaratory Judgment Act did not expand the jurisdiction of the federal courts.

b. There is body of law wrestling with this question, with results too complex to summarize here. But some cases are simple. Suppose a patent-holder believes that a competing business is infringing his patent. He could sue for damages or file for an injunction, and such a suit would "arise under" federal law. Believing that proof of damages or of the requisites for injunctive relief would be expensive, he simply sues for a declaration that the competitor is infringing his patent. The claim for relief arises under federal law.

8. A case can start out as a federal case, but then lose its federal status after a judgment or settlement.

   a. Plaintiff sues defendant on a claim arising under federal law. The parties then settle the case by signing an agreement. The case is dismissed by agreement of the parties in an order that makes no reference to the settlement agreement. Plaintiff then sues defendant for violation of the agreement. Is there federal question jurisdiction? No: The settlement agreement is an ordinary contract whose breach does not arise under federal law; if the conditions for diversity jurisdiction do not exist, the plaintiff will have to go to state court to enforce the agreement. But if the parties had embodied their agreement in a consent decree (which would have been part of the court's judgment), its breach would arise under federal law because federal courts have jurisdiction to enforce their own judgments. Kokkonen v. Guardian Life Ins. Co., 511 U.S. 375 (1994).

   b. Sally borrowed money from Frank, giving him a mortgage as security. She then declared bankruptcy and, in a federal bankruptcy proceeding, Frank's interest was transferred to Joe. (Recall that there is exclusive federal jurisdiction over bankruptcy.) Through an error, however, the transfer to Joe was never properly recorded. Frank now sues Joe in state court, alleging that he still holds a mortgage on the property. Joe seeks to remove the case to federal district court, arguing that Frank's lawsuit calls into question the validity of the federal bankruptcy judgment and thus "arises under" federal law. Held: No, in Rivet v. Regions Bank, 522 U.S. 470 (1998) (claim preclusion based on a prior federal judgment is a defense, so the claim does not arise under federal law, citing *Mottley*).

Procedure as Strategy

Effective lawyers practicing in federal court must learn the sometimes complex boundaries of federal subject matter jurisdiction. They must also learn the consequences of various strategic decisions associated with raising the lack of subject matter jurisdiction in a case. Suppose, for example, you represent a defendant in a case filed in federal district court and you think that there is no basis for federal subject matter jurisdiction over one or more claims in the case. You also think that there's an argument that the claim should be dismissed on Rule 12(b)(6) grounds, for failure to state a claim. You move to dismiss under both Rule 12(b)(1) and Rule 12(b)(6). Does it matter how that motion to dismiss is decided?

- If the federal court grants the motion to dismiss on Rule 12(b)(1) grounds, ruling that the case does not arise under federal law, plaintiff can now refile the same claim in state court. All the dismissal established was that the claim did not arise under federal law; that's entirely consistent with its arising under state law.
- If the federal court grants the Rule 12(b)(6) motion and the plaintiff refiles the same claim in state court, can defendant argue that the federal dismissal requires dismissal of the state claim? As you will see in Chapter 11, except under special circumstances, a federal Rule 12(b)(6) dismissal operates as a judgment on the merits disposing of the claim. A state court is bound to respect that judgment.

Suppose you represent a defendant in a case filed in federal district court and you think that there are grounds to bring a motion to dismiss both for lack of subject matter jurisdiction and for lack of personal jurisdiction. If either challenge is well founded, the case will be dismissed. But a dismissal will have different consequences for a refiled suit, depending on which ground is used for dismissal.

- If a case is dismissed for want of federal subject matter jurisdiction, a plaintiff is free to refile the suit in state court because the judgment establishes only the lack of federal jurisdiction, leaving the state court open.
- If the case is dismissed for want of personal jurisdiction, principles of former adjudication (Chapter 11) preclude plaintiff from refiling in state court in the same state because the federal court's decision that personal jurisdiction is lacking will bind the state court.
- Under those circumstances, should a federal court faced with motions to dismiss on both grounds always take subject matter jurisdiction first, because that will have the narrowest subsequent effect? No, the Supreme Court has said; the discretion of a trial court to handle its docket allows it to dismiss for want of personal jurisdiction if that is the most obvious ground, even though that will preclude subsequent state-court litigation in that state. Ruhrgas AG v. Marathon Oil Co., 526 U.S. 574 (1999).

Now suppose that the defendant does not move to dismiss. Is the objection to subject matter jurisdiction waived? No: As *Mottley* demonstrates, the requirement of subject matter jurisdiction is held to be so fundamental that a court is required to raise the issue *sua sponte* (on the court's own motion) and dismiss if it finds a lack of jurisdiction. In Capron v. Van Noorden, 6 U.S. 126 (1804), plaintiff sued defendant in federal court and lost. On appeal in the Supreme Court, plaintiff suggested a lack of jurisdiction because of lack of diversity. The Supreme Court dismissed the case, leaving the plaintiff free to try again in state court (assuming that the statute of limitations had not yet run).

Given the draconian rules about the nonwaivability of federal subject matter jurisdiction, one might expect it would be easy to mount a collateral attack on a judgment alleged to be without federal jurisdiction. In fact, the answer is "probably not," though the few cases that have dealt with this question have not been resolved consistently. To get a feel for the problem, consider three situations: (1) defendant appears, challenges subject matter jurisdiction and loses; (2) defendant appears, fails to challenge subject matter jurisdiction, but loses on the merits; and (3) defendant defaults. In each case, the question is whether in a second lawsuit the former defendant may seek to avoid the effect of the first judgment by arguing that the court lacked subject matter jurisdiction.

- Parties who appear, challenge the subject matter jurisdiction of a federal court, and lose are bound by that determination; just as with personal jurisdiction, they may not thereafter challenge the judgment in a second action. Stoll v. Gottlieb, 305 U.S. 165 (1938).
- Similarly, and again as with personal jurisdiction, parties who have appeared but failed to challenge the subject matter jurisdiction of a district court may generally not thereafter attack its judgment in another court for lack of diversity or federal question jurisdiction—absent a statute authorizing such a challenge. Chicot County Drainage District v. Baxter State Bank, 308 U.S. 371 (1939); Kalb v. Feuerstein, 308 U.S. 433 (1940).
- What about defendants who entirely default? Were they objecting to personal jurisdiction, they would be entitled to attack collaterally under the doctrine of *Pennoyer*. May they collaterally attack subject matter jurisdiction in the same way? Probably, suggests *V.L. v. E.L.* (infra page 763, in Chapter 11).

WHAT'S NEW HERE?

- Either by negligence or purposely, a defendant can waive her objections to personal jurisdiction. See Rule 12(h).
- Unlike personal jurisdiction, federal subject matter jurisdiction cannot be waived. Not only can a party—even the party who invoked federal jurisdiction in the first place—raise the issue belatedly, but the court can raise it on its own motion, even on appeal—which is what happened in *Mottley*.
- When and whether a defendant raises subject matter jurisdiction may determine whether a case can be refiled in another court.

C. DIVERSITY JURISDICTION

Diversity jurisdiction was among the earliest congressional grants to the lower federal courts. The underlying justification, however, has remained obscure, and the grant has come under regular attack. The following excerpt from a congressional committee report sums up the mystery:

Federal diversity of citizenship jurisdiction is made possible by Article III of the Constitution which was drafted to permit, but not mandate, Federal court jurisdiction based on "controversies between citizens of different States" and "between a State, or the citizens thereof, and foreign States, citizens or subjects." . . .

The debates of the Constitutional Convention are unclear as to why the Constitution made provision for such jurisdiction; nor is pertinent legislative history much aid as to why the First Congress exercised its prerogative to vest diversity jurisdiction in the Federal courts.

> Abolition of Diversity of Citizenship Jurisdiction, H.R. Rep. No. 893,
> 95th Cong., 2d Sess. 2 (1978).

In spite of the gaps in the historical record, the Supreme Court has articulated one commonly asserted understanding of diversity's justification, contrasting it with "arising under" jurisdiction:

> In order to provide a federal forum for plaintiffs who seek to vindicate federal rights, Congress has conferred on the district courts original jurisdiction in federal-question cases—civil actions that arise under the Constitution, laws, or treaties of the United States. 28 U.S.C. §1331. In order to provide a neutral forum for what have come to be known as diversity cases, Congress also has granted district courts original jurisdiction in civil actions between citizens of different States, between U.S. citizens and foreign citizens, or by foreign states against U.S. citizens. §1332.

> Exxon-Mobil Corp. v. Allapattah Servs., Inc., 545 U.S. 546, 552 (2005).

An early case relying on the neutral forum justification while making important law regarding diversity jurisdiction was Strawbridge v. Curtiss, 7 U.S. 267 (1806). Although 28 U.S.C. §1332 does not by its terms require that each plaintiff be diverse from each defendant, that interpretation was attached to the predecessor statute by Chief Justice Marshall in *Strawbridge*, and has been unquestioned law ever since. Thus even in a case with multiple diverse parties the existence of a single party with the same state citizenship as that of an opposing party will destroy diversity. The theory, apparently, was that if citizens of the same state are on both sides of a case, a state court cannot discriminate against an out-of-state party without harming its own. As an opinion written more than 200 years after *Strawbridge* explained it:

> The complete diversity requirement is not mandated by the Constitution, or by the plain text of §1332(a). The Court, nonetheless, has adhered to the complete diversity rule in light of *the purpose of the diversity requirement, which is to provide a federal forum for important disputes where state courts might favor, or be perceived as favoring, home-state litigants.* The presence of parties from the same State on both sides of a case dispels this concern, eliminating a principal reason for conferring §1332 jurisdiction over any of the claims in the action.

> Exxon Mobil Corp. v. Allapattah Servs., Inc., 545 U.S. 546,
> 553 (2005) (emphasis added).

But in some instances Congress has legislated in ways suggesting a broader function for diversity than providing a neutral forum. For example, the Class Action

Fairness Act of 2005 (discussed in more detail, *infra* pages 843-44) appears to depend on a "national case" justification. The idea would be that some cases have national scope and implication and should be heard in a federal court, even if the governing law is state law. For our purposes the question is not whether the "neutral forum" or the "national case" justification for diversity is correct. Instead it is how uncertainty about diversity's purpose plays itself out in the cases.

Redner v. Sanders

2000 WL 1161080 (S.D.N.Y. 2000)

GRIESA, J.

Plaintiff in this action asserts that federal jurisdiction is based on diversity of citizenship. Defendants move under Fed. R. Civ. P. 12(b)(1) to dismiss for lack of jurisdiction. The motion is granted.

The complaint alleges that plaintiff "is, and at all times herein mentioned was, a citizen of the United States residing in France," and that two individual defendants are residents of the State of New York and the corporate defendant has its principal place of business in New York. The complaint avers that diversity jurisdiction exists because plaintiff "is a resident of a foreign state, while defendants are residents of the State of New York." The applicable statute is 28 U.S.C. §1332, which provides in pertinent part:

> (a) The district courts shall have original jurisdiction of all civil actions where the matter in controversy exceeds the sum or value of $75,000, exclusive of interest and costs, and is between—
>
> (1) citizens of different States;
>
> (2) citizens of a State and citizens or subjects of a foreign state. . . .

Plaintiff apparently seeks to invoke subsection (a)(2) as a basis for jurisdiction. However, plaintiff's complaint speaks of *residence* whereas the statute speaks of *citizenship*. The two are not synonymous.

It appears in fact that defendants are citizens of the State of New York. But for jurisdiction to exist under (a)(2) plaintiff would need to be a citizen of a foreign state, not merely a resident, and the complaint itself alleges that plaintiff is a citizen of the United States. Thus the case does not involve an action between citizens of the United States and a citizen of a foreign state. There is no jurisdiction under §1332(a)(2).

In responding to the motion, plaintiff does not really defend the idea of jurisdiction based upon his location in France, but shifts the ground to a discussion of his connection with California. Plaintiff has filed an affidavit stating that he was raised and educated in California commencing in 1948, and that while he has resided in France for the last several years (his attorney's brief says since 1990), he has maintained certain contacts with California, including a license to practice law, and a law office there which he states he has visited at least four times a year since living abroad. He has a California driver's license. He recently solicited two San Francisco law offices for possible employment, although there is no indication of any affirmative response. Plaintiff's affidavit states that he has "not given up the idea of returning to California" and that he considers California as his domicile.

To the extent that plaintiff now argues for a California domicile, it would appear that he might be attempting to lay a basis for jurisdiction under §1332(a)(1). This subsection would, of course, allow a citizen of California to invoke diversity jurisdiction in a suit against citizens of New York. A person is a citizen of a state of the United States within the meaning of 28 U.S.C. §1332 if he is a citizen of the United States and is domiciled within the state in question. Newman-Green Inc. v. Alfonzo-Larrain, 490 U.S. 826, 828 (1989).

However, plaintiff's factual submission is not sufficient to demonstrate a California domicile. Plaintiff's affidavit is entirely lacking in details about what his living in France has involved. Plaintiff provides no information about exactly where he lives, what kind of a residence he has, whether he has any family in France, or what professional activities he carries out in France.

Moreover, despite the discussion of domicile to some extent, neither plaintiff's affidavit nor his attorney's brief actually asserts the claim that there is jurisdiction on the basis of a California domicile or makes a request to amend the complaint to assert such a claim.

The action is dismissed for lack of subject matter jurisdiction. This dismissal is without prejudice.

WHAT'S NEW HERE?

- As with §1331, the federal question statute, the courts read §1332 very carefully. It's not enough that there are "a bunch of people not from the same state." Instead the courts insist that the diversity required exactly match one of the statutory definitions.
- "Citizen" takes on different meanings, depending on which section of §1332 one is reading. To be a "citizen" of France means that one is a French national, with all the political rights and obligations that entails. To be a "citizen" of California, for diversity purposes, means simply that one is a U.S. citizen or permanent resident, present with the intent to remain indefinitely.

Notes and Problems

1. Does this decision mean that Redner cannot sue Sanders in the United States?

2. How did Redner's lawyer make such an elementary mistake? Putting aside the possibility of carelessness or ignorance, consider the possibility that the error was induced by the way in which the underlying statute has been interpreted.

a. On one hand the courts read the statute's sections quite literally; if a given case does not fit into one of §1332's several categories, it does not fall within diversity jurisdiction—regardless of whether one might, in a very loose and intuitive way, perceive the parties as "diverse."

b. On the other hand, because the statute does not define the meaning of state "citizenship," and because, unlike the national government, states do not issue any formal documents to show that one is a "citizen" of California or Florida or Illinois, courts have developed a test of state citizenship. The standard doctrinal formulation says that state citizenship depends on present domicile and intent to remain indefinitely. That test is easy to apply for most people, who have a single clear affiliation.

c. But, like Mr. Redner, many people may reside "temporarily" in a different place for considerable periods. Thus a student who is attending law school in New York might for diversity purposes still be a citizen of Florida. In such cases, much may turn on intent, as demonstrated by external indicia. Consider, for example, *Hawkins v. Masters Farms*, supra page 7. Notice that the factual issues involved in such determinations can require significant inquiry at the outset of the lawsuit, inquiry unrelated to the merits of the case. Does this make the relatively mindless simplicity of the well-pleaded complaint rule look better by comparison?

d. Notice the "neutral forum" justification for diversity lurking in the background of *Redner*: If the original congressional intent lay in the concern that courts of one state might discriminate against the citizens of another— then Redner's residence in France "de-statified" him, and thus eliminated concern that New York courts would discriminate against a Californian (though they may still discriminate against someone from France).

3. Suppose Redner's lawyer explains (with some embarrassment) to his client (also a lawyer!) why his case has been dismissed. Both still believe that federal court is by far the best forum for the case and would like to refile it in federal court. Can they?

a. The time for measuring citizenship for diversity purposes is as of the date on which the complaint is filed in federal court. That is true even if the plaintiff has moved to another state for the sole purpose of establishing diversity:

> On May 5, 1997, plaintiff filed an . . . action in Kansas state court. At the time, plaintiff was domiciled in Kansas. Shortly after filing suit, plaintiff moved to Oklahoma and became domiciled there. Plaintiff voluntarily dismissed his state action on January 10, 2000, then filed this case on February 1, 2000.
>
> Plaintiff alleges that this Court has diversity jurisdiction under 28 U.S.C. §1332. Defendant contends that the parties are not truly diverse. The complaint shows otherwise. Diversity of citizenship is determined at the commencement of the action. Commencement of the action occurs at the time the complaint is filed. When plaintiff filed his complaint here, he was a citizen of Oklahoma. Defendant does not contend otherwise. Rather, defendant argues that the Court must refer back to May 5, 1997, when plaintiff filed his state action. . . .

Defendant notes that plaintiff could not have removed his original state action to federal court and argues that plaintiff should not be allowed the "tactical advantage" of doing essentially the same thing now. . . . Federal subject matter jurisdiction . . . does not focus on whether a party is attempting to gain a tactical advantage. Litigants constantly attempt to gain so-called tactical advantages in various ways, including both removing cases and avoiding removal. Defendant cites no authority for the proposition that subject matter jurisdiction is defeated if it somehow affords one party a tactical advantage. Indeed, defendant's argument that plaintiff is attempting to gain a "tactical advantage" rings entirely hollow because defendant's argument for lack of jurisdiction appears to be nothing more than an attempt to gain his own tactical advantage—a return to state court. . . .

Smith v. Kennedy, 2000 WL 575024 (D. Kan. 2000).

    b. Having absorbed the point above, what would you advise Redner to do if he still wants to invoke diversity jurisdiction?

4. Consider two variations on the facts of the case:
    a. Suppose Redner had been a French citizen. Diversity?
    b. Suppose Redner had been a French citizen who had moved to the United States and, while not becoming a U.S. citizen, had become a permanent resident domiciled in New York. Read §1332(a)(2) and explain how it applies to this situation.

5. Besides the complete diversity requirement, federal courts have narrowed diversity jurisdiction in one more way not suggested by the words of the statute: They have long held that federal courts do not have jurisdiction to grant divorces, adjudicate child custody, or divide marital property between spouses who are citizens of different states. Barber v. Barber, 21 How. 852 (1859). The basis for this judge-made restriction is not entirely clear but is thought to rest on the idea that the federal Constitution grants states broad authority over such matters, with which federal courts should not interfere.

WHAT'S NEW HERE?

- Like the well-pleaded complaint rule for "arising under" jurisdiction, the requirement of complete diversity flows from a judicial interpretation of a jurisdictional statute—not from Article III.
- Like the well-pleaded complaint rule, courts have consistently enforced the complete diversity requirement for a very long time—more than two centuries in the case of complete diversity.
- Like the well-pleaded complaint rule, the long-standing interpretation applies only to the particular jurisdictional statute in question. The analogous constitutional provision and other statutes receive a broader interpretation.

Implications

WHEN "BARE" DIVERSITY IS ENOUGH

The Constitution, as opposed to §1332, requires only minimal diversity, that is, at least one claimant diverse in citizenship from another. State Farm v. Tashire, 386 U.S. 523 (1967). That means that Congress can—in settings other than the general diversity statute—authorize federal courts to hear cases where complete diversity is lacking. Several federal statutes rest on the proposition that minimal diversity satisfies Article III.

- The Federal Interpleader Act, 28 U.S.C. §1335, discussed in Chapter 12 (infra pages 825-28) provides for federal jurisdiction so long as any claimant to a disputed fund is of citizenship different from that of any other and the amount in controversy exceeds $500. The legislative history of this statute suggests that legislators thought that without it, courts of different states could issue conflicting judgments awarding the same property to different claimants.

- The Class Action Fairness Act of 2005 (codified in scattered sections of 28 U.S.C., including §1332(d) and known as CAFA) provides for federal diversity jurisdiction in class actions over amounts in excess of $5 million in which "*any* member" of the class possesses the requisite diversity based on state or foreign citizenship. The legislative history suggests that Congress was concerned that state courts were hearing and deciding class actions in which many or most members of the class came from other states; it reached for diversity jurisdiction as a way to address this problem.

6. Suppose a court faces a case where there is diversity, but also a nondiverse party. Must the entire case be dismissed? No: Newman-Green, Inc. v. Alfonzo-Larrain, 490 U.S. 826 (1989), permitted a court to retain jurisdiction by dismissing a nondiverse party not held to be indispensable. See Rule 19 and infra page 802.

7. Apply the statutory language to the following cases, assuming that in each case, the amount in controversy requirement is met:
   a. A citizen of Mexico sues a citizen of Japan. §1332(a)(2)-(4).
   b. A citizen of California sues citizens of Mexico and Japan. §1332(a)(2).
   c. A citizen of California and a citizen of Mexico sue a citizen of New York and a citizen of Japan. See §1332(a)(3).
   d. Finally, suppose a citizen of California and a citizen of Mexico sue a citizen of Japan. The case does not fall within §1332(a); do you see why? (And if you belong to the "neutral forum" school of thought regarding diversity, that makes sense because, with foreign citizens on both sides of the case, a

state court could not discriminate against foreign citizens.) Should diversity jurisdiction extend to this situation? In what might be called a strong dictum, the Supreme Court has suggested not. Ruhrgas AG v. Marathon Oil, 526 U.S. 574 (1999) ("Marathon joined an alien plaintiff (Norge) as well as an alien defendant (Ruhrgas). If the joinder of Norge is legitimate, the complete diversity required by 28 U.S.C. §1332 (1994 ed. and Supp. III), but not by Article III, . . . is absent.").

8. Section 1359 of 28 U.S.C. deprives district courts of jurisdiction in those cases in which a party has been "improperly or collusively . . . joined" to invoke diversity jurisdiction. For example, a party wishing to invoke diversity jurisdiction cannot achieve it simply by assigning his claim to an out-of-state representative. But the courts are not unanimous in what is "improper." The statute resolves one situation: For diversity purposes the representative of a child, an incompetent, or a deceased person (appointed to administer the estate) has the same citizenship as the individual represented. 28 U.S.C. §1332(c)(2). You saw this principle in operation in *Hawkins v. Masters Farms* (Chapter 1), in which the relevant citizenship was not that of the executor but of the deceased, Mr. Creal.

9. Is a citizen of the District of Columbia (or of Puerto Rico, Guam, or another American territory not a state) a citizen of a "state" for diversity purposes? 28 U.S.C. §1332(e) says so, and its constitutionality was upheld in National Mutual Ins. Co. v. Tidewater Transfer Co., 337 U.S. 582 (1949).

10. Beyond the requirement of complete diversity, the other less than intuitive principle of diversity jurisdiction arises from corporate citizenship. Section 1332(c) provides that, unlike natural persons, corporations can have *two* states of citizenship—that of the state that incorporates them and that of their "principal place of business," if it is different from the state of incorporation. Congress added this provision in 1958 to remedy complaints that too many "home" corporations were able to invoke diversity citizenship by incorporating out of state. For decades thereafter courts struggled with inconsistent tests about how to define the corporation's "principal place of business." After half a century of disagreement, the Supreme Court stepped in to settle the matter.

Hertz Corp. v. Friend
559 U.S. 77 (2010)

BREYER, J., delivered the unanimous opinion of the court.

The federal diversity jurisdiction statute provides that "a corporation shall be deemed to be a citizen of any State by which it has been incorporated *and of the State where it has its principal place of business.*" 28 U.S.C. §1332(c)(1) (emphasis added). We seek here to resolve different interpretations that the Circuits have given this phrase. In doing so, we place primary weight upon the need for judicial administration of a jurisdictional statute to remain as simple as possible. And we conclude that the phrase "principal place of business" refers to the place where the corporation's high level officers direct, control, and coordinate the corporation's activities. Lower federal courts have often metaphorically called that place the corporation's "nerve center." We believe that the "nerve center" will typically be found at a corporation's headquarters. . . .

[The case grew from a class action. Hertz employees in California alleged that Hertz had failed to conform to California's wage and hour laws. Hertz sought to remove to federal court, invoking diversity jurisdiction. The employees resisted with the argument that California was a principal place of business for Hertz, since it derived more revenue from that state than any other and the plurality of its business activities also occurred there. Reasoning that, because of this business activity Hertz was, like them, a citizen of California, the plaintiffs resisted removal. The District Court found that Hertz was a citizen of California, relying on Ninth Circuit precedent instructing "courts to identify a corporation's 'principal place of business' by first determining the amount of a corporation's business activity State by State. If the amount of activity is 'significantly larger' or 'substantially predominates' in one State, then that State is the corporation's 'principal place of business.'" The Ninth Circuit affirmed. The Supreme Court reviewed the history of "principal place of business" and its judicial interpretations.]

V

A

In an effort to find a single, more uniform interpretation of the statutory phrase, we have reviewed the Courts of Appeals' divergent and increasingly complex interpretations. Having done so, we now return to, and expand, Judge Weinfeld's approach, as applied [in a case decided shortly after the 1958 amendment to §1332 created dual corporate citizenship]. We conclude that "principal place of business" is best read as referring to the place where a corporation's officers direct, control, and coordinate the corporation's activities. It is the place that Courts of Appeals have called the corporation's "nerve center." And in practice it should normally be the place where the corporation maintains its headquarters—provided that the headquarters is the actual center of direction, control, and coordination, *i.e.*, the "nerve center," and not simply an office where the corporation holds its board meetings (for example, attended by directors and officers who have traveled there for the occasion).

Three sets of considerations, taken together, convince us that this approach, while imperfect, is superior to other possibilities. First, the statute's language supports the approach. The statute's text deems a corporation a citizen of the "State where it has its principal place of business." 28 U.S.C. §1332(c)(1). The word "place" is in the singular, not the plural. . . .

Second, administrative simplicity is a major virtue in a jurisdictional statute. Complex jurisdictional tests complicate a case, eating up time and money as the parties litigate, not the merits of their claims, but which court is the right court to decide those claims. Complex tests produce appeals and reversals, encourage gamesmanship, and, again, diminish the likelihood that results and settlements will reflect a claim's legal and factual merits. Judicial resources too are at stake. Courts have an independent obligation to determine whether subject-matter jurisdiction exists, even when no party challenges it. So courts benefit from straight-forward rules under which they can readily assure themselves of their power to hear a case.

Third, the statute's legislative history, for those who accept it, offers a simplicity-related interpretive benchmark. The Judicial Conference provided an initial version of its proposal that suggested a numerical test. A corporation would be deemed a citizen of the State that accounted for more than half of its gross income. The Conference changed its mind in light of criticism that such a test would prove too complex and impractical to apply. That history suggests that the words "principal place of business" should be interpreted to be no more complex than the initial "half of gross income" test. A "nerve center" test offers such a possibility. A general business activities test does not.

B

We recognize that there may be no perfect test that satisfies all administrative and purposive criteria. We recognize as well that, under the "nerve center" test we adopt today, there will be hard cases. For example, in this era of tele-commuting, some corporations may divide their command and coordinating functions among officers who work at several different locations, perhaps communicating over the Internet. That said, our test nonetheless points courts in a single direction, towards the center of overall direction, control, and coordination. Courts do not have to try to weigh corporate functions, assets, or revenues different in kind, one from the other. Our approach provides a sensible test that is relatively easier to apply, not a test that will, in all instances, automatically generate a result.

We also recognize that the use of a "nerve center" test may in some cases produce results that seem to cut against the basic rationale for 28 U.S.C. §1332. For example, if the bulk of a company's business activities visible to the public take place in New Jersey, while its top officers direct those activities just across the river in New York, the "principal place of business" is New York. One could argue that members of the public in New Jersey would be *less* likely to be prejudiced against the corporation than persons in New York—yet the corporation will still be entitled to remove a New Jersey state case to federal court. And note too that the same corporation would be unable to remove a New York state case to federal court, despite the New York public's presumed prejudice against the corporation.

We understand that such seeming anomalies will arise. However, in view of the necessity of having a clearer rule, we must accept them. Accepting occasionally counterintuitive results is the price the legal system must pay to avoid overly complex jurisdictional administration while producing the benefits that accompany a more uniform legal system. . . .

Notes and Problems

1. The version of the diversity statute with its dual definition of corporate citizenship came into being in 1958 in response to concerns that the prior law made it too easy for corporations to manipulate jurisdiction (simply by incorporating outside the state where they conducted most of their activities). Unfortunately, it became almost immediately apparent that courts and litigants would be uncertain where the principal place of business was. One might wonder why it took the Court 50 years to resolve the question—with a solution that commanded a unanimous Court.

   a. Is this an obvious solution that the Court simply did not get to for half a century given the importance of other cases on its docket?

   b. Alternatively, was the Court hoping that Congress, which had created the problem in the first place, would get around to clarifying the phrase that had given the lower courts and litigants so much difficulty?

   c. Should we worry that because the Court had left the multiple tests undisturbed for 50 years, litigants might justifiably have come to rely on them? Does this argument have less force when the Court is changing a procedural rule than one that regulates basic conduct?

2. Another question might be whether the Court reached the correct decision. Note that the Court assumes that the purpose of the diversity statute is to guard against local prejudice that might be manifested in state courts. (That is a leading theory of the basis for diversity jurisdiction, but there is as little historical basis for this theory as there is for any other.) But if that is the reason for diversity jurisdiction, does a test that ignores the likelihood of such prejudice (as the Court's New York/New Jersey example illustrates) properly apply the statute?

Implications

DIVERSITY MEETS THE PARTNERSHIP

For diversity purposes, partnerships and other unincorporated entities are not considered as entities but as collections of individuals; thus the citizenship of each of the members of a partnership must be considered. See Americold Realty Trust v. ConAgra Foods, Inc., 136 S. Ct. 1012 (2016) ("[I]t is up to Congress if it wishes to incorporate other entities into 28 U.S.C. §1332(c)'s special jurisdiction rule."). Consider two examples:

Grupo Dataflux v. Atlas Global Group, L.P., 541 U.S. 567 (2004). Atlas, a Texas limited partnership, sued Grupo Dataflux, a Mexican corporation. At the time suit was filed, Atlas had a number of Texan and two Mexican partners. After losing at trial, Dataflux filed a motion to dismiss for want of subject matter jurisdiction. Held: Dismissal required. (Compare this result with that in *Caterpillar Inc. v. Lewis*, at the end of this chapter.)

Coudert Brothers v. Easyfind Intl., Inc., 601 F. Supp. 525 (S.D.N.Y. 1985). Coudert was a law firm based in New York City. Most of its partners were citizens of New York, but a few partners were U.S. citizens living in France and working at their Paris office. Defendants were U.S. and foreign citizens. Coudert filed in state court and defendants sought to remove. Held: case remanded to state court. "If we were dealing with the situation where a partnership had partners who were citizens of New York and citizens of France, there would be diversity jurisdiction under subdivision (3) of the statute. However our case is different. The status of the Coudert partners residing in France is that they are still citizens of the United States and are not citizens of France. If these partners were suing by themselves they would not fit within any of the categories referred to in the statute, since they are neither citizens of a state of the United States nor are they citizens or subjects of a foreign state. . . . It would appear to be a logical extension of the rules of law referred to above that the Coudert partnership is not a party who can sue in federal court under diversity jurisdiction." Id. at 526-27. See also *Redner v. Saunders*.

Note: Amount in Controversy

Besides diversity, §1332 requires an amount greater than $75,000 in controversy. Congress has from time to time increased this amount, most recently in 1997, from $50,000 to the present figure. Given modern understandings of inflation, one can imagine that Congress might "index" the amount in controversy, linking it to some widely accepted measure of inflation. (Congress has pegged post-judgment interest to the rate of widely traded government notes.) What are the arguments for—and against—such a move?

Whatever the dollar figure, the courts have treated this requirement in much the same way as they have the issue of federal question jurisdiction—that is, they have by and large viewed the allegations of the pleading as all but controlling, rather than engaging in judicial guessing about the likelihood that the plaintiff would succeed in collecting as much as he had prayed for. The leading Supreme Court case, St. Paul Mercury Indemnity Co. v. Red Cab Co., 303 U.S. 283, 289 (1938), stated as follows:

> It must appear to a legal certainty that the claim is really for less than the jurisdictional amount to justify dismissal. The inability of plaintiff to recover an amount adequate to give the court jurisdiction does not show his bad faith or oust the jurisdiction. Nor does the fact that the complaint discloses the existence of a valid defense of the claim. But if, from the face of the pleadings, it is apparent, to a legal certainty, that the plaintiff cannot recover the amount claimed, or if, from the proofs, the court is satisfied to a

like certainty that the plaintiff never was entitled to recover that amount, and that his claim was therefore colorable for the purpose of conferring jurisdiction, the suit will be dismissed.

But the courts' trust in the pleadings is not boundless. Consider, for example, a plaintiff who brought a diversity action against a hotel, alleging its security personnel had assaulted him; the likely compensatory damages were small, but the plaintiff relied on a punitive damage count to lift him over the amount in controversy:

> Plaintiff has not provided "competent proof" to meet his burden of demonstrating the requisite amount in controversy. Instead, he argues that he satisfies the jurisdictional requirement because he is entitled to recovery of punitive damages that could result in a verdict in excess of $75,000.
>
> . . . [Plaintiff] has pled that the Defendants acted "intentionally," thus punitive damages are potentially recoverable under Illinois law if [he] can prove what he has alleged.
>
> Even assuming [Plaintiff] can recover punitive damages, [however,] . . . he would have to recover multiple times his actual damages to satisfy the $75,000 amount. Such a recovery certainly would "stretch[] the normal ratio, and would face certain remittitur." Plaintiff's mere hope for an extreme punitive award cannot be the sole basis for jurisdiction. . . .
>
> Salmi v. D.T. Management, Inc., 2002 U.S. Dist. LEXIS 17970 (N.D. Ill. 2002).

In another respect, the Supreme Court has suggested that the amount in controversy requirement differs from the requirement of complete diversity. The issue surfaced in Exxon Mobil Corp. v. Allapattah Servs., Inc., 545 U.S. 546 (2005). In *Allapattah* the Court had to decide whether to include within the supplemental jurisdiction granted by 28 U.S.C. §1367 (discussed infra at pages 232-35) claims held by parties who met the diversity requirement but for less than $75,000. Yes, said the court, in part because the amount in controversy requirement was less central to the idea of diversity jurisdiction:

> To ensure that diversity jurisdiction does not flood the federal courts with minor disputes, §1332(a) requires that the matter in controversy in a diversity case exceed a specified amount, currently $75,000. . . .
>
> [W]e have consistently interpreted §1332 as requiring complete diversity: In a case with multiple plaintiffs and multiple defendants, the presence in the action of a single plaintiff from the same State as a single defendant deprives the district court of original diversity jurisdiction over the entire action. *Strawbridge v. Curtiss.* The Court . . . has adhered to the complete diversity rule in light of the purpose of the diversity requirement, which is to provide a federal forum for important disputes where state courts might favor, or be perceived as favoring, home-state litigants. The presence of parties from the same State on both sides of a case dispels this concern, eliminating a principal reason for conferring §1332 jurisdiction over any of the claims in the action. . . .
>
> In contrast to the diversity requirement, most of the other statutory prerequisites for federal jurisdiction, including the federal-question and amount-in-controversy requirements, can be analyzed claim by claim. . . .

Though the special nature and purpose of the diversity requirement mean that a single nondiverse party can contaminate every other claim in the lawsuit, the contamination does not occur with respect to jurisdictional defects that go only to the substantive importance of individual claims.

Id. at 551, 553, 566.

Other significant issues in determining the amount in controversy for jurisdictional purposes are:

1. What should be done if the plaintiff asks for an injunction rather than money damages? The basic principle is to try to value the injunction, using one of several approaches: Determine the value of the injunction to the plaintiff; determine the cost to the defendant of complying; determine the cost or value to the party invoking federal jurisdiction (the plaintiff, if the action is brought in federal court, and the defendant, if the action was brought in state court and defendant is attempting to remove); and allow jurisdiction if any of the tests above yields a figure above $75,000. For a discussion of these approaches (and an application of the fourth), see McCarty v. Amoco Pipeline Co., 595 F.2d 389 (7th Cir. 1979).

2. May a plaintiff aggregate the amount sought as relief for different claims to reach the statutory minimum? Sometimes: In some circumstances, different claims may be aggregated to meet the statutory amount. Saying when that can happen is harder:

> The law on aggregation . . . is in a very unsatisfactory state. The traditional rules in this area evolved haphazardly and with little reasoning. They serve no apparent policy and "turn on a mystifying conceptual test." . . . Thus it is not altogether easy to say what the law is in this area and it is quite hard to say why it is as it seems to be.
>
> Wright, Federal Courts 210.

Some guidelines from the case law:
a. A single plaintiff with two or more unrelated claims against a single defendant may aggregate claims to satisfy the statutory amount.
b. If two plaintiffs each have claims against a single defendant, they may not aggregate if their claims are regarded as "separate and distinct"—as opposed to a common claim for, say, jointly owned property.
c. If one plaintiff has a claim in excess of the statutory amount and a second plaintiff has the same claim for less than the statutory amount, both against the same defendant, the first plaintiff can sue in federal court. What about the second? Yes: So long as the second plaintiff's claim arises out of the "same case or controversy" as the first there will be supplemental jurisdiction. Exxon Mobil Corp. v. Allapattah Servs., Inc., 545 U.S. 546 (2005).
d. In situations involving multiple plaintiffs or multiple defendants with a common undivided interest and single title or right, the value of the total interest will be used to determine the amount in controversy.

e. The preceding rules have complex application to class actions.

    i. For class actions that meet the criteria of the Class Actions Fairness Act of 2005, codified in part in §1332(d) (discussed more fully in Chapter 12), one can aggregate the claims of all class members; if they reach $5 million, the amount in controversy requirement is met.

    ii. For class actions based on diversity that do not meet the requirements of the Act, one cannot simply add up the claims of all class members. Instead at least some members must have claims that individually satisfy the jurisdictional amount. Snyder v. Harris, 394 U.S. 332 (1969). But if one member meets the amount in controversy requirement, the others can take advantage of supplemental jurisdiction. Exxon Mobil Corp. v. Allapattah Servs., Inc., 545 U.S. 546 (2005).

f. Counterclaims are treated differently, depending on their classification under Rule 13 as either compulsory or permissive. Basically, when a plaintiff's claim exceeds $75,000 (the statutory amount), a compulsory counterclaim may be heard regardless of amount. A permissive counterclaim not arising from the same transaction or occurrence requires an independent jurisdictional basis. The law is unsettled, however, when plaintiff's claim falls short of $75,000 but defendant's counterclaim increases the amount in controversy to more than $75,000. See generally Wright, Federal Courts 217 (reporting "virtually no holdings" addressing the question).

g. Apply these principles to a hypothetical variation on *Louisville & Nashville Railroad v. Mottley*. Suppose the plaintiffs, Erasmus and Annie Mottley, having learned they cannot state an "arising under" claim, still want a federal forum for the trial of their case. So, taking advantage of the fact that diversity is measured at the time of filing, they move out of state and file their action as a diversity case. In each variation, assume that the requisite diversity exists and only the amount in controversy is an issue.

    i. Erasmus sues Railroad for $75,000 for breach of contract.

    ii. Erasmus sues Railroad for $100,000 for breach of contract; Railroad counterclaims for $5,000, alleging that on some occasions Erasmus, in violation of the settlement terms, allowed a friend to use his pass.

    iii. Erasmus sues Railroad on two unrelated claims: breach of the settlement agreement ($72,000) and a due but unpaid Railroad bond ($5,000).

    iv. Annie and Friend sue Railroad. Annie, alleging breach of the settlement agreement, seeks $60,000; Friend, alleging she was riding the train with Annie when a luggage rack fell off and injured her, seeks $40,000.

    v. Erasmus and Annie both sue Railroad for breach of the settlement agreement, each seeking $50,000.

D. SUPPLEMENTAL JURISDICTION

Thus far we have examined aspects of federal subject matter jurisdiction that narrow the doors to federal courts in ways that neither intuition nor the texts of the

Constitution and the statutes might suggest. The resulting picture displays some substantial areas of unexploited constitutional power:

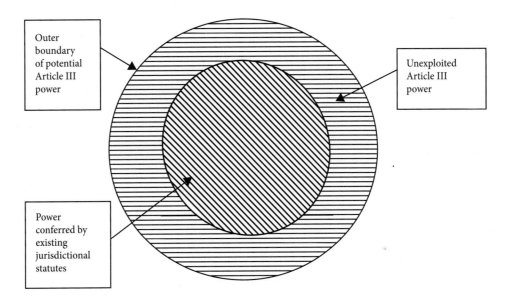

We turn now to a doctrine that broadens federal jurisdiction, filling in selectively some of the area between the inner and the outer rings. This doctrine is known as supplemental jurisdiction. Supplemental jurisdiction originated in case law that stretched federal jurisdiction to cover parts of cases that, if brought independently, would not have fit within the district courts' subject matter jurisdiction. Congress then codified some and modified other case law results. Examine the statute, 28 U.S.C. §1367, and consider its structure and application to some basic problems.

Notes and Problems

---

1. Not all cases described by §1367(a) are covered by §1367(b). What's the key difference?

2. In these problems, assume the litigation occurs in federal district court and that amount in controversy requirements, if they apply, are satisfied. Also assume the joined party or claim would fall within the applicable joinder Rule (see Chapter 12). In working out your analysis, first identify the portion of §1367 that applies, and then apply that section to the facts.

   a. *A*, a citizen of Illinois, sues *B*, also a citizen of Illinois, alleging that *B* violated federal civil rights statutes in firing her. *A* seeks to add a state law claim alleging that her firing also violated a state wrongful discharge law. Is there supplemental jurisdiction?

b. *A*, a citizen of Illinois, sues *B*, also a citizen of Illinois, alleging that *B* violated federal civil rights statutes in firing her. *A* seeks to add a state law claim alleging that *B* negligently caused her injuries when his car backed into hers in the company parking lot. Is there supplemental jurisdiction?

No

c. *A*, a citizen of Illinois, sues *B*, also a citizen of Illinois, alleging that *B* violated federal civil rights statutes by permitting co-workers to engage in sexual harassment. *A* invokes Rule 20 to join *C*, a co-worker from Illinois, who actually engaged in the harassment. State tort law is the basis of *A*'s claim against *C*. Because *C* is not *A*'s employer, the claim against him does not arise under federal law. Is there supplemental jurisdiction over the claim against *C*?

No

d. *A*, a citizen of Illinois, sues *B*, a citizen of Wisconsin, alleging breach of an employment contract and seeking a recovery in excess of $75,000. *A* invokes Rule 20 to join *C*, a citizen of Illinois; *A* alleges that *C* conspired with *B* to breach the employment contract. Is there supplemental jurisdiction over the claim against *C*?

e. Arthur, a citizen of New York, sues Barbara, a citizen of Pennsylvania, in federal district court. He alleges several claims: federal antitrust violations, federal securities law violations, and state law breach of contract. He alleges more than $100,000 in damages for each claim. Will the district court have to analyze how closely related the federal and state law claims are for purposes of deciding whether supplemental jurisdiction exists or whether any of the reasons in §1367(c) for declining to exercise jurisdiction apply? Why not?

3. Having applied the statute to some cases, step back and consider its constitutional underpinnings.

a. A statute that gave federal district courts jurisdiction to decide a case based entirely on state law between two Florida citizens would be unconstitutional—beyond the power granted by Article III. How then can it be constitutional for a district court to hear such a claim when the same parties also are embroiled in litigation over a federal claim?

b. The statute supplies a clue in subsection (a), which speaks of "claims that are so related to claims in the action within such original jurisdiction that they form part of the same case or controversy under Article III of the Constitution." Article III says that federal "judicial Power . . . extend[s] to all Cases" of the sorts enumerated and to "Controversies" of sorts that are further enumerated. From this phrase the courts have drawn the idea that:

> [Supplemental] jurisdiction, in the sense of judicial power, exists whenever there is a claim [within the constitutional jurisdiction], and the relationship between that claim and the [claim outside the constitutionally enumerated jurisdiction of the federal courts] permits the conclusion that the entire action before the court comprises but one constitutional "case." The federal claim must have substance sufficient to confer subject matter jurisdiction on the court. The state and federal claims must derive from a common nucleus of operative fact. But if, considered without regard to their federal or state character, a plaintiff's claims are such that he would ordinarily be expected to try them all in one

judicial proceeding, then, assuming substantiality of the federal issues, there is power in federal courts to hear the whole.[13]

United Mine Workers v. Gibbs, 383 U.S. 715, 725 (1966).

    c. *United Mine Workers v. Gibbs* and §1367 espouse a principle that may look surprising at first glance. Its rationale emerges more clearly if one recalls that a central feature of the Federal Rules is the ease with which they permit joinder of claims. See, e.g., Rule 18(a). It would be logically possible, but awkward, to permit parties to join closely connected claims but then deny the federal courts power over claims that did not bring their own jurisdictional basis with them. In such situations, whichever court (state or federal) tried the related claim second would have to engage in elaborate analyses of which issues were precluded in the first lawsuit. Section 1367 allows some—but not all—of these related claims to come to federal court under the wing of supplemental jurisdiction.

4. Consider the following two cases in which courts wrestle with applying the statute, including their discretionary authority to decline to exercise supplemental jurisdiction.

In re Ameriquest Mortgage Co. Mortgage Lending Practices Litigation

2007 U.S. Dist. LEXIS 70805 (N.D. Ill. 2007)

ASPEN, J.

    Pursuant to Federal Rule of Civil Procedure 12(b)(1) and 28 U.S.C. §§1367(a) and (b), defendant Douglas Trevino now moves to dismiss Counts II and III of plaintiff Barbara Skanes' Amended Complaint. . . .

    We deny Trevino's motion. We find that: a) there is a sufficient nexus between Skanes' state law claims and her TILA claim to support supplemental jurisdiction; and b) the discretionary factors set forth in [§1367(c)] do not weigh in favor of a decision to decline to exercise supplemental jurisdiction.

I. Background

    In her Amended Complaint, Skanes alleges that in April 2004, she consummated a mortgage transaction with Ameriquest. Shortly before the close of the transaction, Ameriquest ordered from co-defendant Homestead Appraisal of Rockford a property appraisal of Skanes' future home. Homestead, through its agent Trevino [appraised the house at] $163,000. . . .

---

[13] While it is commonplace that the Federal Rules of Civil Procedure do not expand the jurisdiction of federal courts, they do embody "the whole tendency of our decisions . . . to require a plaintiff to try his . . . whole case at one time," Baltimore S.S. Co. v. Phillips, [274 U.S. 316,] and to that extent emphasize the basis of pendent [now called supplemental] jurisdiction.

Skanes alleges that the "true value" of her home was much less than the amount reflected in Trevino's report. . . . The reason for this inflation, Skanes contends, was to increase the loan amount for which she could qualify and thereby increase Ameriquest's potential profit. [When the adjustable rate reset, Skanes could not refinance.]

[Count I of the complaint alleged a claim against Ameriquest under the federal Truth in Lending Act (TILA), seeking both rescission of the mortgage and statu-tory damages.] In Count I, her TILA claim, Skanes further states that at the time of her closing, Ameriquest provided her with improper and misleading disclosures of her right to cancel her mortgage. Ameriquest's disclosures, she alleges, triggered an extended right for her to later rescind her mortgage. [Counts II and III alleged state law fraud claims against all defendants.] In addition, Skanes requests that we enter a "judgment declaring what obligation, if any, plaintiff has toward each defendant [following rescission], *taking into account . . . the inflated appraised value*" (emphasis added). . . .

II. Analysis

A. §1367(a) Supplemental Jurisdiction

28 U.S.C. §1367 provides that in any action in which we already have jurisdiction over some federal claim, we also have supplemental jurisdiction over state claims "that are so related to claims in the action within such original jurisdiction that they form part of the same case or controversy under Article III of the United States Constitu-tion.". . . A loose factual connection may be sufficient to confer supplemental jurisdic-tion, so long as those facts are both common and operative. To determine whether the federal and state law claims are connected by common and operative facts, "[c]ourts routinely compare the facts necessary to prove the elements of the federal claim with those necessary to the success of the state claim." We also may ask "whether the state claims can be resolved or dismissed without affecting the federal claims."

Here, Skanes explicitly connected her federal and state claims, such that we cannot now conclude that her state claims could be dismissed or resolved without affecting her TILA claim. As set forth in the Amended Complaint, the facts under-lying her state and federal claims combine to tell one story: Skanes did not fully know of her right to cancel her mortgage at its outset; because that mortgage was overstated, she paid too much during the life of her loan; and—also because of the overstatement—she has not been able to refinance the mortgage. Alleging a [federal] TILA disclosure violation, Skanes now wishes to void her allegedly overstated mort-gage. In doing so, Skanes expressly links her TILA prayer for relief to her state claims. Skanes seeks a judgment voiding her mortgage and a judgment declaring what, if any, payment obligation exists after taking into account Skanes' state law challenge to her home appraisal.

We find this connection operative: if we dismiss Counts II and III, we may be unable to grant the full measure of relief Skanes seeks in Count I: if she is entitled to rescission, and she is correct that her home value was over-appraised, then she may be (or may not be—we do not intend to decide that issue here) entitled to reduce the post-TILA judgment tender amount in light of the over-appraisal. Without a determination of the over-appraisal issue, though, that offset would be unavailable. Because we cannot conclude that the resolution of one of her state claims will have no effect on the resolution on her federal claims, we cannot deny our supplemental jurisdiction here.

B. §1367[(c)] Discretionary Exercise of Supplemental Jurisdiction

Even if we find that we have supplemental jurisdiction over a plaintiff's state law claims, 28 U.S.C. §1367[(c)] provides four instances in which we may choose not to exercise that jurisdiction: "(1) the claim raises a novel or complex issue of State law; (2) the claim substantially predominates over the claim or claims over which the district court has original jurisdiction; (3) the district court has dismissed all claims over which it has original jurisdiction; or (4) in exceptional circumstances, there are other compelling reasons for declining jurisdiction."

We do not perceive a problem with respect to factors (2) through (4): we cannot tell from the face of the Amended Complaint that Skanes' inflated appraisal allegations "substantially predominate" over her TILA claims; we have not dismissed Skanes' TILA claims; and Trevino has not highlighted any persuasive "exceptional circumstances" or "compelling reasons" for us to decline to exercise supplemental jurisdiction. Nor are we persuaded that because the Michigan Mortgage Brokers, Lenders and Servicers Lending Act [a state statute] has not been specifically applied to appraisers or appraisal services, we will not be able to resolve Skanes' claims through reference to existing precedent (which, by the time this case has concluded, could well include applications of the MMBLSLA to appraisers and appraisal services). Accordingly, we choose to exercise our discretion in favor of retaining jurisdiction over Counts II and III of the Amended Complaint. . . .

Szendrey-Ramos v. First Bancorp

512 F. Supp. 2d 81 (D.P.R. 2007)

CASELLAS, J.

[Carmen Szendrey-Ramos, the plaintiff (referred to in the opinion as Szendrey), worked for the defendant bank in Puerto Rico as its general counsel.]

In March 2005, Szendrey received a report from an external law firm that included information about possible ethical and/or legal violations committed by bank officials in relation to the accounting for the bulk purchase of mortgage loans from other financial institutions. Szendrey conducted an investigation into this issue, focusing on the possibility of whether the bank officials' conduct amounted to a violation of law or the bank's Code of Ethics. Upon conclusion of such investigation, Szendrey concluded that there had been irregularities and violations of the Code of Ethics and reported such findings to outside counsel for the bank as well as bank officials. She also divulged her findings to the Board of Directors at a meeting in which she was present. . . .

[After the bank conducted an additional review of its bulk purchase of mortgage loans, it fired Szendrey on the ground that she was responsible for some of the events she had investigated. She sued, alleging violations of federal employment law (Title VII) and additionally stating a number of claims under the laws of Puerto Rico for wrongful discharge, violations of the P.R. Constitution, and for defamation and tortious interference with contracts.]

Applicable Law and Analysis

Upon careful consideration of the issues presented by this case, and the law governing such issues, we decline to exercise supplemental jurisdiction over the P.R. law claims. Accordingly, these claims will be dismissed without prejudice, and Defendants' arguments for dismissal on the merits of such claims are thus moot. As for the Title VII discrimination and retaliation claims, they survive the motion to dismiss. This case thus goes forward solely under Title VII. We explain our reasoning below. . . .

The Court finds that two of §1367(c)'s subsections are at issue here: (1) that the state law claims raise complex or novel issues and (2) that the state-law claims substantially predominate over the federal claim. We start with the latter and work our way back to the former.

Plaintiffs' complaint includes two lonesome claims under Title VII, for discrimination and retaliation thereunder. The remaining claims all arise out of P.R. law. Not only do the P.R. law claims far outnumber the federal claims, but their scope also exceeds that of the federal claims. On that point we note that although some of the P.R. law claims mimic the federal claims . . . the remaining P.R. law claims (wrongful discharge, tortious actions infringing Plaintiff's constitutional rights, tortious interference with contracts, and defamation) are distinct and each has its own elements of proof; proof that is not necessary to establish the Title VII claims. That the state-law claims predominate over the federal claims is, in and of itself, reason enough to decline to exercise supplemental jurisdiction.

Moreover, we note that the P.R. law claims require a much fuller incursion into the performance of Szendrey as General Counsel and any shortcomings she may have had as such. This, in turn, leads us to the other reason for declining to exercise supplemental jurisdiction: the presence of complex or novel issues of state law. The main issue raised by Defendants in their motion to dismiss, that Plaintiffs' prosecution of their claims would run afoul of Canon 21 of the Puerto Rico Code of Professional Ethics, is at its apex in the P.R. law claims. For example, in order to prove that Defendants defamed her, Szendrey would have to establish that what was said about her (i.e., that she participated in wrongful acts) was false. In order to prove such falsity, Szendrey would have to reveal the extent of her participation regarding such wrongful acts, including what information she became aware of as General Counsel, what actions she took after learning such information, and what advice she offered her client with regards to such information. [Defendants argued that Canon 21 of Puerto Rican legal ethics rules forbade a lawyer from disclosing client confidences, even in litigation between lawyer and client.]

Canon 21 undisputably belongs to an exclusively Puerto Rican body of law, and one that deals with the highly sensitive matter of lawyers' conduct, and its relation to society's interest in a fully functioning legal system. The interpretation of the canons is normally the province of the Puerto Rico Supreme Court, which is entrusted with the regulation and supervision of the legal profession. We note, moreover, that Canon 21 is decidedly different to the corresponding Model Rule of the American Bar Association. Unlike this Court and several U.S. jurisdictions, Puerto Rico has not adopted the latest version of the American Bar Association's Model Rules.

Canon 21 is decidedly silent on the issue of a lawyer's claim—whether in-house or not—against his former client, and the possibility of divulging confidential information in order to pursue such a claim. . . . This is an issue of Puerto Rico law that has yet to be addressed by the Puerto Rico courts and which is imbued with important considerations of public policy. . . .

Because the Puerto Rico law claims substantially predominate over the federal claims in this case, and because they posit novel and complex issues of state law, the Court declines to exercise supplemental jurisdiction. Accordingly, the Puerto Rico law claims will be dismissed without prejudice, so that Plaintiffs may re-file them in the Puerto Rico courts. . . .

Notes and Problems

1. Why did *Ameriquest* and *Szendrey-Ramos* reach different results on the question of supplemental jurisdiction?
   a. What key allegation of the complaint convinced the judge in *Ameriquest* to extend supplemental jurisdiction?
   b. Did the judge in *Szendrey-Ramos* have the statutory power to extend supplemental jurisdiction over plaintiff's non-federal claims? What argument of the defendants convinced the judge in *Szendrey-Ramos* not to exercise supplemental jurisdiction?

2. In cases like *Ameriquest*, other courts facing a number of state law claims have taken a stance substantially less hospitable to supplemental jurisdiction.
   a. One district court has in several cases used the following justification in declining to exercise supplemental jurisdiction:

   > Litigation in the federal courts involving both federal law claims and supplemental state law claims has caused procedural and substantive problems. Even if the federal and state claims in this action arise out of the same factual situation, litigating these claims together may not serve judicial economy or trial convenience. Federal and state law each have a different focus, and the two bodies of law have evolved at different times and in different legislative and judicial systems. Because of this, in almost every case with supplemental state claims, the courts and counsel are unduly preoccupied with substantive and procedural problems in reconciling the two bodies of law and providing a fair and meaningful proceeding.
   >
   > The attempt to reconcile these two distinct bodies of law often dominates and prolongs pre-trial practice, complicates the trial, lengthens the jury instructions, confuses the jury, results in inconsistent verdicts, and causes

post-trial problems with respect to judgment interest and attorney fees. Consequently, in many cases the apparent judicial economy and convenience of the parties' interest in the entertainment of supplemental state claims may be offset by the problems they create.

National Fair Housing Alliance, Inc. v. Hobson-Hollowell,
2007 U.S. Dist. LEXIS 66538 (E.D. Mich. 2007).

b. Which section(s) of §1367(c) is the court invoking in so ruling?

3. In *Hobson-Hollowell*, cited in the preceding note, the court appears to have taken a blanket stance toward all or most state law claims. More usual are courts that take varying stances depending on the circumstances of the case. Consider some common variations:

   a. Robert files a federal employment discrimination claim and a state law wrongful discharge claim, which the district court finds to be within the scope of §1367. His federal civil rights claim is dismissed on a Rule 12(b)(6) motion after he fails to plead his membership in any of the racial, religious, or other categories protected by the civil rights statutes as a factor in his dismissal. Should the court continue to exercise supplemental jurisdiction over the state claim?

   b. Same claim, but Robert pleads racial discrimination and the case proceeds to discovery. After substantial discovery, Employer moves for summary judgment on the discrimination claim and the court grants the motion, ruling that Robert has failed to produce evidence that race was a factor in his dismissal. Trial is set to begin two weeks later. Should the court exercise supplemental jurisdiction over the state claim?

   c. Same facts as in 3b, but the state law in question is a newly enacted statute in which it is unclear whether plaintiff must prove that his discharge is wrongful or defendant must show that it was for good cause. Should the court exercise supplemental jurisdiction?

4. Supplemental jurisdiction can create difficult problems for plaintiffs who guess wrong in invoking federal question jurisdiction. Suppose plaintiff believes she has been discriminated against in her employment. Believing she can bring both state and federal law claims and preferring a federal forum, plaintiff files in federal court, invoking supplemental jurisdiction for the state claims. It turns out that plaintiff was wrong about the federal claims: After the state statute of limitations has run, the federal court dismisses the federal claims and declines to exercise jurisdiction over the remaining state law claims. What can plaintiff do?

   a. Some states have "savings" statutes that toll the state statute of limitations under such circumstances, so plaintiff has a limited time to refile in state court.

   b. But not all states have such statutes. In such cases §1367(d) seeks to address the problem by opening a 30-day "window." Suppose our hypothetical plaintiff is in a state that has no "savings" statute; how does §1367(d) help her? What should she do?

   c. The U.S. Supreme Court has held the 30-day extension unconstitutional as applied to a claim against a state agency that had not consented to such a provision. Raygor v. Regents, 534 U.S. 533 (2002).

E. REMOVAL

Jurisdictional statutes give plaintiffs an initial choice of state or federal court for cases in which federal and state court jurisdictions overlap. Congress has also given defendants the power to trump plaintiffs who choose a state court in cases that could have been brought in federal court. The process, known as *removal*, has as its basic text 28 U.S.C. §1441. Read the statute and consider its operation in the following problems.

Notes and Problems

1. Which of the following cases would be removable?
   a. *P* sues *D* for defamation in state court; *D* believes the statement she published is protected under the First Amendment.
   b. *P* sues *D* in state court, alleging violation of *P*'s rights under the Equal Protection Clause of the U.S. Constitution.
   c. *P*, a citizen of Florida, sues *D*, a citizen of New Jersey, on a personal injury claim, in a Florida state court, seeking $100,000 in damages.
   d. *P*, a citizen of Florida, sues *D*, a citizen of New Jersey, on a personal injury claim in New Jersey state court, seeking $100,000 in damages.
   e. The facts are the same as in Problem 1d, except that *P* adds a claim that *D* has violated her federal civil rights.
   f. *P*, a citizen of Florida, sues *D*, a citizen of New Jersey, and *E*, a citizen of New York, on a personal injury claim in New York state court, seeking $100,000 in damages.

2. The procedure for removal is set forth in 28 U.S.C. §1446; that for challenging removal in §1447. Read these statutes and apply them to the following questions.
   a. Plaintiff, a citizen of Pennsylvania, files a complaint in Pennsylvania state court alleging state law violations, naming Danielle as defendant and seeking $100,000 in damages. Danielle is a citizen of Georgia. If Danielle wishes to remove, what must her notice of removal say?
   b. If in her notice of removal Danielle falsely states that she is a citizen of Georgia, what risks does she run?
   c. Danielle files her notice of removal two months after being served with the state court complaint. Assuming that the conditions for diversity exist, can she remove?
   d. Same problem as in 2a, except that plaintiff's initial complaint seeks only $10,000 in damages. Six months later, after some discovery, plaintiff amends his state complaint to add an additional cause of action, so he now seeks $85,000 in damages. May Danielle now remove?
   e. Same problem as in 2a. Defendant removes, invoking diversity. What if plaintiff seeks remand to state court, offering to stipulate that she would seek less than $75,000 in damages? The Sixth Circuit, in Rogers v. Wal-Mart Stores Inc., 230 F.3d 868 (6th Cir. 2000), affirmed a denial of the remand motion, saying that the propriety of removal should be judged by the apparent amount in controversy at the time removal is sought.

f. Plaintiff's complaint seeks $10,000 in damages. Danielle seeks to remove, claiming that if she is liable, which she denies, the damages are far more than the jurisdictional amount alleged. May she remove? What does §1446(c) say about this problem? See *Troupe*, in Chapter 5 (page 300), for an illustration of this problem.

g. Same problem as in 2d, except that plaintiff amends his complaint more than a year after the original complaint. What obstacle to removal does §1446(c) pose?

h. As in 2g, the complaint when first filed alleges less than the amount in controversy and the notice of removal is made over a year after the complaint is filed. Suppose defendant contends that the plaintiff knew from the start that the claim—if it was worth anything, which defendant denies—was worth at least $100,000. Can defendant remove? See §1446(c)(3)(B).

i. Suppose a complaint filed in state court alleges federal employment discrimination and additional state law claims. If the state law claims are so closely related to the federal claim that they fall within supplemental jurisdiction, the entire case may be removed. But suppose they are not—they are contract claims too unconnected with the discrimination count to be part of the "same case or controversy." Read §1441(c) and explain what will happen to the state and federal claims.

PERSPECTIVES

Congress, the Courts, and Diversity

Congress, while unwilling to repeal diversity jurisdiction, has restricted it in a number of small ways.

- It has retained and occasionally increased the amount in controversy requirement.
- It has created dual citizenship for corporations, thus decreasing the number of situations in which they can avail themselves of diversity.
- It has limited diversity removal more than federal question removal, including the one-year time limit on diversity-based removal.
- It has placed more restrictions on supplemental jurisdiction in diversity-only cases.

These restrictions reflect a low-level continuing debate about the contemporary usefulness of diversity jurisdiction. Most observers do not think that discrimination based on state citizenship (as opposed to other characteristics) plays a major role in the United States today. *If* the only reason for diversity jurisdiction were to guard against such discrimination, then one could challenge its contemporary role.

Defenses of diversity jurisdiction take several forms. Some argue that by providing "competition" for state courts, federal diversity cases raise the standards of some state judiciaries. Others argue that by providing a stream of "ordinary" cases (auto accidents, contract disputes), diversity cases prevent federal judges from becoming narrow specialists. Still others argue a variation on traditional justifications for diversity: Even if bias against out-of-staters is not strong, in many regions there *is* a bias in favor of "the home team" and that diversity jurisdiction prevents that type of bias from distorting litigation outcomes.

3. Federal courts are sticklers for the removal rules; they generally require parties rigorously to follow each of the removal statute's procedural requirements and remand those cases that do not comply.

   a. Take, for example, The Formula Inc. v. Mammoth 8050 LLC, 2008 WL 60428 (S.D. Fla. Jan. 3, 2008). Formula filed its complaint in state court in Florida, and served a Summons and Complaint on Mammoth on October 23, 2007. On November 26, 2007, Mammoth removed the case to federal court based on diversity of citizenship. The district court remanded the case to state court on the ground that the removal was untimely.

      > Mammoth erroneously calculated the thirty day time frame so as not to include November 23, 2007 (believing that the Court was closed the day after Thanksgiving) and failed to file a notice of removal until November 26, 2007. Technically, November 23rd is not a legal holiday, as defined for instance in Federal Rule 6(a)(4)—only Thanksgiving Day itself is a legal holiday. Admittedly, the day after Thanksgiving is, for all practical purposes, a day in which many people do not go to work to kickoff the holiday buying-spree season (i.e., Black Friday). It is thus understandable that one may treat that day as a continuation of the Thanksgiving holiday. But no Federal statute, Court Rule, or Court Order deems that Friday as a holiday per se. . . . Mammoth concedes this fact but argues that, under the circumstances, there is good cause to excuse this technical one-day delay. The Court, however, is duty bound to strictly apply and enforce section 1446(b) that is an express statutory requirement for removal. The statute was drafted in mandatory language ("shall be filed within thirty days") and, thus, the failure to comply with the statute "can fairly be said to render the removal 'defective' and justify a remand pursuant to Section 1447(c)."

   b. Or consider Schafer v. Bayer Cropscience LP, 2010 WL 1038518 (E.D. Ark. Mar. 19, 2010). The initial complaint, alleging state law claims, was filed in state court on August 29, 2006. On May 20, 2009, plaintiffs filed an amended complaint, adding Bayer as a defendant. Bayer removed the case on September 17, 2009, but the case was remanded to state court. After the state court severed nondiverse plaintiffs from the case, Bayer again removed the case to federal court on March 16, 2010. This time, the district court remanded the case to state court on the ground that the removal was untimely because it occurred more than one year after the case was first filed. The court acknowledged that Bayer was not a defendant in the case until more than one year after it had been filed.

> [T]he statute is unambiguous that "it plainly prohibits removal on diversity grounds of a case that was commenced in state court more than a year prior to its removal.". . . Although this rule may seem harsh to later added defendants, "Congress accepted a 'modest curtailment in access to diversity jurisdiction' in exchange for avoiding 'substantial delay and disruption' after 'substantial progress in state court.'"

c. One significant exception to this punctilious reading of the removal statutes can be found in the Supreme Court's decision in *Caterpillar, Inc. v. Lewis*. As you read the opinion, consider why.

Caterpillar, Inc. v. Lewis
519 U.S. 61 (1996)

GINSBURG, J., delivered the opinion of the Court. . . .

The question presented is whether the absence of complete diversity at the time of removal is fatal to federal-court adjudication. We hold that a district court's error in failing to remand a case improperly removed is not fatal to the ensuing adjudication if federal jurisdictional requirements are met at the time judgment is entered.

Respondent James David Lewis, a resident of Kentucky, filed this lawsuit in Kentucky state court on June 22, 1989, after sustaining injuries while operating a bulldozer. Asserting state-law claims based on defective manufacture, negligent maintenance, failure to warn, and breach of warranty, Lewis named as defendants both the manufacturer of the bulldozer—petitioner Caterpillar Inc., a Delaware corporation with its principal place of business in Illinois—and the company that serviced the bulldozer—Whayne Supply Company, a Kentucky corporation with its principal place of business in Kentucky.

Several months later, Liberty Mutual Insurance Group, the insurance carrier for Lewis' employer, intervened in the lawsuit as a plaintiff. A Massachusetts corporation with its principal place of business in that State, Liberty Mutual asserted subrogation claims against both Caterpillar and Whayne Supply for workers' compensation benefits Liberty Mutual had paid to Lewis on behalf of his employer.

Pacts

Lewis entered into a settlement agreement with defendant Whayne Supply less than a year after filing his complaint. Shortly after learning of this agreement, Caterpillar filed a notice of removal, on June 21, 1990, in the United States District Court for the Eastern District of Kentucky. Grounding federal jurisdiction on diversity of citizenship, Caterpillar satisfied with only a day to spare the statutory requirement that a diversity-based removal take place within one year of a lawsuit's commencement, see 28 U.S.C. §1446(b).* Caterpillar's notice of removal explained that the case was nonremovable at the lawsuit's start: Complete diversity was absent then because plaintiff Lewis and defendant Whayne Supply shared Kentucky citizenship. Proceeding on the understanding that the settlement agreement between these two Kentucky parties would result in the dismissal of Whayne Supply from the lawsuit, Caterpillar stated that the settlement rendered the case removable.

Lewis objected to the removal and moved to remand the case to state court. Lewis acknowledged that he had settled his own claims against Whayne Supply. But Liberty Mutual had not yet settled its subrogation claim against Whayne Supply, Lewis asserted. Whayne Supply's presence as a defendant in the lawsuit, Lewis urged, defeated diversity of citizenship. Without addressing this argument, the District Court denied Lewis' motion to remand on September 24, 1990, treating as dispositive Lewis' admission that he had settled his own claims against Whayne Supply.

In June 1993, [Liberty Mutual and Whayne settled]. . . . With Caterpillar as the sole defendant adverse to Lewis, the case proceeded to a 6-day jury trial in November 1993, ending in a unanimous verdict for Caterpillar. . . .

We note, initially, two "givens" in this case as we have accepted it for review. First, the District Court, in its decision denying Lewis' timely motion to remand, incorrectly treated Whayne Supply, the nondiverse defendant, as effectively dropped from the case prior to removal. Second, the Sixth Circuit correctly determined that the complete diversity requirement was not satisfied at the time of removal. We accordingly home in on this question: Does the District Court's initial misjudgment still burden and run with the case, or is it overcome by the eventual dismissal of the nondiverse defendant? . . .

Having preserved his objection to an improper removal, Lewis urges that an "all's well that ends well" approach is inappropriate here. He maintains that ultimate satisfaction of the subject-matter jurisdiction requirement ought not swallow up antecedent statutory violations. The course Caterpillar advocates, Lewis observes, would disfavor diligent plaintiffs who timely, but unsuccessfully, move to check improper removals in district court. Further, that course would allow improperly removing defendants to profit from their disregard of Congress' instructions, and their ability to lead district judges into error.

Concretely, in this very case, Lewis emphasizes, adherence to the rules Congress prescribed for removal would have kept the case in state court. Only by removing prematurely was Caterpillar able to get to federal court inside the 1-year limitation set in §1446(b). Had Caterpillar waited until the case was ripe for removal, i.e., until Whayne Supply was dismissed as a defendant, the 1-year limitation would have barred the way, and plaintiff's choice of forum would have been preserved.[14] These

---

* [The relevant provision is now found in §1446(c)—EDS.]

arguments are hardly meritless, but they run up against an overriding consideration. Once a diversity case has been tried in federal court, with rules of decision supplied by state law under the regime of *Erie R. Co. v. Tompkins* [infra page 259] considerations of finality, efficiency, and economy become overwhelming. . . .

Our view is in harmony with a main theme of the removal scheme Congress devised. Congress ordered a procedure calling for expeditious superintendence by district courts. The lawmakers specified a short time, 30 days, for motions to remand for defects in removal procedure, 28 U.S.C. §1447(c), and district court orders remanding cases to state courts generally are "not reviewable on appeal or otherwise," §1447(d). Congress did not similarly exclude appellate review of refusals to remand. But an evident concern that may explain the lack of symmetry relates to the federal courts' subject-matter jurisdiction. Despite a federal trial court's threshold denial of a motion to remand, if, at the end of the day and case, a jurisdictional defect remains uncured, the judgment must be vacated. See Fed. R. Civ. Proc. 12(h)(3) ("Whenever it appears by suggestion of the parties or otherwise that the court lacks jurisdiction of the subject matter, the court shall dismiss the action.") In this case, however, no jurisdictional defect lingered through judgment in the District Court. To wipe out the adjudication postjudgment, and return to state court a case now satisfying all federal jurisdictional requirements, would impose an exorbitant cost on our dual court system, a cost incompatible with the fair and unprotracted administration of justice. Lewis ultimately argues that, if the final judgment against him is allowed to stand, "all of the various procedural requirements for removal will become unenforceable"; therefore, "defendants will have an enormous incentive to attempt wrongful removals." In particular, Lewis suggests that defendants will remove prematurely "in the hope that some subsequent developments, such as the eventual dismissal of nondiverse defendants, will permit the case to be kept in federal court." We do not anticipate the dire consequences Lewis forecasts.

The procedural requirements for removal remain enforceable by the federal trial court judges to whom those requirements are directly addressed. Lewis' prediction . . . rests on an assumption we do not indulge—that district courts generally will not comprehend, or will balk at applying, the rules on removal Congress has prescribed. The prediction furthermore assumes defendants' readiness to gamble that any jurisdictional defect, for example, the absence of complete diversity, will first escape detection, then disappear prior to judgment. The well-advised defendant, we are satisfied, will foresee the likely outcome of an unwarranted removal—a swift and nonreviewable remand order, see 28 U.S.C. §1447(c), (d), attended by the displeasure of a district court whose authority has been improperly invoked. The odds against any gain from a wrongful removal, in sum, render improbable Lewis' projection of increased resort to the maneuver.

For the reasons stated, the judgment of the Court of Appeals is reversed, and the case is remanded for proceedings consistent with this opinion. . . .

---

[14] Lewis preferred state court to federal court based on differences he perceived in, inter alia, the state and federal jury systems and rules of evidence.

PERSPECTIVES

Ruth Bader Ginsburg

Justice Ginsburg, whose Supreme Court nomination was confirmed in 1993, had two careers before assuming her present position, both of which mark her pioneering role as a woman in the legal profession.

Having earned a distinguished record both at Harvard and Columbia Law Schools, Ginsburg found herself highly recommended as a clerk to Justice Felix Frankfurter of the Supreme Court by the dean of Harvard Law School. Frankfurter reportedly turned her down because she was a woman—a practice in which Frankfurter was then not alone among his fellow Justices. Nor, in spite of having been first in her law school class, was she offered a job by any of the 12 New York law firms with whom she interviewed. A similar pattern marked her entry into academia. Initially appointed as a research associate at Columbia Law School, she taught at Rutgers-Newark for ten years before accepting an appointment in 1972 as the first tenured woman in the history of Columbia Law School. Her academic specialties included comparative civil procedure and conflicts of law.

While teaching, Ginsburg co-founded the Women's Rights Project at the American Civil Liberties Union and briefed and argued before the U.S. Supreme Court several pioneering gender discrimination cases. Press accounts credit her with a strategy of small, incremental steps and choosing unthreatening lead plaintiffs—frequently men—in her cases. One account described her strategy as "not expect[ing] to force social change; she wanted [instead] to 'give it a green light' in her words, and she moved the Justices to send that signal through a series of simple, scarcely controversial cases."

Notes and Problems

1. *Caterpillar* splendidly illustrates the pitfalls of removal.
   a. Explain why removal was improper at the time Caterpillar attempted it.
   b. Explain why removal would still have been improper had Caterpillar waited until the point in the lawsuit when complete diversity existed.

2. Removal is not an entirely popular idea, either with states or with plaintiffs who find their initial choice of a forum thwarted.
   a. Why did Congress place a one-year "statute of limitations" on removal petitions in diversity cases—even in cases like *Caterpillar* where the basis for

removal did not present itself until after that date? See §1446(c). Notice that in some cases this time limit allows plaintiffs an opportunity to manipulate jurisdiction, joining nondiverse parties and then dropping them after a year. But note as well that 28 U.S.C. §1446(c)(1) allows removal even after a year if the plaintiff has acted in "bad faith" to block removal.

b. Ohio sought to discourage removal by enacting a statute providing that any out-of-state insurer that removed a case to federal court was barred from doing business in the state for three years. Held: unconstitutional. International Insurance Co. v. Duryee, 96 F.3d 837 (6th Cir. 1996).

3. In *Capron v. Van Noorden*, supra page 217, the plaintiff sued defendant in federal court and lost. On appeal in the Supreme Court, plaintiff argued there was no subject matter jurisdiction over the case because of lack of diversity. The Supreme Court dismissed the case—so the plaintiff won by challenging the very jurisdiction he had invoked! Contrast *Caterpillar*, in which the plaintiff properly and accurately objected to removal. But the Court in *Caterpillar*, acknowledging that diversity did not exist at the time of removal, nevertheless affirmed the federal judgment. Can one distinguish the two cases?

4. Other federal statutes expand or contract the removal power granted by 28 U.S.C. §1441.

a. For example, §1442 permits removal of suits by federal officers or agencies sued for the performance of their duties even when §1441 would not permit removal. A companion section does the same for members of the military. 28 U.S.C. §1442a.

b. The Class Action Fairness Act of 2005, whose minimal diversity provision we have already noted (supra page 224) contains a removal provision in 28 U.S.C. §1453 allowing some claims based entirely on state law and lacking complete diversity nevertheless to be removed to federal court.

c. The Securities Litigation Uniform Standards Act of 1998 (SLUSA) (15 U.S.C. §77p(b)) takes matters one step further—and takes us back to *Mottley*, which began this chapter. First, SLUSA (how's that for an attractive acronym?) preempts state securities class actions alleging fraud in the sales of securities. It provides, in other words, that in such cases federal law displaces otherwise applicable state law. Second, it provides that securities fraud class actions based entirely on state law "shall be removable to the federal district court for the district in which the action is pending." 15 U.S.C. §77p(c). Finally, it orders dismissal of the removed class actions. This three-step process provides a review of much of this chapter. Congress has essentially created a federal defense to state law securities class actions. Think back to *Mottley*, in which a federal defense to a state law claim did not create "arising under" jurisdiction. Congress might have left things there, relying on the state courts and occasional Supreme Court review to enforce this scheme. But SLUSA goes beyond that, using removal jurisdiction to assure that its substantive preemption of state law will be systematically enforced. In this specific category of cases SLUSA creates exactly what *Mottley* rejected: federal jurisdiction, here removal jurisdiction, based on a federal defense to a state law claim.

d. What Congress can give, Congress can take away. As a final reminder of the extent to which federal jurisdiction is a creature of statute, consider 28 U.S.C. §1445. It forbids removal of some actions—among them workers' compensation claims and suits brought under the federal Violence Against Women Act—that otherwise would be removable under §1441. Examine that statute and consider why Congress might have made such actions non-removable and thus allowed plaintiffs to dictate the choice between state and federal court.

* * *

The jurisdictional reach of U.S. federal courts has played an important and often controversial role in the nation's history. Over the past two centuries these courts, sometimes denounced as protectors of powerful national corporations, sometimes denounced and simultaneously hailed as vindicators of racial justice and the rights of women, have also played a homelier role in everyday disputes, ranging from the claim of a worker to his wages to claims arising from auto accidents involving out-of-state tourists. The overlapping jurisdictions of the state and federal courts also figure in lawyers' strategy, as they maneuver to gain (or avoid) a forum with characteristics that often differ from those of the state courts.

Not too long ago, those federal courts also represented an escape from state law, even on claims based on state law. How that happened, how that era ended, and the continuing issues its end created form the subject of the next chapter.

Assessment Questions

Q1. Sue, a resident of Los Angeles, sues the *L.A. Times* for libel. The *Times* believes that the First Amendment to the U.S. Constitution probably protects it from Sue's lawsuit. Which of the following is true?

A. Sue can bring her action in federal district court.

B. The action must be decided by a state trial court.

C. If Sue starts the case in state court the *Times* can remove to federal court.

D. If a state court renders a judgment for Sue, the *Times* can base an appeal to the U.S. Supreme Court on the First Amendment.

Q2. Sue, a resident of New York, sues the *L.A. Times* for libel in a California state court. The *Times* believes that the First Amendment to the U.S. Constitution probably protects it from Sue's lawsuit. Which of the following is true?

A. Sue can bring her action in federal district court no matter what amount of damages she claims.

B. Sue can bring her action in federal district court only if she claims more than $75,000 in damages.

C. If Sue brings her claim in state court in California, the *Times* can remove if she seeks more than $75,000.

D. If Sue is a British citizen who is a lawful permanent resident living in California and seeks more than $75,000, she can sue in federal court.

Q3. Sue (California) sues Ben (New York) alleging breach of contract. In which of the following situations is it clear that Sue *cannot* properly invoke original jurisdiction under 28 U.S.C. §1332?

A. If Sue seeks only an injunction.

B. If Sue seeks $75,000 in damages.

C. If Sue joins Carol (New York) as a plaintiff.

D. If, after the lawsuit is filed, Sue moves to New York.

Q4. Sue (a California resident) sues the *L.A. Times* for libel in federal district court. The *Times* asserts that, even if its story was defamatory, it is protected by the First Amendment to the U.S. Constitution. Which of the following is true?

A. If the *Times* moves to dismiss under Rule 12(b)(1), its motion should be granted.

B. If the *Times* does not move to dismiss for want of jurisdiction, it will have waived the defense.

C. The district court can dismiss the case without a motion.

D. If the case goes to judgment, only the losing party can challenge jurisdiction on appeal.

Q5. In which of the following cases, filed originally in state court, can the defendant remove to federal district court?

A. Sue (California) v. Newspaper (California): libel, with Newspaper invoking the First Amendment in California state court.

B. Sue (California) v. Newspaper (New York): breach of contract, $100,000 in New York state court.

C. Sue (California) v. Newspaper (New York): federal antitrust, $50,000, in New York state court.

D. Sue (California) v. Newspaper (New York): breach of contract, $100,000 in California state court.

Q6. Abe of Illinois sues Barbara of Illinois in federal court alleging that she violated a federal civil rights statute in firing him. Abe seeks to add a state law claim alleging that the firing also violated a state wrongful discharge law. Which of the following is true?

A. Abe's civil rights claim arises under federal law.

B. Abe's state law claim, brought alone, would not fall within federal jurisdiction.

     C. Abe's state law claim falls within the same case or controversy as his civil rights claim.

     D. Abe's state law claim will be within the supplemental jurisdiction of the federal district court hearing his federal civil rights claim.

Q7. Abe of Illinois sues Barbara of Illinois in federal court alleging that she violated a federal civil rights statute in firing him. Abe seeks to add a state law claim alleging that Barbara, a notoriously bad driver, negligently damaged his car backing out of her spot in the company parking lot. Which of the following is true?

     A. Abe's civil rights claim arises under federal law.

     B. Abe's state law claim, brought alone, would not fall within federal jurisdiction.

     C. Abe's state law claim falls within the same case or controversy as his civil rights claim.

     D. Abe's state law claim will be within the supplemental jurisdiction of the federal district court hearing his federal civil rights claim.

Q8. Alice, a citizen of Illinois, sues Ben, a citizen of Wisconsin, alleging breach of an employment contract and damages of $100,000. Alice wants to add Catherine, a citizen of Illinois, to her suit as a second defendant, under Rule 20, on the ground that Catherine allegedly urged Ben to breach his contract with Alice and come to work for her instead. (Assume that Rule 20 properly applies to the joinder of Catherine.) Which of the following is true?

     A. Alice's claim against Ben is within the original jurisdiction of a federal district court.

     B. Alice's claim against Catherine, if brought by itself, would not be within the jurisdiction of the federal district court.

     C. Alice's claim against Catherine is part of the same case or controversy as the claim against Ben.

     D. The court will not have supplemental jurisdiction over Alice's claim against Catherine.

Analysis of Assessment Questions

Q1. B and D are correct responses. A is wrong because the well-pleaded complaint rule (illustrated in *Mottley*) says that Sue's claim—as opposed to the *Times*'s defense—does not arise under federal law. B is correct because the well-pleaded complaint rule operates to put such cases into state courts. C is wrong because removal is available only if the original case could have been brought in federal court—and this one could not. D is correct because the Supreme Court, as in *Mottley*, has jurisdiction to hear and decide any question of federal law, not just claims that arise under federal law.

Q2. B is the only correct response. A is wrong because the diversity statute requires *both* diversity and the stated amount in controversy. C is wrong because a resident of the forum state cannot remove if the only basis for jurisdiction is diversity—as is the case here. D is wrong because the "except" clause of §1332(a)(2) treats lawful permanent residents as citizens of the state where they reside, and so plaintiff and defendant are not diverse.

Q3. B and C are correct responses. A is wrong because an injunction may be "valued," and diversity jurisdiction will lie if that value exceeds $75,000. D is wrong because diversity is measured from the date on which suit is filed; a later move is irrelevant. B is correct (but sneaky) because the statute requires that the amount in controversy *exceed* $75,000. C is correct because the presence of a New York party on both sides of the suit violates the complete diversity rule.

Q4. A and C are correct. A is correct because there is no diversity and the claim (as opposed to the defense) does not arise under federal law. B is wrong because the lack of federal subject matter jurisdiction is not waived (Rule 12(h)(3)). C is correct (12(h)(3)). D is wrong because several cases have held that even a party who invoked the court's subject matter jurisdiction can thereafter challenge it. *Capron v. Van Noorden*, supra page 217.

Q5. C and D are the correct responses. A is wrong because removal is possible only if there would have been original jurisdiction; here there is no federal claim and no diversity—thus no removal. B is wrong because, although there is diversity, a home-state defendant cannot remove. C is correct because the antitrust claim is federal, and thus removable. D is correct because both diversity and the amount in controversy requirements are met and the out-of-state defendant seeks to remove.

Q6. A, B, C, and D are all correct responses. A is correct because federal law creates Abe's claim. B is correct because there's no diversity and the state claim, by definition, does not arise under federal law. C is correct because it's a claim arising from the same facts as the federal claim. D is correct because §1367(a) so provides.

Q7. Only A and B are correct. For A and B see the preceding question. C is wrong because, unlike the preceding question, the state law claim arises from a different set of facts and invokes a distinct body of law. D is wrong: *Because* there's no linkage between the two claims, they do not arise out of the same constitutional case or controversy as required in §1367(a).

Q8. A, B, C, and D are all correct responses. A is correct because there's diversity jurisdiction. B is correct because the claim against Catherine does not arise under federal law and there's no diversity. C is correct because this dispute apparently involves both the employer (who has lost Ben as an employee) and the lurer-away (Catherine), whose actions induced Ben to breach the contract. D is correct because even though the claim against Catherine involves the same constitutional case or controversy, 28 U.S.C. §1367(b) does not permit supplemental jurisdiction to extend to claims by plaintiffs against nondiverse parties joined under Rule 20 when the only basis for jurisdiction is diversity.

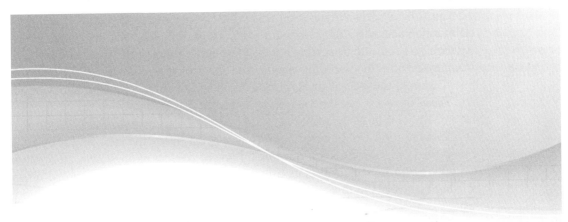

CHAPTER 4

State Law in Federal Courts: *Erie* and Its Entailments

Recall the theme of this section—the constitutional framework for U.S. litigation. The two preceding chapters have illustrated the two principal means by which the Constitution creates that framework: It limits the powers of states over defendants, and it enumerates (thereby limiting) the powers of the federal courts. The first limitation appears in the doctrines of personal jurisdiction, the second in those of federal subject matter jurisdiction. The Constitution thus requires state courts to share power with one another and with a federal judiciary. This chapter explores an entailment of that shared power: How does the Constitution ensure that these two court systems respect each other's spheres of power?

The question arises because state and federal courts not only share power, but they exercise overlapping jurisdiction. For example, under modern understandings of personal jurisdiction, several different states—and the state and federal courts in those states—may have jurisdiction to hear a case against a particular defendant. Similarly, state courts can hear cases arising under federal law, and federal courts, sitting in diversity, can hear cases that arise under state law. Under these circumstances both state and federal courts frequently face a question that arises from this overlapping jurisdiction: What law applies to the case before us?

Consider a fairly simple case: Al (from Arizona) sues Barb (from Texas) on a claim for an allegedly unpaid loan for $100,000; Barb has substantial contacts with Arizona, so she could be sued in a state court either there or in Texas. Moreover, as you have seen in the preceding chapter, the case would also fall under the diversity jurisdiction of the federal courts and so could be filed in federal courts in Arizona and Texas. Suppose that Barb asserts as a defense that the loan violated the lending laws of Texas. Whose law would apply?

This question would arise in whichever court heard the case, and it opens a broad field of inquiry known as *choice of law* or *conflict of laws*. *Erie*, an opinion from which this chapter takes its title, involves a subset of these questions: When a federal court sits in diversity jurisdiction or exercises supplemental jurisdiction, what law does it apply?

This question, though phrased narrowly, opens the door onto a much larger set of questions about the relations of state and federal courts and of constitutional interpretation. Speaking about part of this problem, one distinguished commentator has written, "No issue in the whole field of federal jurisprudence has been more difficult. . . ." Wright, Federal Courts 368. This chapter will seek to explain why someone might take that view—but it also seeks to make the problems much less difficult than this quotation implies.

A. STATE COURTS AS LAWMAKERS IN A FEDERAL SYSTEM

1. The Issue in Historical Context

To understand how the issue arises, one needs a brief historical perspective. The first Judiciary Act provided for federal diversity jurisdiction and also contained a section now codified at 28 U.S.C. §1652 and known as the Rules of Decision Act:

> The laws of the several states, except where the Constitution or Acts of Congress otherwise require or provide, shall be regarded as rules of decisions in civil actions in the courts of the United States, in cases where they apply.

On its face, one might think that that statute, in effect since the earliest days of the Republic, would resolve the question. Since diversity cases are in federal court only because of the parties' citizenship, there isn't any federal law to apply, so one might think that such cases would be "cases where they [i.e., state laws] apply." The story is not that simple, however, because people have disagreed sharply about what "the laws of the several states" means, and beyond that what "law" means.

These issues emerged in Swift v. Tyson, 41 U.S. 1 (1842), the leading pre-*Erie* case, which *Erie* overrules. *Swift* involved a "bill of exchange," a halfway step between a promissory note and a modern check or credit card. With promissory notes, there are numerous defenses available to anyone sued for breach; with their modern analogues those defenses are much more limited. The substantive issue in *Swift* was how many defenses could be asserted and thus how much like an ordinary contract and how much like a modern check or credit card the bill of exchange was. Procedurally and jurisprudentially (the aspects with which we shall be concerned), the issue was which law applied to the substantive question. *Swift* was a diversity case filed in a federal court sitting in New York. New York courts had previously spoken on the substantive issue, ruling that bills were subject to a number of defenses. Were these New York cases part of "the laws" of that state and thus binding on the federal district court? No, held the U.S. Supreme Court in an opinion by Justice Joseph Story, who not only served on the U.S. Supreme Court from 1811-1845 but also taught law and wrote nine influential treatises—all while serving on the Court!

Story's opinion, which, according to the dissent, reached beyond what was necessary for the decision, said that the New York precedents were not "laws"; thus, the federal courts sitting in diversity were free to ignore them:

> But, admitting the doctrine [concerning which defenses could be asserted] to be fully settled in New York, it remains to be considered whether it is obligatory upon this court if it differs from the principles established in the general commercial law. It is observable that the Courts of New York do not found their decisions upon this point upon any local statute, or positive, fixed, or ancient usage; but they deduce the doctrine from the general principles of commercial law. It is, however, contended that [the Rules of Decision Act] furnishes a rule obligatory on this Court to follow the decisions of state tribunals in all cases to which they apply. . . . In order to maintain the argument, it is essential . . . that the word "laws" [in the Rules of Decision Act] includes within the scope of its meaning the decisions of local tribunals. In the ordinary use of language it will hardly be contended that the decisions of Courts constitute laws. They are at most evidence of what the laws are; and are not themselves laws. . . . The laws of a state are more usually understood to mean the rules and enactments promulgated by the legislative authority thereof. . . . [The Court said it would be bound by state statutes and by state judge-made law on matters of peculiarly "local" matters but not on more general topics.] Undoubtedly, the decisions of the local tribunals upon such subjects are entitled to, and will receive, the most deliberate attention and respect of this Court; but they cannot furnish positive rules on conclusive authority. . . .

Swift went on to reach a conclusion different from that reached by the New York courts on the issue at stake.

In the ensuing century, *Swift* came to be seen by many not only as momentous, but also as pernicious, not because of its holding on the negotiability of bills of exchange, but because of its treatment of state law. For many federal courts, *Swift* became a charter of judicial independence, a declaration that they could ignore state case law. Often decisions in the *Swift* line of cases seemed to favor business interests; one elaborate study argued, "As the number of industrial tort suits continued to increase [from the 1890s on] and Americans endured the most severe depression in their nation's history, the Supreme Court [used diversity jurisdiction to] shape[] law in ways that enhanced the litigation position of corporate defendants." Edward A. Purcell, Jr., Litigation and Inequality: Federal Diversity Jurisdiction in Industrial America, 1870-1958, 245 (Oxford 1992).

Notice that *Swift* reached its conclusion as an interpretation of the Rules of Decision Act, which Congress could have amended during the years that followed. Congress did not amend the Act. The next step in the story took matters out of Congress's hands.

2. Constitutionalizing the Issue

The *Erie* doctrine arose from a relatively simple dispute. On Thursday, July 26, 1934, Harry Tompkins visited his mother-in-law's house in Hughestown, a village of 2,800 people in northeastern Pennsylvania. He received a ride part of the way home and walked the remaining distance along the railroad tracks of the Erie Railroad, keeping several feet between himself and the tracks. A train passed, and an open door on a refrigerator car struck him and knocked him partially under the train. His right arm was severed. After recovering from his injuries, he sought a lawyer and found 27-year-old Bernard Nemeroff. Although *Swift v. Tyson* was generally understood to benefit corporations, in this case, Nemeroff and his partner, 21-year-old Aaron Danzig, believed that they could turn *Swift* to Tompkins's strategic advantage if they sued the railroad in the federal District Court for the Southern District of New York.

Under Pennsylvania law, for whose application the railroad's lawyer argued, Tompkins was a trespasser and the railroad was therefore liable only for "wanton" negligence, a finding unlikely given the facts. The judge, relying on the freedom given by *Swift v. Tyson*, instead instructed the jury according to the "general law," that the railroad was liable even if it was guilty of only "ordinary" negligence. The jury returned a verdict for Tompkins in the amount of $30,000 (almost $500,000 in 2019 dollars). The railroad appealed, but the Second Circuit upheld Tompkins's verdict relying on *Swift v. Tyson*. The railroad then sought a writ of certiorari from the Supreme Court. In the meantime the railroad asked Justice Cardozo to stay the judgment until the Supreme Court could consider the certiorari petition, and Justice Cardozo obliged. The railroad then made Tompkins a settlement offer—$7,500 plus the withdrawal of its certiorari petition—but Danzig and Nemeroff talked him out of accepting and then hid him from the railroad's lawyers.

The Supreme Court granted certiorari, even though it rarely did so in negligence cases. On April 25, 1938, the Supreme Court decided the case in one of the last opinions written by Justice Brandeis. The decision went unnoticed until Justice Stone wrote privately to a *New York Times* journalist, calling to his attention "the most important opinion since I have been on the court."

PERSPECTIVES

Louis D. Brandeis is remembered as much for his career before appointment to the U.S. Supreme Court as for his work as a Justice. Successful both as a law reformer and as a private practitioner, Brandeis liked to describe himself as "counsel to the situation," a concept that has drawn both high praise for the idea of the lawyer as problem-solver, and criticism for its suggestion that he was prepared to lay aside the interests of some clients to pursue his own idea of justice. Indeed, some of those on the losing side of Brandeis's legal practice bitterly opposed his nomination by President Wilson to the Supreme Court, and six months of wrangling preceded his confirmation in 1916. Best known during his life for cases upholding social legislation, Brandeis wrote *Erie* as one of his last opinions for the Court. In rejecting a statutory basis for the holding in *Erie*, Brandeis departed from a general principle he otherwise espoused—deciding cases on non-constitutional grounds if possible, a principle that has come to be known as "the *Ashwander* principle," after Ashwander v. Tennessee Valley Authority, 297 U.S. 288 (1936) (Brandeis, J., concurring).

Notice that the opinion opens portentously: "The question for decision is whether the oft-challenged doctrine of *Swift v. Tyson* shall now be disapproved. . . ." That "question" might have come as a shock to the parties, since neither the railroad nor Tompkins had raised or addressed it in their briefs (the railroad simply argued that the law of trespass was sufficiently "local" that under *Swift* the federal courts should follow it).

Erie Railroad v. Tompkins
304 U.S. 64 (1938)

BRANDEIS, J., delivered the opinion of the Court.

The question for decision is whether the oft-challenged doctrine of *Swift v. Tyson* shall now be disapproved. . . .

First. *Swift v. Tyson* held that federal courts exercising jurisdiction on the ground of diversity of citizenship need not, in matters of general jurisprudence, apply the unwritten law of the State as declared by its highest court; that they are free to exercise an independent judgment as to what the common law of the State is—or should be; and that, as there stated by Mr. Justice Story:

> [T]he true interpretation of the [Rules of Decision Act] limited its application to state laws strictly local, that is to say, to the positive statutes of the state, and the construction thereof adopted by the local tribunals, and to rights and titles to things having a

permanent locality, such as the rights and titles to real estate, and other matters immovable and extraterritorial in their nature and character. It never has been supposed by us, that the section did apply, or was intended to apply, to questions of a more general nature, not at all dependent upon local statutes or local usages of a fixed and permanent operation, as, for example, to the construction of ordinary contracts or other written instruments, and especially to questions of general commercial law, where the state tribunals are called upon to perform the like functions as ourselves, that is, to ascertain upon general reasoning and legal analogies, what is the true exposition of the contract of instrument, or what is the just rule furnished by the principles of commercial law to govern the case.

. . . The federal courts assumed, in the broad field of "general law," the power to declare rules of decision which Congress was confessedly without power to enact as statutes. Doubt was repeatedly expressed as to the correctness of the construction given [the Act], and as to the soundness of the rule which it introduced. But it was the more recent research of a competent scholar, who examined the original document, which established that the construction given to it by the Court was erroneous; and that the purpose of the section was merely to make certain that, in all matters except those in which some federal law is controlling, the federal courts exercising jurisdiction in diversity of citizenship cases would apply as their rules of decision the law of the State, unwritten as well as written.[5]

Criticism of the doctrine became widespread after the decision of *Black & White Taxicab Co. v. Brown & Yellow Taxicab Co.* There, Brown and Yellow, a Kentucky corporation owned by Kentuckians, and the Louisville and Nashville Railroad, also a Kentucky corporation, wished that the former should have the exclusive privilege of soliciting passenger and baggage transportation at the Bowling Green, Kentucky, railroad station; and that the Black and White, a competing Kentucky corporation, should be prevented from interfering with that privilege. Knowing that such a contract would be void under the common law of Kentucky, it was arranged that the Brown and Yellow reincorporate under the law of Tennessee, and that the contract with the railroad should be executed there. The suit was then brought by the Tennessee corporation in the federal court for Western Kentucky to enjoin competition by the Black and White; an injunction issued by the District Court was sustained by the Court of Appeals; and this Court, citing many decisions in which the doctrine of *Swift v. Tyson* had been applied, affirmed the decree.

Second. Experience in applying the doctrine of *Swift v. Tyson* had revealed its defects, political and social; and the benefits expected to flow from the rule did not accrue. Persistence of state courts in their own opinions on questions of common law prevented uniformity; and the impossibility of discovering a satisfactory line of demarcation between the province of general law and that of local law developed a new well of uncertainties.

On the other hand, the mischievous results of the doctrine had become apparent. Diversity of citizenship jurisdiction was conferred in order to prevent apprehended

5. Charles Warren, New Light on the History of the Federal Judiciary Act of 1789, 37 Harv. L. Rev. 49, 51-52, 81-88, 108 (1923).

discrimination in State courts against those not citizens of the State. *Swift v. Tyson* introduced grave discrimination by non-citizens against citizens. It made rights enjoyed under the unwritten "general law" vary according to whether enforcement was sought in the state or in the federal court; and the privilege of selecting the court in which the right should be determined was conferred upon the non-citizen. Thus, the doctrine rendered impossible equal protection of the law. In attempting to promote uniformity of law throughout the United States, the doctrine had prevented uniformity in the administration of the law of the State.

The discrimination resulting became in practice far-reaching. This resulted in part from the broad province accorded to the so-called "general law" as to which federal courts exercised an independent judgment. [The opinion cited many fields of law.]

In part the discrimination resulted from the wide range of persons held entitled to avail themselves of the federal rule by resort to the diversity of citizenship jurisdiction. . . .

The injustice and confusion incident to the doctrine of *Swift v. Tyson* have been repeatedly urged as reasons for abolishing or limiting diversity of citizenship jurisdiction. Other legislative relief has been proposed. If only a question of statutory construction were involved, we should not be prepared to abandon a doctrine so widely applied throughout nearly a century. But the unconstitutionality of the course pursued has now been made clear and compels us to do so.

Third. Except in matters governed by the Federal Constitution or by Acts of Congress, the law to be applied in any case is the law of the State. And whether the law of the State shall be declared by its Legislature in a statute or by its highest court in a decision is not a matter of federal concern. There is no federal general common law. Congress has no power to declare substantive rules of common law applicable in a State whether they be local in their nature or "general," be they commercial law or a part of the law of torts. And no clause in the Constitution purports to confer such a power upon the federal courts. As stated by Mr. Justice Field when protesting in Baltimore & Ohio R.R. Co. v. Baugh, 149 U.S. 368, 401, against ignoring the Ohio common law of fellow-servant liability: "[N]otwithstanding the frequency with which the doctrine [of *Swift v. Tyson*] has been reiterated, there stands, as a perpetual protest against its repetition, the constitution of the United States, which recognizes and preserves the autonomy and independence of the states,—independence in their legislative and independence in their judicial departments. Supervision over either the legislative or the judicial action of the states is in no case permissible except as to matters by the constitution specifically authorized or delegated to the United States. Any interference with either, except as thus permitted, is an invasion of the authority of the state, and, to that extent, a denial of its independence."

The fallacy underlying the rule declared in *Swift v. Tyson* is made clear by Mr. Justice Holmes. The doctrine rests upon the assumption that there is "a transcendental body of law outside of any particular State but obligatory within it unless and until changed by statute," that federal courts have the power to use their judgment as to what the rules of common law are; and that in the federal courts "the parties are entitled to an independent judgment on matters of general law":

> [B]ut law in the sense in which courts speak of it today does not exist without some definite authority behind it. The common law so far as it is enforced in a State, whether called

common law or not, is not the common law generally but the law of that State existing by the authority of that State without regard to what it may have been in England or anywhere else. . . . The authority and only authority is the State, and if that be so, the voice adopted by the State as its own [whether it be of its Legislature or of its Supreme Court] should utter the last word.

Thus the doctrine of *Swift v. Tyson* is, as Mr. Justice Holmes said, "an unconstitutional assumption of powers by courts of the United States which no lapse of time or respectable array of opinion should make us hesitate to correct." In disapproving that doctrine we do not hold unconstitutional §34 of the Federal Judiciary Act of 1789 or any other Act of Congress. We merely declare that in applying the doctrine this Court and the lower courts have invaded rights which in our opinion are reserved by the Constitution to the several States.

Fourth. The defendant contended that by the common law of Pennsylvania as declared by its highest court in Falchetti v. Pennsylvania R. Co., 160 A. 859, the only duty owed to the plaintiff was to refrain from willful or wanton injury. The plaintiff denied that such is the Pennsylvania law. In support of their respective contentions the parties discussed and cited many decisions of the Supreme Court of the State. The Circuit Court of Appeals ruled that the question of liability is one of general law; and on that ground declined to decide the issue of state law. As we hold this was error, the judgment is reversed and the case remanded to it for further proceedings in conformity with our opinion.

Reversed.

REED, J.,

I concur in the conclusion reached in this case, in the disapproval of the doctrine of *Swift v. Tyson*, and in the reasoning of the majority opinion except insofar as it relies upon the unconstitutionality of the "course pursued" by the federal courts. . . .

To decide the case now before us and to "disapprove" the doctrine of *Swift v. Tyson* requires only that we say that the words "the laws" [in the Rules of Decision Act] include in their meaning the decisions of the local tribunals. . . . [T]his Court is now of the view that "laws" includes "decisions," [and] it is unnecessary to go further and declare that the "course pursued" was "unconstitutional," instead of merely erroneous.

The "unconstitutional" course referred to in the majority opinion is apparently the ruling in *Swift v. Tyson* that the supposed omission of Congress to legislate as to the effect of decisions leaves federal courts free to interpret general law for themselves. I am not at all sure whether, in the absence of federal statutory direction, federal courts would be compelled to follow state decisions. There was sufficient doubt about the matter in 1789 to induce the first Congress to legislate. . . . If the opinion commits this Court to the position that the Congress is without power to declare what rules of substantive law shall govern the federal courts, that conclusion also seems questionable. The line between procedural and substantive law is hazy but no one doubts federal power over procedure. The Judiciary Article and the "necessary and proper" clause of Article One may fully authorize legislation, such as this section of the Judiciary Act.

In this Court, stare decisis, in statutory construction, is a useful rule, not an inexorable command. It seems preferable to overturn an established construction of an Act of Congress, rather than, in the circumstances of this case, to interpret the Constitution. . . .

[Dissenting opinion of Justices BUTLER and McREYNOLDS is omitted.]

Notes and Problems

---

1. What is the connection between the doctrine announced in the decision and the outcome?

   a. Under the circumstances of this case, why did it matter to Harry Tompkins (or to the Erie Railroad) whether *Swift* was overruled?

   b. Tompkins won in the trial court. The U.S. Supreme Court seems to assume that if the tort law of Pennsylvania applied to the facts of the case, the railroad would owe Tompkins only the duty of refraining from wanton or willful negligence. Tompkins had a better chance of preserving his verdict if the railroad owed him a higher degree of care. Tompkins's lawyers pointed to a different source of law, one requiring such a higher standard of care. What was that source?

2. With the practical consequences framed, turn to the doctrine.

   a. According to the opinion, what is the source of the federal courts' duty to follow Pennsylvania judge-made law in this case? The most obvious answer is to point to the Rules of Decision Act, requiring federal courts to apply state law in appropriate cases.

   b. Yet the opinion states that the Court is overruling *Swift v. Tyson* on constitutional grounds. Notice that the opinion cites no particular phrase or clause of the Constitution, a somewhat unusual omission for a case otherwise insisting that the Constitution provides the basis for its decision.

   c. Consider two sentences from the opinion, at the start of the part labeled "Third": "Except in matters governed by the Federal Constitution or by Acts of Congress, the law to be applied in any case is the law of the State. And whether the law of the State shall be declared by its Legislature in a statute or by its highest court in a decision is not a matter of federal concern." Do those sentences, which some have described as "structural federalism," explain how the decision has constitutional roots? The generally accepted answer is that respect for states includes respect for a state's decision to give part of its lawmaking powers to courts rather than to legislatures. If a state is content to have its judges make some of its laws in the process of adjudicating cases, the federal government—including federal courts—must respect that decision. Those propositions, the argument continues, are inherent in the federal structure of government, a structure expressed throughout the Constitution, and incorporated by allusion in the Tenth Amendment (since the Constitution did not strip the state courts of lawmaking powers, they retain them). Does that explanation illuminate the idea that *Erie* is a constitutional decision even though the opinion does not rest on any particular clause of the Constitution?

d. If *Erie* is not a constitutional decision, Congress could change its result. How?

Procedure as Strategy

Swift v. Tyson was often criticized—by Justice Holmes and others—as allowing corporations to manipulate the substantive law to their advantage. Notice, however, that here Harry Tompkins's lawyers figured out how they could use diversity jurisdiction *against* the railroad. Further notice the irony that Justice Brandeis, often a champion of the "little guy," makes constitutional law at Tompkins's expense.

Implications

THE SURPRISING AFTERLIFE OF FEDERAL COMMON LAW

Erie says that "there is no federal general common law." One can easily understand this sentence to mean more than it does. *Erie* holds only that "*general*" federal common law may not displace that of the states in areas in which the Constitution rests lawmaking power in the states. But—confined to its proper sphere, federal common law continues to flourish: Think of the hundreds of federal causes of action, in which courts must supplement general statutory or constitutional principles with judge-made common law. For example, Congress granted federal jurisdiction over a broad area of labor law—without providing any guiding substantive principles. The Court held that Congress thereby intended to give federal courts common law powers in this area. Textile Workers Union of America v. Lincoln Mills, 353 U.S. 448 (1957). In other fields both state and federal courts rely almost entirely on common law. For example, both state and federal courts consult common law to decide on the principles of former adjudication, which you will study in Chapter 11.

In diversity cases, it will be clear that the only source of substantive law must be that of the states, and *Erie* commands federal courts to respect that law, whether made by legislatures or courts. But the *Erie* principle will also apply whenever states supply the governing law, regardless of the basis for federal subject matter jurisdiction. For example, suppose a federal civil rights claim of employment discrimination is brought in federal district court, with additional state law claims for breach of contract and state employment statutes, brought under the federal supplemental jurisdiction statute explored in Chapter 3. There's no diversity in sight, but the principles of *Erie* still apply: The federal courts will look to state law, including state common law, in deciding the state law claims.

3. If one moves from broad constitutional significance back to a more technical plane, one notes that Tompkins's lawyers filed *Erie* in the Southern District of New York, yet the Court assumed that Pennsylvania law applied. Why?

   a. Each state has a body of law called its choice of law rules, which specify the circumstances in which courts of that state should follow laws of other jurisdictions, such as those of other states, federal law, or foreign law. Two inferences are possible from the *Erie* Court's silence on this point. The Court might have thought it absolutely clear that New York courts would have applied Pennsylvania law, or the Court might have thought that the New York conflict of laws rules were irrelevant.

   b. A few years after *Erie* came Klaxon Co. v. Stentor Elec. Mfg. Co., 313 U.S. 487 (1941), in which the Supreme Court applied *Erie* principles to conflicts rules: Under *Erie* a federal court sitting in diversity must apply the conflicts principles of the *forum state* (legal jargon for the state in which the court sits: In *Erie*, New York was the forum state).

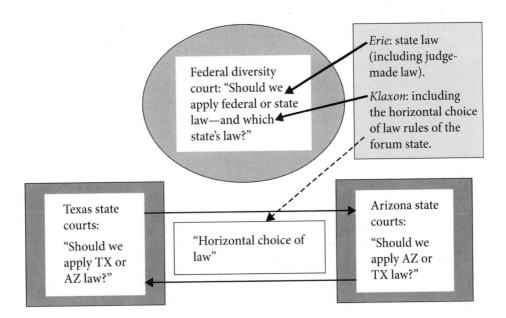

    c. Some have suggested that *Klaxon* was a missed opportunity to refine diversity jurisdiction, arguing that the federal courts, as a neutral forum, would be well suited to decide which state's law should apply. Subsequent cases have, however, suggested that the Supreme Court thinks *Klaxon* well embedded. Van Dusen v. Barrack, 376 U.S. 612 (1964) (holding that even when a case is transferred to a federal court in another state it "takes with it" the substantive law and choice of law rules of the state where it was originally filed).

4. Much of the Court's discussion in *Erie* is devoted to the evils of forum shopping. By "forum shopping" the Court seems to mean the practice of a litigant's selecting one rather than another court in which to sue, in the hope that the court will in some way treat the litigant more favorably than another court that might have heard the case. For example, under *Swift v. Tyson* there were several circumstances in which federal courts would enforce contracts that state courts would have refused to enforce. In such an instance, a plaintiff hoping to enforce such an agreement would "shop" for a forum (in this case the federal courts) that would enforce it.

    a. What's wrong with different outcomes? If a federal judge believes that she has come up with the proper solution to a particular legal problem, doesn't it deny justice to the parties to rule to the contrary simply to imitate the state court's predicted result?

    b. What's wrong with forum shopping? *Erie* seems to assume that forum shopping between state and federal courts is the major problem. At the time of *Erie*, Tompkins could have sued the railroad in Pennsylvania, in New York, and perhaps in several other states where it did business; each of those states would likely have taken a slightly different approach to his case. Seven years after *Erie*, the Court decided *International Shoe*, thus giving its constitutional blessing to an extended jurisdictional reach for state courts. With this extension, plaintiffs will often have a choice of several different states in which to sue a defendant, and those states may have different substantive laws. Moreover, the parties' lawyers have a duty to their clients to find the forum most advantageous to them. So, one might understand *Erie* not as a demonization of forum shopping, but as a limitation on the power of federal courts to decide the law applicable to state law disputes.

5. *Erie* was the first civil case heard by Judge Mandelbaum, the trial judge. Judge Mandelbaum was a product of New York machine politics and, over strong protest from the bar, was appointed to the bench by President Roosevelt. Before his appointment, Mandelbaum had visited the federal courthouse only once, to see what it looked like. His notes, penned in the margin of his copy of the Supreme Court's *Erie* opinion and reported in Irving Younger, *Observation: What Happened in* Erie, 56 Tex. L. Rev. 1011, 1030 (1978), suggest a different perspective on the case: "Because the *Swift Tyson* case[,] although before this case I never knew of its existence to be truthful[,] and for the confusion this decision brought about, it might have been better to leave it alone and stand by good old Swifty."

PERSPECTIVES

1938 Was a Tough Year to Be a Lawyer

Erie—decided in 1938—changed the way federal courts thought about judge-made law. The same year brought another, even bigger, change: 1938 was the year in which the Federal Rules of Civil Procedure became effective. As you will see throughout this course, those rules transformed procedure in many ways. You may have wondered what procedures the federal courts followed before the Rules. The answer comes in two tiers. A federal statute, known as the Conformity Act, ordered the federal courts to follow whatever procedural rules existed in the state where the federal court sat. So a federal court in New York would follow New York procedural rules and a federal court in California would follow that state's procedural regime—*mostly*. It's "mostly" because alongside the state procedures decreed by the Conformity Act existed a separate set of rules for the federal courts when they were "sitting in equity"—considering whether to order an injunction or establish a receivership, to use two common examples. These separate equity rules were necessary because not all state courts had equitable jurisdiction. The Rules Enabling Act, 28 U.S.C. §2072, which empowered the Federal Rules of Civil Procedure, also repealed the Conformity Act and "merged" law and equity, making separate equity rules unnecessary. And—that same year saw *Erie*, which overruled *Swift v. Tyson* and the regime it represented. One imagines a lot of lawyers staying up late on many nights trying to understand the brave new world they had entered.

B. THE LIMITS OF STATE POWER IN FEDERAL COURTS

Having struggled with the constitutional ambiguities, you may be distressed to learn that, constitutional basis aside, *Erie* was an easy case for the application of the principle it announced. The remainder of this chapter will consider decisions in which the issue is how to apply the *Erie* doctrine—decisions that require a more subtle look at what that case held.

Erie established that federal courts sitting in diversity (or exercising supplemental jurisdiction) were bound to replicate state practice in some circumstances. Which circumstances? Though *Erie* did not say so, its setting suggested that at the very least federal courts sitting in diversity or exercising supplemental jurisdiction should observe state substantive law, whether made by legislatures or by courts. But what about other "laws"? For example, were federal courts sitting in diversity bound to apply state statutes of limitations? If the courts of the state in question did not generally enforce arbitration agreements, could federal courts nevertheless do so if authorized by a federal statute? If a suit in state court could be decided only by a judge, was a federal court precluded from using a jury? If a state statute required personal service of process, did that requirement also apply to process served in a federal diversity action? If a state court were bound to refuse to honor a contractual forum selection clause, were federal courts sitting in that state required to do likewise? If a state legislature orders its appellate courts to reduce excessive damages awarded by juries, does a federal appellate court have the same power?

In the years since *Erie*, the Supreme Court has addressed each of these questions (as well as others) in an effort to mediate between opposing principles: that *Erie* requires deference to state courts as lawmaking bodies; and that federal courts are an independent judicial system. Justice Reed's concurrence in *Erie* raised but did not resolve the question: "The line between procedural and substantive law is hazy, but no one doubts federal power over procedure." Notice that many of these questions involve issues that could be described as "procedural." As you read the next cases, consider whether it is true that "no one doubts" federal power over procedure.

1. Interpreting the Constitutional Command of *Erie*

Guaranty Trust Co. v. York
326 U.S. 99 (1945)

FRANKFURTER, J., delivered the opinion of the Court. . . .

[Plaintiffs sued a bond trustee in a federal diversity action alleging misrepresentation and breach of trust. New York substantive law governed. Defendant invoked the New York statute of limitations, which had run. Plaintiffs argued that the statute of limitations did not bar the suit because it was on the "equity side" of federal court. The courts of equity had traditionally considered the length of time elapsing between the maturing of a claim and the bringing of suit but had not thought themselves strictly bound by statutes of limitations. Referring to that equitable tradition, the Second Circuit ruled that plaintiffs' suit was not barred. The Supreme Court disagreed.]

Our starting point must be the policy of federal jurisdiction which *Erie R. Co. v. Tompkins* embodies. In overruling *Swift v. Tyson, Erie R. Co. v. Tompkins* did not merely overrule a venerable case. It overruled a particular way of looking at law which dominated the judicial process long after its inadequacies had been laid bare. Law was conceived as a "brooding omnipresence" of Reason, of which decisions were merely evidence and not themselves the controlling formulations. Accordingly, federal courts deemed themselves free to ascertain what Reason, and therefore Law, required wholly independent of authoritatively declared State law, even in cases where a legal right as the basis for relief was created by State authority and could not be created by federal authority and the case got into a federal court merely because it was "between Citizens of different States" under Art. III, §2 of the Constitution of the United States. . . .

This case reduces itself to the narrow question whether, when no recovery could be had in a State court because the action is barred by the statute of limitations, a federal court in equity can take cognizance of the suit because there is diversity of citizenship between the parties. . . .

And so the question is not whether a statute of limitations is deemed a matter of "procedure" in some sense. The question is whether such a statute concerns merely the manner and the means by which a right to recover, as recognized by the State, is enforced, or whether such statutory limitation is a matter of substance in the aspect that alone is relevant to our problem, namely, does it significantly affect the result of a litigation for a federal court to disregard a law of a State that would be controlling in an action upon the same claim by the same parties in a State court?

It is therefore immaterial whether statutes of limitation are characterized either as "substantive" or "procedural" in State court opinions in any use of those terms unrelated to the specific issue before us. *Erie R. Co. v. Tompkins* was not an endeavor to formulate scientific legal terminology. It expressed a policy that touches vitally the proper distribution of judicial power between State and federal courts. In essence, the intent of that decision was to insure that, in all cases where a federal court is exercising jurisdiction solely because of the diversity of citizenship of the parties, the outcome of the litigation in the federal court should be substantially the same, so far as legal rules determine the outcome of a litigation, as it would be if tried in a State court. . . .

The judgment is reversed and the case is remanded for proceedings not inconsistent with this opinion.

So ordered.

[The dissenting opinion of Justice RUTLEDGE is omitted.]

Notes and Problems

---

1. *Guaranty Trust* displays a ferocity that impedes analysis.

   a. The opinion sharply attacks the proposition that if something is "procedural" it is not governed by the rule in *Erie*. Why? The main opinion in *Erie* had asserted no such proposition; is Justice Frankfurter disputing Justice Reed's concurrence about federal power over procedure?

   b. Even in the midst of this attack, however, Justice Frankfurter conceded that federal courts need not follow state law that "concern[ed] merely the manner and means by which a right to recover is . . . enforced." Isn't this conceding that Justice Reed was right?

   c. As you read the rest of the cases in the *Erie* line, consider whether they don't come down to the question of defining "the manner and means by which a right to recover is . . . enforced." (A procedure casebook can be excused for omitting "merely" from the phrase.)

2. To solve the problem of distinguishing between such "manner and mode" issues and the other "substantive" kind, Guaranty Trust proposed what came to be known as the "outcome-determinative test." A state rule that was out-come-determinative was to be followed, no matter how it might be labeled. What does that mean? The standard paper sizes are 8 1/2" × 11" and 8 1/2" × 14". If a litigant offered the clerk of a federal district court a complaint typed on 8 1/2 × 14-inch paper, but the clerk refused to accept it on the grounds that the rules required shorter paper and the filing cabinets couldn't hold paper 14 inches long, would you call the rule invoked by the clerk substantive because it was outcome-determinative? After all, the plaintiff might very well win in state court but can hardly win in federal court if the complaint can't be filed. If you conclude that the "paper size" rule is not substantive for *Erie* purposes, how would you modify the outcome-determinative rule to exclude cases of this sort?

3. *Guaranty Trust* not only decided a lawsuit; it also asserted that *Erie* marked a revolution in legal thought, a rejection of "Law . . . as a 'brooding omnipres-ence' of Reason," a view presumably attributed to those judges (perhaps espe-cially to Justice Story) who had adhered to *Swift v. Tyson*. *Erie* and *Guaranty Trust* asserted that such a view was not only jurisprudentially bankrupt but historically false—that the understanding of the Rules of Decision Act held by its framers was in accordance with that enunciated by *Guaranty Trust* and *Erie*. That understanding exercised a powerful influence over the *Erie* line of cases following *Guaranty Trust*. Consider four such cases.

Case	Issue	Outcome: State or Federal Law/ Practice?	Opinion's Explanation
Ragan v. Merchants Transfer & Warehouse Co., 337 U.S. 530 (1949)	When does lawsuit begin for statute of limitations purposes; when complaint filed (Rule 3) or when defendant served (KS practice)?	State law followed.	"We cannot give [the claim] longer life in the federal court than it would have had in the state court . . . consistently with *Erie R. Co. v. Tompkins*."
Cohen v. Beneficial Indus. Loan Corp., 337 U.S. 541 (1949)	NJ statute required small shareholder suing corporation to post bond for expenses; Rule 23.1 did not so require.	State law followed.	"[T]his statute is not merely a regulation of procedure. With it or without it the main action takes the same course. However, it creates a new liability

Case	Issue	Outcome: State or Federal Law/ Practice?	Opinion's Explanation
			[for litigation expenses] where none existed before. . . ."
Woods v. Interstate Realty Co., 337 U.S. 535 (1949)	MS statute barred out-of-state corporations not paying MS taxes from suing in state courts; should federal diversity court do so?	State law followed without discussing Rule 17(b), which suggests that the governing law should be that of the state of company's incorporation.	"[W]here in such cases one is barred from recovery in the state court, he should likewise be barred in the federal court."
Bernhardt v. Polygraphic Co. of America, 350 U.S. 198 (1956)	VT barred arbitration of employment practices; federal statute arguably required arbitration.	State law followed.	"If the federal court allows arbitration where the state court would disallow it, the outcome of litigation might depend on the courthouse where suit is brought. For the remedy by arbitration, whatever its merits or shortcomings, substantially affects the cause of action created by the State."

4. The cases in Note 3:

   a. Each involved a conflict between a state practice and an arguably applicable federal statute or rule of procedure. In all cases the state practice prevailed.

   b. Represent a high-water mark of *Erie*-compelled deference to state courts. Starting only two years after *Bernhardt Polygraphic*, the last of the series, the Court began to retreat from its almost reflexive bowing to state law.

   c. Might all be wrongly decided. Later cases have questioned several of these results; see, for example, *Epic Systems v. Lewis*, infra page 559, suggesting the broad scope of the federal arbitration statute. From the late 1950s onward the *Erie* cases broke with the pattern of invariably favoring state practice and suggested a different framework for analyzing the *Erie* problem, in the process retreating from *Guaranty Trust*.

Byrd v. Blue Ridge Rural Electric Cooperative
356 U.S. 525 (1958)

BRENNAN, J., delivered the opinion of the Court.

[Plaintiff was injured while on a construction job for defendant; he sued in tort. Although plaintiff was employed by an independent contractor, defendant contended plaintiff was doing the same work as defendant's regular employees and, therefore, was a "statutory" employee whose exclusive remedy was under the South Carolina Workmen's Compensation Act.]

[Presenting evidence on the statutory employee defense,] respondent's manager testified on direct examination that three of its substations were built by the respondent's own construction and maintenance crews. When pressed on cross-examination, however, his answers left his testimony in such doubt as to lead the trial judge to say, "I understood he changed his testimony, that they had not built three." But the credibility of the manager's testimony, and the general question whether the evidence in support of the affirmative defense presented a jury issue, became irrelevant because of the interpretation given [the state statute] by the trial judge.]

[The Court first decided that the lower courts had incorrectly interpreted the state statute.]

II

A question is also presented as to whether on remand the factual issue is to be decided by the judge or by the jury. The respondent argues on the basis of the decision of the Supreme Court of South Carolina in *Adams v. Davison-Paxon Co.*, that the issue of immunity* should be decided by the judge and not by the jury. . . .

The respondent argues that this state-court decision governs the present diversity case and "divests the jury of its normal function" to decide the disputed fact question of the respondent's immunity under §72-111. This is to contend that the federal court is bound under *Erie R. Co. v. Tompkins* to follow the state court's holding to secure uniform enforcement of the immunity created by the State.

First. It was decided in *Erie R. Co. v. Tompkins* that the federal courts in diversity cases must respect the definition of state-created rights and obligations by the state courts. We must, therefore, first examine the rule in *Adams v. Davison-Paxon Co.* to determine whether it is bound up with these rights and obligations in such a way that its application in the federal court is required.

The Workmen's Compensation Act is administered in South Carolina by its Industrial Commission. The South Carolina courts hold that, on judicial review of actions of the Commission under §72-111, the question whether the claim of an

---

* [The employer would be immune from a tort suit if the worker were covered by workers' compensation, which bars tort actions against employers.—EDS.]

injured workman is within the Commission's jurisdiction is a matter of law for decision by the court, which makes its own findings of fact relating to that jurisdiction. The South Carolina Supreme Court states no reasons in *Adams v. Davison-Paxon Co.* why, although the jury decides all other factual issues raised by the cause of action and defenses, the jury is displaced as to the factual issue raised by the affirmative defense under §72-111. . . . We find nothing to suggest that this rule was announced as an integral part of the special relationship created by the statute. Thus the requirement appears to be merely a form and mode of enforcing the immunity, *Guaranty Trust Co. v. York*, and not a rule intended to be bound up with the definition of the rights and obligations of the parties. . . .

Second. But cases following *Erie* have evinced a broader policy to the effect that the federal courts should conform as near as may be—in the absence of other considerations—to state rules even of form and mode where the state rules may bear substantially on the question whether the litigation would come out one way in the federal court and another way in the state court if the federal court failed to apply a particular local rule. E.g., *Guaranty Trust Co. v. York*; *Bernhardt v. Polygraphic Co.* Concededly the nature of the tribunal which tries issues may be important in the enforcement of the parcel of rights making up a cause of action or defense, and bear significantly upon achievement of uniform enforcement of the right. It may well be that in the instant personal-injury case the outcome would be substantially affected by whether the issue of immunity is decided by a judge or a jury. Therefore, were "outcome" the only consideration, a strong case might appear for saying that the federal court should follow the state practice.

But there are affirmative countervailing considerations at work here. The federal system is an independent system for administering justice to litigants who properly invoke its jurisdiction. An essential characteristic of that system is the manner in which, in civil common-law actions, it distributes trial functions between judge and jury and, under the influence—if not the command[10]—of the Seventh Amendment, assigns the decisions of disputed questions of fact to the jury. The policy of uniform enforcement of state-created rights and obligations, see, e.g., *Guaranty Trust Co. v. York*, supra, cannot in every case exact compliance with a state rule[12]—not bound up with rights and obligations—which disrupts the federal system of allocating functions between judge and jury. Thus the inquiry here is whether the federal policy favoring jury decisions of disputed fact questions should yield to the state rule in the interest of furthering the objective that the litigation should not come out one way in the federal court and another way in the state court.

---

10. Our conclusion makes unnecessary the consideration of—and we intimate no view upon—the constitutional question whether the right of jury trial protected in federal courts by the Seventh Amendment embraces the factual issue of statutory immunity when asserted, as here, as an affirmative defense in a common-law negligence action.

12. This Court held in *Sibbach v. Wilson & Co.* that Federal Rule of Civil Procedure 35 should prevail over a contrary state rule.

We think that in the circumstances of this case the federal court should not follow the state rule. It cannot be gainsaid that there is a strong federal policy against allowing state rules to disrupt the judge-jury relationship in the federal courts. . . . Perhaps even more clearly in light of the influence of the Seventh Amendment, the function assigned to the jury "is an essential factor in the process for which the Federal Constitution provides." . . .

Third. We have discussed the problem upon the assumption that the outcome of the litigation may be substantially affected by whether the issue of immunity is decided by a judge or a jury. But clearly there is not present here the certainty that a different result would follow, cf. *Guaranty Trust Co. v. York*, supra, or even the strong possibility that this would be the case. There are factors present here which might reduce that possibility. The trial judge in the federal system has powers denied the judges of many States to comment on the weight of evidence and credibility of witnesses, and discretion to grant a new trial if the verdict appears to him to be against the weight of the evidence. We do not think the likelihood of a different result is so strong as to require the federal practice of jury determination of disputed factual issues to yield to the state rule in the interest of uniformity of outcome. . . .

Reversed and remanded.

[The opinions of Justices WHITTAKER, FRANKFURTER, and HARLAN are omitted.]

Notes and Problems

---

1. State the holding of *Byrd*.

2. *Byrd* could have been decided under the criterion of *Guaranty Trust*: Unlike previous cases in which the outcome-determinative test had been applied, using a jury rather than a judge in these circumstances might, but would not necessarily, determine the outcome of the case. The Court thus seemed to be going out of its way to find another analysis by which to approach *Erie* problems. That process continued in the next case in this line, to which we now turn.

2. De-constitutionalizing *Erie*

Under both *Guaranty Trust* and *Byrd*, *Erie* questions are constitutional matters; whether federal courts should follow the state practice is a constitutional question. That framing of the issue is consistent with *Erie* itself, which rejected the invitation to reach its decision as an interpretation of the Rules of Decision rather than the Constitution. The next case, while purporting to overrule none of the cases in the *Erie* line, reframes the issue as one of statutory rather than constitutional interpretation. It puts the Rules—and the Rules Enabling Act, 28 U.S.C. §2072—at the front of many *Erie* issues, leaving the Constitution in the background.

Hanna v. Plumer

380 U.S. 460 (1965)

WARREN, C.J., delivered the opinion of the Court.

The question to be decided is whether, in a civil action where the jurisdiction of the United States district court is based upon diversity of citizenship between the parties, service of process shall be made in the manner prescribed by state law or that set forth in Rule 4[(e)(2)(B)] of the Federal Rules of Civil Procedure.

[The case arose out of a diversity suit for personal injuries. The defendant was the estate of one of the drivers involved. The issue arose because Massachusetts law provided that suits against an estate required personal service of process on the estate's executor. Process was instead served under Rule 4[(e)(2)(B)], which allowed for the summons and complaint to be left with a competent adult at the residence of any defendant. Defendant was served by leaving the summons and complaint with his wife at his residence. The district court and First Circuit, citing *Ragan* (see the chart in Note 3 supra page 270), ruled that the claim should be dismissed because plaintiff had failed to comply with the state method of serving process within the applicable statute of limitations.]

We conclude that the adoption of Rule 4[(e)(2)(B)], designed to control service of process in diversity actions, neither exceeded the congressional mandate embodied in the Rules Enabling Act nor transgressed constitutional bounds, and that the Rule is therefore the standard against which the District Court should have measured the adequacy of the service. Accordingly, we reverse the decision of the Court of Appeals.

The [version of the] Rules Enabling Act, 28 U.S.C. §2072 [then in effect] provide[d] in pertinent part:

> The Supreme Court shall have the power to prescribe, by general rules, the forms of process, writs, pleadings, and motions, and the practice and procedure of the district courts of the United States in civil actions.
>
> Such rules shall not abridge, enlarge or modify any substantive right and shall preserve the right of trial by jury. . . .*

Under the cases construing the scope of the Enabling Act, Rule 4[(e)(2)(B)] clearly passes muster. Prescribing the manner in which a defendant is to be notified that a suit has been instituted against him, it relates to the "practice and procedure of the district courts." "The test must be whether a rule really regulates procedure—the judicial process for enforcing rights and duties recognized by substantive law and for justly administering remedy and redress for disregard or infraction of them." *Sibbach v. Wilson & Co.* . . .

Thus, were there no conflicting state procedure, Rule 4[(e)(2)(B)] would clearly control. However, respondent, focusing on the contrary Massachusetts rule, calls to the Court's attention another line of cases, a line which—like the Federal Rules—had its birth in 1938. *Erie R. Co. v. Tompkins*, overruling *Swift v. Tyson*, held that federal courts sitting in diversity cases, when deciding questions of "substantive" law, are

---

* [The current version of §2072 is substantially identical in all respects relevant to this case.—EDS.]

bound by state court decisions as well as state statutes. The broad command of *Erie* was therefore identical to that of the Enabling Act: federal courts are to apply state substantive law and federal procedural law. However, as subsequent cases sharpened the distinction between substance and procedure, the line of cases following *Erie* diverged markedly from the line construing the Enabling Act. . . .

Respondent, by placing primary reliance on *York* and *Ragan*, suggests that the *Erie* doctrine acts as a check on the Federal Rules of Civil Procedure, that despite the clear command of Rule 4[(e)(2)(B)], *Erie* and its progeny demand the application of the Massachusetts rule. . . .

In the first place, it is doubtful that, even if there were no Federal Rule making it clear that in-hand service is not required in diversity actions, the *Erie* rule would have obligated the District Court to follow the Massachusetts procedure. "Outcome-determination" analysis was never intended to serve as a talisman. *Byrd v. Blue Ridge Cooperative*. Indeed, the message of *York* itself is that choices between state and federal law are to be made not by application of any automatic, "litmus paper" criterion, but rather by reference to the policies underlying the *Erie* rule.

The *Erie* rule is rooted in part in a realization that it would be unfair for the character or result of a litigation materially to differ because the suit had been brought in a federal court. . . . The decision was also in part a reaction to the practice of "forum-shopping" which had grown up in response to the rule of *Swift v. Tyson*. That the *York* test was an attempt to effectuate these policies is demonstrated by the fact that the opinion framed the inquiry in terms of "substantial" variations between state and federal litigation. Not only are nonsubstantial, or trivial, variations not likely to raise the sort of constitutional problems which troubled the Court in *Erie*; they are also unlikely to influence the choice of a forum. The "outcome-determination" test therefore cannot be read without reference to the twin aims of the *Erie* rule: discouragement of forum-shopping and avoidance of inequitable administration of the laws.

The difference between the conclusion that the Massachusetts rule is applicable, and the conclusion that it is not, is of course at this point "outcome-determinative" in the sense that if we hold the state rule to apply, respondent prevails, whereas if we hold that Rule 4[(e)(2)(B)] governs, the litigation will continue. But in this sense *every* procedural variation is "outcome-determinative.". . . [I]t is difficult to argue that permitting service of defendant's wife to take the place of in-hand service of defendant himself alters the mode of enforcement of state-created rights in a fashion sufficiently "substantial" to raise the sort of equal protection problems to which the *Erie* opinion alluded.

There is, however, a more fundamental flaw in respondent's syllogism: the incorrect assumption that the rule of *Erie R. Co. v. Tompkins* constitutes the appropriate test of the validity and therefore the applicability of a Federal Rule of Civil Procedure. The *Erie* rule has never been invoked to void a Federal Rule. It is true that there have been cases where this Court has held applicable a state rule in the face of an argument that the situation was governed by one of the Federal Rules. But the holding of each such case was not that *Erie* commanded displacement of a Federal Rule by an inconsistent state rule, but rather that the scope of the Federal Rule was not as broad as the losing party urged, and therefore, there being no Federal Rule which covered the point in dispute, *Erie* commanded the enforcement of state law. . . . (Here, of course, the clash is unavoidable; Rule 4[(e)(2)(B)] says—implicitly, but with unmistakable clarity—that in-hand service is not required in federal courts.) At the same time, in cases adjudicating the validity of Federal Rules, we have not applied the *York* rule or other refinements of *Erie*, but have to this day continued to decide questions concerning the scope of the Enabling Act and the constitutionality of specific Federal Rules in light of the distinction set forth in *Sibbach*.

Nor has the development of two separate lines of cases been inadvertent. The line between "substance" and "procedure" shifts as the legal context changes. . . . It is true that both the Enabling Act and the *Erie* rule say, roughly, that federal courts are to apply state "substantive" law and federal "procedural" law, but from that it need not follow that the tests are identical. For they were designed to control very different sorts of decisions. When a situation is covered by one of the Federal Rules, the question facing the court is a far cry from the typical, relatively unguided *Erie* choice: the court has been instructed to apply the Federal Rule, and can refuse to do so only if the Advisory Committee, this Court, and Congress erred in their prima facie judgment that the Rule in question transgresses neither the terms of the Enabling Act nor constitutional restrictions. . . .

Erie and its offspring cast no doubt on the long-recognized power of Congress to prescribe housekeeping rules for federal courts even though some of those rules will inevitably differ from comparable state rules. . . . Thus, though a court, in measuring a Federal Rule against the standards contained in the Enabling Act and the Constitution, need not wholly blind itself to the degree to which the Rule makes the character and result of the federal litigation stray from the course it would follow in state courts, it cannot be forgotten that the *Erie* rule, and the guidelines suggested in *York*, were created to serve another purpose altogether. To hold that a Federal Rule of Civil Procedure must cease to function whenever it alters the mode of enforcing state-created rights would be to disembowel either the Constitution's grant of power over federal procedure or Congress' attempt to exercise that power in the Enabling Act. Rule 4[(e)(2)(B)] is valid and controls the instant case.

Reversed.

Black, J., concurs in the result.

Harlan, J., concurring. . . .

Erie was something more than an opinion which worried about "forum-shopping and avoidance of inequitable administration of the laws," although to be sure these were important elements of the decision. I have always regarded that decision as one of the modern cornerstones of our federalism, expressing policies that profoundly touch the allocation of judicial power between the state and federal systems. *Erie* recognized that there should not be two conflicting systems of law controlling the primary activity of citizens, for such alternative governing authority must necessarily give rise to a debilitating uncertainty in the planning of everyday affairs.[1] And it recognized that the scheme of our Constitution envisions an allocation of lawmaking functions between state and federal legislative processes which is undercut

---

1. Since the rules involved in the present case are parallel rather than conflicting, this first rationale does not come into play here.

if the federal judiciary can make substantive law affecting state affairs beyond the bounds of congressional legislative powers in this regard. Thus, in diversity cases *Erie* commands that it be the state law governing primary private activity which prevails.

The shorthand formulations which have appeared in some past decisions are prone to carry untoward results that frequently arise from oversimplification. . . . To my mind the proper line of approach in determining whether to apply a state or a federal rule, whether "substantive" or "procedural," is to stay close to basic principles by inquiring if the choice of rule would substantially affect those primary decisions respecting human conduct which our constitutional system leaves to state regulation. If so, *Erie* and the Constitution require that the state rule prevail, even in the face of a conflicting federal rule.

The Court weakens, if indeed it does not submerge, this basic principle by finding, in effect, a grant of substantive legislative power in the constitutional provision for a federal court system, and through it, setting up the Federal Rules as a body of law inviolate. . . . So long as a reasonable man could characterize any duly adopted federal rule as "procedural," the Court, unless I misapprehend what is said, would have it apply no matter how seriously it frustrated a State's substantive regulation of the primary conduct and affairs of its citizens. Since the members of the Advisory Committee, the Judicial Conference, and this Court who formulated the Federal Rules are presumably reasonable men, it follows that the integrity of the Federal Rules is absolute. Whereas the unadulterated outcome and forum-shopping tests may err too far toward honoring state rules, I submit that the Court's "arguably procedural, ergo constitutional" test moves too fast and far in the other direction. . . .

[Justice HARLAN, applying his test to the facts of the case, found the federal rule controlling, not because it was a Rule, but because it would have at most a negligible effect on the parties' out-of-court behavior.]

WHAT'S NEW HERE?

- *Byrd* and *Hanna* reach similar results: Both hold that the federal court need not behave as a state court would if it were hearing the case. Moreover, both enunciate multi-tiered "tests" for determining whether federal or state practice should prevail. And they complement each other in one respect: *Hanna*, narrowly construed, tells a federal court what to do when a Rule or federal statute dictates the federal practice; *Byrd* deals with a federal practice not dictated by a specific federal statute or Rule.
- Though complementary, the two cases diverge sharply in their texture. *Byrd* is nuanced, "soft," and, in many cases, indeterminate—and grounds its analysis directly in the Constitution. *Hanna* is hard-edged and more determinate—and insists that a statute—the Rules Enabling Act—is as important as the Constitution in many *Erie* cases.

Notes and Problems

1. Briefly explain how in *Hanna* the state and federal practices diverged and why the federal court could disregard the state practice.

2. Consider a federal practice flowing from a federal Rule or statute.

   a. *Hanna* says that the analysis in that situation is relatively easy:

      i. Is the statute or Rule constitutional? One can hear in this question an echo of *Erie* with its assertion that Congress could not constitutionally dictate tort law to the states. The converse proposition is that Congress can dictate rules of procedure to the federal courts it creates. If the Rule or statute is constitutional and tells a federal court to do something, the court must follow the provisions of that statute.

      ii. At that point, the *Erie* issue ceases to be directly constitutional, becoming instead a matter of statutory construction: What does the governing statute tell the federal court to do? In the case of a Federal Rule of Civil Procedure, the analysis requires two steps, because the Rules are not themselves statutes but a delegation to the Supreme Court to make statute-like rules.

      iii. Theoretically, one must consider whether the initial delegation (in the Rules Enabling Act, 28 U.S.C. §2072) was constitutional; the few cases to consider the question have said it is. E.g., Sibbach v. Wilson, 312 U.S. 1 (1941).

      iv. One must then ask two questions.
          1. Does the Rule promulgated under the authority of the Rules Enabling Act in fact fit its description: "rules of practice and procedure"?
          2. Is the procedure specified in the Rule constitutional? (For an easy negative example, suppose that Rule 65 allowed seizure of real property without notice or special circumstances; that would violate due process.)

      v. If the Rule passes both these tests, then it must be applied, even if it differs from the state practice in a significant way. If the Rule fails either test (that is, if it is not "procedural" as the Rules Enabling Act uses that term or if it is unconstitutional), then the state practice applies.

   b. Justice Harlan's concurrence expresses skepticism about the "tests" a Rule must pass. In fact, no case has ever held a Rule to be beyond the scope of the Rules Enabling Act, though some have suggested that particular Rules (e.g., Rules 23, 68) come close to the line. Nor has any Rule ever been held unconstitutional, though several have been revised in light of constitutional developments that might have made them subject to attack. See, for example, Rule 65(b), which was revised in the wake of due process cases like *Fuentes v. Shevin*, infra page 324. Does this record prove Harlan correct?

c. To test your understanding of this scheme, apply it to the facts of *Hanna* itself, explaining the source of the conflict between state and federal practice and the reason for following the federal practice.

3. Now suppose the federal practice in question is just that—a "practice," not required by any Rule or statute. What then?
   a. Some examples of such federal "practices":
      i. In many state courts, lawyers are free to roam about the courtroom in addressing a jury, while most federal judges ask lawyers to stay firmly anchored behind the lectern. Many lawyers like the freedom to roam; what if a judge dismissed a diversity case as a sanction for the lawyer's disobedience to instructions to stay put?
      ii. Another might be differences in the manner in which prospective jurors were questioned: Many states, either by law or custom, permit extensive conversations between jurors and lawyers during jury selection; no statute or Rule governs the matter, but in many federal courts judges do all the questioning and do so very quickly. In a diversity case, could a lawyer insist that she be allowed to question jurors extensively?

   b. *Byrd* and *Hanna* would approach that question in different ways. *Byrd* asks whether the practice in question is "bound up with the substantive rights and obligations created by state law" and, if not, whether there is a countervailing interest inherent in the federal system. In the case of the voir dire practice, the answer to the first question will almost always be "no" and to the second "yes." *Hanna* asks first whether the practice in question flows from a Rule (no, for voir dire) and, if not, whether following the federal rule would lead to forum shopping or inequitable administration of the law. For voir dire, the answer is uncertain (in some cases, one can imagine a lawyer believing it very important to get a good feel for the jury); if, however, the answer is no (that lawyers wouldn't choose between state and federal court over such a matter), then *Hanna* arrives at the same outcome—follow federal voir dire practice—by a different route than *Byrd*.

   c. *Hanna* did not overrule *Byrd*, which it cited with approval. Both cases suggest an approach to a federal practice not dictated by a federal statute or Rule. One finds courts citing both.

Implications

In your Constitutional Law course, you will study federal "preemption," a phrase used to describe what happens when federal law occupies a space so completely that it "preempts," that is, displaces or pushes out state law that might otherwise govern. For example, if Congress today passed a statute defining the law of trespass on the tracks of railroads in interstate commerce, that federal statute would preempt the state law that would otherwise govern. It may be helpful to think of *Hanna* as a preemption case: When a federal statute or Rule defines procedure in some area, that federal law preempts state law that might otherwise govern.

For federal law to preempt, the federal law must be constitutional and otherwise valid. To preempt, according to standard doctrine, a federal law must in some sense be intended to displace state law. *Hanna*'s requirement that a Rule must be valid under the Rules Enabling Act sets forth a test of validity for a Rule—a precondition for its preemptive power.

Byrd deals with a softer form of preemption, in which there is no explicit statute or Rule that displaces state practice, only a "custom." *Byrd*'s underlying idea seems to be that for the federal courts to constitute an independent judicial system, they must be free to adopt a series of such "practices" (*Byrd* called them "affirmative countervailing considerations"), even when they depart from what a state court would do. Those might include a number of small matters: *Byrd* thus protects a number of such small customs that do not rise to the level of law, allowing them to displace analogous state court customs that diverge from their federal counterparts.

Erie and its progeny suggest a set of questions that need to be asked before knowing whether state or federal law applies:

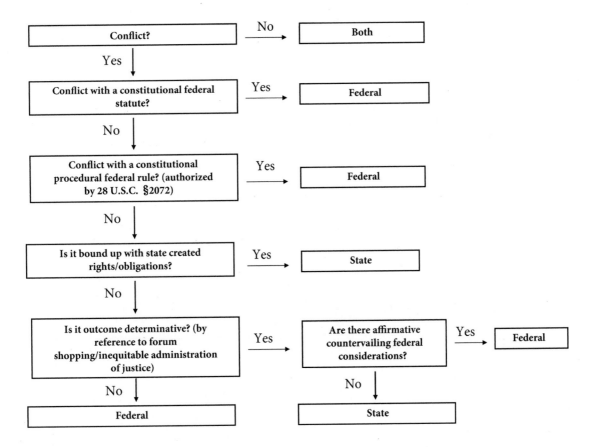

3. Determining the Scope of Federal Law: Avoiding and Accommodating *Erie*

Under *Hanna*'s reading of *Erie*, many "*Erie*" questions will not require resorting to the Constitution because Congress by statute or Rule will have told federal courts what to do in the situation. So long as the statute is constitutional (and the Rule conforms to the Rules Enabling Act), the choice of law problem is solved: Federal procedure governs. The difficulty arises when a federal court has to decide whether a federal statute that *might* occupy the area really does or when, by contrast, a federal statute or Rule should be construed not to conflict with a state practice. A number of pre-*Hanna* cases, described supra at pages 270-71, raised this issue. Consider some post-*Hanna* examples.

- Federal Rule of Appellate Procedure 38 allows—but does not require—an appellate court to punish frivolous appeals with extra costs. Alabama had a statute that automatically added a 10 percent penalty to an unsuccessful appeal of an award of money damages. In Burlington Northern R. v. Woods, 480 U.S. 1 (1987), the Court held that the federal Rule governed in federal courts, reasoning that the discretionary character of Appellate Rule 38 clashed with the mandatory state statute.
- States have varied in their willingness to enforce forum selection clauses. Alabama had a statute making such a clause unenforceable; did that statute govern in federal diversity litigation? No, said Stewart Org. v. Ricoh, 487 U.S. 22 (1988). The state statute was displaced by 28 U.S.C. §1404 (which you met in Chapter 2), which gives the federal courts discretionary power to move litigation to another district in the interests of justice and for the convenience of the parties. The *Stewart* Court said that a federal court considering such a transfer motion should weigh all the factors, including the forum selection clause, rather than giving automatic effect to the state's ban of forum selection clauses. *Atlantic Marine Construction* (supra page 195) suggests that such forum selection clauses should in most cases be enforced—via §1404.
- By contrast, Gasperini v. Center for Humanities, Inc., 518 U.S. 415 (1996), struggled to accommodate both state and federal interests. The Reexamination Clause of the Seventh Amendment prohibits federal Circuit Courts of Appeals from re-examining jury verdicts except as permitted at common law. A New York statute required state appellate courts to decide if jury damage awards exceeded "reasonable compensation" and to adjust them downward if they did. The U.S. Supreme Court held that both state and federal interests could be accommodated by allowing the federal *district* courts to conduct such reviews.
- New York has a statute prohibiting class actions that aggregate statutory penalties—so under New York law an individual can sue for a $1,000 statutory penalty, but ten thousand such persons cannot sue as a class, seeking $10,000,000 in damages. In Shady Grove Orthopedic Assoc., P.A. v. Allstate Ins. Co., 559 U.S. 393 (2010), the Court held that Federal Rule 23, which defines the requirements for bringing federal class actions, displaced

the state statute. As the majority saw it, Rule 23 sets forth the requirements for class certification; because it says nothing about forbidding classes seeking to aggregate statutory penalties, a federal court deciding whether to certify a class should focus exclusively on the Rule's requirements. In dissent, Justice Ginsburg, the author of *Gasperini*, argued that it would be possible to accommodate both the Rule and the state statute, by permitting a class action, but not a class seeking to aggregate statutory penalties.

- The *Erie* line of cases reaches into several areas of procedural law. One, that we'll note here but reserve for a later chapter, is how it interacts with the law of former adjudication. Recall from Chapter 1 (*Ison v. Thomas*) that both state and federal courts have created a law of claim and issue preclusion: Very roughly speaking, a litigant who has brought a case in which a judgment has been entered cannot bring the same case again. But because each state (and the federal system) has its own common law of preclusion, the exact scope of preclusion can vary a bit: A claim that California would preclude from relitigation might not be barred had it been decided in, say, Maryland. To add a wrinkle to this idea, suppose the second case is brought not in California but in Maryland. As you will see in Chapter 11, Maryland would look to California law in deciding the scope of preclusion of the first, California, case. But—to take matters into *Erie*-land—suppose the first case was decided in California by a *federal* court sitting in diversity jurisdiction. In Semtek Intl. Inc. v. Lockheed Martin Corp., 531 U.S. 497 (2001), the Supreme Court held that the scope of a federal judgment rendered in diversity should be the same as that judgment *would have had if it had been rendered by a state court* of the state where the federal court was sitting. In the hypothetical (which tracks the facts of *Semtek*), that would mean that the scope of a judgment of a federal court sitting in diversity jurisdiction in California should be the same as it would be had the action been brought in a California state court. Stay tuned for Chapter 11.

Note: Interpreting State Law: An Entailment of Erie

Erie requires federal courts sitting in diversity to apply state law under various circumstances. Sometimes, it will be easy for federal courts to determine state law: A recent state supreme court case may have carefully defined it, or the matter may be covered in an authoritative statute.

But determining state law can sometimes be difficult. What happens if there is no precedent on point, or the only available precedent is some years old, and the area of law has recently shown signs of change? Or what if the question is complicated by a horizontal choice of law problem like the one that brought forth Judge Henry Friendly's quip: "Our principal task, in this diversity of citizenship case, is to determine what the New York courts would think the California courts would think on an issue about which neither has thought." Nolan v. Transocean Air Lines, 276 F.2d 280, 281 (2d Cir. 1960). For a state trial judge, such uncertainty presents difficulties, but she at least has the assurance that if she is wrong, the state appellate courts will straighten things out. Federal judges, compelled to follow *Erie*, generally lack that assurance, because a federal court's erroneous interpretation of state law cannot be appealed to a state court.

What, then, should the federal district judge do? Should she predict what the state court would probably do under such circumstances? Should she act as she thinks a state court should act in these circumstances, even if she thinks it would not behave that way? For that matter, which state court should the federal district court seek to resemble—the state trial court, which is often hesitant to depart from precedent—or the state supreme court?

The same predicament faces the federal courts of appeals. On appeal from the district court's judgment, a federal court of appeals must do its best to decide what the state appellate courts would do when faced with the same appeal. Nor may the courts of appeals simply defer to the district court—on the ground that a district court judge from that state has a better feel for his own state's law. Salve Regina College v. Russell, 499 U.S. 225 (1991) (federal court of appeals required to review de novo district court's determination of state law).

Under such circumstances, one finds federal courts of appeals making such statements as, "Because we are persuaded by a careful review of the Ohio decisional law, as well as other relevant sources,* that the Supreme Court of Ohio would not construe its statute of limitations so as to preclude recovery in this case, we [do likewise]." McKenna v. Ortho Pharmaceutical Corp., 622 F.2d 657, 659 (3d Cir. 1980). Holdings based on such predictions of state court views are awkward, especially if the predictions later turn out to be wrong.

Consider, for example, the tangle in Pierce v. Cook & Co., 518 F.2d 720 (10th Cir. 1975), cert. denied, 423 U.S. 1079 (1976). Driver and three passengers were involved in a collision with a truck driven by an independent contractor hauling wheat for Cook. Driver and Passengers each brought actions. Two of the suits were removed to federal courts; the third remained in state court. In the federal court actions defendants won a summary judgment on the basis of 30-year-old state-law precedent relieving Cook of responsibility for the negligence of an independent contractor; the case was affirmed on appeal. Meanwhile, the state trial court had also granted summary judgment—on the basis of the same precedent—but plaintiff appealed to the state supreme court, which overruled the precedent. The state supreme court decision became final more than three years after the original federal appeal.

Six months later, the two federal plaintiffs moved to vacate the federal appellate decision under Rule 60(b), which permits the reopening of a final judgment under limited circumstances. See Chapter 11. In setting aside the federal judgment, the

---

* [What other sources could be relevant? Presumably only ones that the Ohio appellate courts themselves would find persuasive.—Eds.]

court of appeals emphasized that there had been "divergent results from a common vehicular accident," that plaintiffs had been forced into the federal courts, and that plaintiffs had received substantially different results in the federal courts than they would have in the state courts, in violation of the *Erie* principle.

Contrast *Pierce* with DeWeerth v. Baldinger, 38 F.3d 1266 (2d Cir.), cert. denied, 513 U.S. 1001 (1994). In 1987, plaintiff invoked diversity jurisdiction to sue a New York art dealer to recover a Monet painting stolen from his family during World War II. The federal court ruled that DeWeerth had failed to satisfy what it understood to be the showing of reasonable diligence in locating stolen property required by state law. Four years later the New York courts in a similar case held that a showing of reasonable diligence was not required under the relevant statute. DeWeerth moved to reopen his federal judgment under Rule 60(b), the same Rule used in *Pierce*. The Second Circuit sharply rejected the attempt:

> *Erie* simply does not stand for the proposition that a plaintiff is entitled to reopen a federal court case that has been closed for several years in order to gain the benefit of a newly announced decision of a state court, a forum in which she specifically declined to litigate her claim.

In an effort to render cases like *Pierce* and *DeWeerth* less frequent, several states have adopted a process called *certification*. In certification the federal court asks the state supreme court for an answer to a question about state law. In cases like *Pierce* and *DeWeerth*, if the state appellate court announced that it was changing the law, a federal diversity court could do likewise. There are, however, several defects in this system. First, the state must have a certification procedure; some do not. Even when the procedure is available and is used, the results are not always satisfactory. Sometimes state courts do not accept the invitation to answer the question about state law. Other times they answer, but in terms that leave the federal courts as perplexed as they were before. Part of the problem flows from the circumstance that the certification process does not simply pass the whole case to the state supreme court (as review, explain why that would violate the premise of diversity jurisdiction). Instead, the federal court frames a question of law that it asks the state court to clarify. But, in a common law system, legal issues often lie deeply embedded in factual contexts, so it is entirely possible for a state court to "answer" a question about state law but leave the federal court entirely unsure how to apply it to the case at hand.

Assessment Questions

Q1. Before *Erie*, which was decided in 1938, federal courts . . .

    A. Followed state procedural law.

    B. In "arising under" cases followed federal law.

    C. In diversity cases felt free to ignore state case law.

    D. Interpreted "laws" in the Rules of Decision Act (28 U.S.C. §1738) to refer only to state statutes.

Q2. When Justice Brandeis wrote in *Erie* of the "unconstitutionality of the course pursued" by the federal courts during the regime of *Swift v. Tyson* . . .

    A. He referred to the Court's recent reinterpretation of the Commerce Clause.

    B. He referred to the Full Faith and Credit Clause.

    C. He wasn't clear what exact portion of the Constitution he had in mind.

Q3. The *Erie* principle—announced in *Erie* and developed in later cases—that federal courts must in appropriate circumstances follow state decisional law as well as state statutes . . .

    A. Applies only in diversity cases.

    B. Applies whenever state law governs a claim or defense.

    C. Does not require a federal court to ignore a Federal Rule of Civil Procedure.

    D. Requires a federal court to observe state choice of law rules as well as state substantive law.

Q4. Cases decided after *Erie* . . .

    A. Have largely ignored its holding.

    B. Have had to wrestle with the border between procedure and substance.

    C. Have read *Erie* as invalidating several Federal Rules of Civil Procedure.

    D. Have displayed varying understandings of its scope and meaning.

Analysis of Assessment Questions

Q1. A, B, C, and D are all correct responses. A is correct because the "Conformity Act," repealed when the Federal Rules came into effect in 1938 (the same year as *Erie*), directed the federal courts to follow the procedural law of the state in which the federal court sat. B is correct—then as now: When federal substantive law governs, a federal court will apply it. C is correct, at least in cases governed by "general law": That's the holding of *Swift v. Tyson*. D is correct because that's how *Swift* interpreted the Rules of Decision Act, and that interpretation stood until it was overruled in *Erie*.

Q2. C is the only correct response. C is correct because most commentators think the best explanation of *Erie*'s constitutional basis rests not on a specific clause but of constitutional "structure": The Constitution assumes that states have broad lawmaking powers and that they're entitled to let their courts (as well as their legislatures) do that lawmaking—and that the federal courts should respect their choices. A and B are wrong because the opinion nowhere references either of these clauses.

Q3. B, C, and D are correct. A is wrong because the *Erie* principle will apply whenever state law supplies a claim or defense—as, for example, in a federal question case that includes state law claims brought in under supplemental jurisdiction. B is correct for the reasons explained in A. C is correct (that's the holding of *Hanna v. Plumer*), though a careful lawyer would note that the courts have sometimes construed Rules in unexpected ways to avoid a conflict with state law (e.g., *Ragan v. Merchants Transfer*, noted at page 270, as well as *Semtek*, noted above). D is correct because that's the holding of *Klaxon v. Stentor*, discussed at page 265.

Q4. B and D are correct. A is wrong because the Court has faithfully adhered to its holding, even when sometimes disagreeing about the scope of that holding. C is wrong because when faced with such a collision, the Court has instead construed the Rule not to pose such a problem.

PART II

THE PROCESS OF LITIGATION

A. APPROACHING CIVIL PROCEDURE

In studying the procedural system used in U.S. courts you can take at least two different paths. One path starts from the bottom, examining the way in which an individual lawsuit develops: how the parties state cases, develop information about them, and bring them to resolution. This approach emphasizes features and problems of the contemporary procedural system, which is in many respects a bold experiment. Studying the process of litigation reveals how these features shape and constrain the litigants' responsibilities and choices. The other path starts from the top, examining the constitutional environment in which the individual lawsuit exists. That approach takes you into both the history and the current interpretation of the Constitution of the United States. Studying that document reveals several limits on the ways in which state and federal court systems conduct their business, limits that have major consequences for individual litigants.

Anyone wanting to become a lawyer has to understand both approaches, comprehending the constitutional environment as well as the modes for processing disputes. This book accordingly contains materials about both, and most courses will examine both. But a course can with equal validity start at the top and work down or begin at the bottom and work up. The three parts of this book are labeled to emphasize those different starting points. Some courses may begin with this section, Part II: The Process of Litigation, comprising Chapters 5-11 and representing the "bottom-up" approach. Other classes may start with Part I: The Constitutional Framework for U.S. Litigation, comprising Chapters 2-4, the "top-down" approach.

The third part of this book, Part III: Probing the Boundaries: Additional Claims and Parties, combines significant elements of both of the other parts and may be studied either at the end of the course, as a reprise, or in conjunction with either of the other two parts.

B. CHOOSING PROCEDURE

Since disputing began (which, according to several religious traditions, was shortly after the first humans appeared on the face of the Earth), disputants and whoever helped them resolve their disputes have been faced with procedural choices. One way of framing the choices is as between speed and quality. Everyone wants disputes to be decided quickly; everyone also wants them to be decided correctly—after full exploration of the facts and careful weighing of the law. But even in a world of unlimited resources these two goals conflict, and we have limited resources. Another way to frame the conflict is as between fairness and justice. Everyone wants the judge to be fair as between the parties; everyone also wants the judge to decide in favor of the party on whose side truth lies. But in some cases these goals will conflict; the side with the best presentation may not be the side where truth resides.

These conflicts force those who design procedure (legislators, lawyers, judges) to choose; moreover, they must choose not just once but at every stage of the process. Should all cases go to trial—on the ground that trials may best uncover the truth—or should we weed out most cases before trial, thus speeding the resolution of disputes while increasing the risk of error? Should plaintiffs at the outset have to state their cases in detail—to sort weak from strong cases at an early stage—or would a requirement of detailed pleading trip up plaintiffs with good cases who need access to facts known only to the defendant? How much post-filing factual investigation should we permit, bearing in mind that greater access will turn up more information but also increase cost and delay? How much autonomy should we give to the parties—which will require fewer judges and less public expense—and how much should we insist on judicial responsibility—which may increase public confidence in the outcome but will increase public cost?

Behind these questions lies another, more generalized issue: Is a lawsuit a quest for truth, or a way to settle a dispute? The more we think litigation is an inquiry into truth, the more likely we are to want judges rather than the adversaries to control the inquiry. The more confident we are that litigation reveals the truth, the more likely we are to think it proper to apply the findings of one judge or jury to similar lawsuits. Conversely, the more we see litigation as a battle between the parties, the greater our comfort with giving the parties control over the terms of that battle, but the less we'll be inclined to think that the personalized battle yields truth.

These and similar questions lie just beneath the surface of contemporary procedural rules: Each rule, and often even innocuous-looking individual words and phrases within the rules, represents a choice among procedural values. In exploring the development of a lawsuit, we shall be doing at least three things: seeing how a procedural system has made particular choices; seeing how judges and other law-makers can have second thoughts about those choices; and looking beneath those choices at the values they imply. That exploration is particularly apt because the procedural system we shall explore—that set forth in the Federal Rules of Civil Procedure—represents a self-conscious choice of flexibility. The drafters of the Rules (and those who have since amended them) sought above all to break free from what they thought were rigidities of earlier procedural systems. They largely succeeded, but critics have begun to ask whether as a result lawsuits have become unstructured, expensive monsters.

C. A ROADMAP FOR EXPLORING CHOICES

This book explores the answers to such questions by following the development of a lawsuit in roughly chronological order. Chapter 5 looks at why people litigate by exploring the demography of contemporary litigation, the arsenal of remedies courts can grant, and how litigation is financed. Chapter 6—on pleading—explores how lawsuits are commenced. At the commencement of the lawsuit a lawyer must decide whether to join additional claims and parties; for teaching purposes one can explore this question in one of two ways. One approach moves from pleading (the setting forth of claims) to the exploration of facts underlying those claims—that is discovery, explored in Chapter 7. The other approach explores how lawyers join additional parties and additional claims to a lawsuit, the topic of Chapter 12, before examining discovery.

Most lawsuits reach the discovery stage; the real question is whether they will go further. Chapter 8 examines a variety of official and unofficial ways in which lawsuits can end during or shortly after the discovery period. If they do not end then, they proceed to trial. Chapter 9 examines who will decide the issues in a lawsuit and what principles limit their freedom of decision. Once the trial is over, the loser may appeal; Chapter 10 examines the availability of and limits on appeals. Whether a lawsuit ends on appeal or at some earlier stage, there may come a quite difficult question: Just what is it that the now-concluded lawsuit has decided? That question, which goes under several doctrinal names, is explored in Chapter 11, Respect for Judgments.

CHAPTER 5

Incentives to Litigate

People don't litigate for fun. Lawsuits cost money. Worse, they are for most participants miserable experiences whether they win or lose. Why would anyone bring a lawsuit? Conversely, plaintiffs almost always seek something in defendant's power to grant; why, instead of paying up, does defendant choose to add the insult of litigation to what may be the eventual injury of an adverse judgment? And to complete the inquiry, one should also ask whether the expense and unpleasantness of litigation are socially desirable. Should it be easier to commence or defend a lawsuit, or is it already too easy? Lawyers give two labels to these inquiries: remedies (what courts can do to and for litigants) and access to justice (whether barriers to litigation are too high or too low).

A. LITIGATION IN THE UNITED STATES AT THE START OF THE TWENTY-FIRST CENTURY

Trying to answer the questions above is silly without knowing a little about the existing litigation system. Whether litigation should be easier—or whether it is already too easy—should turn on facts, not supposition. Legislators, editorial writers, and scholars debate whether litigation is "out of control." Some of this debate turns on factual premises. To participate in this debate or to be a well-informed lawyer one needs to know how much litigation there is, what it consists of, how long it takes, and what its results are.

Because of jurisdictional limits on the federal courts, about 95 percent of litigation in the United States occurs in state courts. In 2008 (the most recent year for which complete data are available), just fewer than 100 million cases were filed in those state courts.* That number represents the outcome of almost two decades (1984-2000) of rising rates of civil litigation, followed by a decade of flat or declining rates, a decline sharpened by the economic downturn. Of those 100 million cases, a bit more than half involve traffic and similar ordinance violations. Some of those cases can significantly affect people's lives—lost driving licenses, towed cars, and increased insurance premiums—but the adjudication of these claims is not typically what we think of as serious litigation.

The remaining 48 million non–traffic ticket cases could be thought of as "serious." They consist of two large groups—civil and criminal cases—and two specialized subsets of the large groupings: Juvenile cases are specialized criminal cases, and family law (sometimes known as domestic relations) cases are a similarly specialized form of civil litigation.

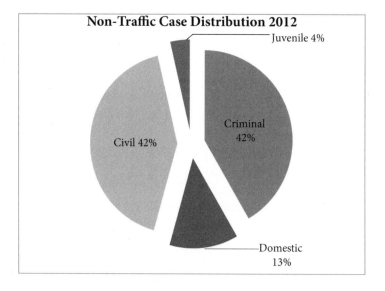

If one excludes the traffic ticket cases and combines domestic relations with general civil cases and juvenile with criminal cases, two large categories emerge, with the civil/domestic cases comprising just over half of the docket and the criminal/juvenile cases just under half.

This course focuses on the civil portion of that litigation. If one includes the domestic relations cases, that's about 25 million cases; if one excludes the domestic relations cases, as most statistical studies of civil litigation do, the number is about

---

* State court statistics in this discussion come from Robert C. LaFountain et al., Examining the Work of State Courts, 2008: A National Perspective from the Court Statistics Project (National Center for State Courts 2012), available online at http://www.courtstatistics.org/~/media/Microsites/Files/CSP/EWSC-2008-Online.ashx. A second, more recent study by the National Center sampled all "non-domestic civil cases disposed of between July 1, 2012 and June 30, 2013," available at https://www.ncsc.org/~/media/Files/PDF/Research/CivilJusticeReport-2015.ashx. Federal statistics come from the Annual Report, Administrative Office of the United States Courts 1998, online at http://www.uscourts.gov/dirrpt98/index.html.

20 million civil lawsuits per year. As noted, over the preceding 50 years that number first grew then shrank. It shrank both absolutely (total number of cases filed) and on a per capita basis (number of cases per 100,000 population).

Why this growth followed by this decline? Experts disagree, but a consensus seems to be forming that civil litigation tracks economic activity. Christian Wollschlager, Exploring Global Landscapes of Litigation Rates (Nomos: 1998) (indicating high litigation rates in developed economies, with Germany, Sweden, Israel, and Austria having higher per capita rates of litigation than the United States). All other things being equal, economic growth produces more civil litigation. Conversely, economic recessions, such as the one the United States has recently passed through, lead to declining rates of civil litigation.

Focusing on the civil lawsuits, one can ask what these 20 million civil disputes were about. Data on this fairly basic question is not definitive, but recent samples suggest the predominance of contract claims. One seven-state sample found the following categories:

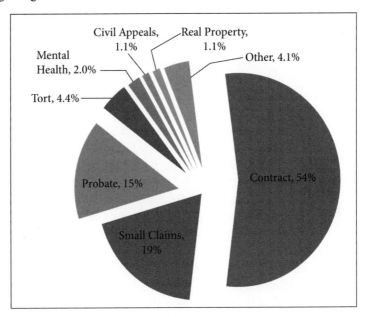

Similar surveys confirm the dominance of contract cases. The leading non-partisan agency collecting state court statistics summarized: "High-value tort and commercial contract disputes are the predominant focus of contemporary debates, but collectively they comprised only a small proportion . . . of the caseload. In contrast nearly two thirds were contract cases and more than half of these were debt collection and landlord/tenant cases." If one reflects on the widespread use of contract as the principal technique for ordering U.S. economic life (including the widespread use of credit), dominance of contract claims makes sense.

At first glance, you might think a litigator trying to predict the fate of her case, or a public official allocating judicial budgets, would care more about how many cases there are than what they are about. But, like some first impressions, this one turns out to be wrong. No sort of case goes to trial at a high rate: The national average hovers around 4 percent, with about 90 percent of those trials coming before a judge rather than a jury.

If all cases went to trial at the same rate, one would expect that most trials would be in contract cases. Not so: Torts, though far less than half of the filings, comprise 60 percent of the trials. In large part this mismatch occurs because so many "contract" cases are essentially debt collection actions, in which there is no real dispute about facts or law. Many of these actions will end not in a trial but in a default judgment.

When trial does occur, the tort/contract distinction also affects the kind of trial: When contract cases do go to trial, most are tried to a judge (called a "bench" trial), while 90 percent of the tort cases that reach trial go before a jury. Because bench trials are a bit easier to schedule and usually a little faster than jury trials, the mean time to judgment in a contract case is between 9 and 10 months; torts take the longest, about 16 months. Actual trials, when they occur, are short: The mean jury trial lasts less than four days, bench trials two days. As with all averages, these conceal wide variations; two New Jersey cases were reported to have been pending for decades!

Who wins? Again, the answer differs depending on whether it is a tort or contract case. In tort trials plaintiffs win (that is, get a judgment for some amount above $0) just about half the time (51 percent of jury cases, 56 percent of bench trials). Plaintiffs do better in contract trials, prevailing in just over two-thirds of the cases. Bear in mind that that "winning" can be a relative term: A plaintiff who recovers a judgment for $10,000 has prevailed in court, but may not feel much like celebrating if he turned down an offer to settle for $15,000 before incurring the expense of trial. When plaintiffs win, how much do they recover? News accounts suggest fabulous sums; reality is different. In data collected before the 2009-2016 "Great Recession," the median recovery in tort cases was between $21,000 and $24,000 (bench and jury verdicts, respectively). In contract cases, the median plaintiff's judgment was $75,000 in jury verdicts and $25,000 in bench-tried cases (suggesting that perhaps parties choose to try the smaller cases to judges). In fewer than 10 percent of all cases won by plaintiffs does the judgment reach $1 million: 8.3 percent of contract cases tried to a jury, 5.7 percent of tort cases similarly tried. In an analogous data set compiled during the recession (2012-2013), the amounts were somewhat different: a median tort recovery (recall we are talking only about successful plaintiffs) of $64,761; for contracts $9,428. Because the two data sets differed one cannot say with any certainty whether they represent changing trends or sample differences.

One fact stands out starkly in the 2012-2013 data: In many cases, the cost of competent representation (lawyer's fees and experts) "likely outstrips the monetary value of the case." If that conclusion is not an artifact of the recession, it presents a serious challenge to the legal profession and to the legal system, about which we'll have more to say when we turn, later in this chapter, to litigation finance.

Seen from a different perspective, these numbers mean that the average stakes in civil litigation lie within $25,000 of the median family income for a year. These are hardly trivial amounts, but neither are they the stuff of urban legend and professional folktales. If there is a serious concern, it would be about litigants who cannot afford competent representation. Still another way to view matters is from the perspective of the lawyers who operate the system on behalf of their clients. A plaintiffs' lawyer, even a competent and successful one, could have a career in which she never recovered a million-dollar verdict. On the other hand, a lawyer representing defendants will spend a good deal of his time trying to make sure that his client does not end up on the wrong side of the less-than-10-percent of cases in which there is a seven-figure verdict.

WHAT'S NEW HERE?

- Like professionals in many fields, lawyers tend to be a lot better at understanding their specialties (civil rights litigation, antitrust, product liability, etc.) than understanding the context within which they practice that specialty. Legislators and the press often have similar difficulties in seeing things in context. This brief introduction should help you in two ways:
  1. in understanding the topics you will be studying in civil procedure—why, for example, procedural changes affecting pleading and discovery will affect more cases than procedural changes that control only jury instructions; and
  2. in understanding and interpreting the legal system as a whole.

Notes and Problems

1. Consider some implications of the statistical picture sketched above:
   a. You walk into a courtroom in a big U.S. city. A civil jury trial is in progress. Without knowing more you can make a very good guess about what kind of case it is. Explain.
   b. You walk into another big-city courtroom, where another civil trial is in progress, this one before a judge without a jury. You can be pretty sure what kind of case it is, who will win, and you can make a prediction about how much the judgment will be for. Explain.
   c. Legislation is introduced to streamline litigation by reducing the amount of time spent in jury selection. Explain why the legislation, though it may make jurors' lives more pleasant and might be a good idea for other reasons, will have no effect on the time of disposition for most cases filed.
   d. State court administrators and judges, staggering under heavy caseloads, sometimes oppose federal legislation that would limit federal diversity jurisdiction on the grounds that the state courts already have too many cases and the "dumped" diversity cases would overwhelm them. Explain why that argument is weak.

2. Is the decline in the proportion of trials a problem? If so, what is the solution? Judges, lawyers, and scholars debate both questions.

   a. On the "it's a problem" side stand those who point out that trials constitute our system's principal public forum for resolving disputes. Some also stress the importance of jury trials in a democracy, which put lay deciders in charge in a way that echoes the use of elections to resolve political questions: Fewer jury trials means a diminished role for such lay decision makers.

   b. On the "why worry?" side stand those who argue that modern discovery naturally leads to increased settlement rates, and we should applaud, not fret over, those who reach consensual resolutions.

   c. For those who think that the decline in trials presents a problem, locating solutions is not easy. Some suggest increased funding for judicial positions and courtrooms, arguing that adjudication plays a critical but underappreciated role in society and the economy. Others look to modern legal culture, which has, they argue, created "litigators" who run the pretrial process but consciously avoid trial—in part because they have had little experience with trial work—and are abetted by judges who themselves may be uneasy with the rapid-fire evidentiary rulings required by trial.

3. Be clear about what trial rates do and do not mean. Although most civil cases will not end in trial, many will end with a judicial decision. Some cases end almost as soon as they begin, with a default judgment: About 14 percent of the total cases and about a quarter of contract cases end with default judgments, probably because a defendant has no defense to a claim for an unpaid debt. For others, the end will come with a pretrial ruling—about jurisdiction, about the sufficiency of pleadings, about discovery issues, or at summary judgment—even though there is no trial. For example, in the federal system, for which we have elaborate statistics, such rulings are dispositive (that is, case-ending) in about one-third of all filings. So a low trial rate does not mean a low adjudication rate. As you will see, a good part of the contemporary litigation process is the pretrial process.

4. Those cases that do not end in trial or a pretrial ruling end in events that are more ambiguous: settlement (often reflected in voluntary dismissal) or abandonment (followed by involuntary dismissal for failure to prosecute).

   a. These terminations may represent a response to the merits: As facts are uncovered, the plaintiff recognizes that what he thought was a strong case has a fatal flaw and gives up rather than throwing good money after bad. Defendant, recognizing that there is only a small chance of a giant plaintiff's verdict, nevertheless decides not to take that chance and settles to eliminate the risk of a catastrophic judgment. These decisions, though they don't result in an official resolution of the dispute, represent the litigants' responses to the merits of the case.

   b. Alternatively, either outcome may represent surrender to financial exigency: A plaintiff gives up a strong case because she cannot afford to litigate any further; a defendant offers something to make a plaintiff with a trumped-up claim go away because winning on the merits will cost more than the settlement offered. When cost rather than the merits of the claim dictates the result, one confronts the central topic of this chapter, the relation of the incentives and costs of litigation to the merits of the claims involved.

B. REASONS TO LITIGATE: DOLLARS, ORDERS, AND DECLARATIONS

The people filing the 20 million civil lawsuits each year want something; the people against whom the lawsuits are filed want to know what they stand to lose. To a lawyer, those questions translate into inquiries about what remedies a court will order—what acts it will require of the defendant if the plaintiff prevails.

Take a very common and very simple lawsuit. D fails to pay her credit card debt. P wants to collect the debt. To get the state's help in collecting the debt, the legal system requires P to file suit, describing the claim and asking for a remedy. If P prevails, he gets a judgment, a statement by the court that P is legally entitled to a certain sum of money. P can then use that judgment to get access to various post-judgment remedies to collect that money from any assets that D has. These may include getting an employer to garnish D's wages, an order attaching D's checking or savings accounts, or putting a lien on any real property D owns, so the property cannot be sold without paying P. The exact scope and procedures for using these post-judgment remedies lie beyond the scope of this course. For now, you need to understand that a judgment is the key that unlocks these remedies.

Remedies embodied in judgments aim to cure a legal harm. Remedies can be divided into two groups—those that seek to provide the plaintiff with a reasonable substitute for whatever was lost (substitutionary remedies) and those that seek to restore directly and specifically that which the defendant has taken from the plaintiff (specific remedies). If, for example, defendant takes plaintiff's car unlawfully, a specific remedy would be an order (either to the defendant or the sheriff) commanding the return of the car. A substitutionary remedy would be a judgment that defendant pay plaintiff enough money to buy an equivalent car. One issue we will examine is the extent to which plaintiffs can choose between specific and substitutionary remedies.

To create the conditions for a lawsuit, plaintiff must want something that defendant is unwilling to give her. Sorting roughly, there are three such things: money; an enforceable order to do (or not to do) something; or a declaration of the parties' respective rights. We'll consider those three remedies, as lawyers call them, in order. We will then consider preliminary relief; remedies ordered before the merits of the case have been adjudicated.

1. Damages

By far the most common remedy awarded by U.S. courts are judgments for money damages. This frequency of money damages has several causes. One is that in a credit economy many claims are for debts, and a successful debt claim will always result in a damage judgment. Second, for many common claims specific remedies are impossible: Defendant cannot replace an injured limb or erase the pain of disfigurement or defamation. Money may be a poor substitute, but only a substitute is possible. Because damages are a substitute, however, sometimes the law encounters difficulty in deciding how to measure them. In settlement negotiations the parties bargain directly about how much (or how little) they would accept to dispose of the case. In trials, judges and juries must resort to less direct methods for estimating the value of a substitute. Many of these methods depend on the existence of a market in which the substitute can be priced, but some substitutionary remedies involve damages for which there is no market.

Even when there is a market, and even when the defendant is clearly liable, the law requires a plaintiff to prove the amount of damages. Sometimes that's easy: The damages for an unpaid promissory note are the principal sum plus accrued interest. Sometimes that's far more difficult: How much is a lifetime of impaired mobility or pain worth? The law insists that judges and juries decide, without a great deal of guidance. The next case displays a judge wrestling with these questions in an unusual context.

As you have seen (or will see) in Chapter 3, under some conditions a defendant can "remove" a case from state to federal court—if there would have been subject matter jurisdiction in federal court. And, as you may already know, there is federal subject matter jurisdiction over cases involving parties from different states when the amount in controversy is more than $75,000. The next case shows the defendant trying to remove—and encountering from plaintiff the argument that damages are insufficient to permit a federal court to hear the case.

Troupe v. C & S Wholesale Grocers, Inc.

2009 WL 1938787 (M.D. Ga. 2009)

ROYAL, J.

Before the Court is Plaintiff's Motion to Remand in which Plaintiff contends that the amount in controversy in the present case does not exceed the minimum amount required by Title 28 U.S.C. §1332(a)(1) and that this Court therefore lacks subject matter jurisdiction. . . . Because Defendant has carried its burden of proving that, if Plaintiff prevails, her damages will "more likely than not" exceed the minimum jurisdictional amount, Plaintiff's Motion to Remand is hereby DENIED.

Factual and Procedural Background

The present action arises from Plaintiff Zelma Troupe's slip and fall on premises owned and operated by Defendant C & S Wholesale Grocers and was originally filed in the State Court of Bibb County, Georgia. In the Complaint filed in the State Court, Plaintiff asserts that she suffered "severe physical injuries" and "excruciating and severe physical distress" as a result of Defendant's negligent inspection and maintenance of its premises. She seeks damages for medical expenses in an amount "in excess of $13,637.00" and prays for an additional award of "all damages allowed under Georgia Law including, but not limited to, recovery for special and general damages, including pain and suffering, both mental and physical, in the amount to be proven at the time of trial." Plaintiff further seeks to recover punitive damages, the cost of litigation, and "such other and further relief as this court deems just and proper." Upon review of the Complaint, Defendant filed a timely Answer and Notice of Removal of the action to this Court. Plaintiff then filed the present motion seeking remand and an award of payment of just costs, actual expenses, and attorney fees incurred.

Discussion

Any action initially brought in state court may be removed if "the district courts of the United States have original jurisdiction." Title 28 U.S.C. §1441(a). "One category of civil actions with such original jurisdiction is those between 'citizens of different states' where the amount in controversy 'exceeds the sum or value of $75,000.'" At issue in this case is whether the amount in controversy exceeds that required for this Court to exercise federal subject matter jurisdiction under Title 28 U.S.C. §1332(a)(1).

The burden of proving any jurisdictional fact rests upon the party seeking to invoke the jurisdiction of the federal courts. . . . Generally, when a complaint does not claim a specific amount of damages, "removal from state court is proper if it is facially apparent from the complaint that the amount in controversy exceeds the jurisdictional requirement." In the event that the jurisdictional amount is not facially apparent on the complaint, "the court should look to the notice of removal and may require evidence relevant to the amount in controversy at the time the case was removed."

The jurisdictional amount may be apparent on the face of the Complaint if the language clearly alleges extensive damages such as long-term medical expenses, mental and physical pain and suffering, loss of enjoyment of life, loss of wages and earning capacity, and permanent disability and disfigurement or other serious injuries. Here, however, the amount in controversy is not so apparent. Simply put, there is no way to determine from the Complaint whether Plaintiff has been so badly injured as to make an award of over $75,000 more likely than not. Plaintiff's Complaint merely asserts that she suffered "severe physical injuries" and "excruciating and severe physical distress" as a result of Defendant's negligence, specifies damages for medical expenses "in excess of $13,637.00," and prays an award of "other special and general damages, including pain and suffering, both mental and physical, in the amount to be proven at the time of trial." There [is] simply nothing on the face of the Complaint to suggest that she will seek recovery for long-term medical expenses, permanent disability and disfigurement, or loss of wages or diminished earning capacity.

Defendant's Notice of Removal provides more assistance, however. The Notice and attached copies of Plaintiff's medical records include additional information about the extent of Plaintiff's injuries: describing the amount of lower back and leg pain Plaintiff endures, detailing her efforts at pain management (including undergoing physical therapy, chiropractic manipulation, and spinal blocks), and showing that her pain continues even a year after the alleged incident. The Court may in fact consider this type of evidence.

According to the medical records, Plaintiff claims to have fallen on her left hip and back while in the Defendant's store and that this incident is believed to have aggravated a pre-existing back injury. The records further indicate that Plaintiff complained of severe, unrelenting pain (sometimes categorized as an 8, 9, or 10 on a 10 point scale) which could not be controlled with medication, that such pain persisted even more than a year after her fall, and that she is possibly still incurring medical expenses for pain management. The records also indicate that Plaintiff lives alone, is self-employed, and owns her own house cleaning service. She has stated that her pain is exacerbated by lifting, bending, stooping, prolonged standing—all of which were required in her profession as a house cleaner. Plaintiff in fact told her physicians that she was forced to reduce the number of houses that she could clean because of her back condition and that she had to discontinue personal activities such as exercising, which also aggravated her pain. Such assertions, if proven, suggest that, if she prevails, Plaintiff will likely be able to recover unspecified damages for long term medical expenses, loss of wages and earning capacity, mental and physical pain and suffering, and loss of enjoyment of life in addition to Plaintiff's specified claim for medical expenses in excess of $13,637.00 and claim for punitive damages.

Given this additional information, the Court concludes that Defendant has satisfied its burden of establishing that the special, general, and punitive damages in this case, if proven, will "more likely than not" exceed the minimum jurisdictional amount. Plaintiff's Motion to Remand is accordingly DENIED.

SO ORDERED.

WHAT'S NEW HERE

- Most of your substantive courses in the first year will focus on liability. For example, is someone who negligently (but unintentionally) makes a misrepresentation liable to one who relied on that misrepresentation? Under what circumstances will the proprietor of a business establishment be liable for harms inflicted by third parties? And so on. Those discussions often abbreviate or omit the question raised here: Assuming liability, what are the damages? That question has, in turn, at least two branches:

  1. What evidence can—or must—be introduced to support each element of damages?

  2. Are certain elements of damages capped or otherwise limited?

- That means that both sides in a lawsuit seeking damages must at a very early stage think about what those damages might be. If the provable damages are low, a plaintiff may think twice about bringing the case; if the provable damages are high, a defendant may consider an early settlement offer and, if that offer is not accepted, be prepared to invest large amounts in defending the case.

Notes and Problems

1. Notice that damages will matter at two stages of this case.

   a. They will of course matter if plaintiff proves liability, at which point a jury (or judge, in a bench trial) will have to calculate the extent of medical expenses, past and future, the amounts to be awarded for pain and suffering, lost wages, and the like.

   b. In addition, the extent of damages may determine which court hears the case. In *Troupe*, defendant, seeking to remove to federal court, was arguing that the damages would be high enough to exceed the $75,000 minimum requisite in a diversity case. Plaintiff, whose lawyer wished to stay in state court, was arguing that the damages would be less than $75,000. (Similar issues might arise in states that have courts of limited jurisdiction, which often have maximum amount in controversy requirements.)

   c. How did the judge resolve the dispute?

2. Further notice that the parties' roles will completely reverse when they proceed from litigating jurisdiction to the merits of the case.

   a. If the case goes to trial, what will be plaintiff's contention about the extent of damages?

   b. What will be defendant's contention about the extent of damages?

   c. Will a jury find out that the parties have reversed the arguments they made to the judge at the jurisdictional stage? No. The parties' briefs and oral arguments at this jurisdictional stage will not be revealed to the jury, which at this preliminary stage of the case has not even been chosen.

a. Damage Amounts: Ceilings and Floors

Because so much civil litigation is about money, any legal rule that limits or increases the amount of damages that can be awarded on a given claim will likely decrease or increase the number of lawsuits brought to vindicate those claims. Some examples illustrate this proposition. In the course of the twentieth century, courts and legislatures expanded the circumstances in which punitive damages were available. The concept behind punitive damages is that they punish defendants for particularly reprehensible behavior—including behavior that does not produce substantial compensatory damages. Punitive damages are generally available for intentional torts—or for behavior falling short of intentionality that is deemed outrageous. That could include behavior ranging from a punch thrown in a fistfight to knowingly selling toxic food products. The potential availability of punitive damages creates a powerful weapon for plaintiffs (and, defendants argue, an unfair advantage). Their power arises because punitives (as they are known in the trade) make the badness of the behavior rather than the damage to plaintiffs the measure of liability, and "badness" is a subjective judgment. And, though punitive damages are awarded in fewer than 10 percent of civil cases where plaintiffs prevail, in some cases involving large institutional defendants, damage awards have been large indeed.

Statutory damages similarly strengthen plaintiffs' claims. These are minimum damage awards decreed by legislation, often in situations in which compensatory damages will be small or difficult to prove. For example, the Copyright Act gives holders whose rights have been infringed a choice between proving lost profits and accepting statutory damages in an amount between $500 and $20,000 for a negligent violation and up to $100,000 for a willful violation. 17 U.S.C. §504(c); Feltner v. Columbia Pictures Television, Inc., 523 U.S. 340 (1998) (holding that a jury must set the amount of statutory damages between the applicable minimum and maximum). Minimum damage provisions (often coupled with separate provisions for attorneys' fees) also arise in the context of small transactions (bad-check statutes provide a common example); they are designed to offset the costs of litigation over matters that are often small in dollar amount and to encourage plaintiffs to enforce public policy by bringing suit.

If punitive and statutory damages have the effect of encouraging litigants to sue in cases where they are available, limiting damages has the opposite effect. In recent decades, some states have sought to curb medical malpractice litigation by putting caps on "noneconomic" damages in such cases. E.g., Cal. Civ. Code §3333.2(b) (capping medical malpractice noneconomic damages at $250,000). Such limitations will, all other things being equal, reduce the number of filings in areas where these limitations apply.

Other damage caps result from judicial decisions. Responding to defendants' arguments that punitive damages were out of control, the U.S. Supreme Court in 2003 ruled that an award of punitive damages more than nine times the compensatory damages in a case will presumptively violate the Due Process Clause. See State Farm Mutual Automobile Insurance v. Campbell, 538 U.S. 408 (2003). Thus, if in *Troupe* plaintiff was awarded punitive damages, they would likely be limited to nine times her compensatory damages (medical expenses, lost wages, and pain and suffering). And all jurisdictions prohibit punitive damages on contract claims.

Finally, consider damages that are, in advance of any lawsuit, negotiated between the parties. Given the difficulty of calculating compensatory damages, in some situations the parties try to agree beforehand about the price of the harm. The most common such situations are contractual, in which the parties may agree to liquidated damages for breach of contract. Their power to so agree is limited in several ways. They may not agree to liquidated damages unless the actual damages would be difficult to calculate. The parties could not, for example, agree to liquidated damages of $1,000 for failure to repay a $500 debt. An example of a statute simultaneously permitting and limiting liquidated damages is Uniform Commercial Code §2-718(1):

> Damages for breach by either party may be liquidated in the agreement but only at an amount which is reasonable in light of the anticipated or actual harm caused by the breach, the difficulties of proof of harm caused by the breach, the difficulties of proof of loss, and the inconvenience or nonfeasibility of otherwise obtaining an adequate remedy. A term fixing unreasonably large liquidated damages is void as a penalty.

b. Categorizing Damages

Troupe also illustrates another aspect of how lawyers think about damages—dividing them into categories. The opinion twice distinguishes between "special" and "general" damages; lawyers also speak of "hard" and "soft" damages and of "economic" and "noneconomic" damages. Several of these categories overlap.

Start with special, economic, hard damages. The case discusses the medical expenses Troupe has already incurred: $13,637.00. Lawyers sometimes call such damages, as to which one can name a precise figure, as "hard" or "special" damages. In *Troupe*, other special damages would include lost income from her house-keeping business: She would presumably have records showing how much she had earned in a typical week and how many weeks she had been out of work. Lawyers would also categorize these as "economic" damages: A damage award would serve to compensate her for specific dollar losses—medical expenses and lost earnings.

By contrast, consider Troupe's claim for pain and suffering. Troupe will not be able to present a receipt for these, but the law treats them as real, compensable injuries. Like pain and suffering, emotional distress may be an element of damages in some cases. So may, in appropriate cases, loss of consortium (harm to a relationship), humiliation, and harm to reputation. These are all examples of general, noneconomic, "soft" damages.

U.S. law uses damages to compensate for these noneconomic harms as well.[*] As you might expect, proving and measuring noneconomic damages presents a challenge. Experienced lawyers and insurance adjusters often use rules of thumb in settling such cases: three times the amount of economic damages for pain and suffering is one common guideline. But these guidelines are not part of law, so juries cannot be instructed to use them. Instead, the parties must offer proof of noneconomic damages. A litigation technique popular among attorneys required to offer such "proof" in physical pain and suffering cases is to ask the jury how much it would take to compensate the plaintiff for a single hour's (or day's) suffering, and then to multiply that number by the expected duration of the pain—sometimes a lifetime. In Beagle v. Vasold, 65 Cal. 2d 166, 417 P.2d 673, 53 Cal. Rptr. 129 (1966), a trial court was reversed for abuse of discretion because it had refused to permit such an argument. Such efforts are in part a result of jury instructions that do not give many guidelines. Following are model jury instructions that offer little guidance to the fact-finder:

> To recover for [past and future physical pain, mental suffering, loss of enjoyment of life, disfigurement, physical impairment, inconvenience, grief, anxiety, humiliation, or emotional distress], [Plaintiff] must prove that [s/he] is reasonably certain to suffer that harm.
>
> No fixed standard exists for deciding the amount of these damages. You must use your judgment to decide a reasonable amount based on the evidence and your common sense.

---

[*] Though we will use the term here, some experienced plaintiffs'-side lawyers avoid saying "noneconomic damages" to a jury, lest jurors treat these damages as less real than other kinds.

Judicial Council of California Civil Jury Instructions, §3905A (2015). To call these general or soft damages is not to minimize their importance: Notice that in *Troupe* only these general damages get the case over the jurisdictional limit.

Notes and Problems

---

1. Test your grasp of the procedural and strategic implications of these principles.

   a. In a breach of contract case, plaintiff asks the court to instruct the jury to award as much damages as it will take to "send the defendant a message" about breaking its promise; what ruling on the request?

   b. Plaintiff's estate and plaintiff's survivors seek to recover damages for the wrongful death of a retired elderly grandparent. There are no lost earnings, and the principal elements of damages will be for the relationships between the deceased and his surviving children and grandchildren. If you represent the plaintiffs, you will want to show a jury the value of the relationships ended by the death—with family pictures, testimony about the frequency of visits to the grandparent, the effect of the grandparent's death on the children's emotional well-being. Whom would you want to testify about what? If you represent the defendant, how, concretely, would you seek to minimize damages—maybe with evidence showing that the children continued to thrive in school and had large networks of family and friends?

   c. Sometimes the need for proof of damages serves not as a barrier but as an aid to recovery. In a claim for personal injuries, the badly injured plaintiff seeks to introduce evidence of her cries of pain during physical therapy; defendant objects that such evidence will prejudice the jury. What is plaintiff's best response?

2. The issues sketched above represent a sample of problems in measuring compensatory damages.

   a. Sometimes the damage in question has no market. In ascertaining such damages courts do not simply ask the plaintiffs how much it would take to compensate them for the harm they have suffered. One reason for not doing so is the parties' understandable temptation to exaggerate the amount.

   b. At other times there is a market, but plaintiff has no access to it. For example, contract doctrines require that the plaintiff mitigate damages by trying to find a substitute for defendant's breach, even if plaintiff has to borrow money to buy the substitute. But what if plaintiff doesn't have good credit? See *Valencia v. Shell Oil Co.*, 23 Cal. 2d 840, 845, 147 P.2d 558, 560 (1944) (plaintiff unable to borrow funds necessary to mitigate damage caused by defendant): "The duty to minimize damages does not require an injured person to do what is unreasonable or impracticable, and, consequently, when expenditures are necessary for minimization of damages, the duty does not run to a person who is financially unable to make such expenditures."

c. A third problem arises from the law's efforts to individualize damages. Such insistence reflects the goal of what might be called the "perfect remedy"— that which provides an exact compensation for the harm suffered by this plaintiff. The goal is noble, but it has its costs, chiefly in the time it takes to establish the precise level of harm. If lawyers and insurance companies regularly use multipliers as rules of thumb, and if predictability is the goal, would statutory schedules (e.g., three times economic damages as pain and suffering in personal injury cases) be a better approach?

3. Courts insisting on such individualization do not mention the cost of vindicating the legal right to compensation—court fees, attorneys' fees, and the like. The reason for this omission is simple: As you will see in Section C of this chapter, American courts do not typically compensate successful litigants for the cost of litigation. This feature of remedial law means that an award of compensatory damages, no matter how precisely calculated, will always fall short of full compensation if plaintiff has to pay her lawyer.

4. As you have seen in the preceding section, lawsuits take time. Time costs money. Courts take account of delay by adding interest to the damages; in cases involving large sums and long delays, the amount of interest and the date at which it starts to accrue will matter. Those rules vary substantially across jurisdictions, making it hard to lay down generally applicable principles. Rules for awarding interest vary depending on whether it is calculated from the time the claim accrues (prejudgment interest) or only during the time between the entry of judgment and the moment when the judgment amount is paid (post-judgment interest).

a. In most jurisdictions, the nature of the harm sued for will determine whether prejudgment interest accrues. The Restatement (Second) of Torts §913 provides for prejudgment interest for the taking of property and for other pecuniary harms if necessary to avoid injustice, but not for bodily injury, emotional distress, or reputational harms. What theory underlies such a distinction? The Restatement (Second) of Contracts §354 provides for prejudgment interest on actions brought to enforce a sum certain (for example, a promissory note), and for interest on other contracts "if justice requires."

b. After judgment is entered, most jurisdictions provide for interest to accrue until the judgment is paid, but the rate of interest varies considerably. Federal law (28 U.S.C. §1961) ties such post-judgment interest to the rate of one-year U.S. Treasury Bills. Some states, however, have fixed rates, which may be above or below the prevailing rate (for example, 10 percent in California. Civ. Proc. Code §685.010 (Matthew Bender 2010)).

2. Specific Relief

Though damages are the most commonly sought remedy, they are not the only available one. Courts may order parties to do things or to refrain from doing them; they also can enlist the help of officials in recapturing personal or real property from defendants wrongfully possessing or occupying it. Lawyers refer to these remedies as specific remedies. Take an agreement for the purchase of a house. If the market drops and the buyers get cold feet, the sellers can sue for the difference between the agreed-on price and the new (lower) market price—a substitutionary remedy. If the market rises and it is the sellers who back away from the agreement, the buyers now have a choice of remedies. They might sue for damages measured by the difference between the contract price and the market price of an identical house—a substitutionary remedy. But another remedy would also be available—an order from the court commanding the sellers, under penalty of contempt, to convey the property. Such a "decree for specific performance" is one among an array of available specific remedies.

Suppose the sellers sign the deed conveying their house, but then refuse to vacate for the new buyers. Under those circumstances the buyers could seek to eject the sellers, getting a court order that required the sheriff to remove them from the premises. Or, suppose when the sellers left, they mistakenly left behind some jewelry. Under those circumstances the sellers could replevy the jewels: A successful action of replevin results in a court order requiring a sheriff to return an item to its owner.

In addition to these specialized remedies, courts have broad power to enter injunctions (court orders directed to parties) commanding them to do or stop doing an act. Some of these orders can be narrow and specific: stop dumping waste on plaintiff's property. Others can be complex and subtle: establish a system of outpatient psychiatric assistance that meets the needs of patients currently institutionalized. In the twentieth century many of the most interesting and controversial remedies were specific: for example, racial integration of schools and places of employment; and changes in the operation of prisons, hospitals, and other institutions.

The power to issue injunctions—as opposed to other forms of specific relief—derives from the jurisdiction exercised by the courts of equity in England and later in the colonies. Since at least the sixteenth century, courts have withheld equitable relief—refusing to grant injunctions and other equitable remedies—unless the plaintiff could demonstrate that the forms of relief offered by the common law were "inadequate." The next case displays a court considering whether and why a legal remedy—damages, in this instance—was inadequate.

Lucy Webb Hayes Natl. Training School v. Geoghegan
281 F. Supp. 116 (D.D.C. 1967)

HOLTZOFF, J.

The plaintiff's prima facie case tends to show the following facts: that defendant Ellen S. Geoghegan has been a patient for a considerable length of time at Sibley

Memorial Hospital, which is maintained and operated by the plaintiff corporation. The hospital is a private hospital. Evidence has been further introduced tending to show that the hospital came to the conclusion that the patient no longer needs hospital care but can be adequately provided for at a nursing home.

After a series of negotiations on June 2nd, 1967 the president of the hospital corporation made a formal demand on the defendant Thomas Geoghegan, the husband of the other defendant, that Ellen Geoghegan, his wife, be transferred from Sibley Memorial Hospital. This demand is worded as follows: "I again request you to make arrangements for the transfer of your wife, Ellen Geoghegan, from Sibley Memorial Hospital." The mere fact that the polite word "request" is used does not detract from the tenor of the letter as a demand.

What, then, is the status of the defendant Ellen Geoghegan when her departure from the hospital has been demanded by the hospital? Manifestly she becomes a trespasser. This action is brought for an injunction to require her removal from the hospital as a trespasser. Obviously an action for damages would be an inadequate remedy.

A private hospital has a right to accept or decline any patient. It has a moral duty to reserve its accommodations for persons who actually need medical and hospital care and it would be a deviation from its purposes to act as a nursing home for aged persons who do not need constant medical care but who need nursing care. There are homes for the aged, there are nursing homes and similar institutions. Hospitals have a duty not to permit their facilities to be diverted to the uses for which hospitals are not intended.

The correspondence introduced in evidence shows that the male defendant takes the position that his wife should remain in the hospital for the remainder of her life. For the hospital to permit that would be to allow a diversion of its facilities to purposes for which they are not intended and would not be in the public interest. An action for damages, of course, would present no solution so far as the plaintiff is concerned because the husband is able and willing to pay whatever the hospital would charge.

It has been established for a great many years that equity will enjoin a continuing trespass or a series of repeated trespasses where an action for damages would not be an adequate remedy. There is a leading English case on that point, London & Northwestern Railway Co. v. Lancashire & Yorkshire Railway Co., Law Reports 4 Equity Cases 174, 179. The Supreme Court has approved and enforced this doctrine on many occasions. . . . This Court had occasion to consider this matter in Potomac Electric Power Co. v. Washington Chapter of the Congress of Racial Equality, 210 F. Supp. 418, 419, and stated, "It is well established that equity may enjoin continuing trespasses, repeated or irreparable injuries to property, or a course of illegitimate interference with business activities, if a remedy by an action for damages is not adequate. This is one of the traditional functions of equity."

It is clear that in this case the damages in an action at law would obviously be inadequate, as has already been stated.

In light of these considerations the defendants' motion to dismiss is denied.

PERSPECTIVES

Equity and the Equitable Tradition

Historically, the power to issue injunctions was lodged not in the courts of common law, but in the Court of Chancery, which administered substantive law and remedies called "equitable." The judge in Chancery was the Lord Chancellor, who was both a judge and a high political official: Imagine that the President's Chief of Staff also ran a judicial system. Because a central function of equity was to solve problems created by the rigidities of common law, and because the Chancellor was, by virtue of his position, sensitive to broader political and social implications of his decisions, equity jurisprudence, as it was called, often took account of factors that a court of common law would not. For example, it often looked to see whether someone seeking an equitable remedy had himself behaved properly—had, as the doctrine put it, "clean hands." It also took explicitly into account the public interest— something you see in *Geoghegan*. And, to a greater extent than common law, it gave substantial discretion to the Chancellor in shaping its rulings. Though equitable remedies in U.S. courts are no longer ordered by gentlemen wearing large wigs, substantive law and the remedies administered still have much of the texture created by centuries of English equity practice.

WHAT'S NEW HERE

- Everyone agrees that the plaintiff hospital is entitled to some remedy; the only argument is about which.
- The discussion revolves around whether damages are an "inadequate remedy." That requirement—through which every request for injunctive relief must pass—leads the court into discussing such matters as the purposes for which hospitals are intended and whether allowing Mrs. Geoghegan to remain in the hospital would be in the "public interest."
- These are not questions that would draw the court's attention were the hospital asking only for damages.
- Notice as well that the inadequacy doctrine puts the defendant husband in the odd position of arguing that, in effect, he wants to pay damages.

Notes and Problems

1. Explain the reasoning that leads the court to conclude that damages—the usual remedy for a trespass—are not adequate. That explanation will lead you out into a discussion of the public interest and then back into a discussion of doctrine as well as the unusual facts of this case.

2. Suppose the Geoghegans remain adamant: He continues to pay the hospital bills, and she remains in her hospital bed. How will the court enforce an injunction?

    a. It could order that the Geoghegans be jailed for contempt of court—a very powerful tool in enforcing injunctions. How likely do you think that is—recalling that the mode of enforcement, like the power to enter an injunction itself, lies in the wise discretion of the court?

    b. Alternatively, it could order that the Geoghegans be fined a set amount for every day during which Mrs. Geoghegan remains in the hospital. Such fines are a common way of enforcing injunctions. Put yourself in the position of the judge: How would you decide on the amount of such a daily fine—keeping in mind that this too is in the broad discretion of the judge?

3. Declaratory Relief

Occasionally, a party has a legal problem that neither damages nor a specific remedy can solve. Imagine, for example, that Alice, whose signature appears on a promissory note due in five years, denies the note's validity. How is Sam, holding the note, to determine whether he has a valuable asset or a worthless piece of paper? He cannot sue for damages until the note is due, and there is no claim for injunctive relief on the facts stated. Meanwhile, witnesses' recollections are fading and Sam, who wants to raise money for a small business, cannot with certainty list the note as an asset. Or suppose Entrepreneur has a potentially important (and profitable) invention he wants to bring to market, but his potential investors are frightened by those in competing industries who contend that his device will infringe their patents. Entrepreneur has as yet suffered no harm and cannot get an injunction or damages—but he wants a court to declare that his invention does not infringe existing patents—allowing him to reassure his would-be investors. Or imagine a theater owner wants to show a film declared obscene by the local prosecutor, who has threatened to prosecute anyone who exhibits the film. Thinking that the film is not obscene, the owner wishes to show it. He wants to abide by the law, however, and doesn't want to risk a jail sentence as the price of guessing wrong about the law of obscenity.

   Once upon a time, Sam, Entrepreneur, and Theater Owner would have been able to rely only on "counsel's opinion" about the legality of their proposed course of action. Under the federal Declaratory Judgment Act, 28 U.S.C. §§2201 and

2202, and similar statutes in almost every state, parties in such circumstances may now seek from a court a declaration of their rights without seeking or being in a position to seek any coercive relief such as damages or an injunction. The procedure for declaratory judgment in the federal courts is governed by Rule 57. Unlike equitable relief, which is available only in the absence of adequate legal remedies, declaratory relief may be chosen by a party even though other remedies are open to her. See Rule 57. In fact, one can see the declaratory judgment statute as designed in part to overcome this limitation.

WHAT'S NEW HERE?

- The plaintiff in an action seeking a declaratory judgment isn't asking either for damages or injunctive relief—just for the court to set forth his legal rights under the circumstances.
- Implicit in every damage judgment or injunction is a declaratory judgment; such judgments say, in effect, "We give judgment in the amount of $X (or enter an injunction) because. . . . " The "because" clause is the implicit declaratory judgment.
- In an action for a declaratory judgment the plaintiff asks only for the "because" clause. Although a plaintiff can seek declaratory relief, damages, and an injunction all in the same case, should she so choose, there are several reasons why a plaintiff might be satisfied with a declaration:
  1. The plaintiff's audience might be a third party—say a bank or potential investor—who just needs to be reassured that the plaintiff is operating within the law.
  2. The plaintiff may be fairly certain the defendant will comply with the law as soon as it has been definitively declared. That will often be the case with governmental defendants.
  3. For strategic reasons a party may want to be the first one to tell her story. If the opposing party has not yet taken an act that would justify coercive relief, an action for a declaratory judgment may allow the party seeking it to lay out her story in the framework she chooses—rather than having to wait and then react to the other side's story.

Who seeks declaratory judgments? "Declaratory judgments are probably sought most often in insurance and patent litigation, but they are available and are used in all types of civil litigation" except state and federal tax disputes, where statutes forbid their use. Wright, Federal Courts 715. Declaratory judgment actions are also used for testing the constitutionality of statutes, though the Supreme Court has proved reluctant to adjudicate public issues without the factual record that often accompanies suits for coercive relief.

Implications

DECLARATORY JUDGMENTS AND THE FEDERAL COURTS

Although Congress passed the federal Declaratory Judgment Act in 1911, the statute has created several knotty problems for the federal courts. Most of these problems lie beyond the boundaries of an introductory course in civil procedure, but brief mention will help connect this topic to other parts of this course and other courses:

- One concerns the line between a hypothetical case and a concrete factual controversy. Article III of the Constitution limits federal courts' jurisdiction to "cases and . . . controversies." Trivially, that means a law student cannot dream up a hypothetical and ask a federal court to resolve it. Because in many declaratory judgment actions no present coercive relief is available, some claims look too much like hypothetical questions—and thus lie outside the boundaries of Article III. In this introductory course we won't probe the line between appropriate and inappropriate actions for declaratory relief.
- Declaratory relief can also raise jurisdictional problems, some of which flow from the interaction of the well-pleaded complaint rule (exemplified in *Louisville & Nashville R.R. v. Mottley*, supra page 210) and the requirements of federal question jurisdiction. The premise of the well-pleaded complaint rule is that courts look at the allegations in a plaintiff's complaint to determine whether federal subject matter jurisdiction exists. Declaratory

judgment actions, however, tend to be brought by potential defendants against those that would sue them (and so are seeking a declaration of their rights regarding the contested issue). How should courts, instructed to follow the well-pleaded complaint rule, view the complaint in a declaratory judgment action that raises a federal question? The courts have said that a party who would assert a federal defense in an action for coercive relief cannot create federal jurisdiction by asserting that defense as a claim for declaratory relief. That means the Mottleys could not have pleaded their way into federal court simply by asking for declaratory relief (even if the statute had existed at the time they brought their case). But the courts have also suggested that if either party could state a claim for coercive relief that would arise under federal jurisdiction, then an action for a declaratory judgment will also "arise under" federal law; it is safe to say that not much more is clear, and that when you study federal jurisdiction in an advanced course you will better understand how vexing the question is.

- Other issues might arise about the interaction between declaratory relief and diversity jurisdiction. Imagine that Insurer, from Texas, sues Joe, from California, in federal court, seeking a declaration that Joe's $100,000 life insurance policy is invalid because he fraudulently misrepresented his medical record in applying for the insurance. Joe challenges diversity jurisdiction, on the grounds that Insurer's complaint does not satisfy the amount in controversy requirement because he seeks no monetary damages. The fact that Insurer does not seek monetary damages does not necessarily mean he cannot sue in federal court. Instead, the court will look to see the value of the declaratory relief. In this case, the value of the declaratory relief would be tied to the amount of insurance that would have to be paid at Joe's death if the policy were valid.

- What about other issues? If P sues D for breach of contract, P bears the burden of producing evidence and the burden of persuasion. But if D sues P for a declaration that D has not violated the contract in question, who should bear these burdens? The case law is again muddled on the subject. And if D sues P for a declaration that D has not breached a contract on which P might have sued either for damages or for specific performance, is either entitled to a jury trial? See Chapter 9.

Notes and Problems

1. Arthur, a citizen of Georgia, agrees that he will build an expensive house for Barbara, a citizen of Florida, using "only top-quality materials." As construction proceeds, Barbara regularly complains that Arthur is skimping on the quality of the materials. Arthur brings an action for declaratory relief in federal court, invoking diversity jurisdiction. Barbara challenges the claim, arguing that there is no case or controversy because she hasn't sued Arthur for breach. What would you decide?

2. Newspaper, about to publish an exposé of corruption in the mayor's office, has concerns about being sued for libel. It believes that its statements are true, and, beyond that, that the "public official" principles of First Amendment doctrine will protect it because none of the statements are recklessly false. Newspaper files an action in federal court for declaratory relief, seeking a declaration that its statements are protected by the First Amendment. What result? Unlike the action for declaratory relief brought by Arthur against Barbara, there is no case or controversy here because there is no actual dispute between the newspaper and the mayor's office. Note, however, that some state courts have more permissive approaches to declaratory judgments—perhaps Newspaper should file in state court instead.

3. Adeline purchases an automobile liability insurance policy. Thereafter she is involved in an accident and asks the insurance company to defend her. During its investigation of the case, insurer learns that Adeline has likely committed fraud on her application (by failing to list a number of traffic violations). Insurer could simply stop defending Adeline, but if its determination that she has committed fraud is incorrect, it will subject itself to a bad faith refusal to

settle the claim, which carries punitive damages. Another alternative is that the insurer could continue to defend her, in which case it might spend many thousands of dollars in unnecessary legal expenses. How might the insurer deploy an action for declaratory judgment to resolve this dilemma?

4. Temporary Remedies

A remedy that comes too late is useless—worse than useless if the client has incurred costs to obtain it. In state and federal courts currently the median time to trial (for those cases that do go to trial) is a bit more than 18 months. Litigants cannot always wait. Interest added to money judgments is one recognition of the importance of delay. But life sometimes demands speed. The battered spouse needs a protective order immediately, not after a year's wait for trial. The small business threatened by a competitor's unlawful action will be bankrupted if it has to wait for trial. Provisional remedies—relief pending final adjudication of the dispute—respond to this need.

Although provisional remedies solve some problems, they create others: Because they must be granted or denied before the case has been heard on the merits, the judge (all temporary relief will be granted by a judge, not a jury) must base her decision on incomplete information and act without the full adversarial exchange that would accompany a trial. This section considers two problems: How should a court decide when to grant temporary relief in the face of incomplete information? And when does the curtailment of ordinary procedures that is necessary to grant temporary relief amount to a denial of due process?

Before addressing these issues notice a spectrum of provisionality created by the Rules and analogous state practices. A final injunction—like that sought in *Lucy Webb Hayes Natl. Training School v. Geoghegan* (page 308)—occurs after a full trial, with all the procedure that entails. But what if time itself will make the eventual remedy meaningless because the threatened harm will already have occurred? In principle, the answer is an order that holds things in place while the court decides whether final relief is appropriate. See Rule 65. Such orders come in three versions with successively smaller procedural protections—and correspondingly greater speed. The preliminary injunction one might think of as "trial lite": It occurs after evidentiary presentations and argument—but with perhaps curtailed discovery and less than complete evidence. Faster—and more temporary—is the temporary restraining order; as the phrase implies, it lasts for a limited time—usually just long enough to have a hearing on the motion for a preliminary injunction. The most dramatic form of the temporary restraining order is the ex parte T.R.O.—ex parte meaning that the order is issued without notice to the opposing party or opportunity for that party to present evidence or argument. Why would a court issue such an order—and why wouldn't it violate the most basic concepts of due process? A careful reading of Rule 65(b) suggests a reason: Suppose that the very act of notifying the opposing party will cause the threatened harm? Perhaps the defendant will spirit the money that might satisfy a damage judgment out of the reach of the court, or retaliate against the spouse or partner seeking the order. In such cases courts issue very short-term orders: Rule 65(b) says no longer than 14 days with a provision for a hearing on two days' notice if sought by the party subject to the order.

a. Preliminary Injunctions and Temporary Restraining Orders: The Basic Problem

Getting from the opening pleading to final relief takes time, and preliminary injunctions (and their siblings, temporary restraining orders) exist to deal with harms that arise from that inevitable delay. But such preliminary relief comes with a built-in problem. First, a court entering such an order necessarily knows less than it would after full evidentiary presentation (that's why it's preliminary). Second, sometimes entering such a temporary order can help the plaintiff only by harming the defendant. The Supreme Court faced such a situation in the next case; did it resolve it correctly? And are the principles it establishes for similar cases the right ones? As you consider these questions, note that, though the case cites various federal statutes, the Court is debating standards that either a state or a federal court might apply in any case seeking a preliminary injunction.

Winter v. Natural Resources Defense Council, Inc.
555 U.S. 7 (2008)

ROBERTS, C.J., delivered the opinion of the Court.

"To be prepared for war is one of the most effectual means of preserving peace." 1 Messages and Papers of the Presidents 57 (J. Richardson comp. 1897). So said George Washington in his first Annual Address to Congress, 218 years ago. One of the most important ways the Navy prepares for war is through integrated training exercises at sea. These exercises include training in the use of modern sonar to detect and track enemy submarines, something the Navy has done for the past 40 years. The plaintiffs complained that the Navy's sonar training program harmed marine mammals, and that the Navy should have prepared an environmental impact statement before commencing its latest round of training exercises. The Court of Appeals upheld a preliminary injunction imposing restrictions on the Navy's sonar training, even though that court acknowledged that "the record contains no evidence that marine mammals have been harmed" by the Navy's exercises.

The Court of Appeals was wrong, and its decision is reversed.

I

[The opinion described the way the Navy uses "mid-frequency active" (MFA) sonar in its training exercises.]

The most effective technology for identifying submerged diesel-electric submarines within their torpedo range is active sonar, which involves emitting pulses of sound underwater and then receiving the acoustic waves that echo off the target. . . .

The waters off the coast of southern California (SOCAL) are an ideal location for conducting integrated training exercises, as this is the only area on the west coast that is relatively close to land, air, and sea bases, as well as amphibious landing areas. . . .

Sharing the waters in the SOCAL operating area are at least 37 species of marine mammals, including dolphins, whales, and sea lions. The parties strongly dispute the extent to which the Navy's training activities will harm those animals or disrupt their behavioral patterns. The Navy emphasizes that it has used MFA sonar during training exercises in SOCAL for 40 years, without a single documented sonar-related injury to any marine mammal. The Navy asserts that, at most, MFA sonar may cause temporary hearing loss or brief disruptions of marine mammals' behavioral patterns.

The plaintiffs are the Natural Resources Defense Council, Jean-Michael Cousteau (an environmental enthusiast and filmmaker), and several other groups devoted to the protection of marine mammals and ocean habitats. They contend that MFA sonar can cause much more serious injuries to marine mammals than the Navy acknowledges, including permanent hearing loss, decompression sickness, and major behavioral disruptions. According to the plaintiffs, several mass strandings of marine mammals (outside of SOCAL) have been "associated" with the use of active sonar. They argue that certain species of marine mammals—such as beaked whales—are uniquely susceptible to injury from active sonar; these injuries would not necessarily be detected by the Navy, given that beaked whales are "very deep divers" that spend little time at the surface.

II

The procedural history of this case is rather complicated. The Marine Mammal Protection Act of 1972 (MMPA), 86 Stat. 1027, generally prohibits any individual from "taking" a marine mammal, defined as harassing, hunting, capturing, or killing it. 16 U.S.C. §§1362(13), 1372(a). The Secretary of Defense may "exempt any action or category of actions" from the MMPA if such actions are "necessary for national defense." §1371(f)(1). In January 2007, the Deputy Secretary of Defense—acting for the Secretary—granted the Navy a 2-year exemption from the MMPA for the training exercises at issue in this case. The exemption was conditioned on the Navy adopting several mitigation procedures. . . .

The National Environmental Policy Act of 1969 (NEPA), 83 Stat. 852, requires federal agencies "to the fullest extent possible" to prepare an environmental impact statement (EIS) for "every . . . major Federal actio[n] significantly affecting the quality of the human environment." 42 U.S.C. §4332(2)(C) (2000 ed.). An agency is not required to prepare a full EIS if it determines—based on a shorter environmental assessment (EA)—that the proposed action will not have a significant impact on the environment. 40 CFR §§1508.9(a), 1508.13 (2007).

In February 2007, the Navy issued an EA concluding that the 14 SOCAL training exercises scheduled through January 2009 would not have a significant impact on the environment. . . .

Shortly after the Navy released its EA, the plaintiffs sued the Navy, seeking declaratory and injunctive relief on the grounds that the Navy's SOCAL training exercises violated NEPA, the Endangered Species Act of 1973 (ESA), and the Coastal Zone

Management Act of 1972 (CZMA). The District Court granted plaintiffs' motion for a preliminary injunction and prohibited the Navy from using MFA sonar during its remaining training exercises. The court held that plaintiffs had "demonstrated a probability of success" on their claims under NEPA and the CZMA. The court also determined that equitable relief was appropriate because, under Ninth Circuit precedent, plaintiffs had established at least a "'possibility'" of irreparable harm to the environment. Based on scientific studies, declarations from experts, and other evidence in the record, the District Court concluded that there was in fact a "near certainty" of irreparable injury to the environment, and that this injury outweighed any possible harm to the Navy.

[After an appeal, the District Court narrowed the terms of its injunction to allow the Navy more flexibility; the Navy continued to challenge the narrowed injunction as unjustified.]

The Court of Appeals further determined that plaintiffs had carried their burden of establishing a "possibility" of irreparable injury. Even under the Navy's own figures, the court concluded, the training exercises would cause 564 physical injuries to marine mammals, as well as 170,000 disturbances of marine mammals' behavior. Lastly, the Court of Appeals held that the balance of hardships and consideration of the public interest weighed in favor of the plaintiffs. The court emphasized that the negative impact on the Navy's training exercises was "speculative," since the Navy has never before operated under the procedures required by the District Court. In particular, the court determined that: (1) the 2,200-yard shutdown zone imposed by the District Court was unlikely to affect the Navy's operations, because the Navy often shuts down its MFA sonar systems during the course of training exercises; and (2) the power-down requirement during [certain] conditions was not unreasonable because such conditions are rare, and the Navy has previously certified strike groups that had not trained under such conditions. The Ninth Circuit concluded that the District Court's preliminary injunction struck a proper balance between the competing interests at stake.

We granted certiorari, and now reverse and vacate the injunction.

III

A

A plaintiff seeking a preliminary injunction must establish that he is likely to succeed on the merits, that he is likely to suffer irreparable harm in the absence of preliminary relief, that the balance of equities tips in his favor, and that an injunction is in the public interest.

The District Court and the Ninth Circuit concluded that plaintiffs have shown a likelihood of success on the merits of their NEPA claim. [The Navy challenged this finding, but the majority opinion found it unnecessary to resolve the parties' disagreement.]

The District Court and the Ninth Circuit also held that when a plaintiff demonstrates a strong likelihood of prevailing on the merits, a preliminary injunction may be entered based only on a "possibility" of irreparable harm. The lower courts held that plaintiffs had met this standard because the scientific studies, declarations, and other evidence in the record established to "a near certainty" that the Navy's training exercises would cause irreparable harm to the environment.

The Navy challenges these holdings, arguing that plaintiffs must demonstrate a likelihood of irreparable injury—not just a possibility—in order to obtain preliminary relief. On the facts of this case, the Navy contends that plaintiffs' alleged injuries are too speculative to give rise to irreparable injury, given that ever since the Navy's training program began 40 years ago, there has been no documented case of sonar-related injury to marine mammals in SOCAL. . . . For their part, plaintiffs assert that they would prevail under any formulation of the irreparable injury standard, because the District Court found that they had established a "near certainty" of irreparable harm.

We agree with the Navy that the Ninth Circuit's "possibility" standard is too lenient. Our frequently reiterated standard requires plaintiffs seeking preliminary relief to demonstrate that irreparable injury is likely in the absence of an injunction. Los Angeles v. Lyons, 461 U.S. 95 (1983). Issuing a preliminary injunction based only on a possibility of irreparable harm is inconsistent with our characterization of injunctive relief as an extraordinary remedy that may only be awarded upon a clear showing that the plaintiff is entitled to such relief.

It is not clear that articulating the incorrect standard affected the Ninth Circuit's analysis of irreparable harm. Although the court referred to the "possibility" standard, and cited Circuit precedent along the same lines, it affirmed the District Court's conclusion that plaintiffs had established a "'near certainty'" of irreparable harm. . . .

As explained in the next section, even if plaintiffs have shown irreparable injury from the Navy's training exercises, any such injury is outweighed by the public interest and the Navy's interest in effective, realistic training of its sailors. A proper consideration of these factors alone requires denial of the requested injunctive relief. For the same reason, we do not address the lower courts' holding that plaintiffs have also established a likelihood of success on the merits.

B

A preliminary injunction is an extraordinary remedy never awarded as of right. In each case, courts "must balance the competing claims of injury and must consider the effect on each party of the granting or withholding of the requested relief." Amoco Production Co., 480 U.S., at 542. "In exercising their sound discretion, courts of equity should pay particular regard for the public consequences in employing the extraordinary remedy of injunction." Romero-Barcelo, 456 U.S., at 312. In this case, the District Court and the Ninth Circuit significantly understated the burden the preliminary injunction would impose on the Navy's ability to conduct realistic training exercises, and the injunction's consequent adverse impact on the public interest in national defense. . . .

This case involves "complex, subtle, and professional decisions as to the composition, training, equipping, and control of a military force," which are "essentially professional military judgments." We "give great deference to the professional judgment of military authorities concerning the relative importance of a particular military interest." As the Court emphasized just last Term, "neither the Members of this

Court nor most federal judges begin the day with briefings that may describe new and serious threats to our Nation and its people." Boumediene v. Bush, 553 U.S. 723, 128 S. Ct. 2229 (2008).

Here, the record contains declarations from some of the Navy's most senior officers, all of whom underscored the threat posed by enemy submarines and the need for extensive sonar training to counter this threat. . . .

[After quoting other military experts the Court continued:] We accept these officers' assertions that the use of MFA sonar under realistic conditions during training exercises is of the utmost importance to the Navy and the Nation.

These interests must be weighed against the possible harm to the ecological, scientific, and recreational interests that are legitimately before this Court. . . .

While we do not question the seriousness of these interests, we conclude that the balance of equities and consideration of the overall public interest in this case tip strongly in favor of the Navy. For the plaintiffs, the most serious possible injury would be harm to an unknown number of the marine mammals that they study and observe. In contrast, forcing the Navy to deploy an inadequately trained antisubmarine force jeopardizes the safety of the fleet. Active sonar is the only reliable technology for detecting and tracking enemy diesel-electric submarines, and the President—the Commander in Chief—has determined that training with active sonar is "essential to national security."

The public interest in conducting training exercises with active sonar under realistic conditions plainly outweighs the interests advanced by the plaintiffs. Of course, military interests do not always trump other considerations, and we have not held that they do. In this case, however, the proper determination of where the public interest lies does not strike us as a close question. . . .

IV

As noted above, we do not address the underlying merits of plaintiffs' claims. While we have authority to proceed to such a decision at this point, doing so is not necessary here. In addition, reaching the merits is complicated by the fact that the lower courts addressed only one of several issues raised, and plaintiffs have largely chosen not to defend the decision below on that ground.

At the same time, what we have said makes clear that it would be an abuse of discretion to enter a permanent injunction, after final decision on the merits, along the same lines as the preliminary injunction. An injunction is a matter of equitable discretion; it does not follow from success on the merits as a matter of course ("a federal judge sitting as chancellor is not mechanically obligated to grant an injunction for every violation of law"). . . .

The judgment of the Court of Appeals is reversed, and the preliminary injunction is vacated to the extent it has been challenged by the Navy.

It is so ordered.

[Justice Breyer's concurring and dissenting opinion is omitted.]

Ginsburg, J., with whom Souter, J., joins, dissenting. . . .

[The first parts of Justice Ginsburg's opinion dealt with the substance of the environmental laws underlying the litigation.]

V

A

Flexibility is a hallmark of equity jurisdiction. "The essence of equity jurisdiction has been the power of the Chancellor to do equity and to mould each decree to the necessities of the particular case. Flexibility rather than rigidity has distinguished it." Weinberger v. Romero-Barcelo, 456 U.S. 305, 312 (1982) (quoting Hecht Co. v. Bowles, 321 U.S. 321, 329 (1944)). Consistent with equity's character, courts do not insist that litigants uniformly show a particular, predetermined quantum of probable success or injury before awarding equitable relief. Instead, courts have evaluated claims for equitable relief on a "sliding scale," sometimes awarding relief based on a lower likelihood of harm when the likelihood of success is very high. 11A C. Wright, A. Miller, & M. Kane, Federal Practice and Procedure §2948.3, p. 195 (2d ed. 1995). This Court has never rejected that formulation, and I do not believe it does so today. . . .

Notes and Problems

---

1. Once one strips away the legal complexities, what's the essentially insoluble problem in this case?

   a. The plaintiffs say what will happen if the Navy proceeds with its training exercises?

   b. The Navy says what will happen if it halts or modifies its training exercises?

   c. That problem, in different guises, is the problem of the preliminary injunction: Sometimes one can't help A without harming B just as irreparably as A says it will be harmed if the order is not entered.

   d. The harm can be of many different kinds. For example, in many business transactions, market conditions will mean that even a short delay makes the transaction financially infeasible. Raider Corporation wants to buy Sluggish Co. for several million dollars. The management of Sluggish seeks a preliminary injunction, alleging that the acquisition will violate securities laws and mean the loss of scores of jobs if Raider tries to cut expenses. Raider opposes the injunction, contending that Sluggish's management is only trying to protect their ill-deserved salaries, and arguing that even a three-week delay (until a fuller hearing can occur) will mean the expiration of their financing for the acquisition. Given the standards for a preliminary injunction articulated in *Winter* how would you, sitting as the district court judge, rule on such a motion?

   e. John Leubsdorf described the "dilemma" of the preliminary injunction as follows:

      > If [the court] does not grant prompt relief, the plaintiff may suffer a loss of his lawful rights that no later remedy can restore. But if the court does grant

immediate relief, the defendant may sustain precisely the same loss of his rights. The dilemma, of course, exists only because the court's interlocutory assessment of the parties' underlying rights is fallible in the sense that it may be different from the decision that ultimately will be reached. The danger of incorrect preliminary assessment is the key to the analysis of interlocutory relief. . . . The court need not consider every harm resulting from an erroneous preliminary decision, but only harm that final relief cannot address.

John Leubsdorf, The Standard for Preliminary Injunctions,
91 Harv. L. Rev. 525, 541 (1978).

If this analysis is valid, does it imply that the more certain a judge is about the correctness of the decision on the merits ("likely to succeed on the merits" in the language of *Winter*), the less she need worry about the special problems of a preliminary injunction?

2. One difficulty arises because often the court—lacking the full development of a record that trial will bring—isn't sure who will finally prevail. What should the judge do then? There are several schools of thought:

   a. The majority opinion succinctly states one approach: "A plaintiff seeking a preliminary injunction must establish that he is likely to succeed on the merits, that he is likely to suffer irreparable harm in the absence of preliminary relief, that the balance of equities tips in his favor, and that an injunction is in the public interest."

   b. Justice Ginsburg's dissenting opinion succinctly states a slightly different approach: "Consistent with equity's character, courts do not insist that litigants uniformly show a particular, predetermined quantum of probable success or injury before awarding equitable relief. Instead, courts have evaluated claims for equitable relief on a 'sliding scale,' sometimes awarding relief based on a lower likelihood of harm when the likelihood of success is very high."

   c. Some lower court opinions express a variation of Justice Ginsburg's sliding scale: "One moving for a preliminary injunction assumes the burden of demonstrating either a combination of probable success and the possibility of irreparable injury or that serious questions are raised and the balance of hardships tips sharply in his favor." Charlie's Girls, Inc. v. Revlon, Inc., 483 F.2d 953 (2d Cir. 1973) (emphasis added).

   d. Does the majority opinion definitively choose one of these approaches? If one construes the holding narrowly, no: The outcome of the case turns on the majority's understanding of the public interest on the facts of the case, rather than the other elements of the standard. After discussing what sounds like the sliding scale standard in disapproving terms ("We agree with the Navy that the Ninth Circuit's 'possibility' standard is too lenient"), the majority opinion then gives two reasons why it need not—and perhaps cannot—base its holding on this aspect of the case:

      i. As the majority notes, the Ninth Circuit's decision did not turn on that standard, since the District Court had found "that plaintiffs had established a 'near certainty' of irreparable harm."

      ii. Instead the Supreme Court could rest its holding on a view of the public interest that sharply diverged from that of the Ninth Circuit—assigning more weight to the military's view of the importance of the sonar exercise for national defense.

3. Focus now on this latter public interest factor, and recall *Lucy Webb Hayes Natl. Training School v. Geoghegan* (supra page 308), which also spoke of the public interest—there of having hospitals devote their care only to patients who need medical attention. Recall that in awarding damages for breach of contract or for negligently inflicted injuries, courts do not debate whether such damages would be in the public interest. Why here?

   a. At one level the answer is fairly simple: For torts and contracts we have concluded, often over centuries, that society functions better if we award damages in such settings, so we don't need to debate the issue anew in each case. By contrast, cases seeking injunctive relief often involve, as do *Winter* and *Geoghegan*, unusual or unique facts—as to which we haven't worked out the public interest.

   b. In a very few categories of injunctive relief cases we've worked that out as well. As you'll learn in Property, courts will almost always order specific performance (a special kind of injunctive relief) for a contract to sell real estate. In cases so ordering one won't find much discussion about the public interest: The court simply decides that if there was a contract the seller will be ordered to convey title.

   c. At another level, the concern about the public interest flows from the equitable tradition (described above at page 310).

4. How did *Winter* get to the U.S. Supreme Court when there was no final judgment? Though appeals in the federal courts generally lie only from final judgments of the district courts (28 U.S.C. §1291), §1292(a)(1) creates an important exception to the final judgment rule, allowing interlocutory appeals from orders "granting, continuing, modifying, refusing or dissolving injunctions, or refusing to dissolve or modify injunctions." Preliminary injunctions are "injunctions" for purposes of the statute. Do the circumstances of *Winter* explain why Congress permitted immediate appeals?

5. Preliminary injunctions are a provisional form of injunctive relief. There are also processes that are in effect provisional monetary relief—attachment and garnishment. The first involves seizure of property (in the case of real property the "seizure" may be accomplished by anything from physical occupation of the land to the symbolic posting of a notice at whatever office keeps track of titles to land). Garnishment involves asking some third party—often the defendant's bank or employer—not to pay defendant money due him because the plaintiff has a claim on it. The justification for these provisional remedies resembles that for the preliminary injunctions: Without them the plaintiff may suffer severe hardship, in some cases extreme enough to render a final remedy meaningless. A plaintiff seeking damages may believe that the defendant will, if given enough time, either dissipate or conceal the assets from which a judgment could be satisfied. Under such circumstances, the plaintiff needs relief before a final judgment. That relief comes, however, at a price to the defendant. As with preliminary injunctive relief, these remedies can work great hardship

on the defendant and give significant power to the plaintiff who obtains such an order. Not only does the attachment or garnishment guarantee the plaintiff that there will be some assets from which a judgment may be satisfied, but it may also provide significant leverage in settlement discussions.

6. Notice who the plaintiff is in *Winter*: an affinity group, discussed in the litigation finance section of this chapter, whose members pay dues to help finance its activities, including its litigation activities. In this case, the NRDC was also probably relying on a fee-shifting statute—the Equal Access to Justice Act, 28 U.S.C. §2412, which grants attorneys' fees in successful actions brought against the United States.

b. Provisional Remedies and Due Process

Preliminary injunctions exist because final remedies can be too slow. Is it possible for provisional remedies to be too fast?

In some situations, the very procedural steps required to obtain a preliminary injunction will cause or exacerbate the threatened harm. For example, a defendant served with notice of an application for an order garnishing her bank account may transfer the money abroad or flee the jurisdiction to avoid service of process. A defendant accused of battering a spouse might inflict new harm if served with a notice of hearing on a preliminary injunction. But the absence of notice collides with another principle: the guarantee of due process. The next case illustrates the collision; it is important in its own right and as a reminder that all procedures are subject to examination under the Due Process Clause. The procedure under scrutiny, replevin, was a common law action more than 800 years old when its modern use was challenged. Historically, replevin arose because feudal landlords, if they thought their tenants were not paying rents and other obligations when due, would, without judicial authorization, seize the tenants' goods, often livestock. The tenants, in turn, would replevy the cattle, by getting an order telling the sheriff to return them until a court had sorted out who owed whom what. Although historically replevin thus represented a debtor's remedy (retrieving the seized cattle from the landlord), in more recent times it has come to be used by creditors—as it is in the next case.

Fuentes v. Shevin

407 U.S. 67 (1972)

STEWART, J., delivered the opinion of the Court.

We here review the decisions of two . . . federal District Courts that upheld the constitutionality of Florida and Pennsylvania laws authorizing the summary seizure of goods or chattels in a person's possession under a writ of replevin. Both statutes provide for the issuance of writs ordering state agents to seize a person's possessions, simply upon the ex parte application of any other person who claims a right to them and posts a security bond. Neither statute provides for notice to be given to the possessor of the property, and neither statute gives the possessor an opportunity to challenge the seizure at any kind of prior hearing. The question is whether these statutory procedures violate the Fourteenth Amendment's guarantee that no State shall deprive any person of property without due process of law.

I

. . . Margarita Fuentes, . . . a resident of Florida[,] . . . purchased a gas stove and service policy from the Firestone Tire and Rubber Co. (Firestone) under a conditional sales contract calling for monthly payments over a period of time. A few months later, she purchased a stereophonic phonograph from the same company under the same sort of contract. The total cost of the stove and stereo was about $500, plus an additional financing charge of over $100. Under the contracts, Firestone retained title to the merchandise, but Mrs. Fuentes was entitled to possession unless and until she should default on her installment payments.

For more than a year, Mrs. Fuentes made her installment payments. But then, with only about $200 remaining to be paid, a dispute developed between her and Firestone over the servicing of the stove. Firestone instituted an action in a small-claims court for repossession of both the stove and the stereo, claiming that Mrs. Fuentes had refused to make her remaining payments. Simultaneously with the filing of that action and before Mrs. Fuentes had even received a summons to answer its complaint, Firestone obtained a writ of replevin ordering a sheriff to seize the disputed goods at once.

In conformance with Florida procedure, Firestone had only to fill in the blanks on the appropriate form documents and submit them to the clerk of the small-claims court. The clerk signed and stamped the documents and issued a writ of replevin. Later the same day, a local deputy sheriff and an agent of Firestone went to Mrs. Fuentes' home and seized the stove and stereo. . . .

Mrs. Fuentes instituted the present action in a federal district court, challenging the constitutionality of the Florida prejudgment replevin procedures under the Due Process Clause of the Fourteenth Amendment. She sought declaratory and injunctive relief against continued enforcement of the procedural provisions of the state statute that authorize prejudgment replevin.

[The second case challenged Pennsylvania's prejudgment replevin process, which, like Florida's, allowed for seizure without prior notice or hearing.]

II

Under the Florida statute challenged here, "[a]ny person whose goods or chattels are wrongfully detained by any other person . . . may have a writ of replevin to recover them. . . ." Fla. Stat. Ann. §78.01 (Supp. 1972-1973). There is no requirement that the applicant make a convincing showing before the seizure that the goods are, in fact, "wrongfully detained." Rather, Florida law automatically relies on the bare assertion of the party seeking the writ that he is entitled to one and allows a court clerk to issue the writ summarily. It requires only that the applicant file a complaint, initiating a court action for repossession and reciting in conclusory fashion that he is "lawfully entitled to the possession" of the property, and that he file a security bond in at least double the value of the property to be replevied conditioned that plaintiff will prosecute his action to effect and without delay and that if defendant recovers judgment against him in the action, he will return the property, if return thereof is adjudged, and will pay defendant all sums of money recovered against plaintiff by defendant in the action. Fla. Stat. Ann. §78.07 (Supp. 1972-1973).

On the sole basis of the complaint and bond, a writ is issued "command[ing] the officer to whom it may be directed to replevy the goods and chattels in possession of defendant . . . and to summon the defendant to answer the complaint." If the goods are "in any dwelling house or other building or enclosure," the officer is required to demand their delivery; but if they are not delivered, "he shall cause such house, building or enclosure to be broken open and shall make replevin according to the writ. . . ." Thus, at the same moment that the defendant receives the complaint seeking repossession of property through court action, the property is seized from him. He is provided no prior notice and allowed no opportunity whatever to challenge the issuance of the writ. After the property has been seized, he will eventually have an opportunity for a hearing, as the defendant in the trial of the court action for repossession, which the plaintiff is required to pursue. And he is also not wholly without recourse in the meantime. For under the Florida statute, the officer who seizes the property must keep it for three days, and during that period the defendant may reclaim possession of the property by posting his own security bond in double its value. But if he does not post such a bond, the property is transferred to the party who sought the writ, pending a final judgment in the underlying action for repossession. . . .

III

For more than a century the central meaning of procedural due process has been clear: "Parties whose rights are to be affected are entitled to be heard; and in order that they may enjoy that right they must first be notified." It is equally fundamental that the right to notice and an opportunity to be heard "must be granted at a meaningful time and in a meaningful manner." . . .

If the right to notice and a hearing is to serve its full purpose, . . . it must be granted at a time when the deprivation can still be prevented. At a later hearing, an individual's possessions can be returned to him if they were unfairly or mistakenly taken in the first place. Damages may even be awarded to him for the wrongful deprivation. But no later hearing and no damage award can undo the fact that the arbitrary taking that was subject to the right of procedural due process has already occurred. "This Court has not . . . embraced the general proposition that a wrong may be done if it can be undone." This is no new principle of constitutional law. . . . Although the Court has held that due process tolerates variances in the form of a hearing "appropriate to the nature of the case," *Mullane v. Central Hanover Tr. Co.*, and "depending upon the importance of the interests involved and the nature of the subsequent proceedings [if any]," *Boddie v. Connecticut*, the Court has traditionally insisted that, whatever its form, opportunity for that hearing must be provided before the deprivation at issue takes effect. "That the hearing required by due process is subject to waiver, and is not fixed in form does not affect its root requirement that an individual be given an opportunity for a hearing before he is deprived of any significant property interest, except for extraordinary situations where some valid governmental interest is at stake that justifies postponing the hearing until after the event." The Florida and Pennsylvania prejudgment replevin statutes fly in the face of this principle. To be sure, the requirements that a party seeking a writ must first post a bond, allege conclusorily that he is entitled to specific goods, and open himself to possible liability in damages if he is wrong, serve to deter wholly unfounded applications for a writ. But those requirements are hardly a substitute for a prior hearing, for they test no more than the strength of the applicant's own belief in his rights.[13] . . .

The minimal deterrent effect of a bond requirement is, in a practical sense, no substitute for an informed evaluation by a neutral official. More specifically, as a matter of constitutional principle, it is no replacement for the right to a prior hearing that is the only truly effective safeguard against arbitrary deprivation of property. While the existence of these other, less effective, safeguards may be among the considerations that affect the form of hearing demanded by due process, they are far from enough by themselves to obviate the right to a prior hearing of some kind. . . .

V

There are "extraordinary situations" that justify postponing notice and opportunity for a hearing. These situations, however, must be truly unusual.[22] Only in a few limited situations has this Court allowed outright seizure[23] without opportunity

---

13. They may not even test that much. For if an applicant for the writ knows that he is dealing with an uneducated, uninformed consumer with little access to legal help and little familiarity with legal procedures, there may be a substantial possibility that a summary seizure of property—however unwarranted—may go unchallenged, and the applicant may feel that he can act with impunity.

22. A prior hearing always imposes some costs in time, effort, and expense, and it is often more efficient to dispense with the opportunity for such a hearing. But these rather ordinary costs cannot outweigh the constitutional right. Procedural due process is not intended to promote efficiency or accommodate all possible interests: it is intended to protect the particular interests of the person whose possessions are about to be taken.

> The establishment of prompt efficacious procedures to achieve legitimate state ends is a proper state interest worthy of cognizance in constitutional adjudication. But the Constitution recognizes higher values than speed and efficiency. Indeed, one might fairly say of the Bill of Rights in general, and the Due Process Clause in particular, that they were designed to protect the fragile values of a vulnerable citizenry from the overbearing concern for efficiency and efficacy that may characterize praiseworthy government officials no less, and perhaps more, than mediocre ones.

Stanley v. Illinois, 405 U.S. 645, 656.

23. Of course, outright seizure of property is not the only kind of deprivation that must be preceded by a prior hearing. In three cases, the Court has allowed the attachment of property without a prior hearing. In one, the attachment was necessary to protect the public against the same sort of immediate harm involved in the seizure cases—a bank failure. Coffin Bros. & Co. v. Bennett, 277 U.S. 29. Another case involved attachment necessary to secure jurisdiction in state court—clearly a most basic and important public interest. Ownbey v. Morgan, 256 U.S. 94. It is much less clear what interests were involved in the third case, decided with an unexplicated per curiam opinion simply citing *Coffin Bros.* and *Ownbey*. McKay v. McInnes, 279 U.S. 820. As far as essential procedural due process doctrine goes, *McKay* cannot stand for any more than was established in the *Coffin Bros.* and *Ownbey* cases on which it relied completely.

for a prior hearing. First, in each case, the seizure has been directly necessary to secure an important governmental or general public interest. Second, there has been a special need for very prompt action. Third, the State has kept strict control over its monopoly of legitimate force: the person initiating the seizure has been a government official responsible for determining, under the standards of a narrowly drawn statute, that it was necessary and justified in the particular instance. Thus, the Court has allowed summary seizure of property to collect the internal revenue of the United States, to meet the needs of a national war effort, to protect against the economic disaster of a bank failure, and to protect the public from misbranded drugs and contaminated food.

The Florida and Pennsylvania prejudgment replevin statutes serve no such important governmental or general public interest. They allow summary seizure of a person's possessions when no more than private gain is directly at stake....

Nor do the broadly drawn Florida and Pennsylvania statutes limit the summary seizure of goods to special situations demanding prompt action. There may be cases in which a creditor could make a showing of immediate danger that a debtor will destroy or conceal disputed goods. But the statutes before us are not "narrowly drawn to meet any such unusual condition." And no such unusual situation is presented by the facts of these cases.

The statutes, moreover, abdicate effective state control over state power. Private parties, serving their own private advantage, may unilaterally invoke state power to replevy goods from another. No state official participates in the decision to seek a writ; no state official reviews the basis for the claim to repossession; and no state official evaluates the need for immediate seizure. There is not even a requirement that the plaintiff provide any information to the court on these matters. The State acts largely in the dark....

VII

We hold that the Florida and Pennsylvania prejudgment replevin provisions work a deprivation of property without due process of law insofar as they deny the right to a prior opportunity to be heard before chattels are taken from their possessor. Our holding, however, is a narrow one. We do not question the power of a State to seize goods before a final judgment in order to protect the security interests of creditors so long as those creditors have tested their claim to the goods through the process of a fair prior hearing. The nature and form of such prior hearings, moreover, are legitimately open to many potential variations and are a subject, at this point, for legislation—not adjudication.[33] Since the essential reason for the requirement of a prior hearing is to prevent unfair and mistaken deprivations of property, however, it is axiomatic that the hearing must provide a real test. "[D]ue process is afforded only by the kinds of 'notice' and 'hearing' that are aimed at establishing the validity, or at least the probable validity, of the underlying claim against the alleged debtor before

---

33. Leeway remains to develop a form of hearing that will minimize unnecessary cost and delay while preserving the fairness and effectiveness of the hearing in preventing seizures of goods where the party seeking the writ has little probability of succeeding on the merits of the dispute.

he can be deprived of his property. . . ." *Sniadach v. Family Finance Corp.* (Harlan, J., concurring).

For the foregoing reasons, the judgments of the District Courts are vacated and these cases are remanded for further proceedings consistent with this opinion.

It is so ordered. Vacated and remanded.

POWELL, J., and REHNQUIST, J., did not participate in the consideration or decision of these cases.

[The dissenting opinion of Justice WHITE is omitted.]

Notes and Problems

---

1. What did the Court hold in *Fuentes*? One way of getting at that answer is to imagine yourself on the staff of a Florida legislative committee shortly after the statutes had been held unconstitutional.

   a. What changes would render the statutes constitutional? One might assume that any revised statute should require a pre-seizure hearing. Such a hearing would obviously satisfy the Due Process Clause. But the opinion does not state that a pre-seizure hearing is required, and states did not interpret the opinion to require one.

   b. Suppose that your legislator-boss tells you that she is under great pressure from finance companies, banks, and large retailers to achieve the necessary changes at minimum disruption of current practices; what is the smallest change in procedures that would render them constitutional?

   c. The least expensive and most widely employed legislative fix was to provide notice and an opportunity for a hearing before seizure. Less than conclusive empirical work in the wake of *Fuentes* suggests that very few debtors availed themselves of such hearings. There is a subsidiary debate about whether this fact demonstrates the lack of plausible objections or simply the absence of adequate counsel for the debtors.

2. *Fuentes* is important in its own right and also as a representative of many circumstances in which due process regulates government actions. In the debtor-creditor context the cases have established the proposition that, except in unusual circumstances, prejudgment seizure of a debtor's property without notice and an opportunity for a hearing is unconstitutional. North Georgia Finishing Inc. v. Di-Chem, Inc., 419 U.S. 601 (1975). But collection attempts do not begin to exhaust the circumstances in which one must consider the meaning of due process.

   a. Connecticut v. Doehr, 501 U.S. 1 (1991), considered a due process challenge to a Connecticut statute permitting the attachment of real estate at the request of a plaintiff in any civil action. The lawsuit was a battery action unrelated to the real estate. The "attachment" consisted of the filing of a lien against the property rather than physical occupation or deprivation of the land; the defendant continued to live in the house throughout the attachment. The Court nevertheless held that, without either a pre-attachment hearing or a bond, there was too serious a risk of error in depriving defendant of a significant asset. On the basis of *Doehr*, some might say that any seizure without the opportunity for a hearing needs special justification.

   b. In United States v. Good, 510 U.S. 43 (1993), the Court held that the exigency of a civil forfeiture action—in which property used for unlawful purposes is seized and forfeited to the government—did not justify the seizure of real property without notice.

3. *Fuentes* says situations in which the state may seize property without prior notice or hearing are "truly unusual." That may overstate the matter; the Court has proved quite flexible about due process, particularly in administrative settings.

   a. Since *Fuentes* the Supreme Court has articulated a generalized framework for deciding when and what sort of hearing is required by due process. Mathews v. Eldridge, 424 U.S. 319 (1976), is the leading case; as described in a subsequent opinion,

> In *Mathews v. Eldridge*, the Court set forth three factors that normally determine whether an individual has received the "process" that the Constitution finds "due": First, the private interest that will be affected by the official action; second, the risk of an erroneous deprivation of such interest through the procedures used, and the probable value, if any, of additional or substitute procedural safeguards; and finally, the Government's interest, including the function involved and the fiscal and administrative burdens that the additional or substitute procedural requirement would entail. By weighing these concerns, courts can determine whether a State has met the "fundamental requirement of due process"—"the opportunity to be heard 'at a meaningful time and in a meaningful manner.'"

   City of Los Angeles v. David, 538 U.S. 715, 716 (2003).

   b. How would you apply the *Mathews v. Eldridge* test to the facts of *City of Los Angeles v. David*? David's car was towed from a tow-away zone. David then paid $134 to retrieve his car, and asked for a hearing to get his money back, contending that his vehicle had been erroneously towed. That hearing occurred 27 days after the towing. Did the length of the delay in the post-seizure hearing violate due process? The Court in *David* concluded it did not. Work through the three *Mathews* factors to think about why the Court came to this conclusion.

   c. Consider another situation. The county health department, in the course of a routine restaurant inspection, finds inadequate refrigeration and rampant rodent infestation, and orders immediate closure. Given the rationale in *Mathews*, is that act unconstitutional because there was no opportunity for a prior hearing? Would the answer be different if the only defect identified by the inspector was a rusty knife blade?

   d. Suppose that a state constitution grants students a "right to an education," a right that would thus be protected against taking by the state without due process. Josephine is a high school student. One day the assistant principal, who has heard that she is disrupting classes, enters her classroom with the school security officers. He orders the officers to remove Josephine from class and tells her she is suspended until she returns with her parents. "What did I do wrong?" shouts Josephine. "You darn well know," replies the assistant principal, and tells her not to come back without her parents. If we assume that a temporary deprivation of schooling is an injury, has the school deprived Josephine of due process?

e. Now vary the preceding scenario slightly. In the changed scenario, the assistant principal responds to Josephine's question by saying, "I heard you've been disrupting classes." Suppose Josephine retorts, "Darn right—except that in this school there's no education to disrupt." On roughly similar facts, the Supreme Court held that the student in question had not been denied due process:

> There need be no delay between the time "notice" is given and the time of the hearing. In the great majority of cases the disciplinarian may informally discuss the alleged misconduct with the student minutes after it has occurred. We hold only that, in being given an opportunity to explain his version of the facts at this discussion, the student first be told what he is accused of doing and what the basis of the accusation is. Since the hearing may occur almost immediately following the misconduct, it follows that as a general rule notice and hearing should precede removal of the student from school. We agree with the District Court, however, that there are recurring situations in which prior notice and hearing cannot be insisted upon. Students whose presence poses a continuing danger to persons or property or an ongoing threat of disrupting the academic process may be immediately removed from school. In such cases, the necessary notice and rudimentary hearing should follow as soon as practicable, as the District Court indicated.

Goss v. Lopez, 419 U.S. 565 (1975).

4. The injunctive equivalent of a seizure without a hearing is a temporary restraining order (or TRO). TROs may be issued with even less process than preliminary injunctions. Indeed, under limited circumstances a TRO may be issued ex parte—that is, without the presence or knowledge of the other party. Situations that might call for such drastic action include those in which there is not time to schedule a hearing (for example, bulldozers are about to excavate an area in which rare and legally protected Native American artifacts have just been discovered) or in which notice itself might trigger the action to be restrained (for example, in the case of a battering spouse).

a. How can such an ex parte TRO be squared with the principles of due process established in *Fuentes* and *Mathews*?

b. Read Rule 65(b), which governs the issuance of TROs in the federal courts. Which of its provisions are constitutionally required?

c. Plaintiff chicken farmer appears in court seeking an ex parte TRO to restrain defendant from conducting excavations by dynamite on defendant's adjacent land. The affidavits submitted with the application say that plaintiff's poultry will have their laying cycles seriously disrupted by such activities and that a two-day delay will enable the plaintiff to move them and prevent this harm. With which requirement of Rule 65(b) does plaintiff's affidavit fail to comply?

5. The *Fuentes* line of cases is based on the Due Process Clause, which forbids only a "state" from denying due process, leaving private action untouched, so long as the private actors do not violate civil or criminal statutes. Self-help repossession, authorized by UCC §9-503 when it can be accomplished without breach of the peace, does not involve state action. Applied to the world of repossession, *Fuentes* will leave those repossessing automobiles largely unaffected but will change the practices of those who sell household appliances and furniture. Why? Because parked cars can be repossessed by private actors from the street without violating any laws. By contrast, household goods will be in households, into which private parties cannot enter—so marshals or the equivalent will be required, thus triggering the state action doctrine.

6. Keep in mind that the issue in *Fuentes* was the constitutionality of prejudgment remedies. Attachment, garnishment, and the like continue to be widely used as means for victorious plaintiffs to collect their judgments.

C. FINANCING LITIGATION

Aside from what courts can do for—or to—them, clients are interested in how much it will cost them to get—or defend against—that relief. Costs of litigation affect clients and lawyers from the very start. The costs of litigation also influence questions about remedies, explored in the prior section of this chapter. Were you to eavesdrop on a conversation between a lawyer and a prospective client, you might be surprised to learn that one of the first things the lawyer wants to know focuses on the remedy sought: What damages are at stake, what injunctive or other relief is sought? The attorney may be trying to understand his client's interests, but will also be thinking about the feasibility of bringing the case. A system that depends on parties to bear the costs of developing the case requires lawyers to think about the amount at stake in relation to the costs of litigating the case. A case that will require thousands of dollars in expert witnesses and hundreds of hours of lawyers' time—but where only $2,000 is at stake—is not viable unless the prevailing party will recover its attorneys' fees from the loser, something that generally happens only when a contract or a statute specifically requires that the loser pay. Similarly, a case in which defendant has a likely meritorious defense that will cost more than the damages claimed is one the lawyer will advise defendant to settle quickly. Conversely, other cases will be inexpensive to bring or defend, even if the amounts at stake are very large.

It is possible (and, we think, illuminating) to think about litigation as an investment. The plaintiff, in bringing his case, is seeking something of value. This could be money in the form of damages. But even in cases seeking entirely equitable relief or a declaratory judgment, the plaintiff is seeking some outcome that is, at a minimum, valuable to him or to a group of similarly situated persons: smaller class sizes in the public schools, increased medical services to low-income patients, cleaner air for the region, or similar outcomes.

The plaintiff who decides to litigate in order to gain something of value must invest his money (and time) in that litigation. This investment decision is actually a series of decisions, as the parties decide whether to begin and then to continue to pursue the case. To understand this investment perspective one must understand two subsidiary points: where the money comes from; and how lawyers and their clients decide whether to continue investing in the suit. We start with the former.

Some costs—the courtroom, the judge, clerical staff, and bailiffs—are borne by society generally, paid for by taxes. This public subsidy is not trivial; in 1993 one state estimated that each "judge-day" of civil litigation cost about $4,000, which is about $6,500 in 2019 dollars. Cal. Code Civ. Proc. §1775(f) (West 2011).

Other expenses are paid by the parties. Some take the form of fees paid directly either to a court or to nonlawyers who perform some service (e.g., expert witnesses, private investigators, court reporters). But attorneys' fees account for much of the cost of litigation in the United States; those fees are often substantial. Relatively high legal fees result in part from the design of the U.S. legal system, which assigns to parties (and their lawyers) responsibility for conducting the suit: Virtually every step of the lawsuit occurs because the lawyer on one side or the other takes some initiative. In other countries a judge or similar official paid by the state assumes some of these responsibilities; that design results in lower legal fees but higher taxes and less party control of litigation strategy.

Legal fees shape contemporary litigation. Any fee system in which the parties bear any costs of litigation will cause cases to be brought, abandoned, or settled on bases other than their legal and factual merits. Financing systems will affect not only how many suits are brought but also which ones; for example, the availability of punitive or statutory damages in a particular case category, combined with contingent fees, will, all other things being equal, move legal resources toward such cases. Conversely, limitations on damage awards will move resources away from such cases. Understanding civil litigation therefore requires comprehending the incentives and barriers to litigation posed by the way in which lawyers are paid. In thinking about fee systems, consider three sorts of incentives: those for the client (when will a prospective litigant be encouraged or discouraged?); those for the lawyer (how will the fee system affect the lawyer's work on the case once it is under way?); and those for the opposing party, who will have their own financing mechanisms and know or can make educated guesses about the financing mechanisms of their adversaries (how will those guesses about financing affect opposition strategy?).

WHAT'S NEW HERE?

- Unlike accidents, lawsuits don't just "happen." Someone has to decide to bring or defend them. Both actions require resources—money. That money can come from the pockets of the parties, insurers, the state, or nonprofit organizations, but someone has to pay. Moreover, conducting a modern lawsuit is a bit like driving a car: The tank needs to filled not just once but repeatedly.
- If you understand litigation finance, you will understand why some lawsuits are brought more frequently than others, why suits settle, why victories or defeats in court are not always what they seem. That knowledge is important no matter where your long-term career interests lie: Lawyers working for legal aid societies or nonprofit organizations need to understand litigation finance just as much as do business lawyers and the plaintiffs' and insurance bars.

1. The "American" and "English" Rules About Attorneys' Fees

Who pays for lawyers' work? Essentially, there are five candidates: the client, the opposing party, third-party financers, society generally (via subsidies or charity), and the lawyer herself (because she does the work for free). Each accounts for a portion of U.S. civil litigation.

The system in which each party pays its own legal fees has come to be known as the American Rule. Under the English Rule (which prevails not only in England but in most of the legal systems of the developed world), the losing party pays both its own fees and those of the other side. In practice, these distinctions are less than absolute: To an increasing extent someone other than the client pays U.S. legal fees, and in Great Britain less than the full amount of actual fees is generally taxed to the other side. Thus these two "rules" do not accurately describe present practice in either country; they serve, however, as useful models and a starting point from which to explore the subject.

The English Rule in its pure form fully compensates a winning plaintiff: She gets both the damages (or other remedy) and the costs of litigation. By contrast, under the pure American Rule, a winning plaintiff has to subtract from any damages recovered the amount charged by his lawyer, and is to that extent made less than whole. Defenders of the American Rule point out that it permits litigants, typically plaintiffs, with tenable but less-than-certain cases to invoke the legal system without fear of having to bear the expense of both their own and the opposition's attorney. That incentive may be particularly important in a political system in which the courts play a significant role (as they do not in Britain) in protecting the constitutional rights of unpopular groups. One might not wish to burden an unsuccessful effort to protect a constitutional right with the legal fees of the victor.

Rule or Practice	*Who Pays the Fees?*	*Resulting Incentives?*
"English"	Loser pays winner's fees	*Encourages* strong but low-damage cases. *Discourages* high-cost "law reform" suits.
"American"	Each party pays own fees	*Encourages* "law reform" suits. *Discourages* strong but low-damage suits.

Let us begin to explore the structure of fee arrangements under the American Rule with a common situation—the client who agrees to pay the lawyer's fee. Often, but not always, agreements take the form of a written contract between lawyer and client, sometimes called a "retainer letter" (from the still-regular practice of requiring a deposit—a retainer—from a client). In some states such written agreements are required in some categories of cases. One common form of agreement calls for the client to pay the lawyer at a specified hourly rate for legal services, plus various costs—photocopying, telephone calls, and the like.

The hourly fee is probably the most common financing mechanism for U.S. litigation. Most contract and commercial litigation, which, as you may recall, accounts for the majority of civil filings, is financed this way. One study done in 2000 found that the median hourly rate for legal fees was about $110 per hour; this average masks very wide variations, with senior lawyers in large urban practices charging over $1,000 per hour and rural solo practitioners charging as little as $75 per hour.

Flat rates mean a lawyer charges a set amount for a particular matter: an uncontested divorce, a will, and so on. Some lawyers use flat rates alone or in combination with other kinds of compensation. Flat rates have the obvious advantage of a predictable, guaranteed fee. Their disadvantages are equally clear. Underestimates are possible: What begins as an uncomplicated conveyance can turn into a nightmare of legal research or title searches, forcing the lawyers to choose between malpractice and very expensive—and uncompensated—work. Yet if the lawyer tries to allow for such contingencies, she risks charging more than the matter warrants or the market will bear. As a consequence, flat rates are most often used for kinds of work that the lawyer thinks will have predictable investments of time: Wills are probably the most common example. Conversely, many lawyers have traditionally resisted handling contested litigation on a flat-rate basis. The last decade, however, has seen erosions of this resistance, and some practice groups that do high volumes of work for a single client have entered into per-case agreements or, sometimes, annual flat rates for all litigation, relying on the law of averages to smooth things out.

Notes and Problems

1. Consider the incentives created by the American Rule.

   a. Andy has a claim for $1,000 arising out of a dispute with a merchant. A competent lawyer estimates that Andy's claim has merit but that handling the claim in even the most economical way will cost $1,500. What will Andy do?

   b. Irma's Grocery is a small family business that does not carry liability insurance. One day Irma receives a summons and complaint from a customer who alleges injuries from a slip and fall. Irma remembers the episode and strongly doubts the customer was injured at all, much less seriously. But when she consults a lawyer she learns that it will cost perhaps $7,000 to defend the claim. The plaintiff's lawyer tells Irma's lawyer his client is willing to settle for $1,500. What will Irma do?

2. How does one defend a legal system in which:

   a. Some meritorious claims and defenses are simply too expensive to vindicate?

   b. A victorious defendant has still "lost" the fees paid to defend her?

2. Insurance, the Contingent Fee, and Alternative Litigation Finance

Thus far, the discussion has assumed that the client will pay legal fees directly out of current assets. Often, however, that will not be the case. Consider an everyday occurrence—an automobile accident like that described in Chapter 1, in which Peters sues Dodge for injuries and property damage. In that common type of litigation in the United States it is unlikely that either side will pay its own legal expenses directly. Both Peters and Dodge will probably have their fees paid through schemes that spread the costs among other similarly situated persons. And recent years have seen an extension of this concept into third-party litigation finance, in which "investors" in a lawsuit will assume major responsibility for its funding.

a. Insurance

Take first Dodge. Suppose he has liability insurance (required in some states and by all auto-finance lenders). In that policy the insurer makes two promises: that it will pay damages up to the policy limit; and that it will provide a lawyer to defend any claim. Most vehicle owners have thus purchased a form of legal insurance. Homeowners' and tenants' insurance policies typically contain similar provisions for claims arising from household accidents, thereby creating a widespread form of legal insurance for potential individual defendants.

Notes and Problems

---

1. Consider how the existence of insurance affects litigation.

   a. You are involved in a vehicle collision in which you sustain substantial uninsured personal injuries and property damage (you carry liability but no collision coverage on your car). You believe it's the other driver's fault, but she declines to pay for your damage and, judging from the looks of her car, probably doesn't have a big bank balance. What determines whether you will sue?

   b. Same scenario, but the other driver is insured for the minimum amount ($10,000 in your state). You consult a lawyer, who concludes that, given contested responsibility for the accident and for the extent of your injuries, it will require at least $8,000 in expert witness fees to bring the case. What likely result?

2. Most standard liability policies that promise to provide the insured's legal defense also give the insurer the power to settle a claim within policy limits without the insured's consent.

   a. Why would an insurance company be reluctant to issue such a policy without a provision giving it control over which lawyer defends the insured?

   b. Why do you suppose the insurers also want to control settlement? Because insurers are paying legal fees for the defense, they want at a minimum to settle cases when legal fees will be more than the proffered settlement. One category of insurance policy where the insured has the right to veto a settlement is, in some states, medical malpractice, where the physician's license may depend on the ability to vindicate her medical judgment in court. Not surprisingly, such medical malpractice insurance policies are more expensive than many other forms of liability policy.

   c. The power to control settlement can also shape litigation. Suppose the same auto accident, this time with a seriously injured plaintiff whose claims, if valid, will warrant high damages. But suppose liability is questionable and the policy limits are $50,000. Plaintiff offers to settle for $50,000; the defendant's insurer declines, litigates on the merits, and loses a $500,000 verdict. In many states, the insured might have an action for "bad faith" refusal to settle the claim within policy limits. If the insured wins such an action, the insurer is liable for the full amount of the verdict and, perhaps, for punitive damages as well. Under such circumstances, one can find insurers settling claims where liability may be questionable, or, sometimes, defending such claims after agreeing in advance to pay any verdict above the policy limit. Suppose you represent a plaintiff in a case where damages will exceed policy limits but the insurer—contesting liability—won't settle. How might you use the threat of bad faith liability to your client's advantage in settlement negotiations?

    d. For some categories of liability insurance, insurers write policies to provide that both legal fees and the amount of the judgment or settlement are subject to the policy limits—this is, for example, a common term in legal malpractice insurance. Under such a policy, $1 million in coverage would support a $200,000 defense and an $800,000 judgment but would not cover all of a $200,000 defense and a $1 million judgment.

    3. In addition to such legal insurance included within liability policies, one finds a small number of "pure" legal insurance policies. Such policies typically provide for a limited amount of prepaid office or telephone consultation and a few standard services at a flat rate. Almost none of them will cover the expenses of any form of litigation, presumably because such expenses are so hard to predict.

Implications

DAMAGES, INSURANCE COVERAGE, AND LITIGATION STRATEGY

Plaintiffs' lawyers will generally be pleased to learn that a defendant has insurance that might cover the damages sought. But complications can arise. Most common forms of liability insurance (auto, homeowners', tenants') cover damages for negligently inflicted injuries—only. Suppose two co-workers, Sally and Ted, are involved in an auto accident in their employer's parking garage. Ted sustains a broken leg, which is expected to heal without lasting effects, and, because of his employer's sick leave, he will not suffer lost wages. Thus far Ted's lawyer will be happy to learn that Sally has auto liability insurance, but he will also understand that in these circumstances compensatory damages are unlikely to be large. Further suppose, however, that Sally and Ted have had a contentious relationship at work (she believes he is trying to undermine her with her supervisor) and that, just before the accident a witness thinks he heard Sally (through her open car window) say something suggesting that she intended to run into Ted. As a matter of law, that opens the door to punitive damages, which could be a multiple of the compensatory damages at stake—a prospect that might at first please Ted's lawyer. But only at first: Many insurance policies do not cover damages for intentionally inflicted injuries or punitive damages. So, if Ted indeed proves that punitive damages are warranted (because Sally acted intentionally), he may thereby have taken the case outside the boundaries of insurance coverage! What should he do?

b. The Contingent Fee

What about Peters, the plaintiff in our hypothetical auto collision case from Chapter 1? His automobile liability policy will provide counsel to defend against any counterclaim the other driver may bring, but it will not pay his attorneys' fees to prosecute his claim as a plaintiff. A peculiarly American fee arrangement—the contingent fee—may, however, perform a similar function. In a contingent fee arrangement, the lawyer typically agrees to represent the client, with the fee to be paid from the proceeds of any settlement or recovery. A standard contingent fee arrangement might award the lawyer 20 percent of a settlement reached before filing suit, 25 percent if suit is filed but no further steps taken, 33 percent if the case goes to trial, and perhaps 50 percent if the case goes to appeal. In return for these hefty chunks taken from the plaintiff's recovery, the lawyer agrees to forgo a fee entirely if there is no recovery: The plaintiff thus eliminates the risk of paying legal fees in a losing cause. For the client with limited funds the idea is often inviting—he pays only if he recovers something. No recovery means no fee.

Most individual plaintiffs seeking damages for personal injuries enter into contingent fee arrangements, even when their finances would permit them to hire a lawyer on an hourly basis and even if they are offered alternatives.

People sometimes praise or malign the contingent fee system without understanding it. To understand it one must consider several perspectives: that of the individual client, the lawyer's other clients, and the lawyer. The client is assured that he will not suffer out-of-pocket expenses for attorney's fees, which may make the client more willing to bring a case where recovery is uncertain. Some have criticized and others have praised the system for this characteristic. This assurance (of a risk-free lawsuit for the client) comes at a cost that becomes apparent if one considers the position of the lawyer and the lawyer's other clients. The lawyer, to be sure, does not charge the plaintiff any fees if the case is lost, but the lawyer has lost the value of his time and incurred expenses—if only such overhead items as rent, payment for digital resources, and paralegal services. Those expenses must be paid, and the only source of payment is the fees generated by clients who have recovered or settled. In setting fees, the lawyer must take the probability of success into account; fees from successful cases must be higher to cover the expenses incurred in unsuccessful cases. To that extent contingent fees cause the successful clients to bear part of the costs attributable to the unsuccessful clients.

To describe it thus is not to condemn the arrangement; the winners are only going to pay legal fees if in fact they recover something, and the guarantee of no fee if they lose may be an assurance for which they would willingly pay the higher fee if they win. Indeed, the prevalence of such arrangements may suggest that all concerned find them satisfactory. An elaborate study of contingent fee lawyers found that their "effective hourly rate" (their mean hourly earnings including both winning and losing cases) was just a few dollars more than their counterparts in the insurance-retained defense bar. Herbert M. Kritzer, The Wages of Risk: The Returns of Contingency Fee Legal Practice, 47 DePaul L. Rev. 267 (1998). A more recent study by the Federal Judicial Center found that plaintiffs' attorneys charging their clients by the hour "reported costs almost 25% higher than those using other billing methods (primarily contingency fee)." Emery G. Lee III & Thomas E. Willging, Federal Judicial Center, Litigation Costs in Civil Cases: Multivariate Analysis, Reporting to the Judicial Conference Advisory Committee on Civil Rules 6 (2010).

One can think of the contingent fee in several ways. For medieval and early modern lawyers it was an antisocial charge that stirred up dissension and disserved society.* This view, still prevalent in parts of the world today, makes a contingent fee a form of criminal activity.

Alternatively, one can see the contingent fee as a form of insurance. The client buys insurance against losing the case; the "premium" is her agreement that if she wins she'll pay a share of her winnings to the lawyer. Just as all drivers who insure with a given insurance company share risks with their fellow-insureds, each contingent fee client pools his risk with that of the other clients of the same lawyer. So long as the lawyer is a good estimator of risks (or has a sufficiently large inventory of cases), the winners and the losers will balance out.

Contingent Fees and Liability Insurance

Financial Arrangement	Who's in the risk pool?	How does the cost get spread?
Liability Insurance	Other policyholders, some of whom will have accidents (or other liability-creating events)	No-accident drivers' premiums subsidize those who have accidents
Contingent Fees	Other clients of that lawyer, some of whom will not recover damages	Fees recovered from winning cases subsidize costs of losing cases

---

*There were three common law crimes, each prohibiting a form of litigation finance now common (and legal); they have names sufficiently exotic that you should learn them if only to impress your relatives with how much you've learned in the first year of law school. Barratry was the "stirring up" of litigation (as, for example, by a lawyer who advertised that certain behavior was actionable). Champerty was the sharing of earnings from litigation (as in a contingent fee). Maintenance was the payment of someone else's litigation expenses (as scores of nonprofit affinity groups do today).

PERSPECTIVES

Changing Attitudes Toward Insurance and the Contingent Fee

In the course of the nineteenth century, U.S. courts struggled with the question of whether either the contingent fee or liability insurance should be lawful.

The case against the contingent fee came from the common law's antipathy to "stirring up trouble," an antipathy that some historians would say was really antipathy about "the wrong sort of people" bringing lawsuits. By the end of the nineteenth century, U.S. courts, unlike their English counterparts, had decided it was lawful, although "careful Victorian[-era] lawyers gave it the same reception they gave ballroom dancing: that the masses engaged in it and the police did not intervene meant only that it was lawful," not desirable. Wolfram, Modern Legal Ethics 527 (1986).

Unease with liability insurance had a different source: Some feared that it would encourage bad behavior. After all, if one takes seriously the idea that negligence is the failure to take reasonable precautions, then negligent defendants had acted in an "unreasonably dangerous" fashion. Some feared that allowing them to insure against the consequences would encourage them to behave in this socially undesirable way. By contrast, many states now require auto drivers and owners to carry liability insurance: Earlier generations might have shaken their heads sadly.

Finally, consider the contingent fee from the lawyer's perspective. Take first the decision to represent a client. For the hourly fee lawyer, each bill-paying client is a source of income, no matter what the merits of her case. Not so for the contingent fee lawyer: For her, only the successful cases will yield any income. Moreover, many cases will require substantial investment by the lawyer—fact investigators, expert witness fees, deposition travel—all of which have to be paid even if there is no recovery. So she may screen her cases more carefully than the hourly fee lawyer, turning away clients for whom recovery is unlikely or damages are likely to be low or uncollectible.

Another incentive may affect the lawyer once she takes the contingent fee case. All lawyers owe their clients the duties of loyalty and competence, but financial self-interest sometimes creates a tension with these ethical obligations. Hourly fee lawyers are paid for their work regardless of the merits of the case; they may, therefore, be tempted to spend more time on the case than it warrants. The contingent fee corrects this problem—by encouraging a lawyer to work as much as necessary to win the case (so that the plaintiff recovers) but not more than is necessary (because doing so would reduce his hourly rate). But the contingent fee creates its own tensions with ethical obligations. The contingent fee can make it far preferable from an attorney's perspective to settle early, even if the plaintiff could recover more were she to wait. Suppose, for example, defendant makes a settlement offer of $10,000 after the plaintiff's lawyer has worked for 10 hours on a case. If the retainer agreement provides that the plaintiff's attorney receives 25 percent of any recovery, the attorney would receive $2,500—meaning that each hour of her time has yielded $250. Imagine that the plaintiff rejects the settlement, the plaintiff's attorney works for another 40 hours on the case, and then defendant makes another settlement offer of $40,000. The plaintiff's attorney's 25 percent fee would amount to $10,000. This amount is larger in absolute terms, but results in a lower per hour fee: $200. The client has ultimate authority to decide whether to accept a settlement agreement, but one can imagine how these financial considerations might affect the lawyer's advice if the client asks, as many clients do, whether the lawyer thinks a settlement offer should be accepted.

Notes and Problems

1. Consider how these arrangements affect actual cases. Suppose an auto accident, with serious injuries but contested liability (was the badly injured plaintiff himself speeding?).

   a. If plaintiff makes a typical fee arrangement with his lawyer, what will it be?
   b. Still supposing such a typical fee arrangement, what considerations should go through the mind of plaintiff's lawyer as she decides whether to represent plaintiff?
   c. If the defendant, who is insured, has a typical fee arrangement with her lawyer, how will that lawyer be paid?
   d. Still supposing a typical fee arrangement, explain why it is very unlikely that defendant's lawyer will need to consider whether to accept defendant as a client.

2. Now suppose the plaintiff is not typical; instead, he's a suspicious law student, who wants from his lawyer a careful explanation of how the lawyer arrives at her fees and whether it might make sense for him to pay an hourly fee instead of the typical arrangement in such a case—a contingent fee. Explain the pros and cons of each arrangement.

3. Suppose the defendant is equally atypical and wants a careful explanation of how the fee arrangements for his lawyer might affect that lawyer's incentives. What would such an explanation sound like—bearing in mind that the insurer is paying the fee of defendant's lawyer?

c. Alternative Litigation Finance

An ordinary banker would not enthusiastically welcome a lawyer applying for a loan with a lawsuit as the only collateral—in part because most bankers are not expert at valuing lawsuits. Over the past decade, however, new forms of litigation finance have emerged in which specialized lenders do essentially that. Some call this form of litigation finance "third-party" finance; others point out that insurers and contingent fee lawyers are themselves third-party financers and prefer "alternative" or "non-traditional" as a more accurate label.

Whatever the label, the field has seen the proliferation of financing mechanisms. Thus far three principal groups of alternative litigation financers have emerged, each with a different business model.*

Consumer Lending.   Some groups lend directly to clients (almost always plaintiffs in personal injury cases), giving them immediate cash in the form of a "loan" that will not be collected if the borrower does not collect a judgment. Moreover, the total repayment will never exceed the amount collected from the judgment or settlement. One study counted nearly 40 such firms in early 2010. If you have recently watched daytime television in any urban area, you will have encountered some of these lenders. They offer rates of interest that vary widely, from about 15 percent upwards and often increase as the time of the "loan" extends. Their business model seems to entail lending only a small percentage (generally 10 percent or less) of what they think might actually be recovered in the underlying lawsuit, often amounting to only a few thousand dollars. Anecdotes suggest that plaintiffs' lawyers are often unhappy when their clients resort to such lenders because the amount that will have to be repaid often can make the client resist what the lawyers think are reasonable settlement offers. Such lenders present alternatives—higher priced alternatives—to an ordinary loan that a consumer might take out. One imagines that many of the borrowers are those who do not have access to ordinary loans, probably because they appear to be bad credit risks. Alternatively, some borrowers who understand the non-recourse feature of these loans may think of them as a

---

* This section relies heavily on the account in Steven Garber, Alternative Litigation Financing in the United States: Issues, Knowns, and Unknowns (RAND 2010, Santa Monica, CA).

way of assuring that they will get some recovery from a lawsuit whose outcome is uncertain; it may be only a thousand dollars, but that's better than nothing, their thinking might go.

Lawyer Lending. Like many businesses large and small, lawyers sometimes borrow to finance expenses incurred while waiting for clients to pay their bills (in the case of hourly fee lawyers) or for judgments and settlements to be paid (in the case of contingent fee lawyers). When the bank lends in such a situation, it is indirectly lending against the expected proceeds, not from a single lawsuit, but from the lawyer's whole portfolio of cases. As one banker who writes loans to lawyers put it:

> One thing we do is to look at a firm's collateral base—its receivables, its inventory, how much it makes. . . . With a plaintiffs' firm, there is no asset base. What they offer is an income stream of several types of cases that will come in over time. So you research their reputation in the marketplace, the size of the organization, the number of cases coming in. . . .
>
> If a lawyer tells you, "I'm going to invest $1 million in this case and it's the only one I have, and I'm sure I'll get paid on June 30," we know that's not how it always works. We are more inclined to lend money to someone who says, "I have seven cases and a business plan that includes a worst-case scenario of what may happen to them."

Michael Grinfeld, Justice on Loan, 19 Cal. Law. 39, 40 (1999). Unlike banks, some lenders lend only to lawyers. These entities usually charge higher interest rates than do banks, for the same reason that the consumer lenders described above charge higher interest rates than banks—because the borrower, here the lawyer, is not a good credit risk. Should a lawyer have to disclose to a client that this is how he is financing his practice?

Direct Investment in Commercial Claims. The preceding two models represent niche-market credit, in which neither lender does much investigation of particular claims. Not so with the third group of alternative financers, who invest directly in lawsuits. They will contract either with parties or with the parties' lawyers, advancing money to finance particular pieces of litigation. Their business model calls for them to assess the merits of commercial litigation offered to them, then to advance sums ranging up to $100 million to finance that litigation; in return they get a share of any recovery. According to the available information (most of the investors in this market are not publicly traded, so information is spotty), they are interested only in major commercial litigation—principally in antitrust, intellectual property, and contract disputes—though one news account described a firm that was investing in divorce litigation of very wealthy individuals. One news report suggested that such funding has attractions both for lawyers and their clients and investors. For lawyers and clients, such funding enables them to undertake high-stakes litigation knowing that they can pursue a case as far as the merits take them. Investors include "pension funds, university endowments family offices and others [that] have collectively pumped more than a billion dollars into the sector in recent years." Sara Randanzo, Litigation Finance Attracts New Set of Investors, Wall St. J. (May 15, 2016).

The questions and the issues raised by this part of the market reverse those of the previous two. The law firms and the entities seeking this form of litigation finance are almost without exception able to finance such litigation themselves, or to borrow at favorable rates to do so. Why, then, might they find this form of finance attractive? Though information is hard to come by, a couple of possibilities suggest themselves. First, the businesses concerned may not want to tie up this much of their working capital in litigation—as the news report just cited put it, such funding "give[s] corporations and law firms a way to shed risk from their balance sheets." They are, after all, in business to make widgets or software or pharmaceuticals and may rather spend their money in an area where they are more familiar with the risks and rewards. An additional attraction might lie in getting a second opinion about the merits of their lawsuit. True, their own lawyers think their case is strong, but it might be reassuring to get another expert to vouch for that—and to back up the assessment by putting millions of dollars behind it. For a law firm the attractions may include the second-opinion feature; for a firm working on a contingent fee basis, accepting an investment of this type also eliminates some of the risk of a zero-recovery outcome.

The broad policy issues involved in this emerging form of finance are quite varied and made more difficult to assess by the circumstance that we have as yet relatively little experience with the form. Moreover, both enthusiasts and critics often make sweeping arguments that fail to distinguish this form of litigation investment from the preceding two.

Alongside the broad policy issues stand some more technical ones. Most states still have on their books prohibitions against champerty and maintenance. Some forms of alternative litigation finance would be unlawful were these laws applied according to their original medieval understandings. Should they be? Probably the strongest argument against such an interpretation emerges if one realizes that both the contingent fee (accepted in every state in the United States) and insurance would also violate the original understanding of these common law crimes. If the contingent fee is lawful, can it be a crime for nonlawyers to do what amounts to the same thing? It's fair to say that working out thoughtful answers to this and other questions will take some time.

Notes and Problems

1. Notice that alongside "alternative" finance lies an entirely accepted form of investment in legal claims: assignment and subrogation.

   a. If you own a patent that you think Evil Infringer is using unlawfully, you can sue the infringer. Or, you can simply sell the patent to Buyer, who then owns it and can sue the alleged infringer: You realize some gain from the patent—whatever Buyer pays you for it—without the expense or uncertainty of a lawsuit. So common is this scenario that the term "patent troll" has come to define an entire business model based on the direct purchase of entire claims. Some bemoan what they believe is excessive litigation generated by such "trolls," but no one proposes that the solution is to make it impossible to sell a patent.

    b. Many insurance contracts contain subrogation clauses. If you are injured in an automobile accident and your health insurer pays your medical bills, it is "subrogated" to your claim against the other driver: If you recover, the health insurer will insist on claiming from the proceeds the amounts it has paid to your doctors and hospital. The existence of subrogated claims ("liens" as they are often called in the trade jargon) may make the prospect of a lawsuit less attractive to your lawyer—because she knows that much of any eventual recovery may be consumed by the claim in subrogation.

2. Of the three forms of alternative finance, direct investment in lawsuits has attracted the most interest and comment. That is in part because the business model is new and in part because some have argued that it violates either professional ethics or good public policy.

    a. Some of the ethics arguments are technical. An investor will want to know a good deal about the lawsuit before it invests. Will disclosure to the investor render information that would otherwise be privileged or protected (see Chapter 7) discoverable by the adversary?

    b. Broader arguments debate the likely effects of direct investment. Will it mean more litigation, which some argue is a bad thing in itself? Will it create better vetting and thus more good—meritorious—litigation?

    c. What effects will it have on the legal profession? At present a limited number of very well-capitalized firms can handle big-stakes litigation on a contingency basis. Direct investment would presumably make that segment of the legal market more competitive. Would that be a good thing?

WHAT'S NEW HERE?

- Maybe nothing, or at least only a little is new here. The firms that extend credit to plaintiffs and to lawyers are simply engaged in a niche of the broader credit market. All the arguments for and against lending in other fields apply here.
- The firms that are making substantial investments directly in individual lawsuits are doing what contingent fee lawyers have been doing for years—investing their time and talent in what they hope will be a profitable outcome. But by making this an explicit investment strategy, these firms have the potential for having wider financial markets share in the risks and potential for profit currently available only to contingent fee lawyers: Two of those firms are publicly traded, making it possible for people to invest directly in other people's lawsuits. That opens a much broader conversation, one that has only begun.

3. Public Subsidies and Professional Charity

Insurance will help only those who have it. Contingent fee systems will help only those who seek to recover money damages (and enough money damages to justify the lawyer's investment of time). Alternative litigation finance will reach only segments of the market for legal services. That leaves substantial numbers of people who could benefit from legal counsel but who have no means to pay for it. But how substantial?

Much depends on how the question is asked. Some would ask how many people would benefit—in the sense of improving their present position—from legal advice or representation but do not think they can spare the money for such assistance. Others would ask how many people handed say, $2,000 (about 20 hours of lawyer's time at about the national median rate), would choose to spend it on legal fees. Legal services organizations often measure need by asking the first question, the response to which yields a picture of widespread unmet legal need. For example, the federally funded Legal Services Corporation (LSC) reported in 2013 that nearly 21 percent of Americans had incomes that qualified them for legal assistance, and the funded agencies are able to assist only a small fraction of that group. The response to the second question suggests that the demand is much lower. Debate occurs over which form of the question is the right one to ask.

However great the need, all agree that it's concentrated in pockets. It helps to separate those needing legal services into plaintiffs and defendants and further to separate plaintiffs into those seeking damages and those seeking relief other than damages. Contingent fee arrangements "cover" people with meritorious claims for significant amounts—providing a market-based form of legal services for plaintiffs seeking money damages. Fee-shifting statutes (infra page 351) can help plaintiffs seeking smaller damages awards or injunctive relief for claims covered by those statutes. Class actions, powered by the common fund theory (infra page 350), can aggregate small claims—though such actions perform better at deterring defendants (and, some would add, compensating lawyers) than at compensating plaintiffs.

What about defendants? In a market economy, people with no insurance and no assets have a grim form of protection against lawsuits: Almost no one intentionally sues a judgment-proof defendant for damages. That leaves two good-sized groups without access to representation: individual plaintiffs with small claims (for whom the legal system has no good answer, regardless of wealth) and persons without liquid assets who are nevertheless sued. This latter group of defendants comprise two large subgroups: holdover tenants (their "asset" is the dwelling they are occupying); and spouses and parents sued for divorce and child custody (one cannot legally end a marriage or establish custody of a child without a court order).

Whatever the measure of need, a range of local, state, and national efforts address it with varying degrees of success. Some of this representation is done by volunteers operating outside a formal organization—lawyers who donate time either as a professional obligation (some bar associations have established minimum amounts of donated time as an obligation of membership) or as a personal act of charity.

At the opposite pole from these individual acts of charity lie the institutions generically referred to as "legal aid." These organizations get their funding from a combination of tax dollars from several levels of government and private philanthropic support. The largest single source of funding comes from the Legal Services Corporation (LSC), a nonprofit organization established by Congress to award grants to legal assistance organizations across the country. In 2016, LSC had a budget of $388 million, and reported that the agencies it funded served 1,760,000 people and closed 736,400 cases. If one does the arithmetic, that amounts to about $200 per person and $516 per case—not an amount that would permit much in the way of legal services.

Legal aid offices typically employ lawyers who deliver assistance directly to clients who seek it. These institutions focus on people of small means faced with eviction, creditors' suits, or domestic violence. They do not take cases that would yield a substantial money recovery, perhaps on the assumption that it is possible to find a lawyer who would take the matter on a contingency basis. Others have argued that such a defensive posture robs legal aid of the ability to challenge the conditions that underlie poverty and oppression in the United States. In the past, such programs have mounted challenges to the existing legal and social order. *Evans v. Jeff D.*, discussed later in this chapter, was financed by legal aid lawyers. Such challenges have sometimes created opposition, especially when publicly subsidized lawyers question some part of the existing political order. In some instances legislatures have responded by trying to limit the kinds of legal work publicly subsidized lawyers can perform for their clients—for example, by forbidding them to sue state and local governments.

If volunteer efforts by individual lawyers mark one end of the spectrum and institutionalized, publicly funded legal aid marks the other, intermediate forms have emerged in recent years that combine features of both systems. In one model, private law firms pledge support, both of money and professional time, to a small organization that functions as a point of client contact and a referral system, matching clients' needs with available professional services. This enables a relatively small organization to deliver legal services many times greater than its budget. It also enables lawyers and firms to participate in pro bono activities with some assurance that they will get a steady flow of such work and that it will match their legal expertise and capacity. Because such organizations are funded by private donations, they also avoid some of the restrictions on practice that governmentally funded aid encounters.

Subsidized legal services formed around a cause—an ethnic, religious, or political group with an agenda for social change—are still another form. The hallmark of such groups is that they solicit funds and memberships with the aim of using those funds to finance litigation that furthers the group's goals. Such groups have been behind major social impact litigation on a range of issues at both ends of the political spectrum. The most prominent example is undoubtedly Brown v. Board of Education, 347 U.S. 443 (1954) (striking down racial segregation in public education), financed largely by the Legal Defense Fund of the National Association for the Advancement of Colored People, a pioneer civil rights group. Analogous affinity groups have funded litigation seeking to advance agendas of reproductive rights, environmental causes, and more. In recent decades, groups from the right side of the political spectrum have mounted their own litigation challenges, sometimes seeking to undo or roll back earlier impact litigation. Almost 50 years after *Brown*, the Supreme Court decided Gratz v. Bollinger, 539 U.S. 244 (2003), striking down a racial preference in admissions for the undergraduate college at the University of Michigan. *Gratz* was financed by the Center for Individual Rights, an organization describing itself as focusing on "defense of individual liberties against the increasingly aggressive and unchecked authority of" government. http://www.cir-usa.org/mission_new.html, visited August 25, 2018.

Finally, recall that every lawsuit receives some public subsidy: the amounts necessary to maintain the judicial establishment—everything from judges' salaries to the electricity bill for the courthouse. Each federal district judgeship (including law clerks, secretarial help, and bailiffs) costs in excess of $500,000 annually just in salaries. This amount does not include real estate costs, the central clerk's office, or general overhead. State judgeships, which are less well supported, would typically have lower costs, but even those costs are substantial. No litigant pays for these direct costs of adjudication. Moreover, the amount of the subsidy falls unevenly. For the great majority of litigants who file a complaint, engage in modest procedural maneuvering, and then settle, the subsidy is small. For litigants who proceed to trial, the subsidy is quite large.

Notes and Problems

---

1. A friend has just separated from her abusive husband and is facing eviction for nonpayment of rent. Unemployed and assetless, she asks you where she can find legal representation. What can you tell her?

2. Just out of law school, you join a small firm in a rapidly expanding suburban area. Because of rapid recent growth, the population has outrun the capacities of a one-person legal aid office largely funded by the county. A number of small law firms have opened practices in this area, and at a Young Lawyers meeting several members raise concerns. Two proposals are made: to lobby the county supervisors for increased legal aid funding; and to organize a system for referring clients to private firms who volunteer to do pro bono representation. You are asked to prepare a short paper outlining the pros and cons of the two proposals. What are your major headings?

4. From Fee Spreading to Fee Shifting

Thus far we have examined means of spreading attorneys' fees, usually the major expense of litigation. Contingent fees and insurance spread fees among particular groups of litigants; public subsidies spread costs among all citizens. There are other "spreading" devices that shade into fee shifting.

a. The Common Fund

Plaintiff brings a lawsuit that benefits him, but in the process also benefits other similarly situated persons. Should those others have an obligation to contribute to the plaintiff's attorneys' fees? Yes, said the U.S. Supreme Court in the late nineteenth century, applying what it took to be a basic principle of equity. Trustees v. Greenough, 105 U.S. 527 (1881). The origin of this theory came in a suit in which a bondholder sued the bond issuer to force payment of the bond. The plaintiff had, by vindicating his interest, helped fellow bondholders to win a valuable legal right. The *Greenough* Court held that the original plaintiff could recover part of his attorney's fee from the fund that his efforts had created—the sum from which the other bondholders would be paid. Notice that this common fund theory requires that the plaintiff's efforts create some fund from which the lawyer's fee can be deducted.

This judicially created doctrine has proved very important in financing class actions, in which one party or a few parties may represent a class of many thousands. If in such a case the class representatives win a judgment or settlement for money damages, they regularly seek a contribution to their fees from the fund created for the benefit of the class. Observe that the common fund theory does not itself shift fees from one party to the other; instead it requires that all who benefit from the recovery share its cost. The common fund theory shares fees among similarly situated persons rather than shifting them to the opposing party in a lawsuit.

Notes and Problems

In which of the following situations will the common fund theory apply?

1. Student A sues the Regents of State University, alleging that they have increased tuition payments without legal authority; she sues on behalf of all students and recovers $4 million in excess tuition payments, to be distributed among those paying the excess tuition.

2. Student B sues the Regents of State University, alleging that the tuition increase about to go into effect is unauthorized. He prevails, and the court enters an injunction forbidding the tuition increase. If Student B had not brought this suit, all students would have been required to pay a higher tuition, the total sum amounting to some $4 million.

You will likely have seen that the common fund applies only in the former case, because there is no pot of money created by the judgment in the latter. Because the common fund theory depends on a fund created by a judgment or settlement against the adversary, it straddles the line between fee spreading and fee shifting. We turn now to purer forms of fee shifting, in which the losing party pays the winner's attorneys' fees. When that happens, the so-called American Rule begins to shade into the English Rule. Since the early 1970s, an increasing amount of U.S. litigation has involved the possibility for such fee shifting, a circumstance that has in turn created sublitigation about the conditions and circumstances for such shifting. Notice that such systems fall into two groups. In their purest form, such fee shifts are symmetrical; that is, the loser pays the winner's fees. But some arrangements only allow some categories of winners to recover their fees from their opponents.

b. By Contract

Today a common form of symmetrical fee shifting arises from contractual agreements. Parties to contracts may provide that if litigation over the contract arises, the loser will pay the winner's legal fees. A lawyer drafting a contract probably commits malpractice if she does not consider such a clause. In theory these provisions may be asymmetrical (tenant pays landlord's lawyer if evicted; landlord doesn't have to pay tenant's lawyer if effort to evict fails), but courts have often interpreted asymmetrical clauses in contracts as symmetrical—loser pays winner's lawyer. Loan agreements and leases often contain such clauses. When a landlord sues a tenant for rent, the tenant may be ordered to pay both the rent and the fee of the landlord's lawyer. The reverse would be true if the tenant sued the landlord for constructive eviction. If the tenant's lease had such a clause, how would it affect her incentives to sue or defend? One often finds such clauses in contracts where the amount in dispute will be relatively small. Do you see why?

c. By Common Law

Even when the parties have not agreed to shift fees, there are exceptions to the American Rule. A well-established situation in which one side may pay the other's legal fee occurs when a plaintiff has groundlessly brought a suit; in most states one element of damages in a subsequent action for malicious prosecution is attorneys' fees for defending the first suit. Beyond any specific statutory authority lies the inherent power of the court to control behavior designed to thwart the just operation of the legal system. Chambers v. NASCO, Inc., 501 U.S. 32 (1991) (upholding imposition of nearly $1 million in fees on party acting in bad faith). In an influential opinion, the U.S. Supreme Court refused to create a generalized common law doctrine shifting fees in "public interest" cases but said that Congress remained free to do so. Alyeska Pipeline Service v. Wilderness Society, 421 U.S. 240, 257 (1975).

d. By Statute

Over the past several decades, state and federal legislatures have enthusiastically accepted the invitation in *Alyeska*. Several hundred federal and several thousand state statutes shift attorneys' fees in various circumstances. Those "exceptions" to the American Rule have grown so numerous that some have asked if the rule still exists in the country that supplied its name. That assessment stretches things—in the most common forms of litigation, fees will still not shift—but it properly highlights the importance of these statutes.

Some such statutes are cast in very broad terms, but most legislatures have been less sweeping, singling out particular substantive areas for fee shifting. These statutes cover many topics—mine safety, truth in lending, consumer product safety, endangered species—but among the most important are those concerning civil rights. The basic provision is in 42 U.S.C. §1988(b):

> In any action or proceeding to enforce . . . [various listed federal civil rights statutes] . . . , the court, in its discretion, may allow the prevailing party, other than the United States, a reasonable attorney's fee as part of the costs.

The statute says a court has "discretion" to award a "prevailing party" fees. Courts have interpreted these terms in ways a casual reader might not suspect. First, the U.S. Supreme Court has held that courts should ordinarily award such fees unless special circumstances render an award unjust—thus sharply limiting the court's discretion. Blanchard v. Bergeron, 489 U.S. 87 (1989). Second, one might think that the statute created a symmetrical entitlement—that an employee who unsuccessfully sued her employer alleging job discrimination would have to pay the defendant's legal fees. Not so, held Christianburg Garment Co. v. Equal Employment Opportunity Commission, 434 U.S. 412 (1978). In light of the legislative history suggesting that Congress wanted to make it easier, not harder, to enforce civil rights, the *Christianburg* Court interpreted the statute to permit routine attorneys' fees awards to prevailing plaintiffs but not to prevailing defendants. A prevailing defendant could get fees only when the plaintiff's claim was "frivolous, unreasonable, or groundless, or that the plaintiff continued to litigate after it clearly became so." Id. at 422. The Supreme Court recently made clear that a defendant can recover fees in a frivolous case resolved in defendant's favor, regardless of whether dismissal was on the merits. CRST Van Expedited, Inc. v. Equal Employment Opportunity Commission, 578 U.S. ___ (2016). Nevertheless, combined, these cases make clear that one-way fee shifting is the rule in civil rights litigation.

Notes and Problems

1. Consider the effect of fee shifting on the filing and conduct of litigation. Client has recently been discharged from her job. Your investigation suggests a breach of the employment contract. There is also a possible racial discrimination claim, which is much more difficult to prove. The potential amounts at stake are not large. How does the choice of which claim to file affect the financing of the case?

2. Suppose you and your client decide to press both claims, with the client agreeing to a contingent fee for any sums recovered in a settlement, and an agreement that you will seek reasonable attorneys' fees from the defendant pursuant to §1988 if you prevail at summary judgment or trial on the racial discrimination claim (there is no fee shifting for the breach of contract claim). In spite of

your best efforts, the employment discrimination claim is dismissed at an early stage. How will this affect your estimate of your potential recovery in the case? Can you tell your client, at this moment, that you are no longer interested in representing her? Ethical rules restrict the ability of a lawyer to withdraw from representation for financial reasons to circumstances in which "the representation will result in an unreasonable financial burden on the lawyer." Model Rule 1.16(a)(5). Losing money on a case in which the lawyer thought he would make money does not qualify as an unreasonable financial burden.

A plaintiff who prevails at trial on a claim for which §1988 applies will be a "prevailing plaintiff" under this statute. Rule 54(d)(2) establishes a procedure for seeking, contesting, and awarding such fees. But most cases will settle before trial. In such cases, the parties can negotiate about fees as well as the portion of the settlement going to the plaintiff. This situation provides an opportunity for the defendant to drive a wedge between lawyer and client, a wedge whose sharpness and power the problem below—based on a seminal Supreme Court case—illustrates.

Problem: How to Lose by Winning

You are a lawyer in a medium-sized firm in a medium-sized city. Wanting to serve the public interest—and maybe get some valuable experience in the process—you volunteer to work on a pro bono case your firm has recently taken on. Your clients are the parents of children with serious developmental disabilities who are cared for in a state institution. The parents seek your firm out because recent work by child psychologists and psychiatrists suggests that, with appropriate treatment, children like these can make far greater educational and social progress than has previously been thought. But the state institution is not giving them such treatment. Federal law gives to all children, including those with special needs, the right to an "appropriate" education. You and your colleagues do research that leads you to believe that the state is failing to provide your clients' children with such an education and that they have a viable legal claim. It will likely cost a good deal to pursue this claim (involving a good deal of expert testimony), and your clients lack the financial resources to fund the case. The pro bono committee of your firm nevertheless authorizes the representation, in part because if your clients prevail, you will be entitled to recover attorneys' fees under the provisions of 42 U.S.C. §1988(b) quoted above. Having obtained your clients' authorization you bring suit in federal district court on their behalf; because there are several hundred parents in the group, you pursue the case as a class action under Rule 23 (more extensively discussed in Chapter 12). The complaint seeks extensive changes in the treatment regime of the children, seeking an injunction that will order those changes. You do not seek damages on behalf of the class. The case progresses, with many motions over the qualifications of various experts, exchanges of reports of experts, depositions, extensive examination of the children's medical records and more, all of which consumes substantial amounts of your firm's time and a considerable amount of money advanced to cover such things as experts' fees.

Just a few weeks before the scheduled trial, the state (the defendant in the case) asks to meet with your firm. At that meeting the state makes an offer to settle. They will agree to make every change sought in your complaint, on one condition: that you waive your entitlement to attorneys' fees. Stunned, you and your colleagues ask for time to talk this over among yourselves and with your client.

Notes and Problems

---

1. First, explain why the lawyers in your firm might find themselves quite upset about this victory. What were they hoping and how have those plans gone awry?

2. As a matter of responsibility, lawyers representing clients are bound to pursue their clients'—not their own—welfare.

3. As a further matter of professional responsibility, clients, not lawyers, have the final authority to accept or reject an offer of settlement. Lawyers who do so without clients' consent risk disbarment. So this is a matter you will have to discuss with your clients (frequently class actions have "named plaintiffs" or a client steering committee that make such decisions).

4. How might plaintiffs' attorneys avoid this situation? Some attorneys have tried through retainer agreements in which their clients promise that they will reject any settlement offer that includes a waiver of fees. But such agreements have been found to be unethical because they restrict a client's ability to accept or reject settlement offers. Another alternative retainer agreement addresses this issue by providing that a client can accept a settlement that does not include fees but then becomes obligated to pay her attorneys a reasonable fee based on their hourly rate and number of hours spent on the case. Such agreements preserve a client's ability to accept a settlement offer that waives the entitlement to attorneys' fees, but imposes significant costs on the client who does so.

5. Why is the state making this offer?

   a. It might be trying to teach lawyers a lesson about not suing it.
   b. Can you articulate another, less vindictive, reason—bearing in mind that it will likely cost a good deal to implement the changes the state is offering?
   c. Such an offer was upheld over the contentions of plaintiffs' counsel that the offer created a conflict of interest and should not be permitted. Evans v. Jeff D., 475 U.S. 717 (1986).

6. Suppose a plaintiff seeks injunctive relief to block some policy of the defendant, and the legal claim is one for which a fee-shifting statute attaches.

   a. If the case goes to judgment and the plaintiff prevails, the court will award the plaintiff injunctive relief and reasonable attorneys' fees.

b. If the case settles, and the defendant is willing to make an allowance for a lawyer's fee, that can be one element of the settlement.

c. Suppose, however, the defendant just gives up, changing whatever policy the lawsuit was challenging. Can the plaintiff claim a fee under the fee-shifting statute? The next case considers that question.

Buckhannon Board and Care Home, Inc. v. West Virginia Department of Health and Human Resources
532 U.S. 598 (2001)

REHNQUIST, C.J., delivered the opinion of the Court.

Numerous federal statutes allow courts to award attorney's fees and costs to the "prevailing party." The question presented here is whether this term includes a party that has failed to secure a judgment on the merits or a court-ordered consent decree, but has nonetheless achieved the desired result because the lawsuit brought about a voluntary change in the defendant's conduct. We hold that it does not.

Buckhannon Board and Care Home, Inc., which operates care homes that provide assisted living to their residents . . . [ran afoul of a state regulation that required residents to be sufficiently ambulatory to get out of burning buildings. Buckhannon and other, similar West Virginia facilities sued, alleging that the state regulation violated several federal housing and disability statutes. Plaintiffs sought injunctive and declaratory relief.].

Respondents agreed to stay enforcement of the cease-and-desist orders pending resolution of the case and the parties began discovery. In 1998, the West Virginia Legislature enacted two bills eliminating the "self-preservation" requirement, and respondents moved to dismiss the case as moot. The District Court granted the motion, finding that the 1998 legislation had eliminated the allegedly offensive provisions and that there was no indication that the West Virginia Legislature would repeal the amendments. Petitioners requested attorney's fees as the "prevailing party" under the FHAA, 42 U.S.C. §3613(c)(2) ("[T]he court, in its discretion, may allow the prevailing party . . . a reasonable attorney's fee and costs"). . . . Petitioners argued that they were entitled to attorney's fees under the "catalyst theory," which posits that a plaintiff is a "prevailing party" if it achieves the desired result because the lawsuit brought about a voluntary change in the defendant's conduct. [Most Courts of Appeals had recognized the "catalyst theory."]

In addition to judgments on the merits, we have held that settlement agreements enforced through a consent decree may serve as the basis for an award of attorney's fees. . . . These decisions, taken together, establish that enforceable judgments on the merits and court-ordered consent decrees create the "material alteration of the legal relationship of the parties" necessary to permit an award of attorney's fees. . . .

We think, however, the "catalyst theory" falls on the other side of the line from these examples. It allows an award where there is no judicially sanctioned change in the legal relationship of the parties. . . . A defendant's voluntary change in conduct, although perhaps accomplishing what the plaintiff sought to achieve by the lawsuit, lacks the necessary judicial imprimatur on the change. . . .

Petitioners nonetheless argue that the legislative history of the Civil Rights Attorney's Fees Awards Act supports a broad reading of "prevailing party" which includes the "catalyst theory." . . .

We think the legislative history cited by petitioners is at best ambiguous as to the availability of the "catalyst theory" for awarding attorney's fees. Particularly in view of the "American Rule" that attorney's fees will not be awarded absent "explicit statutory authority," such legislative history is clearly insufficient to alter the accepted meaning of the statutory term. . . .

Petitioners finally assert that the "catalyst theory" is necessary to prevent defendants from unilaterally mooting an action before judgment in an effort to avoid an award of attorney's fees. They also claim that the rejection of the "catalyst theory" will deter plaintiffs with meritorious but expensive cases from bringing suit. We are skeptical of these assertions, which are entirely speculative and unsupported by any empirical evidence.

Petitioners discount the disincentive that the "catalyst theory" may have upon a defendant's decision to voluntarily change its conduct, conduct that may not be illegal. "The defendant's potential liability for fees in this kind of litigation can be as significant as, and sometimes even more significant than, their potential liability on the merits," *Evans v. Jeff D.*, and the possibility of being assessed attorney's fees may well deter a defendant from altering its conduct.

And petitioners' fear of mischievous defendants only materializes in claims for equitable relief, for so long as the plaintiff has a cause of action for damages, a defendant's change in conduct will not moot the case. . . .[10] We have also stated that "[a] request for attorney's fees should not result in a second major litigation," and have accordingly avoided an interpretation of the fee-shifting statutes that would have "spawn[ed] a second litigation of significant dimension." Among other things, a "catalyst theory" hearing would require analysis of the defendant's subjective motivations in changing its conduct, an analysis that "will likely depend on a highly fact-bound inquiry and may turn on reasonable inferences from the nature and timing of the defendant's change in conduct." . . .

The judgment of the Court of Appeals is Affirmed.

[A concurrence by Justice SCALIA, with whom Justice THOMAS joined, is omitted.]

GINSBURG, J., with whom STEVENS, SOUTER, and BREYER, JJ., joined, dissented.

---

10. Only States and state officers acting in their official capacity are immune from suits for damages in federal court. See, e.g., Edelman v. Jordan, 415 U.S. 651, 94 S. Ct. 1347, 39 L. Ed. 2d 662 (1974). Plaintiffs may bring suit for damages against all others, including municipalities and other political subdivisions of a State, see Mt. Healthy City Bd. of Ed. v. Doyle, 429 U.S. 274, 97 S. Ct. 568, 50 L. Ed. 2d 471 (1977).

The Court today holds that a plaintiff whose suit prompts the precise relief she seeks does not "prevail," and hence cannot obtain an award of attorney's fees, unless she also secures a court entry memorializing her victory. The entry need not be a judgment on the merits. Nor need there be any finding of wrongdoing. A court-approved settlement will do. . . .

In my view, the "catalyst rule," as applied by the clear majority of Federal Circuits, is a key component of the fee-shifting statutes Congress adopted to advance enforcement of civil rights. Nothing in history, precedent, or plain English warrants the anemic construction of the term "prevailing party" the Court today imposes. . . .

Notes and Problems

1. Exactly what was the fight about?

   a. Plaintiffs avoided the threatened shutdown of their nursing homes when the State decided to throw in the towel, either deciding that the plaintiffs' interpretation of federal regulations was correct or that the fight was not worth it. When parties reach that conclusion (and the plaintiffs want the long-term behavior of the defendants to remain as agreed), they sometimes enter into a consent decree, in which the court orders the parties to do what they have already agreed to do. If that had been the end of *Buckhannon*, would the plaintiffs have been able to collect attorneys' fees under the Court's decision?

   b. If so, does it make sense that they cannot collect those fees if the way the State "gives up" is to repeal the offending legislation?

   c. A broader way of asking the preceding question is to ask whether it makes sense to have a rule conditioning attorneys' fees on "judicial imprimatur" in a world in which most cases do not end through judicial action. Most cases end through private settlement agreements, which do not qualify the plaintiffs for fees under §1988. This is true even though settlements will often reflect the law that will be applied if the case was adjudicated.

   d. Suppose the plaintiffs had anticipated the *Buckhannon* principle. Is there any way they could have prevented the dismissal for mootness of their claims?

* * *

This chapter has explored the reasons people litigate. That exploration has taken us from the global and statistical to the minutely doctrinal. We have begun to examine the lawyer's role in litigation by considering the fee system and its potential for linking or separating lawyer and client, but we have not yet begun to examine what lawyers actually do in litigation. The next chapter begins that inquiry by looking at the first step in a lawsuit—the ancient and honorable practice of pleading.

Assessment Questions

Q1. Over the past several decades, civil filings in the United States . . .

   A. Have steadily increased.

   B. Are more likely to involve debt collections than any other type of claim.

   C. Consist mostly of tort cases.

   D. Are concentrated in the federal courts.

Q2. A typical civil lawsuit in the United States . . .

   A. Will be tried to a jury.

   B. Will end in settlement.

   C. Will take two years or less to resolve.

   D. Will, if the plaintiff prevails, likely result in a judgment or settlement in the six-figure range.

Q3. In which of the following cases is it likely that both parties will be paying all of their own lawyers' fees?

   A. Auto accident litigation.

   B. Contract dispute between two small businesses.

   C. Discrimination suit brought under a federal civil rights statute.

   D. Class action suit seeking damages for fraud.

Q4. A pleading alleges "the legal remedy for this injury is inadequate." Such a pleading . . .

   A. Seeks to get the court to dismiss the claim.

   B. Seeks to invoke the court's power to issue an injunction or similar equitable relief.

   C. Describes a case in which the parties will likely at some point argue that a given remedy either is or is not in the public interest.

Q5. Carla sues her employer in federal district court alleging gender discrimination as well as breach of contract. Which of the statements below are correct?

   A. If Carla wins at trial on the employment discrimination claim, the court will order her employer to pay Carla's attorney's fees in addition to any damages or other relief.

   B. If the employer prevails at trial on the employment discrimination claim, the court will order Carla to pay the employer's attorney's fees.

   C. If Carla and the employer settle the case, with the employer offering Carla a check for her claim, the court will order the employer also to pay Carla's attorney's fees.

Q6. In which of the following situations will a court issue an order without even notifying the party against whom the order is issued?

   A. A motion for a preliminary injunction.

   B. A motion for a temporary restraining order.

   C. A motion for an ex parte temporary restraining order.

   D. None: to do so would violate due process.

Q7. Due process . . .

   A. Means that everyone gets a hearing before being deprived of property.

   B. Does not come into question unless the state acts.

   C. Is satisfied so long as the state applies a single procedure to all similarly situated persons.

   D. Is satisfied so long as the state applies the same procedures in a wide range of factual situations.

Analysis of Assessment Questions

Q1. B is the only correct response. Contract cases dominate the civil docket, and more than half of them are actions to collect debts. A is wrong because filings have been flat or decreased in recent years. C is wrong because substantially more contract than tort claims are filed. D is wrong because about 98 percent of civil litigation occurs in state courts.

Q2. B and C are the only correct responses. A is wrong because trials, much less jury trials, will occur only in a small minority of cases. D is wrong because the average case in which the plaintiff prevails results—for both torts and bench-tried contract claims—in judgments between $10,000 and $50,000.

Q3. B is the only correct answer; such parties will typically pay their own lawyers (unless the contract in question calls for the loser to pay the winner's fee). A is wrong because almost all such cases will involve a contingent fee lawyer representing the plaintiff and an insurer-paid lawyer representing the defendant. C is wrong because a fee-shifting statute will give fees to a prevailing plaintiff. D is wrong because under the common fund theory, the plaintiff's lawyer will collect his fee from the award that will be distributed to the plaintiff class.

Q4. B and C are the correct responses. A is wrong because the quoted formula is ancient law jargon contending that the "legal"—meaning available at common law—remedies are inadequate and the court should therefore exercise its equitable powers. Along with those powers comes the court's duty to consider not only the parties' interests but those of the public. See *Lucy Webb Hayes Natl. Training School v. Geoghegan* (supra page 308) and *Winter v. NRDC* (supra page 316).

Q5. Only A is the correct response. B is not correct because, though the federal fee-shifting statute reads as if it contemplated a loser pays winner regime, it has been consistently interpreted to mean that a prevailing plaintiff can collect fees from the defendant, but a prevailing defendant cannot collect from the plaintiff (unless the court finds that the plaintiff's claim was in bad faith). C is incorrect because a fee award requires a judgment; settlement or a change of position by defendant is not enough. *Buckhannon* (supra page 355). Note, however, that the settlement provisions may provide for a fee to the lawyer, or the plaintiff may pay her lawyer from settlement proceeds.

Q6. C is the only correct response. In A and B there will be notice, as well as a hearing—although a truncated one. D is wrong because the courts do allow temporary restraining orders to be issued without notice, though only in the sorts of extreme circumstances contemplated in Rule 65(b).

Q7. B is the only correct response. A is wrong because even when due process does apply, it often requires only the opportunity for a hearing, which will occur only if asked for. C is wrong because, although due process does require the uniform application of procedures, it also requires that the procedures be fundamentally fair—not just that they be uniform. D is spectacularly wrong: The hallmark of the modern Due Process Clause is its flexibility—what process is "due" depends to an extraordinary degree on the circumstances of the case.

CHAPTER 6

Pleading

Our system depends on the parties to move lawsuits forward. Pleadings—the plaintiff's complaint and the defendant's response to that complaint—constitute the first steps. Eighty years ago, the bulk of a course in civil procedure would have consisted of learning the special formulas necessary to bring thirty or so kinds of claims, each of which had a special, formulaic pleading associated with it. Today, for reasons you'll soon see, pleading again stands on center stage, with some claiming that recent judicial interpretations of the Rules have thrown pleading, and, with it, the entire litigation system, into disarray. This chapter aims to describe the changing role of pleading, its current functions, and the sources of the present uncertainty.

Let's start with basics: What *is* a "pleading"? Rule 7(a) defines that term to include the complaint, the answer, and some other initial papers in a lawsuit. Rule 7(b) distinguishes between "pleadings" and "motions," the latter term used to describe any "request for a court order." But, to make things a bit more challenging, sometimes lawyers or judges will describe the "pleading stage" of a lawsuit to include both the papers formally defined as pleadings *and* various motions challenging the sufficiency of the pleadings. This chapter will deal with both.

A. THE STORY OF PLEADING

Pleadings tell the contestants' initial stories. They tell the court why it should bother with the case. They give the other side notice of the disputed terrain. They allow the opposing party to ask the court to sort the dead-on-arrival cases from those that might have merit. They allow the opposing party—via motions—to ask the court to provide rough blueprints for the next steps in litigation. In contemporary practice, pleadings also open the door to the very powerful tools of discovery explored in the next chapter. That's a lot to expect from an initial exchange of documents, and sometimes they fail in one or all of these functions. Moreover, these functions sometimes work at cross-purposes with one another, and the common law system has over the past millennium emphasized now one, now another of these functions.

1. Of Stories and Jurisdiction

The first pleading in a lawsuit—the complaint—lets the plaintiff explain his grievance and asks the court to grant some remedy. Consider two complaints, written 500 years apart:

A Sixteenth-Century Complaint	A Twenty-First-Century Complaint
The King to the Sheriff of Nottinghamshire: greeting. If John Smith shall make you secure to prosecute his claim, then put by gages and safe pledges Richard Jones that he be brought before us on the octave of St. Michael, wheresoever we shall then be in England, to shew wherefore, whereas the same John had delivered a certain horse to the said Richard, at Nottingham, well and sufficiently to shoe, the same Richard fixed a certain nail in the quick of the foot of the aforesaid horse in such a manner that the horse was in many ways made worse, to the damage of him the said John one hundred shillings, as he saith. And have there the names of the pledges and this writ.	Plaintiff John Smith (hereinafter "Plaintiff") alleges: 1. Plaintiff is a citizen of California and Defendant Barbara Jones is a citizen of New York. The matter in controversy exceeds, exclusive of interest and costs, the amount specified by 28 U.S.C. §1332. 2. On July 1, 2018, in a public highway called Wilshire Boulevard in Los Angeles, California, defendant negligently drove a motor vehicle against plaintiff who was then crossing the highway. 3. As a result, plaintiff was thrown down, suffered a concussion, a broken leg and arm and severe internal injuries and was otherwise injured, was prevented from transacting his business, suffered great pain of body and mind, and incurred expenses for medical attention and hospitalization in the amount of $85,000. Wherefore plaintiff demands judgment against defendant in the sum of $125,000.

Notes and Problems

1. The sample on the left is taken from a listing of all the common law writs—some 30-odd different kinds of legal "story"—compiled in 1531, in the reign of Henry VIII. The sample on the right complies with Rule 8 of the Federal Rules

of Civil Procedure, published close to 500 years later. Both tell stories about something that happened (or, more precisely, something that the plaintiff *says* or "alleges" happened) before the lawsuit.

a. Start by describing to yourself, in words you would use in a conversation with a friend, what those two stories are.

b. This elemental story-telling aspect of pleading persists, and a good lawyer never forgets that behind the conventions lie stories. The complaint is the plaintiff's first chance to tell that story, and, within the conventions, an attention-getting story is better than a dull one. Consider what small details in the two complaints might be attributable to this story-telling impulse.

PERSPECTIVES

A Millennium of Pleading

In addition to telling stories about something that happened, both stories also include material you would be unlikely to include if you were describing the stories to your friend. For example, the first complaint contains a greeting to the sheriff of Nottingham (the villain of the Robin Hood legends, but also an actual royal official) and a reference to "gages and safe pledges." The second complaint tells us about the states of which the two parties are "citizens." These extras reveal much about the legal system and provide clues to some of the procedural matters that may be disputed as the case proceeds.

The Court of Common Pleas, Depicted in a Fifteenth-Century Manuscript

The king's greeting to the sheriff provides one example. In medieval England right after the Norman Conquest (in 1066), royal justice (administered by the king, his sheriffs and judges) was special, something extraordinary. Ordinary cases were to be dealt with in local courts and would not involve royal officials. Plaintiffs who wanted to get royal justice—and many did because it quickly gained a reputation as fairer, faster, and generally more efficacious—had to take two steps. First, they had to convince the royal officials that the case was one that warranted royal justice. In early medieval times, this question was debated. Everyone agreed that the royal courts should attend to allegations of breaches of the peace—what today we might call violent crime. Even as royal justice extended to more "peaceful" forms of unlawfulness—failure to pay debts, breach of contract, and negligent injury—the pleadings retained the flavor of outrage. The defendant has not merely failed to keep his word or pay his debt; he has made things worse. Can you see this in the first pleading?

The second thing the plaintiff seeking royal justice had to do was to pay for it. Administering justice was a source of income to the crown, and a plaintiff wanting access to the royal courts had to pay. The writ issued only when the fee was paid, and the "greeting" to the sheriff was also an assurance that the royal coffers had received the right number of shillings—what we would call today a filing fee—from the plaintiff.

Another striking characteristic of medieval royal justice was that—except in cases involving land—there was no such thing as a default judgment: The defendant had to appear for the court to proceed further. Defendants who thought they might lose were understandably reluctant to appear, and so early common law procedure devoted much effort to "encouraging" them to appear. The first stage was, as now, for the sheriff to summon them, and to require that they give him some assurance that they would show up on the date set for trial. The complaint sets the "octave of St. Michael," the week after the feast of St. Michael, on September 29, as the time when the defendant should appear before "us," meaning not the king (though in the Middle Ages the king himself occasionally heard lawsuits) but the royal justices. Defendants assured their appearance in court by two means—by posting what we would now call a bond, called a "gage" (bail bonds are still common in criminal cases, where they assure that defendant will appear) as well as by supplying persons, known as "pledges," who would personally promise to assure defendant's appearance. The writ above thus refers to "gages and safe pledges."

2. Consider now the modern pleading. It is addressed to the court, not to the sheriff, and, because we now have default judgments, it omits gages, pledges, and the like. On the other hand, it begins with a recitation of the state citizenship of the two parties, something that seems quite peripheral to the question of whether Jones's negligence caused Smith's injuries.

   a. In fact, that allegation is analogous to the king's greeting to the sheriff: It establishes the court's jurisdiction. Twenty-first-century federal courts are like medieval royal courts in one respect: They have limited jurisdiction. One basis for that jurisdiction is "diversity of citizenship," defined in the Constitution and in 28 U.S.C. §1332, to which the complaint refers. Note that state court complaints do not generally include a jurisdictional statement as they, in contrast to federal courts, are courts of general jurisdiction—meaning that they can hear all cases, unless a provision of state or federal law restricts their jurisdiction.

   b. If the medieval complaint was focused on getting the defendant to appear, the modern one seems more concerned with the other end of the lawsuit— the nature of injuries and amount of damages claimed by the plaintiff. As we'll see, this "factuality" and a focus on remedies are hallmarks of modern lawsuits.

3. The ingredients of a modern complaint are relatively straightforward. Rule 8(a) contains the recipe—a recitation of the basis for jurisdiction, a "short and plain statement of the claim showing that the pleader is entitled to relief," and "a demand for judgment for the relief sought." The modern recipe is simple. But just as it is deceptively simple to say that a recipe for a soufflé involves only a sauce and some eggs, drafting a complaint requires a bit of art; for most of the rest of this chapter, we'll see instances in which lawyers managed to mess up the recipe and what consequences flowed from their mistakes.

2. Plaintiff's Story, Defendant's Story

Before we go further, keep firmly in mind that the process of pleading, like civil litigation generally, involves *competitive* storytelling. The plaintiff has his tale of woe and outrage, but the defendant typically has a very different version of the events, suggesting that the plaintiff's story is wrong in one of several ways. By far the most common defendant's response, contained in the defendant's first pleading, called the "answer," has been the same for centuries: "I didn't do it" or "That's not what happened." At common law this defense was known as a "traverse" (derived from the Latin sense of "running against"); today it's known as a denial, and finds expression in Rule 8(b).

But both common law and modern procedure offer a set of more technical, "legal" responses. We'll meet most of them in the course of this chapter. Some have to do with the power of the court to hear the case, others with some defect in the way the plaintiff commenced the lawsuit. Rule 12(b) lists a series of such defenses and allows a defendant to assert each as a motion. These motions all have one important feature in common: They do not require the defendant to say whether the allegations of the complaint are true. Instead, they state that the case has some other defect that should cause the court to dismiss it before the defendant has to answer.

One of the more powerful Rule 12(b) motions essentially says that the plaintiff's "story" doesn't matter—doesn't matter because the plaintiff has not told one of the stories that would allow a court to grant a legal remedy. For example, suppose defendant promised to come to plaintiff's party, but failed to show up. However unhappy the disappointed host may be, that story is not one that will cause a court to award damages or other remedy. It's different if the defendant is the caterer and contracted to supply food, but against the invited guest who decides the weather is too bad to attend, the law provides no remedy.

This motion—plaintiff's story doesn't matter, or "so what?"—had the name at common law, and still in some state procedural codes, of "demurrer" (from Latin and French words meaning "delay"); the Rules call this a 12(b)(6) motion. It does two things. First, it admits, for the purposes of the motion, all the facts alleged in the complaint: So if, as in the party invitation example, the plaintiff alleges that he suffered great emotional distress when the defendant failed to show up, a defendant's 12(b)(6) motion admits that distress for the purposes of the motion. Second, the 12(b)(6) motion says that *even if all the facts alleged are true*, the law grants plaintiff no legal remedy—a fancier way of saying that plaintiff's story doesn't matter legally. So when a defendant demurs to a complaint (or, under the Rules, files a 12(b)(6) motion), the question facing the court is whether, assuming the pleaded facts are true, the law provides any remedy. The first several cases in this chapter involve 12(b)(6) motions—and the issue is why the law provides a remedy (or why it doesn't), assuming plaintiff can prove what he alleges—and what the decision of that question tells us about the rules and principles of modern pleading.

3. One Function of Pleading: Establishing the Law

In the United States District Court for the Southern District of Georgia

MICHAEL A. HADDLE,
      Plaintiff

vs.

JEANETTE G. GARRISON [et al.],
      Defendants.

Civ. No. 96-00029-CV-1-AAA

COMPLAINT FOR DAMAGES PURSUANT TO 42 U.S.C. §1985(2) (THE CIVIL RIGHTS ACT OF 1871), THE GEORGIA RICO STATUTE AND GEORGIA LAW OF TORTIOUS INTERFERENCE AND FRAUDULENT CONVEYANCE

NOW COMES Plaintiff MICHAEL A. HADDLE and for this his complaint against Defendants JEANETTE G. GARRISON ("Garrison"), DENNIS KELLY ("Kelly"), PETER MOLLOY ("Molloy"), HEALTHMASTER, INC. ("Healthmaster"), and shows as follows:

Introductory Statement

1. Plaintiff is a citizen and resident of the State of Georgia.
2. Defendant Garrison is a resident of the State of South Carolina.
3. Defendants Molloy [and] Kelly are residents of the Southern District of Georgia.
4. Defendant Healthmaster is a corporation organized and existing under the laws of the State of Georgia with its principal place of business within the Southern District of Georgia.
5. Jurisdiction is proper in this Court over Count I of this Complaint (the Civil Rights Act of 1871) by virtue of 28 U.S.C. §1331. Jurisdiction over Count II (Georgia RICO), Count III (Tortious Interference) and Count IV (Fraudulent Conveyance) is proper in this Court because these Counts are pendent to Count I.
6. Venue is proper in this Court in that most Defendants reside within the Southern District of Georgia and in that the actions of all Defendants as alleged below occurred within the Southern District of Georgia.

General Factual Allegations

7. From September 22, 1986 until approximately April 13, 1995, Plaintiff was employed by Defendant Healthmaster.
8. From approximately April 13, 1995, until his discharge as alleged below, Plaintiff was employed by Healthmaster Home Health Care, Inc., a Georgia corporation whose stock is owned entirely by Defendant Healthmaster.

9. Defendant Garrison has at all relevant times owned 50% of the stock of Healthmaster and controlled Healthmaster until April or May, 1995, when a trustee was appointed for Healthmaster, then a debtor in possession under Chapter II of the federal Bankruptcy Code, by the United States Bankruptcy Court for the Southern District of Georgia.

10. The individual Defendants herein have all served in various capacities as corporate officers and directors of Defendant Healthmaster and of Healthmaster Home Health Care, Inc.

11. Defendant Molloy has at all relevant times been employed by Defendant Healthmaster or Healthmaster Home Health Care, Inc.

12. On March 8, 1995, a grand jury convened in the United States District Court for the Southern District of Georgia, Augusta Division, filed an indictment against Defendants Garrison, Kelly, Healthmaster, and others charging a total of 133 counts of fraud against various defendants, which indictment is enumerated as number CR-195-11 in this Court.

13. Although not indicted, Defendant Molloy was, on information and belief, a target of the ongoing criminal investigation.

14. Plaintiff cooperated with the investigation by federal agents which preceded this indictment and testified pursuant to subpoena before said grand jury and appeared pursuant to subpoena to testify before said grand jury, although his testimony was not actually taken due to the press of time.*

15. As a result of their indictment, Defendants Garrison and Kelly were banned from any participation in the affairs of Healthmaster Home Health Care, Inc., by order of said Bankruptcy Court.

16. On June 21, 1995, after Defendants had become aware that Plaintiff would appear as a witness at the criminal trial of Indictment No. CR 195-11, Defendant Molloy, who was then President of Defendant Healthmaster, having been retained in said position by the trustee, but acting at the direction of Defendants Garrison and Kelly and pursuant to a prior understanding and agreement between these three persons, terminated Plaintiff from his employment at Healthmaster Home Health Care, Inc.

Count I—Conspiracy in Violation of 42 U.S.C. §1985(2) (The Civil Rights Act of 1871)

17. The allegations contained in paragraphs numbered "1" through "16" are incorporated herein by reference.

18. The decision to terminate Plaintiff was made by Defendants and others not in furtherance of the business interests of Defendant Healthmaster, but instead for the purpose of retaliating against Plaintiff for his cooperation with federal agents and his testimony under subpoena to the federal grand jury, and in order to intimidate Plaintiff and others from cooperating with federal agents or testifying in any criminal matters against them including said indictment.

19. Defendants participated in and carried out the decision to terminate Plaintiff, not in furtherance of the business interests of Defendant Healthmaster, but rather to protect themselves as criminal defendants or potential criminal defendants.

20. By means of the described actions, and their agreement and plan to do the same, Defendants have violated 42 U.S.C. §1985(2), in that they have conspired within the State of Georgia to deter, by force, intimidation or threat, a party or witness in the United States District Court for the Southern District of Georgia, from attending such court, or from testifying in any matter pending therein, freely, fully, and truthfully, or to injure such party or witness in his person or property on account of his having so attended or testified, or to influence the verdict, presentment, or indictment of the grand jurors of such court.

---

* [A conversation with plaintiff's lawyer suggested this inconsistent language may be the result of an early draft of the complaint (reflecting some uncertainty about the facts) that then became part of the record on appeal.—Eds.]

21. Plaintiff has been injured in his person and property by the acts of Defendants in violation of 42 U.S.C. §1985(2), and Plaintiff is entitled to recover his damages occasioned by such injury and deprivation against Defendants jointly and severally.

22. Because said Defendants' acts were willful, intentional and malicious, Plaintiff is entitled to recover punitive damages against Defendants jointly and severally.

23. Pursuant to 42 U.S.C. §1988, Plaintiff is entitled to recover his expenses of litigation including a reasonable attorney's fee from said Defendants jointly and severally.

[The counts alleging statutory and common law claims under Georgia law are omitted.]

PRAYER FOR RELIEF

WHEREFORE, Plaintiff demands trial by jury on all counts and judgment as to all Defendants jointly and severally for money damages in such amount for actual damages as the evidence may show and as to all Defendants, jointly and severally, judgment for punitive damages and reasonable attorneys' fees and expenses of litigation, together with all costs of Court and such other and further relief as the Court may deem equitable and just.

WHAT'S NEW HERE?

- This isn't an imagined or a hypothetical pleading. This is the relevant part of a complaint that reached the U.S. Supreme Court and made new law.
- Read it again and ask yourself why the plaintiff's lawyer included each of the sentences in this complaint: What was he trying to do?
- Notice how the complaint shifts back and forth between statements of fact and references to law; the point is to show that the facts alleged fit into the law in such a way as to state a claim.

Notes and Problems

1. As a quick review, start by identifying the three elements required by Rule 8(a).
   a. Where is the jurisdictional allegation?
   b. Where is the "short and plain statement of the claim"?
   c. Where is the prayer for relief?

2. Notice that, though the Rules nowhere require it, the plaintiff has introduced subheadings in the complaint; this practice is quite common, especially in complaints that run more than a paragraph or two. And the plaintiff has obviously supplied a good deal more detail than you might guess from reading the "short and plain statement" requirement of Rule 8(a). Why?

   a. Part of the answer lies in the role of pleading as storytelling. A pleader who has a good story will want to tell it, even if no Rule or case compels him to. This additional detail will show the strengths of the case to the trial judge deciding the case, the defendants, and even, perhaps, the press.

   b. Moreover, this is a case in which many relevant facts will be known to the plaintiff. (Not all: Haddle will have no idea what might have been said about him in discussions of his job performance among defendants.) Since he knows part of the story, why not tell it in a way that puts him in the most attractive—and the defendants in the least attractive—light possible?

3. Haddle has an intuitively attractive story: As he sees it, he was just trying to do the right thing—cooperating with a government investigation of criminal activity—and was fired for it. But not all attractive stories constitute legal claims.

   a. Some states recognize "wrongful discharge" claims; an employee alleging that she was fired without good cause states a wrongful discharge claim. But Georgia at the time of Haddle's case did not recognize such a claim.

   b. So Haddle's lawyer had to look elsewhere. He started with a statute enacted in the wake of the Civil War and aimed at those who sought to intimidate newly freed former slaves by preventing them from using courts to enforce newly granted rights. That statute, now codified as 42 U.S.C. §1985(2), provides:

   > If two or more persons in any State or Territory conspire to deter, by force, intimidation, or threat, any party or witness in any court of the United States from attending such court, or from testifying to any matter pending therein, freely, fully, and truthfully, or to injure such party or witness in his person or property on account of his having so attended or testified . . . the party so injured or deprived may have an action for the recovery of damages, occasioned by such injury or deprivation, against any one or more of the conspirators.

   c. How did Haddle's lawyer turn his grievance into a claim based on §1985(2)? Identify the key sections of the complaint that reframe Haddle's story as a violation of the statute.

4. Now suppose you represent Jeanette Garrison, the defendant. Your client tells you that she did not fire Haddle in retaliation for his grand jury testimony, but for other reasons. You might respond to the complaint by simply filing an answer containing this denial and then proceed toward discovery and trial. But in this case there are two powerful reasons for seeking another solution if it is available.

a. This will be what lawyers call a "he said, she said" case, in which the parties and allied witnesses will present differing versions of the facts and ask a jury to decide whose is most believable. Such factual disputes are both uncertain and expensive to try: There will be depositions of employees, supervisors, and officers of the parties—each deposition likely costing thousands of dollars in lawyer time and deposition expense.

b. Defendants had a special reason for wanting to avoid a "swearing contest" (so called because witnesses are under oath): In the time since the complaint was filed Jeanette Garrison had pleaded guilty to federal felony charges. If defendants go to trial, they will be asking the jury to believe the testimony of a criminal in a case where, on cross-examination, the plaintiff will be able to introduce the following testimony from Jeanette Garrison before the U.S. Senate Committee on Aging:

> My name is Jeanette Garrison. I am a nurse by training. I am married to Joseph Garrison, a now retired anesthesiologist. . . . I was the Chair of the Board and President of Healthmaster, Inc., a Medicare paid home health care company. I also am a convicted felon. I pleaded guilty in July 1995 to ten (10) counts of Medicare fraud. My company and I have repaid the federal and state government sixteen million five hundred thousand dollars ($16,500,000.). I currently am serving a thirty-three (33) month sentence in a federal prison.

So, if there is a defense that will not involve a credibility contest between the defendants and the plaintiff, defendants' lawyers would like to take advantage of it.

c. Is there? Look carefully again at the statute on which the complaint is based, 42 U.S.C. §1985(2). Read it like defendants' lawyers, who are seeking to attack the complaint.

  i. As already noted, the statute requires a conspiracy by two or more persons; clearly Haddle's complaint meets those criteria.

  ii. What is it that the two or more persons must do to trigger liability? Here the statute has two branches: The first focuses on deterring (by force, intimidation, or threat) anyone from testifying in a court proceeding. The second branch speaks of retaliation for having done so.

  iii. Finally, the statute grants a remedy to the party injured "in his person or property."

d. Under Georgia law, any employment agreement that is not for a specified term is considered to be "at will"—that is, terminable by the employer for any reason or for no reason at all. Haddle did not have an employment contract for a specific term. Based on the preceding analysis, defense counsel constructed an argument for the defendants that—however unadmirable their actions may have been—those actions did not violate §1985(2).

WHAT'S NEW HERE?

- The *Notes and Problems* above ask you to act like a lawyer—moving back and forth between a statute creating a civil claim and the facts that a plaintiff bringing such a claim must allege to state a claim.
- That exercise, one that occurs countless times in lawyers' offices every day, is equally important for plaintiff and defendant.
- For the plaintiff it matters because some factual allegation in the complaint has to match each element in the statute or other law creating the claim. For the defendant it matters because if the allegations of the complaint *do not* track the statute or law, then the complaint "fails to state a claim on which relief can be granted" (to quote Rule 12(b)(6)) and will be dismissed by the court if challenged.

Haddle v. Garrison (S.D. Ga. 1996)

Unpublished Opinion, Docket No. 96-00029-CV-1 (S.D. Ga. 1996)

ALAIMO, J.

Plaintiff, Michael A. Haddle, has brought the current litigation seeking damages under Section 1985(2) of Title 42 of the United States Code, and state law. Presently before the Court are four [defendants'] motions to dismiss for failure to state a claim upon which relief can be granted under Rule 12(b)(6) of the Federal Rules of Civil Procedure. For the reasons stated below, Defendants' motions will be Granted.

Facts

Haddle is a former employee of Healthmaster Home Health Care, Inc. He claims that he was improperly discharged from his employment by Defendants in an attempt to deter his participation as a witness in a Federal criminal trial. At the times relevant to this litigation, Haddle concedes that he was an at-will employee.

Discussion

I. Rule 12(b)(6)

Rule 12(b)(6) permits a defendant to move to dismiss a complaint on the grounds that the plaintiff has failed to state a claim upon which relief can be granted. A motion under Rule 12(b)(6) attacks the legal sufficiency of the complaint. In essence, the movant says, "Even if everything you allege is true, the law affords you no relief." Consequently, in determining the merits of a 12(b)(6) motion, a court must assume that all of the factual allegations of the complaint are true. A court should not dismiss a complaint for failure to state a claim unless it is clear that the plaintiff can prove "no set of facts in support of his claim which would entitle him to relief." Conley v. Gibson, 355 U.S. 41, 45-46 (1957).

II. 42 U.S.C. §1985(2)

... In the case at bar, Haddle asserts that he can maintain an action under Section 1985(2) despite the fact that he was defined as an at-will employee during the term of his employment. This is directly contrary to binding precedent of the Eleventh Circuit. Case law states:

> [T]o make out a cause of action under §1985(2) the plaintiff must have suffered an actual injury. Because [Plaintiff] was an at-will employee . . . he has no constitutionally pro-tected interest in continued employment. Therefore, [Plaintiff's] discharge did not con-stitute an actual injury under this statute.

Morast v. Lance, 807 F.2d 926, 930 (11th Cir. 1987). Given the clear language of *Morast*, the Court is required to DISMISS Haddle's claim under Section 1985(2).

[Having dismissed the federal claim, the district court declined to exercise sup-plemental jurisdiction over the state law claims.]

Conclusion

The Court has determined that, under Rule 12(b)(6) Haddle has failed to state a federal claim upon which relief can be granted. His claim under Section 1985(2) is DISMISSED with respect to the above named Defendants. Additionally, all state law claims are DISMISSED WITHOUT PREJUDICE.

Notes and Problems

1. Focus on what is happening here. The court dismisses the case. Why?

    a. Did the district court make a factual determination that Haddle had not been fired? That he had not cooperated with the federal investigation? That he had not agreed to testify before the grand jury? That he had not been fired because of his cooperation with the federal investigation and prosecution?

    b. If not, why was the complaint dismissed?

2. The opinion cites well-settled law that, in deciding a motion under Rule 12(b)(6), the "court must assume that all of the factual allegations of the complaint are true." That phrase provides the key to understanding what a 12(b)(6) motion, or its analogue, the demurrer, is about.

    a. Is the allegation in Paragraph 21 that Haddle was "injured in his person or property" a factual allegation?

    b. If it is a factual allegation, the district court should not have dismissed the complaint. So, if it is not a factual allegation, what is it?

3. The district court's order states that Haddle conceded he was an at-will employee.

    a. Does the complaint itself state that Haddle was an at-will employee?

    b. Is it reasonable to treat the complaint as conceding that Haddle was an at-will employee because it does not allege that his employment was for a specified term? Is it possible that the concession the district court refers to was made somewhere other than in the complaint itself? Imagine oral argument on the motion to dismiss, at which the judge asked Haddle's lawyer if he was contending that his client had some form of protected employment. The lawyer says no. At that point the judge could ask that the complaint be amended to make that clear or could simply treat the concession as part of the pleading as it stood.

4. To distinguish a 12(b)(6) motion from other attacks on plaintiff's claim, imagine some alternative scenarios. Suppose the defendants had moved to dismiss on the ground that Haddle had quit his job and had not been fired, and defendants had submitted in support of the motion a letter signed by Haddle admitting he had quit. Explain why, in such a scenario, the district court could not have granted a motion to dismiss under Rule 12(b)(6). It would, instead, be handled under Rule 12(d), to which we will soon turn.

5. In both state and federal courts, when a complaint fails to state a claim, the court will almost always allow the plaintiff "leave to amend"—meaning a chance to add allegations to the complaint that would render it valid. If the plaintiff seeks leave, and if the court denies it, an appellate court will likely reverse on the grounds that failure to grant leave to amend the complaint is an abuse of discretion.

    a. Yet, in the district court's opinion above, the judge makes no mention of leave to amend. That's very likely because Haddle's lawyer did not seek such leave—because he thought that he had already pleaded all the facts he truthfully could, and it would thus be futile to try to amend the complaint.

    b. For example, if the court had granted leave to amend, Haddle's lawyer could have added allegations that his contract stated he would not be dismissed except for good cause. Given that these allegations are untrue, there's a good reason Haddle's lawyer did not thus amend the complaint (as you will see later in this chapter, when we discuss Rule 11).

6. After the district court's dismissal, the lawyers in *Haddle v. Garrison* might be having quite different reactions to the case.

    a. Defendants' lawyers might be breathing a deep sigh of relief and may be even congratulating themselves a little. Why? Obviously, they won the case, but why might they also be pleased about the way they won?

b. Plaintiff's lawyer would obviously have a different reaction. How bad a loss is this? For a plaintiff and his lawyer, the worst loss is one that has also been expensive, in the sense that lawyer and client have invested heavily in the case before the loss. Do you imagine this loss falls into that category? Why not?

c. What could plaintiff do? Because Haddle admitted he was an at-will employee, there was no way to amend the complaint to avoid dismissal. Instead, the plaintiff appealed.

d. If the law was against plaintiff, why did he appeal? What was he trying to accomplish? On what point of law would the appeal turn?

e. The Court of Appeals gave short shrift to Haddle's appeal. The following is the entire text of its unpublished opinion.

Haddle v. Garrison

Unpublished Opinion, Docket No. 96-8856 (11th Cir. 1997)

PER CURIAM:

Michael A. Haddle appeals following the district court's dismissal of his 42 U.S.C. §1985(2) claim for failure to state a claim. We conclude that Haddle's arguments on appeal are foreclosed by this court's decision in Morast v. Lance, 807 F.2d 926 (11th Cir. 1987). The judgment of the district court is therefore affirmed.

Notes and Problems

---

1. Why might the Eleventh Circuit have thought this was such an easy case that it could be disposed of in a three-sentence per curiam opinion, one perhaps drafted by a law clerk?

2. At this point plaintiff has lost again, but in a much more final way. In recent years, the federal courts have disposed of about 250,000 civil cases annually. The district court dismissal would count as one of those cases. A losing litigant has the right to appeal that loss to a U.S. Court of Appeals. In recent years, the federal Courts of Appeals have disposed of about 55,000 appeals each year; the per curiam affirmance of *Haddle v. Garrison* would count as one of those cases. A litigant who has lost in a Court of Appeals in an ordinary civil case does not have the *right* to have his case heard by the U.S. Supreme Court. He may petition for a writ of certiorari, which the Supreme Court may grant if it believes the question presented is important enough. In recent years, the U.S. Supreme Court has agreed to review and decide fewer than 100 cases each year.

   a. Explain why at this point the plaintiff's lawyer would be telling his client that they still had a chance, but that it was a long shot.

   b. Plaintiff sought a writ of certiorari from the U.S. Supreme Court, which granted certiorari.

   c. With the grant of certiorari the relative strategic advantage of the parties shifted again. One cannot be sure that the Supreme Court will reverse, but in recent years it has reversed or vacated the judgment below approximately twice as often as it has affirmed.

   d. The Supreme Court heard oral argument, and issued the following opinion as one of the 88 cases it decided that year.

Haddle v. Garrison
525 U.S. 121 (1998)

REHNQUIST, C.J., delivered the opinion of the Court.

Petitioner Michael A. Haddle, an at-will employee, alleges that respondents conspired to have him fired from his job in retaliation for obeying a federal grand jury subpoena and to deter him from testifying at a federal criminal trial. We hold that such interference with at-will employment may give rise to a claim for damages under the Civil Rights Act of 1871, Rev. Stat. §1980, 42 U.S.C. §1985(2).

According to petitioner's complaint, a federal grand jury indictment in March 1995 charged petitioner's employer, Healthmaster, Inc., and respondents Jeanette Garrison and Dennis Kelly, officers of Healthmaster, with Medicare fraud. Petitioner cooperated with the federal agents in the investigation that preceded the indictment. He also appeared to testify before the grand jury pursuant to a subpoena, but did not testify due to the press of time. Petitioner was also expected to appear as a witness in the criminal trial resulting from the indictment.

Although Garrison and Kelly were barred by the Bankruptcy Court from participating in the affairs of Healthmaster, they conspired with G. Peter Molloy, Jr., one of the remaining officers of Healthmaster, to bring about petitioner's termination. They did this both to intimidate petitioner and to retaliate against him for his attendance at the federal-court proceedings.

Petitioner sued for damages in the United States District Court for the Southern District of Georgia, asserting a federal claim under 42 U.S.C. §1985(2) and various state-law claims. Petitioner stated two grounds for relief under §1985(2): one for conspiracy to deter him from testifying in the upcoming criminal trial and one for conspiracy to retaliate against him for attending the grand jury proceedings. As §1985 demands, he also alleged that he had been "injured in his person or property" by the acts of respondents in violation of §1985(2) and that he was entitled to recover his damages occasioned by such injury against respondents jointly and severally.

Respondents moved to dismiss for failure to state a claim upon which relief can be granted. Because petitioner conceded that he was an at-will employee, the District Court granted the motion on the authority of Morast v. Lance, 807 F.2d 926 (1987). In Morast, the Eleventh Circuit held that an at-will employee who is dismissed pursuant to a conspiracy proscribed by §1985(2) has no cause of action. The Morast court explained that "to make out a cause of action under §1985(2) the plaintiff must have suffered an actual injury. Because Morast was an at-will employee, he had no constitutionally protected interest in continued employment. Therefore, Morast's discharge did not constitute an actual injury under this statute." Relying on its decision in *Morast*, the Court of Appeals affirmed.

The Eleventh Circuit's rule in *Morast* conflicts with the holdings of the First and Ninth Circuits. We therefore granted certiorari, to decide whether petitioner was "injured in his property or person" when respondents induced his employer to terminate petitioner's at-will employment as part of a conspiracy prohibited by §1985(2).

The statute provides that if one or more persons engaged in such a conspiracy "do, or cause to be done, any act in furtherance of the object of such conspiracy, whereby another is injured in his person or property, . . . the party so injured . . . may have an action for the recovery of damages occasioned by such injury . . . against any one or more of the conspirators." §1985(3).

Petitioner's action was dismissed pursuant to Federal Rule of Civil Procedure 12(b)(6) because, in the Eleventh Circuit's view, he had not suffered an injury that could give rise to a claim for damages under §1985(2). We must, of course, assume that the facts as alleged in petitioner's complaint are true and that respondents engaged in a conspiracy prohibited by §1985(2). Our review in this case is accordingly confined to one question: Can petitioner state a claim for damages by alleging that a conspiracy proscribed by §1985(2) induced his employer to terminate his at-will employment.

We disagree with the Eleventh Circuit's conclusion that petitioner must suffer an injury to a "constitutionally protected property interest" to state a claim for damages under §1985(2). Nothing in the language or purpose of the proscriptions in the first clause of §1985(2), nor in its attendant remedial provisions, establishes such a requirement. The gist of the wrong at which §1985(2) is directed is not deprivation of property, but intimidation or retaliation against witnesses in federal-court proceedings. The terms "injured in his person or property" define the harm that the victim may suffer as a result of the conspiracy to intimidate or retaliate. Thus, the fact that employment at will is not "property" for purposes of the Due Process Clause, does not mean that loss of at-will employment may not "injur[e] [petitioner] in his person or property" for purposes of §1985(2).

We hold that the sort of harm alleged by petitioner here—essentially third-party interference with at-will employment relationships—states a claim for relief under §1985(2). Such harm has long been a compensable injury under tort law, and we see no reason to ignore this tradition in this case. As Thomas Cooley recognized:

> One who maliciously and without justifiable cause, induces an employer to discharge an employee, by means of false statements, threats or putting in fear, or perhaps by means of malevolent advice and persuasion, is liable in an action of tort to the employee for the damages thereby sustained. *And it makes no difference whether the employment was for a fixed term not yet expired or is terminable at the will of the employer.*

2 T. Cooley, Law of Torts 589-591 (3d ed. 1906) (emphasis added).

This Court also recognized in Truax v. Raich, 239 U.S. 33 (1915):

> The fact that the employment is at the will of the parties, respectively, does not make it one at the will of others. The employee has manifest interest in the freedom of the employer to exercise his judgment without illegal interference or compulsion and, by the weight of authority, the unjustified interference of third persons is actionable although the employment is at will.

The kind of interference with at-will employment relations alleged here is merely a species of the traditional torts of intentional interference with contractual relations and intentional interference with prospective contractual relations. See Restatement (Second) of Torts §766, Comment g, pp. 10-11 (1977); see also id., §766B, Comment c, at 22. This protection against third-party interference with at-will employment relations is still afforded by state law today. See W. Keeton, D. Dobbs, R. Keeton & D. Owen, Prosser and Keaton on Law of Torts §129, pp. 995-996, and n. 83 (5th ed. 1984) (citing cases). For example, the State of Georgia, where the acts underlying the complaint in this case took place, provides a cause of action against third parties for wrongful interference with employment relations.

Thus, to the extent that the terms "injured in his person or property" in §1985 refer to principles of tort law, see 3 W. Blackstone, Commentaries on the Laws of England 118 (1768) (describing the universe of common law torts as "all private wrongs, or civil injuries, which may be offered to the rights of either a man's person or his property"), we find ample support for our holding that the harm occasioned by the conspiracy here may give rise to a claim for damages under §1985(2).

The judgment of the Court of Appeals is reversed, and the case is remanded for further proceedings consistent with this opinion.

WHAT'S NEW HERE?

- In deciding that Haddle's complaint did state a claim, the Supreme Court also defines the content of the substantive law involved.
- In doing so, the Court interprets the meaning of "property" and "injury" in 42 U.S.C. §1985(2).
- In that respect, *Haddle* is a classic example of common law development: a statute with some clear applications; a set of facts not within the clear applications; and a judicial opinion stating how the statute applies to this new set of facts. Because this is a Supreme Court opinion interpreting a federal statute, that interpretation now becomes "part of the law"—until Congress amends the statute in question or a subsequent Supreme Court interpretation modifies our understanding of the statute.

Notes and Problems

1. Why did the Supreme Court reverse?

   a. Did the Supreme Court disagree with the district court's application of the standard for granting a motion to dismiss under Rule 12(b)(6)? If not, what aspect of the court's decision was the Supreme Court rejecting?

   b. The Supreme Court's opinion was unanimous. Does that suggest that the Eleventh Circuit was too hasty? Or did the Supreme Court disagree with the Circuit about an issue as to which more deliberate consideration by the circuit court would have made no difference?

2. What will happen now?

   a. This is obviously a victory for the plaintiff. How big and what kind of victory? Explain why Haddle's lawyer, after allowing his colleagues to congratulate him, will be lining up financing for the next stage of the case, which will likely be more expensive than the proceedings up to now.

   b. You represent the defendants. In spite of your best efforts, you have lost in the U.S. Supreme Court. The two main alternatives for your clients? Go to trial or settle. Summary judgment will be unlikely here, as there will likely be factual issues as to the defendants' motivation for firing Haddle.

3. *Haddle v. Garrison* went to a jury after a hard-fought pretrial stage.

   a. A few days before Christmas 1999, the *Augusta (Georgia) Chronicle* carried the following report:

   ### Whistle-Blower Wins Case
   Sandy Hodson, Staff Writer

   A U.S. District Court jury sided with Michael Haddle on Friday afternoon, finding his former bosses fired him for helping uncover corporate crimes that cost taxpayers more than $10 million. But in the same verdict, the jury awarded Mr. Haddle just $65,000 in compensatory damages against Jeannette Garrison, founder and owner of the now-defunct Healthmaster Inc., the company, and her corporate legal counsel and top executive, G. Peter Molloy. "You won again," defense attorney David Hudson told Mrs. Garrison after the jury verdict was announced at the conclusion of a five-day federal court trial. The low amount of damages left the defense team in smiles, extremely pleased with the jury's decision about damages. But they still intend to challenge the verdict, Mr. Hudson said. Afterward, Mr. Haddle smiled, too. "I'm pleased with the verdict. It vindicated me. "Sometimes those things are more important than money."

   The article went on to report that the verdict was several hundred thousand dollars less than plaintiff had sought. Observers speculated that the verdict may have resulted from the jury's conclusion that, even without the retaliatory firing, Mr. Haddle would have lost his job a few months later when the corporation went bankrupt in the wake of the federal investigation and conviction of its president.

b. The defendants may, however, have been a bit premature in their self-congratulation. The statute that provided a basis for the suit carries with it a fee-shifting statute (see ¶23 of Haddle's complaint and supra page 351). Having prevailed in the judgment, the plaintiff's lawyer asked for fees, with the result appearing in the *Augusta Chronicle* on March 30, 2000:

> A federal magistrate judge has recommended that the attorneys who successfully represented Healthmaster whistle-blower Michael Haddle receive $258,113 in legal fees [to be paid by the defendants]. . . . In a report issued Monday, U.S. Magistrate Judge W. Leon Barfield wrote Mr. Haddle's legal team has earned more than a quarter-million dollars for their work during the past four years on Mr. Haddle's behalf—a legal battle that included a successful trip to the U.S. Supreme Court. . . . In addition to the attorneys fees for the work done for Mr. Haddle by Charles C. Stebbins III, C. Thompson Harley and Richard Miley, Judge Barfield recommended that the three receive an additional $15,475 from Atlanta attorneys Phillip A. Bradley and Barry J. Armstrong. Before the civil trial began in December, Judge Alaimo found that Mr. Bradley and Mr. Armstrong, who represented Mrs. Garrison, had violated a specific court order to turn over evidence to Mr. Haddle's attorneys. The judge sanctioned the pair and ordered them [not their clients, as with the other fees] to pay Mr. Haddle's expenses and attorney fees connected with this issue.

Implications

LAW-DEFINING MOMENTS IN PROCEDURE

Haddle shows us the modern equivalent of the demurrer, the 12(b)(6) motion, operating to define the boundaries of substantive law. As you saw in Chapter 1, there are several other procedural moments that require a court to set forth the law: motions for summary judgment and judgments as a matter of law, jury instructions—and more. The 12(b)(6) motion is the first of these moments and has some special characteristics. Notably, a court ruling on a 12(b)(6) motion is uncontaminated by disputed facts. It has the allegations in the complaint, but these are only allegations, and any judge worth her salt understands that the defendant will deny many of these allegations in the answer and contest them in ensuing stages of litigation. But that hasn't yet happened at the 12(b)(6) stage. Consequently, a judge ruling on a 12(b)(6) motion is operating in a hypothetical world: "*If* this were true, how would the law respond?"

4. Another Function of Pleading: Sorting Strong from Weak Cases?

Haddle shows us how complaints and Rule 12(b)(6) challenges to them help define the substantive law. But pleadings sometimes aspire to other tasks as well. Lawsuits take a toll in time, money, and emotions. That toll is worth its price if a suit has merit; if, that is, events have occurred for which the law grants a remedy. If, on the other hand, the suit has no merit because the plaintiff cannot show that the events alleged actually occurred, then the toll of litigation seems excessive. Suppose it were possible to tell from the face of a complaint whether it would ultimately fail: Would it not be a good thing to put such a lawsuit out of its misery at the earliest possible moment?

Over the past several centuries, courts, legislators, and designers of procedural systems have taken several approaches to this problem. At common law, say from 1100 C.E. to the mid-nineteenth century, pleading was in one respect easy: One simply recited the formula for one of the "approved" 30-odd writs, each of which came both with its required allegations and with its own mode of proof. In common law, pleadings problems arose when the pleader tried to prove something that didn't exactly match the allegations of the pleading. Suppose, for example, that, having pleaded a claim of having injured his horse, our medieval John Smith then wanted to prove something a bit more subtle: that the blacksmith had promised "first-class work" (or whatever its Middle English equivalent would be) but that the horse was lamed when the shoe fell off after just one day's riding. Could Smith make that proof having pleaded something else? (The answer mattered a lot because if Smith had pleaded what we would think of as a breach of warranty claim, the defendant Jones would not have to go before a jury, but could defend himself by showing up with a sufficient number of "oath-helpers," who would, perhaps for the price of tankard of ale, swear that Jones had done good work—and that would be the end of the claim.) Locked into the writs' formulae, weak complaints were impossible to distinguish from strong ones before trial.

In reaction to this problem, the great pleading reform of the nineteenth century was to junk the writs and to ask pleaders to state "facts." This result was achieved by "the Field Codes," legislation adopted in many states under the inspiration of David Dudley Field, an influential mid-century lawyer. These Codes directed pleaders to state "facts constituting a cause of action." One of the hopes was that the facts thus recited would enable courts to distinguish early on between strong and weak cases. What could possibly go wrong? Plenty, it turned out. Most saliently for our purposes, courts could not agree what a "fact" was. Some complaints failed because the pleaders recounted excessive detail, each event that might be relevant; courts dismissed these complaints because they contained "mere evidence." Other complaints failed because they erred in the opposite direction, reciting their allegations at a level of generality condemned as "legal conclusions."

a. The "Ordinary" Case: How Much Detail in a Complaint?

The drafters of the Federal Rules took a quite different approach to sorting weak from strong cases. Abandoning the effort to do this at the pleading stage (except for the rare complaint whose allegations failed to state a claim for relief—with which a 12(b)(6) motion would deal), the Rules put the sorting function in the next stage of litigation. In the discovery phase, the thinking went, the plaintiff would dismiss or quickly settle cases with no factual foundation, or would succumb when defendant moved for summary judgment. Under this approach, the basic requirements for complaints could be quite simple:

Federal Rule of Civil Procedure 8(a)

Claim for Relief. A pleading that states a claim for relief must contain

    (1) a short and plain statement of the grounds for the court's jurisdiction unless the court already has jurisdiction and the claim needs no new jurisdictional support;

    (2) a short and plain statement of the claim showing that the pleader is entitled to relief; and

    (3) a demand for judgment for the relief sought, which may include relief in the alternative or different types of relief.

WHAT'S NEW HERE?

- Rule 8(a) tried to avoid "formulas" (the writs) and also "facts" (the rock that had sunk Code pleading).
- To do so, it depended on two elements: "short and plain," suggesting that complaints could be brief and that they should avoid the technical language that characterized the writs; and "statement of the claim," a phrase that studiously avoided words that had been the source of many disputes in the past.

Notes and Problems

1. We have already discussed the requirements of Rule 8(a)(1), setting out the basis for the federal court's subject matter jurisdiction. See Note 2, page 364.

2. Now consider Rule 8(a)(2). The Rule requires only a "short and plain statement of the claim showing that the pleader is entitled to relief." The drafters and subsequent revisers of the Rules appear to have assumed that the details of the claim would be unearthed in discovery and sorted out at summary judgment or trial. To better understand this long-held view about the limited role of pleadings as an obstacle, read or re-read *Bell v. Novick Transfer Co.* at page 19. The court in that case held that the plaintiff's complaint did not need to allege more than that the car he was riding in was struck by a car owned by Defendants, and that it was operated "in a careless, reckless and negligent manner . . . so that" the plaintiff was injured. The court refused to dismiss the complaint for failing to allege defendants' negligence with specificity, reasoning that the details of the claim could be learned during discovery.

    a. Notice that the brevity and conclusory nature of complaints under the Rules will sometimes leave the defendant largely in the dark about the details of plaintiff's case. In *Bell*, the defendant surely wanted to know what kind of negligence the plaintiff was asserting: Did he run a light, fail to stop, have faulty brakes? Did plaintiff think he was drunk, not wearing the glasses required by his driver's license, or something else? The complaint did not say, and the decision did not require him to say.

    b. This brevity can also benefit plaintiffs. Plaintiffs may be happy to tell their story in all its gory details—if they know it. But plaintiffs may not know all the facts at the start of the suit, or they may not be sure which version of the story they want to try to prove, and, of course, some of the "facts" they allege may turn out not to be true. Plaintiff will not know, before discovery, whether the defendant acted negligently because he had faulty brakes or was drunk. Accordingly, plaintiffs will sometimes favor briefer, sketchier recitations of the facts.

    c. For decades, the Supreme Court interpreted Rule 8 to endorse the conclusory brevity considered acceptable by the trial court in *Bell*. Until recently, the leading Supreme Court case was Conley v. Gibson, 355 U.S. 41, 45-46 (1957):

    > In appraising the sufficiency of the complaint we follow, of course, the accepted rule that a complaint should not be dismissed for failure to state a claim *unless it appears beyond doubt that the plaintiff can prove no set of facts in support of his claim which would entitle him to relief* [emphasis added]. Here, the complaint alleged, in part, that petitioners were discharged wrongfully by the Railroad and that the Union, acting according to plan, refused to protect their jobs as it did those of white employees or to help them with their grievances all because they were Negroes. If these allegations are proven there has

been a manifest breach of the Union's statutory duty to represent fairly [all its members]. . . .

[T]he Federal Rules of Civil Procedure do not require a claimant to set out in detail the facts upon which he bases his claim. To the contrary, all the Rules require is "a short and plain statement of the claim" that will give the defendant fair notice of what the plaintiff's claim is and the grounds upon which it rests. . . . Such simplified "notice pleading" is made possible by the liberal opportunity for discovery and the other pretrial procedures established by the Rules to disclose more precisely the basis of both claim and defense and to define more narrowly the disputed facts and issues. Following the simple guide of Rule 8([e]) that "[pleadings must be construed so as to do justice,]"* we have no doubt that petitioners' complaint adequately set forth a claim and gave the respondents fair notice of its basis. The Federal Rules reject the approach that pleading is a game of skill in which one misstep by counsel may be decisive to the outcome and accept the principle that the purpose of pleading is to facilitate a proper decision on the merits.

The corollary of the choice expressed in Rule 8 and *Conley*—endorsing brief and conclusory pleadings—is that discovery, not pleading, will do the major sorting between grounded and ungrounded claims. But deferring this sorting function until discovery has costs, for litigants and for the system as a whole. Good data on the costs of discovery is hard to come by, but in some cases discovery will be a major expense. Worse, a defendant who prevails and gets plaintiff's claim dismissed will still have to pay the costs of discovery and defense. For some plaintiffs, on the other hand, discovery represents the only tool that will uncover evidence of a defendant's liability. The Rules' choice of what is sometimes called "notice pleading" thus represents a fundamental decision: It opens the doors of discovery to some complaints that may not prevail, recognizing that doing so will impose costs on the defendants in such cases. For many years, the Supreme Court stood by this interpretation of Rule 8, with the entailed allocation of costs and risks. Yet, within the past 15 years, the U.S. Supreme Court has twice reconsidered this issue, in the process working what some believe to be a fundamental shift in the landscape of modern litigation.

The first step came in Bell Atlantic Corp. v. Twombly, 550 U.S. 544 (2007). *Twombly* represents one kind of case in which a complaint that turns out to be factually ungrounded will be expensive and time-consuming: an antitrust action. The federal antitrust laws forbid price fixing. So, if five widget manufacturers meet in a hotel room and decide they will all charge $5 per widget, they have thereby subjected themselves both to criminal penalties and civil liability. What, though, if they do not meet but just keep an eye on each other's prices (as all business competitors do), and all, without any overt agreement, hit on $5 as the right price? As the Supreme Court has interpreted the antitrust statutes, such a situation, which antitrust lawyers call "parallel conduct," does not create liability. But, of course, because those

---

* [At the time *Conley* was decided, the text of Rule 8 read: "all pleadings shall be so construed as to do substantial justice."—Eds.]

who have made unlawful agreements want to keep them secret, one can sometimes infer conspiracy from parallel conduct *plus* some other circumstances. (In antitrust jargon, this is termed "parallelism plus.") To make things harder, the courts have held that conclusory allegations of a conspiracy do not suffice; the plaintiff must allege some facts leading to the inference of an unlawful agreement. The problem is that the fact of parallel behavior could be either evidence leading to an inference of conspiracy *or* innocent "parallelism." And many thousands of hours of discovery may be necessary to find out which of these scenarios is closer to the truth.

In *Twombly*, the Supreme Court said that it was going to head the complaint off at the pass. In so doing it re-interpreted *Conley v. Gibson*:

> In applying the[] general standards [of Rule 8] to a[n antitrust] claim, we hold that stating such a claim requires a complaint with enough factual matter (taken as true) to suggest that an agreement was made. . . .
>
> We alluded to the practical significance of the Rule 8 entitlement requirement in Dura Pharmaceuticals, Inc. v. Broudo, 544 U.S. 336, when we explained that something beyond the mere possibility of loss causation must be alleged, lest a plaintiff with "'a largely groundless claim'" be allowed to "'take up the time of a number of other people, with the right to do so representing an *in terrorem* increment of the settlement value.'" . . .
>
> Thus, it is one thing to be cautious before dismissing an antitrust complaint in advance of discovery, but quite another to forget that proceeding to antitrust discovery can be expensive. As we indicated over 20 years ago in Associated Gen. Contractors of Cal., Inc. v. Carpenters, 459 U.S. 519, 528 n.17 (1983), "a district court must retain the power to insist upon some specificity in pleading before allowing a potentially massive factual controversy to proceed." . . .
>
> Plaintiffs do not, of course, dispute the requirement of plausibility and the need for something more than merely parallel behavior . . . , and their main argument against the plausibility standard at the pleading stage is its ostensible conflict with an early statement of ours construing Rule 8. Justice Black's opinion for the Court in *Conley v. Gibson* spoke not only of the need for fair notice of the grounds for entitlement to relief but of "the accepted rule that a complaint should not be dismissed for failure to state a claim unless it appears beyond doubt that the plaintiff can prove no set of facts in support of his claim which would entitle him to relief." This "no set of facts" language can be read in isolation as saying that any statement revealing the theory of the claim will suffice unless its factual impossibility may be shown from the face of the pleadings; and the Court of Appeals appears to have read *Conley* in some such way when formulating its understanding of the proper pleading standard. . . . It seems fair to say that this approach to pleading would dispense with any showing of a "reasonably founded hope" that a plaintiff would be able to make a case; Mr. Micawber's optimism would be enough.
>
> Seeing this, a good many judges and commentators have balked at taking the literal terms of the *Conley* passage as a pleading standard. [The Court then cites several cases holding this view.]
>
> We could go on, but there is no need to pile up further citations to show that *Conley*'s "no set of facts" language has been questioned, criticized, and explained away long enough. To be fair to the *Conley* Court, the passage should be understood in light of the opinion's preceding summary of the complaint's concrete allegations, which the

Court quite reasonably understood as amply stating a claim for relief. But the passage so often quoted fails to mention this understanding on the part of the Court, and after puzzling the profession for 50 years, this famous observation has earned its retirement. The phrase is best forgotten as an incomplete, negative gloss on an accepted pleading standard: once a claim has been stated adequately, it may be supported by showing any set of facts consistent with the allegations in the complaint. *Conley*, then, described the breadth of opportunity to prove what an adequate complaint claims, not the minimum standard of adequate pleading to govern a complaint's survival. . . .

[W]e do not require heightened fact pleading of specifics, but only enough facts to state a claim to relief that is plausible on its face. Because the plaintiffs here have not nudged their claims across the line from conceivable to plausible, their complaint must be dismissed. . . .

After *Twombly*, practitioners and academics debated whether one should understand the case as applying only to antitrust claims (or perhaps to other claims where immense discovery lay ahead if the complaint survived). On that interpretation pleading principles for the rest of the landscape would remain undisturbed. Two years after *Twombly*, the Supreme Court resolved that question in the next case.

Some substantive law background may help readers understand. Well-established law states that a person has a claim against a government official who violates his constitutional rights. Well-established law also provides protection for such officials if those constitutional rights were not clearly established, in which case they enjoy a "qualified immunity" from being sued. If qualified immunity applies, the defendant official is entitled not only to prevail in litigation but to be freed from the burdens of discovery as well. And a denial of a motion to dismiss on qualified immunity grounds is one of those rare non-dispositive decisions subject to interlocutory appeal. The next case, which has its origins in the September 11, 2001 attack on New York's World Trade Center, looked as if it would be another case working out the meaning of qualified immunity—until it suddenly turned into a pleading case instead.

Ashcroft v. Iqbal

556 U.S. 662 (2009)

KENNEDY, J., delivered the opinion of the Court.

Respondent Javaid Iqbal is a citizen of Pakistan and a Muslim. In the wake of the September 11, 2001, terrorist attacks he was arrested in the United States on criminal charges and detained by federal officials. Respondent claims he was deprived of various constitutional protections while in federal custody. To redress the alleged deprivations, respondent filed a complaint against numerous federal officials, including John Ashcroft, the former Attorney General of the United States, and Robert Mueller, the Director of the Federal Bureau of Investigation (FBI). Ashcroft and Mueller are the petitioners in the case now before us. As to these two

Procedural History

Rule 12b6

petitioners, the complaint alleges that they adopted an unconstitutional policy that subjected respondent to harsh conditions of confinement on account of his race, religion, or national origin.

In the District Court petitioners raised the defense of qualified immunity and moved to dismiss the suit, contending the complaint was not sufficient to state a claim against them. The District Court denied the motion to dismiss, concluding the complaint was sufficient to state a claim despite petitioners' official status at the times in question. Petitioners brought an interlocutory appeal in the Court of Appeals for the Second Circuit[, which] affirmed the District Court's decision.

Respondent's account of his prison ordeal could, if proved, demonstrate unconstitutional misconduct by some governmental actors. But the allegations and pleadings with respect to these actors are not before us here. This case instead turns on a narrower question: Did respondent, as the plaintiff in the District Court, plead factual matter that, if taken as true, states a claim that petitioners deprived him of his clearly established constitutional rights. We hold respondent's pleadings are insufficient.

I

Following the 2001 attacks, the FBI and other entities within the Department of Justice began an investigation of vast reach to identify the assailants and prevent them from attacking anew. The FBI dedicated more than 4,000 special agents and 3,000 support personnel to the endeavor. By September 18 "the FBI had received more than 96,000 tips or potential leads from the public."

In the ensuing months the FBI questioned more than 1,000 people with suspected links to the attacks in particular or to terrorism in general. Of those individuals, some 762 were held on immigration charges; and a 184-member subset of that group was deemed to be "of 'high interest'" to the investigation. The high-interest detainees were held under restrictive conditions designed to prevent them from communicating with the general prison population or the outside world.

P facts

Respondent was one of the detainees. According to his complaint, in November 2001 agents of the FBI and Immigration and Naturalization Service arrested him on charges of fraud in relation to identification documents and conspiracy to defraud the United States. Pending trial for those crimes, respondent was housed at the Metropolitan Detention Center (MDC) in Brooklyn, New York. Respondent was designated a person "of high interest" to the September 11 investigation and in January 2002 was placed in a section of the MDC known as the Administrative Maximum Special Housing Unit (ADMAX SHU). As the facility's name indicates, the ADMAX SHU incorporates the maximum security conditions allowable under Federal Bureau of Prison regulations. ADMAX SHU detainees were kept in lockdown 23 hours a day, spending the remaining hour outside their cells in handcuffs and leg irons accompanied by a four-officer escort.

Prison details

Respondent pleaded guilty to the criminal charges, served a term of imprisonment, and was removed to his native Pakistan. He then filed a *Bivens** action in the United States District Court for the Eastern District of New York against 34 current and former federal officials. . . . The defendants range from the correctional officers who had day-to-day contact with respondent . . . all the way to petitioners—officials who were at the highest level of the federal law enforcement hierarchy. . . .

The allegations against petitioners are the only ones relevant here. The complaint contends that petitioners designated respondent a person of high interest on account of his race, religion, or national origin, in contravention of the First and Fifth Amendments to the Constitution. The complaint alleges that "the [FBI], under the direction of Defendant Mueller, arrested and detained thousands of Arab Muslim men . . . as part of its investigation of the events of September 11." It further alleges that "[t]he policy of holding post-September-11th detainees in highly restrictive conditions of confinement until they were 'cleared' by the FBI was approved by Defendants Ashcroft and Mueller in discussions in the weeks after September 11, 2001." Lastly, the complaint posits that petitioners "each knew of, condoned, and willfully and maliciously agreed to subject" respondent to harsh conditions of confinement "as a matter of policy, solely on account of [his] religion, race, and/or national origin and for no legitimate penological interest." The pleading names Ashcroft as the "principal architect" of the policy, and identifies Mueller as "instrumental in [its] adoption, promulgation, and implementation."

Petitioners moved to dismiss the complaint for failure to state sufficient allegations to show their own involvement in clearly established unconstitutional conduct. The District Court denied their motion. Accepting all of the allegations in respondent's complaint as true, the court held that "it cannot be said that there [is] no set of facts on which [respondent] would be entitled to relief as against" petitioners [quoting the lower court opinion, which had in turn relied on *Conley v. Gibson*]. . . . While [this] appeal was pending, this Court decided *Bell Atlantic Corp. v. Twombly*, which discussed the standard for evaluating whether a complaint is sufficient to survive a motion to dismiss.

The Court of Appeals considered *Twombly*'s applicability to this case. . . . It concluded that *Twombly* called for a "flexible 'plausibility standard,' which obliges a pleader to amplify a claim with some factual allegations in those contexts where such amplification is needed to render the claim *plausible*." The court found that petitioners' appeal did not present one of "those contexts" requiring amplification. As a consequence, it held respondent's pleading adequate to allege petitioners' personal involvement in discriminatory decisions which, if true, violated clearly established constitutional law. . . .

---

*[Bivens v. Six Unknown Fed. Narcotics Agents, 403 U.S. 388 (1971), recognized a cause of action arising directly under the Constitution against federal officers alleged to have violated the Constitution.—Eds.]

II

[The Court held that under the collateral-order exception to the final judgment rule of 28 U.S.C. §1291 (see casebook Chapter 10) the Court of Appeals, and thus the Supreme Court, had appellate jurisdiction. Although it was the lower courts' denial of qualified immunity that made the decision immediately appealable, the Court held that it could also address the sufficiency of the pleadings.]

IV

A

We turn to respondent's complaint. Under Federal Rule of Civil Procedure 8(a)(2), a pleading must contain a "short and plain statement of the claim showing that the pleader is entitled to relief." As the Court held in *Twombly*, the pleading standard Rule 8 announces does not require "detailed factual allegations," but it demands more than an unadorned, the-defendant-unlawfully-harmed-me accusation. A pleading that offers "labels and conclusions" or "a formulaic recitation of the elements of a cause of action will not do." Nor does a complaint suffice if it tenders "naked assertion[s]" devoid of "further factual enhancement."

To survive a motion to dismiss, a complaint must contain sufficient factual matter, accepted as true, to "state a claim to relief that is plausible on its face." A claim has facial plausibility when the plaintiff pleads factual content that allows the court to draw the reasonable inference that the defendant is liable for the misconduct alleged. The plausibility standard is not akin to a "probability requirement," but it asks for more than a sheer possibility that a defendant has acted unlawfully. Where a complaint pleads facts that are "merely consistent with" a defendant's liability, it "stops short of the line between possibility and plausibility of 'entitlement to relief.'"

Two working principles underlie our decision in *Twombly*. First, the tenet that a court must accept as true all of the allegations contained in a complaint is inapplicable to legal conclusions. Threadbare recitals of the elements of a cause of action, supported by mere conclusory statements, do not suffice. Rule 8 marks a notable and generous departure from the hyper-technical, code-pleading regime of a prior era, but it does not unlock the doors of discovery for a plaintiff armed with nothing more than conclusions. Second, only a complaint that states a plausible claim for relief survives a motion to dismiss. Determining whether a complaint states a plausible claim for relief will, as the Court of Appeals observed, be a context-specific task that requires the reviewing court to draw on its judicial experience and common sense. But where the well-pleaded facts do not permit the court to infer more than the mere possibility of misconduct, the complaint has alleged—but it has not "show[n]"— "that the pleader is entitled to relief." Fed. Rule Civ. Proc. 8(a)(2).

In keeping with these principles a court considering a motion to dismiss can choose to begin by identifying pleadings that, because they are no more than conclusions, are not entitled to the assumption of truth. While legal conclusions can provide the framework of a complaint, they must be supported by factual allegations. When there are well-pleaded factual allegations, a court should assume their veracity and then determine whether they plausibly give rise to an entitlement to relief.

Our decision in *Twombly* illustrates the two-pronged approach. There, we considered the sufficiency of a complaint alleging that incumbent telecommunications providers had entered an agreement not to compete and to forestall competitive entry, in violation of the Sherman Act, 15 U.S.C. §1. Recognizing that §1 enjoins only anticompetitive conduct "effected by a contract, combination, or conspiracy," the plaintiffs in *Twombly* flatly pleaded that the defendants "ha[d] entered into a contract, combination or conspiracy to prevent competitive entry . . . and ha[d] agreed not to compete with one another." The complaint also alleged that the defendants' "parallel course of conduct . . . to prevent competition" and inflate prices was indicative of the unlawful agreement alleged.

The Court held the plaintiffs' complaint deficient under Rule 8. In doing so it first noted that the plaintiffs' assertion of an unlawful agreement was a "'legal conclusion'" and, as such, was not entitled to the assumption of truth. Had the Court simply credited the allegation of a conspiracy, the plaintiffs would have stated a claim for relief and been entitled to proceed perforce. The Court next addressed the "nub" of the plaintiffs' complaint—the well-pleaded, nonconclusory factual allegation of parallel behavior—to determine whether it gave rise to a "plausible suggestion of conspiracy." Acknowledging that parallel conduct was consistent with an unlawful agreement, the Court nevertheless concluded that it did not plausibly suggest an illicit accord because it was not only compatible with, but indeed was more likely explained by, lawful, unchoreographed free-market behavior. Because the well-pleaded fact of parallel conduct, accepted as true, did not plausibly suggest an unlawful agreement, the Court held the plaintiffs' complaint must be dismissed.

B

Under *Twombly*'s construction of Rule 8, we conclude that respondent's complaint has not "nudged [his] claims" of invidious discrimination "across the line from conceivable to plausible."

We begin our analysis by identifying the allegations in the complaint that are not entitled to the assumption of truth. Respondent pleads that petitioners "knew of, condoned, and willfully and maliciously agreed to subject [him]" to harsh conditions of confinement "as a matter of policy, solely on account of [his] religion, race, and/or national origin and for no legitimate penological interest." The complaint alleges that Ashcroft was the "principal architect" of this invidious policy, and that Mueller was "instrumental" in adopting and executing it. These bare assertions, much like the pleading of conspiracy in *Twombly*, amount to nothing more than a "formulaic recitation of the elements" of a constitutional discrimination claim, namely, that petitioners adopted a policy "'because of,' not merely 'in spite of,' its adverse effects upon an identifiable group." As such, the allegations are conclusory and not entitled to be assumed true. To be clear, we do not reject these bald allegations on the ground that they are unrealistic or nonsensical. We do not so characterize them any more than the Court in *Twombly* rejected the plaintiffs' express allegation of a "'contract, combination or conspiracy to prevent competitive entry,'" because it thought that claim too chimerical to be maintained. It is the conclusory nature of respondent's allegations, rather than their extravagantly fanciful nature, that disentitles them to the presumption of truth.

Conclusionary

Relief

We next consider the factual allegations in respondent's complaint to determine if they plausibly suggest an entitlement to relief. The complaint alleges that "the [FBI], under the direction of Defendant Mueller, arrested and detained thousands of Arab Muslim men . . . as part of its investigation of the events of September 11." It further claims that "[t]he policy of holding post-September-11th detainees in highly restrictive conditions of confinement until they were 'cleared' by the FBI was approved by Defendants Ashcroft and Mueller in discussions in the weeks after September 11, 2001." Taken as true, these allegations are consistent with petitioners' purposefully designating detainees "of high interest" because of their race, religion, or national origin. But given more likely explanations, they do not plausibly establish this purpose.

The September 11 attacks were perpetrated by 19 Arab Muslim hijackers who counted themselves members in good standing of al Qaeda, an Islamic fundamentalist group. Al Qaeda was headed by another Arab Muslim—Osama bin Laden—and composed in large part of his Arab Muslim disciples. It should come as no surprise that a legitimate policy directing law enforcement to arrest and detain individuals because of their suspected link to the attacks would produce a disparate, incidental impact on Arab Muslims, even though the purpose of the policy was to target neither Arabs nor Muslims. On the facts respondent alleges the arrests Mueller oversaw were likely lawful and justified by his nondiscriminatory intent to detain aliens who were illegally present in the United States and who had potential connections to those who committed terrorist acts. As between that "obvious alternative explanation" for the arrests, *Twombly*, and the purposeful, invidious discrimination respondent asks us to infer, discrimination is not a plausible conclusion.

Mueller acted legally

But even if the complaint's well-pleaded facts give rise to a plausible inference that respondent's arrest was the result of unconstitutional discrimination, that inference alone would not entitle respondent to relief. It is important to recall that respondent's complaint challenges neither the constitutionality of his arrest nor his initial detention in the MDC. Respondent's constitutional claims against petitioners rest solely on their ostensible "policy of holding post-September-11th detainees" in the ADMAX SHU once they were categorized as "of high interest." To prevail on that theory, the complaint must contain facts plausibly showing that petitioners purposefully adopted a policy of classifying post-September-11 detainees as "of high interest" because of their race, religion, or national origin.

This the complaint fails to do. Though respondent alleges that various other defendants, who are not before us, may have labeled him a person of "of high interest" for impermissible reasons, his only factual allegation against petitioners accuses them of adopting a policy approving "restrictive conditions of confinement" for post-September-11 detainees until they were "'cleared' by the FBI." Accepting the truth of that allegation, the complaint does not show, or even intimate, that petitioners purposefully housed detainees in the ADMAX SHU due to their race, religion, or national origin. All it plausibly suggests is that the Nation's top law enforcement officers, in the aftermath of a devastating terrorist attack, sought to keep suspected terrorists in the most secure conditions available until the suspects could be cleared of terrorist activity. Respondent does not argue, nor can he, that such a motive would violate petitioners' constitutional obligations. He would need to allege more by way of factual content to "nudg[e]" his claim of purposeful discrimination "across the line from conceivable to plausible." *Twombly*.

It is important to note, however, that we express no opinion concerning the sufficiency of respondent's complaint against the defendants who are not before us. Respondent's account of his prison ordeal alleges serious official misconduct that we need not address here. Our decision is limited to the determination that respondent's complaint does not entitle him to relief from petitioners.

C

Respondent offers three arguments that bear on our disposition of his case, but none is persuasive.

1

Respondent first says that our decision in *Twombly* should be limited to pleadings made in the context of an antitrust dispute. This argument is not supported by *Twombly* and is incompatible with the Federal Rules of Civil Procedure. Though *Twombly* determined the sufficiency of a complaint sounding in antitrust, the decision was based on our interpretation and application of Rule 8. That Rule in turn governs the pleading standard "in all civil actions and proceedings in the United States district courts." Fed. Rule Civ. Proc. 1. Our decision in *Twombly* expounded the pleading standard for "all civil actions," and it applies to antitrust and discrimination suits alike.

2

Respondent next implies that our construction of Rule 8 should be tempered where, as here, the Court of Appeals has "instructed the district court to cabin discovery in such a way as to preserve" petitioners' defense of qualified immunity "as much as possible in anticipation of a summary judgment motion." We have held, however, that the question presented by a motion to dismiss a complaint for insufficient pleadings does not turn on the controls placed upon the discovery process. . . .

Our rejection of the careful-case-management approach is especially important in suits where Government-official defendants are entitled to assert the defense of qualified immunity. The basic thrust of the qualified-immunity doctrine is to free officials from the concerns of litigation, including "avoidance of disruptive discovery." There are serious and legitimate reasons for this. If a Government official is to devote time to his or her duties, and to the formulation of sound and responsible policies, it is counterproductive to require the substantial diversion that is attendant to participating in litigation and making informed decisions as to how it should proceed. Litigation, though necessary to ensure that officials comply with the law, exacts heavy costs in terms of efficiency and expenditure of valuable time and resources that might otherwise be directed to the proper execution of the work of the Government. . . .

It is no answer to these concerns to say that discovery for petitioners can be deferred while pretrial proceedings continue for other defendants. It is quite likely that, when discovery as to the other parties proceeds, it would prove necessary for

Qualified
Immunity

petitioners and their counsel to participate in the process to ensure the case does not develop in a misleading or slanted way that causes prejudice to their position. Even if petitioners are not yet themselves subject to discovery orders, then, they would not be free from the burdens of discovery. . . .

Because respondent's complaint is deficient under Rule 8, he is not entitled to discovery, cabined or otherwise.

3

Respondent finally maintains that the Federal Rules expressly allow him to allege petitioners' discriminatory intent "generally," which he equates with a conclusory allegation (citing Fed. Rule Civ. Proc. 9). It follows, respondent says, that his complaint is sufficiently well pleaded because it claims that petitioners discriminated against him "on account of [his] religion, race, and/or national origin and for no legitimate penological interest." Were we required to accept this allegation as true, respondent's complaint would survive petitioners' motion to dismiss. But the Federal Rules do not require courts to credit a complaint's conclusory statements without reference to its factual context.

It is true that Rule 9(b) requires particularity when pleading "fraud or mistake," while allowing "[m]alice, intent, knowledge, and other conditions of a person's mind [to] be alleged generally." But "generally" is a relative term. In the context of Rule 9, it is to be compared to the particularity requirement applicable to fraud or mistake. Rule 9 merely excuses a party from pleading discriminatory intent under an elevated pleading standard. It does not give him license to evade the less rigid—though still operative—strictures of Rule 8. . . .

4

We hold that respondent's complaint fails to plead sufficient facts to state a claim for purposeful and unlawful discrimination against petitioners. The Court of Appeals should decide in the first instance whether to remand to the District Court so that respondent can seek leave to amend his deficient complaint.

The judgment of the Court of Appeals is reversed, and the case is remanded for further proceedings consistent with this opinion.

It is so ordered.

SOUTER, J., with whom STEVENS, J., GINSBURG, J., and BREYER, J., join, dissenting.

. . . I respectfully dissent from . . . the holding that the complaint fails to satisfy Rule 8(a)(2) of the Federal Rules of Civil Procedure. . . .

. . . Ashcroft and Mueller admit they are liable for their subordinates' conduct if they "had actual knowledge of the assertedly discriminatory nature of the classification of suspects as being 'of high interest' and they were deliberately indifferent to that discrimination." Iqbal alleges that after the September 11 attacks the Federal Bureau of Investigation (FBI) "arrested and detained thousands of Arab Muslim men," that many of these men were designated by high-ranking FBI officials as being "'of high interest,'" and that in many cases, including Iqbal's, this designation was made "because of the race, religion, and national origin of the detainees, and not because of any evidence of the detainees' involvement in supporting terrorist activity." The complaint further alleges that Ashcroft was the "principal architect of the policies and practices challenged," and that Mueller "was instrumental in the adoption, promulgation, and implementation of the policies and practices challenged." According to the complaint, Ashcroft and Mueller "knew of, condoned, and willfully and maliciously agreed to subject [Iqbal] to these conditions of confinement as a matter of policy, solely on account of [his] religion, race, and/or national origin and for no legitimate penological interest." The complaint thus alleges, at a bare minimum, that Ashcroft and Mueller knew of and condoned the discriminatory policy their subordinates carried out. Actually, the complaint goes further in alleging that Ashcroft and Muller affirmatively acted to create the discriminatory detention policy. If these factual allegations are true, Ashcroft and Mueller were, at the very least, aware of the discriminatory policy being implemented and deliberately indifferent to it.

Ashcroft and Mueller argue that these allegations fail to satisfy the "plausibility standard" of *Twombly*. They contend that Iqbal's claims are implausible because such high-ranking officials "tend not to be personally involved in the specific actions of lower-level officers down the bureaucratic chain of command." But this response bespeaks a fundamental misunderstanding of the enquiry that *Twombly* demands. *Twombly* does not require a court at the motion-to-dismiss stage to consider whether the factual allegations are probably true. We made it clear, on the contrary, that a court must take the allegations as true, no matter how skeptical the court may be. The sole exception to this rule lies with allegations that are sufficiently fantastic to defy reality as we know it: claims about little green men, or the plaintiff's recent trip to Pluto, or experiences in time travel. That is not what we have here. . . .

I do not understand the majority to disagree with this understanding of "plausibility" under *Twombly*. Rather, the majority discards the allegations discussed above with regard to Ashcroft and Mueller as conclusory, and is left considering only two statements in the complaint: that "the [FBI], under the direction of Defendant Mueller, arrested and detained thousands of Arab Muslim men . . . as part of its investigation of the events of September 11," and that "[t]he policy of holding post-September-11th detainees in highly restrictive conditions of confinement until they were 'cleared' by the FBI was approved by Defendants Ashcroft and Mueller in discussions in the weeks after September 11, 2001." I think the majority is right in saying that these allegations suggest only that Ashcroft and Mueller "sought to keep suspected terrorists in the most secure conditions available until the suspects could be cleared of terrorist activity," and that this produced "a disparate, incidental impact on Arab Muslims." And I agree that the two allegations selected by the majority, standing alone, do not state a plausible entitlement to relief for unconstitutional discrimination.

But these allegations do not stand alone as the only significant, nonconclusory statements in the complaint, for the complaint contains many allegations linking Ashcroft and Mueller to the discriminatory practices of their subordinates. . . .

Viewed in light of these subsidiary allegations, the allegations singled out by the majority as "conclusory" are no such thing. Iqbal's claim is not that Ashcroft and Mueller "knew of, condoned, and willfully and maliciously agreed to subject" him to a discriminatory practice that is left undefined; his allegation is that "they knew of, condoned, and willfully and maliciously agreed to subject" him to a particular, discrete, discriminatory policy detailed in the complaint. Iqbal does not say merely that Ashcroft was the architect of some amorphous discrimination, or that Mueller was instrumental in an ill-defined constitutional violation; he alleges that they helped to create the discriminatory policy he has described. Taking the complaint as a whole, it gives Ashcroft and Mueller "'fair notice of what the . . . claim is and the grounds upon which it rests.'". . .

I respectfully dissent.

BREYER, J., dissenting.

I agree with Justice Souter and join his dissent. I write separately to point out that, like the Court, I believe it important to prevent unwarranted litigation from interfering with "the proper execution of the work of the Government." But I cannot find in that need adequate justification for the Court's interpretation of *Bell Atlantic Corp. v. Twombly* and Federal Rule of Civil Procedure 8. The law, after all, provides trial courts with other legal weapons designed to prevent unwarranted interference. As the Second Circuit explained, where a Government defendant asserts a qualified immunity defense, a trial court, responsible for managing a case and "mindful of the need to vindicate the purpose of the qualified immunity defense," can structure discovery in ways that diminish the risk of imposing unwarranted burdens upon public officials. A district court, for example, can begin discovery with lower level government defendants before determining whether a case can be made to allow discovery related to higher level government officials. Neither the briefs nor the Court's opinion provides convincing grounds for finding these alternative case-management tools inadequate, either in general or in the case before us. For this reason, as well as for the independently sufficient reasons set forth in Justice Souter's opinion, I would affirm the Second Circuit.

WHAT'S NEW HERE?

- *Iqbal* extends the formula of *Twombly* to all complaints, stating that *Twombly* was not limited to antitrust or any other subcategory of cases.
- *Iqbal* instructs courts facing a challenged complaint first to disregard "conclusory" allegations, then to decide whether the remaining non-conclusory allegations appear "plausible," in "light of judicial experience and common sense."

Notes and Problems

1. *Twombly* and *Iqbal* each hold a complaint insufficient to withstand a 12(b)(6) motion. They also carry the potential to destabilize the regime of civil procedure you are studying. Consider both levels.

2. Why did Iqbal's complaint fail?

   a. Identify the way in which the majority applied the two-step analysis it describes to the facts of *Iqbal*.

      i. Which allegations were ignored because they were considered conclusory?

      ii. Which failed the plausibility test?

   b. Try to hypothesize what additional facts would have satisfied the majority, taking the complaint past the "plausibility" threshold on which it foundered.

   c. How does Justice Souter's application of the plausibility analysis to these same facts differ from that of the majority?

3. The standing committee that considers revisions to the Federal Rules has over the past several decades promulgated (and the Supreme Court approved) a number of changes that restrict or stage discovery. The Civil Rules Advisory Committee could have entertained a proposal that would amend either Rule 8 or Rule 12 to provide for the two-step ignore-conclusory-allegations-then-decide-about-plausibility screening process. No such proposal has come to them. Had there been such a suggestion, the proposed Rule would have been subject to extensive comment by the bar and by the academy, and perhaps to some empirical studies designed to assess the nature and dimensions of the underlying problem. That did not occur except incidentally in the *Iqbal* briefs. Commentators have argued that the Justices should have been more hesitant to reinterpret the civil rules given the available amendment process. Justice Stevens, dissenting in *Twombly*, apparently thought so as well. He wrote: "I would not rewrite the Nation's civil procedure textbooks and call into doubt the pleading rules of most of its States without far more informed deliberation as to the costs of doing so. Congress has established a process—a rulemaking process—for revisions of that order."

4. What does *Iqbal* mean in practice?

   a. Commentators have been trying to answer this question since the opinion was announced in 2009, and have disagreed both regarding the answer and the proper methodology to apply. Some have compared courts' motion to dismiss grant rates before and after *Twombly* and *Iqbal* were decided. Yet, as several scholars have observed, such studies do not take into account the likelihood that litigants' behaviors might change as well:

Some plaintiffs may decide not to file a lawsuit knowing that it cannot withstand a plausibility pleading challenge, or might settle a case soon after filing for fear of a successful motion to dismiss. By the same token, after *Twombly* and *Iqbal*, defendants might be more likely to file a motion to dismiss, believing that the new standard increases their chances of success. Jonah Gelbach, attempting to capture both judicial and litigant effects, found that "[f]or employment discrimination and civil rights cases, switching from *Conley* to *Twombly/Iqbal* negatively affected plaintiffs in at least 15.4% [of employment] and at least 18.1% of [civil rights] cases . . . that faced [motions to dismiss] in the *Iqbal* period. Among cases not involving civil rights, employment discrimination, or financial instruments, *Twombly/Iqbal* negatively affected at least 21.5% of plaintiffs facing [such motions] in the *Iqbal* study period." Jonah B. Gelbach, *Locking the Doors to Discovery? Assessing the Effects of* Twombly *and* Iqbal *on Access to Discovery,* 121 Yale L.J. 2270, 2277-78 (2012). Others argue that pleading should not change dramatically post *Iqbal* because plaintiffs have strong incentives, regardless of pleading rules, to investigate the factual basis for their claims before filing and include those facts in their complaints. See William H.J. Hubbard, *A Fresh Look at Plausibility Pleading,* 83 U. Chi. L. Rev. 693 (2016). Scholars, using a variety of data and a variety of methodologies, have reached wide-ranging results. In 2013, David Engstrom counted 20 studies measuring *Twiqbal*'s impact. David Freeman Engstrom, *The* Twiqbal *Puzzle and Empirical Study of Civil Procedure,* 65 Stan. L. Rev. 1203, 1204 n.7 (2013) (compiling studies).

b. Judges also seem unsure about what *Iqbal* means in practice. Just as Justices Kennedy and Souter appeared to disagree about which allegations in Iqbal's complaint were conclusory, judges have not distinguished between "factual" and "conclusory" allegations in a uniform manner and have assessed "plausibility" in different ways. *Iqbal* in fact encourages this inconsistency, as it instructs judges to assess allegations in light of their "judicial experience and common sense," factors likely to differ from judge to judge.

c. Because the meaning of these two cases has yet to be worked out, and because they seem to offer a powerful new tool to defendants, "the *Twombly-Iqbal* motion" has become a staple of federal civil litigation. Consider a statistic: In the first 32 months after *Twombly* was decided, judges cited it almost twice as many times (22,980) as *Erie Railroad v. Tompkins*—considered a fundamental case in federal civil practice—was cited in the first 72 *years* after it was decided (13,546 citations)!

5. Assuming that *Iqbal* works some important change in pleading practice, in which cases will it matter?

a. In a number of cases the parties will already possess most relevant information. That will be true for many contract claims: The plaintiff won't know *why* the widgets weren't timely delivered, or why they fell apart, but will know *that* it happened, and can allege this in non-conclusory and plausible detail.

b. In other cases the plaintiff will have a plausible theory of, say, negligence, even if that theory turns out not to be the whole story: Defendant appeared to run the red light (though it may later turn out that her brakes were defective or she was under a heavy dose of painkillers that inhibited her reaction time).

c. The cases where *Iqbal* and *Twombly* will cut deepest are those in which the other side, and only the other side, possesses the information that will create or avoid liability. Claims of retaliation, discrimination, and other causes of action dependent on unlawful states of mind may be particularly difficult to plead: How can a plaintiff plausibly allege what a defendant's unspoken intentions were? In those cases, properly conducted discovery could reveal that information, but if, without it, the pleader cannot run the dual gauntlet of non-conclusory statements and plausibility, the case will die at the pleading stage.

b. Special Cases: Requiring and Forbidding Specificity in Pleading

As you have seen in *Twombly* and *Iqbal,* courts, rulemakers, and legislators have long wrestled with the question of how much specificity to require in pleadings. The 1938 Rules sought to avoid this problem with their "short and plain statement" requirement. But, in Rule 9, the drafters carved out some areas where a Rule requires more detail, and statutes have sometimes either required extra specificity or forbidden it. We look at a sample of such special cases.

Stradford v. Zurich Insurance Co.

2002 WL 31027517 (S.D.N.Y. 2002)

BUCHWALD, J.

. . . Dr. Stradford[, the plaintiff] is a dentist who maintains an office in Staten Island, New York. . . . Defendants are affiliated corporate insurers. Northern issued a policy of insurance . . . on Dr. Stradford's office effective August 18, 1999, thereby insuring the premises until August 19, 2000. During this term, Dr. Stradford apparently failed to pay the required insurance premiums, and Northern cancelled the Policy from October 10, 1999 to December 13, 1999. On or about December 6, 1999, however, Dr. Stradford submitted a "no claims" letter certifying that he had no losses from October 19, 1999, to that date. He also apparently resumed paying the premiums, and National reinstated the Policy on or about December 14, 1999. Dr. Stradford was notified of the reinstatement on or about January 9, 2000.

Less than ten days later, Dr. Stradford filed a claim on the Policy. Dr. Stradford notified Northern that, "[o]n January 17, 2000, [he] returned to his office from his vacation and found water dripping from frozen pipes and extensive water damage to his personal property and the interior of his office." He further notified Northern that certain dental implants, worth more than $100,000, which had apparently been stored in his office, "had become wet and [therefore] ruined." Dr. Stradford submitted a claim under the Policy for $151,154.74, and Northern made payments to Dr. Stradford in this amount. After receiving these payments, Dr. Stradford "submitted a revised claim under the Policy totaling $1,385,456.70, consisting of $168,000.00 for property damage, and a business interruption claim of $1,209,456.70." Northern continued to investigate Dr. Stradford's claimed loss. [The insurer concluded that the damage had occurred during the period when the insurance had lapsed because Dr. Stratford had not paid the premium and disclaimed coverage.]

Slightly less than one year later, plaintiffs commenced this suit seeking $1,385,456.70 on the Policy, less the $151,154.74 already paid, or $1,234,301.96. Defendants counterclaimed, asserting, inter alia, that Dr. Stradford "knowingly and willfully devised a scheme and artifice . . . to defraud defendants and obtain money by false pretenses and representations," and seeking the return of the $151,154.74, punitive damages, and investigation expenses. Dr. Stradford now moves, inter alia, to dismiss those counterclaims that are based in fraud for failure to state their claims with sufficient "particularity" under Rule 9(b), and to dismiss certain other counterclaims for failure to state a claim.

Rule 9(b) provides, ["In alleging fraud or mistake, a party must state with particularity the circumstances constituting fraud or mistake. Malice, intent, knowledge, and other conditions of a person's mind may be alleged generally."]* Here, defendants' counterclaims succeed in alleging facts that "give rise to a strong inference of fraudulent intent" as required by the second sentence of Rule 9(b). The timing of Dr. Stradford's claim, just ten days after the policy was reinstated, his alleged refusal to cooperate with National's investigation . . . and the size of his claim can fairly be said to satisfy this requirement.

We find, however, that the counterclaims do not satisfy the first sentence of Rule 9(b), which requires that the "time, place, and nature of the [alleged] misrepresentations" be disclosed to the party accused of fraud. Ross v. Bolton, 904 F.2d 819, 823 (2d Cir. 1990). Here, defendants' counterclaims simply fail to identify the statement made by Dr. Stradford that they claim to be false. Thus, it is unclear from the face of the counterclaims whether defendants assert that Dr. Stradford's claimed losses are improperly inflated, that Dr. Stradford's office never even flooded, or that the offices flooded, but not during the term of the Policy. In essence, defendants claim that Dr. Stradford lied, but fail to identify the lie.

The "primary purpose" of Rule 9(b) is to afford a litigant accused of fraud "fair notice of the[] claim and the factual ground upon which it is based." Here, defendants' counterclaims fail to provide Dr. Stradford with fair notice of precisely which statement, or which aspect of his claim on the Policy, they allege to be false. The counterclaims are therefore insufficient under Rule 9(b), and must be dismissed.

---

* [At the time of the decision the text of Rule 9(b) read: "In all averments of fraud or mistake, the circumstances constituting fraud or mistake shall be stated with particularity. Malice, intent, knowledge, and other condition of mind of a person may be averred generally."—Eds.]

Nevertheless, it is the usual practice in this Circuit, when there was no prior opportunity to replead,[3] to grant a litigant who has suffered a dismissal under Rule 9(b) leave to amend so that he may conform his pleadings to the Rule. Fed. R. Civ. P. 15(a) ("leave [to amend] shall be freely given when justice so requires"). Indeed, defendants have already moved for leave to amend and submitted a proposed amended pleading. This pleading cures the defects we found in the counterclaims dismissed above because it makes clear that defendants allege that Dr. Stradford's office was flooded at a time when he permitted the Policy to lapse, and that Dr. Stradford "misrepresented the date of the loss in an effort to bring the date of loss within the coverage period." Accordingly, we hereby grant defendants leave to amend their counterclaims. . . .

Conclusion

For the reasons stated above . . . [d]efendants are granted leave to serve their proposed Second Amended Answer and Counterclaims, in substantially the same form as presented to the Court. . . .

Furthermore, defendants have requested permission to move for summary judgment pursuant to Fed. R. Civ. P. 56(b). Defendants assert that plaintiffs breached their contractual obligations under the Policy by failing to cooperate in the investigation of the claim, and that this breach precludes plaintiffs from recovering on the Policy. Defendants' request is hereby granted. . . .

Procedure as Strategy

This case did not start as a fraud claim. How and why did fraud come into the picture? The policy and the claims forms contained clauses requiring Dr. Stradford to be truthful in his dealings with the insurer. If he had been untruthful, the insurer would have a defense to the plaintiff's breach of contract claims and could recapture any money already paid out. So why did the insurer allege fraud? Those of you who have read Chapter 5 know that punitive damages are available for fraud but not for breach of contract. Although punitive damages are awarded relatively rarely, the possibility that they might be imposed could strengthen the insurer's hand during settlement negotiations.

Consider an alternative explanation. Disputes like this one will be presented at least to a judge, and perhaps to a jury as well. No one likes an insurance company

---

3. While defendants have already amended their counterclaims once, they did so before receiving notice that Dr. Stradford intended to challenge their claims on Rule 9(b) grounds. In such a circumstance, we see no reason to dismiss defendants' counterclaims with prejudice. The better course, we believe, is to give defendants a chance to properly conform their counterclaims to the requirements of Rule 9(b).

that collects premiums but then fails to pay claims. By turning this case into one about fraud, the insurer can present itself—not Dr. Stradford—as the aggrieved party, the victim of fraud.

Dr. Stradford, the plaintiff, won the first skirmish in the pleading battle, when the court ruled that the insurer defendant had failed to plead fraud with the specificity required by Rule 9. But that victory proved very short-lived, as one can see in the closing sentences of the opinion: The court grants leave to amend and grants the insurer leave to seek summary judgment on plaintiff's original breach of contract claim—when the court granted defendant's summary judgment motion three months later, it left only the fraud claim against Dr. Stradford to be adjudicated.

Notes and Problems

1. Understand what Rule 9(b) requires.

   a. Recall the language of the counterclaim, quoted in the opinion above, that Dr. Stradford "knowingly and willfully devised a scheme and artifice . . . to defraud defendants and obtain money by false pretenses and representations." Why is this allegation insufficient to satisfy Rule 9(b)?

   b. How did the insurer need to amend its pleadings as a result of Rule 9(b)?

   c. Another case summarizes the kind of specificity typically required in Rule 9(b) cases:

   > Taking into consideration all of the allegations in Lanco's answer, defendant nonetheless failed to plead specific facts regarding the fraud such as the identity of Sheraton's agents or employees making the fraudulent representations, the identity of Lanco agents to whom the statements were made, the dates or locations of meetings between the parties, or the exchange of any documents during negotiations. The alleged misrepresentations themselves also are vague and fail to specify the obligations that Sheraton agreed to undertake. Courts have dismissed fraud claims pursuant to Rule 9(b) even where the pleader alleged specific communications because the claims lacked "particularized facts to support the inference that [a party] acted . . . with fraudulent intent." *Shields*, 25 F.3d at 1128-29 (party cited press releases and publicly filed corporate documents to establish fraudulent statements or nondisclosures). See also M.H. Segan Ltd. Partnership v. Hasbro, Inc., 924 F. Supp. 512, 526-27 n.20 (S.D.N.Y. 1996) (holding that plaintiff satisfied Rule 9(b) because party deposition supplemented pleadings to establish time and place of meeting and people who were present). The affidavit that Lanco submitted in connection with this motion provides no additional information regarding the alleged fraud. Moreover, Lanco's general allegation that Sheraton "knew the representations made were false, fraudulent and made with the intent to defraud" is insufficient pleading of scienter. See *Shields*, 25 F.3d at 1129 (holding that

Rule 9(b) was not satisfied where plaintiff alleged that defendants "knew but concealed" some things and "knew or were reckless in not knowing" other things).

> ITT Sheraton Corp. v. Lanco Inns, Inc., 1998 WL 187430
> (N.D.N.Y. 1998).

2. Why does Rule 9(b) require more specificity in pleading?

   a. For the fraud plaintiff the problem is that, if fraud occurred, plaintiff is likely still to be in the dark about some of the salient facts. In the actual case, Northern Insurance was able to get some prefiling "discovery" from Dr. Stradford under the terms of the insurance policy. In most fraud cases that won't be true. In those "average" cases the fraud plaintiff's lawyer wants to get to discovery to uncover information proving that defendant was misrepresenting the facts. But discovery will be unavailable if the complaint is dismissed for failure to plead with sufficient specificity to comply with Rule 9(b).

   b. For the defendant and the legal system the problem is that fraud and mistake cases threaten the legal framework of contract.

      i. Like contract, fraud grows from some dealing between the parties but has consequences quite different from contract. The point emerges perhaps most clearly in cases in which a "contract" plaintiff alleges that the defendant committed fraud because, even "during the negotiation and formation of the contract . . . defendants materially misrepresented facts so as to induce plaintiff . . . to pay for said goods when defendants had no intention of delivering the goods as promised." Event Marketing Concepts, Inc. v. East Coast Logo, Inc., 1998 WL 414657, *2 (E.D. Pa. 1998). Contract disputes can thus easily turn into claims of fraud, exposing the defendant to punitive damages, thwarting the rule of expectation damages typical of contract claims.

      ii. Mistake has similar but less dramatic consequences. A valid claim of mistake regarding the terms of an agreement will void a contract. But one of the bedrock ideas of contract is to settle, in advance, the consequences of some kinds of "mistake." If it is easy to plead mistake, a basic institution of current economic life—contract—is weakened.

3. Although Rule 9(b) is the only federal Rule requiring such specificity, there are other state and federal laws that have adopted special pleading requirements for certain claims.

   a. For example, California Code of Civil Procedure §425.13(a) provides that no complaint may state a claim for punitive damages against a health care provider "unless the court enters an order allowing an amended pleading," and that the court may enter such an order only after "supporting and opposing affidavits [show] that the plaintiff has established that there is a substantial probability that the plaintiff will prevail. . . ." Like Rule 9(b), California's procedure seeks to prevent insubstantial claims from advancing to discovery, but through different means. Is the California approach (amend after presenting evidence) preferable to the federal approach (plead specifically)?

b. In one specialized area involving fraud—securities—Congress has gone well beyond the requirements of Rule 9(b). The Private Securities Litigation Reform Act of 1995 sets forth elaborate pleading requirements that apply only to claims alleging fraud under federal securities statutes. Two of those requirements go beyond Rule 9(b). One provides that the complaint "shall specify each statement alleged to have been misleading, the reason or reasons why the statement is misleading, and, if an allegation regarding the statement or omission is made on information and belief, the complaint shall state with particularity all facts on which that belief is formed." 15 U.S.C. §78u-4(b)(1)(B). The same statute replaces the relative leniency of Rule 9(b) regarding states of mind, requiring instead that a plaintiff "state with particularity facts giving rise to a strong inference that the defendant acted with the required state of mind." 15 U.S.C. §78u-4(b)(2).

4. So far we have examined instances in which courts or statutes have required "extra" specificity. In some areas, courts, legislatures, and drafters of Rules have gone in the other direction, either forbidding specificity or making clear that it was not required. Responding to reports in which defendants fainted or had cardiac episodes after reading the amount of damages demanded in personal injury and wrongful death complaints, the California legislature has forbidden a plaintiff seeking damages in such cases from stating any specific amount in the initial complaint, instead allowing the defendant, after receiving the complaint, to demand a statement of damages. Cal. Code Civ. Proc. §§425.10; 425.11.

5. Allocating the Elements of a Claim

We have considered how pleading helps to define substantive law and, on occasion, aspires to sort strong from weak claims. But we're still missing an important piece of the picture. The substantive law tells the parties in general what issues matter in the lawsuit. The rules of pleading tell the parties the level of detail required.

But in a system driven by party initiative, one must also ask which party has the responsibility for alleging and, ultimately, proving which of those issues. To take a simple example, suppose in a claim for negligently inflicted injuries, the plaintiff alleged an accident, that the accident caused her injuries, and the extent of those injuries; would that complaint stand? You are likely to respond intuitively—no, the plaintiff has failed to allege defendant's negligence. But why is that plaintiff's job; why isn't it defendant's job, in his answer, to allege the absence of negligence? After all, we do not require plaintiff to allege that the statute of limitations has not expired; if defendant so claims, it is his job to allege that in the answer. Why? To take an actual example, why couldn't Joseph Haddle just allege that he was fired, and leave it to the defendant to prove that the firing was justified? Putting this question into technical procedural terms, which elements of the claim must be part of the complaint, and which are defenses, which the defendant must plead in his answer?

In any given case, resolving this issue can be important because, as a general rule, whichever party has the "burden" of pleading an issue must also produce evidence to demonstrate that allegation—or lose the case. If the case is close or the evidence bearing on the element in question difficult to locate, the locating of the burden may determine the outcome of the case. So how does a pleader know which party has the burden of pleading which element? For the great majority of common claims (like the example of negligence given above), either a millennium of common law cases or the applicable statute provide answers. Rule 8(c) sets out a list of affirmative defenses that a party responding to a pleading must assert. But new claims and new twists on old claims arise regularly. The next case displays the Supreme Court confronting a new burden of pleading question that arose after Congress changed the rules for prisoners challenging their conditions of confinement.

Jones v. Bock

549 U.S. 199 (2007)

ROBERTS, C.J., delivered the opinion of the Court. . . .

[Lorenzo Jones was a prisoner held in a Michigan prison. He claimed that, after he suffered injuries in custody in an automobile accident, prison staff refused to change his work assignment despite his complaints that the assignment aggravated his injuries. According to his allegations a prison staff member "told him to do the work or 'suffer the consequences.' Jones performed the required tasks and allegedly aggravated his injuries." Jones sued under 42 U.S.C. §1983. The Court consolidated his case with that of a number of similar prisoner suits, with certiorari limited to the question of pleading described in the opinion.]

I

Prisoner litigation continues to "account for an outsized share of filings" in federal district courts. In 2005, nearly 10 percent of all civil cases filed in federal courts nationwide were prisoner complaints challenging prison conditions or claiming civil rights violations. Most of these cases have no merit; many are frivolous. Our legal system, however, remains committed to guaranteeing that prisoner claims of illegal conduct by their custodians are fairly handled according to law. The challenge lies in ensuring that the flood of nonmeritorious claims does not submerge and effectively preclude consideration of the allegations with merit.

Congress addressed that challenge in the [Prison Litigation Reform Act, 42 U.S.C. §§1997e et seq. (PLRA)]. What this country needs, Congress decided, is fewer and better prisoner suits. To that end, Congress enacted a variety of reforms designed to filter out the bad claims and facilitate consideration of the good. Key among these was the requirement that inmates complaining about prison conditions exhaust prison grievance remedies before initiating a lawsuit.

The exhaustion provision of the PLRA states:

> No action shall be brought with respect to prison conditions under [42 U.S.C. §1983], or any other Federal law, by a prisoner confined in any jail, prison, or other correctional facility until such administrative remedies as are available are exhausted.

Requiring exhaustion allows prison officials an opportunity to resolve disputes concerning the exercise of their responsibilities before being haled into court. This has the potential to reduce the number of inmate suits, and also to improve the quality of suits that are filed by producing a useful administrative record. In an attempt to implement the exhaustion requirement, some lower courts have imposed procedural rules that have become the subject of varying levels of disagreement among the federal courts of appeals.

The first question presented centers on a conflict over whether exhaustion under the PLRA is a pleading requirement the prisoner must satisfy in his complaint or an affirmative defense the defendant must plead and prove. . . .

II

There is no question that exhaustion is mandatory under the PLRA and that unexhausted claims cannot be brought in court. What is less clear is whether it falls to the prisoner to plead and demonstrate exhaustion in the complaint, or to the defendant to raise lack of exhaustion as an affirmative defense. The minority rule, adopted by the Sixth Circuit, places the burden of pleading exhaustion in a case covered by the PLRA on the prisoner; most courts view failure to exhaust as an affirmative defense.

We think petitioners, and the majority of courts to consider the question, have the better of the argument. Federal Rule of Civil Procedure 8(a) requires simply a "short and plain statement of the claim" in a complaint, while Rule 8(c) identifies a nonexhaustive list of affirmative defenses that must be pleaded in response. The PLRA itself is not a source of a prisoner's claim; claims covered by the PLRA are typically brought under 42 U.S.C. §1983, which does not require exhaustion at all. Petitioners assert that courts typically regard exhaustion as an affirmative defense in other contexts, and respondents do not seriously dispute the general proposition. We have referred to exhaustion in these terms, including in the similar statutory scheme governing habeas corpus. The PLRA dealt extensively with the subject of exhaustion, but is silent on the issue whether exhaustion must be pleaded by the plaintiff or is an affirmative defense. This is strong evidence that the usual practice should be followed, and the usual practice under the Federal Rules is to regard exhaustion as an affirmative defense.

In a series of recent cases, we have explained that courts should generally not depart from the usual practice under the Federal Rules on the basis of perceived policy concerns. Thus, in Leatherman v. Tarrant County Narcotics Intelligence and Coordination Unit, 507 U.S. 163 (1993), we unanimously reversed the court of appeals for imposing a heightened pleading standard in §1983 suits against municipalities. We explained that "perhaps if [the] Rules . . . were rewritten today, claims against municipalities under §1983 might be subjected to the added specificity requirement. . . . But that is a result which must be obtained by the process of amending the Federal Rules, and not by judicial interpretation."

In Swierkiewicz v. Sorema N.A., 534 U.S. 506 (2002), we unanimously reversed the court of appeals for requiring employment discrimination plaintiffs to specifically allege the elements of a prima facie case of discrimination. We explained that "the Federal Rules do not contain a heightened pleading standard for employment discrimination suits," and a "requirement of greater specificity for particular claims" must be obtained by amending the Federal Rules. And just last Term, in *Hill v. McDonough*, we unanimously rejected a proposal that §1983 suits challenging a method of execution must identify an acceptable alternative: "Specific pleading requirements are mandated by the Federal Rules of Civil Procedure, and not, as a general rule, through case-by-case determinations of the federal courts." . . .

The argument that screening would be more effective if exhaustion had to be shown in the complaint proves too much; the same could be said with respect to any affirmative defense. . . .

We conclude that failure to exhaust is an affirmative defense under the PLRA, and that inmates are not required to specially plead or demonstrate exhaustion in their complaints. We understand the reasons behind the decisions of some lower courts to impose a pleading requirement on plaintiffs in this context, but that effort cannot fairly be viewed as an interpretation of the PLRA. . . . Given that the PLRA does not itself require plaintiffs to plead exhaustion, such a result "must be obtained by the process of amending the Federal Rules, and not by judicial interpretation." . . .

We are not insensitive to the challenges faced by the lower federal courts in managing their dockets and attempting to separate, when it comes to prisoner suits, not so much wheat from chaff as needles from haystacks. We once again reiterate, however—as we did unanimously in *Leatherman*, *Swierkiewicz*, and *Hill*—that adopting different and more onerous pleading rules to deal with particular categories of cases should be done through established rulemaking procedures, and not on a case-by-case basis by the courts.

WHAT'S NEW HERE?

- Unlike *Haddle v. Garrison* (where the parties disagreed about how to interpret "injury" and "property" in the statute), here everyone agrees that failure to exhaust administrative remedies will defeat Jones's claim.
- The issue before the Court is whether Mr. Jones has the responsibility to allege in his complaint that he exhausted those administrative remedies, or whether Warden Bock must in her answer allege that Jones failed to exhaust those remedies.
- The statute doesn't answer this question, so, as in *Haddle v. Garrison*, the Court must interpret the statute.

Notes and Problems

1. As a starting point be clear that Congress could have specified where it wished the burden of pleading to lie.

   a. The PLRA could have included a sentence or phrase requiring that "as a condition of maintaining suit, each plaintiff must plead exhaustion of administrative remedies, attaching to his complaint documents demonstrating compliance with this requirement."

   b. Alternatively, the statute could have said, "Defendant authorities may defeat any such claim by pleading and proving the prisoner's failure to exhaust administrative remedies."

   c. In either case, the obligations of the parties would have been clear. But neither clarification appears in the statute, thus necessitating the Court's ruling.

2. Why does the outcome of *Jones v. Bock* matter?

   a. In the great majority of cases the pleading rules provide a blueprint for later stages of the suit. Whoever has the burden of pleading an element of the claim will likely also have the burden of producing evidence to demonstrate that allegation. So the issue lurking behind every decision about the burden of pleading is who will ultimately have to prove the thing alleged in the pleading.

   b. Occasionally, the answer to that question will not matter. If Mr. Jones has neatly filed in his prison cell a copy of every grievance he made to the prison authorities, together with their responses, it will make no difference who has the burden. He will produce the documents, and the case will proceed to the merits—did the prison authorities behave with deliberate indifference (the constitutional standard in such suits) or, as they may claim, was the plaintiff just another prisoner trying to shirk?

   c. But that's not likely to be the case here. Suppose Jones has copies of some of his grievances, but not of others. In that case, the burden of pleading may take on great significance. Trial may turn into a swearing contest between the prison staff and Jones. Jones: "I complied with the prison's administrative grievance procedures." Warden: "No he didn't." If the trier of fact is unsure who's telling the truth the outcome may turn on who has the burden of persuasion, which usually follows the burden of pleading.

3. So, how is a court faced with such a problem to decide it, in the absence of legislative guidance? The opinion canvasses the usual sources:

   a. It looks at the words of the statute. Does the Court adequately explain why the opening phrase of the statute ("No action shall be brought with respect to prison conditions" [unless the prisoner has sought an administrative remedy]) does not set forth a pleading requirement? Perhaps because the claim does not arise under the newly enacted PLRA but under a venerable civil rights statute, 42 U.S.C. §1983?

b. The Court also looks at Rule 8(c), which lists common affirmative defenses, and finds that "failure to exhaust administrative remedies" is not among them. But, the Court notes, the list in Rule 8(c) is "nonexhaustive" (is the Chief Justice engaging in word play here?); in other words, there are instances not listed in Rule 8(c) where clearly established law provides that something is an affirmative defense. Does the statute creating Jones's claim so provide?

c. To answer that question, the opinion examines the legislative history of the PLRA ("The PLRA dealt extensively with the subject of exhaustion, but is silent on the issue whether exhaustion must be pleaded by the plaintiff or is an affirmative defense. This is strong evidence that the usual practice should be followed. . . .").

d. It then concludes that the usual practice "is to regard exhaustion as an affirmative defense" and rejects policy arguments in favor of putting the burden on the prisoner.

Implications

THE RULES, THE COURTS, AND THE RULEMAKERS

One aspect of *Jones* connects with *Twombly* and *Iqbal*, and forms part of a debate about whether important Rule changes should occur only through the amendment process or whether courts can "interpret" such changes. *Jones*, echoing a line of cases, says, "We explained that 'perhaps if [the] Rules . . . were rewritten today, claims [of various sorts] might be subjected to the added specificity requirement. . . . But that is a result which must be obtained by the process of amending the Federal Rules, and not by judicial interpretation." It does so after expressing sympathy for the burdens this will place on district courts, but concludes by saying that "adopting different and more onerous pleading rules to deal with particular categories of cases should be done through established rulemaking procedures, and not on a case-by-case basis by the courts."

Twombly, decided four months after *Jones v. Bock*, arguably changed pleading standards and bypassed the Rules amendment process. Seven Justices signed on both to the majority in *Twombly* and the unanimous decision in *Jones*. What values were at stake in both cases that might have persuaded the Justices to dispense with that process in one case, and demand it in the other?

Procedure as Strategy: Consistency in Pleading

Assuming one knows the substantive law and the amount of detail required in a pleading, a third question emerges: What if one has several, perhaps inconsistent, stories to tell?

A common law pleader had to worry about the consistency of his complaint. If Plaintiff alleged Defendant trespassed on Blackacre, Defendant could not simultaneously deny that he had entered Blackacre and assert that he did enter but had an easement. The attractiveness of this insistence on a single consistent story is obvious: We expect people in ordinary life not to vary their version of the facts from moment to moment. A person may legitimately assert either that she made a promise or she didn't; that she kept her promise or she didn't; but not that she didn't make a promise *and* that she kept it.

Yet modern pleading rules, of which Rule 8(d)(2)-(3) is one example, permit just this sort of apparent duplicity: "A party may set out two or more statements of a claim or defense alternately or hypothetically . . . [and a] party may state as many separate claims or defenses as it has, regardless of consistency." As a result, a defendant may deny that she ever entered into a contract with plaintiff and at the same time assert that she kept her side of the bargain; similarly, a plaintiff may seek to recover on the ground that a written contract provides "*X*" and simultaneously seek to have the court reform the contract so that the crucial clause reads "not *X*" rather than "*X*."

Understanding why modern procedure condones behavior that one would condemn in everyday life requires the student to recall the role of the pleadings in the lawsuit. First, pleadings come very early in the case, often before the parties know all that they will by the time the case comes to trial or to the point of serious settlement discussions. The lawyer is therefore often setting forth what seem to her to be the possible versions of the law and the facts that appear plausible at the time the pleading is filed. If discovery reveals that one of the inconsistent stories lacks strong evidentiary support, an amended complaint will drop it. Second, allegations in pleadings are tempered by burdens of proof. Thus, a lawyer who entirely believes her client's story that he had, but lost, a signed, written contract may allege that in her pleadings but, as a safety net, may also seek to recover on a quantum meruit count in case she decides she cannot convince a jury that the written contract existed. Finally, one has to remember that however inconsistent and contradictory the pleadings, the lawyer will often have to settle on a single version of the story before the case comes to trial. Both judge and jury will frown on a case that rests on logically inconsistent versions of the facts. (In a multiparty case the plaintiff might conceivably try different versions of the facts against different defendants, but this tactic has its limits.) Thus, inconsistent pleadings reflect not lawyers' propensity to talk out of both sides of their mouths but a pleading system that requires lawyers to make allegations before they are certain of the facts and the law. Inconsistent pleadings represent alternative drafts of a story, one version of which the advocate hopes ultimately will persuade a judge or jury.

A real-life example of alternate pleading appears in ¶14 of the *Haddle v. Garrison* complaint (at page 367). It alleges both that Haddle testified before the grand jury and that he did not testify but was prepared to do so. Obviously, both of these cannot be true. Presumably, Haddle's lawyer drafted the complaint at a stage where he was not entirely clear what happened, so he included both versions in his complaint. By the time the case reached trial, he would have decided which version to rest on.

B. ETHICAL LIMITATIONS IN PLEADING—AND IN LITIGATION GENERALLY

We have thus far examined pleading as a question of technique: how much detail; what issues are raised by a motion to dismiss; which party bears the responsibility for pleading which element of a claim; and how does modern pleading differ from its predecessors? Lawyers must understand those issues. But pleading raises another, more fundamental question: What responsibilities does the lawyer bear to her client and to the legal system? Many of those issues reach far beyond the scope of procedure, but one Rule requires us to examine these questions at the pleading stage.

We have glimpsed one aspect of this problem in *Haddle*. Haddle's lawyer could have avoided a 12(b)(6) dismissal by alleging that Haddle's contract guaranteed he would not be fired except for good cause. But Haddle's lawyer didn't. Why?

Without regard to ethical responsibilities, such ungrounded allegations are a waste of time and money. The case would survive a Rule 12(b)(6) motion only to collapse when it became clear that the allegations had no factual basis. But there is a second dimension—an ethical dimension. Long-standing rules and codes of professional responsibility forbid a lawyer from making groundless allegations. Consider, for example, Rule 3.1 of the American Bar Association Model Rules of Professional Conduct:

> A lawyer shall not bring or defend a proceeding, or assert or controvert an issue therein, unless there is a basis in law and fact for doing so that is not frivolous. . . .

Since 1983, the Federal Rules of Civil Procedure have incorporated a version of this standard. Read Rule 11.

As you saw in *Bridges v. Diesel Service Inc.* in Chapter 1, Rule 11 allows the court to punish a lawyer who files a pleading when he has no basis to believe that favorable facts or law will emerge as the case progresses. That by itself makes it an unusual Rule of Procedure. Most of the Rules tell lawyers how to operate the system: where to file papers, how to join parties, how to plead, what counts as a pre-answer defense, how to conduct discovery, and the like. Rule 11 is different. It regulates the way lawyers and clients conduct themselves, establishing standards for investigation of law and facts. In so doing, it embodies in a procedural rule a standard that might otherwise be found in a standard of professional conduct, or in the tort of malicious prosecution.

One might ask two questions about such an approach. First, one can ask whether such a principle in a Rule violates the Rules Enabling Act, 28 U.S.C. §2072(b), which provides that the Rules shall not "abridge, enlarge, or modify any substantive right." The Supreme Court considered and somewhat curtly dismissed the Rules Enabling Act challenge:

> This Court[] . . . in Burlington Northern R. Co. v. Woods, 480 U.S. 1 (1987) . . . held, in a unanimous decision, that "Rules which *incidentally* affect litigants' substantive rights

do not violate this provision if reasonably necessary to maintain the integrity of that system of rules." There is little doubt that Rule 11 is reasonably necessary to maintain the integrity of the system of federal practice and procedure, and that any effect on substantive rights is incidental. We held as much only last Term in *Cooter & Gell*: "It is now clear that the central purpose of Rule 11 is to deter baseless filings in district court and thus, consistent with the Rule Enabling Act's grant of authority, streamline the administration and procedure of the federal courts."

> Business Guides v. Chromatic Communications Enterprises,
> 498 U.S. 533, 552 (1991).

Second, one can ask, if professional ethics already condemn such conduct, why duplicate the provision in a procedural rule? One response is that Rule 11 allows courts to enforce the standards in the midst of litigation, rather than in an independent bar disciplinary proceeding that might occur long after the lawsuit was over. That potential can change the balance of power between the parties—and this aspect of Rule 11 has made it controversial, with some arguing that it chills meritorious litigation, others that it fails to deter enough frivolous litigation.

Rule 11 is distinctive in another respect. It establishes an interlocking set of standards, procedures, and sanctions—a miniature regulatory regime all its own, a regime that affects but does not directly regulate the entire conduct of litigation.

We consider Rule 11 in the context of pleading, but it covers every aspect of litigation that involves a written document—with the important exception noted in Rule 11(d). Pleading provides a good example of circumstances in which litigants make assertions about historical facts and the content of legal standards—both of which Rule 11 covers. Read the Rule and respond to the following questions.

Notes and Problems

1. Start with the question of what conduct Rule 11 covers.

   a. Party calls Opponent on the telephone, threatening her with a lawsuit that Party knows to be groundless. May Party be sanctioned under Rule 11?

   b. Is there a different result if Lawyer rather than Party makes the telephone call?

   c. Lawyer files a groundless interrogatory. May Lawyer be sanctioned under Rule 11? (See Rules 11(d) and 26(g).)

2. Client rushes into Lawyer's office, telling him a story of Defendant's actions that suggests several forms of liability. Lawyer drafts and serves a complaint pleading the claims described by Client. Defendant answers, denying all

the significant allegations of the complaint and, in the disclosure required by Rule 26(a)(1)(A), attaches documents, photographs, and affidavits from disinterested persons indicating that most of Client's story was entirely false.

    a. Is there a violation of Rule 11? By whom?

    b. If under these conditions Lawyer has violated Rule 11, how will his stance toward future clients change? Does the Rule in effect require that lawyers be skeptical of their clients' stories?

3. Suppose in the case described in Problem 2 the defendant wanted to seek sanctions under Rule 11.

    a. Could Defendant file a motion for summary judgment (to get the claim dismissed) and include a request with it for the attorney's fees expended in defending the meritless claim? (See Rule 11(c)(2).)

    b. If Defendant drafts a Rule 11 sanctions motion, what must she do before filing it with the court? (See Rule 11(c)(2).)

4. In *Haddle v. Garrison* (supra page 371), the district court opinion accurately stated that a decision of the Eleventh Circuit suggested that an at-will employee could not state a claim under the federal statute in question.

    a. Suppose that Haddle's lawyer did not know about that decision because he had not adequately researched the case. What provision of Rule 11 provides a basis for a sanction?

    b. In the actual *Haddle* case, the plaintiff's lawyer knew all about that Eleventh Circuit precedent. Suppose in the wake of the district court opinion dismissing the case the defendant had sought Rule 11 sanctions against plaintiff's lawyer. What phrase in Rule 11 would provide Haddle's lawyer with grounds to resist the sanctions?

    c. Would your answer to the preceding question change if every federal circuit had reached the same decision as the Eleventh? What if there were a U.S. Supreme Court decision directly on point—but it was from the late nineteenth century?

5. Imagine that Haddle's lawyer learned that the trial judge was going to dismiss the complaint because Haddle had not alleged that he held a job more permanent than at-will employment. Haddle then amended his complaint to allege that he had a written contract guaranteeing that he would be fired only for good cause. Garrison's attorney rightly decides to file a motion for Rule 11 sanctions. On what ground?

6. Lawyer files an answer alleging the statute of limitations as an affirmative defense. At the time Lawyer filed the answer, she reasonably believed that the facts warranted such a response. Lawyer later learns that a salient event occurred later than she previously thought, and that the statute of limitations therefore has not run.

a. Does Lawyer violate the Rule by failing to file an amended answer? (Compare Rule 26(e), which requires supplementation of responses to discovery requests.)

b. Does Lawyer violate the Rule by orally asserting this defense at a subsequent pretrial conference? (See Rule 11(b).)

7. Knowing the structure of the Rule is important, but this does not give the student a sense of the kind of conduct for which lawyers and clients find themselves in trouble. Consider some cases that canvass the range of behavior violating the Rule, the procedural issues raised when enforcing it, and the sanctions available. We start with a case that reminds the student of the risks of not mastering Civil Procedure.

Walker v. Norwest Corp.
108 F.3d 158 (8th Cir. 1996)

GIBSON, J.

Jimmy Lee Walker, III, his guardian, Cynthia Walker, and their attorney, James Harrison Massey, appeal from the district court's award of sanctions against Massey for filing a diversity case in which he failed to plead complete diversity of citizenship, and indeed, pleaded facts which tended to show there was not complete diversity. The Walkers and Massey contend that the district court erred in awarding sanctions at all, in determining the amount of sanctions, and in not allowing the Walkers to amend their complaint. We affirm.

[In a dispute over a minor's trust fund,] Massey filed a complaint in the district court for the District of South Dakota on behalf of the Walkers, alleging breach of fiduciary duty and other state law causes of action . . . [against Norwest Corporation and numerous individual officers and employees]. The complaint stated that jurisdiction was based on diversity, since "the Plaintiff and *some of the Defendants* are citizens of different states." (Emphasis added.) The Walkers are both South Dakotans. The complaint averred that one of the defendants, Norwest Corporation, was a Minnesota corporation. The complaint did not allege the other defendants'[2] citizenship precisely, but stated that many of them were South Dakota "residents." . . .

Upon receiving the complaint, the attorney for Norwest Corporation and its subsidiaries and officers wrote Mr. Massey informing him that his complaint showed on its face that there was no diversity jurisdiction [because long-standing authority requires *complete* diversity under 28 U.S.C. §1332(a)]. The letter asked Massey to dismiss the complaint, and warned that if he did not, Norwest would seek sanctions,

---

2. The defendants are: Norwest Corporation, Richard Kovacevich, Norwest Bank South Dakota, N.A., Gary Olson, Kirk Dean, Norwest Investment Management & Trust, Dennis Hoffman, Tom Naasz, Beal Law Offices, and George Beal. The individual defendants were sued individually and as trustees or corporate agents.

including attorneys' fees. Massey's only answer was a letter that acknowledged Norwest's correspondence, but made no substantive response to the deficiency counsel had pointed out.

After Massey failed to offer any explanation for his defective complaint or to move to amend or dismiss it, Norwest moved to dismiss and for an award of sanctions, as it had promised to do.

The district court granted the Fed. R. Civ. P. 12(b)(1) motion to dismiss for lack of jurisdiction and sanctioned attorney Massey under Fed. R. Civ. P. 11 . . . [awarding $4,800 in fees and expenses]. The Walkers and Massey appeal.

I

They . . . contend that Rule 11 does not require the kind of "complicated, in-depth, and possibly impossible inquiry" that would have been necessary to determine the defendants' citizenship before filing a complaint based on diversity of citizenship.

We review the district court's decision in a Rule 11 proceeding for abuse of discretion. Cooter & Gell v. Hartmarx Corp., 496 U.S. 384, 399-405 (1990). A district court necessarily abuses its discretion if it bases its ruling on an erroneous view of the law.

It was the Walkers' burden to plead the citizenship of the parties in attempting to invoke diversity jurisdiction. . . .

Furthermore, even though it is the Walkers' burden to plead, and if necessary, prove diversity, they did not allege that all of the defendants are domiciled in a state other than South Dakota. Instead, they argue that finding out the defendants' citizenship would be more trouble than they should be expected to take. This is a burden that plaintiffs desiring to invoke diversity jurisdiction have assumed since the days of Chief Justice Marshall. See Strawbridge v. Curtiss, 7 U.S. at 267 [1806]. The fact that the Walkers did not allege the citizenship of the defendants convinces us that the district court did not abuse its discretion in determining that Rule 11 sanctions were appropriate.

II

The Walkers and Massey next contend that the district court abused its discretion in awarding monetary sanctions, since dismissal of the complaint would have been adequate. . . . They also argue that the district court should have inquired into Massey's financial circumstances, and that if it had done so, it would have found that he "is presently experiencing financial hardships and is unable to pay this sanction." Not only did Massey fail to argue this point to the district court, but there is no record evidence to support the argument before this court. . . . We see no abuse of discretion in awarding monetary sanctions.

III

The Walkers and Massey contend that the district court abused its discretion in denying their request to amend their complaint. . . . After the dismissal and denial of the motion to reconsider, the district court held a hearing on the amount of attorneys' fees to be awarded. At that hearing, Massey began to reargue the merits of the dismissal. The court stated that some of the individual defendants were South Dakota residents. Mr. Massey replied: "I think an appropriate step for the Court to have taken would have been to dismiss those individuals that the Court considered that it could not bring into the diversity statute through pendent jurisdiction which is within the discretion of the Court." Massey still had not alleged a citizenship for many of the defendants and did not identify which defendants should be dismissed to create diversity jurisdiction. The district court is not obliged to do Massey's research for him, especially at such a late date.[4] There was no abuse of discretion. . . .

We affirm the district court's entry of Rule 11 sanctions in the amounts provided.

WHAT'S NEW HERE?

- The requirement of complete diversity has been well established for 200 years.
- If the Walkers had lost their case because their lawyer did not know about complete diversity, they might well have had a claim for legal malpractice. But that claim would belong to the Walkers—not to their adversaries.
- The outcome of this case is that the *defendants* get partial compensation for expenses incurred because of the plaintiffs' lawyer's ignorance of the law.

Notes and Problems

1. What portion of Rule 11 did the plaintiffs violate?

2. Who is responsible for paying the fees assessed by the court? The Walkers (Massey's clients)? Or Massey himself? Explain why Rule 11(c)(5)(A) would not permit an order that the Walkers pay this sanction.

3. Did the defendants comply with the steps set forth in Rule 11(c)(2)?

   a. They sent plaintiffs' lawyer a letter with notice of the complaint's deficiencies. But the opinion does not say that they gave the plaintiffs an actual Rule 11 motion, which they then filed with the court after waiting the requisite 21 days.

---

4. Although it is possible for this court to dismiss nondiverse parties on appeal, see Newman-Green, Inc. v. Alfonzo-Larrain, 490 U.S. 826, 836-37 (1989), the Walkers have not asked us to do so and therefore the issue has not been briefed.

b. If the defendants did not comply with this requirement, did the district court err by imposing sanctions? See Rule 11(c)(3). Some courts would so hold. See Arrival Star S.A., et al. v. Meitek Inc., Case No. 12-cv-1225-JVS (RNBx) (C.D. Cal. Jan. 28, 2013) (denying defendant's sanctions motion because it provided plaintiff only with the notice of motion, not "the supporting memorandum or any exhibits" supporting the sanctions motion, during the 21-day "safe harbor" period).

c. Suppose defendants had not raised the issue in any way but the judge had directed his law clerk to scan all complaints for apparent failure of subject matter jurisdiction (as many federal judges do), so he could dismiss them on his own initiative, as Rule 12(h)(3) directs. Read carefully Rule 11(c)(3), (4), and (5) and explain the process by which the judge could order a plaintiff to pay a defendant's attorney's fees under these circumstances.

4. Rule 11 applies to defenses as well as to claims. Consider the fate of a law firm that responded to a complaint of sexual harassment and retaliation claims brought by one of its employees:

> Defendants moved to dismiss the retaliation claims for lack of subject matter jurisdiction and the individual defendants moved to dismiss all claims against them for failure to state a claim. In support of the motion to dismiss for lack of jurisdiction, defendants submitted affidavits from the two individual defendants, other Wilson Elser partners, and Wilson Elser's chief executive officer. These affidavits denied the factual allegations in the Amended Complaint and asserted additional facts which, according to defendants, demonstrated that no adverse employment action had been taken against plaintiff. . . . Defendants contended that all of these facts established that they did not retaliate against plaintiff, and therefore, plaintiff's allegations of retaliation did not amount to a constitutional case or controversy and the court lacked subject matter jurisdiction over the claims. . . . To determine whether Rule 11 has been violated, courts apply an objective standard of reasonableness. Sanctions under Rule 11 may be imposed upon lawyers, law firms, and parties who violate the rule or who are responsible for the violation. Fed. R. Civ. P. 11(c). "Absent exceptional circumstances, a law firm [must] be held jointly responsible for violations committed by its partner[], associate[], or employee[]." Id. 11(c)(1). Monetary sanctions for violation of Rule 11(b)(2) may not be awarded against a represented party. Id. 11(c)([5])(A). Defendants' argument that the court lacked subject matter jurisdiction over plaintiff's retaliation claims was frivolous under an objective standard of reasonableness. Defendants' argument was not a contention about subject matter jurisdiction. It was simply a contention that plaintiff would be unable to prove her claims on the merits. Arguments about the merits of plaintiff's claims, of course, do not go to the court's power to entertain them, and are not appropriately raised on a motion to dismiss the complaint. No competent lawyer, after reasonable inquiry, would have concluded that this argument was warranted by existing law or by a nonfrivolous argument for the extension, modification, or reversal of existing law or the establishment of new law. . . . Because defendants presented to the court a written motion asserting frivolous legal contentions, plaintiff's motion for sanctions under Rule 11(b)(2) is granted. Moreover, I am persuaded that defendants' motion and supporting papers were presented for an improper purpose; namely,

to harass plaintiff and to increase needlessly the cost of litigating her claims.[1] Accordingly, plaintiff's motion for sanctions under Rule 11(b)(1) is also granted. Defendants' motion was submitted and signed by James D. Harmon, Jr. of The Harmon Firm. Accordingly, sanctions are imposed against The Harmon Firm and Mr. Harmon under Rule 11(b)(1) and (2). Sanctions are also imposed against Wilson Elser, Fuerth, and Anesh under Rule 11(b)(1) for presenting papers to the court for an improper purpose. Defendants are experienced lawyers who can fairly be held responsible for papers submitted to the court on their behalf. Moreover, defendants supported their motion with affidavits signed by the individual defendants and other agents of the defendant law firm. . . .

Wright v. Wilson, Elser, Moskowitz, Edelman & Dicker, 71 Fair Empl. Prac. Cas. 902 (S.D.N.Y. 1996).

5. The preceding cases deal with ignorance of well-established law. Probably the most common Rule 11 violation involves the failure to conduct adequate factual investigation. The next case displays that problem.

Christian v. Mattel, Inc.

286 F.3d 1118 (9th Cir. 2003)

McKeown, J.

It is difficult to imagine that the Barbie doll, so perfect in her sculpture and presentation, and so comfortable in every setting, from "California girl" to "Chief Executive Officer Barbie," could spawn such acrimonious litigation and such egregious conduct on the part of her challenger. In her wildest dreams, Barbie could not have imagined herself in the middle of Rule 11 proceedings. But the intersection of copyrights on Barbie sculptures and the scope of Rule 11 is precisely what defines this case.

James Hicks appeals from a district court order requiring him, pursuant to Federal Rule of Civil Procedure 11, to pay Mattel, Inc. $501,565 in attorneys' fees that it incurred in defending against what the district court determined to be a frivolous action. . . .

Mattel is a toy company that is perhaps best recognized as the manufacturer of the world-famous Barbie doll. Since Barbie's creation in 1959, Mattel has outfitted her in fashions and accessories that have evolved over time. . . . Mattel has sought to protect its intellectual property by registering various Barbie-related copyrights, including copyrights protecting the doll's head sculpture. Mattel has vigorously litigated against putative infringers.

---

1. At oral argument, I stated that my preliminary view was that I did not believe that the motion to dismiss was made in bad faith. I always prefer to believe that, but on further reflection, I cannot rationally support that tentative wishful opinion.

In 1990, Claudene Christian, then an undergraduate student at the University of Southern California ("USC"), decided to create and market a collegiate cheerleader doll. The doll, which the parties refer to throughout their papers as "Claudene," had blonde hair and blue eyes and was outfitted to resemble a USC cheerleader. . . .

In the complaint, which Hicks signed, Christian alleged that Mattel obtained a copy of the copyrighted Claudene doll in 1996, the year of its creation,[2] and then infringed its overall appearance, including its face paint, by developing a new Barbie line called "Cool Blue" that was substantially similar to Claudene. Christian sought damages in the amount of $2.4 billion and various forms of injunctive relief. . . .

Two months after the complaint was filed, Mattel moved for summary judgment. In support of its motion, Mattel proffered evidence that the Cool Blue Barbie doll contained a 1991 copyright notice on the back of its head, indicating that it predated Claudene's head sculpture copyright by approximately six years. Mattel therefore argued that Cool Blue Barbie could not as a matter of law infringe Claudene's head sculpture copyright. . . .

At a follow-up counsel meeting required by a local rule, Mattel's counsel attempted to convince Hicks that his complaint was frivolous. During the videotaped meeting . . . Hicks declined Mattel's invitation to inspect the dolls and, later during the meeting, hurled them in disgust from a conference table.

Having been unsuccessful in convincing Hicks to dismiss Christian's action voluntarily, Mattel served Hicks with a motion for Rule 11 sanctions. . . . Hicks declined to withdraw the complaint during the 21-day safe harbor period provided by Rule 11, and Mattel filed its motion. . . .

The district court granted Mattel's motions for summary judgment and Rule 11 sanctions. The court ruled that Mattel did not infringe the 1997 Claudene copyright because it could not possibly have accessed the Claudene doll at the time it created the head sculptures of the Cool Blue (copyrighted in 1991) and Virginia Tech (copyrighted in 1976) Barbies. . . .

As for Mattel's Rule 11 motion, the district court found that Hicks had "filed a meritless claim against defendant Mattel. A reasonable investigation by Mr. Hicks would have revealed that there was no factual foundation for [Christian's] copyright claim." Indeed, the district court noted that Hicks needed to do little more than examine "the back of the heads of the Barbie dolls he claims were infringing," because such a perfunctory inquiry would have revealed "the pre-1996 copyright notices on the Cool Blue and [Virginia Tech] Barbie doll heads." Additionally, the district court made other findings regarding Hicks' misconduct in litigating against Mattel, all of which demonstrated that his conduct fell "below the standards of attorneys practicing in the Central District of California." The district court singled out the following conduct:

- Sanctions imposed by the district court against Hicks in a related action against Mattel for failing, among other things, to file a memorandum of law

---

2. The United States Copyright Office issued a certificate of registration on November 20, 1997, for "Claudene Doll Face and Head." The certificate specified the work's nature as "sculpture," and the "nature of authorship" as "3-dimensional sculpture."

in support of papers styled as a motion to dismiss and failing to appear at oral argument;

- Hicks' behavior during the Early Meeting of Counsel, in which he "toss[ed] Barbie dolls off a table";
- Hicks' interruption of Christian's deposition after Christian made a "damaging admission . . . that a pre-1996 Barbie doll allegedly infringed the later created Claudene doll head. . . ." When asked whether the prior-created Pioneer Barbie doll infringed Claudene, Christian stated, "I think so . . . [b]ecause it's got the look. . . ." At that juncture, Hicks requested an immediate recess, during which he lambasted his client in plain view of Mattel's attorneys and the video camera;
- Hicks' misrepresentations during oral argument on Mattel's summary judgment motion about the number of dolls alleged in the complaint to be infringing and whether he had ever reviewed a particular Barbie catalogue (when a videotape presented to the district court by Mattel demonstrated that Hicks had reviewed it during a deposition);
- Hicks' misstatement of law in a summary judgment opposition brief about the circuit's holdings regarding joint authorship of copyrightable works.

After Mattel submitted a general description of the fees that it incurred in defending against Christian's action, the court requested Mattel to submit a more specific itemization and description of work performed by its attorneys. Mattel complied.

The district court awarded Mattel $501,565 in attorneys' fees. . . .

The district court did not abuse its discretion in concluding that Hicks' failure to investigate fell below the requisite standard established by Rule 11. . . .

Hicks argues that even if the district court were justified in sanctioning him under Rule 11 based on Christian's complaint and the follow-on motions, its conclusion was tainted because it impermissibly considered other misconduct that cannot be sanctioned under Rule 11, such as discovery abuses, misstatements made during oral argument, and conduct in other litigation.

Hicks' argument has merit. While Rule 11 permits the district court to sanction an attorney for conduct regarding "pleading[s], written motion[s], and other paper[s]" that have been signed and filed in a given case, Fed. R. Civ. P. 11(a), it does not authorize sanctions for, among other things, discovery abuses or misstatements made to the court during an oral presentation. . . .

The orders clearly demonstrate that the district court decided, at least in part, to sanction Hicks because he signed and filed a factually and legally meritless complaint and for misrepresentations in subsequent briefing. But the orders, coupled with the supporting examples, also strongly suggest that the court considered extra-pleadings conduct as a basis for Rule 11 sanctions. . . .

The laundry list of Hicks' outlandish conduct is a long one and raises serious questions as to his respect for the judicial process. Nonetheless, Rule 11 sanctions are limited to "paper[s]" signed in violation of the rule. Conduct in depositions, discovery meetings of counsel, oral representations at hearings, and behavior in prior proceedings do not fall within the ambit of Rule 11. Because we do not know for certain whether the district court granted Mattel's Rule 11 motion as a result of an impermissible intertwining of its conclusion about the complaint's frivolity and Hicks' extrinsic misconduct, we must vacate the district court's Rule 11 orders.[10] We decline Mattel's suggestion that the district court's sanctions orders could be supported in their entirety under the court's inherent authority. To impose sanctions under its inherent authority, the district court must "make an explicit finding [which it did not do here] that counsel's conduct constituted or was tantamount to bad faith." Primus Auto. Fin. Serv., Inc. v. Batarse, 115 F.3d 644, 648 (9th Cir. 1997) (internal quotation marks omitted). We acknowledge that the district court has a broad array of sanctions options at its disposal: Rule 11, 28 U.S.C. §1927,[11] and the court's inherent authority. Each of these sanctions alternatives has its own particular requirements, and it is important that the grounds be separately articulated to assure that the conduct at issue falls within the scope of the sanctions remedy. See, e.g., B.K.B. v. Maui Police Dep't, 276 F.3d 1091, 1107 (9th Cir. 2002) (holding that misconduct committed "in an unreasonable and vexatious manner" that "multiplies the proceedings" violates §1927); Fink v. Gomez, 239 F.3d 989, 991-992 (9th Cir. 2001) (holding that sanctions may be imposed under the court's inherent authority for "bad faith" actions by counsel, "which includes a broad range of willful improper conduct"). On remand, the district court will have an opportunity to delineate the factual and legal basis for its sanctions orders. . . .

Procedure as Strategy

Notice how defendant employed Rule 11. Since it had already won its summary judgment motion by the time of the Rule 11 hearing, why did Mattel bother to argue that motion? One answer might be that Mattel wanted its attorneys' fees and that investing a bit more lawyers' time in a motion for such fees would be worthwhile.

But even if sanctions took the form of a fine, it might go to the court rather than the defendant, an outcome that Rule 11(c)(4) explicitly allows—in which case Mattel would have incurred the added expense of a Rule 11 motion with nothing to show for it. Why was Mattel willing to run the risk of throwing good money (in the form of lawyers' time) after bad? Reread the third paragraph of the opinion; does it suggest that the Rule 11 motion was itself part of a long-range litigation strategy? What message does this motion send to other would-be litigants? Should the court have taken that strategy into account in ruling on the motion?

---

10. We emphasize that the district court's underlying order regarding summary judgment is not affected by this opinion. Nor do we disturb the district court's finding that Hicks filed "a case without factual foundation" or its other findings as to Hicks' misconduct.

11. Section 1927 provides for imposition of "excess costs, expenses, and attorneys' fees" on counsel who "multiplies the proceedings in any case unreasonably and vexatiously."

Notes and Problems

1. Note that Hicks's problems may not be over.

    a. Not only does he have to deal with whatever the district court does on remand, but California, like a number of states, requires that lawyers against whom Rule 11 or similar litigation sanctions are levied report that fact to the state bar, which could institute disciplinary proceedings. See Cal. Bus. & Prof. Code §6068(o)(3).

    b. And, using the findings affirmed in the Rule 11 segment of the case, Mattel sued Hicks and his firm for malicious prosecution, a tort in which punitive damages are available; a California appellate court found that the malicious prosecution action could proceed, citing the Ninth Circuit opinion in support of its conclusion. Mattel, Inc. v. Luce, Forward, Hamilton & Scripps, 99 Cal. App. 4th 1179 (2002).

2. *Christian* reveals a court deploying the full power of Rule 11 economic sanctions. Assume that either the judge or the opposition believes a lawyer has violated one of the provisions of Rule 11(b). After the appropriate procedural opportunities (notice, a chance to withdraw the pleading, and the opportunity to respond to charges), the judge finds that the lawyer has violated the Rule. What follows from that finding? See Rule 11(c)(4), (5).

    a. Need the court impose any sanction at all? Rule 11(c) provides that "the court may impose an appropriate sanction. . . ."

    b. The current version of the Rule requires that sanctions be "limited to what suffices to deter repetition" of the offending conduct and mentions nonmonetary sanctions (presumably such as requiring the lawyers to undergo additional training). Some appellate courts have urged trial courts to consider "which sanction 'constitutes the least severe sanction that will adequately deter the undesirable conduct.'" Kirk Capital Corp. v. Bailey, 16 F.3d 1485, 1490 (8th Cir. 1994) (quoting Pope v. Federal Express, 974 F.2d 982, 984 (8th Cir. 1992)).

    c. Faced with the prospect of invoking Rule 11 in this manner, one district court remarked, "This court is disinclined to bring Rule 11's mechanisms into play to consider the imposition of nonmonetary sanctions on [Name of Party] or her lawyer (an action that would most likely compel [Name of Party] to send good money after bad by having to become involved in such proceedings)—it is enough that the publication of this opinion names [Name of Party's] counsel for what it is." Pierre v. Inroads, Inc., 858 F. Supp. 769, 775 (N.D. Ill. 1994). That statement may not be toothless if the lawyer practices in a state that requires lawyers to notify the state bar of the imposition of sanctions. And one imagines that current clients will be unenthusiastic if they learn their lawyer has attracted that kind of judicial attention.

d. Another court, in a child custody case in which one branch of the family sought to challenge a child custody order by filing a federal civil rights suit, dismissed the complaint and invoked Rule 11 to order a lawyer to apologize:

> The court finds that the minimum sanction necessary to deter repetition by Fichtner and others similarly situated is completion of continuing legal education in federal civil rights law and Texas tort law, and submission of letters of apology to Katherine, the Armstrongs, and their counsel for asserting the claims that the court has held above are sanctionable. . . . As the court stated in *Holmes*:
>
> > This court has recognized that requiring counsel to apologize for errant conduct can have an exquisite impact and, in turn, a strong deterrent effect. A learned professional who is required by a tribunal to apologize for his conduct will not soon forget either the requirement that he apologize or the conduct that prompted the sanction. And the obligation that [counsel] fulfill a continuing legal education requirement should serve the salutary purpose of educating him concerning [the applicable] law.
>
> Accordingly, within 30 days of the date this memorandum opinion and order is filed, Fichtner shall submit to defendants, through their counsel of record, and to their counsel of record, letters of apology for asserting the claims that the court has held above are sanctionable. The letters shall not contain qualifying or conditional language. [A footnote gave examples of inadequate apologies: "Because the court has required that I do so, I am apologizing . . ." or "Although I disagree with the court's decision, I am apologizing. . . ."] Within one year of the date of this opinion, Fichtner shall complete 30 hours of continuing legal education in federal civil rights law (at least 15 of the required hours) and Texas tort law. These hours shall be in addition to any other continuing legal education required of him by any state or other licensing authority to which he is subject. None of the hours required by this order may be satisfied by self-study or in-office seminars. Fichtner shall advise the court by letter of the title, date, and sponsoring body of each program attended, and of the number of hours attended at each such program.
>
> Crank v. Crank, 1998 WL 713273 (N.D. Tex. 1998).

e. Rule 11(d) makes clear that the Rule does not apply to discovery requests, responses, and the like; Rules 26 and 37 deal with sanctions during discovery. But, as you will see at pages 515-17, courts can be equally creative when crafting sanctions under those Rules.

C. RESPONDING TO THE COMPLAINT

We now shift our focus from plaintiff to defendant and examine the array of responses available to defendants and the pitfalls and possibilities inherent in each. Suppose a friend comes to you carrying a complaint she was just served. (Chapter 2 gives you more detail about the way in which she might have been served, or how she might have agreed to waive service.) With the complaint, your friend received a summons, telling her to respond or face a default judgment. She asks you what she should do. What do you tell her? You would, of course, need to talk with her about the strength of the claims made against her, her interests and goals, and what money she has available for an attorney. But ultimately, she has just three choices: *default*, make a *pre-answer motion*, or *answer*. Consider them in order.

1. Default

As you will see in more detail in Chapter 8, in *Peralta v. Heights Medical Center* (page 525) a defendant who fails to respond to the complaint can have a default judgment entered against her. Rule 55. There is no reliable estimate of the number of defaults annually, but every year a substantial number of judgments are obtained in this manner. Why? For two reasons, one understandable, the other unfortunate. The understandable reason flows from substantive law. About 60 percent of civil claims are for breach of contract; a large proportion alleges the defendant's failure to make payments required by a loan or credit agreement. The substantive law does not give defendant many defenses to that claim: If she has not paid, a judgment will likely be entered against her. Under these circumstances, hiring a lawyer to defend the claim may not be a sensible move, if the outcome is foreordained. The unfortunate reason is that, though defendant possesses a meritorious defense, either she does not realize it or knows it but cannot afford to hire a lawyer. Chapter 5 addresses funding of legal representation for needy clients and may help explain why someone with a meritorious claim may nonetheless fail to sue or defend a case against her.

2. The Pre-Answer Motion (and a Close Post-Answer Relative)

A defendant who does not default can simply proceed to answer the complaint; this will be defendant's response in the great majority of cases. In her answer, the defendant can include procedural as well as substantive defenses. She can, for example, assert that the court lacks either personal or subject matter jurisdiction, that the allegations of the complaint even if true do not state a claim, and more. But whatever else the defendant does in her answer, she *must* respond to the substantive allegations of the complaint. She must, that is, either admit or deny that she and the plaintiff entered into a contract, that the plaintiff delivered or failed to deliver the widgets, that she was or was not negligent, and so on. An answer sometimes forces a defendant to admit or deny something she would prefer not to address at all, particularly in the earliest stages of the litigation. An answer can also be expensive. Recall that Rule 11 applies to answers as well as complaints; consider the level of factual investigation required to answer the complaint in *Twombly*—a defendant with thousands of employees located in many places. Note also that an answer must state certain counterclaims if they are available. And an answer almost certainly leads to additional expenses in the form of discovery—the next step following an answer. So, if a defendant does not want to default but would also prefer to avoid the expense and time of framing an answer to the complaint and the subsequent stages of litigation, what other course lies open? Read Rule 12(b). The seven defenses there can be included in an answer or in a pre-answer motion.

Unlike a pleading (e.g., a complaint or an answer), a Rule 12 motion does not require a party to set forth her version of the facts alleged in the complaint. Instead, it is a request that the court take some action in regard to the lawsuit. Civil practice is full of motions—to grant summary judgment, a new trial, extend time to answer, award attorneys' fees, and so on. We focus here on a subset of motions—the pre-answer motions—that have particular importance at the pleading stage. We will focus first on the Rule 12(b) motions, which carry special power.

Notes and Problems

1. Consider the list of matters included in Rule 12(b)(1)-(7). What do they have in common?

   a. Historically, they consisted of the old "dilatory" pleas, which would postpone but not end the case—plus the modern-day successor to the demurrer (found at Rule 12(b)(6)). Why, if one were designing a procedural system, would one want to provide an opportunity to get these questions settled before requiring an answer?

   b. Settling most of these matters will not require significant factual investigation. Sometimes they will, though—remember *Hawkins v. Masters Farms*, at page 7, in which the parties took depositions and exchanged discovery in support of a Rule 12(b)(1) motion to dismiss for lack of subject matter jurisdiction? Consider also the amount of discovery involved in some of the personal jurisdiction cases from Chapter 2—these decisions were rendered in response to motions to dismiss.

2. A pre-answer motion under Rule 12(b) can end a case, the court dismissing it without ever having considered the merits.

   a. For a defendant, that idea can be very attractive: It will save the costs of answering, discovery and defense on the merits, and end the suit quickly. For the plaintiff, of course, these features make a successful pre-answer motion a result to be avoided at all costs: It will end the suit without letting her get to discovery and the merits of the claim.

   b. Even a pre-answer motion that eventually fails may provide a defendant other benefits. Rule 12(a)(1) gives a defendant 21 days to answer the complaint, a period extended to 60 days if the defendant waives service of process. Rule 12(a)(1)(A). That period starts to run when the defendant is served, and includes whatever time it takes the defendant to find a lawyer as well as the factual and legal investigation necessary to frame an answer that complies with the requirements of Rule 11. A pre-answer motion stops the clock; see Rule 12(a)(4). Notice though, that because a motion will be in writing, it will thus be subject to Rule 11, so a frivolous pre-answer motion runs the same risk as a frivolous complaint or answer. For an example of a frivolous pre-answer motion, see supra pages 415-16.

Precisely because a Rule 12 motion delays the time for defendant to answer, and delays as well the next stage of the lawsuit, the Rules reflect suspicion that some defendants may use these motions primarily to delay. Rule 12(g) and (h) aim at balancing the availability of these defenses against that possibility. The balance struck poses some traps for the careless defendant's lawyer. Read Rule 12(g) and (h) and vaccinate yourself against malpractice by working through the following problems; be prepared to cite the language in Rule 12 that supports your response.

Notes and Problems

1. Arthur sues Beatrice in federal court for negligently inflicted injuries. Beatrice's lawyer believes that Arthur's suit suffers from several flaws.

    a. Arthur's complaint fails to allege that Beatrice's negligence caused his injuries. What motion should Beatrice make to raise this issue?

    b. Arthur has brought suit in federal district court in Illinois. Beatrice's lawyer believes that Beatrice's contacts with that state are so meager as not to support personal jurisdiction. What motion should Beatrice make to raise this issue?

    c. Can Beatrice combine her two motions—failure to state a claim and lack of personal jurisdiction—in the same motion?

    d. Now move on to consider traps for the unwary. What if Beatrice first moves to dismiss for failure to state a claim and the court denies the motion? Can Beatrice now move to dismiss for lack of personal jurisdiction? Can she include the lack of personal jurisdiction as a defense in her answer?

    e. Reverse the timing: Suppose that Beatrice first moves to dismiss for lack of personal jurisdiction. She now wants to argue that the complaint fails to state a claim. Can she raise this argument? How? When?

2. Andrea sues Bob in federal court for negligently inflicted injuries. Bob moves under Rule 12(b) to dismiss for lack of personal jurisdiction, improper venue, and insufficient service of process. The court denies the motion on all three grounds.

    a. Can Bob include in his answer the defense that Andrea's complaint fails to state a claim?

    b. Can Bob include in his answer the defense that the court lacks subject matter jurisdiction?

    c. Suppose Bob does not raise the lack of subject matter jurisdiction either in a pre-answer motion or in his answer, but the judge hearing the case notices, in reading case documents, that there appears to be no basis for federal subject matter jurisdiction. Is this defense waived? What should the judge do?

Besides the pre-answer motions listed in Rule 12(b), Rule 12 sets forth three other motions related to the pleadings—one of which would logically have to precede the answer, and two of which could come either before or after the answer.

Motion for a More Definite Statement.   Rule 12(e) is best understood in historical terms. Under early common law and Code pleading systems, the complaint bore much of the weight of narrowing the parties' contentions and exposing the issues in dispute. Under such circumstances it was frequently a fair request, as well as a good tactic, to ask the pleader to "make more definite and certain" his contentions. Such motions served as a form of discovery not otherwise permitted. Though it seems inconsistent with the idea of notice pleading, an analogous motion was carried over into the original Rules; there it proved to be the subject of more judicial rulings than any other part of the Federal Rules, often at the hands of judges unfamiliar with the philosophy underlying the Rules. At present, Rule 12(e) is infrequently, and almost never successfully, invoked. (For an example of one unsuccessful effort, see *Bell v. Novick Transfer*, supra page 19.) Some very vague claims will be subject to a 12(b)(6) motion; see *Twombly* and *Iqbal*. In other circumstances, in which the pleader has a fair idea what the claim is about but wants to know more about the precise nature of the pleader's case, discovery beckons.

Motion to Strike.   Rule 12(f) plays two quite different roles:

In its most common use the motion to strike allows a party to challenge a *part* of a pleading that fails under the substantive law, even though the rest of the pleading states a claim or defense. Suppose, for example, *A*'s spouse is killed in an auto accident with *B*, and *A* sues for wrongful death, seeking punitive damages. If the applicable tort law bars punitive damages for negligently inflicted injuries, defendant may move to strike the punitive damages allegations (though not the whole claim). See Mills v. Fox, 421 F. Supp. 519 (E.D.N.Y. 1976). In this use, Rule 12(f) acts like a Rule 12(b)(6) motion directed to a single allegation, or cluster of allegations, rather than to the whole complaint. See Fry v. Lamb Rental Tools, 275 F. Supp. 283 (W.D. La. 1967) (claimed damages for sorrow, grief, loss of love, affection, and companionship not recoverable under state law; motion to strike therefore granted).

In its other, less common, use, the motion to strike forces removal of irrelevant and prejudicial allegations in a pleading. Suppose a complaint or answer, in addition to alleging facts relevant to the claim or defense, makes gratuitously nasty remarks about a party. Under such conditions the court will entertain a motion to strike any "redundant, immaterial, impertinent, or scandalous matter." Courts will grant such a motion if allegations in the complaint have no relation to the case or are unnecessarily confusing; if the complaint is overly long and detailed (especially if it contains excessive evidentiary information); or if allegations are unnecessarily derogatory. See, e.g., Hughes v. Kaiser Jeep Corp., 40 F.R.D. 89, 93 (D.S.C. 1966) (striking reference to car as "death trap"); Budget Dress Corp. v. ILGWU, 25 F.R.D.

506 (S.D.N.Y. 1959) (striking defenses based on alleged conspiracy between plaintiff and underworld elements described as "strong arm men" and "racketeers"). Courts regularly point out that such motions are not favored, waste time, should not be granted as to background information, and should not be granted if the court is at all in doubt. See, e.g., Fuchs Sugars & Syrups, Inc. v. Amstar Corp., 402 F. Supp. 636 (S.D.N.Y. 1975). Accordingly, the decision to strike may depend on whether the allegations are likely to prejudice the moving party, which might occur if the pleadings will be read to the jury, and, if so, whether limiting instructions will be given.

Motion for Judgment on the Pleadings.   Rule 12(c) deserves mention here, though it comes, by definition, after an answer to the complaint. Suppose plaintiff alleges breach of contract, and defendant's answer consists solely of the allegation that he failed to pay his debt because he was supporting a sick parent. Even such an admirable act is not a defense to breach of contract, and defendant hasn't denied any of the allegations of the complaint. Under those conditions the plaintiff could move for judgment on the pleadings. The court would, essentially, match up the allegations of the complaint and those of the answer, and decide whether judgment for the plaintiff should be entered on the basis of the pleadings. On this hypothetical scenario, the answer would be yes: Plaintiff wins because the only "defense" stated is legally insufficient.

Another case suitable for judgment on the pleadings might occur if the complaint's allegations made it clear that the statute of limitations had run on a claim. Defendant might answer, asserting the statute as a defense and move for judgment on the pleadings. See Jin v. Ministry of State Security, 254 F. Supp. 2d 61 (D.D.C. 2003) (dismissing defamation claim against Chinese television program when complaint alleged that most recent broadcast of program had occurred outside the applicable one-year statute of limitations).

The motion for judgment on the pleadings will resolve a case in those relatively rare circumstances in which the parties' pleadings reveal agreement about the relevant facts and only the applicable law is in question. In such instances, slogging through discovery serves no use.

Notes and Problems

---

1. George, a student at a private law school, files a complaint alleging that the school's code of student conduct has violated his First Amendment rights. The school's lawyers intend to argue that the Amendment applies only to state action and thus does not apply to a private institution. What motion should the school file to raise this argument at the earliest possible time?

2. Same facts as in Note 1, except that the school has already filed an answer denying a violation of George's constitutional rights. What motion should the school file to raise its state-action defense?

3. George, having transferred to a public law school, files a similar claim against it, except that one paragraph of the complaint also states that the dean is a "cretinous old fool."

   a. Explain why you would not recommend a 12(b)(6) motion as an expeditious way of dealing with this complaint.

   b. Suppose the defendant answers, denying that it has violated George's constitutional rights. Why will a motion for judgment on the pleadings not dispose of the case?

   c. With what Rule 12 motion might the defendant have success, given the allegations in the complaint?

3. Answer

If the defendant cannot move to dismiss the complaint on Rule 12(b)(6) grounds or dispose of it on any of the other grounds listed in 12(b), she must respond to its factual allegations and can at that time raise some additional matter constituting a defense. Common law pleaders referred to "traverses" (modern-day denials) and "pleas in confession and avoidance" (our modern-day affirmative defenses). Both live on, though under less colorful names.

a. Denials

If you consider what you already intuitively know about the legal system, you will understand why the denial is overwhelmingly the most common response to a complaint. Unlike the situations in *Twombly*, *Iqbal*, or *Haddle*, most complaints do not involve edge-of-the-law allegations or disputes about the required form of pleading. Instead, they involve claims where the defendant agrees that she would be liable if she had done what the plaintiff alleges—but says she didn't do it. Under such circumstances, the right response is to deny one or more of the relevant allegations of the complaint. Rule 8(b) requires the defendant to deny only those allegations that she actually disputes, and Rule 8(b)(6) provides any allegation that is not denied is deemed admitted.

These simple principles, however, conflict with defendants' understandable tendency to "deny everything." At common law, the form of plea called the "general issue" was permitted for many forms of action; this plea placed all allegations of the declaration at issue. The modern analogue is the general denial, an allegation that denies each and every allegation of the complaint. A more limited form of general denial denies each and every allegation of a specific paragraph or group of paragraphs.

There is nothing bad in theory about the general denial. The problem is that extremely few cases arise in which the defendant can plausibly deny every allegation or, as is more common, every allegation not relating to the names and citizenship of the parties. Nevertheless, it is still not uncommon for parties to interpose a general denial when they mean only to deny the major operative allegations of the complaint. Courts condemn casual, blanket denials because they require parties to spend needless time ferreting out the real items in dispute. A defendant who enters such a general denial may well find himself on the wrong end of a Rule 11 inquiry.

The next case deals with the converse problem—a strictly accurate denial that proves to be remarkably deceptive. The case asks you to consider the purpose of denials in litigation.

Zielinski v. Philadelphia Piers, Inc.

139 F. Supp. 408 (E.D. Pa. 1956)

VAN DUSEN, J.

Plaintiff requests a ruling that, for the purposes of this case, the motor-driven fork lift operated by Sandy Johnson on February 9, 1953, was owned by defendant and that Sandy Johnson was its agent acting in the course of his employment on that date. The following facts are established by the pleadings, interrogatories, depositions and uncontradicted portions of affidavits:

1. Plaintiff filed his complaint on April 28, 1953, for personal injuries received on February 9, 1953, while working on Pier 96, Philadelphia, for J.A. McCarthy, as a result of a collision of two motor-driven fork lifts.

2. Paragraph 5 of this complaint stated that "a motor-driven vehicle known as a fork lift or chisel, owned, operated and controlled by the defendant, its agents, servants and employees, was so negligently and carelessly managed . . . that the same . . . did come into contact with the plaintiff causing him to sustain the injuries more fully hereinafter set forth."

3. The "First Defense" of the Answer stated "Defendant . . . (c) denies the averments of paragraph 5. . . ."

4. The motor-driven vehicle known as a fork lift or chisel, which collided with the McCarthy fork lift on which plaintiff was riding, had on it the initials "P.P.I."

5. On February 10, 1953, Carload Contractors, Inc. made a report of this accident to its insurance company, whose policy No. CL 3964 insured Carload Contractors, Inc. against potential liability for the negligence of its employees contributing to a collision of the type described in paragraph 2 above.

6. By letter of April 29, 1953, the complaint served on defendant was forwarded to the above-mentioned insurance company. This letter read as follows:

> Gentlemen:
>
> As per telephone conversation today with your office, we attach hereto "Complaint in Trespass" as brought against Philadelphia Piers, Inc. by one Frank Zielinski for supposed injuries sustained by him on February 9, 1953.
>
> We find that a fork lift truck operated by an employee of Carload Contractors, Inc. also insured by yourselves was involved in an accident with another chisel truck, which, was alleged [sic], did cause injury to Frank Zielinski, and same was reported

to you by Carload Contractors, Inc. at the time, and you assigned Claim Number OL 0153-94 to this claim.

Should not this Complaint in Trespass be issued against Carload Contractors, Inc. and not Philadelphia Piers, Inc.?

We forward for your handling.

7. Interrogatories 1 to 5 and the answers thereto, which were sworn to by defendant's General Manager on June 12, 1953, and filed on June 22, 1953, read as follows:

1. State whether you have received any information of an injury sustained by the plaintiff on February 9, 1953, South Wharves. If so, state when and from whom you first received notice of such injury.

A. We were first notified of this accident on or about February 9, 1953 by Thomas Wilson.

2. State whether you caused an investigation to be made of the circumstances of said injury and if so, state who made such investigation and when it was made.

A. We made a very brief investigation on February 9, 1953 and turned the matter over to (our insurance company) for further investigation. . . .

8. At a deposition taken August 18, 1953, Sandy Johnson testified that he was the employee of defendant on February 9, 1953, and had been their employee for approximately fifteen years.

9. At a pre-trial conference held on September 27, 1955, plaintiff first learned that over a year before February 9, 1953, the business of moving freight on piers in Philadelphia, formerly conducted by defendant, had been sold by it to Carload Contractors, Inc. and Sandy Johnson had been transferred to the payroll of this corporation without apparently realizing it, since the nature or location of his work had not changed. . . .

10. Defendant now admits that on February 9, 1953, it owned the fork lift in the custody of Sandy Johnson and that this fork lift was leased to Carload Contractors, Inc. It is also admitted that the pier on which the accident occurred was leased by defendant.

11. There is no indication of action by either party in bad faith and there is no proof of inaccurate statements being made with intent to deceive. Because defendant made a prompt investigation of the accident . . . its insurance company has been representing the defendant since suit was brought, and this company insures Carload Contractors, Inc. also, requiring defendant to defend this suit, will not prejudice it. Under these circumstances, and for the purposes of this action, it is ordered that the following shall be stated to the jury at the trial:

It is admitted that, on February 9, 1953, the towmotor or fork lift bearing the initials "P.P.I." was owned by defendant and that Sandy Johnson was a servant in the employ of defendant and doing its work on that date.

This ruling is based on the following principles:

1. Under the circumstances of this case, the answer contains an ineffective denial of that part of paragraph 5 of the complaint which alleges that "a motor driven

vehicle known as a fork lift or chisel (was) owned, operated and controlled by the defendant, its agents, servants and employees." Fed. R. Civ. P. 8(b), 28 U.S.C. provides:

> A party shall state in short and plain terms his defenses to each claim asserted and shall admit or deny the averments upon which the adverse party relies. . . . Denials shall fairly meet the substance of the averments denied. When a pleader intends in good faith to deny only a part or a qualification of an averment, he shall specify so much of it as is true and material and shall deny only the remainder.

For example, it is quite clear that defendant does not deny the averment in paragraph 5 that the fork lift came into contact with plaintiff, since it admits, in the answers to interrogatories, that an investigation of an occurrence of the accident had been made and that a report dated February 10, 1953, was sent to its insurance company stating "While Frank Zielinski was riding on bumper of chisel and holding rope to secure cargo, the chisel truck collided with another chisel truck operated by Sandy Johnson causing injuries to Frank Zielinski's legs and hurt head of Sandy Johnson." Compliance with the above-mentioned rule required that defendant file a more specific answer than a general denial. A specific denial of parts of this paragraph and specific admission of other parts would have warned plaintiff that he had sued the wrong defendant.

Paragraph 8.23 of Moore's Federal Practice (2nd Edition) Vol. II, p. 1680, says: "In such a case, the defendant should make clear just what he is denying and what he is admitting." This answer to paragraph 5 does not make clear to plaintiff the defenses he must be prepared to meet. . . .

2. Under the circumstances of this case, principles of equity require that defendant be estopped from denying agency because, otherwise, its inaccurate statements and statements in the record, which it knew (or had the means of knowing within its control) were inaccurate, will have deprived plaintiff of his right of action.

If Interrogatory 2 had been answered accurately by saying that employees of Carload Contractors, Inc. had turned the matter over to the insurance company,[11] it seems clear that plaintiff would have realized his mistake. The fact that if Sandy Johnson had testified accurately, the plaintiff could have brought its action against the proper party defendant within the statutory period of limitations is also a factor to be considered, since defendant was represented at the deposition and received knowledge of the inaccurate testimony.

At least one appellate court has stated that the doctrine of equitable estoppel will be applied to prevent a party from taking advantage of the statute of limitations where the plaintiff has been misled by conduct of such party. See *Peters v. Public Service*

---

11. Pages 73 and 85 of the depositions of October 14, 1955, indicate that the answer to Interrogatory 2 was also inaccurate in saying that defendant made the investigation of the accident; but actually the employees of Carload Contractors, Inc. made the investigation.

Corporation. In that case, the court said, "Of course, defendants were under no duty to advise complainants' attorney of his error, other than by appropriate pleadings, but neither did defendants have a right, knowing of the mistake, to foster it by its acts of omission." This doctrine has been held to estop a party from taking advantage of a document of record where the misleading conduct occurred after the recording, so that application of this doctrine would not necessarily be precluded in a case such as this where the misleading answers to interrogatories and depositions were subsequent to the filing of the answer, even if the denial in the answer had been sufficient.

Since this is a pre-trial order, it may be modified at the trial if the trial judge determines from the facts which then appear that justice so requires.

Notes and Problems

---

1. Start by getting clear about the real problem in this case and how it arose.

    a. For purposes of tort law, an employer is responsible for the negligent torts of an employee while at work. Whoever ran the business—"operated and controlled" the forklift, in the language of the complaint—was therefore responsible if Sandy Johnson had been negligent.

    b. Now read ¶5 of the complaint (quoted in ¶2 of the opinion). What do you suppose the plaintiff *thought* the defendant meant by denying those allegations?

    c. At some point before trial, the confusion about who was responsible for the forklift became obvious to both parties. Why didn't plaintiff at that point simply voluntarily dismiss the suit against Philadelphia Piers (Rule 41(a) permits such dismissals) and file a new complaint naming the correct defendant, Carload Contractors? What prevented this course of action?

2. Now focus on the court's dilemma.

    a. The denial by Philadelphia Piers that it operated and controlled the forklift was true. The judge's order thus forced the defendant at trial to admit something that was false. Why is the judge doing that?

    b. The court's action would be easy to understand if the court had found that the defendant purposely misled the plaintiff, but that explanation fails on two accounts, according to the opinion: "There is no indication of action by either party in bad faith and there is no proof of inaccurate statements being made with intent to deceive."

    c. Did plaintiff make it easy for this defendant to make this deceptive response? Redraft the complaint in a way that would make it much less likely that a hastily drafted answer would unintentionally deceive.

3. In spite of the court's order that Philadelphia Piers admit a fact that wasn't true, the result of the case is probably just. Why? Why does the court's order not harm an innocent party?

4. *Zielinski* illustrates a perennial problem of pleading and in that sense is very much "good law." But two Rule changes since the case was decided would alter the path by which a court could get to a sensible result.

   a. Read Rule 26(e)(1) and Rule 37(c)(1); can you craft an alternative opinion using these Rules?

   b. Read Rule 15(c)(1)(C); can you craft an alternative opinion using this Rule?

5. *Zielinski* is a case in which defendant with complete certainty could have denied the allegation of operation and control, had it focused on that allegation. What happens if defendant is not sure, or if she believes that plaintiff's allegations may be true? Some defendants seek to evade the requirements of Rule 8 by "putting plaintiff to his proof." That practice, at odds with the spirit of Rule 8(b), drew a spirited rebuke from one federal judge who had seen it tried in one case too many:

> This is it. For too many years and in too many hundreds of cases this Court has been reading, and has been compelled to order the correction of, allegedly responsive pleadings that are written by lawyers who are either unaware of or who choose to depart from Rule 8(b)'s plain roadmap. It identifies only three alternatives as available for use in an answer to the allegations of a complaint: to admit those allegations, to deny them or to state a disclaimer (if it can be made in the objective and subjective good faith demanded by Rule 11) in the express terms of Rule 8(b)(5), which then entitles the pleader to the benefit of a deemed denial. Here [defendants'] counsel has engaged in a particularly vexatious violation of that most fundamental aspect of federal pleading. It is hard to imagine, but fully 30 of the Response's 35 paragraphs . . . contain this nonresponse, in direct violation of Rule 8(b)'s express teaching:
>
>> Neither admit nor deny the allegations of said Paragraph—but demand strict proof thereof.
>
> It is time for this Court to follow the Rules itself, in this instance Rule 8[(b)(6)]:
>
>> [An allegation—other than one relating to the amount of damages—is admitted if a responsive pleading is required and the allegation is not denied.]*
>
> . . . Accordingly all of the allegations of Complaint ¶¶6-12, 17, 25-26 and 33-34 are held to have been admitted by [defendants], and this action will proceed on that basis.
>
> King Vision Pay Per View, Ltd. v. J.C. Dimitri's Restaurant, Inc.,
180 F.R.D. 332 (N.D. Ill. 1998).

---

* [At the time the case was decided, the analogous provision, contained in what was then Rule 8(d) read: "Averments in a pleading to which a responsive pleading is required, other than those as to the amount of damage, are admitted when not denied in the responsive pleading."—Eds.]

6. In light of the excerpt above, consider how a defendant should respond in the following situation. Suppose *A*, a jogger, is injured when *B*'s car swerves off the road and hits *A*. *A* sues *B*. After reviewing the text of Rule 11(b), decide how *B* should respond to the following allegations:

   a. The complaint alleges that *B* has not had his car serviced for the past two years. Although this allegation is true, *B* knows that it will be impossible for *A* to prove it.

   b. The complaint alleges that *A* was running north (the same direction *B* was driving). *B* does not doubt that this is true but did not actually see *A* running.

   c. Same facts as in 6b, except that *X*, a friend of *A*, has told *B* that he was standing 20 feet away and saw *A* running north.

b. Affirmative Defenses

Zielinski demonstrates that the traverse lives on in the form of the general or specific denial. This section asks where the borderline lies between a denial and an affirmative defense—the old plea in confession and avoidance. A defense is anything that defeats recovery: A denial of a critical allegation of a complaint is a defense. By contrast, an affirmative defense is an additional allegation—not just a denial of an allegation of the complaint—that defeats liability. For example, in a negligence case, a denial of negligence would be a defense, and an allegation that the statute of limitations had run would be an affirmative defense. Defendants, when they answer a complaint, must include any affirmative defenses they wish to assert in their answer. A nonexhaustive list of affirmative defenses can be found at Rule 8(c). Defendants then bear the burden of persuasion at trial on any affirmative defense they raise. In *Jones v. Bock*, you saw the U.S. Supreme Court sorting out whether the plaintiff/prisoner's exhaustion of administrative remedies was part of a properly pleaded claim or was an affirmative defense. An affirmative defense, held the Court (supra page 403).

Notes and Problems

---

1. As a review of the material thus far, explain why the ruling in *Jones* means that a defendant wishing to rely on Jones's failure to exhaust administrative remedies cannot use a Rule 12(b)(6) motion to raise that issue.

2. Take things one step further. Suppose that after the decision in *Jones v. Bock* a similar case arises, in which the defendant warden intends to rely on the prisoner-plaintiff's failure to exhaust remedies. Prisoner pleads unconstitutional mistreatment. Defendant admits the allegations of the complaint and asserts no affirmative defenses, but intends to introduce at trial evidence concerning failure to exhaust as his sole defense. As a further review, explain what motion the plaintiff should make in order to prevail at this stage of the case.

3. Now suppose that on remand after the decision in *Jones v. Bock*, the warden-defendant is offered a chance to amend the answer. Figuring that everyone understands that he will challenge Jones's exhaustion of remedies, warden does not amend. The case comes on for a hearing, at which the defendant wants to offer evidence tending to show that Jones did not exhaust his administrative remedies. Jones could object to the evidence, arguing that the pleadings failed to raise the issue of exhaustion: By omitting the defense of failure to exhaust administrative remedies in the answer, the defendant had waived the defense, and evidence concerning a waived defense is inadmissible.

4. Take another variation on *Jones*. This time the defendant-warden does amend the answer on remand, alleging failure to exhaust as an affirmative defense.

   a. Read Rule 7(a) and explain why Jones cannot file a pleading denying the warden's allegations of failure to exhaust (unless ordered to by the court).

   b. The case goes to trial, where both plaintiff and defendants offer evidence about the issue of exhaustion. There are some documents, but much of the evidence concerns oral statements that Jones either did or did not make to various prison staff members. With the evidence in this state, the court's instruction to the jury on burdens of persuasion may matter. Such an instruction could say, "On the issue of exhaustion, you should find for the defendants unless you are persuaded by the preponderance of the evidence that plaintiff exhausted his administrative remedies at the prison." Or it could say, "On the issue of exhaustion, you should find for the plaintiff unless you are convinced by a preponderance of the evidence that plaintiff failed to exhaust administrative remedies." In a close case—like this one—it may matter which instruction is given. After *Jones v. Bock*, which instruction should the district judge give?

5. One point of Note 4b is that an element's status as a part of the complaint or as an affirmative defense does not end at the pleading stage but often ripples through the entire lawsuit. That makes it important to know when some element of a case rests on the plaintiff or defendant to plead, whether it is part of plaintiff's claim or an affirmative defense. For the great majority of common claims and defenses the matter is well settled. But this is not always so, and, unfortunately, there are neither clear rules nor well-settled principles for deciding doubtful cases.

   a. Rule 8(c)(1) dodges the matter by coyly telling us that the list of affirmative defenses "include[s]" those it listed; as the Court noted in *Jones v. Bock*, it's understood that this list does not include all such defenses. So one has to trudge through statutes and case law in some instances.

   b. Reading such cases, one occasionally finds unhelpfully broad pronouncements about how one aspect of proof or another is inherently part (or not part) of the elements of the claim—and therefore (or therefore not) put at issue by a general denial. That is of course circular: It's part of the claim if the court so rules and it's an affirmative defense if the court rules otherwise.

c. It may prove more helpful to think of a function of pleading as preventing unfair surprise. Most cases won't involve a statute of limitations defense, for example. If the defendant intends to raise that defense, it should do so in a way that does not surprise the plaintiff—with an affirmative defense. New York State civil procedure rules structure pleading in this manner. See N.Y. Civ. Prac. L. & R. §3018(b) (requiring pleading of "all matters which if not pleaded would be likely to take the adverse party by surprise or would raise issues of fact not appearing on the face of a prior pleading"). Should the Rules adopt such a principle—or would that just lead to litigation over which defenses were "likely to surprise"?

4. Reply

Once upon a time, the dance of pleading could go on and on, as the legal system sought to extract from the parties exact agreement about which questions of law and fact were in dispute. That effort yielded pleadings with wonderfully exotic names: replication, rejoinder (a word that lives on in a colloquial sense), surrejoinder, rebutter, and surrebutter. Today the legal system depends on discovery, the summary judgment motion, and the pretrial process to identify the issues of real contention.

As a consequence, in most cases, the pleadings stop with the answer. This is true whether the answer simply denies certain allegations of the complaint or contains new matter in the form of various affirmative defenses. There are two small exceptions to this principle.

Suppose the answer contains a counterclaim. Rule 7(a)(3) requires an answer by the plaintiff if the defendant's answer contains "a counterclaim designated as a counterclaim." If the defendant's answer contains allegations that are labeled as affirmative defenses, then no reply is required even if the same facts—for example, fraud in a contract dispute—could have supported counterclaims.

Finally, Rule 7(a)(7) allows a judge to order a reply to an answer. When might a judge do so? Suppose an answer contained both denials and several affirmative defenses: Might a judge think that it would clarify the contested terrain if she ordered a reply?

Notes and Problems

As a test of your comfort with the materials on pleading examined thus far, try your hand with some problems.

1. Plaintiff files a complaint against an automobile Dealer and automobile Manufacturer. The complaint, which is properly before the court under diversity

jurisdiction, alleges that Plaintiff was injured in an accident caused by a defect in the vehicle's steering mechanism. Manufacturer believes that the vehicle was not defective when delivered to Dealer and that any defect must have been introduced by Dealer when the vehicle was being prepared for delivery to customer. What pleading, if any, should Manufacturer file?

2. Plaintiff files a complaint against Landlord alleging that Plaintiff was injured when a water heater on Landlord's premises exploded and injured Plaintiff. The complaint invokes diversity jurisdiction, alleging that the water heater was defective and asserts that Landlord is liable for having a defective water heater. Landlord files an answer asserting that the complaint fails to state a claim upon which relief can be granted because the doctrine of strict liability for defective products only applies to manufacturers and sellers of products, not to a landlord. At trial, Plaintiff proves that the heater was defective but Landlord continues to assert that it is not liable because strict liability does not apply to landlords. Plaintiff moves the court to strike this defense on the ground that it should have been made in a Rule 12(b)(6) motion, prior to answering, and was therefore waived. What result?

3. Same facts as Problem 2, except that Landlord's answer denies liability but fails to assert that the complaint fails to state a claim upon which relief can be granted. Is the defense waived?

4. Plaintiff files a complaint for breach of contract. Defendant files an answer asserting, as an affirmative defense, that the complaint is barred by a one-year statute of limitations. Upon receiving the answer, Plaintiff's attorney concludes that the affirmative defense is totally without merit. The statute of limitations applicable to a breach of contract claim is four years; the one-year statute cited in the answer's affirmative defense applies only to negligence claims.

    a. Should Plaintiff file a Rule 12(b) motion to dismiss the affirmative defense?

    b. If not, which Rule 12 motion could Plaintiff file to assert that the affirmative defense is without merit?

5. Plaintiff alleges negligently inflicted injuries in an auto accident; Defendant denies negligence and counterclaims for his own injuries.

    a. Plaintiff believes he was not negligent; what should his response to the counterclaim be?

    b. What should Plaintiff do if the counterclaim alleges negligence but fails to allege causation?

WHAT'S NEW HERE?

- These problems require you to sort out the processes for asserting various defenses.
- Which should take the form of a denial? An affirmative defense? A pre-answer motion? A motion for judgment on the pleadings? A motion to strike?

5. Amendments

Pleadings provide at least a preliminary definition of what a lawsuit is about. But modern civil litigation builds itself around the idea that discovery may cause claims and defenses to change as facts unknown at the time of pleading emerge. Rule 15 both allows such revisions of the parties' original stories and limits the extent and timing of such changes in the plot lines.

A reading of the Rule suggests a tension between two goals: easy amendment, which allows the pleadings to reflect the parties' changed view of the case as it develops; and the notion of "prejudice," which reflects the idea that at some point the other side has to make decisions about how to investigate and present its case, decisions that become difficult if the story it has to meet continually shifts. Before dealing with the difficult issues, read the Rule and use the following problems to orient you to its structure.

Notes and Problems

1. Penelope files a complaint against Fiona for breach of contract. A week later, Penelope's attorney realizes that, in addition to being able to claim breach of contract, Penelope also has a claim for negligence against Fiona.

   a. What should Penelope do?

   b. Alternatively, suppose Fiona answers before Penelope's lawyer realizes she has a claim for negligence against Fiona. What should Penelope's lawyer do?

2. Penelope files a complaint. Fiona answers, denying liability. Ten days after serving the answer, Fiona's lawyer realizes that she negligently failed to include the affirmative defense of statute of limitations in the answer. What should Fiona's lawyer do?

3. The next case arises from a collision between Rule 15 and the statute of limitations. Recall *Zielinski v. Philadelphia Piers* (supra page 428). Suppose that

defendant, making the same mistake plaintiff did, admitted that it operated and controlled the forklift, but denied negligence. A year later, after the statute of limitations had run, defendant discovered its mistake and sought permission to amend its answer to deny operation and control of the forklift. What should the court have done? The next case wrestles with that problem.

a. The Basic Problem: Prejudice

Beeck v. Aquaslide 'N' Dive Corp.
562 F.2d 537 (8th Cir. 1977)

BENSON, J.

This case is an appeal from the trial court's exercise of discretion on procedural matters in a diversity personal injury action.

Jerry A. Beeck was severely injured on July 15, 1972, while using a water slide. He and his wife, Judy A. Beeck, sued Aquaslide 'N' Dive Corporation (Aquaslide), a Texas corporation, alleging it manufactured the slide involved in the accident, and sought to recover substantial damages on theories of negligence, strict liability and breach of implied warranty.

Aquaslide initially admitted manufacture of the slide, but later moved to amend its answer to deny manufacture; the motion was resisted. The district court granted leave to amend. On motion of the defendant, a separate trial was held on the issue of "whether the defendant designed, manufactured or sold the slide in question." This motion was also resisted by the plaintiffs. The issue was tried to a jury, which returned a verdict for the defendant, after which the trial court entered summary judgment of dismissal of the case. Plaintiffs took this appeal, and stated the issues presented for review to be:

Where the manufacturer of the product, a water slide, admitted in its answer and later its answer to interrogatories both filed prior to the running of the statute of limitations that it designed, manufactured and sold the water slide in question, was it an abuse of the trial court's discretion to grant leave to amend to the manufacturer in order to deny these admissions after the running of the statute of limitations?

After granting the manufacturer's motion for leave to amend in order to deny the prior admissions of design, manufacture and sale of the water slide in question, was it an abuse of the trial court's discretion to further grant the manufacturer's motion for a separate trial on the issue of manufacture?

I. Facts

A brief review of the facts found by the trial court in its order granting leave to amend, and which do not appear to have been in dispute, is essential to a full understanding of appellants' claims.

In 1971 Kimberly Village Home Association of Davenport, Iowa, ordered an Aquaslide product from one George Boldt, who was a local distributor handling defendant's products. The order was forwarded by Boldt to Sentry Pool and Chemical

Supply Co. in Rock Island, Illinois, and Sentry forwarded the order to Purity Swimming Pool Supply in Hammond, Indiana. A slide was delivered from a Purity warehouse to Kimberly Village, and was installed by Kimberly employees. On July 15, 1972, Jerry A. Beeck was injured while using the slide at a social gathering sponsored at Kimberly Village by his employer, Harker Wholesale Meats, Inc. Soon after the accident investigations were undertaken by representatives of the separate insurers of Harker and Kimberly Village. On October 31, 1972, Aquaslide first learned of the accident through a letter sent by a representative of Kimberly's insurer to Aquaslide, advising that "one of your Queen Model #Q-3D slides" was involved in the accident. Aquaslide forwarded this notification to its insurer. Aquaslide's insurance adjuster made an on-site investigation of the slide in May 1973, and also interviewed persons connected with the ordering and assembly of the slide. An inter-office letter dated September 23, 1973, indicates that Aquaslide's insurer was of the opinion the "Aquaslide in question was definitely manufactured by our insured." The complaint was filed October 15, 1973.[3] Investigators for three different insurance companies, representing Harker, Kimberly and the defendant, had concluded that the slide had been manufactured by Aquaslide, and the defendant, with no information to the contrary, answered the complaint on December 12, 1973, and admitted that it "designed, manufactured, assembled and sold" the slide in question.[4] The statute of limitations on plaintiff's personal injury claim expired on July 15, 1974. About six and one-half months later Carl Meyer, president and owner of Aquaslide, visited the site of the accident prior to the taking of his deposition by the plaintiff.[5] From his on-site inspection of the slide, he determined it was not a product of the defendant. Thereafter, Aquaslide moved the court for leave to amend its answer to deny manufacture of the slide.

II. Leave to Amend

Amendment of pleadings in civil actions is governed by Rule 15(a)[(2)], F. R. Civ. P., which provides in part that once issue is joined in a lawsuit, a party may amend his pleading ["only with the opposing party's written consent or the court's leave. The court should freely give leave when justice so requires."]* In Foman v. Davis, 371 U.S. 178 (1962), the Supreme Court had occasion to construe that portion of Rule 15(a) set out above:

---

3. Aquaslide 'N' Dive Corporation was the sole defendant named in the complaint.

4. In answers to interrogatories filed on June 3, 1974, Aquaslide again admitted manufacture of the slide in question.

5. Plaintiffs apparently requested Meyer to inspect the slide prior to the taking of his deposition to determine whether it was defectively installed or assembled.

* [At the time of decision the text of this portion of Rule 15 permitted amendment after a responsive pleading "only by leave of court or by written consent of the adverse party; and leave shall be freely given when justice so requires."—Eds.]

Rule 15(a) declares that leave to amend "shall be freely given when justice so requires"[†]; this mandate is to be heeded. . . . If the underlying facts or circumstances relied upon by a plaintiff may be a proper subject of relief, he ought to be afforded an opportunity to test his claim on the merits. In the absence of any apparent or declared reason—such as undue delay, bad faith or dilatory motive on the part of the movant, repeated failure to cure deficiencies by amendments previously allowed, undue prejudice to the opposing party by virtue of allowance of the amendment, futility of amendment, etc.—the leave sought should, as the rules require, be "freely given." Of course, the grant or denial of an opportunity to amend is within the discretion of the district court. . . .

Burden

This court in *Hanson v. Hunt Oil Co.* held that "[p]rejudice *must be shown*." (Emphasis added). The burden is on the party opposing the amendment to show such prejudice. In ruling on a motion for leave to amend, the trial court must inquire into the issue of prejudice to the opposing party, in light of the particular facts of the case.

Certain principles apply to appellate review of a trial court's grant or denial of a motion to amend pleadings. First, as noted in *Foman v. Davis*, allowance or denial of leave to amend lies within the sound discretion of the trial court and is reviewable only for an abuse of discretion. The appellate court must view the case in the posture in which the trial court acted in ruling on the motion to amend.

It is evident from the order of the district court that in the exercise of its discretion in ruling on defendant's motion for leave to amend, it searched the record for evidence of bad faith, prejudice and undue delay which might be sufficient to overbalance the mandate of Rule 15(a), F. R. Civ. P., and *Foman v. Davis*, that leave to amend should be "freely given." Plaintiffs had not at any time conceded that the slide in question had not been manufactured by the defendant, and at the time the motion for leave to amend was at issue, the court had to decide whether the defendant should be permitted to litigate a material factual issue on its merits.

In inquiring into the issue of bad faith, the court noted the fact that the defendant, in initially concluding that it had manufactured the slide, relied upon the conclusions of three different insurance companies,[6] each of which had conducted an investigation into the circumstances surrounding the accident. This reliance upon investigations of three insurance companies, and the fact that "no contention has been made by anyone that the defendant influenced this possibly erroneous conclusion," persuaded the court that "defendant has not acted in such bad faith as to be precluded from contesting the issue of manufacture at trial." The court further found "[t]o the extent that 'blame' is to be spread regarding the original identification, the record indicates that it should be shared equally." In considering the issue of prejudice that might result to the plaintiffs from the granting of the motion for leave to amend, the trial court held that the facts presented to it did not support plaintiffs' assertion that, because of the running of the two-year Iowa statute of limitations on personal

---

† [Quoting the text of Rule 15 at the time of decision.—EDS.]

6. The insurer of Beeck's employer, the insurer of Kimberly Village, as well as the defendant's insurer had each concluded the slide in question was an Aquaslide.

injury claims, the allowance of the amendment would sound the "death knell" of the litigation. In order to accept plaintiffs' argument, the court would have had to assume that the defendant would prevail at trial on the factual issue of manufacture of the slide, and further that plaintiffs would be foreclosed, should the amendment be allowed, from proceeding against other parties if they were unsuccessful in pressing their claim against Aquaslide. On the state of the record before it, the trial court was unwilling to make such assumptions,[7] and concluded "[u]nder these circumstances, the court deems that the possible prejudice to the plaintiffs is an insufficient basis on which to deny the proposed amendment." The court reasoned that the amendment would merely allow the defendant to contest a disputed factual issue at trial, and further that it would be prejudicial to the defendant to deny the amendment.

The court also held that defendant and its insurance carrier, in investigating the circumstances surrounding the accident, had not been so lacking in diligence as to dictate a denial of the right to litigate the factual issue of manufacture of the slide.

On this record we hold that the trial court did not abuse its discretion in allowing the defendant to amend its answer.

▷ admit D was right to correct its answer

III. Separate Trials

After Aquaslide was granted leave to amend its answer, it moved pursuant to Rule 42(b), Fed. R. Civ. P. for a separate trial on the issue of manufacture of the slide involved in the accident. The grounds upon which the motion was based were:

1. a separate trial solely on the issue of whether the slide was manufactured by Aquaslide would save considerable trial time and unnecessary expense and preparation for all parties and the court, and

2. a separate trial solely on the issue of manufacture would protect Aquaslide from substantial prejudice.

The court granted the motion for a separate trial on the issue of manufacture, and this grant of a separate trial is challenged by appellants as being an abuse of discretion.

A trial court's severance of trial will not be disturbed on appeal except for an abuse of discretion.

---

7. The district court noted in its order granting leave to amend that plaintiffs may be able to sue other parties as a result of the substituting of a "counterfeit" slide for the Aquaslide, if indeed this occurred. The court added:

> [A]gain, the court is handicapped by an unclear record on this issue. If, in fact, the slide in question is not an Aquaslide, the replacement entered the picture somewhere along the Boldt to Sentry, Sentry to Purity, Purity to Kimberly Village chain of distribution. Depending upon the circumstances of its entry, a cause of action sounding in fraud or contract might lie. If so, the applicable statute of limitations period would not have run. Further, as defendant points out, the doctrine of equitable estoppel might possibly preclude another defendant from asserting the two-year statute as a defense.

The record indicates that Carl Meyer, president and owner of Aquaslide, designs the slides sold by Aquaslide. The slide which plaintiff Jerry A. Beeck was using at the time of his accident was very similar in appearance to an Aquaslide product, and was without identifying marks. Kimberly Village had in fact ordered an Aquaslide for its swimming pool, and thought it had received one. After Meyer's inspection and Aquaslide's subsequent assertion that it was not an Aquaslide product, plaintiffs elected to stand on their contention that it was in fact an Aquaslide. This raised a substantial issue of material fact which, if resolved in defendant's favor, would exonerate defendant from liability.

Plaintiff Jerry A. Beeck had been severely injured, and he and his wife together were seeking damages arising out of those injuries in the sum of $2,225,000.00. Evidence of plaintiffs' injuries and damages would clearly have taken up several days of trial time, and because of the severity of the injuries, may have been prejudicial to the defendant's claim of non-manufacture. The jury, by special interrogatory, found that the slide had not been manufactured by Aquaslide. That finding has not been questioned on appeal. Judicial economy, beneficial to all the parties, was obviously served by the trial court's grant of a separate trial. We hold the Rule 42(b) separation was not an abuse of discretion.

The judgment of the district court is affirmed.

WHAT'S NEW HERE?

- Defendant admitted it manufactured the allegedly defective product.
- Then, after the statute of limitations had run as to any possible other defendant, Aquaslide sought—and received—permission to amend its answer to deny that allegation.

Notes and Problems

1. Rule 15 says that "[t]he court should freely give leave [to amend] when justice so requires." The courts have read this phrase to mean: (a) that the would-be amender should have a good reason for not getting the pleading right the first time; and (b) that allowing the change now shouldn't hurt the other side

too much. These requirements are often captured in the not very illuminating words "bad faith" and "prejudice."

a. State simply how the *Aquaslide* court concluded that there was no bad faith.

b. Without deciding whether the prejudice to the plaintiffs was too much, explain what it was. How are plaintiffs in a worse position than they would have been if Aquaslide had denied manufacture in its original answer?

2. Is it true, as the court suggests, that the parties are equally to blame for the misidentification of the slide?

a. First assume, as the district court found, that Aquaslide and its insurers acted completely in good faith and that it was in fact difficult to tell the real from the counterfeit slide. Surely the defendant was in a better position to find this out than were the plaintiffs. Moreover, once Aquaslide had admitted manufacture in its answer, could one expect any rational plaintiff to invest additional effort in making sure that the admission was accurate?

b. Another lawsuit between these parties revealed something not discussed in this opinion: that Aquaslide and its president were aware that others had been copying their slides—there had been several other lawsuits in which it had turned out that the slides were made by competitors. Beeck v. Aquaslide 'N' Dive Corp., 350 N.W.2d 149 (Iowa 1984). Suppose that information had been presented to the court in this lawsuit. Under those circumstances would it have been an abuse of discretion had the trial court denied permission to amend?

3. If one accepts the argument implicit in the preceding two notes, the case presents a problem. The defendant has a questionable excuse for having mispleaded in the first place, and the plaintiffs will suffer crushing prejudice if amendment is allowed. The court nevertheless permitted amendment. Perhaps the court was simply wrong. But before you conclude that, consider whether there is another, deeper justification for the court's decision.

a. One answer perhaps appears if one conducts a thought experiment. Assume the amendment had been denied, and Aquaslide had remained in the case. How would defendant have responded to the claim of negligent manufacture? Would it have shown its own design, testing, manufacturing, and safety procedures or those of the actual manufacturer? Assuming the latter, what would happen if it didn't know who manufactured the slide? If the defendant had been forced to stand by its erroneous admission, would the ensuing trial have been a travesty—and, if so, does that justify the decision to permit amendment?

b. Compare *Beeck* to *Zielinski v. Philadelphia Piers*, supra page 428. In that case the court required the defendant to admit an allegation that was demonstrably false. Is *Zielinski* the right analogy? What key fact differed between the circumstances of that case and those of *Beeck*?

Implications

MISPLEADING AS MISREPRESENTATION

The *Beeck* opinion above did not end this litigation. The Beecks filed a second suit in state court, still against Aquaslide. This time, however, they did not claim a defective product but "reckless misrepresentation" made in the pleadings in the federal litigation. Plaintiffs' theory was that misrepresentations in the answer (inaccurately admitting that the product was made by Aquaslide) had caused the Beecks to lose their chance to sue the real manufacturer within the statute of limitations. The Beecks presented evidence summarized in Note 2b—showing that Aquaslide should have been on notice that there were counterfeit slides on the market. Plaintiffs argued that defendant was therefore reckless in admitting manufacture without a more complete investigation.

The case came before the Iowa Supreme Court twice, once in 1981 and again in 1984. In 1984 the court upheld a recovery of over $3 million based on a misrepresentation theory. But, analogizing the Beecks' claim to a legal malpractice action, the court also said that, in order to prevail, the plaintiffs would have to show not only that they would have recovered a judgment against the actual manufacturer but also that the judgment would have been collectible. Beeck v. Aquaslide 'N' Dive Corp., 350 N.W.2d 149 (Iowa 1984). The court remanded the case for yet another trial on the issue of the collectability of the award against the actual manufacturer. Would you expect the Beecks to be able to make this showing?

b. Statutes of Limitations and Relation Back

Zielinski v. Philadelphia Piers derives its bite from the fact that the plaintiff, having suffered a dismissal, would be unable to refile its complaint against the right defendant within the statute of limitations. (The plaintiffs in *Beeck* may also be so barred, although the court leaves open the possibility that the statute of limitations could be tolled if the Beecks found the proper defendant.) Rule 15(c) gives plaintiffs some leeway to name new parties or new claims after the statute of limitations: It allows an amended pleading to be treated as though it was filed on the date of the original pleading. A party seeking to file this type of amended pleading must convince the court that the amendment satisfies both the "when justice so requires" language in Rule 15(a) and that it satisfies the requirements of Rule 15(c).

Central to the decision about whether a new claim or party in an amended pleading should be allowed to relate back pursuant to Rule 15(c) is the question of what constitutes a claim, a question that takes us back to the beginning of this chapter. Compare the approach taken by the next two cases: Are they consistent?

Moore v. Baker

989 F.2d 1129 (11th Cir. 1993)

MORGAN, J.

[Judith Moore consulted Dr. Baker about a blockage of her carotid artery. Baker recommended surgery and warned her about its risks. Moore signed a consent form. The operation went badly and left Moore severely and permanently disabled. Moore sued Dr. Baker. Her initial complaint alleged that he had violated Georgia's informed consent law by failing to advise her of an alternative therapy.] On August 6, 1991, Dr. Baker filed a motion for summary judgment on the issue of informed consent. On August 26, 1991, Moore moved to amend her complaint to assert allegations of negligence by Dr. Baker in the performance of the surgery and in his post-operative care of Moore. . . .

I

Moore claims that the district court abused its discretion by . . . denying Moore's motion to amend her complaint . . . on the ground that the newly-asserted claim was barred by the applicable statute of limitations. . . .

Moore filed her original complaint on the last day permitted by Georgia's statute of limitations. Accordingly, the statute of limitations bars the claim asserted in Moore's proposed amended complaint unless the amended complaint relates back to the date of the original complaint. An amendment relates back to the original filing [when] "[the amendment asserts a claim or defense that arose out of the conduct, transaction, or occurrence set out—or attempted to be set out—in the original pleading."* Fed. R. Civ. P. 15(c)[(2)]. The critical issue in Rule 15(c) determinations is whether the original complaint gave notice to the defendant of the claim now being asserted.

Moore relies heavily on Azarbal v. Medical Center of Delaware, Inc., 724 F. Supp. 279 (D. Del. 1989), which addressed the doctrine of relation back in the context of a medical malpractice case. In *Azarbal*, the original complaint alleged negligence in the performance of an amniocentesis on the plaintiff, resulting in injury to the fetus. After the statute of limitations had expired, the plaintiff sought to amend the complaint to add a claim that the doctor failed to obtain her informed consent prior to performing a sterilization procedure on her because the doctor did not tell her that the fetus had probably been injured by the amniocentesis. The district court [in *Azarbal*] found that "the original complaint provided adequate notice of any claims Ms. Azarbal would have arising from the amniocentesis, including a claim that Dr. Palacio should have revealed that the procedure had caused fetal injury." The instant case is clearly distinguishable from *Azarbal.* Unlike the complaint in *Azarbal*, the

---

* [At the time of the decision the text of Rule 15(c) provided that the amendment related back "whenever the claim or defense asserted in the amended pleading arose out of the conduct, transaction, or occurrence set forth or attempted to be set forth in the original pleading."—EDS.]

allegations asserted in Moore's original complaint contain nothing to put Dr. Baker on notice that the new claims of negligence might be asserted. Even when given a liberal construction, there is nothing in Moore's original complaint which makes reference to any acts of alleged negligence by Dr. Baker either during or after surgery.[1] The original complaint focuses on Baker's actions before Moore decided to undergo surgery, but the amended complaint focuses on Baker's actions during and after the surgery. The alleged acts of negligence occurred at different times and involved separate and distinct conduct. In order to recover on the negligence claim contained in her amended complaint, Moore would have to prove completely different facts than would otherwise have been required to recover on the informed consent claim in the original complaint.

We must conclude that Moore's new claim does not arise out of the same conduct, transaction, or occurrence as the claims in the original complaint. Therefore, the amended complaint does not relate back to the original complaint, and the proposed new claims are barred by the applicable statute of limitations. Since the amended complaint could not withstand a motion to dismiss, we hold that the district court did not abuse its discretion in denying Moore's motion to amend her complaint. . . .

Bonerb v. Richard J. Caron Foundation
159 F.R.D. 16 (W.D.N.Y. 1994)

HECKMANN, M.J.

In this diversity action, plaintiff seeks damages for personal injuries allegedly sustained when he slipped and fell while playing basketball on defendant's recreational basketball court on November 29, 1991. Defendant is a not-for-profit corporation licensed and doing business as a drug and alcohol rehabilitation facility in Westfield, Pennsylvania. Plaintiff is a resident of Western New York.

The original complaint, filed on October 1, 1993, alleges that plaintiff was injured while he was a rehabilitation patient at defendant's Westfield facility, and was participating in a mandatory exercise program. Plaintiff claims that the basketball court was negligently maintained by defendant.

On July 25, 1994, this court granted plaintiff's motion for substitution of new counsel. On September 1, 1994, plaintiff moved to amend his complaint to add a new cause of action for "counseling malpractice." According to plaintiff's counsel,

---

1. Moore's original complaint is very specific and focuses solely on Dr. Baker's failure to inform Moore of EDTA therapy as an alternative to surgery. Although the complaint recounts the details of the operation and subsequent recovery, it does not hint that Dr. Baker's actions were negligent. In fact, the only references in the original complaint relating to the surgery or postoperative care suggest that Dr. Baker acted with reasonable care. The complaint states that "the nurses noticed a sudden onset of right sided weakness of which they *immediately informed* Defendant Baker." (Complaint, P 18). "Upon being informed of this [right-sided weakness], Defendant Baker *immediately* caused Plaintiff to be returned to the operation suite. . . . Although the clot was *promptly removed* by Defendant Baker. . . ." (Complaint, P 19).

investigation and discussions undertaken after his substitution as counsel indicated to him that a malpractice claim was warranted under the circumstances. Defendant objects to the amendment on the grounds that the counseling malpractice claim does not relate back to the original pleading and is therefore barred by Pennsylvania's two-year statute of limitations.

Discussion

Rule 15 of the Federal Rules of Civil Procedure provides that once time for amending a pleading as of right has expired, a party may request leave of court to amend, [and "The court should freely give leave when justice so requires"]. Fed. R. Civ. P. 15(a)[(2)]. . . .

The relation back doctrine is based upon the principle that one who has been given notice of litigation concerning a given transaction or occurrence has been provided with all the protection that statutes of limitation are designed to afford. Thus, if the litigant has been advised at the outset of the general facts from which the belatedly asserted claim arises, the amendment will relate back even though the statute of limitations may have run in the interim.

An amendment which changes the legal theory of the case is appropriate if the factual situation upon which the action depends remains the same and has been brought to the defendant's attention by the original pleading. . . .

In this case, the original complaint alleges that plaintiff was injured when he slipped and fell on a wet, muddy basketball court "while participating in a mandatory exercise program . . ." at defendant's rehabilitation facility. Plaintiff alleges several instances of defendant's negligent conduct, such as failure to maintain the premises safely, failure to warn, failure to inspect and failure to "properly supervise and/or instruct plaintiff. . . ." The proposed amendment seeks to allege that plaintiff "was caused to fall while playing in an outdoor basketball court . . . in an exercise program mandated as part of his treatment in the rehabilitation program, . . ." and that "the rehabilitation and counseling care rendered . . . was negligently, carelessly and unskillfully performed."

The allegations in the original and amended complaints derive from the same nucleus of operative facts involving injury suffered by plaintiff on November 29, 1991. It is true that a claim for professional malpractice invokes an entirely different duty and conduct on the part of the defendant than does a claim for negligent maintenance of the premises. However, the original complaint advised defendant of the same transaction or occurrence giving rise to these different theories of negligence. Indeed, the original complaint alleged that participation in the exercise program was mandatory, and that the injury was caused by defendant's failure to "properly supervise and/or instruct plaintiff. . . ." These allegations not only gave defendant sufficient notice of the general facts surrounding the occurrence, but also alerted defendant to the possibility of a claim based on negligent performance of professional duties. This is all that is required for relation back under Rule 15(c).

Defendant contends that it will be unduly prejudiced by the amendment because it will have to return to the drawing board to prepare an entirely new defense. However, as plaintiff points out, the period for discovery has not yet expired, depositions of defendant's personnel have not yet been taken, and expert witness information has not been exchanged. In addition, the parties have consented to trial before the under-signed, thereby simplifying any further supervision of discovery and the conduct and review of pretrial matters and dispositive motions.

Finally, there has been no showing of undue delay or bad faith on the part of plaintiff. . . .

WHAT'S NEW HERE?

- These cases get their bite from the circumstance that the statute of limitations has run by the time the plaintiffs seek to file their amended complaints.
- But Rule 15(c) allows some amended complaints to "relate back" to the date of the original filing. If they relate back, the court will treat the amended complaint as if it had been filed at the time of the original pleading—and thus within the statute of limitations.
- And—for the amended complaint to relate back—it must assert "a claim or defense that arose out of the conduct, transaction, or occurrence set out . . . in the original pleading."

Notes and Problems

1. Relation-back cases test our belief in statutes of limitations and our idea of a claim. Statutes of limitations are intended to limit the amount of time that a plaintiff has to bring her claim; the relation-back doctrine extends this limit. One could, theoretically, have a doctrine that permitted relation back of any subsequent amendment, no matter how unrelated to the original claim. Such a doctrine would do away altogether with the statute of limitations. Rule 15(c) does something different: It allows relation back only for claims sufficiently related to those described in the original pleading that the defendant should be on notice of the dispute.

2. If one allows relation back for "related" claims, the question becomes how to define relatedness. One possibility would be on the basis of legal theory: Any tort claim could be joined to an initial claim for a tort, and so on. Instead, Rule 15(c) defines the line between permitted and unpermitted amendments in terms of "the conduct, transaction, or occurrence set out—or attempted to be set out—in the original pleading." That language is purposely general, and

courts will inevitably perceive "conduct, transaction, [and] occurrence" in different-sized packages. Yet the language is clearly focused on the factual allegations in the complaint, as opposed to the legal theories.

3. In *Moore v. Baker*, the court finds that the allegations of medical malpractice did not relate back to the allegations of failure to get informed consent for the operation. In *Bonerb v. Richard J. Caron Foundation*, the court finds that the claim of "counseling malpractice" did relate back to the allegations of negligent maintenance of the basketball court.

   a. Are the cases distinguishable? If one focuses just on the "conduct, transaction, or occurrence" language, no. In both cases people presented themselves to health care professionals for treatment and are alleging bad outcomes caused by those professionals. But one plaintiff gets to amend and the other does not. That seems unjustified.

   b. Nor does it help to point out that in *Moore* the plaintiff is trying to change the legal theory of her case while in *Bonerb* the plaintiff is merely shifting from one set of facts to another to support the claim of negligence. Rule 15(c) specifically rejects the idea that amendments should turn on legal theories.

   c. Focus instead on the stage of litigation at which the motions came in the two cases. Articulate an argument that the cases are both correctly decided because of the timing of the motions to amend. Here's a hint: The best argument is based more on the Rule 15(a) requirements you read about in *Beeck* than those in Rule 15(c).

4. Some of the most spectacular relation-back cases occur when the plaintiff wants to change not just a legal theory, but the party sued. One might think that basic ideas of fair notice would prevent such amendments. After all, how could a prospective defendant have fair notice of anything if he didn't know he was being sued? But even such an amendment can relate back under some conditions. Read carefully Rule 15(c)(1)(C).

   a. The ordinary version of such cases involves a corporation sued under the wrong name or an individual whose name is misspelled. In such instances, the "right" defendant was served with process, and thus knows of the suit, and of plaintiff's mistake; the courts have often allowed such amendments to relate back.

   b. Apply Rule 15(c)(1)(C) to the facts of *Zielinski v. Philadelphia Piers*, supra page 428. The present version of this Rule was not in effect at the time *Zielinski* was decided. Suppose it had been. Could the court have avoided the awkward step of forcing the defendant to admit a false statement by instead permitting an amendment to change the defendant?

   c. Now apply Rule 15(c)(1)(C) to the facts of *Beeck v. Aquaslide 'N' Dive Corp.* Imagine that Beeck had discovered the identity of the true manufacturer of the slide after the statute of limitations had run, and equitable estoppel was not an option. Could the plaintiffs have amended the complaint to name the new defendant and have the claim relate back under Rule 15(c)(1)(C)?

* * *

As we have seen, modern pleading has sought to eliminate many of the technicalities and trapdoors that characterized earlier systems. As a result, notice pleading eliminates fewer claims than its predecessors. As a further result, however, false positives—meritless cases that survive pleading and go into expensive discovery—have raised concerns. *Twombly* and *Iqbal* suggest that judges have heard those concerns, and have, by judicial interpretation, tightened the pleading regime for some subset of cases. How large that subset is, how many cases it will eliminate, and how well the plausibility pleading standard does at sorting meritless from meritorious cases will emerge only after many more judicial decisions and their assessment.

The next chapter, on discovery, describes what happens in a case once it gets past the pleading stage. During discovery, parties can spend a great deal of time and money uncovering damaging information about the other side. Efforts to dismiss claims at the pleading stage are in no small part motivated by an interest in avoiding discovery. In other words, discovery explains, in significant part, what all the fuss raised at the pleading stage is really about. Broad discovery is the civil procedure system's response to the scanty information historically conveyed by notice pleading. As you consider the next chapter, bear in mind that the current structure of discovery is in substantial part a response to decisions made long ago about our pleading system.

Assessment Questions

Q1. Plaintiff files a complaint. Defendant answers, denying liability, and the case proceeds. After the close of discovery, at the time the court has set for such motions, Defendant files a motion for summary judgment arguing that the complaint is barred by the statute of limitations. On the merits, Defendant has a strong case. Plaintiff argues, however, that because the statute of limitations was not specifically stated as an affirmative defense in Defendant's answer, it was waived. What result?

    A. The affirmative defense is waived.

    B. The affirmative defense is waived unless defendant is allowed to amend his answer to include the affirmative defense.

    C. The affirmative defense is not waived.

Q2. Paul sues Manufacturer and Retailer in federal district court. The complaint alleges that Plaintiff was injured because of a defect in an appliance. Manufacturer believes that the appliance was not defective when delivered to Retailer and that any defect must have been introduced when Retailer was in possession of the appliance. Manufacturer should:

    A. File a 12(b)(6) motion.

    B. File an answer alleging as an affirmative defense that it was really Retailer's fault.

    C. Deny the allegation of any defect caused by Manufacturer and wait for discovery.

    D. Move under Rule 12(c) to strike the allegation of a defect.

Q3. Plaintiff, injured when a kitchen appliance supplied by his landlord burns him, files a product defect suit against Landlord. Landlord answers, denying liability. At trial, Landlord for the first time asserts that plaintiff has failed to state a claim on which relief can be granted—because a product defect claim lies only against a manufacturer, not a subsequent user like Landlord. Which of the following is true?

    A. Landlord has waived this defense by failing to assert it either in a pre-answer 12(b)(6) motion or in his answer.

    B. Landlord can assert this defense.

Q4. In *Ashcroft v. Iqbal*, the Supreme Court ruled that plaintiff's complaint contained insufficient detail. Choose the answer or answers that best describe the Court's ruling.

    A. The Court based this decision on Rule 9(b).

    B. The Court limited its ruling to complex cases likely to create elaborate discovery.

    C. The Court's decision was consistent with a long line of pleading cases under the Rules.

    D. None of the above.

Q5. Paula sues Dennis on an unpaid promissory note. Dennis answers the complaint, denying breach, and also has two allegations labelled "affirmative defenses": that the one-year statute of limitations has run; and that he failed to repay the debt because he needed the funds to pay for medical care for a sick child. Paula's lawyer determines that neither affirmative defense is valid: The statute of limitations on a promissory note in writing (as this one is) is four years; and the law of contract does not recognize the second defense. Paula's lawyer should:

    A. Apply for an injunction requiring Dennis to amend his answer.

    B. File a Rule 12(f) motion to strike the two affirmative defenses.

    C. File a Rule 12(c) motion for judgment on the pleadings.

    D. File a Rule 12(b)(6) motion.

Q6. In *Haddle v. Garrison*, the U.S. Supreme Court decided:

    A. That Haddle could bring his case in federal court.

    B. That the defendant had treated Haddle unlawfully.

    C. That notice pleading was a correct interpretation of Rule 8.

D. That Haddle had stated a claim because his at-will employment was a form of "property" that had been "injured" by his firing.

Q7. In a complaint under the Rules, plaintiff alleges negligence and injury, but fails to assert causation (a necessary part of her tort claim). Defendant believes that he was not negligent and that the statute of limitations has run. Which of the following is true?

A. Within 21 days of serving the complaint, plaintiff can amend her complaint once without seeking permission of the court.

B. In drafting his answer, defendant must choose between attacking the original complaint for failure to state a claim, denying the allegation of negligence, and raising a statute of limitations defense.

C. If the statute of limitations in fact runs between the filing of the original complaint and an amended complaint (which alleges causation), the amended complaint will "relate back."

D. If plaintiff amends her complaint as stated in C, defendant can still contend that the statute ran before the original complaint was filed.

Analysis of Assessment Questions

Q1. B is correct. The defense is waived unless defendant is allowed to amend his answer to include the affirmative defense. Moreover, a court is likely to deny defendant's request to amend unless defendant can show that information just uncovered in discovery—such as facts showing that plaintiff knew or should have known of his claim earlier than everyone previously assumed—justify amendment.

Q2. Only C is correct. A is wrong because the complaint states a claim if its allegations are true; Manufacturer thinks they are not true, so a 12(b)(6) motion is not the right response. B is wrong because this is not an affirmative defense; it's instead a way of explaining *why* an allegation is false—something that should be done by denying the allegation. D is wrong because the allegation neither fails under substantive law nor is a particularly prejudicial or scandalous assertion.

Q3. B is correct; see Rule 12(h)(2).

Q4. Only D is correct. A is wrong because the case interprets Rule 8, not Rule 9. B is wrong because the opinion specifically rejects this interpretation, insisting that it applies to all cases. C is wrong precisely because *Iqbal* departed from a long line of cases interpreting Rule 8 in a quite different way.

Q5. Only B is correct: A motion to strike will allow the judge to rule on the validity of the two erroneously asserted affirmative defenses and to eliminate them from the case. A is wrong because injunctions are not directed to procedural errors in litigation; a Rule 12(f) motion will have the same effect. C is wrong because, once the affirmative defenses are eliminated, the pleadings reveal a dispute: an allegation of unpaid debts and a denial of that allegation. D is wrong because a 12(b)(6) motion is directed to a claim, not to a defense.

Q6. A (in a roundabout way) and D are correct. Take D first: On a 12(b) motion the court takes as factually true the allegations of the complaint and decides if they state a claim; in *Haddle*, the issue was what two key words in the statute meant. A is correct in a roundabout way because the only basis for federal jurisdiction in the case was *if* the complaint stated a claim arising under federal law, and the only candidate for such a federal law was the statute whose meaning was at stake: Because the Court decided the case for Haddle, that also meant it stayed in federal court. B is wrong because that would require a court to decide whether in fact Haddle had been fired in retaliation, a question not raised by Garrison's 12(b)(6) motion. C is wrong because *Haddle*, a pre-*Iqbal* case, assumed the validity of notice pleading.

Q7. A, C, and D are correct responses. B is wrong because Rule 8(d) permits alternative claims or defenses. A is correct because Rule 15(a)(1) allows amendment of a pleading "as a matter of course" within 21 days of serving it. C is correct because the claim—now with the required allegation of causation—arises from the same occurrence "set out" in the original complaint, and thus will be treated as having been filed on the same date as the original complaint (that's what "relates back" means). D is correct because relation back won't solve plaintiff's problem if in fact the statute had run before the original complaint was filed—and defendant can so contend if he pleads the statute of limitations as an affirmative defense.

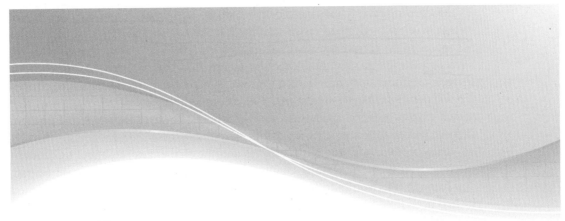

CHAPTER 7

Discovery

A hundred years ago, if a complaint survived a motion to dismiss, the case would go to trial if the plaintiff wanted it to. That is no longer true. In contemporary litigation the chief significance of a complaint's surviving dismissal is that it enables the plaintiff to reach the "pretrial" stage—the intermediate stage between pleading and trial. Today most lawsuits end at this pretrial stage. In part they end at this stage because of the procedural device explored in this chapter—discovery. Discovery ends lawsuits for two reasons. First, discovery produces information about the merits of the lawsuit and permits parties to make informed judgments about the strength of their and their opponent's positions. Such information can hasten a lawsuit's end either through settlement or summary judgment, both explored in the next chapter. Second, because discovery costs time and money, it might enable one party simply to wear the other down—or both sides to wear each other down—without regard to the merits of the case. This chapter explains why discovery has both these potentials and explores how the Rules try to maximize the first reason and minimize the second reason that lawsuits can end at this stage.

A. MODERN DISCOVERY

One hundred years ago, litigants had a limited range of discovery devices that could be used only against some persons, and only in some kinds of actions. Discovery was not always a matter of right, and, as a result, litigants were often surprised by evidence produced at trial. This recipe could produce good courtroom drama, but not, critics argued, truth or justice.

455

Modern discovery has changed that picture. Both state courts and the federal system have adopted broad civil discovery rules that permit a lawyer to uncover, in advance of trial, enormous amounts of information lying solely in the possession of her adversary. Parties can use multiple tools to unearth information. Parties can be required to disclose information damning to their case. And information must be disclosed even if it will not ultimately be used at trial. Courts can limit discovery in various ways that we will explore in this chapter. Even with these limits, however, the scope and depth of modern U.S. discovery practice make it unique among today's legal systems.

To appreciate both the opportunities and the challenges presented by modern discovery, recall the preceding chapter and the dispute between Michael Haddle and Jeanette Garrison (and her company, Healthmaster). Michael Haddle claimed he had been fired from his job at Healthmaster because he cooperated with an FBI investigation of the company and Mrs. Garrison, who was eventually convicted of Medicare fraud. One of his claims is brought pursuant to a Reconstruction-era statute that creates a cause of action against anyone who "injure[s] . . . a person . . . on account of his having . . . testified" in a court proceeding. The plaintiff's theory was that he was fired for cooperating with the FBI investigation, triggering liability under the federal statute.

1. Discovery Before Discovery: Obligations and Spoliation

Even before Haddle's lawyer filed his complaint, Healthmaster and Garrison (and their lawyers) should have thought hard about what documents and other information related to Haddle's work and termination they were required to preserve. Haddle and his attorney should also have given thought to what in Haddle's possession they must preserve. To understand why, consider the next case. Although *Zubulake* concerns a discovery dispute that arose years into litigation, many of the lawyers' and defendants' missteps occurred before the lawsuit even began.

Zubulake v. UBS Warburg LLP

229 F.R.D. 422 (S.D.N.Y. 2003)

Scheindlin, J.

. . . What is true in love is equally true at law: Lawyers and their clients need to communicate clearly and effectively with one another to ensure that litigation proceeds efficiently. When communication between counsel and client breaks down, conversation becomes "just crossfire," and there are usually casualties.

I. Introduction

This is the fifth written opinion in this case, a relatively routine employment discrimination dispute in which discovery has now lasted over two years. Laura Zubulake is once again moving to sanction UBS for its failure to produce relevant information and for its tardy production of such material. . . .

II. Facts

. . . Zubulake is an equities trader specializing in Asian securities who is suing her former employer for gender discrimination, failure to promote, and retaliation under federal, state, and city law.

A. Background

Zubulake filed an initial charge of gender discrimination with the EEOC on August 16, 2001. Well before that, however—as early as April 2001—UBS employees were on notice of Zubulake's impending court action. After she received a right-to-sue letter from the EEOC, Zubulake filed this lawsuit on February 15, 2002.

Fully aware of their common law duty to preserve relevant evidence, UBS's in-house attorneys gave oral instructions in August 2001—immediately after Zubulake filed her EEOC charge—instructing employees not to destroy or delete material potentially relevant to Zubulake's claims, and in fact to segregate such material into separate files for the lawyers' eventual review. . . . [These same instructions were reiterated in August 2001, and again in February, August, and September of 2002. Nevertheless, during discovery, the court found that UBS had deleted relevant e-mails from its active servers, destroyed some backup tapes, and failed to produce responsive e-mails in its possession.] . . .

III. Legal Standard

Spoliation is the destruction or significant alteration of evidence, or the failure to preserve property for another's use as evidence in pending or reasonably foreseeable litigation. The determination of an appropriate sanction for spoliation, if any, is confined to the sound discretion of the trial judge, and is assessed on a case-by-case basis. The authority to sanction litigants for spoliation arises jointly under the Federal Rules of Civil Procedure and the court's inherent powers.

The spoliation of evidence germane to proof of an issue at trial can support an inference that the evidence would have been unfavorable to the party responsible for its destruction. A party seeking an adverse inference instruction (or other sanctions) based on the spoliation of evidence must establish the following three elements: (1) that the party having control over the evidence had an obligation to preserve it at the time it was destroyed; (2) that the records were destroyed with a "culpable state of mind" and (3) that the destroyed evidence was "relevant" to the party's claim or defense such that a reasonable trier of fact could find that it would support that claim or defense.

. . . In *Zubulake IV*, I summarized a litigant's preservation obligations:

> Once a party reasonably anticipates litigation, it must suspend its routine document retention/destruction policy and put in place a "litigation hold" to ensure the preservation of relevant documents. As a general rule, that litigation hold does not apply to inaccessible backup tapes (*e.g.*, those typically maintained solely for the purpose of disaster recovery), which may continue to be recycled on the schedule set forth in the company's policy. On the other hand, if backup tapes are accessible (*i.e.*, actively used for information retrieval), then such tapes *would* likely be subject to the litigation hold.

A party's discovery obligations do not end with the implementation of a "litigation hold"—to the contrary, that's only the beginning. . . .

Once a "litigation hold" is in place, a party and her counsel must make certain that all sources of potentially relevant information are identified and placed "on hold," to the extent required in *Zubulake IV.* To do this, counsel must become fully familiar with her client's document retention policies, as well as the client's data retention architecture. This will invariably involve speaking with information technology personnel, who can explain system-wide backup procedures and the actual (as opposed to theoretical) implementation of the firm's recycling policy. It will also involve communicating with the "key players" in the litigation, in order to understand how they stored information. In this case, for example, some UBS employees created separate computer files pertaining to Zubulake, while others printed out relevant e-mails and retained them in hard copy only. Unless counsel interviews each employee, it is impossible to determine whether all potential sources of information have been inspected. . . .

To the extent that it may not be feasible for counsel to speak with every key player, given the size of a company or the scope of the lawsuit, counsel must be more creative. . . . [I]t is *not* sufficient to notify all employees of a litigation hold and expect that the party will then retain and produce all relevant information. Counsel must take affirmative steps to monitor compliance so that all sources of discoverable information are identified and searched. This is not to say that counsel will necessarily succeed in locating all such sources, or that the later discovery of new sources is evidence of a lack of effort. But counsel and client must take *some reasonable steps* to see that sources of relevant information are located.

. . . The *continuing* duty to supplement disclosures strongly suggests that parties also have a duty to make sure that discoverable information is not lost. Indeed, the notion of a "duty to preserve" connotes an ongoing obligation. Obviously, if information is lost or destroyed, it has not been preserved. . . .

There are thus a number of steps that counsel should take to ensure compliance with the preservation obligation. While these precautions may not be enough (or may be too much) in some cases, they are designed to promote the continued preservation of potentially relevant information in the typical case.

First, counsel must issue a "litigation hold" at the outset of litigation or whenever litigation is reasonably anticipated. The litigation hold should be periodically re-issued so that new employees are aware of it, and so that it is fresh in the minds of all employees.

Second, counsel should communicate directly with the "key players" in the litigation, *i.e.,* the people identified in a party's initial disclosure and any subsequent supplementation thereto. Because these "key players" are the "employees likely to have relevant information," it is particularly important that the preservation duty be communicated clearly to them. As with the litigation hold, the key players should be periodically reminded that the preservation duty is still in place.

Finally, counsel should instruct all employees to produce electronic copies of their relevant active files. Counsel must also make sure that all backup media which the party is required to retain is identified and stored in a safe place. . . .

UBS's in-house counsel issued a litigation hold in August 2001 and repeated that instruction several times from September 2001 through September 2002. Outside counsel also spoke with some (but not all) of the key players in August 2001. Nonetheless, certain employees unquestionably deleted e-mails. Although many of the deleted e-mails were recovered from backup tapes, a number of backup tapes—and the e-mails on them—are lost forever. Other employees, notwithstanding counsel's request that they produce their files on Zubulake, did not do so. . . .

Counsel failed to communicate the litigation hold order to all key players. They also failed to ascertain each of the key players' document management habits. By the same token, UBS employees—for unknown reasons—ignored many of the instructions that counsel gave. This case represents a failure of communication, and that failure falls on counsel and client alike.

At the end of the day, however, the duty to preserve and produce documents rests on the party. Once that duty is made clear to a party, either by court order or by instructions from counsel, that party is on notice of its obligations and acts at its own peril. Though more diligent action on the part of counsel would have mitigated some of the damage caused by UBS's deletion of e-mails, UBS deleted the e-mails in defiance of explicit instructions not to.

[The remainder of the opinion goes on to consider sanctions for destruction of evidence held by the bank/employer.]

WHAT'S NEW HERE?

- *Zubulake* illustrates the scope of a party's duty to preserve evidence even before any formal discovery, or, indeed, before the filing of a suit.
- The obligation to preserve is shared by the attorney (who must take pains to ensure her clients retain relevant documents and physical evidence) and the client (who must comply with those obligations).

Notes and Problems

1. Start by considering the plaintiff's objective in requesting production of the e-mails.

   a. The plaintiff would hope to find e-mails from her boss explicitly stating that he failed to promote Zubulake because of her gender.

   b. Beyond this type of "smoking gun" evidence, what else might Zubulake have hoped to find?

2. Some litigation holds are triggered by a letter from a prospective plaintiff alerting the prospective defendant of possible litigation and warning it to

preserve evidence. As the opinion makes clear, however, even without such a letter the obligation to preserve evidence comes into play. Assume that Garrison and Healthmaster thought there was a possibility that Haddle might sue.

   a. What evidence should Healthmaster's lawyer advise her client to preserve?

   b. What concrete steps should Healthmaster's lawyer take? With whom should she speak, and how should she follow up to ensure those instructions are being followed?

3. Plaintiffs also have a duty to preserve evidence. If you were Haddle's attorney, what evidence would you advise him to preserve?

PERSPECTIVES

The Rules and the Profession Scramble to Keep Up with Technology

Well within the memory of lawyers now in practice, discovery consisted of combing through paper files—sometimes entire warehouses of those files, but more often a much smaller number of documents. The digital revolution has changed that world forever. Even in run-of-the-mill litigation, digital records will usually exist and be critically important to the case. Take an everyday suit arising from an auto accident. Lawyers on both sides will want to capture the drivers' cell-phone records—was either one texting or otherwise distracted? In addition, cars built since 2006 contain versions of the "black box" on airplanes, that capture the vehicle's speed, braking, and perhaps more, depending on the year of manufacture. The lawyers will want to be sure that these recorders are preserved and their data analyzed. If any of the parties received medical attention, those records will likely be in digital form. If the quality of that medical care is in question (did it, for example, exacerbate injuries?), lawyers will want to make sure that those records are preserved and turned over in a form that allows the parties to see if the medical records have been edited in a way designed to cover up lapses in that care. With all this at play in a simple case, you can imagine the mountains of data facing the parties in a complex dispute—say a product liability claim (with vast digital data relating to the design, testing, and marketing of the product) or a complex commercial dispute with multiple drafts of many documents created over years of the now-broken relationship.

   All lawyers today need to know a little about preservation and requests of digital information. Some large firms (and large government and nonprofit legal organizations) have formed sub-groups, usually consisting of some lawyers and some technically adept nonlawyers, which specialize in issues of digital information; firms will rely on those groups for anything beyond routine discovery matters. At the same time, an entire industry has sprung up alongside the bar, companies that offer what they call "litigation support services," assisting lawyers in creating and responding to requests for digital information: For a fee, these companies will search large databases for key words and phrases, the most sophisticated using machine learning to suggest alternative words or phrases that might correspond to the request in question. Some law firms will sub-contract digital discovery to such companies.

One issue that regularly arises in both large and small digital discovery is that of "meta-data." Roughly speaking, meta-data consists of information embedded in a digital file that describes the history of the document in question—including revisions to the document. Think, for example, of a contract that undergoes several drafts, with changes made in response to various comments by those within the drafting organization: The other side would dearly love to know why various changes were made. Sometimes such comments and changes will be protected by lawyer-client privilege or work product (to be discussed a bit later), but not always. Even if they are not protected, the requesting party won't get the comments and ensuing revisions unless it requests records that reflect the meta-data; experienced parties devote part of their pretrial conference to hashing out issues relating to meta-data so they don't end up with mutual recriminations before an annoyed judge. A related problem concerns data that are comprehensible only when read by certain software. Although most parties will be able to open Word documents or PowerPoints, it is not uncommon in many industries to have data files that can only be read by software that is not readily available and not inexpensive. Rule 34 tries to address this problem by permitting parties to request discovery of information that requires "translation by the responding party into reasonably usable form." Note that, as with meta-data, a well-counselled party will ask for such translation as part of an initial request.

2. Getting the Story Straight: Crafting a Discovery Plan

Before beginning discovery, parties must not only preserve evidence in their possession—they must also think carefully about what evidence they will be looking for. In other words, lawyers need an overall discovery strategy. Experienced lawyers tell us that they ask themselves several questions: What information do I need to assemble to prove my claim or defense? What part of that information do I already have? What information might lie in the hands of my adversary (or other parties) and how can I most efficiently acquire that information? And, often just as important, what information now in my possession would I just as soon the other party not know about, and is there a way I can lawfully shield that information? (Often the answer to the last question will be no, but it is worth thinking about.)

To answer these questions, and thus to frame a discovery plan, the lawyer needs to envision two stories—the story she wants to tell concerning her claim or defense, and the story she expects to hear from her adversary. If the lawyer does not have such stories in mind, it is quite likely that she will blunder in two ways. First, she will ask for "everything," a request that will likely be met with resistance and perhaps a motion for sanctions. Second, our hypothetical lawyer with this blunderbuss approach is quite likely to fail to ask the crucial two or three questions necessary for her to tell her story effectively—because she is looking in all directions at once. So—think and sketch story lines before you ask for information.

Two qualifications to this advice are necessary. In some cases there will be several alternative stories, each of which is plausible, but none of which our lawyer possesses enough information to tell convincingly. Remember the preceding chapter with its explanation of alternative pleading (see supra page 408)? You now are in a better position to understand why a lawyer acting in entirely good faith might, at an early stage, want to plead alternative stories—and then pursue discovery that would determine which story she wants to (or plausibly can) settle on.

The second, related qualification is that discovery will sometimes turn up entirely unexpected information that may cause a lawyer to shift stories significantly, not just choosing among already pleaded alternatives but striking out in a new direction. A frequently stated ground for amending a pleading—and a ground on which judges will almost always grant leave to amend—is that discovery produced new information enabling the lawyer to tell a better—that is, more convincing—but different story.

In spite of these two qualifications, the basic point stands: Think and sketch stories before planning discovery. A lawyer who does this can conduct more efficient, more focused, and likely more effective discovery. A lawyer who fails to do this is likely to find himself wandering into many blind passages and may well overlook critical information because he doesn't realize he needs it, as well as a motion by the other side to curtail discovery as disproportionate.

Think again about *Haddle v. Garrison*. You'll recall that Garrison's first preference was not to have to tell any story at all—hence the 12(b)(6) motion—a strategy the Supreme Court ultimately rejected. Now that they are back in the district court, imagine what story Haddle would want to tell and what story Garrison would want to tell. What information would each need in order to tell those stories?

B. THE TOOLS OF DISCOVERY

Now that you know what you're looking for—a story (in fact, at least two stories, yours and theirs)—consider how you might gather the material to tell those stories. Most of attorneys' time in most civil cases is spent not in researching arcane bits of law, but in unearthing the facts of the case. Factual investigation not involving the discovery rules is entirely possible and can sometimes be more important than formal discovery. Telephone calls, informal interviews, examination of public records, online searches, and the like will often yield enormous amounts of information. It is important for the beginning lawyer not to become so mesmerized by the tool kit of formal discovery as to forget the existence of other means of gathering information.

But in the great majority of cases lawyers also need to understand the workings of the discovery tools at their disposal. The easiest way to understand how these tools function is first to read Rules 16 and 26-37; then, refer again to specific Rules as this survey touches on them. As you read, consider why the discovery rules contain more detail than, say, the pleading rules.

Rule 26 is the master rule. It catalogues the types of information subject to discovery and imposes discovery-related requirements on the parties throughout the litigation. (Those details can be found largely in Rule 26(b) and (c), about which we will learn more soon.) Rule 26(f) instructs the parties to confer with each other at the outset of a case about predicted subjects of discovery, anticipated disputes about the discoverability of desired information, and other issues that the judge might be able to resolve at an early stage.

Within two weeks of this planning meeting—and before an initial conference with the judge—the parties must exchange the "initial disclosures" required by Rule 26(a)(1). Once the judge has the initial conference with the parties, and issues a scheduling order (required by Rule 16(b)), further discovery can follow. Typically, that discovery will consist of requests for documents, interrogatories, requests for admission, and depositions, followed by reports of expert witnesses if they are to be used, and, if the case proceeds to trial, another round of disclosures mandated by Rule 26—this time the list of witnesses and other evidence each party will present at trial. Rule 26(a)(3). Finally, Rule 16, whose scheduling conference began the sequence, also closes discovery after a final pretrial conference and order for cases destined for trial. Rule 16(e). Graphically displayed, the sequence looks like this:

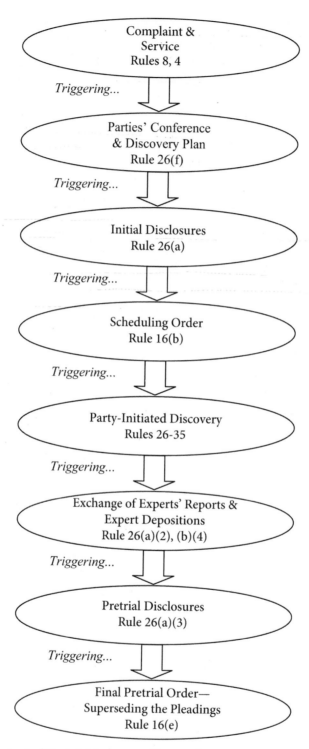

A Prototypical Pretrial Sequence (Focused on Discovery)

This section will survey these tools of discovery, using as its guide the order in which lawyers use them in typical litigation, and the *Haddle v. Garrison* scenario as a way of thinking through how and why parties might deploy these various tools.

1. Required Disclosures—First Round

Rule 26(a) describes the first stage, which it calls "required disclosures." These can be extensive and themselves come in stages, the first of which the Rules call the "Initial Disclosure." Rule 26(a)(1) requires the parties to exchange categories of information "that the disclosing party may use to support its claims or defenses." That information includes the names and locations of witnesses and descriptions and location of documents, as well as calculations of damages and copies of insurance agreements. Each party must offer such information without its having been requested by her opponent and before the initial conference with the judge. Rule 26(a)(1)(C). All this requires cooperation by the lawyers, a timetable, and mechanisms for enforcing discovery and disclosure obligations.

Read Rule 26(a)(1) and answer the questions below.

Notes and Problems

---

1. Once again, think back to *Haddle v. Garrison* in Chapter 6, in which Haddle sued his former employer for retaliatory firing.

   a. Haddle's lawyer has interviewed him and obtained copies of Haddle's W-2 forms (so he can prove damages), his employment contract (which does not contain a "fire-only-for-cause" clause), copies of his employee performance reviews (which are uniformly positive), names of some fellow former employees who, he believes, were also fired for cooperating with the federal investigation, and Haddle's version of a conversation with his supervisor, who told him in connection with the termination that he was "underqualified and overpaid" and that the company could no longer afford him. Which of these potential pieces of evidence should Haddle's lawyer turn over as part of the initial disclosures?

   b. Now consider Haddle's employer, Healthmaster. The company lawyer has interviewed Garrison (the Chair of the Board and President of Healthmaster during the period in question) and learned that she had been "minimally satisfied" with Haddle's work. Garrison brings some documents to the meeting, including a series of generally positive performance reviews, which Garrison characterizes as "boilerplate—everyone gets a positive review unless they're stealing money," and e-mails from Garrison to Human Resources sent two months before Haddle was fired, expressing concern that Haddle was overpaid and exploring the going rate for persons with Haddle's job at comparable firms. Which of these items should her counsel turn over as part of the initial disclosures?

   c. Suppose that Garrison's lawyer fails to disclose the e-mails to Human Resources, and later wants to introduce them at trial in support of a contention that he was fired because his salary was higher than comparable positions in the industry. What objection does Haddle have? Read Rule 37(c)(1).

   d. Garrison also said in her interview with Healthmaster's lawyer that there "might be" some e-mails from Garrison to others in the company expressing anger when she learned of Haddle's cooperation with the investigation. What obligation does the lawyer have to learn more about the e-mails Garrison "might" have sent about Haddle after learning of his cooperation with the investigation? What obligation does the lawyer have to unearth the e-mails that might exist to that effect? Rule 11 and *Zubulake* should provide a blueprint for your answers.

  2. Suppose a party has fully complied with its disclosure requirements, but then learns of an additional witness or document. Read Rule 26(e) and Rule 37(c)(1).

    a. Haddle, suing Garrison for retaliatory firing, supplies her with bills from a psychologist with whom he has consulted regarding emotional distress in the wake of his firing, pursuant to Rule 26(a)(1)(A)(ii). Thereafter, Haddle receives a substantial new bill from the psychologist. What must Haddle's lawyer do?

    b. Haddle fails to inform Garrison of the additional bill, but its existence comes to light during a deposition of the psychologist. Before trial, Garrison seeks to block admission of the bill as part of the evidence on damages. How should the judge rule? Read Rule 37(c)(1).

  3. Disclosure will not occur in all cases. Rule 26(a)(1)(B) exempts a number of cases from initial disclosures—smaller claims and those in which either a well-developed record or the absence of counsel make disclosure unnecessary or potentially unfair. Very large cases, in which close judicial supervision will displace the mandatory disclosure of the Rules, may also be exempted by the court.

WHAT'S NEW HERE?

- The initial round of disclosures asks each party to put its best evidentiary cards on the table—but not those pieces of evidence that will undermine its own case.
- These disclosures help each lawyer form a general idea of the case she will be facing. That *may* produce settlement discussions, and it also gives a very general preview of the main evidentiary attractions at summary judgment and trial.

2. Documents, Things, Land, and Bytes: Requests for Production (Rules 34 and 45)

After the Rule 26(f) meeting between the parties and the mandatory disclosures are out of the way, the parties' lawyers can embark on the next phases of discovery.

Although attorneys will use different discovery tools in different sequences, they will often begin with requests for production. In many cases the lawyers will know at the outset of the suit (perhaps from the initial disclosures) that there are documents or physical objects they want to get their hands on: e-mails, hospital bills, vehicle maintenance records, the wrecked car itself, and so on.

Rule 34 enables such discovery. It has a broad scope, encompassing not only documents but any tangible item, land, or electronically stored information. An e-mail message stored on a computer's hard drive, or on a backup tape made for crash-recovery purposes, is discoverable, as is a photograph or videotape or stored voicemail or text message or Instagram post. So is a software program with embedded accounting data or other information. As we described, supra page 460, the growth of digital data storage has substantially expanded the amount of information subject to discovery in lawsuits, spawned an entire sub-industry devoted to searching electronic records, and complicated attorneys' document requests to include meta-data and translations of material into usable forms.

How exactly must the requester identify the documents in question? In practice, very broad requests are usually allowed because the party propounding the request does not always know what documents the responding party has. A typical request might seek all documents in the custody or control of the responding party that "refer, relate or pertain in any manner" to subject *X*. Such broad requests might end up calling for hundreds, thousands, or even millions of documents, only a small portion of which bear even the remotest potential relevance to the lawsuit. The responding party, faced with such a request, has several choices. It might object to the request as overbroad or not "proportional" to the needs of the case pursuant to Rule 26(b)(1), a rule to which we will soon turn. The party might, in the alternative, assign its employees the time-consuming task of searching all files and digital locations where responsive information might be found. Or the party might point to a warehouse or digital storage of two million files, leaving the requesting party with the daunting challenge of separating wheat from chaff. Read Rule 34(b)(2)(E)(i) and think about how this Rule might justify this third approach.

Thus far, we have focused on requests for production served on parties to the case. Similar requests can be made of a nonparty, but the nonparty must be served with a subpoena issued under Rule 45(a)(1)(A)(iii).

Despite the many complications of Rules 34 and 45, it is critical for lawyers to understand and become adept at using these Rules. In a contract dispute over the interpretation of an ambiguous provision of a contract, for example, each side will want to see any drafts, memos, or notes that might reflect the other side's contemporaneous interpretation of the disputed provision, and will want later to use these documents in deposing the other side's witnesses. These types of documents will often be critical in establishing or disproving liability. Documents can also be critical in establishing damages. Medical records, for example, are central to damage discovery in personal injury cases, and accounting records would be the core of discovery in a case seeking lost profits.

Notes and Problems

---

1. Haddle brings suit against Healthmaster, alleging the claims set forth in the complaint reproduced in Chapter 6 (with the core federal claim being retaliatory firing). Haddle's lawyer makes a Rule 34 request for "all documents, memoranda, and reports relating to the dismissal of Haddle or other employees over the two years preceding Haddle's dismissal until the dissolution of the company." Healthmaster's lawyer learns that on the day of Haddle's firing, Garrison (recall she was Healthmaster's CEO) wrote an e-mail to another employee stating "this should cut down on the number of skunks running to the feds." Must the attorney for Healthmaster produce this e-mail? Which Rule would guide her decision?

2. Suppose that Haddle's request for "all documents, memoranda, and reports relating to the dismissal of Haddle or other employees over the two years preceding Haddle's dismissal until the dissolution of the company" does not specify the format for responses. Healthmaster's lawyer has found hundreds of responsive e-mails and other documents. Can Healthmaster simply produce printouts of these e-mails and documents—which will be hard to search and will not contain evidence of revisions? See Rule 34(b)(2)(E).

3. Does your response to the preceding question change if Haddle's original request specified that each digital document be produced in a format that tracked previous drafts? If so, notice that it becomes critical for the requesting lawyer to have thought about such matters in framing the request.

4. Modern criminal procedure requires that prosecutors turn over to defense counsel information that might tend to exonerate a defendant. Brady v. Maryland, 373 U.S. 83 (1963). Haddle's lawyer believes that as Garrison's prosecution went forward Garrison received from prosecutors information about people who were cooperating with the FBI, that Garrison identified Haddle as a cooperator with this information, and that she fired Haddle based on this information. Haddle requests this information from Garrison, but also wants to request it directly from the FBI. Could Haddle request from the FBI a complete set of the information it turned over to Garrison? How? Rule 45.

3. Asking Questions in Writing, Seeking Admissions: Interrogatories and Admissions (Rules 33 and 36)

While requests for production seek production of documents and things, interrogatories (Rule 33) seek out categories of information that can guide further document requests and depositions. For example, in the suit between Haddle and Healthmaster, interrogatories can be used to learn the names and addresses of all those involved in the decision to fire Haddle, every type of employment review and evaluation conducted by the company, and information about all of the people interviewed for Haddle's job after he was fired.

Interrogatories have some benefits: They can get at information not contained in any document, and they are typically much cheaper than conducting a deposition because one can inexpensively frame a set of appropriate questions, send the requests to an adverse party, and sit back and wait for the answers. A drawback to interrogatories is that, because the questioner cannot follow up evasive answers with a question designed to pin things down, interrogatories that go beyond fairly routine requests for specific information may yield little of value. Another limitation of interrogatories is that parties are presumptively limited to 25 questions (including subparts) to each of their adversaries. Parties must seek permission of the court—or a stipulation from their opponents—before propounding more. A third limitation is that interrogatories may be sent only to a party; nonparty witnesses may be deposed but need not answer written interrogatories. (In contrast, parties can make unlimited requests for production of documents and things, and can make these requests to nonparties through a subpoena.)

Requests for Admissions (Rule 36) share three characteristics with interrogatories. They are usable only against parties, are in writing, and are relatively cheap. One significant difference between the two is that parties can make an unlimited number of requests for admission. This makes sense if one views Rule 36 as much a pleading rule as a discovery device. While interrogatories uncover categories of evidence, requests for admission seek to take issues out of controversy. Suppose Haddle pleads that Healthmaster is a corporation but does so in a paragraph of the complaint that contains other allegations as well, making defendant's denial of the entire paragraph ambiguous. (Cf. *Zielinski v. Philadelphia Piers*, supra page 428.) Plaintiff might well seek an admission as to defendant's corporate status. Because of Rule 37(c)(2), Rule 36 has teeth.

Rule 36 functions best when used to eliminate essentially undisputed issues—for example, that the defendant is incorporated in Georgia or that Haddle received notice of his termination on a particular day. Requests for admission that go to the core of the case will likely be less successful. In this case, such a request might be: "Admit that you fired Michael Haddle as a result of his cooperation with the federal investigation." Rule 36 instructs parties to admit, deny, or explain in detail why they can neither admit nor deny. Healthmaster can deny this request for admission, but if Haddle later proves the statement to be true, he can move for Healthmaster to pay reasonable expenses incurred in making the proof. Rule 37(c)(2). As with answers to pleadings, parties can also admit in part or deny in part. Responding in good faith to requests to admit without showing too much of one's hand is an exercise in subtlety and discretion.

Complications can arise when the party served with a request for admission of critical facts has simply let the time for reply elapse without responding. Read literally, the Rule suggests that the requested facts should be deemed admitted, and courts have so held. Rule 36(a)(3). But courts have also ignored the literal language or have glossed over it when the request for admission concerns a purely legal issue or is ambiguous. Talley v. United States, 990 F.2d 695 (1st Cir. 1993).

Read Rules 33 and 36, together with Rule 37(a)(3) and (b), and apply them to the questions below.

Notes and Problems

---

1. Having been fired in the wake of a criminal indictment of Jeanette Garrison, Haddle sues Garrison and Healthmaster, his employer. The required discovery conference and the ensuing disclosures occur. Haddle then serves 55 interrogatories on Healthmaster and 20 interrogatories on Marcus Wembly, a former employee of Healthmaster who is not named in the case. Both Healthmaster and Wembly refuse to answer.

   a. Explain why Healthmaster needn't answer even if the questions are relevant and not privileged.

   b. What is Wembly's likely objection to Haddle's interrogatories? Can Haddle's lawyer get a court to compel Wembly to answer?

2. One of Haddle's interrogatories asks Healthmaster to specify the compensation for all employees at Haddle's level of seniority from two years before he was fired until the dissolution of the company. Suppose that Healthmaster does not conduct its accounting in a way that would quickly yield an answer to that question. Can it simply produce a flash drive that, it says, contains the payroll and other records that would be required to answer that question, indicating that Haddle is free to consult them? See Rule 33(d).

3. On the day Michael Haddle was fired, several other Healthmaster employees were also terminated. Healthmaster intends to argue that all the firings resulted from the financial stress produced by the criminal case against Jeanette Garrison. Hugh Scott, one of those employees, in a routine "exit interview" conducted by the Human Resources department, tells the interviewer that his immediate supervisor, as he handed him the termination letter, muttered something like, "A pity we have to sacrifice you to get rid of that skunk Haddle." Scott also told Human Resources he had heard rumors that supervisors made similar remarks to other employees terminated at the same time.

   a. Haddle serves an interrogatory seeking the names of anyone who might have information regarding the basis for Haddle's dismissal or the dismissal of other employees. Must Healthmaster identify Scott in its response to the interrogatory?

   b. Plaintiff serves on Healthmaster a Rule 36 notice to admit that several dismissed employees were told that their firings were a pretext to mask the firing of Haddle. Must Healthmaster admit that several employees were told they were fired pretextually?

4. Asking Questions in Person: Depositions (Rule 30) and Physical and Mental Evaluations (Rule 35)

By this point, the parties will likely have accumulated a good deal of information through document requests, interrogatories, and requests for admission. As each of these pieces of information arrives, the lawyers will be trying to join them together with existing information to support their version of the case. Now comes the moment to try to pin down parties' and witnesses' stories before trial. That moment comes in depositions. Rules 27-32 concern issues related to depositions, but it is Rule 30 that sets out the most significant aspects of deposition rules and procedures.

In one respect, a deposition is like questioning a witness at trial without the judge—except that the location will usually be a conference room rather than a courthouse. A lawyer for each party is present, as are the witness and a court reporter or recording device. The lawyer who "noticed" (lawyer-talk for requested) the deposition will ask questions that the witness must answer orally under oath. The witness's lawyer may object to the content or form of the questions and may ask questions of his own when the other lawyer finishes. The court reporter makes a verbatim transcript of the deposition, and the testimony is often visually recorded as well.

In other respects, depositions are quite unlike trials. At trial, a good lawyer will be trying to use questions and other evidence to tell a single, coherent, clear story leading to a favorable verdict or judgment for her client. Accordingly, the lawyer at trial will avoid asking any question that might be distracting or might harm her case. By contrast, at depositions lawyers have opportunities to explore what may turn out to be dead ends, and to ask questions without having the least notion of what the answer might be. A version of the same contrast applies to the treatment of hostile witnesses: At trial, a lawyer will seek to undermine their credibility and expose weaknesses in their testimony. In deposition, the goal is different. Although a lawyer will be delighted if the opposing party admits that his claims or defenses are a pack of lies, she is not expecting or aiming at that goal. Instead, she is meticulously trying to pin down an adverse witness to whatever story that witness wants to tell; once the story is pinned down under oath, the lawyer can decide what to do with it. Finally, depositions free lawyers from some constraints of evidentiary rules. At trial, if a lawyer asks a question whose answer is subject to an evidentiary objection and the other side's lawyer objects, the trial judge will direct the witness not to answer the question. In a deposition, the witness must answer the question (unless the answer would reveal privileged information or information protected by court order). The objection is noted on the record, and the court may prevent this portion of the deposition from being used at later stages of litigation, but the answer is recorded. As a result, some depositions yield a good deal of information that will not be admissible.

The major advantage of a deposition over interrogatories is that the lawyer can ask a series of questions that forces the witness to take a position as to the matters at issue, and the lawyer can immediately follow up with further questions if the witness is evasive or if the testimony opens up new avenues of inquiry. The disadvantage is expense to all concerned. In a deposition, both sides have their lawyers present; if the witness is not one of the parties, he or she may also be represented by a lawyer. In addition, the lawyer who noticed the deposition must arrange for a court reporter to transcribe the deposition and, sometimes, a videographer. In a case with multiple parties, each hour of deposition time may amount to thousands of dollars in attorneys' fees and stenographer's and videographer's time.

As with interrogatories, the Rules place limits on depositions. Without seeking permission, the total number of depositions taken by one side (plaintiff(s), defendant(s), third-party defendant(s)) may not exceed ten; no deposition may exceed a day of seven hours; and no person may be deposed a second time without the permission of the court or the other side. See Rule 30(a)(2)(A)(i).

Conducting depositions of witnesses embedded in large organizations (corporations, governments, universities, etc.) presents special problems. Sometimes the lawyer will want to depose a person with knowledge about a particular area—product design, marketing, curriculum, etc.—without knowing who in the organization has that information. Rule 30(b)(6) allows the requester to identify a topic to be explored, placing the burden on the organization to produce a knowledgeable person.

Parties can undergo an additional, particularly sensitive type of questioning and investigation, this time by doctors instead of lawyers. Rule 35 allows physical and mental examinations of parties and usually is employed only when the physical or mental condition of the party is at stake in the case. Take, for example, *Reise*, in Chapter 1, in which the court orders a psychological evaluation of a plaintiff who alleged emotional injuries resulting from defendants' actions. Similarly, a plaintiff who alleges physical injury might be evaluated by a doctor chosen by the defendant. Unlike other discovery provisions, Rule 35 requires a special application to the court and a showing of "good cause" for such an evaluation. The disputes here focus on what constitutes "good cause," with courts asked to balance need against issues of privacy.

It is well settled that a plaintiff who puts his mental or physical condition at issue by seeking damages for mental or physical injury can be required to undergo a mental or physical examination. The same is true where a defendant has specifically asserted a defense that puts his mental or physical condition at issue. If the defendant in a contract case files an answer that pleads as an affirmative defense that the defendant was mentally incompetent and therefore could not enter into a binding contract, the defendant could be required to undergo an examination regarding his mental capacity.

But the law is much less permissive about allowing physical or mental exams where a party has not clearly put her own physical or mental condition at issue. In the leading case, Schlagenhauf v. Holder, 379 U.S. 104 (1964), a Greyhound bus rear-ended a tractor-trailer. Passengers on the bus were injured and brought suit against Greyhound, the driver, the owner of the tractor, and the owner of the trailer. The tractor and trailer owners sought—and the district judge ordered—vision, neurological, psychiatric, and internal medicine exams of the defendant bus driver. In support of the exams, the tractor owner's counsel submitted an affidavit which stated that the driver had testified at his deposition that he had seen the rear lights of the vehicle ahead of him for 10-15 seconds, but had not slowed down, and had rear-ended the vehicle. The affidavit also established that the bus driver had been involved in a prior similar accident.

A divided Supreme Court held that the record supported at most a vision exam of the driver. The majority concluded that "[n]othing in the pleadings or affidavit would afford a basis for a belief that Schlagenhauf was suffering from a mental or neurological illness warranting wide-ranging psychiatric or neurological examinations. Nor is there anything stated justifying the broad internal medicine examination." The dissenters would have allowed all of the exams ordered by the district court. The dissenting opinion reasoned: "In a collision case like this one, evidence concerning very bad eyesight or impaired mental or physical health which may affect the ability to drive is obviously of the highest relevance. It is equally obvious, I think, that when a vehicle continues down an open road and smashes into a truck in front of it although the truck is in plain sight and there is ample time and room to avoid collision, the chances are good that the driver has some physical, mental or moral defect. When such a thing happens twice, one is even more likely to ask, 'What is the matter with that driver? Is he blind or crazy?'"

Notes and Problems

1. Pursuant to Rule 30(b)(6), Haddle serves on Healthmaster a request to depose an employee or officer responsible for "Human Resources and employee evaluations."

   a. Healthmaster designates Geraldine Chen, a vice president for Human Resources. In part because Healthmaster's lawyer has lodged numerous objections to the questions asked by Haddle's lawyer, the deposition, which started at 9 A.M., ends at 5 P.M. (with a one-hour break for lunch) without Haddle's lawyer having reached his most important questions. When Haddle's lawyer asks that the deposition be continued, Healthmaster's lawyer refuses, citing Rule 30(d)(1), which presumptively limits depositions to seven hours. How can Haddle's lawyer use the same rule to make a strong argument for additional time to continue the deposition?

   b. Suppose Haddle's lawyer finishes deposing Chen on Healthmaster's employee evaluation processes. At trial, Haddle's lawyer introduces Chen's deposition testimony (Rule 32(a) permits such trial use of deposition testimony). Then Healthmaster seeks to present a rebuttal witness, the gist of whose testimony will be that Chen was not really the person in charge of Human Resources and that her deposition testimony was therefore inaccurate. Courts have held that a party generally cannot rebut the testimony of its Rule 30(b)(6) witness. Snapp v. United Transportation Union, 889 F.3d 1088 (9th Cir. 2018) (collecting cases). Why, do you think? On what grounds might Haddle move to exclude the rebuttal witness's testimony?

2. Haddle alleges emotional injuries as a result of his firing. As part of his initial disclosures Haddle identifies the psychologist he has been working with and her bills. As soon as the initial disclosures have been exchanged, Healthmaster seeks to have Haddle examined by a psychologist who will likely testify for Healthmaster.

   a. Should the court grant the request?
   b. If the examination takes place, is Haddle entitled to see a copy of the psychologist's report to Healthmaster? See Rule 35(b).

3. One should not overlook the deposition as a source of unintentional humor. Consider the following excerpts, all but the last collected by Mary Louise Gilman, the editor of *National Shorthand Reporter* and published in Richard Lederer, *Anguished English* (1987):

> *Q:* Doctor, did you say he was shot in the woods?
> *A:* No, I said he was shot in the lumbar region.
>
> *Q:* What is your name?
> *A:* Ernestine McDowell.
> *Q:* And what is your marital status?
> *A:* Fair.
>
> *Q:* When he went, had you gone and had she, if she wanted to and were able, for the time being excluding all the restraints on her not to go, gone also, would he have brought you, meaning you and she, with him to the station?
> *Mr. Brooks:* Objection. That question should be taken out and shot.

Finally, consider what Professor Richard Friedman reports as "an actual trial transcript," whose accuracy he has confirmed with one of the lawyers:

> *The Court:* Next witness.
> *Ms. Olschner:* Your Honor, at this time I would like to swat Mr. Buck in the head with his client's deposition.
> *The Court:* You mean read it?
> *Ms. Olschner:* No, sir. I mean to swat him [in] the head with it. Pursuant to Rule 32[(a)(3)], I may use the deposition [of a party] "for any purpose" and that is the purpose for which I want to use it.
> *The Court:* Well, it does say that.
> (Pause.)

>   ***The Court:*** There being no objection, you may proceed.
>   ***Ms. Olschner:*** Thank you, Judge Hanes.
>   (Whereupon Ms. Olschner swatted Mr. Buck in the head with a deposition.)
>   ***Mr. Buck:*** But Judge . . .
>   ***The Court:*** Next witness.
>   ***Mr. Buck:*** We object.
>   ***The Court:*** Sustained. Next witness.

4. Discussing each of the procedural tools one by one—required disclosures, requests for documents, interrogatories, requests for admission, and depositions—fails to capture the ways in which different types of requests can relate one to the other and inspire further inquiry. Imagine, for example, that Haddle's lawyer conducts her Rule 30(b)(6) deposition of Geraldine Chen, the vice president for Human Resources. Haddle's lawyer learns during Chen's deposition that, a few years before Haddle's dismissal, Healthmaster fired another employee when the firm was under another investigation. Haddle's attorney will most likely submit a document request seeking records concerning that previous firing. Upon reviewing those records, Haddle's attorney might learn that Healthmaster has a previously undisclosed "special employee review" process for employees who cooperated in this prior investigation, and demand production of records reflecting that process. Haddle's attorney might also submit an interrogatory seeking a list of all previous employees dismissed after that special process was invoked. In other words, parties will usually make comprehensive document requests before taking depositions but depositions can prompt additional document requests and interrogatories; those documents and interrogatory responses can prompt additional depositions and requests. The next chart attempts to illustrate the fluidity with which these discovery tools may be used.

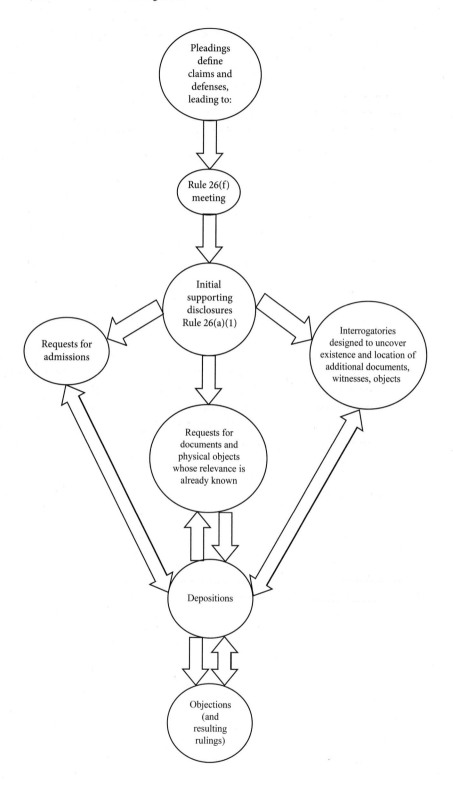

5. Pretrial Witness Lists and the Pretrial Order

The discovery process ends in the way it begins—with a final round of disclosures. These disclosures include a list of the witnesses and other evidence—expert reports, exhibits, documents—that each side proposes to introduce at trial. Rule 26(a)(3). (See *Monfore v. Phillips,* infra page 619, for an illustration of the constraints a final pretrial order can place on trial.) In many cases, these final pretrial disclosures will be set in concrete by the judge's final pretrial conference and the ensuing order. Rule 16(e). Contrary to the impression one might gain from depictions of trials in film and other media, the final pretrial order practically forecloses the possibility of surprise witnesses and evidence.

David and Goliath Do Discovery: A Taxonomy of Problems

Because the parties bear the costs of fact investigation in the U.S. legal system, imbalances in each side's financial resources could affect the outcome of cases regardless of the merits. Note that the problem isn't merely or even primarily "which litigant has the most money." A poor litigant with a strong claim for substantial damages will have plenty of litigation resources if she finds a well-financed lawyer to take her case on a contingent fee basis. As is described in Chapter 5, parties with strong claims can also borrow to finance litigation, including discovery. As a result, a wealthy defendant whose defense is being financed by a liability insurer seeking to reduce litigation expenses may have fewer resources than a poorer plaintiff with strong financial backing. And a defendant who perceives that more is at stake than the individual case suggests—reputation, subsequent similar claims— may be willing to spend more than the case warrants. Although the motivations and resources available to parties vary from case to case, there are undoubtedly many situations in which David is battling Goliath.

What impact does mismatched resources have on discovery? The problem has two versions. First, what happens if one party lacks resources to do adequate discovery? The most troubling case arises when most of the likely evidence is in defendant's hands, and the assembly of evidence would likely be complex—perhaps in a product liability or environmental hazard claim. Without access to discovery, such a claim has no chance of succeeding. Although the Rules nowhere address this problem specifically, several possibilities present themselves. The party with fewer resources may be able to collect evidence from various public sources— government or public documents, press sources, and the like. Digital media and the Internet have made such searches much faster and cheaper than they were 50 years ago. Moreover, a disciplined discovery scheme making maximum use of cheap discovery (such as document requests and interrogatories) may yield a good deal. With large public and private institutions, well-planned document requests can produce rich veins of information. With the information developed from such cheap discovery, a party might be able to approach one of the growing number of firms that advance litigation costs on the basis of their assessment of the merits of an individual case (see supra pages 344-45). It is also worth remembering that in most large institutions there is (a) often another copy of the missing document and (b) someone in whose interest it is to disclose that document or say who destroyed it—if only to avoid blame falling on him.

It may also be possible to freeride on the discovery efforts of others: A deposition conducted by one party will likely yield useful information for a coparty or a future litigation. One Rule makes this avenue more difficult to pursue. Rule 5(d)(1) forbids parties from filing with the court many discovery responses "until they are used in the proceeding or the court orders filing." The motivation behind this amendment was simple: Courts were running out of space to store such documents. But the consequences may be to curtail the availability of discovery materials in separate but factually related cases, making it harder for an ill-funded party to "piggyback" on another's efforts unless the attorneys in the cases coordinate. On the other hand, a party seeking these litigation materials can simply subpoena them from the parties in the other case (assuming they are not covered by a protective order of the kind at issue in *Kalinauskas v. Wong*, at page 546).

The second problem comes if we assume grossly mismatched resources: A modestly financed plaintiff faces an institutional defendant who anticipates many similar cases to come is motivated to spend what appears to be an irrational amount on the particular case. Again, this may be more a problem of litigation finance than of the discovery rules, but a few comments may put the issue in context. If plaintiff's lawyer perceives this to be the case, one possibility is to partner with other lawyers who may be interested in financing this case because they relish the possibility of the future cases the defendant is seeking to avert. Another possibility would be to try to use defendant's fears as leverage for a settlement: An unlitigated case will not yield discovery that can be used in future cases. Parties can also use the Rules to address some of these resource issues. Rule 26(b)(1), amended in 2015, now provides that the scope of discovery be "proportional to the needs of the case," determined, in part, by the parties' resources. And a party might seek to use the provision of Rule 26(g) that requires each lawyer to certify that discovery requests or objections are "neither unreasonable nor unduly burdensome or expensive, considering the needs of the case, prior discovery in the case, the amount in controversy, and the importance of the issues at stake in the action."

C. THE SCOPE OF DISCOVERY

Having now surveyed the types of discovery tools that each side can use to uncover information, we now turn to the breadth of information that can be uncovered with these tools. Both the power and the destructive potential of the discovery tools hinge on the scope of their reach.

Rule 26(b)(1) allows the parties, without court approval, to seek discovery "regarding any nonprivileged matter that is *relevant* to any party's claim or defense." Discoverability does not, however, turn on relevance alone. Even relevant information can be protected from discovery if it is *privileged* (Rule 26(b)(1)); if it is unduly cumulative, duplicative, burdensome, or not proportional to the needs of the case (Rules 26(b)(1) and 26(b)(2)(C)); or if its potential for annoyance, embarrassment, oppression, or undue burden or expense outweigh its evidentiary value (Rule 26(b)(2)(C)). We will consider the scope of each of these terms.

1. Relevance

To be admissible at trial, evidence must be relevant. "Relevance" links admissibility to the substantive law and to common-sense patterns of inference. Start with common sense: How I tie my shoelaces is irrelevant to whether it will rain today; how the sky looks is highly relevant to that question. But legal relevance demands more than this. For a piece of information to be relevant to a legal proposition, that information must tend to prove or disprove something the governing substantive law says matters. If it doesn't matter, the law of evidence will prevent that information from being presented at trial. For example, if, in a contract dispute, the defendant contends that he failed to pay for goods because the goods were defective, the condition of the goods will be relevant and can be offered in evidence. If the defendant instead contends that he failed to pay for the goods because he used the money to support a sick relative, the state of the relative's health would be legally irrelevant. Its irrelevance flows from the law of contract, which says that one's motives for breaching a contract don't matter.

Because the discovery rules aim to unearth information that would be admissible at trial, they too are linked to relevance. But for discovery the links can be more attenuated. The Advisory Committee notes to Rule 26(b) explain that "[i]nformation within this scope of discovery need not be admissible in evidence to be discoverable." For a simple example of information that would be relevant and discoverable—because likely to lead to admissible evidence—but not directly admissible, consider a deposition in an auto accident case. Plaintiff seeks evidence that the light was red when defendant entered the intersection. Witness has already said he did not observe the color of the light. Lawyer asks, "Did you hear anyone say that he or she saw that the light was red?" At trial, a judge would, if defendant objected, tell the lawyer not to ask that question because it calls for hearsay. But in discovery the question is proper because Witness's response may well lead to identification of another witness who can say from personal observation whether the light was red.

Both substantive law and pleading narrow the range of potentially relevant and thus discoverable information. In a claim for breach of contract to deliver goods, suppose the defendant pleaded, as his sole defense, the running of the statute of limitations. On the basis of that pleading, information about whether the plaintiff had fulfilled her part of the agreement would not be "relevant to" the defendant's "defense." By contrast, if in addition to pleading the running of the statute of limitations, defendant admitted that he failed to deliver the goods but asserted that he did so because plaintiff had not paid him for those goods, questions about plaintiff's performance would become relevant and subject to discovery.

The next case illustrates how pleadings define the limits of relevance.

Favale v. Roman Catholic Diocese of Bridgeport

233 F.R.D. 243 (D. Conn. 2005)

SQUATRITO, J.

Now pending in the above-captioned matter is plaintiffs' motion to compel and defendant's motion for a protective order. . . . For the reasons that follow, plaintiffs' motion to compel is DENIED and defendant's motion for a protective order is GRANTED.

Background

Plaintiff Maryann Favale worked as an administrative assistant at Saint Joseph's School in Brookfield, Connecticut, for approximately twenty-one years. During this time period, in November of 2002, Sister Bernice Stobierski became the new interim principal. Then, in May 2003, Sister Stobierski assumed the position of full-time principal. Maryann Favale alleges that Sister Stobierski subjected her to "severe and repeated sexual harassment" in the workplace from December 2002 to June 2003. Specifically, plaintiff alleges that Sister Stobierski touched her inappropriately, made sexually suggestive comments, exhibited lewd behavior, and requested physical affection. Plaintiff first informed her employer, the Roman Catholic Diocese of Bridgeport, ("the Diocese") of the alleged sexual harassment on June 11, 2003. Maryann Favale, who no longer works at Saint Joseph's School, seeks damages against the Diocese for sexual harassment, retaliation, defamation, intentional and negligent infliction of emotional distress, negligent hiring, negligent supervision, and other causes of action. In addition, co-plaintiff Mark Favale asserts a claim for loss of consortium against the defendant. Sister Stobierski is not a party to this case.

Plaintiffs now seek to compel Sister Stobierski to testify to any prior treatment she may have received for her alleged anger management history and psychological or psychiatric conditions. Plaintiffs also move to compel the Diocese to produce any records it has of any such treatment. [The Diocese objects to both motions to compel on relevance grounds, among others.] . . .

Sister Stobierski's Testimony

Plaintiffs assert that Sister Stobierski's testimony regarding the treatment she received for her alleged anger management, psychological, and psychiatric conditions is relevant to their claims of negligent hiring and negligent supervision. To assert a negligent hiring claim under Connecticut law, a plaintiff must "[p]lead and prove that she was injured by the defendant's own negligence in failing to select as its employee a person who was fit and competent to perform the job in question and that her injuries resulted from the employee's unfit or incompetent performance of his work." Roberts v. Circuit-Wise, Inc., 142 F. Supp. 2d 211, 214 n.1 (D. Conn. 2001). Similarly, Connecticut law requires that a plaintiff bringing a negligent supervision claim

[p]lead and prove that he suffered an injury due to the defendant's failure to supervise an employee whom the defendant had a duty to supervise. A defendant does not owe a duty of care to protect a plaintiff from another employee's tortious acts unless the defendant knew or reasonably should have known of the employee's propensity to engage in that type of tortious conduct.

Rule

Abate v. Circuit-Wise, Inc., 130 F. Supp. 2d 341, 344 (D. Conn. 2001). Both negligent hiring and negligent supervision claims turn upon the type of wrongful conduct that actually precipitated the harm suffered by plaintiff. "It is well settled that defendants cannot be held liable for their alleged negligent hiring, training, supervision or retention of an employee accused of wrongful conduct unless they had notice of said employee's propensity for the type of behavior causing the plaintiff's harm." *Elbert v. Connecticut Yankee Council, Inc.*, No. CV010456879S, 2004 WL 1832935, at *13 (Conn. Super. Ct. July 16, 2004) (citations, internal quotation marks, and punctuation omitted).

Plaintiffs allege that the defendant negligently hired and supervised an individual who was not fit to be the principal of an elementary school. They contend that the "defendant knew or reasonably should have known that Sister Stobierski was unfit to be the principal of St. Joseph's School as a result of her prior emotional and anger management issues, and limited school administration experience." . . . Yet, plaintiffs do not allege that Sister Stobierski's prior emotional and anger management issues harmed plaintiff.

Rather, the only type of harm alleged to have been suffered by Maryann Favale was harm resulting from repeated acts of sexual harassment, and plaintiffs do not maintain that Sister Stobierski's alleged anger management and psychological or psychiatric conditions contributed to the sexual harassment. Accordingly, Sister Stobierski's testimony pertaining to the treatment she allegedly received for her anger management, psychological, or psychiatric conditions is not relevant because it does not pertain to the defense or claim of any party.

Indeed, even if the Diocese was aware of Sister Stobierski's alleged anger management history or psychological or psychiatric conditions, this knowledge would have no bearing on plaintiffs' claims for negligent supervision and negligent hiring because the wrongful conduct of which the Diocese would have had notice was not the same type of wrongful conduct that caused Maryann Favale harm. Notice of Sister Stobierski's alleged anger management history or psychological or psychiatric conditions does not equate to notice of Sister Stobierski's propensity to commit acts of sexual harassment. The Diocese's objection to plaintiffs' motion to compel the testimony of Sister Stobierski is sustained, and plaintiffs' motion is denied.

The Production of Defendant's Records Relating to Sister Stobierski

Plaintiffs assert that any documentation that the Roman Catholic Diocese of Bridgeport may have regarding Sister Stobierski's treatment for anger management or psychological and psychiatric conditions is relevant to their claims of negligent hiring and negligent supervision. The elements of these claims are discussed above. . . . [E]ven if the defendant possessed documents relating to treatment Sister Stobierski received for her alleged anger management or psychological and psychiatric conditions, these records would not establish Sister Stobierski's propensity for the type of behavior that caused Maryann Favale harm because they would not demonstrate a propensity for sexual harassment. Again, it is significant that plaintiffs do not allege that Maryann Favale was harmed by Sister Stobierski's alleged inability to control her anger or her alleged psychological or psychiatric conditions. Sexual harassment is the only type of harm alleged by plaintiffs. . . .

Defendant's motion for a protective order is granted. A protective order shall enter barring future discovery into Sister Stobierski's anger management or psychological and psychiatric treatment as the court finds that this information is profoundly personal and, as stated herein, not relevant to the claims in this case.

WHAT'S NEW HERE?

- Relevance is *relational*: It asks whether information is pertinent *given the claim or defense at issue.*
- The question then becomes: Would the information sought in the case help the party seeking it prove or defeat the claim in question?

Notes and Problems

1. One might think that evidence showing the Diocese hired a school principal knowing her to have anger management problems would be relevant to a legal claim about the quality of its hiring and supervision practices. Yet this information was found to be irrelevant to Favale's negligent hiring and supervision claims. Why?

2. To solidify your understanding of the link between relevance and substantive law, imagine that the complaint in this case alleged that Sister Stobierski yelled at and hit Favale. Explain why these changes would render the information sought in *Favale* relevant.

3. Consider the practical finality of this district court's discovery decision. If Favale disagrees with the district court's ruling, can she seek review in the court of appeals? The answer is yes, but not until there is a final judgment in the case. (See *Reise* in Chapter 1.) Realistically, Favale will not appeal the decision unless she loses her case against the Diocese on summary judgment or at trial. If she wins the case, this discovery dispute will no longer matter to her. If the case settles, a condition of settlement would most certainly be to foreclose further litigation of this matter.

4. Assessments of relevance are sometimes counterintuitive when it comes to questions about defendants' financial assets. Consider the following problems:

    a. Albert and Barbara are involved in an automobile collision. Albert sues Barbara, alleging negligence. Barbara denies liability. Albert seeks to discover the size of Barbara's bank account. (He wants to know whether she will be capable of satisfying a damage judgment.) Is this information discoverable? Probably not; the information, while relevant to Albert's ability to recover a damage judgment, is not relevant to whether Barbara was negligent.

    b. Same facts as in 4a, except that in addition to asserting negligence, Albert alleges that Barbara intentionally collided with him. Intentional torts carry with them the possibility of punitive damages, and in many jurisdictions a jury asked to award punitive damages may consider the wealth of the defendant, the idea being that the punishment should be tailored to the defendant's circumstances. Albert again seeks to discover the size of Barbara's bank account. It is now "relevant to a claim or defense" and thus discoverable because the amount of Barbara's assets will determine an appropriate sanction. What has changed here is not the rules of discovery but the substantive law.

    c. Same lawsuit as in 4a—that is, a negligence action, with no allegations of intentional harm. Albert, fearing that Barbara may lack assets to pay damages, seeks to discover whether Barbara has a liability insurance policy that would be available to satisfy a damage judgment if he wins the suit. If one considers only relevance to a claim or defense, the insurance policy would seem irrelevant for the reasons described in the discussion of Problem 4a. Yet Rule 26(a)(1)(A)(iv) requires Barbara to disclose this information. This disclosure requirement, outside the bounds of relevance, appears to reflect a policy choice to discourage litigation pursued in the hope of non-existent assets.

2. Proportionality, Burden, and Privacy

Discovery aims at uncovering truth and permitting lawsuits to be decided on their merits. But the truth sometimes hurts, and a party being asked to disclose information can seek protection from the court if he believes that the burdens of producing the information outweigh the benefits.

Rule 26(b)(1) provides that discovery requested must not only be relevant but also "proportional to the needs of the case, considering the importance of the issues at stake in the action, the amount in controversy, the parties' relative access to relevant information, the parties' resources, the importance of the discovery in resolving the issues, and whether the burden or expense of the proposed discovery outweighs its likely benefit." When parties seek electronically stored information, Rule 26 requires not only that the information sought is proportional, but that it is reasonably accessible. Rule 26(b)(2)(B) provides that "[a] party need not provide discovery of electronically stored information from sources that the party identifies as not reasonably accessible because of undue burden or cost."

Courts can limit a discovery request if it is found not to be proportional to the needs of the case, as provided in Rule 26(b)(1), or if the request is (2) "unreasonably cumulative or duplicative, or can be obtained from some other source that is more convenient, less burdensome, or less expensive"; or (3) "the party seeking discovery has had ample opportunity to obtain the information by discovery." In addition, the court can limit discovery "to protect a party or person from annoyance, embarrassment, [or] oppression." Rule 26(c). The following three cases consider the breadth of these protections.

Cerrato v. Nutribullet, LLC

2017 WL 3608266 (M.D. Fla. 2017)

ORDER ON PLAINTIFF'S MOTION TO COMPEL

SNEED, M.J.

This matter is before the Court on Plaintiff's Motion to Compel Prior Accident/Injury Reports and Consumer Complaints Regarding Product at Issue and Defendant's Response in Opposition. Upon consideration, the Motion to Compel is granted in part and denied in part.

Background

Plaintiffs Phyllis and German Cerrato bring this products liability action against Defendants for injuries allegedly sustained by Plaintiff Phillis Cerrato while using a blender designed and manufactured by Defendants. Plaintiffs allege that the blender exploded and resulted in hot liquids burning Plaintiff Phyllis Cerrato and causing property damage to Plaintiffs' kitchen. Plaintiffs bring negligence, strict liability, and breach of warranty claims against Defendants. . . .

Analysis

. . . Request Number 4 seeks "[a]ll accident reports and records relating to any injury allegedly caused by the product." Request Number 5 seeks "[a]ll consumer complaints of any type relating to the product." Plaintiff defined the term "product" as the "MagicBullet/Nutribullet Pro 900 series that is the subject of this litigation." In response, Defendant objected to both requests as vague, ambiguous, overbroad, not reasonably calculated to lead to the discovery of admissible evidence, [and] not proportional to the needs of the case. . . .

[T]he Court agrees that Plaintiff's requests are overbroad and not proportional to the needs of the case. The requests contain no time limitation and no limitation as to the type of injury at issue, the subject matter of the complaints requested, the alleged defect at issue, or the circumstances of the incident in the materials requested. Defendant asserts that if Plaintiff's Motion to Compel is granted, Plaintiff should only be entitled to discovery of incidents "similar enough" to the incident Plaintiff describes in her deposition. Specifically, Defendant states the requests should be limited to similar incidents where "the Nutribullet Pro 900 cup could not be untwisted from the base to turn it off." Defendant further asserts that Plaintiff should not be entitled to discovery of information concerning other incidents that occurred subsequent to the subject incident as subsequent incidents are irrelevant. Nevertheless, evidence of subsequent incidents is admissible to prove a particular theory of causation, particularly where the exact circumstances of an accident are unknown.

Given the overbroad nature of Plaintiff's requests, the Court finds that the requests are unduly burdensome and seek information that is disproportionate to the needs of this case. However, with an appropriate time limitation, a request for accident reports and consumer complaints concerning incidents where the MagicBullet/Nutribullet Pro 900 Series could not be turned off is relevant and proportional to the needs of the case. The Motion to Compel is therefore granted in part, and Defendant shall supplement its response by producing all accident reports and consumer complaints occurring within five years prior to Plaintiff's incident through the date of Plaintiff's Complaint concerning incidents where the MagicBullet/Nutribullet Pro 900 Series could not be turned off. *See* Moore v. Armour Pharmaceutical Co., 927 F.2d 1194, 1197 (11th Cir. 1991) (stating that the trial court "has wide discretion in setting the limits of discovery"); *Farnsworth*, 758 F.2d at 1547 (same); *Commercial Union Ins. Co.*, 730 F.2d at 731 ("Case law states that a motion to compel discovery is committed to the discretion of the trial court").

Last, Defendant objected to Plaintiff's Requests Number 4 and 5 as seeking confidential and private information, including private information concerning other consumers. The confidential and private information of other consumers is irrelevant to Plaintiffs' claims. Therefore, Defendant shall redact all accident reports and consumer complaints produced to Plaintiffs for the consumers' private and confidential information, including any names, addresses, telephone numbers, and social security numbers. . . .

Wagoner v. Lewis Gale Medical Center, LLC

2016 WL 3893135 (W.D. Va. 2016)

BALLOU, M.J.

Order

Plaintiff, Jim David Wagoner ("Wagoner") seeks to compel defendant Lewis Gale Medical Center, LLC ("Lewis Gale") to conduct a search of its computer systems for certain electronically stored information ("ESI"). Lewis Gale objects because of the "difficulty and unreasonable expense in performing plaintiff's requested searches." Alternatively, Lewis Gale asks that Wagoner pay for the related costs of conducting this search. The motion to compel is GRANTED.

I. Background

Wagoner worked as a security guard for Lewis Gale from April 4, 2014 until he was terminated on June 12, 2014. He worked approximately 16 hours per week and earned $12.49 per hour. He filed suit against Lewis Gale on October 23, 2015, alleging that he suffered from dyslexia and that Lewis Gale wrongfully terminated his employment in violation of the Americans with Disabilities Act ("ADA"). Wagoner asserts claims related to discrimination, retaliation, and failure to accommodate in violation of the ADA.

Wagoner propounded requests for production of documents to Lewis Gale seeking production of ESI maintained by two custodians, Frank Caballos and Bobby Baker, who were Wagoner's supervisors. Wagoner limited the dates for any ESI search to only four months and requested the following search terms:

> Jim OR Wagoner AND dyslexia OR dyslexic OR read OR reading OR slow OR ADA OR disabled OR disability OR security OR schedule OR copy OR copying.

Lewis Gale conceded that it does not have the capability to perform this global search and obtained an estimate of $21,570 from a third-party vendor to collect the requested ESI, with an additional $24,000 estimated to review the documents retrieved. The ESI search would involve seven computers that the two custodians had access to and an exchange server located in Tennessee. Lewis Gale argues that the discovery plaintiff seeks is not proportional because Wagoner only worked for two months as a security guard, and his potential damages are less than the cost to perform the ESI search. Lewis Gale further asserts that it has produced considerable ESI in the form of "e-mails gathered manually from the computers of key custodians."

II. Analysis

A. Relevance

Rule 26 of the Federal Rules of Civil Procedure provides that a party "may obtain discovery regarding any nonprivileged matter that is relevant to any party's claim or defense and proportional to the needs of the case. . . ." Fed. R. Civ. P. 26(b). Thus, as a threshold matter, I must determine whether Wagoner's discovery requests are relevant under Rule 26.

Wagoner contends that his dyslexia caused him to have difficulty reading and copying his posted work schedule, that Lewis Gale denied his request for a written copy of the schedule, and that his termination violated the ADA. E-mails or other memoranda written by Wagoner's supervisors, Frank Caballos and Bobby Baker, between April and July 2014 and containing the search terms listed above are relevant to Wagoner's claim. Indeed, Lewis Gale largely conceded at the hearing that Wagoner's request was relevant, arguing only that the keyword searches were too broad. Accordingly, I find that Wagoner's requested ESI search is relevant to the claims and defenses asserted in this case. . . .

B. Reasonable Accessibility

Lewis Gale argues that the discovery in this case should not be permitted because [it] is not proportional, considering the high cost of performing the ESI search compared to Wagoner's limited potential recovery. Lewis Gale further states that, if the court does order it to obtain the requested discovery, the court should shift the cost of the ESI search to Wagoner. Relevant ESI may still not be discoverable under Rule 26 if the party can show that the information is "not reasonably accessible because of undue burden or cost." Fed. R. Civ. P. 26(b)(2)(B). The court may also specify conditions for the discovery which may include cost sharing. Here I find that Lewis Gale has not shown that the burdens and costs of obtaining the ESI discovery makes the requested information not reasonably accessible, nor has Lewis Gale shown that the requested ESI discovery is not proportional.

Lewis Gale claims that the fact that it cannot perform the requested ESI search in-house, and must contract with a third party vendor at significant cost, requires the court to find that the information is not reasonably accessible. Lewis relies upon the declarations of Karyn Hayes, Systems Manager for HCA Management Services, which provides computer systems services to Lewis Gale, and of Austin Maddox, Senior Litigation Technology Consultant for Document Solutions, Inc., the third-party vendor that provided an estimate to Lewis Gale for performing the ESI search. Ms. Hayes indicated that there were approximately 30,598 [responsive] e-mails. . . . She further stated that a third-party vendor would be required to perform the ESI search on seven computers located at Lewis Gale, and the "computers would require forensic extraction of data, data processing, data hosting, project management, production, and review" with an estimated cost of $45,570.00. Mr. Maddox indicated that Wagoner's ESI request would involve:

> the remote collection of at least seven laptops and email archive data. The data would be processed and loaded into a Catalyst Repository Systems web-hosted review platform. Once the data has been loaded to Catalyst, the [Document Solutions, Inc.] Client Services team would work with the hospital to cull data through objective filters (date range, email domain, file type, etc.) to identify and promote documents for review by counsel.

Mr. Maddox further estimated that, "Reasonable parameters and metrics suggest that after search terms and date filters have been applied, approximately five gigabytes of data consisting of an estimated 3500 documents per gigabyte would need to be reviewed at an estimated 292 hours of expended time, which would cost approximately $24,000."

Rule   Whether production of documents is unduly burdensome or expensive turns primarily on whether the data is kept in an accessible or inaccessible format. Zubulake v. UBS Warburg LLC, 217 F.R.D. 309, 318 (S.D.N.Y. 2003). . . . Lewis Gale has not carried its burden to show that the data on the seven computers or exchange server is inaccessible, i.e. must be restored, de-fragmented, or reconstructed. Instead, Lewis Gale has stated that it is not capable of performing the ESI searches requested by plaintiff in-house, and would be required to contract with an expensive outside vendor.

Moreover, it is difficult to conclude that the ESI sought is not proportional or "not reasonably accessible" due to undue burden and expense because Lewis Gale apparently chose to use a system that did not automatically preserve e-mails for more than three days, and did not preserve e-mails in a readily searchable format, making it costly to produce relevant e-mails when faced with a lawsuit. See AAB Joint Venture v. United States, 75 Fed. Cl. 432, 443 (2007) (noting "the Court cannot relieve Defendant of its duty to produce those documents merely because Defendant has chosen a means to preserve the evidence which makes ultimate production of relevant documents expensive.").

Proportionality consists of more than whether the particular discovery method is expensive. Here, Lewis Gale advances no other reasonable alternative to obtain the requested information. Lewis Gale simply proposes to have the very person who may have authored relevant documents search their computer for responsive information. No insurance exists that this search method would yield any ESI deleted prior to the search. Employment discovery presents particular challenges to the employees where most, and sometimes all, relevant discovery is in the control of the employer. Here, in light of the limited request, restricted by custodian, search terms, and time period, I find the request proportional to the needs of the case.

Finally, because I find that the ESI sought is reasonably accessible without undue burden or expense, cost-shifting is not appropriate. Accordingly, I will not shift the cost of discovery, and the general rule that the party responding to a discovery request bears the cost will apply.

III. Conclusion

Accordingly, Wagoner's motion to compel is GRANTED. . . .
It is so **ORDERED**.

Rengifo v. Erevos Enterprises, Inc.

2007 WL 894376 (S.D.N.Y. Mar. 20, 2007)

ELLIS, M.J.

Plaintiff, Willy Rengifo ("Rengifo") [who brings this action against his former employers to recover unpaid overtime wages under the federal Fair Labor Standards Act (FLSA) and New York Labor Law, among other claims] requests this Court to issue a protective order pursuant to Federal Rule of Civil Procedure 26(c) barring discovery related to his immigration status, social security number, and authorization to work in the United States. . . .

Rule 26(c) authorizes courts, for good cause, to "make any order which justice requires to protect a party or person from annoyance, embarrassment, oppression, or undue burden or expense, including . . . that certain matters not be inquired into, or that the scope of the disclosure or discovery be limited to certain matters. . . ." Fed. R. Civ. P. 26(c). "[T]he burden is upon the party seeking non-disclosure or a protective order to show good cause." Dove v. Atlantic Capital Corp., 963 F.2d 15, 19 (2d Cir. 1992) (citations omitted).

Rengifo argues that discovery related to his immigration status, authorization to work in this country, and social security number are not relevant to his right to recover unpaid wages. Further, Rengifo argues that the intimidating effect of requiring disclosure of immigration status is sufficient to establish "good cause" when the question of immigration status only goes to a collateral issue. Defendants argue that documents containing Rengifo's social security number or tax identification number, such as tax returns, are relevant to the issue of whether he is entitled to overtime wages, which is a central issue in this case. Additionally, defendants argue that the validity of Rengifo's social security number, his immigration status and authorization to work in this country are relevant to his credibility. . . .

Courts have recognized the *in terrorem* effect of inquiring into a party's immigration status and authorization to work in this country when irrelevant to any material claim because it presents a "danger of intimidation [that] would inhibit plaintiffs in pursuing their rights." Liu v. Donna Karan International, Inc., 207 F. Supp. 2d 191, 193 (S.D.N.Y. 2002) (citations omitted). Here, Rengifo's immigration status and authority to work is a collateral issue. The protective order becomes necessary as "[i]t is entirely likely that any undocumented [litigant] forced to produce documents related to his or her immigration status will withdraw from the suit rather than produce such documents and face . . . potential deportation." Topo v. Dhir, 210 F.R.D. 76, 78 (S.D.N.Y. 2002). . . .

Rengifo also seeks to prevent disclosure of his social security number or tax identification number. Defendants note that, in support of his claim for unpaid overtime wages, Rengifo has produced an incomplete set of pay stubs that do not reflect all of the compensation he has received from corporate defendants, and that he has not produced any records regarding the number of hours he has worked on a weekly basis. Defendants contend, therefore, that discovery of documents containing his tax identification number or social security number, such as tax returns, is necessary and relevant to obtain this information. [The court rejects defendants' argument, reasoning that t]he information sought is not relevant to the claims in this case. Even if it were, however, the corporate defendants possess relevant data on hours and compensation, and there is no reason to assume that defendants' records are less reliable than any records maintained by Rengifo. . . .

Defendants also assert that the documents requested would allow them to test the truthfulness of Rengifo's representations to his employer. They argue that by applying for a job and providing his social security number, Rengifo represented to defendants that he was a legal resident and they are entitled to test the truthfulness of that information. Defendants further argue that if Rengifo filed tax returns, this information would be relevant to his overtime claim, but if he failed to file tax returns, this fact would affect the veracity of statements he would potentially make at trial.

While it is true that credibility is always at issue, that "does not by itself warrant unlimited inquiry into the subject of immigration status when such examination would impose an undue burden on private enforcement of employment discrimination laws." Avila-Blum v. Casa de Cambio Delgado, Inc., 236 F.R.D. 190, 192 (S.D.N.Y. 2006). A party's attempt to discover tax identification numbers on the basis of testing credibility appears to be a back door attempt to learn of immigration status. See E.E.O.C. v. First Wireless Group, Inc., 2007 WL 586720, *2 (E.D.N.Y. Feb. 20, 2007). Further, the opportunity to test the credibility of a party based on representations made when seeking employment does not outweigh the chilling effect that disclosure of immigration status has on employees seeking to enforce their rights. "While documented workers face the possibility of retaliatory discharge for an assertion of their labor and civil rights, undocumented workers confront the harsher reality that, in addition to possible discharge, their employer will likely report them to the INS and they will be subjected to deportation proceedings or criminal prosecution." Rivera v. NIBCO, Inc., 364 F.3d 1057, 1064 (9th Cir. 2004). Granting employers the right to inquire into immigration status in employment cases would allow them to implicitly raise threats of such negative consequences when a worker reports illegal practices. *Id.* at 1065.

While defendants suggest a compromise whereby discovery would be limited to the present litigation and not disclosed to any third party for any purpose beyond this litigation, the limitation does not abate the chilling effect of such disclosure. "Even if the parties were to enter into a confidentiality agreement restricting the disclosure of such discovery . . . , there would still remain 'the danger of intimidation, the danger of destroying the cause of action' and would inhibit plaintiffs in pursuing their rights." *Liu,* 207 F. Supp. 2d at 193 (*quoting* Ansoumana v. Gristede's Operating Corp., 201 F.R.D. 81 (S.D.N.Y. 2001)). This Court finds that defendants' opportunity to test the credibility of Rengifo does not outweigh the public interest in allowing employees to enforce their rights.

For the foregoing reasons, Rengifo's application for a protective order barring defendants from inquiring into his immigration status, social security number or tax identification number, and authorization to work in the United States is GRANTED.

WHAT'S NEW HERE?

- The focus in *Cerrato, Wagoner,* and *Rengifo* is not whether the requested information is relevant, but instead whether the benefits of producing the information outweigh the burdens.
- The courts are considering wide-ranging burdens in these cases—time, money, privacy, and even liberty—and weighing those burdens against the likely evidentiary value of the information sought.
- Such weighings are inevitably highly discretionary and highly case-specific.
- Notice that all three cases suggest that one must read in context the sentence in Rule 26(c) that says: "The court may, for good cause, issue an order to protect a party or person from annoyance, embarrassment, oppression, or undue burden or expense. . . ." Much clearly discoverable material is embarrassing to a party or person (I'm embarrassed to admit I ran the red light, but cannot on that ground get a protective order). The sentence needs to be read in conjunction with Rule 26(b)(1)—making much "annoy[ing or] embarrass[ing]" material discoverable so long as it is relevant, unprivileged, and proportional to the needs of the case.

Notes and Problems

1. Be clear about the procedural settings and the nature of the arguments. First consider *Cerrato*.

   a. What information was the plaintiff in *Cerrato* seeking?
   b. Why did plaintiff think that information was relevant?
   c. Was the defendant claiming that the information was privileged?
   d. If not, on what grounds did defendant seek to block discovery?
   e. How did the court fashion an equitable result?

2. Now consider *Wagoner*.

   a. What information is the plaintiff seeking in this case?
   b. Why did the court reject defendant's argument that the electronic discovery sought was unduly burdensome to produce?
   c. Should Lewis Gale Medical Center rethink its document retention policy?

3. Finally, consider *Rengifo*. In this case, it is the defendant who wants information.

   a. What is Erevos Enterprises seeking?
   b. On what ground does Rengifo attempt to block discovery? How does this argument differ from that in *Cerrato* and *Wagoner*?
   c. To ask the question a different way, having read all three cases, how would you distinguish the types of arguments in favor of the discovery limits set forth in Rule 26(b)(2)(C) (raised in *Cerrato*) and Rule 26(b)(2)(B) (raised in *Wagoner*) from those set forth in Rule 26(c) (raised in *Rengifo*)?

4. Protective orders are commonly used, but will not solve all clashes between the broad scope of discovery and parties' interests in keeping certain matters confidential. In *Rengifo* the court considered and then rejected the possibility of using a protective order because disclosure of information about Rengifo's immigration status would be chilling whether or not it was under seal. Another example arose in connection with Coca-Cola Bottling Co. v. Coca-Cola Co., 107 F.R.D. 288 (D. Del. 1985), in which Coca-Cola bottlers sued the manufacturer over the division of profits from Diet Coke. The primary issue in contention was "whether the contractual term 'Coca-Cola Bottler's Syrup' includes the syrup used to make Diet Coke." Id. at 289. The bottlers contended that the question could be resolved by discovering the ingredients used in both drinks. The defendant manufacturer strongly resisted the effort, for reasons the opinion explains:

   > The complete formula for Coca-Cola is one of the best kept trade secrets in the world. . . . The ingredient that gives Coca-Cola its distinctive taste is a secret combination of flavoring oils and ingredients known as "Merchandise 7X." The formula for Merchandise 7X has been tightly guarded since Coca-Cola was first invented and is known by only two persons within The Coca-Cola Company. . . . The only written record of the secret formula is kept in a security vault . . . which can only be opened upon a resolution from the Company's Board of Directors.

The court, ruling that the formula was relevant and unprotected by any privilege, ordered disclosure but also scheduled hearings on ways in which to protect the trade secret from disclosure to third parties. Defendant still refused to comply:

> By letter . . . counsel for the Company informed the Court that the Company would not disclose its formulae, "[i]n light of the overriding commercial importance of the secrecy of the formulae to the entire Coca-Cola system . . . even under the terms of a stringent protective order. . . ."
>
> Coca-Cola Bottling Co. v. Coca-Cola Co., 110 F.R.D. 363, 366 (D. Del. 1986).

The court held a hearing on sanctions, but declined to impose a default judgment, on the grounds that a lesser sanction would be adequate. As that lesser sanction, the court would instruct the jury to infer that the formulas were identical. It also ordered the defendant to pay attorneys' fees and costs on the motion to compel, though not the costs related to its original resistance to discovery.

3. Privilege

Rule 26(b)(1) contains an explicit exception to its broad scope: It makes discoverable only "any *nonprivileged* matter that is relevant . . ." (emphasis added). Claims of privilege differ sharply from those grounded in proportionality and privacy. Unless waived (see below), privileges are absolute—it makes no difference that one party desperately needs the information and that it would cost nothing to disclose it; privilege is an absolute bar to discovery.

So what are privileges? The law of evidence—not discovery rules—creates privileges, and you will study them in Evidence. For now a brief sketch will supply enough information to let us explore how the discovery system protects privileges.

Very briefly, one can say that privileges typically protect information *from certain sources*. For example, in a criminal case the prosecutor cannot call the defendant to the stand and ask her if she committed the crime; such an action would violate the Fifth Amendment privilege against self-incrimination. Privileges would also protect a party's communications with an attorney, a doctor, a member of the clergy, or a spouse. These privileges are premised on the notion that it is important to protect free communication with these sorts of people, no matter how beneficial the information would be to the public. Notice first that a privilege objection has nothing to do with relevance: whether the defendant committed the crime is highly relevant. Second, notice that although privileges typically block information from a particular source, they do not block the underlying facts. Thus, in the prosecution of a criminal case, the prosecutor will be barred by the Fifth Amendment from asking the defendant about her guilt, and barred by the attorney-client privilege from asking similar questions of her lawyer, but can introduce evidence proving the defendant's guilt from other, unprivileged sources.

A notable characteristic of evidentiary privileges is that they are not self-actuating. In other words, privileges will have effect only if a party asserts them. Moreover, privileges, even if asserted, can later be waived. To use (yet another!) illustration from *Haddle v. Garrison*, suppose in a deposition or at trial, Haddle's lawyer asks Garrison, "What did you tell your lawyer about why you fired Michael Haddle?" If Garrison's lawyer objects on privilege grounds, Garrison will not have to answer the question. But if—hard as it is to imagine—no objection is raised and Garrison answers the question, the attorney-client privilege will be waived, and Garrison can be asked additional questions about her communications with her lawyer. And, of course, no question of privilege arises if Garrison is simply asked, "Why did you fire Haddle?" (regardless of whether Garrison discussed this topic with her lawyer).

Waiver can also result from taking some action inconsistent with claiming the privilege—such as disclosing privileged material to a third party. For example, suppose that well before suit was filed, Garrison told a friend about a conversation she had with her lawyer: That action will likely be held to be a waiver of the privilege that would otherwise apply. And, very important for our purposes, parties can waive privileges by taking certain stances in litigation. For example, Haddle waives his doctor-patient privilege with his psychologist because he has put his emotional state at issue in his suit against Garrison. Discussing all of the privileges and the conditions for their invocation and waiver would take us far beyond the scope of a course in Civil Procedure. Our focus instead is on the interaction of privileges and discovery in civil lawsuits.

WHAT'S NEW HERE?

- Privileged information will often be relevant, sometimes acutely so (e.g., "Did you shoot him?"). So the conceptual task—tackled not here but in your Evidence course—is to understand why the law ranks protecting the information higher than getting at the truth.
- But—to understand discovery you do *not* need to master the law of evidentiary privileges. Instead, working with just a few privileges that will be familiar to you in a general way (e.g., privilege against self-incrimination, doctor-patient privilege, attorney-client privilege), the task is to see how these privileges interact with discovery principles.

Notes and Problems

1. Albert and Barbara are involved in an automobile collision. Albert sues Barbara, alleging that Barbara intentionally drove her car into Albert's. Barbara denies liability. In a deposition Albert's lawyer asks Barbara, "Did you intentionally collide with Albert?"

   a. Can Barbara object on the grounds that the question is irrelevant?
   b. Barbara objects on grounds of privilege. What privilege, among those that have just now been described, would be the best fit?

c. Same lawsuit, except that in addition to negligence and battery, Albert alleges that Barbara intentionally inflicted emotional distress. Barbara's answer denies causation and her lawyer plans to argue at trial that Albert has been emotionally unstable for years. During discovery Barbara's lawyer learns that Albert had been in psychotherapy for some time before the accident. (The state in question recognizes a privilege for psychotherapist-patient communications.) Can Albert successfully claim psychotherapist-patient privilege as a basis for refusing to answer questions about his therapy? Why would Albert's assertion of privilege be rejected by the court?

2. The potential for inadvertent waiver of privilege often can turn discovery into a haunted house with trap doors. The general rules on waiver of privilege are straightforward, and are incorporated in Rule 502 of the Federal Rules of Evidence. Any privilege may be waived. Production of a privileged document—even if inadvertent—or testimony about a privileged conversation will operate as a waiver, and prevent a party from asserting the privilege as to any other privileged communications on the same subject matter, with subject matter interpreted very broadly. The purpose of this Rule is to prohibit a party from selectively waiving the privilege—that is, producing some privileged documents that tend to support the party's position, but withholding as privileged other documents that would tend to undercut the party's position.

a. When privileged documents may be mixed in among nonprivileged documents, the possibility of waiver of privilege requires the producing party to review all of the documents before production, and to remove any documents that could be claimed to be privileged. Any documents removed from production based on a claim of privilege must then be listed on a "privilege log" provided to the party requesting the documents. The privilege log must provide sufficient information about the document to allow the requesting party to assess the claim of privilege and decide whether to contest the claim. See Fed. R. Civ. P. 26(b)(5).

b. These principles all worked reasonably smoothly in the world before the copy machine and digital devices. But they create major problems in an information age. In some cases, thousands or millions of documents need to be reviewed before production because of the remote possibility that one or a few of them might be privileged. If any one of the produced documents is deemed to have been privileged, even if innocuous itself, its production could be deemed to constitute a waiver of privilege as to all other documents and oral communications on the same broad subject matter. There are few things a lawyer fears more than a court determining that his production of a privileged document in discovery operated as a waiver of the privilege as to all of his communications with his client.

c. Rule 26(b)(5)(B) tries to address this problem of inadvertent disclosure with what has come to be known in the profession as a "claw-back" provision. Read it while hoping fervently that you will never need to be the party doing the "clawing." Rule 16, dealing with pretrial conferences, scheduling, and case management, also allows the court to consider agreements "for asserting claims of privilege . . . after production."

4. Trial Preparation Material

Privilege forces the discovery rules to accommodate the goals of discovery with larger social values, like free and open communication with one's lawyer, doctor, and spouse. The topic to which we turn balances discovery needs with another social value—an adversarial legal system. Our system requires both that parties disclose potentially harmful information to their adversaries while simultaneously encouraging a competitive stance.

Suppose initial discovery in *Haddle v. Garrison* proceeds, with the parties exchanging disclosures and then conducting predictable document requests and depositions. Garrison asks Haddle's lawyer what documents he reviewed before drafting the complaint. Note that this is not covered by lawyer-client privilege. But, under well-established principles, Garrison will not get those documents absent special circumstances. The next case, still fundamental in the area, tries to explain why. It may be helpful to note that when *Hickman v. Taylor* was decided, the Rules had no provision covering trial preparation materials. (Rule 26(b)(3) did not become effective until 1970.)

Hickman v. Taylor
329 U.S. 495 (1947)

MURPHY, J., delivered the opinion of the Court.

This case presents an important problem under the Federal Rules of Civil Procedure, as to the extent to which a party may inquire into oral and written statements of witnesses, or other information, secured by an adverse party's counsel in the course of preparation for possible litigation after a claim has arisen. . . .

On February 7, 1943, the tug "J.M. Taylor" sank while engaged in helping to tow a car float of the Baltimore & Ohio Railroad across the Delaware River at Philadelphia. The accident was apparently unusual in nature, the cause of it still being unknown. Five of the nine crew members were drowned. Three days later the tug owners and the underwriters employed a law firm, of which respondent Fortenbaugh is a member, to defend them against potential suits by representatives of the deceased crew members and to sue the railroad for damages to the tug.

A public hearing was held on March 4, 1943, before the United States Steamboat Inspectors, at which the four survivors were examined. This testimony was recorded and made available to all interested parties. Shortly thereafter, Fortenbaugh privately interviewed the survivors and took statements from them with an eye toward the anticipated litigation; the survivors signed these statements on March 29. Fortenbaugh also interviewed other persons believed to have some information relating to the accident and in some cases he made memoranda of what they told him. . . .

[One of the survivors sued, and his lawyer] filed 39 interrogatories directed to the tug owners. The 38th interrogatory read: "State whether any statements of the members of the crews of the Tugs 'J.M. Taylor' and 'Philadelphia' or of any other vessel were taken in connection with the towing of the car float and the sinking of the

Tug 'John M. Taylor.' [Plaintiff also asked for] exact copies of all such statements if in writing, and if oral, set forth in detail the exact provisions of any such oral statements or reports."

Supplemental interrogatories asked whether any oral or written statements, records, reports, or other memoranda had been made concerning any matter relative to the towing operation, the sinking of the tug, the salvaging and repair of the tug, and the death of the deceased. If the answer was in the affirmative, the tug owners were then requested to set forth the nature of all such records, reports, statements, or other memoranda.

The tug owners, through Fortenbaugh, answered all of the interrogatories except No. 38 and the supplemental ones just described. While admitting that statements of the survivors had been taken, they declined to summarize or set forth the contents [claiming] that such requests called "for privileged matter obtained in preparation for litigation" and constituted "an attempt to obtain indirectly counsel's private files." It was claimed that answering these requests "would involve practically turning over not only the complete files, but also the telephone records and, almost, the thoughts of counsel." . . . [The district court held that the requested matters were not privileged and ordered Fortenbaugh to produce the requested statements. He refused, and the court ordered him imprisoned until he complied (but stayed the order pending an appeal).]

Procedure

The pre-trial deposition-discovery mechanism established by Rules 26 to 37 is one of the most significant innovations of the Federal Rules of Civil Procedure. . . . Under the prior federal practice, the pre-trial functions of notice-giving issue-formulation and fact-revelation were performed primarily and inadequately by the pleadings. Inquiry into the issues and the facts before trial was narrowly confined and was often cumbersome in method. The new rules, however, restrict the pleadings to the task of general notice-giving and invest the deposition-discovery process with a vital role in the preparation for trial. . . . Thus civil trials in the federal courts no longer need be carried on in the dark. The way is now clear, consistent with recognized privileges, for the parties to obtain the fullest possible knowledge of the issues and facts before trial. . . .

We agree, of course, that the deposition-discovery rules are to be accorded a broad and liberal treatment. No longer can the time-honored cry of "fishing expedition" serve to preclude a party from inquiring into the facts underlying his opponent's case. Mutual knowledge of all the relevant facts gathered by both parties is essential to proper litigation. To that end, either party may compel the other to disgorge whatever facts he has in his possession. The deposition-discovery procedure simply advances the stage at which the disclosure can be compelled from the time of trial to the period preceding it, thus reducing the possibility of surprise. But discovery, like all matters of procedure, has ultimate and necessary boundaries. . . .

We . . . agree that the memoranda, statements and mental impressions in issue in this case fall outside the scope of the attorney-client privilege and hence are not protected from discovery on that basis. . . . [T]he protective cloak of this privilege does not extend to information which an attorney secures from a witness while acting for his client in anticipation of litigation. Nor does this privilege concern the memoranda, briefs, communications and other writings prepared by counsel for his own use in prosecuting his client's case; and it is equally unrelated to writings which reflect an attorney's mental impressions, conclusions, opinions or legal theories.

But the impropriety of invoking that privilege does not provide an answer to the problem before us. Petitioner has made more than an ordinary request for relevant, non-privileged facts in the possession of his adversaries or their counsel. He has sought discovery as of right of oral and written statements of witnesses whose identity is well known and whose availability to petitioner appears unimpaired. He has sought production of these matters after making the most searching inquiries of his opponents as to the circumstances surrounding the fatal accident, which inquiries were sworn to have been answered to the best of their information and belief. Interrogatories were directed toward all the events prior to, during and subsequent to the sinking of the tug. Full and honest answers to such broad inquiries would necessarily have included all pertinent information gleaned by Fortenbaugh through his interviews with the witnesses. Petitioner makes no suggestion, and we cannot assume, that the tug owners or Fortenbaugh were incomplete or dishonest in the framing of their answers. In addition, petitioner was free to examine the public testimony of the witnesses taken before the United States Steamboat Inspectors. We are thus dealing with an attempt to secure the production of written statements and mental impressions contained in the files and the mind of the attorney Fortenbaugh without any showing of necessity or any indication or claim that denial of such production would unduly prejudice the preparation of petitioner's case or cause him any hardship or injustice. For aught that appears, the essence of what petitioner seeks either has been revealed to him already through the interrogatories or is readily available to him direct from the witnesses for the asking. . . .

In our opinion, neither Rule 26 nor any other rule dealing with discovery contemplates production under such circumstances. . . . Not even the most liberal of discovery theories can justify unwarranted inquiries into the files and the mental impressions of an attorney.

Historically, a lawyer is an officer of the court and is bound to work for the advancement of justice while faithfully protecting the rightful interests of his clients. In performing his various duties, however, it is essential that a lawyer work with a certain degree of privacy, free from unnecessary intrusion by opposing parties and their counsel. Proper preparation of a client's case demands that he assemble information, sift what he considers to be the relevant from the irrelevant facts, prepare his legal theories and plan his strategy without undue and needless interference. That is the historical and the necessary way in which lawyers act within the framework of our system of jurisprudence to promote justice and to protect their clients' interests. This work is reflected, of course, in interviews, statements, memoranda, correspondence, briefs, mental impressions, personal beliefs, and countless other tangible and intangible ways—aptly though roughly termed by the Circuit Court of Appeals in this case as the "work product of the lawyer." Were such materials open to opposing counsel on mere demand, much of what is now put down in writing would remain unwritten. An attorney's thoughts, heretofore inviolate, would not be his own. Inefficiency, unfairness and sharp practices would inevitably develop in the giving of legal advice and in the preparation of cases for trial. The effect on the legal profession would be demoralizing. And the interests of the clients and the cause of justice would be poorly served.

We do not mean to say that all written materials obtained or prepared by an adversary's counsel with an eye toward litigation are necessarily free from discovery in all cases. Where relevant and non-privileged facts remain hidden in an attorney's file and where production of those facts is essential to the preparation of one's case, discovery may properly be had. Such written statements and documents might, under certain circumstances, be admissible in evidence or give clues as to the existence or location of relevant facts. Or they might be useful for purposes of impeachment or corroboration. And production might be justified where the witnesses are no longer available or can be reached only with difficulty. . . .

But as to oral statements made by witnesses to Fortenbaugh, whether presently in the form of his mental impressions or memoranda, we do not believe that any showing of necessity can be made under the circumstances of this case so as to justify production. . . .

Denial of production of this nature does not mean that any material, non-privileged facts can be hidden from the petitioner in this case. He need not be unduly hindered in the preparation of his case, in the discovery of facts or in his anticipation of his opponents' position. Searching interrogatories directed to Fortenbaugh and the tug owners, production of written documents and statements upon a proper showing and direct interviews with the witnesses themselves all serve to reveal the facts in Fortenbaugh's possession to the fullest possible extent consistent with public policy. Petitioner's counsel frankly admits that he wants the oral statements only to help prepare himself to examine witnesses and to make sure that he has overlooked nothing. That is insufficient under the circumstances to permit him an exception to the policy underlying the privacy of Fortenbaugh's professional activities. If there should be a rare situation justifying production of these matters, petitioner's case is not of that type. . . .

JACKSON, J., concurring. . . .
Counsel for the petitioner candidly said on argument that he wanted this information to help prepare himself to examine witnesses, to make sure he overlooked nothing. He bases his claim to it in his brief on the view that the Rules were to do away with the old situation where a law suit developed into "a battle of wits between counsel." But a common law trial is and always should be an adversary proceeding. Discovery was hardly intended to enable a learned profession to perform its functions either without wits or on wits borrowed from the adversary.

The real purpose and the probable effect of the practice ordered by the district court would be to put trials on a level even lower than a "battle of wits." I can conceive of no practice more demoralizing to the Bar than to require a lawyer to write out and deliver to his adversary an account of what witnesses have told him. . . .

FRANKFURTER, J., joins in this opinion.

WHAT'S NEW HERE?

- The information sought here was *not* privileged. Instead, it was protected by a Court-made interpretation of the discovery rules.
- The doctrine originally created by the Court goes under the name of "work product" or "trial preparation material."
- That doctrine *conditionally* bars discovery of some information from some sources even though it is relevant and not privileged.
- This conditional protection distinguishes work product from privilege: Unlike work product, privileged information is absolutely protected from discovery, no matter how much the other side may need it.

Notes and Problems

---

1. It is easy to miss the point of *Hickman* unless one focuses on the precise question decided.

   a. What information was sought?
   b. Why wasn't it discoverable?

2. Recall the start of this chapter when we suggested that before commencing discovery the lawyer should consider what story she wants to tell—what the plot is and what information she needs to make that plot persuasive. One way to think of trial preparation material is as rough drafts of that story—drafts that may be discarded or revised as thought and information come to it. Eventually, at summary judgment or trial, the lawyer will need to settle on a coherent story and tell it in public. Until that happens, trial preparation protection lets the lawyer keep the rough drafts to herself—unless special circumstances exist.

3. What does it take to overcome a claim of work product? How "substantial" must be the need, how "undue" the hardship?

   a. What if Fortenbaugh had interviewed the crew members in the hospital, and they had died before giving their testimony to the agency inquiring into the accident?
   b. What if the crew members were still alive but there had been no public hearing on the accident, and the witnesses claimed not to be able to remember events clearly? Does your answer depend on whether the witnesses revealed to Fortenbaugh information that might lead him to admissible evidence concerning the causes of the sinking?

4. At the time of *Hickman*, Rule 26 did not deal specifically with the topic of trial preparation materials. It now does—dealing both with "general" trial preparation

protections in Rule 26(b)(3) and with the special issues of trial preparation protection for expert witnesses (dealt with in the next section of this chapter). The Rules also incorporate the qualified nature of protections for trial preparation materials, allowing disclosure of the information if its substantial equivalent cannot be obtained without significant hardship. See Rules 26(b)(3) and 26(b)(4)(D).

5. Rule 26(b)(3) protects from disclosure "documents and tangible things that are prepared in anticipation of litigation or for trial by or for another party or its representatives." Not surprisingly, disputes arise over whether a document has been prepared "in anticipation of litigation." A diary entry, written by a party, is unlikely to fall in this category; notes from a lawyer's interview of that party most certainly will. Although both may concern the incident that gives rise to litigation, only the latter was prepared in anticipation of that litigation. There are also closer questions concerning whether internal reports of incidents were made as part of the regular course of business or in anticipation of litigation. Suppose that in *Haddle v. Garrison* Healthmaster has a Human Resources department and someone from that department interviewed Haddle shortly before he was fired and wrote a report. Prepared in anticipation of litigation? Compare Rakus v. Erie-Lackawanna Railroad, 76 F.R.D. 145 (W.D.N.Y. 1977) (employees' accident reports to claims department are discoverable) and Nesselrotte v. Allegheny Energy Inc., 242 F.R.D. 338 (W.D. Pa. 2007) (report of an internal investigation that employer hired attorney to conduct in connection with complaint of discrimination made by another employee is protected from disclosure).

6. Just as privilege protects certain sources of information, but not the information itself, trial preparation protections protect documents and things prepared in anticipation of litigation without protecting all the underlying information. Imagine that, preparing for trial, Plaintiff's lawyer hires a private investigator who uncovers an eyewitness to the accident and writes a memo to the lawyer setting out what that witness saw.

   a. If Defendant demanded a copy of the memo in discovery, Plaintiff could successfully protect the memo from disclosure—unless it fell within the exceptions in Rule 26(b)(3)—because it is trial preparation material.
   b. If, on the other hand, defendant served an interrogatory asking for the names of all eyewitnesses, Plaintiff could not protect the identity of the witness from disclosure. The witness's identity is not covered by the trial preparation protection, just the memo itself.

7. Consider *Hickman* from another angle. Like *Bell Atlantic v. Twombly* and *Ashcroft v. Iqbal* (Chapter 6), it represents a gloss—a doctrinal overlay—by the Supreme Court on a Federal Rule of Civil Procedure.

   a. Just nine years after the Rules' promulgation, the *Hickman* Court added to discovery a protection not then present in the Rules. The work product doctrine proved sufficiently workable and functional to be codified in the 1970 amendments to the Rules.

   b. Seventy years after the Rule 8's promulgation, the *Twombly* and *Iqbal* Courts added pleading requirements not contained in the Rules. It remains to be seen how workable and functional the new pleading doctrines will prove.

D. EXPERTS

Another specialized form of trial preparation involves expert witnesses and, as with trial preparation, the Rules call out expert testimony for special treatment. Experts enter civil litigation in two ways. In some cases experts may participate in events that give rise to litigation. Imagine that City designs and builds a bridge over a busy road connecting two parts of a university campus; the bridge later collapses, killing a number of people. Wrongful death litigation may focus on flaws in design and construction. In such a case the engineers and builders who designed and built the bridge, though experts in their fields, will be "fact witnesses" in the same way as those who saw it collapse. These experts will be subject to all the ordinary stages of discovery and will for the most part be treated in the same way as a bystander who witnessed the bridge's collapse.

A second kind of expert—the kind on which the Federal Rules of Civil Procedure focus—enters the picture if parties in the bridge collapse hire experts—to testify, for example, about the design or construction of the bridge. Experts hired (or "retained" in the more elegant language of the Rules) for the purposes of litigation can range from the standard professionals—physicians, accountants, engineers—to experts in "accident reconstruction" and "brand name identification." Such hired experts typically testify to the inferences one can draw about the causes or effects of an event by applying their special knowledge to the information available.

In order to understand the procedural rules applicable to this second type of expert, it may help to have a quick sketch of how lawyers might use them in litigation. Let's return to the bridge collapse scenario as a framework. If litigation ensues, both sides will likely want to use engineers' testimony. The City might want an engineer to support a possible argument the bridge was in all ways properly designed but the contractor it hired cut corners that caused the collapse; the plaintiff will likely want to show that the City's design was based on a new and insufficiently tested concept that proved defective. To support these duelling contentions the parties will seek out independent experts—perhaps from civil engineering faculties of universities (other than the one affected, of course). Locating and hiring such experts is an important part of case preparation: One wants not only someone with impressive credentials but someone who will make a good impression on the trier of fact. Having located such a person, each lawyer will have initial consultations, presenting their expert with information relating to the bridge's design. And here things can go well or badly. Well if the expert's initial impressions support the lawyer's theory; badly if the expert thinks otherwise—or seems unlikely to make the right impression on a judge or jury. Even if all goes well with the expert, her report is likely to go through multiple drafts as the expert and the lawyer shape it to support a persuasive claim or defense. As we'll see, Rule 26(b)(4) now takes account of each of these possibilities.

Just as Rule 26(a) requires parties to disclose witnesses and information they may use to support their claims, Rule 26(a)(2) sets requirements for disclosure of expert witnesses. Rule 26(a)(2)(D) requires that 90 days before trial (or 30 days for rebuttal testimony) the parties identify experts who may testify. This disclosure rule reflects the expectation that lawyers will want to depose the other side's expert—most likely after consulting with their own.

Rule 26(a)(2) then implicitly divides experts into two groups: experts who must provide an elaborate written report (26(a)(2)(B)) and those who need not (26(a)(2)(C)). The division roughly corresponds to the distinction made above—between "fact witness" experts (e.g., the engineers who designed the bridge in the hypothetical above) and those who were hired specially for the lawsuit (e.g., engineers hired to testify about proper bridge design). The latter must produce an elaborate written report, the former not. But, because even non-retained experts are experts, and it will be very difficult for the opposing lawyer effectively to depose or examine them, Rule 26(a)(2)(C) requires, as part of the pretrial disclosures, that even "fact witness" experts summarize "facts and opinions" to which they expect to testify. (The Rule is silent as to who will write this summary, and one imagines that, in practice, it will often be the lawyers who want to call the witnesses.) After producing their report, experts can be deposed by opposing counsel. Rules 26(a)(2), 26(b)(4). These reports and the ensuing depositions will often be the last significant discovery events.

Expert witnesses can serve a third role in litigation: as advisers to the attorney who retained them. Sometimes experts (jury consultants, for example) may be hired in anticipation of litigation but with no expectation of ever testifying at trial. Other times, an expert might be consulted with the expectation that he would testify at trial—he might even prepare a report—but the lawyer might decide not to call him as a witness.

Rule 26(b)(4) addresses work product problems surrounding experts. The Rule contains special provisions for retained experts and their communications with lawyers as they prepare their reports and testimony. Both the defense and plaintiff bars agree that it is important to extend work product protection to drafts of experts' opinions; the current Rule does so. Rule 26(b)(4)(D) protects reports and opinions by witnesses retained in anticipation of litigation who will not testify, with exceptions similar to those in Rule 23(b)(3) for trial preparation materials.

WHAT'S NEW HERE?

- One can think of expert testimony as a special kind of trial preparation or work product: It comes into being only because the parties are anticipating a trial. Because it presents issues not present in ordinary work product disputes, expert testimony gets special treatment—particularly the provision for a testifying expert to prepare a report and submit to a deposition.

- Like work product, experts may generate documents and information that is not going to be used at trial.
- Like work product, experts who will not testify at trial get only qualified protection: Unlike privilege, their opinions can be discovered under some circumstances, if a party makes the requisite showing of special circumstances and need.

Notes and Problems

---

1. Stay with the bridge collapse scenario. Suppose John is seriously injured in the collapse and is taken to Lake Hospital for emergency care. In the emergency room, he is examined by Dr. House, who subsequently operates on John's back. John sues City, which designed and built the bridge.

   a. What information about Dr. House must John's lawyer give to City as part of the initial disclosure required by Rule 26(a)(1)? Dr. House is clearly an "expert" and he is likely to be called as a witness. Does that make him an expert witness who must provide a report as specified by Rule 26(a)(2)(B)? What part of Rule 26(a)(2)(B) does Dr. House not fulfill?

   b. John also wants to depose the head of City's engineering department who designed the bridge, but City has not designated that person as a testifying expert. Does that prevent John from deposing him?

2. Several months later John's lawyer hires Dr. Welby, an orthopedic specialist, to testify at trial. In preparation for that testimony Dr. Welby examines John.

   a. How must John's lawyer go about notifying City's lawyer of Welby's likely testimony? See Rule 26(a)(2).

   b. In the course of preparing to testify, Dr. Welby exchanges several drafts of his proposed report with John's lawyer. As Welby and Lawyer exchange drafts, Lawyer also asks Welby to change some assumptions about the possible kind of future employment John might seek—asking him to suppose, for example, that John might change from an office job to one requiring substantial physical activity. City's lawyer requests all of these exchanges between Welby and Lawyer. Is City's lawyer entitled to these drafts? Rule 26(b)(4)(B).

3. Suppose now that John's lawyer changes his mind (perhaps after reviewing a draft of Welby's report) and decides not to call Dr. Welby at trial. Need John's lawyer supply any information about him as part of the disclosures required by Rule 26(a)(2)?

4. Same situation as in Problem 3, but now suppose that shortly after Dr. Welby examined John, John slipped on a wet sidewalk, exacerbating his back injury. City's lawyer may want to try to show that John's condition at trial was due

at least in part to the fall on the ice, not to his injuries in the bridge collapse. Rule 26(b)(4)(D) may give City's lawyer an argument that he should be able to depose Dr. Welby, a nontestifying expert; what would that argument be? The next two cases deal with analogous situations.

Thompson v. The Haskell Co.

65 Fair Empl. Prac. Cas. (BNA) 1088 (M.D. Fla. 1994)

SNYDER, M.J.

This cause is before the Court on Plaintiff's Motion for Protective Order filed on May 13, 1994 (hereinafter Motion). Plaintiff seeks to shield from discovery documents related to her in the possession of Lauren Lucas, Ph.D., a psychologist. She contends that Rule 26(b)(4) of the Federal Rules of Civil Procedure (FRCP) protects the psychological records in Dr. Lucas' possession. In particular, Plaintiff represents Dr. Lucas was retained by her prior counsel to perform a diagnostic review and personality profile, and that, after seeing Plaintiff on one occasion on June 15, 1992, Dr. Lucas prepared a report for her prior counsel.

Rule 26(b)(4)[(D)] of the FRCP provides:

[Expert Employed Only for Trial Preparation. Ordinarily, a party may not, by interrogatories or deposition, discover facts known or opinions held by an expert who has been retained or specially employed by another party in anticipation of litigation or to prepare for trial and who is not expected to be called as a witness at trial. But a party may do so only:

(i) as provided in Rule 35(b); or

(ii) on showing exceptional circumstances under which it is impracticable for the party to obtain facts or opinions on the same subject by other means.]

Assuming arguendo that Dr. Lucas' report is covered by Rule 26(b)(4), it would nevertheless be discoverable under the circumstances presented in this case. In the instant lawsuit, Plaintiff alleges that, as a result of sexual harassment by co-defendant Zona, a supervisor in the employ of the Defendant, she was "reduced to a severely depressed emotional state and her employment was terminated when she did not acquiesce to the advances of [Zona]." According to a complaint filed with the Jacksonville Equal Opportunity Commission, Plaintiff apparently was terminated from her position with Defendant Haskell Company on June 5, 1992. Thus, her mental and emotional state ten days later on June 15, 1992, the date on which she was examined by Dr. Lucas, is highly probative with regard to the above-quoted allegation, which is essential to her case.

This highly probative information is discoverable notwithstanding Rule 26(b)(4), moreover, given the nature of the report at issue. Apparently, no other comparable report was prepared during the weeks immediately following Plaintiff's discharge. Thus, the Defendant could not obtain the information contained in Dr. Lucas' report by other means. In a case almost on all fours with the instant one, the Court recognized that even "independent examinations . . . pursuant to Rule 35 would not contain equivalent information." Dixon v. Cappellini, 88 F.R.D. 1, 3 (M.D. Pa. 1980). Under these facts, it appears there are exceptional circumstances favoring disclosure of Dr. Lucas' report, and that the Defendant could not obtain comparable information by other means. Accordingly, the Motion [for a protective order] is DENIED. . . .

Chiquita International Ltd. v. M/V Bolero Reefer

1994 U.S. Dist. LEXIS 5820 (S.D.N.Y. 1994)

FRANCIS, M.J.

This is a maritime action in which the shipper, Chiquita International Ltd. ("Chiquita"), sues the carrier, International Reefer Services, S.A. ("International Reefer"), for cargo loss and damage. Chiquita alleges that International Reefer was engaged to transport 154,660 boxes of bananas from Puerto Bolivar, Ecuador to Bremerhaven, Germany aboard the M/V Bolero Reefer. However, because of alleged malfunctions of the vessel's loading cranes and side-ports, only 111,660 boxes were loaded. Thus, 43,000 boxes of bananas were left on the wharf and were later disposed of. The cargo that did arrive in Germany was allegedly in poor condition.

International Reefer has submitted a letter in support of an application to compel discovery of Joseph Winer. Mr. Winer is a marine surveyor [a type of expert familiar with ship design and maintenance] who examined the vessel and loading gear at Chiquita's request shortly after the vessel arrived in Bremerhaven. International Reefer seeks Mr. Winer's deposition and production of the file he assembled in connection with his inspection. Chiquita has objected to these demands on the ground that Mr. Winer is a non-testifying expert as to whom discovery is closely circumscribed by Rule 26(b)(4)([D]) of the Federal Rules of Civil Procedure. International Reefer replies that Mr. Winer is a fact witness rather than an expert. Moreover, even if he is an expert, International Reefer argues that the fact that he is the only surveyor who observed the vessel shortly after it docked is an exceptional circumstance warranting discovery. . . .

[The opinion quotes Rule 26(b)(4)(D).]

[A] non-testifying expert is generally immune from discovery.

Mr. Winer qualifies as such an expert. He is a marine engineer who was specifically engaged by Chiquita to examine the vessel in connection with the cargo loss claim. He is clearly an "expert" in that he brought his technical background to bear in observing the condition of the gear and offering his opinion to Chiquita. He does not forfeit this status merely because he made a personal examination of the vessel and therefore learned "facts," rather than simply offering an opinion based on the observations of others. Rule 26(b)(4)[(D)] generally precludes discovery of "facts known or opinions" held by a non-testifying expert, and so it anticipates that such an expert may make his or her own investigation. Thus, the relevant distinction is not between fact and opinion testimony but between those witnesses whose information was obtained in the normal course of business and those who were hired to make an evaluation in connection with expected litigation. See Harasimowicz v. McAllister, 78 F.R.D. 319, 320 (E.D. Pa. 1978) (medical examiner subject to ordinary discovery on routine autopsy); Congrove v. St. Louis-San Francisco Railway, 77 F.R.D. 503, 504-05 (W.D. Mo. 1978) (treating physician subject to ordinary discovery). Here, Mr. Winer falls into the latter category and Rule 26(b)(4)[(D)] therefore applies.

International Reefer nevertheless contends that discovery should be permitted under the "exceptional circumstances" clause of the rule, since no other marine surveyor viewed the vessel shortly after docking. This argument would have merit if International Reefer had been precluded from sending its own expert to the scene by forces beyond its control. Thus, for example, in [another case] the court found there to be exceptional circumstances where the plaintiff allowed its own expert to examine the item at issue while barring the defendant's experts until the item was no longer accessible.

However, that is not the case here. The vessel and equipment were at least as available to International Reefer as to Chiquita from the time of loading. Indeed, during the three-week voyage to Bremerhaven, International Reefer's employees had the exclusive opportunity to examine the loading cranes. Under these circumstances, the failure of International Reefer to engage its own marine surveyor in a timely manner should not be rewarded by permitting discovery of Chiquita's expert. To do so would permit the exceptional circumstances exception to swallow Rule 26(b)(4)[(D)].

Finally, International Reefer maintains that even if it is foreclosed from deposing Mr. Winer, it should be given access to his file. However, Rule 26(b)(4)[(D)] applies to document discovery as well as to depositions. Nevertheless, International Reefer is correct that information does not become exempt from discovery merely because it is conveyed to a non-testifying expert. Thus, while the file may contain Mr. Winer's recorded observations and opinions which need not be disclosed, it may also include discoverable information provided to Mr. Winer by others. Such documents shall be produced.

Conclusion

For the reasons set forth above, International Reefer's application to take the deposition of Joseph Winer is denied. By May 13, 1994, Chiquita shall produce from Mr. Winer's file those documents that do not reflect his observations and opinions or are otherwise privileged. Chiquita shall prepare a log of any documents withheld, identifying them with the specificity required by Local Rule 46(e).

SO ORDERED.

Notes and Problems

1. Focus first on what was being sought in each case:
   a. What was the defendant seeking in *Thompson*?
   b. What was the defendant seeking in *Chiquita*?

2. *Thompson* and *Chiquita* deal with similar information, which the respective courts concede is relevant and not privileged. But the *Thompson* court orders

disclosure, while the *Chiquita* court denies disclosure (of the expert's observations and conclusions if not the rest of his file).

   a. Why?

   b. What facts would one change about each case to reach a different result?

   c. In *Chiquita*, the views of someone familiar with crucial facts are suppressed. How does one justify that result, given the general thrust toward disclosure in the discovery rules?

3. In *Chiquita*, the court says there is no question that Mr. Winer is an expert "retained or specially employed to provide expert testimony in the case" (Rule 26(b)(4)(D)). In *Thompson*, the court suggests in passing that Dr. Lucas might not be such a specially retained expert: "Assuming arguendo that Dr. Lucas' report is covered by Rule 26[(b)(4)]], it would nevertheless be discoverable under the circumstances presented in this case." If Dr. Lucas was not a specially retained expert, but instead treated Thompson and in the course of that treatment discussed facts related to her sexual harassment claim, would her report be discoverable?

4. Why did the *Chiquita* plaintiff think it mattered that the surveyor/expert had actually inspected the vessel? Because in many, perhaps most, instances an expert testifies on the basis of hypothetical situations. Lawyer: "Doctor, suppose a patient came to you complaining of severe abdominal pain; what would be the preferred course of diagnosis?" Expert: "First one would perform a test to rule out appendicitis; then . . ." In *Chiquita*, the expert examined the actual "patient" (here the ship), and the plaintiff argued that this moved him from the usual expert to a fact witness, an argument the court rejected.

E. ENSURING COMPLIANCE AND CONTROLLING ABUSE OF DISCOVERY

With all this guidance from Rules and case law, what could possibly go wrong? Plenty, it turns out. We do not know how often discovery results in controversy and conflict. A survey conducted by the nonpartisan Federal Judicial Center in 2009 found that lawyers on both sides of the "v" reported that "the disclosure and discovery [in their cases] generated 'the right amount' of information" and that "expenditures for discovery, including attorney fees, amounted at the median 1.6% of the reported stakes for plaintiff[s] and 3.3% [for defendants]."

Nevertheless, even a cursory review of federal district court opinions reveals all sorts of bad behavior during discovery. Delay, evasiveness, abusive use of various discovery devices, use of discovery to buy time or to force a hard-pressed opponent to settle for less, are just some tactics that can be observed. Such depressing behavior has several sources, some of which lie in the design of the discovery system itself. The Federal Rules envisioned discovery would operate largely without judicial supervision, and the Rules therefore speak of lawyers exchanging various discovery requests without intervention by courts. There is a debate within the profession about whether and how much judges should become involved with discovery early in a lawsuit, but at present that remains a judge's choice rather than a command of the Rules.

1. Types of Discovery Disputes

Before assessing the effectiveness of court interventions, it may help to understand some types of disagreements that become full-fledged discovery disputes. One common subject of dispute is the proper scope of discovery. Reverting to the hypothetical in Chapter 1, imagine that Peters has sued Dodge for injuries resulting from an auto accident. Dodge asks Peters for documents reflecting all of Peters's medical treatments for the past ten years. Peters objects: He believes that the request is overbroad—not "proportionate" in the language of Rule 26(b)(1)—and that at least some of the documents requested are privileged. Dodge maintains that the request is appropriate, as past medical records would indicate whether some of the injuries claimed by Peters predated the accident. In Peters's view, Dodge has abused the discovery tools by asking for more information than the claim justifies. In Dodge's view, Peters is stonewalling—resisting appropriate requests for discovery.

A second common subject of dispute concerns whether a party has lost or destroyed important evidence. Until recently, the Rules did not expressly address this type of problem, but the common law did. Now, the Rules do as well, at least concerning electronic discovery. Read Rule 37(e). Under the common law and now the Rules, parties are obligated to preserve evidence relevant to pending or reasonably foreseeable litigation. The failure to preserve or destruction of this type of evidence is called *spoliation*. Recall *Zubulake*, with which this chapter began: an employment discrimination case in which the plaintiff accused the defendant of destroying some e-mails relevant to the case.

2. Ensuring Compliance

All discovery methods need enforcement mechanisms. The Rules provide means of enforcing compliance by both the propounding and the answering party. Rule 26(g), like Rule 11, requires that discovery requests and responses be signed, and states that the signature implies discovery requests are reasonable and discovery responses are complete. Unlike Rule 11, Rule 26(g) suggests that attorneys' fees will be an appropriate sanction for most violations of its obligations.

Rule 37 establishes a system of sanctions for parties violating more specific obligations. Under that Rule, a court may impose punishments ranging from awards of expenses to dismissals of an entire case or the entry of a default judgment. Some sanctions are available on the occurrence of misbehavior. See Rule 37(d), (f). Other sanctions cannot be sought until after the court has ordered a party to comply, but it has refused. See Rule 37(b). And, as we have discussed, the failure to preserve electronically stored information has its own rule regarding sanctions. See Rule 37(e).

Notes and Problems

1. Consider some stages at which the question of sanctions might occur.

   a. Auto accident. Plaintiff makes initial disclosures that include damage calculations, names of treating physicians, and the identity of a witness to the accident. Discovery proceeds on the assumption that these are the relevant witnesses, but when plaintiff discloses the list of trial witnesses as required by Rule 26(a)(3), a new name appears. Are sanctions available? On what theory? What sanctions? See Rule 37(c).

   b. Contract dispute between plaintiff (Supplier) and defendant (Producer), with the parties' understanding of a clause at issue. Supplier serves a request for production requesting "all memoranda, e-mails, and internal correspondence" regarding the contract in question. If Producer believes that the request for production is overbroad, what should it do? See Rule 26(b)(2)(C). If Producer produces only one memo, and Supplier believes there are many more, what should it do? See Rule 37(a). How might this dispute lead to sanctions, according to Rule 37(b)?

   c. Same contract dispute. Supplier asks Producer to admit that the first shipment of goods arrived on time; Producer does not admit this. At trial, Supplier introduces evidence to that effect, and Producer does not challenge it. Is there a sanction available? What? See Rule 37(c)(2).

   d. Same contract dispute. Supplier makes another request for documents. First, suppose that Producer simply fails to respond to the request. What steps must Supplier follow to force Producer either to comply or suffer sanctions? Read carefully Rule 37(a)(1)-(3). See Shuffle Master Inc. v. Progressive Games, Inc., 170 F.R.D. 166 (D. Nev. 1996) (refusing to order sanctions in the absence of a certificate demonstrating good-faith efforts to confer with adversary).

   e. Same contract dispute. Now suppose two of the documents covered by the request happen to be letters from Producer's lawyer to Producer, answering questions about the interpretation of the contract in question; Producer believes that both documents are protected by the attorney-client privilege. How should Producer raise that objection? See Rules 26(c) and 37(a). If the parties cannot agree on whether the documents are privileged, each has an option: Supplier can move to compel production of the document, and Producer can resist by asserting privilege. Or, Producer can move for a protective order under Rule 26(c) and Supplier can resist the motion by arguing that the letters are not privileged. If you were representing Supplier, which path would you prefer? If you were representing Producer?

   f. Same contract dispute. Producer's response to Supplier's request states simply, "The requested documents have not been produced because they are protected by the attorney-client privilege." What should Supplier do? See Rules 26(b)(5)(A), 37(a)(4), 37(a)(3)(B).

2. Having filed a complaint against Baxter Corp. for breach of contract and received the required disclosures, Arthur Corp. sends Baxter a set of interrogatories

seeking some routine information about the details of company organization, such as which officers and employees are responsible for which aspects of the company's affairs. Baxter refuses to answer any of the interrogatories, noting in its response that these matters are not relevant to the claims and defenses of the action. Arthur's lawyer believes that the interrogatories are entirely proper because they enable her to decide which officers to depose.

    a. How should Arthur's lawyer proceed if she wants to get answers to her interrogatories?

    b. Can Arthur seek sanctions? Under which Rule(s)?

    c. Baxter serves a notice to take the deposition of Alice Arthur, the President of Arthur Corp. On the appointed day, Arthur doesn't show up. As attorney for Baxter, what remedies would you seek? See Rule 37(d).

    d. When Baxter seeks sanctions, Arthur claims that Baxter purposefully scheduled the deposition at an extremely inconvenient place and requests that the location be changed. Should that argument, if true, block or mitigate sanctions?

    e. When Baxter deposes Alice Arthur, her lawyer interposes numerous objections, with the result that at the end of seven hours, the deposition is just getting into the core inquiries Baxter has planned. Alice and her lawyer stand, call for the end of the deposition, and draw Baxter's attention to the seven-hour provision of Rule 30(d)(1). What should Baxter do?

    f. Arthur and Baxter serve discovery on each other, including interrogatories, notices of depositions, and requests for the production of documents. Arthur believes that it has responded in good faith to Baxter's requests but that Baxter has been systematically uncooperative, raising many barely tenable objections, declining to produce documents until threatened with a motion seeking a court order, producing incomplete sets of documents, then producing overwhelming quantities of documents in which the relevant material is buried, and similar tactics. What should Arthur do?

3. Finally, consider a court's ability to impose sanctions for discovery-related conduct not flowing directly from any particular discovery Rule. Federal courts have inherent powers "to fashion an appropriate sanction for conduct which abuses the judicial process." Chambers v. NASCO, Inc., 501 U.S. 32, 44-45 (1991). Such abuse might include but is not limited to misconduct in discovery. But—the Supreme Court has held—when a court awards attorneys' fees as part of such a sanction, such fees must be limited to those actually caused by the misconduct, and cannot be awarded as an all-purpose punishment for bad behavior. Goodyear Tire & Rubber Co. v. Haeger, 581 U.S. ___ (2017).

3. Remedies: Management and Sanctions

Having decided that a party has violated its discovery obligations, the court must then decide what sanctions to apply. Read Rule 37(b)(2); it gives courts wide latitude to determine appropriate sanctions for discovery violations, including dismissal of claims, limiting the evidence parties can use at trial, and awards of attorneys' fees. Yet Rule 37 places additional limits on a court's ability to impose sanctions for "electronically stored information that should have been preserved in anticipation of litigation."

The Rule imposes two principal limits: In (e)(1) it specifies that sanctions be "not greater than necessary to cure the prejudice" produced by the missing records; in (e)(2) it requires, for the imposition of the most serious sanctions, a finding that "the party acted with the intent to deprive another party of the information's use in litigation." The latter amendment was criticized at the time of its proposal, on the ground that it encouraged parties to be "merely" negligent in their preservation efforts. Consider how the court applies this new Rule in the next case.

Mueller v. Swift

2017 WL 3058027 (D. Colo. 2017)

Martínez, J.

In this tort action pending under the Court's diversity jurisdiction, 28 U.S.C. §1332, Plaintiff pursues claims against all Defendants for tortious interference with his employment contract and with related business expectancies, while Defendant–Counter Claimant Taylor Swift ("Swift") pursues counterclaims for the torts of assault and battery. Now before the Court is Plaintiff's Motion for Sanctions for Plaintiff's Spoliation of Evidence. As explained below, Defendants' Motion is granted in part, to impose a spoliation sanction that is less harsh than the adverse inference requested by Defendants, but which the Court finds is the most appropriate sanction in the circumstances of this case. . . .

[T]he additional background set out below is both undisputed and supported by evidence in the record. Plaintiff worked as an on-air radio personality for a Denver area radio station, KYGO. On June 2, 2013, he attended a backstage "meet and greet" preceding a concert performed by Swift at Denver's Pepsi Center. As detailed in the summary judgment order, Swift alleges that during a staged photo opportunity at the "meet and greet," Plaintiff purposefully and inappropriately touched her buttocks beneath her dress. Plaintiff denies having done so.

Plaintiff's employer, the company that owned KYGO, was informed of Swift's accusation on the evening of June 2, 2013 and on the following day. On June 3, 2013, Plaintiff met with his superiors at KYGO, including Robert Call ("Call") and Hershel Coomer (a/k/a "Eddie Haskell") ("Haskell"). Unbeknownst to Call and Haskell at the time, Plaintiff made an audio recording of their conversation. The following day, June 4, 2013, Plaintiff was terminated from his employment at KYGO by Call. Call explained that one reason for Plaintiff's termination was because Call perceived Plaintiff had "changed his story that it couldn't have occurred, then that it was incidental."

At some point thereafter, well after having first contacted an attorney regarding potential legal action, Plaintiff edited the audio recording of the June 3, 2013 conversation, and then sent only "clips" of the entire audio file to his attorney. In his deposition testimony, Plaintiff offered the following explanation for these actions: "[t]he audio I recorded was close to two hours long. And the audio that I could provide to [Plaintiff's counsel] was a portion of the entire audio," and "it was so long, that I edited down clips from the recording to provide to [Plaintiff's counsel] to give an idea of what kind of questioning I went . . . through."

According to his testimony, Plaintiff edited the audio file on his laptop computer, on which he also retained a full copy of the original audio file(s). However, sometime thereafter, coffee was spilled on the keyboard of Plaintiff's laptop, damaging it. Plaintiff took the laptop to the Apple Store, and was given "a new machine." He did not keep the original hard drive or recover the files from it. Evidently this occurred sometime in 2015. In addition, although Plaintiff kept an external hard drive "to store audio files and documents," and the complete audio recording was saved on this drive, at some point it "stopped working." At his deposition, Plaintiff testified that he "may have kept" this hard drive, but that because it was "useless" he "[didn't] know if I discarded it because it was junk." It has not been produced.

The end result of all this is that the complete audio recording of the June 3, 2013 conversation among Plaintiff, Call, and Haskell has never been produced. . . . As a result, Defendants move for a Court-imposed sanction for spoliation of evidence, and in particular for the Court to give the jury an adverse inference instruction at trial, to direct the jury "that the entirety of the June 3, 2013 audio recording would have been unfavorable to Plaintiff."

"A spoliation sanction is proper where: '(1) a party has a duty to preserve evidence because it knew, or should have known, that litigation was imminent, and (2) the adverse party was prejudiced by the destruction of the evidence.'" In deciding whether to sanction a party for the spoliation of evidence, courts have considered a variety of factors, but two "generally carry the most weight: (1) the degree of culpability of the party who lost or destroyed the evidence; and (2) the degree of actual prejudice to the other party." . . .

III. Analysis

A. A Spoliation Sanction Is Warranted

The Court concludes that Plaintiff's loss or destruction of the complete recording of the June 3, 2013 conversation constitutes sanctionable spoliation of evidence.

1. Duty to Preserve

Initially, Plaintiff does not dispute that he knew or should have known that litigation was imminent and that he was therefore under a duty to preserve relevant evidence, including the complete audio recording, at the time when he first altered it for his own purposes and then lost or destroyed the unedited file. *See* Zubulake v. UBS Warburg LLC, 220 F.R.D. 212, 216 (S.D.N.Y. 2003). . . .

Indeed, it is quite likely that the reason Plaintiff secretively recorded his conversation with Call and Haskell was because he knew that some form of adversarial legal action was likely to follow.

Moreover, Plaintiff later edited the audio file in order to send "clips" to his own attorney, when it was abundantly clear that litigation was imminent, because Plaintiff himself was actively considering it. . . .

2. Relevance

The Court also readily concludes that the recording of the June 3, 2013 conversation was relevant to numerous disputed facts and issues in this case. For instance, to prevail on his tortious interference claims, Plaintiff must prove that Defendants' communication with KYGO was improper, and that Defendants' conduct caused

KYGO to terminate him. The statements made by Plaintiff and by Messrs. Call and Haskell the day following the incident with Swift and the day before KYGO fired him would plainly be relevant to proving or disproving those facts. Moreover, the record reflects that one of the reasons Mr. Call decided to terminate Plaintiff was because he perceived that Plaintiff had "changed his story" during the course of his communications with KYGO. A recording of this conversation could be invaluable to a jury that will be asked to decide, in part, whether they agree with Mr. Call's assessment that Plaintiff has been inconsistent in his descriptions of the events of June 2, 2013. . . .

3. Prejudice

The Court similarly finds that Defendants were prejudiced by the loss of evidence. At the very least, if the complete recording had been available, it might have saved time and expense in litigation by documenting the June 3, 2013 conversation, allowing for better preparation for depositions and ultimately for trial. Moreover, to the extent there may now be discrepancies in the accounts that Plaintiff and Messrs. Call and Haskill give regarding their June 3, 2013 conversation, the recording would probably have resolved them. . . .

4. Culpability

Finally, the Court finds that the degree of culpability warrants a sanction. Although the Court declines to make a finding that Plaintiff acted in "bad faith" in the sense that he *intended* to destroy the evidence, it also cannot characterize the loss or destruction of evidence in this case as innocent, or as "*mere* negligence." Rather, the spoliation falls higher up on the "continuum of fault." . . .

Plaintiff knew full well that litigation was imminent, since he was pursuing it. He knew that he was the only person in possession of the complete audio recording. He made the decision—inexplicably, in the Court's view—to *alter* the original evidence and to present his lawyer with only "clips" hand-picked from the underlying evidence. This reflects that he obviously intended to make use of portions of the recording to advance his own claims. . . . Plaintiff could and should have made sure that *some* means of backing up the files relevant to litigation was in place, but this was not done.

Moreover, when Plaintiff surrendered his laptop for repair or replacement, he knew that it contained relevant evidence. Depending on whether this occurred before or after the loss of his external hard drive (the record is unclear), the laptop contained either the only remaining copy of the complete audio file or one of only two, as Plaintiff also knew or should have known. Despite this, the record does not reflect that he made any effort to retain the hard drive, to have it returned to him after he surrendered the damaged laptop, or to otherwise recover the lost file(s). The same was true when his external hard drive stopped working. Rather than saving it, seeking to have it repaired, or taking steps to preserve the files stored on it, Plaintiff evidently just set the drive aside, and eventually lost it. . . .

B. Appropriate Sanction

Despite the discussion of Plaintiff's culpability above, the Court rejects Defendants' request to make a finding of bad faith and to give the jury an adverse inference instruction. Having considered various options, and after directing Defendants to brief the issue of alternative sanctions, the Court finds that the following sanction is appropriate: *Notwithstanding any limitations under Federal Rule of Evidence 611(b), Defendants will be permitted to cross-examine Plaintiff in front of the jury regarding the record of his spoliation of evidence, as described above.*

The Court concludes this is the most appropriate sanction for several reasons. *First,* while Plaintiff is culpable, the Court does not find that the nature of that culpability warrants an adverse inference instruction. Although a threshold finding of bad faith is a prerequisite for an adverse inference, the Court does not view bad faith as a binary or "yes/no" issue. . . . [T]he record does not establish—at least not clearly—that Plaintiff was acting with an *intent* to deprive Defendants of relevant evidence. Absent a more clear showing that Plaintiff's conduct reflected his own "consciousness of a weak case," an adverse inference instruction is not appropriate. [Citing case]; *see also* Fed. R. Civ. P. 37(e)(2) (as to electronically stored information, adverse inference jury instruction is permissible "only upon [a] finding that the party acted with the intent to deprive another party of the information's use in litigation."). . . .

[A]llowing Defendants to cross examine Plaintiff about his spoliation of evidence has the benefit of allowing the jury to make its own assessment of Plaintiff's degree of culpability and of the actual prejudice to Defendants. The Court has little doubt that if the jury concludes Plaintiff acted with bad faith or an intention to destroy or conceal evidence, they will draw their own adverse inferences, whether the Court instructs it or not. In this case where Plaintiff's credibility is critical to his claims, allowing cross-examination regarding his spoliation of evidence, including the fact that he personally chose and edited the "clips" now available to the jury is therefore quite a heavy sanction. On the other hand, if the jury is persuaded that Plaintiff's actions were indeed innocent, then the impact of the Court's sanction will be far less harsh. . . .

[T]he remedial and punitive impact of the Court's sanction will follow from the jury's own findings and credibility determinations, rather than from findings by the Court on the basis of only the written record. . . .

For all these reasons, the Court concludes in the exercise of its discretion that among all the many possible sanctions it might impose, the one set forth above is properly suited to the circumstances of this case, is no more onerous than is necessary to serve its purposes, and best serves the interests of justice.

WHAT'S NEW HERE

- At the start of this chapter you saw *Zubulake* lay out the legal standard for spoliation. In *Mueller,* you see a court wrestling with the appropriate sanction once it determines spoliation occurred.
- The case also displays the ubiquity of digital information held in different forms: One does not need to be a giant organization to have multiple digital platforms, each with potentially relevant information.

Notes and Problems

1. On the basis of the facts recited, it's imaginable that the court would have ordered an adverse inference instruction rather than leaving the question to the jury.

   a. Should it have done so?

   b. Why did the court decline to do so?

   c. Given the court's decision, do you suppose that the defendants' lawyers during closing argument could emphasize the "conveniently missing" portions of the recording? Or would that go beyond the approved sanction?

2. Although the court implies that an adverse inference instruction is the most extreme form of sanction for spoliation, that's not quite accurate. In some cases courts have either dismissed the complaint (the ultimate sanction for a plaintiff) or ordered judgment for the plaintiff (the corresponding sanction for a defendant). However you answered the question in the preceding note, can you articulate an argument that such a sanction (dismissal) would have been too extreme on the facts of this case?

3. Consider the behavior of the plaintiff's lawyer. In a footnote edited from the opinion reproduced here, Judge Martínez tersely noted, "The Court takes an even more dim view of Plaintiff's counsel's unexplained failure to obtain, listen to, preserve, and produce the complete audio file, but that is a separate issue from whether Plaintiff should be sanctioned." In *Zubulake*, with which the chapter began, Judge Scheindlin had a good deal more to say about lawyers' continuing obligation to assure that digital evidence be preserved. In the next case, which does not involve e-discovery, the judge focuses on a lawyer's excessive gamesmanship during discovery and crafts a unique sanction to address this behavior.

Security National Bank of Sioux City v. Abbott Laboratories

299 F.R.D. 595 (N.D. Iowa 2014) *rev'd sub nom.* Security Natl.
Bank of Sioux City v. Day, 800 F.3d 936 (8th Cir. 2015)

BENNETT, J.

Something is rotten, but contrary to Marcellus's suggestion to Horatio, it's not in Denmark. Rather, it's in discovery in modern federal civil litigation right here in the United States. . . .

Discovery—a process intended to facilitate the free flow of information between parties—is now too often mired in obstructionism. Today's "litigators" are quick to dispute discovery requests, slow to produce information, and all-too-eager to object at every stage of the process. They often object using boilerplate language containing every objection imaginable, despite the fact that courts have resoundingly disapproved of such boilerplate objections. Some litigators do this to grandstand for their client, to intentionally obstruct the flow of clearly discoverable information, to try and win a war of attrition, or to intimidate and harass the opposing party. Others do it simply because it's how they were taught. . . . Whatever the reason, obstructionist discovery conduct is born of a warped view of zealous advocacy, often formed by insecurities and fear of the truth. This conduct fuels the astronomically costly litigation industry at the expense of "the just, speedy, and inexpensive determination of every action and proceeding." Fed. R. Civ. P. 1. It persists because most litigators and a few real trial lawyers—even very good ones, like the lawyers in this case—have come to accept it as part of the routine chicanery of federal discovery practice.

But the litigators and trial lawyers do not deserve all the blame for obstructionist discovery conduct because judges so often ignore this conduct, and by doing so we reinforce—even *incentivize*—obstructionist tactics. . . . Unless judges impose serious adverse consequences, like court-imposed sanctions, litigators' conditional reflexes will persist. The point of court-imposed sanctions is to stop reinforcing winning through obstruction.

While obstructionist tactics pervade all aspects of pretrial discovery, this case involves discovery abuse perpetrated during depositions. Earlier this year, in preparation for a hard-fought product liability jury trial, I was called upon by the parties to rule on numerous objections to deposition transcripts that the parties intended to use at trial. I noticed that the deposition transcripts were littered with what I perceived to be meritless objections made by one of the defendant's lawyers, whom I refer to here as "Counsel." I was shocked by what I read. Thus, for the reasons discussed below, I find that Counsel's deposition conduct warrants sanctions. . . .

[The court describes "hundreds of unnecessary objections and interruptions" by Counsel during depositions, most of which "completely lacked merit and often ended up influencing how the witnesses responded to questions."]

Based on Counsel's deposition conduct, I would be well within my discretion to impose substantial monetary sanctions on Counsel. But I am less interested in negatively affecting Counsel's pocketbook than I am in positively affecting Counsel's obstructive deposition practices. I am also interested in deterring others who might be inclined to comport themselves similarly to Counsel. . . . Deterrence is especially important given that so many litigators are *trained* to make obstructionist objections. For instance, at trial, when I challenged Counsel's use of "form" objections, Counsel responded, "Well, I'm sorry, Your Honor, but that was my training. . . ." While monetary sanctions are certainly warranted for Counsel's witness coaching and excessive interruptions, a more outside-the-box sanction may better serve the goal of changing improper tactics that modern litigators are trained to use. *See* Matthew L. Jarvey, Note, *Boilerplate Discovery Objections: How They Are Used, Why They Are Wrong, and What We Can Do About Them*, 61 Drake L. Rev. 913, 931-36 (2013) (discussing the importance of unorthodox sanctions in deterring discovery abuse).

In light of this goal, I impose the following sanction: Counsel must write and produce a training video in which Counsel, or another partner in Counsel's firm, appears and explains the holding and rationale of this opinion, and provides specific steps lawyers must take to comply with its rationale in future depositions in any federal and state court. . . . The lawyer in the video must state that the video is being produced and distributed pursuant to a federal court's sanction order regarding a partner in the firm, but the lawyer need not state the name of the partner, the case the sanctions arose under, or the court issuing this order. Upon completing the video, Counsel must file it with this court, under seal, for my review and approval. If and when I approve the video, Counsel must (1) notify certain lawyers at Counsel's firm about the video via e-mail and (2) provide those lawyers with access to the video. The lawyers who must receive this notice and access include each lawyer at Counsel's firm—including its branch offices worldwide—who engages in federal or state litigation or who works in any practice group in which at least two of the lawyers have filed an appearance in any state or federal case in the United States. After providing these lawyers with notice of and access to the video, Counsel must file in this court, under seal, (1) an affidavit certifying that Counsel complied with this order and received no assistance (other than technical help or help from the lawyer appearing in the video) in creating the video's content and (2) a copy of the e-mail notifying the appropriate lawyers in Counsel's firm about the video. . . . Failure to comply with this order within 90 days may result in additional sanctions. . . .

Depositions can be stressful and contentious, and lawyers are bound to make the occasional improper objection. But Counsel's improper objections, coaching, and interruptions went far beyond what judges should tolerate of any lawyer, let alone one as experienced and skilled as Counsel. . . . For the reasons stated in this opinion, I find that sanctions are appropriate in response to Counsel's improper deposition conduct, which impeded, delayed, and frustrated the fair examination of witnesses in the depositions related to this case that Counsel defended. I therefore impose the sanction described above.

Notes and Problems

1. What sanction is ordered in *Abbott Laboratories*?

2. What goal is the judge attempting to achieve through the sanction that he imposes in this case?

3. The court's decision in *Abbott Laboratories* was overturned by the Eighth Circuit Court of Appeals, which concluded that any sanctions should have been ordered within the timeframe of the sanctionable conduct and that the attorney should have had notice of the particular sanction that the court was considering so that she "would have a meaningful opportunity to respond."

   a. Note that the Court of Appeals did not reject the nature of the sanctions, or the district court's conclusion that the conduct was sanctionable.

   b. Note also that five amici, including the American Association of Justice (a plaintiffs' bar organization) and the American Board of Trial Advocates (a group consisting of experienced lawyers from both the defense and plaintiffs' bars), defended the district court's order as an appropriate way to address obstructionist discovery tactics.

c. The Eighth Circuit, in reversing, did not remand the case to the lower court, concluding that "a remand would have little value. Assuming without deciding that there was sanctionable conduct here, defense counsel has already suffered 'inevitable financial and personal costs,' and any additional sanction proceeding so long after the disputed conduct would not usefully serve the deterrent purpose of Rule 30(d)." Security Natl. Bank of Sioux City v. Jones Day, 800 F.3d 936 (8th Cir. 2015).

d. Imagine that you are the attorney who was sanctioned. The district court's sanctions order did not reference you by name but required you to produce a video explaining the basis for the court's sanctions. The court of appeals reversed the district court's sanctions order, but in its opinion referenced you and your firm by name, described, again, your conduct, and assumed that that conduct was sanctionable. Is the Eighth Circuit's reversal of the district court's decision a victory in your mind? Assuming both decisions resulted in a kind of sanction, which do you consider to be harsher?

* * *

Having looked at some of the obstacles to the smooth functioning of discovery, step back and consider its place in the larger scheme. The Supreme Court's recent glosses on Rule 8 (in *Twombly* and *Iqbal*) will prevent some cases from reaching discovery. For those that do, discovery will unearth information the parties need for trial—even as that same discovery may reduce the likelihood that trial will occur. The next two chapters illuminate this paradox. Chapter 8 looks at formal and informal ways in which parties may avoid trial. Chapter 9 looks at what happens during trial itself.

The paradoxical consequences of discovery flow from its dual role. It aims to prevent surprise at trial and to assure that cases will be resolved justly on their merits. Surprise witnesses make good courtroom drama but do not reassure us that justice has been done. To avoid such surprises at trial, discovery aims at laying bare both the parties' positions and the facts of the case.

In its other guise, discovery aims to put the parties in a position from which they can realistically assess the merits. In an ideal world, such assessments would match (that is, the parties would all accurately predict the results of a trial). When that happens, the parties will often settle. The next chapter explores the dynamics of settlement. When the parties' assessments of the merits are mismatched, settlement is unlikely, but other mechanisms, like summary judgment, may use the products of discovery to end the case.

Still other parties may be so averse to the litigation process—including discovery—that they try to take themselves outside the adjudicatory system. U.S. law gives them amazing freedom to do so in recognizing a number of contractual alternatives to litigation.

The next chapter explores both the voluntary and involuntary ways in which litigation may be avoided altogether or in which it can end without a trial.

Assessment Questions

Q1. In a lawsuit brought in federal district court a complaint and an answer have been filed. If the case follows a typical pattern, which of the following discovery events would precede the others?

   A. Exchange of experts' reports

   B. Planning conference

   C. Depositions

   D. Interrogatories

   E. Rule 26(a)(1) disclosures

Q2. Barbara, who operates a small manufacturing business, brings a diversity action against Donald in federal district court, seeking damages for breach of a contract to supply a part used in her product. Barbara has a number of documents she believes support her position. She also has a witness, Ethan (a former employee), and a document that will make it harder for her to prevail on her claim. Which the following statements are accurate?

   A. In her initial disclosure, Barbara must identify Ethan and all of the documents.

   B. In her initial disclosure, Barbara need not reveal Ethan or the unhelpful document, but she must reveal them if she is subsequently sent an interrogatory asking her to identify any relevant document or witness.

   C. If the unhelpful document is a letter from her lawyer advising her about the claim, she need not produce it either in the initial disclosure or at any later stage.

   D. If Donald somehow learns of the existence of Ethan, he is free to interview him.

   E. Whether or not he interviews Ethan, Donald can take his deposition.

Q3. In her initial discovery request after the parties confer and the judge enters a scheduling order, Donald requests copies of "all contracts and agreements" between Barbara and any third party over the preceding five years. Barbara's best objection to such a request would be:

   A. That such a request is not proportional to the case at hand.

   B. That the agreements should be protected under Rule 26(c) because they would be embarrassing.

   C. That the agreements would constitute trial preparation material as to which Donald had not shown any necessity.

   D. That the agreements, because drafted by Barbara's in-house counsel, would be privileged.

Q4. The *Barbara v. Donald* lawsuit continues. Donald, having learned through interrogatories the identity of Ethan, subpoenas him to appear at a deposition. If in the deposition Donald's lawyer asks Ethan about his sexual history, which is irrelevant to the lawsuit, . . .

A. Ethan's lawyer can object on grounds of irrelevance, and if Ethan's lawyer so objects, Donald cannot ask Ethan to answer the question.

B. Ethan's lawyer can object on grounds of irrelevance and, if Donald's lawyer persists in this line of questioning, then recess the deposition to seek a protective order.

C. Ethan's lawyer can instruct the witness not to answer on grounds of irrelevance.

D. If Ethan's lawyer objects but Ethan nevertheless answers the question, it can be used at a later stage of the case because, by answering, Ethan has waived any objection.

Q5. Still *Barbara v. Donald*. Through interrogatories, Donald learns that Barbara's in-house chief financial officer, a certified public accountant, may have relevant information about such matters as damages suffered by Barbara. Which of the following statements are accurate?

A. Because anyone serving as a chief financial officer has expertise in the area of finances and accounting, Donald can expect to receive a written report as specified in Rule 26(a)(2)(B).

B. If Barbara does not plan to call the chief financial officer as a witness, Donald cannot depose him without making a showing of "exceptional circumstances under which it is impracticable for [Donald] to obtain facts or opinions on the subject [of the CFO's testimony] by other means."

C. Donald can depose the CFO whether or not Barbara plans to call him as a witness.

D. Even if Barbara plans to call the CFO as a witness, he need not prepare an elaborate Rule 26(a)(2)(B) report.

Q6. More *Barbara v. Donald*. Donald has his own problems with discovery:

1. When he learned that Barbara was contemplating a lawsuit, he ordered an employee to shred some relevant documents.

2. He failed during initial disclosures to produce a document that he then used as an exhibit in Barbara's deposition.

3. He failed to appear at his properly noticed deposition.

4. In response to a request for documents he failed to produce the document in question, on the (erroneous) ground that it was irrelevant.

As to each of these actions, Barbara wishes to obtain the requested information and to seek sanctions if they are available. Identify which of these statements are true.

A. As to 1, no sanction is available because he shredded the documents before any discovery request had obliged Donald to produce this information.

B. As to 2, Donald will not able to use the document at trial.

C. As to 3, Barbara can expect that at a minimum she would receive the fees and costs attributable to Donald's failure to appear.

D. As to 4, Barbara must first seek a ruling ordering Donald to comply with the request before seeking any sanctions.

Analysis of Assessment Questions

Q1. B is the correct response; see Rule 26(d)(1). A is incorrect; although the parties must early on disclose the identity of experts they plan to use (Rule 26(a)(2)), the exchange of reports typically comes quite late in the process (see Rule 26(a)(2)(D)(i)). C and D are wrong because Rule 26(d)(1) forbids depositions or interrogatories before the parties' planning conference. E is wrong because, although these initial disclosures will be among the first required exchanges of information, they do not come until 14 days *after* the planning conference (Rule 26(a)(1)(C)).

Q2. B, C, D, and E are correct responses. B is correct (and A is incorrect) because at the initial disclosure stage a party need disclose only information *supporting* her claim or defense. C is correct because such a letter would be information protected by the attorney-client privilege and thus undiscoverable unless the privilege were waived. Note, though, that in response to such a request Barbara would have to comply with Rule 26(b)(5), explaining what the document was and why she was claiming privilege. D is correct because the discovery rules do not prohibit informal information gathering. E is correct because, if we assume the employee has relevant, unprivileged information, he can be deposed.

Q3. A is likely the best response. B is wrong because *if* the other contracts were relevant (doubtful but possible), the fact that their terms would embarrass Barbara would not protect them from discovery. C is wrong because the contracts were drafted in the ordinary course of business, not with litigation in mind. D is wrong because while the contracts may be the product of some confidential communications, only those communications themselves are protected by the privilege—the contracts themselves are not protected.

Q4. B is the only correct response. Rule 30(d)(3) permits such a recess, and under the circumstances it seems very likely that the court would issue a protective order. A is wrong because Rule 30(c)(2) provides that for any objection except on grounds of privilege, the question must be answered but the "testimony is taken subject to any objection." C is wrong because Rule 30(c)(2) provides that a person "may instruct a deponent not to answer only when necessary to protect a privilege, enforce [a court-ordered limitation on discovery] or to present a motion under Rule 30(d)(3)." D is wrong because what it means to take testimony "subject to any objection" (Rule 30(c)(2)) is precisely that the objection is preserved and may be renewed if Donald tries to use Ethan's answer in any later stage, say in a motion for summary judgment or during cross-examination at trial; at that point the judge will rule on the objection and exclude the evidence if, as in this case, it is irrelevant.

Q5. C and D are the correct responses. A and B are wrong because their provisions apply only to experts "retained in anticipation of litigation." As a CPA, this witness is certainly an expert, but he was hired to run Barbara's company finances, not specially to testify in this case. Thus, though an expert, he is not an expert hired in anticipation of litigation and thus not subject to the provisions of Rule 26(b)(4). Therefore no report (so A is wrong) and no immunity from deposition (so B is wrong). C is correct because as a witness in possession of relevant unprivileged information he can be deposed. D is correct because the Rule 26(a)(2)(B) report applies only to experts retained in anticipation of litigation.

Q6. C and D are the correct responses. A is wrong because the duty to preserve evidence (enforced through the common law doctrine of spoliation) attaches whenever one is aware (or should be aware) that litigation is reasonably likely. B is wrong because Rule 37(c) states that a court need not sanction a party for failing to disclose a document required by Rule 26(a) if the error is harmless. Here, Barbara has received the document while discovery is still underway and is, therefore, unlikely to be harmed by the earlier failure to disclose. C is correct because Rule 37(d)(3) specifically so provides. D is correct because Barbara needs a specific court order (which is then disobeyed) before one can seek sanctions (Rule 37(a) and (b)).

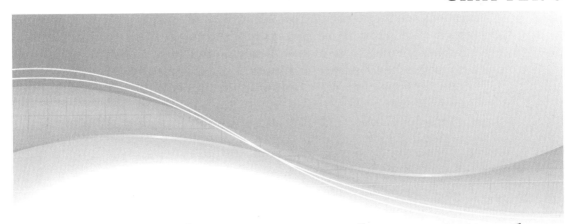

CHAPTER 8

Resolution Without Trial

"A trial is a failure,"* write two lawyers, echoing a sentiment found in many professional and judicial pronouncements. What they might mean and whether they are right will provide the focus of this chapter. Applied to contemporary U.S. litigation, the quoted statement can refer to the parties' failure to settle or otherwise resolve their dispute outside the formal litigation processes. Alternatively, it can refer to a failure to resolve the case through procedural mechanisms that are part of the formal litigation process.

The last few decades have seen renewed interest in resolving disputes outside the litigation process. Such approaches—including arbitration and mediation—have grown in number and interest in them has intensified. The world of private dispute resolution, which some say is replacing ordinary litigation, presents both the best and worst of human creativity. Those who see promise in these alternative systems contend that arbitration and mediation allow parties to resolve disputes economically and imaginatively: We'll see some examples in this chapter. Those who see danger in these alternative systems point to evidence of one-sidedness, greed, and disregard for basic fairness, examples of which we will also see in this chapter.

Some parties do not pursue private dispute resolution and cannot agree on a settlement. What then? A hundred and fifty years ago, the answer was clear: trial. But trials are expensive; even a short trial will cost thousands of dollars in lawyers', witnesses', and jurors' fees, and judicial time—not to mention the time and

---

* Samuel Gross & Kent Syverud, *Getting to No: A Study of Settlement Negotiations and the Selection of Cases for Trial*, 90 Mich. L. Rev. 319 (1991).

emotional toll on the parties. The Federal Rules offer additional opportunities for cases to resolve short of trial in an apparent effort to avoid some of these costs. You have already explored one of these opportunities: Rule 12 motions, which can end a case before the defendant even answers the complaint. In this chapter we consider others, including summary judgment (which allows a court to dismiss a case following discovery).

Procedural changes in the last century have accompanied a substantial decline in the frequency of trials. In the last 75 years, the civil trial rate in the federal courts has fallen from about 20 percent to just less than 2 percent. Figures for the state courts, which handle about 98 percent of civil litigation, are comparable. There is a debate about whether those who designed the new procedures intended this reduction in trials and, whether or not they did, if it is a bad thing.

We start and end with the official litigation system, venturing outside it after we have established some baselines and some points of connection between the official and the alternative systems.

A. THE PRESSURE TO CHOOSE ADJUDICATION OR AN ALTERNATIVE

Why do lawsuits ever proceed beyond the complaint? Defendants accused of wrong-doing might just ignore the allegations if there were no way of forcing a response. Conversely, plaintiffs might file meritless suits that would hang over defendants' heads indefinitely were there not some way of forcing them to a conclusion. Both possibilities are inherent in a system that assigns to the parties rather than the court primary responsibility for the progress of litigation. Two procedural devices force the parties to engage and respond to each other: the default judgment, the threat of which should goad the defendant into action; and the involuntary dismissal, intended to keep the plaintiff from going to sleep at the litigative switch. Versions of such principles are found in Rule 55 (for default judgments) and Rule 41(b) (involuntary dismissal).

1. Default and Default Judgments

How does Rule 55 goad the defendant into action? If a defendant has been properly served with a complaint and then fails to respond, the plaintiff can go to the court clerk with proof of the defendant's delinquency, and the clerk will enter defendant's default. Rule 55(a). Then, the plaintiff can submit proof of her injury to the clerk or court and receive a default judgment that she can use to seize defendant's assets—wages, bank accounts, and real property. Rule 55(c).

Most defaults and default judgments involve creditors' suits over unpaid consumer debts, and the vast majority are not challenged. If a defendant does not have a plausible defense or counterclaim, then the default judgment represents merely a shorter, cheaper route to the right result. If, however, a defendant has a viable defense but cannot find or afford a lawyer, or does not receive adequate notice of the default, the entry of a default judgment represents a reproach to the legal system. No robust empirical studies tell us which possibility occurs more often.

The next case was originally brought in Texas state court—and so does not invoke the federal rules—but shows the Supreme Court balancing the efficiencies of default judgments against defendants' due process protections.

Peralta v. Heights Medical Center
485 U.S. 80 (1988)

WHITE, J., delivered the opinion of the Court.

Heights Medical Center, Inc. (hereafter appellee) sued appellant Peralta in February 1982, to recover some $5600 allegedly due under appellant's guarantee of a hospital debt incurred by one of his employees. Citation issued, the return showing personal, but untimely, service. Appellant did not appear or answer, and on July 20, 1982, default judgment was entered for the amount claimed, plus attorney's fees and costs.

In June 1984, appellant began a bill of review proceeding in the Texas courts to set aside the default judgment and obtain the relief. In the second amended petition, it was alleged that the return of service itself showed a defective service[2] and that appellant in fact had not been personally served at all. The judgment was therefore void under Texas law. It was also alleged that the judgment was abstracted and recorded in the county real property records, thereby creating a cloud on appellant's title, that a writ of attachment was issued, and that, unbeknownst to him, his real property was sold to satisfy the judgment and for much less than its true value. Appellant prayed that the default judgment be vacated, the abstract of judgment be expunged from the county real property records, the constable's sale be voided, and that judgment for damages be entered against the Medical Center and Mr. and Mrs. Paul Seng-Ngan Chen, the purchasers at the constable's sale and appellees here.

Appellee filed a motion for summary judgment asserting that in a bill of review proceeding such as appellant filed, it must be shown that the petitioner had a meritorious defense to the action in which judgment had been entered, that petitioner was prevented from proving his defense by the fraud, accident, or wrongful act of the opposing party, and that there had been no fault or negligence on petitioner's part. Although it was assumed for the purposes of summary judgment that there had been defective service and that this lapse excused proof of the second and third requirement for obtaining a bill of review, it was assertedly necessary, nevertheless, to show a meritorious defense, which appellant had conceded he did not have.

. . . "An elementary and fundamental requirement of due process in any proceeding which is to be accorded finality is notice reasonably calculated, under the

---

2. The petition alleged that the record contained a return of service of process, showing that service was effected more than 90 days after its issuance, contrary to Texas Rule of Civil Procedure 101. . . . Texas courts have held that service after the 90th day is a nullity, depriving the court of personal jurisdiction over the defendant.

circumstances, to apprise interested parties of the pendency of the action and afford them the opportunity to present their objections." *Mullane v. Central Hanover Bank & Trust Co.* [supra page 165]. Failure to give notice violates "the most rudimentary demands of due process of law." Armstrong v. Manzo, 380 U.S. 545, 550 (1965). See also . . . *Pennoyer v. Neff* [supra page 68].

The Texas courts nevertheless held, as appellee urged them to do, that to have the judgment set aside, appellant was required to show that he had a meritorious defense, apparently on the ground that without a defense, the same judgment would again be entered on retrial and hence appellant had suffered no harm from the judgment entered without notice. But this reasoning is untenable. As appellant asserts, had he had notice of the suit, he might have impleaded the employee whose debt had been guaranteed, worked out a settlement, or paid the debt. He would also have preferred to sell his property himself in order to raise funds rather than to suffer it sold at a constable's auction.

Nor is there any doubt that the entry of the judgment itself had serious consequences. It is not denied that the judgment was entered on the county records, became a lien on appellant's property, and was the basis for issuance of a writ of execution under which appellant's property was promptly sold, without notice. Even if no execution sale had yet occurred, the lien encumbered the property and impaired appellant's ability to mortgage or alienate it; and state procedures for creating and enforcing such liens are subject to the strictures of due process. Here, we assume that the judgment against him and the ensuing consequences occurred without notice to appellant, notice at a meaningful time and in a meaningful manner that would have given him an opportunity to be heard. . . .

. . . The Texas court held that the default judgment must stand absent a showing of a meritorious defense to the action in which judgment was entered without proper notice to appellant, a judgment that had substantial adverse consequences to appellant. By reason of the Due Process Clause of the Fourteenth Amendment, that holding is plainly infirm. Where a person has been deprived of property in a manner contrary to the most basic tenets of due process, "it is no answer to say that in his particular case due process of law would have led to the same result because he had no adequate defense upon the merits." Coe v. Armour Fertilizer Works, 237 U.S. 413, 424 (1915). As we observed in *Armstrong v. Manzo*, only "wip[ing] the slate clean . . . would have restored the petitioner to the position he would have occupied had due process of law been accorded to him in the first place." The Due Process Clause demands no less in this case.

The judgment below is reversed.

Notes and Problems

1. First, consider an issue that the Court does not resolve—whether Mr. Peralta received notice of the suit. Mr. Peralta asserted, in his brief to the Court, that he was never served with the complaint. The sheriff claimed to have served

Peralta with the complaint (giving him notice). Regardless, the parties appear to agree that Peralta was not served within 90 days and, as footnote 2 makes clear, untimely service is a nullity in Texas courts.

   a. If Mr. Peralta received no notice of the pending action, the argument for setting aside the default judgment seems easy. Almost all courts hold the defendant's neglect in such circumstances to be excusable.

   b. If one concludes that actual notice—though not timely service—occurred, the case to reopen the default judgment becomes harder. If Mr. Peralta received notice but took no steps to answer or otherwise defend the suit, why does it deny him due process to require that he show a meritorious defense as a prerequisite to setting aside the default judgment?

      i. The Court's answer to that question is phrased in terms of "might haves": Mr. Peralta might have impleaded the employee; he might have worked out a settlement; he might have paid the debt; he might have sold the property himself. How convinced are you by these arguments?

      ii. Does it affect your assessment of Mr. Peralta's position that his real property seized and sold at constable's auction to satisfy the $5,000 debt was valued at $80,000? See Appellate Brief, Peralta v. Heights Medical Center, 1987 WL 880413 (Aug. 7, 1987).

2. *Peralta* demonstrates that courts, while prepared to enter default judgments, greatly prefer to see the parties engage on the merits of the dispute. Although *Peralta* was filed in state court and therefore filed under state procedural rules, the Federal Rules reflect these same interests.

   a. Rule 55(a) and (b) discourage defendants from ignoring the plaintiff's complaint through the threat of a default and default judgment, but Rule 55(c) and Rule 60 grant courts discretion to reopen defaults and default judgments so that parties can resolve their disputes on the merits.

   b. This preference means that parties seeking relief from defaults and default judgments get them set aside if they can show good cause for failing to respond to the summons. See Rule 55(c).

   c. Rule 60(b) also permits the reopening of the case even after judgment is entered on a default, for "any . . . reason that justifies relief." Rule 60(b)(6).

   d. Challenging are the cases in which the defendant is served and retains a lawyer—who then fails to respond to the complaint or to court orders. Theoretically, it would be easy to enter a default judgment and let the plaintiff sue his negligent lawyer for malpractice. In practice, courts don't like that solution—in part because the same lawyers who fail to answer the complaint are unlikely to have bothered to buy malpractice insurance. Or, the problem can lie with the client rather than the lawyer. Consider Honda Power Equip. Mfg., Inc. v. Woodhouse, 219 F.R.D. 2 (D.D.C. 2003). The case arose from a patent dispute between Honda and Mr. Woodhouse, who claimed that some of Honda's engines infringed his patent. Honda filed a declaratory judgment action, seeking a judgment of non-infringement. Woodhouse hired a lawyer, who acknowledged service of process and requested additional time to answer. But Woodhouse then failed to respond to his counsel's inquiries, and an answer was never filed. The court entered a default judgment, but only after writing a six-page opinion reciting defendant's counsel's repeated efforts to get a response from his client, the prejudice to Honda from the delay, and the fact that a UK court had found against Woodhouse in related patent litigation.

3. Honda's willingness to grant Mr. Woodhouse an extension of time to answer in the preceding note is typical. Plaintiffs are often ready to grant such extensions, particularly if they think that defendant will use that time to decide whether to make a settlement offer. Suppose you represent a defendant who comes to you with a complaint.

   a. Time is running: In the absence of an extension, how long do you have to file an answer?

   b. After discussing the case with your client, you call the plaintiff's attorney, with whom you've not previously dealt, and have a relatively cordial conversation, in which she agrees to extend the time to answer for a month. Relieved, you hang up and turn to some other pressing work on your desk. What risk are you running, and what should you have done to avoid it?

4. Assume plaintiff obtains a default judgment. What does it actually accomplish? In some civil law systems, default operates as a general denial—that is, the plaintiff must still satisfy the court that the facts justify granting relief. By contrast, in the United States a default operates as an admission of liability. What does this contrast tell us about party responsibility, the role of the court, and the concept of a lawsuit?

Procedure as Strategy

When a defendant has been served with a complaint, he has three options. He can move to dismiss pursuant to Rule 12; answer the complaint; or ignore the complaint altogether. Consider the financial implications of these three choices and the ways in which these choices implicate other aspects of procedure. If the defendant moves to dismiss the case, he will need to pay his lawyer to research and brief the motion, but could end up having the case dismissed in whole or part if the motion is successful. If the defendant answers the complaint, the answer itself may be relatively inexpensive but the case will proceed to discovery and summary judgment will offer the next likely opportunity for dismissal. Ignoring the complaint is free, but it will likely cause the court to enter a default judgment against him for the value of the plaintiff's claims.

Implications

PERALTA AND *PENNOYER*

If you have already encountered *Pennoyer v. Neff* (in Chapter 2), you know that it stands at the origin of a century and a half of personal jurisdiction doctrine. But Neff, a central figure in *Pennoyer*, is like Mr. Peralta: He apparently was never served with process in the lawsuit filed against him, and—unlike Mr. Peralta—may never have had any knowledge of it until after judgment was entered against him. Suppose the *Pennoyer* Court had taken the approach in *Peralta*. It could have set aside the default judgment without the need to invent the law of personal jurisdiction!

2. Scheduling Orders and Failure to Prosecute: Involuntary Dismissal

Involuntary dismissal does to plaintiffs what default does to defendants: It forces them to pursue the lawsuit to some resolution. In our largest state's court system these dismissals occur in about 5 percent of civil filings. Judicial Council of California, Court Statistics Report (2016), Table 5a, page 93. They sometimes result from plaintiffs realizing that their cases are weaker than previously thought, sometimes from realizing that litigation will be more expensive than thought.

In an ordinary lawsuit, defendant has something that plaintiff wants and can get only if the lawsuit proceeds. One might therefore think that a defendant would be quite happy to face a plaintiff who, after filing and serving the complaint, did nothing. And often defendants are. But consider why a defendant might feel aggrieved if a plaintiff commenced but then did nothing to prosecute the suit for several years. Imagine a variation on the facts in *Peralta*: The plaintiff files the suit, serves the defendant, and puts a lien on his property, but instead of proceeding to a judgment the plaintiff simply sits and waits. Mr. Peralta can't get the suit dismissed on the merits (recall he has no meritorious defense), but meanwhile he can't sell the property or borrow money on it because of the lien.

Add to your picture the role the judge plays in pretrial litigation. You will recall from the preceding chapter on discovery that the event triggering the exchange of disclosures is the "scheduling order." Much of Rule 16 tells the judge what she "may" do, but Rule 16(b) says the judge "*must* issue a scheduling order" (emphasis added) unless the case belongs to an exempt category. That scheduling order "must limit the time to join other parties, amend the pleadings, complete discovery, and file motions" and "may" set other dates. Scheduling orders are supposed to drive the parties along the path to settlement or trial.

Lying behind scheduling orders is a fact that does not often get articulated in judicial opinions: Courts are very busy. In 2016 the federal courts saw about 292,000 civil and 76,000 new criminal cases filed. Congress has authorized 677 district court judgeships. If all those positions were filled, the average federal district judge would have 530 new cases each year for which she was responsible; in practice, there are always a number of unfilled positions, so actual caseloads run higher. Judges in state courts, where most litigation occurs, often have even larger caseloads; in 2008, judges in courts of general jurisdiction (where felonies and large-stake civil litigation occur) had caseloads averaging 2,950 per judge. That national average conceals wide variations, from Massachusetts with about 384 filings per judge to South Carolina, with about 4,842. National Center for State Courts, Examining the Work of State Courts 20 (2008). Such caseloads make for judges who are (a) busy, sometimes to the point of frazzled impatience; and (b) eager to manage their cases in such a way that the backlog does not grow.

What can a defendant do if plaintiff ignores a scheduling order's deadlines or fails to move the lawsuit forward? Rule 41(b) and similar state statutes provide for involuntary dismissal "if the plaintiff fails to prosecute" (as well as on other grounds). Such a dismissal takes the lawsuit off the books. The question is, how lax must a plaintiff be before a judge should enter such a dismissal? In other words, when does "standard" foot-dragging become abandonment? The answer to these questions will be highly context-specific. Consider, though, Caussade v. United States, 293 F.R.D. 625 (S.D.N.Y. 2013) (involuntarily dismissing plaintiff's claim against the United States for injuries at a post office because the plaintiff never made herself available for a deposition, never made initial disclosures, never corrected deficiencies in her responses to interrogatories, did not appear at a pretrial conference, and did not keep in contact with her attorney for months at a time).

3. Voluntary Dismissal

On the basis of the exposition so far, one might assume that both plaintiff and defendant are locked in adversarial combat until a judge or jury enters judgment for one or the other. Not quite. Rule 41(a)(1)(A)(i) allows a plaintiff to dismiss any time before the defendant answers, and Rule 41(a)(1)(A)(ii) permits the plaintiff to dismiss a suit at any time if all the parties agree. Why would they agree? Suppose the parties are close to settling and want more time without distractions like discovery in which to negotiate. Such stipulated dismissals do not bar a later refiling of the suit unless there has been a previous dismissal or the dismissal itself contains a provision that bars refiling. Provisions barring refiling frequently result from successful settlement negotiations: In return for money or other relief, the plaintiff gives up her chance to pursue the suit or to refile it later.

What about the plaintiff who files suit, then realizes she needs to gather more evidence? The defendant is unlikely to agree to a dismissal for such purposes. Rule 41(a)(2) authorizes a voluntary dismissal after defendant answers only by permission of the court.

Notes and Problems

---

1. Why are such cost-free voluntary dismissals ever permitted?

    a. At common law, such dismissals made sense because they enabled a plaintiff who had a good claim but had brought the wrong writ to replead (e.g., to plead trespass instead of trespass on the case, assumpsit instead of debt). The justification for such false starts is much less clear in a system that permits easy joinder of claims and easy amendment. In such a system, one could easily justify a door that locked behind the plaintiff once she had begun a lawsuit: "Either pursue it to a judgment or settlement, or, if you abandon the suit, do so irrevocably."

    b. One possible reason is to give plaintiff a little breathing room to consider changed circumstances. Suppose software Inventor, having sued SoftWare Co. for infringement, learns that Inventor Two is about to sue *him* for infringement. Inventor may need some time to decide whether his suit should be dropped entirely, or, by contrast, whether he should now add Inventor Two as another defendant, perhaps bringing a more complex suit in a different jurisdiction.

2. Rule 41(a)(1)(A)(i) allows the plaintiff voluntarily to dismiss at any time before the defendant has answered; after that point the court's permission or agreement of the other side is necessary. In one notorious case the availability of voluntary dismissal proved catastrophic for the defendant. In corporate control litigation between two giant oil companies, Texaco and Pennzoil—Texaco Inc. v. Pennzoil, 481 U.S. 1 (1987)—the plaintiff filed originally in a Delaware state court seeking a preliminary injunction. Defendant opposed the injunction but did not answer the complaint. When the court denied the request for a preliminary injunction, using language suggesting the plaintiff would eventually lose on the merits, the plaintiff quickly took a voluntary dismissal and refiled in Texas. A Texas jury eventually awarded the plaintiff $10 billion. Voluntary dismissal without court approval would have been unavailable had Texaco answered the Delaware complaint. The defendant's failure to answer has been described as "one of the most expensive tactical errors ever committed in a lawsuit." Timothy Feltham, *Tortious Interference with Contractual Relations: The Texaco Inc. v. Pennzoil Litigation*, 33 N.Y.L. Sch. L. Rev. 111, 117 n.65 (1988). If a voluntary dismissal will harm your client, answer the complaint promptly to lock plaintiff into the forum.

What if a voluntary dismissal without approval of the court or defendant is unavailable? If permission is required, courts routinely require plaintiffs to pay the defendant's attorneys' fees as a condition of granting the motion. The logic is fairly clear: Plaintiff chose the time and place of suit and has caused defendant at least the expense of retaining a lawyer and answering the complaint (recall that voluntary dismissals before an answer do not require leave of court). Now plaintiff has changed his mind, but remains free to sue again. Shouldn't plaintiff have to pay the cost of this vacillation? Should the Rule make this condition explicit?

B. AVOIDING ADJUDICATION

Faced with the products of discovery and kept in engagement by procedural rules, parties may decide that they want to avoid adjudication. Indeed, given foreknowledge about procedural rules, they may decide well before any dispute arises that they wish to avoid litigation. The contemporary U.S. legal regime offers parties a broad set of ways to escape litigation once it has begun or avoid litigation altogether.

1. Negotiation and Settlement: Why Settle? And How?

Since the beginning of recorded legal systems, parties have regularly settled most of their disputes informally, without adjudication. Behind this fact lies a normative question. Settlements are cheaper and faster than trials. Are they also better—or are they merely a capitulation to expediency? Some argue that settlements are not just faster and cheaper but also qualitatively better, because consent is a basic principle of justice, and because settlements can take account of nuances and subtleties in the facts and in the parties' interests that would be lost in adjudication. On the other side are those who argue that settlement leaves the parties less satisfied than if a trier heard their stories, sometimes permits might to triumph over right, and deprives the public of definitive adjudication of issues that may reach beyond the individual case.

Where one falls on this normative question may depend on the case and the reasons it settled. One reason for settlement is unattractive: What if a party simply runs out of funds to pursue the litigation? A settlement, getting something, may be better than getting nothing (which is what will happen if the case is dismissed) or being stuck with a default judgment (if the defendant is the side unable to pursue the case). How often does this happen? There's evidence that cases collapsing without regard to the merits is a much rarer event than it used to be. As the materials in Chapter 5 suggest, modern litigation finance is relatively creative, and the plaintiffs' bar better capitalized; therefore the stock story of the meritorious plaintiff crushed by defendant's vastly superior resources is less true today than it once was. Different dynamics apply to defendants. Defendants who cannot pay a judgment will rarely be sued for damages (hold-over tenants and divorce litigation are significant exceptions here), so when defendants abandon litigation, it will usually be because circumstances have changed since the case began.

That leaves a second, more common and thus more important, reason for settling. Settlements control risk. Trial outcomes have two characteristics that make them risky: (1) They are significantly unpredictable, and (2) they tend to be all-or-nothing. Even experienced lawyers have a hard time predicting how juries will decide a given case—keep in mind that summary judgment (infra page 569) will eliminate the clear cases, so the only cases that make it to trial should be those where the evidence doesn't point clearly in one direction. Substantive law tells judge and jury not to split the difference, but either to hold the defendant liable for all proximately caused damages or to find for the defense. Consequently, trial can result in either a catastrophe or a windfall for both parties, and no one knows for certain which will happen. Exacerbating these risks is the fact that trial is expensive. Not only is lawyers' time in trial expensive, but expert witnesses have to be paid, exhibits prepared, and witnesses' memories refreshed (in most jurisdictions a trial will come at least a year after suit is filed, which may be several years after the events in question). Moreover, in spite of judicial efforts to have parties complete discovery well before trial, in many cases the approach of trial will set off a flurry of additional discovery as lawyers scurry to shore up weak points in their cases. Parties will also submit various pretrial motions to exclude evidence and the like, running expenses even higher. So, for many parties, settlement is appealing because it provides a way of avoiding an expensive and risky trial.

If they are to achieve their goals, whether of risk avoidance or of consensual justice, settlements have to be technically competent. Settlement agreements require both negotiating skill and knowledge of how parties can achieve their goals once they come to agreement in principle. Unlike parties who are negotiating the sale of a building or the terms of an employment agreement, parties who are negotiating in the shadow of litigation and trial are likely to be somewhat annoyed with each other. Lawyers can contribute to negotiations by interposing a professional role that keeps the disputants from each others' throats long enough to work out an agreement. Or they can make things worse by becoming so personally embroiled with their counterparts that they prevent two clients, who might otherwise have agreed, from doing so! Whether they help or hinder agreement, however, lawyers can contribute expertise to the terms and the form of settlement, anticipating problems and preventing the settlement of one dispute from becoming the start of another.

Consider the problems in the context of an example that will provide a framework for the next several sections.

WHAT'S NEW HERE?

This section of the course approaches two topics that will stand at the center of your professional career: risk control and judgment.

- Clients seek lawyers to tell them about risks. Litigation involves one set of such risks: What might be the outcome of this suit? Settlement controls risk. A plaintiff accepting a defendant's settlement offer eliminates the risk of recovering nothing by giving up the possibility of a recovery at trial greater than the settlement amount. For the defendant the risks are reversed: By giving up the possibility of a defense judgment, defendant controls the risk of a verdict greater than the amount paid in settlement.
- Clients seek lawyers to bring skilled and experienced judgment to bear. They will ask you not just "what is the law here?" but also "what's the likely outcome of this case?" They are, in effect, asking for your estimates of risk. That second question is very difficult to answer (and some data suggest that even experienced lawyers are not very accurate in making those estimates). But clients will expect answers, and part of a lawyer's job is to understand the ways in which their client may rank different kinds of risk.

JANE SMART v. GROWCO, INC.

Jane Smart is a plant geneticist. Until recently she worked at GrowCo, a relatively new, profitable, and expanding firm specializing in genetically modified crops. GrowCo has been much in the news recently, with favorable press reports and significant investor interest. Smart has been deeply involved in developing some of GrowCo's most successful crops. A dispute with the Senior Scientist, whom Smart accuses of sexual harassment, leads to her dismissal. Dr. Smart consults a lawyer and threatens to bring an action for unlawful discharge and employment discrimination, invoking state law and Title VII of the federal Civil Rights Act. As the lawyers for both sides speak with their clients, the facts aren't one-sided. Plaintiff's story suggests that Senior Scientist has behaved in ways that are at least obnoxious (and will sound terrible to a jury) and are perhaps unlawful. But plaintiff's story also has some problems. It's not clear that she was an excellent employee before her dismissal, and her past involves some breaches of scientific ethics in testing genetically modified crops on humans that will make it easy for defendant to challenge her testimony and portray her as an untrustworthy person.

a. Contracting to Dismiss

The simplest form of settlement is a contract (sometimes called a release) in which the plaintiff (or prospective plaintiff) agrees not to bring a lawsuit or to drop one already filed. Most plaintiffs want something, typically money, in return for such agreements.

Notes and Problems

---

1. What does a settlement do for the parties?

   a. For GrowCo? Besides the possibility of losing, what risks does a trial hold for this defendant? Conversely, what advantages would settlement hold?

   b. For Smart? Does she have anything to lose besides the lawsuit? And what advantages might accrue to her from a settlement?

2. Notice that there are third parties—not in the lawsuit—that may be affected by a settlement. Consider just two:

   a. Perhaps there are other GrowCo employees who have been subject to similar behavior by Senior Scientist. How might a settlement affect them?

   b. Suppose that Smart does not name Senior Scientist as a defendant in the case but Senior Scientist strongly contests Smart's account of his behavior. Will a settlement leave him without a remedy for a severely damaged reputation?

   c. If a settlement would affect these nonparties, notice that the existing legal framework for settlements does not have a way of taking those interests into account.

3. Clients, not lawyers, are empowered to make settlement decisions, but clients' settlement decisions will impact lawyers' pocketbooks as well. The financial effects of settlements on lawyers will depend on their fee arrangements with their clients. Imagine that Smart's lawyer is working on a contingent fee arrangement such that she will receive one-third of any settlement but nothing if Smart loses, modified by the possibility that a prevailing plaintiff in a Title VII suit can collect reasonable attorneys' fees from the losing defendant. (See Chapter 5, supra.) Imagine GrowCo is paying its lawyer by the hour.

   a. If GrowCo offers Smart $90,000 the day after she files the case, what does this mean for the attorneys? Smart's attorney is poised to earn $30,000 for the relatively few hours it took to investigate Smart's claim and file the complaint. GrowCo's attorney will be paid his hourly rate for the relatively few hours of work needed to settle the case.

   b. Now suppose that Smart declines GrowCo's settlement offer. The parties then each spend $50,000 during discovery. Suppose that GrowCo now offers Smart $120,000 to settle the case. At this point, if Smart accepts the settlement offer, Smart's attorney will earn $40,000 for $50,000 of work. If

Smart rejects the offer, goes to trial, and wins, Smart's attorney will be able to recover her reasonable attorneys' fees—presumably $50,000 plus the cost of her services through trial. If Smart rejects the offer, goes to trial, and loses, Smart's attorney will recover nothing. GrowCo's attorney, in contrast, will be paid for his hourly work regardless of whether his client settles or wins or loses at trial.

4. Suppose, as often happens, that the parties reach a settlement before suit is filed. The parties might do so in a number of ways: a meeting of the lawyers, a series of telephone calls, or an exchange of documents.

   a. Regardless of how they reach agreement, the parties generally do not need the court's approval of their deal. In an ordinary case, the judge need not examine or approve the settlement, though he must grant—usually routinely—plaintiff's request to dismiss the case if that is part of the deal. Plaintiffs needing immediate funds may settle meritorious claims for trivial sums; defendants eager to get on with other matters may offer substantial sums on meritless claims to end litigation. The principal exceptions to this "freedom to settle" arise in class actions (where Rule 23(e) requires judicial approval of settlements); in cases involving minors or incompetent adults, where the court is required to approve settlements; and in some multi-defendant cases. What theory underlies these exceptions to the general rule of judicial indifference to the fairness of settlements?

   b. Is the usual practice of judicial indifference defensible? Should judges be required to scrutinize all settlements for fairness? Before answering, imagine yourself as judge. Suppose a very common case—a rear-end vehicle collision in which plaintiff alleges soft-tissue injuries. Such injuries are common, but also commonly feigned. Defendant, represented by an insurer, has denied liability but has offered a small settlement. You, the judge, are asked to approve or reject the settlement. How would you reach a decision? What information would you want to have? Would your concern be substantive (is the settlement fair?) or procedural (did both parties know the material facts?)? Would the cost of gathering and presenting this information eliminate two of the chief advantages of settlement—speed and efficiency—and place additional burdens on the courts?

   c. As a half-way step between trying to police all settlements and leaving matters entirely to the law of contract, legislators could build procedural protections into settlements of certain kinds of claims. For example, federal legislation regulates settlements releasing Age Discrimination in Employment Act (ADEA) claims: Offers must be clearly written; they must remain in effect for stated periods of time; the employer must advise employees to consult a lawyer; and they must give settling employees at least a week to revoke a signed settlement agreement. 29 U.S.C. §626(f). In Oubre v. Entergy Operations, Inc., 522 U.S. 422 (1998), the Court held that an employee who had released ADEA claims without these procedures could, without tendering back the money paid for a settlement, bring suit under the Act.

   d. Although there is no general doctrine requiring judicial approval of settlements, settlements are contracts and can be attacked on any of the grounds on which one can attack any contract: fraud, duress, mistake, incapacity, unconscionability, and the like.

5. Suppose you represent GrowCo in the hypothetical case of *Smart v. GrowCo*. You think the plaintiff's case is weak, but your client understands that litigating it will require hours of lost time consumed in depositions, and may undermine the morale of other employees, attract similar lawsuits, and frighten off potential investors. GrowCo's general counsel asks you to see if you can settle the case, inquiring what you think it will cost.

   a. How do you answer the question about settlement value? A good deal of it will depend on the merits of the case: How "good" or "bad" are the facts? How sympathetic and credible will the plaintiff and her supervisor be as witnesses? What damages can the plaintiff prove? And would she be entitled to additional attorney's fees should she prevail at trial?

   b. After discussion, your client gives you a dollar figure GrowCo is willing to offer the plaintiff to settle. You contact Smart's lawyer (ethical rules prohibit a lawyer's directly contacting a represented client), discuss a series of depositions you want to take, and, at the end of the conversation, ask whether there's any point in discussing settlement. The plaintiff's attorney says it might be possible, and after some haggling you reach a figure that the plaintiff's counsel is willing to recommend to her client. Assuming the plaintiff accepts, how will you actually effectuate the settlement?

   c. The simplest way would be an oral agreement that plaintiff will drop the suit when she receives your client's check. This route is also an excellent way to assure that your former client sues you for malpractice. Why?

6. Assume now that you think you should draft a written settlement agreement. What should it say? That the plaintiff agrees not to file a threatened lawsuit (if a suit had not yet been filed)? That, having filed suit, the plaintiff will seek a voluntary dismissal and agree not to refile the suit? That, having filed suit, the plaintiff consents to a dismissal with prejudice and, as added assurance, also agrees not to refile the suit? All of these techniques are used to create settlements. Consider some of their advantages and disadvantages and the problems entailed by each.

   a. Take first the prefiling agreement not to sue. In some respects this is the simplest and best form of settlement: By definition it eliminates all litigation costs. But this form of agreement also requires the lawyer to carefully define the scope of the threatened lawsuit. The putative plaintiff must agree not to sue on the same claims in the future, but because there has been no complaint filed, it can be challenging to define the scope of the release.

      Consider the language of a typical insurer-drafted auto accident release entered into before any suit was filed after the parked car belonging to one of the co-authors of this book was hit by a neighbor:

      > KNOW ALL MEN BY THESE PRESENTS: That the Undersigned, being of lawful age, for sole consideration of $2,431.18 TWO THOUSAND FOUR HUNDRED THIRTY ONE AND 18/100 DOLLARS to be paid to Stephen C.

Yeazell does hereby and for his heirs, executors, administrators, successors and assigns release, acquit and forever discharge [Neighbor], her agents, principals, servants, successors, [and a bunch more boilerplate variations] from any and all claims, actions, causes of action, demands, rights, damages, [and more boilerplate variations] whatsoever, which the undersigned now has or which may hereafter accrue on account of or in any way growing out of any and all known and unknown, foreseen and unforeseen bodily and personal injuries and property damage and the consequences thereof resulting from the accident which occurred on or about the 8th day of June 2007, at or near 1ST AT LARCHMONT, LOS ANGELES, CA.

It is understood and agreed that this settlement is the compromise of a doubtful and disputed claim, and that the payment made is not to be construed as an admission of liability on the part of the party or parties hereby released, and that said releasers deny liability therefore and intend merely to avoid litigation and buy their peace.

b. Now suppose an unlikely occurrence: Having signed this release, plaintiff nevertheless files a lawsuit arising out of the same incident. How does defendant get the court to give effect to the release? Read Rule 8(c) to see what defendant should allege in her answer. Then read Rule 56(b) and think about what documents would be attached to defendant's motion for summary judgment.

c. A more difficult problem arises if the parties have several claims, only some of which they want to settle. Suppose that Jane Smart has a claim to a pension whose present value neither side wants to calculate because it depends on several contingent events. In that situation, the lawyers will have to carve the pension claim out of the agreement unless they can reach a global settlement.

7. If settlement is achieved after a suit has been filed, the plaintiff can file a voluntary dismissal to end the case. But recall that Rule 41(a) permits a plaintiff taking a voluntary dismissal to refile the suit—just the result that a settlement seeks to avoid. Accordingly, defense counsel will require the plaintiff to agree, as part of the terms of the settlement agreement, not to refile this or any related lawsuit. If the plaintiff later refiles her suit, defendant can sue for breach of the settlement agreement.

a. An additional way to ensure that the plaintiff cannot refile her claim is to have the dismissal treated as a judgment on the merits (otherwise known as a dismissal with prejudice). As you will see in Chapter 11, under modern doctrines of former adjudication, a claim adjudicated on the merits is interpreted to bar all related claims, whether or not they were stated in the complaint. Such a mode of dismissal also means that if the plaintiff files a second lawsuit, the defendant can invoke not just the contract of settlement but the doctrines of former adjudication to have the suit dismissed. Rule 41(a) voluntary dismissals are treated as dismissals without prejudice "[u]nless the notice or stipulation states otherwise." Accordingly, a savvy defense attorney will ensure that a notice of voluntary dismissal asks the court to dismiss the case "with prejudice."

b. Consider one possible disadvantage of the simple dismissal with prejudice: Imagine that the settlement agreement calls for the parties to take some future action, perhaps to assist the employee to gain other employment, or perhaps to continue medical benefits for some period of time. The employer breaches that duty and the former employee wants to enforce it. How does he do so?

    i. The usual answer is that the party seeking to enforce the settlement must sue for breach of contract, the contract in question being the settlement agreement. That suit must take its place at the back of the line of pending litigation: It gets no special attention by virtue of being a suit to enforce a settlement. Indeed, in federal court it may suffer a disadvantage. Jane Smart's original suit, for employment discrimination, could invoke federal question jurisdiction. But the suit to enforce the settlement contract does not arise under federal law, so the employee can invoke federal jurisdiction only if there is diversity between her and her employer and the amount in controversy is satisfied—probably not the case if only a continuation of medical benefits are at stake. See Langley v. Jackson State University, 14 F.3d 1070 (5th Cir. 1994) (no federal jurisdiction to enforce settlement of federal civil rights claims).

    ii. If one anticipates that problem, there is a solution. Suppose the obligation to pay medical benefits had been embodied in a judgment—usually called a "consent decree," decree because it is a court order; consent because it embodies the parties' consented-to settlement—in those circumstances either party can invoke the court's jurisdiction to enforce its own judgments. The order of dismissal can also include a provision whereby the court "retains jurisdiction" over disputes concerning the terms of the settlement agreement.

8. We have thus far assumed that settlement will end a lawsuit. That's not always so. Recent years have seen the growth of creative forms of settlement, including some that have the effect not of avoiding but of guaranteeing trial. Consider some examples.

    a. The parties can agree—stipulate—to liability, but contest damages, leaving them to be tried. Why would a defendant do that? Consider the facts surrounding the wreck of the Exxon *Valdez*, an oil supertanker that ran aground in Alaskan waters, polluting miles of shoreline and ocean. The captain of the vessel was shown to be drunk in his cabin during the critical time when course should have been changed through the tricky channel; worse, there was evidence suggesting that the defendant knew of the captain's alcoholism but continued to employ him. Why might Exxon want to have a jury consider only the amount of damages and not the circumstances leading to the accident?

    b. Alternatively, the parties can do the opposite, stipulate to damages, trying only the question of liability. Suppose plaintiff is severely injured in an auto accident, but liability is hotly contested. The parties might enter into a "high-low" agreement, in which defendant promises to pay a minimum amount (say $250,000) to plaintiff even if the jury returns a defense verdict. In return, plaintiff agrees that he will accept, say, $750,000 (substantially less than the full cost of lifetime care) if the jury returns a plaintiff's verdict. Explain what each party is gaining from that settlement.

WHAT'S NEW HERE?

- As settlement forms become increasingly complex, this aspect of litigation practice begins to merge with transactional practice—the work done by lawyers who mostly work with "deals" rather than lawsuits.
- As settlement forms become increasingly complex, lawyers need to explain to clients what former risks are being controlled and which new ones are emerging. To take an example from Note 8b above, the high-low agreement eliminates the risk that plaintiff will recover nothing, but incurs a new risk—that of forgoing a jury verdict far higher than the $750,000 maximum called for in the agreement. The defendant is trading equivalent risks.

b. Third-Party Participation in Settlement: Facilitation, Encouragement, and Coercion

Settlement negotiations sometimes fail. Broadly speaking, one can trace the failure of negotiations to two causes: divergent estimates of the case's value and bad communication. In *Smart v. GrowCo*, perhaps either Smart or her lawyer misjudges the likely reaction of a jury to her story and therefore rejects GrowCo's offer. Or GrowCo's general counsel makes no offer, perhaps because he is determined to show the board of directors that he is a strong executive, or to accede to the demands of Senior Scientist who threatens otherwise to quit. Alternatively, the parties may have similar guesses about the outcome of litigation but may not be communicating clearly, perhaps because the parties or their lawyers have taken a dislike to one another. Any of these circumstances can lead to the collapse of negotiations.

Sometimes, however, negotiations that would otherwise fail can succeed if the parties have help. Help comes in several forms, depending on the nature of the problem and the source of help. If the problem is communication, someone who can facilitate those communications may be able to help. Generically, such facilitators are called mediators. What does a mediator do? One vision of "mediation" is as assisted negotiation, an aid in overcoming barriers to agreement.

Another way to describe a mediator's role is to frame it entirely in terms of process: The mediator seeks to engage the parties in a structured set of discussions leading to agreement. Because the goal is an agreement of the parties, the mediator does not rule on the rights and wrongs of the dispute or tell the parties what to do. The mediator's limited role is a function of the fact that she has no coercive power: The mediator succeeds only if the parties agree. A mediator typically talks with the parties (sometimes together, sometimes individually, sometimes both), to ferret out areas of agreement and possible starting points for negotiation, to discover the respective parties' goals, and to suggest ways to accommodate these goals. The success of mediation depends partly on the level of trust the mediator is able to establish and partly on the distance separating the parties' goals.

In recent decades, a cadre of professional mediators—many with legal training—has emerged, who offer their services to parties for a fee. Courts and legislatures have shown significant interest in the power of mediation to achieve settlements, and in some cases have established what sounds like a contradiction: mandatory mediation. Some states require cases to be submitted to mediation before they will set a trial date. In federal law the Alternative Dispute Resolution Act of 1998, 28 U.S.C. §§651 et seq., requires each federal district court to "authorize[], . . . devise, and implement its own alternative dispute resolution program." 28 U.S.C. §651(b). The statute's goal becomes clear from a section instructing district courts to adopt a local rule that "require[s] litigants in all civil cases to consider the use of an alternative dispute resolution process at an appropriate state in the litigation" and to "provide litigants in all civil cases with at least one alternative dispute resolution process. . . ." The statute goes on to require training of "neutrals" to help the parties come to agreement.

Family law—divorce, support, and custody disputes—has been a frequent target for these efforts. In one view, the popularity of mediation in this context reflects the fact that some family conflicts by their nature are ideal for mediation; in another view, it is said to reflect the low importance attached to these cases by some judges and lawyers. Bear in mind, too, that some efforts described as mediation would be more accurately described as settlements arrived at under heavy pressure, in which the mediator threatens to report to the judge that one or another party is behaving unreasonably (sometimes called "muscle mediation," and which is prohibited by some court rules and statutes).

Notes and Problems

1. Imagine that in *Smart v. GrowCo* the two parties, unsure whether to settle, have chosen a mediator, or that a court has assigned one.

   a. To begin work, what would the mediator want to know from the parties?

   b. Some mediators might proceed by asking the parties how much (or how little) they would accept to settle the claim. Such mediation is sometimes called "positional" and treats settlement as a pie to be divided, in which anything gained by one party is lost by the other. Such mediators can be useful if the parties have engaged in significant bluffing, failing to disclose their true settlement positions.

   c. Other mediators will proceed by trying to discover the parties' goals, defining these less in monetary than in other terms. This approach is sometimes called "interest-based" mediation. Suppose, for example, the mediator learns from Jane Smart that she is primarily interested in coming away from this dispute with a clean reference that will enable her to find another job and the dignity of not having been fired for cause. GrowCo, on the other hand, wants to be able to recruit future plant botanists and to continue to attract the interest of investors. Can you think of settlement agreements that would achieve both goals?

2. How should a lawyer conduct herself in mediation? Some approach it like a case—presenting facts and arguments. Many mediators, particularly those employing interest-based mediation (see Note 1c above) resist this, asking lawyers and parties to focus on goals and desired outcomes, not facts and rights.

3. In the course of mediation a party or lawyer makes a statement of fact. If the mediation fails, can the other side later introduce the statement in evidence? Probably not. Mediation agreements and evidentiary rules typically protect such statements from disclosure.

4. How and when should a judge assigned to a case act as a mediator?

   a. One might take the view that they never should—that judges should be adjudicators, and should leave any settlement to the parties or to figures like court-appointed mediators.

   b. Whatever the merits of such a view, current procedural law does not support it. Two bodies of law allow a judge to actively manage litigation, personally and through delegates. Rule 16(a)(5) establishes "facilitating settlement" as one of the goals of pretrial conferences. Rule 16(c) contains a shopping list of management techniques ranging from establishing time limits to encouraging settlement. The Alternative Dispute Resolution Act of 1998, 28 U.S.C. §§651 et seq., requires federal judicial districts to offer the parties, even after they have filed a suit, alternatives to litigation, such as mediation or nonbinding arbitration (described below).

   c. The Act references "early neutral evaluation" as one possible approach. 28 U.S.C. §651(a). Early neutral evaluation embodies a simple idea: Parties tend to have excessively optimistic evaluations of their cases; presenting one's case briefly to a neutral party who assesses its strengths and weaknesses will lead to a more realistic negotiating position. Such evaluators are typically volunteer lawyers or magistrate judges not otherwise involved in the case. By listening to the parties' presentations, they offer each a reality check, enabling each party to see its own case's weaknesses and its adversary's strengths. Notice that with neutral evaluation we are moving away from the world of mediation and toward a sneak preview of litigation.

   d. Another variation is the "summary jury trial" as a settlement device. Summary jury trials are not real trials at all. Instead, lawyers present their cases to a mock "jury" in very abbreviated form (usually narrating what the evidence will show rather than calling actual witnesses). The "jury" is charged, deliberates, and returns its verdict, which, however, is not binding. Instead, the verdict serves as a reality check: The plaintiff who thought his case was worth $250,000 discovers the "jury" was willing to award only $50,000; the defendant who thought she would win a defense verdict finds herself stung by significant damages. The hope underlying all these processes is that actually "losing" a low-cost version of the case (or winning less than was hoped for) may cause the parties to settle.

c. Contracting for Confidentiality

Defendants and plaintiffs sometimes share the goal that any settlement be confidential. Consider again our hypothetical case, *Smart v. GrowCo*. Suppose that Smart files her unlawful discharge action, and GrowCo counterclaims for an injunction forbidding Smart from disclosing any trade secrets. As in many such cases, discovery yields information that makes both sides unhappy. Depositions suggest that Senior Scientist has exhibited behavior toward a number of women that may look quite bad to a jury and that might make it hard to recruit future plant geneticists. Depositions and documents also suggest that Smart, in addition to great talent and skill in plant genetics, has unorthodox work habits and a very free hand with expense accounts that may not endear her to future employers. In addition, there is the matter of the disputed patents and trade secrets. In such a case, both parties might desire some measure of confidentiality concerning both the information unearthed during discovery and the ultimate resolution of the case.

Most commonly, confidentiality agreements seek to bar specific information or documents from public exposure. Can the parties do this—and with what limits?

Notes and Problems

---

1. Consider how a confidentiality agreement might add value to the settlement.

   a. A confidentiality agreement could certainly add value for Jane Smart. Smart would probably like not to publicize the fact that she sued her former employer, for fear that it would cause some prospective employer not to hire her. Although the fact that she filed a suit will always be a matter of public record, a confidentiality agreement can prevent GrowCo from revealing it. Absent such a revelation, only a diligent employer who searched court records would learn about the suit. Return of the documents and records might also prevent others from learning the facts revealed by discovery—such as Smart's unorthodox work habits and expense account use. Discovery requests and responses and depositions are not filed with the court unless included as part of a motion. See Rule 5(d)(1). Therefore, a persistent and diligent employer who searches court records could only learn such facts if they were included in a motion filed with the court.

b. A confidentiality agreement would also add value for GrowCo. The company would be concerned about maintaining confidentiality of any non-patented trade secrets (patents themselves are public records but there are often related unpatented processes). GrowCo would also want to prevent others from learning about certain facts revealed by discovery, such as the sexist behavior of Senior Scientist. Finally, GrowCo wants to discourage other terminated employees from filing suit, and therefore has an interest in maintaining confidential the amount of money it paid to settle Smart's claims.

c. Notice, however, that on these facts, protecting Smart's and GrowCo's interests may impose burdens on others. Suppose there is a group of scientists working for GrowCo who have been subjected to similar behavior by Senior Scientist. They have not brought suit in part because they suspect that no one will believe them. If they knew that Smart had successfully asserted such a claim, they might be emboldened to assert similar claims. How should the law deal with such "collateral damage" from confidential settlements?

2. At a technical level, how might a settlement agreement be drafted to maintain confidentiality? Suppose that one of the parties' lawyers, rummaging in his files, finds the following example and fills in the names of the present parties. He gives it to you for review, asking whether it will fulfill the clients' expectations:

> 7. *Return of Documents.* Both parties agree to return all originals and copies of all documents and data, obtained from Jane Smart or GrowCo, directly or indirectly, at any time, by either party, or any agent, attorney, representative, or anyone else acting or purporting to act on his or her behalf. Insofar as they apply to Jane Smart, the obligations of this Paragraph 7 are cumulative to other existing obligations that Smart has as a result of her employment with GrowCo.

> 8. *Confidentiality.*

> 8.1. Parties and their attorneys, and each of them, expressly agree that this Agreement and the terms and conditions of this Settlement are confidential, and agree not to disclose, publicize, or cause to be disclosed or publicized the fact of settlement or any of the terms or conditions of this Agreement, including but not limited to the amounts received pursuant to Paragraph 1 of this Agreement, except as required by judicial process, or as otherwise required by law. Notwithstanding the foregoing, it is hereby expressly understood and agreed that the parties and their attorneys may need to disseminate certain information concerning the settlement to their accountants, auditors, attorneys, and/or other entities as necessary in the regular course of business. While such disclosures are expressly permitted under the terms of this Agreement, parties and their attorneys shall insure that information deemed confidential under this Agreement is treated as confidential by the recipients thereof. Except as required by judicial process, or as otherwise required by law, if any of the parties or their attorneys or any recipient of information from parties or

their attorneys concerning the Settlement is asked about the disposition of the action, such Party, attorney, or recipient shall state the following in substance: "I am not at liberty to discuss it."

8.2. Each disclosure by Parties or their attorneys or by any recipient of information from Plaintiff or their attorneys concerning this Settlement other than a disclosure expressly permitted by subparagraph 8.1 shall be considered a material breach of this Agreement. For each such breach of the confidentiality provision set forth in subparagraph 8.1, the Party who breaches such confidentiality provision shall be solely liable to the other Party for Twenty-Five Thousand Dollars ($25,000.00) in liquidated damages. Parties, and each of them, agree that said sum represents a reasonable estimate of the actual damages which would be suffered by [Party's Name] as a result of a violation of subparagraph 8.1 and that this sum is not punitive in any way. In the event a Party is required to file suit or otherwise seek judicial enforcement of its rights under this paragraph 8, the Party who breaches such confidentiality provision shall be solely liable for attorneys' fees and costs incurred as a result thereof.

3. Consider the features of this agreement.

   a. The agreement imposes two different obligations on the parties: to return all documents exchanged during the course of litigation, and to not disclose the terms of the settlement or confidentiality agreement. What is each obligation intended to achieve?

   b. Why the liquidated damages provision? How would one enforce such an agreement were there not a liquidated damages clause? One would have to show not only breach of the agreement but also prove damages, and damages may be difficult to establish for the disclosure of confidential information. (Note, though, that under contract law an unreasonable estimate of liquidated damages may void the whole clause.)

4. As matters now stand, such contractual confidentiality agreements are generally enforceable, but what exactly do they protect against? At a minimum, they would prohibit the plaintiff from holding a news conference to announce the terms of the settlement. What could defendant do if, after entering into such a settlement, plaintiff took such an action?

5. Why did the lawyer who drafted the agreement quoted above create an exception for disclosures "as required by judicial process, or as otherwise required by law"? Suppose that one of GrowCo's competitors sues it for abusive deployment of one of its patents—behavior thought by some to violate the antitrust laws. In the course of that lawsuit, the competitor seeks to depose Jane Smart about her lawsuit and the patent dispute she had with GrowCo. Assume that a court rules that GrowCo's treatment of Smart's patent claims is relevant to show a pattern of abusive use of patents. Can Smart refuse to answer on grounds of her confidentiality agreement? Can GrowCo get a court order to prevent Competitor from taking Smart's deposition? Respond after reading the next case, which exemplifies the courts' approach to such agreements when the underlying facts become relevant in a subsequent case.

Kalinauskas v. Wong

151 F.R.D. 363 (D. Nev. 1993)

JOHNSTON, M.J.

This matter was submitted to the undersigned Magistrate Judge on a Motion for a Protective Order filed by defendant Desert Palace, Inc., doing business as Caesars Palace Hotel & Casino (Caesars). . . .

The plaintiff, Ms. Lin T. Kalinauskas (Kalinauskas), a former employee of Caesars, has sued Caesars for sexual discrimination in the instant case. As part of discovery Kalinauskas seeks to depose Donna R. Thomas, a former Caesars employee who filed a sexual harassment suit against Caesars last year. Ms. Thomas's suit settled without trial pursuant to a confidential settlement agreement[,] which the court sealed upon the stipulated agreement of the parties.

This court has examined, in camera, sealed materials relating to Ms. Thomas's case and settlement. The in camera submission included: Stipulation for & Order for Dismissal, Protective Order and Confidentiality Order, Stipulation for Protective Order and Confidentiality Order, and Settlement Agreement. [The Stipulation for a Protective Order provided] that the plaintiff "shall not discuss any aspect of plaintiff's employment at Caesars other than to state the dates of her employment and her job title." Identical language appears in the Protective Order and Confidentiality Order. . . .

Discussion

In general, the scope of discovery is very broad. "Parties may obtain discovery regarding *any [unprivileged matter that is relevant to any party's claim or defense*]*" Fed. R. Civ. P. 26(b)(1) (emphasis added). The primary goal of the court and discovery is "to secure the just, speedy, and inexpensive determination of every action." Fed. R. Civ. P. 1.

The public interest favors judicial policies which promote the completion of litigation. Public interest also seeks to protect the finality of prior suits and the secrecy of settlements when desired by the settling parties. However, the courts also serve society by providing a public forum for issues of general concern. The case at bar presents a direct conflict between these crucial public and private interests.

To allow full discovery into all aspects of Ms. Thomas's case could discourage similar settlements. Confidential settlements benefit society and the parties involved by resolving disputes relatively quickly, with slight judicial intervention, and presumably result in greater satisfaction to the parties. Sound judicial policy fosters and protects this form of alternative dispute resolution. See, e.g., Fed. R. Evid. 408 which protects compromises and offers to compromise by rendering them inadmissible to prove liability. The secrecy of a settlement agreement and the contractual rights of the parties thereunder deserve court protection.

---

* [At the time of the decision in *Kalinauskas* the text of Rule 26(b)(1) read: "Parties may obtain discovery regarding any matter, not privileged, which is relevant to the subject matter involved in the pending action."—EDS.]

On the other hand, to prevent any discovery into Ms. Thomas's case based upon the settlement agreement results in disturbing consequences. First, as pointed out by Kalinauskas, preventing the deposition of Ms. Thomas would condone the practice of "buy[ing] the silence of a witness with a settlement agreement." This court harbors little doubt that preventing the dissemination of the underlying facts which prompted Ms. Thomas to file suit is in Caesars's interest, and formed an important part of the agreement to Caesars. Caesars avers that without the confidentiality order the *Thomas* case would not have settled. Yet despite this freedom to contract, the courts must carefully police the circumstances under which litigants seek to protect their interests while concealing legitimate areas of public concern. This concern grows more pressing as additional individuals are harmed by identical or similar action.

Second, the deposition of Ms. Thomas is likely to lead to relevant evidence. Preventing the deposition of Ms. Thomas or the discovery of documents created in her case could lead to wasteful efforts to generate discovery already in existence. . . .

Caesars['s] motion for a protective order preventing the deposition of Ms. Thomas rests entirely upon the confidential settlement agreement. Caesars . . . maintains that it should be able to rely upon the confidentiality order to protect against [disclosure to] third parties, unless extraordinary circumstances or compelling need justifies some breach of secrecy. . . .

[Caesars's] argument that Kalinauskas must show a compelling need to obtain discovery applies to discovery of the specific terms of the settlement agreement (i.e., the amount and conditions of the agreement), not [to] factual information surrounding Thomas's case. Caesars should not be able to conceal basic facts of concern to Kalinauskas in her case, and of legitimate public concern, regarding employment at its place of business.

Accordingly, keeping in mind the liberal nature of discovery, this court will allow the deposition of Ms. Thomas. . . . The deposition of Ms. Thomas and any further discovery into the Thomas case must not, however, disclose any substantive terms of the Caesars-Thomas settlement agreement. Naturally, Ms. Thomas may answer questions regarding her employment at Caesars and any knowledge of sexual harassment.

Although the terms of the confidential settlement agreement impose penalties upon Ms. Thomas for discussing her past employment at Caesars, those penalties shall not apply to the disclosure of information for discovery purposes in furtherance of Kalinauskas's case. Indeed, the settlement agreement itself makes exception for court ordered release of information.

While settlement is an important objective, an overzealous quest for alternative dispute resolution can distort the proper role of the court. Furthermore, settlement agreements which suppress evidence violate the greater public policy. . . .

Based on the foregoing . . . IT IS HEREBY ORDERED . . . that the Defendant's Motion for Protective Order is granted to the extent that during the deposition of Ms. Donna R. Thomas, no information regarding the settlement agreement itself shall come forth [and] that the Defendant's Motion for Protective Order is denied as to all other requests. . . .

WHAT'S NEW HERE?

- Confidentiality agreements seek to control parties' future actions—what they can say about the lawsuit that the agreement ends.
- Confidentiality agreements can require parties to keep confidential information about the terms of a settlement.
- But, as much as parties might wish otherwise, confidentiality agreements cannot prevent a witness from testifying about past events that are relevant to another lawsuit.

Notes and Problems

1. See the case as a strategic dance.

   a. What did Kalinauskas's lawyer want to do?

   b. How did defendant's lawyer try to stop her?

2. How did the confidentiality-enforcing mechanism in the *Thomas v. Caesars* litigation (the case whose confidential settlement is discussed in *Kalinauskas*) differ from those in the sample confidentiality agreement quoted in the preceding section?

   a. What did the parties do that went beyond a contract to maintain confidentiality regarding the terms of the settlement?

   b. Why did the parties in the *Thomas* litigation seek a protective order? What were they trying to protect from disclosure?

   c. Explain how the outcome in *Kalinauskas* compares with the results under the work product doctrine. Under that doctrine, announced in *Hickman v. Taylor* (supra page 495) and codified in Rule 26(b)(3), a lawyer is protected against disclosure in discovery of information generated by the litigation process itself but not against disclosure of underlying historical facts. Does the ruling in *Kalinauskas* achieve the same result?

3. Apply the *Kalinauskas* ruling to Jane Smart's case. Suppose that while Smart's case is pending she learns through the grapevine that GrowCo has been sued on several former occasions for behavior by Senior Scientist similar to what she alleges—and that they have all settled with agreements like the one in *Kalinauskas*.

   a. Imagine one former employee who sued GrowCo and settled—Sonia Settle—learns of Smart's case. Can Settle approach Smart and her lawyer and tell them about what happened to her?

b.   Suppose Settle does not come forward, but Smart learns about Settle's case through the office grapevine. Can Smart depose Settle? What questions can she ask?

Procedure as Strategy

Understanding cases like *Kalinauskas* opens the door to understanding the larger debate about confidentiality agreements. Why do defendants want them? What do they hope to get from them? And are they good or bad as a matter of public policy?

We now know from *Kalinauskas* and cases like it that a confidentiality agreement or a sealed record cannot "buy silence": Witnesses with relevant information about the underlying facts of a case can testify about those facts regardless of confidentiality agreements. An agreement that tried to forbid such testimony would almost certainly be struck down as a violation of public policy.

Caesars might still stand to gain a great deal through a confidentiality agreement, though. Suppose there are several prospective plaintiffs allegedly harmed by the same actions of defendant—for example, if the same supervisor at Caesars Palace had harassed several other employees. By barring Ms. Thomas from talking about her settlement, Caesars might hope that the settlement might not encourage similarly situated employees to sue. But ordinary workplace gossip occurring well before the confidentiality agreement would likely alert others that Ms. Thomas had sued—indeed her lawyer might well ask her to spread the word in order to elicit others' stories of harassment.

Caesars might also believe that the confidentiality agreement would make it more difficult for other plaintiffs to benefit from the *Thomas* litigation. Suppose there was no confidentiality agreement or sealed record in *Thomas*. A new plaintiff with a similar claim might simply call Ms. Thomas's lawyer and request the discovery exchanged in her case to save the cost and trouble of doing her own investigation and discovery. The confidentiality agreement requires future plaintiffs to absorb the full costs of investigation and discovery.

Plaintiffs' lawyers are of two minds about confidentiality agreements. In any given case, accepting a confidentiality agreement may be the key to settlement, or may result in the client getting more money, sometimes referred to as a "confidentiality premium." On the other hand, confidentiality agreements and sealed discovery may delay public knowledge of dangerous or unlawful situations, or repeated bad behavior by the same defendant. Suppose a defendant repeatedly dumps toxic chemicals into a residential area, or engages in serial harassment. Even if some plaintiffs come forward, settlements requiring confidentiality and sealed discovery prevent the knowledge about these harms from spreading quickly. Arguably, courts should not be in the business of abetting such concealment. Moreover, if discovery in prior cases is available, it will reduce the expense of subsequent, similar lawsuits—a desirable outcome if such suits will force a defendant to change unlawful practices. Some states have captured this idea in legislation; in Washington, a statute declares that the public has a right to information from products liability or hazardous substance cases "necessary for a lay member of the public to understand the nature, source, and extent of the risk from alleged hazards" and requires a court considering a protective order to weigh that public interest. Wash. Rev. Code Ann. §4.24.611(1)(c)(2). Should a statute similarly mandate transparency in sexual harassment cases?

2. Contracting for Private Adjudication: Arbitration and Its Variants

a. The Idea and Practice of Arbitration

Parties can enter into contracts to settle lawsuits, and they can employ mediators to help them reach such settlements. But what if the parties cannot agree, even with the help of a mediator, or can agree only that they want to have their disputes decided by a third party. Is their only choice to resort to the courts? No. Arbitration is one of the oldest and best-established alternatives to litigating in court. Unlike a mediator, an arbitrator decides a dispute after having heard from both sides. Arbitration, in other words, closely resembles adjudication—private, nonjudicial adjudication, but still adjudication.

Why, if it is so much like adjudication, do the parties not simply proceed through the court system? Sometimes the reasons are purely practical; for example, the parties may be able to arrange hearing dates and locations that are more convenient for counsel and witnesses. But arbitration can have more fundamental differences—differences that, depending on the case, may advantage one party and disadvantage the other:

- Unlike court adjudication, binding arbitration results in an award that is essentially final and not subject to further challenge, with very limited exceptions, such as proof that the arbitrator was corrupt or the agreement to arbitrate was unconscionable. The absence of appeal prevents the case from dragging on, but may also protect from reversal an arbitrary, unfair result.
- Parties can choose the arbitrator. The choice may simply be someone who has a reputation for being fair and reasonable. Or, the parties may arrange that the arbitrator will be someone who is experienced in the subject matter of the dispute (be it medical malpractice, engineering, or securities) in the expectation that this will produce a fairer result than could be obtained before even a highly qualified, but generalist, judge or a lay jury. Again, this might be viewed as a disadvantage to a party whose case contravenes conventional wisdom in that subject area, or a party whose case is long on emotion but short on the facts and the law.
- Arbitration permits the parties to determine what substantive rules apply— they can insist, for example, that the arbitrator will not refer to the ordinary rules of contract but instead will adhere to the traditions that have developed

around this particular commercial relationship. As a result, the arbitrator, though deciding the dispute, may decide it more "softly" than a court:

> It is said of the American commercial arbitrator that he may "do justice as he sees it, applying his own sense of the law and equity to the facts as he finds them to be and making an award reflecting the spirit rather than the letter of the agreement." Many awards resulting from such proceedings might also be described as Solomonic, halving the objects in dispute.
>
> Paul Carrington & Paul Haagen, *Contract and Jurisdiction*, 1996 Sup. Ct. Rev. 331, 345, quoting Silverman v. Benmor Coats, 61 N.Y.2d 299 (1984).

- Parties can also dictate which procedural rules apply in the arbitration. Sometimes that results in processes that are scarcely distinguishable from judicial adjudication—full discovery followed by a hearing that looks very much like a trial. In other cases, the parties may agree to depart dramatically from legal process (*Ferguson v. Writer's Guild of America, West*, infra page 567, is an example). As you will see in *Epic Systems*, infra page 559, a current issue in arbitration agreements is the extent to which the parties may contract out of class actions and class arbitrations.
- Arbitration *can* be less expensive than adjudication. The parties can take several steps that may make the process cheaper: dispensing with, or substantially curtailing, the rules of discovery; agreeing that most (or all) witnesses can testify by affidavit rather than in person; truncating the hearing through agreed-upon time limits. The one service that is usually more expensive in arbitration is the time of the arbitrator. Taxpayers pay the salaries of judges; the construction and upkeep of the courthouse are also expenses largely borne by taxpayers. Arbitrators, in contrast, charge by the hour—often at rates in excess of those charged by attorneys. And one common form of arbitration uses three arbitrators (one chosen by each party, with the third chosen by the first two); in such a case each day of arbitration can cost $10,000—just for the arbitrators.
- Arbitration is more confidential than ordinary adjudication. The public, including the press, normally have the right to attend judicial proceedings. Unless protected by judicial order, documents filed in court and transcripts of judicial proceedings are normally public records. In contrast, arbitration hearings are normally not open to the public, and the parties can even agree that the outcome of the arbitration be kept private.
- Arbitration may avoid the vagaries in outcome that a jury may introduce, although one has to be careful here: If a jury acts in a lawless way, its verdict is subject to reversal, while arbitration "awards" are not subject to judicial review except for the most extreme reasons.

Agreements to arbitrate can occur at several points in a dispute. Sometimes they come after the parties have already begun litigation. A post-dispute agreement to arbitrate is uncontroversially enforceable—a party cannot commence arbitration and then back out.

But arbitration agreements often come long before any dispute, much less a lawsuit, has arisen. In recent years, an increasing number of organizations have included arbitration provisions in their contracts for a wide range of products and services: employment, credit cards, cell phones, medical care, financial services, and software—to name just a few. Judicial attitudes toward enforcement of pre-dispute arbitration agreements have undergone a swing historically, and the pendulum appears still to be moving. In the nineteenth and early twentieth centuries, some courts refused to enforce pre-dispute arbitration agreements under any circumstances. By case law and statute, however, the rule has generally been changed in favor of their enforcement. For example, the U.S. Supreme Court, which once viewed with suspicion the arbitration of claims arising under federal statutes, has enforced agreements to arbitrate many kinds of statutory claims—for example, antitrust claims, securities law claims and, most recently, employment discrimination claims—so long as the arbitration procedure does not effectively prevent the claimant from vindicating her statutory rights.

Some of these arbitration agreements arise in situations where one party essentially dictates the terms of the contract (including the terms of the arbitration agreement) to the other party on a "take-it-or-leave-it" basis. The employer, for example, makes acceptance of an employer-drafted arbitration agreement a condition of employment. In recent years, courts have looked more closely at the fairness of the arbitration process before enforcing an arbitration agreement in such contexts.

b. *Federalism and Arbitration: Herein of Preemption*

To understand the framework for courts' scrutiny of arbitration agreements, one has to understand the relation of state and federal law in this area: Very roughly speaking, federal law declares the general enforceability of agreements to arbitrate, but allows state law to set some limits on those agreements. Inside those boundaries, states are allowed to regulate arbitration, but if they step over those boundaries, federal law displaces ("preempts" in lawyer-talk) that of the states.

The Federal Arbitration Act (FAA), 9 U.S.C. §§2 et seq., enacted in 1925 to counter judicial hostility to pre-dispute arbitration agreements, has three basic sections.

- Section 2 consists of substantive law, broadly declaring agreements to arbitrate valid as a matter of federal law: "A written provision in any . . . contract evidencing a transaction involving commerce to settle by arbitration a controversy thereafter arising out of such contract or transaction . . . shall be valid, irrevocable, and enforceable, save upon such grounds as exist at law or in equity for the revocation of any contract." This section has been held to be binding on both federal and state courts, so that a state legislature or court may not, for example, declare that arbitration clauses in employment contracts are unenforceable under any circumstances. And the "involving commerce" provision has been given an expansive definition.

- Section 3 tells the courts what to do if a party, in spite of an arbitration agreement, instead files a lawsuit: "If any suit or proceeding be brought in any of the courts of the United States upon any issue referable to arbitration . . . , the court in which such suit is pending . . . shall on application of one of the parties stay the trial of the action until such arbitration [occurs], providing the applicant for the stay is not in default in proceeding with such arbitration."

- Section 4 tells the federal courts what to do if a party neither invokes arbitration nor files suit: "A party aggrieved by the alleged failure, neglect, or refusal of another to arbitrate under a written agreement for arbitration may petition any United States district court which, save for such agreement, would have jurisdiction under Title 28 . . . , for an order directing that such arbitration proceed in the manner provided for in such agreement."

That structure provides a roadmap for a party seeking an order to enforce an arbitration agreement, but it leaves out one ingredient that will doubtless have occurred to the civil procedure student—the ordering court's jurisdiction.

> The Arbitration Act is something of an anomaly in the field of federal-court jurisdiction. It creates a body of federal substantive law establishing and regulating the duty to honor an agreement to arbitrate, yet it does not create any independent federal-question jurisdiction under 28 U.S.C. §1331 or otherwise. Section 4 provides for an order compelling arbitration only when the federal district court would have jurisdiction over a suit on the underlying dispute; hence, there must be diversity of citizenship or some other independent basis for federal jurisdiction before the order can issue. Section 3 likewise limits the federal courts to the extent that a federal court cannot stay a suit pending before it unless there is such a suit in existence. Nevertheless, although enforcement of the Act is left in large part to the state courts, it nevertheless represents federal policy to be vindicated by the federal courts where otherwise appropriate.
>
> Moses H. Cone Memorial Hosp. v. Mercury Constr. Corp.,
> 460 U.S. 1, 24 (1983).

The Supreme Court has also made clear that state courts are bound to enforce this national policy in favor of enforcement of arbitration agreements. Demonstrating that it meant what it said, the Court has required state courts to enforce arbitration agreements even when they contravene state law if the underlying transaction involves commerce. In such situations the Court has said that the Arbitration Act, not state law, controls and that the states are bound to enforce the Act and permit arbitration to proceed.

Over the near-century since the passage of the Federal Arbitration Act, the Supreme Court has interpreted it to apply to a widening range of cases—not just business-to-business contract disputes that were likely at the front of Congress's mind when the Act was adopted, but to a variety of other claims, including those arising under federal securities laws, antitrust laws, employment discrimination claims, and more. As a result, some claims that once would have been triable to a jury and subject to appellate review have become subject to arbitration.

In many of these types of cases, agreements to arbitrate were not negotiated by both parties to the agreement—instead, they were provisions in standard consumer and employment contracts that were drafted by companies with limited or no opportunity for negotiation by the consumer or employee. Consumers and employees subject to these arbitration agreements have repeatedly challenged them as unenforceable; in recent years federal courts have often rejected those challenges.

When, under §2 of the Arbitration Act, could an agreement to arbitrate be unenforceable? Only, says the Act, on a ground that would apply to all contracts, not just contracts to arbitrate. Thus if I sign an agreement to arbitrate only because of a threat of violence, it—like all contracts entered under duress—is unenforceable. The portion of general contracts doctrine most frequently deployed to challenge arbitration clauses is unconscionability. Indeed, some claim that recent unconscionability decisions around the country arise almost entirely from arbitration contexts. Consider just one example, where a federal court applied a state's law of unconscionability to strike down an arbitration agreement.

Ferguson v. Countrywide Credit Industries, Inc.

298 F.3d 778 (9th Cir. 2002)

Pregerson, J.

Misty Ferguson filed a complaint against Countrywide Credit Industries, Inc. and her supervisor, Leo DeLeon, alleging causes of action under federal and state law for sexual harassment, retaliation, and hostile work environment. Countrywide filed a petition for an order compelling arbitration of Ferguson's claims. The district court denied Countrywide's petition on the grounds that Countrywide's arbitration agreement is unenforceable based on the doctrine of unconscionability.

I. Factual and Procedural History

When Ferguson was hired she was required to sign Countrywide's Conditions of Employment, which states in relevant part: "I understand that in order to work at Countrywide I must execute an arbitration agreement."

The district court denied Countrywide's petition to compel arbitration. It ruled that the arbitration agreement is unenforceable because it is unconscionable under Armendariz v. Foundation Health Psychcare Services, Inc., 24 Cal. 4th 83 (2000).

II. Unconscionability

The FAA compels judicial enforcement of a wide range of written arbitration agreements. Section 2 of the FAA provides, in relevant part, that arbitration agreements "shall be valid, irrevocable, and enforceable, save upon such grounds that exist at law or in equity for the revocation of any contract." 9 U.S.C. §2. In determining the validity of an agreement to arbitrate, federal courts "should apply ordinary state-law principles that govern the formation of contracts." First Options of Chicago,

Inc. v. Kaplan, 514 U.S. 938, 944 (1995). "Thus, generally applicable defenses, such as unconscionability, may be applied to invalidate arbitration agreements without contravening the FAA." Doctor's Assocs., Inc. v. Casarotto, 517 U.S. 681, 687 (1996). California courts may invalidate an arbitration clause under the doctrine of unconscionability. This doctrine, codified by the California Legislature in California Civil Code 1670.5(a), provides:

> if the court as a matter of law finds the contract or any clause of the contract to have been unconscionable at the time it was made, the court may refuse to enforce the contract, or may enforce the remainder of the contract without the unconscionable clause, or it may so limit the application of any unconscionable clause as to avoid any unconscionable result.

This statute, however, does not define unconscionability. Instead, we look to the California Supreme Court's decision in *Armendariz*, which provides the definitive pronouncement of California law on unconscionability to be applied to mandatory arbitration agreements, such as the one at issue in this case. In order to render a contract unenforceable under the doctrine of unconscionability, there must be both a procedural and substantive element of unconscionability. These two elements, however, need not both be present in the same degree. Thus, for example, the more substantively oppressive the contract term, the less evidence of procedural unconscionability is required to come to the conclusion that the term is unenforceable.

1. Procedural Unconscionability

Procedural unconscionability concerns the manner in which the contract was negotiated and the circumstances of the parties at that time. A determination of whether a contract is procedurally unconscionable focuses on two factors: oppression and surprise. Oppression arises from an inequality of bargaining power which results in no real negotiation and an absence of meaningful choice. Surprise involves the extent to which the supposedly agreed-upon terms of the bargain are hidden in the prolix printed form drafted by the party seeking to enforce the disputed terms.

In Circuit City Stores, Inc. v. Adams, 279 F.3d 889, 892 (9th Cir.), cert. denied, 535 U.S. 1112 (2002), we held that the arbitration agreement at issue satisfied the elements of procedural unconscionability under California law. We found the agreement to be procedurally unconscionable because Circuit City, which possesses considerably more bargaining power than nearly all of its employees or applicants, drafted the contract and uses it as its standard arbitration agreement for all of its new employees. The agreement is a prerequisite to employment, and job applicants are not permitted to modify the agreement's terms—they must take the contract or leave it.

2. Substantive Unconscionability

Substantive unconscionability focuses on the terms of the agreement and whether those terms are so one-sided as to shock the conscience. Just before oral argument was heard in this case, the California Court of Appeal held in another case that Countrywide's arbitration agreement was unconscionable. See Mercuro v. Superior Court, 96 Cal. App. 4th 167 (2002).

a. One-Sided Coverage of Arbitration Agreement

Countrywide's arbitration agreement specifically covers claims for breach of express or implied contracts or covenants, tort claims, claims of discrimination or harassment based on race, sex, age, or disability, and claims for violation of any federal, state, or other governmental constitution, statute, ordinance, regulation, or public policy. On the other hand, the arbitration agreement specifically excludes claims for workers' compensation or unemployment compensation benefits,[6] injunctive and/or other equitable relief for intellectual property violations, unfair competition and/or the use and/or unauthorized disclosure of trade secrets or confidential information. We adopt the California appellate court's holding in *Mercuro*, that Countrywide's arbitration agreement was unfairly one-sided and, therefore, substantively unconscionable because the agreement "compels arbitration of the claims employees are most likely to bring against Countrywide . . . [but] exempts from arbitration the claims Countrywide is most likely to bring against its employees."

b. Arbitration Fees

In *Armendariz*, the California Supreme Court held that:

> when an employer imposes mandatory arbitration as a condition of employment, the arbitration agreement or arbitration process cannot generally require the employee to bear any type of expense that the employee would not be required to bear if he or she were free to bring the action in court. This rule will ensure that employees bringing [discrimination] claims will not be deterred by costs greater than the usual costs incurred during litigation, costs that are essentially imposed on an employee by the employer.

Countrywide's arbitration agreement has a provision that requires the employee to "pay to NAF [National Arbitration Forum] its filing fee up to a maximum of $125.00 when the Claim is filed. The Company shall pay for the first hearing day. All other arbitration costs shall be shared equally by the Company and the Employee." Countrywide argues that this provision is not so one-sided as to "shock the conscience" and, therefore, is enforceable.

However, *Armendariz* holds that a fee provision is unenforceable when the employee bears any expense beyond the usual costs associated with bringing an

---

6. In *Mercuro*, the court concluded that the inclusion of workers' compensation or unemployment compensation benefits among those claims that are exempt from the arbitration agreement did not "turn what is essentially a unilateral arbitration agreement into a bilateral one." The California court reasoned that both these areas are governed by their own adjudicatory systems rendering them an improper subject matter for arbitration. In its opening brief, Countrywide acknowledges that workers' compensation or unemployment compensation benefits are different and concludes: "The agreement could not encompass these claims as a matter of law."

action in court. NAF imposes multiple fees which would bring the cost of arbitration for Ferguson into the thousands of dollars.[7] . . .

Because the only valid fee provision is one in which an employee is not required to bear any expense beyond what would be required to bring the action in court, we affirm the district court's conclusion that "the original fee provision . . . appears clearly to violate the *Armendariz* standard."

c. One-Sided Discovery Provision

Ferguson also argues that the discovery provision in the arbitration agreement is one-sided and, therefore, unconscionable. The discovery provision states that "a deposition of a corporate representative shall be limited to no more than four designated subjects," but does not impose a similar limitation on depositions of employees. Ferguson also notes that the arbitration agreement sets mutual limitations (e.g., no more than three depositions) and mutual advantages (e.g., unlimited expert witnesses) which favor Countrywide because it is in a superior position to gather information regarding its business practices and employees' conduct, and has greater access to funds to pay for expensive expert witnesses.

Ferguson urges this court to affirm the district court's ruling that the discovery provision is unconscionable on the ground that the limitations and mutual advantages on discovery are unfairly one-sided and have no commercial justification other than "maximizing employer advantage," which is an improper basis for such differences under *Armendariz*. Countrywide argues to the contrary that the arbitration agreement provides for ample discovery by employees.

In *Armendariz*, the California Supreme Court held that employees are "at least entitled to discovery sufficient to adequately arbitrate their statutory claims, including access to essential documents and witnesses." Adequate discovery, however, does not mean unfettered discovery. As *Armendariz* recognized, an arbitration agreement might specify "something less than the full panoply of discovery provided in the California Code of Civil Procedure."

In *Mercuro*, the California Court of Appeals applied the parameters set forth in *Armendariz* to Countrywide's discovery provisions. It concluded that "without evidence showing how these discovery provisions are applied in practice, we are not prepared to say they would not necessarily prevent Mercuro from vindicating his statutory rights." *Mercuro* relied heavily on the ability of the arbitrator to extend the discovery

---

7. Amicus Curiae National Employment Lawyers Association ("NELA") discusses at length the significant forum costs associated with arbitration. Parties to arbitration are often charged two or three thousand dollars per day in arbitration "forum fees," since arbitrators typically charge $300-400 per hour. We are concerned by the significant deterrent effect that such fees will have on employees who are required to arbitrate their civil rights claims. [In a subsequent footnote, the court added: "Our conclusion that Countrywide's fee provision is unconscionable is not affected by the fact that, under Countrywide's arbitration agreement, 'the arbitrator may in his or her discretion permit the prevailing party to recover fees and costs.' As is clear on its face, this provision is *discretionary* and, therefore, there is no guarantee that the prevailing party will, in fact, recover fees. Moreover, the significant up-front costs associated with bringing a claim in an arbitral forum may prevent individuals with meritorious claims from even pursuing these claims in the first place."]

limits for "good cause." In fact, *Mercuro* ultimately left it up to the arbitrator to balance the need for simplicity in arbitration with the discovery necessary for a party to vindicate her claims. Following the Court in *Mercuro*, we too find that Countrywide's discovery provisions may afford Ferguson adequate discovery to vindicate her claims.

Nevertheless, we recognize an insidious pattern in Countrywide's arbitration agreement. Not only do these discovery provisions appear to favor Countrywide at the expense of its employees, but the entire agreement seems drawn to provide Countrywide with undue advantages should an employment-related dispute arise. Aside from merely availing itself of the cost-saving benefits of arbitration, Countrywide has sought to advantage itself substantively by tilting the playing field.

While many of its arbitration provisions appear equally applicable to both parties, these provisions may work to curtail the employee's ability to substantiate any claim against the employer. We follow *Mercuro* in holding that the discovery provisions alone are not unconscionable, but in the context of an arbitration agreement which unduly favors Countrywide at every turn, we find that their inclusion reaffirms our belief that the arbitration agreement as a whole is substantively unconscionable.

Conclusion

The district court's denial of Countrywide's petition to compel arbitration on the ground that Countrywide's arbitration agreement is unenforceable under the doctrine of unconscionability is AFFIRMED.

Notes and Problems

1. Do not assume that *Ferguson*'s outcome—invalidating the arbitration agreement on grounds of unconscionability—is typical. For an almost contemporaneous case upholding the same clause in the same employment contract—applying the Texas rather than the California unconscionability precedents—see Carter v. Countrywide Credit Industries, Inc., 362 F.3d 294 (5th Cir. 2004).

2. What is typical about *Ferguson* is the framework it deploys. Consider first the procedural framework. The *Ferguson* plaintiff contended the arbitration agreement was unenforceable, so she simply filed her lawsuit as if the arbitration agreement didn't exist.

   a. What procedure did the defendants then use to attempt to force the claims into arbitration?
   b. What will happen if the losers persist? If Countrywide appears before an arbitrator in California and wins a default judgment because Ferguson does not appear? California courts would not enforce the arbitration award because the agreement was held unconscionable and therefore unenforceable.

3. Next consider the analytic framework, of "procedural" and "substantive" unconscionability. What do these terms mean as they are revealed in *Ferguson*?

4. Apply this framework to *Smart v. GrowCo*. Suppose that Jane Smart, the botanical geneticist, and GrowCo, the biotechnology firm, entered into an employment contract which contains a provision that "all disputes arising out of this agreement shall be referred to arbitration conducted under the rules of the American Arbitration Association." Suppose GrowCo fires Smart.

   a. Smart brings a state court lawsuit alleging unlawful discharge. If GrowCo wants to arbitrate rather than litigate the suit, it would file a motion in the state court to stay the action pending arbitration. By filing for a stay rather than for a dismissal, the stayed action can become the vehicle for enforcing the arbitrator's award. Seeking a stay rather than a dismissal also takes care of the situation in which there are issues not resolved by the arbitration award.

   b. If Smart has moved away from GrowCo's home state, can GrowCo ask a federal court to enforce the arbitration clause? If Smart is still in GrowCo's state, can it do so? The answer depends on whether there is subject matter jurisdiction in federal court. As noted above, the FAA does not, on its own, grant any party federal court jurisdiction to enforce arbitration agreements. Even if GrowCo cannot invoke federal jurisdiction, however, it can still enforce the FAA in state courts, which are substantively bound by the provisions of the FAA.

   c. Suppose Smart wants to challenge the arbitration clause as unconscionable. What additional factual details—about the clause and the context in which it was agreed to—would you want to know?

5. In *Ferguson v. Countrywide*, the court found that the California law of unconscionability squeezed inside the exceptions clause of the Arbitration Act because it was based on "such grounds as exist at law or in equity for the revocation of any contract." In 2011, the Supreme Court reached the opposite conclusion in *AT&T v. Concepcion*, a 5-4 decision involving a cell phone contract, finding that California law's interpretation of unconscionability was preempted by the FAA. In the next case, the U.S. Supreme Court again came to a similar conclusion in a closely divided case (upholding the arbitration clause against challenge)—this time considering a federal statute rather than state law as a possible escape from arbitration. The majority and dissenting opinions offer good summaries of competing histories of the FAA.

Epic Systems v. Lewis
584 U.S. ___ (2018)

GORSUCH, J., delivered the opinion of the Court.

Should employees and employers be allowed to agree that any disputes between them will be resolved through one-on-one arbitration? Or should employees always be permitted to bring their claims in class or collective actions, no matter what they agreed with their employers?

As a matter of policy these questions are surely debatable. But as a matter of law the answer is clear. In the Federal Arbitration Act, Congress has instructed federal courts to enforce arbitration agreements according to their terms—including terms providing for individualized proceedings. Nor can we agree with the employees' suggestion that the National Labor Relations Act (NLRA) offers a conflicting command. It is this Court's duty to interpret Congress's statutes as a harmonious whole rather than at war with one another. And abiding that duty here leads to an unmistakable conclusion. The NLRA secures to employees rights to organize unions and bargain collectively, but it says nothing about how judges and arbitrators must try legal disputes that leave the workplace and enter the courtroom or arbitral forum. This Court has never read a right to class actions into the NLRA—and for three quarters of a century neither did the National Labor Relations Board. Far from conflicting, the Arbitration Act and the NLRA have long enjoyed separate spheres of influence and neither permits this Court to declare the parties' agreements unlawful.

I

The three cases before us differ in detail but not in substance. Take *Ernst & Young LLP v. Morris*. There Ernst & Young and one of its junior accountants, Stephen Morris, entered into an agreement providing that they would arbitrate any disputes that might arise between them. The agreement stated that the employee could choose the arbitration provider and that the arbitrator could "grant any relief that could be granted by . . . a court" in the relevant jurisdiction. The agreement also specified individualized arbitration, with claims "pertaining to different [e]mployees [to] be heard in separate proceedings."

After his employment ended, and despite having agreed to arbitrate claims against the firm, Mr. Morris sued Ernst & Young in federal court. He alleged that the firm had misclassified its junior accountants as professional employees and violated the federal Fair Labor Standards Act (FLSA) and California law by paying them salaries without overtime pay. Although the arbitration agreement provided for individualized proceedings, Mr. Morris sought to litigate the federal claim on behalf of a nationwide class under the FLSA's collective action provision, 29 U.S.C. §216(b). He sought to pursue the state law claim as a class action under Federal Rule of Civil Procedure 23.

Ernst & Young replied with a motion to compel arbitration. The district court granted the request, but the Ninth Circuit reversed this judgment. The Ninth Circuit recognized that the Arbitration Act generally requires courts to enforce arbitration agreements as written. But the court reasoned that the statute's "saving clause," see 9 U.S.C. §2, removes this obligation if an arbitration agreement violates some other federal law. And the court concluded that an agreement requiring individualized arbitration proceedings violates the NLRA by barring employees from engaging in the "concerted activit[y]," of pursuing claims as a class or collective action. . . .

Although the Arbitration Act and the NLRA have long coexisted—they date from 1925 and 1935, respectively—the suggestion they might conflict is something quite new. Until a couple of years ago, courts more or less agreed that arbitration agreements like those before us must be enforced according to their terms. . . .

II

We begin with the Arbitration Act and the question of its saving clause.

Congress adopted the Arbitration Act in 1925 in response to a perception that courts were unduly hostile to arbitration. No doubt there was much to that perception.

Before 1925, English and American common law courts routinely refused to enforce agreements to arbitrate disputes. But in Congress's judgment arbitration had more to offer than courts recognized—not least the promise of quicker, more informal, and often cheaper resolutions for everyone involved. So Congress directed courts to abandon their hostility and instead treat arbitration agreements as "valid, irrevocable, and enforceable." 9 U.S.C. §2. The Act, this Court has said, establishes "a liberal federal policy favoring arbitration agreements."

Not only did Congress require courts to respect and enforce agreements to arbitrate; it also specifically directed them to respect and enforce the parties' chosen arbitration procedures.

On first blush, these emphatic directions would seem to resolve any argument under the Arbitration Act. The parties before us contracted for arbitration. They proceeded to specify the rules that would govern their arbitrations, indicating their intention to use individualized rather than class or collective action procedures. And this much the Arbitration Act seems to protect pretty absolutely. See AT&T Mobility LLC v. Concepcion, 563 U.S. 333 (2011); *Italian Colors, supra*; DIRECTV, Inc. v. Imburgia, 577 U.S. ___ (2015). You might wonder if the balance Congress struck in 1925 between arbitration and litigation should be revisited in light of more contemporary developments. You might even ask if the Act was good policy when enacted. But all the same you might find it difficult to see how to avoid the statute's application.

Still, the employees suggest the Arbitration Act's saving clause creates an exception for cases like theirs. By its terms, the saving clause allows courts to refuse to enforce arbitration agreements "upon such grounds as exist at law or in equity for the revocation of any contract." §2. That provision applies here, the employees tell us, because the NLRA renders their particular class and collective action waivers illegal. In their view, illegality under the NLRA is a "ground" that "exists at law . . . for the revocation" of their arbitration agreements, at least to the extent those agreements prohibit class or collective action proceedings.

The problem with this line of argument is fundamental. . . .

[The clause] can't [apply] because the saving clause recognizes only defenses that apply to "any" contract. In this way the clause establishes a sort of "equal-treatment" rule for arbitration contracts. The clause "permits agreements to arbitrate to be invalidated by 'generally applicable contract defenses, such as fraud, duress, or unconscionability.' " *Concepcion*. At the same time, the clause offers no refuge for "defenses that apply only to arbitration or that derive their meaning from the fact that an agreement to arbitrate is at issue." Under our precedent, this means the saving clause does not save defenses that target arbitration either by name or by more subtle methods, such as by "interfer[ing] with fundamental attributes of arbitration."

This is where the employees' argument stumbles. They don't suggest that their arbitration agreements were extracted, say, by an act of fraud or duress or in some other unconscionable way that would render *any* contract unenforceable. Instead, they object to their agreements precisely because they require individualized arbitration proceedings instead of class or collective ones. And by attacking (only) the individualized nature of the arbitration proceedings, the employees' argument seeks to interfere with one of arbitration's fundamental attributes.

We know this much because of *Concepcion*. There this Court faced a state law defense that prohibited as unconscionable class action waivers in consumer contracts.

The Court readily acknowledged that the defense formally applied in both the litigation and the arbitration context. But, the Court held, the defense failed to qualify for protection under the saving clause because it interfered with a fundamental attribute of arbitration all the same. It did so by effectively permitting any party in arbitration to demand classwide proceedings despite the traditionally individualized and informal nature of arbitration. This "fundamental" change to the traditional arbitration process, the Court said, would "sacrific[e] the principal advantage of arbitration—its informality—and mak[e] the process slower, more costly, and more likely to generate procedural morass than final judgment." . . .

Of course, *Concepcion* has its limits. The Court recognized that parties remain free to alter arbitration procedures to suit their tastes, and in recent years some parties have sometimes chosen to arbitrate on a classwide basis. But *Concepcion*'s essential insight remains: courts may not allow a contract defense to reshape traditional individualized arbitration by mandating classwide arbitration procedures without the parties' consent. Just as judicial antagonism toward arbitration before the Arbitration Act's enactment "manifested itself in a great variety of devices and formulas declaring arbitration against public policy," *Concepcion* teaches that we must be alert to new devices and formulas that would achieve much the same result today. And a rule seeking to declare individualized arbitration proceedings off limits is, the Court held, just such a device. . . .

Illegality [the term used by the NLRA statute], like unconscionability, may be a traditional, generally applicable contract defense in many cases, including arbitration cases. But an argument that a contract is unenforceable *just because it requires bilateral arbitration* is a different creature. A defense of that kind, *Concepcion* tells us, is one that impermissibly disfavors arbitration whether it sounds in illegality or unconscionability. The law of precedent teaches that like cases should generally be treated alike, and appropriate respect for that principle means the Arbitration Act's saving clause can no more save the defense at issue in these cases than it did the defense at issue in *Concepcion*. At the end of our encounter with the Arbitration Act, then, it appears just as it did at the beginning: a congressional command requiring us to enforce, not override, the terms of the arbitration agreements before us.

[The remainder of the opinion deals with the question of whether the later-enacted NLRA statute overrode or qualified the FAA; after canvassing the principles for harmonizing apparently conflicting statutes, the majority said that the NLRA did not change its interpretation of the FAA.]

IV

The dissent sees things a little bit differently. In its view, today's decision ushers us back to the *Lochner* era when this Court regularly overrode legislative policy judgments. The dissent even suggests we have resurrected the long-dead "yellow dog" contract. But like most apocalyptic warnings, this one proves a false alarm. . . .

Our decision does nothing to override Congress's policy judgments. As the dissent recognizes, the legislative policy embodied in the NLRA is aimed at "safeguard[ing], first and foremost, workers' rights to join unions and to engage in collective bargaining." Those rights stand every bit as strong today as they did yesterday. And rather than revive "yellow dog" contracts against union organizing that the NLRA outlawed back in 1935, today's decision merely declines to read into the NLRA a novel right to class action procedures that the Board's own general counsel disclaimed as recently as 2010. . . .

* * *

The policy may be debatable but the law is clear: Congress has instructed that arbitration agreements like those before us must be enforced as written. While Congress is of course always free to amend this judgment, we see nothing suggesting it did so in the NLRA—much less that it manifested a clear intention to displace the Arbitration Act. Because we can easily read Congress's statutes to work in harmony, that is where our duty lies. The judgments in *Epic* and *Ernst & Young* are reversed, and the cases are remanded for further proceedings consistent with this opinion. The judgment in *Murphy Oil* is affirmed.

So ordered.

[Justice Thomas's concurrence joined the majority but argued that the case could have been decided on narrower grounds—that the FAA's saving clause referred only to traditional contract defenses such as duress and fraud.]

Ginsburg, J., with whom Breyer, J., Sotomayor, J., and Kagan, J., join, dissenting.

The employees in these cases complain that their employers have underpaid them in violation of the wage and hours prescriptions of the Fair Labor Standards Act of 1938 (FLSA) and analogous state laws. Individually, their claims are small, scarcely of a size warranting the expense of seeking redress alone. But by joining together with others similarly circumstanced, employees can gain effective redress for wage underpayment commonly experienced. To block such concerted action, their employers required them to sign, as a condition of employment, arbitration agreements banning collective judicial and arbitral proceedings of any kind. The question presented: Does the Federal Arbitration Act permit employers to insist that their employees, whenever seeking redress for commonly experienced wage loss, go it alone, never mind the right secured to employees by the National Labor Relations Act (NLRA) "to engage in . . . concerted activities" for their "mutual aid or protection"? The answer should be a resounding "No."

In the NLRA and its forerunner, the Norris-LaGuardia Act (NLGA), 29 U.S.C. §101 *et seq.*, Congress acted on an acute awareness: For workers striving to gain from their employers decent terms and conditions of employment, there is strength in numbers. A single employee, Congress understood, is disarmed in dealing with an employer. The Court today subordinates employee-protective labor legislation to the Arbitration Act. In so doing, the Court forgets the labor market imbalance that gave rise to the NLGA and the NLRA, and ignores the destructive consequences of diminishing the right of employees "to band together in confronting an employer." Congressional correction of the Court's elevation of the FAA over workers' rights to act in concert is urgently in order.

To explain why the Court's decision is egregiously wrong, I first refer to the extreme imbalance once prevalent in our Nation's workplaces, and Congress' aim in the NLGA and the NLRA to place employers and employees on a more equal footing. I then explain why the Arbitration Act, sensibly read, does not shrink the NLRA's protective sphere. . . .

The end of the 19th century and beginning of the 20th was a tumultuous era in the history of our Nation's labor relations. Under economic conditions then prevailing, workers often had to accept employment on whatever terms employers dictated. Aiming to secure better pay, shorter workdays, and safer workplaces, workers increasingly sought to band together to make their demands effective. . . .

Early legislative efforts to protect workers' rights to band together were unavailing. . .

In the 1930's, legislative efforts to safeguard vulnerable workers found more receptive audiences. As the Great Depression shifted political winds further in favor of worker-protective laws, Congress passed two statutes aimed at protecting employees' associational rights. First, in 1932, Congress passed the NLGA, which regulates the employer-employee relationship indirectly. Section 2 of the Act declares:

> "Whereas . . . the individual unorganized worker is commonly helpless to exercise actual liberty of contract and to protect his freedom of labor, . . . it is necessary that he have full freedom of association, self-organization, and designation of representatives of his own choosing, . . . and that he shall be free from the interference, restraint, or coercion of employers . . . in the designation of such representatives or in self-organization or in other concerted activities for the purpose of collective bargaining or other mutual aid or protection." 29 U.S.C. §102. . . .

But Congress did so three years later, in 1935, when it enacted the NLRA. Relevant here, §7 of the NLRA guarantees employees "the right to self-organization, to form, join, or assist labor organizations, to bargain collectively through representatives of their own choosing, *and to engage in other concerted activities for the purpose of collective bargaining or other mutual aid or protection.*" 29 U.S.C. §157 (emphasis added). Section 8(a)(1) safeguards those rights by making it an "unfair labor practice" for an employer to "interfere with, restrain, or coerce employees in the exercise of the rights guaranteed in [§7]." §158(a)(1). . . .

Despite the NLRA's prohibitions, the employers in the cases now before the Court required their employees to sign contracts stipulating to submission of wage and hours claims to binding arbitration, and to do so only one-by-one. When employees subsequently filed wage and hours claims in federal court and sought to invoke the collective-litigation procedures provided for in the FLSA and Federal Rules of Civil Procedure, the employers moved to compel individual arbitration. The Arbitration Act, in their view, requires courts to enforce their take-it-or-leave-it arbitration agreements as written, including the collective-litigation abstinence demanded therein.

In resisting enforcement of the group-action foreclosures, the employees involved in this litigation do not urge that they must have access to a judicial forum. They argue only that the NLRA prohibits their employers from denying them the right to pursue work-related claims in concert in any forum. If they may be stopped by employer-dictated terms from pursuing collective procedures in court, they maintain, they must at least have access to similar procedures in an arbitral forum. . . .

Suits to enforce workplace rights collectively fit comfortably under the umbrella "concerted activities for the purpose of . . . mutual aid or protection." 29 U.S.C. §157. "Concerted" means "[p]lanned or accomplished together; combined." American Heritage Dictionary 381 (5th ed. 2011). "Mutual" means "reciprocal." *Id.,* at 1163. When employees meet the requirements for litigation of shared legal claims in joint, collective, and class proceedings, the litigation of their claims is undoubtedly "accomplished together." By joining hands in litigation, workers can spread the costs of litigation and reduce the risk of employer retaliation. . . .

In face of the NLRA's text, history, purposes, and longstanding construction, the Court nevertheless concludes that collective proceedings do not fall within the scope of §7. None of the Court's reasons for diminishing §7 should carry the day. . . .

The inevitable result of today's decision will be the underenforcement of federal and state statutes designed to advance the well-being of vulnerable workers. . . .

* * *

If these untoward consequences stemmed from legislative choices, I would be obliged to accede to them. But the edict that employees with wage and hours claims may seek relief only one-by-one does not come from Congress. It is the result of take-it-or-leave-it labor contracts harking back to the type called "yellow dog," and of the readiness of this Court to enforce those unbargained-for agreements. The FAA demands no such suppression of the right of workers to take concerted action for their "mutual aid or protection." Accordingly, I would reverse the judgment of the Fifth Circuit in No. 16-307 and affirm the judgments of the Seventh and Ninth Circuits in Nos. 16-285 and 16-300.

WHAT'S NEW HERE?

- Unlike *Ferguson* and *Concepcion* (the latter of which is discussed in the Court's decision in *Epic Systems*), this conflict involves not the state law of unconscionability but an exception to the FAA implied—the plaintiffs said—by a pair of federal statutes passed after the FAA. No, the Court said, these statutes created no such exception.

- Just below that level is another disagreement: What is the purpose underlying the FAA? For the dissent, that statute merely removed hostility to the enforcement of arbitration clauses, hostility said to have been embedded in state law. For the majority, the FAA went further—not just permitting but *encouraging* arbitration, and in close cases it should be read to achieve that goal. It's fair to say that most of the academic commentary embraces the dissent's view of FAA history, but the Supreme Court gets the last word here.

- At a third level down, the Court faced a very difficult problem: that of deciding how several Congresses (that had passed first the FAA and then the pair of labor statutes involved) would have felt about class action waivers. The class action technically existed at the time of these statutes but had taken nothing like its present form—which it assumed only in 1966 with the amendment of Rule 23. Would the Congresses that passed these statutes have smiled or frowned upon the use of collective litigation to enforce the wage statutes, and would they have smiled or frowned upon the use of arbitration clauses to avoid such collective litigation?

Notes and Problems

1. The majority and dissent implicitly agree that Congress could either expand or narrow the scope of disputes subject to the FAA. They disagree about what Congress meant when it passed the Act, and, as in many preemption cases, Congress has been silent on the question.

2. Congress could, of course, clarify—or change—its meaning with an amendment either to the FAA or to the relevant labor statutes. One proposal, pending through several recent Congresses, would exempt certain categories of disputes from arbitration—consumer contracts and employment contracts being two groups often suggested. Such legislation has to date not passed.

3. A narrower pathway, one at play in *Epic Systems*, would be for a federal agency charged with oversight of a part of the economy to promulgate a regulation that forbade arbitration in disputes subject its purview.

    a. The National Labor Relations Board had done just that as to wage and hour disputes. In a part of opinion excised above, the Court held that the Board's interpretation of the relevant statute was not plausible (and contravened long-standing practice to the contrary).

    b. Another federal agency, the relatively new Consumer Financial Protection Board (created in the wake of the financial crises commencing in 2009), relying on a large empirical study of banks that did and did not have arbitration agreements with their customers—forbade financial institutions from requiring such clauses. Congress responded by passing a statute that overrode that regulation, so that such clauses are again valid.

4. Although arbitration clauses are quite common in contracts between companies and their employees and consumers, such clauses first developed in intra-business commercial contexts, where the contract terms may be bilaterally negotiated. Yet an empirical study of the frequency of arbitration provisions in a sample of contracts of large public companies indicates that the perceived desirability of arbitration may be ebbing in these large companies. As the authors explained:

    > [L]arge corporate actors do not systematically embrace arbitration. International contracts include arbitration clauses more than domestic contracts, but also at a surprisingly low rate. Our results have implications for the justifications for the widespread use of arbitration clauses in consumer contracts. If the reasons that some have advanced to support the use of arbitration in the consumer context—that it is simpler and cheaper than litigation—are correct, it is surprising that public companies do not seek these advantages in disputes among themselves. In the simple economic view, our results suggest that corporate representatives believe that litigation can add value over arbitration.

    > Theodore Eisenberg & Geoffrey P. Miller, *The Flight from Arbitration: An Empirical Study of Ex Ante Arbitration Clauses in the Contracts of Publicly Held Companies*, 56 DePaul L. Rev. 335 (2007).

Do these findings call into question assumptions made by the Supreme Court about the desirability of mandated arbitration in consumer contracts?

5. *Ferguson* and *Epic Systems* both portray arbitration as a form of dispute resolution that might be called "litigation lite"—limited discovery, abbreviated presentation of evidence, and then argument by lawyers before a neutral arbiter who would render an often quite brief written decision. But consider a quite different—more creative—form of arbitration that bears no resemblance to adjudication and has been in place in the entertainment industry for decades.

   a. Screenwriting credits—the names that scroll on the screen at the start or end of a film or similar production—can be worth hundreds of thousands of dollars in future writing engagements as well as a larger share of profits from screenings, DVDs, and online sales. Writers, directors, and producers of such entertainment sometimes disagree about who should get credit. Writers have a union—called in Hollywood parlance a "guild"—that has worked out a way of arbitrating such credits when there is a disagreement. As a case described it:

   > The basic agreement contains, in a section entitled theatrical schedule A, detailed provisions concerning writing credits for feature-length theatrical photo-plays. Under schedule A, the production company must notify all participating writers of its tentative credits determination. Any of the writers may then file with the production company and the Writers Guild a written request for arbitration of credits. . . .
   >
   > The credits manual, discussed below, sets forth the procedures the Writers Guild has adopted. . . . The credit arbitration is administered by the Writers Guild's credit arbitration secretary. When a credit arbitration is requested, this officer sends the parties to the arbitration a screen arbiter's list, containing the names of all potential arbitrators. These are Writers Guild members with credit arbitration experience or with at least three screenplay credits of their own. This list comprised at least 400 names in 1987. Each party can peremptorily disqualify a reasonable number of persons from the list. From the remaining potential arbitrators, the secretary selects three, endeavoring to select individuals experienced in the type of writing involved in the particular case.
   >
   > The secretary delivers to the three arbitrators all script, outline, and story material prepared or used in the creation of the screenplay, together with source material (writings upon which the screenplay or story is based). These documents are supplied to the Writers Guild by the production company, and each participant in the credit arbitration may examine them to assure the inclusion of everything he or she has written. Any dispute over the "authenticity, identification, sequence, authorship or completeness" of literary material to be included is resolved by a special three-member committee, which conducts for that purpose a prearbitration hearing, at which all affected writers may present testimony and other evidence.
   >
   > The arbitrators also receive the production company's statement of tentative credits; a copy of the credits manual; and the statements of the parties, which are confidential. The secretary designates a member of the Writers Guild's Screen Writers' credits committee to act as consultant to the arbitrators

on procedure, precedent, policies, and rules, and to aid the arbitrators toward a majority decision.

The three arbitrators hold no hearing, and they deliberate independently of each other. Indeed, each remains unaware of the identity of the other two (unless, after they reach their decisions, the consultant convenes a meeting with the three). Each arbitrator notifies the secretary of his or her determination. The secretary then informs the parties of the decision of the majority of the arbitrators.

Within 24 hours thereafter, any party may request the convening of a policy review board, consisting of three members of the Writers Guild's credits committee including that committee's chairman or vice-chairman. The policy review board does not examine the script, story, or source material; indeed, its members are forbidden to read these. Its function is solely to detect any substantial deviation from the policy of the Writers Guild or from the procedure set forth in the credits manual. The policy review board has authority to direct the arbitration committee to reconsider the case or to order a fresh arbitration by a new triumvirate. The policy review board is not empowered to reverse the decision of an arbitration committee in matters of judgment. A decision of the policy review board approving a credit determination is final.

> Ferguson v. Writers' Guild of America,
> West, 226 Cal. App. 3d 1382, 277 Cal. Rptr. 450 (1991).

b. Imagine that a state legislature adopted the Writers Guild procedure for its court system: litigants limited to written submission to an anonymous panel of judges; no opportunity to appear, summon witnesses, or present testimony; and the court's judgment rendered without explanation. Such a process would presumably violate due process. What, then, makes it permissible in this setting—as it has been for years?

6. If a judge renders a decision, in most U.S. jurisdictions the decision can be appealed. What about arbitrators' awards? The general proposition is that appeal to a court is possible but not generally useful because the court will narrowly restrict the scope of its review: Was the arbitrator bribed or did the procedure violate fundamental fairness? For some parties the inability to appeal an arbitration award is an advantage: It eliminates a source of delay. For others, it is a disadvantage: It puts the parties at the mercy of an arbitrator who may be interpreting a new statute or an especially unusual contract.

a. Some arbitration organizations are now advertising that they offer such appellate review—which will, of course, lengthen the process.

b. Could the parties provide that an appellate court would review an arbitrator's award? In the federal courts the answer is almost certainly no. The basic jurisdictional statute of the circuit courts limits their power to the review of "final decisions of the district courts of the United States." 28 U.S.C. §1291. But that statute does not control states' appellate process, and one can imagine a state legislature allowing its courts to hear such cases.

C. ADJUDICATION WITHOUT TRIAL: SUMMARY JUDGMENT

Suppose there is no arbitration agreement, or that it is unenforceable. Litigation ensues. Your client is open to settlement, but negotiations prove fruitless. Or your client wants something that only adjudication can deliver—for example, a binding public declaration of rights. Is trial inevitable? No. A court can grant summary judgment in cases in which there is no material factual dispute. The key provision, in Rule 56(a), provides that "the court shall grant summary judgment if the movant shows that there is no genuine dispute as to any material fact and the movant is entitled to judgment as a matter of law." Courts interpret this provision to mean that summary judgment should be granted if, given the evidence presented, no reasonable jury could find for the nonmoving party. Summary judgment may be appropriate because the critical dispute concerns the law—does the First Amendment forbid a school district from requiring pupils to recite the Pledge of Allegiance? Or summary judgment may be appropriate in a case where the law was clear but one party lacked evidence supporting a critical element of her case. In either circumstance, trial is pointless because no reasonable jury could find for one side or the other. This section explores the possibilities and limits of summary judgment.

Notes and Problems

---

1. One way of understanding summary judgment is to consider the ways in which it differs from a pre-answer motion to dismiss for failure to state a claim. Imagine that a plaintiff sues a defendant, alleging that the defendant signed a promissory note that he did not pay when due.

   a. The defendant files a Rule 12(b)(6) motion. That motion will be denied. Why?

   b. Now explain why the denial of the Rule 12(b)(6) motion does not mean that the plaintiff will prevail at trial. What does a trial require that a 12(b)(6) motion does not?

2. Assume that the defendant answers the complaint by denying liability.

   a. Unlike a 12(b)(6) motion, a denial puts the facts of the case at issue.

   b. Under the governing substantive law, only a few facts are relevant on this type of claim: Did defendant sign the note? Was it paid when due? (Note that other responses the defendant might make—that the plaintiff had previously sued on this same note; that the parties had agreed to arbitrate their dispute; or that the plaintiff fraudulently misrepresented facts in order to get defendant to sign the note—are specified as affirmative defenses under Rule 8(c) and therefore are not raised by an answer that simply denies liability.)

    c. If you were the plaintiff faced with the defendant's denial of liability, what information would you want to find out during discovery?

3. Assume that disclosure and discovery yield the note itself, whose validity the defendant does not contest, and the defendant's response to requests for admission in which he admits signing the note and admits he has not repaid the sum.

    a. If the parties go to trial, the plaintiff will presumably introduce the note and defendant's admissions, and testify that the defendant has not paid the money owed under the note. At that point the plaintiff will rest his case. Unless the defendant changes his story from that revealed in his responses to requests for admission, he has no defense because he acknowledges having signed the note and does not claim to have repaid it. Accordingly, the plaintiff would prevail at trial because no reasonable jury could find in the defendant's favor.

    b. Under these circumstances summary judgment prevents a futile trial. If the plaintiff properly moved for summary judgment on these facts, the court would grant it, entering judgment in the plaintiff's favor. The court would take this action because no reasonable jury could find for the defendant or, in the language of Rule 56(a), "there is no genuine dispute as to any material fact and the movant is entitled to judgment as a matter of law."

WHAT'S NEW HERE?

- Except to the extent required by *Iqbal*, pleading does not test whether evidence supports a claim or defense. Pleading practice—including motions under Rule 12(b)(6)—asks whether, *if* allegations were true, they would be legally sufficient.
- By contrast, at summary judgment a party can use evidence unearthed during discovery and other informal investigation to challenge the truth of assertions made in pleadings ("You say there was a contract, and I denied it. Now—do you have evidence of an agreement?").
- Summary judgment motions also "match up" evidence with the substantive law. ("To recover for negligently inflicted injuries, you need to show *X* things: Do you have admissible evidence on each of those things? If not, you lose.")

4. How would a plaintiff in the promissory note case make a summary judgment motion? What would he have to present to the court?

    a. Courts decide summary judgment motions on the basis of various documents (affidavits, deposition transcripts, copies of relevant documents). Rule 56(c)(1)(A). No witnesses testify in court, and no jury is present.

b. One common document in summary judgment practice is an affidavit. An affidavit is a written document in which the affiant swears under penalty of perjury that the statements made are true. Typically, an affidavit is drafted by a lawyer who reviews it with the affiant, who then signs it, attesting that its statements are true. Rule 56(c)(4) sets out the requirements for affidavits to be used in summary judgment motions.

5. What types of information can serve as evidence supporting a summary judgment motion or opposition? As Rule 56(c)(2) makes clear, a court cannot consider information that would not be admissible at trial. You will better understand the full impact of this rule after studying Evidence. Consider, though, its impact as it relates to our hypothetical case regarding the promissory note.

   a. Recall that one of the issues in the case was whether the defendant had signed the promissory note. Suppose the plaintiff's lawyer presented to the court an affidavit in which the lawyer swore, "Plaintiff told me he watched the defendant personally sign the promissory note." Although the plaintiff could properly submit an affidavit asserting that he saw the defendant sign the promissory note, the lawyer's statement would not be admissible as evidence because it is inadmissible hearsay.

   b. Suppose the plaintiff signs an affidavit whose core statement is, "I know that defendant signed the promissory note." The problem here is that the plaintiff does not explain the basis for this knowledge.

   c. Suppose the plaintiff's lawyer has learned from interviewing his client that the plaintiff watched the defendant sign the note. Given the problems with the evidence identified in 5a and b, above, what statements do you think the plaintiff's affidavit should contain to support the contention that the defendant signed the note?

6. Finally, consider what the party resisting summary judgment must present to avoid it. In our hypothetical case, assume that plaintiff has presented evidence sufficient to warrant a grant of summary judgment. That evidence includes an affidavit from the plaintiff stating that he watched the defendant sign the promissory note and further that it remains unpaid. The defendant tells his lawyer that he did not sign the note.

   a. To defeat the motion for summary judgment, can he submit an affidavit saying, "I can prove I didn't sign the note"? Why not?

   b. What should the affidavit say?

   c. Notice a crucial point: If in opposition to a plaintiff's motion for summary judgment, the defendant submits an affidavit denying that he signed the note, the judge should deny the plaintiff's motion. That is true even if the plaintiff bolsters his own affidavit with affidavits of 26 disinterested witnesses, each of whom swears to having watched the defendant sign the note. So long as there is a material factual dispute, a court should leave it to a jury to resolve.

d. Note also that, even if the defendant prevails at summary judgment, it does not mean that defendant will prevail at trial. It simply means that there is something to have a trial about—here, about the defendant's credibility in denying that he signed the note and about the accuracy of perception and credibility of the witnesses contradicting the defendant.

1. Summary Judgment in Action: The Burdens on the Moving and Nonmoving Parties

Having considered the role of summary judgment and the ways in which parties seek and defend against summary judgment motions, we turn to the application of the summary judgment standard. Just as the standards of pleading have changed in recent years, the standards for summary judgment have shifted since the initial promulgation of the Rules. Before 1938, summary judgment was available only under limited circumstances; the Federal Rules promulgated in 1938 made summary judgment available to all parties and claims. It was, though, used sparingly by judges, who may have perceived summary judgment as infringing on parties' right to a trial. In three cases decided in 1986—*Celotex, Anderson,* and *Matsushita*—the Supreme Court interpreted the summary judgment standard in ways that gave courts broader authority to grant summary judgment. Since 1986, parties—usually though not always defendants—have brought summary judgment motions with increasing frequency. Today, more cases end at summary judgment than at trial. In the remainder of this chapter, we will consider the impact of each of these cases on summary judgment practice.

The first, *Celotex Corp. v. Catrett,* focuses on what the party moving for summary judgment must do, in the absence of any opposition, to justify a court's granting its motion. Before *Celotex,* the leading case on federal summary judgment was Adickes v. S.H. Kress & Co., 398 U.S. 144 (1970). *Adickes* grew out of a civil rights demonstration in which plaintiff, refused service at a racially segregated lunch counter, sued the restaurant owner. At the time, the federal public accommodations laws provided no damages remedy for private discrimination, and the liability of the business therefore depended on whether it had acted in concert with the local authorities, thereby fulfilling the state action requirement of 42 U.S.C. §1983. All agreed that there had been a police officer in the store at the time service was refused, but plaintiff produced no evidence showing communication between the officer and any store employee. The defendant submitted affidavits and deposition transcripts from the store manager and the police officer that they had not communicated with each other and that the manager had refused service because he was concerned about "a riot." The Supreme Court said: "Our own scrutiny of the factual allegations of petitioner's complaint, as well as the material found in the affidavits and depositions presented by Kress to the District Court, however, convinces us that summary judgment was improper here, for we think *respondent* [the defendant store] *failed to carry its burden of* *showing the absence of any genuine* issue of fact."* Id. at 153 (emphasis added). After reviewing the evidence presented at the motion for summary judgment the Court summarized:

> We think that on the basis of this record, it was error to grant summary judgment. As the moving party, respondent had the burden of showing the absence of a genuine issue as to any material fact, and for these purposes the material it lodged must be viewed in the light most favorable to the opposing party. Respondent here did not carry its burden because of its failure to *foreclose the possibility* that there was a policeman in the Kress store while petitioner was awaiting service, and that this policeman reached an understanding with some Kress employee that petitioner not be served.

398 U.S. at 157 (emphasis added). For the *Adickes* Court, then, the defendant moving for summary judgment had the burden of "foreclos[ing] the possibility" that plaintiff could prevail at trial.

The *Celotex* case asserts that it does not overrule *Adickes*. Is that correct?

Celotex Corp. v. Catrett
477 U.S. 317 (1986)

REHNQUIST, J.

> *Celotex moved for summary judgment*

. . . Respondent commenced this lawsuit in September 1980, alleging that the death . . . of her husband . . . resulted from his exposure to products containing asbestos manufactured or distributed by 15 named corporations. . . . Petitioner's motion [for summary judgment] . . . argued that summary judgment was proper because respondent had "failed to produce evidence that any [Celotex] product . . . was the proximate cause of the injuries alleged. . . ." In particular, petitioner noted that respondent had failed to identify, in answering interrogatories specifically requesting such information, any witnesses who could testify about the decedent's exposure to petitioner's asbestos products. In response to petitioner's summary judgment motion, respondent then produced three documents which she claimed "demonstrate that there is a genuine material factual dispute" as to whether the decedent had ever been exposed to petitioner's asbestos products. The three documents included a transcript of a deposition of the decedent, a letter from an official of one of the decedent's former employers whom petitioner planned to call as a trial witness, and a letter from an insurance company to respondent's attorney, all tending to establish that the decedent had been exposed to petitioner's asbestos products in Chicago.

> *Evidence P was going to introduce*

---

* [The quoted language constituted the text of Rule 56 at the time *Adickes* was decided. The Advisory Committee Note to the current text indicates that the change in wording does not constitute any change in the meaning of the standard.—EDS.]

Petitioner, in turn, argued that the three documents were inadmissible hearsay and thus could not be considered in opposition to the summary judgment motion.

Procedure

. . . The District Court granted . . . the motion . . . because "there [was] no showing that the plaintiff was exposed to the defendant Celotex's product in the District of Columbia or elsewhere within the statutory period." [The court of appeals reversed.] According to the majority, Rule 56(e) of the Federal Rules of Civil Procedure, and this Court's decision in Adickes v. S.H. Kress & Co., 398 U.S. 144, 159 (1970), establish that "the party opposing the motion for summary judgment bears the burden of responding *only after* the moving party has met its burden of coming forward with proof of the absence of any genuine issues of material fact." 244 U.S. App. D.C., at 163, 756 F.2d, at 184 (emphasis in original; footnote omitted). The majority therefore declined to consider petitioner's argument that none of the evidence produced by respondent in opposition to the motion for summary judgment would have been admissible at trial.

. . . We think that the position taken by the majority of the Court of Appeals is inconsistent with the standard for summary judgment set forth in Rule 56[(a)] of the Federal Rules of Civil Procedure. . . . In our view, the plain language of Rule 56[(a)] mandates the entry of summary judgment, after adequate time for discovery . . . against a party who fails to make a showing sufficient to establish the existence of an element essential to that party's case, and on which that party will bear the burden of proof at trial. In such a situation, there can be "no genuine [dispute] as to any material fact," since a complete failure of proof concerning an essential element of the nonmoving party's case necessarily renders all other facts immaterial. The moving party is "entitled to judgment as a matter of law" because the nonmoving party has failed to make a sufficient showing on an essential element of her case with respect to which she has the burden of proof. "[The] standard [for granting summary judgment] mirrors the standard for a directed verdict under Federal Rule of Civil Procedure 50(a). . . ." Anderson v. Liberty Lobby, 477 U.S. 242, 250 (1986).

Of course, a party seeking summary judgment always bears the initial responsibility of informing the district court of the basis for its motion, and identifying those portions of ["particular parts of materials in the record, including depositions, documents, electronically stored information, affidavits or declarations, stipulations . . . admissions, interrogatory answers [quoting Rule 56(c)(1)]"] which it believes demonstrate the absence of a genuine [dispute]. But unlike the Court of Appeals, we find no express or implied requirement in Rule 56 that the moving party support its motions with affidavits or other similar materials *negating* the opponent's claim. On the contrary, Rule 56(c), which refers to "pleadings, depositions, answers to interrogatories and admission on file, together with the affidavits if *any*"* (emphasis added), suggests the absence of such a requirement. . . . One of the principal purposes of the summary judgment rule is to isolate and dispose of factually unsupported claims or defenses, and we think it should be interpreted in a way that enables it to accomplish this purpose. . . .

---

* [Quoting the text of Rule 56(c) at the time of the *Celotex* decision.—Eds.]

We do not mean that the nonmoving party must produce evidence in a form that would be admissible at trial in order to avoid summary judgment. Obviously, Rule 56 does not require the nonmoving party to depose her own witness. Rule 56[(a)] permits a proper summary judgment motion to be opposed by any of the kinds of evidentiary materials listed in Rule 56(c), except the mere pleadings themselves. . . .

The Court of Appeals in this case felt itself constrained, however, by language in Adickes v. S. H. Kress & Co., 398 U.S. 144 (1970). There we held that summary judgment had been improperly entered in favor of the defendant. . . . Adickes . . . said . . . "both the commentary on and the background of the 1963 Amendment conclusively show that it was not intended to modify the burden of the moving party . . . to show initially the absence of a genuine issue concerning any material fact." We think that this statement is accurate in a literal sense. . . . But we do not think the Adickes language quoted above should be construed to mean that the burden is on the party moving for summary judgment to produce evidence showing the absence of a genuine issue of material fact, even with respect to an issue on which the nonmoving party bears the burden of proof. Instead, as we have explained, the burden on the moving party may be discharged by "showing"—that is, pointing out to the District Court— that there is an absence of evidence to support the nonmoving party's case. . . .

Our conclusion is bolstered by the fact that district courts are widely acknowledged to possess the power to enter summary judgments sua sponte, so long as the losing party was on notice that she had to come forward with all of her evidence. It would surely defy common sense to hold that the District Court could have entered summary judgment sua sponte in favor of petitioner in the instant case, but that petitioner's filing of a motion requesting such a disposition precluded the District Court from ordering it.

Respondent commenced this action in September 1980, and petitioner's motion was filed in September 1981. The parties had conducted discovery, and no serious claim can be made that the respondent was in any sense "railroaded" by a premature motion for summary judgment. Any potential problem with such premature motions can be adequately dealt with under Rule 56[(d)], which allows a summary judgment motion to be denied, or the hearing on the motion to be continued, if the nonmoving party has not had an opportunity to make full discovery.

In this Court, respondent's brief and oral argument have been devoted as much to the proposition that an adequate showing of exposure to petitioner's asbestos products was made as to the proposition that no such showing should have been required. But the Court of Appeals declined to address either. . . . We think the Court of Appeals . . . is better suited than we are to make these determinations in the first instance. . . . Summary judgment procedure is properly regarded not as a disfavored procedural shortcut, but rather as an integral part of the Federal Rules as a whole, which are designed "to secure the just, speedy and inexpensive determination of every action." Fed. Rule Civ. Proc. 1. Before the shift to "notice pleading" accomplished by the Federal Rules, motions to dismiss a complaint or to strike a defense were the principal tools by which factually insufficient claims or defenses could be isolated and prevented from going to trial. . . . But with the advent of "notice pleading," the motion to dismiss seldom fulfills this function any more, and its place has been taken by the motion for summary judgment. . . .

The judgment of the Court of Appeals is accordingly reversed, and the case is remanded for further proceedings consistent with this opinion.

WHITE, J., concurring.

[I agree with the holding, but] the movant must discharge the burden the rules place upon him: It is not enough to move for summary judgment without supporting the motion in any way or with a conclusory allegation that the plaintiff has no evidence to prove his case. . . .

. . . Celotex does not dispute that if respondent has named a witness to support her claim, summary judgment should not be granted without Celotex['s] somehow showing that the named witness' possible testimony raises no genuine issue of material fact. It asserts, however, that respondent has failed on request to produce any basis for her case. Respondent, on the other hand, does not contend that she was not obligated to reveal her witnesses and evidence but insists that she has revealed enough to defeat the motion for summary judgment. Because the Court of Appeals found it unnecessary to address this aspect of the case, I agree that the case should be remanded for further proceedings.

[Dissents by Justices BRENNAN and STEVENS are omitted.]

WHAT'S NEW HERE?

- Before *Celotex*, burdens of production differed depending on whether one was talking about trial or summary judgment, and depending on whether one was moving for or resisting summary judgment.
- After *Celotex*, the burden of production at the summary judgment stage is the same as at trial. Your job is to understand the implications of that statement.

Notes and Problems

1. What was the fight about in *Celotex*?

   a. Everyone agreed that in order to recover Mrs. Catrett had to show that her husband had been exposed to asbestos manufactured by Celotex. (A subsidiary issue concerned the date of that exposure. Had it been within the statute of limitations?)

   b. Everyone agreed that Celotex could defeat recovery by showing that Mr. Catrett had not been exposed to asbestos manufactured by it (or one of its predecessors).

   c. So what were the parties disagreeing about?

2. What did *Celotex* do to summary judgment standards? Why does it matter? One way of understanding the answers to these questions is to consider the burdens on the parties at trial. At trial, Celotex, the defendant, could prevail in two ways. It could prove that Mr. Catrett was not exposed to its asbestos by demonstrating that neither it nor its predecessor companies had ever manufactured asbestos—unlikely given that asbestos was a principal part of its business at that time. Or it could prevail if Mrs. Catrett *failed to show* that Mr. Catrett was exposed to its asbestos, perhaps by convincing a jury that the sole testimony linking Mr. Catrett to Celotex asbestos was not credible because the witness had been bribed.

   a. Explain why these two routes lead to the same result.

   b. As a matter of practice (if we eliminate the dramatic and unlikely examples above and suppose that one of Celotex's predecessor firms did distribute asbestos but that the evidence linking Celotex to Mr. Catrett is thin), which standard—that in *Adickes* or *Celotex*—is likely to be easier for Celotex to meet?

   c. According to *Celotex*, the defendant Celotex can certainly win its summary judgment motion by showing that Mr. Catrett was not exposed to its product. That is no news: *Adickes* had said as much. Can Celotex also win by showing that Mrs. Catrett has failed to show that Mr. Catrett was exposed? The answer in *Adickes* was no. Consider this quotation from *Adickes*:

> [Defendant] here did not carry its burden because of its failure to foreclose the possibility that there was a policeman in the Kress store while petitioner was awaiting service, and that this policeman reached an understanding with some Kress employee that [plaintiff] not be served.

Now consider this quotation from *Celotex*:

> [T]he burden on the moving party [at summary judgment] may be discharged by "showing"—that is, pointing out to the District Court—that there is an absence of evidence to support the nonmoving party's case. . . .

Explain how this shift in emphasis could affect the number of cases in which courts will grant summary judgment.

3. *Celotex* focuses on the state of evidence at the time of summary judgment: It will not suffice for the party resisting summary judgment to say, "I'm planning to look into that before trial, and I'm sure I'll come up with evidence on that point." Unless the party can show that it has had insufficient time for discovery, it will lose. How would a party that believed it had had insufficient opportunity for discovery ward off summary judgment? See Rule 56(d).

Procedure as Strategy

Celotex is about summary judgment. But both in the federal courts and in the state courts that have taken the same path, it will affect how and when parties use discovery. Before *Celotex*, a party with the burden of production at trial could wait until quite late in the pretrial stage to assemble all its evidence, resting fairly secure in the knowledge that it would be very difficult for the opposing party to *disprove* the claim or defense. After *Celotex*, waiting until just before trial to assemble the evidence will be too late: If the basic evidence supporting your claim or defense is not available at the summary judgment stage, you lose.

4. Notice the *Celotex* formulation: The party that will have the burden of proof at trial has the equivalent burden at summary judgment—the burden of "mak[ing] a showing" of evidence sufficient to let a rational trier of fact find in its favor. This alignment of burdens at summary judgment with burdens at trial means that the standard for summary judgment will apply differently depending on which party is moving for summary judgment. To see this point, suppose that one of the issues in contention is whether asbestosis (as opposed to some other disease) caused Mr. Catrett's death. Mrs. Catrett's complaint alleges that asbestosis caused her husband's death; Celotex denies that allegation in its answer. Mrs. Catrett as the plaintiff will have the burden of proof at trial on that issue.

   a. First suppose that Celotex, the defendant, moves for summary judgment on this issue of causation. In its supporting papers, it points out that no medically qualified expert has opined that asbestosis caused Mr. Catrett's death. In her response, Mrs. Catrett produces the affidavit of a pathologist who recites his professional qualifications, describes his examination of the relevant tissue samples, and comes to the conclusion that the laboratory findings are "consistent with Mr. Catrett's having died as a result of asbestosis." Explain why the court should deny Celotex's motion for summary judgment.

   b. Now suppose that it is Mrs. Catrett, not Celotex, who moves for summary judgment on the issue of causation. In support of this motion she produces the same affidavit. In response, Celotex produces no affidavit or other evidence contradicting plaintiff's expert. Explain why the court should deny Mrs. Catrett's motion for summary judgment.

   c. Why does the same affidavit lead to the same result (denial of summary judgment) even though different parties are moving for summary judgment?

5. The Court in *Celotex* did not actually decide who should prevail on the defendant's motion for summary judgment. It contented itself instead with setting out a new standard for summary judgment and remanding for the lower courts to decide the case using that new standard. Suppose that Celotex had made an adequate initial showing under that new standard to justify the grant of summary judgment—unless plaintiff in response produced evidence that would entitle a rational trier of fact to find in her favor. Such a situation would frame

a question for the lower court: Did the material presented by Mrs. Catrett in response to the motion for summary judgment suffice? We next consider how courts should approach this question.

2. Summary Judgment in Action: How Courts Should Assess the Evidence

The other two cases in the so-called summary judgment trilogy—*Anderson* and *Matsushita*—set out the Supreme Court's view about how courts should assess competing information offered by opposing sides at summary judgment. The Court in *Anderson* explained that "summary judgment will not lie if the dispute about a material fact is 'genuine,' that is, if the evidence is such that a reasonable jury could return a verdict for the nonmoving party" and that, in making this assessment, "[t]he evidence of the nonmovant is to be believed, and all justifiable inferences are to be drawn in his favor." The Court in *Matsushita* gave district courts discretion to assess the plausibility of the parties' contentions and grant summary judgment if the nonmoving party could show only "some metaphysical doubt as to the material facts." Consider the ways in which the next two decisions interpret and apply these standards.

Tolan v. Cotton
134 S. Ct. 1861 (2014)

Per Curiam.
During the early morning hours of New Year's Eve, 2008, police sergeant Jeffrey Cotton fired three bullets at Robert Tolan; one of those bullets hit its target and punctured Tolan's right lung. At the time of the shooting, Tolan was unarmed on his parents' front porch about 15 to 20 feet away from Cotton. Tolan sued, alleging that Cotton had exercised excessive force in violation of the Fourth Amendment. The District Court granted summary judgment to Cotton. In articulating the factual context of the case, the Fifth Circuit failed to adhere to the axiom that in ruling on a motion for summary judgment, "[t]he evidence of the nonmovant is to be believed, and all justifiable inferences are to be drawn in his favor." Anderson v. Liberty Lobby, Inc., 477 U.S. 242, 255 (1986). For that reason, we vacate its decision and remand the case for further proceedings consistent with this opinion.

I

A

The following facts, which we view in the light most favorable to Tolan, are taken from the record evidence and the opinions below. At around 2:00 on the morning of December 31, 2008, John Edwards, a police officer, was on patrol in Bellaire, Texas, when he noticed a black Nissan sport utility vehicle turning quickly onto a residential street. The officer watched the vehicle park on the side of the street in front of a house. Two men exited: Tolan and his cousin, Anthony Cooper.

Edwards attempted to enter the license plate number of the vehicle into a computer in his squad car. But he keyed an incorrect character; instead of entering plate number 696BGK, he entered 695BGK. That incorrect number matched a stolen vehicle of the same color and make. This match caused the squad car's computer to send an automatic message to other police units, informing them that Edwards had found a stolen vehicle.

Edwards exited his cruiser, drew his service pistol and ordered Tolan and Cooper to the ground. He accused Tolan and Cooper of having stolen the car. Cooper responded, "That's not true." And Tolan explained, "That's my car." Tolan then complied with the officer's demand to lie face-down on the home's front porch.

As it turned out, Tolan and Cooper were at the home where Tolan lived with his parents. Hearing the commotion, Tolan's parents exited the front door in their pajamas. In an attempt to keep the misunderstanding from escalating into something more, Tolan's father instructed Cooper to lie down, and instructed Tolan and Cooper to say nothing. Tolan and Cooper then remained face-down.

Edwards told Tolan's parents that he believed Tolan and Cooper had stolen the vehicle. In response, Tolan's father identified Tolan as his son, and Tolan's mother explained that the vehicle belonged to the family and that no crime had been committed. Tolan's father explained, with his hands in the air, "[T]his is my nephew. This is my son. We live here. This is my house." Tolan's mother similarly offered, "[S]ir this is a big mistake. This car is not stolen. . . . That's our car."

While Tolan and Cooper continued to lie on the ground in silence, Edwards radioed for assistance. Shortly thereafter, Sergeant Jeffrey Cotton arrived on the scene and drew his pistol. Edwards told Cotton that Cooper and Tolan had exited a stolen vehicle. Tolan's mother reiterated that she and her husband owned both the car Tolan had been driving and the home where these events were unfolding. Cotton then ordered her to stand against the family's garage door. In response to Cotton's order, Tolan's mother asked, "[A]re you kidding me? We've lived her[e] 15 years. We've never had anything like this happen before."

The parties disagree as to what happened next. Tolan's mother and Cooper testified during Cotton's criminal trial that Cotton grabbed her arm and slammed her against the garage door with such force that she fell to the ground. Tolan similarly testified that Cotton pushed his mother against the garage door. In addition, Tolan offered testimony from his mother and photographic evidence to demonstrate that Cotton used enough force to leave bruises on her arms and back that lasted for days. By contrast, Cotton testified in his deposition that when he was escorting the mother to the garage, she flipped her arm up and told him to get his hands off her. He also testified that he did not know whether he left bruises but believed that he had not.

The parties also dispute the manner in which Tolan responded. Tolan testified in his deposition and during the criminal trial that upon seeing his mother being pushed, he rose to his knees. Edwards and Cotton testified that Tolan rose to his feet. Both parties agree that Tolan then exclaimed, from roughly 15 to 20 feet away, "[G]et your fucking hands off my mom." The parties also agree that Cotton then drew his pistol and fired three shots at Tolan. Tolan and his mother testified that these shots came with no verbal warning. One of the bullets entered Tolan's chest, collapsing his right lung and piercing his liver. While Tolan survived, he suffered a life-altering injury that disrupted his budding professional baseball career and causes him to experience pain on a daily basis.

B

In May 2009, Cooper, Tolan, and Tolan's parents filed this suit in the Southern District of Texas, alleging claims under Rev. Stat. §1979, 42 U.S.C. §1983. Tolan claimed, among other things, that Cotton had used excessive force against him in violation of the Fourth Amendment. After discovery, Cotton moved for summary judgment.

The District Court granted summary judgment to Cotton. It reasoned that Cotton's use of force was not unreasonable and therefore did not violate the Fourth Amendment. The Fifth Circuit affirmed.

In reaching this conclusion, the Fifth Circuit began by noting that at the time Cotton shot Tolan, "it was . . . clearly established that an officer had the right to use deadly force if that officer harbored an objective and reasonable belief that a suspect presented an 'immediate threat to [his] safety.'" The Court of Appeals reasoned that Tolan failed to overcome th[at] bar because "an objectively-reasonable officer in Sergeant Cotton's position could have . . . believed" that Tolan "presented an 'immediate threat to the safety of the officers.'" In support of this conclusion, the court relied on the following facts: the front porch had been "dimly-lit"; Tolan's mother had "refus[ed] orders to remain quiet and calm"; and Tolan's words had amounted to a "verba[l] threa[t]." Most critically, the court also relied on the purported fact that Tolan was "moving to intervene in" Cotton's handling of his mother, and that Cotton therefore could reasonably have feared for his life. Accordingly, the court held, Cotton did not violate clearly established law in shooting Tolan. . . .

II

B

In holding that Cotton's actions did not violate clearly established law, the Fifth Circuit failed to view the evidence at summary judgment in the light most favorable to Tolan with respect to the central facts of this case. By failing to credit evidence that contradicted some of its key factual conclusions, the court improperly "weigh[ed] the evidence" and resolved disputed issues in favor of the moving party, *Anderson*, 477 U.S., at 249.

First, the court relied on its view that at the time of the shooting, the Tolans' front porch was "dimly-lit." The court appears to have drawn this assessment from Cotton's statements in a deposition that when he fired at Tolan, the porch was "'fairly dark,'" and lit by a gas lamp that was "'decorative.'" In his own deposition, however, Tolan's father was asked whether the gas lamp was in fact "more decorative than illuminating." He said that it was not. Moreover, Tolan stated in his deposition that two floodlights shone on the driveway during the incident, and Cotton acknowledged that there were two motion-activated lights in front of the house. And Tolan confirmed that at the time of the shooting, he was "not in darkness."

Second, the Fifth Circuit stated that Tolan's mother "refus[ed] orders to remain quiet and calm," thereby "compound[ing]" Cotton's belief that Tolan "presented an immediate threat to the safety of the officers." But here, too, the court did not credit directly contradictory evidence. Although the parties agree that Tolan's mother repeatedly informed officers that Tolan was her son, that she lived in the home in front of which he had parked, and that the vehicle he had been driving belonged to her and her husband, there is a dispute as to how calmly she provided this information. Cotton stated during his deposition that Tolan's mother was "very agitated" when she spoke to the officers. By contrast, Tolan's mother testified at Cotton's criminal trial that she was neither "aggravated" nor "agitated."

Third, the Court concluded that Tolan was "shouting," and "verbally threatening" the officer, in the moments before the shooting. The court noted, and the parties agree, that while Cotton was grabbing the arm of his mother, Tolan told Cotton, "[G]et your fucking hands off my mom." But Tolan testified that he "was not screaming." And a jury could reasonably infer that his words, in context, did not amount to a statement of intent to inflict harm. Tolan's mother testified in Cotton's criminal trial that he slammed her against a garage door with enough force to cause bruising that lasted for days. A jury could well have concluded that a reasonable officer would have heard Tolan's words not as a threat, but as a son's plea not to continue any assault of his mother.

Fourth, the Fifth Circuit inferred that at the time of the shooting, Tolan was "moving to intervene in Sergeant Cotton's" interaction with his mother. The court appears to have credited Edwards' account that at the time of the shooting, Tolan was on both feet "[i]n a crouch" or a "charging position" looking as if he was going to move forward. Tolan testified at trial, however, that he was on his knees when Cotton shot him, a fact corroborated by his mother. Tolan also testified in his deposition that he "wasn't going anywhere," and emphasized that he did not "jump up."

Considered together, these facts lead to the inescapable conclusion that the court below credited the evidence of the party seeking summary judgment and failed properly to acknowledge key evidence offered by the party opposing that motion. And while "this Court is not equipped to correct every perceived error coming from the lower federal courts," Boag v. MacDougall, 454 U.S. 364, 366 (1982) (O'Connor, J., concurring), we intervene here because the opinion below reflects a clear misapprehension of summary judgment standards in light of our precedents.

The witnesses on both sides come to this case with their own perceptions, recollections, and even potential biases. It is in part for that reason that genuine disputes are generally resolved by juries in our adversarial system. By weighing the evidence and reaching factual inferences contrary to Tolan's competent evidence, the court below neglected to adhere to the fundamental principle that at the summary judgment stage, reasonable inferences should be drawn in favor of the nonmoving party.

Applying that principle here, the court should have acknowledged and credited Tolan's evidence with regard to the lighting, his mother's demeanor, whether he shouted words that were an overt threat, and his positioning during the shooting. . . . The judgment of the United States Court of Appeals for the Fifth Circuit is vacated, and the case is remanded for further proceedings consistent with this opinion.

[The concurring opinion of Justice ALITO is omitted.]

Notes and Problems

---

1. There are several facts in this case that appear not to be in dispute. Tolan and his cousin were pulled over in front of Tolan's house; the officer believed Tolan's car was stolen and ordered the two men to the ground; Tolan's parents came out and identified their son; and Cotton came on the scene, drew his pistol, and ordered Tolan's mother to stand against the garage. What facts are disputed?

2. What, in the Supreme Court's view, did the District Court and Court of Appeals do wrong in granting summary judgment for Cotton?

3. Is this a case in which summary judgment should, instead, be granted to Tolan?

4. Note that in this case the Court is not announcing a new legal rule but, instead, correcting an error from the lower courts. The decision makes note of the fact that the Supreme Court cannot grant certiorari in every case in which there was an error by the lower court. Why do you think the Court chose to intervene in this case?

Bias v. Advantage International, Inc.

905 F.2d 1558 (D.C. Cir. 1990)

SENTELLE, J.

This case arises out of the tragic death from cocaine intoxication of University of Maryland basketball star Leonard K. Bias ("Bias"). James Bias, as Personal Representative of the Estate of Leonard K. Bias, deceased ("the Estate"), appeals an order of the District Court for the District of Columbia which granted summary judgment to defendants Advantage International, Inc. ("Advantage") and A. Lee Fentress. . . . For the reasons which follow, we affirm. . . .

I. Background

On April 7, 1986, after the close of his college basketball career, Bias entered into a representation agreement with Advantage whereby Advantage agreed to advise and represent Bias in his affairs. Fentress was the particular Advantage representative servicing the Bias account. On June 17 of that year Bias was picked by the Boston Celtics in the first round of the National Basketball Association draft. On the morning of

June 19, 1986, Bias died of cocaine intoxication. The Estate sued Advantage and Fentress for . . . injuries allegedly arising out of the representation arrangement between Bias and the defendants.

Issue

[T]he Estate alleges that, prior to Bias's death, Bias and his parents directed Fentress to obtain a one-million dollar life insurance policy on Bias's life, that Fentress represented to Bias and Bias's parents that he had secured such a policy, and that in reliance on Fentress's assurances, Bias's parents did not independently seek to buy an insurance policy on Bias's life. . . . [D]efendants . . . did not secure any life insurance coverage for Bias prior to his death. . . .

Procedure

The District Court awarded the defendants summary judgment. . . . With respect to the [life insurance] claim, the District Court held, in effect, that the Estate did not suffer any damage from the defendants' alleged failure to obtain life insurance for Bias because, even if the defendants had tried to obtain a one-million dollar policy on Bias's life, they would not have been able to do so. The District Court based this conclusion on the facts, about which it found no genuine issue, that Bias was a cocaine user and that no insurer in 1986 would have issued a one-million dollar life insurance policy, or "jumbo" policy, to a cocaine user unless the applicant made a misrepresentation regarding the applicant's use of drugs, thereby rendering the insurance policy void. . . .

The Estate appeals . . . the District Court's conclusions, arguing that there is a genuine issue as to Bias's insurability. . . .

II. Summary Judgment Standard

SJ Rule

The Supreme Court has stated that the moving party always bears the initial responsibility of informing the district court of the basis for its motion and identifying those portions of the record which it believes demonstrate the absence of a genuine issue of material fact. *Celotex Corp. v. Catrett*. The Supreme Court also explained that summary judgment is appropriate, no matter which party is the moving party, where a party fails to make a showing sufficient to establish the existence of an element essential to that party's case, and on which that party will bear the burden of proof at trial. Thus, the moving party must explain its reasons for concluding that the record does not reveal any genuine issues of material fact, and must make a showing supporting its claims insofar as those claims involve issues on which it will bear the burden at trial.

Once the moving party has carried its burden, the responsibility then shifts to the nonmoving party to show that there is, in fact, a genuine issue of material fact. The Supreme Court has directed that the nonmoving party "must do more than simply show that there is some metaphysical doubt as to the material facts." Matsushita Elec. Industrial Co. v. Zenith Radio, 475 U.S. 574, 586 (1986). The nonmoving party "must come forward with 'specific facts showing that there is a *genuine issue for trial*.'" (emphasis in original). In evaluating the nonmovant's proffer, a court must of course draw from the evidence all justifiable inferences in favor of the nonmovant. Anderson v. Liberty Lobby, Inc., 477 U.S. 242, 255 (1986).

III. The Insurance Issue

The District Court's determination that there was no genuine issue involving Bias's insurability rests on two subsidiary conclusions: First, the District Court concluded that there was no genuine issue as to the fact that Bias was a drug user. Second, the District Court held that there was no dispute about the fact that as a drug user, Bias could not have obtained a jumbo life insurance policy. We can only affirm the District Court's award of summary judgment to the defendants on the insurance issue if both of these conclusions were correct.

A. Bias's Prior Drug Use

The defendants in this case offered the eyewitness testimony of two former teammates of Bias, Terry Long and David Gregg, in order to show that Bias was a cocaine user during the period prior to his death. Long and Gregg both described numerous occasions when they saw Bias ingest cocaine, and Long testified that he was introduced to cocaine by Bias and that Bias sometimes supplied others with cocaine.

Although on appeal the Estate attempts to discredit the testimony of Long and Gregg, the Estate did not seek to impeach the testimony of these witnesses before the District Court, and the Estate made no effort to depose these witnesses. Instead, the Estate offered affidavits from each of Bias's parents stating that Bias was not a drug user; the deposition testimony of Bias's basketball coach, Charles "Lefty" Driesell, who testified that he knew Bias well for four years and never knew Bias to be a user of drugs at any time prior to his death; and the results of several drug tests administered to Bias during the four years prior to his death which may have shown that, on the occasions when the tests were administered, there were no traces in Bias's system of the drugs for which he was tested.

Because the Estate's generalized evidence that Bias was not a drug user did not contradict the more specific testimony of teammates who knew Bias well and had seen him use cocaine on particular occasions, the District Court determined that there was no genuine issue as to the fact that Bias was a drug user. We agree.

There is no question that the defendants satisfied their initial burden on the issue of Bias's drug use. The testimony of Long and Gregg clearly tends to show that Bias was a cocaine user. We also agree with the District Court that the Estate did not rebut the defendants' showing. The testimony of Bias's parents to the effect that they knew Bias well and did not know him to be a drug user does not rebut the Long and Gregg testimony about Bias's drug use on particular occasions. The District Court properly held that rebuttal testimony either must come from persons familiar with the particular events to which the defendants' witnesses testified or must otherwise cast more than metaphysical doubt on the credibility of that testimony. Bias's parents and coach did not have personal knowledge of Bias's activities at the sorts of parties and gatherings about which Long and Gregg testified. The drug test results offered by the Estate may show that Bias had no cocaine in his system on the dates when the tests were administered, but, as the District Court correctly noted, these tests speak only to Bias's abstention during the periods preceding the tests. The tests do not rebut the

Long and Gregg testimony that on a number of occasions Bias ingested cocaine in their presence.

The Estate could have deposed Long and Gregg, or otherwise attempted to impeach their testimony. The Estate also could have offered the testimony of other friends or teammates of Bias who were present at some of the gatherings described by Long and Gregg, who went out with Bias frequently, or who were otherwise familiar with his social habits. The Estate did none of these things. The Estate is not entitled to reach the jury merely on the supposition that the jury might not believe the defendants' witnesses. We thus agree with the District Court that there was no genuine issue of fact concerning Bias's status as a cocaine user.

B. The Availability of a Jumbo Policy in Light of Bias's Prior Drug Use . . .

The defendants offered evidence that *every* insurance company inquires about the prior drug use of an applicant for a jumbo policy at *some point* in the application process. . . . The Estate's evidence that some insurance companies existed in 1986 which did not inquire about prior drug use at certain particular stages in the application process does not undermine the defendant's claim that at *some* point in the process *every* insurance company did inquire about drug use, particularly where a jumbo policy was involved. The Estate failed to name a single particular company or provide other evidence that a single company existed which would have issued a jumbo policy in 1986 without inquiring about the applicant's drug use. Because the Estate has failed to do more than show that there is "some metaphysical doubt as to the material facts," *Matsushita Elec.*, the District Court properly concluded that there was no genuine issue of material fact as to the insurability of a drug user. . . .

In order to withstand a summary judgment motion once the moving party has made a prima facie showing to support its claims, the nonmoving party must come forward with specific facts showing that there is a genuine issue for trial. Fed. R. Civ. P. 56(e). The Estate has failed to come forward with such facts in this case, relying instead on bare arguments and allegations or on evidence which does not actually create a genuine issue for trial. For this reason, we affirm the District Court's award of summary judgment to the defendants in this case.

Notes and Problems

1. Start by framing the claim and defense around which the summary judgment motion revolves.

   a. Bias's estate sues for breach of contract. What contract? What are the damages sought?

   b. How did defendants respond? What parts of the claim did defendants attack?

   c. How did plaintiff seek to rebut defendants' response?

2. Explain how defendants used evidence unearthed during discovery to attack plaintiff's claim. Explain how *Celotex* enabled them to make such an attack.

3. Once defendants made this motion for summary judgment, *Celotex* and its companion cases allow the nonmoving party (here the plaintiff) to respond in either of two ways. He can argue that the party moving for summary judgment has not adequately demonstrated a deficiency in the evidence available to the party resisting summary judgment. Or, he can present evidence to counter the movant's evidence, in the hope of demonstrating the existence of an issue of fact.

   a. The plaintiff in *Bias* obviously took the latter course. Explain why that was almost certainly the right move to make, even though it did not succeed.

   b. Why does the plaintiff lose? Is the court correctly interpreting the rule and case law?

   c. The best demonstration of what constitutes a "genuine dispute as to [a] material fact," as well as of how close the decision in *Bias* comes to the line, emerges if we think about some variations on the facts of the case. Start by supposing that the sole evidence of drug use presented by the defendants was the testimony of Bias's friends, who said under oath that they had on several specific dates seen Bias use cocaine. Further suppose that plaintiff had presented evidence of other persons, present at the same times, who unequivocally testified that they had been in Bias's company the whole time and that he had not used drugs. Explain why summary judgment would not be appropriate.

   d. Now come closer to the actual case, in which there was testimony that Bias had ingested cocaine on specific dates and that he had provided drugs for others; there was also evidence (the negative drug tests) that he had been drug-free on other days, and that close associates and family did not believe him to have used drugs. Why does this state of evidence not create a similar conflict for a trier of fact to resolve?

   e. The court's answer to that question is that the evidence of drug use was specific, while the evidence of non-use was general, and that the specific trumps the general—such that there really isn't a conflict for the trier to resolve. Suppose that Bias had died when he was struck by a car while crossing the street. Under those circumstances if the defendants had moved for summary judgment by introducing evidence of drug use and arguing that he would not have been able to obtain a life insurance policy, do you suppose the case would have come out the same way? Or would plaintiff have been able to argue, first, that, at worst, defendants' evidence showed occasional exposure to the drug and, second, that the defendants were trying to avoid their own breach of contract by posthumously smearing the name of a great African-American athlete? Moreover, the defendants were doing so with the testimony of persons who, by their own account, were habitual drug users; shouldn't Bias's estate be able to put them on the stand before a jury and probe their veracity?

   f. In the real world, we know that Bias did not die in a car accident, but from a drug overdose. Is the court, without explicitly saying so, inferring from the cocaine-related death that Bias must have been a *habitual* user, that drugs would inevitably have showed up in any insurance physical, and that he was therefore uninsurable? If so, are such inferences permissible?

4. Given the facts, could plaintiff have avoided summary judgment?

    a. We are told that Bias was given "several" drug tests, all of which were negative. The court says that this demonstrates only that Bias had not used drugs recently on the days the tests were given and that is not enough to overcome specific testimony by the associates of drug use. But suppose the tests had been administered randomly, some of them in the same months where the other witnesses testified to drug use. Would that be enough to cast doubt on the picture of habitual drug use? Recall that the question on summary judgment is whether there is an issue of fact to try.

    b. We are also told that plaintiff's counsel did not depose the two friends who testified as to Bias's drug use or attack their credibility. What sort of deposition questions might have shed enough doubt on their credibility to create a triable issue of fact? What if they admitted that they felt Bias's parents had mistreated and taken advantage of Bias, and that they didn't like the parents and would be happy if the parents lost the suit? Would that be enough?

    c. What other facts would you, as plaintiff's counsel, attempt to unearth during discovery and use in your opposition to defendant's summary judgment motion?

* * *

As you have seen, most lawsuits filed in U.S. courts will end by the time they have reached the stages described in this chapter. But don't stop reading: Those suits will end because the parties understand the processes discussed in the next several chapters. One can, therefore, think about those processes in two ways. From one point of view, they will yield results so predictable that parties can settle without regret. From another point of view, they are so unpredictable and so dangerous that parties will settle even strong cases to avoid them. As you read the next chapters, consider which point of view seems closest to the truth.

Assessment Questions

Q1. Properly invoking federal diversity jurisdiction, Abe sues Barbara in federal district court alleging a breach of contract. Before the suit goes far, the parties agree to settle the suit: Barb will pay Abe $100,000 and Abe will drop his claim. If, after voluntarily dismissing his claim, Abe refiles an identical one . . .

    A. Abe's suit will automatically be barred by the prior case.

    B. Barb must answer Abe's claim by invoking the settlement as an affirmative defense.

    C. Abe's suit will be barred only if the settlement is in writing.

    D. Abe's suit will be barred only if the judge approved the settlement.

Q2. Mediation, arbitration, and settlement all resolve lawsuits without trial. Identify all of the following statements about the relation among these approaches that are correct.

    A. Mediation aims at helping parties come to settlement.

    B. Mediation usually follows a successful arbitration.

    C. An unsuccessful mediation might lead to arbitration.

    D. Parties must choose at the beginning of their case whether they will arbitrate or mediate.

Q3. Jane, as a condition of her employment with GrowCo, signs an agreement to arbitrate any dispute between her and her employer. Such a dispute arises. The state where Jane is employed has a new statute barring arbitration of employment disputes.

    A. The state statute will have no effect on the arbitrability of this dispute.

    B. The statute will bar arbitration of this dispute.

    C. Whether this dispute is arbitrable will depend on the state's contract law.

    D. Jane does not need to arbitrate unless her claim arises under federal law.

Q4. Plaintiff sues for negligently inflicted injuries. Defendant's answer denies causation and asserts as an affirmative defense the two-year statute of limitations that applies to such claims. If, at the close of discovery, defendant moves for summary judgment . . .

    A. The court will enter summary judgment for the defendant if the defendant argues that discovery has yielded no evidence that would permit a jury to find for plaintiff on causation, and the plaintiff does not offer evidence of causation in her opposition.

    B. The court will not enter summary judgment for the defendant if the defendant argues that discovery has yielded no evidence that would permit a jury to find that plaintiff's claim is within the statute of limitations, and the plaintiff does not offer evidence regarding the statute of limitations in her opposition.

    C. Neither of the above.

Q5. After *Celotex, Anderson,* and *Matsushita* . . .

    A. Parties are under pressure to use available discovery devices before the date on which the court's scheduling order tells them to expect motions for summary judgment.

    B. So long as a party opposing summary judgment puts forth evidence supporting her claim, the motion will be denied.

    C. Judges must draw all inferences in favor of the party opposing summary judgment.

Analysis of Assessment Questions

Q1. B is the only correct response. Rule 8(c) lists "accord and satisfaction," the archaic term for settlement, as an affirmative defense. A is wrong: Since accord and satisfaction is an affirmative defense, defendant must raise it. C is wrong because, like oral contracts of other sorts, an oral settlement agreement is perfectly valid; because it will be harder to prove, prudence suggests getting these agreements written down, but that's a matter of prudence, not legal validity. D is wrong because judicial approval of settlements is not required except in a few types of cases—those involving minors or incompetent persons and those involving class actions.

Q2. A and C are the correct responses. A is correct because mediation is assisted negotiation. C is correct because even if the parties cannot agree on settlement terms (the unsuccessful mediation), they might be able to agree on a process to resolve the dispute (arbitration). B is wrong because if arbitration is successful, the dispute settles and there would be nothing for a mediator to decide. D is wrong because parties can decide at any point during—or before—litigation to mediate or arbitrate their claims.

Q3. A and C are the correct responses. A is correct because the Federal Arbitration Act, which governs arbitration agreements, preempts state law, providing that arbitration agreements may be avoided only on grounds applicable to *all* contracts; this statute, which singles out arbitration in employment agreements, fails the test of being generally applicable to all contracts. C is correct for the converse reason: If this agreement fails under the state's general law of unconscionability, courts may refuse to enforce it, but not otherwise. B is wrong for the same reasons listed under A. D is wrong because the FAA governs all agreements to arbitrate involving "commerce," which has been very broadly interpreted—including state law claims.

Q4. A and B are correct. They are correct because the *plaintiff* has the burden of production on the question of causation, and if the evidence to date hasn't yielded such evidence, after *Celotex* defendant wins on this showing. B is correct because the burdens of production are reversed: *Defendant* has the burden of production on an affirmative defense and can prevail only by making a positive showing that the statute has run. C is wrong because A and B are correct.

Q5. A and C are correct. A is correct because *Celotex* tells judges to view the evidence presented as of the time of summary judgment and to grant summary judgment if the party with the burden of production has not collected and presented enough evidence to allow a rational trier of fact to find in its favor. That instruction tells parties with the burden of production that they must be able to present such a collection of evidence at the moment of summary judgment—and thus makes it critical to deploy available discovery tools to gather that evidence. C is correct because *Anderson* tells us so—at summary judgment, evidence must be viewed in the light most favorable to the nonmoving party. The district court and Fifth Circuit did not do so in *Tolan v. Cotton* and were reversed as a result. B is incorrect because the party opposing summary judgment has not avoided judgment simply by presenting evidence in her opposition. Instead, that evidence must create a material factual dispute. In the *Bias* case, both sides did offer evidence supporting their claims, but the court found that the information offered by the plaintiff in opposition to defendants' summary judgment motion did not create a factual dispute.

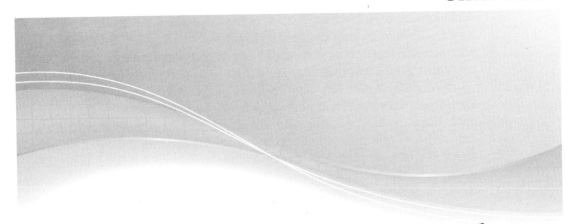

CHAPTER 9

The Trier and the Trial

We now come to the only part of civil procedure about which you thought you knew something before starting law school. Trials are a familiar part of our general social knowledge. They have been the stuff of drama for centuries, and of the scriptures of several religious traditions for millennia. In this tradition, trial, the culminating moment of every lawsuit, brings truth to light as witnesses blurt out surprising statements, or juries do justice in the face of apparently overwhelming adverse evidence. And when the verdict arrives, the case is over: Victors beam, losers slink away.

Unfortunately, most of that knowledge turns out to be wrong. First: Despite the ubiquity of trials in books and movies, there are at present very few trials in real life. As you have already gathered from earlier chapters, in the federal courts fewer than 2 percent of civil cases reach this point; in state courts the proportion is somewhat higher, but still small. Second, when civil cases do get to trial, they look very little like the edge-of-the-seat versions you read about and watch. Instead, there are few surprises and little drama, at least if lawyers have conducted appropriate discovery. In well-prepared civil litigation both sides will know what every witness or document will say, and if a witness's testimony varies from that given in deposition, he will be promptly impeached with prior sworn testimony. Dramatic revelations, if they occur, may even provide the basis for a new trial, at least if the information disclosed at trial was sought by one of the parties but not revealed in discovery. The parties may not know how the case will be decided, but they will know well the conflicting versions of the story. This phase of litigation differs from popular depictions for a third reason: Trial is not the end of the saga, or at least not always. As we will see in the next chapter, there may well be an appeal, but even if there is not, there will certainly be post-verdict motions for judgment as a matter of law or, alternatively, for a new trial.

Why, then, study a rare and usually dull intermediate stage of civil litigation? First, trials, rare though they have come to be, shape almost every aspect of procedure. The elaborate provisions for discovery have as one of their primary goals the uncovering of information to be presented at trial. Much of the law of evidence is aimed at controlling the flow of information during trial. Likewise, the emphasis on the presentation of live witnesses (rather than depositions or other documentary evidence)—which brings with it the opportunity for theatrical displays by lawyers—stems from a conception of the trial as the culmination of litigation. Even the adversarial stance of the lawyers—perhaps more marked in Anglo-American law than in other systems—may flow in part from the realization that the whole case rides on a single presentation in a comparatively short time span before a judge or jury.

Second, although trials do not display the kind of drama that you have come to expect, there is, nevertheless, a certain kind of drama in trials. But the drama goes on behind the scenes, as the parties battle over which judge and which jurors should be allowed to decide the case, what they should be allowed to hear, and whether the judge's or jurors' decision should be allowed to stand. This chapter goes behind the scenes to examine the actors in these concealed struggles for power that can make all the difference in the outcome of the case.

This chapter will tackle the topic by asking (and answering) just two questions: *Who* will decide the case? (Sections A and B, dealing with choosing judges and juries); and *How* will they decide the case? (Sections C-G, about the procedures that shape trial). We begin with who.

A. CHOOSING AND CHALLENGING JUDGES

Whether or not there will be a jury in your case, there will be a judge. That judge may rule on whether you are entitled to a jury. And if you are entitled to a jury, that judge will rule on your challenges to the jury pool and individual jurors. And long before you get to the trial stage, that judge—in almost all federal courts and in many state courts—will have likely ruled on various aspects of the litigation, from the sufficiency of pleadings to motions to dismiss to discovery disputes and summary judgment motions. So a great deal turns on the wisdom, knowledge, fairness, and diligence of the judge. Litigators will tell you that, next to the merits of the case, the identity of the judge is the most important factor in predicting the outcome of the case.

How do judges get to be judges? Broadly speaking, they get to their offices in one of two ways: by appointment or by election. Federal judges are nominated by the President and confirmed by the U.S. Senate; once appointed they can be removed only by impeachment. Most state judges owe their initial place on the bench to gubernatorial appointment. Thereafter they are subject to occasional electoral exposure, sometimes by facing a challenge in a reconfirmation election. A minority of state judges will first take the bench as a winner of an electoral contest. These elections are usually nonpartisan, but in some states judges run as candidates of a given political party. Both the appointive and the electoral process leave their imprints.

Let's start with the imprint of a President, governor, or other appointing authority. Though these executives may have run on a platform promising to appoint judges of a certain cast of mind, all will want to appoint judges who will not embarrass them. That means a very thorough background check, which will be devoted partly to ascertaining the skill, professional standing, and reputation of the nominee, and partly to looking into nooks and crannies of her past with an eye to discovering anything that might block her confirmation or cast the appointing authority in a bad light. Electoral contests may also turn up such information—and may pressure the judicial candidate to take positions on issues of concern to the voters. If the judge has to face voters in a reconfirmation election, she may also be wary about rulings that will be unpopular or easily mischaracterized by opponents. That is not to say that judges will not make such rulings—they do every day—but it is to say that the consequences of such a ruling may lurk in the back of the judicial mind.

Beyond these features lie those of background. Almost all judges will be trained as lawyers; only a few states do not require lower judicial officers (magistrates or justices of the peace) to have legal training. Judges will thus bring with them to the bench all the knowledge and habits of thought such training implies; even at this early stage of your career you are likely learning that lawyers think about many matters differently than nonlawyers. And because they have half a career as lawyers behind them, judges will not likely have had significant experience in ballet dancing, heavy construction, cab-driving, or elementary school teaching and therefore lack the knowledge and sense of the world that each of these occupations might bring. Moreover, they are distinguished even from the million or so people in the United States who are licensed to practice law: They belong to the subset of about 20,000 who hold judicial offices.

Such professional training helps keep judges focused on factors the law defines as legally relevant, but judges are human, and humans are fallible. How does the system seek to protect litigants against biased judges? There are two answers to that question: judicial discipline and recusal.

Most states and the federal judiciary have procedures for disciplining judges who, though unbiased, fail to comply with the Judicial Canons of Ethics. States have various mechanisms for receiving, investigating, and acting upon complaints against state judges. In the federal judiciary, 28 U.S.C. §§351 et seq. permits persons to file complaints against judges, and requires the chief judge of each circuit to investigate the charges and to take various actions—including dismissal of the complaint, a declaration that the judge in question is disabled, censure or reprimand, and referral of the case to the House of Representatives for impeachment proceedings. But violation of the Canons, while perhaps cause for complaint and discipline against a judge, does not remove that judge from your particular case. Only recusal does that.

There are two forms of recusal: peremptory and for cause. About a third of the states, mostly midwestern and western, permit peremptory challenges of judges. A party wishing to make such a challenge simply files a timely affidavit alleging in conclusory terms that the judge is prejudiced against the party. James Sample, David Posen & Michael Young, Fair Courts: Setting Recusal Standards 8 (Brennan Center for Justice 2008). Actual prejudice need not be shown, but each side gets only one such challenge. The words of one federal statute, 28 U.S.C. §144, appear to require peremptory recusal in the federal courts,* but the Supreme Court has interpreted that statute to require cause.

What cause might look like is defined in 28 U.S.C. §455, which closely tracks the ABA Model Code of Judicial Conduct, a code likewise echoed by most state recusal statutes. Section 455 establishes two broad categories for disqualifying a judge. One contains specific guidelines barring, for example, a judge's hearing a case "where he has served as lawyer in the matter in controversy" before becoming a judge or "[w]here he has served in governmental employment and . . . expressed an opinion concerning the merits of the particular case or controversy." It also bars decisions in cases in which a judge or her family has a financial interest. 28 U.S.C. §455(b). The other category is much broader: "Any justice, judge, or magistrate of the United States shall disqualify himself in any proceeding in which his impartiality might reasonably be questioned." 28 U.S.C. §455(a). As a build-up to the case law, use the following problems to familiarize yourself with the statute.

Notes and Problems

1. In most federal and state courts there is more than one judge, and so the clerk's office will randomly assign each case to a judge (unless the case is connected with a pending action—if so, it will go to the judge already managing the related matter).

2. Student leads a demonstration protesting the university's alleged failure to address sexual harassment on campus. Invoking diversity jurisdiction, University sues Student, alleging that she unlawfully destroyed University property in the course of the demonstration. Suppose that the case of *University v. Student* is assigned to Judge Michael López. The statute calls for the judge to recuse himself when he realizes a ground for recusal exists, or when one is brought to his attention by motion. Read §455 and analyze its application to the following three scenarios.

---

* "Whenever a party to any proceeding in a district court makes and files a timely and sufficient affidavit that the judge before whom the matter is pending has a personal bias or prejudice either against him or in favor of any adverse party, such judge shall proceed no further therein, but another judge shall be assigned to hear such proceeding."

    a. When he was in private practice, López represented the University in two lawsuits alleging medical malpractice in its hospital. Recusal? §455(b)(2).

    b. López's daughter, a student at the University, was involved in the demonstration that led to the suit and appears on a party's witness list. Recusal? §455(b)(1) and (b)(4).

    c. Before his appointment as a federal judge, Judge López served on the state bench, a position to which he was elected. During one of his state electoral campaigns, he distributed pamphlets calling for "tough enforcement" of the laws "to remind young people that they have obligations as well as rights," a statement that some in the student community interpreted as calling for special severity against students. Recusal? §455(a).

3. Suppose you represent a small business owner—a local franchisee of a national firm—in a contract claim where you have drawn one of the two following judges; the question is whether either judge is subject to recusal under a state statute identical to §455.

    a. Judge Hott, whose name strikes dread in lawyers' hearts, is intemperate, abusive to lawyers, not given to reading briefs or listening to oral argument, and thought not to have studied law carefully either during or after law school. Lawyers with whom you practice report that Judge Hott appears to issue rulings almost randomly. Do you have good grounds for a recusal motion?

    b. Judge Wize is well liked by lawyers, listens carefully even to ill-prepared arguments, rules promptly, and, even the losers concede, usually correctly. As required by Rule 7.1 you have filed a Disclosure Statement indicating that 45 percent of your client is owned by Franchisor Corp. Judge Wize indicates that she owns ten shares of Franchisor Corp. Both you and your adversary would be happy to keep Judge Wize on the case; can you? Analytically, that question has two parts. First, locate the portion of §455 that says she has a problem—which clause applies? Second, read §455(e); does it provide a way for the parties to allow Judge Wize to sit?

4. The most difficult applications of §455 are situations involving the general standard—"might reasonably be questioned"—of §455(a). The next case involves a state with a recusal statute similar to §455(a); it asks when a judge's refusal to recuse himself can amount to a violation of due process.

Caperton v. A.T. Massey Coal Co.
556 U.S. 868 (2009)

KENNEDY, J., delivered the opinion of the Court.

In this case the Supreme Court of Appeals of West Virginia reversed a trial court judgment, which had entered a jury verdict of $50 million. Five justices heard the case, and the vote to reverse was 3 to 2. The question presented is whether the Due Process Clause of the Fourteenth Amendment was violated when one of the justices in the majority denied a recusal motion. The basis for the motion was that the justice had received campaign contributions in an extraordinary amount from, and through the efforts of, the board chairman and principal officer of the corporation found liable for the damages.

Under our precedents there are objective standards that require recusal when "the probability of actual bias on the part of the judge or decisionmaker is too high to be constitutionally tolerable." Applying those precedents, we find that, in all the circumstances of this case, due process requires recusal.

I

In August 2002 a West Virginia jury returned a verdict that found respondents A.T. Massey Coal Co. and its affiliates (hereinafter Massey) liable for fraudulent misrepresentation, concealment, and tortious interference with existing contractual relations. The jury awarded petitioners Hugh Caperton . . . (hereinafter Caperton) the sum of $50 million in compensatory and punitive damages. . . .

Don Blankenship is Massey's chairman, chief executive officer, and president. After the verdict but before the appeal, West Virginia held its 2004 judicial elections. Knowing the Supreme Court of Appeals of West Virginia would consider the appeal in the case, Blankenship decided to support an attorney who sought to replace Justice McGraw[,] a candidate for reelection to that court. The attorney who sought to replace him was Brent Benjamin.

In addition to contributing the $1,000 statutory maximum to Benjamin's campaign committee, Blankenship donated almost $2.5 million to "And For The Sake Of The Kids," a political organization formed under 26 U.S.C. §527[, a section of the Internal Revenue Code permitting tax-exempt political organizations]. The §527 organization opposed McGraw and supported Benjamin. Blankenship's donations accounted for more than two-thirds of the total funds it raised. This was not all. Blankenship spent, in addition, just over $500,000 on independent expenditures—for direct mailings and letters soliciting donations as well as television and newspaper advertisements—"'to support . . . Brent Benjamin.'"

To provide some perspective, Blankenship's $3 million in contributions were more than the total amount spent by all other Benjamin supporters and three times the amount spent by Benjamin's own committee. Caperton contends that Blankenship spent $1 million more than the total amount spent by the campaign committees of both candidates combined.

Benjamin won. He received 382,036 votes (53.3%), and McGraw received 334,301 votes (46.7%).

In October 2005, before Massey filed its petition for appeal in West Virginia's highest court, Caperton moved to disqualify now-Justice Benjamin under the Due Process Clause and the West Virginia Code of Judicial Conduct, based on the conflict caused by Blankenship's campaign involvement. Justice Benjamin denied the motion [at several points in the litigation, before casting the decisive vote against Caperton in a 3-2 decision reversing the $50 million verdict against Massey. He also delivered an opinion stating] that he [had] "carefully considered the bases and accompanying exhibits proffered by the movants." But he found "no objective information . . . to show that this Justice has a bias for or against any litigant, that this Justice has pre-judged the matters which comprise this litigation, or that this Justice will be anything but fair and impartial" . . . [and] that he had no "'direct, personal, substantial, pecuniary interest' in this case." Adopting "a standard merely of 'appearances,'" he concluded, "seems little more than an invitation to subject West Virginia's justice system to the vagaries of the day—a framework in which predictability and stability yield to supposition, innuendo, half-truths, and partisan manipulations."

We granted certiorari.

II

It is axiomatic that "[a] fair trial in a fair tribunal is a basic requirement of due process." As the Court has recognized, however, "most matters relating to judicial disqualification [do] not rise to a constitutional level." The early and leading case on the subject is Tumey v. Ohio, 273 U.S. 510 (1927). There, the Court stated that "matters of kinship, personal bias, state policy, remoteness of interest, would seem generally to be matters merely of legislative discretion."

The *Tumey* Court concluded that the Due Process Clause incorporated the common-law rule that a judge must recuse himself when he has "a direct, personal, substantial, pecuniary interest" in a case. This rule reflects the maxim that "[n]o man is allowed to be a judge in his own cause; because his interest would certainly bias his judgment, and, not improbably, corrupt his integrity." . . .

As new problems have emerged that were not discussed at common law, however, the Court has identified additional instances which, as an objective matter, require recusal. These are circumstances "in which experience teaches that the probability of actual bias on the part of the judge or decisionmaker is too high to be constitutionally tolerable." To place the present case in proper context, two instances where the Court has required recusal merit further discussion.

A

The first involved the emergence of local tribunals where a judge had a financial interest in the outcome of a case, although the interest was less than what would have been considered personal or direct at common law.

This was the problem addressed in *Tumey*. There, the mayor of a village had the authority to sit as a judge (with no jury) to try those accused of violating a state law prohibiting the possession of alcoholic beverages. Inherent in this structure were two potential conflicts. First, the mayor received a salary supplement for performing judicial duties, and the funds for that compensation derived from the fines assessed in a case. No fines were assessed upon acquittal. The mayor-judge thus received a salary supplement only if he convicted the defendant. Second, sums from the criminal fines were deposited to the village's general treasury fund for village improvements and repairs.

The Court held that the Due Process Clause required disqualification. . . .

This concern with conflicts resulting from financial incentives was elaborated in Ward v. Monroeville, 409 U.S. 57 (1972), which invalidated a conviction in another mayor's court. In *Monroeville*, unlike in *Tumey*, the mayor received no money; instead, the fines the mayor assessed went to the town's general fisc. The Court held that "[t]he fact that the mayor [in *Tumey*] shared directly in the fees and costs did not define the limits of the principle." The principle, instead, turned on the "'possible temptation'" the mayor might face; the mayor's "executive responsibilities for village finances may make him partisan to maintain the high level of contribution [to those finances] from the mayor's court." As the Court reiterated in another case that Term, "the [judge's] financial stake need not be as direct or positive as it appeared to be in *Tumey*." . . .

[In another case] the Court stressed that it was "not required to decide whether in fact [the justice] was influenced." The proper constitutional inquiry is "whether sitting on the case then before the Supreme Court of Alabama "would offer a possible temptation to the average . . . judge to . . . lead him not to hold the balance nice, clear and true." The Court underscored that "what degree or kind of interest is sufficient to disqualify a judge from sitting 'cannot be defined with precision.'" In the Court's view, however, it was important that the test have an objective component.

B

The second instance requiring recusal that was not discussed at common law emerged in the criminal contempt context, where a judge had no pecuniary interest in the case but was challenged because of a conflict arising from his participation in an earlier proceeding. This Court characterized that first proceeding (perhaps pejoratively) as a "'one-man grand jury.'"

In that first proceeding, and as provided by state law, a judge examined witnesses to determine whether criminal charges should be brought. The judge called the two petitioners before him. One petitioner answered questions, but the judge found him untruthful and charged him with perjury. The second declined to answer on the ground that he did not have counsel with him, as state law seemed to permit. The judge charged him with contempt. The judge proceeded to try and convict both petitioners.

This Court set aside the convictions on grounds that the judge had a conflict of interest at the trial stage because of his earlier participation followed by his decision to charge them. The Due Process Clause required disqualification. The Court recited the general rule that "no man can be a judge in his own case," adding that "no man is permitted to try cases where he has an interest in the outcome." It noted that the disqualifying criteria "cannot be defined with precision. Circumstances and relationships must be considered." These circumstances and the prior relationship required recusal: "Having been a part of [the one-man grand jury] process a judge cannot be, in the very nature of things, wholly disinterested in the conviction or acquittal of those accused." That is because "[a]s a practical matter it is difficult if not impossible for a judge to free himself from the influence of what took place in his 'grand-jury' secret session." . . .

III

Based on the principles described in these cases we turn to the issue before us. This problem arises in the context of judicial elections, a framework not presented in the precedents we have reviewed and discussed.

Caperton contends that Blankenship's pivotal role in getting Justice Benjamin elected created a constitutionally intolerable probability of actual bias. Though not a bribe or criminal influence, Justice Benjamin would nevertheless feel a debt of gratitude to Blankenship for his extraordinary efforts to get him elected. That temptation, Caperton claims, is as strong and inherent in human nature as was the conflict the Court confronted . . . when a mayor-judge (or the city) benefited financially from a defendant's conviction, as well as the conflict identified . . . when a judge was the object of a defendant's contempt.

Justice Benjamin was careful to address the recusal motions and explain his reasons why, on his view of the controlling standard, disqualification was not in order. In four separate opinions issued during the course of the appeal, he explained why no actual bias had been established. He found no basis for recusal because Caperton failed to provide "objective evidence" or "objective information," but merely "subjective belief" of bias. Nor could anyone "point to any actual conduct or activity on [his] part which could be termed 'improper.'" In other words, based on the facts presented by Caperton, Justice Benjamin conducted a probing search into his actual motives and inclinations; and he found none to be improper. We do not question his subjective findings of impartiality and propriety. Nor do we determine whether there was actual bias. . . .

The difficulties of inquiring into actual bias, and the fact that the inquiry is often a private one, simply underscore the need for objective rules. Otherwise there may be no adequate protection against a judge who simply misreads or misapprehends the real motives at work in deciding the case. The judge's own inquiry into actual bias, then, is not one that the law can easily superintend or review, though actual bias, if disclosed, no doubt would be grounds for appropriate relief. In lieu of exclusive reliance on that personal inquiry, or on appellate review of the judge's determination respecting actual bias, the Due Process Clause has been implemented by objective standards that do not require proof of actual bias. In defining these standards the Court has asked whether, "under a realistic appraisal of psychological tendencies and human weakness," the interest "poses such a risk of actual bias or prejudgment that the practice must be forbidden if the guarantee of due process is to be adequately implemented."

We turn to the influence at issue in this case. Not every campaign contribution by a litigant or attorney creates a probability of bias that requires a judge's recusal, but this is an exceptional case. We conclude that there is a serious risk of actual bias—based on objective and reasonable perceptions—when a person with a personal stake in a particular case had a significant and disproportionate influence in placing the judge on the case by raising funds or directing the judge's election campaign when the case was pending or imminent. The inquiry centers on the contribution's relative size in comparison to the total amount of money contributed to the campaign, the total amount spent in the election, and the apparent effect such contribution had on the outcome of the election. . . .

Whether Blankenship's campaign contributions were a necessary and sufficient cause of Benjamin's victory is not the proper inquiry. Much like determining whether a judge is actually biased, proving what ultimately drives the electorate to choose a particular candidate is a difficult endeavor, not likely to lend itself to a certain conclusion. This is particularly true where, as here, there is no procedure for judicial factfinding and the sole trier of fact is the one accused of bias. Due process requires an objective inquiry into whether the contributor's influence on the election under all the circumstances "would offer a possible temptation to the average . . . judge to . . . lead him not to hold the balance nice, clear and true." . . .

Justice Benjamin did undertake an extensive search for actual bias. But, as we have indicated, that is just one step in the judicial process; objective standards may also require recusal whether or not actual bias exists or can be proved. Due process "may sometimes bar trial by judges who have no actual bias and who would do their very best to weigh the scales of justice equally between contending parties." The failure to consider objective standards requiring recusal is not consistent with the imperatives of due process. We find that Blankenship's significant and disproportionate influence—coupled with the temporal relationship between the election and the pending case—"offer a possible temptation to the average . . . judge to . . . lead him not to hold the balance nice, clear and true." On these extreme facts the probability of actual bias rises to an unconstitutional level.

IV

Our decision today addresses an extraordinary situation where the Constitution requires recusal. Massey and its amici predict that various adverse consequences will follow from recognizing a constitutional violation here—ranging from a flood of recusal motions to unnecessary interference with judicial elections. We disagree. The facts now before us are extreme by any measure. The parties point to no other instance involving judicial campaign contributions that presents a potential for bias comparable to the circumstances in this case.

It is true that extreme cases often test the bounds of established legal principles, and sometimes no administrable standard may be available to address the perceived wrong. But it is also true that extreme cases are more likely to cross constitutional limits, requiring this Court's intervention and formulation of objective standards. This is particularly true when due process is violated. . . .

* * *

The judgment of the Supreme Court of Appeals of West Virginia is reversed, and the case is remanded for further proceedings not inconsistent with this opinion.

ROBERTS, C.J., with whom SCALIA, J., THOMAS, J., and ALITO, J., join, dissenting.

I, of course, share the majority's sincere concerns about the need to maintain a fair, independent, and impartial judiciary—and one that appears to be such. But I fear that the Court's decision will undermine rather than promote these values. . . .

Today . . . the Court enlists the Due Process Clause to overturn a judge's failure to recuse because of a "probability of bias." Unlike the established grounds for disqualification, a "probability of bias" cannot be defined in any limited way. The Court's new "rule" provides no guidance to judges and litigants about when recusal will be constitutionally required. . . .

With little help from the majority, courts will now have to determine:

1. How much money is too much money? What level of contribution or expenditure gives rise to a "probability of bias"? . . .

7. How long does the probability of bias last? Does the probability of bias diminish over time as the election recedes? Does it matter whether the judge plans to run for reelection?

8. What if the "disproportionately" large expenditure is made by an industry association, trade union, physicians' group, or the plaintiffs' bar? Must the judge recuse in all cases that affect the association's interests? Must the judge recuse in all cases in which a party or lawyer is a member of that group? Does it matter how much the litigant contributed to the association?

9. What if the case involves a social or ideological issue rather than a financial one? Must a judge recuse from cases involving, say, abortion rights if he has received "disproportionate" support from individuals who feel strongly about either side of that issue? If the supporter wants to help elect judges who are "tough on crime," must the judge recuse in all criminal cases? . . .

[Chief Justice Roberts's dissent listed 40 questions thought to be unanswered by the majority opinion, concluding with: "40. What if the parties settle a *Caperton* claim as part of a broader settlement of the case? Does that leave the judge with no way to salvage his reputation?"]

It is an old cliché, but sometimes the cure is worse than the disease. I am sure there are cases where a "probability of bias" should lead the prudent judge to step aside, but the judge fails to do so. Maybe this is one of them. But I believe that opening the door to recusal claims under the Due Process Clause, for an amorphous "probability of bias," will itself bring our judicial system into undeserved disrepute, and diminish the confidence of the American people in the fairness and integrity of their courts. I hope I am wrong.

I respectfully dissent.

SCALIA, J., dissenting.

The principal purpose of this Court's exercise of its certiorari jurisdiction is to clarify the law. As The Chief Justice's dissent makes painfully clear, the principal consequence of today's decision is to create vast uncertainty with respect to a point of law that can be raised in all litigated cases in (at least) those 39 States that elect their judges. This course was urged upon us on grounds that it would preserve the public's confidence in the judicial system.

The decision will have the opposite effect. What above all else is eroding public confidence in the Nation's judicial system is the perception that litigation is just a game, that the party with the most resourceful lawyer can play it to win, that our seemingly interminable legal proceedings are wonderfully self-perpetuating but incapable of delivering real-world justice. The Court's opinion will reinforce that perception, adding to the vast arsenal of lawyerly gambits what will come to be known as the *Caperton* claim. . . .

A Talmudic maxim instructs with respect to the Scripture: "Turn it over, and turn it over, for all is therein." The Babylonian Talmud, Tractate Aboth, Ch. V, Mishnah 22 (I. Epstein ed. 1935). Divinely inspired text may contain the answers to all earthly questions, but the Due Process Clause most assuredly does not. The Court today continues its quixotic quest to right all wrongs and repair all imperfections through the Constitution. Alas, the quest cannot succeed—which is why some wrongs and imperfections have been called nonjusticiable. In the best of all possible worlds, should judges sometimes recuse even where the clear commands of our prior due process law do not require it? Undoubtedly. The relevant question, however, is whether we do more good than harm by seeking to correct this imperfection through expansion of our constitutional mandate in a manner ungoverned by any discernable rule. The answer is obvious.

WHAT'S NEW HERE?

● 28 U.S.C. §455 and analogous state statutes already require a judge to recuse himself if his impartiality might reasonably be questioned. Judge Benjamin had declined to do so.
● *Caperton* holds that under some circumstances refusal to recuse is a denial of due process. Potentially, that makes every refusal to recuse a constitutional violation.

Notes and Problems

1. Notice that the majority and the dissent do not fundamentally disagree about whether Judge Benjamin should have recused himself. They disagree instead about whether the Court has started down a treacherous path—whether, as one dissent has it, "the cure," constitutionalizing recusals, is worse than the "disease."

   a. The dissent predicts a flood of appeals from refusals to recuse. The majority, defending itself against this charge, suggests that few cases will present facts as extreme as those in *Caperton*. Intuitively, what outcome would you predict?

   b. Suppose that you are a state judge asked to recuse yourself on what you think are marginal grounds. Does *Caperton* push you toward recusal?

2. Why is there little disagreement about whether Judge Benjamin should have recused himself?

   a. He apparently had no personal ties to Blankenship, and was an experienced lawyer who was running for his office on his own "platform" before Blankenship made the campaign contributions.

b. Under the majority's view of things, would a U.S. Supreme Court Justice, elevated by a President to the nation's highest court, be therefore bound to recuse himself in all cases important to the appointing administration, or to the President personally? Historically, the Justices have not done so. How would you distinguish *Caperton*?

3. The day after *Caperton* was handed down, three major national newspapers made the decision the subject of editorials.

   a. The *Wall Street Journal* bemoaned the decision as ham-handed meddling by the Supreme Court in state judiciaries, asserting that the author of the majority opinion favored judicial elitism over citizen voice in judicial selection.

   b. The *New York Times* applauded the decision as having secured the right to "honest justice," opining that "the only truly alarming thing about [the] decision is that it was not unanimous."

   c. *USA Today* took a third path, generally supporting the outcome and expressing the hope that the dangers exposed by the case would lead states to abandon judicial elections in favor of other selection systems.

4. Suppose that in addition to seeking to recuse Judge Benjamin, Hugh Caperton had filed a complaint with the Judicial Investigation Commission of West Virginia, the public body charged with policing the judiciary. Suppose you are a member of the Commission. One canon requires a judge to "act at all times in a manner that promotes public confidence in the integrity and impartiality of the judiciary." The Commission launches an investigation. It finds that the undisputed facts are as recited in *Caperton v. A.T. Massey Coal Co.* Would you vote to find that Judge Benjamin had violated the quoted standard? Assume that a majority of the Commission voted that Judge Benjamin had violated the standard. The Commission has the power to impose sanctions ranging from a confidential letter of reproval to public censure to removal from office. What sanction would you vote for?

5. A subsequent case, Williams v. Pennsylvania, 579 U.S. ___ (2016), addressed one of the questions posed in the *Caperton* dissent: how the passage of time might affect the due process calculation. An elected Pennsylvania district attorney, Ronald Castille, approved his office's seeking the death penalty against Terrance Williams, who was convicted and sentenced to death. Thirty-two years later, Ronald Castille had been elected to the Pennsylvania Supreme Court, when Williams's post-conviction appeal came before that tribunal. The substantive issue was whether one of Castille's prosecutors had improperly withheld exculpatory evidence from the defense. When that question came before the Pennsylvania Supreme Court, Williams's lawyers asked that Justice Castille recuse himself; he declined and voted to deny Williams's petition. The U.S. Supreme Court, in a 5-3 decision (a seat was vacant) reversed, citing *Caperton* for the proposition that because Justice Castille had a "significant, personal involvement" in the underlying case, due process compelled him to recuse himself.

B. SHARING POWER WITH A JURY

All through the pretrial process, the parties propose, and the judge disposes—ruling on pre-answer motions, on discovery requests, on motions for summary judgment, and similar matters. If the judge's ruling creates a final judgment, the loser can appeal. If it does not, the loser can reconsider settlement (now at a less attractive value) or hunker down to wait for the end. With a jury, matters are different: There is now another source of power in the room, a source to whom both parties can speak. They can speak only of certain matters and only in certain ways, matters and ways the judge controls. But the existence of the jury changes everything—from lawyers' propensity to speak in jargon and shorthand, to their calculations of ultimate success. Experienced lawyers will say that some cases are winnable only with a jury. Good empirical research tells us, however, that juries are not pushovers, and judges not stern deniers: Plaintiffs prevail in only half of the tort cases that go to a jury trial, and in some cases judges are more likely than juries to award high damages.*

1. When May a Jury Decide?

Whichever party a jury may favor, the presence of a jury will often matter, sometimes critically. But juries do not sit in all cases. They will be present only if two conditions are met: (1) at least one party asks for a jury; and (2) it is a case of the sort in which the parties are entitled to a jury. This section sorts out the second requirement.

The civil trial jury flourishes only in the United States. Although we inherited the institution from English law, it is available there only in a few specialized cases (for example, in libel actions). But in the United States, civil jury trials are widely available in both state and federal courts. This availability results from provisions in state and the federal Constitutions granting the right to jury trial in certain cases. We will focus on the federal courts. In the debates attending the adoption of the federal Constitution in 1789 and the Bill of Rights in 1791, much attention was paid to the jury trial. Some opponents of the Constitution cited the omission of a civil jury trial provision (in the Constitution as it existed before the Bill of Rights) as an argument for not ratifying that document:

> [T]he crux of the objection lay in the political significance of the jury trial. While an adequate representation in at least one branch of the legislature was indispensable at the top, law-making level, the jury trial provided the people's safeguard at the bottom, administrative, level. A [Maryland] Farmer argued, indeed, that the jury trial is more important than representation in the legislature, because "those usurpations, which

---

* For example, one elaborate study found that in claims against individual (non-institutional) defendants, judges were significantly more likely than juries to award punitive damages. Theodore Eisenberg et al., *Juries, Judges, and Punitive Damages: An Empirical Study*, 87 Cornell L. Rev. 744, 763 (2002).

silently undermine the spirit of liberty, under the sanctions of law, are more dangerous than direct and open legislative attacks. . . ."

> H.J. Storing, What the Anti-Federalists Were For:
> The Political Thought of the Opponents of the Constitution 18-19 (1981).

Beyond its place in the structure of government, those seeking to include the right to jury trial in the Constitution believed that it would affect the outcome of certain cases. In particular, many of the jury's champions believed that juries would be sympathetic to the claims of rural debtors when sued by big-city or foreign creditors. As one authority points out:

> [I]nconveniences [of jury trial were] accepted precisely because, in important instances, through its ability to disregard substantive rules of law, the jury would reach a result that the judge either could not or would not reach. Those who favored the civil jury were not misguided tinkerers. [T]hey were, for their day, libertarians who avowed that important areas of protection for litigants . . . would be placed in grave danger unless it were required that juries sit in civil cases.

> Charles W. Wolfram, *The Constitutional History of the Seventh Amendment*,
> 57 Minn. L. Rev. 639 (1973).

The proponents of civil jury trial won an important battle: The Seventh Amendment became part of the Bill of Rights. They did not win the war, however, because the Amendment did not make all cases triable to a jury. Instead, it compromised between those who thought jury trial at best a nuisance, at worst an invitation to lawlessness, and those who thought it a vital structural and substantive principle of government. The compromise is embedded in the deceptively short text of the Seventh Amendment:*

> In suits at common law, where the value in controversy shall exceed twenty dollars, the right of trial by jury shall be preserved, and no fact tried by a jury shall otherwise be reexamined in any Court of the United States, than according to the rules of the common law.

Courts and lawyers typically divide the Amendment into two roughly equal halves: the "right to jury trial" clause, comprising the text up through the word "preserved"; and the "reexamination" clause, comprising the rest of the Amendment. Both parts empower and limit the civil jury. We begin with the part of the Amendment granting the right to a civil jury.

The first part of the Seventh Amendment reflects the great compromise in two phrases: "suits at common law" and "shall be preserved." The Seventh Amendment purports to "preserve" a right but does not indicate the scope of the right being preserved. The English judicial system, whose organization was echoed by colonial courts in the period immediately before the Revolution, was divided into several jurisdictions. In courts of common law, jury trial was widely available on most of the writs commonly in use by the eighteenth century. A full list is not possible here,

---

* The right to a jury trial in criminal cases appears in the Sixth Amendment.

but some of the more common writs will give the student a flavor: trespass (with several subcategories); debt (to recover sums owed); covenant (to remedy breaches of written, sealed contracts); ejectment (to recover land unlawfully occupied); trover and replevin (to recover for unlawful takings of personal property); and assumpsit (meaning "he (or she) promised," to recover for breaches of informal, usually oral, contracts).

In courts of chancery (which oversaw some important substantive areas, e.g., the law of trusts, and also administered various equitable remedies, e.g., injunctions), however, the judge (the chancellor) sat without a jury. The constitutional compromise, then, "preserved" as triable to a jury those cases that could have been brought in a court of common law. If, however, the claim would have fallen into the jurisdiction of the court of chancery, the Seventh Amendment did not extend the right to jury trial. Courts dealing with this issue distinguish between legal and equitable claims and remedies. By doing so, they are simply using a shorthand form of reference: "Legal" in this context means a claim recognized by a court of law (where juries sat), and "equitable" means that the claim or remedy would have been in chancery (where no juries sat).

In Chapter 5, we noted the development of elaborate doctrine concerning which cases could be brought in equity. The result was that equity had exclusive jurisdiction over some substantive areas (trusts are a good example) and shared jurisdiction when plaintiffs sought remedies such as injunctions, specific performance, rescission, and accountings and procedural devices such as derivative suits, class actions, bills of peace, and bills of interpleader. A given plaintiff had to show either that equity had exclusive jurisdiction over, say, the law of trusts, or that the traditional legal remedy of money damages was inadequate and that plaintiff otherwise qualified for equitable relief. See *Lucy Webb Hayes Natl. Training School v. Geoghegan*, in Chapter 5 (page 308) for an example of a court administering an equitable remedy (injunction) on a common law claim (trespass).

Remember: Cases within equity jurisdiction did not wind up there because of anyone's conviction that the judge was better suited than a jury to decide a particular type of claim. Although the judge may have been more qualified to sort out fiduciary relationships, probate matters, or multiparty actions, many other branches of equity jurisdiction involved the same questions of fact—what happened, how it happened, and who was telling the truth—as legal actions. For example, injunctive actions frequently involved questions of land ownership or commission of a tort, and specific performance claims usually involved the construction and meaning of contracts. Moreover, as time went on, distinctions between the two jurisdictions blurred even further: Legal claims in general assumpsit (money had and received) tended to parallel equitable remedies for restitution, and traditionally equitable defenses such as fraud, duress, and illegality came to be recognized at law. As a result, the law-equity jurisdictional distinction was far from hard and fast, and whatever distinction existed was more a result of history than of logic or function.

Given the constitutional language "preserving" the right to a jury trial for suits at "common law," it is not surprising that the courts have adopted a historical test for deciding the right to jury trial under the Seventh Amendment. Under the historical test, courts seek to give parties the same right of jury trial as they had in

1791. Presumably, the drafters of the Seventh Amendment were thinking of a world in which there were separate courts of law and equity, a world in which one could only "preserve" a right to jury trial in suits at common law. Because there had never been a right to jury trial in equity, there was nothing to preserve and no right to jury trial.

Consequently, courts applying the historical test do not directly inquire about jury trial. Instead, they ask a related question: whether a given claim and remedy lay within the jurisdiction of the common law courts in 1791. If so, the parties have the right to a jury; if not—if only a court of equity would have heard the claim or administered that remedy—there is no right to a jury. Equitable jurisdiction generally turned on whether the plaintiff wanted injunctive or other relief available only in equity, wanted to use a procedural device that was available only in equity, or had a claim that could be brought only in equity. Before you despair of sorting all this out, be comforted by the thought that a very large portion of claims fit neatly into well-established historical patterns. Having mastered that pattern, you will have answers for the great majority of jury trial questions you will ever encounter.

Finally, note that the U.S. Supreme Court has never held that the Seventh Amendment applies to the states—which are therefore free to decide the right to jury trial in civil cases without recourse to the U.S. Constitution.

WHAT'S NEW HERE?

- In this and other courses, you have likely taken jury trials largely for granted. In fact, they are one of the most distinctive features of U.S. civil lawsuits: No other nation in the world uses them to the extent we do.
- Historically, the insistence on the right to civil jury trials was an important part of the fight to ratify the U.S. Constitution. But—because there was a fight over the jury issue—the right to jury trial does not extend over the whole realm of civil litigation.
- Functionally, the institution of the civil jury de-professionalizes and decentralizes many important government decisions. Judges are bureaucrats whose careers involve interpreting and applying law, which they have studied for most of their adult lives. Jurors are amateurs, drafted to perform, temporarily, a governmental function.

When deciding whether long-standing types of claims are legal or equitable, one must assess whether, in 1791, the claim would have been brought in a court of law or in a court of equity. That may require refreshing one's historical memory, but it presents no conceptual difficulties.

Knottier problems emerge when one considers claims that did not exist at the time the Bill of Rights was adopted, often those created by statute. In a series of cases the Supreme Court has said that when facing such a case, the court should first try to locate the closest historical analogy. Thus, in a case involving union members' right to fair representation by their union—a claim that could not have existed in 1791 because unions were illegal—the Court examined analogies to a malpractice action against one's lawyer (which would have been a legal claim triable to a jury), a motion to vacate an arbitration order (equitable; no jury), and an action by the beneficiary of a trust against the trustee for breach of fiduciary duty (equitable; no jury). Chauffeurs, Teamsters, & Helpers, Local No. 391 v. Terry, 494 U.S. 558 (1990). Finding no analogy close enough to satisfy it entirely, the majority then took a second, tie-breaking step, to look at the remedy sought in the case, money damages, and decided that it most resembled the remedy typical in legal claims triable to a jury, and that a jury was thus required. A concurring opinion complained that the Court was not at its best when "rattling through the dusty attics of ancient writs." A dissent, by contrast, thought that the Court had discovered just the right analogue in that attic (the suit by the beneficiary of a trust) and that the Court should have stopped there and denied a jury trial. Again, recall that for the vast majority of claims the question of the right to trial by jury will be well established either in federal courts, which apply the Seventh Amendment, or in state courts, which apply their own constitutions and statutes.

Notes and Problems

---

1. For the litigator, a well-established right to trial by jury does not end matters. Like other constitutional rights, the parties can waive it by failing to raise the issue. In the case of the right to trial by jury, Rule 38 reaffirms the constitutional status of jury trial while insisting on a timely demand and establishing waiver as the penalty for failing to do so.

   a. Plaintiff sues, seeking damages for breach of contract. Within the time limits set forth in Rule 12(a)(1), defendant answers, denying various allegations. If the only pleadings in the case are the complaint and answer, how long do the parties have in which to demand a jury trial?

   b. A party can insert a demand for a jury directly into its pleading. In Note 1a, for example, the plaintiff who sought damages for breach could have in his complaint demanded a jury trial, and the defendant could equally have done so in her answer.

2. The law-equity jury trial issue also arises in state courts. Unlike the Sixth Amendment (dealing with criminal juries), the Seventh Amendment does not apply to the states. As a consequence, there is no *federal* constitutional requirement that states accord the right of jury trial in any civil case tried in state

courts. State courts may thus reach conclusions under their own laws that differ from those reached by the federal courts under the Seventh Amendment.

a. In many instances, state courts have proved substantially less enthusiastic about jury trials in civil cases than have the federal courts. As examples of cases in which state courts rejected claims of entitlement to a jury, consider C&K Engineering Contractors v. Amber Steel Co., 23 Cal. 3d 1 (1978) (contract actions based on promissory estoppel); Strauss v. Summerhays, 157 Cal. App. 3d 806 (1984) (quiet-title actions); Robair v. Dahl, 80 Mich. App. 458 (1978) (constructive trusts); State ex rel. Willman v. Sloan, 574 S.W.2d 421 (Mo. 1978) (calculation of damages after breach of a contractual covenant not to compete); Pelfrey v. Bank of Greer, 270 S.C. 691 (1978) (explicitly rejecting, as a matter of state law, Ross v. Bernhard, 396 U.S. 531 (1970), which held that shareholders' derivative actions were triable to a jury); State Bank of Lehi v. Woolsey, 565 P.2d 413 (Utah 1977) (mortgage foreclosure).

b. Why have state courts embraced the civil jury less warmly than the federal courts have? Two possibilities—one political, one practical—come to mind. First, the history of the Seventh Amendment, whose absence was thought by some to be so important as nearly to scuttle the ratification of the federal Constitution, might cause the federal courts to err on the side of the jury when in doubt. There was no equivalent controversy in most state constitutional debates: Civil juries were taken to be a matter of course. Second, federal courts can more easily absorb the costs of additional jury trials; federal courts are generally better financed than their state counterparts. Every time a state court creates a new right to civil jury trial, it is adding a strain on court budgets.

New claims create one set of jury trial problems for litigants and courts. Changing procedures creates another. At the time of the Seventh Amendment there were separate courts of law and equity. If a litigant needed relief from both (for example, first the reformation of a contract, then suit for damages on the reformed agreement), he would have to file two suits. Moreover, a good deal of adversarial jockeying could arise, with one party seeking remedies at law while the other sought equitable relief. In such cases, which court took precedence?

The Federal Rules merged law and equity. Rules 1 and 2. Claims that were formerly legal or equitable could now be pleaded in the same suit, and the courts were given little guidance as to when a jury trial was required in a merged procedure. The constitutional right to jury trial still applied. The trouble was that the right that was "preserved" came from a system that no longer existed—that is, the right was preserved but the underlying procedural system was not. There was no particular difficulty in applying the historical approach to actions that could be denominated as clearly legal or equitable. For example, the typical personal injury suit was cognizable at law, and a suit seeking only injunctive relief was cognizable in equity. In such cases, a jury trial was granted or denied in accordance with the pre-merger practice.

But what happened when legal and equitable claims and defenses found their way into the same case? Some examples might be helpful:

1. Plaintiff joins legal and equitable claims. For example, plaintiff might sue to enjoin a nuisance and simultaneously seek damages for past harm.

2. Plaintiff brings a legal claim; defendant has an equitable defense. For example, plaintiff might sue for breach of contract, and defendant might claim mistake and seek reformation of the instrument.

3. Plaintiff brings an equitable claim; defendant brings a legal counterclaim. For example, plaintiff might seek specific performance of a contract while defendant counterclaims for damages.

Notice that in each of these situations the legal and equitable phases of the case had common issues: For example, did the defendant's behavior constitute a nuisance? The merger of law and equity forced courts to think about jury trial in situations such as these with little guidance from the rulemakers who had preserved the right but destroyed the system.

The Supreme Court has offered a clear answer—though it rests on shaky historical and logical grounds. When a case blends equitable and legal claims—*and* there are overlapping factual issues—the judge should defer to the jury. He can do so by holding the equitable claims in abeyance until the jury renders its verdict. (If the equitable claims are pressing, the judge can grant a preliminary injunction, revisiting the matter in the light of the jury's verdict.) Beacon Theatres, Inc. v. Westover, 359 U.S. 500 (1959); Dairy Queen, Inc. v. Wood, 369 U.S. 469 (1962); see also Amoco Oil Co. v. Torcomian, 722 F.2d 1099 (3d Cir. 1983).

WHAT'S NEW HERE?

Because the courts have interpreted the Seventh Amendment historically, they have to deal with two problems created by the passage of time and by procedural reform:

- What to do with new claims—claims that did not exist at the time the Seventh Amendment was ratified?
- How to cope with modern joinder rules, which allow parties to combine equitable and legal claims in the same lawsuit?

2. Choosing Jurors

We have looked at how judges are selected and challenged; we now turn to jurors. The battle over whether there will be a jury assumes that the jury—as an institution—matters. In part that is true because jurors typically won't look or think like judges. Part of the reason lies in the number of jurors: Groups make decisions differently than individuals do. And laypeople, drafted for temporary service, will see things differently than professionals for whom this is "another malpractice case" rather than a rare exposure to litigation. One sees these assumptions at work in the processes by which jurors are selected.

Jurors are selected in ways that contrast sharply with the selection of judges. At common law, the sheriff was given very wide discretion in summoning jurors, and it was understood that he would summon people with both feet firmly planted in the established order. A medieval sheriff would have greeted the idea of a jury reflecting a demographic cross section first with incomprehension, then with horror. That outlook long prevailed. Not long ago, racial minorities, women, and members of the working class were often omitted from juries. The past 50 years have seen vast changes in these practices, both in the states and in the federal system. It is unconstitutional to discriminate on the basis of race or gender in compiling the list from which jurors are summoned. Most jurisdictions go further by statutorily requiring jury selection pools that represent broad cross sections of the community. The federal courts' policy about jury pools appears at 28 U.S.C. §1861: "[L]itigants . . . entitled to trial by jury shall have the right to . . . juries selected at random from a fair cross section of the community. . . ."

A persistent piece of lawyers' lore—a view sometimes expressed in press accounts of juries—is that juries, unlike judges, are more easily fooled, swayed by emotion, or otherwise likely to decide a case on the basis of something other than the evidence. Empirical studies cast doubt on this perception. One careful study concluded:

> Indeed, one of the more remarkable lessons that empirical study has to offer the law is that virtually no evidence exists to support the prevailing ingrained intuitions about juries. In fact, existing evidence is to the contrary. . . . [T]he evidence . . . consistently supports a view of the jury as generally unbiased and competent, at least so compared to a judge. . . .
>
> Research . . . indicates that the strength of the trial evidence is the most important determinant of the verdict. Evaluating over the run of cases, juries are good factfinders. More specifically, the research does not support a view of the jury as overly generous on awards, frequently ignoring the law, or institutionally unable to handle complex cases.

> Kevin Clermont & Theodore Eisenberg, *Trial by Jury or Judge: Transcending Empiricism*, 77 Cornell L. Rev. 1124, 1151-52 (1992).

A trial jury is the result of a process involving several steps: defining a jury pool, assembling from that pool a subset of prospective jurors to hear the case (sometimes called an "array"), then from that array selecting the actual jury, which emerges from voir dire after lawyers have been permitted to challenge jurors peremptorily and for cause.

To assemble a pool of prospective jurors, one has to decide whom to call to the courthouse. While it is clear that no group of mentally competent adult citizens can be systematically excluded from selection,* the general composition of the jury can differ substantially, depending on the type of list used and the method of choosing whom to summon. For example, summoning jurors exclusively from voters' rolls, lists of Social Security recipients, auto registrations, welfare lists, or college registration rolls would yield juries with substantially different characteristics. The manner in which the federal courts create cross-sectional summonses appear at 28 U.S.C. §§1863-1864 and §1866. The method for challenging a jury pool appears at 28 U.S.C. §1867(c). Notice that the federal statute, and most state analogues, do not entitle litigants to an actual jury representing a demographic cross section; instead they require that the entire list of potential jurors—consisting of thousands or tens of thousands of names (depending on the size of the district from which they are drawn) have those cross-sectional characteristics. Moreover, challenges to the pool as a whole must be made long before the actual jury is selected.

At one time many jury service statutes categorically exempted large groups of people, ranging from police officers to mothers to physicians. In recent decades state and federal statutes have dramatically reduced these occupational exemptions. The current federal list exempts only active members of the armed services, public safety officers, and some public officials, including judges. Some state statutes exclude even fewer categories (including, for example, judges as potential jurors), though all statutes allow jurors to be excused for individual hardship. The result is that contemporary jury pools reflect a broad array of age, occupation, education, and wealth. As a consequence, challenges to jury pools—more common at times when many persons were categorically excluded from jury service—are now rare.

3. Challenging Jurors

From the pool of all prospective jurors the clerk of the court or jury commissioner will send summonses to a number of jurors asking them to report for duty on a particular day. From among these prospective jurors a certain number—perhaps 30 or 40 for a 12-person jury (fewer for a 6-person jury)—are randomly selected and sent to a particular courtroom. From those in the courtroom 6 or 12 are selected to sit in the jury box for initial questioning, a process called *voir dire*.† This stage provides the parties a basis for exercising challenges to individual jurors.

The goal of voir dire is to identify unbiased jurors who can fairly hear and decide the case. Both the lawyers and the judge participate in the screening process. Typically, the judge will tell the parties a little bit about the case, identifying the parties and counsel and asking whether anyone on the jury panel is personally acquainted with or related to parties or counsel; if so, those jurors are excused.

---

* In Thiel v. Southern Pacific Co., 328 U.S. 217 (1946), the Supreme Court held that the practice of excluding all persons who worked for a daily wage from the jury list was improper. As a consequence, the Court exercised its supervisory power to reverse a judgment for defendant railroad; the fact that the actual jury contained five persons "of the laboring class" was considered immaterial.

† The term comes from "law French," an artificial blend of English and French terms used in medieval English courts; it means "to speak the truth" and dates to an age when jurors were as much witnesses as they were deciders of fact.

The judge then typically asks each member of the potential jury briefly to describe their area of residence, occupation, and that of their spouse or partner. This questioning lays the groundwork for additional questioning by the lawyers. Here practice varies widely: In most federal courts, the individual lawyers submit questions to the judge who screens them and asks those she thinks helpful. In some state courts, by contrast, the lawyers are given a free hand to engage in detailed questioning. No matter who asks these questions, the answers provide the lawyers with a basis for challenging jurors. For some challenges—those "for cause"—the lawyers explain their basis for thinking the juror unsuitable for this case. For other challenges—"peremptory" challenges—the lawyers need not supply a reason—though, as we shall see, in recent years the courts have developed rules designed to prevent peremptory challenges from being used in ways that discriminate on the basis of race or gender.

Procedure as Strategy

Where lawyers are allowed to question prospective jurors directly in voir dire, they have two goals—one obvious, the other below the surface. The obvious one is to identify any bias against their client or her cause. The less obvious one is to begin to "educate" jurors about their client's case—by asking questions that emphasize the points they will later make during the formal presentation of evidence. ("[Prospective juror] Jones, do you believe that when someone has been injured because of another's negligence, she is entitled to full compensation for her injuries?"—from plaintiff's lawyer. "Ms. Jones, do you believe that before someone is required to turn his hard-earned dollars over to another, that other should have to prove that her injuries were in fact caused by the defendant?"—from defendant's counsel.) There are limits to lawyers' ability to use voir dire in this way: The judge will step in if the efforts are blatant, but lawyers will often approach this line as closely as they can, figuring that the chance to make a good first impression during voir dire is too good to pass up.

No statute defines the standards governing challenges for cause. A representative case describing the judicially developed principles stated:

> We review the district court's refusal to strike a juror for cause for an abuse of discretion, keeping in mind that the district court is in the best position to observe the juror and to make a first-hand evaluation of his ability to be fair. The district court must grant a challenge for cause, however, if a prospective juror shows actual prejudice or bias. Actual bias can be shown either by the juror's own admission of bias or "by proof of specific facts which show the juror has such a close connection to the facts at trial that bias is presumed."
>
> In our recent *Vasey* decision, we noted that "courts have presumed bias in extraordinary situations where a prospective juror has had a *direct* financial interest in the trial's outcome." As examples of such extraordinary situations, we cited a case in which a prospective juror was a stockholder in or an employee of a corporation that was a

party to the suit. "In these situations, the relationship between the prospective juror and a party to the lawsuit 'point[s] so sharply to bias in [the] particular juror' that even the juror's own assertions of impartiality must be discounted in ruling on a challenge for cause."

Getter v. Wal-Mart Stores, Inc., 66 F.3d 1119, 1122 (10th Cir. 1995).

In the cited case, the prospective juror owned stock in defendant Wal-Mart, which also employed his wife; the court held that in spite of the prospective juror's statement that he would base his decision on the law and the facts, it was an abuse of discretion to refuse to dismiss him for cause. Some other clear-cut examples of justified challenges for cause might be instances where a juror was related to a party (or its lawyer) or where the juror was currently involved in similar litigation.

What if jurors conceal or lie on voir dire? The first question is how a lawyer would find out. Jurors answer the voir dire questions under oath, but there is no official investigation of their accuracy. Consequently, lawyers find out about anomalies mostly by chance. Once a lawyer determines that a juror was not candid during voir dire, what recourse does she have? Procedurally, the route is to move for a new trial; but when will one be granted? The leading case on that question, McDonough Power Equipment v. Greenwood, 464 U.S. 548 (1984), established the standard for challenging a verdict on the basis of inaccurate answers on voir dire:

> We hold that to obtain a new trial in such a situation, a party must first demonstrate that a juror *failed to answer honestly a material question* on voir dire, and then further show that *a correct response would have provided a valid basis for a challenge for cause.*

Id. at 555 (emphasis added). Would you expect many verdicts to be upset under this standard?

In addition to an unlimited number of challenges for cause, parties are also permitted a limited number of peremptory challenges—challenges the party need not justify in any way. In civil cases in federal court (where the Rules provide that juries consist of 6 to 12 people), parties are entitled to three peremptory challenges. 28 U.S.C. §1870. States establish various numbers of peremptory challenges. What justifies peremptory challenges? One view is that peremptories in effect allow the parties to choose their juries, thus giving any ensuing verdict greater legitimacy in their eyes. A softer justification is that peremptories allow parties to excuse a juror about whom they have a hunch that does not rise to the level of a challenge for cause, or whom they may have offended through vigorous (but unsuccessful) voir dire questioning. Still a third justification, if it is that, holds that peremptories allow lawyers to exercise various hunches about the characteristics of social groups: Are blue-collar, rural whites of northern European descent likely to be more defense-oriented than African-American Catholics? Are elderly accountants less generous than young race car drivers? And so on.

Taken to the extreme, however, peremptories conflict with the ideas of the cross-sectional jury embodied in statutes like 28 U.S.C. §1861. If society believes that juries composed of many different viewpoints are desirable, does it make sense to allow parties to negate that goal through the use of peremptories? In recent decades the Supreme Court (as well as statutes and common law decisions in many states) has changed the law and the landscape regarding peremptory challenges. The U.S. Supreme Court has held that unaccountability in peremptories stops when race and gender enter the picture. In Batson v. Kentucky, 476 U.S. 79 (1986), the Court in a criminal case held that the prosecution's systematic striking of Black jurors without a justification based on nonracial factors violated the defendant's and jurors' rights to equal protection, and harmed the community at large. Edmonson v. Leesville Concrete Co., 500 U.S. 614 (1991), extended *Batson* to civil cases, and subsequent cases have expanded the impermissible categories to include gender. J.E.B. v. Alabama, 511 U.S. 127 (1994).

Notes and Problems

1. *Batson, Edmonson*, and *J.E.B.* open the door for one party to object to the other's use of peremptory challenges. How do such objections to challenges work? According to *Batson*, a party must first make an initial showing (a "prima facie case") that allows a court to infer a pattern based on race or gender; that showing then requires the party exercising the peremptory challenge to offer a satisfactory reason—one not based on race or gender. Suppose that Betty, a dismissed employee of a state university, sues, alleging wrongful discharge. After voir dire comes the time for the parties to exercise their peremptory challenges.

   a. Defendant (the state university) exercises its first peremptory challenge against a male African-American juror. Betty objects, citing *Edmonson*. Her objection will likely be overruled because there is, as of yet, no pattern.

   b. Defendant then challenges a second African-American juror. Betty renews her objection, now citing the pattern of peremptory challenges. Defendant may now be required to justify the challenges in nonracial terms.

   c. Notice that Betty can raise such a *Batson* challenge even if she does not belong to the group asserted to be the target of the peremptory challenges.

2. *Batson, Edmonson*, and *J.E.B.* open a previously closed procedural door, permitting opponents to question the exercise of peremptories and forcing the parties to give nondiscriminatory justifications. But none of those cases devotes much consideration to what ought to count as an acceptable alternative reason for an apparently unacceptable use of a peremptory challenge.

   a. Imagine a *Batson* challenge to a peremptory challenge. Asked to justify what is an apparently race- or gender-based pattern, the lawyer responds, "I didn't like the way she looked at me during voir dire." If the court accepts that justification, then *Edmonson* and *J.E.B.* do little to constrain the jury selection process.

   b. Alternatively, suppose that counsel replies, "Yes, it's true that both challenged jurors were women [or African Americans], but my real reason was that they occupied managerial positions, and I am therefore concerned that they will not be sympathetic to my client's claim of wrongful discharge from her job." If courts refuse to accept that justification, they will effectively eliminate peremptory challenges. When voir dire is brief, counsel will rarely have any but stereotypical information on which to base their challenges.

3. Consider a case displaying the interaction of challenges for cause with a peremptory challenge. The underlying case was a Title VII action in which plaintiff alleged employment discrimination. During voir dire, one juror, Ms. Leiter, expressed skepticism about such suits: "Leiter raised her hand and explained that she has 'been an owner of a couple of businesses and am currently an owner of a business, and I feel that as an employer and owner of a business that will definitely sway my judgment in this case.' The judge asked her whether 'if I instructed you as to what the law is that you would be able to apply the law recognizing that you are a business owner?' To which she replied, 'I think my experience will cloud my judgment, but I can do my best.'" One of the parties' lawyers then asked Leiter "whether she was concerned 'that if somebody doesn't get them [benefits sought from their employer] they're going to sue you,' and she answered, 'Of course.' Asked then whether 'you believe that people file lawsuits just because they don't get something they want?', she answered, 'I believe there are some people that do.'" Thompson v. Altheimer & Gray, 248 F.3d 621 (7th Cir. 2003).

a. The plaintiff's lawyer moved to strike Ms. Leiter for cause, but the judge declined to do so. The plaintiff's lawyer used all of her three peremptory challenges on jurors other than Leiter. The jury returned a defense verdict.

b. Was it error not to remove Leiter for cause? The Seventh Circuit equivocated, holding not that Leiter should have been removed for cause but reversing because the trial judge did not get from Ms. Leiter a stronger assurance that she would decide entirely on the basis of the evidence and the law: "Had the judge pushed Leiter and had she finally given unequivocal assurances that he deemed credible, his ruling could not be disturbed. But he failed to do that. The venire contained 20 prospective jurors, and more than enough were left to make up a full jury of 8 when he refused to excuse her. A candid and thoughtful person, if one may judge from the transcript, Leiter would probably have made an excellent juror—in another case. . . ."

c. The Seventh Circuit holds that the judge's failure to elicit from Leiter a statement that she could be open-minded was reversible error. What assumptions about human psychology underlie such a ruling?

i. The most cynical view holds that people are incapable of overcoming biases but that it is for public relations purposes important to have them pledge allegiance to fairness. In such a view, the "error" would be one only of appearance, since the juror would behave the same regardless of what she said.

ii. A different view, supported by some empirical evidence, is that, when their possible biases are brought to their attention, people can to some extent overcome them, and that the public commitment to open-mindedness itself will reinforce this commitment. On this view, it is important that the judge elicit the public commitment, and the failure is significant.

C. WHAT WILL TRIAL BE ABOUT? THE FINAL PRETRIAL CONFERENCE AND ORDER

At this point our examination of trial pivots from "Who?" to "How?" Up to now, the chapter has examined the law surrounding the people who will hear and decide a case if it goes to trial. We now turn to the rules that structure the trial, beginning with a process that one can with equal accuracy describe as the end of pleading or the start of trial—the final pretrial conference.

One would expect that the question posed by this section's heading would long since have been answered. Isn't that what pleadings are for? And, if some of the allegations in those pleadings lacked factual or legal support, would they not have disappeared in motions on the pleadings and summary judgment?

Perhaps. But because discovery will not resolve all factual questions, and because counsel may wish to leave open as late as possible alternative legal theories of their claims and defenses, there may still be some question about what issues trial will address. Modern civil litigation does not leave these questions open until the trial itself. One way in which the Federal Rules force answers to these questions is by requiring, through Rule 16(e), a "final pretrial conference and order."

Other conferences with the court, including the scheduling conference mandated by Rule 16(b) and optional pretrial conferences the judge may hold to discuss various matters, focus primarily on the pretrial stage of the case and, perhaps, efforts to settle or dismiss before trial. The final pretrial conference, in contrast, assumes a trial will occur—and soon. The final pretrial conference aims solely at clarifying the issues that trial will be about—"to formulate a trial plan," as the Rule puts it. As Rule 16(e) states, the "conference must be held as close to the start of the trial as is reasonable," and goes on to state that "[t]he court may modify the order issued after a final pretrial conference only to prevent manifest injustice." Contrast that rather stern statement with the permissive standard for amending pleadings ("The court should freely give leave [to amend a pleading] when justice so requires." Rule 15(a)). A final pretrial order—and an unsuccessful effort to convince the court to allow an amendment—is at stake in the next case.

Monfore v. Phillips

778 F.3d 849 (10th Cir. 2015)

GORSUCH, J.

Sherman Shatwell went to the hospital complaining of neck pain. Tests showed he probably had throat cancer. It was treatable but required immediate attention. Thanks to a variety of bureaucratic blunders the news never made it to him. Instead, Mr. Shatwell was sent home with a prescription for antibiotics. By the time he learned the truth a year later, it was too late.

Eventually, his widowed wife pursued negligence claims against the doctors and hospital. Through twenty months of motions practice and discovery and all the way through their submissions for the final pretrial order the defendants maintained a unified front, denying any negligence by anyone. Then, two weeks before trial, some of the defendants settled. Dr. Kenneth Phillips wasn't one of those. Left to stand trial and with just days before jury selection, he sought permission to amend the pretrial order so he could revamp his trial strategy. Now he wanted to pursue a defense pinning the blame on the absent settling defendants, arguing that they were indeed negligent and that they—not he—should be held responsible for any damages. Dr. Phillips's motion to amend the final pretrial order sought permission to introduce new jury instructions, exhibits, and witnesses aimed at advancing this new defense. But the district court denied the motion and at the trial's end the jury found him liable for damages of a little over $1 million. Dr. Phillips now asks us to overturn the judgment, contending that the district court's refusal to amend the final pretrial order and allow his new defense amounts to reversible error.

Final pretrial orders seek to "formulate a trial plan." Fed. R. Civ. P. 16(e). In their complaints and answers lawyers and parties today often list every alternative and contradictory claim or defense known to the law; during discovery they sometimes depose every potential witness still breathing and collect every bit and byte of evidence technology, time, and money will allow. Final pretrial orders seek to tame such exuberant modern pretrial practices and focus the mind on the impending reality of trial. "The casual pleading [and discovery] indulged by the courts under the Federal Rules . . . has quite naturally led to"—some might say required—"more and more emphasis on pre-trial hearings and statements to define the issues" for trial. Meadow Gold Prods. Co. v. Wright, 278 F.2d 867, 868-69 (D.C. Cir. 1960). Leaving the reins so loose at the front end of the case requires some method of gathering them up as the end approaches. At trial you just can't argue every contradictory and mutually exclusive claim or defense you were able to conjure in your pleadings: juries would lose faith in your credibility. Neither can you present the millions of documents and the scores of witnesses you were able to dig up in discovery: no sensible judge would tolerate it. Final pretrial orders encourage both sides to edit their scripts, peel away any pleading and discovery bluster, and disclose something approximating their real trial intentions to opposing counsel and the court. Toward those ends, the parties are often asked—as they were in this case—to specify the witnesses and exhibits, supply the proposed jury instructions, and identify the claims and defenses they actually intend to introduce at trial.

While pretrial orders entered earlier in the life of a case often deal with interstitial questions like discovery staging and motions practice and are relatively easy to amend as a result, a final pretrial order focused on formulating a plan for an impending trial may be amended "only to prevent manifest injustice." Fed. R. Civ. P. 16(e). Even that standard isn't meant to preclude any flexibility—trials are high human dramas; surprises always emerge; and no judge worth his salt can forget or fail to sympathize with the challenges the trial lawyer confronts. For all our extensive pretrial procedures, even the most meticulous trial plan today probably remains no more reliable a guide than the script in a high school play—provisional at best and with surprising deviations guaranteed. At the same time, the standard for modifying a final pretrial order is as high as it is to ensure everyone involved has sufficient incentive to fulfill the order's dual purposes of encouraging self-editing and providing reasonably fair disclosure to the court and opposing parties alike of their real trial intentions. This court will review a district court's decision to amend or not to amend a pretrial order only for abuse of discretion.

We see nothing like that here. Dr. Phillips says that he was surprised when his co-defendants left him to stand trial and that the court was insufficiently sympathetic to his desire to revamp his trial strategy in light of the last-minute settlement. But can a partial settlement really come as a surprise in an age when virtually all cases settle in part or in whole, many on the eve of trial? Especially in multiparty litigation, where an incentive exists to break ranks, settle relatively cheaply, and leave others on the hook before the jury? The truth is, what happened in this case was hardly unforeseeable. Like many before him in multi-defendant cases, Dr. Phillips initially saw profit in presenting a united front with his co-defendants only to regret the decision later. United front defenses often present a tempting choice at the outset of multiparty cases and through discovery. Parties can pool their resources and efforts in joint defense arrangements. Besides, no one likes to throw overboard someone else in the same boat. But the complications associated with this strategic choice often come home to roost as trial nears. An attractive partial settlement may be dangled before one defendant and not others. The settling defendant may get a good deal, replenish an opponent's litigation coffers depleted through exhausting pretrial litigation, and leave others exposed at trial for the bulk of the plaintiff's damages. Remaining defendants can be left wishing for a defense or evidence or witnesses forgone. If a remaining defendant's attorney counted on a colleague working for a settling party to do the heavy lifting at trial he may feel flat-footed when it comes to examining witnesses and arguing motions. Even if all the defendants do go to trial, failing to obtain experts and gather evidence to show contributory negligence by co-defendants can exact its toll and lead to regret. Multiparty litigation presents a variety of collective action problems and other strategic pitfalls and those Dr. Phillips encountered here are well known, not the stuff of surprise.

It's hard, as well, to ignore the prejudice the other side can experience in these circumstances. Dr. Phillips effectively sought to force the plaintiff to prepare for an entirely different trial on a few days' notice. For the better part of two years the defendants presented a united front. Even in their final pretrial order submissions they didn't designate experts to suggest one or another of the codefendants acted unprofessionally. They didn't submit documents to prove such a claim. They didn't propose jury instructions asking that someone else be held accountable. The closest they came to suggesting contributory negligence was to prepare boilerplate blaming unspecified others for Mr. Shatwell's injuries. Beyond that, through the long months of discovery and into their final Rule 16(e) submissions, nothing. In these circumstances, the plaintiff and her lawyers had some reasonable expectations about what trial would look like and the sort of evidence they would—and would not—need. They knew they'd need to prove negligence by the defendants who chose to go to trial but they wouldn't have to worry about finger pointing between defendants; trial would present one set of challenges but not another.

It may be that the district court could have allowed Dr. Phillips to rejigger his defense at the last minute and afforded the plaintiff more time to prepare for it. But we do not see why that outcome was mandatory. A district court does not abuse its discretion in holding a party to a long-scheduled trial and to the strategy he articulated though pleading and discovery and in the face of such obvious risks, especially when indulging an eleventh-hour strategic shift would mean either imposing prejudice on the other side or inviting more delay. So beware: when a fellow litigant settles on the eve of trial you can't bank on the right to claim surprise and rewrite your case from top to bottom.

Many of Dr. Phillips's remaining arguments echo his Rule 16 complaint and fail with it. . . .

Affirmed.

WHAT'S NEW HERE?

- Modern procedure is flexible, but at some point the flexibility ends: The parties are locked into their respective stories. And they will be stopped at trial if they try to tell a story different from the one they have identified at the pretrial conference.
- This is so even if a party's companions have changed their story at the last minute by settling their claims.

Notes and Problems

1. By the time trial began, Dr. Phillips was between a rock and a hard place; understand what got him there.

   a. What was Dr. Phillips's defense throughout the pretrial phase of litigation, and in the Rule 16(e) final pretrial order?

   b. Days before trial began, Dr. Phillips attempted to amend his final pretrial order. What changes did he wish to make?

   c. What prompted Dr. Phillips's desire to make these changes?

2. The district court denied Dr. Phillips's request to amend his pretrial order and the court of appeals was similarly unsympathetic. Why? What does the Court of Appeals' decision tell you about the role of final pretrial orders? What does the decision tell you about the potential pitfalls of coordinating with codefendants?

Procedure as Strategy

Dr. Phillips ended up losing big in this case. From one standpoint, he was hung out to dry by his codefendants, who settled, leaving him to defend the case alone. From another point of view—the one adopted by the court—Phillips's lawyer wasn't looking far enough ahead, thinking about the possibility that the some or all of the codefendants would settle.

Suppose Phillips's lawyer had contemplated this possibility. (Phillips's lawyer may well have been hired by a liability insurer and, if so, was likely to be familiar with such multi-defendant cases.) What could she have done? If you look back to Chapter 8, two possibilities present themselves. One is an agreement among defendants about how, if they are held liable, they will apportion the costs among themselves. Another is a sliding scale agreement with the plaintiff, spelling out how liability will be apportioned given various settlements and adjudicated outcomes.

D. JUDGES GUIDING JURIES

Once a jury—a second potential decision maker—enters the picture, one needs principles defining judges' and juries' respective spheres of competence and power. At trial, lawyers will present witnesses and evidence and offer their most compelling description of their clients' claims and defenses to the jurors deciding the case. Yet jurors are, by definition, laypeople who may have little clue about the law underlying the stories they will hear from the parties, how to weigh the information at their disposal, or how many of them must agree to render a verdict. Accordingly, judges must instruct and guide juries at several points before and during their deliberations.

1. Instruction and Comment

Jurors will often not know the substantive law, so the judge teaches that law through jury instructions. See Rule 51. Notice that like so much else in U.S. procedure, this too depends on the parties, who must request instructions, and, in the absence of an objection, may not complain that the judge has wrongly instructed the jury. As you approach your first trial, work out proposed jury instructions way in advance of anything else—otherwise they will sneak up and bite you from behind.

Instructions explain the substantive law that applies to the case, and the judge explains in a sequential way the decisions the jury must reach in a given case. For example, if the jury determines that the defendant was negligent, it must then decide whether the defendant's negligence caused the injury of which the plaintiff is complaining.

Jury instructions have two audiences. Their first audience is the jury itself, who may have an intuitive understanding of the law (quite likely in a negligence case) or none at all (as, for example, in antitrust). The second audience for jury instructions is the appellate court, which will reverse a case if an instruction misstates the law in a material way. These audiences have essentially incompatible requirements. The jury wants a simplified, easy-to-follow path through the wilderness of evidence to help it distinguish the central from the peripheral and to explain what factors should go into its decision on each question. The appellate court wants a nuanced, perfectly balanced, all-inclusive statement of the law. The clash between these contradictory requirements means that most instructions are compromises. Traditionally, juries received no instructions until the case was finished, at which point jurors sometimes learned they had been paying attention to the wrong things. Today some courts are experimenting with staged instructions, instructing juries on aspects of the law pertinent to particular parts of evidence as it comes in; preliminary information suggests the staged instructions are helpful.

Besides telling the jury what the law is, the judge may tell the jury what she thinks of the evidence. Here the law speaks to the judge with a mixed voice. In federal courts at least, the judge has the theoretical power to comment on the evidence. That power is hedged, however, with many qualifications and with exhortations that the judge not trespass onto the jury's autonomous decision-making space. Judges who do so egregiously—like the judge who solemnly informed a jury that in his experience witnesses who wiped their hands while testifying were liars, Quercia v. United States, 289 U.S. 466, 468 (1933)—are reversed.

2. Excluding Improper Influences

Early medieval juries were supposed already to know the relevant facts (Was John seised of Blackacre on the day the Old King died?). Modern juries are supposed to know nothing about the case except what they learn at trial; a juror who said he'd been at the intersection at the time of the accident and was familiar with both parties' driving records—making him an ideal medieval juror—would immediately be excused for cause.

Besides proper instructions about the law, juries need insulation from improper influences. The process starts well before trial gets under way. Screening the jury through voir dire (see supra page 614) seeks to eliminate jurors whose sympathies or inability to understand the evidence might cause them to reach irrational verdicts. During the trial, judges try to ensure that jurors will consider only information screened through the law of evidence (many of whose parts can be explained as efforts to insulate jurors from information that might be misleading).

Even good-faith efforts by jurors to bring their fellow jurors information not filtered through the evidentiary and adversarial screens may result in reversal. For example, in a case that turned on whether aluminum electrical wiring was dangerous, one juror, after hearing testimony to that effect, went home, examined the wiring in his own home, and reported his findings to his fellow jurors the next day. The appellate court ordered a new trial. In re Beverly Hills Fire Litigation, 695 F.2d 207 (6th Cir. 1982).

Judges try to avoid such outcomes by instructing the jurors not to discuss the case with others and to decide only on the basis of evidence presented in the courtroom. In extreme instances, where the case is the subject of much public discussion, the judge can sequester the jury. In recent years the wide availability of web-based information has posed another problem. Lawyers and judges report juries "contaminated" by jurors who research matters at issue in the trial (What does the intersection look like? Have others reported injuries from this product? Has defendant been sued by others?), and judges will often instruct jurors not to use such tools.

3. Size and Decision Rules

Still another way of preventing juries from reaching aberrant conclusions involves jury size and jury decision rules. The underlying ideas are that groups will render decisions that cancel out aberrant views of one or two members, and that requiring consensus assures full discussion of the evidence. At early common law a jury consisted of 12 persons; the verdict was required to be unanimous; and the verdict could be attacked only by "attaint," a process in which a second jury, twice as large, considered charges that the first jury had been deliberately untruthful in its verdict. Those rules have changed—in the federal courts—in recent decades.

In the widely criticized decision of Colgrove v. Battin, 413 U.S. 149 (1973), the Supreme Court constitutionalized six-person civil juries, which are now in widespread use in federal courts and in some states. What difference does it make? Fundamentally, a smaller jury is less "average," less representative. Smaller juries are less likely to include any given point of view or social characteristic—race, political views, economic status, and so on. Just as a single individual is more likely to be eccentric than a large group, so smaller juries are more likely to render aberrant verdicts than are larger juries.

In the federal system, unanimous verdicts in civil cases are still required unless the parties agree to accept a nonunanimous verdict. See Rule 48. Some states permit nonunanimous verdicts, usually allowing two or three opposing votes on a 12-person jury. Again one can ask what difference it makes. Rules of unanimity will result in more hung juries (a single holdout can block a verdict), requiring a retrial. Balanced against this loss of efficiency are some studies suggesting that groups where unanimity is required discuss the evidence with more intensity and in more detail than do groups where unanimity is not required.

Notice that, combined, these changes in size and decision rules can magnify each other. Decreasing the size of the jury reduces the likelihood that any given social characteristic will be reflected in the jury's membership. Moreover, abolishing the unanimity requirement lessens the effect that social diversity will have on the jury's verdict: If jurors do not have to render a unanimous verdict, the majority can simply ignore the point of view of one or two individuals.

* * *

If the procedures described in the preceding sections work as planned, the litigants will face a judge and a jury who can approach the case without bias. But even an unbiased fact-finder can go wrong. The system therefore worries about two problems: juries reaching verdicts unsustainable in logic; and, conversely, judges improperly seizing control of litigation from juries. The next two sections examine the procedures and doctrines designed to prevent either of these from happening. At the outset, it's worth noting that judges and juries appear to agree with each other in the very great majority of cases.* So the cases and principles examined here apply in the cases where judge and jury disagree. Who then prevails—and how?

Several circumstances make it difficult to police the boundary between these shared responsibilities. First, in modern civil procedure only closely balanced cases will come to trial. Summary judgment will have weeded out most of the rest. Accordingly, every case should be a close one. Second, we have aspirations for the jury beyond simple fact-finding, although finding facts in the midst of conflict and perjury is hardly simple. The jury also serves as the voice of the community, tempering and making acceptable applications of law that might otherwise be resented or resisted. Finally, it is a temporary, lay, and democratic institution that stands at the core of a permanent, professional, and elite institution—the judiciary. The two latter roles conflict at times with fact-finding, at least if that task is understood in a limited way. To ask juries to decide cases, then, is to permit them—or even to require them—to do something more than find facts. If one accepts these propositions, the task of procedure becomes more difficult. The litigation system is dedicated to rationality. It is also, however, committed to a model of fact-finding that blends rationality with other goals. How does one frame procedural rules that give juries sufficient leeway to perform the tasks we have set for them without irreparably compromising the rationality of verdicts?

E. JUDGES CONTROLLING JURIES: JUDGMENT AS A MATTER OF LAW

Suppose that, in spite of carefully conducted voir dire and perfect instructions on the law, a jury uncontaminated by outside influences reaches—unanimously—an insupportable conclusion. In a negligence case, the plaintiff presents no evidence that the defendant's negligence caused the accident. Or in a case where the defense rests solely on the statute of limitations, the only evidence points to the critical events having occurred within the statute. In such cases the opposing party can ask the judge to grant "judgment as a matter of law." Read Rule 50(a). If the court grants such a motion, the jury will not receive the case (or that part of it as to which the motion is granted). Historically, the grant of such a motion was called a "directed verdict,"† a term that many state courts and lawyers continue to use.

---

* An 80 percent agreement rate is most commonly cited. Roselle L. Wissler et al., *Decisionmaking About General Damages: A Comparison of Jurors, Judges, and Lawyers*, 98 Mich. L. Rev. 751 (1999).
† It was so called because the judge ordered ("directed") the jury to return a verdict conforming with the evidence. Juries were usually delighted to be spared the task of deliberating, but every so often one balked, and refused to return the requested verdict, leading in the rare case to the court's holding them in contempt until they complied. Rule 50 eliminates such episodes and changes its terminology to conform to actual practice.

Although the wording of Rule 56 (summary judgment) and Rule 50(a) (directed verdict) differ, the Supreme Court has made clear that "the standard for granting summary judgment 'mirrors' the standard for judgment as a matter of law, such that 'the inquiry under each is the same.'" Reeves v. Sanderson Plumbing Products, Inc., 530 U.S. 133 (2000). At both summary judgment and directed verdict, the question is whether—drawing all inferences in favor of the nonmoving party and avoiding credibility determinations or weighing of the evidence—the party with the burden of production has put forth sufficient evidence for a reasonable jury to find for that party on that issue.

Notes and Problems

1. Courts say that they grant judgments as a matter of law when the party with the *burden of production* has failed to carry that burden. This phrase captures an essential implication of party responsibility for proof. The system assigns to the parties—more precisely to one of the parties—the responsibility for investigating, discovering, marshaling evidence, and presenting that evidence to the trier of fact. If that party fails to carry the burden assigned, she loses the case. You have already seen the burden of production operating in summary judgment. At the heart of *Celotex Corp. v. Catrett*, supra page 573, lies a hard truth: A party with the burden of production can lose even before trial if she fails to demonstrate, among the facts uncovered by investigation and discovery, sufficient evidence to allow a rational trier of fact to find in her favor.

   a. To understand why lawyers care about burdens of production, take an example from a simple auto accident case. Plaintiff has the burden of production on negligence. What does that mean in practice? First, the plaintiff has to decide how she is going to show defendant's negligence: Will she base it on faulty maintenance, speeding, inebriation, failure to watch opposing traffic, driving in spite of a disabling medical condition, or some other breach of care? This initial decision will flow in large measure from plaintiff's sense of the facts: One would risk sanctions as well as failure on the merits if one based one's case on defendant's inebriation without having any factual foundation.

   b. Let's assume that plaintiff reports that defendant ran the red light. That would provide an adequate basis for pleading negligence while meeting the factual foundation requirements of Rule 11. Discovery might, of course, turn up other information—faulty maintenance of defendant's brakes, say—and it might cast doubt on the original theory: Plaintiff thinks she saw defendant run the light, but other, disinterested witnesses deny it. Whatever plaintiff's theory of negligence, she has the responsibility for gathering and presenting evidence on that theory. Let's assume that plaintiff thinks her strongest case is the "defendant ran the light" story. To carry her burden of production on the question of whether the defendant ran the red light, it is up to plaintiff to find the witnesses, interview or depose them, get their affidavits (to avoid summary judgment), make sure they come to court on the day of trial, and conduct the direct examination in a way that makes their statements admissible. If the plaintiff fails in any of these steps, she loses—even though, as a matter of historical fact, the defendant did run the red light. The plaintiff loses because she has failed to satisfy the burden of production—of coming forward with evidence from which a rational trier of fact could conclude some proposition of material fact.

2. Notice that in our red light hypothetical case, plaintiff has the burden of proving negligence. But defendant will have the responsibility (let's not call it a burden, lest we confuse ourselves hopelessly) of making the motion that tests whether plaintiff has carried that burden.

   a. At the pretrial stage, how would defendant challenge plaintiff's ability to satisfy the burden of production? See pages 569-72.
   b. At trial, how would defendant raise the challenge?
   c. What if plaintiff's evidence, in the words of Rule 50(a)(1), would not give "a reasonable jury . . . a legally sufficient evidentiary basis to find for" plaintiff—but defendant fails to make the appropriate motion?
      i. Can the court just enter judgment on its own motion? Not according to Rule 50(a).
      ii. But neither does the Rule forbid a judge from holding a sidebar conference at which she says something like, "At this time, counsel, I would be happy to entertain any relevant pre-verdict motions." Counsel who do not respond to this hint deserve to lose both the case and the ensuing malpractice suit.

3. Different parties may have the burden of production on different issues. For example, in a negligence case, the plaintiff will have the burden of production on the defendant's negligence. By contrast, if the defendant pleads the statute of limitations as a defense, the defendant will have the burden of producing facts to support that defense. Suppose that the plaintiff was exposed to some allegedly toxic chemicals, perhaps as a result of the defendant's negligence. The statute of limitations is one year, and under state law the statute runs from the time the plaintiff should reasonably have realized that she was injured. Plaintiff filed suit more than a year after exposure alleging injuries from the exposure.

   a. The plaintiff has the burden of producing evidence that the defendant negligently handled or used the chemicals in question and that the exposure caused the symptoms complained of.
   b. The defendant has the burden of producing evidence that the plaintiff should reasonably have realized that she was injured more than a year before the case was filed.
   c. Under those circumstances, both parties have the burden of producing evidence about material facts best known to the adversary—and have the risk of losing if they fail to do so. Whether they can meet their burdens may depend on how well they have used discovery.

WHAT'S NEW HERE?

- To have the burden of production on a claim or defense means that you bear responsibility not only for deciding which story to try to tell in court, but for assembling all the bits and pieces of evidence that will make that story persuasive. Failing to gather even one critical piece of evidence could result in the collapse of your client's entire case.
- Procedural devices enforce that burden. Summary judgment is one; judgment as a matter of law is the other.
- Although Rule 50 and Rule 56 are worded differently, they have been interpreted to impose the same burden on the party with the burden of production at trial.

1. Judgment as a Matter of Law in Action: How Courts Should Assess the Evidence

With these foundational matters to one side, the great and difficult question in directing verdicts lies before us: When may a court interfere with the jury's fact-finding and law-applying role? We have already explored these questions as they relate to summary judgment. In *Houchens* (supra page 38), we saw a situation in which the court granted summary judgment because there was no evidence from which a rational fact-finder could have found for Mrs. Houchens. But what if there's *some* evidence? Can a judge decide whom to believe? The well-established law in this area says that a judge may never make a credibility determination in granting judgment as a matter of law—credibility is a matter for the jury. Nor may a judge "weigh" the evidence, as opposed to finding whether there *is* any evidence from which the jury could find for the party against whom the motion is directed. When you read *Tolan* and *Bias* (in Chapter 8), you considered whether the courts had followed these tenets in the summary judgment context. In the next case, an appeal of a directed verdict, decide whether the U.S. Supreme Court is adhering to these standards or fudging them.

Pennsylvania Railroad v. Chamberlain
288 U.S. 333 (1933)

SUTHERLAND, J., delivered the opinion of the Court.

This is an action brought by respondent against petitioner to recover for the death of a brakeman, alleged to have been caused by petitioner's negligence. The complaint alleges that the deceased, at the time of the accident resulting in his death,

Facts

was assisting in the yard work of breaking up and making up trains and in the classifying and assorting of cars operating in interstate commerce; that in pursuance of such work, while riding a cut of cars, other cars ridden by fellow employees were negligently caused to be brought into violent contact with those upon which deceased was riding, with the result that he was thrown therefrom to the railroad track and run over by a car or cars, inflicting injuries from which he died.

Procedure

At the conclusion of the evidence, the trial court directed the jury to find a verdict in favor of petitioner. Judgment upon a verdict so found was reversed by the court of appeals, Judge Swan dissenting.

That part of the yard in which the accident occurred contained a lead track and a large number of switching tracks branching therefrom. The lead track crossed a "hump," and the work of car distribution consisted of pushing a train of cars by means of a locomotive to the top of the "hump," and then allowing the cars, in separate strings, to descend by gravity, under the control of hand brakes, to their respective destinations in the various branch tracks. Deceased had charge of a string of two gondola cars, which he was piloting to track 14. Immediately ahead of him was a string of seven cars, and behind him a string of nine cars, both also destined for track 14. Soon after the cars ridden by deceased had passed to track 14, his body was found on that track some distance beyond the switch. He had evidently fallen onto the track and been run over by a car or cars.

The case for respondent rests wholly upon the claim that the fall of deceased was caused by a violent collision of the string of nine cars with the string ridden by deceased. Three employees, riding the nine-car string, testified positively that no such collision occurred. They were corroborated by every other employee in a position to see, all testifying that there was no contact between the nine-car string and that of the deceased. The testimony of these witnesses, if believed, establishes beyond doubt that there was no collision between these two strings of cars, and that the nine-car string contributed in no way to the accident. The only witness who testified for the respondent was one Bainbridge; and it is upon his testimony alone that respondent's right to recover is sought to be upheld. His testimony is concisely stated, in its most favorable light for respondent, in the prevailing opinion below by Judge Learned Hand, as follows:

> The plaintiff's only witness to the event, one Bainbridge, then employed by the road, stood close to the yardmaster's office, near the "hump." He professed to have paid little attention to what went on, but he did see the deceased riding at the rear of his cars, whose speed when they passed him he took to be about eight or ten miles. Shortly thereafter a second string passed which was shunted into another track and this was followed by the nine, which, according to the plaintiff's theory, collided with the deceased's. After the nine cars had passed at a somewhat greater speed than the deceased's, Bainbridge paid no more attention to either string for a while, but looked again when the deceased, who was still standing in his place, had passed the switch and onto the assorting track where he was bound. At that time his speed had been checked to about three miles, but the speed of the following nine cars had increased. They were just passing the switch, about four or five cars behind the deceased. Bainbridge looked away again and soon heard what he described as a "loud crash," not however an unusual event in a switching yard. Apparently this did not cause him at once to turn, but he did so shortly thereafter,

and saw the two strings together still moving, and the deceased no longer in sight. Later still his attention was attracted by shouts and he went to the spot and saw the deceased between the rails. Until he left to go to the accident, he had stood fifty feet to the north of the track where the accident happened, and about nine hundred feet from where the body was found.

The court, although regarding Bainbridge's testimony as not only "somewhat suspicious in itself, but its contradiction . . . so manifold as to leave little doubt," held, nevertheless, that the question was one of fact depending upon the credibility of the witnesses, and that it was for the jury to determine, as between the one witness and the many, where the truth lay. The dissenting opinion of Judge Swan proceeds upon the theory that Bainbridge did not testify that in fact a collision had taken place, but inferred it because he heard a crash, and because thereafter the two strings of cars appeared to him to be moving together. It is correctly pointed out in that opinion, however, that the crash might have come from elsewhere in the busy yard and that Bainbridge was in no position to see whether the two strings of cars were actually together; that Bainbridge repeatedly said he was paying no particular attention; and that his position was such, being 900 feet from the place where the body was found and less than 50 feet from the side of the track in question, that he necessarily saw the strings of cars at such an acute angle that it would be physically impossible even for an attentive observer to tell whether the forward end of the nine-car cut was actually in contact with the rear end of the two-car cut. The dissenting opinion further points out that all the witnesses who were in a position to see testified that there was no collision; that respondent's evidence was wholly circumstantial, and the inferences which might otherwise be drawn from it were shown to be utterly erroneous unless all of petitioner's witnesses were willful perjurers. "This is not a case," the opinion proceeds, "where direct testimony to an essential fact is contradicted by direct testimony of other witnesses, though even there it is conceded a directed verdict might be proper in some circumstances. Here, when all the testimony was in, the circumstantial evidence in support of negligence was thought by the trial judge to be so insubstantial and insufficient that it did not justify submission to the jury." We thus summarize and quote from the prevailing and dissenting opinions, because they present the divergent views to be considered in reaching a correct determination of the question involved. It, of course, is true, generally, that where there is a direct conflict of testimony upon a matter of fact, the question must be left to the jury to determine, without regard to the number of witnesses upon either side. But here there really is no conflict in the testimony as to the *facts*. The witnesses for petitioner flatly testified that there was no collision between the nine-car and the two-car strings. Bainbridge did not say there was such a collision. What he said was that he heard a "loud crash," which did not cause him at once to turn, but that shortly thereafter he did turn and saw the two strings of cars moving together with the deceased no longer in sight; that there was nothing unusual about the crash of cars—it happened every day; that there was nothing about this crash to attract his attention except that it was extra loud; that he paid no attention to it; that it was not sufficient to attract his attention. The record shows that there was a continuous movement of cars over and down the "hump," which were distributed among a large number of branch tracks within the yard, and that any two strings of these cars moving upon the same track might have come together and caused the crash which Bainbridge heard. There is no direct evidence that *in fact* the crash was occasioned by a collision of the two strings in question; and it is perfectly clear that no such fact was brought to Bainbridge's attention as a perception of the physical sense of sight or of hearing. At most there was an inference to that effect drawn from observed facts which gave equal support to the opposite inference that the crash was occasioned by the coming together of other strings of cars entirely away from the scene of the accident, or of the two-car string ridden by deceased and the seven-car string immediately ahead of it.

We, therefore, have a case belonging to that class of cases where proven facts give equal support to each of two inconsistent inferences; in which event, neither of them being established, judgment, as a matter of law, must go against the party upon whom rests the necessity of sustaining one of these inferences as against the other, before he is entitled to recover.

The rule is succinctly stated in Smith v. First National Bank in Westfield, 99 Mass. 605, 611-612, quoted in the *Des Moines National Bank* case [United States F. & G. Co. v. Des Moines National Bank, 145 F. 273, 280 (8th Cir. 1906)]:

> There being several inferences deducible from the facts which appear, and equally consistent with all those facts, the plaintiff has not maintained the proposition upon which alone he would be entitled to recover. There is strictly no evidence to warrant a jury in finding that the loss was occasioned by negligence and not by theft. When the evidence tends equally to sustain either of two inconsistent propositions, neither of them can be said to have been established by legitimate proof. A verdict in favor of the party bound to maintain one of those propositions against the other is necessarily wrong.

That Bainbridge concluded from what he himself observed that the crash was due to a collision between the two strings of cars in question is sufficiently indicated by his statements. But this, of course, proves nothing, since it is not allowable for a witness to resolve the doubt as to which of two equally justifiable inferences shall be adopted by drawing a conclusion, which, if accepted, will result in a purely gratuitous award in favor of the party who has failed to sustain the burden of proof cast upon him by the law.

And the desired inference is precluded for the further reason that respondent's right of recovery depends upon the existence of a particular fact which must be inferred from proven facts, and this is not permissible in the face of the positive and otherwise uncontradicted testimony of unimpeached witnesses consistent with the facts actually proved, from which testimony it affirmatively appears that the fact sought to be inferred did not exist. . . .

Not only is Bainbridge's testimony considered as a whole suspicious, insubstantial and insufficient, but his statement that when he turned shortly after hearing the crash the two strings were moving together is simply incredible, if he meant thereby to be understood as saying that he saw the two in contact; and if he meant by the words "moving together" simply that they were moving at the same time in the same direction but not in contact, the statement becomes immaterial. As we have already seen he was paying slight and only occasional attention to what was going on. The cars were 800 or 900 feet from where he stood and moving almost directly away from him, his angle of vision being only 3°03 from a straight line. At that sharp angle and from that distance, near dusk of a misty evening (as the proof shows), the practical impossibility of the witness being able to see whether the front of the nine-car string was in contact with the back of the two-car string is apparent. And, certainly, in the light of these conditions, no verdict based upon a statement so unbelievable reasonably could be sustained as against the positive testimony to the contrary of unimpeached witnesses, all in a position to see, as this witness was not, the precise relation of the cars to one another. The fact that these witnesses were employees of the petitioner, under the circumstances here disclosed, does not impair this conclusion. Chesapeake & Ohio Ry. v. Martin, 283 U.S. 209, 216-220. . . .

Leaving out of consideration, then, the inference relied upon, the case for respondent is left without any substantial support in the evidence, and a verdict in her favor would have rested upon mere speculation and conjecture. This, of course, is inadmissible.

The judgment of the Circuit Court of Appeals is reversed and that of the District Court is affirmed.

Stone, J., and Cardozo, J., concur in the result.

Notes and Problems

1. Focus first on the procedural steps that frame the issue.

   a. A trial typically consists of the plaintiff's presentation of her case, the defendant's of its case, closing arguments, and jury instructions. When in the course of this sequence did the court grant a directed verdict, which would today be called judgment as a matter of law? Locate the portion of Rule 50 that permits a party to make a motion at this point.

   b. Could the defendant have moved for a directed verdict earlier? When?

2. To understand the force of *Chamberlain*, consider a variation on the facts.

   a. Suppose at the time of the accident Bainbridge had not been standing several hundred feet away from the scene on a misty evening but instead had been standing ten feet away. He testifies that he clearly saw the collision, and that Chamberlain's death had been caused by the following cars overtaking his and crushing him between the cars. But suppose further that at the time of the accident a group of clergy had been taking a tour of the rail yards. These clergy also saw the accident clearly, and all testify under oath that the following string did not come near Chamberlain's and that the deceased fell onto the tracks when he waved to a friend. Would this testimony warrant granting a judgment for defendant?

   b. The commonly accepted answer to this question is no. This answer is a result of the courts' insistence that in directing verdicts they not make judgments about the credibility of witnesses, even when the case seems strongly one-sided.

c. Review the facts described by the Court and construct the evidence presented into a pattern that makes it reasonable to infer that the fellow workers' negligence caused Chamberlain's death. In constructing such a story, consider a snippet from the opinion below, by Judge Learned Hand:

> It does not appear to us impossible, or indeed improbable, that one in [Bainbridge's] position could tell whether the two strings were together. The intervals between cars in a train are uniform; they may be detected by the straight sides. Certainly a gap of four or five car lengths, when the nine cars came to rest, would have been easily observable; and this was the story of the defendant. What Bainbridge saw, coupled with what he had heard, if uncontradicted, would be enough to support a finding that the nine cars had collided with the deceased's and thrown him off. There is no inherent impossibility in the story.

> Chamberlain v. Pennsylvania R.R., 59 F.2d 986, 987 (2d Cir. 1932).

d. Does the Supreme Court make a comparative assessment of witness credibility? As the Supreme Court describes the case, Bainbridge's testimony is suspicious because of his inadequate opportunity to observe, while the fellow workers' contrary testimony is taken at face value. Is there reason to suspect the workers' testimony? Is there reason to credit Bainbridge's inference that the two strings collided?

3. Cases such as *Chamberlain* have been thought to raise two related issues. The first is the precise standard for taking the case from the jury—more particularly, which evidence should be considered by the court when deciding whether to do so. There is general agreement that the court should consider all evidence favorable to the nonmoving party, all inferences from that evidence, and all undisputed evidence. But should the court also consider testimonial and disputed evidence in favor of the moving party? Closely related is the matter of evaluating the evidence. Many courts have stated that the basic test is whether reasonable persons could differ; if they could, the court should defer to the jury on the ground that its members are reasonable persons whose verdict represents one of several reasonable views. A leading case articulating the prevailing view is Boeing Co. v. Shipman, 411 F.2d 365, 374-75 (5th Cir. 1969):

> On motions for directed verdict and for judgment notwithstanding the verdict [both now called judgment as a matter of law] the Court should consider all of the evidence—not just that evidence which supports the non-mover's case—but in the light and with all reasonable inferences most favorable to the party opposed to the motion. If the facts and inferences point so strongly and overwhelmingly in favor of one party that the Court believes that reasonable men could not arrive at a contrary verdict, granting of the motions is proper. On the other hand, if there is substantial evidence opposed to the motions, that is, evidence of such quality and weight that reasonable and fair-minded men in the exercise of impartial judgment might reach different conclusions, the motions should be denied, and the case submitted to the jury. A mere scintilla of evidence is insufficient to present

a question for the jury. The motions for [judgment as a matter of law] should not be decided by which side has the better of the case, nor should they be granted only when there is a complete absence of probative facts to support a jury verdict. There must be a conflict in substantial evidence to create a jury question. However, it is the function of the jury as the traditional finder of the facts, and not the Court, to weigh conflicting evidence and inferences, and determine the credibility of witnesses.

4. In *Chamberlain*, the Court has to avoid questions of credibility because the jury is the undoubted arbiter of credibility. But we ask jurors to do much more than to decide who is telling the truth. We also give to the jury many questions that require them to apply general, open-ended standards to specific facts of the case. Was it negligent under these circumstances to be driving five miles faster than the speed limit? Was the behavior of one of the contracting parties unreasonable? To arrive at answers to such questions, juries may have to decide questions of fact. But even after doing so they must then apply the open texture of law to those facts.

   a. Because of this role, courts often give to juries cases where the facts are undisputed. A classic example is Railroad Co. v. Stout, 84 U.S. 657 (1873). A child was injured while playing on a railroad turntable located at the edge of a sparsely populated rural settlement. The turntable was not locked or fenced. No one contested any of these facts; the case went to the jury, which found negligence. Rejecting the railroad's contentions that the judge should have taken the case from the jury, the Supreme Court wrote:

   > Upon the facts proven in such cases, it is a matter of judgment and discretion, of sound inference, what is the deduction to be drawn from the undisputed facts. Certain facts we may suppose to be clearly established from which one sensible, impartial man would infer that proper care had not been used, and that negligence existed; another man equally sensible and equally impartial would infer that proper care had been used, and that there was no negligence. It is this class of cases and those akin to it that the law commits to the decision of a jury. Twelve men of the average of the community, comprising men of education and men of little education, men of learning and men whose learning consists only in what they have themselves seen and heard, the merchant, the mechanic, the farmer, the laborer; these sit together, consult, apply their separate experience of the affairs of life to the facts proven, and draw a unanimous conclusion. This average judgment thus given it is the great effort of the law to obtain. It is assumed that twelve men know more of the common affairs of life than does one man, that they can draw wiser and safer conclusions from admitted facts thus occurring than can a single judge.

   > Railroad Co. v. Stout, 84 U.S. at 663.

   Note that the assumption about the gender of jurors rests on premises since held to be unconstitutional. See supra page 613.

   b. Given this practice, describing the jury as merely a fact-finding body is deceptive. Isn't the jury's role in such cases very close to making "law"?

Implications

SUMMARY JUDGMENT AND JUDGMENT AS A MATTER OF LAW

After *Celotex* (discussed in Chapter 8), there should, in a world of perfect theory, never be an occasion for judgment as a matter of law. Put another way, in the same world of perfect theory, a judgment as a matter of law suggests that someone made a mistake in failing to move for or failing to grant summary judgment.

Why? *Celotex* said that at the summary judgment stage, parties have the same burden of production they will have at trial. If parties have made good use of discovery, they will, by the time for summary judgment, have assembled all the evidence that they will use at trial. A summary judgment motion asks whether this evidence would be sufficient to allow a reasonable jury to find in favor of the party with the burden of production. If not, the court should grant summary judgment against that party. So, if summary judgment is doing its job, all the cases where judgment as a matter of law might be granted will be screened out at the summary judgment stage, never reaching trial.

We do not live in that perfect world of theory. For example, witnesses can change their stories or be unavailable to testify at trial, thus depriving a party of some critical piece of evidence. When that happens, motions for judgment as a matter of law serve as a backstop.

2. Judgment as a Matter of Law in Action: Judgments and Renewed Judgments

Thus far, we have focused on how judges should assess the evidence when considering a motion for judgment as a matter of law. But Rule 50 is also a procedurally complex rule that sets traps for unwary litigants and judges. Read Rule 50(a) and (b) and consider the obligations they place on parties.

Notes and Problems

1. Return to the facts of the *Chamberlain* case. When is the earliest that defendant could move for judgment as a matter of law under Rule 50(a)? When is the latest that defendant could move under Rule 50(a)?

2. Suppose that at the close of the evidence, defendant moves for judgment as a matter of law. The court denies the motion and submits the case to the jury, which returns

a plaintiff's verdict. The defendant still firmly believes that there was no evidence from which "a reasonable jury would . . . have a legally sufficient evidentiary basis to find" that the negligence of Chamberlain's fellow workers caused his death. What should the defendant do? See Rule 50(b). Also review *Norton v. Snapper Power Equipment*, supra page 43, in which just this procedure was used.

a. Notice one egregious error the moving party might make in such a situation. Suppose that, in the heat of trial, defendant fails to make a Rule 50(a) motion before the case goes to the jury. Awaiting the verdict, defendant's counsel thinks he has now identified a fatal gap in plaintiff's case. May he make a post-verdict motion for judgment as a matter of law under Rule 50(b)? No, the Supreme Court has held, and that holding has the force of the Seventh Amendment behind it. The reasoning is that at the time the Amendment was adopted, courts permitted such post-verdict motion only as a renewal of a similar pre-verdict motion. Because the Amendment forbids "reexamin[ing]" a verdict except as was permitted at common law, a post-verdict motion for judgment as a matter of law standing alone would be unconstitutional. Baltimore & Carolina Line v. Redman, 295 U.S. 654 (1935).

b. Suppose that a defendant makes a Rule 50(a) motion and the jury enters a verdict for the plaintiff. Can the defendant appeal the Rule 50(a) denial without bringing a post-verdict motion pursuant to Rule 50(b)? The Supreme Court answered this question in the next case, and in doing so offered some insight into—and disagreement about—the procedural framework of Rule 50.

Unitherm Food Systems, Inc. v. Swift-Eckrich, Inc.

546 U.S. 394 (2006)

THOMAS, J.

Ordinarily, a party in a civil jury trial that believes the evidence is legally insufficient to support an adverse jury verdict will seek a judgment as a matter of law by filing a motion pursuant to Federal Rule of Civil Procedure 50(a) before submission of the case to the jury, and then (if the Rule 50(a) motion is not granted and the jury subsequently decides against that party) a motion pursuant to Rule 50(b). In this case, however, the respondent filed a Rule 50(a) motion before the verdict, but did not file a Rule 50(b) motion after the verdict. Nor did respondent request a new trial under Rule 59. The Court of Appeals nevertheless proceeded to review the sufficiency of the evidence and, upon a finding that the evidence was insufficient, remanded the case for a new trial. Because our cases addressing the requirements of Rule 50 compel a contrary result, we reverse.

I

The genesis of the underlying litigation in this case was ConAgra's attempt to enforce its patent for "A Method for Browning Precooked Whole Muscle Meat

Products." [In 2000, ConAgra issued a warning to companies who sold equipment and processes for browning precooked meats and its direct competitors in the precooked meat business. Unitherm, which had invented a similar process six years before ConAgra filed its patent application, sued ConAgra, alleging that ConAgra's patent was invalid and that ConAgra had violated §2 of the Sherman Act "by attempting to enforce a patent that was obtained by committing fraud on the Patent and Trademark Office"—what is referred to as a *Walker Process* claim. The district court found that ConAgra's patent was invalid and allowed the *Walker Process* antitrust claim to go to trial.]

Prior to the court's submission of the case to the jury, ConAgra moved for a directed verdict under Rule 50(a) based on legal insufficiency of the evidence. The District Court denied that motion. The jury returned a verdict for Unitherm, and ConAgra neither renewed its motion for judgment as a matter of law pursuant to Rule 50(b), nor moved for a new trial on antitrust liability pursuant to Rule 59.

On appeal to the Federal Circuit [the court that hears appeals of cases arising under the Patent Act], ConAgra maintained that there was insufficient evidence to sustain the jury's *Walker Process* verdict. Although the Federal Circuit has concluded that a party's "failure to present the district court with a post-verdict motion precludes appellate review of sufficiency of the evidence," in the instant case it was bound to apply the law of the Tenth Circuit. *Unitherm Food Sys.*, 375 F.3d at 1365 n.7 ("On most issues related to Rule 50 motions . . . we generally apply regional circuit law unless the precise issue being appealed pertains uniquely to patent law"). Under Tenth Circuit law, a party that has failed to file a postverdict motion challenging the sufficiency of the evidence may nonetheless raise such a claim on appeal, so long as that party filed a Rule 50(a) motion prior to submission of the case to the jury. Notably, the only available relief in such a circumstance is a new trial.

Freed to examine the sufficiency of the evidence, the Federal Circuit concluded that, although Unitherm had presented sufficient evidence to support a determination that ConAgra had attempted to enforce a patent that it had obtained through fraud on the PTO, Unitherm had failed to present evidence sufficient to support the remaining elements of its antitrust claim. Accordingly, it vacated the jury's judgment in favor of Unitherm and remanded for a new trial. We granted certiorari, and now reverse.

II

Federal Rule of Civil Procedure 50 sets forth the procedural requirements for challenging the sufficiency of the evidence in a civil jury trial and establishes two stages for such challenges—prior to submission of the case to the jury, and after the verdict and entry of judgment. Rule 50(a) allows a party to challenge the sufficiency of the evidence prior to submission of the case to the jury, and authorizes the district court to grant such motions at the court's discretion. Rule 50(b), by contrast, sets forth the procedural requirements for renewing a sufficiency of the evidence challenge after the jury verdict and entry of judgment.

This Court has addressed the implications of a party's failure to file a postverdict motion under Rule 50(b) on several occasions and in a variety of procedural contexts.

This Court has concluded that, "[i]n the absence of such a motion" an "appellate court [is] without power to direct the District Court to enter judgment contrary to the one it had permitted to stand." *Cone v. West Virginia Pulp & Paper Co.*, 330 U.S. 212, 218 (1947). This Court has similarly concluded that a party's failure to file a Rule 50(b) motion deprives the appellate court of the power to order the entry of judgment in favor of that party where the district court directed the jury's verdict, *Globe Liquor Co. v. San Roman*, 332 U.S. 571 (1948), and where the district court expressly reserved a party's preverdict motion for a directed verdict and then denied that motion after the verdict was returned. A postverdict motion is necessary because "[d]etermination of whether a new trial should be granted or a judgment entered under Rule 50(b) calls for the judgment in the first instance of the judge who saw and heard the witnesses and has the feel of the case which no appellate printed transcript can impart." Moreover, the "requirement of a timely application for judgment after verdict is not an idle motion" because it "is . . . an essential part of the rule, firmly grounded in principles of fairness."

The foregoing authorities lead us to reverse the judgment below. Respondent correctly points out that these authorities address whether an appellate court may enter judgment in the absence of a postverdict motion, as opposed to whether an appellate court may order a new trial (as the Federal Circuit did here). But this distinction is immaterial. This Court's observations about the necessity of a postverdict motion under Rule 50(b), and the benefits of the district court's input at that stage, apply with equal force whether a party is seeking judgment as a matter of law or simply a new trial. In *Cone*, this Court concluded that, because Rule 50(b) permits the district court to exercise its discretion to choose between ordering a new trial and entering judgment, its "appraisal of the bona fides of the claims asserted by the litigants is of great value in reaching a conclusion as to whether a *new trial* should be granted." Similarly, this Court has determined that a party may only pursue on appeal a particular avenue of relief available under Rule 50(b), namely, the entry of judgment *or a new trial*, when that party has complied with the Rule's filing requirements by requesting that particular relief below. . . .

[T]he text and application of Rule 50(a) support our determination that respondent may not challenge the sufficiency of the evidence on appeal on the basis of the District Court's denial of its Rule 50(a) motion. . . . [W]hile a district court is permitted to enter judgment as a matter of law when it concludes that the evidence is legally insufficient, it is not required to do so. To the contrary, the district courts are, if anything, encouraged to submit the case to the jury, rather than granting such motions. As Wright and Miller explain:

> "Even at the close of all the evidence it may be desirable to refrain from granting a motion for judgment as a matter of law despite the fact that it would be possible for the district court to do so. If judgment as a matter of law is granted and the appellate court holds that the evidence in fact was sufficient to go to the jury, an entire new trial must be had. If, on the other hand, the trial court submits the case to the jury, though it thinks the evidence insufficient, final determination of the case is expedited greatly. If the jury agrees with the court's appraisal of the evidence, and returns a verdict for the party who moved for judgment as a matter of law, the case is at an end. If the jury brings in a different verdict, the trial court can grant a renewed motion for judgment as a matter of law. Then if the

appellate court holds that the trial court was in error in its appraisal of the evidence, it can reverse and order judgment on the verdict of the jury, without any need for a new trial. For this reason the appellate courts repeatedly have said that it usually is desirable to take a verdict, and then pass on the sufficiency of the evidence on a post-verdict motion." 9A Federal Practice §2533, at 319 (footnote omitted).

Thus, the District Court's denial of respondent's preverdict motion cannot form the basis of respondent's appeal, because the denial of that motion was not error. It was merely an exercise of the District Court's discretion, in accordance with the text of the Rule and the accepted practice of permitting the jury to make an initial judgment about the sufficiency of the evidence. The only error here was counsel's failure to file a postverdict motion pursuant to Rule 50(b).

* * *

For the foregoing reasons, we hold that since respondent failed to renew its preverdict motion as specified in Rule 50(b), there was no basis for review of respondent's sufficiency of the evidence challenge in the Court of Appeals. The judgment of the Court of Appeals is reversed.

It is so ordered.

STEVENS, J., with whom KENNEDY, J., joins, dissenting.

Murphy's law applies to trial lawyers as well as pilots. Even an expert will occasionally blunder. For that reason Congress has preserved the federal appeals courts' power to correct plain error, even though trial counsel's omission will ordinarily give rise to a binding waiver. This is not a case, in my view, in which the authority of the appellate court is limited by an explicit statute or controlling rule. The spirit of the Federal Rules of Civil Procedure favors preservation of a court's power to avoid manifestly unjust results in exceptional cases. Moreover, we have an overriding duty to obey statutory commands that unambiguously express the intent of Congress even in areas such as procedure in which we may have special expertise.

Today, relying primarily on a case decided in March 1947, *Cone,* and a case decided in January 1948, *Globe Liquor Co.,* the Court holds that the Court of Appeals was "powerless" to review the sufficiency of the evidence supporting the verdict in petitioner's favor because respondent failed to file proper postverdict motions pursuant to Rules 50(b) and 59 of the Federal Rules of Civil Procedure in the trial court. The majority's holding is inconsistent with a statute enacted just months after *Globe Liquor* was decided. That statute, which remains in effect today, provides:

> "The Supreme Court or any other court of appellate jurisdiction may affirm, modify, vacate, set aside or reverse any judgment, decree, or order of a court lawfully brought before it for review, and may remand the cause and direct the entry of such appropriate judgment, decree, or order, or require such further proceedings to be had as may be just under the circumstances." 28 U.S.C. §2106.

Nothing in Rule 50(b) limits this statutory grant of power to appellate courts; while a party's failure to make a Rule 50(b) motion precludes the *district court* from directing a verdict in that party's favor, the Rule does not purport to strip the courts of appeals of the authority to review district court judgments or to order such relief as "may be just under the circumstances.". . .

I respectfully dissent.

Notes and Problems

---

1. The Federal Circuit concluded that Unitherm had not met its burden of proving its antitrust claim. The Supreme Court does not take issue with this conclusion but nevertheless reverses the circuit decision and reinstates a jury verdict for Unitherm. Why?

2. Having read Rule 50, students of civil procedure might think it obvious that both parties would move for a directed verdict under Rule 50(a) before the jury receives the case, and that the losing party would renew its motion after the verdict is entered. Yet temporary amnesia about the importance of making and re-making Rule 50 motions appears to afflict even seasoned attorneys at trial.

    a. As one recent and high-profile example, a 2015 trial concerned whether Robin Thicke and Pharrell Williams's "Blurred Lines" infringed the copyright of "Got to Give it Up," a song written by Marvin Gaye. The jury found that Thicke and Williams infringed Gaye's copyright and awarded over $6 million in damages and profits. Thicke and Williams moved, after the verdict, under Rule 50(b) for judgment as a matter of law but were denied because they had failed to move for judgment as a matter of law under Rule 50(a).

    b. To complicate matters further, the district court had told the parties that it was not going to grant a Rule 50 motion before the jury rendered a verdict. Thicke and Williams argued that this admonition from the court excused their failure to so move, but the district court was unpersuaded. "Even if such a motion is denied, it serves the important procedural functions of preserving claims of error and alerting the responding party to any claimed deficiencies in its proof. By remaining silent, the Thicke Parties failed to apprise the Gaye Parties of 'the judgment sought and the law and facts that entitle the movant to the judgment,' as required by Rule 50(a)." *Williams v. Bridgeport Music, Inc.* 2015 WL 4479500 (C.D. Cal. July 14, 2015), aff'd *Williams v. Gaye*, 885 F.3d 1150 (9th Cir. 2018).

3. Attorneys not only need to remember to make a Rule 50(a) motion, but must be able to anticipate the arguments they might want to raise after trial: A Rule 50(b) motion can only renew the arguments that were made in the Rule 50(a) motion.

4. Notice that the *Unitherm* decision discusses Unitherm's failure both to bring a Rule 50(b) motion for renewed judgment as a matter of law, and a Rule 59

motion for a new trial. A court can order a new trial as a remedy under either Rule, but the procedural requirements and standards of proof differ, as the next section will make clear.

F. JUDGES UNDOING VERDICTS: THE NEW TRIAL

Suppose two variations on the trial of *Peters v. Dodge* in Chapter 1—a suit for injuries resulting from an auto accident—assuming in both that the parties have made all appropriate pre-verdict motions. In the first variation, imagine that Peters produced a witness—a witness who was near the intersection when the accident occurred and testified that Dodge's light was red. Further suppose that the trial judge thought the witness's testimony was very weak: The witness happens to work with Peters's mother, and so might be biased; moreover, she suffered from macular degeneration, making her ability to perceive the events suspect. Nevertheless, the jury returned a plaintiff's verdict. In the second variation, suppose that unbiased and clear-sighted but contradictory witnesses testify about whether Peters or Dodge was in the wrong. In this version, however, the judge realizes after the jury has returned a defendant's verdict that he failed to give a requested instruction on the substantive law, forgetting to make it clear that Peters had to show not only Dodge's negligence, but that the negligence (rather, say than a preexisting injury) caused Peters's medical condition.

As review, explain why—

- in the first case, the judge could not grant judgment as a matter of law for defendant;
- in the second case, the judge could not grant judgment as a matter of law for the plaintiff.

1. The Justifications for New Trials

In both cases the procedural remedy is not judgment as a matter of law, but an order for a new trial, governed by Rule 59. Rule 59 does not specify the grounds for which a new trial may be ordered, stating only that the court may do so "for any reason for which a new trial has heretofore been granted in an action at law in federal court." Do you see the Reexamination Clause of the Seventh Amendment lurking behind that phrasing? A fairly well-developed body of common law suggests two principal reasons for granting new trials, one focusing on the procedure leading up to the verdict, the other on the correctness of the verdict itself.

a. Flawed Procedures

New trials may be granted when the judge concludes that the process leading up to the verdict has been flawed, as in the second variation on *Peters v. Dodge* above.

Other examples: The judge may conclude that a lawyer has made an impermissible argument to the jury; or, on reflection after the trial is over, the judge may conclude that she erred in admitting a piece of evidence; or a judge may discover that a juror, although properly selected, misbehaved during the trial by visiting the accident scene himself. Ordering a new trial gives the judge a chance to fix the flawed process. And, unlike Rule 50, Rule 59(d) explicitly gives the judge power to order a new trial even if neither party so moves.

b. *Flawed Verdicts*

Even if the trial was perfect, the judge may conclude that the result of that trial—the verdict—is unjustifiable. Probably the most common ground for granting a new trial is that the verdict is against the great weight of the evidence. Understanding this idea requires a glance back at judgments as a matter of law. Although both judgments as a matter of law and new trials result from verdicts with little or no evidentiary support, it is important to understand the difference between them. The consequences of each reflect their different rationales. In granting judgment as a matter of law, a court is saying that the winner of the verdict had no evidentiary support for at least one essential element of his claim or defense. Judgment as a matter of law results in an immediate entry of judgment for the loser of the verdict. By contrast, the grant of a new trial does not make a winner out of a loser; it merely begins the contest again. The standard is accordingly lower: As most courts would put it, a judge may grant a new trial when the verdict is "against the great weight of the evidence." Those same courts would agree, however, that in considering whether to grant a new trial the trial judge may not simply decide how she would have voted as a juror. Where the standard lies between these two poles is harder to say.

WHAT'S NEW HERE?

- Rule 59 results in a do-over rather than a final judgment for one party.
- Such do-overs represent a solution to two quite different problems. In one form, the grant of a new trial is an almost-but-not-quite version of judgment as a matter of law: One cannot say that there was *no* evidence for the prevailing side, but it was very thin. In its other form, the court grants a new trial because the jury didn't have the right information before it, and a new trial gives a new jury the chance to decide on the basis of the right evidence and law.

Lind v. Schenley Industries

278 F.2d 79 (3d Cir. 1960)

BIGGS, J.

[Lind, a sales manager for the defendant liquor company, alleged that it had promised him an increase in pay and a share of commissions but had then breached that promise. The alleged promises were oral. Lind and his then-secretary, Mrs. Kennan, testified to such promises. Schenley's agents denied making them. The jury found a contract; a damage award followed. Schenley filed a renewed motion for judgment as a matter of law and, alternatively, for a new trial. The trial judge granted the 50(b) motion and, in the alternative, a new trial (see Rule 50(c), which mandates such contingent rulings). The plaintiff appealed. The court of appeals first held that it was error for the trial judge to grant the Rule 50(b) motion. It then considered the motion for a new trial.]

The district court granted the alternative motion for a new trial because it found the jury's verdict (1) contrary to the weight of the evidence, (2) contrary to law and (3) a result of error in the admission of evidence. . . .

[The court ruled on points (2) and (3) above, holding that it had been error to grant a new trial for Schenley on these grounds.]

The remaining basis for ordering a new trial is that the verdict was against the weight of the evidence. It is frequently stated that a motion for a new trial on this ground ordinarily is nonreviewable because within the discretion of the trial court. But this discretion must still be exercised in accordance with ascertainable legal standards and if an appellate court is shown special or unusual circumstances which clearly indicate an abuse of discretion in that the trial court failed to apply correctly the proper standards, reversal is possible. Concededly appellate courts rarely find that the trial court abused its discretion.

In *Commercial Credit Corp. v. Pepper*, Judge Borah stated:

> It is a principle well recognized in the federal courts that the granting or refusing of a new trial is a matter resting within the discretion of the trial court. The term "discretion," however, when invoked as a guide to judicial action, means a sound discretion, exercised with regard to what is right and in the interests of justice. And an appellate court is not bound to stay its hand and place its stamp of approval on a case when it feels that injustice may result. Quite to the contrary, it is definitely recognized in numerous decisions that an abuse of discretion is an exception to the rule that the granting or refusing of a new trial is not assignable as error.

Thus an appellate court must still rule upon the propriety of an order for a new trial, even though the grounds for reversal are exceedingly narrow. But before any rational decision can be made, the reviewing court must know what standards the trial judge is bound to apply when ruling upon a motion for a new trial. These standards necessarily vary according to the grounds urged in support of the new trial. There is, however, little authority on what standards are to be applied in ruling on a motion for new trial on the grounds that the verdict is against the weight of the evidence beyond the simple maxim that the trial judge has wide discretion. The few available authorities are conflicting. Professor Moore concludes that while the trial judge has a responsibility for the result at least equal to that of the jury he should not set the verdict aside as contrary to the weight of the evidence and order a new trial simply because he would have come to a different conclusion if he were the trier of the facts. Professor Moore states in this connection:

> [S]ince the credibility of witnesses is peculiarly for the jury it is an invasion of the jury's province to grant a new trial merely because the evidence was sharply in conflict. The trial judge, exercising a mature judicial discretion, should view the verdict in the overall setting of the trial; consider the character of the evidence and the complexity or simplicity of the legal principles which the jury was bound to apply to the facts; and abstain from interfering with the verdict unless it is quite clear that the jury has reached a seriously erroneous result. The judge's duty is essentially to see that there is no miscarriage of justice. If convinced that there has been then it is his duty to set the verdict aside; otherwise not.

Professor Moore's views are logical and persuasive and buttressed by some decisional authority. . . .

What we have stated demonstrates that there is no consensus of opinion as to the exact standards to be used by a trial court in granting a new trial and that the criteria to be employed by an appellate tribunal charged with reviewing the trial judge's decision in this respect are equally indefinite. New trials granted because (1) a jury verdict is against the weight of the evidence may be sharply distinguished from (2) new trials ordered for other reasons: for example, evidence improperly admitted, prejudicial statements by counsel, an improper charge to the jury or newly discovered evidence. In the first instance given it is the jury itself which fails properly to perform the functions confided to it by law. In the latter instances something occurred in the course of the trial which resulted or which may have resulted in the jury receiving a distorted, incorrect, or an incomplete view of the operative facts, or some undesirable element obtruded itself into the proceedings creating a condition whereby the giving of a just verdict was rendered difficult or impossible. In the latter instances, (2), supra, the trial court delivered the jury from a possibly erroneous verdict arising from circumstances over which the jury had no control. Under these conditions there is no usurpation by the court of the prime function of the jury as the trier of the facts and the trial judge necessarily must be allowed wide discretion in granting or refusing a new trial.

But where no undesirable or pernicious element has occurred or been introduced into the trial and the trial judge nonetheless grants a new trial on the ground that the verdict was against the weight of the evidence, the trial judge in negating the jury's verdict has, to some extent at least, substituted his judgment of the facts and the credibility of the witnesses for that of the jury. Such an action effects a denigration of the jury system and to the extent that new trials are granted the judge takes over, if he does not usurp, the prime function of the jury as the trier of the facts. It then becomes the duty of the appellate tribunal to exercise a closer degree of scrutiny and supervision than is the case where a new trial is granted because of some undesirable or pernicious influence obtruding into the trial. Such a close scrutiny is required in order to protect the litigants' right to jury trial.

Where a trial is long and complicated and deals with a subject matter not lying within the ordinary knowledge of jurors a verdict should be scrutinized more closely by the trial judge than is necessary where the litigation deals with material which is familiar and simple, the evidence relating to ordinary commercial practices. An example of subject matter unfamiliar to a layman would be a case requiring a jury to pass upon the nature of an alleged newly discovered organic compound in an infringement action. A prime example of subject matter lying well within the comprehension of jurors is presented by the circumstances at bar.

The subject matter of the litigation before us is simple and easily comprehended by any intelligent layman. The jury's main function was to determine the veracity of the witnesses: i.e., what testimony should be believed. If Lind's testimony and that of Mrs. Kennan, Kaufman's secretary, was deemed credible, Lind presented a convincing, indeed an overwhelming case. We must conclude that the jury did believe this testimony and that the court below substituted its judgment for that of the jury on this issue and thereby abused its legal discretion.

The judgment of the court below will be reversed and the case will be remanded with the direction to the court below to reinstate the verdict and judgment in favor of Lind.

HASTIE, J., with whom KALODNER, J., joins (dissenting).

. . . I think the majority make a serious mistake when they take the extraordinary additional step of reversing the alternative order of the trial judge, granting a new trial because he considered the verdict against the weight of the evidence. . . .

Under [the traditional understanding of trial courts' power to grant new trials] the only function of a reviewing court, once the trial court has ordered a new trial, is to see whether there can have been any basis in reason for the trial judge's conclusion as to the weight of the evidence and the injustice of the verdict. The majority do not challenge this view, though they do not state explicitly what their understanding of our role is.

The present record discloses a sharp conflict of testimony whether Kaufman, the metropolitan sales manager, ever promised plaintiff, his subordinate district manager, a 1% commission on all gross sales of agents working under plaintiff. There are several remarkable aspects of this alleged promise which could reasonably have influenced the trial judge on this decisive issue. This commission would have more than quadrupled plaintiff's salary of $150 per week, making him much higher paid than his immediate superior, Kaufman, or any other company executive, except the president. No other sales manager or supervisor received any such commission at all. Moreover, after the alleged promise was made, month after month elapsed with no payment of the 1% commission or indication of any step to fulfill such an obligation. Yet plaintiff himself admits that he made no formal demand for or inquiry about the large obligation for several years, and said nothing even informally about it to anyone for many months save for an occasional passing verbal inquiry said to have been addressed to Kaufman. The trial court may have reasoned that the amount said to have been promised was so abnormally large and plaintiff's concern about nonpayment so unnaturally small as to make it incredible that the promise ever was made. In addition, the very vagueness of the alleged promise and the absence of any mention of time in it may have increased the incredulity of the judge who heard the evidence.

In such circumstances it was neither arbitrary nor an abuse of discretion for the trial judge to grant a new trial. Whether in the same circumstances some other trial judge or any member of this court would have let the verdict stand is beside the point.

The majority thinks the trial judge usurped the function of the jury. I think it is we who are impinging upon the function and discretion of the trial judge in a way that is serious, regrettable and without precedent in this court.

Notes and Problems

---

1. Why did the trial court grant a new trial?

2. Why did the appellate court reverse the grant of a new trial?

3. The *Lind* opinion addresses three issues: (1) what standard the trial court should apply in setting aside verdicts as being against the weight of the evidence, (2) how the trial court should apply that standard to the case at hand, and (3) what standard the appellate court should apply in reviewing new trial rulings. How does the *Lind* opinion resolve each of these issues?

4. The *Lind* opinion also illustrates another part of the relationship between directed verdicts and orders for new trials. Notice that defendant, having lost the verdict, made both motions, and the trial court granted both.

    a. Why? If the trial judge granted defendant judgment as a matter of law under Rule 50(b) that would end the case. Why bother also ruling on a motion for a new trial? Rule 50(c) contains the answer, permitting a party making a renewed motion for judgment as a matter of law to make a conditional motion for a new trial, and requiring the court to rule on that conditional motion if she grants the Rule 50(b) motion. This conditional ruling comes into play only if "the judgment [notwithstanding the verdict] is later vacated or reversed." *Lind* illustrates the need for such a conditional ruling because the judgment as a matter of law was in fact reversed. Without Rule 50(c), the defendant would have had to return to the trial court and, perhaps some years after the trial, make its motion for a new trial, long after perhaps-critical details had faded from the trial judge's memory. Rule 50(c) allows the trial judge to rule on all post-trial motions with the case still fresh in mind and allows the appellate court to consider all of them at once—as it did in *Lind.* You can see the U.S. Supreme Court endorsing this reasoning toward the end of the opinion in *Unitherm Food Systems, Inc. v. Swift-Eckrich, Inc.* (supra page 637).

    b. Notice that while the grant of a judgment as a matter of law constitutes a final judgment from which an appeal may be taken, the grant of a new trial, standing alone, does not create a final judgment—there will be no final judgment until after completion of the new trial. Accordingly, a party cannot appeal the grant of a new trial until after the second trial has occurred! You will see this procedural posture in *Peterson*, infra page 650.

5. Suppose a jury returns a defense verdict. The judge, believing that the evidence strongly favored the plaintiff, orders a new trial. The second jury agrees with the first. Should the judge order still a third trial or simply conclude that he was wrong about the weight of the evidence? Because the new trial order is not appealable, the length of such a sequence is theoretically indefinite. Worry not: In practice, one of four things is likely to happen: The judge may finally get a jury that agrees with him, or the judge may decide that the juries were right and he was wrong. If neither of these occurs, the parties may well decide to settle rather than continue pouring money into repeated trials. Or, finally, defendant might eventually get an appellate court to grant a writ of mandamus (see infra page 689) to put him out of his misery.

2. Conditional New Trials

Up to now, we have dealt with situations in which grants of new trials involved retrying the entire case. Consider a judge who concludes that the jury reasonably could have reached a verdict for the plaintiff but that its damage calculations are unreasonably low or high. May the judge grant a new trial limited to the issue of damages? The answer is yes, though the problems involved in reaching that answer are considerable.

a. New Trial Limited to Damages

Consider the logical underpinnings of such a ruling. To be prepared to order a new trial limited to the issue of damages, the judge must be convinced that whatever influences led the jury astray on damages did not infect the judgment on liability as well. Take, for example, a verdict for the plaintiff combined with clearly insufficient damages. Can the judge be certain that the low award did not reflect considerable jury uncertainty that the plaintiff should recover at all—uncertainty that should have been reflected in a verdict for the defendant? The same doubt can exist in the case of clearly excessive damages; a jury passionately disposed toward the plaintiff regarding damages may have been so influenced on the issue of liability as well.

Yet courts do order such partial new trials. Pingatore v. Montgomery Ward & Co., 419 F.2d 1138 (6th Cir. 1969), cert. denied, 398 U.S. 928 (1970), serves as an example. A rat leapt on and bit plaintiff's knee while she was leaving a department store's premises. She developed complications leading to partial paralysis in an arm and leg. Testimony divided over whether the damage was attributable to the treatment for the bite (a series of rabies inoculations), to "conversion hysteria" or "psychosis," or to "malingering." After a trial in which the plaintiff's attorney ranted and swore at the defendant corporation, the jury awarded plaintiff $126,000 in damages and $25,000 to her husband. The court of appeals reversed the judgment on account of the plaintiff's attorney's misbehavior. But, without explaining more than that "there is substantial evidence to support the verdict of the jury on the question of liability," the court limited the new trial to damages. Why was liability so clear? Because it was obvious that the plaintiff should get *something* for being bitten by a rat?

b. *Remittitur and Additur*

Instead of ordering a new trial on damages, could the *Pingatore* court simply have reduced the amount of the damage award to one it thought reasonable? The answer is yes—under some circumstances. In such an action, known as *remittitur*, the judge orders a new trial unless the plaintiff agrees to accept reduced damages. Its damage-increasing analogue is *additur*. Both involve many of the problems inherent in the partial new trial as well as some special difficulties.

If the jury renders a verdict that is arguably excessive, the trial judge faces several questions. These questions apply, in reverse, to additur, the less common of the two devices. Essentially, the questions are: First, when should one grant such a reduction (or addition) in damages? And, second, how does one calculate the amount?

Consider the choice to which the grant of remittitur puts a plaintiff. Assume a verdict of $150,000 for plaintiff that the court orders remitted to $75,000. If plaintiff refuses the remittitur, the consequence is, of course, that the court will grant a new trial. The Supreme Court has held that a plaintiff must get a choice between a new trial and accepting reduced compensatory damages. Hetzel v. Prince William County, 523 U.S. 208 (1998). What about punitive damages? In several cases (see Chapter 5), the Supreme Court has held that due process requires judicial scrutiny and reduction of some punitive damage awards. A number of courts have found that this line of cases overcomes what would otherwise be a Seventh Amendment requirement that the court give plaintiff a choice between reduced punitive damages and a new trial—plaintiff simply has to accept the reduced punitives. E.g., Johansen v. Combustion Engineering, Inc., 170 F.3d 1320 (11th Cir. 1999).

Suppose the plaintiff accepts the remittitur of compensatory damages. May she condition her acceptance on a right to appeal? If not, may the plaintiff at least raise the matter if the defendant appeals the remitted verdict? The Supreme Court has blocked the attempt of lower courts to permit appeals from conditionally accepted verdicts. According to the Court, the plaintiff had a choice: Accept the remittitur or prepare for a new trial. Donovan v. Penn Shipping Co., 429 U.S. 648, 649 (1977).

Are remittitur and additur constitutional? Some years ago, the Supreme Court held that additur violates the Seventh Amendment but that remittitur does not. The theory was that remittitur simply involves modifying a decision actually made by a jury—lopping off the excess—while additur involves making an award that no jury has ever made. See Dimick v. Schiedt, 293 U.S. 474, 483 (1935). Critics have suggested that this is a distinction without a difference, but it is still the law in federal courts. Many states permit additur as well as remittitur.

G. THE LIMITS OF JUDICIAL POWER: THE REEXAMINATION CLAUSE AND THE JURY AS A BLACK BOX

What happens if the evidence admitted at trial provides some basis for finding for either side? Recall that the second half of the Seventh Amendment provides: "[N]o fact tried by a jury, shall be otherwise reexamined in any court of the United States, than according to the rules of the common law." What does that mean? At a minimum, as we have already seen, it prevents a judge from overturning a jury verdict merely because she, as a juror, would have voted differently than the actual jury did. How much further does it restrict judicial control over jury verdicts?

Suppose the jury is properly instructed in the law, proceeds to deliberate, and then returns a verdict. Suppose the losing party's attorney interviews all the jurors after the verdict. (Jurors have no obligation to speak with the lawyers about the case, but lawyers are interested and jurors are frequently willing.) From these interviews it appears that the jurors misunderstood the jury instructions. Suppose the jurors further say that they would have decided the case for the losing party if they had understood the instructions. Suppose the jurors go one step further, and each executes a sworn affidavit to that effect. Should the court grant judgment notwithstanding the verdict or grant a new trial to ensure a rational result under the applicable law?

Peterson v. Wilson
141 F.3d 573 (5th Cir. 1998)

WIENER, J. . . .

I. Facts and Proceedings

Peterson filed this suit in district court under 42 U.S.C. §§1983 and 1988, as well as the First, Fifth, and Fourteenth Amendments of the United States Constitution after he was fired as grant director at Texas Southern University (TSU). He claims that his property interest in his employment at TSU was damaged or destroyed when it was arbitrarily and capriciously terminated. . . . After five days of trial, conducted by the magistrate judge with the consent of the parties, the jury found for Peterson and awarded him $152,235 for lost pay and benefits and $35,000 for past and future mental anguish. Following the verdict, Wilson renewed his motion for j.m.l. and supplemented it with his bare-bones alternative motion for a new trial.

Some four months later, in January 1996, the district court granted the new trial, ostensibly in response to Wilson's motion, but in actuality on its own motion: The substantive language of the district court's order granting a new trial eschews any conclusion other than that the ruling was granted sua sponte, and that it was not granted for insufficiency of the evidence or because the jury verdict was against the great weight of the evidence, but rather for the following reason:

The court concludes, based on the jury's verdict and *comments the jurors made to the court after returning the verdict* [and outside the presence of the parties and their respective counsel], that the jury completely disregarded the Court's instructions. Instead, it appears that the jury considered improper factors in reaching its verdict. Accordingly, the Court deems it in the interest of justice to grant a new trial (emphasis added).

. . . The inference is inescapable that, to impeach the jury's verdict, the district court relied on information gleaned from the jurors themselves during the court's post-verdict, ex parte meeting with the jury. The court voided the verdict because, in the court's own words, the jury "completely disregarded the Court's instructions." Peterson timely filed a motion for reconsideration, which the district court did not grant. The case was re-tried in June 1996, and ended in a jury verdict in favor of Wilson, rejecting Peterson's claims. . . .

The jury, as the finder of facts and the maker of all credibility calls, reached its verdict in the first trial on the basis of the following record facts and inferences.

Peterson is well educated, well trained, and widely experienced in his field of concentration, which is grant administration for institutions of higher education. When Peterson joined TSU in 1983 he assumed responsibility for administering grants, principally Title III grants. In addition, he was in charge of student affairs and was responsible for determining the residency status of foreign students. Peterson also supervised finances of the university and was in charge of Institutional Research. As Title III Director, Peterson generally reported directly to the Vice President for Academic Affairs: first Clarkson, then Moore, and eventually, Wilson. The programs supported by Title III grants included faculty development, equipment purchases, and institutional research, providing millions of dollars annually for expenditures at TSU. . . .

Without reiterating every detail of the relevant testimony and documents, it suffices that the evidence heard and obviously credited by the jury painted a picture of Peterson as a highly principled, apolitical, objective grant administrator who repeatedly refused to "play ball" with high ranking TSU administrators when they attempted to obtain expensive equipment for unauthorized personal use or sought to have unauthorized job positions created and funded with grant money for their special "friends." The jury also heard and obviously credited testimony of both direct and implied threats by Wilson of adverse job actions, including firing, that Peterson was in jeopardy of incurring if, on reflection, he should fail or refuse to accede to requests that would require the unauthorized expenditure of grant funds.

The termination letter of January 3, 1991, from Wilson to Peterson purported to outline nine items constituting "cause" for the firing, each of which was set forth in a report prepared and submitted on request by one Joyce Deyon with whom, it turned out, Wilson never conferred after receiving the report. Wilson testified that he accepted the report and made his judgment based on it.

The jury heard testimony and saw documents which, if believed—as the jury apparently did—methodically refuted or explained away each of the nine purported causes for termination and revealed that Wilson did not even understand some of the items. The jury also heard evidence which, if credited, was sufficient to support a conclusion that the termination and its purported causes were pretext intended to cover Wilson's retaliation and desire to accomplish his actual or implied threats of getting rid of Peterson and replacing him with a grant director who would be more of a team player, i.e., would be more amenable to funding equipment purchases and job creations for "friends" of the higher-ups in the TSU administration with grant money.

That the jury unquestionably credited the testimony and documentation supporting Peterson's version of the facts and rejected Wilson's is confirmed by the "Yes" answer to Interrogatory No. I-A, "Do you find from a preponderance of the evidence that Dr. Bobby Wilson acted arbitrarily and capriciously in terminating Dr. Peterson?" In the interrogatory that followed, the jury awarded Peterson $152,235 in lost pay and benefits, and $35,000 for past and future mental anguish.

II. Analysis

. . . We review the district court's grant of a new trial for abuse of discretion. "It is a well-settled rule in this circuit that 'a verdict can be against the "great weight of the evidence," and thus justify a new trial, even if there is substantial evidence to support it.'" What courts cannot do—and what the district court here never purported to do—is to grant a new trial "simply because [the court] would have come to a different conclusion than the jury did." . . .

The district court's succinct but cryptic, three-sentence explanation for granting a new trial demonstrates beyond question that, following the verdict, the court impermissibly met with and interrogated the jurors outside the presence of the parties and their respective counsel, and then proceeded to act in direct reliance on the jurors' comments as though they constituted newly discovered evidence of a kind that the court could properly consider. It was not. The conclusion is inescapable that, in impeaching the jury's verdict in this case, the district court relied on information obtained from the jurors in the court's post-verdict, ex parte meeting with them and that, by definition, any information thus obtained had to come directly from their internal deliberations qua jurors.

1. Jury Impeachment

Rule 606(b) of the Federal Rules of Evidence (F.R.E.) tightly controls impeachment of jury verdicts. This rule states, in pertinent part:

> Upon an inquiry into the validity of a verdict . . . , a juror may not testify as to any matter or statement occurring during the course of the jury's deliberations or to the effect of anything upon that or any other juror's mind or emotions as influencing the juror to assent to or dissent from the verdict . . . or concerning the juror's mental processes in connection therewith, except that a juror may testify on the question whether extraneous prejudicial information was improperly brought to the jury's attention or whether any outside influence was improperly brought to the jury's attention or whether any outside influence was improperly brought to bear upon any juror. Nor may a juror's affidavit or evidence of any statement by the juror concerning a matter about which the juror would be precluded from testifying be received for these purposes. . . .

The landmark Supreme Court case on this issue is *Tanner v. United States*. After acknowledging that "[b]y the beginning of this century, if not earlier, the near-universal and firmly established common-law rule in the United States flatly prohibited the admission of juror testimony to impeach a jury verdict," the Court observed that "Federal Rule of Evidence 606(b) is grounded in the common-law rule against admission of jury testimony to impeach a verdict and the exception for juror testimony relating to extraneous influences." Following *Tanner*, and more closely on point, we held in *Robles v. Exxon Corp.* that receiving testimony from the jurors after they have returned their verdict, for the purpose of ascertaining that the jury misunderstood its instructions, is absolutely prohibited by F.R.E. 606(b). We underscored that holding by noting that "the legislative history of the rule unmistakably points to the conclusion that Congress made a conscious decision to disallow juror testimony as to the jurors' mental processes or fidelity to the court's instructions." What is pellucid here, from the court's own unequivocal and unambiguous words, is that the jurors' statements to the court related directly to matters that transpired in the jury room, that these matters comprehended the mental processes of the jurors in their deliberations on the case, and that the jurors' statements formed the foundation of the court's impeachment of the verdict grounded in the jury's lack of "fidelity to the court's instructions." We cannot conceive of an example more explicitly violative of *Robles*. . . .

[The Court of Appeals concluded that the district court did not find that the verdict was against the great weight of the evidence and that, even if it had, such a decision was contrary to the record.] We are thus left with no choice but to reverse the district court's grant of a new trial, vacate the court's judgment rendered on the basis of the jury verdict in the second trial, and reinstate the results of the first trial. We therefore remand this case to the district court for entry of judgment in favor of Peterson and against Wilson in the principal sum of $187,235 ($152,235 for lost pay and benefits and $35,000 for past and future mental anguish), and for the assessment of appropriate interest and costs, including reasonable attorneys' fees incurred by Peterson in both trials and on appeal.

WHAT'S NEW HERE?

- We ask judges to make findings of fact and law explaining how they arrived at a given result. Rule 52. The appellate court reversed the trial judge's new trial order precisely because it could trace his reasoning in making that order.
- In contrast, we do not require such findings from a jury. Indeed, we make it impossible to use evidence of jury deliberations to overturn a verdict that is otherwise reasonable. Instead, the appellate court reconstructs the path by which the jury *could have* reached its verdict.

Notes and Problems

1. *Peterson* serves both as a review of the preceding chapter and as an embodiment of an important principle about jury integrity. Begin with reviewing some fundamental propositions:

   a. Explain why plaintiff could not appeal after the first trial.

   b. Explain why the result would have been different had the appellate court found—as defendant urged it to—that the trial court had granted a new trial because the first verdict was "against the great weight of the evidence."

   c. Explain why the trial judge, after interviewing the jurors in the first trial and ascertaining that they had misunderstood the instructions, could not simply grant judgment as a matter of law for defendant.

2. The principle elaborated in *Peterson* has to do with the inviolability of jury deliberations, but also with the limits on the law's insistence on rationality.

   a. Why, having learned through these interviews that the jury misunderstood instructions, could the trial court not grant a new trial on that basis?

   b. Distinguish *Peterson* from *In re Beverly Hills Fire Litigation*, noted at page 624. In the latter case, a juror performed home experiments on aluminum electrical wiring (the dangerousness of which was a contested issue at trial) and reported his findings to the other jurors. The appellate court held it an abuse of discretion not to grant a new trial. Why is it erroneous to grant a new trial when a juror misunderstands instructions and erroneous not to grant a new trial when a juror performs such experiments? Explain the distinction.

3. Two bodies of law guard the integrity of jury verdicts (as the winner of a case might put it), or (as the loser would see it) the jury's ability to reach erroneous verdicts.

   a. The Reexamination Clause of the Seventh Amendment (and similar state provisions) provides substantive protections. A federal statute providing that whenever a judge disagreed with a verdict it could be overturned would be unconstitutional.

   b. Federal Rule of Evidence 606 (and similar state provisions) provides procedural protection—by blocking evidence that might otherwise be used to challenge verdicts. Note, though, that not all states have such a rule, some allowing juror testimony about deliberations.

4. What interests are served by prohibiting impeachment of a jury's verdict through post-verdict statements by the jurors regarding their deliberations?

   a. One can explain Federal Rule of Evidence 606 cynically: Too many jury verdicts would fall if we delved into jury deliberations deeply.

b. A different and more optimistic explanation is also possible. As you have already seen, if summary judgment and judgment as a matter of law are operating properly, only close cases—cases that could rationally be decided either way—will go to the jury. In such cases, any verdict should be sustainable. And, some would add, in such cases the soft variables that constitute the jury's sense of justice should come into play, even when those variables are hard to justify from the lofty plane of rationalism. By preventing too close an inquiry into a jury's decision processes, one allows these considerations some free play.

c. Finally, one can justify the Rule as a matter of court administration. Many people are reluctant to serve on a jury: It disrupts lives and schedules and involves them in making difficult decisions. If one added to these inconveniences the possibility that one could be questioned by a disappointed loser about jury deliberations, it might become very difficult to fill jury boxes.

5. Distinguish two issues that courts sometimes conflate: what constitutes jury conduct sufficiently improper to require a new trial; and when the court will hear evidence about jury conduct from a *juror*. Rule 606 governs the latter but has nothing to say about the former.

a. To sharpen the distinction, imagine a case in which evidence of jury conduct came from two sources—a bailiff who overheard deliberations while stationed outside the room and a juror herself. Rule 606 bars testimony from the latter but not from the former.

b. In fact, because juries deliberate in private, only in the very rare case will anyone other than the jurors know what happened in the jury room.

6. In contrast to information about jury deliberations, Rule 606 does allow a verdict to be impeached by evidence that there was some improper "outside influence" on the jury.

a. Bribery obviously meets that criterion. So do threats to jurors by outsiders. (As a review, explain why presenting evidence of a bribed jury does not constitute an unconstitutional reexamination of a jury verdict.)

b. What about evidence that a majority of jurors badgered a holdout juror until the holdout caved in and went along with the majority? Is there any basis for treating an outside threat to a juror differently from a threat by a fellow juror? A survey found the courts divided and could offer only the not very helpful observation that the decisions seemed fact-specific. Impeachment of Verdict by Juror's Evidence That He Was Coerced or Intimidated by Fellow Juror, 39 A.L.R.4th 800 (1996).

c. The U.S. Supreme Court recently faced a collision between Rule 606 and the apparent racial prejudice of a juror. In Peña-Rodriguez v. Colorado, 580 U.S. ___ (2017), the Court ruled that a juror's clear expression of racial stereotype as a basis for voting to convict required that a court allow a fellow juror to testify as to that bias in spite of Rule 606. The Court cited the Sixth

Amendment, which applies only to criminal cases; one imagines, however, that if the same circumstance arose in a civil case the Due Process Clause might require a similar result.

7. It may already have occurred to you that one might make jury verdicts less opaque by asking the jury to explain how it reached its verdict. There are in fact two ways to do just that—the special verdict and the general verdict with special interrogatories. See Rule 49.

    a. Which of these procedures was used in *Peterson*?
    b. In a special verdict the jury does not render a general verdict at all. Instead, it answers a series of questions about the evidence: "Was the defendant negligent? If so, did the defendant's negligence cause the plaintiff's injuries? If so, was the plaintiff also negligent? If so, did the plaintiff's negligence in some part contribute to his injuries?" When the jury has answered all the questions—or all those that are necessary—it delivers them as the verdict. In a general verdict with interrogatories, the jury renders a general verdict but also answers particular questions.
    c. The concept of the special verdict and general verdict with interrogatories is simple: One gives the jurors a road map of the relevant legal issues, helping them to focus on each question as (and if) it becomes relevant.
    d. The practice surrounding these procedures has been much less happy. Jurors can become confused by the questions. The nightmare outcome—one too often realized in the cases—is that juries give inconsistent answers. In one notorious case, the jury said (a) that the defendant was negligent but (b) that it was impossible for the defendant to have foreseen any danger from a particular condition on its property—that condition being the only way in which the jury could have found the defendant negligent! Gallick v. Baltimore & Ohio Railroad, 372 U.S. 108 (1963). As a consequence of these problems, judges, in whose discretion the decision to allow a special verdict lies, often avoid them.

* * *

Though trial by ordeal—drowning, burning, and the like—was abolished by the Lateran Council of 1215, lawyers tell us that even ordinary trials are ordeals of anxiety, weariness, and, for at least one side, disappointment. The one thing most civil trials are not is dramatic. Witnesses can change their stories and an occasional surprise will appear, but a well-prepared civil trial where both sides have made effective use of discovery will not look like a "Perry Mason" episode.

Real trials differ from those in drama in another respect. In drama, the trial is the end of the road: The winners rejoice; the losers slink away in shame or anger. In litigation, the trial is a rare event, but even when it occurs, it may not be the end. Perhaps because trials are so rare, parties who have been unable to resolve their differences beforehand may not do so just because a judge or jury has announced a winner. For some, an appeal lies ahead.

Assessment Questions

Q1. Jeffrey sues his former employer, Giant Software Co., for employment discrimination based on race. The trial judge can be recused from the case . . .

   A. If in practice she exclusively represented employers in such cases.

   B. If her adult daughter works for the company.

   C. For no reason at all if the case is filed in state court in a state that allows peremptory challenges of judges.

   D. If she has strongly criticized plaintiff's counsel for a "sloppy brief."

Q2. Same employment discrimination case proceeds in federal district court. Plaintiff presents evidence that supervisor disliked him, but no evidence that animus was racial—as required by law. Parties make various evidentiary objections, but no other motions.

   A. Judge cannot enter judgment as a matter of law.

   B. Judge should enter judgment as a matter of law because plaintiff has failed to prove racial motivation—an essential element of the case.

   C. Judge should let case go to jury, then enter judgment notwithstanding the verdict if jury returns a plaintiff's verdict.

Q3. Same employment discrimination case. Both parties present contested evidence on all elements of the claim. The judge charges the jury on all elements of substantive law, but fails to charge on burden of persuasion. Both parties make Rule 50 motions before the case goes to jury: denied. Jury returns a plaintiff's verdict.

   A. Judge can order a new trial.

   B. Judge can enter judgment as a matter of law for defendant.

   C. Judge must enter judgment on verdict because there was disputed evidence on both sides.

   D. Judge can order a new trial only if defendant so moves.

Q4. Same employment discrimination case. Both parties present contested evidence on all elements of the claim. As the judge hears testimony, she becomes convinced that the plaintiff has far more persuasive evidence than the defendant.

   A. If plaintiff makes the proper motion, the judge can grant judgment as a matter of law for plaintiff.

   B. Even if plaintiff makes the proper motion, the judge cannot grant judgment as a matter of law for plaintiff.

   C. If the jury returns a defense verdict, the judge could order a new trial.

Q5. Civil trial for wrongful death. Defendant wants to move for judgment as a matter of law. She can do so . . .

A. Only after plaintiff has presented his evidence and before defendant presents his defense.

B. Only after both sides have presented their evidence.

C. At either or both times.

Q6. Employment discrimination case. Jury, properly charged, returns a verdict for the defendant. Lawyers speak with jurors after the trial. Which of the following information would supply a basis for moving for a new trial?

A. Jurors misunderstood instruction on burden of persuasion—thinking plaintiff had to convince them beyond a reasonable doubt.

B. One juror spoke with plaintiff in restroom during trial—and reported to fellow jurors that "he could see why the guy lost his job—he is really rude."

C. One juror reported during deliberations that he had experienced some of the same on-the-job treatment as plaintiff, but that it was "just part of life, and not the basis for a lawsuit."

Analysis of Assessment Questions

Q1. C is the only correct response; it is correct because some states permit "peremptory" recusal of judges. A is wrong because 28 U.S.C. §455(b)(2) (and analogous state law provisions) requires recusal only when the lawyer has served as counsel "in the matter" in controversy—meaning this very case. B is (probably) wrong unless the daughter's employment gave the judge knowledge of disputed, material facts. D is wrong because except in the rare case in which the judge becomes so embroiled with the parties that she loses perspective, recusal is required only when biases preexist the litigation itself.

Q2. A is the only correct response. Rule 50(a) requires a motion by a party. B is wrong for the same reason: Defendant has not made a Rule 50 motion. C is wrong because for a federal court to grant a Rule 50(b) motion, a party must have made a pre-verdict Rule 50(a) motion.

Q3. A is the only correct response. A new trial is in order because there was a procedural mistake—the failure to charge on the burden of persuasion; Rule 59(d) permits a judge to make such an order either on her own motion or on a motion by a party. B is wrong because both parties have presented conflicting evidence on all the elements of the claim. C is wrong because Rule 59 permits a new trial order. D is wrong because Rule 59, unlike Rule 50, permits the judge to order a new trial on her own motion.

Q4. B and C are the correct responses. B is correct because the question specifies that both sides have presented conflicting evidence on all the elements of the claim, and judges are not permitted to resolve questions of weight of the evidence or credibility of witnesses in ruling on directed verdicts. C is correct because a judge can grant a new trial if the verdict is against "the great weight of the evidence."

Q5. C is the correct response. A is wrong because, although Rule 50 allows a motion at such time it does not limit a motion to that time. B is wrong for the same reason.

Q6. Only B is a correct response—this brings "outside" information, not subject to evidentiary objections or cross-examination, into the deliberations. A is wrong because one would have to learn this from a juror—who under Fed. R. Evid. 606(b) cannot testify about jury deliberations. C is wrong for two reasons: As with B it would be excluded under 606(b); moreover, this is just the sort of common life experience we expect jurors to bring to their deliberations.

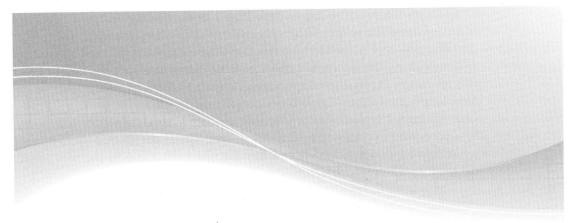

CHAPTER 10

Appeal

Appeals in U.S. litigation are a booming business. Over the past 50 years, federal civil appeals have increased at a rate one and one-half times faster than the increase in lawsuits filed. This increase has come even though one may appeal only from a judgment and, as we have seen, fewer than one-third of federal civil cases end in a judgment. Moreover, this increase has come even though fewer than 10 percent of federal cases are reversed on appeal.

Appeals are the setting for particularly fierce battles between two goals of civil procedure: fairness and justice. Fairness dictates that parties should win or lose depending on their compliance with procedural rules and the quality of their arguments. Justice dictates that the "right" party should prevail, regardless of such technicalities. Because the system embraces both goals, one must frequently yield to the other, and the conflict appears starkly in appellate litigation.

Unlike some other legal systems, the U.S. litigation system operates with a heavy presumption that most trial court decisions are correct. U.S. appellate courts do not supervise trial courts. They do not have jurisdiction to review many trial court decisions and orders that might have been erroneously decided. And when they can review trial court decisions, they may reverse only if an error appears in the record of the trial court proceedings, only if it is an error the appealing party pointed out below, and only if the error in question is harmful—that is, if it is likely to have changed the outcome of the case.

Both practical and doctrinal walls insulate trial court decisions. A word about some of the practical ones is in order. Strategic decisions can turn out to be wrong: You think you have a fine venue, so pass on an objection to it, only to find that the judge seems to hate you. Having made so many evidentiary objections that the jury is becoming irritated, you make a tactical decision to pass on one—only to find out too late that the jury thought that document fatal to your cause. Page limits for appellate briefs require you to focus on one or two erroneous rulings—perhaps passing on one that the appellate court would have found substantial. These types of strategic decisions can make or break a case but cannot be appealed if they do not involve an error by the trial court. In a particularly egregious case, a disappointed party might be able to bring a malpractice action against her attorney, but she cannot appeal the trial court's decision on these grounds.

This chapter focuses instead on errors by the trial court, and the doctrinal walls that shield U.S. trial court decisions. It will answer three questions about the availability of review: *Who*—which persons can seek review of a trial court decision? *When*—at what moment may one appeal a trial court decision? And *how*—with what depth will an appellate court scrutinize an appealable decision?

Understanding these doctrines has two virtues. It is obviously essential for any lawyer who wants to appeal a trial court decision. It is equally important for another reason: Understanding the barriers to appellate review helps one to comprehend that, as a practical matter, the trial court's decision will likely be the *only* decision on most procedural and substantive matters. This practical autonomy of the trial court puts great weight on the trial judge—to make the right decision—and on the lawyers—to give the trial judge all the information needed to make the right decision.

A. WHO CAN APPEAL?

In theory, one could imagine appellate courts functioning as the supervisors of trial courts, automatically reviewing cases to assure both that the results are correct and that the trial judges are following appropriate procedures. Or one might imagine a judicial inspector general who would have the power and duty to bring to the attention of appellate courts instances in which either the process or the result of a trial court decision seems questionable. Administrative systems follow such models, and some civil law systems approximate them.

The U.S. courts do not. Even a blatantly erroneous decision may be appealed only by a party to the lawsuit; a party, that is, who has not settled. A settlement agreement will invariably prevent further litigation of a claim. So, if a defendant grudgingly agrees to a settlement because he believes the trial court wrongly denied his motion to dismiss, he loses his right to appeal that decision by settling the case. Even more striking, a losing party who has not settled may nevertheless be unable to gain appellate reversal of a clearly erroneous trial court decision. Two doctrines create this result: those that allow appeals only by parties who have suffered an adverse outcome in the case, and those that deter appeals with various penalties.

WHAT'S NEW HERE?

- In most of your courses—including this one—discussion in appellate opinions will focus on what the court did with the case rather than how it got there. This chapter reverses that emphasis.
- By understanding the constraints on appellate review, you will better understand what an appellate case decides—and what it leaves open—because of those constraints.

1. A Losing Party: Adversity

A hallmark of modern procedure is the ease with which parties can join multiple claims in a single lawsuit. This poses a problem for appellate review: If plaintiff wins on one claim but loses on others, may plaintiff appeal the unsuccessful claims? Conversely, if a defendant prevails on one of several defenses, may he appeal his loss on the others? Contemporary appellate review is result-oriented, so the answer to this question requires one to look at the relief sought by the party prevailing on one but not all claims or defenses. If the relief sought under the losing theories was identical to that awarded in the winning claim, no appeal will lie, even if the appellate court thinks the trial court erred. If, on the other hand, the rejected claim or defense would have entitled the appealing party to more or different relief—to a different judgment—then the party can appeal. One can describe the principle as the requirement of an "adverse" judgment, a judgment granting relief less than what one requested.

Notes and Problems

1. Apply the "adversity" principle to the cases below:

   a. Tenant is injured when she slips in a pool of water formed in her apartment resulting from a leaky roof. She sues landlord for personal injuries, invoking two theories under which the landlord had a duty to repair the roof—a duty arising under the lease, and a duty arising under the municipal housing code. Both allow for compensatory damages, and the municipal housing code authorizes prevailing plaintiffs to recover reasonable attorneys' fees. Suppose the trial court rules that a duty is owed under the lease but that there is no duty under the municipal housing code. The court awards damages for personal injury. May plaintiff appeal, contending that a duty arose under the housing code as well?

   b. Plaintiff sues, alleging that automobile dealer sold her a used car when she paid for a new one. She alleges two theories: that the dealer (1) breached a contract and (2) committed fraud. Contract damages call for the plaintiff to recover the difference between the value of the car she received and a new one—$3,000 in this instance. Punitive damages are available for fraud, and are measured not by plaintiff's loss but by the magnitude of the wrong committed by defendant. The court dismisses the plaintiff's fraud claim, but awards plaintiff damages for breach of contract. May plaintiff appeal?

   c. Consider the plaintiffs in the two preceding problems. They have "won" parts of both cases. Yet they may still appeal, because each has suffered an adverse judgment—winning less than the law permitted.

2. The "losing party" principle described above comes under tension when a party has won the judgment but where a theory rejected by the trial court will have collateral consequences. That happened in the next case, which provides a stylized framework useful for understanding several issues of appellate review.

Aetna Casualty & Surety Co. v. Cunningham
224 F.2d 478 (5th Cir. 1955)

[In large building projects, the owner or developer frequently requires that its main contractor take out an insurance policy to cover the possibility that the contractor will be unable to complete the project. If this happens, the policy provides funds so others can complete the project. In *Cunningham*, the contractor failed to complete the project, and Aetna, the insurer, stepped in. After the dust settled (so to speak) and the project was completed with Aetna's money, Aetna tried to recover $32,000—the amount of its loss—from the contractor. At trial Aetna presented two claims: that the contractor/insured violated its contractual obligation to indemnify Aetna for these losses; and that, without regard to the policy terms, the contractor/insured had committed fraud in applying for the policy and that Aetna's loss was traceable to that fraud. (Aetna did not seek punitive damages on the fraud claim.) The district court found for Aetna on the contract claim but ruled that the contractor had not committed fraud. Both Aetna and the contractor appealed; an issue on appeal was which party could raise which contentions of error on appeal. Note that (1) failed construction contractors often file for bankruptcy protection from their creditors and (2) under some conditions liabilities incurred as a result of fraud are not discharged in bankruptcy.]

At the outset there is some doubt as to whether Aetna can appeal from the judgment which was in its favor in the amount prayed. If the relief granted was all to which Aetna was entitled, the mere fact that it was granted on one ground rather than on another would not make Aetna an aggrieved party on appeal. But amount is not the sole measure of the relief to which a party may be entitled. The judgment may have different qualities and legal consequences dependent on the claim on which it is based. At the beginning of the trial, Aetna's counsel, in response to an inquiry from the court, frankly stated his reason for insisting on the tort claim for fraud and deceit, "Because if we get a straight contract judgment it would be dischargeable in bankruptcy." . . .

It would be premature for us to pass upon the effect of bankruptcy on a judgment on either claim, or upon whether the finding that Cunningham's representations were not fraudulent would be *res judicata* as to the operation of a discharge in bankruptcy. It is enough at this time for us to hold that, if Aetna was denied judgment of the quality to which it laid claim [i.e., the fraud claim], it is a party aggrieved on appeal. . . .

The law is fashioned to work substantial justice in real transactions. We hold, therefore, that when, as a practical matter, the denial of any one claim results in the plaintiff not getting the relief to which it claims to be entitled, whether in the amount or in the quality of the judgment, it has a right to be heard on appeal. . . .

Notes and Problems

1. The insurer won on the contract theory but lost on the fraud theory. May the insurer appeal?

   a. Applying the principle of the adverse judgment, the answer would be no. The insurer was seeking only compensatory damages, so the amount of recovery on the contract claim was identical to that under the fraud claim. Winning on the fraud count would therefore not have increased the judgment.

   b. Nevertheless, the court allows the insurer to appeal the unsuccessful fraud claim. Why? Key to the answer is the fact that fraud liabilities may not be discharged in bankruptcy, but contract liabilities will be.

   c. How could the plaintiff have framed the prayer for damages so as to assure appealability if the plaintiff lost on the fraud count?

2. In cases with counterclaims and cross-appeals, a party can prevail and suffer an adverse judgment in the same case. Imagine that Retailer sues Customer for nonpayment of a bill. Customer counterclaims for breach of warranty on the product involved. The trial court enters judgment for Retailer on its claim but also awards damages to Customer on its warranty claim. Customer appeals. On appeal, Retailer will argue the correctness of the trial court's rulings on the claim of nonpayment. Retailer may also *cross-appeal*, arguing that the court erred in upholding the counterclaim for breach of warranty against it. As to that part of the case Retailer has suffered an adverse judgment.

3. Another aspect of the requirement that the judgment be adverse is the doctrine of mootness, which holds that one may not appeal from a judgment when circumstances have changed in such a way that relief is no longer possible. The doctrine affects not only appeals but also the justiciability of the suit because mootness undercuts the existence of an actual case or controversy required by Article III of the Constitution. There are, however, numerous exceptions to the doctrine.

a. One of the most important exceptions is the case in which the plaintiff's claim has been satisfied despite an adverse ruling by the lower court, but the question raised by the claim is likely to recur, and application of the mootness doctrine would effectively prevent the question from ever receiving appellate review. In *Sosna v. Iowa*, 419 U.S. 393 (1975), for example, the plaintiff challenged Iowa's one-year residency requirement for obtaining a divorce. The lower court upheld the requirement, but during the litigation the year passed and the plaintiff became able to obtain her divorce. The Supreme Court nevertheless refused to dismiss the case as moot, reasoning that other plaintiffs would find themselves in the same situation.

b. Mootness can also result from settlement. Suppose a case goes to judgment in the trial court and the loser appeals. While the appeal is pending, the parties settle. That settlement moots the appeal and, on being notified, the appellate court will dismiss the case without deciding the issues raised by the appeal.

2. Who Raised the Issue Below: Of Waivers and Sandbags

Consider the framework of *Aetna v. Cunningham* (supra page 664) once more. Suppose that at trial the insurer's evidence of fraud consisted not of misstatements by the contractor but of his failure to disclose the extent of his debts. Some jurisdictions recognize nondisclosure as a form of fraud. Suppose the contractor's lawyer does not object to the evidence. If the trial court enters judgment against the contractor on the fraud count, may the contractor on appeal argue that nondisclosure was not sufficient to show fraud?

Generally not: A party must present to the trial court the contentions on which it wants rulings. Failure to do so results in waiver. A century ago the party had not only to raise the contention below but then to make a formal "exception" to the trial court ruling in order to preserve the issue for appeal. Rule 46 did away with the need for exceptions; the "party need only state the action that it wants the court to take or objects to, along with the grounds. . . ." The abolition of the formal requirement did not, however, abolish the doctrine of waiver.

Courts try to walk a narrow path here. On one hand, they want to avoid hypertechnicality and preserve the ability to do justice. On the other hand, they want to prevent a litigant from "sandbagging" opposing counsel or the trial court—by vaguely expressing opposition to a trial court's decision, then proceeding through trial, hoping to win on the merits but thinking it has "banked" an appellate reversal in case of a loss. The doctrine of waiver on appeal prevents such a strategy. Think about how it should apply in the circumstances in the problems below.

WHAT'S NEW HERE?

- In the trial court parties make motions, objections, and arguments. The first objective of these contentions is obvious—to persuade the trial judge to rule in one's favor.
- We now see a second objective lurking in the background: "making a record" of contentions that, if the trial court rejects them, can be the basis for appeal.

Notes and Problems

---

1. How persistently must a party object?

    a. Suppose that in *Aetna v. Cunningham* the defendant filed a 12(b)(6) motion challenging the complaint on the grounds that it alleged only failure to disclose, not affirmative misrepresentation. Having lost the 12(b)(6) motion, does the defendant also have to object to the plaintiff's evidence at trial to preserve the point for appeal? Yes, at least to be on the safe side:

> To preserve the point the moving party can, and in general is required, upon the trial to renew and support his pleaded objections by objections to evidence, and by requesting rulings and instructions from the Court to the jury which he deems necessary to protect and preserve the point asserted by his motion to dismiss or to strike. In the present case the points asserted by motion were not again presented by any request for instructions, or by any effort to have the Court direct the jury to pass separately upon the question of whether the actions should be merely abated or determined upon its merits. Therefore, since the point was not properly urged and presented, there is no occasion to determine the validity of the . . . defense. Likewise, as to the objections now urged to the charge (which in some portions apparently gave effect to this defense) since no objection was presented to the trial Court, the appellant cannot here properly complain of the alleged erroneous instruction. We cannot accept the contention that the assertion of the objection by motion to strik[e] properly presented and preserved the point throughout the proceedings of the subsequent trial.
>
> Mims v. Central Mfrs. Mut. Ins. Co., 178 F.2d 56, 59 (5th Cir. 1949).

This approach has special salience in a world of pretrial conferences and final pretrial orders: A judge needs to know that a litigant has not abandoned an objection to the pleadings made during a pretrial conference held a year before the trial.

b. The advocate may also need to be tactful in preserving the record for appeal. Having once rejected a set of contentions, the judge may express irritation at having them renewed. For this reason one frequently hears lawyers prefacing renewed objections with such phrases as "With all respect, your honor, and to preserve the issue for appeal. . . ."

2. Not only must a litigant object, but, in the words of Rule 46, the litigant must state "the grounds for the request or objection."

    a. Thus, an appellant cannot raise an argument on appeal that was not made below. Justify such a rule on the basis of the "no sandbagging" principle.

    b. How about an appellee, the party seeking affirmance of the judgment? If appellee lost on a defense or claim below and wants to preserve the objection in case the decision is reversed, he must cross-appeal. But suppose appellee wants to use a new argument in *support* of the judgment? For an example, recall again the facts of *Aetna v. Cunningham*. Suppose that the insurer contended that the insured's fraud had consisted of failure to disclose certain information. Further suppose there was a question of whether the law of Connecticut (the insurer's base) or Texas (the insured's) applied. At trial, insurer argued that Connecticut law applied and that it recognized non-disclosure as fraud. Insurer wins a judgment on the fraud claim and the defendant appeals. On appeal, appellee insurer wants to argue in support of the judgment that Texas also recognizes nondisclosure as fraud so that an appellate ruling that Texas law applies would not require reversal of the judgment. Can it do so? Yes:

> It is true that a party who does not appeal from a final decree of the trial court cannot be heard in opposition thereto when the case is brought here by appeal of the adverse party. In other words, the appellee may not attack the decree with a view either to enlarging his own rights thereunder or of lessening the rights of his adversary, whether what he seeks is to correct an error or to supplement the decree with respect to a matter dealt with below. But it is likewise settled that the appellee may, without taking a cross-appeal, urge in support of a decree any matter appearing in the record, although his argument may involve an attack upon the reasoning of the lower court or an insistence upon a matter overlooked or ignored by it.

> United States v. American Ry. Express Co., 265 U.S. 425, 435 (1923).

Can you justify this apparent exception to the "no sandbagging" principle? Consider that U.S. appellate courts affirm judgments, not reasoning: If a judgment below is correct it will be affirmed, even if the trial court reached that judgment for the wrong reasons.

3. Another test of the courts' adherence to the requirement that an appellate issue be raised below comes when there has been a change in the law between the entry of judgment and the time of appeal.

    a. Arthur applies for Social Security disability benefits and his claim is denied. He sues, challenging the determination that he is not disabled. He loses in trial court and appeals. While his appeal is pending, a case comes down holding that the administrative procedure by which such claims are determined is unconstitutional. May Arthur on appeal raise this constitutional issue, which he did not raise below? A hard-nosed advocate of the adversary system would say no—that Arthur could have raised such a claim below and cannot now seek to ride on the coattails of a more enterprising or imaginative litigant.

    b. Courts are not always this hard-nosed, however, and will sometimes permit such late-maturing grounds for appeal. If the change in law is sufficiently fundamental, they may hear an argument on appeal that was not raised below. See Carson Products Co. v. Califano, 594 F.2d 453 (5th Cir. 1979) (drug company challenges FDA determination that product ingredient is not a trade secret; on appeal permitted to raise contention that FDA procedures denied due process). But no litigant should count on this grace.

4. The "plain error" rule is another exception to the general requirement that an issue must be raised in the trial court as a predicate to having it addressed on appeal.

    a. The doctrine is most commonly applied in criminal cases, where the courts are thought to have a special duty to assure that defendants are not convicted unfairly. In that context, the Supreme Court has explained that the error in the trial court must not have been intentionally waived, must have been obvious, and must have affected substantial rights of the appellant. United States v. Olano, 507 U.S. 725 (1990).

    b. Before you conclude that this doctrine will save you from a failure to object, be warned that courts in civil cases are inclined to apply the plain-error rule "sparingly and only in exceptional cases or under peculiar circumstances to prevent a clear miscarriage of justice." Smith v. Massachusetts Institute of Technology, 877 F.2d 1106 (1st Cir. 1989).

    c. The plain-error rule tests how appellate courts balance the principle of fairness to the parties against the correctness of the result. To say that the failure to object is excused (because an error is "plain") is to say that the appellate courts assume some degree of responsibility for assuring the correctness of the outcome, not just fairness to the parties.

    d. Having virtually assaulted the student with the proposition that appellate courts will not consider arguments not made at trial, we should note a glaring exception: *Erie Railroad v. Tompkins*, supra page 259. In that landmark decision, neither party had raised the choice of law question, nor had the Supreme Court granted certiorari to consider it. The Court thus made its landmark decision on a basis not argued or briefed by either party. One can reconcile *Erie* with the preceding discussion: A court may decide on a basis not raised by the parties, but a party must consistently raise an issue he wants to argue. Nevertheless, one might think that the concept of fair notice that applies to the parties might also apply to the courts.

5. Recall from Chapter 3 that there is one issue—the court's subject matter jurisdiction—that the federal courts are required to raise on their own and that may be raised for the first time on appeal by either party or the appellate court.

Louisville & Nashville Railroad v. Mottley, supra page 210, is an example of this principle.

3. Who Was Not Deterred from Appealing

Both legislatures and appellate courts take ambivalent stances toward appeal. We all want to correct erroneous outcomes, but appeals take time and money and we are just as eager to discourage ill-grounded appeals. In many respects the urge to discourage fruitless appeals mirrors the struggle over ungrounded complaints: Is there a way to discourage the unmeritorious appeals without burdening merito-rious ones?

The Supreme Court has never held that there is a constitutional right to appeal a civil case, so a jurisdiction could in theory either forbid civil appeals absolutely or, less dramatically, make all civil appeals a matter of discretion rather than of right. Most jurisdictions, though, grant the right to at least one appeal in civil cases; fur-ther appeal is often discretionary.

Although legislatures permit appeals, they sometimes try to discourage them. The U.S. Supreme Court has explored the limits of such discouragement in sev-eral cases in which state statutes put special burdens on some appeals. In Lindsey v. Normet, 405 U.S. 56 (1972), the Court invalidated a state statute that required tenants appealing an eviction judgment to post a bond twice as great as the rent expected to accrue during the appeal. By contrast, in Bankers Life & Casualty Co. v. Crenshaw, 486 U.S. 71 (1988), the Court rejected a challenge to a Mississippi statute that imposed a 15 percent penalty on an unsuccessful appeal of a judg-ment for money damages. The penalty was imposed regardless of the merits of the appeal so long as the appellate court affirmed the damages award without alter-ation. Bankers Life suffered a $1.6 million punitive damage judgment, which it unsuccessfully appealed, with the appellate court adding a $243,000 penalty to the judgment because the original award was affirmed. Bankers Life argued that the statute had denied it equal protection of the law "because it singles out appellants from money judgments, and because it penalizes all such appellants who are unsuc-cessful, regardless of the merits of their appeal." 486 U.S. at 81. The Supreme Court rejected this contention in language that revealed its general stance toward appeals:

> Under this Court's equal protection jurisprudence, Mississippi's statute is "presumed to be valid and will be sustained if the classification . . . is rationally related to a legiti-mate state interest." The state interests assertedly served by the Mississippi statute were detailed by the Mississippi Supreme Court in Walters v. Inexco Oil Co., 440 So. 2d 268 (1983). The penalty statute . . . "expresses the state's interest in discouraging frivolous appeals. It likewise expresses a bona fide interest in providing a measure of compensation for the successful appellee, compensation for his having endured the slings and arrows of successful appellate litigation." In a similar vein the statute protects the integrity of judgments by discouraging appellant-defendants from prolonging the litigation merely to "squeeze a favorable settlement out of an impecunious" appellee. Also, the penalty statute "tells the litigants that the trial itself is a momentous event, the

centerpiece of litigation, not just a first step weighing station en route to endless rehearings and reconsiderations." Finally, in part because it serves these other goals, the penalty statute furthers the State's interest in conserving judicial resources.

Id. at 81-82. The *Bankers Life* Court distinguished *Lindsey* on the grounds that the Oregon statute in *Lindsey* arbitrarily discriminated against tenants (because it applied only to them among all appellants) and was not needed to effectuate the state's purpose of preserving the property at issue.

Lindsey and *Bankers Life* involved "extra" appellate costs. What about ordinary costs that rest on all litigants? Can they ever be unconstitutional? In M.L.B. v. S.L.J., 519 U.S. 102 (1996), the indigent petitioner sought to appeal from a trial court order terminating her parental rights on the grounds she was unfit as a mother. To appeal the state court decision, M.L.B. would have had to pay filing and transcript fees of about $2,300. The state supreme court refused to waive the fees. The U.S. Supreme Court reversed, basing its decision on a combination of due process ("a family association so undeniably important is at stake") and equal protection; the 6-3 majority held "that Mississippi may not withhold from M.L.B. a record of sufficient completeness to permit proper consideration of her claims."

Lest you think that appellate costs burden only the poor, consider Pennzoil Co. v. Texaco, Inc., 481 U.S. 1 (1987). Many states require appellants to post *supersedeas* bonds to prevent judgment winners from executing the trial court judgment immediately while the case is on appeal. These bonds, which allow appeal to proceed, are often posted by insurers in return for a premium that is a fraction of the bond amount. Texaco suffered a $10 billion jury verdict in a takeover fight with a business rival. Although it was at the time the fifth-largest corporation in the United States, Texaco lacked the funds to post such a bond or to pay the premium for an insurer to do so—and was consequently unable to appeal the verdict. It argued to the U.S. Supreme Court that the size of the *supersedeas* bond violated the Equal Protection and Due Process Clauses; the Court rejected the case on jurisdictional grounds without reaching the constitutional claims. Read together, *Lindsey, Bankers Life, M.L.B.,* and *Texaco* suggest that some burden on appeals is constitutional, even when those burdens fall heavily on particular litigants.

Should legal systems seek generally to discourage appeals by requiring, for example, that the loser pay the winner's attorneys' fees? Federal Rule of Appellate Procedure (Fed. R. App. P.) 38 permits a court of appeals to award "just damages and single or double costs to the appellee" if the appellate court "determine[s] that an appeal is frivolous." One finds occasional invocation of this Rule, but it is used far less frequently than is Rule 11, its analogue at the district court level. A quite different sort of sanction for meritless appeals that is increasingly used by state and federal appellate courts is the summary affirmance or unpublished decision. Such orders, which go under different names in different systems, often involve denial of the right to oral argument, a decision on the briefs and record alone, and either a one-word order ("affirmed") or a short unpublished opinion. For an example, see *Haddle v. Garrison,* supra page 374. Some would argue that such "appeals" exist in name only.

B. WHEN A DECISION MAY BE REVIEWED: "FINALITY"

The single most significant doctrine of appellate procedure in the United States is one that purports to be only about the timing of appeal. Under 28 U.S.C. §1291, appeals can be brought only after there is a final decision by the district court (with some significant exceptions). Most, but not all, states follow a similar pattern. *Reise v. Board of Regents of the University of Wisconsin*, supra page 51, shows an appellate court refusing to review the trial court's discovery decision on this ground.

The final judgment rule affects not just the timing of appeal but its availability. To see why, consider how modern procedure has altered the center of gravity in civil litigation. Once upon a time, most trial court decisions were made at trial. In such a system, decisions were promptly reviewable because the trial resulted in a judgment from which an appeal would lie. Modern procedure changes that pattern: Discovery and the pretrial process now dominate the procedural landscape. Many rulings entered during the pretrial stage do not immediately produce final judgments; they are "interlocutory." An interlocutory decision cannot be appealed until there is a final judgment in the case, and many cases will never have final judgments because they settle. Under such circumstances, the final judgment rule does not just defer but eliminates appellate review.

So to note is not to condemn. The unavailability of appeal may be a good thing: Appeals take time, and most are unsuccessful. The unavailability of appeal may merely make justice faster and cheaper. Alternatively, one can see it as empowering trial judges to be petty dictators who can be secure in the knowledge that most of their rulings will never reach appellate scrutiny.

Any rule that has such effects will generate tensions and exceptions. This section explores the contours of the basic rule and some exceptions generated by the pressure to escape it.

WHAT'S NEW HERE?

- Given the pattern of modern litigation, a timing rule (wait to appeal until a final judgment) becomes a rule that eliminates appeal entirely for many trial court decisions in many cases—because settlement means there will never *be* a final judgment.

1. The Final Judgment Rule

A final decision "is one which ends the litigation on the merits and leaves nothing for the court to do but execute the judgment." Catlin v. United States, 324 U.S. 229, 233 (1945). That's the easy part; the hard part is determining which decisions are "final." Although at first glance the problem may seem to center on premature attempts at appeal, which entail unnecessary cost and delay, the more serious problem is late appeals: There are cases in which litigants waited for a document labeled as a "final judgment" only to learn that earlier orders disposing of their claims were deemed to be a final judgment and that the time for appeal had run in the meantime.

a. Appellate Jurisdiction and the Final Judgment Rule

Section 1291, which contains the final judgment rule as it applies to federal courts, has two functions: It defines the moment at which an appeal is proper; and it grants jurisdiction for the appellate courts to hear that appeal. The next case demonstrates the consequences that a wrong guess about the first function can have on the second. A bit of context may explain why this decision embarrassed the Court at least slightly. In the mid-1970s, the law regarding discrimination involving pregnancy was in flux. Some cases had ruled that it was a form of gender discrimination banned by civil rights legislation. Other cases had said that, although only women could become pregnant, discrimination on account of pregnancy was not gender discrimination. The Supreme Court had granted certiorari on several related cases to resolve the dispute—only to discover that it could not decide one of the cases on the merits.

Liberty Mutual Insurance Co. v. Wetzel
424 U.S. 737 (1976)

REHNQUIST, J., delivered the opinion of the Court.

Respondents filed a complaint in the United States District Court for the Western District of Pennsylvania in which they asserted that petitioner's employee insurance benefits and maternity leave regulations discriminated against women in violation of Title VII of the Civil Rights Act of 1964, as amended by the Equal Employment Opportunity Act of 1972. The District Court ruled in favor of respondents on the issue of petitioner's liability under that Act, and petitioner appealed to the Court of Appeals for the Third Circuit. That court held that it had jurisdiction of petitioner's appeal under 28 U.S.C. §1291, and proceeded to affirm on the merits the judgment of the District Court. We granted certiorari and heard argument on the merits. Though neither party has questioned the jurisdiction of the Court of Appeals to entertain the appeal, we are obligated to do so on our own motion if a question thereto exists. Because we conclude that the District Court's order was not appealable to the Court of Appeals, we vacate the judgment of the Court of Appeals with instructions to dismiss petitioner's appeal from the order of the District Court.

Respondents' complaint, after alleging jurisdiction and facts deemed pertinent to their claim, prayed for a judgment against petitioner embodying the following relief:

> (a) requiring that defendant establish non-discriminatory hiring, payment, opportunity, and promotional plans and programs;
> (b) enjoining the continuance by defendant of the illegal acts and practices alleged herein;
> (c) requiring that defendant pay over to plaintiffs and to the members of the class the damages sustained by plaintiffs and the members of the class by reason of defendant's

illegal acts and practices, including adjusted back pay, with interest, and an additional equal amount as liquidated damages, and exemplary damages;

(d) requiring that defendant pay to plaintiffs and to the members of the class the costs of this suit and a reasonable attorney's fee, with interest; and

(e) such other and further relief as the Court deems appropriate.

After extensive discovery, respondents moved for partial summary judgment only as to the issue of liability. Fed. Rule Civ. Proc. 56[(a)]. The District Court on January 9, 1974, finding no issues of material fact in dispute, entered an order to the effect that petitioner's pregnancy-related policies violated Title VII of the Civil Rights Act of 1964. It also ruled that Liberty Mutual's hiring and promotion policies violated Title VII. Petitioner thereafter filed a motion for reconsideration which was denied by the District Court. Its order of February 20, 1974, denying the motion for reconsideration, contains the following concluding language:

> In its Order the court stated it would enjoin the continuance of practices which the court found to be in violation of Title VII. The Plaintiffs were invited to submit the form of the injunction order and the Defendant has filed Notice of Appeal and asked for stay of any injunctive order. Under these circumstances the court will withhold the issuance of the injunctive order and amend the Order previously issued under the provisions of Fed. R. Civ. P. 54(b), as follows:
>
>> And now this 20th day of February, 1974, it is directed that final judgment be entered in favor of Plaintiffs that Defendant's policy of requiring female employees to return to work within three months of delivery of a child or be terminated is in violation of the provisions of Title VII of the Civil Rights Act of 1964; that Defendant's policy of denying disability income protection plan benefits to female employees for disabilities related to pregnancies or childbirth is in violation of Title VII of the Civil Rights Act of 1964 and that it is expressly directed that Judgment be entered for the Plaintiffs upon these claims of Plaintiffs' Complaint; there being no just reason for delay.

It is obvious from the District Court's order that respondents, although having received a favorable ruling on the issue of petitioner's liability to them, received none of the relief which they expressly prayed for in the portion of their complaint set forth above. They requested an injunction, but did not get one; they requested damages, but were not awarded any; they requested attorneys' fees, but received none.

Counsel for respondents when questioned during oral argument in this Court suggested that at least the District Court's order of February 20 amounted to a declaratory judgment on the issue of liability pursuant to the provisions of 28 U.S.C. §2201. Had respondents sought only a declaratory judgment, and no other form of relief, we would of course have a different case. But even if we accept respondents' contention that the District Court's order was a declaratory judgment on the issue of liability, it nonetheless left unresolved respondents' requests for an injunction, for compensatory and exemplary damages, and for attorneys' fees. It finally disposed of none of respondents' prayers for relief.

The District Court and the Court of Appeals apparently took the view that because the District Court made the recital required by Fed. Rule Civ. Proc. 54(b) that final judgment be entered on the issue of liability, and that there was no just reason for delay, the orders thereby became appealable as a final decision pursuant to 28 U.S.C. §1291. We cannot agree with this application of the Rule and statute in question.

Rule 54(b)[2] "does not apply to a single claim action. . . . It is limited expressly to multiple claims actions in which 'one or more but less than all' of the multiple claims have been finally decided and are found otherwise to be ready for appeal." *Sears, Roebuck & Co. v. Mackey.*[3] Here, however, respondents set forth but a single claim: that petitioner's employee insurance benefits and maternity leave regulations discriminated against its women employees in violation of Title VII of the Civil Rights Act of 1964. They prayed for several different types of relief in the event that they sustained the allegations of their complaint, see Fed. Rule Civ. Proc. 8(a)(3), but their complaint advanced a single legal theory which was applied to only one set of facts.[4] Thus, despite the fact that the District Court undoubtedly made the findings required under the Rule had it been applicable, those findings do not in a case such as this make the order appealable pursuant to 28 U.S.C. §1291.

We turn to consider whether the District Court's order might have been appealed by petitioner to the Court of Appeals under any other theory. The order, viewed apart from its discussion of Rule 54(b), constitutes a grant of partial summary judgment limited to the issue of petitioner's liability. Such judgments are by their term interlocutory, and where assessment of damages or awarding of other relief remains to be resolved have never been considered to be "final" within the meaning of 28 U.S.C. §1292. Thus the only possible authorization for an appeal from the District Court's order would be pursuant to the provisions of 28 U.S.C. §1292.

If the District Court had granted injunctive relief but had not ruled on respondents' other requests for relief, this interlocutory order would have been appealable under §1292(a)(1).[5] As noted above, the court did not issue an injunction. It might be

---

2. [The current text of Rule 54 reads:

> **Judgment on Multiple Claims or Involving Multiple Parties.** When an action presents more than one claim for relief—whether as a claim, counterclaim, crossclaim, or third-party claim—or when multiple parties are involved, the court may direct entry of a final judgment as to one or more, but fewer than all, claims or parties only if the court expressly determines that there is no just reason for delay. Otherwise, any order or other decision, however designated, that adjudicates fewer than all the claims or the rights and liabilities of fewer than all the parties does not end the action as to any of the claims or parties and may be revised at any time before the entry of a judgment adjudicating all the claims and all the parties' rights and liabilities.]

3. Following Mackey, the Rule was amended to insure that orders finally disposing of some but not all of the parties could be appealed pursuant to its provisions. That provision is not implicated in this case, however, to which Mackey's exposition of the Rule remains fully accurate.

4. We need not here attempt any definitive resolution of the meaning of what constitutes a claim for relief within the meaning of the Rules. It is sufficient to recognize that a complaint asserting only one legal right, even if seeking multiple remedies for the alleged violation of that right, states a single claim for relief.

5. [Except as provided in subsections (c) and (d) of this section,] the courts of appeals shall have jurisdiction of appeals from:

> (1) Interlocutory orders of the district courts of the United States, the United States District Court for the District of the Canal Zone, the District Court of Guam, and the District Court of the Virgin Islands, or of the judges thereof, granting, continuing, modifying, refusing or dissolving injunctions, or refusing to dissolve or modify injunctions, except where a direct review may be had in the Supreme Court.

argued that the order of the District Court, insofar as it failed to include the injunctive relief requested by respondents, is an interlocutory order refusing an injunction within the meaning of §1292(a)(1). But even if this would have allowed respondents to then obtain review in the Court of Appeals, there was no denial of any injunction sought by Petitioner and it could not avail itself of that grant of jurisdiction.

Nor was this order appealable pursuant to 28 U.S.C. §1292(b).[6] Although the District Court's findings made with a view to satisfying Rule 54(b) might be viewed as substantial compliance with the certification requirement of that section, there is no showing in this record that petitioner made application to the Court of Appeals within the 10 days therein specified. And that court's holding that its jurisdiction was pursuant to §1291 makes it clear that it thought itself obliged to consider on the merits petitioner's appeal. There can be no assurance that had the other requirements of §1292(b) been complied with, the Court of Appeals would have exercised its discretion to entertain the interlocutory appeal.

Were we to sustain the procedure followed here, we would condone a practice whereby a district court in virtually any case before it might render an interlocutory decision on the question of liability of the defendant, and the defendant would thereupon be permitted to appeal to the court of appeals without satisfying any of the requirements that Congress carefully set forth. We believe that Congress, in enacting present §§1291 and 1292 of Title 28, has been well aware of the dangers of an overly rigid insistence upon a "final decision" for appeal in every case, and has in those sections made ample provision for appeal of orders which are not "final" so as to alleviate any possible hardship. We would twist the fabric of the statute more than it will bear if we were to agree that the District Court's order of February 20, 1974, was appealable to the Court of Appeals.

The judgment of the Court of Appeals is therefore vacated, and the case is remanded with instructions to dismiss the petitioner's appeal. It is so ordered.

BLACKMUN, J., took no part in the consideration or decision of this case.

WHAT'S NEW HERE?

● For the federal courts the final judgment rule is jurisdictional: If there is no final judgment (and the case doesn't fall into any of the exceptions discussed in the next section), the Court of Appeals has no *jurisdiction* to hear the case.

---

6. "When a district judge, in making in a civil action an order not otherwise appealable under this section, shall be of the opinion that such order involves a controlling question of law as to which there is substantial ground for difference of opinion and that an immediate appeal from the order may materially advance the ultimate termination of the litigation, he shall so state in writing in such order. The Court of Appeals may thereupon, in its discretion, permit an appeal to be taken from such order, if application is made to it within ten days after the entry of the order: Provided, however, That application for an appeal hereunder shall not stay proceedings in the district court unless the district judge or the Court of Appeals or a judge thereof shall so order."

- And, if the Court of Appeals has no jurisdiction, then the U.S. Supreme Court also lacks jurisdiction to consider the case.
- You have, in fact, met a version of this issue before: In *Louisville & Nashville Railroad v. Mottley* (supra page 210) we saw a case in which the jurisdictional problem was deeper—the trial court lacked jurisdiction, therefore the court of appeals lacked jurisdiction, and therefore the Supreme Court lacked jurisdiction—but the result was the same: dismissal of the case without reaching the merits.

Notes and Problems

1. For federal courts, the final judgment rule is jurisdictional; if there has not been a final judgment, the appellate court does not have jurisdiction to hear the case. This has been so since the Judiciary Act of 1789. Note, however, that the final judgment rule does not always apply—as you will learn when you encounter the "practical finality" doctrine, infra page 682.

2. Moreover, some states allow interlocutory appeals in a wide range of situations. New York, for example, has formally rejected the final judgment rule. Its procedural code makes appealable by right "any final or interlocutory judgment" and further specifies a series of pretrial orders from which a losing party may take immediate appeal, including such broad categories as any order that "involves some part of the merits or . . . affects a substantial right." N.Y. Civ. Prac. L. & R. 5701. Other states may, less formally, have created substantial loopholes by manipulating the availability of the extraordinary writs of mandamus and prohibition (see infra page 689).

3. A salient characteristic of modern procedure is its allowance of multiple claims and parties. How has the final judgment rule adapted to this reality?

   a. One option would have been to allow no appeal until after all claims of all parties had been resolved. As noted in *Wetzel*, Rule 54(b) rejects this solution: "[T]he court may direct entry of a final judgment as to one or more, but fewer than all, claims or parties only if the court expressly determines that there is no just reason for delay." If such a judgment is entered, it becomes appealable.

   b. Rule 54(b) requires that the "court expressly determine[s] that there is no just reason for delay" in making the decision immediately appealable. Suppose a case involving several plaintiffs against a single defendant. The court grants summary judgment against one of the plaintiffs. Or imagine a case involving one plaintiff against several defendants in which the court grants summary judgment in favor of one defendant. If the court so certifies under Rule 54(b), the loser can immediately appeal. What should guide the judge's discretion in deciding whether to issue a Rule 54(b) certification in such a case? There are efficiency considerations: If the potential appeal contains an issue that persists in the remaining claims, an appellate decision may clarify it before trial. Or a judge might decide to allow an interlocutory appeal on precisely the opposite grounds—that the issues involved as to the loser are entirely different from those for the remaining case—such that a decision won't complicate the case for the remaining parties.

c. Finally, suppose a more ordinary case, in which a plaintiff has several claims against a defendant—perhaps a claim of copyright infringement and several state law contract claims. The defendant wins partial summary judgment on the copyright claim, which the plaintiff would like to appeal. But the judge does not certify that claim under Rule 54(b). Can the plaintiff voluntarily dismiss the remaining claims and thus create an appealable final judgment? Held: Yes, absent evidence of intent to manipulate appellate jurisdiction. *James v. Price Stern Sloan, Inc.*, 283 F.3d 1064 (9th Cir. 2002). Consider how a court might assess whether there was an intent to manipulate appellate jurisdiction.

4. Cases in which the trial judge is particularly likely to be wrong also pose an exception to the final judgment rule. Under 28 U.S.C. §1292(b), discussed in *Wetzel*, in *Mosley*, infra page 788, and at further length later in this section, the trial judge may certify (among other things) that her order involves "a controlling question of law as to which there is substantial ground for difference of opinion" and "that an immediate appeal from the order may materially advance the ultimate termination of the litigation." If the Court of Appeals agrees, it may hear an appeal from a non-final order.

Implications

WHY THE FINAL JUDGMENT RULE?

The basic argument for the final judgment rule involves a cost-benefit calculation. The costs of allowing interlocutory appeals are the costs of an unnecessary extra appeal if the trial judge turns out to have been correct. The costs of not allowing interlocutory appeals are those of an unnecessary or an unnecessarily long trial if the trial judge turns out to have been wrong.

Advocates of the final judgment rule would argue that the costs of interlocutory appeal are too high. If we assume that the costs of an unnecessary extra appeal are approximately the same as the costs of an unnecessary or unnecessarily long trial, the overall costs are proportional to the number of times the trial judge is right versus the number of times he is wrong. If trial judges are right more often than they are wrong (measured by eventual reversal when appeal finally occurs), then the general policy should disfavor interlocutory appeals. In fact, trial judges are reversed far less often than they are affirmed (the federal courts report a reversal rate of between 10-20 percent), and many decisions are not even appealed. From this perspective, the general policy seems wise.

Those opposed to the final judgment rule might argue that some of these premises are wrong. First, trials, which require elaborate pretrial preparation, witnesses, and sometimes juries, will generally be more expensive than appeals. Second, in some undetermined number of cases, parties will abandon meritorious positions (that is, settle the case) because they cannot afford to wait for vindication on appeal. To point to the absence of appeal in such cases as evidence of a satisfactory trial is to ignore the realities of litigation.

Beyond that, one can make a historical argument. Whatever one thinks of the original merits of the final judgment rule, its effect has changed dramatically with the advent of modern procedure. Before the Federal Rules (and equivalent state systems' rules of procedure) came into effect, there were essentially two stages in litigation, pleading and trial. If a case ended at the pleading stage, appeal was immediately available. If it didn't, trial would follow shortly, after which appeal was again available to the loser. Modern procedure, with its emphasis on discovery and a multistage pretrial process, adopts many of the main features of equity practice. Unlike the common law, equity permitted appeal from all interlocutory rulings. By adopting equity procedure but retaining the common law rule for appealability, modern process has delegated substantial amounts of unreviewable power to the trial court. That might be a good idea, but it has to be defended in light of the current structure of litigation.

b. Defining the Moment of Judgment

Even when one is alert to the dire jurisdictional consequences of failure to heed the final judgment rule, it is not always easy to locate the precise point at which a judgment becomes final—or even, for that matter, to identify the judicial act that constitutes a judgment. One difficulty is that the judge's belief that she is entering a judgment can be second-guessed by the appellate court. Recall that in *Wetzel* both parties understandably thought that the judge's announcement that "final judgment be entered" meant what it said, but the Supreme Court ruled otherwise.

Consider the matter from the perspective of a party wishing to appeal. The only step required to bring an appeal from a ruling of the district court is the timely filing of a notice of appeal with the clerk of the district court. Fed. R. App. P. 3(a)(1). That notice must be filed within the time allowed by Fed. R. App. P. 4(a)(1)(A)—30 days for the typical appeal; 60 days for an appeal involving the United States. The issue of timing is critical because, as you have seen, the courts of appeals have repeatedly held that the time limits are jurisdictional—that is, that the court of appeals has no jurisdiction to hear the appeal if the notice of appeal is filed too late. Two provisions of 28 U.S.C. §2107 and the appellate rules slightly alleviate the problem of late filings. Section 2107 and Fed. R. App. P. 4(a)(6) empower the district court to extend this time for a party who did not receive notice of the entry of the judgment in question if no prejudice to other parties results. Section 2107 and Fed. R. App. P. 4(a)(5) also allow the district court to extend the time for filing the notice of appeal up to 30 days on a showing of "excusable neglect or good cause."

An equally serious problem confronts litigants who file their appeals *too early*. As we have seen, under 28 U.S.C. §1291, appeals lie "from all final decisions of the district courts." By negative implication appeals do not lie from decisions of the district courts that are not final. In the distinction lies what the comments to Fed. R. App. P. 4 term "a trap for an unsuspecting litigant." Before the Rule was amended, the trap was sprung if the appellant filed a notice of appeal after the judgment but while a post-trial motion for judgment as a matter of law or new trial was pending. Until these motions are decided, the final outcome—and judgment—in the case has not occurred. A number of unfortunate would-be appellants discovered this point in sorrow-producing ways. The amended rule, Fed. R. App. P. 4(a)(4)(B), alleviates the difficulty by providing that when a party seeks to appeal from an order that would be final but for the interposition of one of these common post-trial motions, the appeal is held in abeyance until the disposition of these motions, at which point it becomes effective, thus preserving the jurisdiction of the court of appeals.

Even with these provisions, timing remains critical, and rulemakers have therefore tried to make the moment of judgment extremely clear. Rule 58 requires that "[e]very judgment and amended judgment must be set out in a separate document. . . ." In United States v. Indrelunas, 411 U.S. 216 (1973), the Court said that the separate-document requirement must be "mechanically applied." The problem is that the separate document rule applies not to litigants but to court clerks and judges. These officials don't always do what the Rules require, and when they fail, the litigants, not the officials, suffer the consequences. As the Rules Advisory Committee noted in 2002, "This simple separate document requirement has been ignored in many cases . . . [with the result that] there have been many and horridly confused problems under Appellate Rule 4(a)." The current version of Rule 58 tries to set guidelines for some of the worst problems.

Notes and Problems

1. Suppose the judge announces what she and the parties intend as a final judgment; the clerk duly enters that judgment on the docket (as required by Rule 79(a)); but the "separate document" required by Fed. R. Civ. P. 58 never appears. The parties appeal.

   a. What result?
   b. Read Fed. R. Civ. P. 58(c)(2); does this solve the appellant's problem at least as to timing?

2. FirsTier Mortgage Co. v. Investors Mortgage Insurance Co., 498 U.S. 269, 272 (1991), deals with the opposite problem—the premature appeal. In *FirsTier* the trial judge announced that he would grant summary judgment on all counts

for the defendant and asked the parties to submit proposed findings of fact. Before the trial judge had issued his findings, the plaintiff appealed—"close to a month before the entry of judgment."

a. The Court held that Fed. R. App. P. 4(a)(2) ("A notice of appeal filed after the court announces a decision or order but before the entry of the judgment or order is treated as filed on the date of and after the entry") applied, even though the judge had announced only his intent to enter summary judgment, not the summary judgment itself, much less the separate document embodying the judgment.

b. The *FirsTier* opinion evinces a certain amount of nervousness about the implications of its holding:

> This is not to say that [Fed.] Rule [App. P.] 4(a)(2) permits a notice of appeal from a clearly interlocutory decision—such as a discovery ruling or a sanction order under Rule 11 of the Federal Rules of Civil Procedure—to serve as a notice of appeal from the final judgment. A belief that such a decision is a final judgment would *not* be reasonable.

Id. (Emphasis added.)

c. It appears that the rule now is that a premature notice of appeal is saved by Fed. R. App. P. 4(a)(2) if the appellant reasonably believed that what the judge had issued was a final order. Is that a workable standard?

3. Many statutes and a number of contracts now have fee-shifting provisions attached to them (see supra pages 349-57). Rule 54(d)(2) establishes a procedure for claiming and proving such fees. Suppose a judgment on the merits of the case has been entered, but there is a pending motion for attorney's fees; can the losing party appeal the case? Or does the pendency of the fees motion mean that the judgment is not yet final? (Note that, in almost all cases, the answer matters because most fee disputes will take longer to resolve than the 30 days in which Fed. R. App. P. 4(a) requires that a notice of appeal must be filed.) In a pair of cases the U.S. Supreme Court has answered that question: "Whether the claim for attorney's fees is based on a statute, a contract, or both, the pendency of a ruling on an award for fees and costs does not prevent, as a general rule, the merits judgment from becoming final for purposes of appeal." Ray Haluch Gravel Co. v. Central Pension Fund, 134 S. Ct. 773 (2014). The consequence in the cited case was that the appellant, who had waited to appeal until the ruling on fees was entered, was far too late, and the appellate court therefore lacked jurisdiction to hear the appeal.

2. Exceptions to the Final Judgment Rule

The adoption of the Federal Rules—and state codes that tracked the Rules' innovations—greatly increased the importance of the stage between pleading and trial, in which substantial numbers of important but non-final rulings would occur. That circumstance placed substantial pressure on legislatures and courts to carve out appropriate exceptions to the final judgment rule. The efforts to define exceptions without abandoning the rule have not been easy. We survey the major exceptions below, starting with the one that has caused the greatest difficulty.

a. Practical Finality

Lauro Lines s.r.l. v. Chasser
490 U.S. 495 (1989)

BRENNAN, J., delivered the opinion of the Court.

We granted certiorari to consider whether an interlocutory order of a United States District Court denying a defendant's motion to dismiss a damages action on the basis of a contractual forum-selection clause is immediately appealable under 28 U.S.C. §1291 as a collateral final order. We hold that it is not.

I

The individual respondents were, or represent the estates of persons who were, passengers aboard the cruise ship Achille Lauro when it was hijacked by terrorists in the Mediterranean in October 1985. Petitioner Lauro Lines s.r.l., an Italian company, owns the Achille Lauro. Respondents filed suits against Lauro Lines in the District Court for the Southern District of New York to recover damages for injuries sustained as a result of the hijacking, and for the wrongful death of passenger Leon Klinghoffer. Lauro Lines moved before trial to dismiss the actions, citing the forum-selection clause printed on each passenger ticket. This clause purported to obligate the passenger to institute any suit arising in connection with the contract in Naples, Italy, and to renounce the right to sue elsewhere.

The District Court denied petitioner's motions to dismiss, holding that the ticket as a whole did not give reasonable notice to passengers that they were waiving the opportunity to sue in a domestic forum. Without moving for certification for immediate appeal pursuant to 28 U.S.C. §1292(b), Lauro Lines sought to appeal the District Court's orders. The Court of Appeals for the Second Circuit dismissed petitioner's appeal on the ground that the District Court's orders denying petitioner's motions to dismiss were interlocutory and not appealable under §1291. The court held that the orders did not fall within the exception to the rule of nonappealability carved out for collateral final orders in Cohen v. Beneficial Industrial Loan Corp., 337 U.S. 541 (1949). We granted certiorari to resolve a disagreement among the Courts of Appeals. We now affirm.

II

Title 28 U.S.C. §1291 provides for appeal to the courts of appeals only from "final decisions of the district courts of the United States." For purposes of §1291, a final judgment is generally regarded as "a decision by the District Court that 'ends the litigation on the merits and leaves nothing for the court to do but execute the judgment.'" Van Cauwenberghe v. Biard, 486 U.S. 517, 521 (1988), quoting Catlin v. United States, 324 U.S. 229, 233 (1945). An order denying a motion to dismiss a civil action on the ground that a contractual forum-selection clause requires that such suit be brought in another jurisdiction is not a decision on the merits that ends the litigation. On the contrary, such an order "ensures that litigation will continue in the District Court."

Gulfstream Aerospace Corp. v. Mayacamas Corp., 485 U.S. 271, 275 (1988). Section 1291 thus permits an appeal only if an order denying a motion to dismiss based upon a forum-selection clause falls within the "narrow exception to the normal application of the final judgment rule [that] has come to be known as the collateral order doctrine." Midland Asphalt Corp. v. United States, 489 U.S. 794, 798 (1989). That exception is for a "small class" of prejudgment orders that "finally determine claims of right separable from, and collateral to, rights asserted in the action, [and that are] too important to be denied review and too independent of the cause itself to require that appellate consideration be deferred until the whole case is adjudicated." *Cohen*, supra, at 546. We have held that to fall within the *Cohen* exception, an order must satisfy at least three conditions: "It must 'conclusively determine the disputed question,' 'resolve an important issue completely separate from the merits of the action,' and 'be effectively unreviewable on appeal from a final judgment.'" Richardson-Merrell Inc. v. Koller, 472 U.S. 424, 431 (1985), quoting Coopers & Lybrand v. Livesay, 437 U.S. 463, 468 (1978). For present purposes, we need not decide whether an order denying a dismissal motion based upon a contractual forum-selection clause conclusively determines a disputed issue, or whether it resolves an important issue that is independent of the merits of the action, for the District Court's orders fail to satisfy the third requirement of the collateral order test.

We recently reiterated the "general rule" that an order is "effectively unreviewable" only "where the order at issue involves 'an asserted right the legal and practical value of which would be destroyed if it were not vindicated before trial.'" *Midland Asphalt Corp.*, quoting United States v. MacDonald, 435 U.S. 850, 860 (1978). If it is eventually decided that the District Court erred in allowing trial in this case to take place in New York, petitioner will have been put to unnecessary trouble and expense, and the value of its contractual right to an Italian forum will have been diminished. It is always true, however, that "there is value . . . in triumphing before trial, rather than after it," *MacDonald*, supra, at 860, n.7, and this Court has declined to find the costs associated with unnecessary litigation to be enough to warrant allowing the immediate appeal of a pretrial order. See *Richardson-Merrell Inc.*, supra, at 436 ("the possibility that a ruling may be erroneous and may impose additional litigation expense is not sufficient to set aside the finality requirement imposed by Congress" in §1291). Instead, we have insisted that the right asserted be one that is essentially destroyed if its vindication must be postponed until trial is completed.

We have thus held in cases involving criminal prosecutions that the deprivation of a right not to be tried is effectively unreviewable after final judgment and is immediately appealable. Similarly, in civil cases, we have held that the denial of a motion to dismiss based upon a claim of absolute immunity from suit is immediately appealable prior to final judgment, "for the essence of absolute immunity is its possessor's entitlement not to have to answer for his conduct in a civil damages action." Mitchell v. Forsyth, 472 U.S. 511, 525 (1985). And claims of qualified immunity may be pursued by immediate appeal, because qualified immunity too "is an immunity from suit." On the other hand, we have declined to hold the collateral order doctrine applicable where a district court has denied a claim, not that the defendant has a right not to be sued at all, but that the suit against the defendant is not properly before the particular court because it lacks jurisdiction. In Van Cauwenberghe v. Biard, 486 U.S. 517 (1988), a civil defendant moved for dismissal on the ground that he had been immune from service of process because his presence in the United States had been compelled by extradition to face criminal charges. We noted that, after *Mitchell*, "[t]he critical question . . . is whether 'the essence' of the claimed right is a right not to stand trial," 486 U.S., at 524, and held that the immunity from service of process defendant asserted did not amount to an immunity from suit—even though service was essential to the trial court's jurisdiction over the defendant.

Lauro Lines argues here that its contractual forum-selection clause provided it with a right to trial before a tribunal in Italy, and with a concomitant right not to be sued anywhere else. This "right not to be haled for trial before tribunals outside the agreed forum," petitioner claims, cannot effectively be vindicated by appeal after trial in an improper forum. There is no obviously correct way to characterize the right embodied in petitioner's forum-selection provision: "all litigants who have a meritorious pretrial claim for dismissal can reasonably claim a right not to stand trial." *Van Cauwenberghe*. The right appears most like that to be free from trial if it is characterized—as by petitioner—as a right not to be sued at all except in a Neapolitan forum. It appears less like a right not to be subjected to suit if characterized—as by the Court of Appeals—as "a right to have the binding adjudication of claims occur in a certain forum." Even assuming that the former characterization is proper, however, petitioner is obviously not entitled under the forum-selection clause of its contract to avoid suit altogether, and an entitlement to avoid suit is different in kind from an entitlement to be sued only in a particular forum. Petitioner's claim that it may be sued only in Naples, while not perfectly secured by appeal after final judgment, is adequately vindicable at that stage—surely as effectively vindicable as a claim that the trial court lacked personal jurisdiction over the defendant—and hence does not fall within the third prong of the collateral order doctrine.

Petitioner argues that there is a strong federal policy favoring the enforcement of foreign forum-selection clauses, citing The Bremen v. Zapata Off-Shore Co., 407 U.S. 1 (1972), and that "the essential concomitant of this strong federal policy . . . is the right of immediate appellate review of district court orders denying their enforcement." A policy favoring enforcement of forum-selection clauses, however, would go to the merits of petitioner's claim that its ticket-agreement requires that any suit be filed in Italy and that the agreement should be enforced by the federal courts. Immediate appealability of a prejudgment order denying enforcement, insofar as it depends upon satisfaction of the third prong of the collateral order test, turns on the precise contours of the right asserted, and not upon the likelihood of eventual success on the merits. The Court of Appeals properly dismissed petitioner's appeal, and its judgment is affirmed.

SCALIA, J., concurring.

I join the opinion of the Court, and write separately only to make express what seems to me implicit in its analysis.

The reason we say that the right not to be sued elsewhere than in Naples is "adequately vindicable," by merely reversing any judgment obtained in violation of it is, quite simply, that the law does not deem the right important enough to be vindicated by, as it were, an injunction against its violation obtained through interlocutory appeal. The importance of the right asserted has always been a significant part of our collateral order doctrine. When first formulating that doctrine in *Cohen v. Beneficial Industrial Loan Corp.* we said that it permits interlocutory appeal of final determinations of claims that are not only "separable from, and collateral to, rights asserted in the action," but also, we immediately added, "*too important* to be denied review" (emphasis added). Our later cases have retained that significant requirement. . . .

While it is true, therefore, that the "right not to be sued elsewhere than in Naples" is not fully vindicated—indeed, to be utterly frank, is positively destroyed—by permitting the trial to occur and reversing its outcome, that is vindication enough because the right is not sufficiently important to overcome the policies militating against interlocutory appeals. We have made that judgment when the right not to be tried in a particular court has been created through jurisdictional limitations established by Congress or by international treaty. The same judgment applies—if anything, a fortiori—when the right has been created by private agreement.

Procedure as Strategy

The cruise line spent a good deal of money trying to get the appellate courts to treat this order as a final judgment—only to find out that it had spent the money in vain. A competent appellate lawyer could have told the appellant that this was a very long shot, given the existing law. Why did the appellant nevertheless think it was a shot worth taking? Without knowing for sure, we offer two speculations. First, if this case ends like most, it will settle—in which case no appeal is possible. Second, the underlying events would make the cruise line extremely reluctant to try the case to a New York jury. The pirates had singled out Leon Klinghoffer, the deceased passenger, as a Jew, then shot him to death and pushed him in his wheelchair into the ocean. Klinghoffer was a New York native. The issue before the jury would be whether the cruise line had taken adequate security measures to prevent these acts. Does that explain why the appellant may have thought that the long odds of an appeal were nevertheless its best odds?

WHAT'S NEW HERE?

- Given the decisive importance of some pretrial rulings, it was almost inevitable that courts interpreting the final judgment requirement of §1291 would create a class of exceptions.
- They did, calling those exceptions "collateral final orders." A ruling that falls into this category is immediately appealable even though one would not intuitively think the order was final.
- The courts' struggle has been to define with any clarity the line between non-appealable, non-final orders (like that in *Lauro Lines*) and those that have been held to be appealable even though not final (see below).

Notes and Problems

1. *Lauro Lines* tells us that it is one of a series of cases delineating judicially created exceptions to the final judgment rule.

   a. The attraction of such an exception is easy to understand: Some non-final rulings seem to cry out for reversal before trial is over.

   b. The difficulties of creating exceptions are equally obvious: How can one define a coherent set of cases that will be entitled to review before the final judgment?

2. The Court in *Lauro Lines* held that the order was not appealable and therefore did not decide whether the forum selection clause was valid. That ruling will often have the same practical effect as holding the order appealable but affirming the trial court decision on the merits. In some cases it is difficult to overcome the sense that denials of review are made with at least an over-the-shoulder glance at the merits. Such a glance may be particularly important in a case like *Lauro Lines*. Such cases are very unlikely to go to trial, and a settlement will not be appealable. Thus, the interlocutory review of the court order is likely to be the only review. Might this be the point of Justice Scalia's concurrence?

   Concerns about "practical finality" often arise in cases concerning the official immunity defense for government officials. Government officials sued for violating the constitutional rights of citizens have a powerful defense: "official immunity"—both absolute and qualified, as *Lauro Lines* describes. These doctrines intend not only to shield them from liability but also to shield them from the obligation to stand trial—including the necessity to endure discovery. As *Lauro Lines* recognizes, the "right not to stand trial" can only be vindicated if immediate appeal lies from a trial court order that—erroneously—holds that official immunity does not apply. See Nixon v. Fitzgerald, 457 U.S. 731 (1982) (allowing immediate appeal of trial court's refusal to dismiss claim against President of the United States on grounds of absolute official immunity); Mitchell v. Forsyth, 472 U.S. 511 (1985) (allowing immediate appeal of trial court's refusal to dismiss a suit against a former United States Attorney General on qualified immunity grounds). *Ashcroft v. Iqbal* in Chapter 6 is another case that was appealed up to the Supreme Court following the denial of a motion to dismiss on qualified immunity grounds. (Note, however, that the Supreme Court's opinion in *Iqbal* focused not on qualified immunity—the immediately appealable issue—but on pleading standards, which are not subject to collateral review.)

   a. *Nixon* and *Mitchell* arguably opened Pandora's box. Like *Lauro Lines*, they deal with defendants who argue that they have the "right not to stand trial." If one conceives of such a right, then its vindication *after* trial and final judgment seems futile and self-defeating. But one could describe many defendants in such terms. For example, any defendant who moves to dismiss on any of the grounds listed in Rule 12(b) (and loses the motion) could argue that her "right not to stand trial" has been violated. Likewise, so could a defendant who made an unsuccessful motion for summary judgment. The defendant in *Lauro Lines* unsuccessfully made such an argument, to the effect that it had, at least, the right not to stand trial anywhere but in Naples.

b. The Court has not explained why government officials, but not other defendants, should be entitled to this particular protection.

3. An incomplete list of other orders that have been held to be practically final under the *Cohen* doctrine includes:

a. Orders declining to apply in federal court a state statute requiring the posting of a bond in shareholder derivative actions brought by plaintiffs owning small amounts of stock. Cohen v. Beneficial Industrial Corp., 337 U.S. 541 (1949) (cited in *Lauro Lines*, supra).

b. Orders vacating the attachment of a vessel. Swift & Co. v. Compania Colombiana de Caribe, 339 U.S. 684 (1950).

c. Orders denying a party leave to proceed *in forma pauperis*. Roberts v. United States District Court, 339 U.S. 844 (1950).

d. Orders refusing to dismiss actions against government agencies on grounds of Eleventh Amendment immunity from suit. Puerto Rico Aqueduct & Sewer Auth. v. Metcalf & Eddy, 506 U.S. 139 (1993).

e. Orders remanding diversity actions on grounds of abstention. Quackenbush v. Allstate Insurance Co., 517 U.S. 706 (1996).

4. Contrast with the cases listed in Note 3 a partial series of examples in which the Court, as in *Lauro Lines*, has held the order in question not to be practically final:

a. Orders refusing to certify class actions. Coopers & Lybrand v. Livesay, 437 U.S. 463 (1978). As the next section explains, this ruling has been partly reversed by an amendment to Rule 23(f).

b. Orders disqualifying or refusing to disqualify trial counsel for alleged conflicts of interest. Richardson-Merrell v. Koller, 472 U.S. 424 (1985); Flanagan v. United States, 465 U.S. 259 (1984); Firestone v. Risjord, 449 U.S. 368 (1981).

c. Orders denying permission to intervene as of right under Rule 24(a) while granting permissive intervention under Rule 24(b). Stringfellow v. Concerned Neighbors in Action, 480 U.S. 370 (1987).

d. Orders denying a motion to dismiss on the ground that the person is immune from service of process and on the ground of forum non conveniens. Van Cauwenberghe v. Biard, 486 U.S. 517 (1988).

e. Orders requiring class action defendants to bear the cost of notifying members of the class. Eisen v. Carlisle & Jacquelin, 417 U.S. 156 (1974). (See Chapter 12.)

f. Orders rescinding a dismissal pursuant to settlement. Digital Equipment Corp. v. Desktop Direct, Inc., 511 U.S. 863 (1994).

g. Orders refusing to apply the "judgment bar" rule blocking a constitutional suit against the United States after a previous suit based on the Federal Tort Claims Act had been dismissed. Will v. Hallock, 546 U.S. 345 (2006).

5. And there is, predictably, a list of topics on which the circuits have split on the question of appealability. One example: the appealability of an order denying *pro se* plaintiffs the right to counsel. In 2017, the Supreme Court denied certiorari in *Sai v. Transportation Security Administration*, a case in which the Court could have resolved the question.

6. The difficulty of satisfactorily distinguishing between the cases in the three preceding notes may have led to a 1990 amendment to 28 U.S.C. §2072. Congress extended the Supreme Court's rulemaking power under the Rules Enabling Act to include Rules "defin[ing] when a ruling of a district court is final for the purposes of appeal under section 1291 of this title." One might interpret this provision as a subtle suggestion that, in writing the Rules, rulemakers eliminate some of the twists and turns in the collateral order doctrine by overruling some decisions in this line. If so, the rulemakers have not taken the hint: No Rule has to date taken up Congress's challenge.

b. Injunctions

An important exception to the final judgment rule appears in 28 U.S.C. §1292(a), which allows appeals from interlocutory orders of the district courts "granting, continuing, modifying, refusing or dissolving injunctions, or refusing to dissolve or modify injunctions." Recall that this was one of the argued grounds for appealability in *Wetzel*, supra page 673. Such review is thought to be appropriate because of the special nature of injunctions and their potential for harm. It may also be a historical artifact: In equity, *all* rulings (including grants and denials of injunctions) were immediately appealable.

Notes and Problems

---

1. Section 1292(a)(1) does not apply to a temporary restraining order, though it does to a preliminary injunction. Presumably, the basis for this distinction is the short duration of a TRO—14 days under Rule 65(b).

2. The Supreme Court has held that denial of summary judgment in favor of one seeking a permanent injunction does not give rise to the right to immediate appeal under this section because the ruling is simply a step on the way to trial rather than a rejection of the claim on the merits. Switzerland Cheese Association v. E. Horne's Market, Inc., 385 U.S. 23 (1966).

3. Courts require parties to act or refrain from acting repeatedly during the course of litigation. Suppose, for example, a district court, acting pursuant to Rule 16, orders the parties to refrain from any discovery while they discuss settlement or submit to court-ordered mediation. Is that an injunction? Or just an unappealable pretrial order?

c. Interlocutory Appeals

Additional efforts to release some of the tension created by the final judgment rule are found in several statutes. The terms of 28 U.S.C. §1292(b) permit a district court to certify interlocutory appeals from non-final judgments. A district court judge wishing to create the possibility for such an interlocutory appeal must certify that the order "involves a controlling question of law as to which there is a substantial ground for difference of opinion" and that "an immediate appeal from the order may materially advance the ultimate termination of the litigation." For the interlocutory appeal to occur, not only must the district court judge so certify, but the appellate court must agree.

The statute is infrequently used. A study at the close of the 1980s, a period when overall appeals increased dramatically, revealed that out of the 40,000+ federal appeals in an average year only about 300 were certified by district courts, and of those only about one-third, 100 cases, were accepted by the courts of appeals. Michael Solomine, *Revitalizing Interlocutory Appeals in the Federal Courts*, 58 Geo. Wash. L. Rev. 1165 (1990). Note that one of the cases you may soon read, *Mosley v. General Motors Corp.*, infra page 788, was one of those relatively few exceptions.

Another approach appears in Rule of Civil Procedure 23(f). Acting under the authority granted by 28 U.S.C. §2072(c), which permits the Rules to define "when a ruling of a district court is final for purposes of appeal," Rule 23(f) now provides: "A court of appeals may permit an appeal from an order granting or denying class-action certification under this rule if a petition for permission to appeal is filed with the circuit clerk within fourteen days after the order is entered." The district court need not agree. Do you think §1292(b) should be amended in a similar fashion?

d. Mandamus

A *writ of mandamus* is not quite an interlocutory appeal, but it has a similar function. A party seeking a writ of mandamus essentially brings suit in an appellate court against the trial judge in the case, seeking an order that that judge perform an act required by law. For example, in LaBuy v. Howes Leather, 352 U.S. 249 (1957), where the district court had declined to try an antitrust case, instead referring it to a special master, the defendants sought a writ of mandamus from the court of appeals, ordering the district court to try the case. The court of appeals issued the writ and the writ was upheld by the Supreme Court. The Seventh Circuit had previously expressed its displeasure with referral of such cases to masters, and the Supreme Court was even more emphatic in describing the district court's action as an "abdication of the judicial function." The difficulty with mandamus arises because it can become a tempting route for the avoidance of the rules against interlocutory appeals explored in the preceding material. To prevent this evasion of the final judgment rule, the availability of the writ must be limited, as courts regularly remind:

> The remedy of mandamus is a drastic one, to be invoked only in extraordinary situations. As we have observed, the writ "has traditionally been used in the federal courts only 'to confine an inferior court to a lawful exercise of its prescribed jurisdiction or

to compel it to exercise its authority when it is its duty to do so.'" And, while we have not limited the use of mandamus by an unduly narrow and technical understanding of what constitutes a matter of "jurisdiction," the fact still remains that "only exceptional circumstances amounting to a judicial 'usurpation of power' will justify the invocation of this extraordinary remedy."

Kerr v. United States District Court, 426 U.S. 394, 402 (1976).

In spite of such limitations, one does find cases where appellate courts are prepared to issue writs of mandamus. One area in which mandamus seems freely available, with little discussion of the usual stated limitations, is that in which the trial judge has denied a jury trial. Thus, in Beacon Theatres v. Westover, 359 U.S. 500 (1959) (granting a writ of mandamus and ordering a jury trial in a case combining legal and equitable claims), the propriety of interlocutory appellate review was largely assumed. Another exception to the general stinginess of the courts in issuing the writ is to prevent the transfer of a case, under 28 U.S.C. §1404(a), out of the circuit. The rationale is that the statutory basis for the writ, 28 U.S.C. §1651, authorizes writs to be issued by courts "in aid of their respective jurisdictions." Because a transfer out of the circuit would deprive the court of appeals of its eventual jurisdiction on appeal, the appellate court has jurisdiction to consider the propriety of such a transfer order. The Seventh Circuit has adopted an apparently unique use of mandamus. In seeking the recusal of judges under 28 U.S.C. §455(a) (on the broad ground that "impartiality might reasonably be questioned"), that Circuit requires parties to use mandamus rather than appeal. The Circuit's theory is that in such broadly based recusal motions, an aggrieved party who waits to appeal until after trial will have great difficulty demonstrating an effect on his "substantial rights." As you will see in the next section, only an effect on "substantial rights" can constitute reversible error; therefore, in order to create some avenue by which denial of a §455(a) motion can be reviewed, mandamus is available. However tortured the Seventh Circuit's reasoning, the result makes sense: In most cases mandamus on these grounds will be sought early in the case, before time has been wasted on proceedings that must be set aside.

Notes and Problems

1. One way in which an appellate court might have its cake and eat it too—refuse to issue a writ of mandamus but achieve the same practical effect—is to write an opinion refusing to grant the writ and in the process discuss the course it "hopes" the district court will take. Several Supreme Court opinions take such a tack.

   a. In *Kerr v. United States District Court*, supra, the Supreme Court upheld the Ninth Circuit's refusal to issue a writ of mandamus requiring the district court to vacate a discovery order that would have required the California prison system to turn over all of its personnel files. The defendant prison system resisted on grounds that the files were covered by various privileges. The Supreme Court "upheld" the refusal of the writ in terms that came close to granting it:

> Petitioners ask in essence only that the District Court review the challenged documents in camera before passing on whether each one individually should or should not be disclosed. But the Court of Appeals' opinion dealing with the Adult Authority files did not foreclose the possible necessity of such in camera review. . . . The court apparently left open the opportunity for petitioners to return to the District Court, assert the privilege more specifically . . . and then have their request for an in camera review . . . reconsidered in a different light. . . .

Theoretically, the district court remained free after this opinion to refuse in-camera review of the files. How likely is the district court judge to so refuse after reading this Supreme Court opinion?

b. A similar approach was used in *Schlagenhauf v. Holder*, noted supra page 472. The principal issue in *Schlagenhauf* was whether the district court could order a series of mental and physical examinations of a defendant bus driver whose bus had collided with another vehicle that he later claimed he did not see. The Supreme Court ruled that, of the numerous examinations ordered by the district court, only the eye examination was justified. The court of appeals had refused to issue a writ of mandamus ordering the district court to rescind its order for the additional examinations. One would therefore expect the Supreme Court to remand to the court of appeals for it to issue the writ of mandamus. Instead, the Court remanded the case to the district court for proceedings consistent with its opinion. (The Court did not note that the mandamus action before it, being an original action in the court of appeals, could not be remanded to the district court and that the original action was still in the district court.)

C. SCOPE OF REVIEW

Even if a decision is final or otherwise reviewable, and even if the lower court decision is flawed, it does not follow that an appellate court will reverse the judgment. Reversal is appropriate only if the trial court's error is sufficiently grave and leads to an erroneous result. Whether an error is sufficiently grave depends upon whether it concerned a question of "law" or "fact," as *Anderson*, the next case, illuminates. And the meaning of "harmless error" becomes clearer after reading *Van Zee v. Hanson*, infra.

1. Law and Fact

Courts of appeals must apply different standards on appeal depending on whether the trial court's decision concerned an issue of "law" or "fact." Issues of law get de novo review; in other words, the court of appeals can consider purely legal questions—like whether at-will employees have a property interest in their jobs (see *Haddle v. Garrison*, Chapter 6)—without deference to the trial court's earlier analysis. Courts of appeals grant more deference to trial courts' decisions on issues of fact, reversing only if the trial courts' decision was "clearly erroneous." The meaning of that standard will be clearer after reading the next case.

Anderson v. Bessemer City

470 U.S. 564 (1985)

WHITE, J., delivered the opinion of the Court.

[A] District Court's finding of discriminatory intent in an action brought under Title VII of the Civil Rights Act of 1964 . . . is a factual finding that may be overturned on appeal only if it is clearly erroneous. In this case, the Court of Appeals for the Fourth Circuit concluded that there was clear error in a District Court's finding of discrimination and reversed. Because our reading of the record convinces us that the Court of Appeals misapprehended and misapplied the clearly-erroneous standard, we reverse.

I

[Bessemer City sought a new Recreation Director. Ms. Anderson was the only woman to apply for the job. A five-member committee interviewed the eight applicants and chose a male, and Ms. Anderson sued, alleging discrimination.]

. . . After a 2-day trial, during which the court heard testimony from petitioner, Mr. Kincaid [the successful applicant], and the five members of the selection committee, the court issued a brief memorandum of decision setting forth its finding that petitioner . . . had been denied the position . . . on account of her sex. . . . [The judge also requested] that petitioner's counsel submit proposed findings of fact and conclusions of law expanding upon those set forth in the memorandum. . . . [This procedure led to several rounds of proposed findings by plaintiff and objections by defendant. Finally,] the court issued its own findings of fact and conclusions of law.

. . . [T]he court's finding that petitioner had been denied employment . . . because of her sex rested on a number of subsidiary findings[: (1) that Ms. Anderson "had been better qualified than Mr. Kincaid" (the court detailed the careers of each); (2) that "male committee members had in fact been biased against" Ms. Anderson because she was a woman, a finding based "in part on the testimony of one of the committee members that he believed it would have been 'real hard' for a woman to handle the job and that he would not want his wife to have to perform" its duties; (3) that Ms. Anderson "alone among the applicants . . . had been asked whether she realized the job would involve night work and travel and whether her husband approved of her applying for the job" (there was some dispute about whether Mr. Kincaid was asked an analogous question but the trial court concluded that it was "not a serious inquiry"); and (4)] that the reasons offered by the male committee members for their choice of Mr. Kincaid were pretextual. The court rejected the proposition that Mr. Kincaid's degree in physical education justified his choice, as the evidence suggested that where male candidates were concerned, the committee valued experience more highly than formal education. . . .

The Fourth Circuit reversed . . . [holding that three of] the District Court's crucial findings were clearly erroneous: the finding that petitioner was the most qualified candidate, the finding that petitioner had been asked questions that other applicants were spared, and the finding that the male committee members were biased against hiring a woman. . . .

II

We must deal at the outset with the Fourth Circuit's suggestion that "close scrutiny of the record in this case [was] justified by the manner in which the opinion was prepared"—that is, by the District Court's adoption of petitioner's proposed findings of fact and conclusions of law.

We too, have criticized courts for their verbatim adoption of findings of fact prepared by prevailing parties. . . . Nonetheless, our previous discussions of the subject suggest that even when the trial judge adopts the proposed findings verbatim, the findings are those of the court and may be reversed only if clearly erroneous. . . .

In any event, the District Court in this case does not appear to have uncritically accepted findings prepared without judicial guidance. . . .

III

Because a finding of intentional discrimination is a finding of fact, the standard governing appellate review . . . is that set forth in Federal Rule of Civil Procedure 52(a): "Findings of fact shall not be set aside unless clearly erroneous, and due regard shall be given to the opportunity of the trial court to judge the credibility of the witnesses." . . .

Although the meaning of the phrase "clearly erroneous" is not immediately apparent, certain general principles . . . may be derived from our cases. The foremost of these principles, as the Fourth Circuit itself recognized, is that a "finding is 'clearly erroneous' when although there is evidence to support it, the reviewing court on the entire evidence is left with the definite and firm conviction that a mistake has been committed." United States v. United States Gypsum Co., 333 U.S. 364, 395 (1948). . . . Where there are two permissible views of the evidence, the factfinder's choice between them cannot be clearly erroneous.

This is so even when the district court's findings do not rest on credibility determinations, but are based instead on physical or documentary evidence or inferences from other facts. To be sure, various Courts of Appeals have on occasion asserted the theory that an appellate court may exercise de novo review over findings not based on credibility determinations. . . .

The rationale for deference to the original finder of fact is not limited to the superiority of the trial judge's position to make determinations of credibility. The trial judge's major role is the determination of fact, and with experience in fulfilling that role comes expertise. Duplication of the trial judge's efforts in the court of appeals would very likely contribute only negligibly to the accuracy of fact determination at a huge cost in diversion of judicial resources. . . . As the Court has stated in a different context, the trial on the merits should be "the 'main event' . . . rather than a 'tryout on the road.'" Wainwright v. Sykes, 433 U.S. 72, 90 (1977). . . .

IV

Application of the foregoing principles to the facts of the case lays bare the errors committed. . . . [T]he Fourth Circuit improperly conducted what amounted to a de novo weighing of the evidence in the record. The District Court's finding was based on essentially undisputed evidence regarding the respective backgrounds of petitioner and Mr. Kincaid and the duties . . . of Recreation Director. The District Court, after considering the evidence, concluded that the position . . . carried with it broad responsibilities for creating and managing a recreation program involving not only athletics, but also other activities for citizens of all ages and interests. The court determined that petitioner's more varied educational and employment background and her extensive involvement in a variety of civic activities left her better qualified to implement such a rounded program. . . .

The Fourth Circuit, reading the same record, concluded that the basic duty of Recreation Director was to implement an athletic program. . . . Accordingly, it seemed evident to the Court of Appeals that Mr. Kincaid was in fact better qualified than [Ms. Anderson].

Based on our reading of the record, we cannot say that either interpretation of the facts is illogical or implausible. Each has support in inferences that may be drawn from the facts in the record. . . . The question we must answer, however, is not whether the Fourth Circuit's interpretation of the facts was clearly erroneous, but whether the District Court's finding was clearly erroneous. . . .

Somewhat different concerns are raised by the Fourth Circuit's treatment of the District Court's finding that petitioner, alone among the applicants . . . , was asked questions regarding her spouse's feelings. . . . Here the error of the Court of Appeals was its failure to give due regard to the ability of the District Court to interpret and discern the credibility of oral testimony. . . . The Court of Appeals rested its rejection of the District Court's finding . . . on its own interpretation of testimony by Mrs. Boone. . . .

Mrs. Boone's testimony on this point, which is set forth in the margin,[3] is certainly not free from ambiguity. But Mrs. Boone several times stated that other candidates had not been questioned about the reaction of their wives—at least "not in the same

---

3. **Q:** Did the committee members ask that same kind of question of the other applicants?
   A: Not that I recall. . . .
   Q: Do you deny that the other applicants, aside from the plaintiff, were asked about the prospect of working at night in that position?
   A: Not to my knowledge.
   Q: Are you saying they were not asked that?
   A: They were not asked, not in the context that they were asked of Phyllis. I don't know whether they were worried because Jim wasn't going to get his supper or what. You know that goes both ways.
   Q: Did you tell Phyllis Anderson that Donnie Kincaid was not asked about night work?
   A: He wasn't asked about night work.
   Q: That answers one question. Now, let's answer the other one. Did you tell Phyllis Anderson that, that Donnie Kincaid was not asked about night work?

context.". . . Whether the judge's interpretation is actually correct is impossible to tell from the paper record, but it is easy to imagine that the tone of voice in which the witness related her comment, coupled with her immediate denial that she had questioned Mr. Kincaid on the subject, might have conclusively established that the remark was a facetious one. We therefore cannot agree that the judge's conclusion that the remark was facetious was clearly erroneous. . . .

The Fourth Circuit's refusal to accept the District Court's finding that the committee members were biased against hiring a woman was based to a large extent on its rejection of the finding that petitioner had been subjected to questioning that the other applicants were spared. Given that that finding was not clearly erroneous, the finding of bias cannot be termed erroneous. . . .

Our determination that the findings of the District Court regarding petitioner's qualifications, the conduct of her interview, and the bias of the male committee members were not clearly erroneous leads us to conclude that the court's finding that petitioner was discriminated against on account of her sex was also not clearly erroneous. . . .

In so holding, we do not assert that our knowledge of what happened 10 years ago in Bessemer City is superior to that of the Court of Appeals; nor do we claim to have greater insight than the Court of Appeals into the state of mind of the men on the selection committee. . . . Even the trial judge, who has heard the witnesses directly . . . cannot always be confident that he "knows" what happened. Often, he can only determine whether the plaintiff has succeeded in presenting an account of the facts that is more likely to be true than not. Our task—and the task of appellate tribunals generally—is more limited still: we must determine whether the trial judge's conclusions are clearly erroneous. On the record before us, we cannot say that they are. Accordingly, the judgment of the Court of Appeals is reversed.

[The concurring opinions of Justice POWELL and Justice BLACKMUN are omitted.]

WHAT'S NEW HERE?

- Appellate courts insulate factual findings from review: Facts found at the trial level are the basis for reversal only if "clearly erroneous."
- That was long true for jury findings; *Anderson* applies the same rule to factual findings by a judge.

A: Yes, after the interviews—I think the next day or sometime, and I know—may I answer something?

Q: If it's a question that has been asked; otherwise no. It's up to the Judge to say.

A: You asked if there was any question asked about—I think Donnie was just married, and I think I made the comment to him personally—and your new bride won't mind.

Q: So you asked him yourself about his wife's reaction?

A: No, no.

Q: That is what you just said.

Mr. Gibson: Objection, Your Honor.

[The] Court: Sustained. You don't have to rephrase the answer.

App. 108a, 120a-121a.

Notes and Problems

1. Consider two readings of *Anderson*:

   a. The Court's holding might rest on the empirical belief that the trial judge is more likely than an appellate court to be correct in his judgments about which witnesses are telling the truth. If so, then the holding could be challenged by a showing that people in general, even judges, are in fact rather bad at detecting lies, even when they see the witness face to face. There is some empirical evidence that many people lack the capacity to detect untruth. Indeed, that same evidence suggests that people are *better* at detecting lies when they read a transcript than when they hear and see the witnesses. Guy Wellborn, *Demeanor*, 76 Cornell L. Rev. 1075 (1991) (reviewing a substantial body of essentially unanimous social science literature). If the clearly erroneous rule rests on such an empirical belief, it is itself clearly erroneous.

   b. Alternatively, the holding may have a different justification. Under Rule-driven procedure, cases that get to trial will have evidence supporting both sides; otherwise summary judgment would have occurred. So in such cases a rational trier of fact could come down on either side. Notwithstanding this uncertainty, a judgment has to be rendered. Precisely because of this uncertainty, it makes sense to adopt the view of the first hearer of the case unless there is powerful reason for thinking him wrong. Perhaps that is what the "clearly erroneous" rule is about.

2. Rule 52(a)(6) now codifies one of *Anderson*'s points: "Findings of fact, *whether based on oral or other evidence*, must not be set aside unless clearly erroneous." (Emphasis added.)

3. Many decisions are up to the sound discretion of the trial judge: Think of how many sections of the Rules say "may" rather than "must." Appellate courts can review such decisions for abuse of discretion. As in *Anderson*'s insistence that factual findings be reversed only if clearly erroneous, the Supreme Court has expressed its impatience with appellate courts that "cheat" on the abuse-of-discretion standard by applying it too stringently. In General Electric v. Joiner, 522 U.S. 136 (1997), a trial court had refused to allow some expert witnesses to testify. Such decisions are within the court's discretion. The Eleventh Circuit reversed, citing a generalized preference for admissibility, and conceding that it was applying a particularly stringent standard of review. The Supreme Court reversed, ordering that the usual abuse-of-discretion standard be applied.

4. When a jury rather than a judge has found the fact in question, the principle of *Anderson*, or even a more stringent standard, may be constitutionally required. The "reexamination clause" of the Seventh Amendment provides that "no fact, tried by a jury, shall be otherwise reexamined in any Court of the United States, than according to the rules of common law." The Supreme Court has said that this clause permits trial court scrutiny of jury verdicts via Rule 50 and Rule 59 motions. The Court has also suggested, however, that the same reexamination

by an appellate court, because it has not been historically sanctioned, is at least doubtful. Does this suggest that jury verdicts get even more insulation than do judges' factual findings?

5. In one area the Court has not only permitted but required searching appellate review of facts and their application to law: punitive damage awards. In a pair of cases, the Supreme Court held that due process requires (a) that a state or federal appellate court must review a jury award of punitive damages, Honda Motor Co. v. Oberg, 512 U.S. 415 (1994); and (b) that the appellate review must be de novo, Cooper Industries, Inc. v. Leatherman Tool Group, Inc., 532 U.S. 424 (2001), thus stripping both jury and trial judge of the deference granted to such fact-finding and law-application.

6. *Anderson* deals with one side of the law-fact distinction, holding that findings of fact are entitled to a deferential standard of review. The other side of that distinction is equally important: the proposition that trial court conclusions of law are not entitled to any deference. What does it tell us about the function of appellate review that a trial court may be "a little wrong" about facts, but not about law?

2. Harmless Error

Even if an appellate court applying the appropriate standard of review determines that the trial court committed error, it will not necessarily reverse. Federal courts are forbidden to reverse for "errors or defects that do not affect the substantial rights of the parties." 28 U.S.C. §2111. This statute was enacted to reverse the so-called Exchequer Rule,* which had presumed that any error was harmful and required reversal. As a consequence of §2111, a court must, after concluding there was error, also decide whether that error was harmful.

Courts typically do so by speculating about the likely outcome of the case in the absence of the error; consider whether the next case correctly applies the principle.

Van Zee v. Hanson
630 F.3d 1126 (8th Cir. 2011)

BENTON, J.

Joseph S. Van Zee sued Marilyn Hanson under 42 U.S.C. §1983, alleging that she violated his Fourteenth Amendment rights by disclosing his juvenile records to an Army recruiter. The district court dismissed the complaint for failure to state a claim upon which relief could be granted. This court affirms.

Van Zee enlisted in the Army in early 2008. In June, his recruiter advised him that he could begin basic training after completion of a background check. Van Zee

---

* So called from the name of the English court that had originated the practice.

then executed two blank release forms: one for law enforcement records, the other for probation officer and court records. The Army recruiter sent these forms to law enforcement and court agencies where Van Zee had resided, including to the Court Services Office of the Sixth Judicial District of South Dakota. The Chief Court Services Officer responded on July 2 that under South Dakota Law, Van Zee's juvenile records could not be disclosed. On July 9, the recruiter contacted Hanson, Clerk of Courts for Hyde County, South Dakota, requesting Van Zee's juvenile records. After Hanson disclosed Van Zee's juvenile records, the recruiter notified him that his enlistment was canceled.

The district court ruled that Van Zee did not state a claim under 42 U.S.C. §1983 because Hanson's actions did not violate his right of privacy. This court reviews de novo the grant of a motion to dismiss for failure to state a claim, granting all reasonable inferences in favor of the non-moving party.

To state a claim under §1983, a plaintiff must allege (1) that the defendant acted under color of state law, and (2) that the alleged conduct deprived the plaintiff of a constitutionally protected federal right.

Van Zee claims that Hanson's conduct violated his right of privacy under the Fourteenth Amendment. "[T]o violate the constitutional right of privacy the information disclosed must be either a shocking degradation or an egregious humiliation. . . , or a flagrant bre[a]ch of a pledge of confidentiality which was instrumental in obtaining the personal information." Cooksey v. Boyer, 289 F.3d 513, 516 (8th Cir. 2002) (internal quotation omitted). "To determine whether a particular disclosure satisfies this exacting standard, we must examine the nature of the material . . . to assess whether the person had a legitimate expectation that the information would remain confidential while in the state's possession." Eagle v. Morgan, 88 F.3d 620, 625 (8th Cir. 1996). The district court concluded that Van Zee lacked a legitimate expectation of privacy in his juvenile records due to his signed release forms, and that Hanson's disclosure was neither shockingly degrading nor egregiously humiliating.

Van Zee argues that because the pleadings do not include his release forms, the district court's reliance on them converted Hanson's motion to dismiss into a motion for summary judgment, without permitting him the opportunity to respond. "If, on a motion under Rule 12(b)(6). . . , matters outside the pleadings are presented to and not excluded by the court, the motion must be treated as one for summary judgment under Rule 56." Fed. R. Civ. P. 12(d). "All parties must be given a reasonable opportunity to present all the material that is pertinent to the motion." Id. "[C]onstructive notice that the court intends to consider matters outside the complaint can be sufficient." Country Club Estates, L.L.C. v. Town of Loma Linda, 213 F.3d 1001, 1005 (8th Cir. 2000). "Consideration of matters outside the pleading is harmless where the nonmoving party had an adequate opportunity to respond to the motion and material facts were neither disputed nor missing from the record." BJC Health Sys. v. Columbia Cas Co., 348 F.3d 685, 688 (8th Cir. 2003) (internal quotation omitted).

Van Zee had (at least) constructive notice that the district court intended to consider matters outside the complaint when the court, by memorandum to counsel in August 2009, requested copies of any release forms Van Zee signed when enlisting in the Army. Van Zee's counsel responded, forwarding copies of Van Zee's signed forms.

The court dismissed Van Zee's complaint in February 2010. Van Zee had an adequate opportunity to respond to the motion.

According to Van Zee, the district court deprived him of the opportunity to dispute whether Hanson received a copy of the release, and if so, the legal effect of it. While these issues might affect whether Hanson committed a common-law tort or violated South Dakota law, they have no effect on whether she violated Van Zee's Fourteenth Amendment rights. To demonstrate a breach of privacy amounting to a constitutional violation, Van Zee must allege facts showing a legitimate expectation that his juvenile records would not be disclosed to the recruiter. Van Zee does not dispute that he told the recruiter he had a juvenile record and signed forms requesting the release of his juvenile records to the recruiter. The undisputed facts indicate Van Zee expected his juvenile records to be disclosed as part of his background check. Any Rule 12(d) error committed by the district court was harmless. . . .

The judgment of the district court is affirmed.

Notes and Problems

1. According to the plaintiff, what error did the district court commit?

2. How does the court of appeals address the arguable error?

3. If there was no error—as the opinion implies—why does the court of appeals go on to conclude that "any Rule 12(d) error was harmless"? What would be the basis for such a ruling?

4. Should certain kinds of errors be considered intrinsically more serious than others? Consider the following three cases, each concerning errors involving juries, and think about why the first and third were reversed but the second was not.

    a. In Gertz v. Bass, 59 Ill. App. 180, 208 N.E.2d 113 (1965), the appellate court reversed because a jury asked to decide whether defendant's behavior was "willful" or "wanton" had obtained from a bailiff a dictionary containing definitions of those terms that differed from the definitions in the jury instructions.

    b. In Aetna Casualty & Surety Co. v. Perez, 360 S.W.2d 157 (Tex. Civ. App. 1962), the judgment of the lower court was affirmed even though the bailiff had said to some of the jurors, "If you guys are just a couple of thousand dollars apart why don't you settle it?" and "What in the world is the matter with you in there; are you fighting over two or three thousand dollars?" None of the jurors discussed these comments with each other.

    c. In Javis v. Board of Education, 393 Mich. 689, 227 N.W.2d 543 (1975), the Michigan Supreme Court ruled that failure to give any of the Michigan Standard Jury Instructions that are (1) requested by a party, (2) relevant to the case, and (3) a correct statement of the law is presumed to be prejudicial (and therefore reversible error) even if another instruction, otherwise correct and adequate, is given.

Assessment Questions

Q1. Which of the following federal district court rulings can the losing party immediately appeal?

A. The grant of a motion to compel discovery.

B. The denial of a motion to compel discovery.

C. The grant of a motion to dismiss for failure to state a claim.

D. The denial of a motion to dismiss for failure to state a claim.

E. The grant of a motion for a new trial.

F. The denial of a motion for a preliminary injunction.

Q2. Customer sues Retailer alleging a defective product. Customer has three theories of liability: express warranty, implied warranty of merchantability, and misrepresentation. The first two claims would yield the same damages (the price of a non-defective product); the third could yield punitive damages. The case is tried to a judge who makes findings of fact. If the ensuing judgment is for Customer on the express warranty claim but for Retailer on all other claims . . .

A. Customer can appeal its loss on the implied warranty theory.

B. Retailer can appeal its loss on the express warranty theory.

C. Customer can appeal its loss on the misrepresentation theory.

D. Both parties can appeal on any theory on which they lost.

Q3. Same situation as in Q2. If the court of appeals disagrees with the district judge's . . .

A. Findings of fact, it will reverse (so long as the error was not harmless).

B. Findings of fact, it will reverse only if those findings are clearly erroneous (and the error was not harmless).

C. Conclusions of law, it will reverse (so long as the error was not harmless).

D. Conclusions of law, it will reverse only if those conclusions are clearly erroneous (and the error was not harmless).

Q4. Same situation as in Q2 but on the last day of trial the judge announces that he is finding for Customer on all claims and will enter judgment shortly. He also announces that because the contract so provides, he will award Customer attorneys' fees. Which of the following are true?

A. Retailer can appeal.

B. Retailer cannot appeal until the court enters judgment.

C. Retailer cannot appeal until the court enters judgment and awards attorneys' fees because only then will the judgment be final.

D. Retailer can appeal when the court enters judgment, or, if the court fails to do so, 150 days after the clerk enters the ruling on the civil docket.

Q5. Government Official is sued for violating a citizen's civil rights. Official believes she is protected by the qualified immunity doctrine, which she pleads in response to the complaint. To her disappointment the judge rules against her at the pleading stage and discovery is scheduled to commence. Which is true?

   A. Official cannot appeal because no final judgment has been entered.

   B. Official can appeal even though no final judgment has been entered.

Analysis of Assessment Questions

Q1. C and F are the only correct responses. Under 28 U.S.C. §1291 the courts of appeals have jurisdiction only to hear appeals from final judgments; 28 U.S.C. §1292(a)(1) expands that jurisdiction to make certain interlocutory judgments—including either the grant or denial of a preliminary injunction or similar order—immediately appealable. The remaining choices all result in non-final orders that would not be appealable until a final judgment in the case.

Q2. B and C are the only correct responses. A is incorrect because the outcome—the quantum of damages—on the implied warranty theory is the same as for the express warranty; Customer therefore did not suffer an adverse judgment: He got exactly what he would have gotten had he prevailed on the implied warranty theory. D is incorrect, because only a party who suffers an "adverse" judgment—one that yielded a worse result than he was arguably entitled to—can appeal. B is correct because the Retailer did suffer an adverse judgment. C is correct because the measure of damages on the misrepresentation claim might be greater than on the warranty claims (given the availability of punitive damages for the misrepresentation claim), and to that extent Customer suffered an adverse outcome.

Q3. B and C are the only correct responses. A is wrong because findings of fact, whether made by a judge or jury, are protected by the clearly erroneous standard (see Rule 52(a)(6) and *Anderson v. Bessemer City*, supra page 692). D is wrong because reviewing courts hold trial courts to a higher standard on questions of law than for those of fact: A trial court that gets a salient legal standard wrong will be reversed, even if it's just a "little" wrong, unless the error had no effect on the outcome of the case.

Q4. B and D are the correct responses. A is wrong for reasons explained in *Liberty Insurance Co v. Wetzel*, supra page 673. B is correct; the entry of judgment starts the time to appeal running. C is incorrect for the reasons explained supra page 681. D is correct because the Rules drafters have provided this as an alternate route designed to protect litigants from judges who fail to carry through by providing the "separate document" embodying the judgment. See Rule 52(c)(2)(B).

Q5. B is the correct response. Under the "practical finality" doctrine described in *Lauro Lines s.r.l. v. Chasser*, supra page 682, the denial of an official immunity defense to a civil rights claim is one of those "collateral final orders" that are immediately appealable even though it does not fit comfortably within either §1291 or §1292(a)(1).

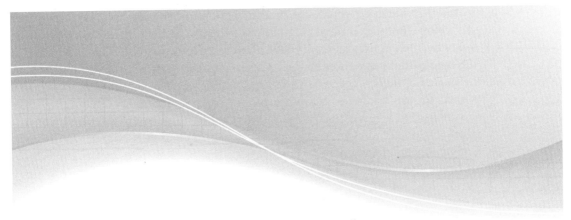

CHAPTER 11

Respect for Judgments

Procedural rules serve two masters. They aim to air disputes completely and to reach an accurate and just outcome. They also seek to end disputes—even if the resting condition is less than optimal. Writers sometimes loftily describe this second goal as "finality" or "repose." Several branches of law serve the goal of finality. Statutes of limitations bar litigation that begins too late. Precedent limits dispute about governing legal principles. And appellate courts have only limited power to overturn trial court findings. This chapter focuses on two other common law doctrines that serve to bring lawsuits to an end: *claim preclusion* and *issue preclusion.*

Both doctrines form part of the broader topic of *former adjudication*—the effect of judgments on subsequent litigation. These doctrines answer a pair of related questions: What does it mean for a lawsuit to be over? What does a concluded lawsuit decide? Suppose, for instance, that Pamela sues Donald for injuries sustained in an auto accident, and the case goes to a final judgment. The loser can, of course, appeal. But can there be a second lawsuit? For example, may Pamela bring a second suit concerning the same accident, this time seeking recovery for damage to her automobile? Today most courts would say no, based on claim preclusion. See, for example, *Ison v. Thomas*, in Chapter 1 (supra page 48). Claim preclusion forbids a party from litigating a claim that was, or could and should have been, raised in former litigation.

Issue preclusion comes into play when a claim is not barred from subsequent litigation, but some issue involved in that claim was actually previously litigated. Suppose Pamela and Donald had the misfortune to become involved in a second collision the week after the first. Pamela's suit against Donald for injuries sustained in the first accident would not prevent her from bringing suit concerning the second one. But she and Donald might find themselves prevented from relitigating issues decided in that first suit that are relevant to the second, such as whether at the time of the accidents either was required to wear glasses while driving.

Much of this chapter will be devoted to exploring the conditions that enable a party to invoke issue or claim preclusion. You will find that in examining these questions courts sometimes use an older set of terminology to refer to these concepts. They refer to claim preclusion as *res judicata* and to issue preclusion as *collateral estoppel*. They also occasionally use *res judicata* to refer to the entire topic of former adjudication. The underlying ideas are identical; only the terminology varies.

A. CLAIM PRECLUSION

Claim preclusion—barring an entire second action—occurs when the case concerns the same claim as a prior action, is litigated by the same parties to the prior action, and when the first action resulted in a final judgment on the merits. In this section, we will consider the meaning of each of these phrases: "same claim," "same parties," "final judgment," and "judgment on the merits." As we do, we will explore the underlying goals of claim preclusion: efficiency, finality, and the avoidance of inconsistency.

1. Precluding the "Same" Claim

The standard doctrinal formulation says that claim preclusion bars the same claim from relitigation. Thus stated, the principle sounds both uncontroversial and obvious. In practice, matters become much more interesting because claim preclusion has two goals—the fostering of efficiency and the prevention of inconsistency. In pursuit of these goals, claim preclusion goes much further than that simple statement might suggest.

a. Efficiency

Claim preclusion grows from pleading. A common law pleader could not combine different writs in a single suit. Because it seemed unfair to block a second suit if the pleader's only mistake lay in selecting the wrong writ, common law courts precluded a plaintiff only from bringing a second claim on the same writ; the plaintiff remained free to try a different writ on the same facts.

The two great pleading reforms of the past 150 years, the Field Codes in the nineteenth century and the Rules in the twentieth, freed pleaders from the confines of the writs. But to the extent they thereby made pleading easier, they made claim preclusion broader. A pleader under the Codes or the Rules was free to combine claims resting on different legal theories and different facts. Did she therefore *have* to do so at the risk of finding them precluded? To put the problem at its most extreme, under Rules 8 and 18, a pleader may state as many claims as she has against the opposing party. If she brings only one such claim, are all others forever precluded? No court has ever gone this far, but, short of this extreme, how broadly should preclusion sweep? In the next case the court contrasts two answers to that question.

Frier v. City of Vandalia

770 F.2d 699 (7th Cir. 1985)

EASTERBROOK, J.

The City of Vandalia is fairly small (the population is less than 2,500), and apparently its police have maintained informal ways. When Charles Frier parked one of his cars in a narrow street, which forced others to drive on someone else's lawn to get around Frier's car, the police left two notes at Frier's house asking him to move the car. That did not work, so an officer called a local garage, which towed the car back to the garage. The officer left a note, addressed to "Charlie," telling him where he could find the car. The officer did not issue a citation for illegal parking, however; he later testified that he wanted to make it easier for Frier to retrieve the car.

Frier balked at paying the $10 fee the garage wanted. He also balked at keeping his cars out of the street. The police had garages tow four of them in 1983—a 1963 Ford Falcon, a 1970 Plymouth Duster, a 1971 Opal GT, and a 1971 Dodge van. Instead of paying the garages, Frier filed suits in the courts of Illinois seeking replevin. Each suit named as defendants the City of Vandalia and the garage that had towed the car.

One of the suits (which sought to replevy two cars) was dismissed voluntarily when Frier got his cars back. We do not know whether he paid for the tows and the subsequent daily storage fees or whether the garage thought it cheaper to surrender the cars than to defend the suit. The other two cases were consolidated and litigated. The police testified to the circumstances under which they had called for the tows. The court concluded that the police properly took the cars into the City's possession to remove obstructions to the alley, and it declined to issue the writ of replevin because the City had the right to remove the cars from the street. Frier then retrieved another car;[1] so far as we can tell, a garage still has the 1970 Plymouth Duster.

After losing in state court, Frier turned to federal court. His [federal] complaint maintained that the City had not offered him a hearing either before or after it took the cars and that it is the "official policy" of the City not to do so. The complaint invoked the Due Process Clause of the Fourteenth Amendment and 42 U.S.C. §1983, and it sought equitable relief in addition to $100,000 in compensatory and $100,000 in punitive damages. The district court, after reviewing the transcript of the replevin action, dismissed the complaint for failure to state a claim on which relief may be granted. (Because the judge considered the transcript he should have treated the

---

1. One garage told Frier he could come and get his car anytime he wanted, without paying a fee.

motion to dismiss as one for summary judgment. We analyze the decision as if he had done so.) The court found that Frier had notice of each tow and knew how to get his cars back. Frier also had a full hearing in the replevin action on the propriety of the tows. Although the judicial hearing came approximately one month after the tows, the court thought the delay permissible.

A month is a long wait for a hearing when the subject is an automobile. The automobile is "property" within the meaning of the Due Process Clause, and the City therefore must furnish appropriate process. Sutton v. City of Milwaukee, 672 F.2d 644 (7th Cir. 1982), holds that a hearing is not necessary before the police tow a car but suggests that one must be furnished promptly after the tow. *Sutton* also suggests, in line with many other cases, that the City must establish the process and tender an opportunity for a hearing; it may not sit back and wait for the aggrieved person to file a suit.

The City, for its part, maintains that a few isolated tows without hearings are not the "policy" of the City and may not be imputed to it, and that anyway a month's delay in holding a hearing about seized property is permissible. . . .

A court ought not resolve a constitution[al] dispute unless that is absolutely necessary. Here it is not. Frier had his day in court in the replevin action. The City has argued that this precludes further suits. (The City raised this argument in the motion to dismiss, which is irregular but not fatally so. See Fed. R. Civ. P. 8(c).) The district court bypassed this argument because, it believed, Frier could not have asserted his constitutional arguments in a replevin action. This is only partially correct.

Frier could not have obtained punitive damages or declaratory relief in a suit limited to replevin. But he was free to join one count seeking such relief with another seeking replevin. See Welch v. Brunswick Corp., 10 Ill. App. 3d 693 (1st Dist. 1973), revd. in part on other grounds, 57 Ill. 2d 461 (1974); Hanaman v. Davis, 20 Ill. App. 2d 111 (2d Dist. 1959), both of which allow one count seeking replevin to be joined with another count seeking different relief. As we show below, the law of Illinois, which under 28 U.S.C. §1738 governs the preclusive effect to be given to the judgment in the replevin actions, see Marrese v. American Academy of Orthopaedic Surgeons, 470 U.S. 373 (1985), would bar this suit. The City therefore is entitled to prevail on the ground of claim preclusion, although the district court did not decide the case on that ground. See Massachusetts Mutual Life Insurance Co. v. Ludwig, 426 U.S. 479 (1976).

Illinois recognizes the principles of claim preclusion (also called *res judicata* or estoppel by judgment). Jones v. City of Alton, 757 F.2d 878, 884-85 (7th Cir. 1985) (summarizing the law of preclusion in Illinois). One suit precludes a second "where the parties and the cause of action are identical." "Causes of action are identical where the evidence necessary to sustain a second verdict would sustain the first, i.e., where the causes of action are based upon a common core of operative facts." Two suits may entail the same "cause of action" even though they present different legal theories, and the first suit "operates as an absolute bar to a subsequent action . . . 'not only as to every matter which was offered and received to sustain or defeat the claim or demand, but as to any other admissible matter which might have been offered for that purpose.'" . . .

The City was a defendant in each replevin action. Frier could have urged constitutional grounds as reasons for replevin.[2] He also could have joined a constitutional claim seeking punitive damages and declaratory relief to his demand for replevin, and therefore he had a full and fair opportunity to litigate (unlike *Jones v. City of Alton*, where procedural obstacles impeded litigation of the federal claim). The actions also involve both the same "common core of operative facts" and the same transactions. Frier argues that the City towed his cars wrongfully. Each complaint seeking replevin asserted [that] Frier owned each car and that it had not been "seized under lawful process"—in other words, that there had been no citation and no hearing at which anyone had found that the cars were illegally parked. The replevin statute requires a plaintiff to show that the property was taken without "lawful process." Ill. Rev. Stat., ch. 110, §19-104. "Process," even in its technical sense, initiates or follows a hearing. Had there been process and a hearing at which a magistrate found the cars to have been illegally parked, Frier would have had no claim for replevin no matter how strongly he contested the substantive issue. The "operative facts" in the replevin and §1983 actions therefore are the same. Frier urges that he owned the car (the property interest) and that the City did not offer him a hearing to adjudicate the legality of his parking (the absence of due process).

The replevin actions diverged from the path of this §1983 suit only because the state judge adjudicated on the merits the propriety of the seizures. Having found the seizures proper, the judge had no occasion to determine whether the City should have offered Frier an earlier hearing. But this divergence does not mean that the two legal theories require a different "core of operative facts." . . .

To the extent there is any doubt about this, we look . . . to the purpose of doctrines of preclusion. Claim preclusion is designed to impel "parties to consolidate all closely related matters into one suit." This prevents the oppression of defendants by multiple cases, which may be easy to file and costly to defend. There is no assurance that a second or third case will be decided more accurately than the first and so there is no good reason to incur the costs of litigation more than once. When the facts and issues of all theories of liability are closely related, one case is enough. Here the replevin theory contained the elements that make up a due process theory, and we are therefore confident that the courts of Illinois would treat both theories as one "cause of action." The final question is whether it makes a difference that only two of the replevin actions went to judgment, while here Frier challenges the towing of four cars. Under Illinois law the answer is no. The defendant may invoke claim preclusion when the plaintiff litigated in the first suit a subset of all available disputes between the parties. See Baird & Warner, Inc. v. Addison Industrial Park, Inc., 70 Ill. App. 3d 59 (1st Dist. 1979), which holds that a suit on three of six disputed parcels of land precludes a subsequent suit on all six. We doubt that Illinois would see difference between three lots out of six and two cars out of four.

---

2. At one point in the argument before the state court, Frier's lawyer invoked the Constitution, saying that the towing was "the taking of a man's property without due process of law and . . . they have taken [the cars] illegally and are holding [them] illegally" (Tr. 48). This is too fleeting to amount to a formal request for a constitutional ruling, but it does show the pertinence of the Constitution to the replevin action.

If Frier had filed the current suit in state court, he would have lost under the doctrine of claim preclusion. Under 28 U.S.C. §1738 he therefore loses in federal court as well.

AFFIRMED.

SWYGERT, Senior Circuit Judge, concurring in the result.

In my view, the majority has simply applied the wrong analysis to the problem at hand. Rather than trying to squeeze a *res judicata* solution into a mold that does not fit, I would review the facts to determine whether Frier's procedural due process claims could withstand a summary judgment motion. Because I believe the City was entitled to summary judgment, I concur in the result.

I

In determining whether the disposition of a claim in State court precludes a subsequent suit on the same claim in federal court, the federal court must apply the State's law of *res judicata*. Because Illinois continues to adhere to the narrow, traditional view of claim preclusion, as opposed to the broader approach codified in the Restatement (Second) of Judgments §§24, 25 (1982), I would hold that Frier's substantive traffic law claim does not preclude this subsequent procedural due process claim. Under the more modern view of the new Restatement, all claims arising from a single "transaction"—broadly defined to include matters related in time, space, origin, and motivation—must be litigated in a single, initial lawsuit, or be barred from being raised in subsequent litigation. There was only one transaction in the case at bar: the seizure of Frier's cars. Accordingly, Frier should have raised both his substantive and procedural objections to the seizure in one initial lawsuit.

Illinois, however, has not adopted the view of the new Restatement.[1] Rather, as the majority recognizes, the Illinois courts focus on the similarities between the causes of action alleged in both suits, not on whether there is a common factual transaction. One suit precludes a second "where the parties and the cause of action are identical." Redfern v. Sullivan, 111 Ill. App. 3d 372, 444 N.E.2d 205, 208 (1983). "Causes of action are identical where the evidence necessary to sustain a second verdict would sustain the first, i.e., where the causes of action are based upon a common core of operative facts." Id. . . .

In sum, the common set of facts that must be shown to invoke Illinois' doctrine of claim preclusion is defined as those facts necessary to sustain the cause of action, not as those facts that could be conveniently litigated in one lawsuit. This focus on the elements of the causes of action and the proofs at trial—rather than on the policy advantages of trying both actions in one suit—dooms any attempt to invoke claim preclusion in the case at bar. To be sure, both actions arise from the same seizure of the same cars. Yet, both the theory of recovery and focus of factual inquiry are dramatically different in each case. Frier's replevin claim was substantive in nature; to replevy property, the claimant must show his superior possessory rights. Frier's

---

1. No Illinois court has ever cited the new Restatement. The first Restatement, which follows the traditional "cause of action" approach, see Restatement of Judgments §61 (1942), has been cited several times.

possessory rights turned on the legality of his parking. Because the trial court found that "the officer reasonably believed and had a right to believe that . . . [Frier's] vehicle obstructed the free use and passage way of that street at that time," it concluded that, therefore, Frier did not enjoy the "superior right to possession of the property" necessary to sustain a replevin action.

Frier's procedural due process claim requires an entirely different factual showing. The legality or reasonableness of the seizure is irrelevant. Because of the "risk of error inherent in the truth-finding process," an individual is entitled to certain procedural safeguards regardless of whether the deprivation of property was substantively justified. The focus of the inquiry, then, is the adequacy of procedures attending the seizure, not the seizure itself.

The majority urges that Frier could have joined a separate constitutional claim to his replevin action. This precise argument was rejected in *Fountas*, 455 N.E.2d at 204. . . . Illinois law focuses on the similarities and differences between the various causes of action. That two wholly different causes of action arising out of the same transaction could be joined together as one convenient trial unit is irrelevant for the purposes of Illinois law, though this would be dispositive under the new Restatement.

II

It was established at Frier's replevin trial that the City police caused various service station owners to tow four of Frier's cars and, in lieu of a traffic citation, left written notice of the reason for the towing and the whereabouts of the cars. Frier eventually recovered two of his cars. Thus, the replevin action, and this action, concern only two of the cars. Frier could have recovered one of those cars immediately by paying a $10.00 towing fee to the owner of the service station that towed the car. However, Frier was informed that any further delay in reclaiming the car would result in a $2.50 per day storage charge. Frier was free to reclaim the other car without paying any fee. I would hold that, on the basis of these uncontested facts, the City was entitled to summary judgment against Frier's procedural due process claim. . . .

[Judge Swygert analyzed the line of cases interpreting the Due Process Clause as they related to plaintiff's claim.]

I would hold, then, that notice of towing, the availability of an expedited State tort suit that can make the petitioner whole, and the ability to reclaim the towed cars immediately at a cost of $10.00 together constitute adequate postdeprivation process as long as the $10.00 fee does not present a financial hardship. This holding would not necessarily conflict with recent decisions of other courts requiring more immediate and elaborate postdeprivation process. More elaborate process may well be required in those cases because the towing practices of the various municipalities were more burdensome on the respective petitioners: Immediate reclamation required significantly more than $10.00 and the litigants had standing to represent indigents who could afford no fee. We need not reach such troublesome issues in the case at bar.

I would find, as a matter of law, no procedural due process violation under these facts. Accordingly, I concur with the majority's decision to affirm the judgment below.

WHAT'S NEW HERE?

- Claim preclusion bars not only claims previously litigated but also some claims closely related to a litigated claim.
- The difficult problem in most claim preclusion cases lies in defining *how* closely related the claims are.

Notes and Problems

1. Why does Frier lose?

   a. Does the majority reject his constitutional claim?

   b. Does anyone assert that he actually litigated his constitutional claim in the first lawsuit?

   c. If not, why is it fair to prevent him from doing so in a second action?

2. The majority and concurrence debate the difference (if any) between the Illinois definition of "claims" for purposes of preclusion and that of the Restatement (Second) of Judgments §24.

   a. The Restatement (Second) of Judgments, which seeks to summarize the common law of claim and issue preclusion, sets forth a broad definition of "claims":

   > (1) When a valid and final judgment rendered in an action extinguishes a plaintiff's claim . . . , the claim extinguished includes all rights of the plaintiff to remedies against the defendant with respect to all or any part of the transaction, or series of connected transactions, out of which the claim arose.
   >
   > (2) What factual grouping constitutes a "transaction," and what groupings constitute a "series," are to be determined pragmatically, giving weight to such considerations as whether the facts are related in time, space, origin, or motivation, whether they form a convenient trial unit, and whether their treatment as a unit conforms to the parties' expectations or business understanding or usage.

   b. The concurrence in *Frier* argues that Illinois does not follow the Restatement (Second) definition of "same claim" and, instead, uses a narrower definition. What, according to the concurrence, is Illinois's definition of "same claim" and how does it differ from that in Restatement (Second)?

   c. In a case decided 13 years after *Frier*, the Illinois Supreme Court clarified that the transactional test should apply. River Park, Inc. v. City of Highland Park, 184 Ill. 2d 290 (1998). The court observed that Illinois courts had for years used both the "transactional" and "same evidence" tests, which "resulted in courts having to engage in lengthy analyses of claims under both tests" and "created confusion as to the proper application of these tests." Id. at 310. In *River Park*, the Illinois Supreme Court instructed lower courts to follow the transactional approach, which it described as "more pragmatic." Id. at 309.

    d. What considerations ought to determine whether a given jurisdiction adopts a transactional test or a narrower one?

    e. Notice that the doctrines of claim preclusion discussed in *Frier* do not flow from the Constitution, Rules, or statute but from common law. One could imagine an amendment to Rule 8 stating that a final judgment on a claim barred the refiling of that claim or any other arising from the same transaction or occurrence. Should the Rules explicitly so state? Would such an amendment violate the Rules Enabling Act, 28 U.S.C. §2072(b), which specifies that the Rules may not "abridge, enlarge, or modify any substantive right"?

3. The opinion identifies some of the justifications for claim preclusion:

> Claim preclusion is designed to impel "parties to consolidate all closely related matters into one suit[.]" This prevents the oppression of defendants by multiple cases, which may be easy to file and costly to defend. There is no assurance that a second or third case will be decided more accurately than the first and so there is no good reason to incur the costs of litigation more than once.

Would any of these principles be violated by permitting Frier to bring a second case asserting his constitutional challenge to Vandalia's towing practices?

4. If the purpose of claim preclusion is to prevent inefficiency by forcing a party to bring all its closely related claims together, who is the intended beneficiary of this efficiency—the courts, the opposing party, or both?

    a. Rule 8(c) lists claim preclusion (which the Rule calls *res judicata*) as an affirmative defense: Failure to plead and prove an affirmative defense results in waiving it. If the doctrine of claim preclusion is intended to protect the courts, why can it be waived by the opposing side?

    b. If the concern is fairness to the opposing party, why can't a litigant avoid preclusion by paying all the expenses of the first lawsuit? The law contains no such exception.

5. Many states and the federal court system use the transactional definition of "claim" for preclusion purposes. Both *Frier* opinions agree that, under the transactional test, Frier's second claim would have been precluded. Is this a sensible result? Assuming that plaintiff wants to challenge the city's entire procedure for towing cars, should he have had to do so when he tried to retrieve his car from the garage? Would it make more sense to permit him to get his car back and then bring a second, broad-based constitutional challenge to the underlying process?

6. The standard answer to the questions posed in the preceding note is that forcing a plaintiff to put into his complaint all the claims arising out of a transaction does not mean the court will try all those claims in a single suit. Rule 42(b) (and equivalent state rules) give trial courts authority to sever claims for trial. One can imagine a court would wish to separate Frier's claim seeking his car back from the claim that the city's towing process was unconstitutional. If that is so, however, it casts some doubt on whether the two claims should be treated as one for preclusion purposes. Notice that Restatement (Second) of Judgments §24(b) specifies that "whether [the claims] form a convenient trial unit" is one of the factors to be considered in deciding whether to preclude them.

7. Having grasped the counterintuitive idea that unlitigated claims can be precluded, do not overstate the principle.

   a. Before a claim can be precluded from being raised, it must have *been* a claim at the time of the first suit. For example, if after the *Frier* litigation ended Vandalia again towed one of Frier's vehicles, new due process and replevin claims would arise, ones not barred by claim preclusion.

   b. A similar principle prevents claim preclusion from applying if the court rendering the first judgment lacked jurisdiction over the allegedly precluded claim. For example, suppose Frier appeared in traffic court to contest his cars being towed. That court could not have awarded him damages sought for his constitutional claim, so *res judicata* would not bar that claim.

   c. Nor does the transactional definition extend to claims arising from the same episode but belonging to different parties. For example, if Husband and Wife were injured when their car was hit by *T*'s truck, each can sue *T*, so a suit by Wife will not preclude a later suit by Husband. While a compulsory joinder of parties rule might be desirable in certain cases, in Reid v. Spadone Machine Co., 119 N.H. 198 (1979), the court, noting that no such compulsory joinder rule exists, allowed a wife to sue for loss of consortium after her husband had won a claim for an employment-related injury. For another example, see *Illinois Central Gulf R. v. Parks*, infra page 738.

8. The majority in *Frier* states the generally accepted law when it says that in trying to decide the preclusive effect of a judgment one should look to the jurisdiction that rendered that judgment in the first case.

   a. For the *Frier* court, the question was whether the courts of Illinois, which rendered the first judgment, would bar the civil rights claim. That is almost always the right analysis. So if Frier had first brought his civil rights claim in federal court, then brought a state law replevin action, the Illinois state court would have faced the question of what preclusive effect a federal court would assign to its judgment in the first case. (As a quick review of this chapter so far, explain what the answer to that question is. Hint: Note 5, supra, provides key information.)

   b. Suppose, however, the first case is brought in a federal court sitting in diversity jurisdiction. Such a court is bound by the holding in *Erie Railroad v. Tompkins* (see Chapter 4), to apply the substantive law of the state where it sits. Does that substantive law include the state's law of preclusion? The U.S. Supreme Court answered that question—yes—in the next case.

Semtek Intl. Inc. v. Lockheed Martin Corp.

531 U.S. 497 (2001)

SCALIA, J., delivered the opinion of the Court.

This case presents the question whether the claim-preclusive effect of a federal judgment dismissing a diversity action on statute-of-limitations grounds is determined by the law of the State in which the federal court sits.

I

Petitioner filed a complaint against respondent in California state court, alleging breach of contract and various business torts. Respondent removed the case to the United States District Court for the Central District of California on the basis of diversity of citizenship, and successfully moved to dismiss petitioner's claims as barred by California's 2-year statute of limitations. In its order of dismissal, the District Court, adopting language suggested by respondent, dismissed petitioner's claims "in [their] entirety on the merits and with prejudice." . . . Petitioner [then] . . . brought suit against respondent in the State Circuit Court for Baltimore City, Maryland, alleging the same causes of action, which were not time barred under Maryland's 3-year statute of limitations. . . . Following a hearing, the Maryland state court granted respondent's motion to dismiss on the ground of *res judicata*. . . . The [Maryland] Court of Special Appeals affirmed, holding that, regardless of whether California would have accorded claim-preclusive effect to a statute-of-limitations dismissal by one of its own courts, the dismissal by the California federal court barred the complaint filed in Maryland, since the *res judicata* effect of federal diversity judgments is prescribed by federal law, under which the earlier dismissal was on the merits and claim preclusive. . . .

II

Petitioner contends that the outcome of this case is controlled by Dupasseur v. Rochereau, 88 U.S. 130, 135 (1875), which held that the *res judicata* effect of a federal diversity judgment "is such as would belong to judgments of the State courts rendered under similar circumstances," and may not be accorded any "higher sanctity or effect." Since, petitioner argues, the dismissal of an action on statute-of-limitations grounds by a California state court would not be claim preclusive, it follows that the similar dismissal of this diversity action by the California federal court cannot be claim preclusive. While we agree that this would be the result demanded by *Dupasseur*, the case is not dispositive because it was decided under the Conformity Act of 1872 [the pre-Rules legislation] which required federal courts to apply the procedural law of the forum State in nonequity cases. . . .

Respondent, for its part, contends that the outcome of this case is controlled by Federal Rule of Civil Procedure 41(b), which provides as follows:

[Involuntary Dismissal; Effect. If the plaintiff fails to prosecute or to comply with these rules or a court order, a defendant may move to dismiss the action or any claim against it. Unless the dismissal order states otherwise, a dismissal under this subdivision (b) and any dismissal not under this rule—except one for lack of jurisdiction, improper venue, or failure to join a party under Rule 19—operates as an adjudication on the merits.*]

Since the dismissal here did not "[state] otherwise" (indeed, it specifically stated that it *was* "on the merits"), and did not pertain to the excepted subjects of jurisdiction, venue, or joinder, it follows, respondent contends, that the dismissal "is entitled to claim preclusive effect."

Implicit in this reasoning is the unstated minor premise that all judgments denominated "on the merits" are entitled to claim-preclusive effect. That premise is not necessarily valid [as the meaning of the phrase has evolved]. . . .

In short, it is no longer true that a judgment "on the merits" is necessarily a judgment entitled to claim-preclusive effect; and there are a number of reasons for believing that the phrase "adjudication upon the merits" does not bear that meaning in Rule 41(b). . . .

And even apart from the purely default character of Rule 41(b), it would be peculiar to find a rule governing the effect that must be accorded federal judgments by other courts ensconced in rules governing the internal procedures of the rendering court itself. Indeed, such a rule would arguably violate the jurisdictional limitation of the Rules Enabling Act: that the Rules "shall not abridge, enlarge or modify any substantive right," 28 U.S.C. §2072(b). . . . In the present case, for example, if California law left petitioner free to sue on this claim in Maryland even after the California statute of limitations had expired, the federal court's extinguishment of that right (through Rule 41(b)'s mandated claim-preclusive effect of its judgment) would seem to violate this limitation.

Moreover, as so interpreted, the Rule would in many cases violate the federalism principle of Erie R. Co. v. Tompkins, 304 U.S. 64, 78-80 (1938), by engendering "'substantial' variations [in outcomes] between state and federal litigation" which would "likely . . . influence the choice of a forum," *Hanna v. Plumer*. See also *Guaranty Trust Co. v. York*. With regard to the claim-preclusion issue involved in the present case, for example, the traditional rule is that expiration of the applicable statute of limitations merely bars the remedy and does not extinguish the substantive right, so that dismissal on that ground does not have claim-preclusive effect in other jurisdictions with longer, unexpired limitation periods. Out-of-state defendants sued on stale claims in California and in other States adhering to this traditional rule would systematically remove state-law suits brought against them to federal court—where, unless other-

---

* [At the time of the decision, the text of Rule 41(b) read:

Involuntary Dismissal: Effect Thereof

   For failure of the plaintiff to prosecute or to comply with these rules or any order of court, a defendant may move for dismissal of an action or of any claim against the defendant. Unless the court in its order for dismissal otherwise specifies, a dismissal under this subdivision and any dismissal not provided for in this rule, other than a dismissal for lack of jurisdiction, for improper venue, or for failure to join a party under Rule 19, operates as an adjudication upon the merits.

—Eds.]

wise specified, a statute-of-limitations dismissal would bar suit everywhere.[1] We think the key to a more reasonable interpretation of the meaning of "operates as an adjudication upon the merits" in Rule 41(b) is to be found in Rule 41(a)[(1)(B)], which, in discussing the effect of voluntary dismissal by the plaintiff, makes clear that an "adjudication upon the merits" is the opposite of a "dismissal without prejudice":

> [Unless the notice or stipulation states otherwise, the dismissal is without prejudice. But if the plaintiff previously dismissed any federal- or state-court action based on or including the same claim, a notice of dismissal operates as an adjudication on the merits.*]

The primary meaning of "dismissal without prejudice," we think, is dismissal without barring the defendant from returning later, to the same court, with the same underlying claim. That will also ordinarily (though not always) have the consequence of not barring the claim from *other* courts, but its primary meaning relates to the dismissing court itself. . . .

We think, then, that the effect of the "adjudication upon the merits" default provision of Rule 41(b)—and, presumably, of the explicit order in the present case that used the language of that default provision—is simply that, unlike a dismissal "without prejudice," the dismissal in the present case barred refiling of the same claim in the United States District Court for the Central District of California. That is undoubtedly a necessary condition, but it is not a sufficient one, for claim-preclusive effect in other courts.[2]

III

Having concluded that the claim-preclusive effect, in Maryland, of this California federal diversity judgment is dictated neither by *Dupasseur v. Rochereau*, as petitioner contends, nor by Rule 41(b), as respondent contends, we turn to consideration of what determines the issue. Neither the Full Faith and Credit Clause, U.S. Const.,

---

1. Rule 41(b), interpreted as a preclusion-establishing rule, would not have the two effects described in the preceding paragraphs—arguable violation of the Rules Enabling Act and incompatibility with *Erie R. Co. v. Tompkins*—if the court's failure to specify an other-than-on-the-merits dismissal were subject to reversal on appeal whenever it would alter the rule of claim preclusion applied by the State in which the federal court sits. No one suggests that this is the rule, and we are aware of no case that applies it.

* [At the time of the decision, the text of Rule 41(b) read:

> Unless otherwise stated in the notice of dismissal or stipulation, the dismissal is without prejudice, except that a notice of dismissal operates as an adjudication upon the merits when filed by a plaintiff who has once dismissed in any court of the United States or of any state an action based on or including the same claim.

—EDS.]

2. We do not decide whether, in a diversity case, a federal court's "dismissal upon the merits" (in the sense we have described), under circumstances where a state court would decree only a "dismissal without prejudice," abridges a "substantive right" and thus exceeds the authorization of the Rules Enabling Act. We think the situation will present itself more rarely than would the arguable violation of the Act that would ensue from interpreting Rule 41(b) as a rule of claim preclusion; and if it is a violation, can be more easily dealt with on direct appeal.

Art. IV, §1, nor the full faith and credit statute, 28 U.S.C. §1738, addresses the question. By their terms they govern the effects to be given only to state-court judgments (and, in the case of the statute, to judgments by courts of territories and possessions). And no other federal textual provision, neither of the Constitution nor of any statute, addresses the claim-preclusive effect of a judgment in a federal diversity action. . . .

It is left to us, then, to determine the appropriate federal rule. And despite the sea change that has occurred in the background law since *Dupasseur* was decided—not only repeal of the Conformity Act but also the watershed decision of this Court in *Erie*—we think the result decreed by *Dupasseur* continues to be correct for diversity cases. Since state, rather than federal, substantive law is at issue there is no need for a uniform federal rule. And indeed, nationwide uniformity in the substance of the matter is better served by having the same claim-preclusive rule (the state rule) apply whether the dismissal has been ordered by a state or a federal court. This is, it seems to us, a classic case for adopting, as the federally prescribed rule of decision, the law that would be applied by state courts in the State in which the federal diversity court sits. See *Gasperini v. Ctr. for Humanities, Inc.* As we have alluded to above, any other rule would produce the sort of "forum-shopping . . . and . . . inequitable administration of the laws" that *Erie* seeks to avoid, since filing in, or removing to, federal court would be encouraged by the divergent effects that the litigants would anticipate from likely grounds of dismissal. See *Guaranty Trust Co. v. York.*

This federal reference to state law will not obtain, of course, in situations in which the state law is incompatible with federal interests. If, for example, state law did not accord claim-preclusive effect to dismissals for willful violation of discovery orders, federal courts' interest in the integrity of their own processes might justify a contrary federal rule. No such conflict with potential federal interests exists in the present case. Dismissal of this state cause of action was decreed by the California federal court only because the California statute of limitations so required; and there is no conceivable federal interest in giving that time bar more effect in other courts than the California courts themselves would impose.

Because the claim-preclusive effect of the California federal court's dismissal "upon the merits" of petitioner's action on statute-of-limitations grounds is governed by a federal rule that in turn incorporates California's law of claim preclusion (the content of which we do not pass upon today), the Maryland Court of Special Appeals erred in holding that the dismissal necessarily precluded the bringing of this action in the Maryland courts. The judgment is reversed, and the case remanded for further proceedings not inconsistent with this opinion.

It is so ordered.

WHAT'S NEW HERE?

- An early post-*Erie* case, *Klaxon v. Stentor*, noted supra at page 265, found in *Erie* the command that a federal court applying state substantive law should also apply that state's choice of law rules.

- *Semtek* takes the idea one step further—and finds that the scope of a federal judgment based on state law should be the same as that judgment *would have had* if a state court had entered it.
- Before *Semtek* many would have said that Rule 41(b)—with its provision that such dismissals "operate[] as an adjudication on the merits"—did what the opinion says it doesn't: require that such dismissals had claim-preclusive effect, as they indeed do in nondiversity cases.
- Instead, the opinion says, this language only prevents the plaintiff from refiling a claim in *that same* court. Whether or not you find this interpretation convincing, note that it's part of the holding: The opinion can get to the common law of preclusion only after it has steered around the Rule 41 issue.

Notes and Problems

---

1. Understand the issue before the Court.

   a. Unlike other *Erie* cases encountered in Chapter 4, this was not a question of the law to be applied by a federal court in a diversity action. It was instead a question of how a state court, in a subsequent case, should understand a federal judgment in a diversity action. Specifically, the question was whether the state court should look to federal preclusion doctrine in deciding the scope of the federal diversity judgment. Held: No; instead the second court should give the diversity judgment the same scope *as if* it had been rendered by a state rather than a federal court.

   b. Further, bear in mind that in claims that might plausibly be brought in several states, states often apply their own statute of limitations (instead of looking to the rules governing the prior court). So, if the *Semtek* claim had remained in a California state court, which had concluded that the statute of limitations had run, one can imagine the plaintiffs refiling in Maryland and having Maryland decide to apply its longer statute of limitations.

2. The preceding note leaves Rule 41 out of the discussion.

   a. The Maryland court thought Rule 41 required it to give broad application to a federal judgment. Moreover, the Maryland court was correct in one respect. Federal courts have regularly said that involuntary dismissals under Rule 41(b) bar not only the claim pleaded but all claims arising from the transaction or occurrence behind the pleaded claim. To see the breadth of this doctrine, suppose the claim in question had arisen under federal law, the federal court had dismissed with prejudice, and the plaintiff then sought to bring a related claim under state law in a state court. The state court would be required to bar the claim. Federated Dept. Stores v. Moitie, 452 U.S. 394 (1981), so holds.

   b. Note that federal common law, according to *Semtek*, has some flexibility: "This federal reference to state law will not obtain, of course, in situations in which the state law is incompatible with federal interests. If, for example, state law did not accord preclusive effect to dismissals for willful violations of discovery orders, federal courts' interest in the integrity of their own processes might justify a contrary federal rule."

b. Consistency—The Logical Implications of the Former Judgment

Notice something about one commonly offered justification for preclusion—that it is efficient. It certainly can be. For example, on the facts of *Ison v. Thomas*, considered in Chapter 1, it might well have saved time for George Ison to combine his property damage and personal injury claims in the same lawsuit: The witnesses, jury, and judge would have had to consider the same evidence—the defendant's negligence, whether that negligence caused Ison's injuries, and the extent if any of Ison's own negligence—only once.

But the facts of *Frier v. City of Vandalia* should also make us just a bit wary about accepting efficiency as the sole justification for preclusion doctrines. Would it really have been more efficient to try Charles Frier's replevin and due process claims in the same lawsuit? Except for the fact of towing the cars, the evidence presented by the parties would overlap very little: In the replevin action, the central question would be who owned the cars; in the due process claim, the relevant inquiry would center on the circumstances leading to the towing (did the cars pose a hazard or a significant obstruction to traffic) and on the post-towing procedures available to Frier. So one might wonder whether more was at work than efficiency. And, in fact, the cases suggest that besides efficiency, preclusion aims at preventing inconsistent judgments. Consider a very simple case, in which Creditor sues Debtor on an unpaid promissory note and prevails. Could Debtor now turn around and sue Creditor for fraud, claiming that the very note on which Creditor had just won a judgment was the product of fraud? No; in the words of an often-cited case:

> [A judgment on the merits] is a finality as to the claim or demand in controversy, concluding parties and those in privity with them, not only as to every matter which was offered and received to sustain or defeat the claim or demand, but as to any *other admissible matter which might have been offered for that purpose*. Thus, for example, a judgment rendered on a promissory note is conclusive as to the validity of the instrument and the amount due upon it, although it be subsequently alleged that perfect defenses actually existed, of which no proof was offered, such as forgery, want of consideration, or payment. If such defenses were not presented in the action, and established by competent evidence, *the subsequent allegation of their existence is of no consequence*.

Cromwell v. County of Sac, 94 U.S. 351, 352 (1876) (emphasis added).

County of Sac and cases like it stand for the proposition that matters that could have been offered as a defense in Lawsuit #1 cannot become the basis for Lawsuit #2. To that extent preclusion blocks inconsistent outcomes, in which Creditor recovers on the promissory note, which is then said to be the product of fraud. Preclusion doctrines say to Defendant/Debtor that she must assert that defense in the first suit—or lose it. We will not permit Defendant/Debtor to prevail on a claim that would undermine the integrity of the first judgment: That rule surely has to be based on preventing inconsistency rather than on efficiency.

Modern rules of procedure take matters one step further. Consider Rule 13:

Rule 13. Counterclaim and Crossclaim

(a) Compulsory Counterclaim.

(1) *In General.* A pleading must state as a counterclaim any claim that—at the time of its service—the pleader has against an opposing party if the claim:

(A) arises out of the transaction or occurrence that is the subject matter of the opposing party's claim; and

(B) does not require adding another party over whom the court cannot acquire jurisdiction.

(2) *Exceptions.* The pleader need not state the claim if:

(A) when the action was commenced, the claim was the subject of another pending action; or

(B) the opposing party sued on its claim by attachment or other process that did not establish personal jurisdiction over the pleader on that claim, and the pleader does not assert any counterclaim under this rule.

Notes and Problems

---

1. Consider a simple application of Rule 13(a), based on a variation on *Frier*. Suppose that Vandalia, like many cities with financial problems, imposes a series of fees for city services—including towing. Further suppose that Illinois has a compulsory counterclaim statute like Rule 13.

   a. Frier sues Vandalia in replevin, seeking the return of his cars. Vandalia answers and the case goes to judgment. Can Vandalia now sue Frier to collect towing charges?

   b. Suppose that, when it receives Frier's complaint, the city—wishing to economize on legal fees—doesn't bother to draft an answer, but just phones Frier to tell him he can come and pick up his cars. Read 13(a)(1) carefully and explain why on these facts Vandalia will *not* be barred from bringing a subsequent claim for towing fees.

2. Rule 13 means that in a jurisdiction using a transactional test for claim preclusion, plaintiff and defendant will have symmetrical incentives.

   a. Plaintiff will have an incentive to bring all transactionally related claims in the same lawsuit, understanding that the failure to do so means he will thereafter be precluded on those claims.

   b. Defendant will have the same incentive—in the form of an explicit command in Rule 13(a)—to bring all counterclaims that arise out of the same transaction or occurrence. Although the Rule does not say so explicitly, the penalty is that "unbrought" transactionally related counterclaims are waived.

3. Why does Rule 13 contain an explicit command to bring related counterclaims while Rules 8 and 18 contain no such explicit instruction? Historically, the scope of preclusion had been a judicially developed doctrine; it wasn't necessary to spell it out in the Rules, which implicitly assume the common law background. Historically, counterclaims were either forbidden or sharply limited; the drafters may have thought it necessary to define their scope at the same time as they enabled them.

2. Between the "Same" Parties

Most commonly, claim preclusion will operate only between those who were the parties to both the first and second lawsuits; by contrast, different parties possess different claims for preclusion purposes, even when those claims arise out of the same transaction. To use *Frier* again as an example, suppose Charles Frier had a roommate, who also parked cars in the alley, and they were similarly towed. The decision in *Frier* would not bar roommate's claim (though Frier's case might provide a precedential barrier to roommate's claim).

The proposition that claim preclusion operates only between the same parties has, however, several exceptions. Imagine, for example, that the owner of Suburbanacre sues Neighbor for trespass, and the court rules that Neighbor enjoys a permanent easement over Owner's land. If Owner sells Suburbanacre to Buyer, Buyer will be bound by the judgment, even though he was not a party to the action. In buying the land, he "buys" the result of litigation defining the nature of Owner's rights. Courts describe Buyer as being bound because he is "in privity" with Owner, a phrase that makes sense given the transaction between Owner and Buyer. Courts have sometimes gone even further than this, finding that someone not formally named as a party is so closely connected to a suit that it is appropriate to treat her as if she were named. When they do so, they use the same phrase, "in privity," to describe the party bound by the first suit. That term is harmless as long as one understands that it merely expresses the conclusion that the person whose name was not on the caption of the first case should nevertheless be bound. When that should happen is the issue before the court in the next case.

Taylor v. Sturgell

553 U.S. 880 (2008)

GINSBURG, J., delivered the opinion of the Court.

"It is a principle of general application in Anglo-American jurisprudence that one is not bound by a judgment in personam in a litigation in which he is not designated as a party or to which he has not been made a party by service of process." Hansberry v. Lee, 311 U.S. 32, 40 (1940) [infra page 831]. Several exceptions, recognized in this Court's decisions, temper this basic rule. In a class action, for example, a person not named as a party may be bound by a judgment on the merits of the action, if she was adequately represented by a party who actively participated in the litigation. In this case, we consider for the first time whether there is a "virtual representation" exception to the general rule against precluding nonparties. Adopted by a number of courts, including the courts below in the case now before us, the exception so styled is broader than any we have so far approved. . . .

We disapprove the doctrine of preclusion by "virtual representation," and hold, based on the record as it now stands, that the judgment against Herrick does not bar Taylor from maintaining this suit.

I

The Freedom of Information Act (FOIA) accords "any person" a right to request any records held by a federal agency. 5 U.S.C. §552(a)(3)(A) (2006 ed.). No reason need be given for a FOIA request, and unless the requested materials fall within one of the Act's enumerated exemptions, see §552(a)(3)(E), (b), the agency must "make the records promptly available" to the requester, §552(a)(3)(A). If an agency refuses to furnish the requested records, the requester may file suit in federal court and obtain an injunction "order[ing] the production of any agency records improperly withheld." §552(a)(4)(B).

The courts below held the instant FOIA suit barred by the judgment in earlier litigation seeking the same records. Because the lower courts' decisions turned on the connection between the two lawsuits, we begin with a full account of each action.

A

The first suit was filed by Greg Herrick, an antique aircraft enthusiast and the owner of an F-45 airplane, a vintage model manufactured by the Fairchild Engine and Airplane Corporation (FEAC) in the 1930's. In 1997, seeking information that would help him restore his plane to its original condition, Herrick filed a FOIA request asking the Federal Aviation Administration (FAA) for copies of any technical documents about the F-45 contained in the agency's records.

To gain a certificate authorizing the manufacture and sale of the F-45, FEAC had submitted to the FAA's predecessor, the Civil Aeronautics Authority, detailed specifications and other technical data about the plane. Hundreds of pages of documents produced by FEAC in the certification process remain in the FAA's records. The FAA denied Herrick's request, however, upon finding that the documents he sought are subject to FOIA's exemption for "trade secrets and commercial or financial information obtained from a person and privileged or confidential," 5 U.S.C. §552(b)(4) (2006 ed.). . . .

[When Herrick filed suit,] the District Court granted summary judgment to the FAA [rejecting Herrick's argument that a 1955 letter from Fairchild to a government agency had waived any protection.] [T]he Tenth Circuit . . . affirmed. . . .

B

Less than a month later, on August 22, petitioner Brent Taylor—a friend of Herrick's and an antique aircraft enthusiast in his own right—submitted a FOIA request seeking the same documents Herrick had unsuccessfully sued to obtain. When the FAA failed to respond, Taylor filed a complaint in the U.S. District Court for the

District of Columbia. Like Herrick, Taylor argued that FEAC's 1955 letter had stripped the records of their trade-secret status. But Taylor also sought to litigate . . . two issues concerning recapture of protected status that Herrick had failed to raise in his appeal to the Tenth Circuit.

After Fairchild intervened as a defendant, the District Court in D.C. concluded that Taylor's suit was barred by claim preclusion; accordingly, it granted summary judgment to Fairchild and the FAA. . . .

The record before the District Court in Taylor's suit revealed the following facts about the relationship between Taylor and Herrick: Taylor is the president of the Antique Aircraft Association, an organization to which Herrick belongs; the two men are "close associate[s]"; Herrick asked Taylor to help restore Herrick's F-45, though they had no contract or agreement for Taylor's participation in the restoration; Taylor was represented by the lawyer who represented Herrick in the earlier litigation; and Herrick apparently gave Taylor documents that Herrick had obtained from the FAA during discovery in his suit. . . .

Applying this test to the record in Taylor's case, the D.C. Circuit found both of the necessary conditions for virtual representation well met. . . .

II

The preclusive effect of a federal-court judgment is determined by federal common law. See Semtek Int'l Inc. v. Lockheed Martin Corp., 531 U.S. 497, 507-508 (2001). For judgments in federal-question cases—for example, Herrick's FOIA suit—federal courts participate in developing "uniform federal rule[s]" of *res judicata*, which this Court has ultimate authority to determine and declare. Id. at 508.[3] The federal common law of preclusion is, of course, subject to due process limitations. See Richards v. Jefferson County, 517 U.S. 793, 797 (1996).

Taylor's case presents an issue of first impression in this sense: Until now, we have never addressed the doctrine of "virtual representation" adopted (in varying forms) by several Circuits and relied upon by the courts below. Our inquiry, however, is guided by well-established precedent regarding the propriety of nonparty preclusion. We review that precedent before taking up directly the issue of virtual representation.

A

The preclusive effect of a judgment is defined by claim preclusion and issue preclusion, which are collectively referred to as "*res judicata*."[4] . . . By "preclud[ing] parties from contesting matters that they have had a full and fair opportunity to litigate," these two doctrines protect against "the expense and vexation attending

3. For judgments in diversity cases, federal law incorporates the rules of preclusion applied by the State in which the rendering court sits. See Semtek Int'l Inc. v. Lockheed Martin Corp., 531 U.S. 497, 508 (2001).

4. These terms have replaced a more confusing lexicon. Claim preclusion describes the rules formerly known as "merger" and "bar," while issue preclusion encompasses the doctrines once known as "collateral estoppel" and "direct estoppel." See Migra v. Warren City School Dist. Bd. of Ed., 465 U.S. 75, 77, n.1 (1984).

multiple lawsuits, conserv[e] judicial resources, and foste[r] reliance on judicial action by minimizing the possibility of inconsistent decisions."

A person who was not a party to a suit generally has not had a "full and fair opportunity to litigate" the claims and issues settled in that suit. The application of claim and issue preclusion to nonparties thus runs up against the "deep-rooted historic tradition that everyone should have his own day in court." *Richards.* Indicating the strength of that tradition, we have often repeated the general rule that "one is not bound by a judgment in personam in a litigation in which he is not designated as a party or to which he has not been made a party by service of process." *Hansberry*; Martin v. Wilks, 490 U.S. 755, 761 (1989).

B

Though hardly in doubt, the rule against nonparty preclusion is subject to exceptions. For present purposes, the recognized exceptions can be grouped into six categories.[5] [The Court listed (1) agreement by the parties to be bound by a prior action; (2) preexisting "substantive legal relationships" (such as preceding and succeeding owners of property); (3) adequate representation by someone with the same interests who was a party (such as trustees, guardians, and other fiduciaries); (4) a party "assuming control" over prior litigation; (5) a party who loses an individual suit then sues again, this time as the representative of a class; and (6) special statutory schemes such as bankruptcy and probate proceedings, provided those proceedings comport with due process.]

III

Reaching beyond these six established categories, some lower courts have recognized a "virtual representation" exception to the rule against nonparty preclusion. Decisions of these courts, however, have been far from consistent. . . .

The D.C. Circuit, the FAA, and Fairchild have presented three arguments in support of an expansive doctrine of virtual representation. We find none of them persuasive.

A

The D.C. Circuit purported to ground its virtual representation doctrine in this Court's decisions stating that, in some circumstances, a person may be bound by a judgment if she was adequately represented by a party to the proceeding yielding that judgment. But the D.C. Circuit's definition of "adequate representation" strayed from the meaning our decisions have attributed to that term. . . .

---

5. The established grounds for nonparty preclusion could be organized differently. See, e.g., 1 & 2 Restatement (Second) of Judgments §§39-62 (1980) (hereinafter Restatement); D. Shapiro, Civil Procedure: Preclusion in Civil Actions 75-92 (2001); 18A C. Wright, A. Miller, & E. Cooper, Federal Practice and Procedure §4448, pp. 327-329 (2d ed. 2002) (hereinafter Wright & Miller). The list that follows is meant only to provide a framework for our consideration of virtual representation, not to establish a definitive taxonomy.

The D.C. Circuit misapprehended *Richards*. . . . [O]ur holding [in *Richards*] that the Alabama Supreme Court's application of *res judicata* to nonparties violated due process turned on the lack of either special procedures to protect the nonparties' interests or an understanding by the concerned parties that the first suit was brought in a representative capacity. . . .

B

Fairchild and the FAA do not argue that the D.C. Circuit's virtual representation doctrine fits within any of the recognized grounds for nonparty preclusion. Rather, they ask us to abandon the attempt to delineate discrete grounds and clear rules altogether. Preclusion is in order, they contend, whenever "the relationship between a party and a non-party is 'close enough' to bring the second litigant within the judgment." Courts should make the "close enough" determination, they urge, through a "heavily fact-driven" and "equitable" inquiry. . . .

We reject this argument for three reasons. First, our decisions emphasize the fundamental nature of the general rule that a litigant is not bound by a judgment to which she was not a party. . . .

Our second reason for rejecting a broad doctrine of virtual representation rests on the limitations attending nonparty preclusion based on adequate representation. A party's representation of a nonparty is "adequate" for preclusion purposes only if, at a minimum: (1) the interests of the nonparty and her representative are aligned, see *Hansberry*; and (2) either the party understood herself to be acting in a representative capacity or the original court took care to protect the interests of the nonparty, see *Richards*. In addition, adequate representation sometimes requires (3) notice of the original suit to the persons alleged to have been represented.[6] In the class-action context, these limitations are implemented by the procedural safeguards contained in Federal Rule of Civil Procedure 23.

An expansive doctrine of virtual representation, however, would "recogniz[e], in effect, a common-law kind of class action." That is, virtual representation would authorize preclusion based on identity of interests and some kind of relationship between parties and nonparties, shorn of the procedural protections prescribed in *Hansberry*, *Richards*, and Rule 23. These protections, grounded in due process, could be circumvented were we to approve a virtual representation doctrine that allowed courts to "create de facto class actions at will."

Third, a diffuse balancing approach to nonparty preclusion would likely create more headaches than it relieves. Most obviously, it could significantly complicate the task of district courts faced in the first instance with preclusion questions. An all-things-considered balancing approach might spark wide-ranging, time-consuming, and expensive discovery tracking factors potentially relevant under seven- or five-prong tests. . . .

---

6. *Richards* suggested that notice is required in some representative suits, *e.g.*, class actions seeking monetary relief. See 517 U.S., at 801 (citing Hansberry v. Lee, 311 U.S. 32 (1940), Eisen v. Carlisle & Jacquelin, 417 U.S. 156 (1974), and Mullane v. Central Hanover Bank & Trust Co., 339 U.S. 306, 319 (1950)). But we assumed without deciding that a lack of notice might be overcome in some circumstances. See *Richards*, 517 U.S., at 801.

C

Finally . . . the FAA maintains that nonparty preclusion should apply more broadly in "public-law" litigation than in "private-law" controversies. To support this position, the FAA offers two arguments. First, the FAA urges, our decision in *Richards* acknowledges that, in certain cases, the plaintiff has a reduced interest in controlling the litigation "because of the public nature of the right at issue." . . .

[W]e said in *Richards* only that, for the type of public-law claims there envisioned, [state and federal legislatures] are free to adopt procedures limiting repetitive litigation [involving public rights]. . . . It hardly follows, however, that this Court should proscribe or confine successive FOIA suits by different requesters. Indeed, Congress' provision for FOIA suits with no statutory constraint on successive actions counsels against judicial imposition of constraints through extraordinary application of the common law of preclusion.

The FAA next argues that "the threat of vexatious litigation is heightened" in public-law cases because "the number of plaintiffs with standing is potentially limitless." . . .

But we are not convinced that this risk justifies departure from the usual rules governing nonparty preclusion. First, *stare decisis* will allow courts swiftly to dispose of repetitive suits brought in the same circuit. Second, even when *stare decisis* is not dispositive, "the human tendency not to waste money will deter the bringing of suits based on claims or issues that have already been adversely determined against others." This intuition seems to be borne out by experience: The FAA has not called our attention to any instances of abusive FOIA suits in the Circuits that reject the virtual-representation theory respondents advocate here.

IV

For the foregoing reasons, we disapprove the theory of virtual representation on which the decision below rested. The preclusive effects of a judgment in a federal-question case decided by a federal court should instead be determined according to the established grounds for nonparty preclusion described in this opinion. . . .

We now turn back to Taylor's action to determine whether his suit is such a case, or whether the result reached by the courts below can be justified on one of the recognized grounds for nonparty preclusion.

A

It is uncontested that four of the six grounds for nonparty preclusion have no application here. . . .

That leaves only the fifth category: preclusion because a nonparty to an earlier litigation has brought suit as a representative or agent of a party who is bound by the prior adjudication. Taylor is not Herrick's legal representative and he has not purported to sue in a representative capacity. He concedes, however, that preclusion would be appropriate if respondents could demonstrate that he is acting as Herrick's "undisclosed agen[t]." . . .

We therefore remand to give the courts below an opportunity to determine whether Taylor, in pursuing the instant FOIA suit, is acting as Herrick's agent. Taylor concedes that such a remand is appropriate. . . .

* * *

For the reasons stated, the judgment of the United States Court of Appeals for the District of Columbia Circuit is vacated, and the case is remanded for further proceedings consistent with this opinion.

It is so ordered.

WHAT'S NEW HERE?

- The U.S. Supreme Court says the doctrine of "virtual representation" is a nonstarter in the federal courts except in well-defined circumstances.

Notes and Problems

1. The doctrine of virtual representation takes a hit in *Taylor*. What kind of hit?

   a. Suppose Landowner sues Alleged Trespasser for using a path across his land; Trespasser defends, alleging a prescriptive easement—and wins. When Landowner subsequently sells the property, Buyer wants to know if he will be burdened by the same prescriptive easement. In the past a number of courts have said yes, citing as an explanation the doctrine of virtual representation—that Buyer was "virtually represented" by Landowner. Does *Taylor* change that outcome?

   b. Minor is injured in an accident and sues Defendant through an appointed guardian ad litem. Minor loses. When Minor becomes an adult can he, assuming the statute of limitations has not run, institute a new suit against Defendant for the same injuries? In the past, courts have said no, citing virtual representation. Does *Taylor* change that outcome?

2. Consider the source of law in *Taylor*.

   a. *Taylor* is not a case like *Frier v. City of Vandalia* (supra page 705), in which the federal court was trying to apply the state's law of preclusion. This is a federal claim, and some variety of federal law will therefore govern.

   b. The Court explains that it is guided in its analysis by the federal common law of preclusion as well as the Due Process Clause.

3. In several cases, the U.S. Supreme Court has held that the Due Process Clause does in fact place limits on state courts' use of virtual representation. An earlier case cited in *Taylor*, *Richards v. Jefferson County*, 517 U.S. 793 (1996), arose

from an Alabama county's imposition of an "occupation tax" to finance construction of a new civic center. Several lawsuits challenging the legality of the tax were filed. The first of these, Bedingfield v. Jefferson County, 520 So. 2d 1270 (Ala. 1988), went to the Alabama Supreme Court, which upheld the tax. When Richards filed a separate action, raising federal law challenges to the tax, the Alabama Supreme Court held "that the federal claims as well as the state claims were barred by the adjudication in *Bedingfield* . . . [because a] judgment is generally '*res judicata* not only as to all matters litigated and decided by it, but as to all relevant issues which could have been but were not raised and litigated in the suit,'" (quoting Jefferson County v. Richards, 662 So. 2d 1127 (Ala. 1995)).

a. As a quick review, explain why the Alabama Supreme Court was on solid ground in this part of its ruling. Which case in this chapter is most squarely on point?

b. Even though the Alabama Supreme Court was entirely conventional in its statement of claim preclusion doctrine, the U.S. Supreme Court reversed. It did so because Alabama had applied claim preclusion not to the original parties in the suit but to new parties on the grounds that there was "substantial identity of the parties" in the first and second lawsuits.

> State courts are generally free to develop their own rules for protecting against the relitigation of common issues or the piecemeal resolution of disputes. We have long held, however, that extreme applications of the doctrine of *res judicata* may be inconsistent with a federal right that is "fundamental in character." . . .
>
> The limits on a state court's power to develop estoppel rules reflect the general consensus "'in Anglo-American jurisprudence that one is not bound by a judgment in personam in a litigation in which he is not designated as a party or to which he has not been made a party by service of process.' *Hansberry v. Lee* [infra page 831]. . . . This rule is part of our 'deep-rooted historic tradition that everyone should have his own day in court.'" *Martin v. Wilks* [infra page 819]. . . .
>
> Of course, these principles do not always require one to have been a party to a judgment in order to be bound by it. Most notably, there is an exception when it can be said that there is "privity" between a party to the second case and a party who is bound by an earlier judgment. For example, a judgment that is binding on a guardian or trustee may also bind the ward or the beneficiaries of a trust. Moreover . . . the term "privity" is now used to describe various relationships between litigants that would not have come within the traditional definition of that term. See generally Restatement (Second) of Judgments, ch. 4 (1980). . . . [The Court said the procedure followed in this case did not satisfy the conditions for "privity."]
>
> We begin by noting that the parties to the *Bedingfield* case failed to provide petitioners with any notice that a suit was pending which would conclusively resolve their legal rights. That failure is troubling because, as we explained in *Mullane v. Central Hanover Bank & Trust Co.* [supra page 165], the right to be heard ensured by the guarantee of due process "has little reality or worth unless one is informed that the matter is pending and can choose for himself whether to appear or default, acquiesce or contest." . . .
>
> Nevertheless, respondents ask us to excuse the lack of notice on the ground that petitioners, as the Alabama Supreme Court concluded, were adequately represented in *Bedingfield*. . . .

. . . [O]ur opinion in *Hansberry* . . . explained that a prior proceeding, to have binding effect on absent parties, would at least have to be "so devised and applied as to insure that those present are of the same class as those absent and that the litigation is so conducted as to insure the full and fair consideration of the common issue." It is plain that the *Bedingfield* action . . . does not fit such a description. . . .

. . . [T]here is no reason to suppose that the *Bedingfield* court took care to protect the interests of petitioners in the manner suggested in *Hansberry*. Nor is there any reason to suppose that the individual taxpayers in *Bedingfield* understood their suit to be on behalf of absent county taxpayers. Thus, to contend that the plaintiffs in *Bedingfield* somehow represented petitioners, let alone represented them in a constitutionally adequate manner, would be "to attribute to them a power that it cannot be said that they had assumed to exercise." *Hansberry*. . . .

Of course, we are aware that governmental and private entities have substantial interests in the prompt and determinative resolution of challenges to important legislation. We do not agree with the Alabama Supreme Court, however, that, given the amount of money at stake, respondents were entitled to rely on the assumption that the *Bedingfield* action "authoritatively established" the constitutionality of the tax. A state court's freedom to rely on prior precedent in rejecting a litigant's claims does not afford it similar freedom to bind a litigant to a prior judgment to which he was not a party. That general rule clearly applies when a taxpayer seeks a hearing to prevent the State from subjecting him to a levy in violation of the Federal Constitution.

Id. at 797-805.

c. Notice that, although the *Richards* Court was applying the Due Process Clause, rather than the common law of preclusion, its concerns and its language sound remarkably like *Taylor v. Sturgell*. It may be helpful to imagine that when a judge or justice thinks about applying preclusion to someone not a party to the prior lawsuit, the judge imagines that the Due Process Clause is peering over her shoulder as she shapes the common law of preclusion.

Implications

PRECLUSION AND PRECEDENT

The *Taylor v. Sturgell* opinion in passing distinguishes *stare decisis* from virtual representation or other forms of preclusion. Just what is the distinction?

Even though the Court holds that Taylor was not "virtually represented" in the previous law- suit, the FAA and Fairchild will be free to argue on remand that the Tenth Circuit has just decided a closely related case and that the D.C. Circuit should be persuaded by the Tenth Circuit's analysis of the Freedom of Information Act as applied to the design specifications for this aircraft.

What's the difference between such an application of precedent (also called *stare decisis*) and the position for which the FAA and Fairchild were arguing? Virtual representation (and claim preclusion) would entirely bar Taylor's claim. By contrast, the doctrine of precedent allows Taylor to argue that his case is distinguishable from the Tenth Circuit case or that the Tenth Circuit was simply wrong in interpreting the law.

The Court addresses the distinction just drawn when the opinion notes "'the human tendency not to waste money will deter the bringing of suits based on claims or issues that have already been adversely determined against others.' This intuition seems to be borne out by experience: The FAA has not called our attention to any instances of abusive FOIA suits in the Circuits that reject the virtual-representation theory respondents advocate here." Explain why this passage addresses the difference between preclusion and precedent.

4. Apply *Taylor* and *Richards* to the following case. A divorcing Utah couple, Edlean and Woodey Searle, were litigating the division of marital property. One asset was a second home known as Slaugh House. Woodey, the husband, contended that the property was not in fact entirely a marital asset, claiming that he and the couple's two sons, Randy and Rhett, held Slaugh House as a partnership—though there was no document recording that co-ownership. Randy and Rhett testified at trial in support of Woodey's contention concerning the partnership, but the trial court was not persuaded, and divided the property as if it had been wholly owned by the couple. After the divorce was final, Randy and Rhett sued their mother, contending—again—that the property was partly theirs because they owned it in partnership with their father. Edlean argued that her sons' lawsuit was barred, because they had been "virtually represented" by Woodey in the divorce litigation.

   a. The case came before the Utah Supreme Court. Searle Bros. v. Searle, 588 P.2d 689 (Utah 1978). Applying the teachings of *Taylor v. Sturgell,* how, as a matter of the common law of virtual representation, should the case have been decided?

   b. If the Utah Supreme Court had decided that the brothers' claim had been precluded as a result of virtual representation, consider how they could have framed an appeal to the U.S. Supreme Court; what case should their petition for certiorari have cited prominently?

3. After a Final Judgment

Courts and treatises sometimes say that claim preclusion requires a prior final judgment. Like the proposition that claim preclusion applies only between the same parties, courts do not literally interpret the final judgment requirement. For example, some administrative determinations may be entitled to claim-preclusion effect if the procedure employed contains sufficient due process protections.

More important is the effect of an appeal on a judgment's status. The usual rule is that a judgment is final even though an appeal is pending. What should be done if a judgment is given claim-preclusive effect and then reversed on appeal? Some courts solve the problem by postponing the decision on claim preclusion until the appeal is resolved. For another approach see Rule 60(b)(5), which lists among the grounds for reopening a judgment that "it is based on an earlier judgment that has been reversed or vacated."

4. After a Judgment "on the Merits"

Not all final judgments, even though they involve the same claim and the same parties, receive preclusive effect. All agree that a judgment after a full trial is undoubtedly entitled to preclusive effect. Short of that, however, when ought preclusive effect to attach? The problem is difficult because courts might want to assign preclusive effect to a judgment for two quite different reasons. One reason, of course, is that the court considered and decided the merits of the lawsuit. A different reason would be that the party had misbehaved (for example, refused to obey court orders) and the court dismissed the suit as a sanction. Such a dismissal would have nothing to do with the merits of the complaint, but the sanction would be futile unless it barred the refiling of the suit. Unfortunately, courts sometimes discuss this problem by stating that preclusive effect ought to attach only to judgments "on the merits." Like "in privity," this phrase conceals more than it explains, because it begs the real question: For what reasons and under what circumstances should we attach preclusive effect to a judgment? In studying this question, try to put the deceptive "on the merits" phrase out of your mind.

Notes and Problems

---

1. As a matter of principle, which of the following stages of litigation ought to preclude filing of a second suit by the same party on the same claim?

   a. Full jury trial.
   b. Judgment as a matter of law (i.e., a directed verdict or j.n.o.v.).
   c. Summary judgment.
   d. Dismissal after a Rule 12(b)(6) motion for failure to state a claim.
   e. Dismissal after a Rule 12(b)(2) motion for want of personal jurisdiction.
   f. Dismissal for failure to prosecute.

2. Chapters 2 and 3 should have hinted at the answer to 1e: dismissal for want of jurisdiction does *not* result in claim preclusion. A case dismissed because a court lacked personal jurisdiction can be brought in a different state that has jurisdiction over the defendant. Similarly, a case dismissed because a federal court lacks subject matter jurisdiction can be brought in a state court.

WHAT'S NEW HERE?

So far this chapter has dealt with preclusion instances in which the first lawsuit ended in a trial on the merits (or something very close to that).
● Now we're looking at situations in which courts attach preclusive effect to something less—maybe far less—than a trial. What's the logic behind that?

3. How did you answer Problem 1d? This problem—how to treat a judgment following a dismissal for failure to state a claim upon which relief can be granted under Rule 12(b)(6)—presents an issue that calls one's entire understanding of procedure into question. On the one hand, such a dismissal can be for essentially formal reasons: The plaintiff's lawyer forgot that one must allege an agreement as part of a breach of contract suit. If the underlying facts suggest an agreement, it seems unjust to preclude when a sentence added to the pleading would have cured the problem. On the other hand, if the plaintiff's lawyer has alleged all that can truthfully be alleged and the complaint is still dismissed, isn't that a statement about the merits of a claim?

    a. One might think that one reason to treat Rule 12(b)(6) dismissals as preclusive flows from the ease of amending pleadings. It is axiomatic that a trial court should not dismiss a pleading for failure to state a claim without granting plaintiff at least one opportunity to amend; a trial court's dismissal without leave to amend would be strong grounds for reversal. Suppose plaintiff does amend, and the trial court nevertheless dismisses the amended complaint. Is the opportunity to amend—after being instructed by the trial court what was wrong with the original complaint—a sufficient assurance that plaintiff has stated any possible claim, and therefore justification for assigning preclusive effect? In Federated Department Stores v. Moitie, 452 U.S. 394 (1981), the Supreme Court apparently accepted such reasoning, in a footnote that, in its entirety, reads: "The dismissal for failure to state a claim under Fed. Rule Civ. Proc. 12(b)(6) is a 'judgment on the merits.'" Id. at 399 n.3. The statement was necessary to the decision of the case and is thus a holding, but the Court did not explain its justification for this conclusion.

    b. Not all states follow the same rule. For example, see In re Estate of Cochrane, 72 Ill. App. 3d 812, 391 N.E.2d 35 (1979) (under Illinois procedural law, dismissal for failure to plead enough facts to state a claim does not bar a second suit with the necessary facts added; presumably it would bar bringing a suit based on an identically worded complaint); Keidatz v. Albany, 39 Cal. 2d 826, 249 P.2d 264 (1952) (dismissal on demurrer bars subsequent action on complaint alleging same facts but does not bar claim raising new issues or new facts in support of same claim). Is it possible to decide which rule is preferable without taking into account the pleading regime of the jurisdiction in question? Recall that after *Semtek Intl. Inc. v. Lockheed Martin Corp.* (supra page 713) the judgment of a federal court sitting in diversity jurisdiction will be the same as that of a state court in that state. Thus a federal diversity judgment by a federal court in Illinois or California would get the same scope as a state court judgment—so that the federal judgment would not preclude a second complaint on the same claim, properly alleged.

c. Should the federal courts continue to follow *Moitie* (finding that a Rule 12(b)(6) dismissal is a final judgment on the merits for claim preclusion purposes) in the wake of *Ashcroft v. Iqbal* (supra page 385)?

  i. You will recall that *Iqbal* tightened federal pleading standards, saying that in considering a 12(b)(6) motion a court should ignore all conclusory allegations in the complaint and should dismiss unless the remaining statements considered "in the light of judicial experience and common sense" appeared to be "plausible."

  ii. Suppose a federal district court, applying that standard rigorously, grants a 12(b)(6) motion to dismiss. Thereafter, before the relevant statute of limitations has run, new information comes to light that enables the plaintiff to plead with greater particularity and to avoid conclusory statements. *Moitie* says the claim should be barred; can you construct an argument that this result should be different after *Iqbal*?

d. The next case tries to extract itself from the quicksand of the opposite situation: a *state court* dismissal of a claim for noncompliance with discovery, with the added feature that the claim dismissed ought not to have been in state court in the first place. A bit of background: Congress has given the federal courts exclusive jurisdiction over federal securities fraud claims. If such a claim is filed in state court, the state court should therefore dismiss it. Apparently neither the state judge nor the parties appearing before him knew that principle, and the resulting mess came before the Sixth Circuit to be sorted out.

Gargallo v. Merrill Lynch, Pierce, Fenner & Smith

918 F.2d 658 (6th Cir. 1990)

RYAN, J.

This case presents the interesting dual questions 1) whether a federal court must apply federal or state claim preclusion law in deciding 2) whether a prior state court judgment upon subject matter over which only a federal court has jurisdiction is a bar to a subsequent federal court claim upon the identical cause of action. . . . The district court dismissed the suit below on grounds of *res judicata* as to Merrill Lynch. . . .

I

Miguel Gargallo opened a "margin brokerage account" with Merrill Lynch in 1976. He maintained the account until 1980, when his investments apparently went awry and losses occurred, resulting in a debt of some $17,000 owed to Merrill Lynch. . . . When the obligation was not paid, the brokerage firm filed suit for collection in the

Court of Common Pleas, Franklin County, Ohio. In response, Mr. Gargallo filed an answer and counterclaim against Merrill Lynch, alleging that Merrill Lynch caused his losses through "negligence, misrepresentations, and churning," and that the firm had violated . . . federal securities laws. After a considerable history of discovery difficulties, the state court dismissed Mr. Gargallo's counterclaim "with prejudice," citing Ohio Civil Rule 37 [substantially identical to Federal Rule 37], for refusal to comply with Merrill Lynch's discovery requests and the court's discovery orders. . . .

Mr. Gargallo . . . then filed a complaint in the United States District Court, Southern District of Ohio, charging Merrill Lynch and its account executive, Larry Tyree, with violating [federal securities laws] . . . based on the same transactions at issue in the state litigation. After preparing a thoughtful written opinion, the district court dismissed the suit against Merrill Lynch on *res judicata* grounds, finding that the "issues, facts and evidence to sustain this action are identical to the claims asserted [against the brokerage firm] in [Mr. Gargallo's] counterclaim that was dismissed with prejudice by the state court." This appeal followed.

II

There is no dispute in this case about the essential facts relating to the summary judgment, and the ultimate issue is: whether the district court correctly dismissed the plaintiff's claims on *res judicata* . . . grounds. . . .

A. Claim Preclusion

The federal securities law violations asserted against Merrill Lynch . . . in this litigation are the same, for all practical purposes, as those Mr. Gargallo previously asserted in the counterclaim he filed in the Franklin County court. For reasons we shall discuss shortly, Ohio claim preclusion law ultimately determines the outcome of this case. Consequently, we must decide whether the Franklin County court judgment dismissing Mr. Gargallo's first lawsuit would operate as a bar, under Ohio claim preclusion rules, to the action brought in the district court, now under review, had it been brought in an Ohio court. . . .

In Ohio, the requirements for application of the doctrine of claim preclusion, or *res judicata* as the earlier Ohio court termed it, are the same as those applicable in a federal court:

> The doctrine of *res judicata* is that an existing final judgment rendered upon the merits, without fraud or collusion, by a court of competent jurisdiction, is conclusive of rights, questions and facts in issue, as to the parties and their privies, in all other actions in the same or any other judicial tribunal of concurrent jurisdiction.

Norwood v. McDonald, 142 Ohio St. 299, 305, 52 N.E.2d 67, 71 (1943).

Under Ohio law, the dismissal with prejudice of Mr. Gargallo's Common Pleas Court counterclaim for noncompliance with Ohio's Civil Rule 37 was a "final judgment rendered upon the merits."

. . . We agree with the district court that the "issues, facts, and evidence to sustain this action are identical to the claims asserted . . . in [plaintiff's state] counterclaim," and we are satisfied that the federal claim or cause of action giving rise to this appeal is the same claim or cause of action that was asserted in the counterclaim dismissed in the state court litigation.

Thus, we have no question that, absent any regard for subject matter jurisdiction, Ohio claim preclusion law would bar the claim asserted in Mr. Gargallo's district court complaint had it been filed in an Ohio court.

B. Federal Exclusivity

However, the district court in which plaintiff brought his claim is not an Ohio court but a federal tribunal. Consequently, we are faced with the more difficult issue of whether a federal district court may give claim preclusive effect to an Ohio judgment regarding federal securities laws that are within the exclusive jurisdiction of the federal courts. The first rule in determining whether a prior state court judgment has preclusive effect in a federal court is that the full faith and credit statute, 28 U.S.C. §1738,[3] requires a federal court to give a state court judgment the same preclusive effect such judgment would have in a state court. . . . And the rule is no less applicable in a case in which the state court was without jurisdiction to entertain the exclusively federal claim it adjudicated. . . .

Marrese v. [American] Academy of Orthopaedic Surgeons, 470 U.S. 373 (1985) . . . requires . . . that a federal court must determine whether to give claim preclusive effect to a state court judgment upon a cause of action over which the state court had no subject matter jurisdiction by determining whether the state court would give preclusive effect to such a judgment. . . .

Ohio appears to subscribe to the Restatement (Second) of Judgments position that a judgment rendered by a court lacking subject matter jurisdiction ought not be given preclusive effect. Addressing whether an Ohio judgment in an action commenced after expiration of the applicable limitations period was entitled to claim preclusive effect, the Ohio Supreme Court stated:

> It is not contended that the judgment in the prior action [in this case] was void because of some defect relating to the jurisdiction of either court therein, *in which case the judgment could not operate as an estoppel as to a particular fact or issue; nor could it operate as* res judicata *as to a cause of action.*

LaBarbera v. Batsch, 227 N.E.2d 55, 59 (1967) (citing Horovitz v. Shafer, 94 N.E.2d 201 (1950)) (emphasis added).

It seems clear, therefore, that in Ohio a final judgment by a court of that state, upon a cause of action over which the adjudicating court had no subject matter jurisdiction, does not have claim preclusive effect in any subsequent proceedings. . . .

In summary, we hold that the Ohio court judgment, dismissing, with prejudice, Mr. Gargallo's federal securities law claims against Merrill Lynch . . . may not be given claim preclusive effect in a subsequent federal court action asserting those same

---

3. In pertinent part, 28 U.S.C. §1738 provides that "the Acts of the legislature of any State, Territory, or Possession of the United States" and "the records and judicial proceedings of any court of any such State, Territory or Possession . . . shall have the same full faith and credit in every court within the United States and its Territories and Possessions as they have by law or usage in the courts of such State, Territory or Possession from which they are taken."

claims because Ohio courts would not give claim preclusive effect to a prior final judgment upon a cause of action over which the Ohio court had no subject matter jurisdiction. . . .

[Reversed and remanded.]

Notes and Problems

---

1. *Gargallo* has two aspects: (1) whether the original dismissal was "on the merits" for purposes of claim preclusion; and (2) how the jurisdictional defect in the first proceeding ought to affect claim preclusion.

2. Start with the first aspect. Cases like *Gargallo* are easier to understand if one does not become distracted by the misleading phrase "on the merits."

   a. Explain why it is fair—and probably necessary—to assign preclusive effect to the dismissal for failure to comply with discovery orders.

   b. Explain why it is fair to do so although no one in his right mind would say that the prior suit determined the merits of Gargallo's claim in the ordinary sense of that phrase.

3. To understand the force of the principle illustrated in *Gargallo*, suppose that Mr. Gargallo had not waited to be sued by his brokerage and had instead brought his federal securities claims against Merrill Lynch in a federal court. Further imagine that Mr. Gargallo had been uncooperative in discovery in federal court and suffered a dismissal under Rules 37 and 41 for failure to comply with discovery orders. Now suppose he refiled that suit in federal court—what result?

4. Turn now to the jurisdictional defect in Gargallo's state court counterclaim. The principle that federal courts have exclusive jurisdiction over federal securities claims has been clearly established for more than half a century. Gargallo should not have brought this claim in state court. When he did, Merrill Lynch's lawyer should have challenged it promptly. Or the state court should have dismissed the counterclaim on its own motion for lack of jurisdiction. When all the dust has settled, Gargallo's securities claim is in federal court—where it should have been in the first place. Given the multiple failures to apply well-established law, does the result in this case make sense?

B. ISSUE PRECLUSION

Issue preclusion has narrower but deeper bite than claim preclusion. If the conditions for claim preclusion are met, a party will find all her contentions barred from relitigation—those she actually advanced in the first case as well as those that she did not advance. The preclusive effect, however, extends at most to claims that are part of the same transaction. By contrast, issue preclusion bars from relitigation only those issues actually litigated and determined. But they will be barred from relitigation in all subsequent claims between the parties regardless of whether they concern the same transaction—and, according to recent doctrine, in some claims that do not involve both parties.

The black letter of issue preclusion is simple: When

1. an issue of fact or law is
2. actually litigated and determined by
3. a valid and final judgment, and
4. the determination is essential to the judgment,

the determination is conclusive in a subsequent action between the parties, whether on the same or a different claim. Restatement (Second) of Judgments §27.

As you will see, case law has added a fifth requirement: that the party burdened with issue preclusion have had an "adequate opportunity and incentive" to litigate the issue in the earlier proceeding.

Each of these five conditions involves some difficulties that we will examine in turn. We will first look briefly at what it means for an issue to be the same in successive cases. Second comes an exploration of the boundaries between issue and claim preclusion and an effort to define the conditions under which one can say that an issue has been "actually litigated and determined." Then we examine the meaning of "essential to the judgment." Then we turn to a body of doctrine that severely limits a longstanding requirement—that the subsequent case be "between the [same] parties." Finally, as a continuing theme in these cases, we will explore what it means to have an adequate opportunity and incentive to litigate an issue.

WHAT'S NEW HERE?

- We've stopped talking about precluding entire claims.
- In this section, the cases all assume that the claim in the second case can be brought, but that some *issue* embedded in the new claim may be precluded as a result of prior litigation.

1. The Same Issue

A threshold question in all issue-preclusion cases is the nature of the issue to be precluded. Sometimes the analysis of that question will be easy. For example, suppose the United States sues Student civilly, seeking nonpayment of two student loans, both signed on the same day and containing an identical, allegedly fraudulent statement regarding Student's assets. Student defends on the grounds that the statements in the loan documents are true. If Student loses the first lawsuit, the fraudulence of the statement in question will be precluded in a second suit as well.

But matters can be subtler. Suppose that the government prevails in the student loan lawsuits, establishing fraudulent misstatements. The United States then prosecutes Student criminally, basing its charge on the proposition that Student obtained the loans fraudulently. Student defends on grounds that the statements are true. Does the government's previous victory in the civil lawsuit preclude Student from his defense? No: Civil and criminal proceedings operate under different burdens of proof. To prevail, as the government did, on a civil burden of preponderance of the evidence* does not mean that one can establish the same issue beyond a reasonable doubt. One must, then, build into one's definition of the "issue" not only its substantive contours but also the procedural conditions under which it was determined.

And, of course, be aware that in this area, as in many areas of law, the same word or phrase can shift meanings in different contexts. For example, many state universities charge different rates of tuition to "resident" students and others. But the fact that you are a "resident" of a state for tuition purposes may not establish your residence for purposes, say, of diversity jurisdiction.

Notes and Problems

1. The federal government criminally prosecutes an IRS agent, accusing her of stealing tax revenues. She is acquitted. The government then sues Agent in a civil suit to recover funds allegedly embezzled in the same criminal acts. Agent seeks to invoke preclusion on the grounds that the previous case demonstrates the acts did not occur. Preclusion?

2. Reverse the order of the civil and criminal actions in the preceding problem. Suppose the civil action came first, and the government prevailed, winning a judgment against Agent on the ground that she had embezzled funds. The government now prosecutes Agent criminally, charging her with the same acts of embezzlement. Why doesn't the first case preclude Agent from relitigating the question of embezzlement?

3. Suppose in Problem 1 Agent had been convicted in the criminal prosecution. In the subsequent civil case could the government take advantage of preclusion against Agent?

2. An Issue "Actually Litigated and Determined"

Even if one concludes that the issue at stake in the first and second lawsuits is identical, one must ask a further question: Was that issue actually litigated and determined in the first case? Unlike claim preclusion, in which an unlitigated theory—like Frier's due process claim—can be precluded, issue preclusion insists that the issue to be precluded actually have been litigated and decided in the prior

---

* Or, as some jurisdictions require it for fraud, by "clear and convincing" evidence.

case. For example, in *Gargallo v. Merrill Lynch et al.,* supra page 732, when Larry Tyree, the Merrill Lynch stockbroker sued by Gargallo, sought to use the issues established in the first suit against Gargallo in the second, federal suit, the court's answer was swift and clear:

> With respect to the summary judgment in favor of Larry Tyree, since Mr. Gargallo's counter claim was dismissed in the state court as a sanction for discovery violations, none of the factual or legal issues he raised were actually litigated and decided. Consequently, the doctrine of collateral estoppel, or issue preclusion, is not applicable.
>
> Gargallo v. Merrill Lynch et al., 918 F.2d 658, 664 (6th Cir. 1990).

The answer is not always so easy, as the next case illustrates. One preliminary note may help. At one time many states treated negligence by the plaintiff as not simply reducing the amount of defendant's liability, but as a complete defense to any recovery: Against a plaintiff asserting negligence, "contributory negligence" was a complete bar to recovery—as in the next case.

Illinois Central Gulf Railroad v. Parks
181 Ind. App. 141, 390 N.E.2d 1078 (1979)

LYBROOK, J.

[Jessie and Bertha Parks were injured when a car driven by Jessie in which Bertha was a passenger collided with an Illinois Central train. Bertha and Jessie sued Illinois Central; Bertha sought compensation for her injuries, and Jessie sought damages for loss of Bertha's services and consortium. Bertha recovered a $30,000 judgment on her claim, and judgment was rendered for Illinois Central on Jessie's claim.

Jessie then sued Illinois Central for his own injuries. On Illinois Central's motion for summary judgment, the trial court held that Jessie's claim was not barred by claim preclusion and that the prior action did not preclude Jessie on the issue of contributory negligence. Illinois Central appealed the interlocutory order pursuant to the trial court's certification of the appeal under state law.]

... Illinois Central Gulf's first allegation of error is an attempt to apply estoppel by judgment [the court's term for claim preclusion] in the case at bar, but the railroad concedes its own argument by admitting that Jessie's cause of action for loss of services and consortium as a derivative of Bertha's personal injuries is a distinct cause of action from Jessie's claim for damages for his own personal injuries.

Estoppel by judgment precludes the relitigation of a *cause of action* finally determined between the parties, and decrees that a judgment rendered is a complete bar to any subsequent action on *the same claim or cause of action.* Jessie's cause of action in the case at bar is a different cause of action from the one he litigated in the companion case; therefore, estoppel by judgment does not apply.

Estoppel by verdict [the court's term for issue preclusion], however, does apply. Using Judge Shake's terminology, the causes of action are not the same but, if the case at bar were to go to trial on all the issues raised in the pleadings and answer, some facts or questions determined and adjudicated in the companion case would again be put in issue in this subsequent action between the same parties.

To protect the integrity of the prior judgment by precluding the possibility of opposite results by two different juries on the same set of facts, the doctrine of estoppel by verdict allows the judgment in the prior action to operate as an estoppel as to those facts or questions actually litigated and determined in the prior action. The problem at hand, then, is to determine what facts or questions were actually litigated and determined in the companion case.

We agree with three concessions made by Illinois Central Gulf as to the effect of the verdict in the prior case: (1) that the verdict in favor of Bertha established, among other things, that the railroad was negligent and that its negligence was a proximate cause of the accident and Bertha's injuries; (2) that, inasmuch as Jessie's action for loss of services and consortium was derivative, if Jessie sustained any such loss it was proximately caused by the railroad's negligence; and (3) that, in order for the jury to have returned a verdict against Jessie, it had to have decided that he either sustained no damages or that his own negligence was a proximate cause of his damages.

This third proposition places upon the railroad the heavy burden outlined by Judge Shake in [Flora v. Indiana Service Co., 222 Ind. App. 253, 256-57 (1944)]:

> . . . [W]here a judgment may have been based upon either or any of two or more distinct facts, a party desiring to plead the judgment as an estoppel by verdict or finding upon the particular fact involved in a subsequent suit must show that it went upon that fact, or else the question will be open to a new contention. The estoppel of a judgment is only presumptively conclusive, when it appears that the judgment could not have been rendered without deciding the particular matter brought in question. It is necessary to look to the complete record to ascertain what was the question in issue.

The railroad argues that, because Jessie's evidence as to his loss of services and consortium was uncontroverted, the jury's verdict had to be based upon a finding of contributory negligence. Illinois Central Gulf made this same argument in the companion case[*] in relation to a related issue and Jessie countered, as he does here, with his contention that, although the evidence was uncontroverted, it was minimal and, thus, could have caused the jury to find no compensable damages. We reviewed the complete record in the companion case and held that the jury verdict against Jessie in that cause could mean that he had failed his burden of proving compensable damages. . . .

We hold that Illinois Central Gulf has failed its burden of showing that the judgment against Jessie in the prior action could not have been rendered without deciding that Jessie was contributorily negligent in the accident which precipitated the two

---

* [The appeal from the first suit, in which Bertha had recovered for her injuries.—EDS.]

lawsuits. Consequently, the trial court was correct in granting partial summary judgment estopping the railroad from denying its negligence and in limiting the issues at trial to whether Jessie was contributorily negligent, whether any such contributory negligence was a proximate cause of the accident, and whether Jessie sustained personal injuries and compensable damages. . . .

Notes and Problems

---

1. Though it does not dwell on this point, *Parks* serves as a fine vehicle for distinguishing between claim and issue preclusion.

    a. If one had just completed study of the preceding section on claim preclusion and were told the facts in the first lawsuit (*Bertha and Jessie v. Railroad*) and were further told that the railroad asserted a defense of former adjudication in the second suit, what would one expect that defense to be?

    b. Why wasn't Jessie's claim precluded? Because Indiana applies a definition of claim preclusion narrower than that set forth in Restatement (Second) of Judgments §24, supra page 710. See also Afolabi v. Atl. Mortg. & Inv. Corp., 849 N.E.2d 1170 (Ind. Ct. App 2006) (applying the "same evidence" test). So, in Indiana, Jessie's personal injury claim survived, even though it was related to his prior claim for loss of consortium.

2. Now focus on why Jessie was not precluded from relitigating the issue of his contributory negligence in the second lawsuit. Why did the court reject the railroad's contention that the jury's verdict demonstrated that Jesse was contributorily negligent?

    a. Isn't it plausible—even likely—that the jury decided that Jessie was contributorily negligent? So why doesn't the court so conclude?

    b. How else could the jury have reached its verdict in the first suit?

3. Assume that Illinois Central had not asserted Jessie's contributory negligence in the first action. Would Illinois Central be precluded from asserting it when Jessie sued for his own injuries? Most courts would say no. Unlike claim preclusion, under which claims are barred even if not raised, issue preclusion only applies to issues actually decided in the prior action. Why, so long as it's not the same claim, is it fair to preclude only those issues in the previous suit that were actually litigated?

4. Should a litigant be allowed to use evidence extrinsic to the record to establish what issues were actually determined in the previous litigation? The answer is yes, according to Restatement (Second) of Judgments §27 comment f. What kind of extrinsic evidence would be useful to show which issues were determined by previous litigation?

Implications

WHAT IS THE PURPOSE OF ISSUE PRECLUSION?

As a typical opinion explains, "[a]pplication of the doctrine of [issue preclusion] represents a decision that the needs of judicial finality and efficiency outweigh the possible gains of fairness or accuracy from continued litigation of an issue that previously has been considered by a competent tribunal." Nasem v. Brown, 595 F.2d 801 (D.C. Cir. 1979).

Efficiency? Maybe it saves time not to relitigate an issue, but against that one has to count the time figuring out whether issue preclusion should apply.

Consider another explanation: Professor Martin Shapiro has argued that "it must always

be remembered that the basic aim of a trial is to resolve a conflict or to impose social controls, not to find the facts. Much of what may appear to be unsatisfactory as pure fact-finding, if we were applying general scientific canons for empirical inquiry, may be quite satisfactory in the specific context of trials." Shapiro, Courts: A Comparative and Political Analysis 44 (1981). If Professor Shapiro's analysis is correct, courts are understandably hesitant to transplant the "findings" to a second dispute because it is a different dispute. The requirements that hedge issue preclusion thus grow from courts' understandable reluctance to equate "findings" with "facts."

3. An Issue "Essential to the Judgment"

In *Illinois Gulf Central R. v. Parks,* the court declined to apply preclusion because the opacity of the general verdict made it difficult to determine what the first judgment had decided. Sometimes courts face the opposite problem: too many findings in support of a judgment. In a trial to the bench, Rule 52(a) requires the judge to set forth findings of fact and conclusions of law. Imagine that the trial in *Parks* had taken place before a judge, who had determined (1) that Illinois Central had not been negligent and (2) that Jessie Parks had been contributorily negligent. Under these circumstances, should the court in a subsequent claim between the same parties hold Jessie precluded from relitigating both those issues? Or neither one? That question, though it occurs infrequently, reveals the values underlying the doctrine. The first Restatement of Judgments took the position that when alternative grounds for decision existed, *both* should be precluded in subsequent litigation. The Restatement (Second) of Judgments §27 comment i says that *neither* determination should be binding in subsequent litigation. The Reporters' note to the Restatement (Second) explained their thinking:

> First, a determination in the alternative may not have been as carefully or rigorously considered as it would have if it had been necessary to the result, and in that sense it has some of the characteristics of dicta. Second, and of critical importance, the losing party, although entitled to appeal from both determinations, might be dissuaded from doing

so because of the likelihood that at least one of them would be upheld and the other not even reached. If he were to appeal solely for the purpose of avoiding the application of the rule of issue preclusion, then the rule might be responsible for increasing the burdens of litigation on the parties and the courts rather than lightening those burdens.

Yet, as if to show just how close the question is, a later comment to the same section qualifies the suggested rule:

[Comment] o [to §27]. Effect of an Appeal . . .

If the judgment of the court of first instance was based on a determination of two issues, either of which standing independently would be sufficient to support the result, and the appellate court upholds both of these determinations as sufficient, and accordingly affirms the judgment, the judgment is conclusive as to both determinations. In contrast to the case discussed in Comment i, the losing party has here obtained an appellate decision on the issue, and thus the balance weighs in favor of preclusion.

If the appellate court upholds one of these determinations as sufficient but not the other, and accordingly affirms the judgment, the judgment is conclusive as to the first determination.

If the appellate court upholds one of these determinations as sufficient and refuses to consider whether or not the other is sufficient and accordingly affirms the judgment, the judgment is conclusive as to the first determination.

To get a grasp of the issues in an actual high-stakes case, imagine that in federal district court a defendant makes a pretrial motion seeking to dismiss a case, citing alternative grounds for its decision—lack of federal subject matter jurisdiction and lack of personal jurisdiction. Ruhrgas AG v. Marathon Oil, 526 U.S. 574 (1999), noted supra page 217. The district court dismisses and the plaintiff refiles the suit in state court. When he does so, the defendant invokes issue preclusion based on the prior decision. The next problems consider what might happen next.

Notes and Problems

---

1. Begin with the simplest variation on *Ruhrgas*. Suppose the district court had ruled solely on grounds that federal subject matter jurisdiction was lacking. Under those conditions, what effect will the prior decision have on the state court suit?

2. Now suppose that the federal district court had dismissed solely on grounds that personal jurisdiction was lacking. What effect will the prior decision have on the state court suit?

3. Now suppose, as in the actual case, the district court had dismissed, citing both grounds, ruling in a written opinion that personal and subject matter jurisdiction were both lacking. What effect should that ruling have in the second lawsuit?

4. Finally, suppose that after the federal district court had dismissed, citing both grounds, the plaintiff had appealed. Suppose the court of appeals affirms.

   a. If the appellate court affirms the absence of subject matter jurisdiction without reaching the question of personal jurisdiction, what effect in the second lawsuit?

   b. If the appellate court affirms both grounds for dismissal, what effect in the second suit?

5. Who's winning the battle between the positions of the Restatement First and the Restatement Second? A case from the Third Circuit nicely summarized the state of play:

   > There is no consensus among the courts of appeals as to whether the First or Second Restatement offers the better approach. The Courts of Appeals for the Second, Seventh, Ninth, and Eleventh Circuits generally give preclusive effect to alternative findings. . . . By contrast, the Courts of Appeals for the Tenth and Federal Circuits have refused to give preclusive effect to alternative findings that were each independently sufficient to support a judgment.

   > Jean Alexander Cosmetics, Inc. v. L'Oreal USA, Inc., 458 F.3d 244
   > (3d Cir. 2006) (holding that the Third Circuit would adopt the majority view).

   As of 2018, the Circuit split on this issue had not been resolved.

Implications

WHAT'S BEHIND THE WAR BETWEEN RESTATEMENTS?

What idea lies behind the importance that the Restatement (Second) attaches not just to the opportunity to appeal but to actual appellate litigation of alternative grounds? Put yourself in the position of the plaintiff in the hypothetical lawsuit. You have just lost big in federal district court, with the judge throwing your lawsuit out of court on two alternative grounds. One of those grounds was that the defendant had insufficient contacts with the state to permit personal jurisdiction. You think that finding rests on very flimsy grounds, so you say to your lawyer, "We should appeal."

Your lawyer will explain why an appeal claiming that the personal jurisdiction ruling was erroneous isn't worth his time or your money. Even if you're right about the personal jurisdiction ruling, the court of appeals will affirm the judgment—because the other ground for dismissal stands. Recall that appellate courts in the United States do not review the correctness of each trial court ruling—just whether the resulting judgment was justified—and here it was.

Consider that the Restatement (Second) position is based on an image of litigation not as a search for truth but as a set of incentives and disincentives. In that world, a judge will have less reason to be careful about any particular finding if there are other independent grounds leading to the same result. The losing litigant will have less incentive to appeal any particular finding if it seems likely that the appellate court will affirm on the basis of the other, independent grounds for decision. Under those circumstances, the theory goes, too few people have an incentive to make sure the findings are accurate. That being the case, we should be reluctant to import those findings into a second lawsuit.

4. Between Which Parties?

We have thus far dealt with situations in which the former and the present lawsuits involve the same parties. Common law required this identity of parties (called "mutuality") for both claim preclusion and issue preclusion. It continues to be a requirement for claim preclusion; in recent decades, however, many courts have abandoned this requirement for issue preclusion.

To see how such a scheme might operate, consider a variation on the facts in *Illinois Central Gulf Railroad v. Parks.* Wife alone sues Railroad for injuries suffered in a crossing collision. Wife wins a judgment. Husband now sues for his injuries sustained in the same accident. Railroad cannot argue that his claim is precluded by the first lawsuit: Biologically separate individuals possess separate claims, and no rule compels such individuals, even when married to each other, to prosecute their claims together. So Husband's suit can go forward.

In *Husband v. Railroad*, can either party take advantage of issue preclusion? Seventy-five years ago, the answer was a clear no. Like claim preclusion, issue preclusion applied only if the parties in the second suit both had been parties in the first suit, and, because Husband was not a party to that first lawsuit, the conditions for issue preclusion were not met: "Mutuality"—conditions under which both parties could benefit from or be burdened with preclusion—did not exist. The last several decades have seen that principle of mutuality erode. Many courts today would permit Husband, even though he had not been a party to the first suit, to take advantage of an issue fully litigated and determined in that suit. In such a case Railroad's negligence, causation, and proximate causation would all be candidates for preclusion in the second action. The rationale for that extension of issue preclusion is that the victim of issue preclusion (here, Railroad) had a full and fair opportunity to litigate those issues in the first suit.

Now change one factor: What if Railroad had won the first suit, demonstrating to the jury's satisfaction that it was not negligent? Could it take advantage of that determination in a second action brought by Husband? The answer is no. Whether they attribute this result to simple fairness or to due process, all agree that a party who has never had an opportunity to litigate an issue cannot be precluded from doing so. (*Taylor v. Sturgell,* supra page 720, illustrates these principles in the claim preclusion context.) The abandonment of mutuality thus creates a potential asymmetry: If Railroad loses the first case brought by Wife, it will be saddled by that loss in subsequent litigation with Husband. If it wins against Wife, however, it must still defend against Husband. The anomaly has its logic; as one pioneering decision put it:

> The criteria for determining who may assert a plea of [issue preclusion] differ fundamentally from the criteria for determining against whom [such] a plea . . . may be asserted. The requirements of due process of law forbid the assertion of a plea of . . . [issue preclusion] against a party unless he was bound by the earlier litigation in which the matter was decided. He is bound by that litigation only if he has been a party thereto or in privity with a party thereto. There is no compelling reason, however, for requiring that the party asserting the plea . . . must have been a party, or in privity with a party, to the earlier litigation.
>
>   No satisfactory rationalization has been advanced for the requirement of mutuality. Just why a party who was not bound by a previous action should be precluded from asserting it as *res judicata* against a party who was bound by it is difficult to comprehend.

> Bernhard v. Bank of America, 19 Cal. 2d 807, 811-12 (1942) (Traynor, J.).

Despite this reasoning, the asymmetrical availability of nonmutual preclusion has made some courts and commentators uneasy. The next case explores the problem.

Parklane Hosiery Co. v. Shore
439 U.S. 322 (1979)

STEWART, J., delivered the opinion of the Court.

This case presents the question whether a party who has had issues of fact adjudicated adversely to it in an equitable action may be collaterally estopped from relitigating the same issues before a jury in a subsequent legal action brought against it by a new party.

The respondent brought this stockholder's class action against the petitioners in a Federal District Court. The complaint alleged that the petitioners, Parklane Hosiery Co., Inc. (Parklane), and 13 of its officers, directors, and stockholders, had issued a materially false and misleading proxy statement in connection with a merger.[1] The proxy statement, according to the complaint, had violated §§14(a), 10(b), and 20(a) of the Securities Exchange Act of 1934, as well as various rules and regulations promulgated by the Securities and Exchange Commission (SEC). The complaint sought damages, rescission of the merger, and recovery of costs.

Before this action came to trial, the SEC filed suit against the same defendants in the Federal District Court, alleging that the proxy statement that had been issued by Parklane was materially false and misleading in essentially the same respects as those that had been alleged in the respondent's complaint. Injunctive relief was requested. After a four-day trial, the District Court found that the proxy statement was materi-

---

1. The amended complaint alleged that the proxy statement that had been issued to the stockholders was false and misleading because it failed to disclose (1) that the president of Parklane would financially benefit as a result of the company's going private; (2) certain ongoing negotiations that could have resulted in financial benefit to Parklane; and (3) that the appraisal of the fair value of Parklane stock was based on insufficient information to be accurate.

ally false and misleading in the respects alleged, and entered a declaratory judgment to that effect. The Court of Appeals for the Second Circuit affirmed this judgment.

The respondent in the present case then moved for partial summary judgment against the petitioners, asserting that the petitioners were collaterally estopped from litigating the issues that had been resolved against them in the action brought by the SEC.[2] The District Court denied the motion on the ground that such an application of collateral estoppel would deny the petitioners their Seventh Amendment right to a jury trial. The Court of Appeals for the Second Circuit reversed, holding that a party who has had issues of fact determined against him after a full and fair opportunity to litigate in a nonjury trial is collaterally estopped from obtaining a subsequent jury trial of these same issues of fact. The appellate court concluded that "the Seventh Amendment preserves the right to jury trial only with respect to issues of fact, [and] once those issues have been fully and fairly adjudicated in a prior proceeding, nothing remains for trial, either with or without a jury." Because of an inter-Circuit conflict, we granted certiorari.

I

The threshold question to be considered is whether quite apart from the right to a jury trial under the Seventh Amendment, the petitioners can be precluded from litigating facts resolved adversely to them in a prior equitable proceeding with another party under the general law of collateral estoppel. Specifically, we must determine whether a litigant who was not a party to a prior judgment may nevertheless use that judgment "offensively" to prevent a defendant from relitigating issues resolved in the earlier proceeding.[4]

A

Collateral estoppel, like the related doctrine of *res judicata*,[5] has the dual purpose of protecting litigants from the burden of relitigating an identical issue with the same party or his privy and of promoting judicial economy by preventing needless litigation. Until relatively recently, however, the scope of collateral estoppel was limited by the doctrine of mutuality of parties. Under this mutuality

---

2. A private plaintiff in an action under the proxy rules is not entitled to relief simply by demonstrating that the proxy solicitation was materially false and misleading. The plaintiff must also show that he was injured and prove damages. Mills v. Electric Auto-Lite Co., 396 U.S. 375, 386-390. Since the SEC action was limited to a determination of whether the proxy statement contained materially false and misleading information, the respondent conceded that he would still have to prove these other elements of his prima facie case in the private action. The petitioners' right to a jury trial on those remaining issues is not contested.

4. In this context, offensive use of collateral estoppel occurs when the plaintiff seeks to foreclose the defendant from litigating an issue the defendant has previously litigated unsuccessfully in an action with another party. Defensive use occurs when a defendant seeks to prevent a plaintiff from asserting a claim the plaintiff has previously litigated and lost against another defendant.

5. Under the doctrine of *res judicata*, a judgment on the merits in a prior suit bars a second suit involving the same parties or their privies based on the same cause of action. Under the doctrine of collateral estoppel, on the other hand, the second action is upon a different cause of action and the judgment in the prior suit precludes relitigation of issues actually litigated and necessary to the outcome of the first action.

doctrine, neither party could use a prior judgment as an estoppel against the other unless both parties were bound by the judgment. Based on the premise that it is somehow unfair to allow a party to use a prior judgment when he himself would not be so bound,[7] the mutuality requirement provided a party who had litigated and lost in a previous action an opportunity to relitigate identical issues with new parties.

By failing to recognize the obvious difference in position between a party who has never litigated an issue and one who has fully litigated and lost, the mutuality requirement was criticized almost from its inception.[8] Recognizing the validity of this criticism, the Court in *Blonder-Tongue Laboratories, Inc. v. University of Illinois Foundation*, supra, abandoned the mutuality requirement. . . . The "broader question" before the Court, however, was "whether it is any longer tenable to afford a litigant more than one full and fair opportunity for judicial resolution of the same issue." . . .

B

The *Blonder-Tongue* case involved defensive use of collateral estoppel—a plaintiff was estopped from asserting a claim that the plaintiff had previously litigated and lost against another defendant. The present case, by contrast, involves offensive use of collateral estoppel—a plaintiff is seeking to estop a defendant from relitigating the issues which the defendant previously litigated and lost against another plaintiff. In both the offensive and defensive use situations, the party against whom estoppel is asserted has litigated and lost in an earlier action. Nevertheless, several reasons have been advanced why the two situations should be treated differently.

First, offensive use of collateral estoppel does not promote judicial economy in the same manner as defensive use does. Defensive use of collateral estoppel precludes a plaintiff from relitigating identical issues by merely "switching adversaries." *Bernhard v. Bank of America Natl. Trust & Savings Assn.*[12] Thus defensive collateral estoppel gives a plaintiff a strong incentive to join all potential defendants in the first action if possible. Offensive use of collateral estoppel, on the other hand, creates precisely the opposite incentive. Since a plaintiff will be able to rely on a previous judgment against a defendant but will not be bound by that judgment if the defendant wins, the plaintiff has every incentive to adopt a "wait and see" attitude, in the hope that the first action by another plaintiff will result in a favorable judgment.

---

7. It is a violation of due process for a judgment to be binding on a litigant who was not a party or a privy and therefore has never had an opportunity to be heard. Blonder-Tongue Laboratories, Inc. v. University of Illinois Foundation, [402 U.S. 313 (1971)].

8. This criticism was summarized in the Court's opinion in *Blonder-Tongue Laboratories, Inc. v. University of Illinois Foundation*, supra. The opinion of Justice Traynor for a unanimous California Supreme Court in *Bernhard v. Bank of America Natl. Trust & Savings Assn.*, made the point succinctly: "No satisfactory rationalization has been advanced for the requirement of mutuality. Just why a party who was not bound by a previous action should be precluded from asserting it as *res judicata* against a party who was bound by it is difficult to comprehend."

12. Under the mutuality requirement, a plaintiff could accomplish this result since he would not have been bound by the judgment had the original defendant won.

Thus offensive use of collateral estoppel will likely increase rather than decrease the total amount of litigation, since potential plaintiffs will have everything to gain and nothing to lose by not intervening in the first action.[13] A second argument against offensive use of collateral estoppel is that it may be unfair to a defendant. If a defendant in the first action is sued for small or nominal damages, he may have little incentive to defend vigorously, particularly if future suits are not foreseeable. The *Evergreens v. Nunan*; cf. *Berner v. British Commonwealth Pac. Airlines* (application of offensive collateral estoppel denied where defendant did not appeal an adverse judgment awarding damages of $35,000 and defendant was later sued for over $7 million). Allowing offensive collateral estoppel may also be unfair to a defendant if the judgment relied upon as a basis for the estoppel is itself inconsistent with one or more previous judgments in favor of the defendant.[14] Still another situation where it might be unfair to apply offensive estoppel is where the second action affords the defendant procedural opportunities unavailable in the first action that could readily cause a different result.[15]

C

We have concluded that the preferable approach for dealing with these problems in the federal courts is not to preclude the use of offensive collateral estoppel, but to grant trial courts broad discretion to determine when it should be applied.[16] The general rule should be that in cases where a plaintiff could easily have joined in the earlier action or where, either for the reasons discussed above or for other reasons, the application of offensive estoppel would be unfair to a defendant, a trial judge should not allow the use of offensive collateral estoppel.

In the present case, however, none of the circumstances that might justify reluctance to allow the offensive use of collateral estoppel is present. The application of

_____

13. The Restatement (Second) of Judgments §88(3) (Tent. Draft No. 2, Apr. 15, 1975) provides that application of collateral estoppel may be denied if the party asserting it "could have effected joinder in the first action between himself and his present adversary."

14. In Professor Currie's familiar example, a railroad collision injures 50 passengers all of whom bring separate actions against the railroad. After the railroad wins the first 25 suits, a plaintiff wins in suit 26. Professor Currie argues that offensive use of collateral estoppel should not be applied so as to allow plaintiffs 27 through 50 automatically to recover. Currie, [Mutuality of Collateral Estoppel: Limits of the *Bernhard* Doctrine], 9 Stan. L. Rev. [281, 304 (1957)]. See Restatement (Second) of Judgments §88(4).

15. If, for example, the defendant in the first action was forced to defend in an inconvenient forum and therefore was unable to engage in full scale discovery or call witnesses, application of offensive collateral estoppel may be unwarranted. Indeed, differences in available procedures may sometimes justify not allowing a prior judgment to have estoppel effect in a subsequent action even between the same parties, or where defensive estoppel is asserted against a plaintiff who has litigated and lost. The problem of unfairness is particularly acute in cases of offensive estoppel, however, because the defendant against whom estoppel is asserted typically will not have chosen the forum in the first action. See id., at §88(2) and Comment d.

16. This is essentially the approach of [the Restatement (Second) of Judgments] at §88, which recognizes that "the distinct trend if not the clear weight of recent authority is to the effect that there is no intrinsic difference between 'offensive' as distinct from 'defensive' issue preclusion, although a stronger showing that the prior opportunity to litigate was adequate may be required in the former situation than the latter." Id. Reporter's Note, at 99.

offensive collateral estoppel will not here reward a private plaintiff who could have joined in the previous action, since the respondent probably could not have joined in the injunctive action brought by the SEC even had he so desired.[17] Similarly, there is no unfairness to the petitioners in applying offensive collateral estoppel in this case. First, in light of the serious allegations made in the SEC's complaint against the petitioners, as well as the foreseeability of subsequent private suits that typically follow a successful Government judgment, the petitioners had every incentive to litigate the SEC lawsuit fully and vigorously.[18] Second, the judgment in the SEC action was not inconsistent with any previous decision. Finally, there will in the respondent's action be no procedural opportunities available to the petitioners that were unavailable in the first action of a kind that might be likely to cause a different result.[19] We conclude, therefore, that none of the considerations that would justify a refusal to allow the use of offensive collateral estoppel is present in this case. Since the petitioners received a "full and fair" opportunity to litigate their claims in the SEC action, the contemporary law of collateral estoppel leads inescapably to the conclusion that the petitioners are collaterally estopped from relitigating the question of whether the proxy statement was materially false and misleading.

II

The question that remains is whether, notwithstanding the law of collateral estoppel, the use of offensive collateral estoppel in this case would violate the petitioners' Seventh Amendment right to a jury trial. . . . The Seventh Amendment has never been interpreted in the rigid manner advocated by the petitioners. On the contrary, many procedural devices developed since 1791 that have diminished the civil jury's historic domain have been found not to be inconsistent with the Seventh Amendment. . . .

The law of collateral estoppel, like the law in other procedural areas defining the scope of the jury's function, has evolved since 1791. Under the rationale of [an earlier] case, these developments are not repugnant to the Seventh Amendment simply for the reason that they did not exist in 1791. Thus if, as we have held, the law of collateral estoppel forecloses the petitioners from relitigating the factual issues determined against them in the SEC action, nothing in the Seventh Amendment dictates a

---

17. *SEC v. Everest Management Corp.* ("the complicating effect of the additional issues and the additional parties outweighs any advantage of a single disposition of the common issues"). Moreover, consolidation of a private action with one brought by the SEC without its consent is prohibited by statute. 15 U.S.C. §78u(g).

18. After a four-day trial in which the petitioners had every opportunity to present evidence and call witnesses, the District Court held for the SEC. The petitioners then appealed to the Court of Appeals for the Second Circuit, which affirmed the judgment against them. Moreover, the petitioners were already aware of the action brought by the respondent, since it had commenced before the filing of the SEC action.

19. It is true, of course, that the petitioners in the present action would be entitled to a jury trial of the issues bearing on whether the proxy statement was materially false and misleading had the SEC action never been brought—a matter to be discussed in Part II of this opinion. But the presence or absence of a jury as factfinder is basically neutral, quite unlike, for example, the necessity of defending the first lawsuit in an inconvenient forum.

different result, even though because of lack of mutuality there would have been no collateral estoppel in 1791. . . .

[The Court went on to hold that the Seventh Amendment was not a bar to successful assertion of issue preclusion.

Justice REHNQUIST dissented on the ground that preclusion under these circumstances violated the Seventh Amendment.]

WHAT'S NEW HERE?

- Shore was not a party to the litigation between Parklane and the SEC. If the SEC had lost, Shore would still have had the right to bring his lawsuit and argue that the proxy was misleading.
- Shore here gets to use as preclusive the ruling in a lawsuit to which he was not a party.

Notes and Problems

1. Think of *Parklane* as a variation on *Illinois Central Gulf Railroad v. Parks.*

   a. Without joining her husband Jessie, suppose Bertha Parks sues the railroad, alleging its negligence as a cause of her injuries. Bertha wins. In *Parklane*, which party is Bertha and which is the railroad?

   b. Jessie Parks now sues the railroad, alleging its negligence as a cause of his injuries. Jessie wants to treat the determination of the railroad's negligence and causation as precluded from relitigation. That issue is identical, was actually litigated and determined, and was essential to the judgment in the first case. In *Parklane*, which party to the second lawsuit is in the same position as Jessie, and what issue did that party want to preclude from relitigation?

   c. In fact, the *Parklane* opinion suggests a reason for thinking that *Parks* is a *weaker* case for preclusion than is *Parklane* itself. What opportunity did Jessie Parks have that Shore (the plaintiff in the second *Parklane* suit) did not have? Under *Parklane*, would that opportunity have been sufficient reason for denying Jessie the use of nonmutual issue preclusion?

2. Consider the following situations in which parties might wish to take advantage of preclusion. In which should they be able to do so?

   a. Mr. and Mrs. Rush, riding on a motorcycle, are thrown off when the cycle hits a pothole. Mrs. Rush, the owner of the cycle, sues the city for $1,000 in damages to the machine. Mrs. Rush brings the suit in municipal court, which uses an abbreviated system of discovery and has a jurisdictional limit of $5,000. City loses. Mr. Rush sues for disabling spinal injuries suffered in the same accident; he seeks damages of $1.5 million. Mr. Rush seeks to invoke preclusion on the issue of City's negligence.

b. The federal government accuses an IRS agent of criminal embezzlement. She is acquitted. The government then sues Accomplice to recover funds allegedly embezzled in the same criminal acts. Accomplice seeks to invoke preclusion on the grounds that the previous case demonstrates the acts did not occur. Standefer v. United States, 447 U.S. 10 (1980) (no preclusion).

c. These hypothetical cases emphasize a point that should by now be familiar: Lawsuits do not decide "what happened" in the abstract; instead, they decide who, given the procedural setting of the case, made a better showing. If one keeps this point in mind, it is easier to understand why procedural settings that differ significantly may supply a reason not to apply preclusion.

3. *Parklane* joins a number of state cases in permitting nonmutual preclusion. Like *Parklane*, these cases generally cite both efficiency and fairness as grounds for applying preclusion.

4. The widespread move to various forms of comparative negligence raises several questions of issue preclusion.

a. Consider a fairly simple case. Two cars collide; Passenger is riding in one of them. The two drivers sue each other and the case goes to judgment. The jury finds that both drivers were negligent and apportions fault at 70 percent to Driver A and 30 percent to Driver B. If Passenger now sues (assuming the state permits such claims), the apportionment of fault from the former suit will bind both drivers. The reasoning is that both had a fair opportunity to litigate an issue essential to the judgment.

b. But what happens if Passenger sues only one driver, perhaps because she is uncertain about the other's negligence and wishes not to complicate an otherwise clear case? May Passenger take advantage of the finding of negligence as against Driver A alone? Presumably so. Is she limited to collecting only 70 percent of her damages? That will depend on the state's regime of joint and several liability, but in many states Passenger (assuming no fault on her part) will be able to collect her total damage bill from Driver A, who may have an action for equitable indemnification against Driver B.

c. Suppose Passenger is in a state that has modified the common law rules of joint and several liability so that she may collect from each driver only in proportion to his fault. Must Passenger accept the finding that Driver A was only 70 percent at fault, or is she free to show that his proportion was greater? Should Passenger get the sweet without the bitter—the determination of liability without the limitation as to its amount?

Implications

NONMUTUAL PRECLUSION AND THE U.S. GOVERNMENT

There is a glaring exception to the Court's endorsement of nonmutual preclusion: the federal government. In United States v. Mendoza, 464 U.S. 154 (1984), the Court held that the United States could not be subjected to nonmutual issue preclusion. The ordinary rules of issue preclusion apply if Party and the United States are involved in two successive lawsuits, but if *A* sues the United States and prevails, *B* may not in a later suit use against the United States those issues determined in *A*'s favor. Otherwise put, the principles of *Parklane* do not apply to the United States. Why not? The *Mendoza* Court did not do a very good job of justifying its result, but one can imagine two reasons.

There is a practical problem. At present the United States appeals selectively, choosing only those cases in which some principle of law or fact important to the United States is at stake. (The office of the Solicitor General makes these discretionary judgments.) The *Mendoza* Court worried that applying *Parklane* to the United States would force the government to appeal virtually every case it lost, for fear of its effect in subsequent cases. Note that this same problem afflicts other large litigants—state governments, Microsoft, General Motors, large insurers—but no such exception has been carved out for them.

The United States faces another problem. Some of the suits to which it is a party involve constitutional questions. As things now stand, an unappealed decision of a district court involving a constitutional question affects only the parties involved in the case itself. It does not even bind other courts in the same district. If one applied *Parklane* to the United States, all that would change. A single district court decision against the United States on a constitutional issue would become—by virtue of issue preclusion—super-precedent that would bind all other courts, including the U.S. Supreme Court. For example, suppose a district court in the course of a criminal trial ruled that all searches of automobiles without a warrant were unconstitutional. If that ruling stood, it could be applied against the United States by all subsequent defendants. Moreover, unlike ordinary precedent, the ruling would not be subject to reconsideration or "overruling" by the U.S. Supreme Court. Is this a good enough reason not to extend *Parklane* to the United States? Or does it suggest a narrower exception involving only questions of constitutional law?

5. Those who favor the *Parklane* principle must confront a nightmare case: a number of plaintiffs with essentially identical claims against the same defendant. The typical example is a bus or train crash, with multiple suits brought by injured passengers. Why is this example a nightmare? Because it emphasizes the extent to which everything turns on the outcome of the first case.

   a. If a plaintiff won the first case and the second through fiftieth plaintiffs now seek to invoke preclusion, what result under the doctrine of *Parklane*?

b. If the defendant won the first case and now seeks to invoke preclusion against subsequent plaintiffs, what result?

c. Lest you think such situations are confined to the teeming brains of law teachers, consider the facts of State Farm Fire & Casualty Co. v. Century Home Components, 275 Or. 97, 550 P.2d 1185 (1976). A fire broke out in a light-industrial strip mall, burning a number of businesses. Fifty of those businesses sued Century Home Components (one of the strip-mall tenants), alleging that its negligent treatment of a dumpster full of sawdust and oil had caused the fire to break out. The first two cases tried resulted in defense verdicts. On appeal the first judgment was reversed on account of defendant's failure to produce a document in discovery. The third case tried resulted in a plaintiff's verdict, as did the first case on retrial. At that point the remaining litigants moved to preclude defendant on the issues of negligence and causation, leaving only damages to be tried. Plaintiffs reasoned that there were two plaintiff's verdicts, the issues were identical, and because Oregon had adopted nonmutual preclusion, they were entitled to take advantage of preclusion. The Oregon Supreme Court thought otherwise:

> The "multiple-claimant anomaly" was first hypothesized by Brainerd Currie as one instance where, absent mutuality, the unrestrained application of collateral estoppel might produce unfair results. Currie, Mutuality of Collateral Estoppel: Limits of the Bernhard Doctrine, 9 Stan. L. Rev. 281 (1957). Currie posed the situation of a train wreck resulting in 50 separate claims being filed against the railroad for negligence. If the defendant railroad won the first 25 cases and subsequently lost the 26th, Currie characterized as an "absurdity" the notion that the remaining 24 claimants could ride in on the strength of the 26th plaintiff's judgment and estop the defendant on the issue of negligence. The reason was that the 26th judgment would clearly seem to be an aberration. Currie then reasoned that, if we should be unwilling to give preclusive effect to the 26th judgment, we should not afford such effect to an adverse judgment rendered in the *first* action brought because "we have no warrant for assuming that the aberrational judgment will not come as the first in the series." Currie, supra. Currie thus concluded that, absent mutuality, collateral estoppel should not be applied where a defendant potentially faces more than two successive actions.
>
> Those courts which have discarded the rule of mutuality and permit the offensive assertion of collateral estoppel have generally rejected Currie's solution to the multiple-claimant anomaly in situations where the *first* judgment is adverse to the defendant, and have precluded a defendant from relitigating multiple claims where it has been concluded that the defendant had in actuality the incentive and complete opportunity to contest the issue fully in the first action. Currie's reservations were based on the apprehension that the first judgment might well be an aberration, but this view failed to recognize that the very notion of collateral estoppel demands and assumes a certain confidence in the integrity of the end result of our adjudicative process. . . .
>
> As the foregoing discussion would indicate, however, we are not free to disregard incongruous results when they are looking us in the eye. If the circumstances are such that our confidence in the integrity of the determination is severely undermined, or that the result would likely be different in a second trial, it would work an injustice to deny the litigant another chance. Thus,

where it is apparent that the verdict was the result of a jury compromise, the losing party should not be precluded by the judgment. . . . It has also been held that if the prior determination was manifestly erroneous the judgment should not be given preclusive effect. Restatement (Second) of Judgments §88(7) and Comment i. (Tent. Draft No. 2, 1975). And the existence of newly discovered or crucial evidence that was not available to the litigant at the first trial would provide a basis for denying preclusion where it appears the evidence would have a significant effect on the outcome.

We agree with the commentators to the extent at least that, where there are extant determinations that are inconsistent on the matter in issue, it is a strong indication that the application of collateral estoppel would work an injustice. There seems to be something fundamentally offensive about depriving a party of the opportunity to litigate the issue again when he has shown beyond a doubt that on another day he prevailed. . . .

Id. at 105-10.

WHAT'S NEW HERE?

- One might have thought the facts of *Century Home Components* presented a good case for nonmutual preclusion. By the time the case reached appeal there were several lawsuits—most pointing in one direction (liability).
- But, because the verdicts were inconsistent, the court backed away from preclusion.

6. The position of the Restatement (Second) of Judgments on mutuality is as follows:

§29. Issue Preclusion in Subsequent Litigation with Others

A party precluded from relitigating an issue with an opposing party, in accordance with §§27 and 28,* is also precluded from doing so with another person unless he lacked full and fair opportunity to litigate the issue in the first action or other circumstances justify affording him an opportunity to relitigate the issue. The circumstances to which considerations should be given include those enumerated in §28 and also whether:

(1) Treating the issue as conclusively determined would be incompatible with an applicable scheme of administering the remedies in the actions involved;

(2) The forum in the second action affords the party against whom preclusion is asserted procedural opportunities in the presentation and determination of the issue that were not available in the first action and that could likely result in the issue being differently determined;

---

* See supra page 736 and infra page 757.

(3) The person seeking to invoke favorable preclusion, or to avoid unfavorable preclusion, could have effected joinder in the first action between himself and his present adversary;

(4) The determination relied on as preclusive was itself inconsistent with another determination of the same issue;

(5) The prior determination may have been affected by relationships among the parties to the first action that are not present in the subsequent action, or apparently was based on a compromise verdict or finding;

(6) Treating the issue as conclusively determined may complicate determination of issues in the subsequent action or prejudice the interests of another party thereto;

(7) The issue is one of law and treating it as conclusively determined would inappropriately foreclose opportunity for obtaining reconsideration of the legal rule upon which it was based;

(8) Other compelling circumstances make it appropriate that the party be permitted to relitigate the issue.

Which of these factors justify the result in *Century Home Components*? Is there a common thread running through these exceptions?

7. One solution to the problem posed by *Century Home Components* lies in judicial control of dockets. In many jurisdictions, claims arising out of the same episode—a large building fire, an airplane crash—will be assigned to the same judge for consolidated proceedings. That judge's management of the case can have substantial implications for the application of preclusion.

   a. Suppose such consolidation had occurred in *Century Home Components* and that the first case tried resulted in a plaintiff's verdict. At that point, preclusion might have seemed like an attractive possibility.

   b. To avoid the premature use of preclusion, some judges faced with these circumstances will purposely set several cases for trial to see if the results are inconsistent or if a pattern develops. Is this a better approach?

C. THE BOUNDARIES OF PRECLUSION

With the *Century Home Components* case noted above, we have already begun to approach the topic of this section—the point at which preclusion doctrines should yield. Both claim and issue preclusion are judge-made doctrines, and neither is engraved in stone. With the exception of full faith and credit issues, to be considered in the next section, and the due process restrictions on the excessive use of either doctrine, neither has significant constitutional dimensions. Thus, it is not surprising that other policies should occasionally challenge the applications of either doctrine.

1. Claim Preclusion

Claim preclusion, or *res judicata*, presents fewer opportunities for anomalous results than does issue preclusion. Section 26 of the Restatement (Second) of

Judgments lists some straightforward reasons for declining to apply claim preclusion: where the parties have expressly or implicitly agreed to allow claim splitting; where a court has in the first action reserved plaintiff's right to bring the second; or where jurisdictional limitations prevented plaintiff from seeking certain forms of relief now sought. Past that point, the Restatement enters uncertain ground:

§26. Exceptions to the General Rule Concerning Splitting

(1) When any of the following circumstances exists, the general rule of §24 does not apply to extinguish the claim, and part or all of the claim subsists as a possible basis for a second action by the plaintiff against the defendant: . . .

(d) The judgment in the first action was plainly inconsistent with the fair and equitable implementation of a statutory or constitutional scheme, or it is the sense of the scheme that the plaintiff should be permitted to split his claim; or

(e) For reasons of substantive policy in a case involving a continuing or recurrent wrong, the plaintiff is given an option to sue once for the total harm, both past and prospective, or to sue from time to time for the damages incurred to the date of suit, and chooses the latter course; or

(f) It is clearly and convincingly shown that the policies favoring preclusion of a second action are overcome for an extraordinary reason, such as the apparent invalidity of a continuing restraint or condition having a vital relation to personal liberty or the failure of the prior litigation to yield a coherent disposition of the controversy.

The situation imagined in (d) typically involves a broadly applicable law as to which interpretation has changed. Imagine that in the years before Brown v. Board of Education, 347 U.S. 483 (1954), a school child sues seeking racial integration of her school. She loses. The next year *Brown* is decided. It has to be possible for the plaintiff, otherwise bound by the now rejected interpretation of the Constitution, to take advantage of the changed law. Or, for a more contemporary application, suppose that a same-sex couple wishing to marry challenges a state's ban on such marriages and loses. Thereafter, in another case, the U.S. Supreme Court overrules the prior case, allowing such marriages. Obergefell v. Hodges, 135 S. Ct. 2584 (2015). It can't be that every other same-sex couple in the nation can marry, but not the couple who first challenged the law. Section 26(e) seeks the same result for situations involving repeated interactions between the same parties. The final catchall exception is designed to help courts out of messes that inconsistent prior decisions can lead to.

Apart from these rather unusual circumstances, courts take claim preclusion very seriously, even when the prior decision has obviously been erroneous. Recall *Gargallo v. Merrill Lynch et al.*, supra page 732, in which the lower court gave preclusive effect to a state court judgment on a claim over which federal courts have exclusive jurisdiction.

2. Issue Preclusion

Exceptions to the application of issue preclusion, or collateral estoppel, are more numerous than exceptions to claim preclusion. The Restatement (Second) of Judgments §28, excerpts of which are reprinted below, provides a guide to the terrain:

§28. Exceptions to the General Rule of Issue Preclusion

Although an issue is actually litigated and determined by a valid and final judgment, and the determination is essential to the judgment, relitigation of the issue in a subsequent action between the parties is not precluded in the following circumstances:

(1) The party against whom preclusion is sought could not, as a matter of law, have obtained review of the judgment in the initial action. . . .

(2) The issue is one of law and

(a) the two actions involve claims that are substantially unrelated, or

(b) a new determination is warranted in order to take account of an intervening change in the applicable legal context or otherwise to avoid inequitable administration of the laws. . . .

(3) A new determination of the issue is warranted by differences in the quality or extensiveness of the procedures followed in the two courts or by factors relating to the allocation of jurisdiction between them. . . .

(4) The party against whom preclusion is sought had a significantly heavier burden of persuasion with respect to the issue in the initial action than in the subsequent action; the burden has shifted to his adversary; or the adversary has a significantly heavier burden than he had in the first action. . . .

(5) There is a clear and convincing need for a new determination of the issue

(a) because of the potential adverse impact of the determination on the public interest or the interests of persons not themselves parties in the initial action,

(b) because it was not sufficiently foreseeable at the time of the initial action that the issue would arise in the context of a subsequent action, or

(c) because the party sought to be precluded, as a result of the conduct of his adversary or other special circumstances, did not have an adequate opportunity or incentive to obtain a full and fair adjudication in the initial action.

Consider whether any of these exceptions would apply to cases you have encountered—for example, *Parklane Hosiery* and *Century Home Components.*

D. REPOSE: COLLATERAL ATTACK AND REOPENED JUDGMENTS

This chapter has focused on a pair of common law doctrines that prevent subsequent lawsuits from undermining judgments. Claim preclusion, by preventing subsequent litigation of the same claim, requires the parties to include related grievances in the same suit. Issue preclusion prevents inconsistent findings when subsequent litigation is permitted. We turn now to two principles that ensure that courts heed the doctrines of former adjudication without producing unfair hardship.

To see their relationship, consider a hypothetical case. Motorists from New York and New Jersey collide with each other. New Jersey plaintiff sues New York defendant in New Jersey state court and loses. Could plaintiff try again by going to New York and suing there in either state or federal court? Or suppose that after the original case has gone to judgment, plaintiff discovers a witness who supplies the crucial missing evidence of defendant's negligence; moreover, plaintiff discovers that defendant knew of the witness but failed to reveal his existence in response to interrogatories. Can plaintiff somehow bring this evidence before the court? The doctrines of claim preclusion do not answer the first question because, as common law doctrines under state law, they speak only to the courts of a given jurisdiction: On the facts given, they tell the New Jersey courts that N.J. Motorist cannot bring a second suit in that state; but they say nothing to the courts of New York. As the next section shows, principles of full faith and credit back up the common law by insisting that courts of one jurisdiction heed the judgments of another, here telling N.Y. courts to heed the N.J. judgment. But the doctrines of former adjudication, reinforced by full faith and credit, have the potential to work injustice if, for example, they perpetuate defendant's fraudulent concealment of evidence in the second hypothetical. To prevent that, legislatures have created the opportunity, in very limited circumstances, to reopen a judgment.

1. Full Faith and Credit as a Bar to Collateral Attack

The common law doctrines of claim and issue preclusion require courts of any given political unit to heed the judgments of courts of that unit. They give, however, no guidance respecting the judgments of sister jurisdictions—other states or the federal government. Two provisions of law fill that silence. The Constitution, in Article IV, obligates state courts to recognize sister-state judgments—to give them, in the Constitution's words "Full Faith and Credit." Section 1738 of 28 U.S.C. demands that all courts, state and federal, give the same full faith and credit to state court judgments as those states would themselves give. This rule makes sense: Parties litigating in the courts of one state should know in advance what the preclusive effects of any ruling will be.

Though §1738 does not mention full faith and credit to federal court judgments, that requirement has always been assumed and is not questioned, either as a proposition of federal common law or, as some would have it, an implication of the Supremacy Clause, found in Article VI ("This Constitution and the Laws of the United States which shall be made in Pursuance thereof . . . shall be the supreme Law of the Land; and the Judges in every State shall be bound thereby. . . .").

If one puts these provisions together with the common law of preclusion, they create an apparently seamless web. Within any given political unit, the applicable common law doctrine of preclusion prevents attacks on the judgment. Although, as we have seen, the doctrine of preclusion may differ in certain ways from state to state (for example, some states recognize the "same transaction or occurrence" test for the scope of claim preclusion, while others may recognize a "same evidence" test), the generally applied doctrine is clear: Any claim that was or could have been litigated in the previous case may not be relitigated, and any issue that was litigated may not be relitigated in a second proceeding by a disappointed litigant. Put in legal terms, "collateral attack" on the outcome of Case 1 is not available in Case 2. Across the boundaries of political units—what is called "interjurisdictional preclusion"—the principles of full faith and credit require that the courts of one unit give to sister courts' judgments the same effect they would have in the unit that rendered them. We have already seen these principles in operation in *Gargallo v. Merrill Lynch et al.*, supra page 732, and *Frier v. City of Vandalia*, supra page 705.

There is, however, a hole—of indeterminate size—in this doctrinal tapestry: Under some circumstances one may collaterally attack a judgment—that is, contest the enforceability in Case 2 of a judgment reached in Case 1—on the ground that the court rendering the judgment lacked jurisdiction to decide it. (That is one of the holdings of *Pennoyer v. Neff*, supra page 68.) In principle, this makes sense: A party should not be bound by a judgment reached by a court that lacked power to render it. Nineteenth-century courts often asserted this proposition in sweeping terms, saying that a judgment entered without jurisdiction was "void." One implication of that proposition was that such a judgment was not entitled to full faith and credit—and that giving it full faith and credit might itself violate the Constitution. Again, *Pennoyer v. Neff*, where personal jurisdiction over the defendant was lacking in the first case, is a classic example of this proposition.

Put in the most general terms, the objection that a judgment was invalid for want of jurisdiction created a significant exception to the doctrines of finality. More recent decisions have clarified and limited this "jurisdictional" exception, helping to maintain the power of the doctrine of preclusion to produce genuine finality in litigation. For example, *Pennoyer v. Neff* makes clear that lack of personal jurisdiction in Case 1 can be a legitimate basis for collaterally attacking the judgment reached in that case in Case 2. Can the same be said when the problem in Case 1 is the absence of *subject matter* jurisdiction? The next case (involving the subject matter jurisdiction of a state rather than a federal court) considers that question.

V.L. v. E.L.
136 S. Ct. 1017 (2016)

PER CURIAM.

A Georgia court entered a final judgment of adoption making petitioner V.L. a legal parent of the children that she and respondent E.L. had raised together from birth. V.L. and E.L. later separated while living in Alabama. V.L. asked the Alabama courts to enforce the Georgia judgment and grant her custody or visitation rights. The Alabama Supreme Court ruled against her, holding that the Full Faith and Credit Clause of the United States Constitution does not require the Alabama courts to respect the Georgia judgment. That judgment of the Alabama Supreme Court is now reversed by this summary disposition.

I

V.L. and E.L. are two women who were in a relationship from approximately 1995 until 2011. Through assisted reproductive technology, E.L. gave birth to a child named S.L. in 2002 and to twins named N.L. and H.L. in 2004. . . .

V.L. and E.L. eventually decided to give legal status to the relationship between V.L. and the children by having V.L. formally adopt them. To facilitate the adoption, the couple rented a house in Alpharetta, Georgia. V.L. then filed an adoption petition in the Superior Court of Fulton County, Georgia. E.L. also appeared in that proceeding. While not relinquishing her own parental rights, she gave her express consent to V.L.'s adoption of the children as a second parent. The Georgia court determined that V.L. had complied with the applicable requirements of Georgia law, and entered a final decree of adoption allowing V.L. to adopt the children and recognizing both V.L. and E.L. as their legal parents.

V.L. and E.L. ended their relationship in 2011, while living in Alabama. . . . V.L. later filed a petition in the Circuit Court of Jefferson County, Alabama, alleging that E.L. had denied her access to the children and interfered with her ability to exercise her parental rights. She asked the Alabama court to register the Georgia adoption judgment and award her some measure of custody or visitation rights. . . . That court entered an order awarding V.L. scheduled visitation with the children. . . .

The Alabama Supreme Court reversed. It held that the Georgia court had no subject-matter jurisdiction under Georgia law to enter a judgment allowing V.L. to adopt the children while still recognizing E.L.'s parental rights. As a consequence, the Alabama Supreme Court held Alabama courts were not required to accord full faith and credit to the Georgia judgment.

II

The Constitution provides that "Full Faith and Credit shall be given in each State to the public Acts, Records, and judicial Proceedings of every other State." That Clause requires each State to recognize and give effect to valid judgments rendered by the courts of its sister States. It serves "to alter the status of the several states as independent foreign sovereignties, each free to ignore obligations created under the laws or by the judicial proceedings of the others, and to make them integral parts of a single nation."

With respect to judgments, "the full faith and credit obligation is exacting." "A final judgment in one State, if rendered by a court with adjudicatory authority over the subject matter and persons governed by the judgment, qualifies for recognition throughout the land." A State may not disregard the judgment of a sister State because it disagrees with the reasoning underlying the judgment or deems it to be wrong on the merits. On the contrary, "the full faith and credit clause of the Constitution precludes any inquiry into the merits of the cause of action, the logic or consistency of the decision, or the validity of the legal principles on which the judgment is based."

A State is not required, however, to afford full faith and credit to a judgment rendered by a court that "did not have jurisdiction over the subject matter or the relevant parties." "Consequently, before a court is bound by [a] judgment rendered in another State, it may inquire into the jurisdictional basis of the foreign court's decree." That jurisdictional inquiry, however, is a limited one. "[I]f the judgment on its face appears to be a 'record of a court of general jurisdiction, such jurisdiction over the cause and the parties is to be presumed unless disproved by extrinsic evidence, or by the record itself.'"

Those principles resolve this case. Under Georgia law, as relevant here, "[t]he superior courts of the several counties shall have exclusive jurisdiction in all matters of adoption." Ga. Code Ann. §19-8-2(a) (2015). That provision on its face gave the Georgia Superior Court subject-matter jurisdiction to hear and decide the adoption petition at issue here. The Superior Court resolved that matter by entering a final judgment that made V.L. the legal adoptive parent of the children. Whatever the merits of that judgment, it was within the statutory grant of jurisdiction over "all matters of adoption." The Georgia court thus had the "adjudicatory authority over the subject matter" required to entitle its judgment to full faith and credit.

The Alabama Supreme Court reached a different result by relying on Ga. Code Ann. §19-8-5(a). That statute states (as relevant here) that "a child who has any living parent or guardian may be adopted by a third party . . . only if each such living parent and each such guardian has voluntarily and in writing surrendered all of his or her rights to such child." The Alabama Supreme Court concluded that this provision prohibited the Georgia Superior Court from allowing V.L. to adopt the children while also allowing E.L. to keep her existing parental rights. It further concluded that this provision went not to the merits but to the Georgia court's subject-matter jurisdiction. . . .

That analysis is not consistent with this Court's controlling precedent. Where a judgment indicates on its face that it was rendered by a court of competent jurisdiction, such jurisdiction "is to be presumed unless disproved." There is nothing here to rebut that presumption. The Georgia statute, on which the Alabama Supreme Court relied, does not speak in jurisdictional terms; for instance, it does not say that a Georgia court "shall have jurisdiction to enter an adoption decree" only if each existing parent or guardian has surrendered his or her parental rights. . . .

Section 19-8-5(a) does not become jurisdictional just because it is "mandatory" and "must be strictly construed." This Court "has long rejected the notion that all mandatory prescriptions, however emphatic, are properly typed jurisdictional." Indeed, the Alabama Supreme Court's reasoning would give jurisdictional status to *every* requirement of the Georgia adoption statutes, since Georgia law indicates those requirements are all mandatory and must be strictly construed. That result would comport neither with Georgia law nor with common sense.

As Justice Holmes observed more than a century ago, "it sometimes may be difficult to decide whether certain words in a statute are directed to jurisdiction or to merits." In such cases, especially where the Full Faith and Credit Clause is concerned, a court must be "slow to read ambiguous words, as meaning to leave the judgment open to dispute, or as intended to do more than fix the rule by which the court should decide." That time-honored rule controls here. The Georgia judgment appears on its face to have been issued by a court with jurisdiction, and there is no established Georgia law to the contrary. It follows that the Alabama Supreme Court erred in refusing to grant that judgment full faith and credit.

The petition for writ of certiorari is granted. The judgment of the Alabama Supreme Court is reversed, and the case is remanded for further proceedings not inconsistent with this opinion. *It is so ordered.*

WHAT'S NEW HERE?

- The Court holds that the Constitution requires Alabama to enforce a judgment of a court in a sister state—even when that sister state may not have correctly applied its own law in entering the judgment.
- Put another way, the Court forbids a collateral attack on a substantive ruling made in conformity with the jurisdictional rules governing it: So long as the court rendering the original judgment appeared to have authority to enter it, the inquiry is at an end.

Notes and Problems

1. To see the force of the opinion, begin by stating the loser's (E.L.'s) argument and then the unanimous opinion's response to it. Why, according to E.L., should the Georgia court not have entered the order allowing V.L. to adopt? The Supreme Court does not determine whether the Georgia court properly followed the requirements of Georgia law. Why does it nevertheless order enforcement of the Georgia judgment?

2. Instead of resisting enforcement in a later proceeding in an Alabama court, what might E.L. have done had she wanted to contest the ruling in the Georgia case? She could have appealed the initial ruling in the Georgia Superior Court through the appellate courts in Georgia, and perhaps even to the U.S. Supreme Court if her argument raised a federal constitutional question.

   a. This is the general choice faced by losing litigants; they can appeal the loss through the appellate courts of their state, or instead try to attack the judgment collaterally by later litigating in the courts of another state, knowing that (in the absence of fraud) the *only* basis for collaterally attacking the earlier judgment is the absence of jurisdiction in the court that rendered it. Ironically, the choice of appealing in timely fashion the Georgia adoption decree through the Georgia appellate system was not realistically available to E.L., because at that time she was actually in support of the adoption decree. In reality, once that decree was entered by the Georgia court, E.L. never had a legally recognized opportunity to attack or contest it.

   b. Does the U.S. Supreme Court adequately recognize that there was no genuine adversarial quality to the adoption proceeding, and whether that should militate in favor of permitting collateral attack once the relationship dissolved and E.L. took a different position on the validity of the adoption?

3. The analysis and result in *V.L. v. E.L.* demonstrates that the requirement of full faith and credit to sister-state judgments is, as Justice Ginsburg has put

it, "exacting." Baker v. General Motors Corp., 522 U.S. 222, 233 (1998). Apart from collateral attacks on jurisdiction and the reopening of judgments as discussed below, full faith and credit is due to sister-state judgments, period. In particular, the fact that the court in the first case may have made an obvious error—basing its decision on an incorrect reading of the facts, or misapplying the law governing the case—is not a basis for the courts of another state to deny full faith and credit to the judgment. This has been the rule at least since Justice Holmes's opinion for the Court in Fauntleroy v. Lum, 210 U.S. 230 (1908), which is quoted briefly in *V.L. v. E.L.*

4. *Pennoyer v. Neff* establishes that a party over whom the court lacks personal jurisdiction, and who does not appear in the case, may collaterally challenge the resulting judgment. That proposition is still good law. After all, in the case of such a default judgment, the validity of personal jurisdiction was never explicitly found, and no defendant was there to raise the issue. The opposite proposition—that a party who appears and contests personal jurisdiction is bound by the court's decision on the jurisdictional question—was decided in Baldwin v. Iowa State Traveling Men's Assn., 283 U.S. 522 (1931). So collateral attack is not available simply because the losing party disagrees with the first court's decision on personal jurisdiction. If the first court explicitly found that it had jurisdiction over the defendant, that finding may not be relitigated.

5. In Durfee v. Duke, 375 U.S. 106 (1963), the Supreme Court established the same basic principle when it is subject matter jurisdiction that was allegedly lacking in the first case: Lack of subject matter jurisdiction may, in principle, be a basis for collateral attack, but if the defendant has appeared in the first case and the court has actually found that it had subject matter jurisdiction, no collateral attack is available. It is worth noting that, whereas the U.S. Constitution itself holds that a judgment entered in the absence of constitutionally valid personal jurisdiction is void, the kinds of subject matter jurisdiction issues that arise in state court do not always raise such grandiose constitutional issues; often they simply concern state rules directing various types of litigation to different state courts or determining what kinds of remedies a court can issue. Thus, while state court judgments rendered without proper subject matter jurisdiction are not, as a general matter, entitled to full faith and credit in the courts of other states, that is not necessarily because the initial assertion of subject matter jurisdiction itself violated the Constitution.

6. With these principles as background, what made E.L. think she could proceed as she did—mounting a collateral attack on the Georgia court's ruling on adoption? Suppose that the question a party sought to relitigate was an ordinary factual one: the date of a purported deed conveying land. If a court in State *A* had decided that question, ordinary preclusion doctrine would bar its relitigation in any subsequent action between the same parties. The Full Faith and Credit Clause (and 28 U.S.C. §1738) would require that the court of a sister state (or a federal court) give the same effect to that decided issue as a court in State *A*.

7. Armed with the knowledge that lack of jurisdiction in Case 1 is an exception to the full faith and credit obligation, E.L. simply tried to argue in the Alabama

courts (initially with some success) that the Georgia courts had lacked jurisdiction to enter the adoption decree. You can see that the U.S. Supreme Court did not buy the argument. The Georgia statute cited by E.L. (and allegedly ignored or wrongly applied by the Georgia court) was not one regulating the jurisdiction of the Georgia trial court; it was one that simply established the prerequisites for granting an adoption under the circumstances faced by V.L. and E.L. Given the prevailing doctrine of full faith and credit, losing parties will have an incentive to characterize laws that were allegedly improperly applied by the first court as *jurisdictional* in nature, even if such a characterization is dubious.

   a. *V.L. v. E.L.* takes the doctrine of *Durfee v. Duke* one small step further, holding that one who appears and fails to challenge subject matter jurisdiction is bound by the resulting judgment, unless she can "rebut that presumption" that the court had jurisdiction. In other words, it is not necessary that the court explicitly rule that it had subject matter jurisdiction in order for its ruling on the merits to be entitled to full faith and credit; if the court proceeds to exercise such jurisdiction under a statute that appears to grant it that power, the validity of the first court's jurisdiction will be presumed (unless the presumption can be rebutted) in any later collateral attack on the judgment. Thus, E.L. did technically have the opportunity in the Alabama case to collaterally challenge the Georgia courts' subject matter jurisdiction, but the "rebuttable presumption" approach taken by the Supreme Court unquestionably set a high bar for E.L.

   b. Defendants who appear but fail to raise a challenge to personal jurisdiction, proceeding to litigate on the merits, are treated in every jurisdiction as having waived their objections to personal jurisdiction, whether they seek to raise them in the first case itself or collaterally. In the federal courts, this principle is embodied in Fed. R. Civ. P. 12(h). The state judicial systems have various procedures for attaining the same result.

8. There remain a few rare but complex variations on the full faith and credit principles summarized above.

   a. In its most significant recent decision on full faith and credit, Baker v. General Motors Corp., 522 U.S. 222 (1998), the U.S. Supreme Court held that the courts in State *B* are not required by the Full Faith and Credit Clause or the federal statute to enforce according to its terms an injunction entered by a court in State *A*. Ronald Elwell, a former GM engineer who testified against GM in a Georgia state case, reached a settlement with GM in their ensuing legal dispute; that settlement included Elwell's agreement to a permanent injunction barring Elwell from testifying against GM in other product liability cases. When Elwell nevertheless testified in such a case in a federal court in Missouri, GM sought interstate enforcement of the injunction. The Supreme Court held that full faith and credit did not require enforcement of the injunction by the federal court in Missouri: "Enforcement measures [such as injunctions] do not travel with the sister state judgment as preclusive effects do; such measures remain subject to the even-handed control of forum law." Of course, the duty of enforcing sister-state money judgments remains firm.

b. One may not collaterally attack subject matter jurisdiction for failure of diversity, Des Moines Navigation & Railroad v. Iowa Homestead Co., 123 U.S. 552 (1887), even though a court may dismiss *sua sponte* for lack of diversity on appeal in the original case, Capron v. Van Noorden, 6 U.S. 126 (1804).

c. Conversely, states may choose to declare judgments of their own courts void when they lack subject matter jurisdiction; such judgments are subject to attack at any time. See the discussions in *Gargallo v. Merrill Lynch et al.*, supra page 732. Under the full faith and credit statute, 28 U.S.C. §1738, and its requirement to give the "same" full faith and credit as the rendering state, the second state must look to the effect that the first state gives its own judgments from courts lacking subject matter jurisdiction.

d. Even if a court has jurisdiction over the defendant and the subject matter, the defendant may collaterally attack the judgment in another state by showing that it was procured fraudulently, Bondeson v. Pepsico, Inc., 573 S.W.2d 842 (Tex. Civ. App. 1978) (summary judgment in favor of plaintiff to enforce Florida judgment reversed where defendant alleged that plaintiff had promised to dismiss the Florida action and not prosecute it further).

9. Foreign country judgments present special problems. If the United States and the foreign nation entered into a treaty requiring reciprocal enforcement of each other's judgments, that treaty would bind state and federal courts. But the United States has to date never signed such a treaty. In the absence of such a treaty, neither state nor federal courts are required to give full faith and credit to a foreign judgment under the terms of 28 U.S.C. §1738 or Article IV of the Constitution.

a. The United States has, however, signed a treaty providing for easy enforcement of international arbitration awards. Convention on the Recognition and Enforcement of Foreign Arbitral Awards, 21 U.S.T. 2517, 330 U.N.T.S. 3 (1959). As a result, many international transactions contain arbitration clauses—precisely to allow for reciprocal enforcement.

b. And many states have adopted the Uniform Foreign Money-Judgments Recognition Act, 13 U.L.A. 261. That Act has substantially more exceptions than does the Full Faith and Credit Clause, including, for example, a provision that a judgment need not be enforced if the underlying claim "is repugnant to the public policy of this state." §4(a)(3). The Act nevertheless allows many foreign money judgments to be enforced in state courts.

2. The Reopened Judgment as an Alternative to Collateral Attack

Claim and issue preclusion combine with requirements of full faith and credit to force litigants and courts to honor judgments. In the great majority of cases, litigants wishing to challenge the correctness of a judgment must appeal the decision to a higher court rather than file a second lawsuit. This principle, intended to force challenges into regular channels, can itself work injustice. Consider the case of a litigant who discovers that her opponent has won a victory by unlawful means: Perhaps he failed to serve her with process and thus obtained a default judgment; perhaps he concealed a crucial piece of evidence by failing to produce it in response to an appropriate discovery request. In such a case, appeal will not work because the original court committed no error; the complaint is instead about evidence that never reached the court's attention. But if the plaintiff simply begins a second lawsuit, she will face the defense of claim preclusion.

The escape from this dilemma lies in the opportunity to reopen a judgment. See Rule 60(b). We approach this subject carefully because any discussion of it tends to overstate its practical availability. The basic mechanisms for correcting errors are post-trial motions in the trial court and appeals. To the extent that another post-judgment remedy is available, it necessarily undercuts the appellate system. For this reason, courts insist repeatedly that relief under Rule 60(b) is not a substitute for appeal.

Scan Rule 60(b) and note the different grounds for which relief may be granted. Consider its effort to define the line between interests in finality of adjudication and the inclination to correct injustices when they occur. Now consider what should happen, under Rule 60, if, after a final judgment, the losing litigant discovers that the opposition has failed during discovery to produce highly relevant, perhaps dispositive, materials in its possession. Compare your intuition to the results of the next case.

United States v. Beggerly
524 U.S. 38 (1998)

REHNQUIST, C.J., delivered the opinion of the Court.

[In assembling the lands for a National Seashore, the federal government in 1979 brought a quiet title action (the *Adams* litigation) in the Southern District of Mississippi against respondents. *Adams* turned on whether, before the date of the Louisiana Purchase in 1803, Horn Island had been deeded to a private individual. If so, it would belong to Beggerly, and the United States would have to purchase it; if not, the U.S. government would already own it. That case settled on the eve of trial for a relatively modest sum, reflecting the uncertainty of Beggerly's title.] Judgment was entered based on this settlement agreement. In 1994, some 12 years after that judgment, respondents sued in the District Court to set aside the settlement agreement and obtain a damage award for the disputed land. . . .

During discovery in the *Adams* litigation, respondents sought proof of their title to the land. Government officials searched public land records and told respondents that they had found nothing proving that any part of Horn Island had ever been granted to a private landowner. Even after the settlement in the *Adams* litigation, however, respondents continued to search for evidence of a land patent that supported their claim of title. In 1991 they hired a genealogical record specialist to conduct research in the National Archives in Washington. The specialist found materials that, according to her, showed that on August 1, 1781, Bernardo de Galvez, then the Governor General of Spanish Louisiana, granted Horn Island to [a private party].

Armed with this new information, respondents filed a complaint in the District Court on June 1, 1994. They asked the court to set aside the 1982 settlement agreement and award them damages. . . . The District Court concluded that it was without jurisdiction to hear respondents' suit and dismissed the complaint.

The Court of Appeals reversed. It concluded that there were two jurisdictional bases for the suit. First, the suit satisfied the elements of an "independent action," as the term is used in Federal Rule of Civil Procedure 60(b). . . .

The Government's primary contention is that the Court of Appeals erred in concluding that it had jurisdiction over respondents' 1994 suit. It first attacks the lower court's conclusion that jurisdiction was established because the suit was an "independent action" within the meaning of Rule 60(b). . . . [The Government argued that although] the District Court had jurisdiction over the original *Adams* litigation because the United States was the plaintiff, 28 U.S.C. §1345, there was no statutory basis for the Beggerlys' 1994 action, and the District Court was therefore correct to have dismissed it.

We think the Government's position is inconsistent with the history and language of Rule 60(b). Prior to the 1937 adoption of the Federal Rules of Civil Procedure, the availability of relief from a judgment or order turned on whether the court was still in the same "term" in which the challenged judgment was entered. . . . If the term had expired, resort had to be made to a handful of writs, the precise contours of which were "shrouded in ancient lore and mystery." . . .

The 1946 Amendment [to Rule 60] . . . made clear that nearly all of the old forms of obtaining relief from a judgment, i.e., coram nobis, coram vobis, audita querela, bills of review, and bills in the nature of review, had been abolished. The revision made equally clear, however, that one of the old forms, i.e., the "independent action,"[2] still survived. The Advisory Committee notes confirmed this, indicating that "if the right to make a motion is lost by the expiration of the time limits fixed in these rules, the only other procedural remedy is by a new or independent action to set aside a judgment upon those principles which have heretofore been applied in such an action." . . .

The Government is therefore wrong to suggest that an independent action brought in the same court as the original lawsuit requires an independent basis for jurisdiction. This is not to say, however, that the requirements for a meritorious independent action have been met here. If relief may be obtained through an independent action in a case such as this, where the most that may be charged against the Government is a failure to furnish relevant information that would at best form the basis for a Rule 60(b)(3) motion, the strict 1-year time limit on such motions would be set at naught. Independent actions must, if Rule 60(b) is to be interpreted as a coherent whole, be reserved for those cases of "injustices which, in certain instances, are deemed sufficiently gross to demand a departure" from rigid adherence to the doctrine of *res judicata*. Hazel-Atlas Glass Co. v. Hartford-Empire Co., 322 U.S. 238 (1944).

---

2. This form of action was also referred to as an "original action."

Such a case was Marshall v. Holmes, 141 U.S. 589 (1891), in which the plaintiff alleged that judgment had been taken against her in the underlying action as a result of a forged document. The Court said:

> According to the averments of the original petition for injunction . . . the judgments in question would not have been rendered against Mrs. Marshall but for the use in evidence of the letter alleged to be forged. The case evidently intended to be presented by the petition is one where, without negligence, laches or other fault upon the part of petitioner, [respondent] has fraudulently obtained judgments which he seeks, against conscience, to enforce by execution.

Id., at 596.

The sense of these expressions is that, under the Rule, an independent action should be available only to prevent a grave miscarriage of justice. In this case, it should be obvious that respondents' allegations do not nearly approach this demanding standard. Respondents allege only that the United States failed to "thoroughly search its records and make full disclosure to the Court" regarding the Boudreau grant. Whether such a claim might succeed under Rule 60(b)(3) we need not now decide; it surely would work no "grave miscarriage of justice," and perhaps no miscarriage of justice at all, to allow the judgment to stand. We therefore hold that the Court of Appeals erred in concluding that this was a sufficient basis to justify the reopening of the judgment in the *Adams* litigation.

The judgment of the Court of Appeals is therefore reversed, and the case is remanded for further proceedings consistent with this opinion.

[Justice STEVENS's concurring opinion is omitted.]

WHAT'S NEW HERE?

- The Court declines to reopen a judgment even in the face of newly discovered information suggesting that the original judgment did not reflect the relevant facts.
- The Court declines to do so because the motion to reopen was made more than a year after the original judgment, and the error does not rise to the level of a "grave miscarriage of justice."

Notes and Problems

1. *Beggerly* deals with several distinct problems in reopening judgments. Start with the issue that faced the plaintiff and the Supreme Court. The plaintiffs had found significant evidence not disclosed by their adversary in the prior litigation that might well have led to the award of damages many times the amount for which they had settled 12 years previously.

a. Examine Rule 60(b) carefully and explain why "an independent action," described in the Court's opinion, was the only avenue of relief open to them under the Rule.

b. Now explain the basis for the federal district court's jurisdiction to hear this "independent action."

c. Finally, approach the merits. Why does the Court conclude that these facts do not satisfy the criteria for reopening the judgment under the murky criteria for an independent action? Why does it not work a "grave miscarriage of justice" for the federal government to have taken the plaintiffs' land for an alleged fraction of its value?

d. The materials bearing on the case were apparently in the National Archives, which are open to anyone armed with the determination, and bibliographic and linguistic skills to make use of them. Should the case have come out differently if the same information had existed solely in confidential or secret files, such as those of the Federal Bureau of Investigation or Central Intelligence Agency?

2. Return now to the text of Rule 60(b) and consider how it might have applied had the Beggerlys uncovered the archival evidence within months after the first judgment.

a. Which sections of the Rule might apply?

b. The opinion mentions Rule 60(b)(3). Is that the most obvious one?

3. What principles or values justify holdings like those in *Beggerly*? It is easy to pillory the courts for adhering to mindless technicalities in upholding unjust judgments.

a. Consider the consequences of an opposite rule: that a judgment could be reopened at any time a party had additional relevant information to present.

b. Once one rejects such a rule, there is going to be a difficult line-drawing problem. Does Rule 60 put the lines in the right places?

4. Underlying some decisions in the Rule 60 area is realism about the limits of adversarial fact-finding and advocacy—a line between, if you will, litigation and science. In scientific inquiry, no evidence ever comes in too late, and no conclusion is barred from reexamination; indeed one might say that the essence of scientific research is to raise challenges to long-held assumptions.

a. Litigation is different. We bring some disputes to an end not because we're sure we're right, but because we're sure there has to be an end to the dispute so people can move on with their lives. In such a view, only a genuinely egregious mistake (and perhaps one that the other side caused) is enough to upset the judgment.

b. Moreover, the passage of time itself confers legitimacy: Old law is good law in part because we come to rely on it.

5. Such responses seem most convincing, however, only if the litigant seeking relief has had at least one fair shot at the adversarial system. Perhaps as a consequence, although the Rule itself does not make any distinction between judgments entered at different stages of the litigative process, the courts have in practice made a very sharp distinction between default judgments and others. The effect has been to make it comparatively easy to open a default judgment

on the showing of some negligence and meritorious defense. (See *Peralta*, supra page 525, for an example.) Numerous decisions state, in one way or another, a very strong policy against judgments without consideration of the merits. Indeed, this policy is so strong that some practitioners advise against taking a default judgment unless there is absolutely no alternative. These lawyers have seen too many default judgments taken and defended in clear and justifiable circumstances, only to be set aside in the trial court or on appeal. The net result is considerable expense and a multiyear delay in the litigation.

Assessment Questions

Q1. Jane is a plant geneticist working for GrowCo, a bioengineering company. She sues GrowCo alleging employment discrimination. The case settles and Jane signs an agreement not to pursue this or any related claim. Thereafter, Jane sues GrowCo alleging breach of her employment contract. Which of the following is true?

  A. GrowCo can successfully defend the second suit if the jurisdiction in which the first suit was brought bars subsequent claims "arising from the same transaction or occurrence."

  B. Regardless of the rule applied in the first jurisdiction, GrowCo cannot successfully defend on grounds of claim preclusion.

  C. GrowCo has a valid defense to Jane's second suit regardless of the rule applied in the first jurisdiction.

Q2. Jane sues GrowCo in federal district court, invoking diversity jurisdiction and alleging that GrowCo breached an employment contract calling for her to receive a share of the profits from genetically modified crops she has helped to develop. GrowCo answers the complaint, denying breach of the agreement. The case goes to trial, Jane prevailing. GrowCo then files its own suit, alleging that during her employment Jane stole trade secrets involving the newly developed crops, which violated the terms of her employment contract. Which is true?

  A. Jane has a valid procedural defense to GrowCo's suit.

  B. GrowCo's suit must be allowed to proceed because its claims were not adjudicated in the first lawsuit.

Q3. Student borrows money for educational expenses from the United States, which thereafter concludes that Student has committed fraud in the representations made in her loan application. Lawsuit #1: *United States v. Student* (a civil case seeking to have the loan rescinded). Judgment for the United States with a finding of fraud. Lawsuit #2: *United States v. Student* (a criminal prosecution alleging fraud on the loan application). Does the outcome in the first case preclude Student from relitigating the issue of her fraud?

  A. Yes.

  B. No.

Q4. Lawsuit #1: Borrower sues Lender in federal court, invoking a federal statute regulating the disclosures that must be made on loan documents. Lender makes a Rule 12(b)(6) motion challenging the complaint; motion granted and case dismissed. Lawsuit #2: Borrower sues Lender in state court, invoking a state statute with provisions similar to that of those in the federal statute. The effect of Lawsuit #1 on Lawsuit #2 is . . .

   A. Borrower's second claim is precluded.

   B. Borrower can bring the second claim, but only in state court.

   C. If Borrower is allowed to bring the second claim he will nevertheless lose because Lawsuit #1 determined that Lender did not violate the disclosure law.

Q5. Lawsuit #1: Borrower *A* sues Lender in federal court under a federal statute regulating loans, asserting fraud. Lender denies fraud. Verdict and judgment for Lender. Lawsuit #2: Borrower *B* brings suit on same grounds, involving same alleged misrepresentations. The effect of Lawsuit #1 on Lawsuit #2 is . . .

   A. Borrower *B* can bring the claim.

   B. Borrower *B*'s claim is precluded.

Q6. Lawsuit #1: Borrower *A* sues Lender in federal court under a federal statute regulating loans, asserting fraud. Summary judgment for Borrower *A*. Lawsuit #2: Borrower *B* brings suit on same grounds, involving a different loan for an amount similar to that in first case, and alleging same misrepresentations. The effect of Lawsuit #1 on Lawsuit #2 is . . .

   A. Borrower *B*'s claim is precluded because he should have joined with *A*.

   B. Borrower *B* can bring a claim.

   C. If Borrower *B* is allowed to bring a second claim, Lender will likely be precluded from contesting fraud.

Q7. Lawsuit #1: *Frier v. Vandalia*, seeking replevin of his towed cars. Judgment for Frier. Lawsuit #2: *Frier's Roommate v. Vandalia*, seeking damages for violation of due process when his cars were towed under identical circumstances. The effect of Lawsuit #1 on Lawsuit #2 is . . .

   A. Claim preclusion: Because Frier had the chance to litigate his due process claim in Lawsuit #1, Roomate is precluded.

   B. Issue preclusion: Because Lawsuit #1 resolved whether City violated due process, Roommate cannot relitigate it.

   C. Precedent: Roommate can raise his claim, but it will be bound by the precedent established in Lawsuit #1.

   D. None of the above.

Q8. Lawsuit #1: *Frier v. Vandalia*, with Frier including both replevin and due process claims. Judgment for Vandalia. Lawsuit #2: *Frier's Roommate v. Vandalia*, alleging that City's towing procedures violated due process. The effect of Lawsuit #1 on Lawsuit #2 is . . .

   A. Precedential only.

   B. Claim precluded because Roommate could have joined Frier's suit.

   C. Issue preclusion on question of whether City's procedures violated due process.

Analysis of Assessment Questions

Q1. B and C are correct. A is wrong because claim preclusion requires a judgment, and a settlement is not a judgment—and thus B is correct. C is correct because, if the release was properly drafted, GrowCo can plead it as an affirmative defense and bar Jane's second suit.

Q2. A is correct. Because there was an answer (which is a "pleading"—see Rule 7), Rule 13(a) comes into play. Because Jane's complaint alleged claims surrounding intellectual property in new plant strains, most courts would find that GrowCo's claim concerning trade secrets involved the same transaction or occurrence or series of transactions or occurrences—and was therefore a compulsory counterclaim, waived when omitted from the answer.

Q3. B is correct. The civil case determined only that it was more likely than not that Student committed fraud. The issue in the criminal case will be whether a fact-finder can conclude beyond a reasonable doubt that fraud was committed—a different issue.

Q4. Only A is correct. A is correct because federal courts not sitting in diversity attach broad preclusive effect to 12(b)(6) dismissals—precluding not only the claim brought but transactionally related claims that could be brought. (Here the state law claim could have come into federal court under supplemental jurisdiction.) The second court—state or federal—must give the federal judgment the scope the rendering court would give it. B is wrong because a state court is bound to give the federal judgment the same preclusive effect as the court that rendered it. C is wrong because a 12(b)(6) motion addresses only whether the complaint states a claim.

Q5. A is the correct response. Borrower *B* can bring her claim because she has not had an opportunity to present her claim. B is wrong because the first lawsuit established only that Borrower *A* did not so persuade the court; Borrower *B* is entitled to her own day in court.

Q6. B and C are correct. A is wrong because Borrower *B* has a right to bring his own claim; there is no requirement of joinder. B is correct for the reason just stated. C is correct because federal courts have allowed nonmutual issue preclusion; so long as Lender's opportunity and incentive to litigate were similar in the first and second suits, and Borrower *B* could not have joined Borrower *A*'s suit, preclusion on this issue will apply.

Q7. D is the only correct response. A is wrong because although Frier's due process claim might be precluded (as the court held), Roommate's isn't. B is wrong because Lawsuit #1 established only whether Frier was entitled to get his car back. C is wrong because Frier's entitlement to get his car back will have no bearing on whether the City violated due process.

Q8. Only A is correct. The court's decision in Frier's case will have precedential effect (whether that effect is binding or only persuasive will depend on what court issued the ruling). B is wrong because the ability to join Frier's claim is not sufficient to warrant claim preclusion (see *Taylor v. Sturgell*). C is wrong because issue preclusion cannot be asserted against one not a party to the prior suit.

PART III

PROBING THE BOUNDARIES: ADDITIONAL CLAIMS AND PARTIES

This section combines the approaches taken in the two sections that precede it. Part I took a top-down view, looking at the ways in which the U.S. Constitution establishes constraints for civil litigation. Part II started at the bottom, taking the individual lawsuit as its unit of examination.

We turn now to opportunities and problems that arise when procedural rules expand the confines of a lawsuit. Our forum for that examination is the rules of joinder, the principles that allow parties to modern civil litigation to combine claims and add additional parties. Those principles constitute one of the respects in which contemporary civil litigation differs sharply from its predecessors: A modern lawsuit can, to a large extent, aim at resolving an entire dispute by encompassing all the claims and all the parties involved.

Those same principles, however, challenge both the jurisdictional scheme elaborated in Part I and the litigation process explored in Part II. In many cases jurisdictional problems will either limit or defeat joinder that would otherwise be available. From one standpoint, these limitations are undesirable restrictions on a lawsuit that would otherwise provide a comprehensive resolution to a dispute. From another standpoint, jurisdictional limits prevent what might otherwise become a monster from devouring both the court system and the litigants swept into it. Joinder poses a similar issue for the design of the procedural system. Flexible joinder rules permit parties to frame issues broadly and to include everyone who has a stake in the resolution of those issues. Carried to its logical conclusion, however, this principle of inclusion can create a lawsuit that cannot resolve anything—because it is unmanageable. The Rules consequently walk a fine line, seeking broad inclusion but trying to keep inclusiveness from preventing resolution of the dispute.

The issues thus raised provide a review of much of this course. At the threshold of many cases will be both a pleading problem and a jurisdictional problem. The pleading problem will require you to consider whether the party or claim fits within the joinder rule's definition. If it does, there will sometimes be a second level of inquiry: Assuming that the party or claim can be joined as a matter of pleading, does the court's jurisdictional reach extend far enough to allow joinder of this claim or this party? Just beyond the pleading and jurisdictional inquiries may lie a question about claim or issue preclusion—one party seeking to achieve it, another to avoid it by manipulating joinder rules. This interplay among principles already explored makes joinder challenging—and useful as a test of your grasp of the preceding material.

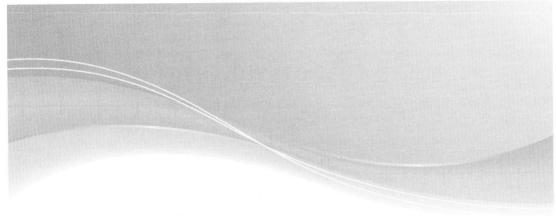

CHAPTER 12

Joinder

Modern civil procedure in the United States has three distinguishing features. One, notice pleading (to the extent it survives *Iqbal*), allows plaintiffs to start lawsuits with less than complete information. The second, discovery, increases the factual depth of any given lawsuit. The third, broad joinder of claims and parties, increases the breadth of a suit. To achieve this breadth, modern process turned from the single-mindedness of common law procedure to focus on the transaction rather than on the writ or legal theory. This focus permits parties to combine various claims. A larger litigative package confers advantages: It allows a court in a single suit to adjudicate multiple claims against multiple parties and for litigation to reflect some of life's complexity. Disadvantages can also flow from this freedom: Litigation can become intricate, and considerable procedural skirmishing can occur long before the merits come into view, as parties dispute whether a particular party or claim is properly joined.

A. JOINDER OF CLAIMS

In our exploration of procedure up to this point, we have for the most part assumed a simple case in which one plaintiff pleads a claim against one defendant, and the defendant does not assert a claim against the plaintiff. But, as you have already seen, many lawsuits are not that simple: A plaintiff often has more than one claim against a defendant, and a defendant may have claims against the plaintiff. We first consider joinder issues in the context of a lawsuit between a single plaintiff and a single defendant. Then we examine the questions that arise when additional parties are joined, either in the initial pleadings or by a later amendment.

1. Joinder of Claims by Plaintiff

a. Historical Background

At common law the rules governing joinder of claims were simple: Plaintiff could join only claims using the same writ but could do so regardless of whether the claims were factually related. For example, plaintiff could join claims for assaults on two separate occasions or a slander on one day and an act of negligence months later (because both used the same writ), but could not join a claim for assault with a claim for slander, even if both arose from the same incident, because slander and assault required different writs. Plaintiff also could join alternative versions of the same grievance by alleging each in a separate count, as if each count referred to a separate occurrence. But, again, each version had to be within the same form of action; plaintiff could not set forth one count in assumpsit and another in trover, even if both arose from the same allegedly wrongful taking. This principle becomes more understandable if one remembers that different writs used different forms of pretrial and trial processes and that the goal of much common law procedure was to frame a single, straightforward question for the jury. Also bear in mind that the scope of former adjudication was correspondingly narrow (see supra page 704).

At common law, a mistake in joinder had severe consequences. Misjoinder could lead to dismissal or even the upsetting of a verdict; the defect was not waived by failure to make an early objection. One can still find cases from the early twentieth century throwing out verdicts because of misjoinder.

As noted in Chapters 5 and 6, as England emerged into the modern era there were separate courts for law and equity. Each operated its own system: If, for example, one wanted specific performance of a contract, one went to Chancery, the court system that administered equitable remedies, such as injunctions. If one wanted instead damages as a remedy for breach of contract, one went to the courts of common law—King's (or Queen's) Bench and Common Pleas, as they were known. For present purposes, the critical point is that courts of equity were more relaxed than courts of law regarding joinder; indeed, its broader scope was one reason for parties' resort to claims for relief that brought claims into courts of equity. Although standards for joinder in equity were never made completely clear, joinder was generally permitted when claims shared a transactional relationship and raised common issues. There were limits, however, and a bill in equity could be found objectionable for *multifariousness*, meaning that it combined too many claims.

b. The Federal Rules

The Rules changed all this: They eliminated all barriers to joinder of claims by a plaintiff. Read Rule 18. A single plaintiff can join any and all claims he has against a single defendant. This freedom can create trial management problems. If one imagines a case between Amazon or Microsoft and one of its major business partners, the possibilities are mind-boggling. The Rules solve this problem by permitting the judge, under Rule 42(b), to sever claims for trial convenience. Such severed claims may be as distinct for pretrial and trial purposes as if the plaintiff had brought entirely separate suits.

Although Rule 18 permits joinder, it does not compel it. So far as the *Rules* are concerned, there is no compulsory joinder of claims. The Rules do not, however, tell the whole story. The principles of claim preclusion, explored in Chapter 11, force a plaintiff to join related claims: If the plaintiff fails to join a claim, and a later court finds it is related to one adjudicated, it will be barred. Moreover, plaintiff will often want to join all claims, or at least all related claims, he has against a defendant for efficiency's sake. The combination of these two factors creates a powerful incentive for plaintiffs to join claims, even in the absence of a Rule requiring that they do so.

c. Joinder and Jurisdiction

Although preclusion and strategy encourage broad joinder, jurisdiction sometimes presents an obstacle. Review of a few fundamental propositions may be helpful in setting the stage.

Assume Ann, a citizen of Illinois, sues Barbara, also a citizen of Illinois, on a federal claim. Can *A* join a state claim against *B*? That question poses two subquestions: (1) Do the Rules permit combining these claims?; and (2) Assuming the Rules allow joinder, does the federal court have jurisdiction over the state claim thus joined?

Rule 18 creates no joinder problem in this situation because it permits a plaintiff to join as many claims as she wishes, whether related or unrelated. The problem is jurisdictional: The court may lack subject matter jurisdiction over Ann's state law claim.

Recall that federal courts have limited jurisdiction: They do not have jurisdiction unless a provision of the Constitution and a statute grant it to them. In the example above, the basis for jurisdiction over the plaintiff's original claim is straightforward: It arises under federal law, over which Article III and 28 U.S.C. §1331 confer jurisdiction.

Jurisdiction over the state law claim is more difficult. There is no diversity of citizenship between plaintiff and defendant. The claim arises under state rather than federal law, so there is no federal question jurisdiction. If there is jurisdiction, it exists only by virtue of the supplemental jurisdiction conferred by 28 U.S.C. §1367. Read that statute and consider what question would have to be answered to resolve the jurisdictional issue here.

Section 1367 has a particularly important feature for our exploration of joinder. Its grant of supplemental jurisdiction depends on four variables: (1) the relationship between the original claim and the claim to be joined; (2) the basis of the original jurisdiction over the case; (3) the identity of the party—plaintiff or defendant—seeking to invoke supplemental jurisdiction; and (4) the Rule authorizing the joinder of the party or claim over whom supplemental jurisdiction is sought.

In the sections below, we will have repeated occasion to explore these variables; in order to gain a basic orientation, consider some elementary problems. In answering each, be prepared to explain which provision of §1367 governs and how you believe that section resolves the question.

Notes and Problems

1. In this and the next four problems, assume the litigation occurs in federal district court. Ann, a citizen of Illinois, sues Barbara, also a citizen of Illinois, alleging that Barbara violated federal civil rights statutes in firing her. Ann seeks to add a state law claim alleging that her firing also violated a state wrongful discharge law. Is there supplemental jurisdiction?

2. Ann, a citizen of Illinois, sues Barbara, also a citizen of Illinois, alleging that Barbara violated federal civil rights statutes in firing her. Ann seeks to add a state law claim alleging that Barbara caused her injuries when Barbara negligently backed her car into Ann's in the company parking lot. Is there supplemental jurisdiction?

3. The same statute blends joinder of additional parties with joinder of claims, as the next two questions illustrate. Ann, a citizen of Illinois, sues Barbara, also a citizen of Illinois, alleging that Barbara violated federal civil rights statutes by permitting co-workers to engage in sexual harassment. Ann seeks to join Charles, a co-worker, who is also a citizen of Illinois and actually engaged in the harassment. Because Charles is not Ann's employer, the claim against him does not arise under federal law, but state tort law supplies a basis for that claim. Assume that the claim against Charles presents sufficiently common issues to qualify for joinder under Rule 20. Is there supplemental jurisdiction over the claim against Charles?

4. Ann, a citizen of Illinois, sues Barbara, a citizen of Wisconsin, alleging breach of an employment contract and seeking a recovery in excess of $75,000. Ann seeks to join Charles, a citizen of Illinois; Ann alleges that Charles conspired with Barbara to breach the employment contract. Assume that the claim against Charles presents sufficiently common issues to qualify for joinder under Rule 20. Is there supplemental jurisdiction over the claim against Charles?

5. State courts also see issues of subject matter jurisdiction arising as a result of joinder.

   a. Suppose in a state court that has adopted the Federal Rules plaintiff sues a publisher for breach of contract, alleging defendant failed to publish her book as promised. After filing this claim, plaintiff proposes an amended complaint that includes a copyright infringement claim (for which there is exclusive federal jurisdiction). Does Rule 18 pose any problem? What is defendant's likely objection to this claim? See 28 U.S.C. §1338(a); cf. *Gargallo v. Merrill Lynch et al.*, supra page 732.

b. Suppose Homeowner sues Neighbor for damages incurred when tree branches fell into Homeowner's yard, bringing the claim in a municipal court whose limited jurisdiction permits it to hear only money damage claims below a set amount. After filing, Homeowner seeks to add a claim for injunctive relief—an order that Neighbor trim similar trees. The new claim may be perfectly proper as a matter of pleading but may lie beyond the jurisdiction of the court.

6. So far we have focused on the interplay between joinder rules and subject matter jurisdiction. What about personal jurisdiction? Suppose that Doug, a citizen of California, wants to sue Edith, a citizen of Nevada, and Frank, a citizen of California, on a federal civil rights claim.

a. Joinder will present no problem if the claims against the two defendants arise from the same transaction and share common questions of law and fact. Nor will federal subject matter jurisdiction: The claim arises under federal law.

b. But if the suit is brought in California, there may be a question of whether the court has personal jurisdiction over Edith, the citizen of Nevada. Such problems of personal jurisdiction will affect the ability of both state and federal courts to hear joined claims. As a quick review of jurisdictional concepts, explain why §1367 will not help with such problems of personal jurisdiction. The litigants and the courts must apply the ordinary principles of personal jurisdiction: If Edith lacks sufficient contacts with California, she can't be joined to a suit brought in that state.

c. In a few instances, however, Rules and statutes offer a "boost" for the personal jurisdiction of the federal courts in a way somewhat analogous to the supplemental jurisdiction extended by §1367. Examine Rule 4(k)(1)(B) and 28 U.S.C. §2361; each will be discussed in connection with the specific joinder devices to which they apply—Rule 4(k)(1)(B) as it relates to impleader and necessary parties, and 28 U.S.C. §2361 as it applies to interpleader.

WHAT'S NEW HERE?

- We're looking at how Parts I and II of this book interact: Chapters 2 through 4, describing constitutional limits on litigation; and the Rules and common law principles that shape the adjudication of contested issues (discussed in Chapters 5 through 11).

2. Claims by the Defendant: Counterclaims and Crossclaims

In examining pleading, we considered the responses that defendant might make to plaintiff's complaint, but we did not much explore the possibility that defendant might have claims against plaintiff. At common law, the rules governing defendant's claims were simple: They did not exist. The defendant who had a claim against plaintiff could bring a separate suit or, in a limited number of cases, "set off" her claim against the plaintiff's (that is, reduce the plaintiff's recovery) but could not herself recover in the original action. Today Rule 13 permits—and sometimes requires—defendants to assert such claims. Rule 13 divides counterclaims into two categories, *compulsory* and *permissive*. Read the Rule and then read the next case. As you do, consider what it means for a counterclaim to be compulsory and why it matters.

WHAT'S NEW HERE?

- Counterclaims change the game. Plaintiffs thinking about a lawsuit have to realize that they cannot entirely define the terms of engagement. Defendants can fire back with claims that can exceed the value of plaintiffs' claims.
- As a result, any plaintiff contemplating a lawsuit has to consider not only the merits of her claim, but the likelihood that defendant may assert counterclaims.

Cordero v. Voltaire, LLC

2013 WL 6415667 (W.D. Tex. Dec. 6, 2013)

Report and Recommendation of the United States Magistrate Judge
AUSTIN, M.J.

TO: THE HONORABLE LEE YEAKEL UNITED STATES DISTRICT JUDGE
. . .

I. General Background

Plaintiffs Carlos Cordero, Omar Benitez, Cory Harvey, Remi Harvey and Toby Marrujo sue their former employer, Defendant Voltaire, LLC ("Defendant"), a construction company, to recover unpaid overtime wages allegedly due under the Fair Labor Standards Act ("FLSA"), 29 U.S.C. §201 et seq. Plaintiffs Cory Harvey, Toby Marrujo, Remi Harvey and Omar Benitez were employed as laborers with Defendant, while Carlos Cordero was employed as Vice President of Construction. Plaintiffs allege that Defendant willfully failed to pay them at least one and one-half times their regular rate of pay for overtime hours worked as is required under the FLSA.

P argues

In response, Defendant alleges that Plaintiffs cannot recover under the FLSA, or that any recovery should be reduced, because Plaintiffs have falsified and inflated the hours they allegedly worked. Specifically, Defendant alleges that "[Plaintiff-Laborers] and numerous other contractors working at Defendant's job sites would provide their time to Carlos Cordero who would then accumulate that time and provide it to Defendant. Cordero was involved in a scheme to defraud and steal from Defendant which included falsifying and inflating the time [they] claimed to work for Defendant and also conspiring with the other workers to falsify and inflate their time that was turned in to Defendant." In addition, Defendant alleges that Plaintiffs took valuable materials and equipment from it. Based upon the foregoing, Defendant has asserted . . . counterclaims for fraud, theft, conversion and breach of fiduciary duty. . . .

Δ argues

Δ has a counterclaim

II. Analysis

Cordero, Remi Harvey, Corey Harvey, and Marrujo have each moved to dismiss the counterclaims . . . pursuant to Federal Rules of Civil Procedure 12(b)(1). . . .

A. Plaintiffs' Rule 12(b)(1) Motion to Dismiss Defendant's Counterclaims

Cordero argues that the counterclaims for theft, conversion, fraud and breach of fiduciary duty are permissive counterclaims under Federal Rule of Civil Procedure 13(b) and, therefore, must "be supported by independent grounds of federal jurisdiction." . . . Although the Court disagrees with some of the legal reasoning, it agrees that some of Voltaire's counterclaims should be dismissed for lack of jurisdiction. . . .

∏ lacks SMJ

2. Supplemental Jurisdiction and Rule 13

As noted, federal courts are courts of limited jurisdiction, and absent jurisdiction conferred by statute, they lack the power to adjudicate claims. Supplemental jurisdiction permits a federal court to entertain a claim over which it would not have an independent basis of subject matter jurisdiction. In 1990, Congress passed the supplemental jurisdiction statute, 28 U.S.C. §1367, which provides that in any case properly brought in federal court, the district court "shall have supplemental jurisdiction over all other claims that are so related to claims in the action within such original jurisdiction that they form part of the *same case or controversy* under Article III." §1367(a) (emphasis added).

Plaintiffs focus their argument on the contention that because the counterclaims are permissive under Rule 13, the counterclaims must have an independent basis for jurisdiction to be brought in this action. Rule 13 divides counterclaims into two basic categories: compulsory and permissive. If the counterclaim "arises out of the transaction or occurrence that is the subject matter of the opposing party's claim," then the party must either assert it under the compulsory counterclaim provision in Rule 13(a) or waive the right to recover on it. It is well established that federal courts have supplemental jurisdiction over compulsory counterclaims because to be compulsory counterclaims in the first place, they have already passed the more stringent test of arising out of the same "transaction or occurrence" as the jurisdiction-invoking claim, and therefore, by definition, satisfy §1367(a)'s "same case or controversy" standard.

If the defendant's claim is independent of the plaintiff's claim, however, then the defendant has the option of bringing it in a separate suit or of asserting it under Rule 13(b) as a permissive counterclaim. In contrast to compulsory counterclaims, permissive counterclaims must either be supported by independent grounds of federal jurisdiction *or* fall within the supplemental jurisdiction of the court under 28 U.S.C. §1367.

Plaintiffs' argument ignores §1367. Before Section 1367 was passed in 1990, courts, including the Fifth Circuit, routinely held that permissive counterclaims required an independent jurisdictional basis before a federal court could exercise subject matter jurisdiction over such claims. . . . Although the Fifth Circuit has not addressed the issue, the consensus among the courts of appeals and the numerous district courts that have considered the issue is that §1367 supersedes case law on supplemental jurisdiction, and it is no longer the case that permissive counterclaims must be supported by an independent basis for jurisdiction, but rather must only meet the test for supplemental jurisdiction under §1367(a). Thus . . . "the appropriate focus should be whether the counterclaims satisfy the requirements of §1367—that is, whether the state law claims are so related to a federal claim as to form part of the same case or controversy under Article III of the Constitution—rather than on whether the counterclaim is compulsory or permissive." . . .

3. Are Defendant's Counterclaims Compulsory? . . .

[I]t appears that the only counterclaim which is compulsory in this case is the counterclaim against Cordero for fraud. Voltaire alleges that Cordero committed fraud by submitting work statements to it with "falsified and inflated hours," and that he submitted bills for time and expenses that were expended on personal and private projects. . . . To prove his FLSA claim, Cordero will have to present evidence showing how many hours he worked, how much he was paid for those hours and how much he should have been paid for those hours. Similarly, to prove its fraud counterclaim, Voltaire will have to present evidence showing that Cordero billed it for false and/or inflated hours and for work expended on personal and private projects. Thus, both claims focus on whether Cordero is owed overtime compensation under the Act and if so, the amount actually owed. . . . Based upon the foregoing, the Court recommends that the District Court deny Plaintiff Cordero's Motion to Dismiss Defendant's fraud counterclaim for lack of jurisdiction.

In contrast to the fraud counterclaim, the evidence needed to prove Defendant's counterclaims for theft, conversion, and breach of fiduciary duty is entirely different than the evidence needed to prove Plaintiffs' FLSA claim. Defendant's allegations that Plaintiffs committed theft and conversion by unlawfully taking valuable equipment and materials and the resulting breach of their fiduciary duties plainly does not rest on the same operative facts as Plaintiffs' FLSA claim that Defendant failed to pay them overtime wages. . . .

4. Does the Court Have Supplemental Jurisdiction over the Permissive Counterclaims?

There is no claim that Voltaire's state law counterclaims of theft, conversion and fiduciary duty are supported by independent grounds of federal jurisdiction. The only question is thus whether those counterclaims fall within the supplemental jurisdiction of the court under 28 U.S.C. §1367. . . .

Voltaire's counterclaims for theft, conversion, and breach of fiduciary duty do not arise from the same set of facts as the FLSA claims. Voltaire's counterclaims do not share common facts with the FLSA claims and a different body of evidence will be required to prove those claims. The only nexus between the FLSA claims and Voltaire's counterclaims is the employment relationship between the parties. "The mere fact that the parties were once linked by an employer-employee relationship is insufficient when the claims would stir such different issues and rely on such different facts and evidence." Thus, numerous courts have found that there was no supplemental jurisdiction over unrelated counterclaims in FLSA actions.

Even if the counterclaims did fall within the court's supplemental jurisdiction, the Court would recommend that the district judge decline to exercise jurisdiction over them because "there are other compelling reasons for declining jurisdiction." 28 U.S.C. §1367(c). "[C]ourts have been hesitant to permit an employer to file counterclaims in FLSA suits for money the employer claims the employee owes it, or for damages the employee's tortious conduct allegedly caused." Thus . . . the Fifth Circuit [explained:]

> The federal courts were not designated by the FLSA to be either collection agents or arbitrators for an employee's creditors. Their sole function and duty under the Act is to assure to the employees of a covered company a minimum level of wages. Arguments and disputations over claims against those wages are foreign to the genesis, history, interpretation, and philosophy of the Act. The only economic feud contemplated by the FLSA involves the employer's obedience to minimum wage and overtime standards. To clutter these proceedings with the minutiae of other employer-employee relationships would be antithetical to the purpose of the Act.

. . . The Court therefore recommends that the District Court grant Plaintiff Cordero's Motion to Dismiss Defendant's counterclaims for theft, conversion, and breach of fiduciary duty under Rule 12(b)(1), but deny the Motion with regard to Voltaire's fraud counterclaim. The Court further recommends that the District Court grant Plaintiffs Remi Harvey, Cory Harvey, and Marrujo's Motion to Dismiss Defendant's counterclaims for theft and conversion under Rule 12(b)(1). . . .

Notes and Problems

1. What is the practical significance of this decision?
   a. If plaintiffs had inflated their hours worked and stolen materials and equipment from Voltaire LLC, why hadn't Voltaire LLC already sued them? To put

the same question another way, what does Voltaire stand to gain by being able to assert a counterclaim that it couldn't achieve by bringing a stand-alone lawsuit in state court?

b. The court concludes that defendant's fraud counterclaim is compulsory. Why does the court reach that conclusion, and why does it matter?

c. The court concludes that defendant's other counterclaims are permissive. Why does the court reach that conclusion, and why does it matter?

d. How does the determination of whether a counterclaim is compulsory or permissive relate to the question of whether the court has subject matter jurisdiction to hear the claim?

2. *Cordero* posits that two consequences flow from deciding a counterclaim is compulsory.

a. First, it must be brought at the risk of losing it. This is an implication of calling a counterclaim compulsory. Some say that an unbrought counterclaim later held to be compulsory is precluded by doctrines of former adjudication. Others, believing that a Rule that specified claim preclusion principles would violate the Rules' Enabling Act ban on altering substantive rights, reach the same conclusion by arguing that a defendant who fails to assert a compulsory counterclaim has thereby waived it.

b. Second, if it is brought, supplemental jurisdiction extends to cover it.

c. Under those circumstances, there is a penalty for omitting a counterclaim that is later held to be compulsory, but no penalty for including a counterclaim that is found not to be compulsory.

d. As a result of this asymmetrical penalty, defense counsel are likely to hedge their bets and include all possible counterclaims, with the result that most cases presenting the issue whether a counterclaim is compulsory or permissive do not arise when defendant has omitted the counterclaim in one action and attempted to assert it in a later action. Instead, most cases are like *Cordero*: Plaintiffs assert a federal claim; defendant interposes counterclaims under state law for which there is no independent federal jurisdiction; plaintiffs move to dismiss the counterclaims for lack of subject matter jurisdiction; and defendant argues that the counterclaims are compulsory and, thus, within the supplemental jurisdiction of the federal court.

5. It is less clear what consequences befall a counterclaim that is determined permissive. As the *Cordero* opinion recites, at one time, courts agreed that there is no supplemental jurisdiction over permissive counterclaims. But more recently courts have taken an increasingly nuanced perspective about the relationship between Rule 13(b) permissive counterclaims and supplemental jurisdiction. As the magistrate in *Cordero* concludes, a claim may not arise out of the same transaction or occurrence for Rule 13 purposes, but can still form part of the same case or controversy for §1367 purposes.

6. Whether a counterclaim is compulsory may depend on when the suit is brought.

a. In January 2018, *B* purchased a house from *S* and gave a promissory note for $100,000, payable on January 2, 2019, for the unpaid balance of the purchase price. In November 2018, alleging numerous defects in the house, *B* sued *S* for breach of contract and breach of warranty. Reread Rule 13(a) and explain why *S*'s claim on the unpaid promissory note is not a compulsory counterclaim.

b. Same facts as in 6a, except that Buyer brought his breach of contract and warranty case on February 1, 2019. Buyer did not pay the $100,000 he owed to Seller on January 2, 2019. On February 15, 2019, Seller includes in his answer a counterclaim on the unpaid note. Explain why the Seller's counterclaim is now compulsory. Rule 12(a)(1) and Rule 13(a)(1).

7. Rule 13 also allows a defendant to bring what the Rules call a crossclaim against a codefendant. Assume Passenger is injured in a collision between Driver One and Driver Two and brings suit against both. Driver One may have no counterclaim against Passenger but may have a claim against Driver Two.

a. The Rules refer to Driver One's claim against Driver Two as a *crossclaim.* See Rule 13(g).

b. Note that an initial crossclaim under Rule 13(g) can only be brought if it concerns the same transaction or occurrence as the original claim, or if it concerns property that is the subject matter of the original action. But note also that once Driver One has brought a crossclaim against Driver Two, Rule 18 allows Drivers One and Two to assert any claims they have against each other.

c. Some states do not make such fine distinctions in their joinder terminology. California, for example, uses "crossclaim" to refer both to what a federal court would call a "counterclaim" and to what a federal court would call a "crossclaim."

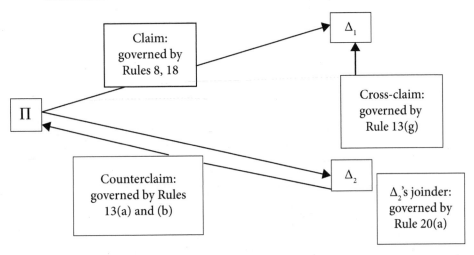

8. Counter- and crossclaims are an important point of modern joinder, but don't assume they apply to all situations. They function as a way of *asserting* liability, not as a way of avoiding it; they are a way of bringing a claim against another,

not defending against one. So if one wants simply to avoid liability, denial and affirmative defenses are the routes to take. Counter- and crossclaims are the tools to use when one wants to obtain some affirmative relief from another party. Consider the following problems. Plaintiff files a complaint against an automobile Dealer and an automobile Manufacturer. The complaint, which is properly before the court under diversity jurisdiction, alleges that Plaintiff was injured in an accident caused by a defect in the vehicle's steering mechanism.

a. Manufacturer wants to assert that the vehicle was not defective when delivered to Dealer and that any defect must have been introduced by Dealer when the vehicle was being prepared for delivery to customer. What pleading, if any, should Manufacturer file?

b. Manufacturer wants to assert that Dealer has failed to pay for several vehicles that Manufacturer delivered to Dealer (not including the vehicle at issue in the action). Can it bring a claim against Dealer in this case?

c. Dealer wants to assert that Plaintiff owes Dealer money for a breach of contract that has no relationship whatsoever to the vehicle or accident at issue in Plaintiff's complaint (perhaps a repair to another vehicle owned by Plaintiff). Can Dealer do so? What pleading, if any, should it use?

d. Dealer and Manufacturer both want to assert that there was no defect in the vehicle and that the accident was solely the result of Plaintiff's negligence. What pleading, if any, should Dealer and Manufacturer use?

B. JOINDER OF PARTIES

1. By Plaintiffs

Mosley v. General Motors Corp.
497 F.2d 1330 (8th Cir. 1974)

Ross, J.

Nathaniel Mosley and nine other persons joined in bringing this action individually and as class representatives alleging that their rights guaranteed under 42 U.S.C. §2000e et seq. and 42 U.S.C. §1981 were denied by General Motors and Local 25, United Automobile, Aerospace and Agriculture Implement Workers of America [Union] by reason of their color and race. . . . Each of the ten named plaintiffs had, prior to the filing of the complaint, filed a charge with the Equal Employment Opportunity Commission [EEOC] asserting the facts underlying these claims. Pursuant thereto, the EEOC made a reasonable cause finding that General Motors, Fisher Body Division and Chevrolet Division, and the Union had engaged in unlawful employment practices in violation of Title VII of the Civil Rights Act of 1964. Accordingly, the charging parties were notified by EEOC of their right to institute a civil action in the appropriate federal district court. . . .

In each of the first eight counts of the twelve-count complaint, eight of the ten plaintiffs alleged that General Motors, Chevrolet Division, had engaged in unlawful employment practices by: "discriminating against Negroes as regards promotions, terms and conditions of employment"; "retaliating against Negro employees who protested actions made unlawful by Title VII of the Act and by discharging some because they protested said unlawful acts"; "failing to hire Negro employees as a class on the basis of race"; "failing to hire females as a class on the basis of sex"; "discharging Negro employees on the basis of race"; and "discriminating against Negroes and females in the granting of relief time." Each additionally charged that the defendant Union had engaged in unlawful employment practices "with respect to the granting of relief time to Negro and female employees" and "by failing to pursue . . . grievances." The remaining two plaintiffs made similar allegations against General Motors, Fisher Body Division. All of the individual plaintiffs requested injunctive relief, back pay, attorneys' fees and costs. Counts XI and XII of the complaint were class action counts against the two individual divisions of General Motors. They also sought declaratory and injunctive relief, back pay, attorneys' fees and costs. . . .

The district court ordered that "insofar as the first ten counts are concerned, those ten counts shall be severed into ten separate causes of action," and each plaintiff was directed to bring a separate action based upon his complaint, duly and separately filed. The court also ordered that the class action would not be dismissed, but rather would be left open "to each of the plaintiffs herein, individually or collectively . . . to allege a separate cause of action on behalf of any class of persons which such plaintiff or plaintiffs may separately or individually represent."

In reaching this conclusion on joinder, the district court followed the reasoning of *Smith v. North American Rockwell Corp.* which, in a somewhat analogous situation, found there was no right to relief arising out of the same transaction, occurrence or series of transactions or occurrences, and that there was no question of law or fact common to all plaintiffs sufficient to sustain joinder under Federal Rule of Civil Procedure 20(a). Similarly, the district court here felt that the plaintiffs' joint actions against General Motors and the Union presented a variety of issues having little relationship to one another; that they had only one common problem, i.e., the defendant; and that as pleaded the joint actions were completely unmanageable. Upon entering the order, and upon application of the plaintiffs, the district court found that its decision involved a controlling question of law as to which there is a substantial ground for difference of opinion and that any of the parties might make application for appeal under 28 U.S.C. §1292(b). We granted the application to permit this interlocutory appeal and for the following reasons we affirm in part and reverse in part.

Rule 20(a) of the Federal Rules of Civil Procedure provides:

> [(1) *Plaintiffs.* Persons may join in one action as plaintiffs if:
> (A) they assert any right to relief jointly, severally, or in the alternative with respect to or arising out of the same transaction, occurrence, or series of transactions or occurrences; and
> (B) any question of law or fact common to all plaintiffs will arise in the action.*]

---

* [At the time of the decision, the relevant portion of Rule 20 read: "All persons may join in one action as plaintiffs if they assert any right to relief jointly, severally, or in the alternative in respect of or arising out of the same transaction, occurrence, or series of transactions or occurrences and if any question of law or fact common to all these persons will arise in the action. . . ."—EDS.]

Additionally, Rule 20(b) and Rule 42(b) vest in the district court the discretion to order separate trials or make such other orders as will prevent delay or prejudice. In this manner, the scope of the civil action is made a matter for the discretion of the district court, and a determination on the question of joinder of parties will be reversed on appeal only upon a showing of abuse of that discretion. To determine whether the district court's order was proper herein, we must look to the policy and law that have developed around the operation of Rule 20.

The purpose of the rule is to promote trial convenience and expedite the final determination of disputes, thereby preventing multiple lawsuits. 7 C. Wright, Federal Practice and Procedure §1652, at 265 (1972). Single trials generally tend to lessen the delay, expense and inconvenience to all concerned. Reflecting this policy, the Supreme Court has said: "Under the Rules, the impulse is toward entertaining the broadest possible scope of action consistent with fairness to the parties; joinder of claims, parties and remedies is strongly encouraged." United Mine Workers of America v. Gibbs, 383 U.S. 715 (1966).

Permissive joinder is not, however, applicable in all cases. The rule imposes two specific requisites to the joinder of parties: (1) a right to relief must be asserted by, or against, each plaintiff or defendant relating to or arising out of the *same transaction or occurrence, or series of transactions or occurrences;* and (2) *some question of law or fact common* to all the parties must arise in the action.

In ascertaining whether a particular factual situation constitutes a single transaction or occurrence for purposes of Rule 20, a case by case approach is generally pursued. 7 C. Wright, Federal Practice and Procedure §1653, at 270 (1972). No hard and fast rules have been established under the rule. However, construction of the terms "transaction or occurrence" as used in the context of Rule 13(a) counterclaims offers some guide to the application of this test. For the purposes of the latter rule, "'Transaction' is a word of flexible meaning. It may comprehend a series of many occurrences, depending not so much upon the immediateness of their connection as upon their logical relationship." Moore v. New York Cotton Exchange, 270 U.S. 593 (1926). Accordingly, all "logically related" events entitling a person to institute a legal action against another generally are regarded as comprising a transaction or occurrence. 7 C. Wright, Federal Practice and Procedure §1653, at 270 (1972). The analogous interpretation of the terms as used in Rule 20 would permit all reasonably related claims for relief by or against different parties to be tried in a single proceeding. Absolute identity of all events is unnecessary.

This construction accords with the result reached in United States v. Mississippi, 380 U.S. 128 (1965), a suit brought by the United States against the State of Mississippi, the election commissioners, and six voting registrars of the State, charging them with engaging in acts and practices hampering and destroying the right of black citizens of Mississippi to vote. The district court concluded that the complaint improperly attempted to hold the six county registrars jointly liable for what amounted to nothing more than individual torts committed by them separately against separate applicants. In reversing, the Supreme Court said:

But the complaint charged that the registrars had acted and were continuing to act as part of a state-wide system designed to enforce the registration laws in a way that would

> inevitably deprive colored people of the right to vote solely because of their color. On such an allegation the joinder of all the registrars as defendants in a single suit is authorized by Rule 20(a) of the Federal Rules of Civil Procedure. . . . These registrars were alleged to be carrying on activities which were part of a series of transactions or occurrences the validity of which depended to a large extent upon "question[s] of law or fact common to all of them."

Here too, then, the plaintiffs have asserted a right to relief arising out of the same transactions or occurrences. Each of the ten plaintiffs alleged that he had been injured by the same general policy of discrimination on the part of General Motors and the Union. Since a "state-wide system designed to enforce the registration laws in a way that would inevitably deprive colored people of the right to vote" was determined to arise out of the same series of transactions or occurrences, we conclude that a company-wide policy purportedly designed to discriminate against blacks in employment similarly arises out of the same series of transactions or occurrences. Thus the plaintiffs meet the first requisite for joinder under Rule 20(a).

The second requisite necessary to sustain a permissive joinder under the rule is that a question of law or fact common to all the parties will arise in the action. The rule does not require that *all* questions of law and fact raised by the dispute be common. Yet, neither does it establish any qualitative or quantitative test of commonality. For this reason, cases construing the parallel requirement under Federal Rule of Civil Procedure 23(a) provide a helpful framework for construction of the commonality required by Rule 20. In general, those cases that have focused on Rule 23(a)(2) have given it a permissive application so that common questions have been found to exist in a wide range of contexts. 7 C. Wright, Federal Practice and Procedure §1763 at 604 (1972). Specifically, with respect to employment discrimination cases under Title VII, courts have found that the discriminatory character of a defendant's conduct is basic to the class, and the fact that the individual class members may have suffered different effects from the alleged discrimination is immaterial for the purposes of the prerequisite. *Hicks v. Crown Zellerbach Corp.* In this vein, one court has said:

> [A]lthough the actual effects of a discriminatory policy may thus vary throughout the class, the existence of the discriminatory policy threatens the entire class. And whether the Damoclean threat of a racially discriminatory policy hangs over the racial class is a question of fact common to all the members of the class.

The right to relief here depends on the ability to demonstrate that each of the plaintiffs was wronged by racially discriminatory policies on the part of the defendants General Motors and the Union. The discriminatory character of the defendants' conduct is thus basic to each plaintiff's recovery. The fact that each plaintiff may have suffered different effects from the alleged discrimination is immaterial for the purposes of determining the common question of law or fact. Thus, we conclude that the second requisite for joinder under Rule 20(a) is also met by the complaint.

For the reasons set forth above, we conclude that the district court abused its discretion in severing the joined actions. The difficulties in ultimately adjudicating damages to the various plaintiffs are not so overwhelming as to require such severance. If appropriate, separate trials may be granted as to any particular issue after the determination of common questions.

The judgment of the district court disallowing joinder of the plaintiffs' individual actions is reversed and remanded with directions to permit the plaintiffs to proceed jointly. . . .

Notes and Problems

1. Why did the litigants think the joinder question so important? If you were the plaintiffs' lawyer, would you rather try these cases together or separately? If you were General Motors's lawyer, which would you prefer? It may be helpful to consider whether *Mosley* involves the same strategic considerations at play in *Fisher v. Ciba Specialty Chemicals Corp.*, Chapter 1, supra page 28.

2. Note the unusual procedural posture in *Mosley*: The district court's ruling on joinder did not produce an appealable final judgment, but the district and appellate courts thought the issue of joinder important enough to certify an interlocutory appeal, something that at present happens only about 100 times each year among the 250,000 civil suits filed annually in the federal system.

3. The court says that "[e]ach of the ten plaintiffs alleged that he had been injured by the same general policy of discrimination on the part of General Motors and the Union."

   a. Consider who the plaintiffs are:
      - African Americans employed by GM alleging they had not been promoted;
      - African Americans employed by GM alleging they had been punished for protesting GM's unlawful actions;
      - African Americans who had applied for but not been hired by GM;
      - Women (presumably both African-American and white) who had applied for jobs but not been hired by GM;
      - African-American employees who had been fired;
      - African-American male and female employees and white female employees who alleged they had not been granted "relief time" on the same terms as white males.

   What "question of law or fact common to all plaintiffs will arise in the action"? Rule 20(a)(1).

   b. Although joinder here seems like a victory for the plaintiffs, it can also limit their rights going forward. Suppose the case proceeds, with discovery focusing on the defendants' alleged refusal to hire or promote African Americans and women. Imagine the ten plaintiffs prevail after trial (or, more likely, there is a settlement that is embodied in a consent decree, which has the same preclusive effect as a judgment). Thereafter, one of the ten female plaintiffs brings a second suit alleging that GM's maternity leave policies during the period at issue in the first lawsuit constituted a violation of Title VII, the same statute invoked in the first suit. Couldn't GM argue that the breadth of joinder in the first suit meant that it precluded relitigation of any claim involving prohibited race- or gender-based discrimination?

   c. What would have happened in *Mosley* if the court had found joinder improper? See Rule 21.

4. Courts are not always as flexible as *Mosley* in finding common links among plaintiffs:

> The Plaintiffs in this case, all female, are employed by or were formerly employed by AT&T as sales persons in a small, distinct business organization within AT&T known as the Profile Initiative Program (PIP). The Plaintiffs are residents of five different cities and four different states who worked in four separate AT&T offices located in three states. While the Plaintiffs were directly supervised by different managers in each office, it appears they were indirectly supervised by the same centralized PIP upper management group. The Plaintiffs contend the PIP management systematically discriminated against them because of their sex and allege discriminatory actions by some of the same individuals in PIP management. However, the Plaintiffs identify no specific discriminatory policy or practice to which they were all subjected. In addition to the claims of sex discrimination, Plaintiff Harryman asserts claims of race, age, and national origin discrimination, while Plaintiff Bryan asserts a claim of age discrimination. All the Plaintiffs also assert various state law claims against the Defendants. Thus, AT&T is faced with five individual Plaintiffs asserting a total of more than twenty claims against it. . . .
>
> AT&T contends the Plaintiffs are misjoined and request that this Court sever the claims of each Plaintiff and proceed with five separate trials. . . . AT&T argues the jury may improperly conclude that it is guilty of wrongdoing simply because so many Plaintiffs will complain of discrimination and so many different witnesses will testify in support of the Plaintiffs' claims. AT&T further contends that in a single trial, the jury will hear evidence that may be relevant to the claims of one Plaintiff, but that is completely irrelevant and prejudicial to the claims of the remaining Plaintiffs. According to AT&T, a single trial will unnecessarily complicate evidentiary rulings and will deprive this Court of its discretion to rule on the admissibility of marginally relevant but highly prejudicial evidence.

Henderson v. AT&T Corp., 918 F. Supp. 1059, 1061 (S.D. Tex. 1996).

Recognizing that *Mosley* was the leading case on joinder of plaintiffs in employment discrimination cases, the court allowed the joinder under Rule 20 but went on to sever three of the five cases for pretrial and trial.

5. *Henderson* (supra) reminds us that joinder is a game that three can play.

   a. Initially, plaintiff has the choice, subject to the constraints of Rule 20(a)(1).

   b. As in *Mosley* and *Henderson*, defendant can challenge joinder of parties, with the result, under Rule 21, that the parties found to be improperly joined will have their cases severed.

   c. The third player is the judge, who rules on any challenges to joinder under Rule 20, but also exercises independent power to consolidate and sever claims under Rule 42. Suppose that the *Mosley* plaintiffs had filed ten separate lawsuits and the trial judge had concluded that they were in fact closely related and should be consolidated. Under Rule 42(a), the judge can "join for hearing or trial any or all matters at issue in the actions."

d. Conversely, even if the parties are content with the party structure as it stands, a court acting under the authority of Rule 42(b) may sever claims.

e. Finally, in many federal districts there are local rules that require parties to identify a case that is factually related to any other case currently pending in the district. The purpose of this identification is to allow consolidation of related claims—and to prevent judge-shopping by filing several similar claims and then dismissing all but the one that draws the friendliest judge. Note, though, that this rule can also have the opposite effect. If a case is pending before a friendly judge, an attorney with a similar case can try to get his case before that same judge by arguing that it is related.

6. Given broad judicial discretion to consolidate and hold separate trials, one might ask whether Rules 20 and 21 are necessary. In other words, there could be unlimited joinder of parties—just as there is of claims—with the question of joinder treated, through Rule 42, as one of trial convenience. Assume *A* has similar claims against *B* and *C*. What is the practical difference between one action by *A* against *B* and *C* and consolidation of separate actions by *A* vs. *B* and *A* vs. *C* under Rule 42(a)? Some possible differences include requirements of serving papers, Rules 5(a), 30(b)(1); right to cross-examine at depositions, cf. Rule 30(c); and right of discovery by *B* against *C* and vice versa, Rules 33, 34, 35. In practice, the court consolidating the two cases may order that *B* and *C* be treated as coparties for such matters, thus minimizing these differences.

2. By Defendants: Third-Party Claims

Modern economic life is full of contingent liabilities: If John has an auto accident, his insurers will indemnify him; if Jane overdraws her checking account her bank will cover the overdraft (up to a stated amount); if a roof collapses because Supplier sold Builder defective materials, the Supplier must pay for the damages. But notice that in each of these cases the immediate defendant may be John, Jane, or Builder. The next case illustrates a party's ability to defend itself by passing on liability—and the joinder device that permits it.

Price v. CTB, Inc.
168 F. Supp. 2d 1299 (M.D. Ala. 2001)

DE MENT, J., . . .

[Price, a chicken farmer, hired Latco to build a new chicken house. Alleging that the structure was defective, Price sued multiple defendants, including] Latco . . . in the underlying action concerning the quality of its workmanship when it constructed chicken houses for various Alabama farmers. The causes of action against Latco include breach of the construction contract, fraudulent misrepresentation of the caliber of materials to be used, and negligence and wantonness in the construction. Latco moved to file a Third Party Complaint against, inter alios, ITW on February 21, 2001, approximately six months after the case had been removed to the Middle District of Alabama. . . . In the Third Party Complaint, Latco alleges that ITW, a nail manufacturer, defectively designed the nails used in the construction of the chicken houses. The specific causes of action include breach of warranty, violation of the Alabama Extended Manufacturer's Liability Doctrine, and common law indemnity. ITW argues that it was improperly impleaded under Rule 14 of the Federal Rules of Civil Procedure, or, alternatively, that the Third Party Complaint is barred by the equitable doctrine of laches.

Under Rule 14(a), a defendant may assert a claim against anyone not a party to the original action if that third party's liability is in some way dependent upon the outcome of the original action. There is a limitation on this general statement, however. Even though it may arise out of the same general set of facts as the main claim, a third party claim will not be permitted when it is based upon a separate and independent claim. Rather, the third party liability must in some way be derivative of the original claim; a third party may be impleaded only when the original defendant is trying to pass all or part of the liability onto that third party.

Latco argues that ITW is the prototypical third party defendant under Rule 14. It asserts that ITW can be found liable for the warranty surrounding its products if Latco is first found liable for faulty construction. Furthermore, insists Latco, this derivative liability merely involves a shift in the overall responsibility of the allegedly defective chicken houses. ITW contends, however, that because Rule 14 is merely a procedural rule, the propriety of its application depends upon the existence of a right to indemnity under the substantive law. ITW accurately states the law in this regard, but its conclusion that there is no viable substantive claim under Alabama law is incorrect.

Conceding that Alabama does not recognize a right to contribution among joint tortfeasors, Latco directs the court's attention to the concept of implied contractual indemnity. Under this doctrine, Alabama courts recognize that a manufacturer of a product has impliedly agreed to indemnify the seller when 1) the seller is without fault, 2) the manufacturer is responsible, and 3) the seller has been required to pay a monetary judgment. Under Latco's theory, should it be found liable for its construction of the chicken houses, it can demonstrate that the true fault lies with the nail guns and the nails manufactured by ITW.

Alabama case law, not to mention the parties' briefs, is especially sparse with respect to the contours of the doctrine of implied indemnity. . . . [The opinion went on to find that Alabama's law resembled that of Illinois on the point in question and that Illinois would permit a claim for implied indemnity under the circumstances of the case.] The court finds that Alabama law provides Latco a cause of action under common law indemnity against ITW.

It must be noted, however, that, under Alabama law, the doctrine permits recovery only when the party to be indemnified is "without fault." Whether, in fact, such a factual scenario will be proven at trial is irrelevant for present purposes. The only issue before the court is whether there exists a legal basis to implead ITW, not whether ITW is, in fact, liable to Latco. Since Rule 14 permits Latco to implead any party who "may be liable," Fed. R. Civ. P. 14(a), it follows that the court must permit development of the factual record so the extent of that liability may be determined. . . .

Furthermore, since Latco has established a basis upon which it may properly implead ITW, the court need not address the applicability of Rule 14 to the other claims in Latco's Third Party Complaint. It is well established that a properly impleaded claim may serve as an anchor for separate and independent claims under Rule 18(a).[3] . . . In short, the court finds that Latco has properly impleaded ITW under Rule 14(a). [The opinion went on to reject ITW's claim of laches, finding there had been no undue delay in filing the claim and no prejudice to ITW.]

Accordingly, it is CONSIDERED and ORDERED that ITW's Motion to Dismiss be and the same is hereby DENIED.

WHAT'S NEW HERE?

- Impleader depends on an interesting defensive maneuver: The person sued (in addition to denying liability) can say that "*if* I am adjudged liable, there's someone else who has to pay all or part of the damages."
- That "derivative liability," as it's sometimes called, arises because of some relationship between the defendant and the impleaded party. That relation can be contractual (an insurance policy, for example) or imposed because of some relation between the parties (for example, joint tortfeasors).
- Impleader (exemplified in Rule 14) does not create the derivative liability; instead, it offers a procedural channel through which that liability can be asserted in the main lawsuit rather than in a separate action.

---

3. The court finds it necessary to dispel any worry that its rule might permit defendants to improperly encumber ongoing lawsuits by simply asserting claims of implied contractual indemnity. Rule 14(a) grants federal courts discretion in determining the propriety of a third party complaint, and in making its determination, a court may consider the burden upon the litigation that might ensue, as well as the merit of the third party complaint. . . . Rules 21 and 42 further provide original plaintiffs protection against vexatious litigation by permitting the court to drop parties or to sever claims. In the present matter, the court deems it appropriate to allow the factual record to develop so that the role of ITW's products in the allegedly defective chicken houses can be determined. Under the rationale that a stitch in time saves nine, the court considers it more efficient to determine liability presently rather than to risk potential relitigation on all the issues at a later date. This conclusion is underscored given that forty identical suits were filed against Latco.

Notes and Problems

1. To understand the possibilities and limits of impleader, consider a world in which it did not exist.

   a. Mr. Price, a chicken farmer, sues Latco for damages suffered when the structures fell apart and the chickens died or fell ill. If Latco wins, there's no problem—at least no procedural problem (Mr. Price will be unhappy).

   b. Suppose, however, Latco loses, with a judgment that finds the houses defective and awards damages. In a world without impleader, Latco could still sue the nail manufacturer. But, because the nail manufacturer wasn't a party to the first suit, it would be able in the second suit to argue, for example, that the chicken houses weren't defective at all, or that it was, for example, Mr. Price's poor maintenance that destroyed them. The two lawsuits could thus result in opposed findings—that the houses were defective and that they weren't—with Latco left holding the bag. Or the jury in the first case might find that Mr. Price suffered very substantial damages—when all his chickens died—while the jury in the second case might find that damages were limited to the cost of a new structure, because the chickens' death had been due to Mr. Price's failure to mitigate.

   c. Impleader provisions like those found in Rule 14 solve the problems just described. By bringing the nail manufacturer into the lawsuit, impleader assures that the manufacturer will be bound by a judgment in the original case.

2. With this understanding, refocus on what is at stake for ITW, the nail manufacturer, now that impleader has been held to be proper.

   a. Obviously, it has to defend this case.

   b. What do you imagine the stakes are for ITW in this case? Reread the last sentence of footnote 3. How might a loss in this case implicate those 40 identical suits? How does ITW's problem present a situation that Mr. Price's lawyer might exploit?

   c. With this new problem in mind, suppose that, as litigation proceeds, ITW's lawyer decides that things are not going well. The judge has made a number of rulings that ITW thinks will make it hard to mount a really effective defense at trial; moreover, he is concerned about how a local jury might react to an out-of-state defendant corporation (the *I* in ITW stands for Illinois). Can you recommend a course of action that might minimize ITW's litigation exposure in this and the 40 other cases?

Procedure as Strategy

Rule 14 has two attractions for parties defending against claims. First, and obviously, it gives them a way of bringing into the suit anyone else who might help them foot all or part of the damage bill. Less obviously, it gives such defendants a way of delaying the case and making litigation more expensive for the plaintiff by adding another party. Inevitably, a three-party case will take longer than a two-party case: For the added party there will be a flurry of pleadings and related motions; there will be additional discovery; scheduling three sets of lawyers' meetings increases time conflicts exponentially; and so on. Moreover, from the plaintiff's standpoint, this added delay and expense does nothing for her, so long as she has identified a solvent defendant and has a strong claim. Impleader is for defendant's benefit. Not surprisingly, then, plaintiffs are often unenthusiastic about defendant's impleading additional parties. (Footnote 3 of *Price* exemplifies the concerns that plaintiffs may have.)

Like all tactics, impleader also has some drawbacks for defendants. Consider *Price*. Yes, the construction company now has someone who may pay all or part of the damages if the chicken houses are judged defective. But the construction company now has *two* parties who will bend their litigative efforts to showing that the construction was shoddy: In addition to the plaintiff, the nail manufacturer will want to show that poor construction practices, not bad nails, caused the houses to fail.

3. To reinforce your understanding of the principle represented by impleader, imagine that when Mr. Price sued Latco for the collapsed chicken house, Latco investigated and found evidence that the house was in fact destroyed by Farmer Jones, a rival neighbor chicken raiser who sneaked onto Price's property at night and vandalized the house.

   a. Latco could *not* implead Jones. This outcome looks at first surprising, but it is well established:

   > It is no longer possible . . . to implead a third party claimed to be solely liable to the plaintiff. . . . A proposed third-party plaintiff must allege facts sufficient to establish the derivative or secondary liability of the proposed third-party defendant. . . . Thus, under Rule 14(a), a third-party complaint is appropriate only in cases where the proposed third-party defendant would be secondarily liable to the original defendant in the event the latter is held to be liable to the plaintiff.

   > Barab v. Menford, 98 F.R.D. 455, 456 (E.D. Pa. 1983) (citations omitted).

   > Numerous courts have echoed this principle. . . . Derivative liability is central to the operation of Rule 14. It cannot be used as a device to bring into a controversy matters which merely happen to have some relationship to the original action. . . . In other words, a third party claim is not appropriate where the defendant and putative third party plaintiff says, in effect, "It was him, not me." [Impleader] is viable only where a proposed third party plaintiff says, in effect, "If I am liable to plaintiff, then my liability is only technical or secondary or partial, and the third party defendant is derivatively liable and must reimburse me for all or part of anything I must pay plaintiff."

   > Watergate Landmark Condominiums Unit Owners' Ass'n v. Wiss, Janey, Elstner Assocs., 117 F.R.D. 576, 578 (E.D. Va. 1987).

    b. How, then, can Latco raise and litigate the issue of Jones's responsibility for the damage?

4. Impleader typically has two substantive foundations, one in tort and the other in contract, both mentioned in the case.

    a. The tort doctrine is that of "contribution," a claim that allows one tortfeasor to demand that another fellow wrongdoer "contribute" to the damages payable to the harmed plaintiff. Nineteenth-century law often limited or forbade entirely such contribution on the grounds that no one should be able to avoid the consequences of his own wrongdoing. Legislatures and courts in the twentieth and twenty-first centuries have often been more forgiving, permitting such actions for contribution among joint tortfeasors. But not always; notice that Alabama at the time of *Price v. CTB* did not allow for such an action of contribution.

    b. The contract doctrine is of indemnity. Suppose Mr. Price, the farmer who sued Latco, did not own the chicken houses but instead leased them from AgriBiz. The lease contains a provision that Price will indemnify and hold AgriBiz harmless from any claim arising out of Price's use of the premises. Price's employee, who works in the building in question, develops lung disease and sues AgriBiz, claiming that his injury is caused by the asbestos-lined ventilation system in the structures. Employee can't bring that claim against his employer, Price, because workers' compensation statutes block suits against the employer. But he can sue AgriBiz, a third party, claiming its installation and maintenance of the ventilation system caused his injuries. AgriBiz, when sued by Employee, can then implead Price, invoking his indemnity agreement.

5. Now consider who can file a third-party complaint, and when impleader can be challenged.

    a. Price sues Latco for defectively constructed chicken houses. Latco promptly impleads Nails, the manufacturer of the nails and nail guns used in constructing the houses, contending that Nails's products were defective. The court permits the impleader of Nails. After a six-month investigation of the claims, Nails seeks leave to implead SteelCo, the manufacturer who supplied the metal used in making Latco's nails; Nails's third-party complaint alleges that the metal supplied during the time in question had impurities that caused the nails to corrode when exposed to the weather. Successive impleader of this nature is allowed by the Rules. On what grounds might a party object to Nails's motion to implead SteelCo?

    b. In the case described in 5a, when Price sues Latco, Latco counterclaims against Price for unpaid construction bills, alleging that Price failed to pay the agreed-upon contract price for the construction. In response to Latco's counterclaim, Price seeks to implead Bank, which, Price alleges, failed to fund Price's line of credit as it had agreed. Rule 14 permits a *plaintiff* to use impleader in this fashion: Any "defending party" may use impleader to pass on all or part of the liability.

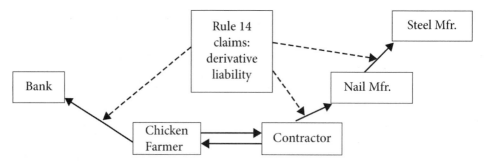

Chickens (and Impleader) Run Wild: Variation on *Price*

6. As we have just seen, parties already in the case may be able to object to a motion to implead either on the grounds that impleader doesn't lie (because the substantive law doesn't allow an action for indemnity or contribution under the circumstances) or because allowing impleader will unjustifiably increase delay or expense. Parties can also object on jurisdictional grounds.

    a. Personal jurisdiction over an impleaded third-party defendant (like the nail manufacturer) will usually lie because in many circumstances the third-party defendant will have been involved in the occurrence or transaction that led to the original claim and will thus be subject to personal jurisdiction. If that isn't enough, Rule 4(k)(1)(B) gives an extra 100-mile boost to the court's jurisdiction. Read that provision and apply it to the following situation. Plaintiff sues Defendant, a Pennsylvania corporation, in federal court in Philadelphia, alleging a breach of contract arising out of some work Defendant performed in Wilmington, Delaware, about 35 miles south of Philadelphia. Defendant wants to implead Employee, who lives and works in Wilmington, and has insufficient contacts with Pennsylvania to subject him to personal jurisdiction there. Employee does not have a jurisdictional objection to his joinder. Use Rule 4(k)(1)(B) to explain why.

    b. Joinder can also implicate questions of subject matter jurisdiction. If a claim carries with it an independent jurisdictional basis, that question is quickly resolved. For example, if a crossclaim arises under federal law, there will be no problem. Similarly, if a defendant/third-party plaintiff and a third-party defendant meet the requirements of diversity of citizenship, there will be no difficult jurisdictional issue. But what happens if the federal court would not otherwise have jurisdiction over a compulsory counterclaim, third-party claim, or crossclaim? Does supplemental jurisdiction extend to cover these essentially defensive claims? In many circumstances, the answer is yes. Section 1367 permits many, but not all, defensive claims to come in under the umbrella of supplemental jurisdiction. Reread that provision and explain why a federal district court will always have subject matter jurisdiction over Nails and SteelCo in the hypothetical in Note 5.

    c. Supplemental jurisdiction over third-party claims can, however, get complicated. What if Price sues Latco, Latco impleads Nails, and then Price decides he wants to sue Nails as well. If Price's claim raises a federal question, there is independent subject matter jurisdiction over the claim. If Price and Nails are diverse parties with an amount in controversy over $75,000, there is also independent subject matter jurisdiction. But what if Price and Nails are citizens of the same state? No supplemental jurisdiction. To understand why, look at §1367(b), which precludes supplemental jurisdiction in diversity-only cases "over claims by plaintiffs against persons made parties under Rule 14 . . ." if doing so would defeat diversity. This restriction predated the statute; the Supreme Court made clear, in Owen Equipment & Erection Co. v. Kroger, 437 U.S. 365 (1978), that allowing such a claim would "[d]estroy complete diversity just as surely as if [the plaintiff] had sued the [third-party defendant] initially." As the Court reasoned:

> It is a fundamental precept that federal courts are courts of limited jurisdiction. The limits upon federal jurisdiction, whether imposed by the Constitution or by Congress, must be neither disregarded nor evaded. Yet [if supplemental jurisdiction over such a claim were allowed], a plaintiff could defeat the statutory requirement of complete diversity by the simple expedient of suing only those defendants who were of diverse citizenship and waiting for them to implead nondiverse defendants.

Id. at 374.

Congress's enactment of §1367 in 1990 codified the outcome in *Kroger* (thus making supplemental jurisdiction for a plaintiff's claim against a third-party defendant unavailable in a diversity case when the claim would defeat diversity); while it also instructed courts to reach the opposite result when the basis for jurisdiction over the original claim was a federal question.

d. Consider the reach of supplemental jurisdiction in another hypothetical variation on *Price v. CTB*, supra page 794, in which the chicken farmer, when sued by the contractor for unpaid bills, impleaded his bank (located in the same state as Price), alleging it had failed to fund a line of credit as it had promised to do. Imagine that the amount in controversy is less than $75,000.

i. Rule 14(a)(1) permits a plaintiff against whom a counterclaim is asserted to bring in a third party to the same extent a defendant may do so.

ii. But what about supplemental jurisdiction over that claim? Were the third-party claim asserted by a defendant, say the contractor, supplemental jurisdiction would apply. But §1367(b) precludes supplemental jurisdiction in diversity-only cases "over claims by plaintiffs against persons made parties under Rule 14. . . . when exercising supplemental jurisdiction over such claims would be inconsistent with the jurisdictional requirements of section 1332." Read literally, the statute seems to deny supplemental jurisdiction over the plaintiff's claim against Bank in the case imagined, even though the chicken farmer is in the position of a defendant as to the counterclaim. Several courts and commentators have suggested that the drafters of the statute did not intend to preclude supplemental jurisdiction under these circumstances. But, so far, courts have held that the plain language of the statute controls, and Farmer is out of luck.

3. Compulsory Joinder

This chapter has thus far concentrated on who can be joined in a suit if someone already a party seeks joinder. We now consider whether there are those who must be joined—even if neither they nor those already in the suit desire to see them there. The topic, sometimes rather confusingly described in terms of "necessary and indispensable parties," has its roots in eighteenth-century equity practice. Chancery developed the perfectly sensible notions that (1) litigation sometimes affected people who weren't formal parties; and (2) if the effects were serious enough and the affected persons could be joined, they should be. Rule 19 now embodies these propositions. Reading the Rule might leave one with the impression that it requires courts in every case to consider the most efficient and effective party structure for a lawsuit. That is not how courts have interpreted it.

WHAT'S NEW HERE?

- Up to now we have explored joinder devices that someone in the lawsuit can use: joining additional claims or counterclaims, adding additional parties, adding third-party defendants, and the like.
- We now encounter a doctrine, and a Rule, that imagines a situation in which someone not a party to the lawsuit—and perhaps a party that no one in the lawsuit wants to have involved—must nevertheless be added, on pain of the suit's being dismissed in its entirety.
- If you think this doctrine sounds as if it came from a parallel universe, you're right. It came, in fact, from the English Court of Chancery, a court that administered a body of law called equity. You have met equity in this course—think injunctions—and will meet it in other courses. For present purposes, courts of equity came from a tradition in which judges did not just decide which party had presented the stronger case, but tried, as best they could, to assure that justice was done. Out of this quest came the idea that sometimes there was a party not presently in the suit who should be. As you will see, the concept does not fit smoothly within a tradition of party responsibility—and autonomy—that otherwise characterizes the U.S. legal system.

Temple v. Synthes Corp.
498 U.S. 5, reh'g denied, 498 U.S. 1092 (1990)

PER CURIAM.

Petitioner Temple, a Mississippi resident, underwent surgery in October 1986 in which a "plate and screw device" was implanted in his lower spine. The device was manufactured by respondent Synthes, Ltd. (U.S.A.) (Synthes), a Pennsylvania corporation. Dr. S. Henry LaRocca performed the surgery at St. Charles General Hospital in New Orleans, Louisiana. Following surgery, the device's screws broke off inside Temple's back.

Temple filed suit against Synthes in the United States District Court for the Eastern District of Louisiana. The suit, which rested on diversity jurisdiction, alleged defective design and manufacture of the device. At the same time, Temple filed a state administrative proceeding against Dr. LaRocca and the hospital for malpractice and negligence. At the conclusion of the administrative proceeding, Temple filed suit against the doctor and the hospital in Louisiana state court.

Synthes did not attempt to bring the doctor and the hospital into the federal action by means of a third-party complaint, as provided in Federal Rule of Civil Procedure 14(a). Instead, Synthes filed a motion to dismiss Temple's federal suit for failure to join necessary parties pursuant to Federal Rule of Civil Procedure 19. Following a hearing, the District Court ordered Temple to join the doctor and the hospital as defendants within twenty days or risk dismissal of the lawsuit. According to the court, the most significant reason for requiring joinder was the interest of judicial economy. The court relied on this Court's decision in Provident Tradesmens Bank & Trust Co. v. Patterson, 390 U.S. 102 (1968), wherein we recognized that one focus of Rule 19 is "the interest of the courts and the public in complete, consistent, and efficient settlement of controversies." When Temple failed to join the doctor and the hospital, the court dismissed the suit with prejudice.

Temple appealed, and the United States Court of Appeals for the Fifth Circuit affirmed. The court deemed it "obviously prejudicial to the defendants to have the separate litigations being carried on," because Synthes' defense might be that the plate was not defective but that the doctor and the hospital were negligent, while the doctor and hospital, on the other hand, might claim that they were not negligent but that the plate was defective. The Court of Appeals found that claims overlapped and that the District Court therefore had not abused its discretion in ordering joinder under Rule 19. A petition for rehearing was denied.

In his petition for certiorari to this Court, Temple contends that it was error to label joint tortfeasors as indispensable parties under Rule 19(b) and to dismiss the lawsuit with prejudice for failure to join those parties. We agree. Synthes does not deny that it, the doctor, and the hospital are potential joint tortfeasors. It has long been the rule that it is not necessary for all joint tortfeasors to be named as defendants in a single lawsuit. Nothing in the 1966 revision of Rule 19 changed that principle. The Advisory Committee Notes to Rule 19(a) explicitly state that "a tortfeasor with the usual 'joint-and-several' liability is merely a permissive party to an action against another with like liability." Advisory Committee's Notes on Fed. Rule Civ. Proc. 19. There is nothing in Louisiana tort law to the contrary.

The opinion in *Provident Bank*, supra, does speak of the public interest in limiting multiple litigation, but that case is not controlling here. There, the estate of a tort victim brought a declaratory judgment action against an insurance company. We assumed that the policyholder was a person "who, under . . . [Rule 19](a), should be joined if 'feasible'" and went on to discuss the appropriate analysis under Rule 19(b), because the policyholder could not be joined without destroying diversity. After examining the factors set forth in Rule 19(b), we determined that the action could proceed without the policyholder; he therefore was not an indispensable party whose absence required dismissal of the suit.

Here, no inquiry under Rule 19(b) is necessary, because the threshold requirements of Rule 19(a) have not been satisfied. As potential joint tortfeasors with Synthes, Dr. LaRocca and the hospital were merely permissive parties. The Court of Appeals erred by failing to hold that the District Court abused its discretion in ordering them joined as defendants and in dismissing the action when Temple failed to comply with the court's order. For these reasons, we grant the petition for certiorari, reverse the judgment of the Court of Appeals for the Fifth Circuit, and remand for further proceedings consistent with this opinion.

It is so ordered.

Notes and Problems

1. The opinion does not dispute the lower courts' conclusion that it would be more efficient to have all the claims in a single forum. It nevertheless holds that it was reversible error to dismiss the case. Moreover, the opinion was *per curiam* (by the Court as a whole, rather than signed by an individual Justice). These brief, anonymous opinions are often used when the Court believes the principles so clear that they require no extended discussion. What principle is the Court valuing more highly than the obvious efficiency of consolidating the cases?

2. What does the Court mean by saying that "Synthes did not attempt to bring the doctor and the hospital into the federal action by means of a third-party complaint, as provided in Federal Rule of Civil Procedure 14(a)"?

   a. As a review of impleader, recall that Synthes could *not* implead the doctor on the basis that his negligence rather than a defective product caused Billy Temple's injury. (Such a claim would constitute a forbidden "it's him, not me" use of impleader.)

   b. So what factual or legal relations would have had to exist for Synthes to be able to implead the doctor or hospital?

3. As further review, consider whether, if the plaintiff had wanted to sue both defendants in the same action, he could have done so.

   a. As a matter of pleading?

   b. As a matter of jurisdiction?

4. Ordinarily, one expects that plaintiffs will be eager to sue as many plausible defendants as possible. The strategy in such a case is to have one defendant—perhaps the surgeon—argue that he was not negligent, but the product was defective, while Synthes contends that its product was fine but that the medical defendants were negligent. In such circumstances the defendants, pointing

fingers at each other, do part of plaintiff's work. What risks was Temple's lawyer running by filing separate lawsuits against the two defendants?

5. *Temple* stands at least for the proposition that Rule 19 does not require the most efficient possible packaging of lawsuits. Nor does it require the joinder of anyone who might be affected by precedent. E.g., Janney Montgomery Scott, Inc. v. Shepard Niles, Inc., 11 F.3d 399, 407 (3d Cir. 1993).

6. Given these background understandings, the "necessary parties" rules therefore typically operate only when "there is some connection of property ownership, contract rights, or obligations between those who are initially made parties and those who have not been joined." James, Hazard & Leubsdorf at 285. Common situations include:

   a. Cases involving an obligation on which more than one person is benefitted or burdened by the obligation but not all joint obligees or joint obligors are parties.

   b. Cases involving interests in real or personal property in which a person claiming an interest (for example, a joint owner, lessee, or mortgagee) is not included as a party.

   c. Cases involving representative parties in which either the representative or the party being represented is not included.

   d. Cases involving claims to a limited fund or pool of assets, such that a potential claimant not a party will find the fund depleted by the time her case is heard.

7. Rule 19 seeks to describe when courts should overcome the ordinary presumptions of party autonomy. Read it and apply it to some elementary problems.

   a. Larry is the income beneficiary of a spendthrift trust (which limits the amount of trust funds that a beneficiary can spend), and his children have the remainder interest (whatever remains when Larry dies). The trustee has power to appoint the trust to Larry at any time—allowing him to spend whatever he wants. Larry, a California resident, sues the trustee, an Illinois resident, seeking a declaration that the trustee abused his power by not appointing the trust to him. Any problems?

   b. Prior to 2006, Husband was married to *W1* and procured insurance from InsCo payable to "my wife." In 2008 Husband procures a divorce in Mexico and marries *W2*. After Husband's death in 2010, *W1* brings an action against InsCo claiming: (a) Husband and she were never properly divorced; and (b) even if she and Husband were divorced, his intention was to have the policy payable to her. InsCo moves to dismiss for failure to join *W2*. What result?

8. Who can raise an issue of compulsory joinder? Obviously, a party can (see *Temple*). What about the court on its own motion? Rule 19(a)(1) says: "A person who is subject to service of process and whose joinder will not deprive the court of subject-matter jurisdiction must be joined as a party if . . ." the conditions are met. Does this suggest the court has independent power (and

perhaps a duty) to make inquiry—see the vestige of equity's seeking to "do justice"? In practice, courts will often not know enough about the facts to enter such an order, relying instead on the defendant's incentives to raise an objection that may derail the lawsuit.

9. How might Rule 19 derail a lawsuit? Rule 19(a) requires a necessary party to be joined if it can be served and joining it does not deprive the court of subject matter jurisdiction over the case. Rule 19(b) considers what a court should do if a party is necessary but cannot be joined for jurisdictional reasons: The options are to continue on with the current parties or to dismiss the case. In the next case, the court considers just this sort of situation—perhaps coming up with the wrong solution.

Helzberg's Diamond Shops v. Valley West Des Moines Shopping Center

564 F.2d 816 (8th Cir. 1977)

ALSOP, J.

On February 3, 1975, Helzberg's Diamond Shops, Inc. (Helzberg), a Missouri corporation, and Valley West Des Moines Shopping Center, Inc. (Valley West), an Iowa corporation, executed a written Lease Agreement. The Lease Agreement granted Helzberg the right to operate a full line jewelry store at space 254 in the Valley West Mall in West Des Moines, Iowa. Section 6 of Article V of the Lease Agreement provides:

> [Valley West] agrees it will not lease premises in the shopping center for use as a catalog jewelry store nor lease premises for more than two full line jewelry stores in the shopping center in addition to the leased premises. This clause shall not prohibit other stores such as department stores from selling jewelry from catalogs or in any way restrict the shopping center department stores.

Subsequently, Helzberg commenced operation of a full line jewelry store in the Valley West Mall.

Between February 3, 1975 and November 2, 1976 Valley West and two other corporations entered into leases for spaces in the Valley West Mall for use as full line jewelry stores. Pursuant to those leases the two corporations also initiated actual operation of full line jewelry stores. On November 2, 1976, Valley West and Kirk's Incorporated, Jewelers, an Iowa corporation, doing business as Lord's Jewelers (Lord's), entered into a written Lease Agreement. The Lease Agreement granted Lord's the right to occupy space 261 in the Valley West Mall. Section I of Article V of the Lease Agreement provides that Lord's will use space 261

> . . . only as a retail specialty jewelry store (and not as a catalogue or full line jewelry store) featuring watches, jewelry (and the repair of same) and incidental better gift items.

However, Lord's intended to open and operate what constituted a full line jewelry store at space 261.

In an attempt to avoid the opening of a fourth full line jewelry store in the Valley West Mall and the resulting breach of the Helzberg-Valley West Lease Agreement, Helzberg instituted suit seeking preliminary and permanent injunctive relief restraining Valley West's breach of the Lease Agreement. The suit was filed in the United States District Court for the Western District of Missouri. Subject matter jurisdiction was invoked pursuant to 28 U.S.C. §1332 based upon diversity of citizenship between the parties and an amount in controversy which exceeded [the statutory amount]. Personal jurisdiction was established by service of process on Valley West pursuant to the Missouri "long arm" statute, Rev. Stat. Mo. §506.500 et seq. (1977). Rule 4(e), Fed. R. Civ. P.

Valley West moved to dismiss pursuant to Rule 19 because Helzberg had failed to join Lord's as a party defendant. That motion was denied. The district court went on to order that

> pending the determination of [the] action on the merits, that [Valley West] be, and it is hereby, enjoined and restrained from allowing, and shall take all necessary steps to prevent, any other tenant in its Valley West Mall (including but not limited to Kirk's Incorporated, Jewelers, d/b/a Lord's Jewelers) to open and operate on March 30, 1977, or at any other time, or to be operated during the term of [Helzberg's] present leasehold, a fourth full line jewelry store meaning a jewelry store offering for sale at retail a broad range of jewelry items at various prices such as diamonds and diamond jewelry, precious and semi-precious stones, watches, rings, gold jewelry, costume jewelry, gold chains, pendants, bracelets, belt buckles, tie tacs, tie slides and earrings, provided, however, nothing contained herein shall be construed to enjoin [Valley West] from allowing the opening in said Valley West Mall of a small store, known by [Valley West] as a boutique, which sells limited items such as only Indian jewelry, only watches, only earrings, or only pearls.

From this order Valley West appeals.

It is clear that Valley West is entitled to appeal from the order granting preliminary injunctive relief. 28 U.S.C. §1292(a)(1). However, Valley West does not attack the propriety of the issuance of a preliminary injunction directly; instead, it challenges the District Court's denial of its motion to dismiss for failure to join an indispensable party and argues that the District Court's order fails for lack of specificity in describing the acts of Valley West to be restrained. . . .

Because Helzberg was seeking and the District Court ordered injunctive relief which may prevent Lord's from operating its jewelry store in the Valley West Mall in the manner in which Lord's originally intended, the District Court correctly concluded that Lord's was a party to be joined if feasible. See Rule 19(a)[(1)(b)*](i), Fed. R. Civ. P. Therefore, because Lord's was not and is not subject to personal jurisdiction in the Western District of Missouri, the District Court was required to determine whether or not Lord's should be regarded as indispensable. After considering the

---

* [Renumbered to reflect the current position of the relevant provision in Rule 19.—Eds.]

factors which Rule 19(b) mandates be considered, the District Court concluded that Lord's was not to be regarded as indispensable. We agree. . . .

Rule 19(b) requires the court to look first to the extent to which a judgment rendered in Lord's absence might be prejudicial to Lord's or to Valley West. Valley West argues that the District Court's order granting preliminary injunctive relief does prejudice Lord's and may prejudice Valley West. We do not agree.

It seems axiomatic that none of Lord's rights or obligations will be ultimately determined in a suit to which it is not a party. Even if, as a result of the District Court's granting of the preliminary injunction, Valley West should attempt to terminate Lord's leasehold interest in space 261 in the Valley West Mall, Lord's will retain all of its rights under its Lease Agreement with Valley West. None of its rights or obligations will have been adjudicated as a result of the present proceedings, proceedings to which it is not a party. Therefore, we conclude that Lord's will not be prejudiced in a way contemplated by Rule 19(b) as a result of this action.

Likewise, we think that Lord's absence will not prejudice Valley West in a way contemplated by Rule 19(b). Valley West contends that it may be subjected to inconsistent obligations as a result of a determination in this action and a determination in another forum that Valley West should proceed in a fashion contrary to what has been ordered in these proceedings.

It is true that the obligations of Valley West to Helzberg, as determined in these proceedings, may be inconsistent with Valley West's obligations to Lord's. However, we are of the opinion that any inconsistency in those obligations will result from Valley West's voluntary execution of two Lease Agreements which impose inconsistent obligations rather than from Lord's absence from the present proceedings.

Helzberg seeks only to restrain Valley West's breach of the Lease Agreement to which Helzberg and Valley West were the sole parties. Certainly, all of the rights and obligations arising under a lease can be adjudicated where all of the parties to the lease are before the court. Thus, in the context of these proceedings the District Court can determine all of the rights and obligations of both Helzberg and Valley West based upon the Lease Agreement between them, even though Lord's is not a party to the proceedings.

Valley West's contention that it may be subjected to inconsistent judgments if Lord's should choose to file suit elsewhere and be awarded judgment is speculative at best. In the first place, Lord's has not filed such a suit. Secondly, there is no showing that another court is likely to interpret the language of the two Lease Agreements differently from the way in which the District Court would. Therefore, we also conclude that Valley West will suffer no prejudice as a result of the District Court's proceeding in Lord's absence. Any prejudice which Valley West may suffer by way of inconsistent judgments would be the result of Valley West's execution of Lease Agreements which impose inconsistent obligations and not the result of the proceedings in the District Court.

Rule 19(b) also requires the court to consider ways in which prejudice to the absent party can be lessened or avoided. The District Court afforded Lord's an opportunity to intervene in order to protect any interest it might have in the outcome of this litigation. Lord's chose not to do so. In light of Lord's decision not to intervene we conclude that the District Court acted in such a way as to sufficiently protect Lord's interests.

Similarly, we also conclude that the District Court's determinations that a judgment rendered in Lord's absence would be adequate and that there is no controlling significance to the fact that Helzberg would have an adequate remedy in the Iowa courts were not erroneous. It follows that the District Court's conclusion that in equity and good conscience the action should be allowed to proceed was a correct one.

In sum, it is generally recognized that a person does not become indispensable to an action to determine rights under a contract simply because that person's rights or obligations under an entirely separate contract will be affected by the result of the action. This principle applies to an action against a lessor who has entered into other leases which also may be affected by the result in the action in which the other lessees are argued to be indispensable parties. We conclude that the District Court properly denied the motion to dismiss for failure to join an indispensable party. . . .

In view of the foregoing, it follows that the judgment of the District Court is affirmed.

Procedure as Strategy

Notice the striking—though unsuccessful—stance taken by Valley West. Faced with defending a lawsuit against Helzberg's, it argued that *more* people should be suing it, but then with what one imagines were crocodile tears, regretfully noted that Lord's could not be joined for jurisdictional reasons—and therefore the entire suit should be dismissed. The *Helzberg's* court rejected this argument, but one regularly finds this stance taken in Rule 19 cases. A defendant argues (a) that to do perfect justice someone else should be joined to the lawsuit, (b) that for jurisdictional or other reasons that party cannot be joined, and (c) that the suit should therefore be dismissed. In so arguing, the litigants are echoing the views of eighteenth-century Lord Chancellors, who sometimes seemed to be saying that if their courts could not do perfect justice (by joining all who might have an interest in the suit), they would do none at all. The current Rule 19 was drafted in part to avoid this stance; see Rule 19(b).

Notes and Problems

1. Consider *Helzberg's* as a fight about former adjudication.

    a. Assume the suit proceeds without Lord's, and the court enters a permanent injunction forbidding Valley West to rent to Lord's. When Valley West tries to evict Lord's, Lord's sues, alleging that the eviction will be a breach of its lease with Valley West. Valley West points to the injunction, arguing that the court's construction of the lease is binding. As a review of the preceding chapter on former adjudication, what is Lord's winning response to that contention?

b. Suppose that in Lord's suit against Valley West the court construes the lease differently from the first court and holds that Lord's is entitled to conduct its business in the mall and decrees specific performance. At this point Valley West is under two conflicting court orders: one requiring that it evict Lord's, the other that it honor its lease with Lord's. Both decrees are valid; what should Valley West do?

c. The opinion in *Helzberg's* seems to concede implicitly that the scenario just sketched is possible. What is its response to the dilemma in which Valley West may find itself?

d. What would have been the alternative to proceeding with the suit in federal district court in Missouri?

e. In light of this alternative, articulate an argument that the court improperly applied Rule 19 and therefore came to the wrong result.

2. *Helzberg's* proceeded in the absence of a party whose joinder would have been desirable. Contrast a case that instead dismissed the suit in the face of similar objections. Clinton v. Babbitt, 180 F.3d 1081 (9th Cir. 1999), involved a three-cornered dispute: the Hopi Tribe and Navajo Nation and the U.S. Secretary of the Interior. As background, bear in mind that many Indian tribes have for some purposes the status of sovereign nations. The lawsuit turned on conflicting "claims to exclusive use [of land] . . . between the Hopi Tribe and the Navajo Nation, producing what became known as 'the greatest title problem in the West.'"

a. Members of the Navajo Nation living on lands that a settlement had awarded to the Hopi Tribe sued the Secretary of the Interior, alleging unconstitutional discrimination in the terms of the leases given them as part of the settlement. The Secretary argued that the Hopi Tribe, which stood to lose large sums of money if the settlement fell apart, was a necessary party. But, the argument continued, the Hopi Tribe could not be joined because of sovereign immunity—and the suit must therefore be dismissed. The Ninth Circuit agreed:

> The plaintiffs seek, at a minimum, a declaration that Secretary Babbitt cannot constitutionally approve any individual leases between the Navajos and the Hopi Tribe that use the standard terms of the [settlement]. Such a declaration would prohibit the Tribe from fulfilling its obligations under the Settlement Agreement to enter into such leases and would deprive the Tribe of substantial compensation from the United States (over $25 million and the creation of additional trust lands), which is conditioned on Secretary Babbitt's approval of certain numbers of such leases. The Hopi Tribe, therefore, has a legally protected interest relating to the subject of the action as defined by Rule 19(a)[(1)(B)]. . . .
>
> . . . Although no alternative forum exists for the plaintiffs to seek relief, we conclude that the Hopi Tribe's interest in maintaining its sovereign immunity outweighs the interest of the plaintiffs in litigating their claim. See *Quileute*, 18 F.3d at 1460-61 ("'[A p]laintiff's interest in litigating a claim may be outweighed

by a tribe's interest in maintaining its sovereign immunity [because] society has consciously opted to shield Indian tribes from suit without congressional or tribal consent.'" (citations omitted)). . . .

Clinton v. Babbitt, 180 F.3d at 1089-90.

b. Notice the striking result of Rule 19 in such conditions: Because the court cannot do perfect justice, it decides it will do nothing at all. Before it takes such an action, should a court be sure that it is not doing a worse injustice to the existing parties by dismissing than it would do to the unjoined party by proceeding in its absence? Consider a footnote in *Clinton*:

> Whether the allegations of the plaintiffs' equal protection claim are sufficient to state a claim upon which relief may be granted is a question we need not reach in this appeal. We note, however, the apparent lack of substance to the claim. First, the plaintiffs admit they are in the unique position of being offered free leases to remain on land to which they have no right, and fail to allege that they are being treated less favorably than any similarly situated individuals. Second, even if the plaintiffs make the threshold showing of disparate treatment they fail to show that this treatment is not rationally related to legitimate legislative goals, such as the peaceful settlement of the Navajo-Hopi land dispute:
>
> > [The 1996 Settlement Act] will implement a settlement [which is] a consensual resolution of an age-old problem. It creates a way for Navajo families now residing on Hopi land to lawfully remain at the home sites where their families have lived for many generations. At the same time, it preserves the Hopi Tribe's right to exercise jurisdiction over its land. It is based on principles of self-determination for the Tribes and human dignity for all tribal members. With this settlement, both tribes now will be able to devote their efforts and resources to important educational, health, and economic developments for the Navajo and Hopi people.

Id. at 1087 n.4 (quoting Navajo-Hopi Land Dispute Settlement Act of 1996: Signing Statement of President William J. Clinton, 32 Weekly Comp. Pres. Doc. 2042 (Oct. 14, 1996). Does this footnote constitute an effort to assure readers that the court has not lost sight of what Rule 19(b) calls "equity and good conscience"?

3. In *Helzberg's*, the asserted jurisdictional obstacle to joinder was personal jurisdiction. In *Clinton*, the obstacle was the sovereign immunity of an Indian tribe. Because claims of sovereign immunity will be rare, and the reach of modern long-arm jurisdiction is long, the more common objection is want of subject matter jurisdiction.

a. Take, for example, a variation on the facts of *Helzberg's*. Suppose that Helzberg's and Lord's were both Missouri corporations. Under those circumstances Helzberg's could invoke diversity jurisdiction in its suit against Valley West (an Iowa corporation); joining Lord's as a defendant would, however, destroy diversity.

b. In cases relying entirely on diversity jurisdiction, 28 U.S.C. §1367(b) explicitly excludes from supplemental jurisdiction "claims by plaintiffs against persons made parties under Rule 14, 19, 20, or 24 . . . or over claims by persons proposed to be joined as plaintiffs under Rule 19 . . . or seeking to intervene as plaintiffs under Rule 24 . . . when exercising supplemental jurisdiction over such claims would be inconsistent with the jurisdictional requirements of section 1332." What is the theory underlying denial of supplemental jurisdiction under these circumstances? Sometimes it is said that permitting supplemental jurisdiction in this situation would open the door to collusive manipulation of jurisdiction: *A*, wishing to sue *B* and *C* but lacking complete diversity, would sue just *B*, hoping that *B* would plead *C*'s absence and insist on joinder under Rule 19; if supplemental jurisdiction extended to cover this situation, *A* could achieve an otherwise impermissible lawsuit.

c. Another section of the same statute (28 U.S.C. §1367(a)), however, allows supplemental jurisdiction to extend to such parties if the plaintiff is not asserting claims against them or if there is a ground for federal jurisdiction other than diversity. Is there a theory justifying such discrepancies?

4. Should federal courts be more willing under Rule 19(b) to dismiss cases in which the reason for nonjoinder is a problem with subject matter jurisdiction than when the difficulty is personal jurisdiction? The argument for such a result would be that there will always be a state court where subject matter jurisdiction is not a problem, but (because the state and federal courts have substantially identical reaches under personal jurisdiction) there may not be a court that can resolve the lawsuit if the difficulty is personal jurisdiction.

C. INTERVENTION

The joinder devices thus far explored have a common characteristic: They serve to bring into a lawsuit a party who does not want to be there. We turn now to a doctrine with the opposite function: to permit an unjoined person to elbow her way into a suit where no one wants her. Like the doctrines of compulsory joinder, the principles of intervention flow from a recognition that lawsuits may have effects on persons not joined. The effects will not be those of formal preclusion—due process forbids binding one who was not a party—but judgments have broader ripple effects than the formal binding effect of the decree.

To take a common example, suppose that Developer and City Zoning Board are engaged in litigation over whether Developer can build an office building on a plot of land bordering a residential area. If Developer wins the suit, Homeowner, whose property lies next to the plot in question, will be affected. If Developer loses the suit, Landowner, who owns another adjacent plot of land that would be more valuable if it can be commercially developed, will be adversely affected. The resulting judgment will not formally bind either Homeowner or Landowner, but it will affect them. Both might wish to influence the outcome of the suit. If they were entitled to intervene, they would thereby become parties to the suit, with the right to present evidence and arguments in the same way as Developer and Zoning Board.

Notice that Developer and Zoning Board (and perhaps the judge as well) may be notably unenthusiastic about intervention. From the standpoint of the existing parties, it complicates and perhaps weakens their litigating strategy. Even an intervenor who seeks the same outcome as one of the parties will have a different perspective and perhaps a different strategy. Moreover, additional parties may make the lawsuit more expensive and settlement more difficult. Conceptually, intervention means further erosion of the principle of party autonomy, and, carried to a logical extreme, turns every lawsuit into a town meeting at which anyone even distantly "interested" in the topic of litigation becomes a party. The principles of intervention seek to allow some—but not all—who might wish to be involved in a lawsuit to join it. Read Rule 24.

Note the structure of the Rule. It is subdivided into two major categories: intervention of right (Rule 24(a)) and permissive intervention (Rule 24(b)). Intervention of right is designed to give to those with strong interests in the litigation the power to insist on joinder. The words of Rule 24(a)(2) echo those of Rule 19(a)(1)(B)—"an interest relating to . . . the subject of the action . . . so situated that disposing of the action may as a practical matter impair or impede" the interests of would-be intervenor. Permissive intervention is the weaker counterpart, as it is designed to capture those with weaker bases for insisting on joinder. As the words imply, an applicant who meets the criteria of Rule 24(a) must be allowed to join the lawsuit. An applicant who meets only the criteria of Rule 24(b) may be allowed to join, with the judge's decision reviewed only for abuse of discretion.

Most of the reported cases focus on Rule 24(a), the general criteria for intervention as of right. That section contains four requirements. The intervention must be timely—the intervenor may not lie in wait until the litigation is on the brink of resolution. Second, the intervenor must have an "interest" in the property or transaction that is the subject of the suit, and, third, that interest must be in some strong way at risk. Finally, even an applicant meeting all these criteria will be denied intervention if those already in the lawsuit are adequately representing the interest. The next case assumes that intervention is timely and analyzes the other three criteria.

Natural Resources Defense Council v. United States Nuclear Regulatory Commission

578 F.2d 1341 (10th Cir. 1978)

DOYLE, J.

The American Mining Congress and Kerr-McGee Nuclear Corporation seek review of the order of the United States District Court for the District of New Mexico denying their motions to intervene [as] a matter of right or on a permissive basis, pursuant to Rule 24(a)(2) and (b), Fed. R. Civil Proc.

The underlying action in which the movants requested intervention was instituted by the Natural Resources Defense Council, Inc., and others. In the action, declaratory and injunctive relief is directed to the United States Nuclear Regulatory Commission (NRC) and the New Mexico Environmental Improvement Agency (NMEIA), prohibiting those agencies from issuing licenses for the operation of uranium mills in New Mexico without first preparing environmental impact statements. Kerr-McGee and United Nuclear are potential recipients of the licenses.

Congress, in the Atomic Energy Act of 1954, has authorized the NRC to issue such licenses. NMEIA is involved because under §274(b) of the Act, the NRC is authorized to enter into agreements with the states allowing the states to issue licenses. Such agreements have been made with about 25 states including New Mexico. Thus, the action below in effect seeks to prevent the use of §274(b) of the Act so as to avoid the requirement of an impact statement for which provision is made in the National Environmental Policy Act. . . .

The relief sought by the plaintiffs' complaint is, first, that NRC's involvement in the licensing procedure in New Mexico is, notwithstanding the delegation to the state, sufficient to constitute major federal action, whereby the impact statement requirement is not eliminated. Second, that if an impact statement is not required in connection with the granting of licenses, the New Mexico program is in conflict with §274(d)(2) of the Atomic Energy Act of 1954.

The motion of United Nuclear Corporation to intervene is not opposed by the parties and was granted. On May 3, 1977, the date that the complaint herein was filed, NMEIA granted a license to United Nuclear to operate a uranium mill at Church Rock, New Mexico. The complaint seeks to enjoin the issuance of the license thus granted.

It was after that that Kerr-McGee Nuclear Corporation, Anaconda Company, Gulf Oil Corporation, Phillips Petroleum Company, and the American Mining Congress filed motions to intervene. These motions, insofar as they sought intervention as of right, were denied on the ground that the interests of the parties or movants would be adequately represented by United Nuclear. Permissive intervention was also denied. Kerr-McGee and the American Mining Congress both appeal denial of both intervention as of right and permissive intervention.

Our issue is a limited one. We merely construe and weigh Rule 24(a) of the Fed. R. Civ. P. (intervention as of right) and decide in light of the facts and considerations presented whether the denial of intervention was correct. [The court quoted Rule 24(a).] We do not have a subsection (1) situation involving a statutory conferring of right to intervene. Accordingly, we must consider the standards set forth in subsection (2), which are:

1. Whether the applicant claims an interest relating to the property or transaction which is the subject of the action.

2. Whether the claimants are so situated that the disposition of the action may as a practical matter impair or impede their ability to protect that interest.

3. Whether their interest is not adequately represented by existing parties.

[The district court decided that, even if the first two tests were satisfied,] the interests of the movants were adequately protected by United Nuclear [and therefore denied the motion to intervene]. Our conclusion is that the interests of movants in the subject matter is sufficient to satisfy the requirements of Rule 24 and that the threat of loss of their interest and inability to participate is of such magnitude as to impair their ability to advance their interest.

I

... Strictly to require that the movant in intervention have a direct interest in the outcome of the lawsuit strikes us as being too narrow a construction of Rule 24(a)(2). ...

In our case the matter of immediate interest is, of course, the issuance and delivery of the license sought by United Nuclear. However, the consequence of the litigation could well be the imposition of the requirement that an environmental impact statement be prepared before granting any uranium mill license in New Mexico, or, secondly, it could result in an injunction terminating or suspending the agreement between NRC and NMEIA. Either consequence would be felt by United Nuclear and to some degree, of course, by Kerr-McGee, which is said to be one of the largest holders of uranium properties in New Mexico. It operates a uranium mill in Grants, New Mexico, pursuant to an NMEIA license, which application for renewal is pending. A decision in favor of the plaintiffs, which is not unlikely, could have a profound effect upon Kerr-McGee. Hence, it does have an interest within the meaning of Rule 24(a)(2). This interest of Kerr-McGee is in sharp contrast to the minimal interest which was present in *Allard*, wherein it was an interest of environmental groups in the protection of living birds. This was considered insufficient to justify intervention in a case involving feathers which are part of Indian artifacts. Their interest was said to be limited to a general interest in the public. The interest asserted on behalf of Kerr-McGee and the American Mining Congress is one which is a genuine threat to Kerr-McGee and the members of the American Mining Congress to a substantial degree.

We do not suggest that Kerr-McGee could expect better treatment from state authorities than federal. We do recognize that a change in procedure would produce impairing complications.

II

The next question is whether, assuming the existence of an interest, the chance of impairment is sufficient to fulfill the requirement of Rule 24(a)(2).

... If the relief sought by the plaintiffs is granted, there can be little question but that the interests of the American Mining Congress and of Kerr-McGee would be affected. Plaintiffs contend, however, that appellants would not be bound by such a result if they are not participants. Kerr-McGee points out that even though it may not be *res judicata*, still it would have a stare decisis effect. Moreover, with NRC and NMEIA as parties, the result might be more profound than stare decisis.

It should be pointed out that the Rule refers to impairment "as a practical matter." Thus, the court is not limited to consequences of a strictly legal nature. The court may consider any significant legal effect in the applicant's interest and it is not restricted to a rigid *res judicata* test. Hence, the stare decisis effect might be sufficient to satisfy the requirement. It is said that where, as here, the case is of first impression, the stare decisis effect would be important.

Finally, the considerations for requiring an environmental impact statement will be relatively the same in respect to the issuance of a uranium mining license in every instance. Hence, to say that it can be repeatedly litigated is not an answer, for the chance of getting a contrary result in a case which is substantially similar on its facts to one previously adjudicated seems remote.

We are of the opinion, therefore, that appellants have satisfied the impairment criterion.

III

The final question is whether the trial court was correct in its conclusion that United Nuclear would adequately represent Kerr-McGee and the American Mining Congress.

The finding and conclusion was that the representation would be adequate because United Nuclear, a fellow member of the industry, has interests which were the same as those of the appellants and possessed the same level of knowledge and experience with the ability and willingness to pursue the matter and could adequately represent Kerr-McGee and the members of the American Mining Congress. . . .

United Nuclear is situated somewhat differently in this case than are the other members of the industry since it has been granted its license. From this it is urged by Kerr-McGee that United Nuclear may be ready to compromise the case by obtaining a mere declaration that while environmental impact statements should be issued, this requirement need be prospective only, whereby it would not affect them. While we see this as a remote possibility, we gravely doubt that United Nuclear would opt for such a result. It is true, however, that United Nuclear has a defense of laches that is not available to Kerr-McGee or the others.

7A C. Wright & A. Miller, Federal Practice & Procedure, §1909, at 524 (1972), says:

> [I]f [an applicant's] interest is similar to, but not identical with, that of one of the parties, a discriminating judgment is required on the circumstances of the particular case, but he ordinarily should be allowed to intervene unless it is clear that the party will provide adequate representation for the absentee.

While the interest of the two applicants may appear similar, there is no way to say that there is no possibility that they will not be different and the possibility of divergence of interest need not be great in order to satisfy the burden of the applicants under *National Farm Lines*.

There are other reasons for allowing intervention. There is some value in having the parties before the court so that they will be bound by the result. American Mining Congress represents a number of companies having a wide variety of interests. This can, therefore, provide a useful supplement to the defense of the case. The same can be said of Kerr-McGee.

The trial court was concerned that the addition of these movants would make the litigation unwieldy. If the intervenors are limited to this group, unwieldiness does not become a problem which the trial court cannot control. It does not appear that there would be a need for additional parties in view of the presence of the American Mining Congress. While we do not express an opinion on the possibilities of further additions, we wish to make clear that the present holdings that the two applicants should be allowed to intervene does not say that others should be added. . . .

The order of the district court is reversed and the cause is remanded with instructions to the trial court to grant the appellants, Kerr-McGee's and American Mining Congress', motions to intervene.

Notes and Problems

---

1. Focus on each of the intervenors separately.

    a. United Nuclear's motion to intervene was granted without objection. Why? Analyze United Nuclear's position and explain why it met the criteria of Rule 24.

    b. Kerr-McGee sought to intervene as of right; the trial court denied the motion. Why? How does the Court of Appeals deal with the trial court's reason for denying Kerr-McGee's motion?

    c. How was the position of the American Mining Congress different from that of the other intervenors? How does its case for intervention compare to that of Kerr-McGee?

    d. Construct an argument that the correct result on these facts was to grant intervention to United Nuclear and the American Mining Congress, but to deny Kerr-McGee's motion.

    e. The court holds that both of the would-be intervenors met the criteria of Rule 24(a). Suppose it had come to a different decision. It would then have had to review the decision of the trial court to deny the intervenors permissive intervention under Rule 24(b). Explain why it is likely that the appellate court would have affirmed the trial court's denial of permissive intervention.

2. Rule 24 applies not only to competing claimants to property but, as *Natural Resources Defense Council* indicates, goes far beyond such a situation. How far?

    a. Assume *A* and *B* were both injured in a fireworks display held at Memorial Stadium. *A* sues Memorial Stadium and alleges that the stadium was negligent in handling the fireworks, and, in the alternative, that the fireworks display was an extrahazardous activity for which the stadium has strict liability. *B* seeks to intervene, claiming liability on similar grounds and asserting, as her "interest," her hope to establish a favorable precedent. Intervention will be denied; the mere hope for a favorable precedent cannot be the basis for intervention.

    b. Plaintiff sues Auto Manufacturer, claiming that a defective design led to her injury. Substantial discovery occurs, followed by a settlement agreement that includes a provision requiring that the materials uncovered by plaintiff in discovery remain confidential. Sixteen persons, each claiming injuries in unrelated accidents involving the same design feature, seek to intervene to challenge the protective order that is part of the settlement. See Jochims v. Isuzu Motors, Ltd., 148 F.R.D. 624 (S.D. Iowa 1993) (permissive intervention granted for limited purpose of challenging motion for protective order).

c. In Town of Chester v. Laroe Estates, Inc., 137 S. Ct. 1645 (2017), the Supreme Court held unanimously that an intervenor must meet the standing requirements of Article III unless the intervenor is seeking the same relief that the plaintiff requested.

3. Consider the relationship between Rule 19 and Rule 24. The texts of the two Rules closely resemble each other; more fundamentally, the two Rules address similar issues, Rule 19 from the viewpoint of those already in the lawsuit, Rule 24 from that of those outside it.

a. How should a court address the problem that arises when someone who might have been joined—but was not—and might have intervened—but did not—now complains of harm suffered from the judgment entered without her participation?

b. Occasionally, courts have hinted that knowledge of a pending action in which one could intervene would suffice to make the judgment binding on such a person, even though she had not in fact intervened. *Helzberg's Diamond Shops*, supra page 806, has language so suggesting. In Provident Tradesmens Bank & Trust Co. v. Patterson, 390 U.S. 102, 114 (1968), the Court remarked:

> [I]t might be argued that [a certain nonparty] should be bound by the previous decision because, although technically a nonparty, he had purposely bypassed an adequate opportunity to intervene. We do not now decide whether such an argument would be correct. . . .

Parklane Hosiery v. Shore, supra page 745, contained a similar hint, involving not intervention but the failure to join a prior action. Explaining why it was prepared to allow nonmutual-issue preclusion, the *Parklane* Court noted:

> The application of offensive collateral estoppel will not here reward a private plaintiff who could have joined in the previous action, since the respondent probably could not have joined in the injunctive action brought by the SEC even had he so desired.

439 U.S. at 331.

In spite of these hints, neither *Provident Tradesmens* nor *Parklane* decided squarely whether one could bind parties who had knowledge of a suit in which their interests were at stake in a lawsuit but who failed to intervene. The next case does so—saying "no."

Martin v. Wilks

490 U.S. 755 (1989)

REHNQUIST, C.J., delivered the opinion of the Court. . . .

The litigation [that gave rise to the present lawsuit] began in 1974, when the Ensley Branch of the NAACP and seven black individuals filed separate class-action complaints against the City [of Birmingham] and the Board [that made hiring decisions for public employees]. They alleged that both had engaged in racially discriminatory hiring and promotion practices in various public service jobs in violation of Title VII of the Civil Rights Act of 1964 and other federal law. After a bench trial on some issues, but before judgment, the parties entered into two consent decrees, one between the black individuals and the City and the other between them and the Board. These proposed decrees set forth an extensive remedial scheme, including long-term and interim annual goals for the hiring of blacks as firefighters. The decrees also provided for goals for promotion of blacks within the department. The District Court entered an order provisionally approving the decrees and directing publication of notice of the upcoming fairness hearings. Notice of the hearings, with a reference to the general nature of the decrees, was published in two local newspapers. At that hearing, the Birmingham Firefighters Association (BFA) appeared and filed objections as amicus curiae. After the hearing, but before final approval of the decrees, the BFA and two of its members also moved to intervene on the ground that the decrees would adversely affect their rights. The District Court denied the motions as untimely and approved the decrees. Seven white firefighters, all members of the BFA, then filed a complaint against the City and the Board seeking injunctive relief against enforcement of the decrees. The seven argued that the decrees would operate to illegally discriminate against them; the District Court denied relief. . . .

A new group of white firefighters, the *Wilks* respondents, then brought suit against the City and the Board in District Court. They too alleged that, because of their race, they were being denied promotions in favor of less qualified blacks in violation of federal law. The Board and the City admitted to making race conscious employment decisions, but argued the decisions were unassailable because they were made pursuant to the consent decrees. A group of black individuals, the *Martin* petitioners, were allowed to intervene in their individual capacities to defend the decrees.

The defendants moved to dismiss the reverse discrimination cases as impermissible collateral attacks on the consent decrees. . . . After trial the District Court granted the motion to dismiss. . . .

On appeal, the Eleventh Circuit reversed. It held that "[b]ecause . . . [the *Wilks* respondents] were neither parties nor privies to the consent decrees, . . . their independent claims of unlawful discrimination are not precluded." . . .

We granted certiorari and now affirm the Eleventh Circuit's judgment. All agree that "[i]t is a principle of general application in Anglo-American jurisprudence that one is not bound by a judgment in personam in a litigation in which he is not designated as a party or to which he has not been made a party by service of process." Hansberry v. Lee, 311 U.S. 32, 40 (1940) [see infra page 831]. This rule is part of our "deep-rooted historic tradition that everyone should have his own day in court." 18 C. Wright, A. Miller & E. Cooper, Federal Practice and Procedure §4449, p. 417 (1981) (18 Wright). A judgment or decree among parties to a lawsuit resolves issues as among them, but it does not conclude the rights of strangers to those proceedings.[2] Petitioners argue that, because respondents failed to timely intervene in the initial proceedings, their current challenge to actions taken under the consent decree constitutes an impermissible "collateral attack." They argue that respondents were aware that the underlying suit might affect them and if they chose to pass up an opportunity to intervene, they should not be permitted to later litigate the issues in a new action. The position has sufficient appeal to have commanded the approval of the great majority of the Federal Courts of Appeals, but we agree with the contrary view expressed by the Court of Appeals for the Eleventh Circuit in this case.

We begin with the words of Justice Brandeis in Chase National Bank v. Norwalk, 291 U.S. 431 (1934):

> The law does not impose upon any person absolutely entitled to a hearing the burden of voluntary intervention in a suit to which he is a stranger. . . . Unless duly summoned to appear in a legal proceeding, a person not a privy may rest assured that a judgment recovered therein will not affect his legal rights.

Id. at 441.

While these words were written before the adoption of the Federal Rules of Civil Procedure, we think the Rules incorporate the same principle; a party seeking a judgment binding on another cannot obligate that person to intervene; he must be joined. . . . Against the background of permissive intervention set forth in *Chase National Bank*, the drafters cast Rule 24, governing intervention, in permissive terms. See Fed. Rule Civ. Proc. 24(a) (intervention as of right) ("[on timely motion, the court must permit anyone to intervene"]); Fed. Rule Civ. Proc. 24(b) (permissive intervention) (["on timely motion, the court may permit anyone to intervene"]).* They determined that the concern for finality and completeness of judgments would be "better [served] by mandatory joinder procedures." 18 Wright §4452, p. 453. Accordingly, Rule 19(a) provides for mandatory joinder in circumstances where a judgment rendered in the absence of a person may "leave [an existing party] subject

---

2. We have recognized an exception to the general rule when, in certain limited circumstances, a person, although not a party, has his interests adequately represented by someone with the same interests who is a party. See Hansberry v. Lee, 311 U.S. 32, 41-42 (1940) ("class" or "representative" suits); Fed. Rule Civ. Proc. 23 (same); Montana v. United States, 440 U.S. 147, 154-155 (1979) (control of litigation on behalf of one of the parties in the litigation). Additionally, where a special remedial scheme exists expressly foreclosing successive litigation by nonlitigants, as for example in bankruptcy or probate, legal proceedings may terminate pre-existing rights if the scheme is otherwise consistent with due process. See NLRB v. Bildisco & Bildisco, 465 U.S. 513, 529-530, n.10 (1984) ("proof of claim must be presented to the Bankruptcy Court . . . or be lost"); Tulsa Professional Collection Services, Inc. v. Pope, 485 U.S. 478 (1988) (nonclaim statute terminating unsubmitted claims against the estate). Neither of these exceptions, however, applies in this case.

* [At the time of the decision, the relevant portions of Rule 19(a) and (b) read, respectively, "Upon timely application anyone shall be permitted to intervene" and "Upon timely application anyone may be permitted to intervene."—Eds.]

to a substantial risk of incurring . . . inconsistent obligations. . . ." Rule 19(b) sets forth the factors to be considered by a court in deciding whether to allow an action to proceed in the absence of an interested party.

Joinder as a party, rather than knowledge of a lawsuit and an opportunity to intervene, is the method by which potential parties are subjected to the jurisdiction of the court and bound by a judgment or decree.[6] The parties to a lawsuit presumably know better than anyone else the nature and scope of relief sought in the action, and at whose expense such relief might be granted. It makes sense, therefore, to place on them a burden of bringing in additional parties where such a step is indicated, rather than placing on potential additional parties a duty to intervene when they acquire knowledge of the lawsuit. The linchpin of the "impermissible collateral attack" doctrine—the attribution of preclusive effect to a failure to intervene—is therefore quite inconsistent with Rule 19 and Rule 24. . . .

Petitioners . . . rely on our decision in *Provident Tradesmans Bank*, supra, as authority for the view which they espouse. In that case we discussed Rule 19 shortly after parts of it had been substantially revised, but we expressly left open the question of whether preclusive effect might be attributed to a failure to intervene.

Petitioners contend that a different result should be reached because the need to join affected parties will be burdensome and ultimately discouraging to civil rights litigation. Potential adverse claimants may be numerous and difficult to identify; if they are not joined, the possibility for inconsistent judgments exists. Judicial resources will be needlessly consumed in relitigation of the same question.

Even if we were wholly persuaded by these arguments as a matter of policy, acceptance of them would require a rewriting rather than an interpretation of the relevant Rules. But we are not persuaded that their acceptance would lead to a more satisfactory method of handling cases like this one. It must be remembered that the alternatives are a duty to intervene based on knowledge, on the one hand, and some form of joinder, as the Rules presently provide, on the other. No one can seriously contend that an employer might successfully defend against a Title VII claim by one group of employees on the ground that its actions were required by an earlier decree entered in a suit brought against it by another, if the later group did not have adequate notice or knowledge of the earlier suit.

The difficulties petitioners foresee in identifying those who could be adversely affected by a decree granting broad remedial relief are undoubtedly present, but they arise from the nature of the relief sought and not because of any choice between mandatory intervention and joinder. Rule 19's provisions for joining interested parties are designed to accommodate the sort of complexities that may

---

6. The dissent argues on the one hand that respondents have not been "bound" by the decree but rather, that they are only suffering practical adverse affects from the consent decree. On the other hand, the dissent characterizes respondents' suit not as an assertion of their own independent rights, but as a collateral attack on the consent decree which, it is said, can only proceed on very limited grounds. Respondents in their suit have alleged that they are being racially discriminated against by their employer in violation of Title VII: either the fact that the disputed employment decisions are being made pursuant to a consent decree is a defense to respondents' Title VII claims or it is not. If it is a defense to challenges to employment practices which would otherwise violate Title VII, it is very difficult to see why respondents are not being "bound" by the decree.

arise from a decree affecting numerous people in various ways. We doubt that a mandatory intervention rule would be any less awkward. As mentioned, plaintiffs who seek the aid of the courts to alter existing employment policies, or the employer who might be subject to conflicting decrees, are best able to bear the burden of designating those who would be adversely affected if plaintiffs prevail; these parties will generally have a better understanding of the scope of likely relief than employees who are not named but might be affected. Petitioners' alternative does not eliminate the need for, or difficulty of, identifying persons who, because of their interests, should be included in a lawsuit. It merely shifts that responsibility to less able shoulders.

Nor do we think that the system of joinder called for by the Rules is likely to produce more relitigation of issues than the converse rule. The breadth of a lawsuit and concomitant relief may be at least partially shaped in advance through Rule 19 to avoid needless clashes with future litigation. And even under a regime of mandatory intervention, parties who did not have adequate knowledge of the suit would relitigate issues. Additional questions about the adequacy and timeliness of knowledge would inevitably crop up. We think that the system of joinder presently contemplated by the Rules best serves the many interests involved in the run of litigated cases, including cases like the present one. . . .

STEVENS, J., with whom BRENNAN, J., MARSHALL, J., and BLACKMUN, J., join, dissenting.

As a matter of a law there is a vast difference between persons who are actual parties to litigation and persons who merely have the kind of interest that may as a practical matter be impaired by the outcome of a case. Persons in the first category have a right to participate in a trial and to appeal from an adverse judgment; depending on whether they win or lose, their legal rights may be enhanced or impaired. Persons in the latter category have a right to intervene in the action in a timely fashion, or they may be joined as parties against their will. But if they remain on the sidelines, they may be harmed as a practical matter even though their legal rights are unaffected. One of the disadvantages of sideline-sitting is that the bystander has no right to appeal from a judgment no matter how harmful it may be.

In this case the Court quite rightly concludes that the white firefighters who brought the second series of Title VII cases could not be deprived of their legal rights in the first series of cases because they had neither intervened nor been joined as parties. The consent decrees obviously could not deprive them of any contractual rights, such as seniority or accrued vacation pay, or of any other legal rights, such as the right to have their employer comply with federal statutes like Title VII. There is no reason, however, why the consent decrees might not produce changes in conditions at the white firefighters' place of employment that, as a practical matter, may have a serious effect on their opportunities for employment or promotion even though they are not bound by the decrees in any legal sense. The fact that one of the effects of a decree is to curtail the job opportunities of nonparties does not mean that the nonparties have been deprived of legal rights or that they have standing to appeal from that decree without becoming parties. . . .

PERSPECTIVES

Martin v. Wilks takes on special significance due to its location. Birmingham, Alabama was the site of dramatic struggles in the 1960s as the city resisted desegregation. At one point, police dogs were turned on unarmed demonstrators. At another point, the city's fire department was deployed to turn fire hoses on demonstrators, an incident captured in the adjacent picture. As you can imagine, that gave the continuing legal efforts to integrate that fire department deep salience.

Notes and Problems

1. Consider both the sequence of litigative events and the identity of the parties involved. The basic lawsuit involved one "entity plaintiff" (the NAACP) and seven individual plaintiffs suing a pair of entity defendants (the city and the county personnel board, which was responsible for staffing firehouse positions).

   a. The plaintiffs and defendants engaged in considerable litigation—including a trial of some issues—before arriving at a settlement.

   b. There were then three separate efforts to challenge the settlement, each by a slightly different set of individual and entity parties. Be sure you understand which groups took which actions at which stages of the lawsuit. Why, as the Court saw matters, did none of these prior challenges bind the *Wilks* respondents from bringing their claims?

2. Put yourself in the position of the original parties. They have fought each other to exhaustion and have arrived at a settlement that they are prepared to live with. Now comes a group not previously involved in the litigation—but standing on its sidelines—who contend that the terms of the settlement disadvantage them in an unlawful way.

   a. Explain why the original parties to the suit would be unhappy about this development.

b. Describe the argument—ultimately rejected by the Court—that the original parties used to explain why the white firefighters should be bound by the settlement agreement, even though they had not participated in the lawsuit or in the settlement negotiations. Though it was rejected by the majority, this argument got four votes. Why?

3. *Wilks* can be understood as a question of who has the responsibility to ensure that the requisite interests are represented in the lawsuit. One view, rejected by the majority, is that the absentees have the burden of invoking Rule 24 to intervene if they have notice of the lawsuit. On this view the penalty for failing to intervene is that one must subsequently suffer under any unfavorable result. The other view, adopted in *Wilks*, is that those in the suit share with the court the responsibility for joining the absentees. On this view the penalty for failing to locate and join all absentee interests is that one must face the prospect of subsequent litigation when the absentees do assert their interests. As a matter of either good judicial administration or due process, is the choice between the two paths clear?

4. Notice the connection between *Wilks* and *Taylor v. Sturgell*, supra page 720, which decided that someone who knew of litigation—and was deeply interested in its outcome—was nevertheless not bound by its outcome because not a party. *Taylor* was a case decided under the common law of former adjudication, but it breathes the same air as *Wilks*.

5. What is the source of law for the decision in *Wilks*? Is it an interpretation of Rule 19 or is it based on the Due Process Clause? The decision itself does not answer this question. Note, though, its import: If *Wilks* is based on the Due Process Clause, a statute purporting to overrule *Wilks* would be unconstitutional.

   a. Congress apparently concluded that *Wilks* was not based on the Due Process Clause, because after *Wilks*, Congress enacted and the President signed legislation aimed at, among other things, reversing the holding of the case. 42 U.S.C. §2000e2(n). The statute prohibits a collateral challenge to a consent decree in a civil rights case complaining of employment discrimination if the challenger is "a person who, prior to the entry of [the consent decree] had—(i) actual notice . . . of the proposed judgment . . . ; and (ii) a reasonable opportunity to present objections to such judgment or order; or (iii) . . . a person whose interests were adequately represented" in the first action. Explain why, on the facts of *Wilks*, this statute would lead to a result different from that decision.

   b. The legislation applies only to employment discrimination consent decrees. It would not apply, for example, to a school desegregation decree or an antitrust consent judgment that adversely affected nonparties. Is there something about employment discrimination litigation that led Congress to dictate a special procedural rule? Or did Congress, focused on overturning the holding of *Wilks*, overlook the application of its holding to other contexts?

D. INTERPLEADER

In discussing necessary parties, we considered briefly a case in which a husband made a life insurance policy payable to "my wife." Suppose the couple subsequently divorced, Husband remarried and later died. Suppose both wives claim the proceeds of the policy. If they bring separate suits on the policy, it is possible that, to the consternation of the insurance company, both will win. The same situation could occur if a bank held an account of a small business, whose members had a falling out. Suppose two competing claimants appear at the bank, each wanting to withdraw the entire account. In both cases, the "stakeholder"—the insurer or the bank—concedes that it owes the money—but it wants some way to bind everyone to an adjudication of the dispute. The stakeholder wants a procedure that will bind all claimants.

In the past, any possible resolution of the stakeholder's dilemma had to overcome two difficulties: (1) the unavailability of an effective procedural device to join both claimants, and (2) possible jurisdictional and venue limitations. *Interpleader* provides a procedure by which a stakeholder—often a bank or insurer—can require the competing claimants to litigate their rights to the fund or property in question. Rule 22 typifies such a joinder provision; note that it allows interpleader even if the stakeholder asserts some claim on the assets itself—as might be the case if a bank wanted to reduce the balance of the account by the amount of an unpaid loan. Typically, the stakeholder invokes interpleader, joining the claimants as parties.

Such a proceeding will, however, fail to yield a stable resolution of the dispute if the forum lacks jurisdiction over the claimants. As an illustration of the jurisdictional difficulties such limitations could pose, consider New York Life Insurance Co. v. Dunlevy, 241 U.S. 518 (1916). Father, in Pennsylvania, bought an insurance policy that paid a lump sum amount after a set number of years. The sum came due, but Father and Daughter disagreed about whether he or she was entitled to the sum. One of Daughter's creditors brought suit in Pennsylvania. The insurer, knowing of the dispute between Father and Daughter, interpleaded Father, Daughter, and Creditor. The Pennsylvania court ruled that Father was entitled to the proceeds. Daughter, dissatisfied by this result, sued the insurer in California. Insurer contended that the Pennsylvania suit precluded Daughter's claim. Wrong, held the U.S. Supreme Court—because Pennsylvania had not acquired personal jurisdiction over Daughter, who lived in California. The insurer was thus liable—a second time—for the policy proceeds.

Congress responded to the procedural uncertainties and the jurisdictional issues presented in cases like *Dunlevy* by enacting the Federal Interpleader Act, codified at 28 U.S.C. §§1335, 1397, and 2361. This legislation accomplishes several tasks:

- The Interpleader Act broadens the circumstances in which interpleader is available, eliminating some restrictions that older equity doctrines had imposed. See §1335.
- The Act removes limitations on federal subject matter jurisdiction. How does it do this? See §1335(a).

- The Act permits nationwide service of process—a phrase interpreted to mean nationwide personal jurisdiction. See §2361. Thus, in *Dunlevy*, Daughter would be subject to the jurisdiction of the federal courts in Pennsylvania, which could thus resolve all the parties' conflicting claims.
- The Act expands venue provisions to permit venue where any claimant resides. See §1397.

Rule 22 closely resembles the Interpleader Act. But Rule 22 interpleader actions are subject to the normal rules for subject matter jurisdiction (diversity between all plaintiffs and all defendants; amount in controversy); personal jurisdiction (jurisdiction within the state); and venue (residency of all defendants, or where the claim arises). In practice, Rule 22 interpleader is used when the stakeholder is a citizen of one state and all claimants are citizens of a second state. In such a case, there is no jurisdiction under the Interpleader Act because no two claimants are of diverse citizenship. In such cases, however, the normal rules for jurisdiction and venue can be satisfied by an action in the state of all claimants.

The table below illustrates some differences between statutory interpleader and Rule 22 interpleader.

Issue	"Statutory" Interpleader	"Rule" Interpleader
Federal Subject Matter Jurisdiction —Diversity	Minimal diversity, determined as between claimants	Complete diversity, determined as between stakeholder and claimants
—Amount	$500	$75,000+
Personal Jurisdiction	Nationwide service of process	Must meet ordinary jurisdiction rules; contacts with claimants required; service under Rule 4
Venue	Residence of one or more claimants	Ordinary venue rules under 28 U.S.C. §1391
Injunctions (typically to freeze assets or require their delivery to a claimant)	Specifically provided for interpleader cases in 28 U.S.C. §2361	No specific basis; courts have used 28 U.S.C. §2361 ("where necessary in aid of . . . jurisdiction")

The next case is a straightforward illustration of interpleader and the different jurisdictional hoops one must pass through to bring a claim pursuant to the statute and Rule.

Southern Farm Bureau Life Ins. Co. v. Davis

2010 WL 1245024 (W.D. La. 2010)

MINALDI, J.

Presently before the court is a Motion to Dismiss filed by the defendant, Robyn Little Davis ("Ms. Davis"). The motion is opposed by the plaintiff, Southern Farm Bureau Life Insurance Company ("Farm Bureau"). For the reasons stated herein, the Motion to Dismiss will be denied.

Facts

The plaintiff, Farm Bureau [a corporation with its principal place of business in Mississippi], filed this interpleader action naming as defendant, Ms. Davis and the unopened succession [meaning the as-yet unknown heirs] of her husband, Mr. Davis. [Ms. Davis is a citizen of Louisiana and the estate of Mr. Davis is treated as a citizen of Louisiana.] At issue is a life insurance policy with a face value of $95,000.00 insuring the life of Mr. Davis.

The named beneficiary of the policy, Ms. Davis, has been arrested and charged with killing Mr. Davis. Pursuant to Louisiana law, a beneficiary of the life insurance policy cannot recover proceeds if she is deemed to have been criminally responsible for the death, disablement, or injury of the insured, or judicially determined to have participated in the intentional, unjustified killing of the insured. If a primary beneficiary is disqualified to receive the benefits of the policy and there is no contingent beneficiary, the life insurance proceeds are to be paid to the estate of the insured. La. R.S. 22:901.

Law

. . . In any case in federal court, federal subject matter jurisdiction must be present before the court may properly consider the claim. *Cf.* Richmond, Fredericksburg & Potomac R. Co. v. United States, 945 F.2d 765, 768 (4th Cir. 1991). Plaintiff initiated this interpleader action in order to fulfill its obligations under the insurance policy insuring the life of Mr. Davis and to be discharged from any future actions involving the policy. The concept of interpleader is that, where two or more persons are engaged in a dispute over some property, and the subject of that dispute is in the hands of a third party who is willing to give up the property, the third person is not obliged to incur the expense and risk of defending the action. Rather, the third party may give up the property and be relieved from further actions concerning the matter, leaving the court to resolve the dispute between the persons claiming an interest in the disputed property.

In the instant case, the plaintiff is the third party willing to give up the subject of the dispute, namely the $95,000 insurance policy amount. The defendants are those persons with a presumed interest in the property held by the plaintiff. Through this interpleader action, the plaintiff is surrendering the value of the policy to the court in order to be relieved of all its obligations under the policy.

To determine whether there is jurisdiction, this court must examine the two central interpleader provisions, statutory interpleader, 28 U.S.C. §1335, and rule interpleader, Fed. R. Civ. P. 22. While the concept of interpleader under both statutory and rule interpleader is similar, their jurisdictional differences are significant. "The central distinction between statutory interpleader and rule interpleader is the basis for a federal court's subject matter jurisdiction under each."

Statutory interpleader under 28 U.S.C. §1335 confers on federal courts jurisdiction over certain interpleader claims. §1335 declares that "district courts shall have original jurisdiction of any civil action of interpleader," as long as the amount in controversy equals $500 or more and the *claimants* are at least minimally diverse. 28 U.S.C. §1335(a). In other words, assuming the requisite jurisdictional amount is met, statutory interpleader still requires that two or more of the adverse claimants to a contested fund be "of diverse citizenship as defined in section 1332 of this title." 28 U.S.C. §1335(a)(1). In the present case, although the amount in controversy exceeds $500, there is no diversity between the defendant claimants. Therefore, there is no jurisdiction under statutory interpleader.

Rule interpleader is a procedural device that does not alone confer federal jurisdiction over a claim. An interpleader brought under Rule 22 must fall within one of the general statutory grants of federal jurisdiction. This may include diversity jurisdiction, provided that the complete diversity and amount in controversy requirements are met. In the instant case, the amount in controversy is over $75,000.00, and there is diversity between the plaintiff and the defendants. Because the requirements for general diversity jurisdiction are satisfied, the court has jurisdiction over plaintiff's interpleader action under Rule 22.

Notes and Problems

---

1. First, understand the underlying action. Why did the insurance company file this interpleader action? What was it worried about and what did it hope to accomplish by filing the lawsuit? Who are the potential claimants of the insurance policy proceeds?

2. Now, make sure that you understand the different requirements of statutory interpleader and rule interpleader. The trial concludes that it has jurisdiction over the case under Rule 22 but not §1335. Why?

3. As the opinion notes, interpleader is one of the instances in which a statute has based diversity jurisdiction on minimal diversity rather than the complete diversity required under §1332(a). As you will see in the next section, the class action provides another instance.

E. CLASS ACTIONS

1. Introduction

A class action permits, in the words of Rule 23, one or more parties to "sue or be sued as representative parties on behalf" of all those similarly situated. The underlying concept is simple: If many persons find themselves in the same situation, advantages may flow from aggregating their many lawsuits into one. But one side's advantage may be another's nightmare as it now faces numerous similarly situated persons rather than a single plaintiff. In practice, the class action has stimulated comments as favorable as "one of the most socially useful remedies in history" and as negative as "legalized blackmail."* Technically a joinder device, the class action has a potential effect on the judicial system and the substantive law unmatched by other joinder devices discussed in this chapter. The class action repays study: It raises some of the most challenging procedural issues on the current legal scene, and it raises questions that lie close to the heart of civil litigation—the nature of representation and the purpose of a lawsuit.

Although one can trace collective litigation into the mists of the common law, the modern class action traces its immediate pedigree only to 1966. See generally Stephen C. Yeazell, From Medieval Group Litigation to the Modern Class Action (Yale Univ. Press 1987). The revision of Rule 23 in that year sparked a new interest in and widespread use of class actions, prompting reaction of the type quoted above. Class actions clearly differ from the normal litigation model in which an individual plaintiff seeks redress from an individual defendant. The difference is not merely quantitative. For reasons that will become clear in the following materials, the ability to aggregate large numbers of litigants tends to shift the focus from the client to the lawyer, from damages to attorneys' fees, and from litigation to settlement.

The effect of class actions on the substantive law is subtler. It is not that the availability of class actions literally changes the statutes or the content of the case law, but, rather, that rules devised for one-on-one litigation have different effects in the context of mass litigation. As you saw in Chapter 5's discussion of litigation finance, the legal system makes some claims and defenses uneconomical to bring or defend. If your cell phone carrier overcharges you by $2, you might call or e-mail to complain. But if the carrier does not reverse the charge, few of us would bring a lawsuit: The amount at stake would not begin to justify the expense of a suit. By the same token, if—defying economic rationality—you did sue, the carrier would likely settle; the suit would not be worth defending. Now suppose the carrier made similar overcharges to a million customers. If they could join together in a single lawsuit, the economics of litigation would change dramatically: The suit is worth bringing, and it's worth defending. Is that a good thing? That question, in

---

* The former comment comes from Pomerantz, *New Developments in Class Actions—Has Their Death Knell Been Sounded?*, 25 Bus. Law. 1259 (1970); the latter characterization appears in Handler, *The Shift from Substantive to Procedural Innovations in Anti-Trust Suits*, 71 Colum. L. Rev. 1, 9 (1971).

various forms, poses the debate surrounding the class action. When the availability of class actions increases the number of claims that are brought rather than simply facilitating the bringing of large numbers of claims that would have been brought separately, the impact of the underlying substantive law may be greatly heightened. Some have argued that this effect is a regrettable aspect of the Rule. Others have argued that the increased potential for deterring wrongdoers and forcing wider compliance with the law is a powerful argument in favor of the device.

Alongside the debate about whether the class action is a good thing stands a second issue—that of legal representation. In most of the litigation you have thus far studied, someone hires a lawyer (or finds one to take the case on a contingent basis). As the lawyer conducts the suit, rules of professional responsibility require her to let her client make major litigation decisions—whether to sue and whether and on what terms to settle being among the most important. In class actions, however, there is no client in the ordinary sense of the word. There is a class of people—say cell phone users from the hypothetical case above—and there are representative parties (a few of those who have been overcharged, who are identified as plaintiffs by name in the complaint). But these representatives have no legal authority to make litigation decisions on behalf of the million members of the class. That means that the class's lawyer stands in a position of enormous responsibility: She must act in the best interests of the class without being able to discuss the case with them. Increasing that burden is the circumstance that the lawyer will often be negotiating her own fee at the same time that she is negotiating the terms of the settlement on behalf of the class. This very difficult professional situation provides a second focus for the debate over the class action, as you will see.

We start with a pair of cases that provide the constitutional grounding for the modern class action; from there we move to the current statutory requirements and problems of settlement and representation.

2. The Class Action and the Constitution

Above the controversy surrounding the class action stand a pair of constitutional arguments that both enable and limit the procedure. Both flow from the Due Process Clause. One argument inquires whether a party can be bound by litigation to which he is not a party. The other asks whether due process requires certain procedures within the class action in order for it to be a valid adjudication of the absentees' rights.

a. Representative Adequacy

Fundamental to the class action is the idea that a suit, conducted by a representative on behalf of a number of persons who are not formal parties, may nevertheless bind the entire represented class. In that respect it represents a departure from the ordinary proposition that one may be bound only by litigation to which one is a party. One might cite any number of cases for this proposition, including *Taylor v. Sturgell*, supra page 720, and *Martin v. Wilks*, supra page 819. The next case works out the conditions under which such a representative may bind those who are not parties. It limits the class action, but at the same time it gives the class action, thus limited, great potential power.

PERSPECTIVES

A biography of the named party's daughter sets the stage, while demonstrating that one person's "legal technicality" can be another's leading constitutional case:

> [Lorraine Hansberry] was the youngest of Nannie Perry Hansberry and Carl Augustus Hansberry's four children. Her father founded Lake Street Bank, one of the first banks for blacks in Chicago[,] and ran a successful real estate business. . . .
>
> Despite their middle-class status, the Hansberrys were subject to segregation. When she was eight years old, Hansberry's family deliberately attempted to move into a restricted neighborhood. Restrictive covenants, in which white property owners agreed not to sell to blacks, created a ghetto known as the "Black Belt" on Chicago's South Side. Carl Hansberry, with the help of Harry H. Pace, president of the Supreme Liberty Life Insurance Company and several white realtors, secretly bought property at 413 East Sixtieth Street and 6140 South Rhodes Avenue. The Hansberrys moved into the house on Rhodes Avenue in May 1937. The family was threatened by a white mob, which threw a brick through a window, narrowly missing Lorraine. The Supreme Court of Illinois upheld the legality of the restrictive covenant and forced the family to leave the house. The U.S. Supreme Court reversed the decision on a legal technicality. The result was the opening of thirty blocks of South Side Chicago to African Americans. . . .
>
> In *A Raisin in the Sun*, the first play written by an African American to be produced on Broadway, [Lorraine Hansberry] drew upon the lives of the working class people who rented from her father and who went to school with her on Chicago's South Side. . . .

Chicago Public Library, Lorraine Hansberry: A Brief Biography, available at www.chipublib. org/003cpl/oboc/raisin/biography.html.

Hansberry v. Lee
311 U.S. 32 (1940)

STONE, J., delivered the opinion of the Court.

The question is whether the Supreme Court of Illinois, by its adjudication that petitioners in this case are bound to a judgment rendered in an earlier litigation to which they were not parties, has deprived them of the due process of law guaranteed by the Fourteenth Amendment. . . .

[The case was decided before *Shelley v. Kraemer*, 334 U.S. 1 (1948), holding racially restrictive covenants unenforceable. The Hansberrys, a black family, bought a house in an area of Chicago allegedly covered by a racially restrictive covenant. The covenant said it did not take effect unless signed by owners of 95 percent of the frontage. In fact, the signers represented only 54 percent. Lee brought an action to enjoin breach of the covenant, naming as defendants both the Hansberrys, who had purchased a home allegedly in violation of the covenant, and the people from whom the Hansberrys had bought the property. One of the Hansberrys' defenses was that the covenant was unenforceable because not enough owners had signed it. Plaintiff countered by referring to *Burke v. Kleiman*, an earlier suit to enforce the same covenant. In *Burke*, a property owner "on behalf of herself and other property owners in like situation" sued four named individuals allegedly in violation of the covenant. *Burke* was litigated in the Illinois courts, where the parties had *stipulated* (falsely) that the requisite 95 percent had signed, and the earlier court had adopted that stipulation in its findings. *Burke* upheld the covenant. The Supreme Court of Illinois in the present case determined that *Burke* had been a class action, that the Hansberrys and their vendors were members of the class of plaintiffs in *Burke*, and that they were therefore bound by the findings in the previous action even though those findings were factually erroneous.]

To the defense that the agreement had never become effective because owners of 95 per cent of the frontage had not signed it, respondents pleaded that that issue was *res judicata* by the decree in an earlier suit. To this petitioners pleaded, by way of rejoinder, that they were not parties to that suit or bound by its decree, and that denial of their right to litigate, in the present suit, the issue of performance of the condition precedent to the validity of the agreement would be a denial of due process of law guaranteed by the Fourteenth Amendment. It does not appear, nor is it contended that any of petitioners is the successor in interest to or in privity with any of the parties in the earlier suit.

The [state] . . . court, after a trial on the merits, found that owners of only about 54 per cent of the frontage had signed the agreement, and that the only support of the judgment in the *Burke* case was a false and fraudulent stipulation of the parties that owners of 95 per cent had signed. But it ruled that the issue of performance of the condition precedent to the validity of the agreement was *res judicata* as alleged and entered a decree for respondents. . . .

From this the Supreme Court of Illinois concluded in the present case that *Burke v. Kleiman* was a "class" or "representative" suit, and that in such a suit, "where the remedy is pursued by a plaintiff who has the right to represent the class to which he belongs, other members of the class are bound by the results in the case unless it is reversed or set aside on direct proceedings"; that petitioners in the present suit were members of the class represented by the plaintiffs in the earlier suit and consequently were bound by its decree. . . .

State courts are free to attach such descriptive labels to litigations before them as they may choose and to attribute to them such consequences as they think appropriate under state constitutions and laws, subject only to the requirements of the Constitution of the United States. But when the judgment of a state court, ascribing to the judgment of another court the binding force and effect of *res judicata*, is challenged for want of due process it becomes the duty of this Court to examine the course of procedure in both litigations to ascertain whether the litigant whose rights have thus been adjudicated has been afforded such notice and opportunity to be heard as are requisite to the due process which the Constitution prescribes.

It is a principle of general application in Anglo-American jurisprudence that one is not bound by a judgment in personam in a litigation in which he is not designated as a party or to which he has not been made a party by service of process. *Pennoyer v. Neff*. A judgment rendered in such circumstances is not entitled to the full faith and credit which the Constitution and statutes of the United States prescribe, *Pennoyer v. Neff*; and judicial action enforcing it against the person or property of the absent party is not that due process which the Fifth and Fourteenth Amendments require.

To these general rules there is a recognized exception that, to an extent not precisely defined by judicial opinion, the judgment in a "class" or "representative" suit, to which some members of the class are parties, may bind members of the class or those represented who were not made parties to it.

The class suit was an invention of equity to enable it to proceed to a decree in suits where the number of those interested in the subject of the litigation is so great that their joinder as parties in conformity to the usual rules of procedure is impracticable. Courts are not infrequently called upon to proceed with causes in which the number of those interested in the litigation is so great as to make difficult or impossible the joinder of all because some are not within the jurisdiction or because their whereabouts is unknown or where if all were made parties to the suit its continued abatement by the death of some would prevent or unduly delay a decree. In such cases where the interests of those not joined are of the same class as the interests of those who are, and where it is considered that the latter fairly represent the former in the prosecution of the litigation of the issues in which all have a common interest, the court will proceed to a decree. . . .

[T]here is scope within the framework of the Constitution for holding in appropriate cases that a judgment rendered in a class suit is *res judicata* as to members of the class who are not formal parties to the suit. Here, as elsewhere, the Fourteenth Amendment does not compel state courts or legislatures to adopt any particular rule for establishing the conclusiveness of judgments in class suits, nor does it compel the adoption of the particular rules thought by this Court to be appropriate for the federal courts. With a proper regard for divergent local institutions and interests, this Court is justified in saying that there has been a failure of due process only in those cases where it cannot be said that the procedure adopted, fairly insures the protection of the interests of absent parties who are to be bound by it.

It is familiar doctrine of the federal courts that members of a class not present as parties to the litigation may be bound by the judgment where they are in fact adequately represented by parties who are present, or where they actually participate in the conduct of the litigation in which members of the class are present as parties, or where the interest of the members of the class, some of whom are present as parties, is joint, or where for any other reason the relationship between the parties present and those who are absent is such as legally to entitle the former to stand in judgment for the latter.

In all such cases, so far as it can be said that the members of the class who are present are, by generally recognized rules of law, entitled to stand in judgment for those who are not, we may assume for present purposes that such procedure affords a protection to the parties who are represented, though absent, which would satisfy the requirements of due process and full faith and credit. Nor do we find it necessary for the decision of this case to say that, when the only circumstance defining the class is that the determination of the rights of its members turns upon a single issue of fact or law, a state could not constitutionally adopt a procedure whereby some of the members of the class could stand in judgment for all, provided that the procedure were so devised and applied as to insure that those present are of the same class as those absent and that the litigation is so conducted as to insure the full and fair consideration of the common issue. We decide only that the procedure and the course of litigation sustained here by the plea of *res judicata* do not satisfy these requirements.

The restrictive agreement did not purport to create a joint obligation or liability. If valid and effective its promises were the several obligations of the signers and those claiming under them. The promises ran severally to every other signer. It is plain that in such circumstances all those alleged to be bound by the agreement would not constitute a single class in any litigation brought to enforce it. Those who sought to secure its benefits by enforcing it could not be said to be in the same class with or represent those whose interest was in resisting performance, for the agreement by its terms imposes obligations and confers rights on the owner of each plot of land who signs it. If those who thus seek to secure the benefits of the agreement were rightly regarded by the state Supreme Court as constituting a class, it is evident that those signers or their successors who are interested in challenging the validity of the agreement and resisting its performance are not of the same class in the sense that their interests are identical so that any group who had elected to enforce rights conferred by the agreement could be said to be acting in the interest of any others who were free to deny its obligation.

Because of the dual and potentially conflicting interests of those who are putative parties to the agreement in compelling or resisting its performance, it is impossible to say, solely because they are parties to it, that any two of them are of the same class. Nor without more, and with the due regard for the protection of the rights of absent parties which due process exacts, can some be permitted to stand in judgment for all.

It is one thing to say that some members of a class may represent other members in a litigation where the sole and common interest of the class in the litigation, is either to assert a common right or to challenge an asserted obligation. It is quite another to hold that all those who are free alternatively either to assert rights or to challenge them are of a single class, so that any group, merely because it is of the class so constituted, may be deemed adequately to represent any others of the class in litigating their interests in either alternative. Such a selection of representatives for purposes of litigation, whose substantial interests are not necessarily or even probably the same as those whom they are deemed to represent, does not afford that protection to absent parties which due process requires. The doctrine of representation of absent parties in a class suit has not hitherto been thought to go so far. Apart from the opportunities it would afford for the fraudulent and collusive sacrifice of the rights of absent parties, we think that the representation in this case no more satisfies the requirements of due process than a trial by a judicial officer who is in such situation that he may have an interest in the outcome of the litigation in conflict with that of the litigants.

The plaintiffs in the *Burke* case sought to compel performance of the agreement in behalf of themselves and all others similarly situated. They did not designate the defendants in the suit as a class or seek any injunction or other relief against others than the named defendants, and the decree which was entered did not purport to bind others. In seeking to enforce the agreement the plaintiffs in that suit were not representing the petitioners here whose substantial interest is in resisting performance. The defendants in the first suit were not treated by the pleadings or decree as representing others or as foreclosing by their defense the rights of others; and, even though nominal defendants, it does not appear that their interest in defeating the contract outweighed their interest in establishing its validity. For a court in this situation to ascribe to either the plaintiffs or defendants the performance of such functions on behalf of petitioners here, is to attribute to them a power that it cannot be said that they had assumed to exercise, and a responsibility which, in view of their dual interests it does not appear that they could rightly discharge.

Reversed.

McREYNOLDS, J., ROBERTS, J., and REED, J., concur in the result.

WHAT'S NEW HERE?

- The Supreme Court held that a member of a class could not be bound by a judgment involving the class unless that member was "adequately represented."
- That holding has a negative and a positive implication. The negative: Because the Court held that Hansberry had not been adequately represented, he was not bound by the judgment in the purported class action.
- The positive: *If* one could construct a procedure that would result in adequate representation, a class member would be bound, even though she did not appear as a formal party to the lawsuit. (Scattered prior cases involving class-like equity suits had so implied, but it had never arisen as a sharply defined constitutional question.)

Notes and Problems

1. How does the principle of (in)adequate representation apply to the facts of *Hansberry*?

   a. Were the Hansberrys and their vendors "represented" in the earlier class action, according to the Illinois courts?

   b. On which side? The only plausible class was a group of persons seeking to enforce the covenant *against* those who wished to buy or sell property free of racial restrictions. Surely the Hansberrys weren't represented by this class.

   c. If there had been a defendant class in *Burke v. Kleiman* as well—a class consisting of all those who challenged the validity of the covenant—one could at least begin to discuss whether the Hansberrys were members of that class. But the defendants in *Burke* were four named individuals who purported to represent only themselves. So, on its face, it represents massive confusion to describe *Burke v. Kleiman* as a class suit that bound the Hansberrys.

2. At this point, the U.S. Supreme Court had a problem. The Court doesn't have jurisdiction to correct confusion, even massive confusion, within state courts unless that confusion falls within its jurisdiction. The only way the Court could reach the Illinois judgment was to find a constitutional error.

   a. What was the constitutional error?

   b. The *Hansberry* opinion tells us that the Illinois Supreme Court deemed the earlier action to have been a class action even though it was not conducted with any real attention to the interests of the "class" members. Couldn't the result in *Hansberry* have rested on the much narrower ground that due process is denied when binding effect is given to a judgment in an action in which no attempt was made to consider the problems of representing a group of absentees? Isn't the real problem that no one tried to represent the Hansberrys' interests in the earlier suit?

3. In explaining why the prior litigation did not bind the Hansberrys, the Court contrasted appropriate class actions with inappropriate ones:

   > It is one thing to say that some members of a class may represent other members in a litigation where the sole and common interest of the class in the litigation is either to assert a common right or to challenge an asserted obligation. It is quite another to hold that all those who are free alternatively either to assert rights or to challenge them are of a single class, so that any group, merely because it is of the class so constituted, may be deemed adequately to represent any others of the class in litigating their interests in either alternative.

311 U.S. at 44-45.

In the context of the *Hansberry* case itself, the statement has special force. Professor Allen Kamp's research revealed that the Burke family, who sold to the

Hansberrys, had been the leaders of the plaintiff class in the first lawsuit and then later changed their minds about the covenant:

> The Court's words, "free to assert or deny" [rights] did not refer to an abstract possibility—that is exactly what had happened. The party enforcing the covenant in *Burke* was the wife of the person who had sold his house to Carl Hansberry. . . . Although the language is so sweeping it could apply to and invalidate every class action, what actually happened in *Burke* and *Hansberry* was unique—that husband of the class representative in the first action had become a defendant and sought to subvert the goals of the plaintiff class.

> Allen Kamp, The History Behind *Hansberry v. Lee*,
> 20 U.C. Davis L. Rev. 481, 497 (1987).

4. The problem of the binding power of a class action usually boils down to a question of fairness to parties who may not have been adequately represented. Although the court in the first action can help to ensure adequate representation of such parties, no ruling to that effect in the first action should bind them if in fact they were not adequately represented. Thus, *Hansberry* can also be cited for the proposition that a person asserted to be bound by former class litigation has the right collaterally to challenge the adequacy of the representation in the class suit.

   Gonzales v. Cassidy, 474 F.2d 67 (5th Cir. 1973), nicely illustrated this point: An unnamed member of a class was not precluded from bringing a later action even though an earlier class action had failed. The named plaintiff in the earlier action had succeeded in securing relief for himself; at that point, the second court ruled, he had become an inadequate representative of the class by failing to appeal. Failure of the plaintiff in the second action to intervene in the first action for the purpose of appealing was held not to be fatal to his argument that the first decision should not bind him.

b. Personal Jurisdiction

Hansberry tells us that for a class action to bind absentees the representation of the class must be adequate. Does due process place further constraints on the operation of the class action?

Phillips Petroleum v. Shutts

472 U.S. 797 (1985)

Rehnquist, J.

[Phillips produces and sells natural gas. Some of this gas came from land leased from others. Phillips paid royalties on the gas it extracted from each parcel of leased land. The royalty was based on the price for which the gas was finally sold; increases in the selling price required approval by a federal agency. While regulatory approval was pending, however, Phillips sold the gas at higher prices but paid royalties only on the lower, already-approved prices, releasing the funds accumulated from the increased royalties only when the increase met with regulatory approval. Phillips's defense of this practice rested on the difficulty of obtaining rebates from the royalty owners if the price increases were not approved. Phillips paid the royalty owners no interest on the money it held (and invested) pending regulatory approval.

Plaintiff Irl Shutts filed a suit on behalf of himself and 33,000 small royalty owners, claiming that they were entitled to interest on the money during the period when Phillips was awaiting approval of its price increases. The average claim of the class members was $100. Suit was filed in Kansas state court, which certified the action under a state provision substantially resembling Federal Rule of Civil Procedure 23.]

After the class was certified respondents provided each class member with notice through first-class mail. The notice described the action and informed each class member that he could appear in person or by counsel; otherwise each member would be represented by Shutts and the Andersons, the named plaintiffs. The notices also stated that class members would be included in the class and bound by the judgment unless they "opted out" of the lawsuit by executing and returning a "request for exclusion" that was included with the notice. The final class as certified contained 28,100 members; 3,400 had "opted out" of the class by returning the request for exclusion, and notice could not be delivered to another 1,500 members, who were also excluded. Less than 1,000 of the class members resided in Kansas. Only a minuscule amount, approximately one quarter of one percent, of the gas leases involved in the lawsuit were on Kansas land. [After some procedural skirmishing over the class action issue, the case went to trial. On the merits, the Kansas court held "as a matter of Kansas equity law" that Phillips owed the royalty owners interest and entered judgment for the plaintiff class.]

Petitioner raised two principal claims in its appeal to the Supreme Court of Kansas. It first asserted that the Kansas trial court did not possess personal jurisdiction over absent plaintiff class members as required by *International Shoe Co. v. Washington* and similar cases. Related to this first claim was petitioner's contention that the "opt-out" notice to absent class members, which forced them to return the request for exclusion in order to avoid the suit, was insufficient to bind class members who were not residents of Kansas or who did not possess "minimum contacts" with Kansas. Second, petitioner claimed that Kansas courts could not apply Kansas law to every claim in the dispute. The trial court should have looked to the laws of each State where the leases were located to determine, on the basis of conflict of laws principles, whether interest on the suspended royalties was recoverable, and at what rate. . . .

Reduced to its essentials, petitioner's argument is that unless out-of-state plaintiffs affirmatively consent, the Kansas courts may not exert jurisdiction over their claims. Petitioner claims that failure to execute and return the "request for exclusion" provided with the class notice cannot constitute consent of the out-of-state plaintiffs; thus Kansas courts may exercise jurisdiction over these plaintiffs only if the plaintiffs possess the sufficient "minimum contacts" with Kansas as that term is used in cases involving personal jurisdiction over out-of-state defendants. E.g., *International Shoe Co. v. Washington, Shaffer v. Heitner, World-Wide Volkswagen Corp. v. Woodson.* Since Kansas had no prelitigation contact with many of the plaintiffs and leases involved, petitioner claims that Kansas has exceeded its jurisdictional reach and thereby violated the due process rights of the absent plaintiffs. . . .

Although the cases like *Shaffer* and *Woodson* which petitioner relies on for a minimum contacts requirement all dealt with out-of-state defendants or parties in the procedural posture of a defendant, petitioner claims that the same analysis must apply to absent class-action plaintiffs. In this regard petitioner correctly points out that a chose in action is a constitutionally recognized property interest possessed by each of the plaintiffs. *Mullane v. Central Hanover Bank & Trust Co.* An adverse judgment by Kansas courts in this case may extinguish the chose in action forever through *res judicata.* Such an adverse judgment, petitioner claims, would be every bit as onerous to an absent plaintiff as an adverse judgment on the merits would be to a defendant. Thus, the same due process protections should apply to absent plaintiffs: Kansas should not be able to exert jurisdiction over the plaintiffs' claims unless the plaintiffs have sufficient minimum contacts with Kansas.

We think petitioner's premise is in error. The burdens placed by a State upon an absent class-action plaintiff are not of the same order or magnitude as those it places upon an absent defendant. An out-of-state defendant summoned by a plaintiff is faced with the full powers of the forum State to render judgment *against* it. The defendant must generally hire counsel and travel to the forum to defend itself from the plaintiff's claim, or suffer a default judgment. The defendant may be forced to participate in extended and often costly discovery, and will be forced to respond in damages or to comply with some other form of remedy imposed by the court should it lose the suit. The defendant may also face liability for court costs and attorney's fees. . . .

A class-action plaintiff, however, is in quite a different posture. . . .

In sharp contrast to the predicament of a defendant haled into an out-of-state forum, the plaintiffs in this suit were not haled anywhere to defend themselves upon pain of a default judgment. As commentators have noted, from the plaintiffs' point of view a class action resembles a "quasi-administrative proceeding, conducted by the judge." A plaintiff class in Kansas and numerous other jurisdictions cannot first be certified unless the judge, with the aid of the named plaintiffs and defendant, conducts an inquiry into the common nature of the named plaintiffs and the absent plaintiffs' claims, the adequacy of representation, the jurisdiction possessed over the class, and any other matters that will bear upon proper representation of the absent plaintiffs' interest. See, e.g., Kan. Stat. Ann. §60-223 (1983), Fed. Rule Civ. Proc. 23. Unlike a defendant in a civil suit, a class-action plaintiff is not required to fend for himself. See Kan. Stat. Ann. §60-223(d) (1983). The court and named plaintiffs protect his interest. Indeed, the class-action defendant itself has a great interest in ensuring that the absent plaintiffs' claims are properly before the forum. . . .

The concern of the typical class-action rules for the absent plaintiffs is manifested in other ways. Most jurisdictions, including Kansas, require that a class action, once certified, may not be dismissed or compromised without the approval of the court. In many jurisdictions such as Kansas the court may amend the pleadings to ensure that all sections of the class are represented adequately. Kan. Stat. Ann. §60-223(d) (1983); see also e.g., Fed. Rule Civ. Proc. 23(d).

Besides this continuing solicitude for their rights, absent plaintiff class members are not subject to other burdens imposed upon defendants. They need not hire counsel or appear. They are almost never subject to counterclaims or crossclaims, or liability for fees or costs.[2] Absent plaintiff class members are not subject to coercive or punitive remedies. Nor will an adverse judgment typically bind an absent plaintiff for any damages, although a valid adverse judgment may extinguish any of the plaintiff's claim which was litigated. . . .

In most class actions an absent plaintiff is provided at least with an opportunity to "opt out" of the class, and if he takes advantage of that opportunity he is removed from the litigation entirely. This was true of the Kansas proceedings in this case. . . .

Because States place fewer burdens upon absent class plaintiffs than they do upon absent defendants in nonclass suits, the Due Process Clause need not and does not afford the former as much protection from state-court jurisdiction as it does the latter. The Fourteenth Amendment does protect "persons," not "defendants," however, so absent plaintiffs as well as absent defendants are entitled to some protection from the jurisdiction of a forum State which seeks to adjudicate their claims. In this case we hold that a forum State may exercise jurisdiction over the claim of an absent class-action plaintiff, even though that plaintiff may not possess the minimum contacts with the forum which would support personal jurisdiction over a defendant. If the forum State wishes to bind an absent plaintiff concerning a claim for money damages or similar relief at law,[3] it must provide minimal procedural due process protection. The plaintiff must receive notice plus an opportunity, to be heard and participate in the litigation, whether in person or through counsel. The notice must be the best practicable, "reasonably calculated, under all the circumstances, to apprise interested parties of the pendency of the action and afford them an opportunity, to present their objections." *Mullane.* The notice should describe the action and the plaintiffs' rights in it. Additionally, we hold that due process requires at a minimum that an absent plaintiff be provided

---

2. Petitioner places emphasis on the fact that absent class members might be subject to discovery, counterclaims, crossclaims or court costs. Petitioner cites no cases involving any such imposition upon plaintiffs, however. We are convinced that such burdens are rarely imposed upon plaintiff class members, and that the disposition of these issues is best left to a case which presents them in a more concrete way.

3. Our holding today is limited to those class actions which seek to bind known plaintiffs concerning claims wholly or predominantly for money judgments. We intimate no view concerning other types of class-action lawsuits, such as those seeking equitable relief. Nor, of course, does our discussion of personal jurisdiction address class actions where the jurisdiction is asserted against a defendant class.

with an opportunity to remove himself from the class by executing and returning an "opt out" or "request for exclusion" form to the court. Finally, the Due Process Clause of course requires that the named plaintiff at all times adequately represent the interests of the absent class members. . . .

We think that the procedure followed by Kansas, where a fully descriptive notice is sent first-class mail to each class member, with an explanation of the right to "opt out," satisfies due process. . . .

The Kansas courts applied Kansas contract and Kansas equity law to every claim in this case, notwithstanding that over 97 percent of the gas leases and some 97 percent of the plaintiffs in the case had no apparent connection to the State of Kansas except for this lawsuit. Petitioner protested that the Kansas courts should apply the laws of the States where the leases were located, or at least apply Texas and Oklahoma law because so many of the leases came from those States. The Kansas courts disregarded this contention and found petitioner liable for interest on the suspended royalties as a matter of Kansas law, and set the interest rates under Kansas equity principles. . . .

. . . We make no effort to determine for ourselves which law must apply to the various transactions involved in this lawsuit, and we reaffirm our observation in *Allstate* that in many situations a state court may be free to apply one of several choices of law. But the constitutional limitations laid down in cases such as *Allstate* and *Home Insurance Co. v. Dick* must be respected even in a nationwide class action.

We therefore affirm the judgment of the Supreme Court of Kansas insofar as it upheld the jurisdiction of the Kansas courts over the plaintiff class members in this case, and reverse its judgment insofar as it held that Kansas law was applicable to all of the transactions which it sought to adjudicate. We remand the case to that Court for further proceedings not inconsistent with this opinion.

POWELL, J., took no part in the decision of this case.

STEVENS, J., [concurred with the majority opinion on the class action issue and dissented only on the choice of law question].

WHAT'S NEW HERE?

- Because Kansas had a class action rule that closely tracked Rule 23, and the defendant argued that the notice and opt-out provisions of that Rule denied the class members due process, *Shutts* had to decide whether those provisions were enough to render the binding effect constitutional. Held: yes.
- In so doing, *Shutts* raised a question it didn't decide: Were the less rigorous notice provisions of Rule 23(b)(1) and (2) constitutional?

Notes and Problems

1. Start by admiring the defendant's clever argument.

    a. According to the defendant, how did the plaintiff class members in this case resemble defendants in ordinary cases?

    b. According to the defendant, what implication did that resemblance have for the conduct of the class action?

    c. How did the Supreme Court disagree with defendant?

2. Now turn to *Shutts*'s implications for our understanding of due process and the class action. At the time of *Shutts*, Rule 23 was silent about whether any notice was required for (b)(1) and (b)(2) classes. Rule 23(c)(2)(A) now provides that "the court may direct appropriate notice" to (b)(1) and (b)(2) classes. Does *Shutts* shed any light on when a court should require notice?

3. Suppose that Kansas, instead of excluding the 1,500 royalty owners who could not be located, had included them in the class. Would these unnotified absentees have been bound by the resulting judgment? *Shutts* suggests not, but recall the facts of *Mullane v. Central Hanover Bank & Trust* (Chapter 2). In that case, the Court held that a number of unnotified trust beneficiaries would be bound by a judgment because they had been adequately represented by those who were notified. If *Mullane* is good law, then notice to those who can't easily be located is not required. This is how lower courts and commentators have read *Shutts* and *Mullane*: So long as notice was reasonably calculated to reach class members, class members who did not actually receive notice of the action are still bound.

4. *Shutts*, besides raising issues of notice and due process, reminds us that, under the influence of Rule 23, class actions have taken deep root in state courts. It also reminds us that nationwide classes, whether in state or federal courts, present very difficult issues of choice of law: Recall that one of the questions facing the Kansas and U.S. Supreme Courts was what law—that of Kansas or of some other state—should apply to the leases. Many of the issues raised by *Shutts* are very much alive today.

3. The Class Action and Federalism

Besides its lessons on personal jurisdiction, *Shutts* touches on two other important features of the modern class action. First, though not all states provide for class actions, many do, and thus state as well as federal courts can entertain class actions—including class actions in which, as in *Shutts*, most members of the class reside outside the state in question.

Second, in spite of its multistate class membership *Shutts* was stuck in Kansas courts because of the way in which the Supreme Court had applied its subject matter jurisdiction doctrine to class actions. When a class suit is based on a federal statute, jurisdiction will arise under federal law and §1331 (or some other more specific jurisdiction statute).

But what about diversity cases? To take a concrete example, what if *Shutts* had been filed in a federal court invoking diversity jurisdiction? Or what if Phillips Petroleum had sought to remove the case from Kansas state court to a federal court? Class members were scattered over 50 states, and the defendant, incorporated in Delaware, had its headquarters in Oklahoma. The federal courts have seemed uncertain about how to think about diversity jurisdiction and class actions. Well before the Federal Rules, Supreme Tribe of Ben-Hur* v. Cauble, 255 U.S. 356 (1921), held that for purposes of diversity, courts should look to the citizenship only of the class representatives and ignore the class members. *Supreme Tribe* thus created an exception to the complete diversity rule for class actions, and to that extent lowered jurisdictional barriers to the multistate diversity-based class action. So far, things would look good for diversity jurisdiction in *Shutts.*

Forty years later, as class actions grew in the wake of the 1966 Rules revisions, the Supreme Court had what appeared to be second thoughts. In a pair of cases, it held that both the named plaintiff and each member of the class had to satisfy the amount in controversy requirement. So our hypothetical *Shutts* diversity action would have been doomed in 1985 because many of those entitled to royalty payments had only small amounts at stake.

But two recent developments—one from the courts, the other from Congress—change the picture again. In Exxon Mobil Corp. v. Allapattah Services, Inc., 545 U.S. 546 (2005), the Court interpreted the supplemental jurisdiction statute, 28 U.S.C. §1367, to allow such smaller-claims actions under the basic diversity statute, so long as the named party satisfied the amount in controversy requirement. What would this do to our hypothetical *Shutts* diversity action? The answer is we don't know; since amount in controversy was not an issue in the Kansas court, the opinions do not tell us whether the named party (or any of the claimants) met the requisite amount; if they had, *Shutts* would have met the requirements for diversity jurisdiction.

In the same year *Allapattah* was decided, Congress entered the scene. Responding to complaints that a few state courts had certified some large class actions of questionable merits—suits that could not be removed to the federal courts because they failed to satisfy the requirements of diversity jurisdiction—Congress enacted the Class Action Fairness Act of 2005. Referred to by lawyers as CAFA, the Act is codified in a new Chapter 114 of 28 U.S.C., in amendments to 28 U.S.C. §1332, and in a new removal provision 28 U.S.C. §1453.

---

* The colorfully named Supreme Tribe was a fraternal organization whose life insurance program was the subject of the lawsuit.

The Act makes broad use of the principle that Article III requires only minimal diversity. It grants original jurisdiction to the federal courts in class actions in which "any member of the class of plaintiffs" possesses the requisite diversity with respect to "any defendant." This invocation of bare diversity is coupled with the ability to aggregate claims of all class members to reach the $5 million amount in controversy requirement. 28 U.S.C. §1332(d)(2). Such suits may be brought under original jurisdiction or, under the provisions of §1453, may be removed by "any defendant," whether or not a citizen of the state in which the action arose.

These provisions use diversity jurisdiction to "federalize" many class actions previously within the exclusive jurisdiction of the state courts. Displaying some uncertainty about how far this federalization should go, the Act both allows and commands federal courts to remand actions in which state interests seem to predominate. It does so by providing that a federal court whose jurisdiction is thus invoked "may . . . decline" to exercise it under some circumstances and "shall . . . decline" to exercise it in others. Section 1332(d)(3) defines the factors relevant to the discretionary power to decline federal jurisdiction. Those factors include the relative size of the in-state and out-of-state class membership, "whether the claims asserted involve matters of national or interstate interest," which state's law will apply to the claims, and the connection of the forum to the class members, the harm, and the defendant. 28 U.S.C. §1332(d)(3). Recall that these factors bear not on certification but on federal diversity jurisdiction.

Section 1332(d)(4) delineates the circumstances in which a federal court must decline jurisdiction: if two-thirds or more of the members of the proposed plaintiff class are citizens of the state in which the action was brought and either (1) the primary defendants are also citizens of that state or (2) at least one defendant is a citizen of that state and the principal injuries also occurred there.

The next case illustrates an effort by a litigant who wished to remain in state court to evade the grasp of CAFA; in the process it lays bare some fundamental features of representative litigation.

Standard Fire Ins. Co. v. Knowles

568 U.S. 588 (2013)

BREYER, J., delivered the opinion of the Court.

The Class Action Fairness Act of 2005 (CAFA) provides that the federal "district courts shall have original jurisdiction" over a civil "class action" if, among other things, the "matter in controversy exceeds the sum or value of $5,000,000." The statute adds that "to determine whether the matter in controversy exceeds the sum or value of $5,000,000," the "claims of the individual class members shall be aggregated."

The question presented concerns a class-action plaintiff who stipulates, prior to certification of the class, that he, and the class he seeks to represent, will not seek damages that exceed $5 million in total. Does that stipulation remove the case from CAFA's scope? In our view, it does not.

I

In April 2011 respondent, Greg Knowles, filed this proposed class action in an Arkansas state court against petitioner, the Standard Fire Insurance Company. Knowles claimed that, when the company had made certain homeowner's insurance loss payments, it had unlawfully failed to include a general contractor fee. And Knowles sought to certify a class of "hundreds, and possibly thousands" of similarly harmed Arkansas policyholders. In describing the relief sought, the complaint says that the "Plaintiff and Class stipulate they will seek to recover total aggregate damages of less than five million dollars." An attached affidavit stipulates that Knowles "will not at any time during this case . . . seek damages for the class . . . in excess of $5,000,000 in the aggregate."

On May 18, 2011, the company, pointing to CAFA's jurisdictional provision, removed the case to Federal District Court [where the judge accepted the stipulation as binding and remanded to state court.] 28 U.S.C. §1332(d); §1453. . . .

The company appealed from the remand order, but the Eighth Circuit declined to hear the appeal. See 28 U.S.C. §1453(c)(1) (2006 ed., Supp. V) (providing discretion to hear an appeal from a remand order). [The Supreme Court granted the insurer's petition for certiorari.]

II

CAFA provides . . . "the claims of the individual class members shall be aggregated" [in calculating the amount in controversy.] And those "class members" include "persons (named or unnamed) who fall within the definition of the *proposed* or certified class." §1332(d)(1)(D) (emphasis added). . . .

The District Court in this case found that resulting sum would have exceeded $5 million *but for* the stipulation. And we must decide whether the stipulation makes a critical difference.

In our view, it does not. Our reason is a simple one: Stipulations must be binding. See 9 J. Wigmore, Evidence §2588, p. 821 (J. Chadbourn rev. 1981) (defining a "judicial admission or stipulation" as an "express waiver made . . . by the party or his attorney conceding for the purposes of the trial the truth of some alleged fact" (emphasis deleted)); 9 Wigmore, *supra*, §2590, at 822 (the "vital feature" of a judicial admission is "universally conceded to be its *conclusiveness* upon the party making it"). The stipulation Knowles proffered to the District Court, however, does not speak for those he purports to represent.

That is because a plaintiff who files a proposed class action cannot legally bind members of the proposed class before the class is certified. Because his precertification stipulation does not bind anyone but himself, Knowles has not reduced the value of the putative class members' claims. For jurisdictional purposes, our inquiry is limited to examining the case "as of the time it was filed in state court." At that point, Knowles lacked the authority to concede the amount-in-controversy issue for the absent class members. The Federal District Court, therefore, wrongly concluded that Knowles' precertification stipulation could overcome its finding that the CAFA jurisdictional threshold had been met.

Knowles concedes that "[f]ederal jurisdiction cannot be based on contingent future events." Brief for Respondent 20. Yet the two legal principles to which we have just referred—that stipulations must be binding and that a named plaintiff cannot bind precertification class members—mean that the amount to which Knowles has stipulated is in effect contingent.

If, for example, as Knowles' complaint asserts, "hundreds, and possibly thousands" of persons in Arkansas have similar claims, and if each of those claims places a significant sum in controversy, the state court might certify the class and permit the case to proceed, but only on the condition that the stipulation be excised. Or a court might find that Knowles is an inadequate representative due to the artificial cap he purports to impose on the class' recovery. . . . Even were these possibilities remote in Knowles' own case, there is no reason to think them farfetched in other cases where similar stipulations could have more dramatic amount-lowering effects. . . .

The strongest counterargument, we believe, takes a syllogistic form: First, *this* complaint contains a presently nonbinding stipulation that the class will seek damages that amount to less than $5 million. Second, if the state court eventually certifies that class, the stipulation will bind those who choose to remain as class members. Third, if the state court eventually insists upon modification of the stipulation (thereby permitting class members to obtain more than $5 million), it will have in effect created a new, *different* case. Fourth, CAFA, however, permits the federal court to consider only the complaint that the plaintiff has filed, *i.e., this* complaint, not a new, modified (or amended) complaint that might eventually emerge.

Our problem with this argument lies in its conclusion. We do not agree that CAFA forbids the federal court to consider, for purposes of determining the amount in controversy, the very real possibility that a nonbinding, amount-limiting, stipulation may not survive the class certification process. This potential outcome does not result in the creation of a new case not now before the federal court. To hold otherwise would, for CAFA jurisdictional purposes, treat a nonbinding stipulation as if it were binding, exalt form over substance, and run directly counter to CAFA's primary objective: ensuring "Federal court consideration of interstate cases of national importance." It would also have the effect of allowing the subdivision of a $100 million action into 21 just-below-$5-million state-court actions simply by including nonbinding stipulations; such an outcome would squarely conflict with the statute's objective. . . .

Knowles also points out that federal courts permit individual plaintiffs, who are the masters of their complaints, to avoid removal to federal court, and to obtain a remand to state court, by stipulating to amounts at issue that fall below the federal jurisdictional requirement. That is so. But the key characteristic about those stipulations is that they are legally binding on all plaintiffs. That essential feature is missing here, as Knowles cannot yet bind the absent class. . . .

In sum, the stipulation at issue here can tie Knowles' hands, but it does not resolve the amount-in-controversy question in light of his inability to bind the rest of the class. For this reason, we believe the District Court, when following the statute to aggregate the proposed class members' claims, should have ignored that stipulation.

Because it did not, we vacate the judgment below and remand the case for further proceedings consistent with this opinion.

It is so ordered.

WHAT'S NEW HERE?

- At one level this is a routine amount in controversy case dealing with the same issues one confronts in individual litigation. You may recall from Chapter 3 that Congress has passed legislation dealing with similar efforts by parties to manipulate the amount in controversy in non-class litigation. See, for example, the provisions of 28 U.S.C. §1446(c), permitting a court considering a removal petition to hold a hearing to decide whether the amount in controversy in fact exceeds the statutory limit.
- But the case gets its bite from the circumstances that (a) the class has not been certified, and (b) if the stipulation is allowed to stand Knowles might become an inadequate representative of the class. You will see both of these themes played out in more detail in the next section, which deals with the standards for class certification.

Procedure as Strategy

As in other settings, both lawyers are using procedural rules for strategic and tactical reasons. We don't know why Knowles believed that an Arkansas state court would be more hospitable to his claim than a federal court sitting in Arkansas, but he must have strongly so believed—so much that he was willing to leave money on the table by his stipulation (although perhaps he was willing just to leave other class members' money on the table—thus the Court's concern about his ability to adequately represent the interests of those class members). Similarly, we don't know why Standard Fire Insurance's lawyers felt strongly enough about litigating in the federal system that they were prepared to spend many tens of thousands of dollars appealing the district judge's remand ruling. As with many other jurisdictional battles lawyers often have strong intuitions about which forum will be more hospitable to their claims or defenses. Those intuitions can be based on factors ranging from guesses about how a state's highest court will view their case—if it gets that far—to knowledge about the predilections of the state judiciary (or perhaps even a single state or federal judge) to thoughts about the demography of a prospective jury. In jurisdictional cases, these intuitions rarely get articulated in an opinion, but you can be sure that the lawyers on both sides have thought about them.

Notes and Problems

1. As you unpack the case, begin with the mechanics.

    a. It began as a state court filing.

    b. What did defendant then do? (And what section of which federal statute permitted it to do so?)

    c. What happened in the federal district court?

    d. Ordinarily, decisions of a district court to remand to state court are not appealable. 28 U.S.C. §1447(d). If this had been an individual case, the defendant would have been stuck back in state court. But one of CAFA's provisions, codified at 28 U.S.C. §1453(c), gives the courts of appeals discretion to hear an appeal of a CAFA remand order ("may accept an appeal"). As you will see in the next section, the Rules as well as CAFA create special avenues for the discretionary appeals of some preliminary class actions rulings.

    e. How did the Eighth Circuit exercise that discretion?

    f. And how did the insurer challenge the Eighth Circuit's decision?

2. Now to the merits of the case—at least the procedural merits.

    a. Be sure you understand why, in ordinary, two-party litigation, had Knowles filed a complaint stipulating a damages ceiling, that stipulation would have been dispositive and likely welcomed by the defendant (because it would reduce the risk of a higher verdict).

    b. Then, explain how the "classness" of the case rendered Knowles's stipulation not dispositive.

    c. Finally, looking ahead to the next section, see if you understand why Knowles's stipulation might—but might not—have been dispositive had the class been certified before he made the stipulation. (Don't worry if you're unsure of this point: All will become clear in the course of the next few pages.)

3. Recall that federal courts in diversity cases are bound to apply the law of the state in which the case was filed, including that state's choice of law principles. (See supra page 265.)

    a. So, although *Knowles* will be litigated in federal district court, that court will be applying the substantive law of Arkansas to the claims involved. (You will recall that in *Shutts* one of the issues the Court was asked to decide was whether Kansas violated the Constitution by applying its law to the claims of the many class members outside Kansas. Held: no, though the majority seemed to think Kansas had come close to the constitutional line and Justice Stevens dissented on this point.)

    b. As the Class Action Fairness Act made its way through Congress, some proposed amendments would have specified how federal courts should approach choice of law problems in multistate class actions like *Shutts*. The theory underlying those amendments was that CAFA, with its national-ization of large multistate diversity actions, gives a federal court in such a case more latitude to apply general, neutral choice of law principles. Those amendments did not become part of the statute as enacted, in part because Congress could not agree on what those neutral choice of law principles should be.

4. None of the cases or legislation thus far noted affects class actions based on federal law; CAFA and *Allapattah* concern only diversity actions. Congress, however, has spoken sharply in one such area in which state and federal law intersect.

   a. For several years class actions based on alleged violations of federal securi-ties laws have proved controversial. In 1995 Congress, believing that some of these suits lacked merit, acted to tighten pleading requirements for claims alleging violations of federal securities laws. 15 U.S.C. §78u4(b)(1)(B).

   b. Three years later, citing evidence that plaintiffs had reacted to this change by alleging violations not of federal but of state securities laws and bringing their suits in state courts, Congress enacted the Securities Litigation Uniform Standards Act of 1998, 15 U.S.C. §77p(c). That Act uses an interesting reper-tory of procedural devices to restrict state law securities class actions. First, it states that federal law preempts state securities laws, but only in class actions alleging fraud in the purchase and sale of securities. Second, it provides that all class actions filed in state courts and alleging securities fraud shall be removable to federal district courts without regard to diversity or amount in controversy. Then, the Act requires the dismissal of the removed claims, unless they fall into a narrow range of permitted claims. The result of this two-step procedure—removal followed by dismissal—essentially eliminates all class actions based on violations of state securities laws.

   c. The student of procedure will find several features of the statute remark-able. Congress undoubtedly has the power to preempt state securities laws. Here, however, Congress has achieved both more and less than preemp-tion. The Act achieves less than preemption because it applies only to class actions rather than to all state law securities claims. It achieves more than ordinary preemption because it assures that all preempted claims will be dismissed. With ordinary substantive preemption, Congress relies on state courts to recognize and enforce the preemptive effect of federal law. The Supreme Court acts as the only federal enforcer of preemptive federal law by granting certiorari if state courts fail to recognize federal preemption. But the Supreme Court can hear only about 100 cases a year and thus allows for considerable slippage in the enforcement of preemptive federal laws. In the Act's scheme, removal solves this slippage problem. The federal district courts, not the Supreme Court, enforce federal preemption. Every class action involving state securities laws is removable, thus assuring a federal forum for this federal defense. The Act demonstrates both the significance of the class action and the use of federal jurisdiction to control it.

5. Considered as a pair, the Securities Litigation Uniform Standards Act and the Class Action Fairness Act deploy federal jurisdiction in interesting, innovative—and controversial—ways. Together, they funnel selected categories of civil suits from state to federal courts. Both involve areas where Congress might legislate substantively under its Commerce Clause and related powers. But Congress has not, relying instead on the federal courts to achieve congressional aims. This use of federal judicial power is particularly interesting because, by statutory definition, it applies only to cases involving substantial numbers of people—at least enough to constitute a class.

4. Statutory Requirements

Hansberry (together with *Mullane v. Central Hanover Bank & Trust,* supra page 165) gave the class action a constitutional basis. *Shutts* helped sort out additional issues of due process, and the Class Action Fairness Act of 2005, interpreted in cases like *Knowles,* extended diversity jurisdiction to many class actions that, like *Shutts,* would otherwise have fallen under state jurisdiction. But none of these decisions explains the level of debate surrounding the class action.

Major businesses and other institutions will tell you that they see the class action as a dreadful scourge, forcing them to settle even unjustified suits. With equal fervor the plaintiffs' bar and public interest groups say that the class action has proved to be a major force for good, achieving institutional reform and requiring powerful institutions to comply with the law. One can find evidence supporting both points of view. This debate has been occurring sporadically since the 1966 revisions to Rule 23 created the modern class action and has occasionally led to such dueling characterizations of the device as those quoted in the introduction to this section: "legalized blackmail" and "one of the most socially useful remedies in history."

To understand this debate, one has to see how the 1966 revisions to Rule 23 opened new possibilities for the class action. Courts have for the past 50 years been working out those possibilities—and their limits. The starting point is, as always, the text of the Rule. That text establishes a series of hurdles for class actions to surmount on their way to "certification," a process described in Rule 23(c). To become certified, a class action must meet both the requirements of Rule 23(a) and also fit into one of the three categories of Rule 23(b).

Practitioners refer to the four requirements of Rule 23(a) as numerosity, commonality, typicality, and adequacy of representation. To establish a case as a class action, the person seeking to represent the class must show that each of these requirements is satisfied.

- Numerosity (Rule 23(a)(1)) is established if the class representative can show that enough persons are in the class to make joining them as individuals impractical. Courts occasionally certify classes as small as a few score, but typically classes consist of at least hundreds of persons.
- Commonality (Rule 23(a)(2)) captures the idea that the class should be a class—that it should consist of persons who share characteristics that matter

in terms of the substantive law involved. We have already encountered this idea in *Mosley v. General Motors*, supra page 788. *Mosley* discussed commonality as a requirement for joining individual plaintiffs under Rule 20. A similar requirement of cohesiveness recurs in class actions. For example, a "class" consisting of all persons who have claims against the United States would not have much in common: One person would be seeking an income tax refund, another compensation for an accident involving a postal truck, and a third might be seeking Social Security benefits. A much-litigated question is whether the members of the class have *enough* in common to justify class certification. Since virtually all classes proposed will have some characteristics in common and some unshared characteristics, there is much room for argument. This requirement is one focus of *Wal-Mart v. Dukes*, infra page 855.

- Typicality (Rule 23(a)(3)) is the requirement that class representatives stand, in significant respects, in the same shoes as the average class member. For example, in a case alleging mismanagement of a pension plan, if most members of the class have lost a few hundred dollars, it would raise a typicality problem if the class representative alleged losses of tens of thousands—or vice versa. The premise underlying the typicality requirement is that the class's lawyers will be making litigation decisions with the representative in mind. In order to protect the interests of the absent class members, one would want the representative clients to have the same incentives and motivations as the average class members. In practice, the class representatives have proved far less significant than the lawyers, and judges have consequently been willing to bend the requirements of typicality if they are assured that the last requirement—adequacy of representation—is fulfilled.

- Adequacy (Rule 23(a)(4)) has two dimensions. One focuses on the class representatives, the other on the class's prospective lawyer. Let us start with the representatives. To take an obvious point, a class representative should not be an employee or a relative of the lawyer—relationships that would conflict with the representative's decisions about the litigation. Class representatives have been found inadequate because their real reason for pursuing the class action was to gain leverage for their own case. Still other class representatives have been found inadequate for reasons like those in *Hansberry*: Their interests conflicted in some way with those of some or all of the class members. In *Hansberry*, you will recall the problem was that the class in which Hansberry was supposed to be included consisted of people trying to enforce the racially restrictive covenant that Hansberry was attacking. But more subtle conflicts can also doom a representative. Consider *Knowles*, supra page 844, where the court rejected Knowles's stipulation concerning damages because it might have put him at odds with class members if it appeared that the insurer's payment policies had damaged the class members by *more* than $5 million.

The second branch of the "adequacy" determination requires courts to focus on the class's lawyer—recognizing that the lawyer will be making many of the most significant decisions. Rule 23(g) enumerates factors a court should consider in selecting class counsel. The lawyer should have no conflicts that would cloud the representation. The lawyer has to be sufficiently skillful and equipped with sufficient support and resources to handle the case. To use an extreme example, it is unlikely that a young lawyer with the ink still drying on her bar certificate would be found to be an adequate representative in a complex class action. Conversely, courts finding adequacy typically recite the lawyer's experience with previous similar cases. Decisions also note the lawyer's and firm's ability to finance protracted litigation—many class actions will be long and expensive. Looking in a different direction, Rule 23(g)(1)(A)(i) tells the court to consider "work [prospective] counsel has done in identifying or investigating potential claims in the action"—thus crediting the entrepreneurial activity of counsel. Rule 23(g) also empowers the court to ask prospective counsel what fees it might eventually ask for—because in most class actions the court must approve lawyers' fees.

Although Rule 23(a) does not list it, some circuits have additionally required plaintiffs demonstrate the ascertainability of the class. The Third Circuit has the most demanding test, requiring plaintiffs to show that "(1) the class is defined with reference to objective criteria; and (2) there is a reliable and administratively feasible mechanism for determining whether putative class members fall within the class definition." Byrd v. Aaron's Inc. 784 F.3d 154, 163 (3d Cir. 2015). Other circuits have rejected a heightened precertification ascertainability requirement, finding it incompatible with the language of Rule 23. See Briseno v. ConAgra Foods Inc., 844 F.3d 1121 (9th Cir. 2017).

Having surmounted the hurdles of Rule 23(a), the lawyer seeking class certification still has to show that the litigation fits within one of the three categories of Rule 23(b). One might ask why: If the case fits the requirements of Rule 23(a), should it not be a class action? The answer lies in the law's uncertainty about the goals of the class action. The drafters of the Rule were understandably unsure about the potential of the class action—for good or for ill. They had two fairly clear cases in mind that they thought should usually be treated as class actions—the situations described in Rule 23(b)(1) and 23(b)(2)—and a residual category—the (b)(3) cases—where they wanted courts to proceed cautiously.

The first situation—the 23(b)(1) class—is essentially a mass-production version of Rule 19. For example, suppose a city proposes to issue bonds to build a new civic auditorium. One group of citizens sues to block the issuance of the bonds; another group sues the city to insist that it go forward with the bonds and the project. If those suits proceed separately, the city might find itself the subject of incompatible judicial rulings: Issue the bonds; do not issue the bonds. By grouping the challengers and the supporters into classes, the court prevents a situation in which "varying adjudications with respect to individual class members" (the taxpayers) "would establish incompatible standards of conduct for the party opposing the class" (the city). Or, to take another example, suppose that a number of claimants all seek to collect on claims that exceed insurance coverage. Under such circumstances, Rule 23(b)(1) provides a way to assure that similarly situated parties are treated alike.

Rule 23(b)(2) provides for class actions where the party opposing the class has acted or refused to act "on grounds that apply generally to the class." The

Advisory Committee notes to the Rule make clear that the drafters had in mind civil rights claims, although the notes reflect that subdivision (b)(2) is not limited to such claims. Courts have glossed Rule 23(b)(2) by limiting it to cases in which the plaintiffs are primarily seeking injunctive or declaratory relief. Again, such a description fits the standard civil rights case, where the typical relief sought is an injunction requiring some action—voter registration, school integration, changes in employment practices—by a defendant. An often litigated question is how much incidental monetary relief a Rule 23(b)(2) class can seek before the action ceases to be primarily injunctive and therefore ineligible for Rule 23(b)(2) treatment; you will see that issue coming to the surface in *Wal-Mart v. Dukes*, the next case.

The final category of class actions—those brought under Rule 23(b)(3)—has proved the most controversial. It comprises all class actions not captured in Rules 23(b)(1) and 23(b)(2). In particular, it includes all claims in which the plaintiffs are seeking primarily money damages. Rule 23(b)(3) provides that a court can certify such a class only if it meets two criteria in addition to those in 23(a): that the issues common to the class members "predominate" over those affecting only individual class members; and that a class action is "superior" to any other method for "fairly and efficiently" adjudicating the controversy. Rule 23(b)(3) also sets forth factors a court should consider in certifying a (b)(3) class, one of which is the "likely difficulties in managing a class action." That last factor can be important; class actions typically require active court management and can consume substantial amounts of judicial time.

In practice, (b)(3) actions can be subdivided into two groups. One group consists of what one might call "small claims" lawsuits: actions in which many persons allege small amounts of damage. Examples include the hypothetical cell phone overcharge described earlier in this section. Typically, such claims are not worth any individual plaintiff's time or money to bring and only the class action device makes them viable. Because of this feature, lawyers sometimes refer to this group of class actions as "negative value" cases—meaning that to pursue claims on an individual basis would cost more than the case could yield. As a result, in such actions the defendant is, as a practical matter, immune from liability unless a class is certified.

At the other end of the scale of Rule 23(b)(3) actions lies what is often called the "mass tort"—an airplane crash, a hotel fire, the exposure of hundreds of thousands of workers to asbestos. Notice that, unlike the negative value cases, each individual claim has substantial damages attached to it. The drafters of Rule 23 suggested in the Advisory Committee notes that such cases would not usually be appropriate for class treatment, but in recent decades courts have increasingly—and controversially—certified class actions in mass torts. In these suits, the incentives for a class action change. To plaintiffs, they continue to offer the increased bargaining power that comes from aggregation and the prospect of a single overwhelming damage judgment. In contrast to the small claims cases, they also offer some advantages to defendants—consolidation (of suits that would have been brought even without the class action), efficiency, and the possibility of a global settlement.

Placing a class action in one of the Rule 23 categories is more than a matter of analytical neatness. Whole cases may stand or fall as a result of the classification. This unexpected consequence flows from two sources. First, Rule 23(b)(3) requires the certifying judge to engage in a complicated weighing of advantages and disadvantages, unnecessary for (b)(1) and (b)(2) classes—as a result of which he may rule against certification.

Second, Rule 23(c)(2)(B) requires individual notice to all members of Rule 23(b)(3) classes who can be identified through reasonable effort; by contrast, Rule 23(c)(2)(A) allows, but does not require, "appropriate notice" to the class in 23(b)(1) and (b)(2) cases. Because the Supreme Court has held that the representative plaintiff must initially pay for such notice, inability to bear these costs may end the suit. Eisen v. Carlisle & Jacquelin, 417 U.S. 156 (1974). There is a third significant difference between the class types: Members of a Rule 23(b)(3) class, when notified of the action, must also be given an opportunity to opt out of the class. Rule 23(b)(3) class members may get another opportunity to opt out when the case is settled. Members of (b)(1) and (b)(2) classes, in contrast, are unable to opt out.

The notes that follow ask you to apply what you have learned in this elementary description of Rule 23.

Notes and Problems

1. The regents of State University announce a tuition increase that applies only to out-of-state students. Two thousand such students stand to have their tuition increased. The president of the Student Association, an in-state student, announces that she is filing suit on behalf of the affected students to enjoin the regents from implementing the increase.

   a. With which of the requirements of Rule 23(a) will the prospective class action have the most difficulty?

   b. What additional information will the court likely require about the student's attorney in order to decide whether the suit meets the criteria of Rule 23(a)?

   c. Suppose that after some rearrangement, the court rules that the class meets the requirements of Rule 23(a); into which category of Rule 23(b) would it fall?

2. Assume that the tuition increase described in the preceding note has gone into effect and has been paid by the out-of-state students. One enterprising such student discovers that the regents adopted the increase at a closed meeting—in violation of state law—and that it is therefore unlawful. He proposes to file suit as representative of a class of all out-of-state students.

   a. Student (as class representative) proposes to seek an injunction ordering reduced tuition in the following school year. Do you see why such a plan for relief may cause the court to find Student an inadequate representative (and perhaps an atypical one) for at least some members of the class?

   b. Suppose Student proposes to remedy the adequacy of representation problems exposed in 2a by seeking cash refunds to all students, present and former, who paid the allegedly unlawful higher fees. What will this change in remedy do to the classification of the lawsuit under Rule 23(b)? Which consequences will that change in classification have on the costs of litigating the claim? See Rule 23(c)(2)(B).

    c. Suppose Student finally decides to seek certification of a Rule 23(b)(3) class seeking cash refunds to all students who paid the higher fees. The costs of notifying the class are estimated to be in the neighborhood of $30,000. How might this fact cause a court that was otherwise satisfied that Student met the criteria of Rule 23(a)(4) to reconsider its decision and to decertify the class?

3. Rule 23 can seem, at first glance, like a laundry list of complex and interrelated requirements without any particular rhyme or reason. Yet the drafters of this Rule, and those who have debated its efficacy, would tell you that these requirements balance multiple conflicting interests and pressures related to class actions.

    a. In litigation, as with so much else in life, those with more economic and social power are at an advantage. Procedural rules have the potential to shift those power relations in dramatic ways. The class action puts the power-shifting potential of procedure into sharp relief. In a case brought by an individual consumer against a large public or private institution, the institution will often have the upper hand. But in a case brought by a class of thousands of consumers, financed by a group of plaintiffs' attorneys, the economic and social dynamics shift. Business groups argue that this financial shift causes plaintiff classes to seek "blackmail settlements" for meritless claims. Certification requirements, particularly those in Rule 23(b)(3), limit the kinds of disputes that can be certified as class actions, and thereby limit the reach of class actions' power-shifting potential.

    b. Class action rules also aim to guide the complex relationship between a lawyer and a class. When a lawyer represents a single client, communication, consultation, and lines of authority are generally well established. In a class action, each of these areas becomes more difficult to maneuver. Rules governing commonality and adequacy at the class certification stage, and notice at multiple stages of the litigation process, aim to address some of these problems of legal representation endemic to the class action.

4. Now consider a case in which both Rules 23(a) and 23(b) posed what turned out to be insurmountable obstacles for one of the largest class actions ever brought. The decision both provides a guided application of Rule 23, and an articulation of common concerns about the class action.

Wal-Mart Stores, Inc. v. Dukes
564 U.S. 338 (2011)

Scalia, J., delivered the opinion of the Court.

We are presented with one of the most expansive class actions ever. The District Court and the Court of Appeals approved the certification of a class comprising about one and a half million plaintiffs, current and former female employees of petitioner Wal-Mart who allege that the discretion exercised by their local supervisors over pay and promotion matters violates Title VII by discriminating against women. In addition to injunctive and declaratory relief, the plaintiffs seek an award of backpay. We consider whether the certification of the plaintiff class was consistent with Federal Rules of Civil Procedure 23(a) and (b)(2).

I

A

Petitioner Wal-Mart is the Nation's largest private employer. It operates four types of retail stores throughout the country: Discount Stores, Supercenters, Neighborhood Markets, and Sam's Clubs. Those stores are divided into seven nationwide divisions, which in turn comprise 41 regions of 80 to 85 stores apiece. Each store has between 40 and 53 separate departments and 80 to 500 staff positions. In all, Wal-Mart operates approximately 3,400 stores and employs more than one million people.

Pay and promotion decisions at Wal-Mart are generally committed to local managers' broad discretion, which is exercised "in a largely subjective manner." Local store managers may increase the wages of hourly employees (within limits) with only limited corporate oversight. As for salaried employees, such as store managers and their deputies, higher corporate authorities have discretion to set their pay within preestablished ranges.

Promotions work in a similar fashion. Wal-Mart permits store managers to apply their own subjective criteria when selecting candidates as "support managers," which is the first step on the path to management. Admission to Wal-Mart's management training program, however, does require that a candidate meet certain objective criteria, including an above-average performance rating, at least one year's tenure in the applicant's current position, and a willingness to relocate. But except for those requirements, regional and district managers have discretion to use their own judgment when selecting candidates for management training. Promotion to higher office—*e.g.*, assistant manager, co-manager, or store manager—is similarly at the discretion of the employee's superiors after prescribed objective factors are satisfied.

B

The named plaintiffs in this lawsuit, representing the 1.5 million members of the certified class, are three current or former Wal-Mart employees who allege that the company discriminated against them on the basis of their sex by denying them equal pay or promotions, in violation of Title VII of the Civil Rights Act of 1964. . . .

These plaintiffs, respondents here, do not allege that Wal-Mart has any express corporate policy against the advancement of women. Rather, they claim that their local managers' discretion over pay and promotions is exercised disproportionately in favor of men, leading to an unlawful disparate impact on female employees. And, respondents say, because Wal-Mart is aware of this effect, its refusal to cabin its managers' authority amounts to disparate treatment. Their complaint seeks injunctive and declaratory relief, punitive damages, and backpay. It does not ask for compensatory damages.

Importantly for our purposes, respondents claim that the discrimination to which they have been subjected is common to *all* Wal-Mart's female employees. The basic theory of their case is that a strong and uniform "corporate culture" permits bias against women to infect, perhaps subconsciously, the discretionary decision-making of each one of Wal-Mart's thousands of managers—thereby making every woman at the company the victim of one common discriminatory practice. Respondents therefore wish to litigate the Title VII claims of all female employees at Wal-Mart's stores in a nationwide class action.

C

Class certification is governed by Federal Rule of Civil Procedure 23. [The opinion quoted Rule 23(a), noting that all class actions must satisfy those requirements.]

[T]he proposed class must satisfy at least one of the three requirements listed in Rule 23(b). Respondents rely on Rule 23(b)(2), which applies when "the party opposing the class has acted or refused to act on grounds that apply generally to the class, so that final injunctive relief or corresponding declaratory relief is appropriate respecting the class as a whole."

Invoking these provisions, respondents moved the District Court to certify a plaintiff class consisting of "'[a]ll women employed at any Wal-Mart domestic retail store at any time since December 26, 1998, who have been or may be subjected to Wal-Mart's challenged pay and management track promotions policies and practices.'" As evidence that there were indeed "questions of law or fact common to" all the women of Wal-Mart, as Rule 23(a)(2) requires, respondents relied chiefly on three forms of proof: statistical evidence about pay and promotion disparities between men and women at the company, anecdotal reports of discrimination from about 120 of Wal-Mart's female employees, and the testimony of a sociologist, Dr. William Bielby, who conducted a "social framework analysis" of Wal-Mart's "culture" and personnel practices, and concluded that the company was "vulnerable" to gender discrimination.

Wal-Mart unsuccessfully moved to strike much of this evidence. It also offered its own countervailing statistical and other proof in an effort to defeat Rule 23(a)'s requirements of commonality, typicality, and adequate representation. Wal-Mart further contended that respondents' monetary claims for backpay could not be certified under Rule 23(b)(2), first because that Rule refers only to injunctive and declaratory relief, and second because the backpay claims could not be manageably tried as a class without depriving Wal-Mart of its right to present certain statutory defenses. With one limitation not relevant here, the District Court granted respondents' motion and certified their proposed class. [Invoking Rule 23(f), which permits a Court of Appeals to accept an appeal from an order "granting or denying class-action certification," Wal-Mart appealed.]

D

A divided en banc Court of Appeals substantially affirmed the District Court's certification order. . . .

[As part of its ruling,] the Court of Appeals determined that the action could be manageably tried as a class action because the District Court could adopt the approach the Ninth Circuit approved in Hilao v. Estate of Marcos, 103 F.3d 767, 782-787 (1996). There compensatory damages for some 9,541 class members were calculated by selecting 137 claims at random, referring those claims to a special master for valuation, and then extrapolating the validity and value of the untested claims from the sample set. . . .

II

The class action is "an exception to the usual rule that litigation is conducted by and on behalf of the individual named parties only." In order to justify a departure from that rule, "a class representative must be part of the class and 'possess the same interest and suffer the same injury' as the class members." Rule 23(a) ensures that the named plaintiffs are appropriate representatives of the class whose claims they wish to litigate. The Rule's four requirements—numerosity, commonality, typicality, and adequate representation—"effectively 'limit the class claims to those fairly encompassed by the named plaintiff's claims.'"

A

The crux of this case is commonality—the rule requiring a plaintiff to show that "there are questions of law or fact common to the class." Rule 23(a)(2).[5] That language is easy to misread, since "[a]ny competently crafted class complaint literally raises common 'questions.'" Nagareda, Class Certification in the Age of Aggregate Proof, 84 N.Y.U. L. Rev. 97, 131-132 (2009). For example: Do all of us plaintiffs indeed work for Wal-Mart? Do our managers have discretion over pay? Is that an unlawful employment practice? What remedies should we get? Reciting these questions is not sufficient to obtain class certification. Commonality requires the plaintiff to demonstrate that the class members "have suffered the same injury." This does not mean merely that they have all suffered a violation of the same provision of law. Title VII, for example, can be violated in many ways—by intentional discrimination, or by

---

5. We have previously stated in this context that "[t]he commonality and typicality requirements of Rule 23(a) tend to merge. Both serve as guideposts for determining whether under the particular circumstances maintenance of a class action is economical and whether the named plaintiff's claim and the class claims are so interrelated that the interests of the class members will be fairly and adequately protected in their absence. Those requirements therefore also tend to merge with the adequacy-of-representation requirement, although the latter requirement also raises concerns about the competency of class counsel and conflicts of interest." In light of our disposition of the commonality question, however, it is unnecessary to resolve whether respondents have satisfied the typicality and adequate-representation requirements of Rule 23(a).

hiring and promotion criteria that result in disparate impact, and by the use of these practices on the part of many different superiors in a single company. Quite obviously, the mere claim by employees of the same company that they have suffered a Title VII injury, or even a disparate-impact Title VII injury, gives no cause to believe that all their claims can productively be litigated at once. Their claims must depend upon a common contention—for example, the assertion of discriminatory bias on the part of the same supervisor. That common contention, moreover, must be of such a nature that it is capable of classwide resolution—which means that determination of its truth or falsity will resolve an issue that is central to the validity of each one of the claims in one stroke.

> "What matters to class certification . . . is not the raising of common 'questions'—even in droves—but, rather the capacity of a classwide proceeding to generate common *answers* apt to drive the resolution of the litigation. Dissimilarities within the proposed class are what have the potential to impede the generation of common answers."

Nagareda, *supra*, at 132.

Rule 23 does not set forth a mere pleading standard. A party seeking class certification must affirmatively demonstrate his compliance with the Rule—that is, he must be prepared to prove that there are *in fact* sufficiently numerous parties, common questions of law or fact, etc. We recognized in *Falcon* that "sometimes it may be necessary for the court to probe behind the pleadings before coming to rest on the certification question," and that certification is proper only if "the trial court is satisfied, after a rigorous analysis, that the prerequisites of Rule 23(a) have been satisfied." Frequently that "rigorous analysis" will entail some overlap with the merits of the plaintiff's underlying claim. That cannot be helped. "'[T]he class determination generally involves considerations that are enmeshed in the factual and legal issues comprising the plaintiff's cause of action.'" *Falcon, supra*.[6] Nor is there anything unusual about that consequence: The necessity of touching aspects of the merits in order to resolve preliminary matters, *e.g.*, jurisdiction and venue, is a familiar feature of litigation.

In this case, proof of commonality necessarily overlaps with respondents' merits contention that Wal-Mart engages in a *pattern or practice* of discrimination.[7] That

---

6. A statement in one of our prior cases, Eisen v. Carlisle & Jacquelin, 417 U.S. 156, 177 (1974), is sometimes mistakenly cited to the contrary: "We find nothing in either the language or history of Rule 23 that gives a court any authority to conduct a preliminary inquiry into the merits of a suit in order to determine whether it may be maintained as a class action." But in that case, the judge had conducted a preliminary inquiry into the merits of a suit, not in order to determine the propriety of certification under Rules 23(a) and (b) (he had already done that), but in order to shift the cost of notice required by Rule 23(c)(2) from the plaintiff to the defendants. To the extent the quoted statement goes beyond the permissibility of a merits inquiry for any other pretrial purpose, it is the purest dictum and is contradicted by our other cases. . . .

7. In a pattern-or-practice case, the plaintiff tries to "establish by a preponderance of the evidence that . . . discrimination was the company's standard operating procedure[,] the regular rather than the unusual practice." If he succeeds, that showing will support a rebuttable inference that all class members were victims of the discriminatory practice, and will justify "an award of prospective relief," such as "an injunctive order against the continuation of the discriminatory practice."

is so because, in resolving an individual's Title VII claim, the crux of the inquiry is "the reason for a particular employment decision." Here respondents wish to sue about literally millions of employment decisions at once. Without some glue holding the alleged *reasons* for all those decisions together, it will be impossible to say that examination of all the class members' claims for relief will produce a common answer to the crucial question *why was I disfavored.*

<h2 style="text-align:center">B</h2>

This Court's opinion in *Falcon* describes how the commonality issue must be approached[:]

> "Conceptually, there is a wide gap between (a) an individual's claim that he has been denied a promotion [or higher pay] on discriminatory grounds, and his otherwise unsupported allegation that the company has a policy of discrimination, and (b) the existence of a class of persons who have suffered the same injury as that individual, such that the individual's claim and the class claim will share common questions of law or fact and that the individual's claim will be typical of the class claims."

Falcon suggested two ways in which that conceptual gap might be bridged. First, if the employer "used a biased testing procedure to evaluate both applicants for employment and incumbent employees, a class action on behalf of every applicant or employee who might have been prejudiced by the test clearly would satisfy the commonality and typicality requirements of Rule 23(a)." Second, "[s]ignificant proof that an employer operated under a general policy of discrimination conceivably could justify a class of both applicants and employees if the discrimination manifested itself in hiring and promotion practices in the same general fashion, such as through entirely subjective decisionmaking processes." We think that statement precisely describes respondents' burden in this case. The first manner of bridging the gap obviously has no application here; Wal-Mart has no testing procedure or other company-wide evaluation method that can be charged with bias. The whole point of permitting discretionary decisionmaking is to avoid evaluating employees under a common standard.

The second manner of bridging the gap requires "significant proof" that Wal-Mart "operated under a general policy of discrimination." That is entirely absent here. Wal-Mart's announced policy forbids sex discrimination, and as the District Court recognized the company imposes penalties for denials of equal employment opportunity. The only evidence of a "general policy of discrimination" respondents produced was the testimony of Dr. William Bielby, their sociological expert. Relying on "social framework" analysis, Bielby testified that Wal-Mart has a "strong corporate culture," that makes it "'vulnerable'" to "gender bias." He could not, however, "determine with any specificity how regularly stereotypes play a meaningful role in employment decisions at Wal-Mart. At his deposition . . . Dr. Bielby conceded that he could not calculate whether 0.5 percent or 95 percent of the employment decisions at Wal-Mart might be determined by stereotyped thinking. . . . Bielby['s testimony] is worlds away from "significant proof" that Wal-Mart "operated under a general policy of discrimination."

C

The only corporate policy that the plaintiffs' evidence convincingly establishes is Wal-Mart's "policy" of *allowing discretion* by local supervisors over employment matters. On its face, of course, that is just the opposite of a uniform employment practice that would provide the commonality needed for a class action. . . .

To be sure, we have recognized that, "in appropriate cases," giving discretion to lower-level supervisors can be the basis of Title VII liability under a disparate-impact theory—since "an employer's undisciplined system of subjective decisionmaking [can have] precisely the same effects as a system pervaded by impermissible intentional discrimination." But the recognition that this type of Title VII claim "can" exist does not lead to the conclusion that every employee in a company using a system of discretion has such a claim in common. . . .

Respondents have not identified a common mode of exercising discretion that pervades the entire company—aside from their reliance on Dr. Bielby's social frameworks analysis that we have rejected. In a company of Wal-Mart's size and geographical scope, it is quite unbelievable that all managers would exercise their discretion in a common way without some common direction. Respondents attempt to make that showing by means of statistical and anecdotal evidence, but their evidence falls well short.

The statistical evidence consists primarily of regression analyses performed by Dr. Richard Drogin, a statistician, and Dr. Marc Bendick, a labor economist. After considering regional and national data, Drogin concluded that "there are statistically significant disparities between men and women at Wal-Mart . . . [and] these disparities . . . can be explained only by gender discrimination." Bendick compared workforce data from Wal-Mart and competitive retailers and concluded that Wal-Mart "promotes a lower percentage of women than its competitors."

Even if they are taken at face value, these studies are insufficient to establish that respondents' theory can be proved on a classwide basis. . . . As Judge Ikuta observed in her dissent, "[i]nformation about disparities at the regional and national level does not establish the existence of disparities at individual stores, let alone raise the inference that a companywide policy of discrimination is implemented by discretionary decisions at the store and district level." A regional pay disparity, for example, may be attributable to only a small set of Wal-Mart stores, and cannot by itself establish the uniform, store-by-store disparity upon which the plaintiffs' theory of commonality depends. . . . [For these and other reasons, the Court found this expert testimony insufficient to suggest a common practice.]

Respondents' anecdotal evidence suffers from the same defects, and in addition is too weak to raise any inference that all the individual, discretionary personnel decisions are discriminatory. . . . Here . . . respondents filed some 120 affidavits reporting experiences of discrimination—about 1 for every 12,500 class members—relating to only some 235 out of Wal-Mart's 3,400 stores. . . . Even if every single one of these accounts is true, that would not demonstrate that the entire company "operate[s] under a general policy of discrimination." . . .

In sum, we agree with Chief Judge Kozinski that the members of the class:

> "held a multitude of different jobs, at different levels of Wal-Mart's hierarchy, for variable lengths of time, in 3,400 stores, sprinkled across 50 states, with a kaleidoscope of supervisors (male and female), subject to a variety of regional policies that all differed. . . . Some thrived while others did poorly. They have little in common but their sex and this lawsuit." (dissenting opinion).

III

We also conclude that respondents' claims for backpay were improperly certified under Federal Rule of Civil Procedure 23(b)(2). Our opinion in Ticor Title Ins. Co. v. Brown, 511 U.S. 117, 121 (1994) (*per curiam*) expressed serious doubt about whether claims for monetary relief may be certified under that provision. We now hold that they may not, at least where (as here) the monetary relief is not incidental to the injunctive or declaratory relief.

A

Rule 23(b)(2) allows class treatment when "the party opposing the class has acted or refused to act on grounds that apply generally to the class, so that final injunctive relief or corresponding declaratory relief is appropriate respecting the class as a whole." One possible reading of this provision is that it applies *only* to requests for such injunctive or declaratory relief and does not authorize the class certification of monetary claims at all. We need not reach that broader question in this case, because we think that, at a minimum, claims for *individualized* relief (like the backpay at issue here) do not satisfy the Rule. The key to the (b)(2) class is "the indivisible nature of the injunctive or declaratory remedy warranted—the notion that the conduct is such that it can be enjoined or declared unlawful only as to all of the class members or as to none of them." Nagareda, 84 N.Y.U. L. Rev. at 132. In other words, Rule 23(b)(2) applies only when a single injunction or declaratory judgment would provide relief to each member of the class. It does not authorize class certification when each individual class member would be entitled to a *different* injunction or declaratory judgment against the defendant. Similarly, it does not authorize class certification when each class member would be entitled to an individualized award of monetary damages.

That interpretation accords with the history of the Rule. Because Rule 23 "stems from equity practice" that predated its codification, in determining its meaning we have previously looked to the historical models on which the Rule was based. As we observed in *Amchem*, "[c]ivil rights cases against parties charged with unlawful, class-based discrimination are prime examples" of what (b)(2) is meant to capture. In particular, the Rule reflects a series of decisions involving challenges to racial segregation—conduct that was remedied by a single classwide order. In none of the cases cited by the Advisory Committee as examples of (b)(2)'s antecedents did the plaintiffs combine any claim for individualized relief with their classwide injunction.

Permitting the combination of individualized and classwide relief in a (b)(2) class is also inconsistent with the structure of Rule 23(b). Classes certified under (b)(1) and (b)(2) share the most traditional justifications for class treatment—that individual adjudications would be impossible or unworkable, as in a (b)(1) class, or that the relief sought must perforce affect the entire class at once, as in a (b)(2) class. For that reason these are also mandatory classes: The Rule provides no opportunity for (b)(1) or (b)(2) class members to opt out, and does not even oblige the District Court to afford them notice of the action. Rule 23(b)(3), by contrast, is an "adventuresome innovation" of the 1966 amendments, framed for situations "in which 'class-action treatment is not as clearly called for'" (quoting Advisory Committee's Notes, 28 U.S.C. App., p. 697 (1994 ed.)). It allows class certification in a much wider set of circumstances but with greater procedural protections. Its only prerequisites are that "the questions of law or fact common to class members predominate over any questions affecting only individual members, and that a class action is superior to other available methods for fairly and efficiently adjudicating the controversy." Rule 23(b)(3). And unlike (b)(1) and (b)(2) classes, the (b)(3) class is not mandatory; class members are entitled to receive "the best notice that is practicable under the circumstances" and to withdraw from the class at their option. See Rule 23(c)(2)(B).

Given that structure, we think it clear that individualized monetary claims belong in Rule 23(b)(3). The procedural protections attending the (b)(3) class—predominance, superiority, mandatory notice, and the right to opt out—are missing from (b)(2) not because the Rule considers them unnecessary, but because it considers them unnecessary *to a (b)(2) class*. When a class seeks an indivisible injunction benefitting all its members at once, there is no reason to undertake a case-specific inquiry into whether class issues predominate or whether class action is a superior method of adjudicating the dispute. Predominance and superiority are self-evident. But with respect to each class member's individualized claim for money, that is not so—which is precisely why (b)(3) requires the judge to make findings about predominance and superiority before allowing the class. Similarly, (b)(2) does not require that class members be given notice and opt-out rights, presumably because it is thought (rightly or wrongly) that notice has no purpose when the class is mandatory, and that depriving people of their right to sue in this manner complies with the Due Process Clause. In the context of a class action predominantly for money damages we have held that absence of notice and opt-out violates due process. While we have never held that to be so where the monetary claims do not predominate, the serious possibility that it may be so provides an additional reason not to read Rule 23(b)(2) to include the monetary claims here. . . .

B

Against that conclusion, respondents argue that their claims for backpay were appropriately certified as part of a class under Rule 23(b)(2) because those claims do not "predominate" over their requests for injunctive and declaratory relief. They rely upon the Advisory Committee's statement that Rule 23(b)(2) "does not extend to cases in which the appropriate final relief relates *exclusively or predominantly* to money damages." . . .

Respondents' predominance test . . . creates perverse incentives for class representatives to place at risk potentially valid claims for monetary relief. In this case, for example, the named plaintiffs declined to include employees' claims for compensatory damages in their complaint. That strategy of including only backpay claims made it more likely that monetary relief would not "predominate." But it also created the possibility (if the predominance test were correct) that individual class members' compensatory-damages claims would be *precluded* by litigation they had no power to hold themselves apart from. If it were determined, for example, that a particular class member is not entitled to backpay because her denial of increased pay or a promotion was *not* the product of discrimination, that employee might be collaterally estopped from independently seeking compensatory damages based on that same denial. That possibility underscores the need for plaintiffs with individual monetary claims to decide *for themselves* whether to tie their fates to the class representatives' or go it alone—a choice Rule 23(b)(2) does not ensure that they have. . . .

C

The Court of Appeals believed that it was possible to replace such proceedings with Trial by Formula. A sample set of the class members would be selected, as to whom liability for sex discrimination and the backpay owing as a result would be determined in depositions supervised by a master. The percentage of claims determined to be valid would then be applied to the entire remaining class, and the number of (presumptively) valid claims thus derived would be multiplied by the average backpay award in the sample set to arrive at the entire class recovery—without further individualized proceedings. We disapprove that novel project. Because the Rules Enabling Act forbids interpreting Rule 23 to "abridge, enlarge or modify any substantive right," 28 U.S.C. §2072(b); a class cannot be certified on the premise that Wal-Mart will not be entitled to litigate its statutory defenses to individual claims. And because the necessity of that litigation will prevent backpay from being "incidental" to the classwide injunction, respondents' class could not be certified even assuming, *arguendo*, that "incidental" monetary relief can be awarded to a 23(b)(2) class.

* * *

The judgment of the Court of Appeals is *Reversed.*

GINSBURG, J., with whom BREYER, J., SOTOMAYOR, J., and KAGAN, J., join, concurring in part and dissenting in part.

The class in this case, I agree with the Court, should not have been certified under Federal Rule of Civil Procedure 23(b)(2). The plaintiffs, alleging discrimination in violation of Title VII, seek monetary relief that is not merely incidental to any injunctive or declaratory relief that might be available. A putative class of this type may be certifiable under Rule 23(b)(3), if the plaintiffs show that common class questions "predominate" over issues affecting individuals—*e.g.*, qualification for, and the amount of, backpay or compensatory damages—and that a class action is "superior" to other modes of adjudication.

Whether the class the plaintiffs describe meets the specific requirements of Rule 23(b)(3) is not before the Court, and I would reserve that matter for consideration and decision on remand.[1] The Court, however, disqualifies the class at the starting gate, holding that the plaintiffs cannot cross the "commonality" line set by Rule 23(a)(2). In so ruling, the Court imports into the Rule 23(a) determination concerns properly addressed in a Rule 23(b)(3) assessment. . . .

* * *

The Court errs in importing a "dissimilarities" notion suited to Rule 23(b)(3) into the Rule 23(a) commonality inquiry. I therefore cannot join Part II of the Court's opinion.

Procedure as Strategy

Consider the impact of the *Wal-Mart* decision on the parties to this case. The Court does not hold that the plaintiffs have suffered no discrimination. But the effect of the procedural ruling in this case changed dramatically the nature of the litigation they could pursue. A million individual suits would have been difficult or impossible to maintain. Instead, following the Court's decision, the plaintiffs' counsel filed regional class actions in California, Texas, Tennessee, Florida, and Wisconsin. The class certification motions have been winding their ways through the courts.

Consider also what would have happened if the Supreme Court had affirmed the decision to certify the class. The likely result would not have been trial but intense settlement negotiations. Faced with a certified class of this size, even a defendant with Wal-Mart's resources would likely decide that settlement was the most rational approach, regardless of its view of the merits of the case.

Consequently, in this and similar class actions, the decision on certification is often the most important event in the litigation.

Notes and Problems

1. The majority gives two reasons the class should not have been certified, citing different portions of Rule 23. What are the reasons and what are the sections of Rule 23 that the majority says prevent certification?

---

1. The plaintiffs requested Rule 23(b)(3) certification as an alternative, should their request for (b)(2) certification fail.

2. All nine Justices agree as to one of those reasons.

    a. What is it?
    b. Why, in the view of a unanimous Court, did the class fail to meet that requirement?
    c. What would have been the consequence if the Court had limited itself to the ground on which all the Justices agreed? Where would that have left the plaintiffs?

3. Failed litigation strategies are always easy to pick apart in hindsight. Instead, as a way of better understanding Rule 23, try to reconstruct the choices made by the plaintiffs' lawyers and to understand them in light of the structure of the Rule. All class actions have to jump through Rule 23(a) hoops, demonstrating numerosity, typicality, commonality, and adequacy of representation.

    a. Numerosity was not going to pose a problem.
    b. Nor was adequacy of representation going to pose a problem so far as the lawyers were concerned. Plaintiffs were represented by a joint venture of law firms and nonprofit pro bono affinity groups with a special interest in gender equality. They were skilled and experienced lawyers and were adequately financed—two areas of special concern to judges certifying classes.
    c. Though it proved unsuccessful, they also had a strategy for addressing the typicality and commonality requirements. Describe that strategy. The majority opinion suggests that the plaintiffs should have gathered statistical evidence about gender disparities at each store. Imagine a strategy conference early in the case at which someone suggested that course of action: What would have been the objections?
    d. Battles over expert evidence have become increasingly important in class certification. Older decisions suggested that it would suffice for plaintiffs pursuing class certification to present evidence that—if believed—would justify class treatment. Some recent cases have applied a more demanding standard: The certifying court must weigh the testimony of experts and certify the class only if it decides by a preponderance of the evidence that the testimony supporting the commonality and typicality of the class outweighs the defendant's challenge to that evidence. In re Hydrogen Peroxide Antitrust Litigation, 552 F.3d 305 (3d Cir. 2008). *Wal-Mart* does not directly address this question, but its treatment of the plaintiff's expert testimony may suggest that it is leaning in the direction of the *Hydrogen Peroxide* court.

4. The second fateful decision was to seek certification as a Rule 23(b)(2) class. A unanimous Court rejects that approach on the ground that individualized claims (primarily for back pay) were too significant a part of the case to make a Rule 23(b)(2) class appropriate.

    a. Class action lawyers will tell you that, on the whole, Rule 23(b)(2) cases are easier to bring than Rule 23(b)(3) class actions.
        i. First, the case does not have to leap through the additional hoops posed by Rule 23(b)(3), hoops that lawyers abbreviate by referring to

the "superiority" requirements of that subsection. In a number of cases, courts have found that class actions that meet the requirements of Rule 23(a) fail those of Rule 23(b)(3). In a case this large manageability might present an especially significant challenge. So, if the plaintiffs' lawyers could avoid Rule 23(b)(3), they would want to.

  ii. Second, as the majority opinion notes, Rule 23(c)(2)(b) requires that in all Rule 23(b)(3) cases each plaintiff who can be identified through reasonable effort (hear the echo of *Mullane* here?) must be individually notified and given a chance to withdraw ("opt out") of the class (see *Shutts*). Prior cases held that the plaintiffs must bear the entire expense of that notice—here involving a million and a half present and former Wal-Mart employees.

  b. So, on both grounds, Rule 23(b)(2) must have looked like the way to go—if they could.

5. Having made that choice, why did the plaintiffs' lawyers add claims for back pay, claims that led a unanimous Court to hold that a Rule 23(b)(2) class could not be certified?

  a. Look back at Rule 23(a)(4) and (g)(4) and consider the plaintiffs' lawyers' problem.

  b. If they dropped the claims for back pay, they might have a "clean" Rule 23(b)(2) class. But if they dropped the claims for back pay, they would have much less settlement leverage: Back pay for 1.5 million women would add up to a large number, and might encourage Wal-Mart to settle and implement the structural changes sought by plaintiffs. The possibility of a back pay award could also entice for-profit attorneys to join the plaintiffs' team. Moreover, dropping the back pay claim could imperil or prevent certification: Could they look the court in the eye and say they were adequately representing over a million clients, many of whom, if the allegations in the complaint could be proved, had lost money in wages?

6. *Wal-Mart* does not hold that it is impossible to bring a large employment discrimination class action, but it does suggest that future such efforts will have to be more focused, and will perhaps require deeper pre-filing investigation and investment and more discovery and investment at the certification stage.

5. Settlement of Class Actions and the "Settlement Class"

The student will already have understood that the effect of the class action is more than the simple gathering together of similar cases. That proposition is particularly true at the settlement stage—the way in which most class actions, like other lawsuits, end. Settlement presents several difficult problems unique to the class action. Most of those problems flow from the circumstance that, in many class actions (especially those created by Rule 23(b)(1) and (b)(3)), the litigative group is organized only for purposes of the lawsuit. In the most extreme cases the "group" may exist only in the abstract—as, for example, the sharers of some hypothesized interest. Yet many of the ordinary rules of litigation assume a client who hires a lawyer, guides the case, authorizes settlement, and benefits directly from any relief. Exacerbating the situation is that the class's lawyers, on whom we have been counting to represent the class adequately, are typically negotiating their own fees at the same time as relief for the class. So the law has to worry about the potential conflict of interest: the temptation to trade a tiny bit of relief for the class for a large fee agreement. In some notorious cases preceding the enactment of the Class Action Fairness Act of 2005, settlements involved large fees for the plaintiffs' lawyers, whose clients got only coupons that might be of no value unless they chose to purchase a sometimes expensive product. Several bodies of law address these problems, taking two approaches—requiring lots of transparent process to expose conflicts and simply forbidding some forms of settlements.

To approach the problem, suppose counterfactually that the Supreme Court had approved the certification of a class in *Wal-Mart v. Dukes* and that, after an unsuccessful motion for summary judgment, the parties began to talk about settlement. Further suppose that the proposed settlement involved offering new promotion opportunities to existing Wal-Mart female employees, establishing a fund that would be used to give those employees additional training and education (thus enabling them to advance more quickly), and a public outreach campaign, funded by Wal-Mart, that, while not conceding any violations of law, made it known that the company had improved its practices in regard to women and was making special efforts to hire and promote women managers. Finally, suppose that the plaintiffs' lawyers submitted a proposed fees bill of $1,500,000; you may recall that in civil rights actions like this one, a prevailing plaintiff may claim a fee from the opposing party.

Start with Rule 23(e), which requires court approval of a settlement of a class action. To order such approval, the judge must first "direct notice in a reasonable manner to all class members who would be bound by the proposal." Rule 23(e)(1). This notice must occur without regard to what sort of class action is involved, but Rule 23(e) does not require individual notice. So sometimes such notices take the form of newspaper ads, online postings, radio spots, and the like. Given that some of the members of the class would have left Wal-Mart's employment, it's very likely that they could be reached only through such non-individualized means.

Such notices include information about the terms of settlement and that those objecting to the terms of the settlement may do so to the court. If the settlement involves a Rule 23(b)(3) class, it may offer a second chance for individual members to opt out of the class and the settlement. And, to prevent objectors being "bought off" by the settling parties, objections may not be withdrawn without court approval. Rule 23(e)(5). In each of these ways, class settlements look very different from ordinary settlements.

After such notice, the court must conduct a hearing at which it hears arguments from the settling parties about why the settlement is fair to the class members.

At this hearing, the Rule permits class members to come forward to object to the settlement terms. The idea is that they will have an incentive to do so because, at least in common fund cases, the lawyer's fee is coming out of a fund, the remainder of which will be distributed to the class. In a number of cases, objectors have come forward. Indeed, some critics say that the fairness hearings have spawned a group of professional "objectors," who are themselves hoping to win fees by raising objections that cause the parties to add a bit to the settlement terms.

The Class Action Fairness Act of 2005 adds additional features. For example, CAFA requires that, if the defendant is subject to state or federal regulation, that the regulatory authorities be notified of the suit and a pending settlement. 28 U.S.C. §1715. In the *Wal-Mart* case, both state and federal agencies that regulate labor and employment would have to be notified. Although the statute does not directly so state, the idea seems to be that a regulator could appear at a settlement hearing and offer an opinion about the appropriateness of the settlement, given its expertise regarding the unlawful acts alleged. The same notice could presumably trigger greater regulatory scrutiny if the regulator thought that the acts involved suggested other forms of unlawful behavior. Consider how the Rule and statutes interact in some hypothetical cases.

Notes and Problems

1. A manufacturer of "scrubber" equipment that removes environmentally harmful residues from smokestack emissions has its plant and headquarters in Arizona. The manufacturer has been sued in federal court by a class consisting of present and former female employees; the complaint alleges gender discrimination in employment and promotion and invokes both state and federal statutes. In particular, it alleges that women employees have not been offered the highest-paying jobs in the production division on the grounds that some of the chemicals used in production pose special health problems for women. The court certifies a Rule 23(b)(2) class. The parties work out a proposed settlement involving some additional job opportunities for women and some changes in manufacturing practices.

   a. To whom does Rule 23 require that notice of the settlement be given?
   b. Must the members of the class be given an opportunity to opt out of the settlement?

2. In such a settlement, 28 U.S.C. §1715 would also require that notice be sent to the Attorney General of the United States (because the complaint alleged violation of federal law) and to "the person in the State [here Arizona] who has the primary regulatory or supervisory authority with respect to the defendant." One imagines that the parties might be unsure whether that would mean the state official with primary responsibilities over labor conditions or the state official charged with regulating manufacturing or environmental conditions.

In case of uncertainty, the statute allows the parties to notify the state's attorney general, on the theory that he or she can figure out who else to notify.

3. One member of the class receives notice of the settlement, consults her own lawyer, and files an objection that the proposal does not remove the discriminatory practices to which she has been subjected. After her objection is received, she is promoted, and seeks to withdraw her objection. Can she? Under what circumstances?

a. Fees

In class actions, fee agreements and disputes are closely bound with settlements— because of the inherent conflict between the class and the lawyers in some settlements. In most litigation, the client pays the lawyer's fee because she has agreed to do so, and the lawyer may not settle without the client's agreement. Neither holds true for the class action. While the named representative party in a class action may have such an agreement, that contract does not bind absentees. Yet it may seem that the lawyer whose work has benefited the class should be paid for that work. In class actions that recover money damages, courts apply the "common fund" doctrine, described supra page 350. According to this doctrine, a plaintiff whose efforts create a fund is entitled to have those who benefit contribute to his lawyer's fee. In class actions that create funds for distribution to class members, the doctrine is applied more directly: Courts regularly award the class lawyer a fee taken directly from the fund created by the litigation.

How should the court calculate such a fee? One school of thought is that a simple percentage is appropriate, using the analogy of contingent fee arrangements. Others point out that the key ingredient in a contingent fee calculation—the agreement between lawyer and client—is missing in the class action context. They argue instead that the proper way to calculate fees is to start with the appropriate hourly rate of the lawyer taking into account such factors as special risks, novelty of the issues, and the like. This latter method—often called "the lodestar" method, because the hourly rate provides a point of reference by which the court can "steer"—is used in federal courts, but not all states adhere to it. In practice, the two methods may often arrive at similar results.

Setting these fees presents problems because most class actions settle and the fee award is made in the context of a settlement approval hearing required by Rule 23(e). At that hearing the representatives of the class and defendant, who will have agreed on an appropriate amount of fees, are unlikely to raise questions casting doubt on the agreed amount or on the vigorousness of the litigation leading to the settlement. Moreover, because the fees are negotiated at the same time as the relief going to the class members, lawyers for the class and the defendant may be tempted to put more dollars into the fees than into relief for the class, thus buying off the plaintiffs' lawyer. A special version of this problem has arisen in so-called coupon settlements, in which members of the class get coupons—good for some discount on future purchases of cars, software, etc.—but the plaintiffs' lawyers are paid in cash. All of these issues replicate the fundamental structural feature of the class action—that the class's lawyer is representing a diffuse group, who cannot directly instruct or monitor the lawyer's actions.

The law addresses these problems in two ways. For all class actions, Rule 23(e) requires notice to the absent class members and a hearing and judicial finding that the proposed settlement is "fair, reasonable, and adequate." And Rule 23(h) creates a process the court must use to approve any attorneys' fees—including those embodied in a settlement: It requires notice, hearing, findings, and an opportunity to object to fees. Congress has specifically addressed aspects of the coupon settlement in 28 U.S.C. §1712, part of the Class Action Fairness Act of 2005. That section provides that fee awards in such a settlement must be based on the value of the coupons actually redeemed, not on the hypothetical value of the settlement if all such coupons were redeemed. Consider how some representative fee problems should be solved.

Notes and Problems

---

1. Solo Practitioner brings a class action on behalf of a group of plaintiffs, alleging they were overcharged for their automobiles. The case is settled after three years, during which time Solo has devoted a third of her professional hours to it. The suit grants injunctive relief and $100,000 in compensatory damages. The 200 members of the class will share in whatever remains of the proceeds after Solo's fee is paid. The judge finds that Solo spent more than 1,500 hours on the case. The court also finds that in her other legal work Solo billed clients at $75 an hour. Finally, the court finds that similarly skilled lawyers working in larger firms typically bill for such work at not less than $150 per hour.

   a. Should the court use Solo's actual hourly rate or the higher rate for comparable big-firm lawyers?

   b. This was Solo's first piece of comparably complex litigation. The judge finds that a more experienced practitioner would have devoted 200 fewer hours to the case. Should the judge subtract this amount from the hours Solo actually expended?

   c. Even using the lower billing rate and fewer hours, multiplying the hours times the rate will yield a sum nearly as great as the $100,000 recovery. What should the court do?

2. In a class action seeking several millions of dollars in damages, the defendant offers to settle for a total sum of $100,000, with $95,000 allocated to lawyers' fees and $5,000 to the 500 plaintiffs.

   a. Such separately negotiated attorneys' fees are ethical, but they are also not binding on the court. The trial judge has the power to assess the proposed attorneys' fees award for fairness.

   b. How should the judge decide whether to approve such an offer?

3. In a suit against a software manufacturer, the plaintiff alleged that the defendant created software that would block users from downloading free software that competed with that of the defendant. A proposed settlement would give coupons to the members of the class good for purchases of future software from defendant, and enjoins defendant to "unblock" existing software in one of its periodic downloads. If all the coupons were redeemed, the class would get discounts of $10 million.

   a. How should the court decide on the value of the coupons for fee-setting purposes? See 28 U.S.C. §1712(d).

   b. Suppose the court decides that the value of the redeemed coupons is likely to be about $1 million. How should the court value the injunctive relief for fee-setting purposes?

4. Finally, in other class actions that involve no money damages (likely brought under Rule 23(b)(2)), the injunctive relief will justify a fee—to be paid by defendant—based on a fee-shifting statute (e.g., 42 U.S.C. §1988(b)). Setting fees in such cases presents challenges—how, for example, does one calculate the "going rate" for various practice specialties?—but in principle these fees pose fewer challenges than do those in money damages cases.

b. Damages and Injunctive Relief

In class actions, damages pose an issue that rarely arises in ordinary cases: making sure that the class recovery finds its way into the hands of the class members. Class members often are unaware of the class action and subsequent recovery and consequently don't claim damages. The nature of some types of class actions makes notice difficult. One proposed solution to the problem is the *fluid class recovery*, under which, in the case of a class consisting of past consumers that dealt with a company, damages would be distributed to future consumers through rate reductions lasting long enough to exhaust the recovery. Or the proposed relief may run to those who currently occupy the position of now-departed members of the class. The terms of the hypothetical settlement in the *Wal-Mart* case contain some such elements—training designed to benefit current employees, which will not help those who have moved to other jobs. Note that the ordinary purpose of litigation—compensation of the plaintiff for a wrong suffered—is not served by the fluid class recovery because some of the beneficiaries are not the people who have suffered the harm but merely people similar to them. Fluid class recovery thus serves to deter the defendants but not to compensate the plaintiffs. Is that a problem? Or is it a virtue?

c. Settlement and Dismissal

Class actions gain their power, and their controversial status, because they combine groups for litigation that are often not otherwise organized. Suddenly confronted not by scattered claimants, each with a paltry amount at stake, but instead by a giant group claiming many millions of dollars in damages, defendants sometimes claim unfairness—that they are forced to settle regardless of the merits of the case because bankruptcy looms if they lose. But the tables can turn. Suppose a class with great potential liability could be certified—and the claims then settled for far less than they were worth. Such a settlement might, through the doctrines of former adjudication, bar its members from individual suits. In such a situation the class action would have turned from defendant's nightmare ("legalized blackmail" in the quotation at the start of this section) into a lawyers' conspiracy against the class members. Is that a fair description of the next case? Or does it instead embody both fairness and creativity in the highest traditions of the legal system?

Amchem Products, Inc. v. Windsor
521 U.S. 591 (1997)

GINSBURG, J., delivered the opinion of the Court.

This case concerns the legitimacy under Rule 23 of the Federal Rules of Civil Procedure of a class-action certification sought to achieve global settlement of current and future asbestos-related claims. The class proposed for certification potentially encompasses hundreds of thousands, perhaps millions, of individuals tied together by this commonality: each was, or some day may be, adversely affected by past exposure to asbestos products manufactured by one or more of 20 companies. Those companies, defendants in the lower courts, are petitioners here. . . .

I

A

The settlement-class certification we confront evolved in response to an asbestos-litigation crisis. A United States Judicial Conference Ad Hoc Committee on Asbestos Litigation, appointed by The Chief Justice in September 1990, described facets of the problem in a 1991 report:

> [This] is a tale of danger known in the 1930s, exposure inflicted upon millions of Americans in the 1940s and 1950s, injuries that began to take their toll in the 1960s, and a flood of lawsuits beginning in the 1970s. On the basis of past and current filing data, and because of latency period that may last as long as 40 years for some asbestos related diseases, a continuing stream of claims can be expected. The final toll of asbestos related injuries is unknown. Predictions have been made of 200,000 asbestos disease deaths before the year 2000 and as many as 265,000 by the year 2015.
>
> The most objectionable aspects of asbestos litigation can be briefly summarized: dockets in both federal and state courts continue to grow; long delays are routine; trials are too long; the same issues are litigated over and over; transaction costs exceed the victims' recovery by nearly two to one; exhaustion of assets threatens and distorts the process; and future claimants may lose altogether.

Report of the Judicial Conference Ad Hoc Committee on Asbestos Litigation 2-3 (Mar. 1991).

Real reform, the report concluded, required federal legislation creating a national asbestos dispute-resolution scheme. . . . To this date, no congressional response has emerged.

In the face of legislative inaction, the federal courts—lacking authority to replace state tort systems with a national toxic tort compensation regime—endeavored to work with the procedural tools available to improve management of federal asbestos litigation. Eight federal judges, experienced in the superintendence of asbestos cases, urged the Judicial Panel on Multidistrict Litigation (MDL Panel), to consolidate in a single district all asbestos complaints then pending in federal courts. Accepting the recommendation, the MDL Panel transferred all asbestos cases then filed, but not yet on trial in federal courts to a single district, the United States District Court for the Eastern District of Pennsylvania; pursuant to the transfer order, the collected cases were consolidated for pretrial proceedings before Judge Weiner. The order aggregated pending cases only; no authority resides in the MDL Panel to license for consolidated proceedings claims not yet filed.

B

After the consolidation, attorneys for plaintiffs and defendants formed separate steering committees and began settlement negotiations. . . . Settlement talks . . . concentrated on devising an administrative scheme for disposition of asbestos claims not yet in litigation. In these negotiations, counsel for masses of inventory plaintiffs* endeavored to represent the interests of the anticipated future claimants, although those lawyers then had no attorney-client relationship with such claimants.

Once negotiations seemed likely to produce an agreement purporting to bind potential plaintiffs, CCR[, a consortium of defendants,] agreed to settle, through separate agreements, the claims of plaintiffs who had already filed asbestos-related lawsuits. . . . After settling the inventory claims, CCR, together with the plaintiffs' lawyers CCR had approached, launched this case, exclusively involving persons outside the MDL Panel's province—plaintiffs without already pending lawsuits.[3]

C

The class action thus instituted was not intended to be litigated. Rather, within the space of a single day, January 15, 1993, the settling parties—CCR defendants and the representatives of the plaintiff class described below—presented to the District Court a complaint, an answer, a proposed settlement agreement, and a joint motion for conditional class certification.

---

* [As the opinion elsewhere explained, the steering committees referred to persons who had already filed claims as "inventory plaintiffs," distinguishing them from those who had not yet experienced illness or filed any claim, to whom they referred as "exposure-only" cases.—Eds.]

3. It is basic to comprehension of this proceeding to notice that no transferred case is included in the settlement at issue, and no case covered by the settlement existed as a civil action at the time of the MDL transfer.

The complaint identified nine lead plaintiffs, designating them and members of their families as representatives of a class comprising all persons who had not filed an asbestos-related lawsuit against a CCR defendant as of the date the class action commenced, but who (1) had been exposed—occupationally or through the occupational exposure of a spouse or household member—to asbestos or products containing asbestos attributable to a CCR defendant, or (2) whose spouse or family member had been so exposed. Untold numbers of individuals may fall within this description. All named plaintiffs alleged that they or a member of their family had been exposed to asbestos-containing products of CCR defendants. More than half of the named plaintiffs alleged that they or their family members had already suffered various physical injuries as a result of the exposure. The others alleged that they had not yet manifested any asbestos-related condition. The complaint delineated no subclasses; all named plaintiffs were designated as representatives of the class as a whole.

The complaint invoked the District Court's diversity jurisdiction. . . .

A stipulation of settlement accompanied the pleadings; it proposed to settle, and to preclude nearly all class members from litigating against CCR companies, all claims not filed before January 15, 1993, involving compensation for present and future asbestos-related personal injury or death. An exhaustive document exceeding 100 pages, the stipulation presents in detail an administrative mechanism and a schedule of payments to compensate class members who meet defined asbestos-exposure and medical requirements. The stipulation describes four categories of compensable disease: mesothelioma; lung cancer; certain "other cancers" (colon-rectal, laryngeal, esophageal, and stomach cancer); and "non-malignant conditions" (asbestosis and bilateral pleural thickening). Persons with "exceptional" medical claims—claims that do not fall within the four described diagnostic categories—may in some instances qualify for compensation, but the settlement caps the number of "exceptional" claims CCR must cover. . . .

For each qualifying disease category, the stipulation specifies the range of damages CCR will pay to qualifying claimants. Payments under the settlement are not adjustable for inflation. Mesothelioma claimants—the most highly compensated category—are scheduled to receive between $20,000 and $200,000. The stipulation provides that CCR is to propose the level of compensation within the prescribed ranges; it also establishes procedures to resolve disputes over medical diagnoses and levels of compensation.

Class members are to receive no compensation for certain kinds of claims, even if otherwise applicable state law recognizes such claims. . . . Although not entitled to present compensation, exposure-only claimants and pleural claimants may qualify for benefits when and if they develop a compensable disease and meet the relevant exposure and medical criteria. Defendants forgo defenses to liability, including statute of limitations pleas.

Class members, in the main, are bound by the settlement in perpetuity, while CCR defendants may choose to withdraw from the settlement after ten years. A small number of class members—only a few per year—may reject the settlement and pursue their claims in court. Those permitted to exercise this option, however, may not assert any punitive damages claim or any claim for increased risk of cancer. Aspects of the administration of the settlement are to be monitored by the AFL-CIO and class counsel. Class counsel are to receive attorneys' fees in an amount to be approved by the District Court.

D

On January 29, 1993, as requested by the settling parties, the District Court conditionally certified, under Federal Rule of Civil Procedure 23(b)(3), an encompassing opt-out class. . . . Judge Weiner assigned to Judge Reed, also of the Eastern District of Pennsylvania, "the task of conducting fairness proceedings and of determining whether the proposed settlement is fair to the class." [The district court approved the settlement.]

E

The Court of Appeals [reversing] . . . found that "serious intra-class conflicts precluded the class from meeting the adequacy of representation requirement" of Rule 23(a)(4). . . .

III

To place this controversy in context, we briefly describe the characteristics of class actions for which the Federal Rules provide. Rule 23, governing federal-court class actions, stems from equity practice and gained its current shape in an innovative 1966 revision. . . .

In the decades since the 1966 revision of Rule 23, class action practice has become ever more "adventuresome" as a means of coping with claims too numerous to secure their "just, speedy, and inexpensive determination" one by one. See Fed. Rule Civ. Proc. 1. The development reflects concerns about the efficient use of court resources and the conservation of funds to compensate claimants who do not line up early in a litigation queue. . . .

Among current applications of Rule 23(b)(3), the "settlement only" class has become a stock device. Although all Federal Circuits recognize the utility of Rule 23(b)(3) settlement classes, courts have divided on the extent to which a proffered settlement affects court surveillance under Rule 23's certification criteria. . . .

IV

We granted review to decide the role settlement may play, under existing Rule 23, in determining the propriety of class certification. . . .

Confronted with a request for settlement-only class certification, a district court need not inquire whether the case, if tried, would present intractable management problems, see Fed. Rule Civ. Proc. 23(b)(3)(D), for the proposal is that there be no trial. But other specifications of the rule—those designed to protect absentees by blocking unwarranted or overbroad class definitions—demand undiluted, even heightened, attention in the settlement context. Such attention is of vital importance, for a court asked to certify a settlement class will lack the opportunity, present when a case is litigated, to adjust the class, informed by the proceedings as they unfold. See Fed. Rule Civ. Proc. 23(c), (d).[16] And, of overriding importance, courts must be mindful that the rule as now composed sets the requirements they are bound to enforce. Federal Rules take effect after an extensive deliberative process involving many reviewers: a Rules Advisory Committee, public commenters, the Judicial Conference, this Court, the Congress. The text of a rule thus proposed and reviewed limits judicial inventiveness. Courts are not free to amend a rule outside the process Congress ordered, a process properly tuned to the instruction that rules of procedure "shall not abridge . . . any substantive right." 28 U.S.C. §2072(b).

Rule 23(e) [at the time of the decision,] on settlement of class actions, read[] in its entirety: "A class action shall not be dismissed or compromised without the approval of the court, and notice of the proposed dismissal or compromise shall be given to all members of the class in such manner as the court directs." This prescription was designed to function as an additional requirement, not a superseding direction, for the "class action" to which Rule 23(e) refers is one qualified for certification under Rule 23(a) and (b). . . . The safeguards provided by the Rule 23(a) and (b) class-qualifying criteria, we emphasize, are not impractical impediments—checks shorn of utility—in the settlement class context. . . .

Federal courts, in any case, lack authority to substitute for Rule 23's certification criteria a standard never adopted—that if a settlement is "fair," then certification is proper. Applying to this case criteria the rulemakers set, we conclude that the Third Circuit's appraisal is essentially correct. Although that court should have acknowledged that settlement is a factor in the calculus, a remand is not warranted on that account. The Court of Appeals' opinion amply demonstrates why—with or without a settlement on the table—the sprawling class the District Court certified does not satisfy Rule 23's requirements. . . .

A

We address first the requirement of Rule 23(b)(3) that "[common] questions of law or fact . . . predominate over any questions affecting only individual members." The District Court concluded that predominance was satisfied based on two factors: class members' shared experience of asbestos exposure and their common "interest in receiving prompt and fair compensation for their claims, while minimizing the risks and transaction costs inherent in the asbestos litigation process as it occurs presently in the tort system." . . .

---

16. Portions of the opinion dissenting in part appear to assume that settlement counts only one way—in favor of certification. To the extent that is the dissent's meaning, we disagree. Settlement, though a relevant factor, does not inevitably signal that class action certification should be granted more readily than it would be were the case to be litigated. For reasons the Third Circuit aired, proposed settlement classes sometimes warrant more, not less caution on the question of certification.

The predominance requirement stated in Rule 23(b)(3), we hold, is not met by the factors on which the District Court relied. The benefits asbestos-exposed persons might gain from the establishment of a grand-scale compensation scheme is a matter fit for legislative consideration, but it is not pertinent to the predominance inquiry. That inquiry trains on the legal or factual questions that qualify each class member's case as a genuine controversy, questions that preexist any settlement. . . .

B

Nor can the class approved by the District Court satisfy Rule 23(a)(4)'s requirement that the named parties "will fairly and adequately protect the interests of the class." The adequacy inquiry under Rule 23(a)(4) serves to uncover conflicts of interest between named parties and the class they seek to represent. . . .

As the Third Circuit pointed out, named parties with diverse medical conditions sought to act on behalf of a single giant class rather than on behalf of discrete subclasses. In significant respects, the interests of those within the single class are not aligned. Most saliently, for the currently injured, the critical goal is generous immediate payments. That goal tugs against the interest of exposure-only plaintiffs in ensuring an ample, inflation-protected fund for the future. . . .

The settling parties, in sum, achieved a global compromise with no structural assurance of fair and adequate representation for the diverse groups and individuals affected. Although the named parties alleged a range of complaints, each served generally as representative for the whole, not for a separate constituency. . . .

The Third Circuit found no assurance here—either in the terms of the settlement or in the structure of the negotiations—that the named plaintiffs operated under a proper understanding of their representational responsibilities. That assessment, we conclude, is on the mark.

C

Because we have concluded that the class in this case cannot satisfy the requirements of common issue predominance and adequacy of representation, we need not rule, definitively, on the notice given here. In accord with the Third Circuit, however, we recognize the gravity of the question whether class action notice sufficient under the Constitution and Rule 23 could ever be given to legions so unselfconscious and amorphous.

V

The argument is sensibly made that a nationwide administrative claims processing regime would provide the most secure, fair, and efficient means of compensating victims of asbestos exposure. Congress, however, has not adopted such a solution. And Rule 23, which must be interpreted with fidelity to the Rules Enabling

Act and applied with the interests of absent class members in close view, cannot carry the large load CCR, class counsel, and the District Court heaped upon it. As this case exemplifies, the rulemakers' prescriptions for class actions may be endangered by "those who embrace [Rule 23] too enthusiastically just as [they are by] those who approach [the rule] with distaste." C. Wright, Law of Federal Courts 508 (5th ed. 1994). . . .

O'CONNOR, J., took no part in the consideration or decision of this case.

BREYER, J., with whom STEVENS, J., joins, concurring in part and dissenting in part.

Although I agree with the Court's basic holding that "settlement is relevant to a class certification," I find several problems in its approach that lead me to a different conclusion. First, I believe that the need for settlement in this mass tort case, with hundreds of thousands of lawsuits, is greater than the Court's opinion suggests. Second, I would give more weight than would the majority to settlement-related issues for purposes of determining whether common issues predominate. Third, I am uncertain about the Court's determination of adequacy of representation, and do not believe it appropriate for this Court to second-guess the District Court on the matter without first having the Court of Appeals consider it. Fourth, I am uncertain about the tenor of an opinion that seems to suggest the settlement is unfair. And fifth, in the absence of further review by the Court of Appeals, I cannot accept the majority's suggestions that "notice" is inadequate. . . .

WHAT'S NEW HERE?

- Unlike *Wal-Mart v. Dukes*, in which the defendant vigorously fought class certification, the *Amchem* defendants supported class certification. They did so because certification (and an approved settlement) would at one fell swoop eliminate not only pending lawsuits but also those that had not yet been brought.
- In the ordinary case when both sides support a settlement, that is the end of the matter. In this one, the Supreme Court overturned a settlement supported by both sides.
- The Court says it did so because the way in which the settlement was achieved strongly suggested a conflict of interest between the set of plaintiffs with existing claims and the set of plaintiffs with latent claims—with the same lawyers seeking to represent both.

Notes and Problems

1. *Amchem* exposes numerous issues, some of which challenge the most basic assumptions about the nature of civil litigation. In that respect it is a fitting close both to this chapter on joinder and to the student's exploration of civil procedure.

2. Start by defining the respects in which *Amchem* is an unusual case, even within the category of class actions, which are themselves unusual if measured by ordinary litigation standards.

   a. In a typical class action the plaintiff files a complaint; there is a battle over class certification, followed (if the class is certified) by discovery, perhaps a summary judgment motion, and settlement discussions. What happened in *Amchem*?

   b. In many ordinary, single-plaintiff/single-defendant cases, the parties settle before suit is filed. To use the asbestos context, a lawyer for a former shipyard worker alleging injuries from inhalation of asbestos dust could approach an asbestos manufacturer and settle the claim without ever filing a complaint. Why didn't the parties do so in *Amchem*? Why *couldn't* they do so if they wanted the settlement to have the intended effect?

   c. What did the parties—in particular the defendants—want to get from class certification that they could not have gotten in any other way?

3. To answer Problem 2c, one must be clear about the definition of the class. The persons involved in the *Amchem* litigation comprised two groups.

   a. There were individual claimants who had filed complaints against various asbestos manufacturers (the so-called inventory claimants). These cases had been consolidated (under the provision for Multidistrict Litigation, 28 U.S.C. §1407). These claims could have been settled without regard to class certification; indeed, it was the discussion of their settlement that led to the proposed class action.

   b. Who, then, were the other members of the class?

   c. Put yourself in the position of a defendant. Why would you have wanted the class certification and settlement before being willing to settle the "inventory" of individual cases?

   d. The Supreme Court has emphasized that it meant what it said in *Amchem* about the avoidance of conflicts of interest by lawyers representing classes. Striking down another asbestos settlement class in Ortiz v. Fibreboard Corp., 527 U.S. 815 (1999), the Court said:

   > One may take a settlement amount as good evidence of the maximum available if one can assume that parties of equal knowledge and negotiating skill agreed upon the figure through arms-length bargaining, unhindered by any considerations tugging against the interests of the parties ostensibly represented in the negotiation. But no such assumption may be indulged in this case, or probably in any class action settlement with the potential for gigantic fees. In this case,

certainly, any assumption that plaintiffs' counsel could be of a mind to do their simple best in bargaining for the benefit of the settlement class is patently at odds with the fact that at least some of the same lawyers representing plaintiffs and the class had also negotiated the separate settlement of 45,000 pending claims, the full payment of which was contingent on a successful global settlement agreement or the successful resolution of the insurance coverage dispute. . . . Class counsel thus had great incentive to reach any agreement in the global settlement negotiations that they thought might survive a Rule 23(e) fairness hearing, rather than the best possible arrangement for the substantially unidentified global settlement class. . . . The resulting incentive to favor the known plaintiffs in the earlier settlement was, indeed, an egregious example of the conflict noted in *Amchem* resulting from divergent interests of the presently injured and future claimants.

Id. at 852-53.

4. In spite of *Amchem* and *Ortiz* there have been both settlement classes and procedures that achieved some of the goals of the settlement class without using that form.

   a. For an example of an approved settlement class, see Hanlon v. Chrysler Corp., 150 F.3d 1011, 1020-21 (9th Cir. 1997), in which plaintiffs sued an auto manufacturer alleging a defective latch in a van's door. Affirming the district court's approval of a settlement class, the Ninth Circuit carefully distinguished *Amchem*:

>   At the heart of *Amchem* was concern over settlement allocation decisions; asbestos manufacturers had a designated amount of money that was not fairly distributed between present and future claimants. The *Amchem* settlement eliminated all present and future claims against asbestos manufacturers, with class counsel attempting to represent both groups of plaintiffs. The Supreme Court found this dual representation to be particularly troubling, given that present plaintiffs had a clear interest in a settlement that maximized current funds, while future plaintiffs had a strong interest in preserving funds for their future needs and protecting the total fund against inflation.
>
>   Unlike the class in *Amchem*, this class of minivan owners does not present an allocation dilemma. Potential plaintiffs are not divided into conflicting discrete categories, such as those with present health problems and those who may develop symptoms in the future. Rather, each potential plaintiff has the same problem: an allegedly defective rear latchgate which requires repair or commensurate compensation. The differences in severity of personal injury present in *Amchem* are avoided here by excluding personal injury and wrongful death claims. Similarly, there is no structural conflict of interest based on variations in state law, for the named representatives include individuals from each state, and the differences in state remedies are not sufficiently substantial so as to warrant the creation of subclasses. Representatives of other potential subclasses are included among the named representatives, including owners of every minivan model. However, even if the named representatives did not include a broad cross-section of claimants, the prospects for irreparable conflict of interest are minimal in this case because of the relatively small differences in damages and potential remedies.

Is this an adequate response?

b. For an example of a settlement device that achieves many of the goals of the settlement class without the defects found in *Amchem*, consider a settlement between a pharmaceutical house and plaintiffs not certified as a class. Merck manufactured a widely prescribed pain medicine, Vioxx, which was withdrawn from the market after it was alleged to increase the risk of heart disease. Twenty-six thousand lawsuits followed, some from survivors of those who had died of heart disease after taking the drug, others from those who had suffered some identifiable health harm, and still others who alleged only increased anxiety and stress from fear of future effects. As in *Amchem*, many of these were consolidated before a single federal district judge pursuant to the multidistrict litigation provisions. Merck defended the claims initially, trying a number, losing some big verdicts but winning the majority of the cases (15 out of 20, according to one news report). Plaintiffs' and defendant's lawyers then negotiated a global settlement, providing a total of $5 billion to be disbursed according to a schedule, with claimants suffering death or serious injury receiving amounts in excess of $1 million, but those with less serious injuries far less. The part of the settlement that resembles the *Amchem* settlement class are three provisions: (1) that the plaintiffs' lawyers recommend it to their clients; (2) that the settlement would not go into effect unless 85 percent of all claimants accepted the settlement; and (3) that the plaintiffs' lawyers agreed not to represent any plaintiff who chooses not to accept the settlement. Are the first and third provisions consistent with the lawyer's duty to his client?

5. As one can gather from the disagreement between majority and dissent, the judiciary, academia, and the bar are divided on the desirability of settlements like *Amchem* and *Ortiz*—and perhaps that in the Vioxx case just described.

   a. One experienced observer of the legal scene described such cases as violations of due process and "the sale of *res judicata* at a bargain basement price."

   b. Others have praised them as embodying the highest traditions of judicial creativity and lawyers' cooperation.

   c. In part, one's assessment may depend on one's assumptions about the alternatives. If one thinks that the alternative is an expeditiously conducted civil trial, much of the straining to find that the settlement did not breach either the principles of due process or of professional ethics will seem unnecessary and undesirable. One can find some evidence to support the thesis that the "ordinary" litigation system was developing methods of coping with the asbestos cases.

   d. If one thinks that the alternative is the death or financial destitution of those waiting in line for such a civil trial, then the district courts' rulings in *Amchem* and *Ortiz* will seem both humane and sensible. One can find some evidence that the litigation system was drowning in asbestos litigation and that litigation expenses, including lawyers' fees, were consuming two-thirds of the amounts recovered.

6. Beyond this level of debate is a subsidiary one about legal institutions. Some who would accept the argument that courts were doing badly with asbestos litigation would nevertheless say that there were other institutions that could have and should have responded.

   a. One candidate was Congress, which could have created an administrative system (like that for workers' compensation) for dealing with the asbestos claims. The Black Lung Benefits Act, 30 U.S.C. §§901 et seq., might have provided a model. Under the Act, funded by a tax on coal, miners who show disability produced by exposure to coal dust collect benefits from a federal agency. As the opinion in *Amchem* noted, Congress has not acted in a similar way in the case of asbestos. Does that mean that the courts should act on their own? Or has the courts' search for solutions taken the political heat off Congress and thereby thwarted a legislative solution?

   b. Another candidate was the bankruptcy courts. Some have argued that bankruptcy courts are in the business of collective litigation: They regularly resolve cases in which large numbers of creditors have claims against an entity. Moreover, they are expressly vested with the power to do the sort of quasi-administrative tasks achieved by the proposed settlement. One theoretical objection to the settlement class in *Ortiz* was that by using Rule 23(b)(1) and a limited fund rationale, the defendants were seeking the sort of protection they might have achieved in bankruptcy without subjecting themselves to the powers of a bankruptcy proceeding that might have dug much more deeply into their pockets.

7. As a nice summation of your grasp of civil procedure, be prepared either to defend or to attack the *Amchem* settlement—and explain your grounds for doing so—both as a matter of procedural law and of political theory.

Assessment Questions

Q1. Plaintiff files a complaint against an automobile Dealer and an automobile Manufacturer. The complaint, which is properly before the court under diversity jurisdiction, alleges that Plaintiff was injured in an accident caused by a defect in the vehicle's steering mechanism. The following questions ask you about what pleading(s) should be filed. Your options in answering are (1) an answer; (2) a crossclaim; (3) a counterclaim; (4) a third-party claim; and (5) none of the above.

   A. Dealer wants to assert that Manufacturer is contractually obligated to indemnify Dealer for any liability that Dealer may have to Plaintiff in the action. What pleading, if any, should Dealer file?

   B. Manufacturer wants to assert that the vehicle was not defective when delivered to Dealer and that any defect must have been introduced by Dealer when the vehicle was being prepared for delivery to customer. What pleading, if any, should Manufacturer file?

   C. Manufacturer wants to assert that Dealer has failed to pay for several vehicles that Manufacturer delivered to Dealer (not including the vehicle at issue in the action). Can it do so? What pleading, if any, should Manufacturer file?

   D. Dealer wants to assert that Plaintiff owes Dealer money for a breach of contract that has no relationship whatsoever to the vehicle or accident at issue in Plaintiff's complaint. Can Dealer do so? What pleading, if any, should it use?

   E. Dealer and Manufacturer both want to assert that there was no defect in the vehicle and that the accident was solely the result of Plaintiff's negligence. What pleading, if any, should Dealer and Manufacturer use?

Q2. Joinder of claims and parties in contemporary civil litigation . . .

   A. Substantially departs from the preceding common law regime.

   B. Is controlled by the Federal Rules.

   C. Is both facilitated and limited by jurisdictional statutes and doctrines.

Q3. Imagine a car purchase that has gone sour. Buyer sues Dealer in a diversity action, alleging Buyer was injured by a design defect. Dealer denies the defect, joins Manufacturer as a third-party defendant, and files a counterclaim against Buyer for unpaid repair bills on the vehicle in question. Buyer believes that his online billpay service should have paid these bills and is liable for its failure to do so. Which of the following are true?

   A. If there is a legal basis for Dealer's third-party claim against Manufacturer, supplemental jurisdiction will extend to this claim.

   B. Rule 14 permits Buyer to join Online Billpay Service as a third-party defendant on the counterclaim.

   C. If there is a legal basis for Buyer's third-party complaint against Online, supplemental jurisdiction will extend to this claim.

Q4. California Buyer purchases from Nevada Dealer a vehicle made by California Manufacturer. In San Francisco, Buyer becomes involved in a collision with Oregon Driver. Buyer invokes diversity jurisdiction to sue Dealer in federal district court in Nevada. Identify the correct statement(s).

   A. Manufacturer can intervene as of right, on the basis that Dealer is likely to try to cast the blame on Manufacturer.

   B. Dealer will succeed if he argues that where there are three plausibly liable parties (Manufacturer and Driver, in addition to Dealer), Rule 19 requires that all they be joined—or, at a minimum, the court should explain why not.

   C. Driver can intervene as of right, on the ground that if Dealer prevails, it will make Buyer more likely to come after him.

   D. On these facts, no nonparty has plausible grounds for required joinder or intervention as of right.

Q5. Regents of State University raise tuition, and current students sue to challenge this action. In response Regents propose a settlement that they won't charge the current students the increased tuition, but that they will have to curtail future academic programs to offset the cost. Identify the correct statement(s).

   A. Just-admitted students (who will be freshmen next year) have grounds to intervene in this suit as a class.

   B. The Regents can invoke Rule 19 to join the just-admitted students.

Q6. Joe files a claim against General Motors, seeking damages for injuries resulting from a defective ignition switch. GM answers, asserting former adjudication as a defense, and then moves for summary judgment attaching papers showing a judgment in a (b)(3) class action brought on behalf of those injured under similar circumstances. Joe can avoid preclusion if . . .

   A. He can show that he received notice of the class suit and chose to opt out of it.

   B. He can show that, although his address was available in the GM files, plaintiff's counsel failed to mail him notice of the suit.

   C. He can show that he was not adequately represented in the former suit.

   D. None of the above: Joe is bound by the former suit.

Q7. A group of ten parents sue on behalf of all parents in the community to force a local elementary school to close on the basis that its grounds—a former landfill—are contaminated. Assume that the requisites of subject matter jurisdiction are satisfied. In its current form the suit might nevertheless fail to be certified as a class if . . .

   A. A substantial number of parents that would be part of the class wanted the school to remain open while on-site remediation occurred.

   B. The class's lawyer was just out of law school.

   C. The class representatives could not afford to send individual mail notice to all the class members.

   D. Neither the class nor its lawyers had substantial assets.

Analysis of Assessment Questions

Q1A. The correct response is 2—a cross-claim. This is a claim for indemnification. If Manufacturer were not already a party, a Rule 14 third-party claim would be appropriate. But because Manufacturer is already a party (and this claim arises out of the same transaction or occurrence), a cross-claim is the correct route to go.

Q1B. The correct response is 1—an answer, in which the Manufacturer would simply deny liability; in the course of litigation it could tell its version of events—that the Dealer must have done it.

Q1C. The correct response is 5—none of the above. Because this crossclaim does not arise from the same transaction or occurrence as the main claim, Rule 13(g) does not permit its assertion. Manufacturer will need to file a separate action against Dealer.

Q1D. The correct response is 3—a counterclaim. Because this counterclaim is not transactionally related, it is permissive and therefore no supplemental jurisdiction will attach, but Rule 13(b) permits its assertion.

Q1E. The correct response is 1—an answer, in which both defendants would deny liability.

Q2. A, B, and C are the correct responses.

Q3. A and B are the correct responses. A is correct because the third-party claim falls within 28 U.S.C. §1367(a) and does not fall within the exclusions of §1367(b). B is correct because as to the counterclaim Buyer is a "defending party" within the meaning of Rule 14. C is wrong: By the plain language of §1367(b), language the courts have interpreted according to its literal meaning, no supplemental jurisdiction extends to claims by plaintiffs (here Buyer) against persons made parties under Rule 14 (here Online) if doing so would defeat diversity. So, if Buyer and Online are citizens of the same state, there is no supplemental jurisdiction. The drafters may well have meant to extend supplemental jurisdiction in this situation, but the courts have said that the statute means what its language says.

Q4. D is the only correct response. A is incorrect because Dealer can cast all the blame it likes but the judgment won't bind Manufacturer and won't impair or impede Manufacturer's ability to defend its interests: Defendants regularly try to cast blame on some absent party. B is wrong because, as *Temple v. Synthes* demonstrates, Rule 19 does not require plaintiffs to package their lawsuits in the most efficient possible form. C is wrong because, though Buyer may sue Driver, his exclusion from the first suit doesn't impair or impede his ability to defend himself if that suit does occur.

Q5. Both A and B are correct. A is correct because the new students can make a plausible case that "as a practical matter" the Regents' action will decrease the funds available for their education. (The new students would be a Rule 23(b)(2) class.) B is correct because, if they have read *Martin v. Wilks* and want to bind both current and future students, the Regents will want to join them.

Q6. A, B, and C are the correct responses. A is correct because one of the consequences of opting out of a class action is that one neither receives its benefits, if any, nor its burdens. B is correct because, since this was a Rule 23(b)(3) suit, plaintiff's counsel was obligated by Rule 26(c)(2)(B), as well as *Mullane v. Central Hanover Bank & Trust*, to provide individual notice to "all members who can be identified through reasonable effort." C is correct because *Hansberry v. Lee* permits collateral attack on a class judgment by one alleging inadequate representation.

Q7. A, B, and D are all correct responses. A is correct because the apparently conflicting wishes of the parents might well defeat both the typicality and the adequacy representation requirements of Rule 23(a). B is correct because such a lawyer would be very unlikely to be able—as a matter of professional competence—adequately to represent the class. D is very likely correct because part of representative adequacy includes the ability to finance the lawsuit. C is wrong because this will be a (b)(2) class, which would not require individual notice to all class members (though some form of notice would likely be required).

Table of Cases

Principal cases are italicized.

Table of Citations to the Judicial Code (28 U.S.C.)

§133(a)	182	§1391(c)	182
§144	596	§1391(d)	182
§§351 et seq.	595	§1397	182, 825, 826
§455	596, 597, 604	§1404	188, 195, 199, 200, 282
§455(a)	596, 597, 690	§1404(a)	188, 189, 690
§455(b)	596, 597, 658	§1406	183, 186, 195, 199, 200, 202
§455(e)	597	§1407	880
§§651 et seq.	541, 542	§1441	241, 248, 249
§651(a)	542	§1441(c)	242
§651(b)	541	§1442	248
§§1253-1258	55	§1442(a)	248
§1253	55	§1445	249
§1254	55	§1446	241
§1255	55	§1446(c)	242, 245, 248, 847
§1256	55	§1447	241
§1257	55	§1447(d)	848
§1258	55	§1453	248, 843, 844
§1291	51, 52, 323, 388, 568, 672-673, 680, 685, 701, 702	§1453(c)	848
§1292(a)	323, 688, 701, 702	§1651	690
§1292(b)	678, 689	§1652	256
§1331	7, 206, 208, 210, 213, 214, 221, 779, 843	§1712	871
		§1712(d)	872
§1332	7, 10, 206, 208, 219, 221, 222, 224, 225, 226, 229, 250, 362, 364, 843	§1715	869
		§1738	71, 286, 758, 763, 765
§1332(a)	7, 223, 224, 252, 412, 828	§1861	613, 616
§1332(c)	225	§§1863-1864	614
§1332(d)	224, 232, 844	§1863	614
§1332(e)	225	§1864	614
§1333	208	§1866	614
§1334	208	§1867(c)	614
§1335	175, 224, 825, 828	§1870	616
§1335(a)	825	§1961	307
§1338	208	§2072	16, 267, 274, 275, 279, 281, 688
§1338(a)	781	§2072(b)	16, 409, 689, 711
§1341	208	§2072(c)	689
§1346(b)	208	§§2073-2077	17
§1350	133	§2073	17
§1359	225	§2074	17
§1367	230, 233, 235, 240, 779, 780, 781, 786, 800, 801, 843	§2075	17
		§2076	17
§1367(a)	233, 234, 252, 812, 886	§2077	17
§1367(b)	233, 253, 801, 811, 886	§2107	679
§1367(c)	234, 235, 240	§2111	697
§1367(d)	240	§§2201-2202	215
§1391	181, 182, 183, 202, 826	§2201	215, 311
§1391(a)	182	§2202	215, 312
§1391(b)	182, 186	§2361	110, 172, 181, 781, 825, 826
		§2412	324

Table of Citations to the Federal Rules of Civil Procedure

Table of Authorities

Index